A-Z MERSEYSIDE

C000003728

CONTENTS

REFERENCE

Motorway	M57
A Road	A580
Proposed	
Tunnel	
B Road	B5202
Dual Carriageway	
One-way Street — Traffic flow on A Roads is indicated by a heavy line on the driver's left. All one-way streets are shown on Large Scale Pages 4-5	
Restricted Access	
Pedestrianized Road	
Track & Footpath	
Railway — Station / Level Crossing / Tunnel	
Built-up Area	STONE ST.
Local Authority Boundary	
Posttown Boundary	
Postcode Boundary within Posttown	

Map Continuation 7	Large Scale City Centre 4
Car Park (selected)	P
Church or Chapel	†
Cycleway (selected)	
Fire Station	■
Hospital	H
House Numbers A and B Roads only	18 25
Information Centre	i
National Grid Reference	^{3}40
Park & Ride	The Esplanade P+
Police Station	▲
Post Office	★
Toilet: without facilities for the Disabled	▽
with facilities for the Disabled	▽
for exclusive use by the Disabled	▽
Viewpoint	
Educational Establishment	
Hospital or Hospice	
Industrial Building	
Leisure or Recreational Facility	
Place of Interest	
Public Building	
Shopping Centre or Market	
Other Selected Buildings	

SCALE

Map Pages 6-173	Map Pages 4-5
1:14908 4¼ inches to 1 mile	1:10560 6 inches to 1 mile
½ Mile	⅜ Mile
750 Metres	500 Metres
6.7 cm to 1km 10.8 cm to 1 mile	9.46 cm to 1km 15.24 cm to 1 mile

Copyright of Geographers' A-Z Map Company Ltd.

Head Office:
Fairfield Road, Borough Green, Sevenoaks, Kent, TN15 8PP
Telephone: 01732 781000 (Enquiries & Trade Sales)
01732 783422 (Retail Sales)
www.a-zmaps.co.uk

Ordnance Survey® This product includes mapping data licensed from Ordnance Survey® with the permission of the Controller of Her Majesty's Stationery Office.
© Crown Copyright 2004. All Rights Reserved. Licence number 100017302

Edition 2 2005

IRISH SEA

LIVERPOOL BAY

6	**7**	**8** Marshside	**9** Banks
SOUTHPORT		Churchtown	
10 Hillside	**11** Birkdale	**12** High Park Brown Edge	**13** Carr Cross
14 Ainsdale-on-sea Ainsdale	**15** Woodvale	**16** Scarisbrick	**17** Bescar Pinfold

Rufford

Burscough

18	**19** Freshfield	**20**	**21**	**22** Halsall Haskayne	**23** Primrose Hill Clieves Hills	**24** ORMSKIRK
FORMBY						

25 Westhead **26** Lathom

28	**29**	**30** Lady Green	**31** Great Altcar	**32** Lydiate	**33** Aughton	**34** Town Green Royal Oak

35 Scarth Hill Bickerstaffe **36** Pennyland

Inset Page 29

40 Hightown Little Crosby	**41** Ince Blundell Homer Green Thornton	**42** MAGHULL Sefton Netherton	**43** Moss Side Melling	**44** Melling Mount Tower Hill	**45** Barrow Nook

46 Rainford Junction

Crosby Channel

52 CROSBY Seaforth	**53** Litherland	**54**	**55** Aintree Fazakerley	**56** Southdene	**57** KIRKBY Knowsley Industrial Park

Buckley Hill **58**

64	**65** New Brighton	**66** BOOTLE	**67**	**68** Kirkdale Anfield	**69** WALTON West Derby	**70**

Norris Green **71** Knowsley **72** Gillar's Green

PRESCOT

LARGE SCALE **4** **5** LIVERPOOL CITY CENTRE

82	**83** HOYLAKE	**84** WALLASEY Moreton	**85** Bidston	**86** Egremont Liscard Seacombe (Kingsway) Mersey Tunnel (Queensway)	**87**	**88** Everton

89 Old Swan LIVERPOOL	**90** Huyton-with-Roby Knotty Ash	**91** Huyton

92 Whiston

Meols

102 West Kirby	**103** Grange Frankby	**104** Upton Greasby Woodchurch	**105** Oxton	**106** Claughton BIRKENHEAD Prenton	**107** Tranmere Rock Ferry	**108** Toxteth Wavertree

109 Sefton Park Mossley Hill	**110** Childwall Allerton	**111** Gateacre Woolton

112 Tarbock Green

122	**123** Caldy Thurstaston	**124** Irby Pensby	**125** Thingwall Barnston	**126** Storeton Brimstage	**127** Port Sunlight	**128** New Ferry BEBINGTON

129 Aigburth Grassendale Bromborough	**130** Garston Hunt's Cross	**131** SPEKE

132 Halewood

Point of Ayr

142 HESWALL Gayton	**143**	**144** Thornton Hough Raby	**145** Poulton Brookhurst	**146** Eastham Ferry Eastham	**147**	**148** Liverpool John Lennon Airport

149 Speke **150** Hale

156	**157** Parkgate NESTON	**158** Wirral Hill Ness	**159** Willaston	**160** Hooton Little Sutton	**161** Overpool Whitby	**162** ELLESMERE PORT

163 Stanlow Ince Banks **164** Elton CHESTER

168 Woodbank	**169** Capenhurst Great Sutton Whitbyheath	**170** Little Stanney Stoak	**171** Thornton-le-Moors Croughton	**172** Elton Green

Holywell (Treffynnon)

Bagillt

Flint (Y Fflint)

ENGLAND WALES

Connah's Quay

RIVER DEE (AFON DYFRDWY)

RIVER MERSEY

A59 A565 B5246 A59 A5147 A565 A570 M58 A59 M57 M58 A580 M53 A41 M53 M56 A548 A550 A540 A494 A5117 A5026 A55 A5119 A548 B5122 A5026 B5121 B5123 A541

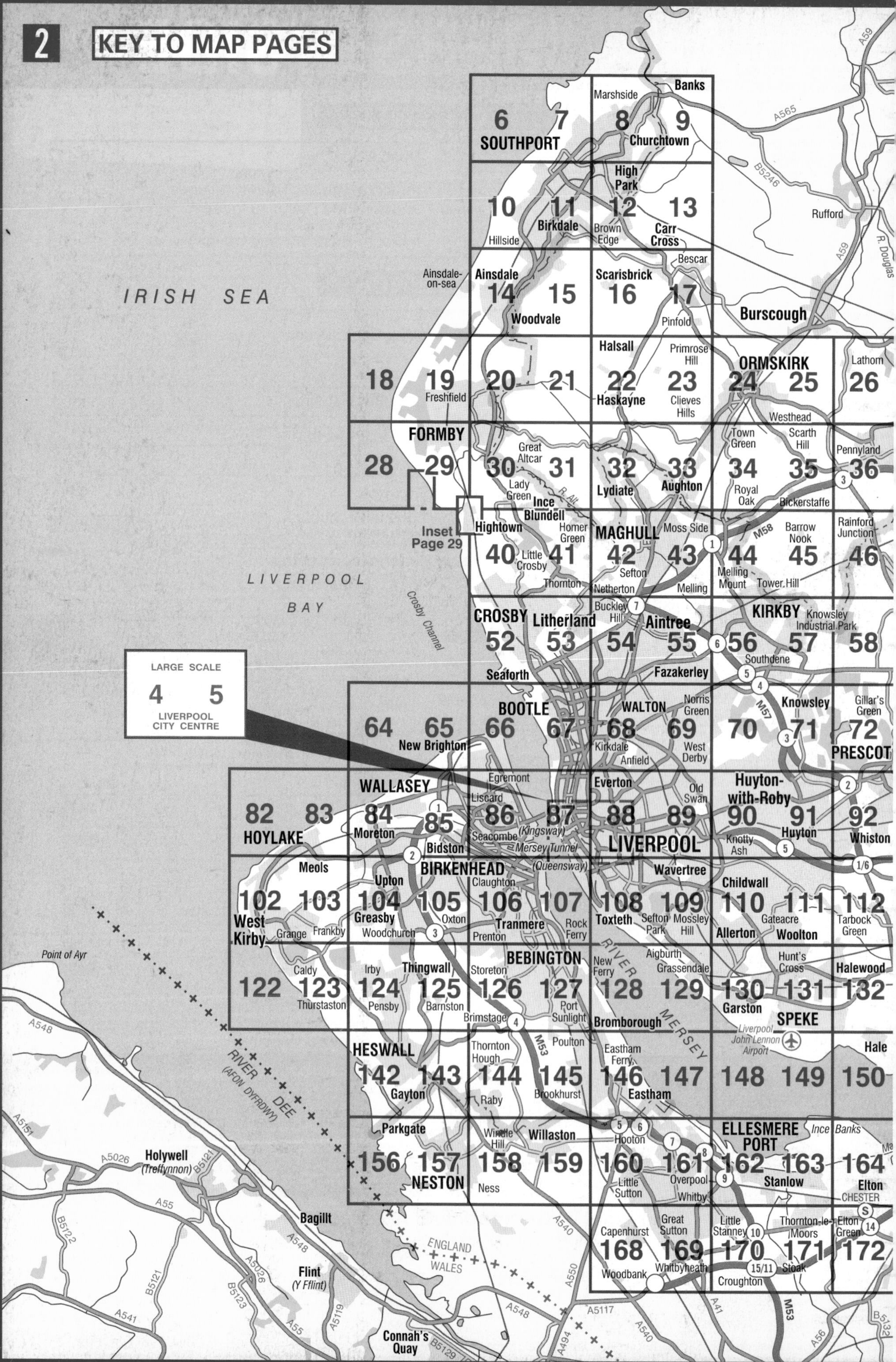

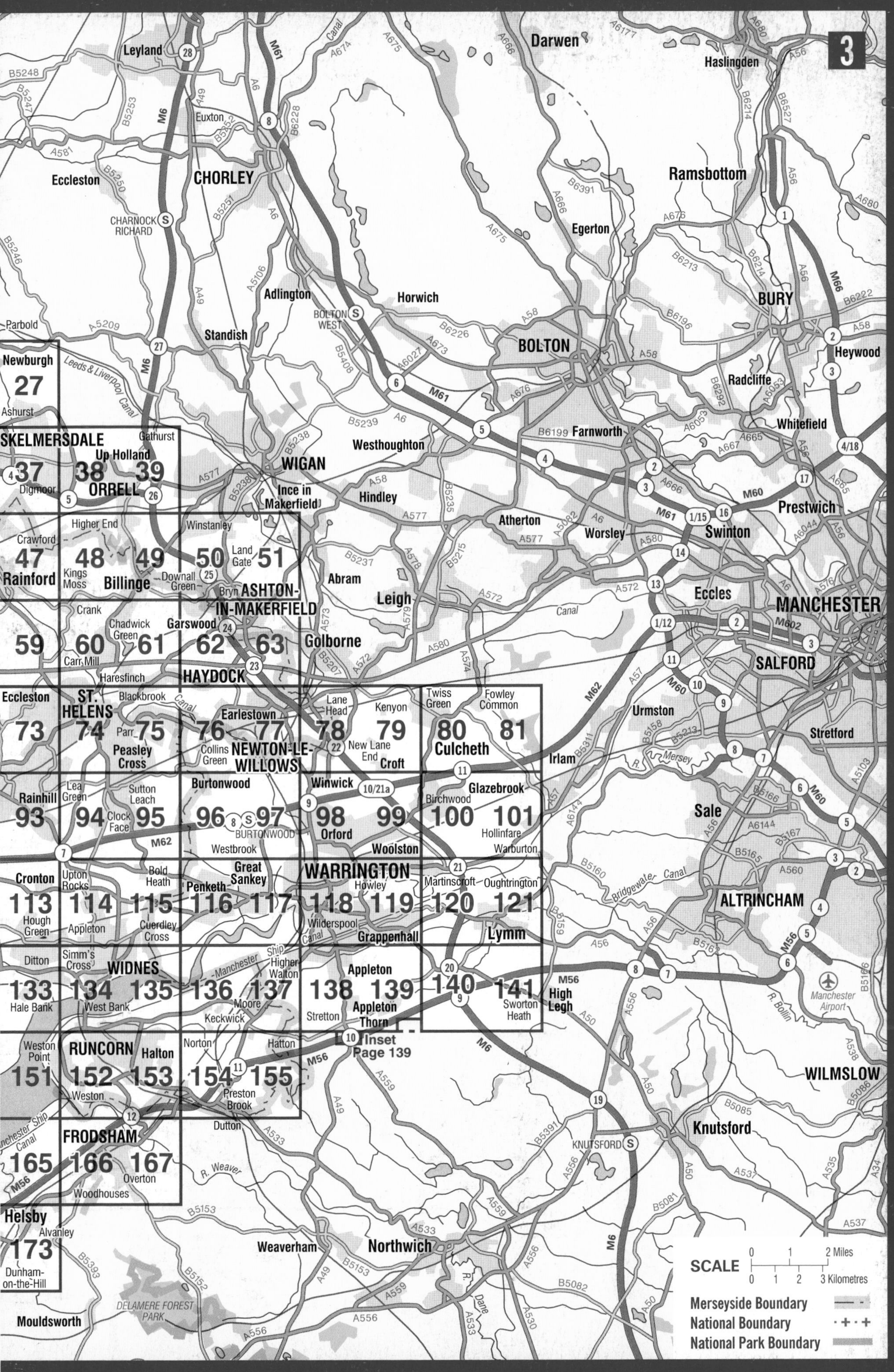
Leyland
Darwen
Haslingden
Euxton
CHORLEY
Eccleston
CHARNOCK RICHARD
Ramsbottom
Egerton
Adlington
Horwich
BOLTON WEST
BURY
Parbold
Standish
BOLTON
Heywood
Newburgh
27
Ashurst
Radcliffe
Westhoughton
Whitefield
SKELMERSDALE
Gathurst
Up Holland
37
38
39
Digmoor
ORRELL
WIGAN
Farnworth
Ince in Makerfield
Hindley
Prestwich
Atherton
Worsley
Swinton
Higher End
Winstanley
Crawford
47
48
49
50
51
Rainford
Kings Moss
Billinge
Downall Green
Land Gate
Bryn
ASHTON-IN-MAKERFIELD
Abram
Leigh
Eccles
MANCHESTER
Crank
Chadwick Green
Garswood
59
60
61
62
63
Carr Mill
Golborne
SALFORD
Haresfinch
HAYDOCK
Eccleston
ST. HELENS
Blackbrook
Earlestown
Lane Head
Kenyon
Twiss Green
Fowley Common
Urmston
73
74
75
76
77
78
79
80
81
Parr
Peasley Cross
Collins Green
NEWTON-LE-WILLOWS
New Lane End
Croft
Culcheth
Stretford
Irlam
Rainhill
Lea Green
Sutton Leach
Burtonwood
Winwick
Birchwood
Glazebrook
Sale
93
94
95
96
97
98
99
100
101
Clock Face
BURTONWOOD
Orford
Hollinfare
Westbrook
Woolston
Warburton
Cronton
Upton Rocks
Bold Heath
Penketh
Great Sankey
WARRINGTON
Howley
Martinscroft
Oughtrington
ALTRINCHAM
113
114
115
116
117
118
119
120
121
Hough Green
Appleton
Cuerdley Cross
Wilderspool
Grappenhall
Lymm
Ditton
Simm's Cross
WIDNES
Higher Walton
Appleton
133
134
135
136
137
138
139
140
141
High Legh
Hale Bank
West Bank
Moore
Keckwick
Stretton
Appleton Thorn
Sworton Heath
Manchester Airport
Weston Point
RUNCORN
Halton
Norton
Hatton
Inset Page 139
151
152
153
154
155
WILMSLOW
Weston
Preston Brook
Dutton
Knutsford
KNUTSFORD
FRODSHAM
165
166
167
Overton
Woodhouses
Helsby
Alvanley
173
Dunham-on-the-Hill
Weaverham
Northwich
DELAMERE FOREST PARK
Mouldsworth
Leeds & Liverpool Canal
Manchester Ship Canal
Bridgewater Canal
R. Mersey
R. Weaver
R. Bollin
R. Dane
M6
M61
M62
M60
M602
M56
M66
SCALE
0 1 2 Miles
0 1 2 3 Kilometres
Merseyside Boundary
National Boundary
National Park Boundary

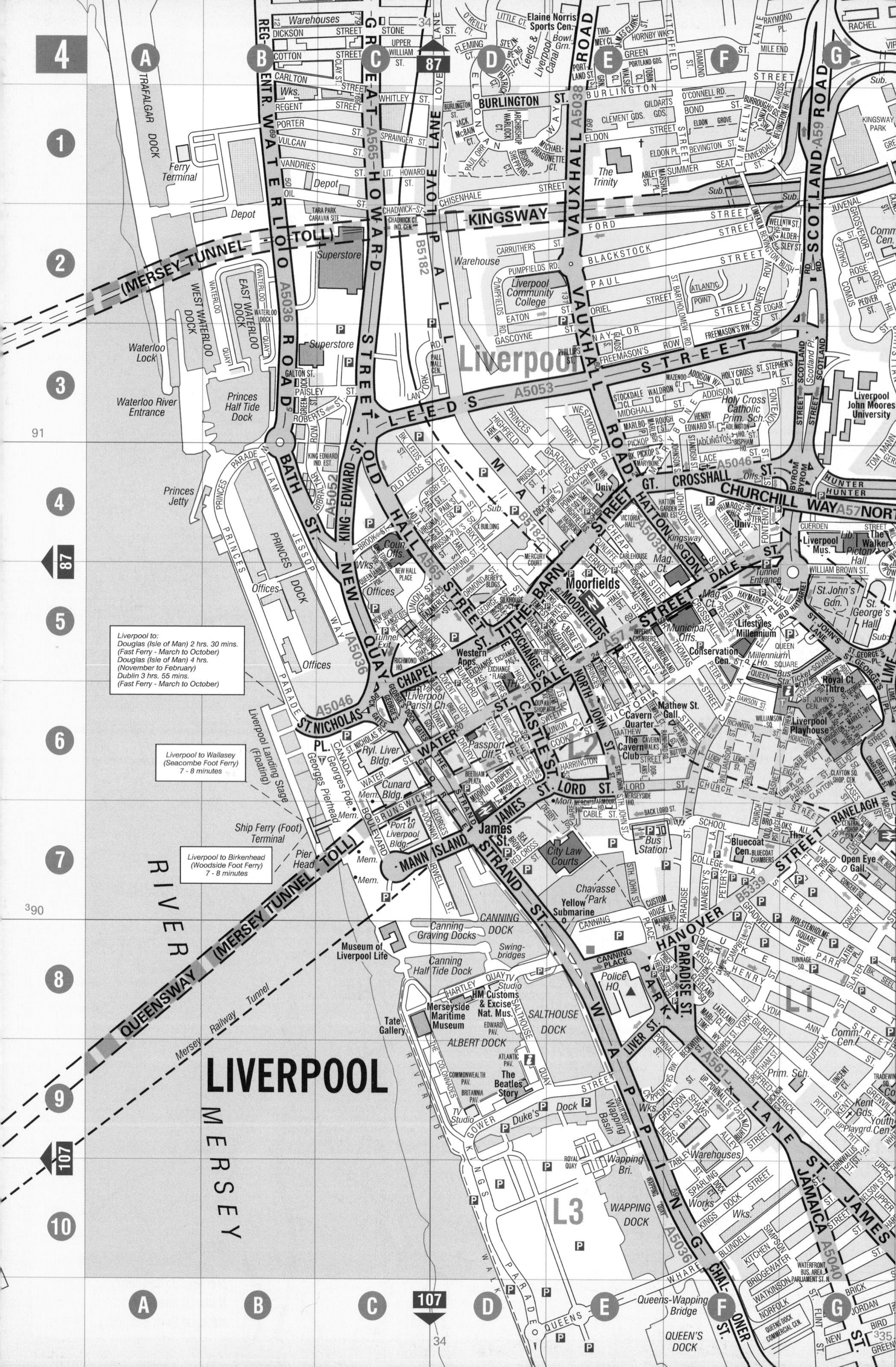
A
B
C
D
E
F
G
1
2
3
4
5
6
7
8
9
10
87
107
34
35
91
390
LIVERPOOL
Liverpool
RIVER
MERSEY
Liverpool to:
Douglas (Isle of Man) 2 hrs. 30 mins.
(Fast Ferry - March to October)
Douglas (Isle of Man) 4 hrs.
(November to February)
Dublin 3 hrs. 55 mins.
(Fast Ferry - March to October)
Liverpool to Wallasey
(Seacombe Foot Ferry)
7 - 8 minutes
Liverpool to Birkenhead
(Woodside Foot Ferry)
7 - 8 minutes
TRAFALGAR DOCK
Ferry Terminal
Depot
(MERSEY TUNNEL - TOLL)
WEST WATERLOO DOCK
EAST WATERLOO DOCK
Waterloo Lock
Waterloo River Entrance
Princes Half Tide Dock
Princes Jetty
PRINCES DOCK
Offices
Liverpool Landing Stage (Floating)
Ship Ferry (Foot) Terminal
Pier Head
Georges Pierhead
QUEENSWAY (MERSEY TUNNEL TOLL)
Mersey Railway Tunnel
Museum of Liverpool Life
Canning Graving Docks
CANNING DOCK
Canning Half Tide Dock
Swing-bridges
Merseyside Maritime Museum
HM Customs & Excise Nat. Mus.
Tate Gallery
ALBERT DOCK
SALTHOUSE DOCK
The Beatles Story
Duke's Dock
Wapping Basin
Wapping Bri.
WAPPING DOCK
Queens-Wapping Bridge
QUEEN'S DOCK
L1
L2
L3
WATERLOO ROAD
BATH ST.
NEW QUAY
GREAT HOWARD STREET
OLD HALL STREET
LEEDS STREET
KINGSWAY
VAUXHALL ROAD
SCOTLAND ROAD
BYROM ST.
CHURCHILL WAY
TITHEBARN STREET
DALE STREET
CHAPEL ST.
WATER ST.
CASTLE ST.
LORD ST.
JAMES ST.
STRAND ST.
MANN ISLAND
HANOVER STREET
PARADISE ST.
PARK LA.
WAPPING
ST. JAMES ST.
JAMAICA ST.
WHITECHAPEL
RANELAGH ST.
ST. JOHN'S LANE
A5036
A565
A5052
B5182
A5053
A5038
A5046
A59
A57
B5339
A561
A5040
Superstore
The Trinity
Liverpool Community College
Liverpool John Moores University
Holy Cross Catholic Prim. Sch.
Univ.
Coun. Offs.
Moorfields
Mag. Ct.
Municipal Offs.
Lifestyles Millennium
Conservation Cen.
Liverpool Mus.
The Walker
Picton Hall
St. John's Gdn.
St. George's Hall
Royal Ct. Thtre.
Liverpool Playhouse
Western Apps
Liverpool Parish Ch.
Ryl. Liver Bldg.
Cunard Bldg.
Port of Liverpool Bldg.
Passport Off.
Cavern Quarter
The Cavern Club
Mathew St. Gall.
Bus Station
City Law Courts
Chavasse Park
Yellow Submarine
Police HQ
Bluecoat Cen.
Open Eye Gall.
Comm. Cen.
Prim. Sch.
Warehouses
Elaine Norris Sports Cen.
Leeds & Liverpool Canal
Tunnel Entrance
Tunnel Exit
Mem.

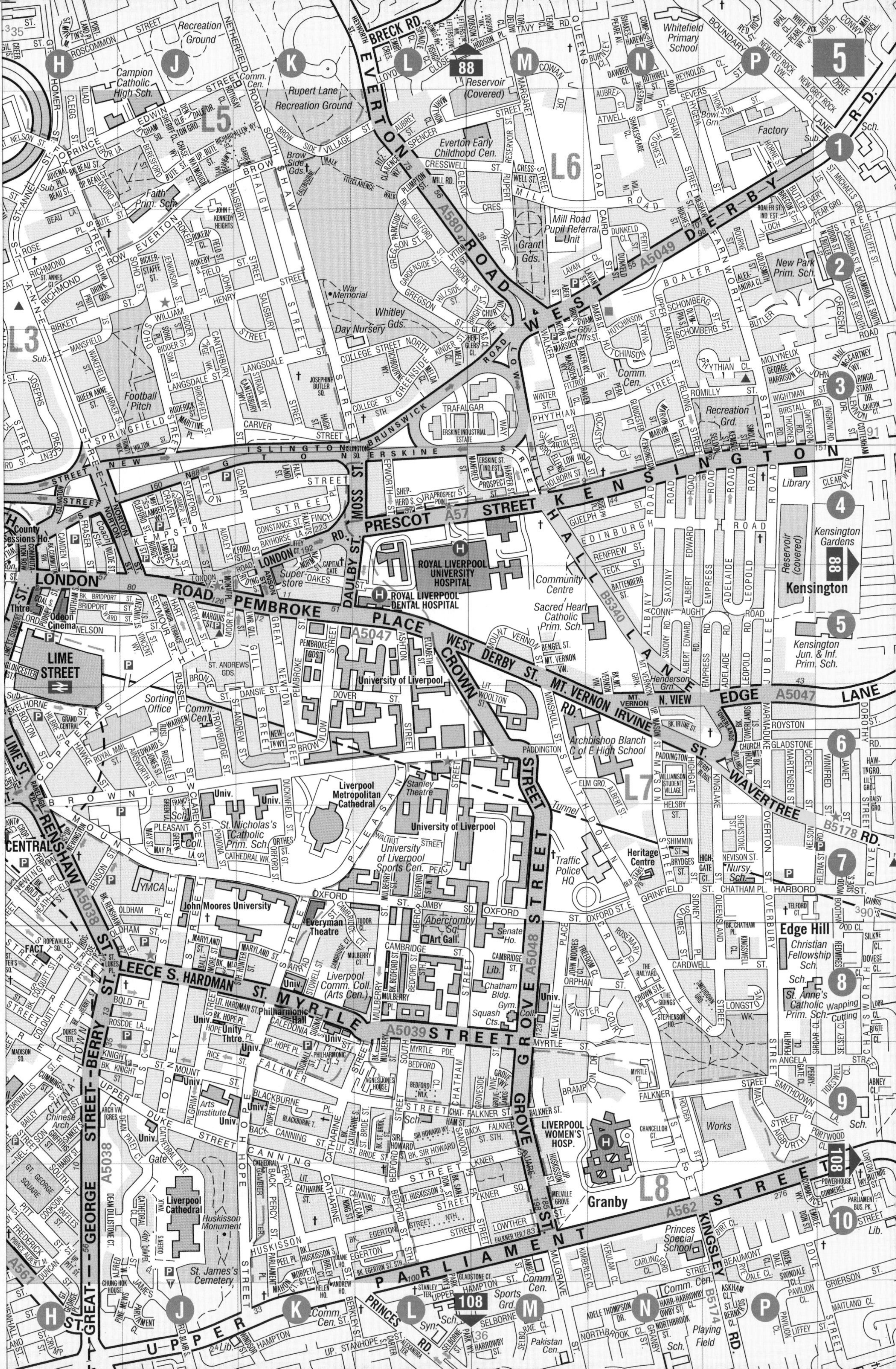

5
88
108
L3
L5
L6
L7
L8
EVERTON ROAD
A580
WEST DERBY ROAD
A5049
KENSINGTON
A57
PRESCOT STREET
LONDON ROAD
PEMBROKE PLACE
A5047
WEST DERBY ST.
EDGE LANE
WAVERTREE RD.
B5178
CROWN STREET
GROVE STREET
A5048
MYRTLE STREET
A5039
LEECE S. HARDMAN ST.
PARLIAMENT STREET
A562
UPPER PARLIAMENT ST.
GREAT GEORGE ST.
BERRY ST.
RENSHAW ST.
A5038
LIME ST.
ISLINGTON
SHAW STREET
ST. ANNE STREET
SMITHDOWN LANE
MOUNT PLEASANT
BROWNLOW HILL
HOPE STREET
RODNEY STREET
DUKE STREET
UPPER DUKE ST.
CATHARINE ST.
PRINCES RD.
KINGSLEY RD.
B5174
B5340
LODGE LANE
Recreation Ground
Campion Catholic High Sch.
Rupert Lane Recreation Ground
Reservoir (Covered)
Whitefield Primary School
Everton Early Childhood Cen.
Brow Side Gds.
Faith Prim. Sch.
Mill Road Pupil Referral Unit
Grant Gds.
Factory
New Park Prim. Sch.
War Memorial
Whitley Gds.
Day Nursery
Football Pitch
Recreation Grd.
Comm. Cen.
Library
Kensington Gardens
Kensington
Reservoir (covered)
County Sessions Ho.
Super-store
ROYAL LIVERPOOL UNIVERSITY HOSPITAL
ROYAL LIVERPOOL DENTAL HOSPITAL
Community Centre
Sacred Heart Catholic Prim. Sch.
Kensington Jun. & Inf. Prim. Sch.
Odeon Cinema
LIME STREET
University of Liverpool
Henderson Grn.
Sorting Office
Royal Mail
Archbishop Blanch C of E High School
Williamson Student Village
Liverpool Metropolitan Cathedral
Stanley Theatre
Tunnel
CENTRAL
St. Nicholas's Catholic Prim. Sch.
University of Liverpool Sports Cen.
Traffic Police HQ
Heritage Centre
YMCA
John Moores University
Everyman Theatre
Abercromby Sq.
Art Gall.
Senate Ho.
Edge Hill
Christian Fellowship Sch.
FACT
Liverpool Comm. Coll. (Arts Cen.)
Chatham Bldg.
Squash Cts.
Gym.
St. Anne's Catholic Prim. Sch.
Wapping Cutting
Philharmonic Hall
Unity Thtre
Arts Institute
Chinese Arch
CHINA TOWN
Works
LIVERPOOL WOMEN'S HOSP.
Granby
GT. GEORGE SQUARE
Liverpool Cathedral
Huskisson Monument
St. James's Cemetery
Princes Special School
Sports Grd.
Comm. Cen.
Pakistan Cen.
Playing Field
Syn.
Lib.

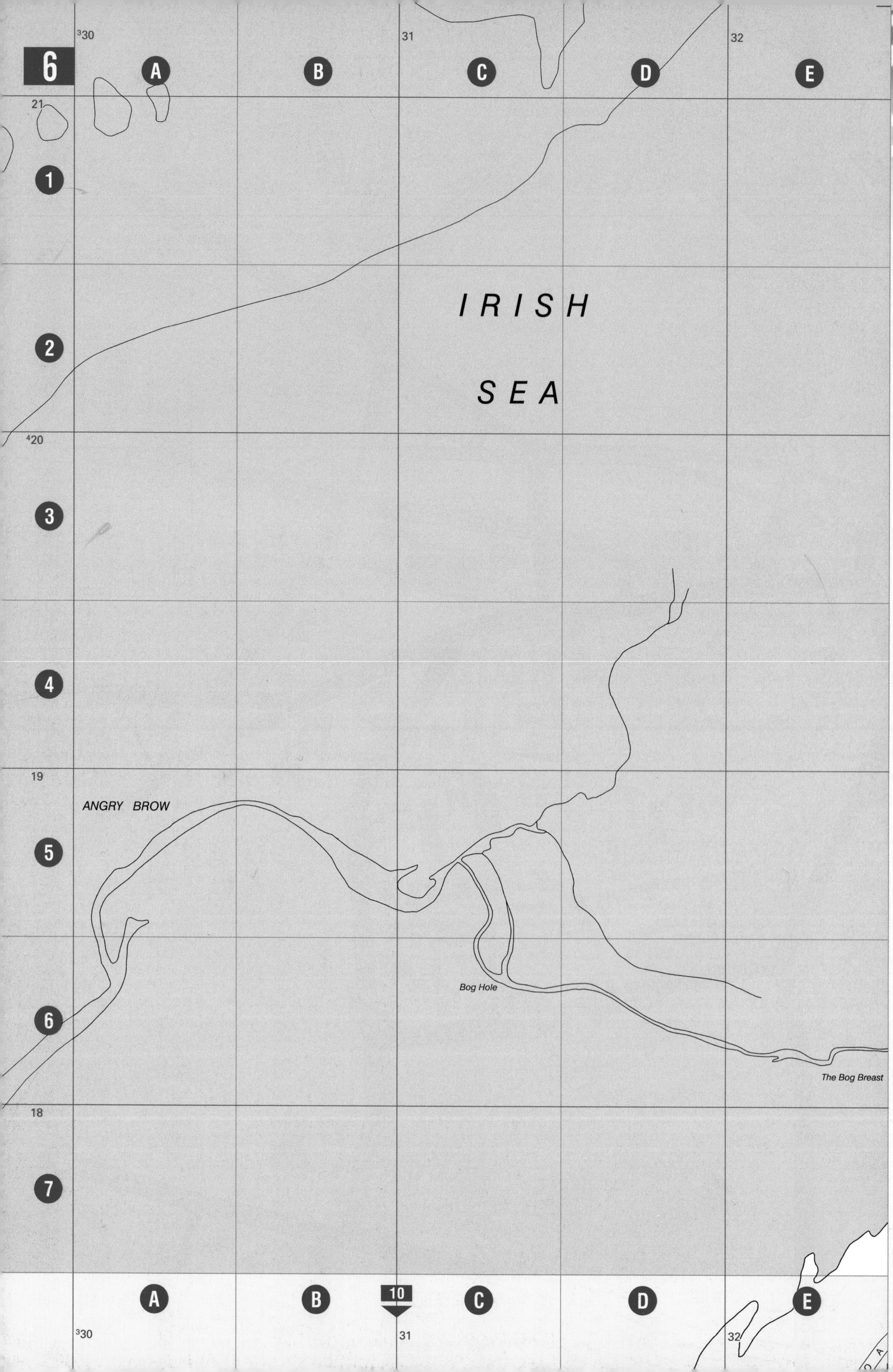

6

21

1

2

I R I S H

S E A

⁴20

3

4

19

ANGRY   BROW

5

Bog Hole

6

The Bog Breast

18

7

A   B   10   C   D   E

³30   31   32

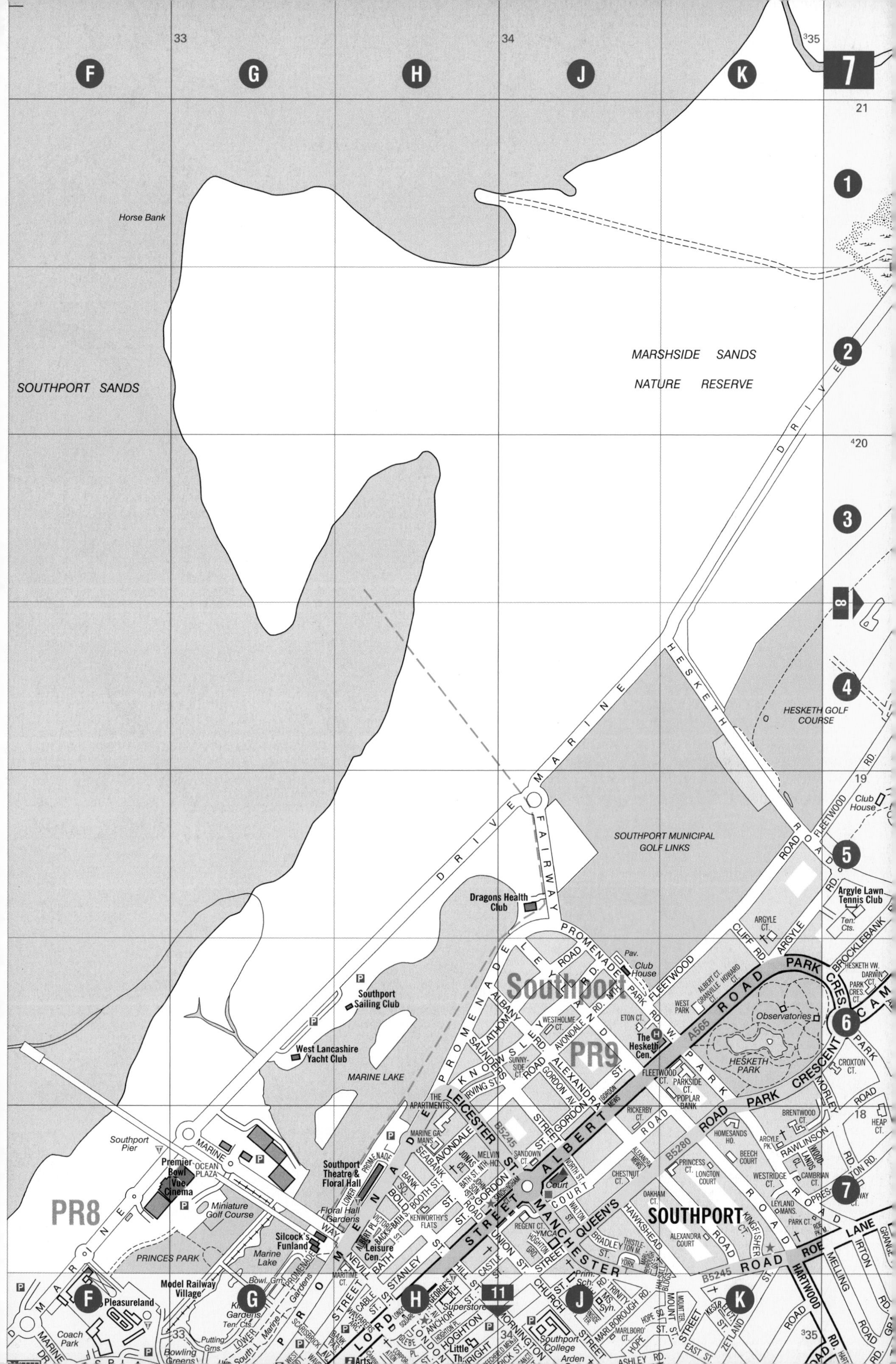
F
G
H
J
K
33
34
35
21
20
19
18
1
2
3
4
5
6
7
8
Horse Bank
SOUTHPORT SANDS
MARSHSIDE SANDS
NATURE RESERVE
MARINE DRIVE
HESKETH DRIVE
HESKETH GOLF COURSE
SOUTHPORT MUNICIPAL GOLF LINKS
FAIRWAY
Dragons Health Club
Southport Sailing Club
West Lancashire Yacht Club
MARINE LAKE
Southport
PR9
PR8
SOUTHPORT
Club House
Argyle Lawn Tennis Club
Observatories
HESKETH PARK
Southport Pier
Premier Bowl
Vue Cinema
OCEAN PLAZA
Miniature Golf Course
PRINCES PARK
Silcock's Funland
Marine Lake
Southport Theatre & Floral Hall
Floral Hall Gardens
Leisure Cen.
Model Railway Village
Pleasureland
Coach Park
Superstore
Southport College
PROMENADE
LEICESTER ST.
LORD STREET
ALBERT ROAD
QUEEN'S ROAD
MANCHESTER ROAD
PARK CRESCENT
PARK ROAD
FLEETWOOD ROAD
HESKETH ROAD
ROE LANE
HARTWOOD ROAD
CAMBRIDGE ROAD
ALEXANDRA ROAD
KNOWSLEY ROAD
LEYLAND ROAD
ARGYLE ROAD
A565
B5280
B5245
11

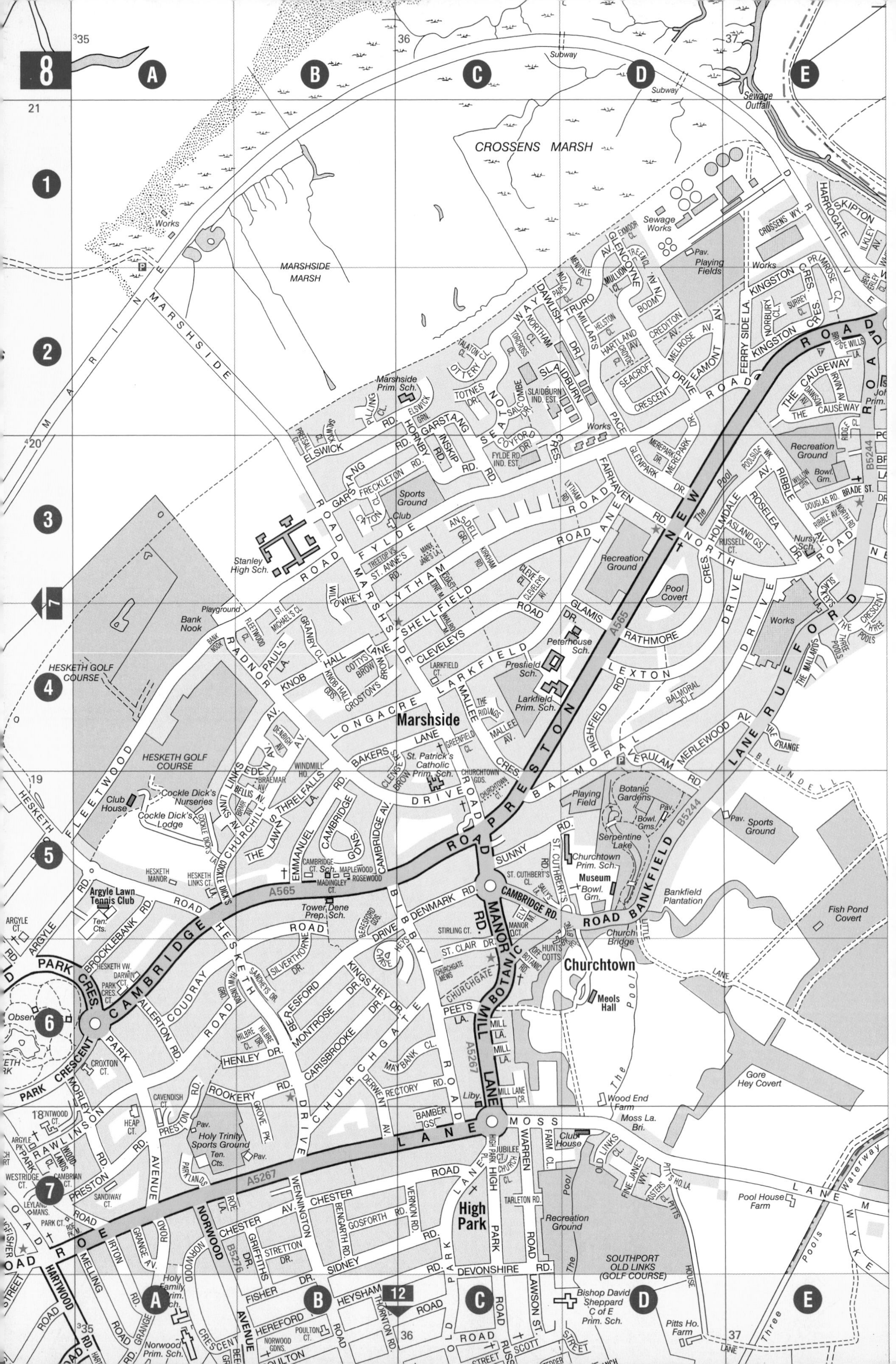

CROSSENS MARSH
MARSHSIDE MARSH
Subway
Sewage Outfall
Sewage Works
Playing Fields
Works
MARINE DRIVE
MARSHSIDE
Marshside Prim. Sch.
Stanley High Sch.
Sports Ground
Club
Bank Nook
Playground
HESKETH GOLF COURSE
Club House
Cockle Dick's Nurseries
Cockle Dick's Lodge
Marshside
St. Patrick's Catholic Prim. Sch.
Peterhouse Sch.
Presfield Sch.
Larkfield Prim. Sch.
Recreation Ground
Pool Covert
Botanic Gardens
Playing Field
Serpentine Lake
Churchtown Prim. Sch.
Museum
Bankfield Plantation
Church Bridge
Churchtown
Meols Hall
Fish Pond Covert
Gore Hey Covert
Wood End Farm
Moss La. Bri.
Pool House Farm
SOUTHPORT OLD LINKS (GOLF COURSE)
Bishop David Sheppard C of E Prim. Sch.
Pitts Ho. Farm
High Park
Holy Trinity Sports Ground
Holy Family Prim. Sch.
Norwood Prim. Sch.
Argyle Lawn Tennis Club
Tower Dene Prep. Sch.
Cambridge Ct. Sch.
Liby.
PRESTON NEW ROAD
A565
CAMBRIDGE ROAD
ROE LANE
A5267
MILL LANE
BOTANIC RD.
MANOR RD.
FYLDE ROAD
BALMORAL DRIVE
RUFFORD ROAD
BANKFIELD LANE
B5244
B5276
MOSS LANE
NORWOOD AVENUE
PARK CRESCENT
HESKETH ROAD
FLEETWOOD ROAD
NORTH ROAD
THE CAUSEWAY
KINGSTON CRES.

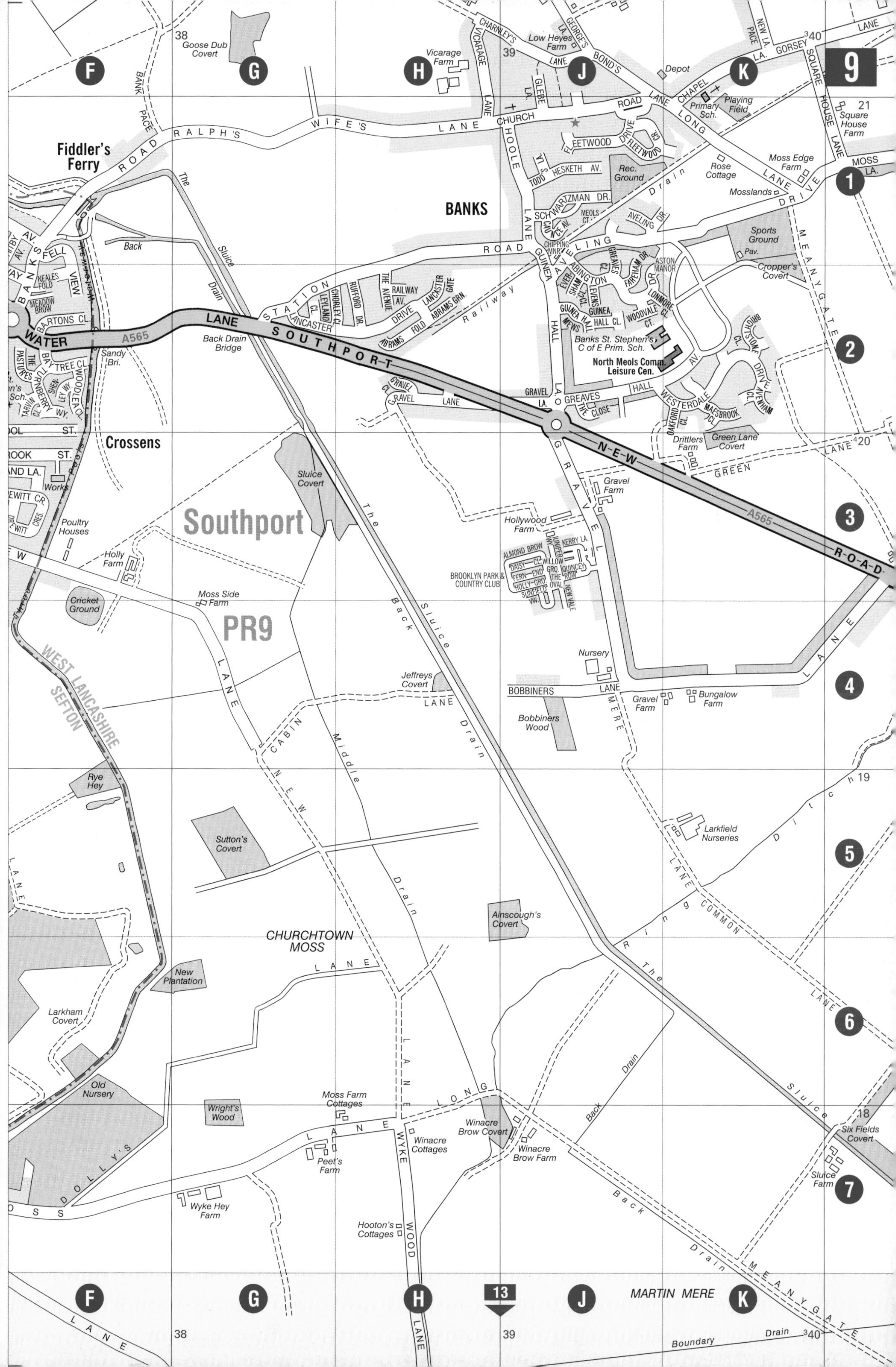

9
Fiddler's Ferry
BANKS
Crossens
Southport
PR9
CHURCHTOWN MOSS
MARTIN MERE
WEST LANCASHIRE
SEFTON
A565
SOUTHPORT NEW ROAD
WATER LANE
RALPH'S WIFE'S LANE
CHURCH ROAD
Goose Dub Covert
Vicarage Farm
Low Heyes Farm
Depot
Primary Sch.
Playing Field
Square House Farm
Moss Edge Farm
Rose Cottage
Mosslands
Rec. Ground
Sports Ground
Pav.
Cropper's Covert
Banks St. Stephen's C of E Prim. Sch.
North Meols Comm. Leisure Cen.
Back Drain Bridge
Sandy Bri.
Drittlers Farm
Green Lane Covert
Gravel Farm
Hollywood Farm
BROOKLYN PARK & COUNTRY CLUB
Sluice Covert
Poultry Houses
Holly Farm
Moss Side Farm
Cricket Ground
Works
Nursery
Jeffreys Covert
BOBBINERS LANE
Gravel Farm
Bungalow Farm
Bobbiners Wood
Rye Hey
Sutton's Covert
Larkfield Nurseries
Ainscough's Covert
New Plantation
Larkham Covert
Old Nursery
Wright's Wood
Moss Farm Cottages
Peet's Farm
Winacre Cottages
Winacre Brow Covert
Winacre Brow Farm
Six Fields Covert
Sluice Farm
Wyke Hey Farm
Hooton's Cottages
The Sluice
The Back Sluice Drain
Middle Drain
Back Drain
Ring Ditch
Boundary Drain
LONG LANE
WYKE LANE
WYKE WOOD LANE
MEANYGATE
RING COMMON LANE
CABIN LANE
NEW LANE
GRAVEL LANE
GREEN LANE
MERE LANE
DOLLY'S LANE
MOSS LANE
13
38
39
340
21
20
19
18

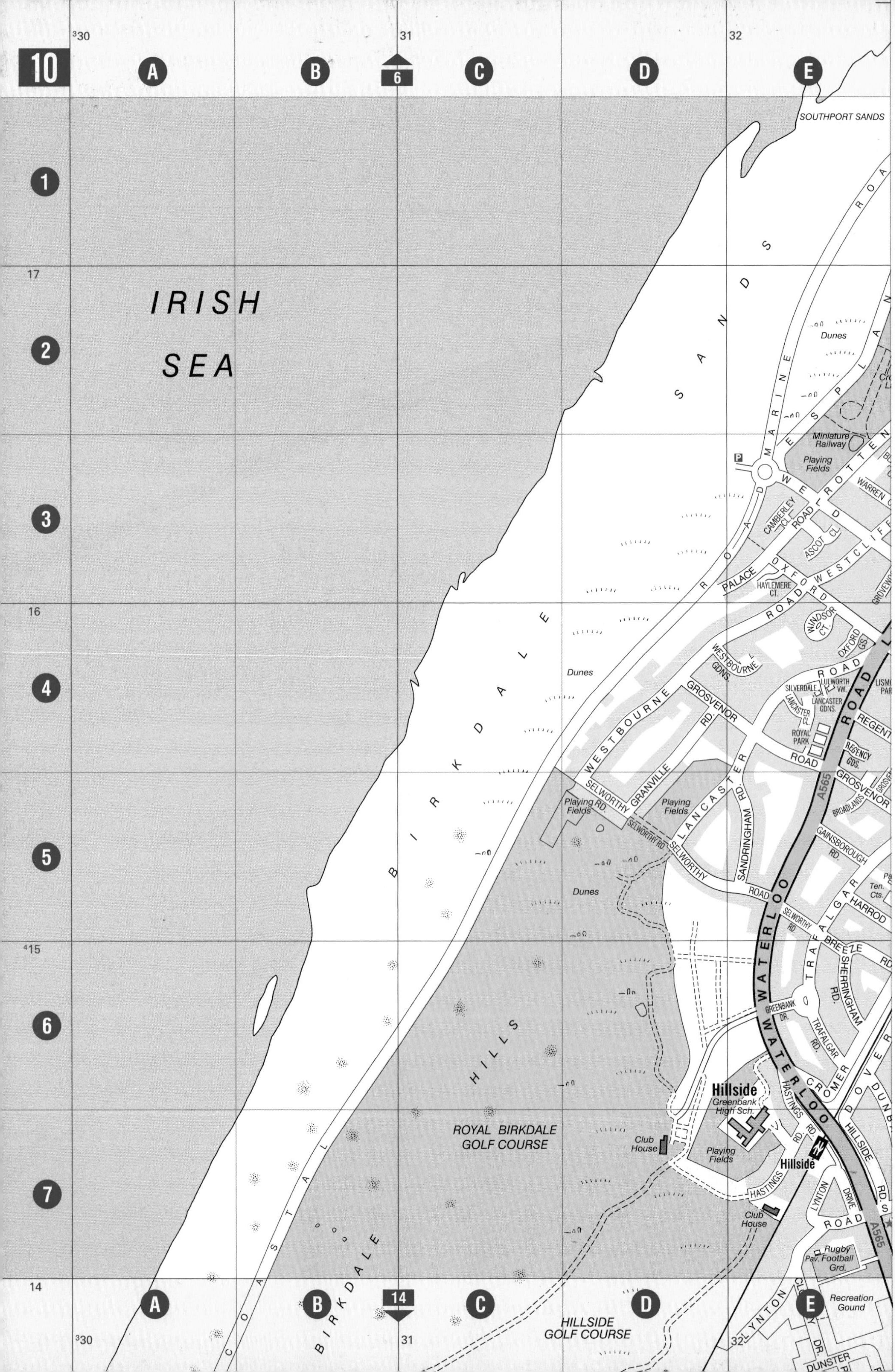

IRISH

SEA

SOUTHPORT SANDS

SANDS

Dunes

Miniature
Railway

Playing
Fields

WARREN

CAMBERLEY

ASCOT CL.

PALACE

HAYLEMERE
CT.

WINDSOR
CT.

OXFORD

WESTBOURNE
GDNS.

Dunes

SILVERDALE
LANCASTER
CL.
LULWORTH
VW.
LANCASTER
GDNS.

ROYAL
PARK

ROAD

REGENCY
GDS.

A565

GROSVENOR

BROADLANDS

WESTBOURNE

GROSVENOR
RD.

Playing
Fields

GAINSBOROUGH
RD.

SELWORTHY RD.

GRANVILLE

Playing
Fields

LANCASTER RD.

SANDRINGHAM RD.

WATERLOO

TRAFALGAR

HARROD

Ten.
Cts.

SHERRINGHAM
RD.

Playing
Fields

SELWORTHY
RD.

SELWORTHY

ROAD

BREEZE

Dunes

HILLS

GREENBANK
DR.

TRAFALGAR
RD.

CROMER

DOVER

BIRKDALE

HILLS

Hillside
Greenbank
High Sch.

Playing
Fields

HASTINGS
RD.

HILLSIDE

RD.

ROYAL BIRKDALE
GOLF COURSE

Club
House

Hillside

Club
House

HASTINGS

LYNTON

DRIVE

COASTAL

BIRKDALE

Rugby
Pav. Football
Grd.

Recreation
Gound

HILLSIDE
GOLF COURSE

LYNTON
ROAD

A565 S

DUNSTER

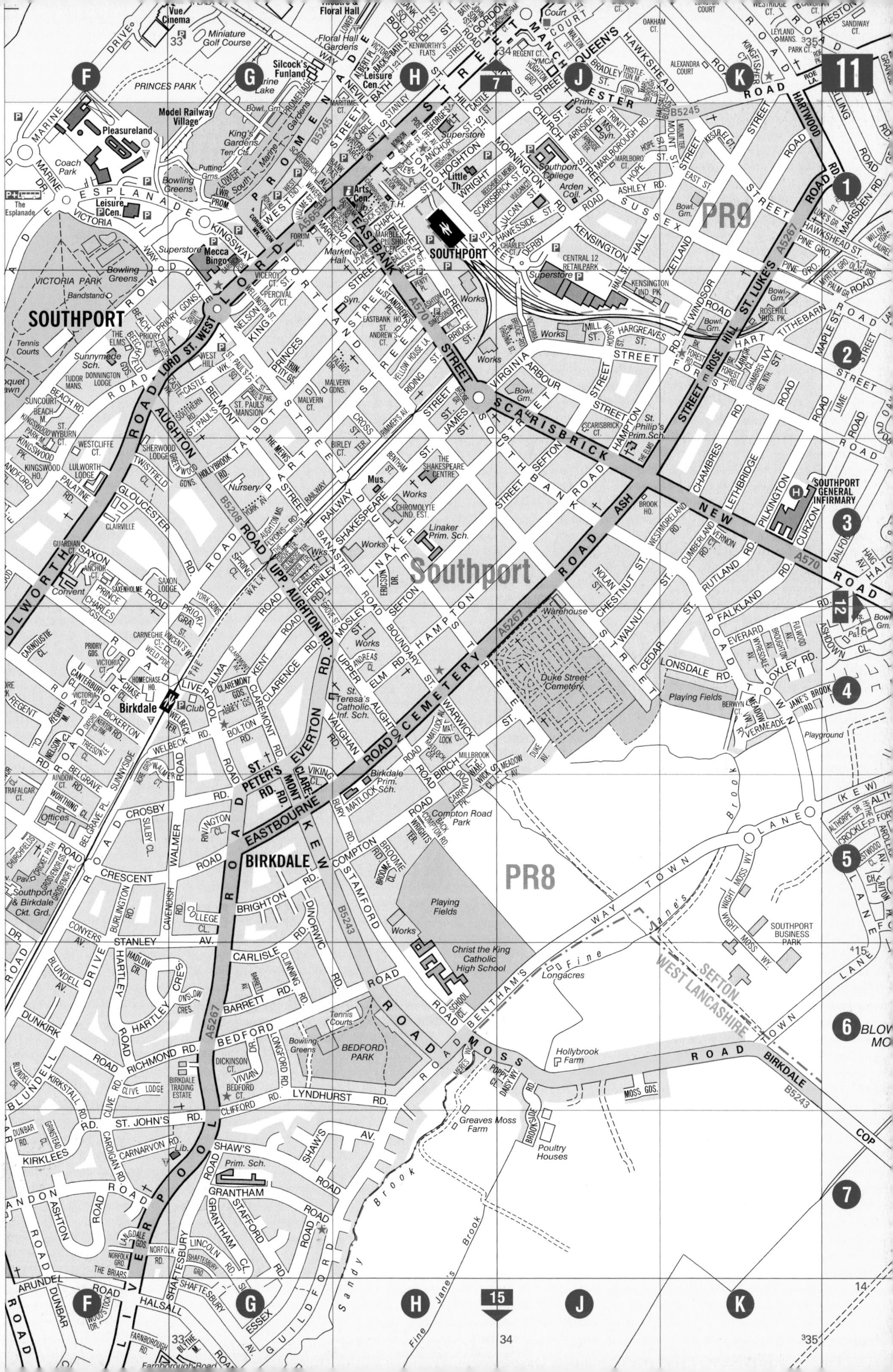
SOUTHPORT
Southport
BIRKDALE
PR9
PR8
Pleasureland
PRINCES PARK
VICTORIA PARK
Model Railway Village
Miniature Golf Course
Vue Cinema
Silcock's Funland
Floral Hall Gardens
Leisure Cen.
Mecca Bingo
Arts Cen.
Market Hall
SOUTHPORT
Southport College
Arden Coll.
Little Th.
CENTRAL 12 RETAIL PARK
KENSINGTON IND. PK.
ROSEHILL BUS. PK.
SOUTHPORT GENERAL INFIRMARY
THE SHAKESPEARE CENTRE
CHROMOLYTE IND. EST.
Linaker Prim. Sch.
St. Philip's Prim. Sch.
St. Teresa's Catholic Inf. Sch.
Birkdale Prim. Sch.
Duke Street Cemetery
Playing Fields
Compton Road Park
Christ the King Catholic High School
BEDFORD PARK
Hollybrook Farm
Greaves Moss Farm
Poultry Houses
Longacres
SOUTHPORT BUSINESS PARK
SEFTON
WEST LANCASHIRE
Southport & Birkdale Ckt. Grd.
BIRKDALE TRADING ESTATE
Birkdale
LORD STREET
LORD ST. WEST
PROMENADE
ESPLANADE
KINGSWAY
EASTBANK STREET
SCARISBRICK NEW ROAD
ASH STREET
ROSE HILL
ST. LUKE'S ROAD
HARTWOOD RD.
QUEEN'S ROAD
MANCHESTER ROAD
CEMETERY ROAD
EASTBOURNE ROAD
LIVERPOOL ROAD
WATERLOO ROAD
AUGHTON ROAD
UPP. AUGHTON RD.
EVERTON RD.
KEW ROAD
BEDFORD ROAD
MOSS ROAD
BIRKDALE ROAD
TOWN LANE
WAY TOWN LANE
BENTHAM'S WAY
A565
A570
A5267
B5245
B5208
B5243
F
G
H
J
K
1
2
3
4
5
6
7
7
12
15
33
34
35
14

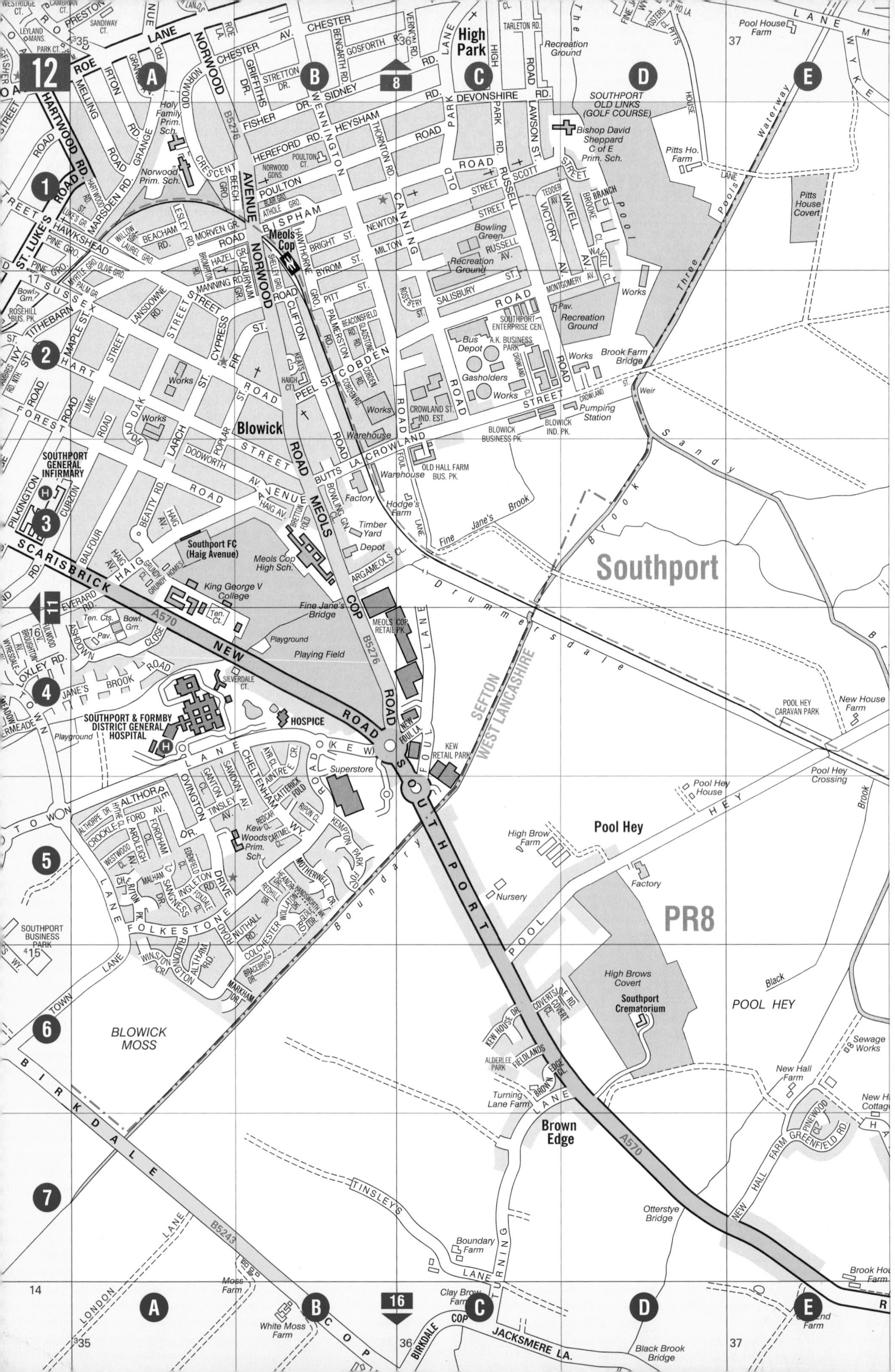
12
8
11
16
A
B
C
D
E
1
2
3
4
5
6
7
35
36
37
14
15
16
17
High Park
Blowick
Southport
PR8
Pool Hey
POOL HEY
Brown Edge
BLOWICK MOSS
SOUTHPORT OLD LINKS (GOLF COURSE)
Bishop David Sheppard C of E Prim. Sch.
Holy Family Prim. Sch.
Norwood Prim. Sch.
Meols Cop
SOUTHPORT GENERAL INFIRMARY
Southport FC (Haig Avenue)
Meols Cop High Sch.
King George V College
SOUTHPORT & FORMBY DISTRICT GENERAL HOSPITAL
HOSPICE
Kew Woods Prim. Sch.
SOUTHPORT BUSINESS PARK
MEOLS COP RETAIL PK.
KEW RETAIL PARK
Superstore
SOUTHPORT ENTERPRISE CEN.
A.K. BUSINESS PARK
Bus Depot
Gasholders
CROWLAND ST. IND. EST.
BLOWICK BUSINESS PK.
BLOWICK IND. PK.
OLD HALL FARM BUS. PK.
Pumping Station
Brook Farm Bridge
Fine Jane's Bridge
Playing Field
Recreation Ground
Bowling Green
High Brows Covert
Southport Crematorium
Pitts House Covert
Pitts Ho. Farm
Pool House Farm
New House Farm
POOL HEY CARAVAN PARK
Pool Hey Crossing
Pool Hey House
High Brow Farm
Nursery
Factory
Sewage Works
New Hall Farm
Turning Lane Farm
Otterstye Bridge
Boundary Farm
Clay Brow Farm
Moss Farm
White Moss Farm
Black Brook Bridge
SEFTON
WEST LANCASHIRE
Three Pools Waterway
Drummersdale
Sandy Brook
Fine Jane's Brook
Boundary
A570
B5276
B5243
NEW ROAD
SCARISBRICK NEW ROAD
SOUTHPORT ROAD
MEOLS COP ROAD
NORWOOD AVENUE
NORWOOD ROAD
HARTWOOD RD.
ST. LUKE'S ROAD
BIRKDALE COP
JACKSMERE LA.
TOWN LANE
POOL HEY LANE
TURNING LANE
NEW HALL FARM

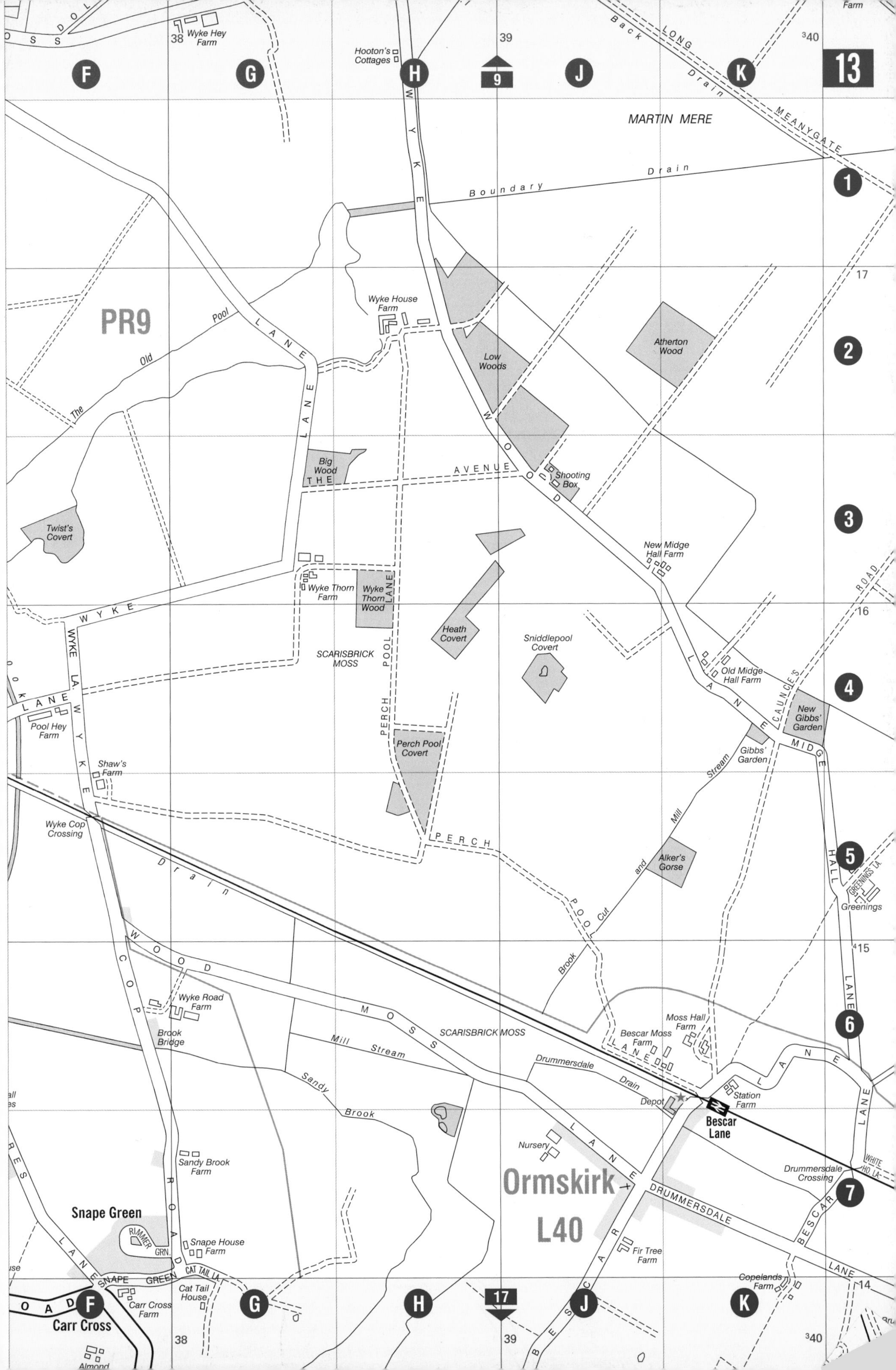

Wyke Hey Farm
Hooton's Cottages
MARTIN MERE
Back Long Drain
MEANYGATE
Boundary Drain
PR9
The Old Pool
WYKE LANE
Wyke House Farm
Low Woods
Atherton Wood
Big Wood
THE AVENUE
Shooting Box
WOOD
Twist's Covert
New Midge Hall Farm
Wyke Thorn Farm
Wyke Thorn Wood
PERCH POOL LANE
Heath Covert
Sniddlepool Covert
SCARISBRICK MOSS
WYKE LA.
Pool Hey Farm
Old Midge Hall Farm
CAUNCE'S ROAD
New Gibbs' Garden
Gibbs' Garden
MIDGE HALL LANE
Shaw's Farm
Perch Pool Covert
Wyke Cop Crossing
PERCH POOL
Mill Stream and Pool Cut
Alker's Gorse
Greenings
GREENINGS LA.
Drain
WOOD
COP ROAD
Brook
Wyke Road Farm
Brook Bridge
MOSS LANE
SCARISBRICK MOSS
Moss Hall Farm
Bescar Moss Farm
Mill Stream
Drummersdale Drain
Sandy Brook
Depot
Station Farm
Bescar Lane
Nursery
Sandy Brook Farm
Ormskirk
L40
Drummersdale Crossing
WHITE HO. LA.
DRUMMERSDALE LANE
Snape Green
RIMMER GRN.
Snape House Farm
Fir Tree Farm
BESCAR LANE
BESCAR
SNAPE GREEN
CAT TAIL LA.
Cat Tail House
Copelands Farm
Carr Cross Farm
Carr Cross
Almond
F
G
H
J
K
1
2
3
4
5
6
7
9
17
38
39
340
17
16
415
14

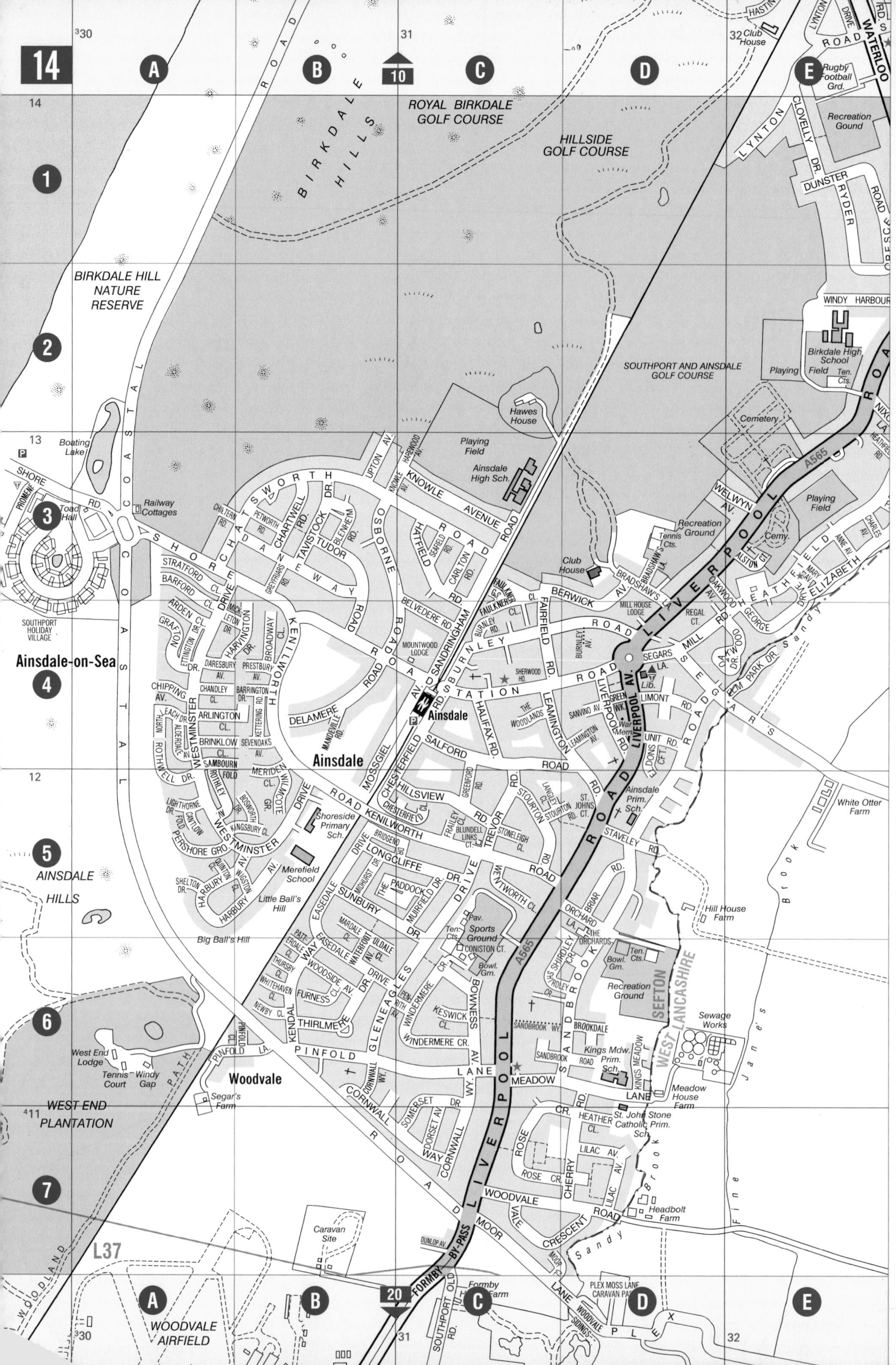

ROYAL BIRKDALE GOLF COURSE
HILLSIDE GOLF COURSE
BIRKDALE HILLS
BIRKDALE HILL NATURE RESERVE
SOUTHPORT AND AINSDALE GOLF COURSE
Birkdale High School
Playing Field
Ainsdale High Sch.
Hawes House
Ainsdale-on-Sea
SOUTHPORT HOLIDAY VILLAGE
Boating Lake
Toad Hall
Railway Cottages
Ainsdale
Shoreside Primary Sch.
Merefield School
Little Ball's Hill
Big Ball's Hill
AINSDALE HILLS
Sports Ground
Recreation Ground
Ainsdale Prim. Sch.
Kings Mdw. Prim. Sch.
St. John Stone Catholic Prim. Sch.
SEFTON
WEST LANCASHIRE
Sewage Works
Meadow House Farm
Hill House Farm
White Otter Farm
Headbolt Farm
Woodvale
West End Lodge
WEST END PLANTATION
Segar's Farm
Caravan Site
WOODVALE AIRFIELD
PLEX MOSS LANE CARAVAN PARK
Formby Hall Farm
FORMBY BY-PASS
LIVERPOOL ROAD
COASTAL ROAD
SHORE RD.
KENILWORTH ROAD
STATION ROAD
BURNLEY ROAD
WOODVALE ROAD
PINFOLD LANE
MEADOW LANE
MOOR LANE
A565
L37

10
20

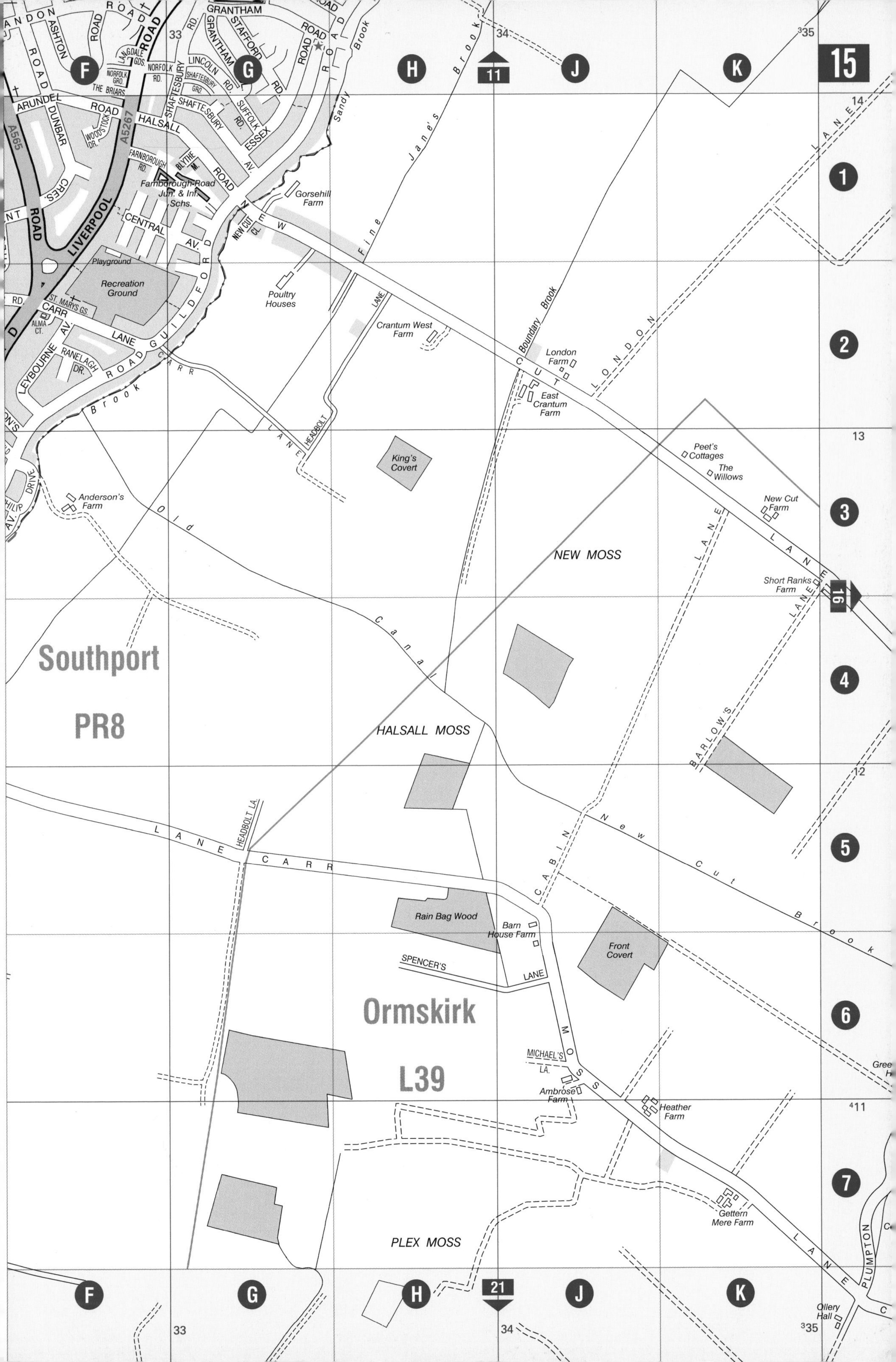
Southport
PR8
Ormskirk
L39
NEW MOSS
HALSALL MOSS
PLEX MOSS
Recreation Ground
Playground
Farnborough Road Jun. & Inf. Schs.
Gorsehill Farm
Poultry Houses
Crantum West Farm
London Farm
East Crantum Farm
King's Covert
Peet's Cottages
The Willows
New Cut Farm
Short Ranks Farm
Anderson's Farm
Rain Bag Wood
Barn House Farm
Front Covert
Ambrose Farm
Heather Farm
Gettern Mere Farm
Ollery Hall
NEW CUT LANE
LONDON LANE
BARLOW'S LANE
CABIN LANE
MOSS LANE
CARR LANE
HEADBOLT LANE
HEADBOLT LA.
SPENCER'S LANE
MICHAEL'S LA.
PLUMPTON
Old Canal
New Cut Brook
Fine Jane's Brook
Boundary Brook
Sandy Brook
Carr Brook
LIVERPOOL ROAD
A5267
A565
GUILDFORD ROAD
HALSALL ROAD
CENTRAL AV.
CARR LANE
ARUNDEL ROAD
DUNBAR CRES.
WOODSTOCK DR.
FARNBOROUGH RD.
BLYTHE M.
SHAFTESBURY RD.
SHAFTESBURY GRO.
LINCOLN RD.
SUFFOLK RD.
ESSEX AV.
GRANTHAM RD.
STAFFORD RD.
ASHTON ROAD
LANGDALE GDS.
NORFOLK RD.
NORFOLK GRO.
THE BRIARS
ST. MARYS GS.
ALMA CT.
LEYBOURNE AV.
RANELAGH DR.
NEW CUT CL.
F G H J K
1 2 3 4 5 6 7
33 34 35
11 12 13 14
11 16 21

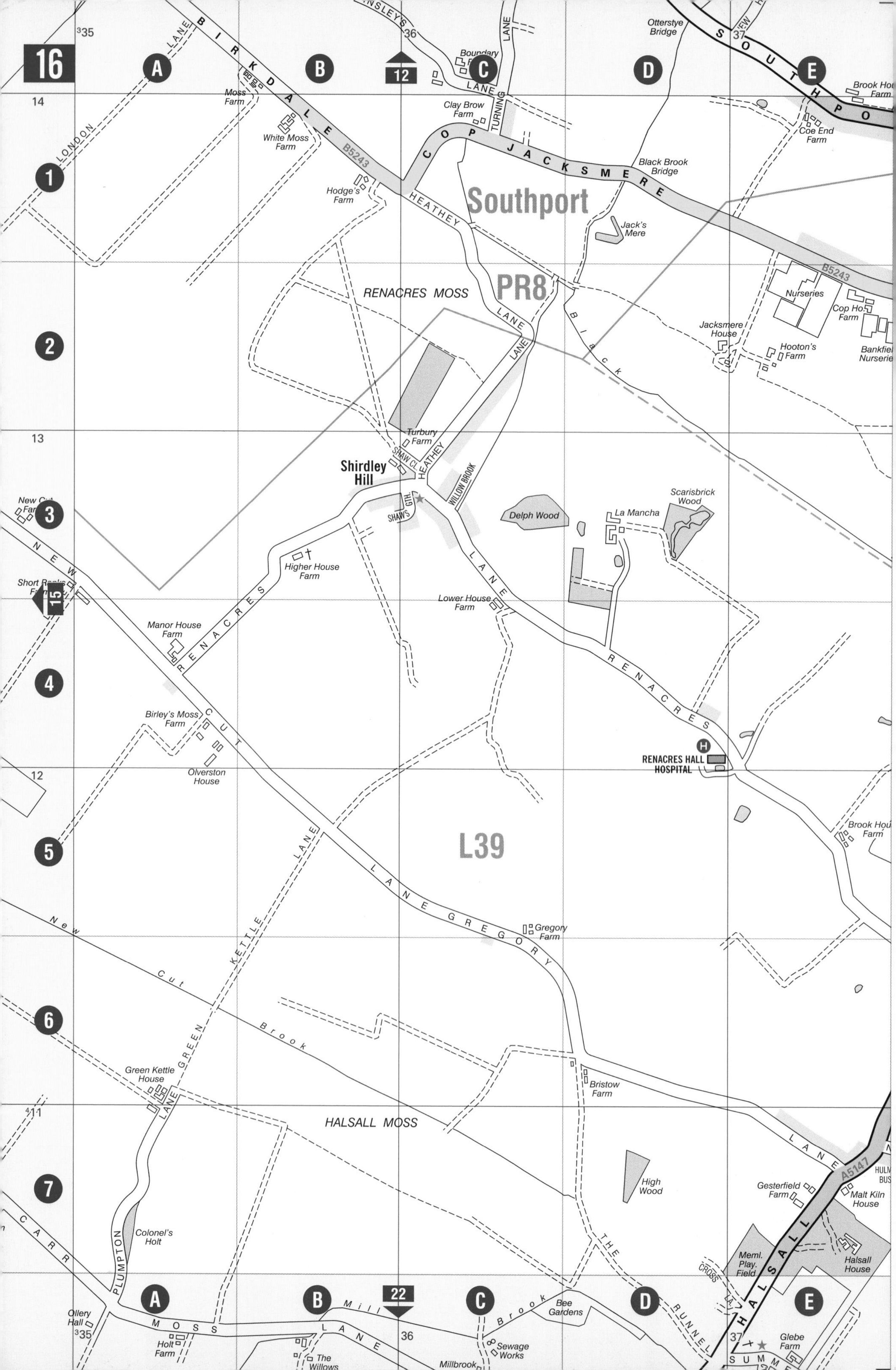

Southport
PR8
L39
RENACRES MOSS
HALSALL MOSS
Shirdley Hill
Moss Farm
White Moss Farm
Hodge's Farm
Clay Brow Farm
Boundary Farm
Otterstye Bridge
Black Brook Bridge
Jack's Mere
Coe End Farm
Brook House Farm
Nurseries
Cop House Farm
Jacksmere House
Hooton's Farm
Bankfield Nurseries
Turbury Farm
New Cut Farm
Short Ranks Farm
Delph Wood
La Mancha
Scarisbrick Wood
Higher House Farm
Lower House Farm
Manor House Farm
Birley's Moss Farm
Olverston House
RENACRES HALL HOSPITAL
Brook House Farm
Gregory Farm
Green Kettle House
Bristow Farm
High Wood
Gesterfield Farm
Malt Kiln House
Colonel's Holt
Meml. Play. Field
Halsall House
Ollery Hall
Holt Farm
The Willows
Bee Gardens
Sewage Works
Millbrook
Glebe Farm
BIRKDALE LANE
LONDON LANE
COP JACKSMERE
HEATHEY LANE
TURNING LANE
B5243
A5147
SHAW CL.
WILLOW BROOK
SHAWS GTH.
RENACRES LANE
NEW CUT LANE
GREGORY LANE
GREEN KETTLE LANE
PLUMPTON LANE
MOSS LANE
CARR
New Cut Brook
Mill Brook
THE RUNNEL
HALSALL
CROSS LA.
SOUTHPORT
NEW
Black Brook
12
15
22

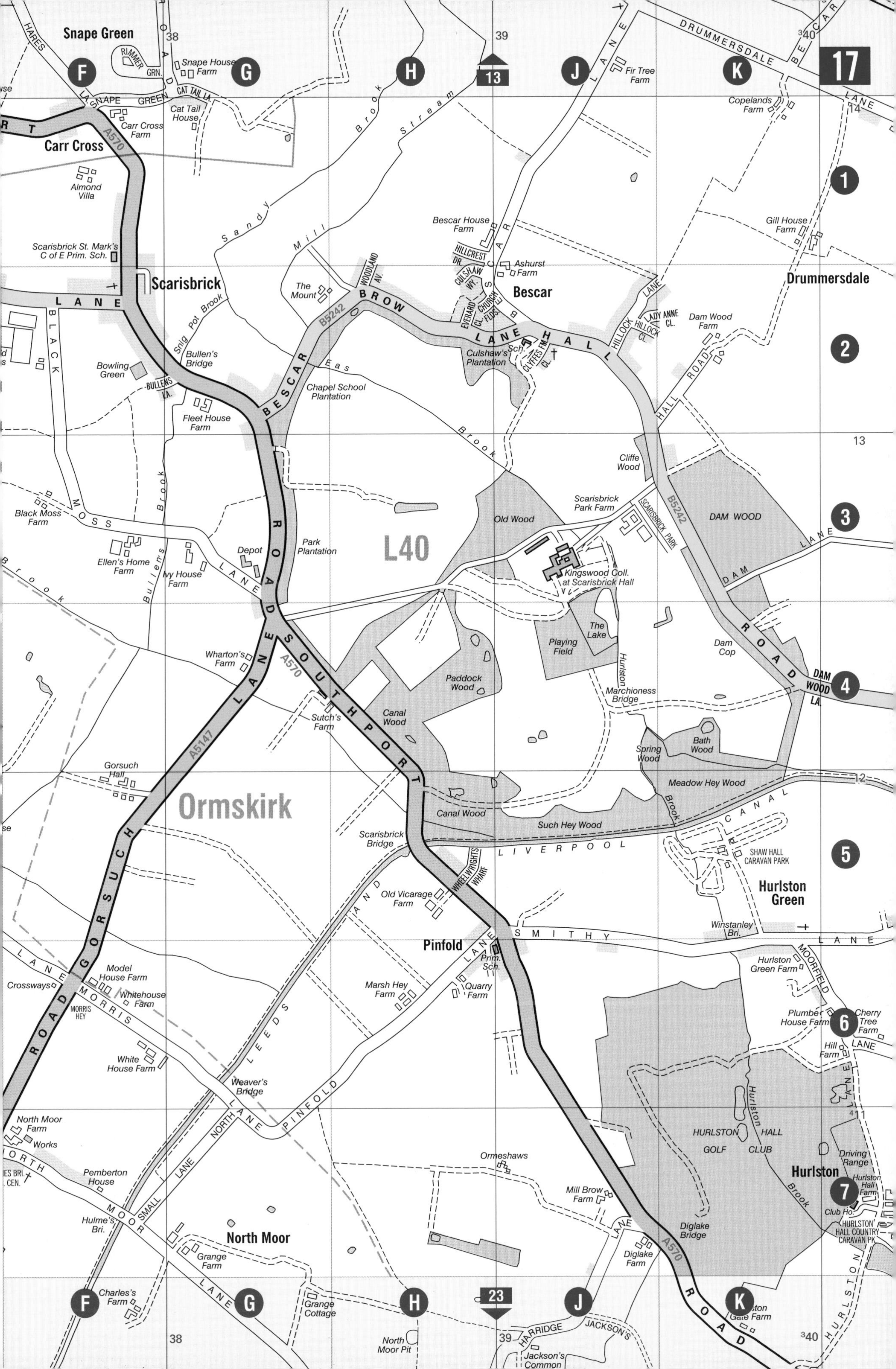

Snape Green
Carr Cross
Almond Villa
Scarisbrick St. Mark's C of E Prim. Sch.
Scarisbrick
Bowling Green
Bullen's Bridge
Fleet House Farm
Black Moss Farm
Ellen's Home Farm
Ivy House Farm
Depot
Park Plantation
Chapel School Plantation
The Mount
Bescar House Farm
Ashurst Farm
Bescar
Culshaw's Plantation
Drummersdale
Gill House Farm
Copelands Farm
Fir Tree Farm
Dam Wood Farm
Cliffe Wood
Scarisbrick Park Farm
Old Wood
DAM WOOD
L40
Kingswood Coll. at Scarisbrick Hall
The Lake
Playing Field
Dam Cop
Wharton's Farm
Paddock Wood
Canal Wood
Sutch's Farm
Marchioness Bridge
Spring Wood
Bath Wood
Meadow Hey Wood
Gorsuch Hall
Ormskirk
Canal Wood
Such Hey Wood
Scarisbrick Bridge
SHAW HALL CARAVAN PARK
Hurlston Green
Old Vicarage Farm
Winstanley Bri.
Pinfold
Prim. Sch.
Quarry Farm
Marsh Hey Farm
Hurlston Green Farm
Plumbe Farm House
Cherry Tree Farm
Hill Farm
Model House Farm
Crossways
Whitehouse Farm
MORRIS HEY
White House Farm
Weaver's Bridge
HURLSTON GOLF
HALL CLUB
Driving Range
Hurlston
Hurlston Hall Farm
Club Ho.
HURLSTON HALL COUNTRY CARAVAN PK
North Moor Farm
Works
Pemberton House
Ormeshaws
Mill Brow Farm
Hulme's Bri.
North Moor
Grange Farm
Diglake Bridge
Diglake Farm
Charles's Farm
Grange Cottage
North Moor Pit
Jackson's Common
Gate Farm
HARES LA
RIMMER GRN.
SNAPE GREEN
CAT TAIL LA.
Snape House Farm
Cat Tail House
Carr Cross Farm
A570
LANE
BLACK
BULLENS LA.
MOSS LANE
Bullen's Brook
Snig Pot Brook
Sandy Brook
Mill Brook Stream
Eas Brook
B5242
BESCAR BROW LANE
WOODLAND AV.
HILLCREST DR.
CULSHAW WY.
EVERARD CL.
CHURCH FLDS.
CLYFFES FM. CL.
Sch.
HALL
HILLOCK LANE
LADY ANNE CL.
HILLOCK CL.
HALL ROAD
DRUMMERSDALE LANE
BESCAR LANE
SCARISBRICK PARK
DAM LANE
DAM WOOD LA.
ROAD
SOUTHPORT ROAD
A5147
GORSUCH LANE
GORSUCH ROAD
LIVERPOOL CANAL
WHEELWRIGHTS WHARF
LEEDS AND
SMITHY LANE
MOORFIELD
LANE
MORRIS LANE
PINFOLD
NORTH LANE
SMALL LANE
NORTH MOOR LANE
HARRIDGE
JACKSON'S
HURLSTON LANE
Hurlston Brook
Brook
F G H J K
1 2 3 4 5 6 7
13
23
38 39 340
14 13 12 411

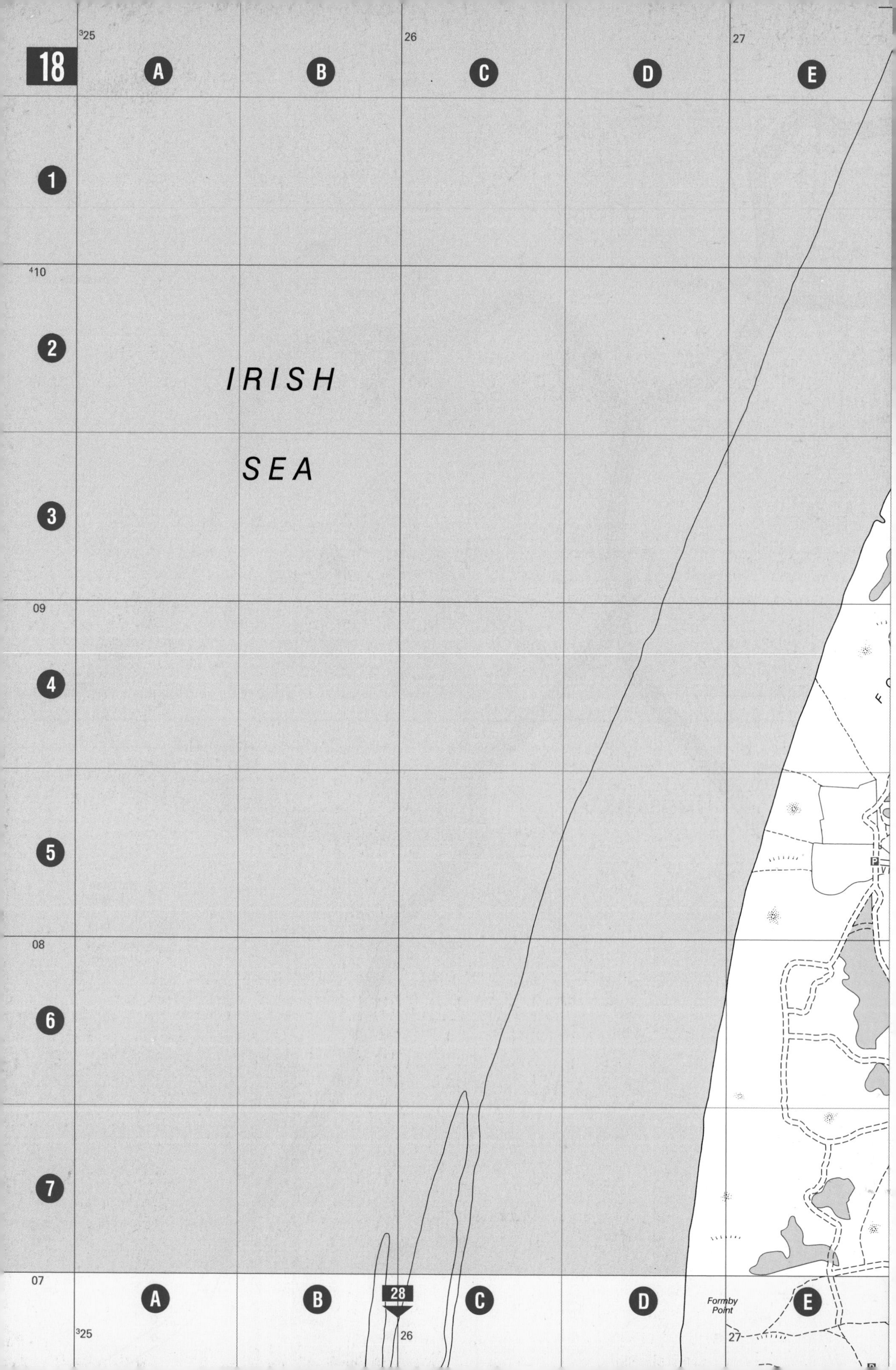

18

A　B　C　D　E

³25　26　27

1

⁴10

2

IRISH

SEA

3

09

4

5

08

6

7

07

A　B　28　C　D　*Formby Point*　E

³25　26　27

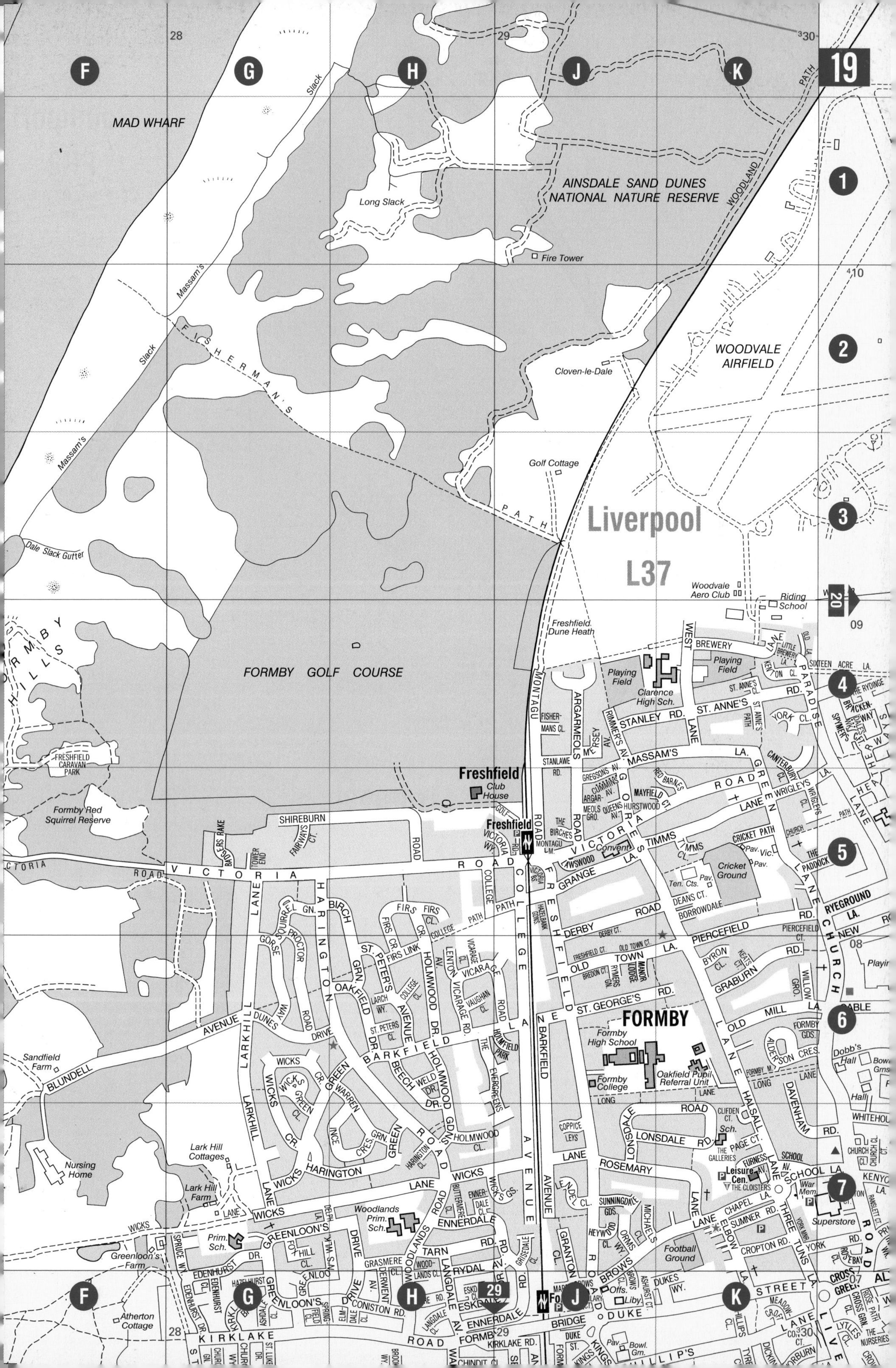

28
29
30
F
G
H
J
K
1
2
3
4
5
6
7
10
09
08
07
20
MAD WHARF
Slack
Long Slack
AINSDALE SAND DUNES
NATIONAL NATURE RESERVE
Fire Tower
WOODLAND PATH
Massam's Slack
FISHERMAN'S PATH
WOODVALE
AIRFIELD
Cloven-le-Dale
Golf Cottage
Liverpool
L37
Dale Slack Gutter
FORMBY HILLS
Woodvale
Aero Club
Riding
School
Freshfield
Dune Heath
FORMBY GOLF COURSE
FRESHFIELD CARAVAN PARK
Formby Red
Squirrel Reserve
Freshfield
Club
House
Freshfield
SHIREBURN
BADGERS RAKE
FAIRWAYS CT.
TOWER END
VICTORIA ROAD
VICTORIA WY.
MONTAGU ROAD
WEST LANE
BREWERY
LITTLE BREWERY LA.
SIXTEEN ACRE LA.
PARADISE LANE
Playing Field
Clarence
High Sch.
Playing
Field
ST. ANNE'S RD.
ST. ANNE'S CL.
STANLEY RD.
FISHERMANS CL.
ARGARMEOLS
MERSEY AV.
RIMMER'S AV.
MASSAM'S LA.
GREEN LANE
STANLAWE RD.
GREGSONS AV.
CUMMINS AV.
MAYFIELD CT.
RED BARNES
ROAD
MEOLS GRO.
QUEENS AV.
HURSTWOOD CT.
WRIGLEYS LA.
THE BIRCHES
VICTORIA ROAD
Convent
TIMMS LA.
TIMMS CL.
CRICKET PATH
Cricket
Ground
THE PADDOCK
GRANGE
Ten. Cts.
DEANS CT.
BORROWDALE
RYEGROUND LA.
NEW RD.
DERBY ROAD
PIERCEFIELD RD.
OLD TOWN LA.
BYRON CL.
KEATS CT.
GRABURN RD.
WILLOW GRO.
CHURCH ROAD
ST. GEORGE'S RD.
FORMBY
Formby
High School
OLD MILL LA.
ALDERSON CRES.
Formby
College
Oakfield Pupil
Referral Unit
LONG LANE
DAVENHAM
ROAD
LONSDALE RD.
CLIFDEN CT.
Sch.
THE GALLERIES
PAGE CT.
ROSEMARY LANE
COPPICE LEYS
SUNNINGDALE GDS.
MICHAELS
HALSALL LANE
FURNESS AV.
Leisure
Cen.
THE CLOISTERS
SCHOOL LA.
War Mem.
Superstore
CHAPEL LA.
SUMNER RD.
THREE TUNS LA.
ELBOW LANE
CROPTON RD.
YORK RD.
Football
Ground
BROWS LANE
DUKES WY.
DUKE STREET
Offs.
Liby.
Formby
BRIDGE
DUKE ST.
KINGS RD.
Pav.
Bowl. Grn.
CROSS GREEN
COLLEGE AVENUE
FRESHFIELD ROAD
BARKFIELD LANE
BARKFIELD AVENUE
COLLEGE PATH
HARINGTON ROAD
BIRCH GN.
SQUIRREL GN.
GORSE WAY
PROCTOR ROAD
FIRS CR.
FIRS CL.
FIRS LINK
ST. PETER'S AVENUE
HOLMWOOD DR.
LENTON AV.
VICARAGE RD.
VAUGHAN CL.
OAKFIELD DR.
LARCH WY.
BEECH DR.
WELD DR.
HOLMFIELD PARK
THE EVERGREENS
LARKHILL LANE
DUNES DRIVE
BLUNDELL AVENUE
Sandfield
Farm
WICKS CR.
WICKS GREEN CL.
WARREN GREEN
INCE CRES.
HOLMWOOD CL.
HARINGTON CL.
WICKS LANE
HARINGTON
Lark Hill
Cottages
Nursing
Home
Lark Hill
Farm
Woodlands
Prim.
Sch.
ENNERDALE
WOODLANDS ROAD
TARN RD.
LANGDALE
RYDAL AV.
GRISEDALE
GRASMERE AV.
DERWENT AV.
GREENLOON'S DR.
FOX HILL CL.
DELPH LA.
Prim.
Sch.
SPRUCE WY.
EDENHURST DR.
Greenloon's
Farm
GREENLOON'S
HAZELHURST
ASHDALE
CONISTON RD.
ESKDALE
ENNERDALE RD.
Atherton
Cottage
KIRKLAKE ROAD
ENNERDALE
FORMBY
GRANTON CL.
ST. PHILIP'S
TYRER
MEADOW CROFT
LIVERPOOL
THE NURSERIES

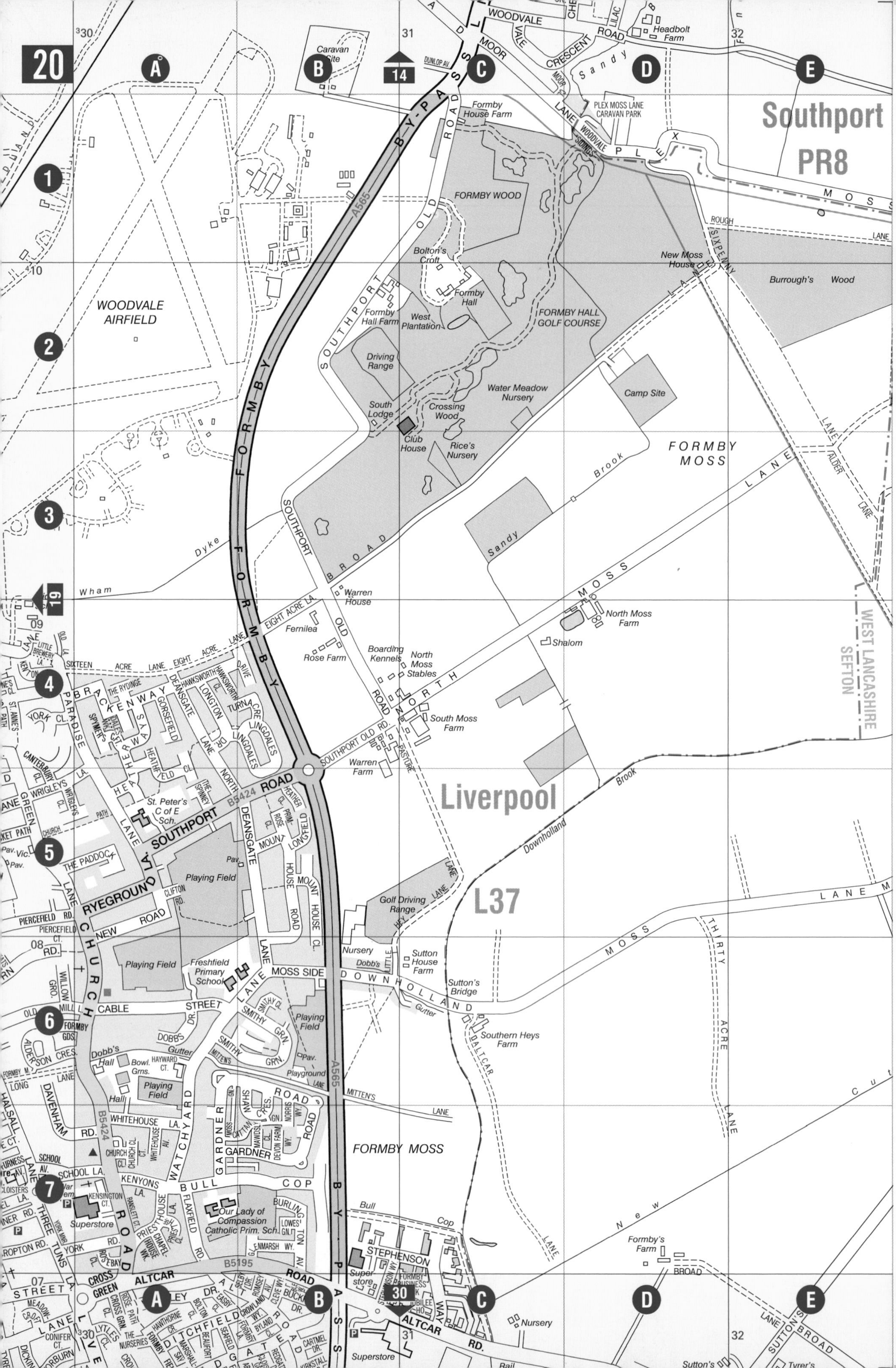
WOODVALE AIRFIELD
FORMBY BY-PASS
A565
Formby House Farm
FORMBY WOOD
Bolton's Croft
Formby Hall
Formby Hall Farm
West Plantation
FORMBY HALL GOLF COURSE
Driving Range
South Lodge
Club House
Crossing Wood
Water Meadow Nursery
Rice's Nursery
Camp Site
New Moss House
Burrough's Wood
PLEX MOSS LANE CARAVAN PARK
Headbolt Farm
Southport
PR8
FORMBY MOSS
Warren House
Fernilea
Rose Farm
Boarding Kennels
North Moss Stables
North Moss Farm
Shalom
South Moss Farm
Warren Farm
Liverpool
L37
WEST LANCASHIRE
SEFTON
Golf Driving Range
Nursery
Sutton House Farm
Sutton's Bridge
Southern Heys Farm
FORMBY MOSS
Formby's Farm
St. Peter's C of E Sch.
Playing Field
Freshfield Primary School
Our Lady of Compassion Catholic Prim. Sch.
Superstore
Wham Dyke
Downholland Brook
New Cut
SOUTHPORT ROAD
B5424
B5195
ALTCAR ROAD
MOSS SIDE
DOWNHOLLAND
CABLE STREET
BULL COP
STEPHENSON WAY
THIRTY ACRE LANE
SIXPENNY LANE
NORTH MOSS LANE
MOSS LANE
SIXTEEN ACRE LANE
EIGHT ACRE LANE
CHURCH ROAD
RYEGROUND LA.
SOUTHPORT OLD RD.
WOODVALE ROAD
14
19
30

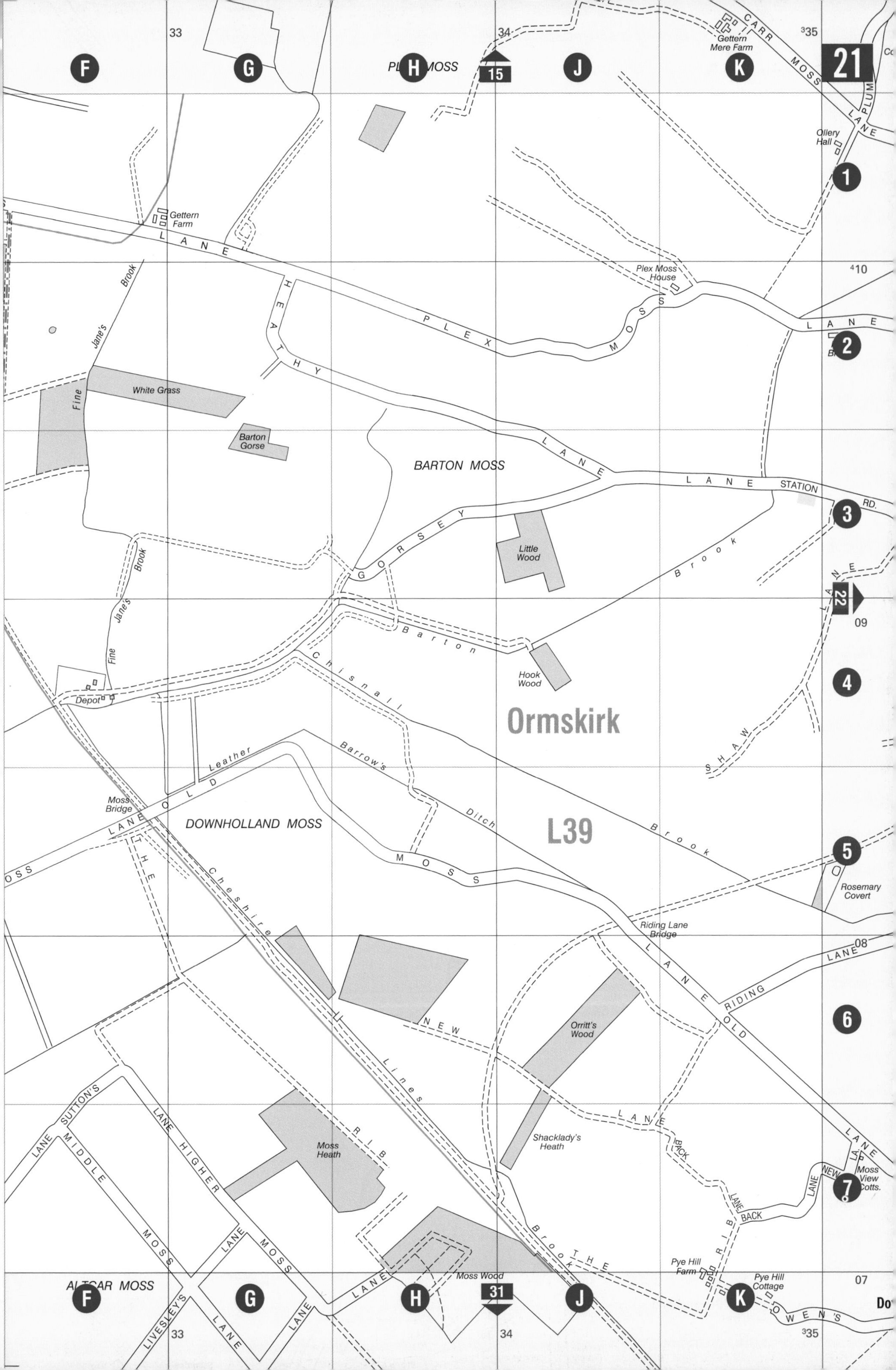

F G PLEX MOSS H 15 J Gettern Mere Farm K

Carr Moss Lane

Plum Lane

Co

33 34 335

Ollery Hall

1

Gettern Farm

LANE

HEATHY LANE

PLEX MOSS LANE

Plex Moss House

410

2

Br

Jane's Brook

Fine Brook

White Grass

Barton Gorse

BARTON MOSS

GORSEY LANE

LANE STATION RD.

Brook

3

LANE

22
09

Jane's Brook

Fine Lane

Little Wood

Barton

4

Depot

CHISNALL LANE

Hook Wood

Ormskirk

Moss Bridge

OLD LANE

Leather

Barrow's

Ditch

MOSS

Ormskirk

SHAW

L39

Brook

5

Rosemary Covert

HETHE

Cheshire

DOWNHOLLAND MOSS

Riding Lane Bridge

RIDING LANE

OLD LANE

Lane 08

6

SUTTON'S LANE

MIDDLE MOSS LANE

HIGHER LANE

Lines

NEW

Orritt's Wood

BACK LANE

Moss Heath

RIBI

Shacklady's Heath

NEW LANE

RIB

Moss View Cotts.

7

ALTCAR MOSS F

LIVESLEYS LANE

MOSS LANE G

MOSS LANE

Moss Wood

H 31 THE Brook J

Pye Hill Farm

BACK LANE

OWEN'S

Pye Hill Cottage

K

07

Do

07

33 34 335

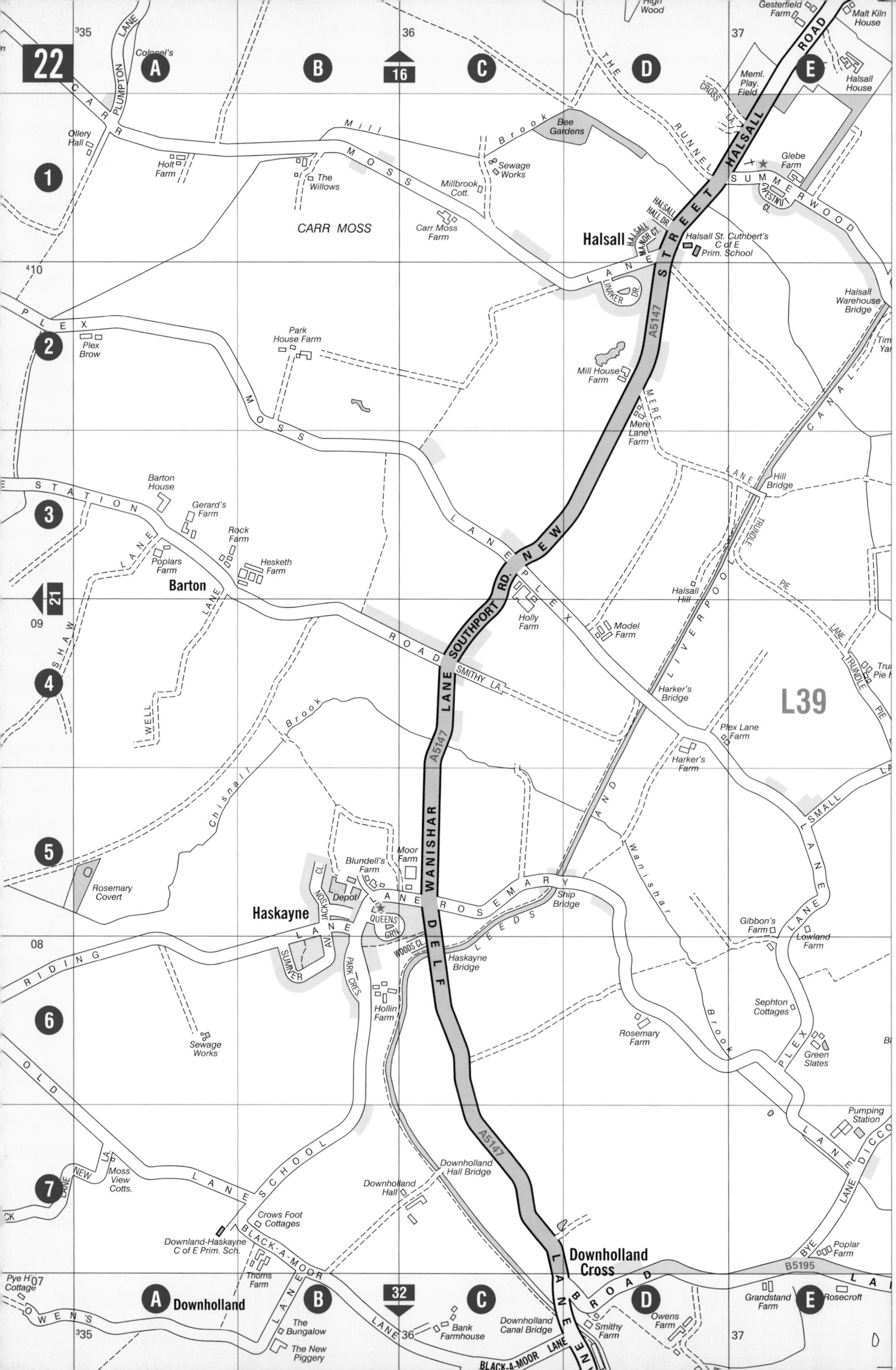

Colonel's
Gesterfield Farm
Malt Kiln House
High Wood
Meml. Play. Field
Halsall House
Ollery Hall
Holt Farm
The Willows
Bee Gardens
Sewage Works
Millbrook Cott.
Glebe Farm
CARR MOSS
Carr Moss Farm
Halsall
Halsall St. Cuthbert's C of E Prim. School
Halsall Warehouse Bridge
Plex Brow
Park House Farm
Mill House Farm
Mere Lane Farm
Hill Bridge
Barton House
Gerard's Farm
Rock Farm
Poplars Farm
Hesketh Farm
Barton
Halsall Hill
Holly Farm
Model Farm
Harker's Bridge
L39
Plex Lane Farm
Harker's Farm
Rosemary Covert
Blundell's Farm
Moor Farm
Depot
Haskayne
Ship Bridge
Gibbon's Farm
Lowland Farm
Haskayne Bridge
Hollin Farm
Sephton Cottages
Rosemary Farm
Sewage Works
Green Slates
Pumping Station
Moss View Cotts.
Downholland Hall Bridge
Downholland Hall
Crows Foot Cottages
Downland-Haskayne C of E Prim. Sch.
Downholland Cross
Poplar Farm
Thorns Farm
Pye H. Cottage
Downholland
Grandstand Farm
Rosecroft
Owens Farm
The Bungalow
The New Piggery
Bank Farmhouse
Downholland Canal Bridge
Smithy Farm
CARR LANE
PLUMPTON LANE
MILL
MOSS LANE
BROOK
THE RUNNEL
CROSS LA.
HALSALL ROAD
STREET
SUMMERWOOD
CHESTNUT CL.
HALSALL HALL DR.
HALSALL MANOR CT.
LINAKER DR.
PLEX MOSS LANE
NEW SOUTHPORT RD.
A5147
MERE LANE
LIVERPOOL AND LEEDS CANAL
STATION ROAD
BARTON LANE
SHAW LANE
WELL LANE
SMITHY LA.
TRUNDLE PIE LANE
PLEX LANE
SMALL LANE
WANISHAR LANE
DELF LANE
ROSEMARY LANE
Chisnall Brook
Wanishar Brook
JACKSON CL.
JACKSON AVE.
QUEENS GRN.
WOODS CL.
SUMMER
PARK CRES.
RIDING LANE
OLD SCHOOL LANE
NEW LA.
BLACK-A-MOOR LANE
DICCONSON LANE
BYE LANE
B5195
OWEN'S LANE
BROAD LANE
16
21
32
35
36
37
410
09
08
07

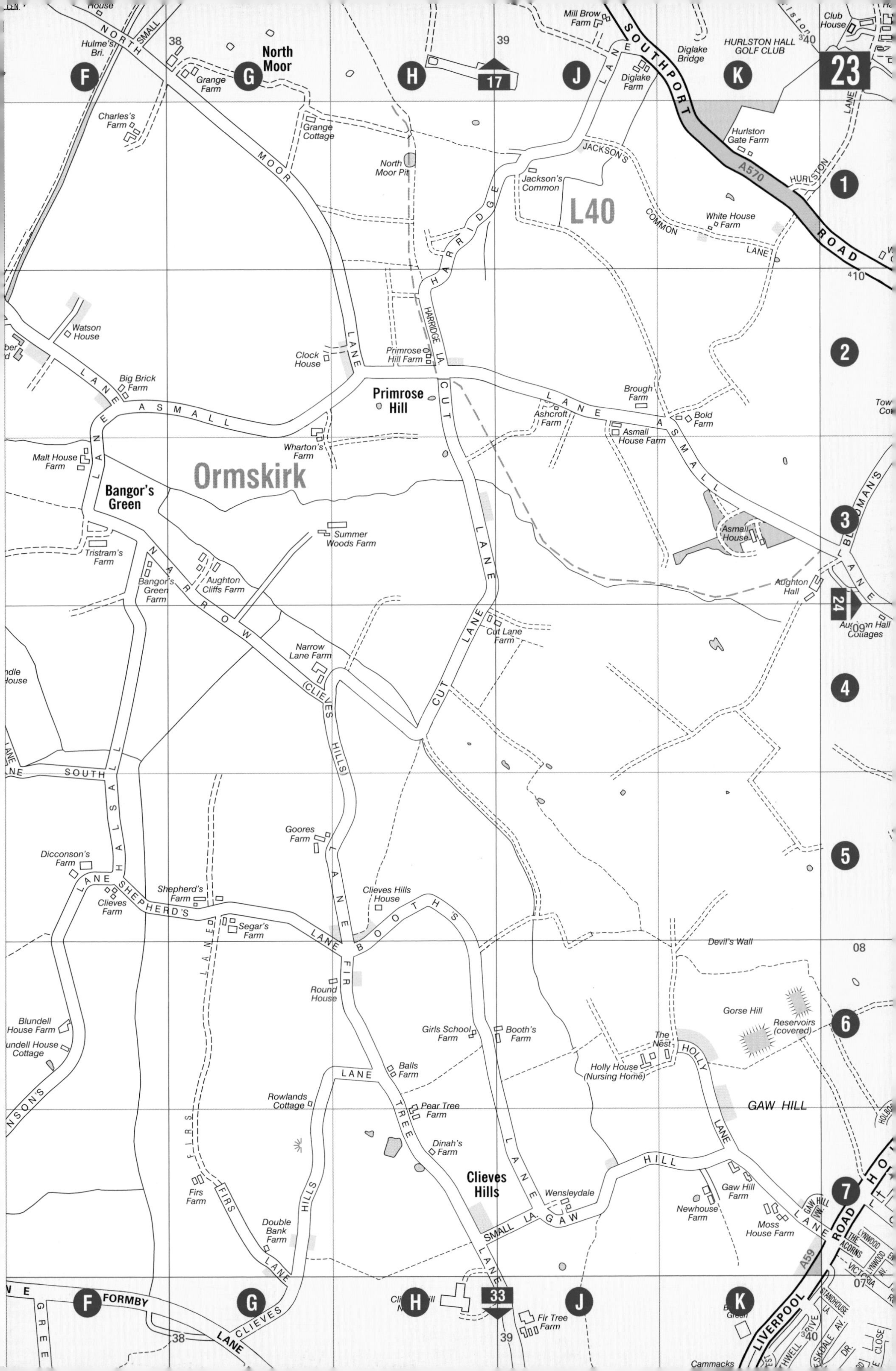
23
North Moor
Grange Farm
Charles's Farm
Hulme's Bri.
NORTH MOOR LANE
SMALL
Grange Cottage
North Moor Pit
17
Mill Brow Farm
Diglake Bridge
Diglake Farm
HURLSTON HALL GOLF CLUB
Club House
SOUTHPORT ROAD
A570
Hurlston Gate Farm
HURLSTON
Jackson's Common
JACKSON'S COMMON LANE
L40
White House Farm
HARRIDGE LA.
Watson House
Big Brick Farm
Clock House
Primrose Hill Farm
Primrose Hill
Brough Farm
Bold Farm
Ashcroft Farm
Asmall House Farm
ASMALL LANE
Wharton's Farm
Malt House Farm
Ormskirk
Bangor's Green
Summer Woods Farm
Tristram's Farm
Bangor's Green Farm
Aughton Cliffs Farm
NARROW LANE
Asmall House
Aughton Hall
BLOWMAN'S LANE
24
Aughton Hall Cottages
Cut Lane Farm
CUT LANE
Narrow Lane Farm
(CLIEVES HILLS)
SOUTH
HALSALL LANE
Goores Farm
Dicconson's Farm
Clieves Farm
Shepherd's Farm
SHEPHERD'S LANE
Segar's Farm
Clieves Hills House
BOOTH'S LANE
Devil's Wall
FIR LANE
Round House
Gorse Hill
Reservoirs (covered)
Blundell House Farm
Girls School Farm
Booth's Farm
The Nest
HOLLY LANE
Holly House (Nursing Home)
Balls Farm
Rowlands Cottage
Pear Tree Farm
TREE LANE
GAW HILL
Dinah's Farm
Clieves Hills
GAW HILL
Firs Farm
FIRS LANE
HILLS
Wensleydale
Newhouse Farm
Gaw Hill Farm
Moss House Farm
Double Bank Farm
SMALL LA.
GAW HILL LANE
A59
LIVERPOOL ROAD
FORMBY
CLIEVES LANE
33
Fir Tree Farm
Cammacks
38
39
40
410
08
07
09
F
G
H
J
K
1
2
3
4
5
6
7

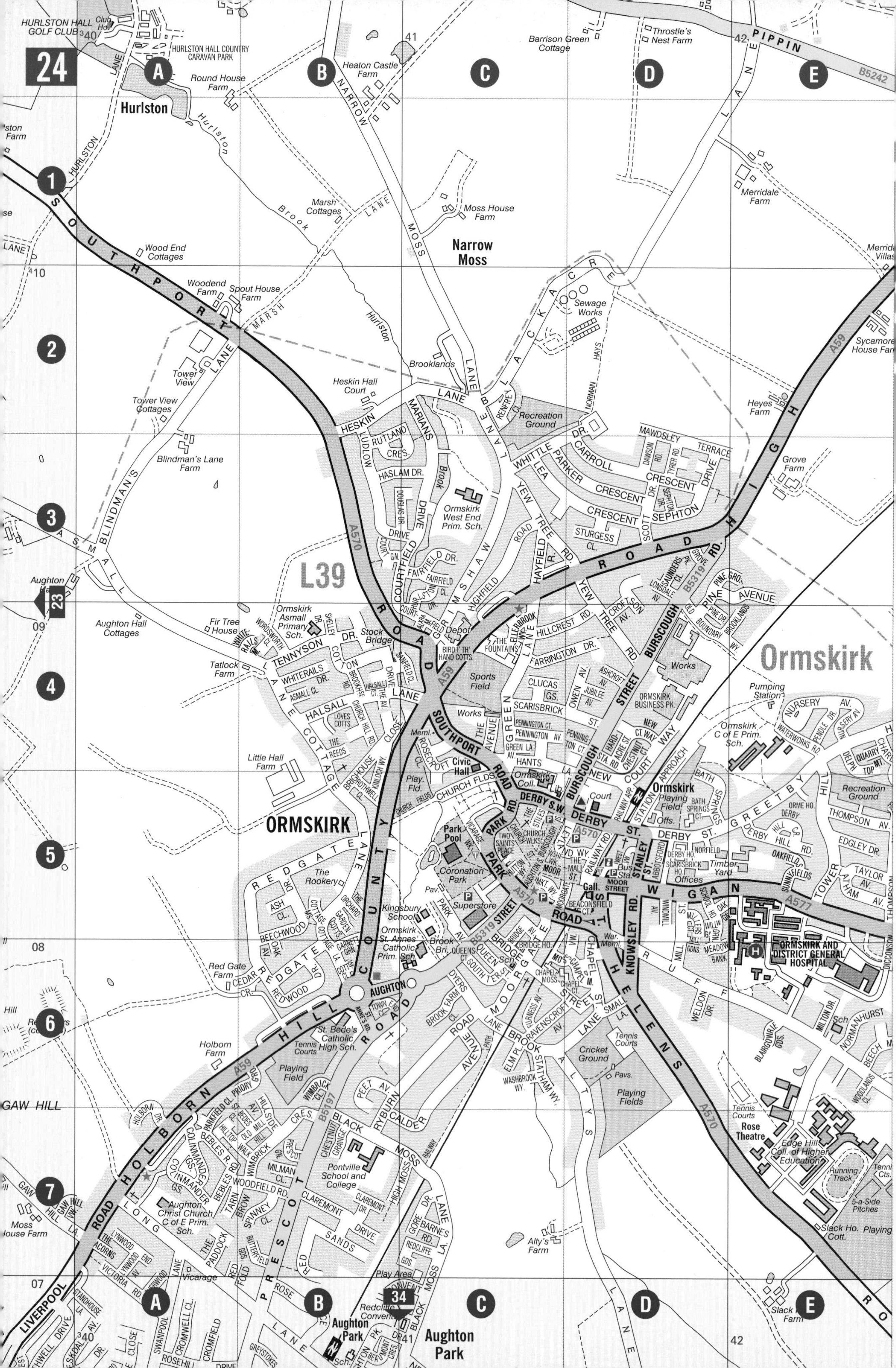

24
HURLSTON HALL GOLF CLUB
HURLSTON HALL COUNTRY CARAVAN PARK
Hurlston
Round House Farm
Heaton Castle Farm
Barrison Green Cottage
Throstle's Nest Farm
PIPPIN
B5242
Merridale Farm
Marsh Cottages
Moss House Farm
Narrow Moss
Wood End Cottages
Woodend Farm
Spout House Farm
Sewage Works
Brooklands
Heskin Hall Court
Tower View
Tower View Cottages
Blindman's Lane Farm
Recreation Ground
Heyes Farm
Grove Farm
Sycamore House Farm
Ormskirk West End Prim. Sch.
L39
Aughton Hall Cottages
Fir Tree House
Ormskirk Asmall Primary Sch.
Tatlock Farm
Sports Field
Ormskirk
Pumping Station
Ormskirk C of E Prim. Sch.
Ormskirk Business Pk.
Works
Little Hall Farm
Civic Hall
Ormskirk Coll.
Court
Ormskirk Playing Field
Recreation Ground
ORMSKIRK
Park Pool
Coronation Park
The Rookery
Superstore
Kingsbury School
Ormskirk St. Annes' Catholic Prim. Sch.
Timber Yard
Offices
ORMSKIRK AND DISTRICT GENERAL HOSPITAL
Red Gate Farm
St. Bede's Catholic High Sch.
Holborn Farm
Playing Field
Tennis Courts
Cricket Ground
Playing Fields
GAW HILL
Pontville School and College
Aughton Christ Church C of E Prim. Sch.
Moss House Farm
Rose Theatre
Edge Hill Coll. of Higher Education
Running Track
5-a-Side Pitches
Slack Ho. Cott.
Alty's Farm
Slack Farm
Vicarage
Play Area
Redcliffe Convent
Aughton Park
34
23
A570
A59
A577
B5319
B5197
SOUTHPORT ROAD
COUNTY ROAD
HIGH ROAD
WIGAN ROAD
DERBY ST.
BURSCOUGH STREET
ST. HELENS ROAD
HOLBORN HILL
PRESCOT ROAD
MOOR STREET
AUGHTON STREET

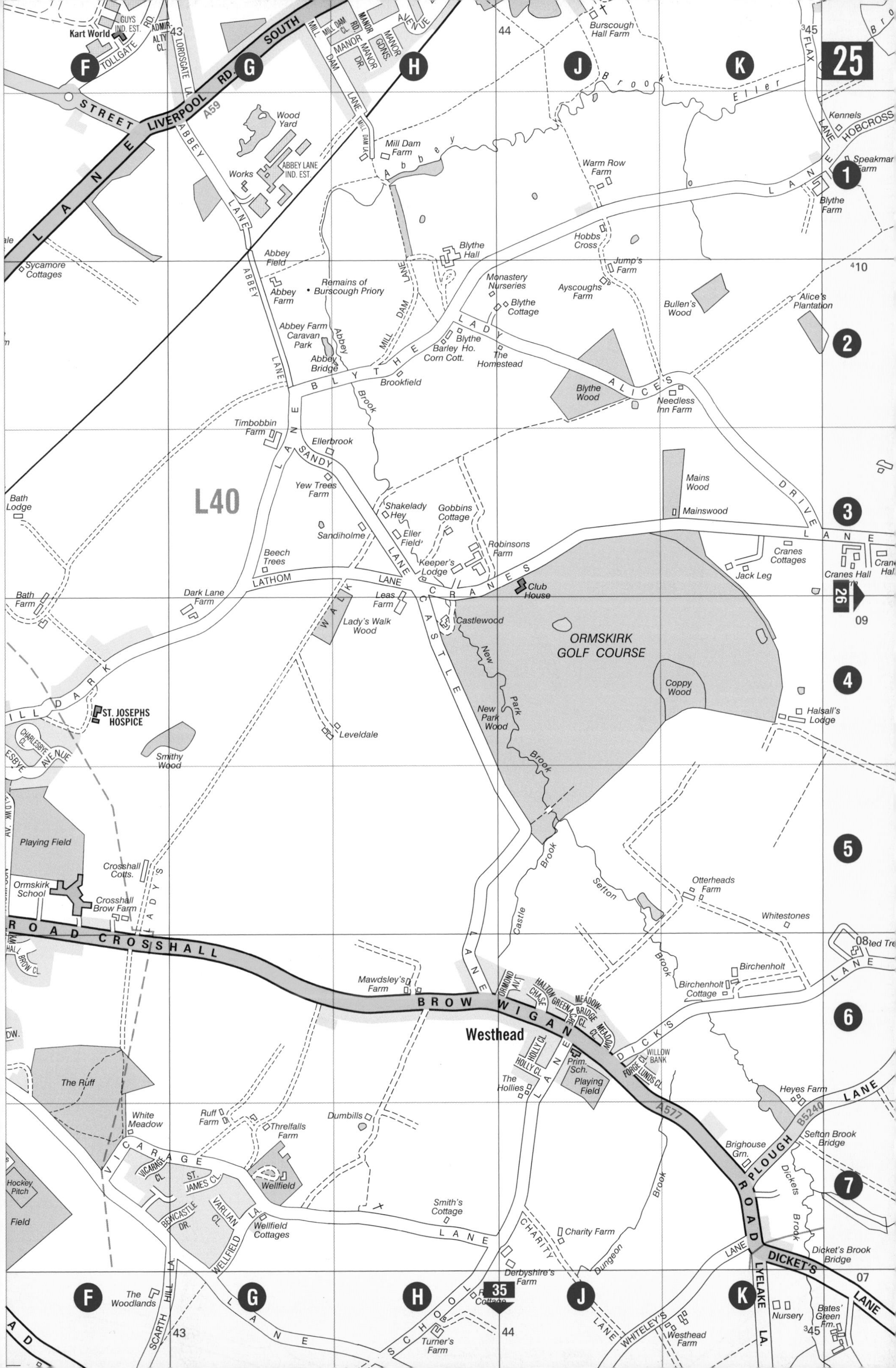
Kart World
GUYS IND. EST.
TOLLGATE
ADMIRALTY CL.
LORDSGATE LA.
LIVERPOOL RD. SOUTH
STREET LANE
A59
MILL DAM CL.
MANOR RD.
MANOR GDNS.
MANOR DR.
MANOR AVENUE
MILL DAM LANE
Wood Yard
ABBEY LANE IND. EST.
Works
Mill Dam Farm
Abbey Brook
Burscough Hall Farm
Eller Brook
Kennels
HOBCROSS LANE
FLAX LANE
Speakman Farm
Blythe Farm
Warm Row Farm
Hobbs Cross
Jump's Farm
Blythe Hall
Abbey Field
Sycamore Cottages
Remains of Burscough Priory
Abbey Farm
Abbey Farm Caravan Park
Abbey Bridge
Monastery Nurseries
Blythe Cottage
Ayscoughs Farm
Bullen's Wood
Alice's Plantation
Blythe Ho.
Barley Corn Cott.
The Homestead
BLYTHE LANE
LADY ALICE'S DRIVE
Brookfield
Blythe Wood
Needless Inn Farm
Timbobbin Farm
Ellerbrook
SANDY LANE
Yew Trees Farm
L40
Bath Lodge
Shakelady Hey
Gobbins Cottage
Mains Wood
Mainswood
Eller Field
Sandiholme
Robinsons Farm
Cranes Cottages
Beech Trees
Keeper's Lodge
Jack Leg
Cranes Hall Farm
LATHOM LANE
CRANES LANE
Club House
Bath Farm
Dark Lane Farm
Leas Farm
LADY'S WALK
Lady's Walk Wood
Castlewood
ORMSKIRK GOLF COURSE
CASTLE LANE
New Park Brook
Coppy Wood
DARK LANE
ST. JOSEPHS HOSPICE
New Park Wood
Halsall's Lodge
CHARLESBYE CL.
CHARLESBYE AVENUE
Smithy Wood
Leveldale
Playing Field
Crosshall Cotts.
Ormskirk School
Crosshall Brow Farm
Otterheads Farm
Sefton Brook
Castle Brook
Whitestones
CROSSHALL ROAD
CROSSHALL BROW CL.
Birchenholt
Birchenholt Cottage
Mawdsley's Farm
WIGAN ROAD
BROW
ORMOND AV.
HALTON CHASE
GREENACRE
MEADOW BRIDGE CL.
MEADOW
Westhead
HOLLY CL.
DICK'S LANE
WILLOW BANK
FORGE CL.
LUNDS CL.
Prim. Sch.
Playing Field
The Hollies
The Ruff
Heyes Farm
White Meadow
Ruff Farm
Threlfalls Farm
Dumbills
A577
B5240
PLOUGH LANE
Sefton Brook Bridge
Brighouse Grn.
VICARAGE LANE
VICARAGE CL.
ST. JAMES CL.
Wellfield
Dickets Brook
Hockey Pitch
Field
BEWCASTLE DR.
VARLIAN CL.
Wellfield Cottages
WELLFIELD LANE
Smith's Cottage
Charity Farm
CHARITY LANE
Dungeon
Dicket's Brook Bridge
DICKET'S LANE
Derbyshire's Farm
The Woodlands
SCARTH HILL LA.
SCHOOL LANE
Cottage
WHITELEY'S LANE
LYELAKE LA.
Nursery
Bates' Green Fm.
Westhead Farm
Turner's Farm
F G H J K
1 2 3 4 5 6 7
43 44 345 410 09 08 07
26
35

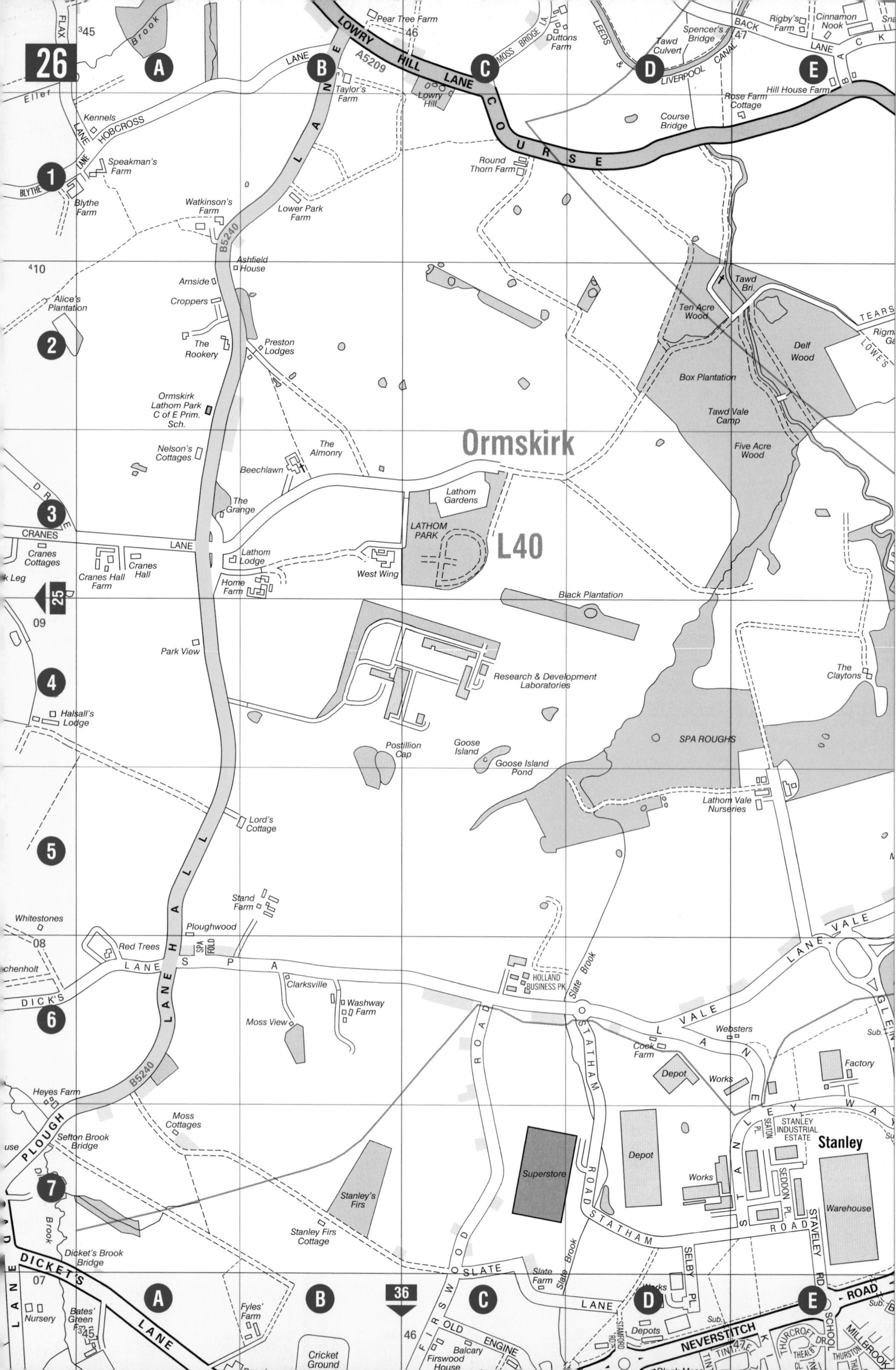
Ormskirk
L40
Stanley
LOWRY HILL LANE
A5209
COURSE LANE
B5240
HALL LANE
SPA LANE
VALE LANE
STATHAM ROAD
SLATE LANE
NEVERSTITCH ROAD
DICKETS LANE
PLOUGH LANE
CRANES LANE
HOBCROSS LANE
LEEDS & LIVERPOOL CANAL
Pear Tree Farm
Taylor's Farm
Lowry Hill
Duttons Farm
Tawd Culvert
Spencer's Bridge
Rigby's Farm
Cinnamon Nook
Hill House Farm
Rose Farm Cottage
Course Bridge
Round Thorn Farm
Kennels
Speakman's Farm
Blythe Farm
Watkinson's Farm
Lower Park Farm
Ashfield House
Arnside
Croppers
Alice's Plantation
The Rookery
Preston Lodges
Ormskirk Lathom Park C of E Prim. Sch.
Nelson's Cottages
The Almonry
Beechlawn
The Grange
Lathom Gardens
LATHOM PARK
Lathom Lodge
West Wing
Home Farm
Cranes Cottages
Cranes Hall Farm
Cranes Hall
Black Plantation
Tawd Bri.
Ten Acre Wood
Delf Wood
Box Plantation
Tawd Vale Camp
Five Acre Wood
Park View
Research & Development Laboratories
Halsall's Lodge
Postillion Cap
Goose Island
Goose Island Pond
SPA ROUGHS
The Claytons
Lathom Vale Nurseries
Lord's Cottage
Stand Farm
Whitestones
Ploughwood
Red Trees
SPA FOLD
Clarksville
Washway Farm
Moss View
HOLLAND BUSINESS PK
Slate Brook
Websters
Cook Farm
Depot
Works
Factory
Heyes Farm
Moss Cottages
Sefton Brook Bridge
STANLEY INDUSTRIAL ESTATE
Superstore
Warehouse
Stanley's Firs
Stanley Firs Cottage
Dicket's Brook Bridge
Slate Farm
Fyles' Farm
Nursery
Bates' Green Fm
Depots
Cricket Ground
Balcary
Firswood House
FIRSWOOD ROAD
OLD ENGINE
SELBY PL.
STAVELEY RD
SEDDON PL.
STANLEY WAY
SCHOOL
THURCROFT DR.
MILLBROOK
Sub.
25
36

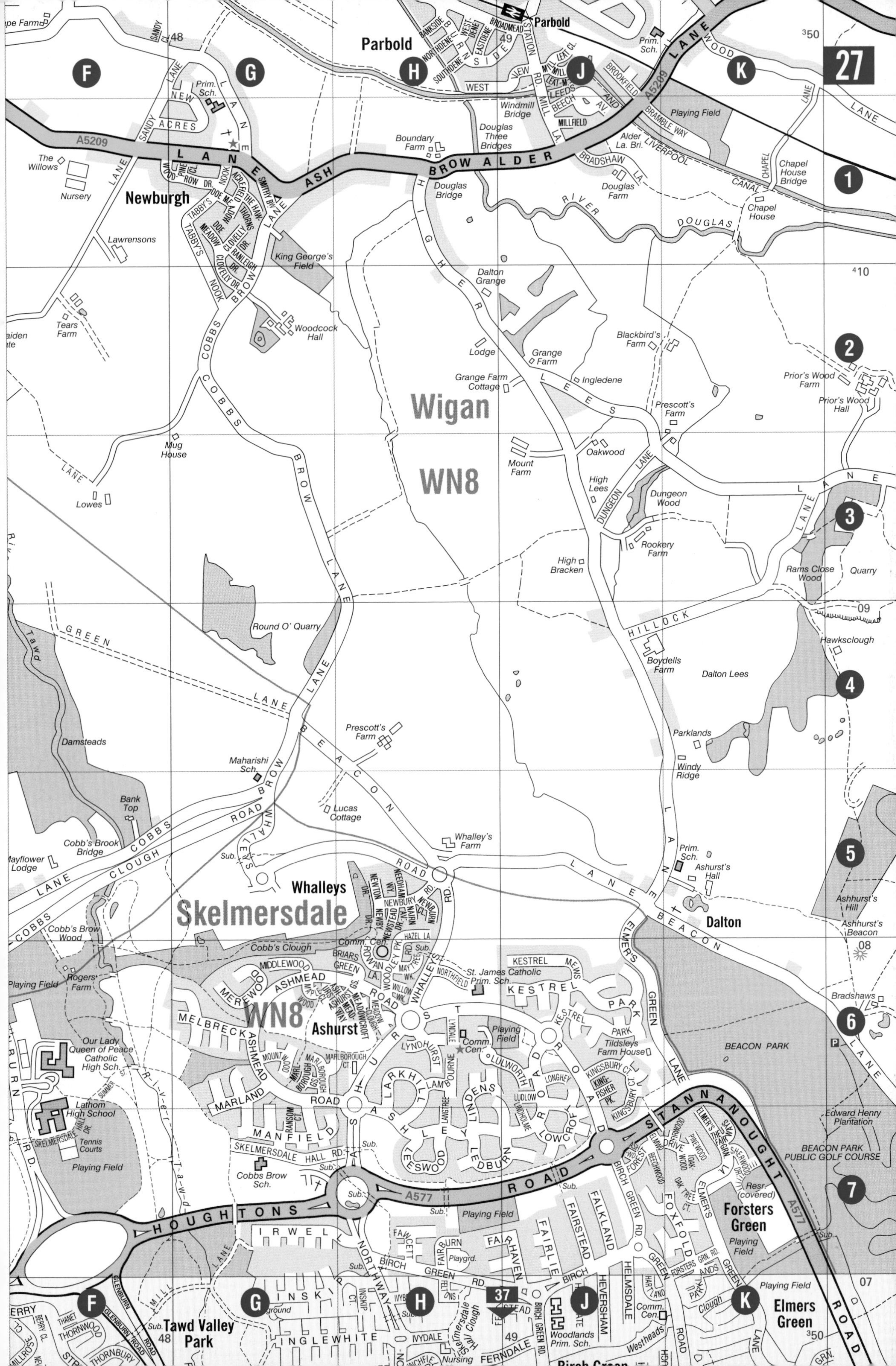
Parbold
Newburgh
Wigan
WN8
Skelmersdale
Whalleys
Ashurst
Dalton
Forsters Green
Elmers Green
Tawd Valley Park
A5209
A577
Douglas Bridge
King George's Field
Woodcock Hall
Dalton Grange
Grange Farm
Lodge
Mug House
Lowes
Mount Farm
High Lees
Dungeon Wood
Rookery Farm
High Bracken
Round O' Quarry
Damsteads
Prescott's Farm
Maharishi Sch.
Bank Top
Lucas Cottage
Whalley's Farm
Boydells Farm
Dalton Lees
Parklands
Windy Ridge
Hawksclough
Rams Close Wood
Quarry
Prior's Wood Farm
Prior's Wood Hall
Chapel House Bridge
Chapel House
Ashurst's Hill
Ashurst's Beacon
Ashurst's Hall
Bradshaws
BEACON PARK
Edward Henry Plantation
BEACON PARK PUBLIC GOLF COURSE
Our Lady Queen of Peace Catholic High Sch.
Lathom High School
Cobbs Brow Sch.
Woodlands Prim. Sch.
St. James Catholic Prim. Sch.
Tildsleys Farm House
Cobb's Brook Bridge
Mayflower Lodge
Rogers' Farm
Cobb's Brow Wood
Cobb's Clough
Douglas Three Bridges
Boundary Farm
Windmill Bridge
Douglas Farm
Blackbird's Farm
Ingledene
Oakwood
Grange Farm Cottage
Lawrensons
Tears Farm
The Willows
Nursery
Playing Field
37

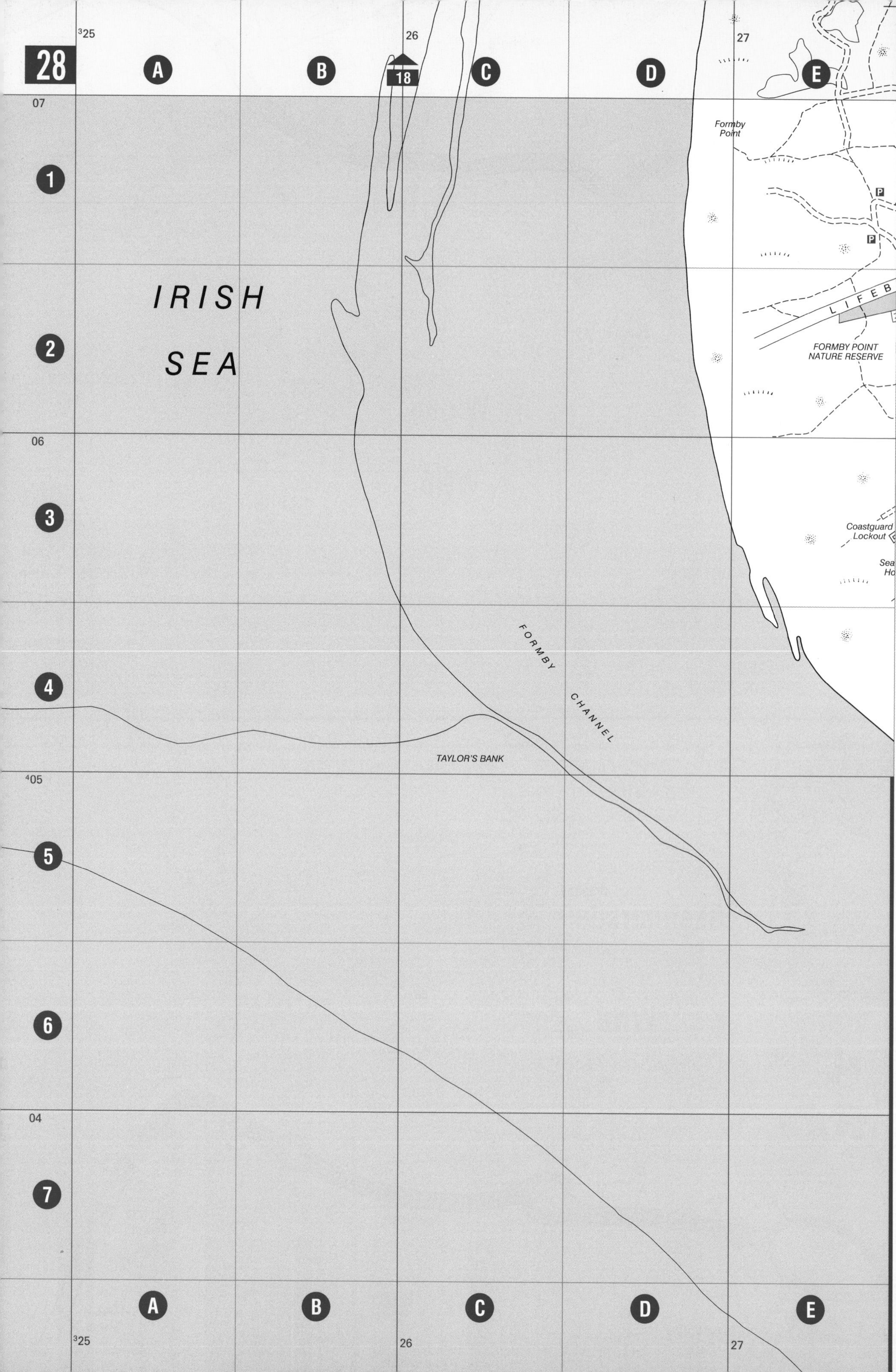

³25   26   27

07

18

1

IRISH

SEA

2

06

3

*Formby
Point*

P

P

L I F E B

*FORMBY POINT
NATURE RESERVE*

*Coastguard
Lookout*

Sea
Ho

4

FORMBY   CHANNEL

TAYLOR'S BANK

⁴05

5

6

04

7

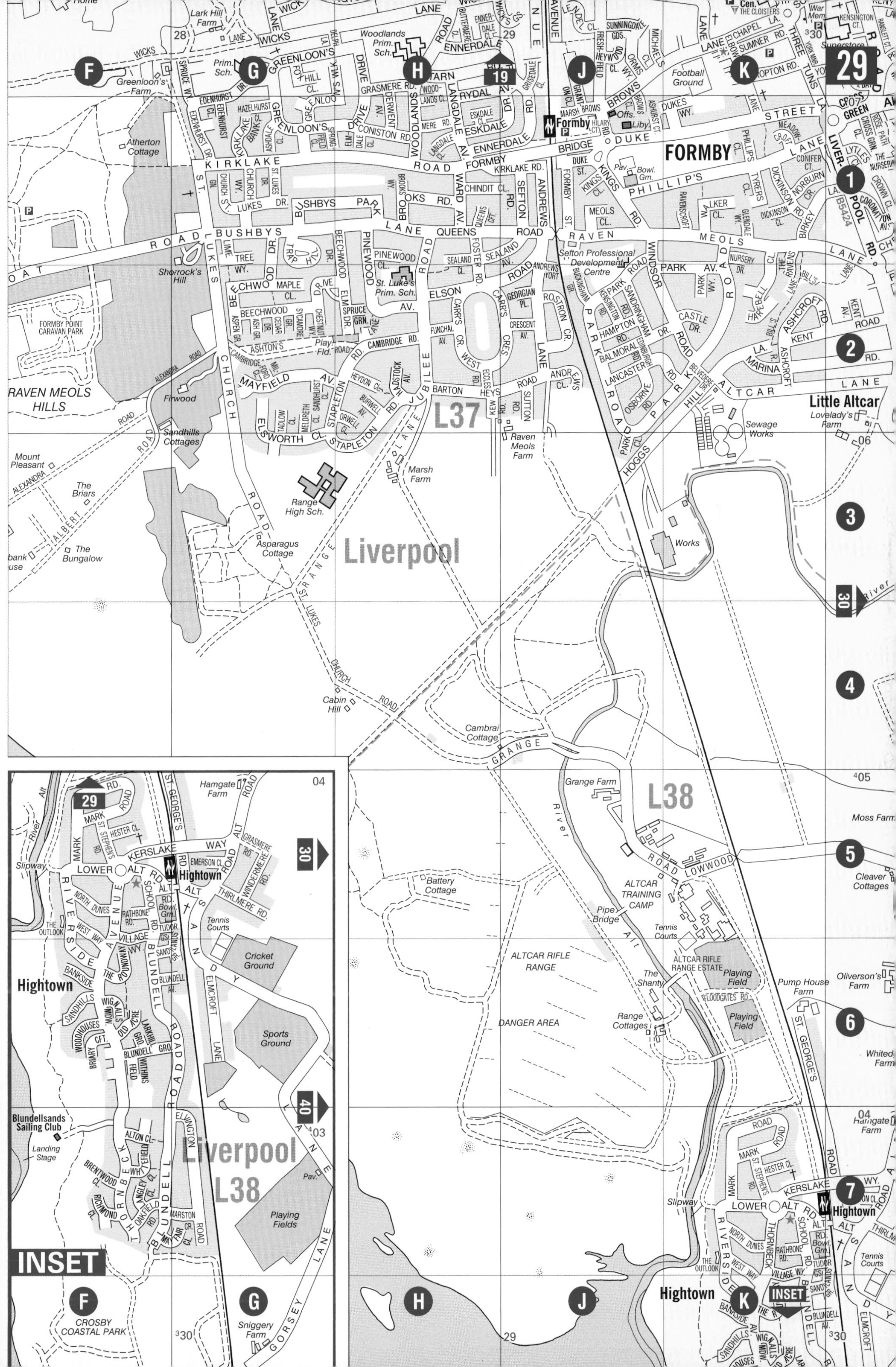
FORMBY
Formby
Little Altcar
RAVEN MEOLS HILLS
Liverpool
L37
L38
ALTCAR RIFLE RANGE
DANGER AREA
ALTCAR TRAINING CAMP
ALTCAR RIFLE RANGE ESTATE
Hightown
Grange Farm
Range High Sch.
St. Luke's Prim. Sch.
Woodlands Prim. Sch.
Sefton Professional Development Centre
Sewage Works
Works
Cabin Hill
Cambrai Cottage
Battery Cottage
Asparagus Cottage
Marsh Farm
Raven Meols Farm
Shorrock's Hill
FORMBY POINT CARAVAN PARK
Firwood
Sandhills Cottages
Mount Pleasant
The Briars
The Bungalow
Atherton Cottage
Greenloon's Farm
Lark Hill Farm
Pipe Bridge
The Shanty
Range Cottages
Playing Field
Pump House Farm
Oliverson's Farm
Cleaver Cottages
Moss Farm
Hamgate Farm
Slipway
Lovelady's Farm
INSET
Blundellsands Sailing Club
Landing Stage
Cricket Ground
Sports Ground
Playing Fields
Tennis Courts
CROSBY COASTAL PARK
Sniggery Farm
Liverpool L38
Hightown

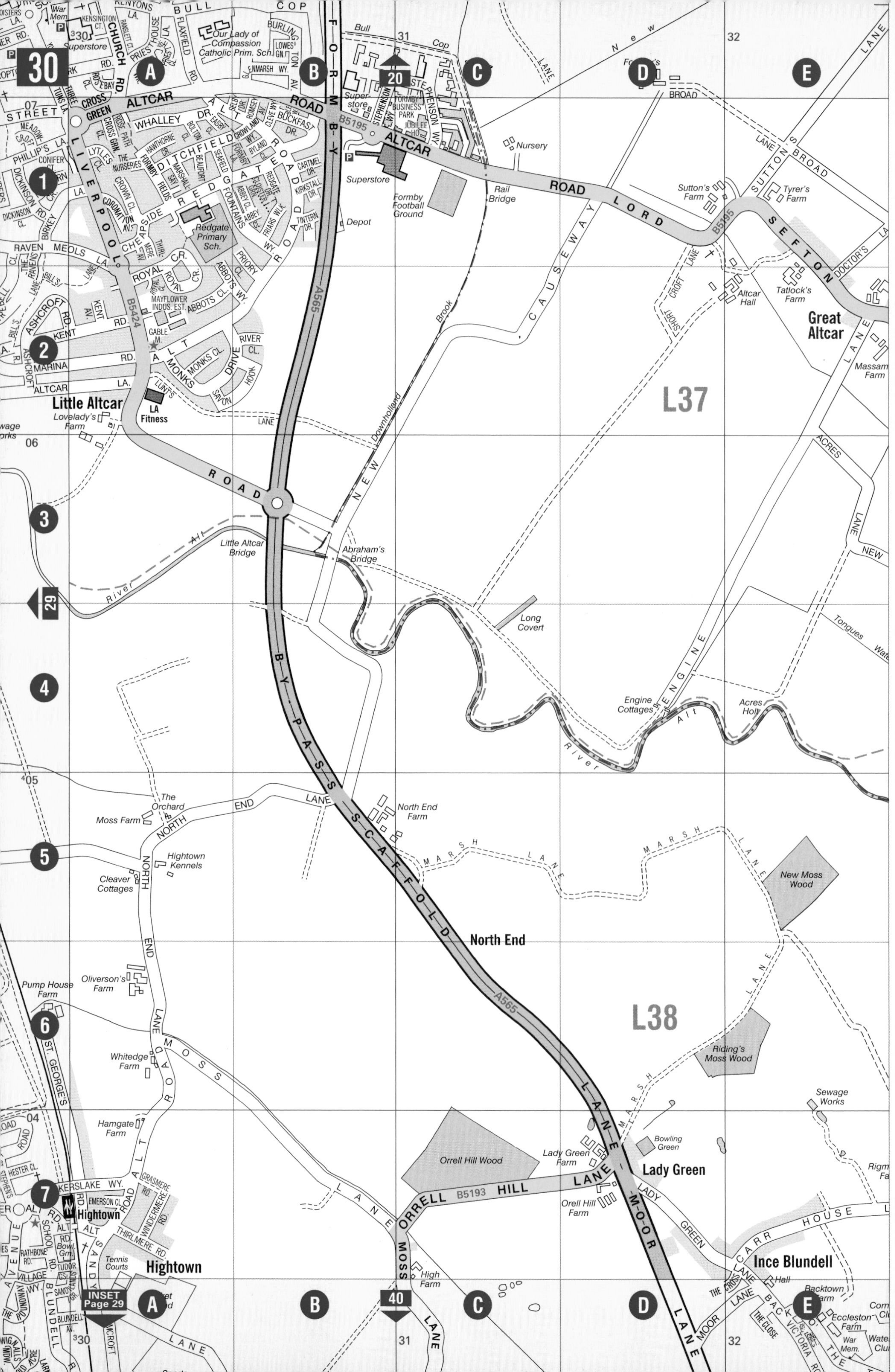

A
B
C
D
E
1
2
3
4
5
6
7
20
29
40
INSET Page 29
31
32
30
07
06
05
04
Our Lady of Compassion Catholic Prim. Sch.
Superstore
Formby Business Park
Jubilee Ho.
Nursery
Rail Bridge
Formby Football Ground
Depot
Redgate Primary Sch.
Mayflower Indus. Est.
Gable M.
LA Fitness
Little Altcar
Lovelady's Farm
Sewage Works
Little Altcar Bridge
Abraham's Bridge
River Alt
Brook
New Downholland
Long Covert
Sutton's Farm
Tyrer's Farm
Altcar Hall
Tatlock's Farm
Great Altcar
Massam Farm
L37
Tongues Water
Engine Cottages
Acres Holt
The Orchard
Moss Farm
North End Farm
Hightown Kennels
Cleaver Cottages
North End
New Moss Wood
Pump House Farm
Oliverson's Farm
L38
Whitedge Farm
Riding's Moss Wood
Sewage Works
Hamgate Farm
Orrell Hill Wood
Lady Green Farm
Bowling Green
Lady Green
Orrell Hill Farm
Hightown
Tennis Courts
High Farm
Ince Blundell
Hall
Backtown Farm
Eccleston Farm
War Mem.
ALTCAR ROAD
LORD SEFTON WAY
SEFTON LANE
B5195
B5424
A565
FORMBY BY-PASS
SCAFFOLD LANE
MOOR LANE
ORRELL HILL LANE
B5193
MOSS LANE
NORTH END LANE
MARSH LANE
ALT ROAD
MOSS ROAD
LADY GREEN LANE
CARR HOUSE LANE
NEW CAUSEWAY
ENGINE LANE
ACRES LANE
NEW LANE
BROAD LANE
SHORT CROFT LANE
LIVERPOOL ROAD
REDGATE
DITCHFIELD
CHEAPSIDE
ROYAL CR.
KENT RD.
MARINA RD.
ALTCAR LA.
RAVEN MEOLS LA.
ASHCROFT RD.
MONKS DRIVE
RIVER CL.
ABBOTS WY.
PRIORY CL.
WHALLEY DR.
GREEN CROSS
ST. GEORGE'S RD.
KERSLAKE WY.
GRASMERE RD.
WINDERMERE RD.
THIRLMERE RD.
EMERSON CL.
SANDY LA.
BLUNDELL AV.
THE CROSS
THE CLOSE
VICTORIA RD.

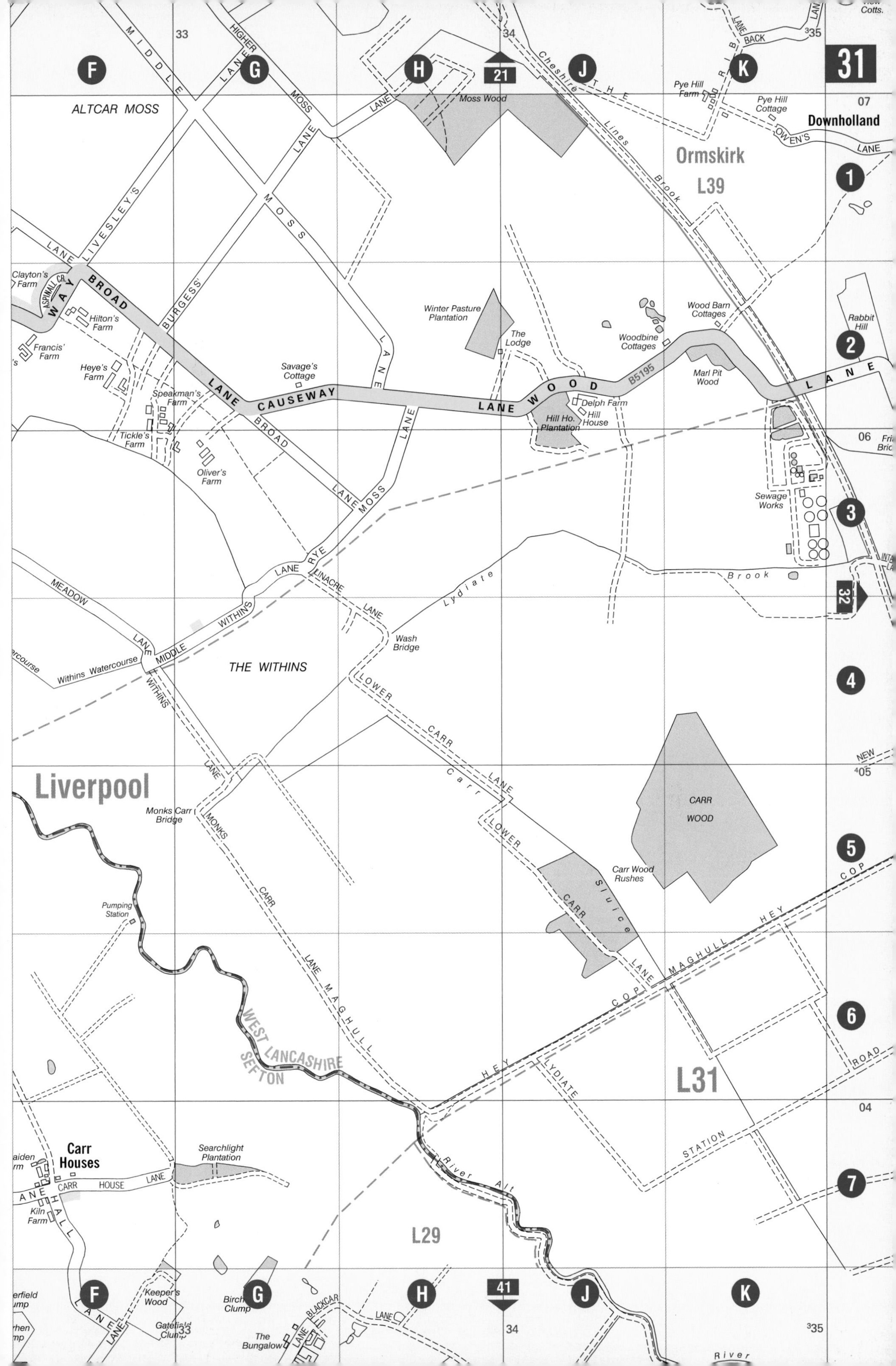

31

F · **G** · **H** · **21** · **J** · **K**

New Cotts.

MIDDLE LANE · 33 · HIGHER LANE · 34 · Cheshire Lines Brook · RIB LANE · BACK LANE · 35 · 07

ALTCAR MOSS · Moss Wood · Pye Hill Farm · Pye Hill Cottage

Downholland

Ormskirk L39

1

MOSS LANE · LIVESLEYS LANE · BROAD WAY · ASPINALL CR · BURGESS LANE

Clayton's Farm · Hilton's Farm · Francis' Farm · Heye's Farm · Speakman's Farm · Tickle's Farm · Oliver's Farm · Savage's Cottage

BROAD LANE · CAUSEWAY LANE · MOSS LANE

Winter Pasture Plantation · The Lodge · Woodbine Cottages · Wood Barn Cottages

Rabbit Hill

2

WOOD LANE · B5195 · Marl Pit Wood · LANE

Hill Ho. Plantation · Delph Farm · Hill House · Fri Bric · 06

3

Sewage Works · Brook · 32

MEADOW LANE · WITHINS LANE · RYE LANE · LINACRE LANE · MOSS LANE · Lydiate Brook

Withins Watercourse · MIDDLE LANE · THE WITHINS · Wash Bridge · LOWER CARR LANE

4

NEW · 05

Liverpool

Monks Carr Bridge · MONKS CARR LANE · Carr · LOWER CARR LANE · CARR WOOD · Carr Wood Rushes · COP

5

Pumping Station · LANE MAGHULL · CARR LANE · Sluice · COP HEY · MAGHULL

6

ROAD · 04

WEST LANCASHIRE · SEFTON · L31 · HEY LANE · LYDIATE LANE · STATION

Carr Houses · Searchlight Plantation · CARR HOUSE LANE · Kiln Farm · River Alt

7

F · **G** · **H** · **41** · **J** · **K**

Keeper's Wood · Birch Clump · Gatefield Clump · The Bungalow · BLACKCAR LANE · LANE · L29 · 33 · 34 · 35

River

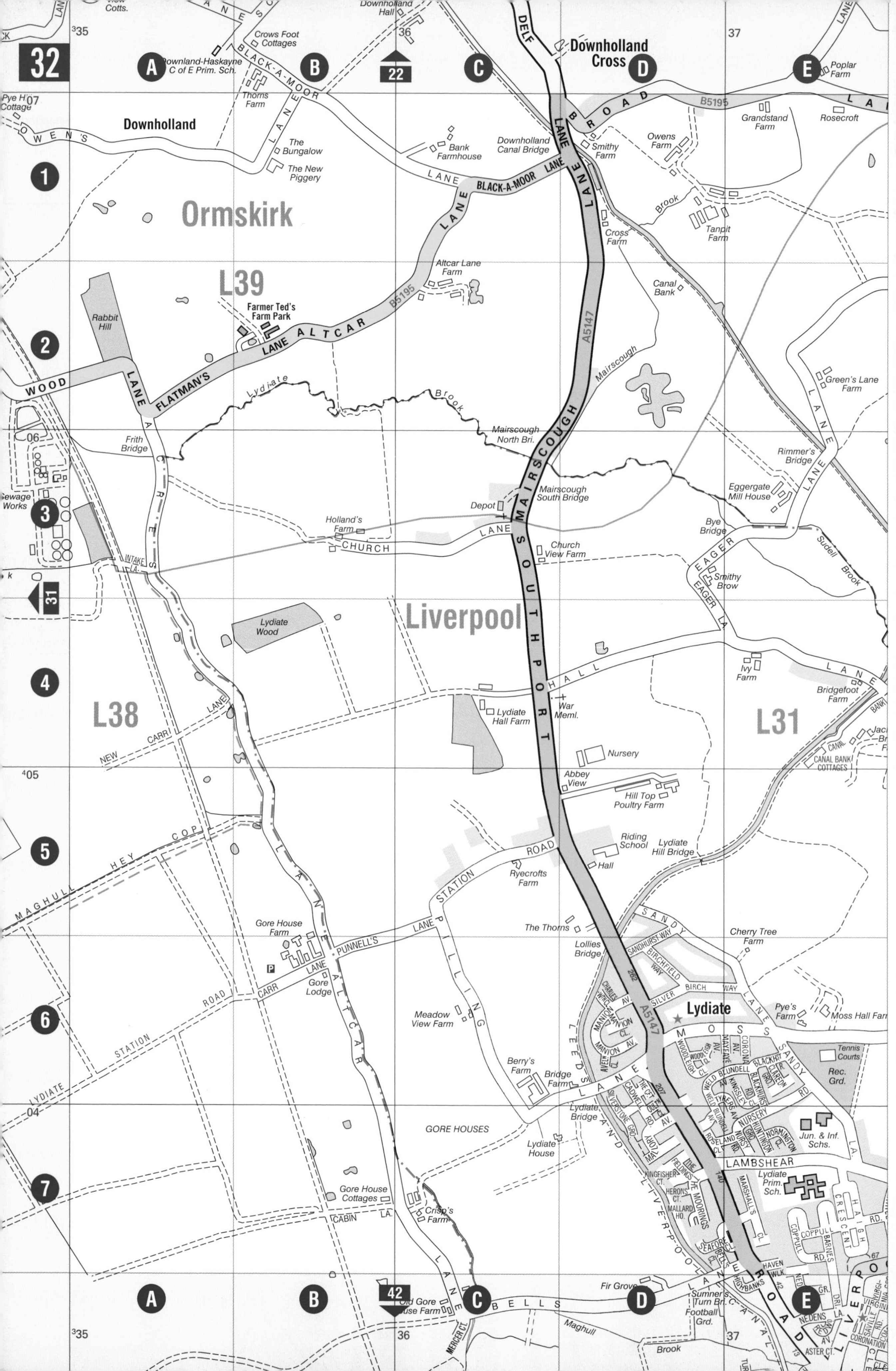
Downholland Cross
Downholland
Ormskirk
L39
Liverpool
L38
L31
Lydiate
Crows Foot Cottages
Downland-Haskayne C of E Prim. Sch.
Thorns Farm
The Bungalow
The New Piggery
Bank Farmhouse
Downholland Canal Bridge
Smithy Farm
Owens Farm
Grandstand Farm
Rosecroft
Poplar Farm
Tanpit Farm
Cross Farm
Canal Bank
Altcar Lane Farm
Farmer Ted's Farm Park
Rabbit Hill
Green's Lane Farm
Mairscough North Bri.
Mairscough South Bridge
Rimmer's Bridge
Eggergate Mill House
Frith Bridge
Sewage Works
Depot
Holland's Farm
Church View Farm
Bye Bridge
Smithy Brow
Lydiate Wood
Ivy Farm
Bridgefoot Farm
Lydiate Hall Farm
War Meml.
Nursery
Canal Bank Cottages
Abbey View
Hill Top Poultry Farm
Riding School
Lydiate Hill Bridge
Hall
Ryecrofts Farm
The Thorns
Cherry Tree Farm
Lollies Bridge
Gore House Farm
Gore Lodge
Meadow View Farm
Pye's Farm
Moss Hall Farm
Tennis Courts
Rec. Grd.
Berry's Farm
Bridge Farm
Lydiate Bridge
Jun. & Inf. Schs.
GORE HOUSES
Lydiate House
Lydiate Prim. Sch.
Gore House Cottages
Crisp's Farm
Old Gore House Farm
Fir Grove
Sumner's Turn Br.
Football Grd.
Maghull
Brook
B5195
A5147
BLACK-A-MOOR LANE
OWEN'S LANE
ALTCAR LANE
FLATMAN'S LANE
WOOD LANE
MAIRSCOUGH LANE
DELF LANE
BROAD LANE
CHURCH LANE
INTAKE LA.
CARR LANE
NEW CARR LANE
SOUTHPORT ROAD
HALL LANE
EAGER LANE
STATION ROAD
PUNNELL'S LANE
PILLING LANE
COP LANE
MAGHULL HEY
LYDIATE STATION ROAD
CABIN LA.
BELLS LANE
SANDY LANE
MOSS LANE
LAMBSHEAR LA.
LIVERPOOL ROAD
LEEDS AND LIVERPOOL CANAL
HAIGH CRESCENT
Lydiate Brook
Mairscough Brook
Sudell Brook
22
31
42
335
36
37
07
06
405
04

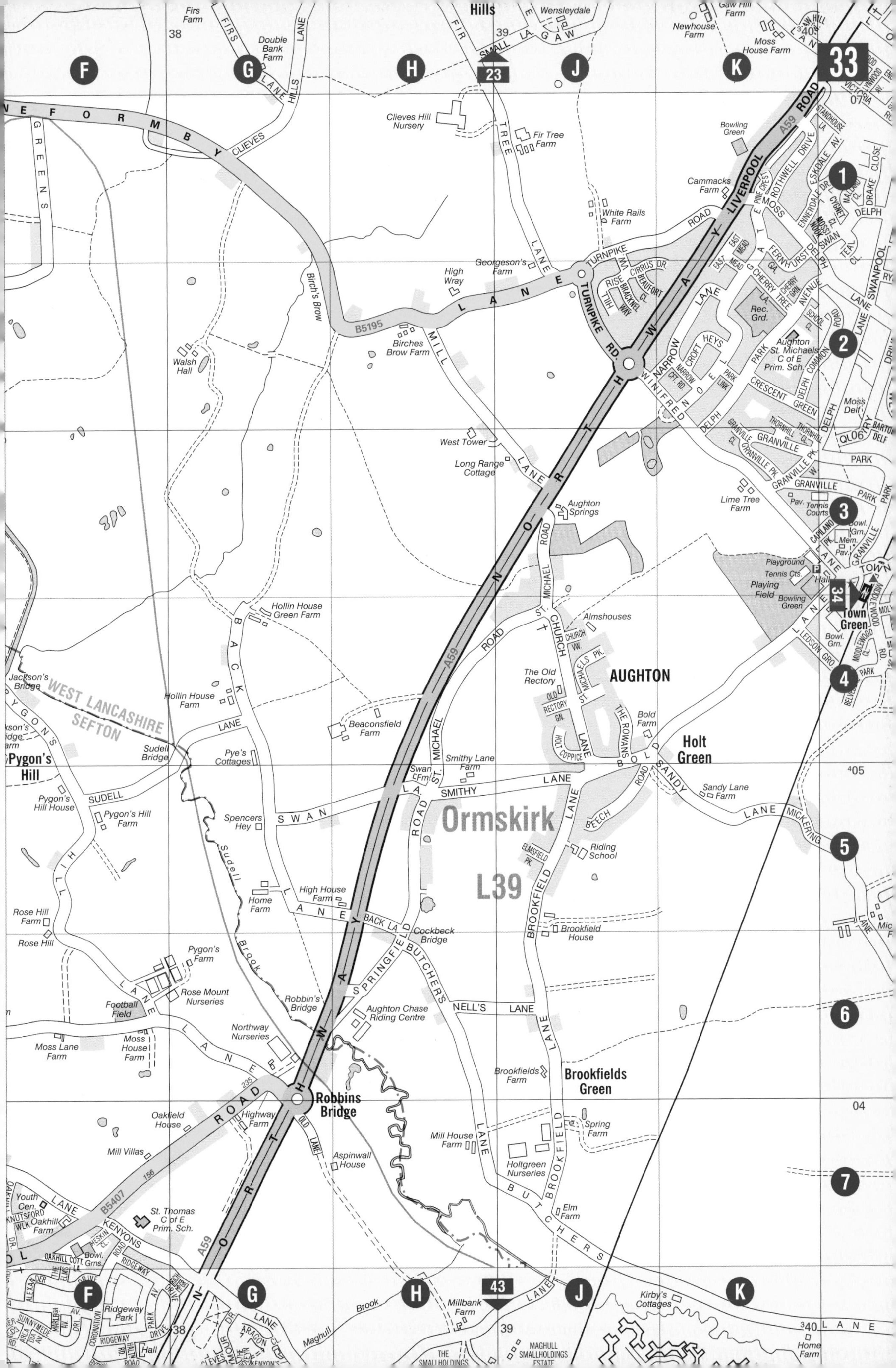
33
23
43
34
Ormskirk
L39
AUGHTON
Holt Green
Town Green
Robbins Bridge
Brookfields Green
Pygon's Hill
Clieves Hills
WEST LANCASHIRE
SEFTON
FORMBY CLIEVES
LIVERPOOL ROAD
NORTH WAY
A59
B5195
B5407
TURNPIKE RD.
SMITHY LANE
SWAN LA.
BACK LANE
SUDELL LANE
MILL LANE
BIRCH'S BROW
FIR TREE LANE
ST. MICHAEL ROAD
CHURCH LANE
BROOKFIELD LANE
BUTCHERS LANE
NELL'S LANE
SPRINGFIELD ROAD
SANDY LANE
MICKERING LANE
OLD LANE
Clieves Hill Nursery
Fir Tree Farm
White Rails Farm
Georgeson's Farm
High Wray
Birches Brow Farm
Walsh Hall
West Tower
Long Range Cottage
Aughton Springs
Hollin House Green Farm
Hollin House Farm
Beaconsfield Farm
Pye's Cottages
Sudell Bridge
Jackson's Bridge
Spencers Hey
Smithy Lane Farm
Swan Fm.
High House Farm
Home Farm
Cockbeck Bridge
Pygon's Hill House
Pygon's Hill Farm
Rose Hill Farm
Rose Hill
Pygon's Farm
Rose Mount Nurseries
Football Field
Robbin's Bridge
Aughton Chase Riding Centre
Northway Nurseries
Moss Lane Farm
Moss House Farm
Oakfield House
Highway Farm
Mill Villas
Aspinwall House
Mill House Farm
Holtgreen Nurseries
Brookfields Farm
Spring Farm
Elm Farm
Brookfield House
Riding School
Sandy Lane Farm
Bold Farm
Almshouses
The Old Rectory
Lime Tree Farm
Cammacks Farm
Bowling Green
Playing Field
Tennis Cts.
Playground
Rec. Grd.
Aughton St. Michaels C of E Prim. Sch.
St. Thomas C of E Prim. Sch.
Youth Cen.
Oakhill Farm
Ridgeway Park
Millbank Farm
Kirby's Cottages
Home Farm
Firs Farm
Double Bank Farm
Newhouse Farm
Moss House Farm
Gaw Hill Farm
Wensleydale
Maghull Brook
Sudell Brook
THE SMALLHOLDINGS
MAGHULL SMALLHOLDINGS ESTATE
F G H J K
1 2 3 4 5 6 7
38 39 340 405 04

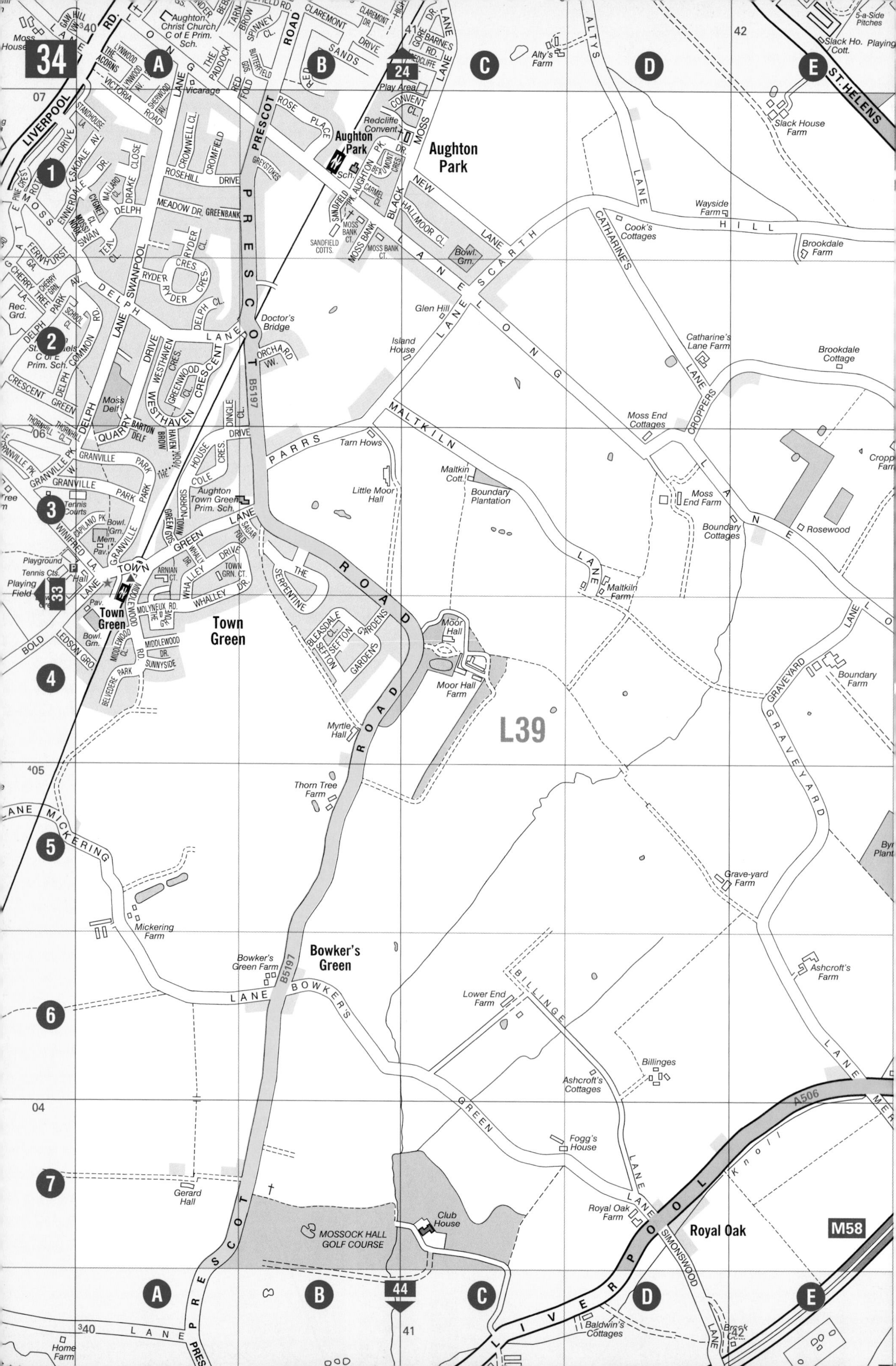
Aughton Park
Town Green
Bowker's Green
Royal Oak
L39
Prescot Road
B5197
Liverpool Road
A506
M58
St. Helens Road
Long Lane
Maltkiln Lane
Catharine's Lane
Croppers Lane
Graveyard Lane
Billinge Lane
Green Lane
Bowker's Lane
Mickering Lane
Simonswood Lane
Parrs Lane
Scarth Hill
Moss Lane
New Lane
Black Moss Lane
Mossock Hall Golf Course
Club House
Moor Hall
Moor Hall Farm
Little Moor Hall
Tarn Hows
Myrtle Hall
Thorn Tree Farm
Mickering Farm
Gerard Hall
Bowker's Green Farm
Lower End Farm
Ashcroft's Cottages
Fogg's House
Royal Oak Farm
Billinges
Grave-yard Farm
Ashcroft's Farm
Boundary Farm
Boundary Cottages
Rosewood
Moss End Farm
Moss End Cottages
Maltkiln Farm
Maltkiln Cott.
Boundary Plantation
Catharine's Lane Farm
Brookdale Cottage
Brookdale Farm
Wayside Farm
Cook's Cottages
Slack House Farm
Alty's Farm
Glen Hill
Island House
Doctor's Bridge
Aughton Town Green Prim. Sch.
Aughton Christ Church C of E Prim. Sch.
Redcliffe Convent
Baldwin's Cottages
Home Farm

24
33
44

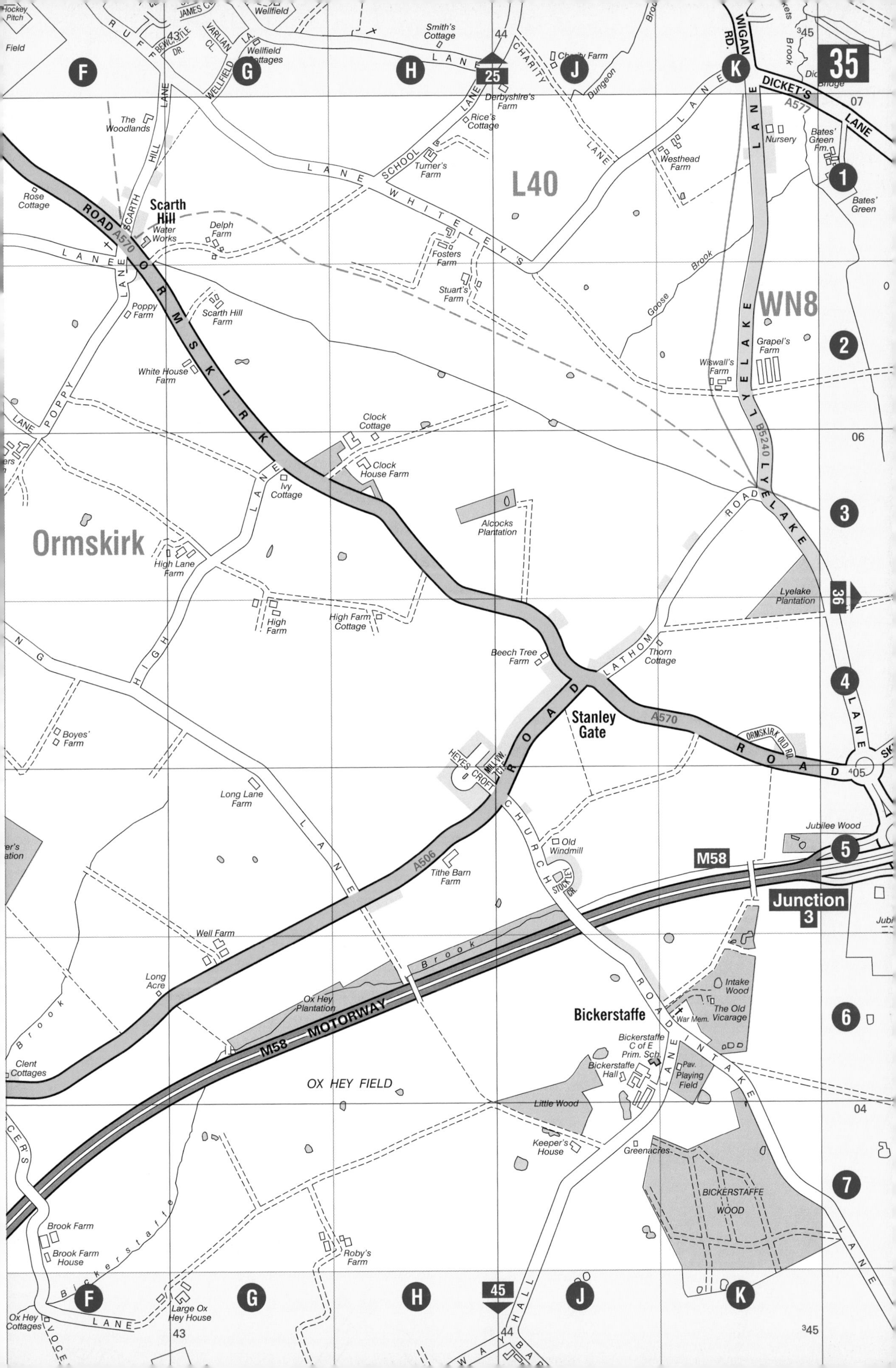
Ormskirk
Scarth Hill
Stanley Gate
Bickerstaffe
L40
WN8
ORMSKIRK ROAD
A570
A506
M58 MOTORWAY
Junction 3
LYELAKE LANE
B5240
WHITELEY'S LANE
SCHOOL LANE
CHARITY LANE
DICKET'S LANE
A577
WIGAN RD.
LATHOM ROAD
HIGH LANE
LONG LANE
POPPY LANE
SCARTH HILL LANE
CHURCH ROAD
INTAKE LANE
HALL LANE
BICKERSTAFFE LANE
Scarth Hill Farm
Delph Farm
Poppy Farm
White House Farm
Clock Cottage
Clock House Farm
Ivy Cottage
Alcocks Plantation
High Lane Farm
High Farm
High Farm Cottage
Beech Tree Farm
Thorn Cottage
Boyes' Farm
Long Lane Farm
Old Windmill
Tithe Barn Farm
Well Farm
Long Acre
Ox Hey Plantation
OX HEY FIELD
Clent Cottages
Brook Farm
Brook Farm House
Large Ox Hey House
Ox Hey Cottages
Roby's Farm
Keeper's House
Little Wood
Greenacres
BICKERSTAFFE WOOD
Bickerstaffe Hall
Bickerstaffe C of E Prim. Sch.
Playing Field
The Old Vicarage
Intake Wood
War Mem.
Jubilee Wood
Lyelake Plantation
Grapel's Farm
Wiswall's Farm
Westhead Farm
Nursery
Bates' Green Fm.
Bates' Green
Fosters Farm
Stuart's Farm
Turner's Farm
Rice's Cottage
Derbyshire's Farm
Charity Farm
Smith's Cottage
Wellfield Cottages
The Woodlands
Rose Cottage
Water Works
Goose Brook
Dungeon
Hockey Pitch
Field
HEYES CROFT
STOCKLEY CR.
ORMSKIRK OLD RD.
Brook
25
36
45
43
44
345
405
07
06
04
F
G
H
J
K
1
2
3
4
5
6
7

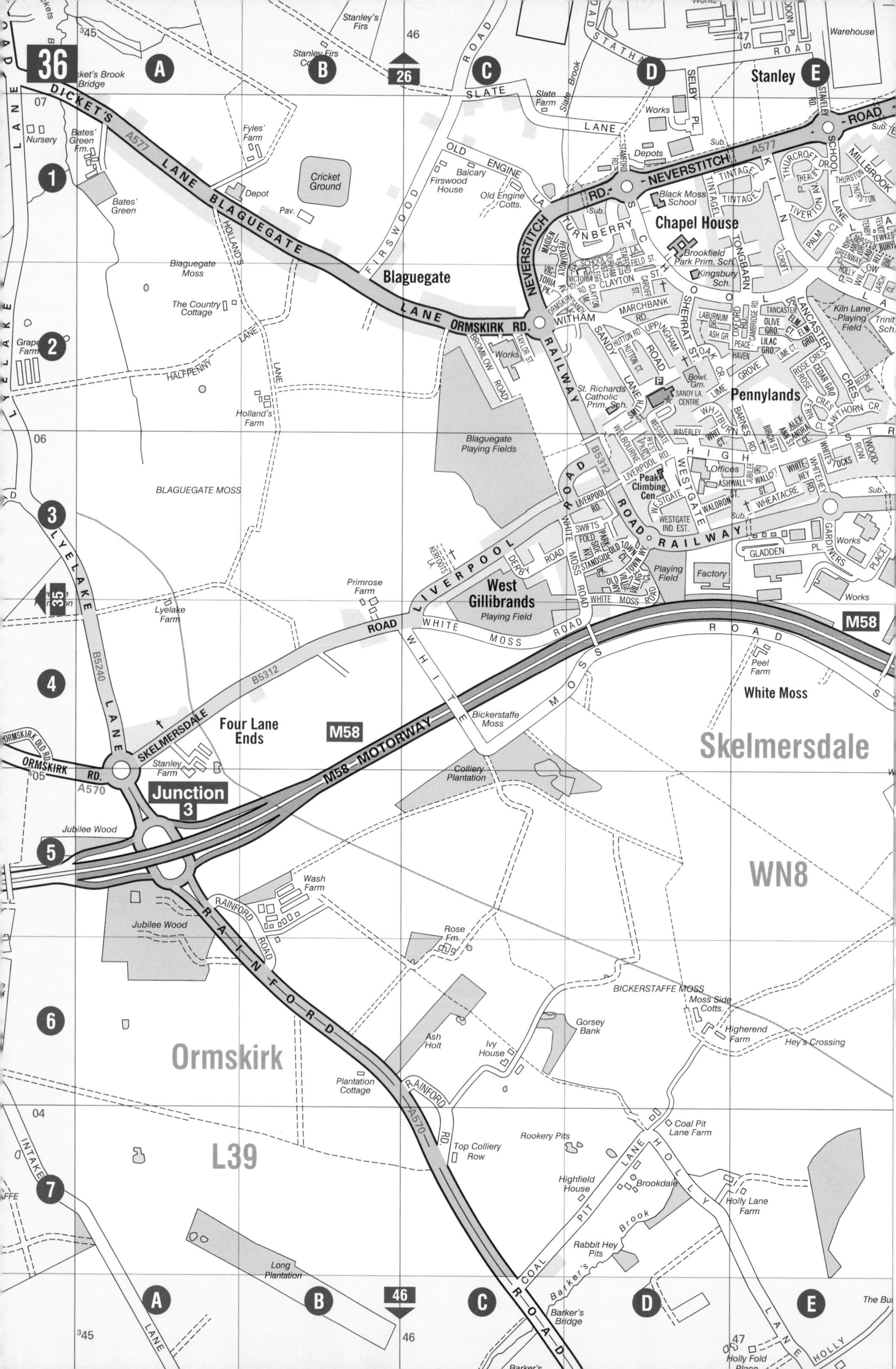
Dicket's Brook Bridge
Bates' Green Fm.
Nursery
Bates' Green
DICKET'S LANE
BLAGUEGATE LANE
A577
Stanley's Firs
Stanley Firs Cott.
Fyles' Farm
Cricket Ground
Depot
Pav.
Blaguegate Moss
The Country Cottage
HOLLANDS LANE
HALFPENNY LANE
Holland's Farm
Grape Farm
LYELAKE LANE
BLAGUEGATE MOSS
Lyelake Farm
B5240
Blaguegate
ORMSKIRK RD.
SLATE LANE
Slate Farm
Slate Brook
OLD ENGINE LA.
Balcary
Firswood House
Old Engine Cotts.
FIRSWOOD ROAD
STATHAM ROAD
Works
Depots
SELBY PL.
Stanley
NEVERSTITCH RD.
NEVERSTITCH ROAD
SCHOOL LANE
Black Moss School
Chapel House
Brookfield Park Prim. Sch.
Kingsbury Sch.
TONGBARN
TINTAGEL
THURCROFT DR.
MILLBROOK
Kiln Lane Playing Field
Trinity Sch.
Pennylands
SANDY LANE
SHERRAT ST.
WITHAM RD.
MARCHBANK RD.
CLAYTON ST.
St. Richards Catholic Prim. Sch.
SANDY LA. CENTRE
Bowl. Grn.
Blaguegate Playing Fields
Works
BROMILOW ROAD
TAYLOR ST.
RAILWAY ROAD
HIGH STREET
WESTGATE
Offices
Peak Climbing Cen.
WESTGATE IND. EST.
LIVERPOOL RD.
B5312
RAILWAY ROAD
GLADDEN PL.
GARDINERS PLACE
Works
Factory
Playing Field
White Moss Road
West Gillibrands
Playing Field
DERBY ROAD
LIVERPOOL ROAD
KERFOOTS LA.
Primrose Farm
M58
WHITE MOSS ROAD
Peel Farm
White Moss
Bickerstaffe Moss
Skelmersdale
M58 MOTORWAY
SKELMERSDALE ROAD
Four Lane Ends
Stanley Farm
ORMSKIRK RD.
ORMSKIRK OLD RD.
A570
Junction 3
Colliery Plantation
WN8
Jubilee Wood
Wash Farm
RAINFORD ROAD
Rose Fm.
BICKERSTAFFE MOSS
Moss Side Cotts.
Higherend Farm
Hey's Crossing
Gorsey Bank
Ash Holt
Ivy House
Ormskirk
Plantation Cottage
RAINFORD RD.
Top Colliery Row
Rookery Pits
Coal Pit Lane Farm
L39
INTAKE LANE
Highfield House
Brookdale
Holly Lane Farm
HOLLY LANE
COAL PIT LANE
Rabbit Hey Pits
Brook
Long Plantation
Barker's Bridge
Holly Fold Place
The Bu
26
35
46

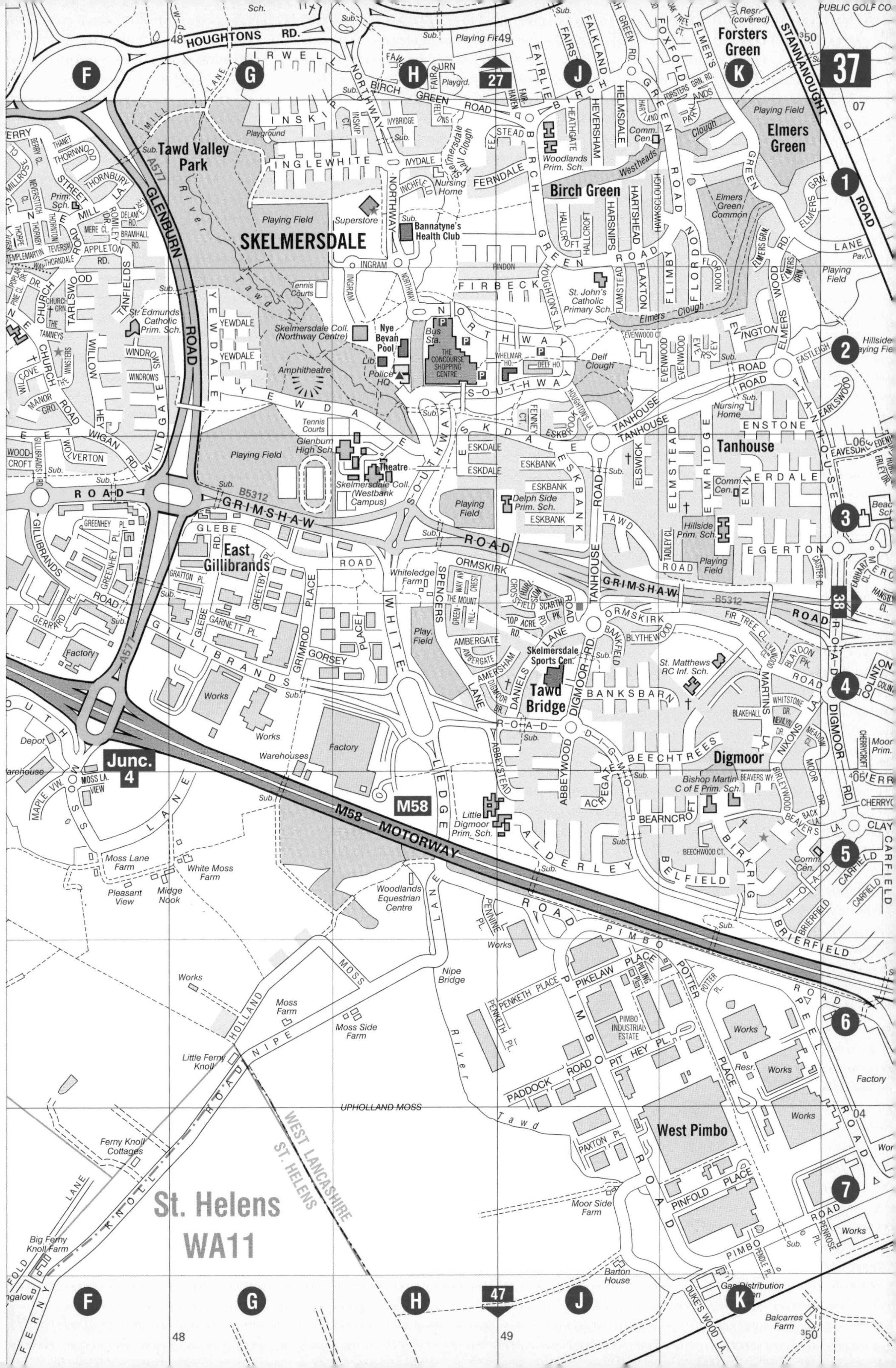
HOUGHTONS RD.
Forsters Green
Elmers Green
Tawd Valley Park
SKELMERSDALE
Birch Green
Bannatyne's Health Club
Superstore
Playing Field
Skelmersdale Coll. (Northway Centre)
Nye Bevan Pool
THE CONCOURSE SHOPPING CENTRE
Bus Sta.
Police HQ
Amphitheatre
Glenburn High Sch.
Theatre
Skelmersdale Coll. (Westbank Campus)
Delph Side Prim. Sch.
Tanhouse
Hillside Prim. Sch.
East Gillibrands
GRIMSHAW ROAD
B5312
GLENBURN ROAD
A577
Tawd Bridge
Skelmersdale Sports Cen.
St. Matthews RC Inf. Sch.
Digmoor
Bishop Martin C of E Prim. Sch.
Little Digmoor Prim. Sch.
Junc. 4
M58
M58 MOTORWAY
Works
Factory
Warehouses
Woodlands Equestrian Centre
Moss Lane Farm
White Moss Farm
Pleasant View
Midge Nook
Moss Farm
Moss Side Farm
Little Ferny Knoll
Ferny Knoll Cottages
Big Ferny Knoll Farm
UPHOLLAND MOSS
WEST LANCASHIRE
ST. HELENS
St. Helens WA11
PIMBO INDUSTRIAL ESTATE
West Pimbo
Moor Side Farm
Barton House
Gas Distribution Station
Balcarres Farm
St. John's Catholic Primary Sch.
Woodlands Prim. Sch.
St. Edmunds Catholic Prim. Sch.
Elmers Green Common
Nipe Bridge
27
38
47
F
G
H
J
K
1
2
3
4
5
6
7
48
49
350

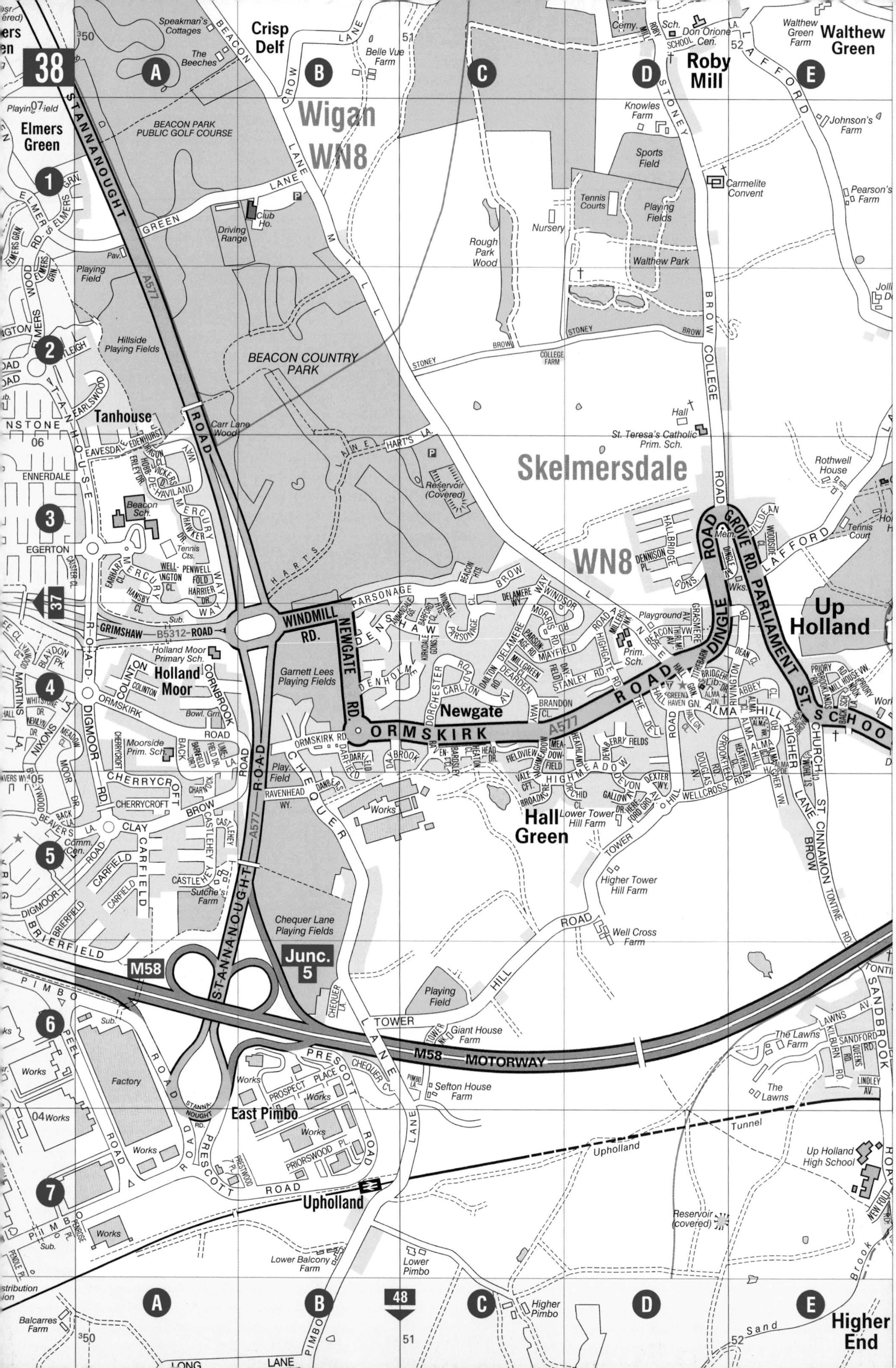
Crisp Delf
Wigan
WN8
Roby Mill
Walthew Green
Elmers Green
Speakman's Cottages
The Beeches
Belle Vue Farm
Don Orione Cen.
Walthew Green Farm
Knowles Farm
Johnson's Farm
BEACON PARK PUBLIC GOLF COURSE
Sports Field
Carmelite Convent
Pearson's Farm
Tennis Courts
Playing Fields
Club Ho.
Driving Range
Rough Park Wood
Nursery
Walthew Park
Playing Field
Hillside Playing Fields
BEACON COUNTRY PARK
Tanhouse
Carr Lane Wood
College Farm
Hall
St. Teresa's Catholic Prim. Sch.
Skelmersdale
Rothwell House
Reservoir (Covered)
Beacon Sch.
Tennis Cts.
WN8
Tennis Court
Up Holland
Holland Moor Primary Sch.
Holland Moor
Garnett Lees Playing Fields
Playground
Prim. Sch.
Newgate
Moorside Prim. Sch.
Play. Field
Works
Hall Green
Lower Tower Hill Farm
Comm. Cen.
Sutche's Farm
Higher Tower Hill Farm
Chequer Lane Playing Fields
Well Cross Farm
Junc. 5
M58
Playing Field
Giant House Farm
M58 MOTORWAY
The Lawns Farm
The Lawns
Factory
East Pimbo
Sefton House Farm
Tunnel
Upholland
Up Holland High School
Reservoir (covered)
Lower Balcony Farm
Lower Pimbo
Higher Pimbo
Balcarres Farm
Higher End
STANNANOUGHT ROAD
A577
ORMSKIRK ROAD
DINGLE ROAD
PARLIAMENT ST.
SCHOOL
B5312
GRIMSHAW ROAD
WINDMILL RD.
NEWGATE RD.
DIGMOOR RD.
CHEQUER LANE
TOWER HILL ROAD
PRESCOTT ROAD
PIMBO ROAD
STONEY BROW
COLLEGE ROAD
LAFFORD LA.
MILL LANE
HARTS LA.
37
48
A B C D E
1 2 3 4 5 6 7
350 51 52
07 06 05 04

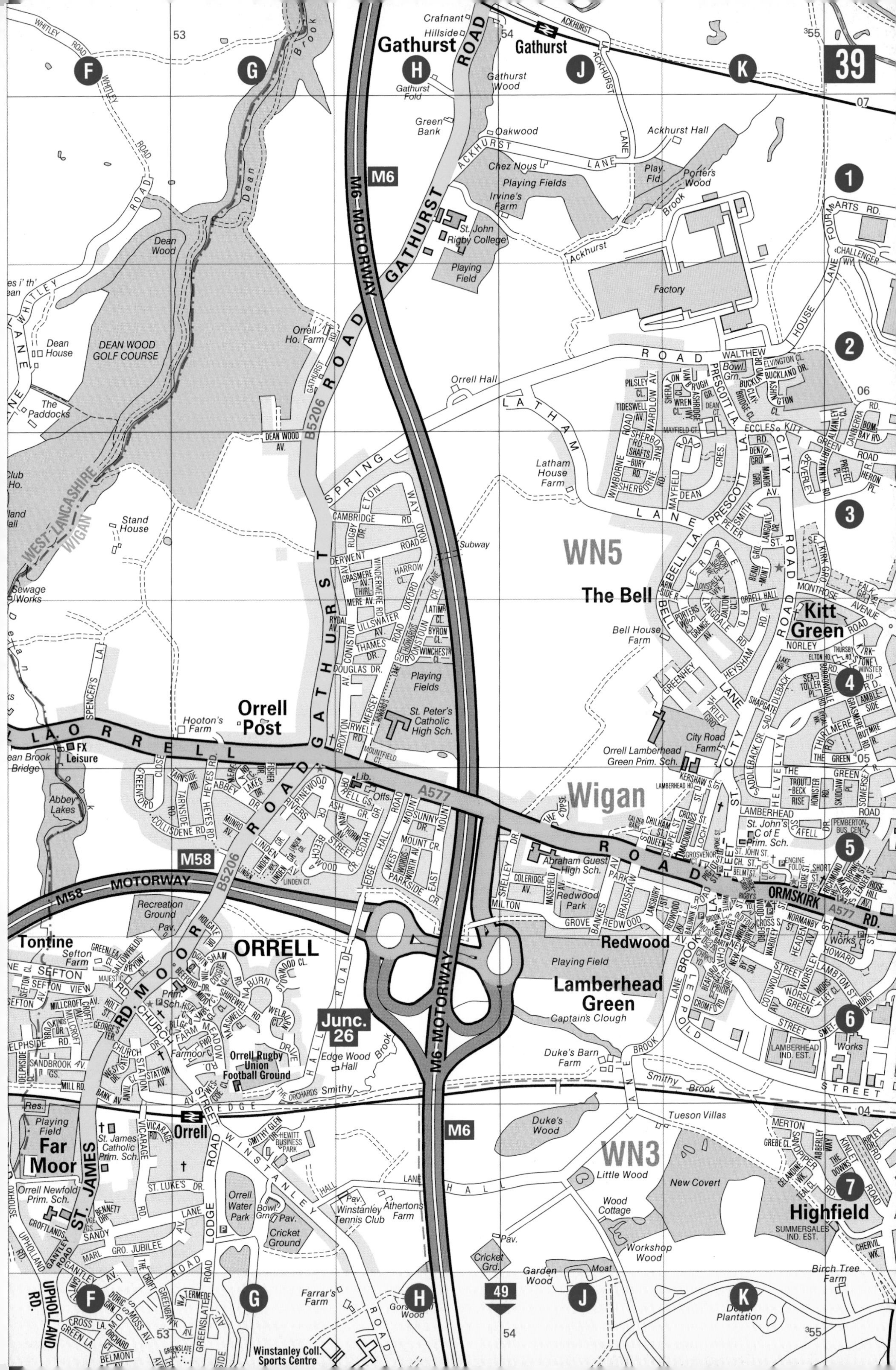
Gathurst
Gathurst Road
Gathurst Wood
Gathurst Fold
Crafnant
Hillside
Green Bank
Oakwood
Ackhurst Lane
Ackhurst Hall
Ackhurst Road
Chez Nous
Playing Fields
Irvine's Farm
Play. Fld.
Porters Wood
St. John Rigby College
Playing Field
Factory
Four Arts Rd.
Challenger Wy.
House Lane
Whitley Road
Whitley Lane
Dean Brook
Dean Wood
Dean House
Dean Wood Golf Course
The Paddocks
Dean Wood Av.
Orrell Ho. Farm
Orrell Hall
B5206
M6
M6 Motorway
Spring Road
Latham Lane
Latham House Farm
Walthew Road
Stand House
West Lancashire
Wigan
Sewage Works
Subway
WN5
The Bell
Bell House Farm
Kitt Green
Montrose Avenue
Norley Road
Orrell Lamberhead Green Prim. Sch.
City Road Farm
City Road
Heysham Road
Cambridge Rd.
Derwent
Rydal Av.
Coniston Av.
Ullswater Av.
Thames Dr.
Douglas Dr.
Harrow Cl.
Oxford Road
Playing Fields
St. Peter's Catholic High Sch.
Orrell Post
Hooton's Farm
Spencer's La.
Orrell Lane
FX Leisure
Dean Brook Bridge
Abbey Lakes
Orrell Road
A577
Lib.
Offs.
Wigan
Ormskirk Road
Lamberhead Road
St. John's C of E Prim. Sch.
Pemberton Bus. Cen.
Abraham Guest High Sch.
Redwood Park
Redwood
Playing Field
Lamberhead Green
Captain's Clough
Duke's Barn Farm
Brook Lane
Leopold
Lamberhead Ind. Est.
Works
M58
M58 Motorway
Recreation Ground
Pav.
Tontine
Sefton Farm
Sefton View
ORRELL
Moor Road
Church St.
Prim. Sch.
Farmoor Cl.
Orrell Rugby Union Football Ground
Junc. 26
Edge Wood Hall
Hall Road
Smithy Brook
Edge Hall
Orrell
Far Moor
St. James Catholic Prim. Sch.
St. James
Orrell Newfold Prim. Sch.
Upholland Road
Gantley Road
Winstanley Road
Orrell Water Park
Bowl. Grn.
Cricket Ground
Winstanley Tennis Club
Atherton's Farm
Hall Lane
Lodge Road
Smithy Glen
Hewitt Business Park
Duke's Wood
Tueson Villas
WN3
Little Wood
Wood Cottage
New Covert
Workshop Wood
Cricket Grd.
Garden Wood
Moat
Farrar's Farm
Gorse Hall Wood
Winstanley Coll. Sports Centre
Highfield
Summersales Ind. Est.
Birch Tree Farm
Dean Plantation
Merton Street
49
53
54
55
04
05
06
07
F
G
H
J
K
1
2
3
4
5
6
7

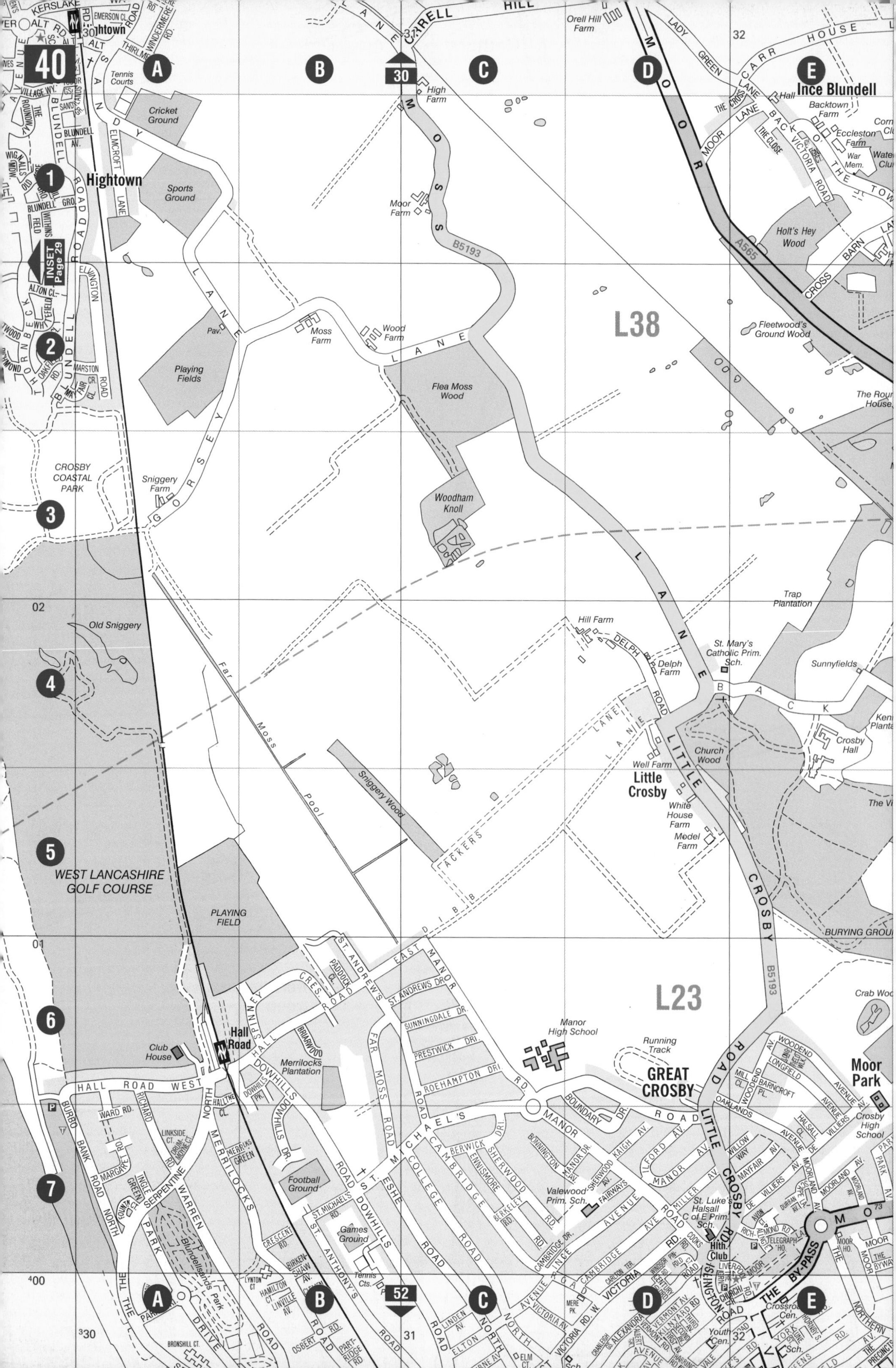
Hightown
Ince Blundell
Tennis Courts
Cricket Ground
Sports Ground
Playing Fields
Pav.
Orell Hill Farm
High Farm
Moor Farm
Moss Farm
Wood Farm
Flea Moss Wood
Woodham Knoll
Holt's Hey Wood
Fleetwood's Ground Wood
Backtown Farm
Eccleston Farm
War Mem.
L38
CROSBY COASTAL PARK
Sniggery Farm
Old Sniggery
WEST LANCASHIRE GOLF COURSE
Far Moss Pool
Sniggery Wood
Hill Farm
Delph Farm
St. Mary's Catholic Prim. Sch.
Sunnyfields
Trap Plantation
Church Wood
Crosby Hall
Well Farm
Little Crosby
White House Farm
Model Farm
PLAYING FIELD
L23
Manor High School
Running Track
GREAT CROSBY
Moor Park
Crosby High School
Club House
Hall Road
Merrilocks Plantation
Football Ground
Games Ground
Blundellsands Park
Valewood Prim. Sch.
St. Luke's Halsall C of E Prim. Sch.
Hlth. Club
Youth Cen.
HALL ROAD WEST
MOSS LANE
B5193
LITTLE CROSBY ROAD
GORSEY LANE
A565
INSET Page 29
30
52
A B C D E
1 2 3 4 5 6 7

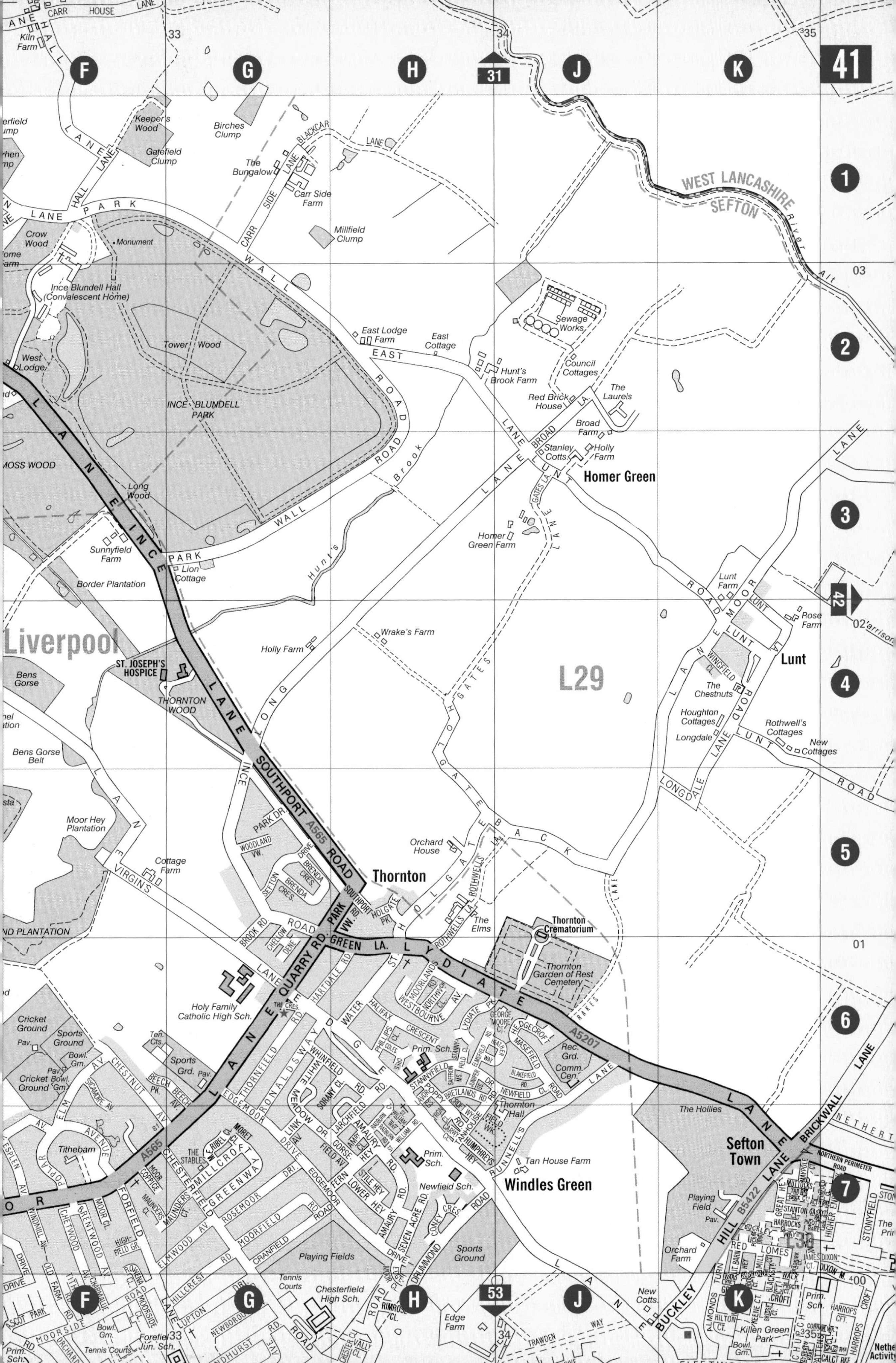

Homer Green
Thornton
Lunt
Windles Green
Sefton Town
Liverpool
L29
INCE BLUNDELL PARK
Ince Blundell Hall (Convalescent Home)
Tower Wood
Crow Wood
West Lodge
Monument
Birches Clump
Keeper's Wood
Gatefield Clump
The Bungalow
Carr Side Farm
Millfield Clump
East Lodge Farm
East Cottage
Sewage Works
Council Cottages
Hunt's Brook Farm
Red Brick House
The Laurels
Broad Farm
Stanley Cotts.
Holly Farm
Homer Green Farm
Wrake's Farm
Lunt Farm
Rose Farm
The Chestnuts
Houghton Cottages
Longdale
Rothwell's Cottages
New Cottages
ST. JOSEPH'S HOSPICE
THORNTON WOOD
Sunnyfield Farm
Lion Cottage
Border Plantation
Long Wood
MOSS WOOD
Bens Gorse
Bens Gorse Belt
Moor Hey Plantation
Cottage Farm
Orchard House
The Elms
Thornton Crematorium
Thornton Garden of Rest Cemetery
Holy Family Catholic High Sch.
Cricket Ground
Sports Ground
Tithebarn
Prim. Sch.
Newfield Sch.
Thornton Hall
Tan House Farm
The Hollies
Playing Field
Orchard Farm
Playing Fields
Sports Ground
Chesterfield High Sch.
Tennis Courts
Edge Farm
New Cotts.
Killen Green Park
WEST LANCASHIRE
SEFTON
River Alt
SOUTHPORT ROAD A565
LYDIATE LANE A5207
BRICKWALL LANE
HILL B5422
NORTHERN PERIMETER ROAD
EAST LANE
LONG LANE
PARK WALL ROAD
CARR SIDE LANE
CARR HOUSE LANE
HALL LANE
BLACKCAR LANE
BROAD LA.
LUNT ROAD
LUNT LANE
MOOR LANE
GATES LANE
HOLGATE
BACK LANE
INCE LANE
VIRGIN'S LANE
QUARRY RD.
GREEN LA.
EDGEMOOR DRIVE
BUCKLEY HILL
41
42
31
53
33
34
35
01
02
03
F
G
H
J
K
1
2
3
4
5
6
7

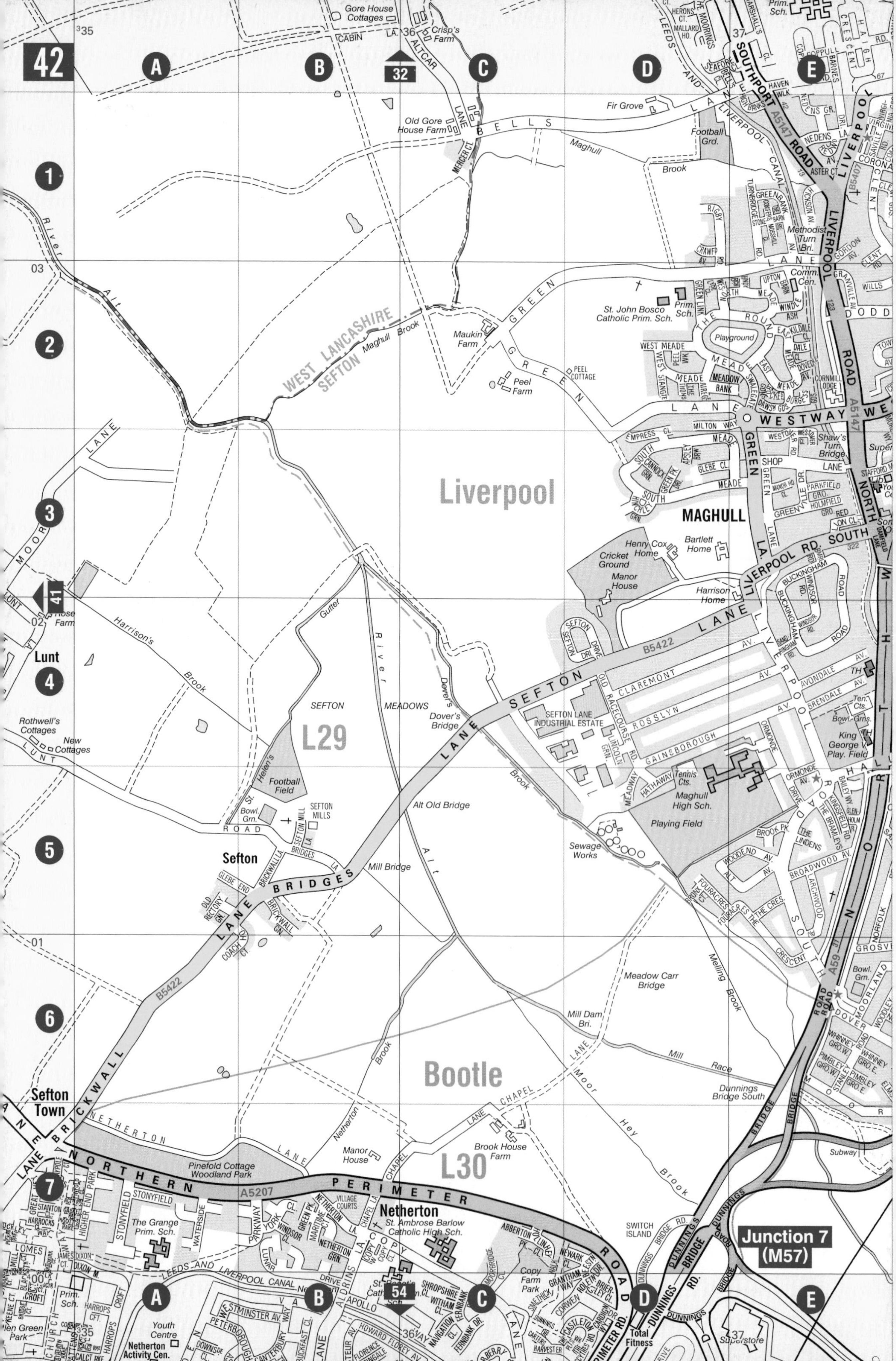
A
B
C
D
E
1
2
3
4
5
6
7
32
41
54
Gore House Cottages
Crisp's Farm
Old Gore House Farm
Fir Grove
Football Grd.
Maghull Brook
Methodist
Turn Bri.
Comm. Cen.
St. John Bosco Catholic Prim. Sch.
Prim. Sch.
Playground
Maukin Farm
Peel Farm
PEEL COTTAGE
WEST LANCASHIRE
SEFTON
Liverpool
MAGHULL
Henry Cox Home
Bartlett Home
Cricket Ground
Manor House
Harrison Home
Shaw's Turn Bridge
WESTWAY
SEFTON LANE INDUSTRIAL ESTATE
Maghull High Sch.
Playing Field
Tennis Cts.
Sewage Works
King George V Play. Field
Ten. Cts.
Bowl. Grns.
Dover's Bridge
SEFTON
MEADOWS
L29
Football Field
SEFTON MILLS
Sefton
Alt Old Bridge
Mill Bridge
Harrison's Brook
Lunt
Rothwell's Cottages
New Cottages
Rose Farm
River Alt
Meadow Carr Bridge
Mill Dam Bri.
Mill Race
Dunnings Bridge South
Melling Brook
Bootle
Sefton Town
Pinefold Cottage Woodland Park
Manor House
Brook House Farm
L30
Netherton
St. Ambrose Barlow Catholic High Sch.
The Grange Prim. Sch.
Copy Farm Park
SWITCH ISLAND
Junction 7 (M57)
Subway
Superstore
Total Fitness
Youth Centre
Netherton Activity Cen.
Prim. Sch.
LEEDS AND LIVERPOOL CANAL
NORTHERN PERIMETER ROAD
A5207
B5422
A5147
A59
B5407
SOUTHPORT ROAD
LIVERPOOL ROAD NORTH
BELLS LANE
GREEN LANE
SEFTON LANE
BRIDGES LANE
BRICKWALL LANE
LIVERPOOL RD. SOUTH
DUNNINGS BRIDGE RD.
MOOR LANE
CHAPEL LANE
NETHERTON LANE
Moor Hey Brook

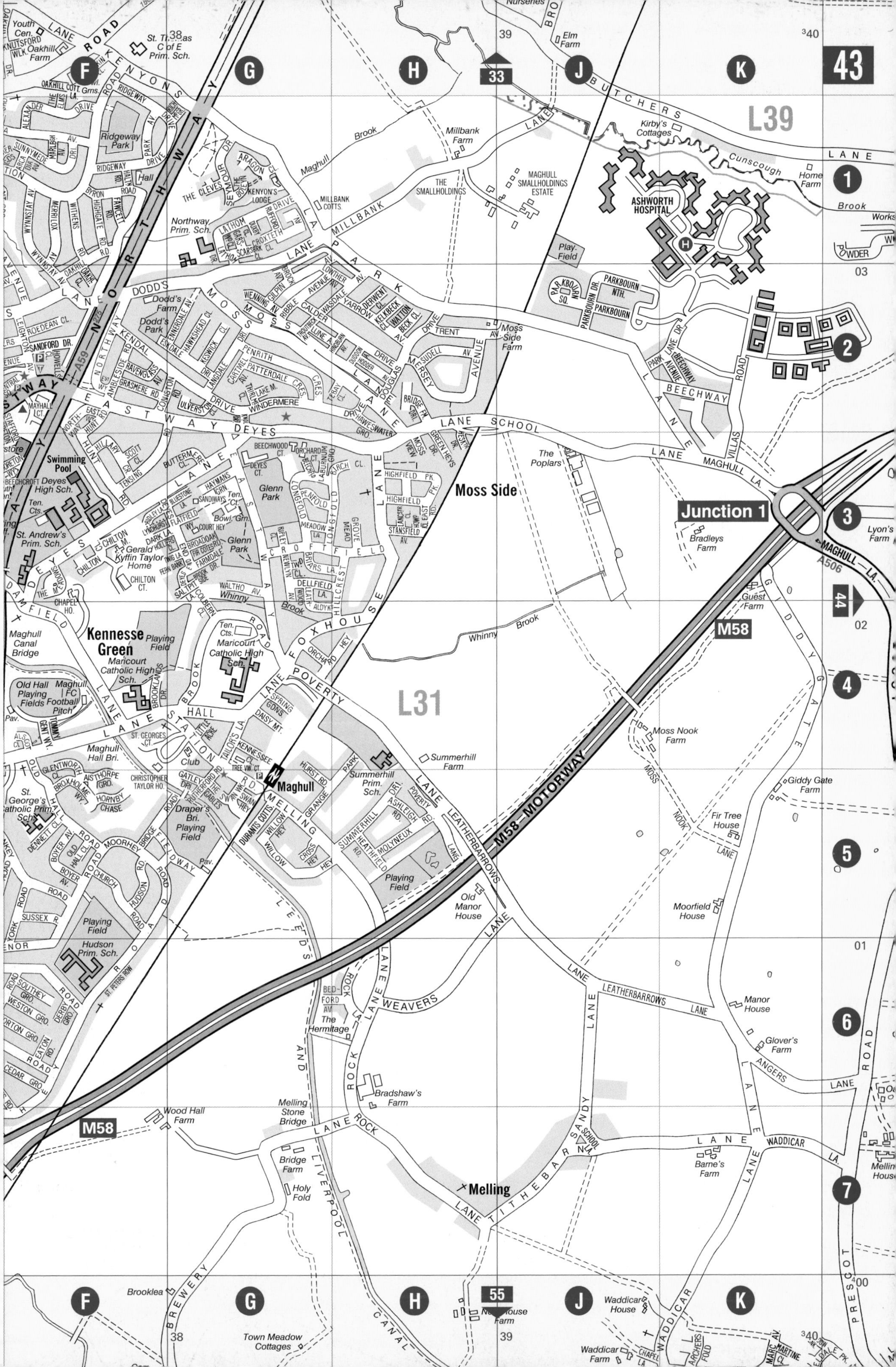
F
G
H
J
K
33
55
44
38
39
340
L39
L31
1
2
3
4
5
6
7
03
02
01
400
Butchers Lane
Cunscough Brook
Home Farm
Kirby's Cottages
Ashworth Hospital
Play. Field
Parkbourn Sq.
Parkbourn Nth.
Parkbourn Dr.
Parkbourn
Beechway
Park Lane Dr.
Maghull La.
Junction 1
Lyon's Farm
A506
Bradleys Farm
Guest Farm
M58
Giddy Gate
Giddy Gate Farm
Moss Nook Farm
Moss Nook Lane
Fir Tree House
Moorfield House
Manor House
Glover's Farm
Angers Lane
Prescot Road
Waddicar La.
Waddicar Lane
Barne's Farm
Waddicar House
Waddicar Farm
Leatherbarrows Lane
Sandy Lane
School Lane
Tithebarn Lane
Melling
Rock Lane
Weavers Lane
Bradshaw's Farm
The Hermitage
Melling Stone Bridge
Bridge Farm
Holy Fold
Brewery Lane
Brooklea
Town Meadow Cottages
Leeds and Liverpool Canal
Wood Hall Farm
M58 Motorway
Old Manor House
Summerhill Farm
Summerhill Prim. Sch.
Playing Field
Maghull
Melling Grange
Poverty Lane
Foxhouse Lane
Moss Side
The Poplars
Whinny Brook
School Lane
Maghull Lane
Moss Side Farm
Trent Av.
Mersey Avenue
Millbank Farm
The Smallholdings
Maghull Smallholdings Estate
Maghull Brook
Millbank
Millbank Cotts.
Park Lane
Moss Lane
Dodd's Lane
Dodd's Farm
Dodd's Park
Northway Prim. Sch.
Kenyon's Lodge
The Cleves
Kenyons Lane
Ridgeway Park
Ridgeway
St. Thomas C of E Prim. Sch.
Youth Cen.
Oakhill Farm
Northway
A59
Eastway
Deyes Lane
Swimming Pool
Deyes High Sch.
St. Andrew's Prim. Sch.
Gerald Kyffin Taylor Home
Glenn Park
Kennesse Green
Maricourt Catholic High Sch.
Maghull Canal Bridge
Old Hall Playing Fields
Maghull FC Football Pitch
Hall Lane
Station Road
Maghull Hall Bri.
Christopher Taylor Ho.
Draper's Bri. Playing Field
Moorhey Road
St. George's Catholic Prim. Sch.
Church Road
Hudson Prim. Sch.
Sussex R.
Derby Road
St. Peters Row

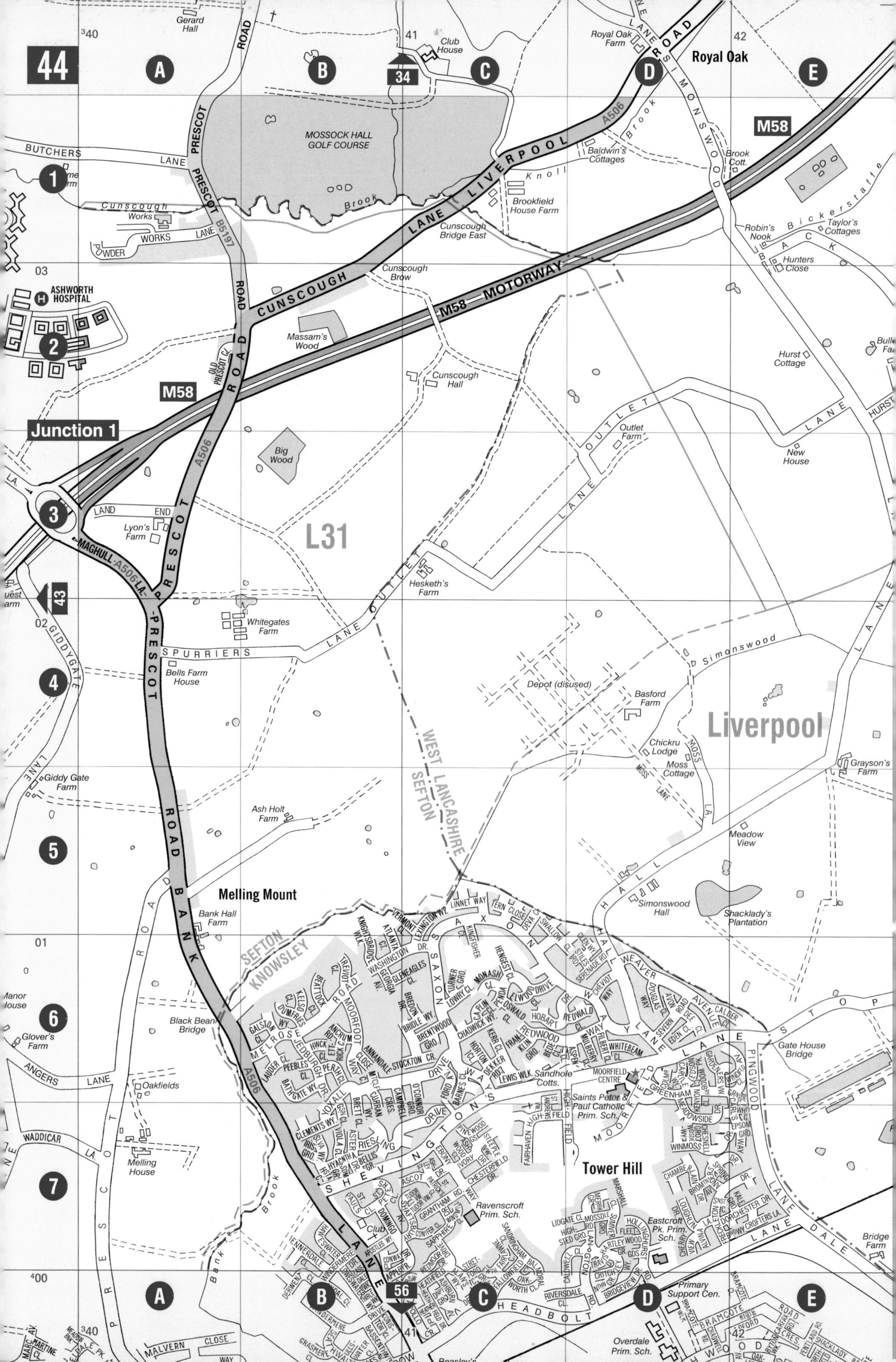

Gerard Hall
Club House
Royal Oak Farm
Royal Oak
MOSSOCK HALL GOLF COURSE
BUTCHERS LANE
PRESCOT ROAD
LIVERPOOL ROAD
A506
M58
Cunscough Works
WORKS LANE
POWDER
B5197
Baldwin's Cottages
Brookfield House Farm
Brook Cott.
Cunscough Bridge East
Robin's Nook
Taylor's Cottages
Hunters Close
ASHWORTH HOSPITAL
CUNSCOUGH LANE
Cunscough Brow
M58 MOTORWAY
Massam's Wood
Cunscough Hall
OLD PRESCOT CL.
Hurst Cottage
Junction 1
Big Wood
OUTLET LANE
Outlet Farm
New House
HURST LANE
LAND END
Lyon's Farm
MAGHULL LA.
L31
Hesketh's Farm
Whitegates Farm
SPURRIERS
GIDDYGATE LANE
Bells Farm House
Simonswood
Depot (disused)
Basford Farm
Liverpool
Chickru Lodge
Moss Cottage
MOSS LANE
Grayson's Farm
Giddy Gate Farm
WEST LANCASHIRE
SEFTON
Ash Holt Farm
Meadow View
PRESCOT ROAD
BANK LANE
Melling Mount
Simonswood Hall
Shacklady's Plantation
Bank Hall Farm
SEFTON
KNOWSLEY
Manor House
Black Bean Bridge
Glover's Farm
ANGERS LANE
Oakfields
WADDICAR LA.
Melling House
Gate House Bridge
STOPGATE LANE
SANDHOLE Cotts.
MOORFIELD CENTRE
Saints Peter & Paul Catholic Prim. Sch.
PINGWOOD LANE
Tower Hill
Ravenscroft Prim. Sch.
Eastcroft Pk. Prim. Sch.
DALE LANE
Bridge Farm
SHEVINGTON'S LANE
HEADBOLT LANE
Primary Support Cen.
Overdale Prim. Sch.
MALVERN CLOSE

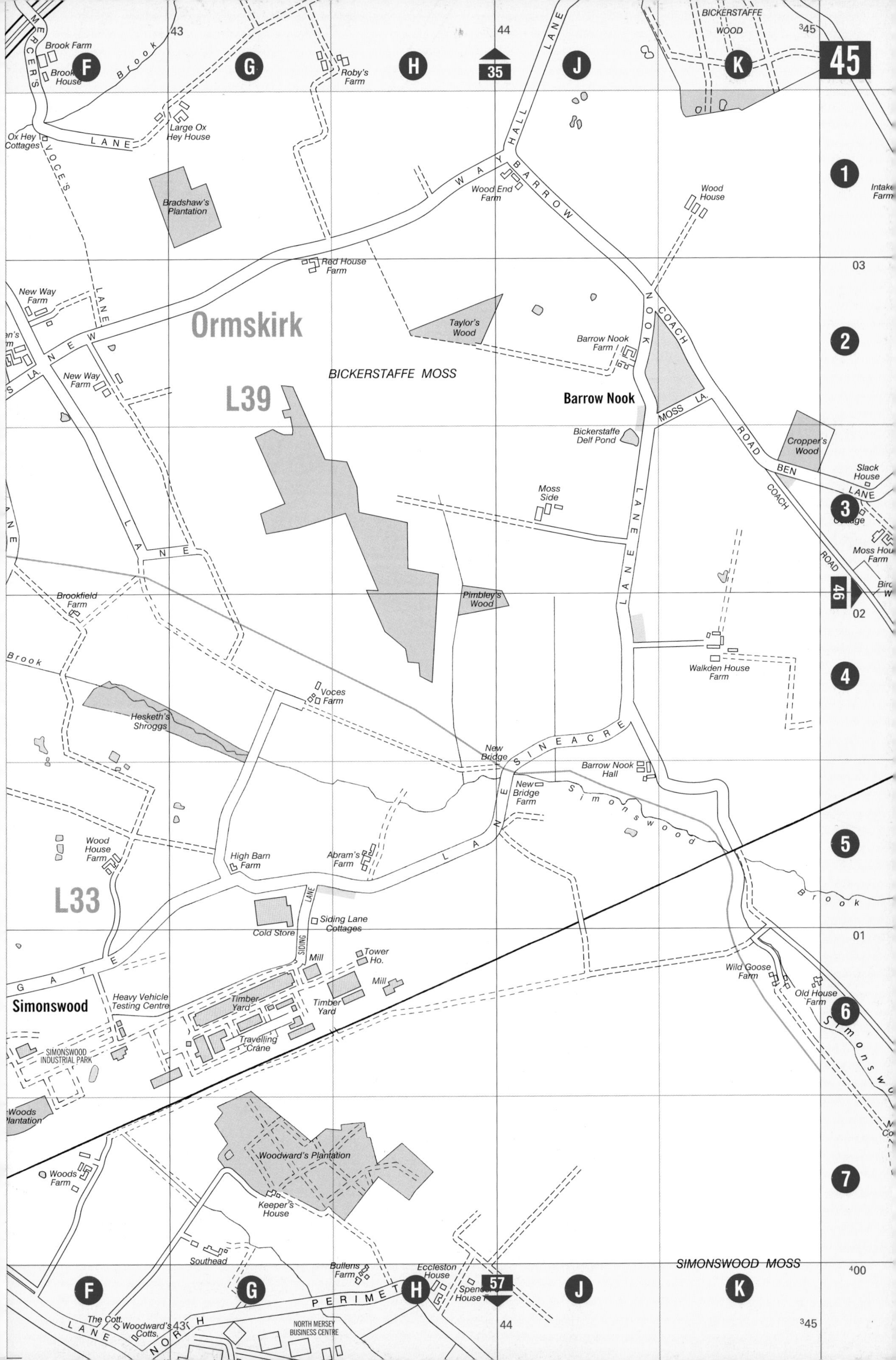

Brook Farm
Brook House
Large Ox Hey House
Ox Hey Cottages
Roby's Farm
Bradshaw's Plantation
Wood End Farm
Wood House
Red House Farm
New Way Farm
Ormskirk
Taylor's Wood
Barrow Nook Farm
BICKERSTAFFE MOSS
Barrow Nook
L39
Bickerstaffe Delf Pond
Cropper's Wood
Slack House
Moss Side
Brookfield Farm
Pimbley's Wood
Walkden House Farm
Voces Farm
Hesketh's Shroggs
New Bridge
Barrow Nook Hall
New Bridge Farm
Wood House Farm
High Barn Farm
Abram's Farm
L33
Siding Lane Cottages
Cold Store
Tower Ho.
Mill
Wild Goose Farm
Old House Farm
Simonswood
Heavy Vehicle Testing Centre
Timber Yard
Travelling Crane
SIMONSWOOD INDUSTRIAL PARK
Woods Plantation
Woodward's Plantation
Woods Farm
Keeper's House
Southead
Bullens Farm
Eccleston House
Spencer House
SIMONSWOOD MOSS
The Cott.
Woodward's Cotts.
NORTH MERSEY BUSINESS CENTRE
BICKERSTAFFE WOOD
Intake Farm
Moss House Farm

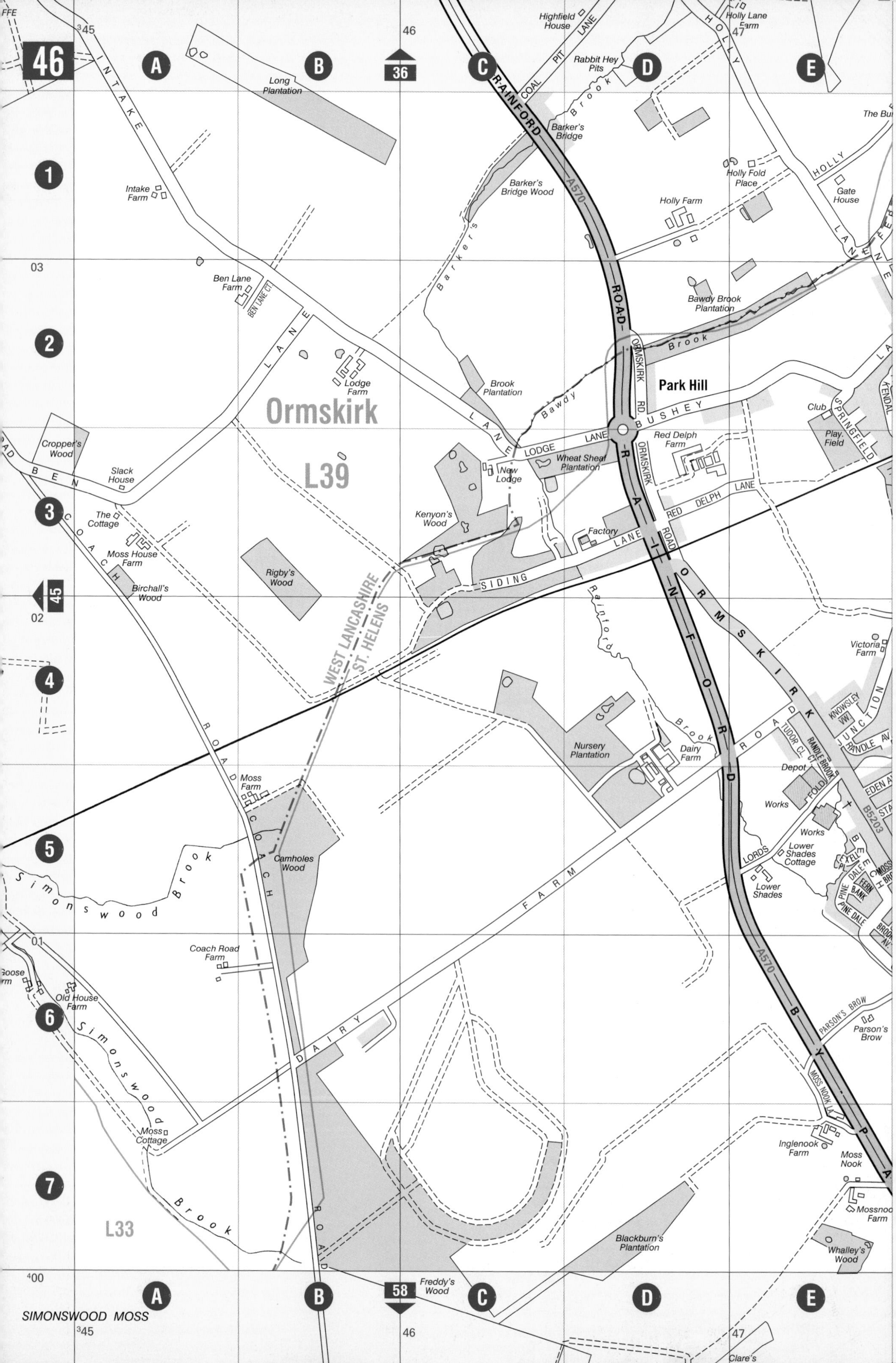
Ormskirk
L39
L33
Park Hill
SIMONSWOOD MOSS
RAINFORD ROAD
A570
ORMSKIRK ROAD
B5203
BY PASS
INTAKE LANE
BEN LANE
BEN LANE CT.
COACH ROAD
LODGE LANE
SIDING LANE
BUSHEY LANE
RED DELPH LANE
ORMSKIRK RD.
COAL PIT LANE
HOLLY LANE
DAIRY FARM ROAD
LORDS FOLD
TUDOR CL.
RANDLE BROOK CT.
RANDLE AV.
KNOWSLEY VW.
JUNCTION
SPRINGFIELD
PINE DALE
FERN BANK
PARSON'S BROW
MOSS NOOK LA.
WEST LANCASHIRE
ST. HELENS
Long Plantation
Intake Farm
Ben Lane Farm
Lodge Farm
Cropper's Wood
Slack House
The Cottage
Moss House Farm
Birchall's Wood
Rigby's Wood
Moss Farm
Camholes Wood
Coach Road Farm
Old House Farm
Moss Cottage
Simonswood Brook
Highfield House
Rabbit Hey Pits
Holly Lane Farm
Barker's Bridge
Barker's Bridge Wood
Barkers Brook
Holly Fold Place
Holly Farm
Gate House
Bawdy Brook Plantation
Bawdy Brook
Brook Plantation
New Lodge
Wheat Sheaf Plantation
Kenyon's Wood
Red Delph Farm
Factory
Club
Play. Field
Rainford Brook
Victoria Farm
Nursery Plantation
Dairy Farm
Depot
Works
Lower Shades Cottage
Lower Shades
Parson's Brow
Inglenook Farm
Moss Nook
Mossnook Farm
Whalley's Wood
Blackburn's Plantation
Freddy's Wood
Clare's Wood
A B C D E
1 2 3 4 5 6 7
36
45
58
345
46
47
03
02
01
400

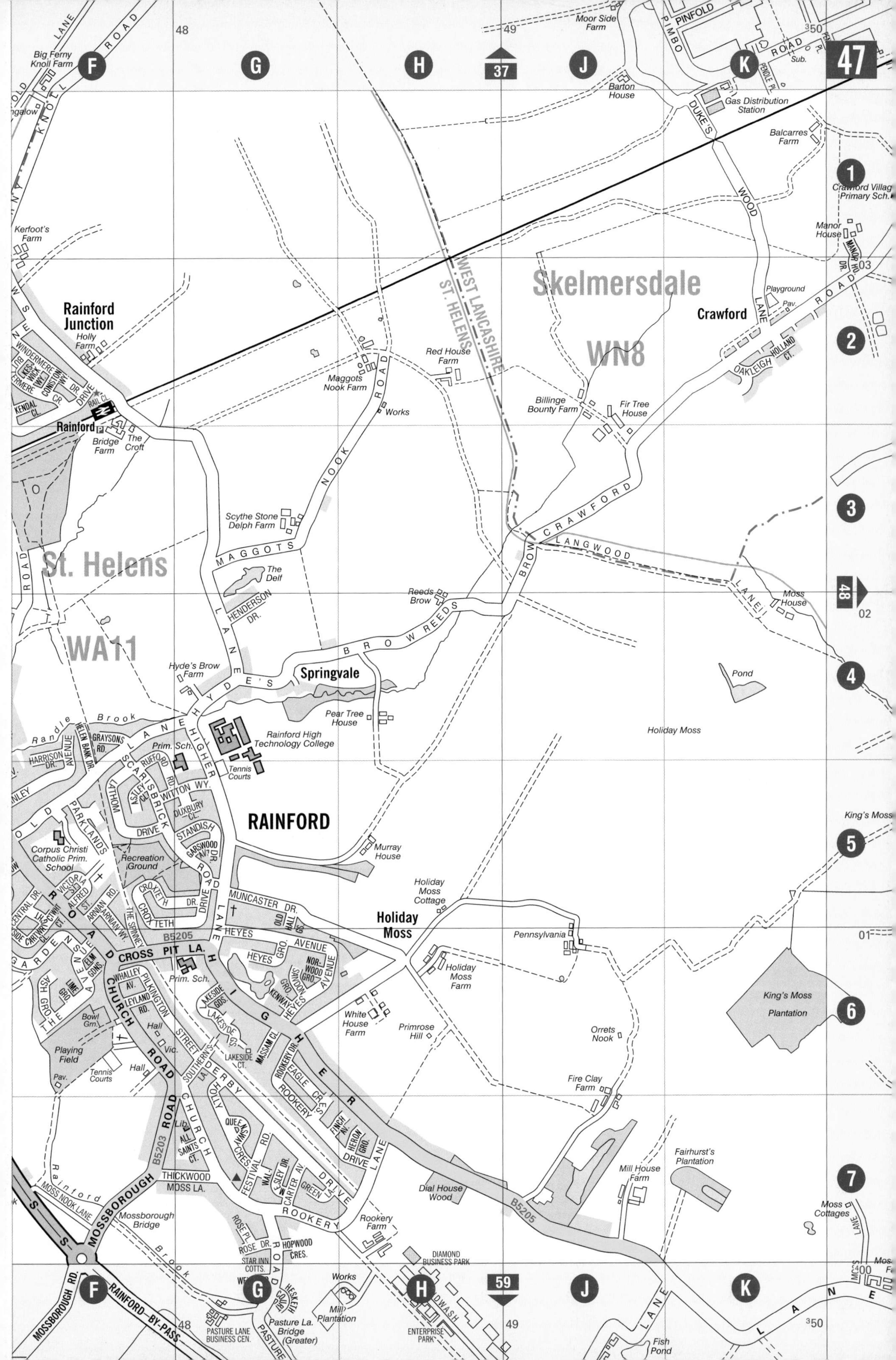
Skelmersdale
WN8
Crawford
St. Helens
WA11
RAINFORD
Rainford Junction
Springvale
Holiday Moss
Rainford
Moor Side Farm
Barton House
Gas Distribution Station
Balcarres Farm
Crawford Village Primary Sch.
Manor House
Playground
Kerfoot's Farm
Holly Farm
Bridge Farm
The Croft
Red House Farm
Maggots Nook Farm
Works
Billinge Bounty Farm
Fir Tree House
Scythe Stone Delph Farm
The Delf
Reeds Brow
Moss House
Hyde's Brow Farm
Pond
Pear Tree House
Rainford High Technology College
Tennis Courts
Prim. Sch.
Holiday Moss
Corpus Christi Catholic Prim. School
Recreation Ground
Murray House
Holiday Moss Cottage
Pennsylvania
Holiday Moss Farm
King's Moss Plantation
King's Moss
White House Farm
Primrose Hill
Orrets Nook
Playing Field
Tennis Courts
Fire Clay Farm
Fairhurst's Plantation
Mill House Farm
Dial House Wood
Rookery Farm
Mossborough Bridge
Moss Cottages
DIAMOND BUSINESS PARK
Mill Plantation
Pasture La. Bridge (Greater)
PASTURE LANE BUSINESS CEN.
ENTERPRISE PARK
Fish Pond
WEST LANCASHIRE
ST. HELENS
CRAWFORD BROW
LANGWOOD LANE
REEDS BROW
HYDE'S BROW
MAGGOTS NOOK ROAD
HIGHER LANE
CROSS PIT LA.
CHURCH ROAD
MOSSBOROUGH ROAD
RAINFORD-BY-PASS
B5205
B5203
WOOD LANE
DUKE'S
PINFOLD
PIMBO
37
48
59
F G H J K
1 2 3 4 5 6 7
48 49 350
02 03 01

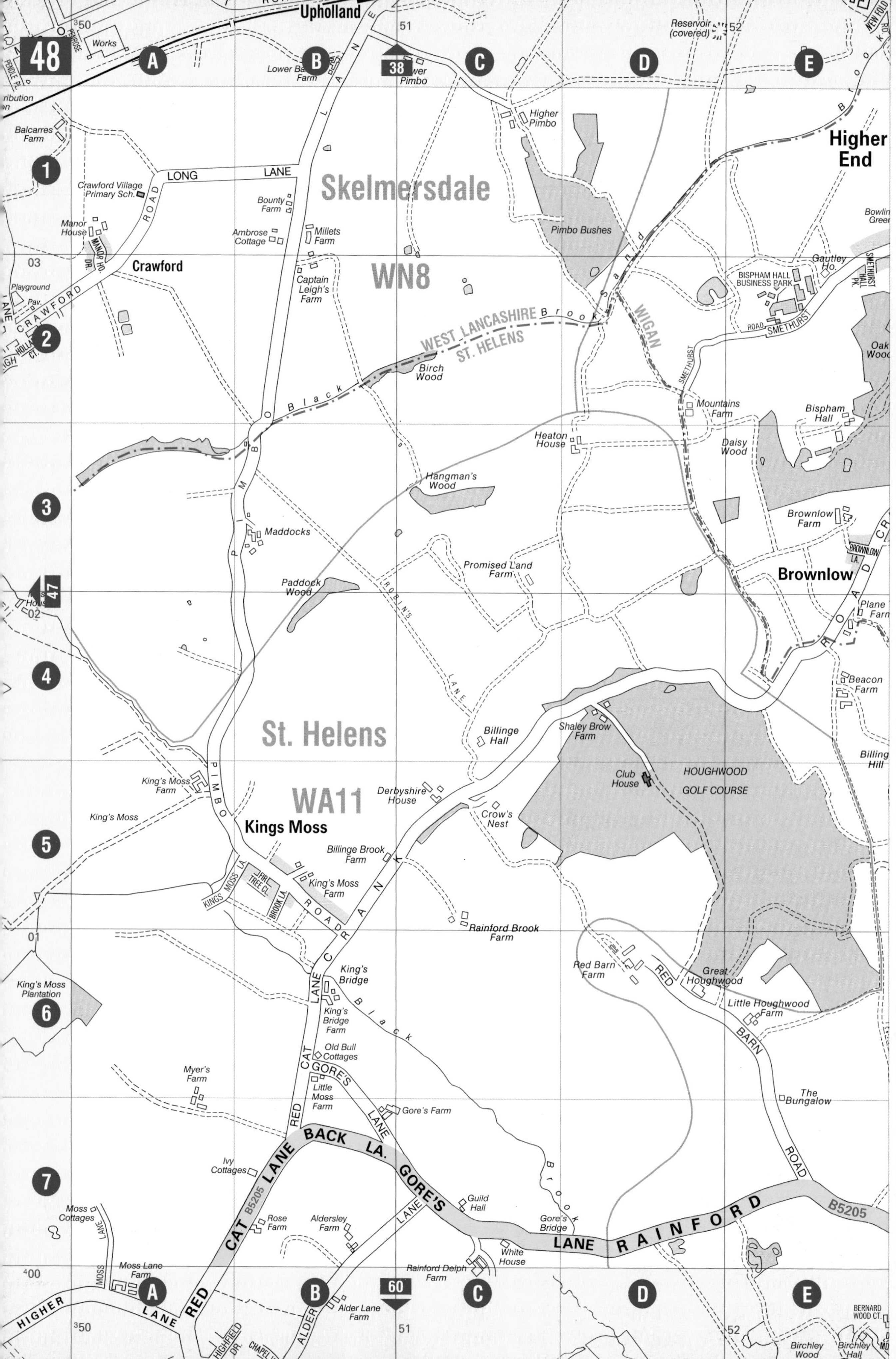
Upholland
ROAD
Works
Lower Barn Farm
38
Lower Pimbo
Reservoir (covered)
Higher Pimbo
Higher End
Balcarres Farm
Crawford Village Primary Sch.
LONG LANE
Skelmersdale
Bounty Farm
Manor House
Ambrose Cottage
Millets Farm
Pimbo Bushes
Crawford
Captain Leigh's Farm
WN8
Playground
Pav.
CRAWFORD
Gautley Ho.
BISPHAM HALL BUSINESS PARK
SMETHURST ROAD
WEST LANCASHIRE
ST. HELENS
WIGAN
Black Brook
Birch Wood
Sand Brook
Oak Wood
Mountains Farm
Bispham Hall
Heaton House
Daisy Wood
Hangman's Wood
Brownlow Farm
Maddocks
Promised Land Farm
Brownlow
Paddock Wood
ROBIN'S LANE
Plane Farm
PIMBO ROAD
Beacon Farm
St. Helens
Billinge Hall
Shaley Brow Farm
Billinge Hill
King's Moss Farm
Club House
HOUGHWOOD GOLF COURSE
WA11
Derbyshire House
King's Moss
Crow's Nest
Kings Moss
Billinge Brook Farm
King's Moss Farm
KINGS MOSS LA.
FIR TREE CL.
BROOK LA.
Rainford Brook Farm
CRANK ROAD
King's Bridge
Red Barn Farm
Great Houghwood
King's Moss Plantation
King's Bridge Farm
Little Houghwood Farm
Old Bull Cottages
Myer's Farm
Little Moss Farm
GORE'S LANE
Gore's Farm
RED BARN ROAD
The Bungalow
BACK LA.
RED CAT LANE
B5205
Ivy Cottages
Guild Hall
Moss Cottages
Rose Farm
Aldersley Farm
Gore's Bridge
RAINFORD
Moss Lane Farm
White House
Rainford Delph Farm
60
47
HIGHER LANE
ALDER LANE
Alder Lane Farm
HIGHFIELD DR.
CHAPEL VW.
BERNARD WOOD CT.
Birchley Wood
Birchley Hall
A
B
C
D
E
1
2
3
4
5
6
7
350
51
52
03
02
01
400

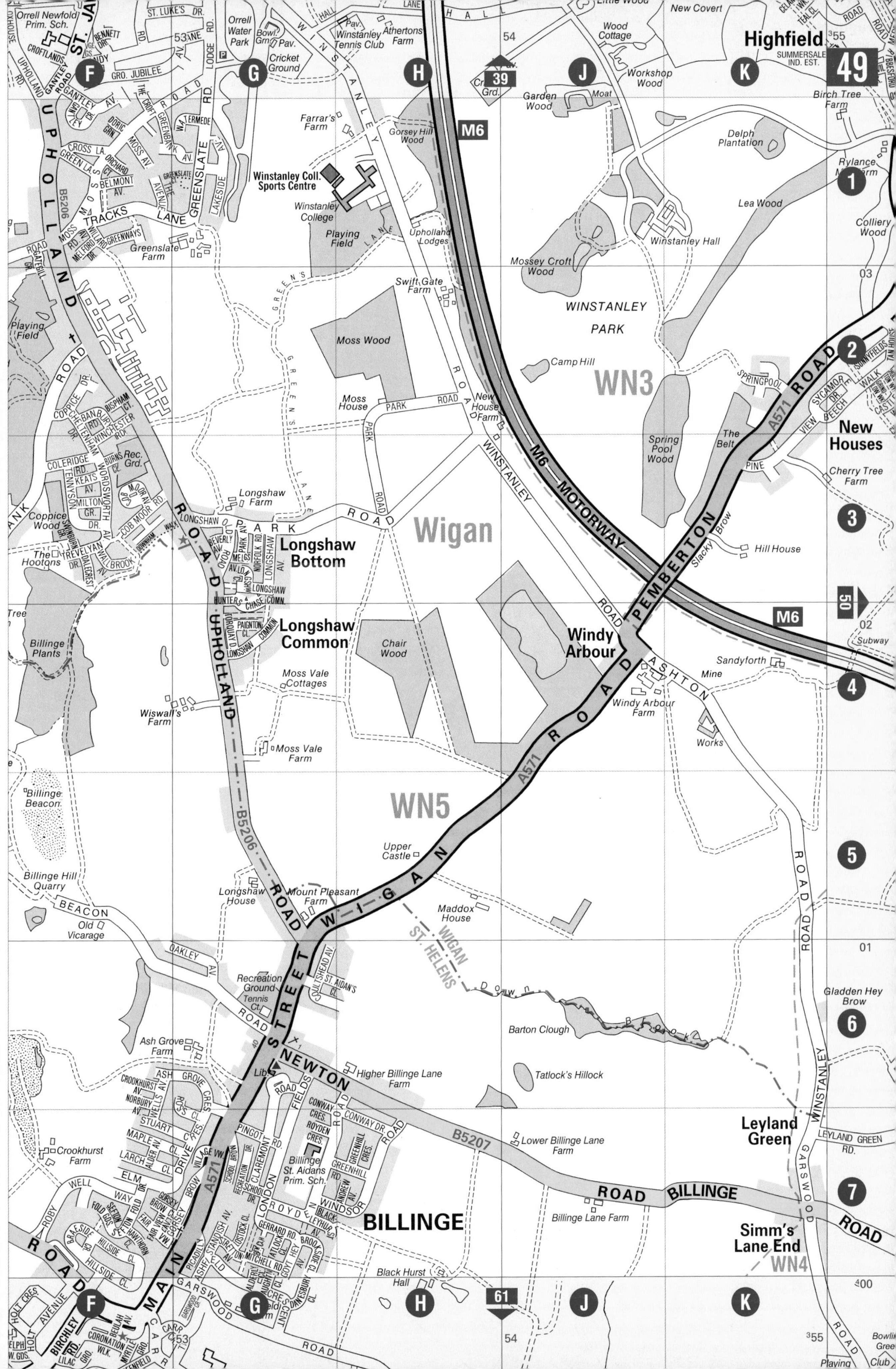

49
Highfield
SUMMERSALE IND. EST.
New Covert
Wood Cottage
Workshop Wood
Garden Wood
Moat
Birch Tree Farm
Delph Plantation
Rylance Farm
Lea Wood
Colliery Wood
Winstanley Hall
Mossey Croft Wood
WINSTANLEY PARK
Camp Hill
WN3
Spring Pool Wood
The Belt
SPRINGPOOL
SYCAMORE DR.
BEECH
PINE
VIEW
WALK
New Houses
Cherry Tree Farm
Hill House
Slacky Brow
PEMBERTON ROAD
A571
M6
M6 MOTORWAY
39
50
Subway
Sandyforth
Mine
Windy Arbour
Windy Arbour Farm
ASHTON
Works
Wigan
WN5
Chair Wood
Moss Wood
Moss House
PARK ROAD
WINSTANLEY ROAD
New House Farm
Swift Gate Farm
Upholland Lodges
Winstanley Coll. Sports Centre
Winstanley College
Playing Field
Farrar's Farm
Gorsey Hill Wood
Winstanley Tennis Club
Athertons Farm
Pav.
Orrell Water Park
Bowl. Grn.
Cricket Ground
Orrell Newfold Prim. Sch.
ST. LUKE'S DR.
GRO. JUBILEE
CROFTLANDS
GANTLEY
UPHOLLAND ROAD
B5206
CROSS LA.
GREEN LA.
MOSS AV.
ORCHARD
BELMONT AV.
GREENSLATE RD.
LAKESIDE
WATERMEDE
GREENBANK AV.
TRACKS LANE
GREENWAYS
MELFORD DR.
Greenslate Farm
GREEN'S LANE
Playing Field
COPPICE DR.
BANBURY RD.
BISPHAM CT.
CHELTENHAM
WINCHESTER
COLERIDGE RD.
TENNYSON
KEATS AV.
MILTON GR.
BURNS CL.
WORDSWORTH AV.
Rec. Grd.
MOOR AV.
COB MOOR RD.
Coppice Wood
The Hootons
TREVELYAN DR.
WALBROOK
LONGSHAW PARK ROAD
Longshaw Farm
Longshaw Bottom
LONGSHAW AV.
NORFOLK RD.
HUNTERS CHASE
LONGSHAW COMMON
PAIGNTON CL.
TORQUAY DR.
Longshaw Common
Billinge Plants
Moss Vale Cottages
Wiswall's Farm
Moss Vale Farm
Billinge Beacon
Billinge Hill Quarry
BEACON
Old Vicarage
Upper Castle
Longshaw House
Mount Pleasant Farm
Maddox House
WIGAN ROAD
WIGAN STREET
ST. HELENS
OAKLEY AV.
Recreation Ground
Tennis Ct.
ST. AIDAN'S CL.
Down Brook
Barton Clough
Tatlock's Hillock
Ash Grove Farm
ASH GROVE
NEWTON ROAD
B5207
Higher Billinge Lane Farm
Lower Billinge Lane Farm
CONWAY DR.
GREENHILL
Billinge St. Aidans Prim. Sch.
ROYDEN CRES.
LONDON
CLAREMONT
WINDSOR AV.
BILLINGE
BILLINGE ROAD
Billinge Lane Farm
Black Hurst Hall
Crookhurst Farm
CROOKHURST AV.
NORBURY AV.
STUART
MAPLE AV.
LARCH
ELM
WELL WAY
HILLSIDE CL.
BRAESIDE
MAIN STREET
GARSWOOD
HOLT CRES.
AVENUE
BIRCHLEY RD.
BEULAH AV.
CORONATION WLK.
LILAC GRO.
CARR
WINSTANLEY ROAD
Gladden Hey Brow
Leyland Green
LEYLAND GREEN RD.
GARSWOOD ROAD
Simm's Lane End
WN4
61
Bowling Green
Club
Playing

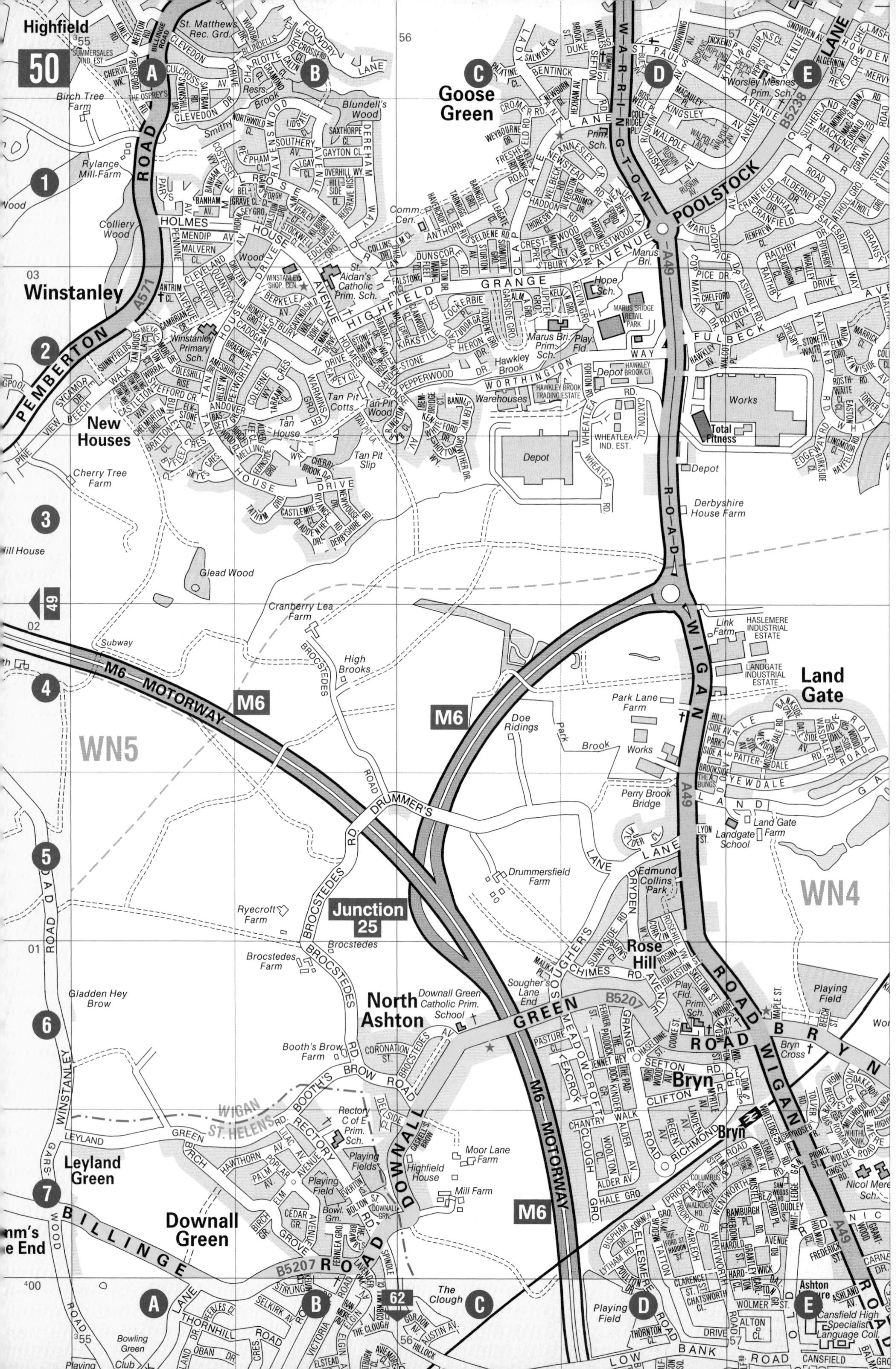
Highfield
Goose Green
Winstanley
New Houses
Land Gate
WN5
WN4
North Ashton
Bryn
Leyland Green
Downall Green
Junction 25
M6 MOTORWAY
WARRINGTON ROAD
WIGAN ROAD
POOLSTOCK LANE
PEMBERTON ROAD
BILLINGE ROAD
GREEN ROAD
Marus Bridge Retail Park
Hawkley Brook Trading Estate
Wheatlea Ind. Est.
Haslemere Industrial Estate
Landgate Industrial Estate
Winstanley Primary Sch.
St. Aidan's Catholic Prim. Sch.
Downall Green Catholic Prim. School
Rectory C of E Prim. Sch.
Landgate School
Nicol Mere Sch.
Cansfield High Specialist Language Coll.
Glead Wood
Cranberry Lea Farm
High Brooks
Doe Ridings
Drummersfield Farm
Ryecroft Farm
Brocstedes Farm
Booth's Brow Farm
Moor Lane Farm
Highfield House
Mill Farm
Edmund Collins Park
Perry Brook Bridge
Park Lane Farm
Link Farm
Derbyshire House Farm
Total Fitness
Birch Tree Farm
Rylance Mill Farm
Colliery Wood
Cherry Tree Farm
Gladden Hey Brow
The Clough
Bryn Cross

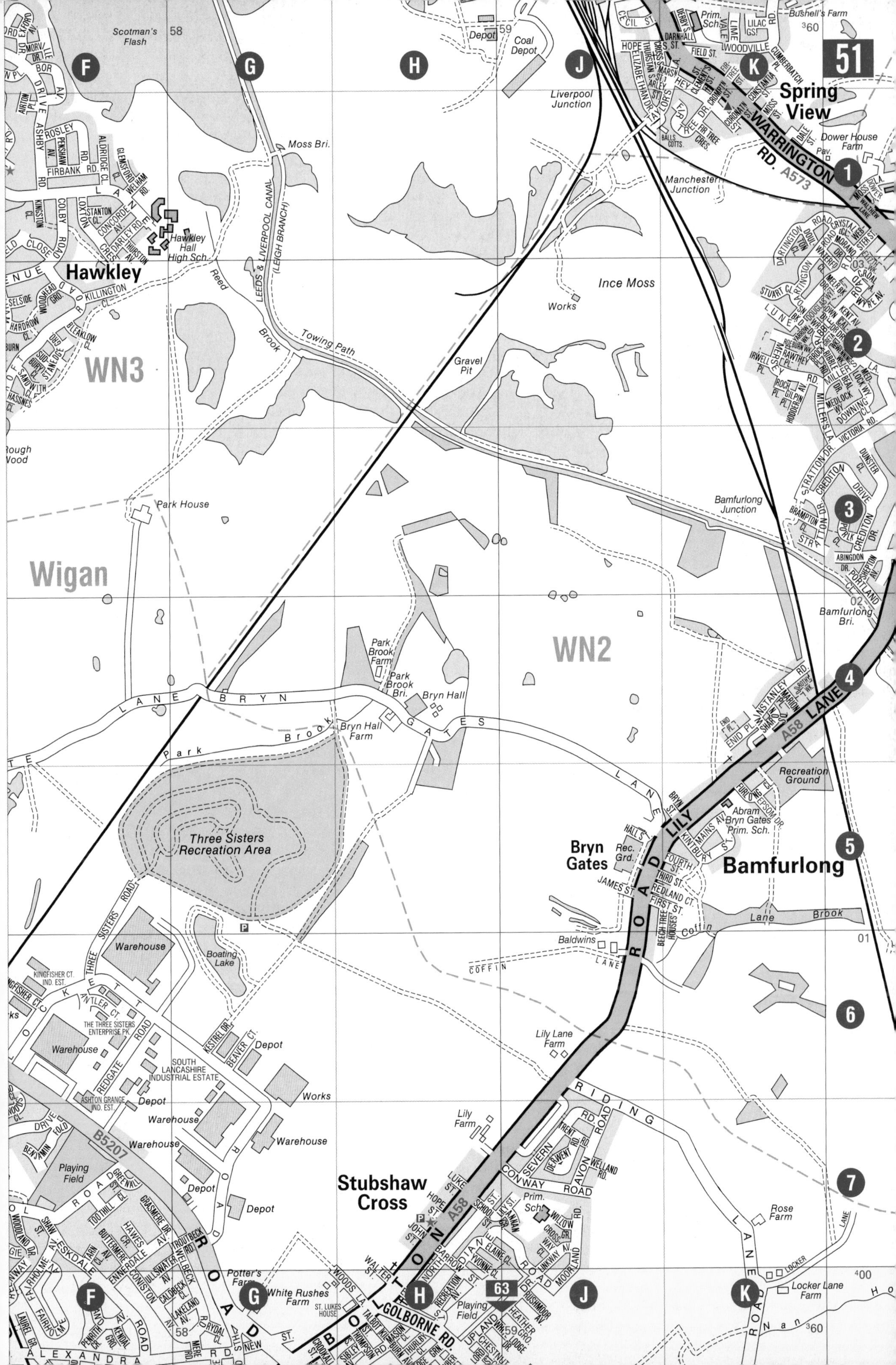
Scotman's Flash
Hawkley
Hawkley Hall High Sch.
WN3
Wigan
Park House
Moss Bri.
LEEDS & LIVERPOOL CANAL (LEIGH BRANCH)
Towing Path
Reed Brook
Depot
Coal Depot
Liverpool Junction
Manchester Junction
Ince Moss
Works
Gravel Pit
Bamfurlong Junction
Bamfurlong Bri.
WN2
Park Brook Farm
Park Brook Bri.
Bryn Hall
Bryn Hall Farm
BRYN LANE
GATES LANE
Park Brook
Three Sisters Recreation Area
Boating Lake
Warehouse
KINGFISHER CT. IND. EST.
THE THREE SISTERS ENTERPRISE PK.
SOUTH LANCASHIRE INDUSTRIAL ESTATE
ASHTON GRANGE IND. EST.
Depot
Works
Playing Field
Spring View
WARRINGTON RD. A573
Dower House Farm
Bushell's Farm
Recreation Ground
Abram Bryn Gates Prim. Sch.
Bryn Gates
Rec. Grd.
Bamfurlong
Lane Brook
Coffin
Baldwins
COFFIN LANE
LILY LANE A58
Lily Lane Farm
Lily Farm
RIDING LANE
Rose Farm
Locker Lane Farm
Stubshaw Cross
BOLTON ROAD A58
GOLBORNE RD.
Potter's Farm
White Rushes Farm
Playing Field
B5207
ALEXANDRA
63
F
G
H
J
K
1
2
3
4
5
6
7

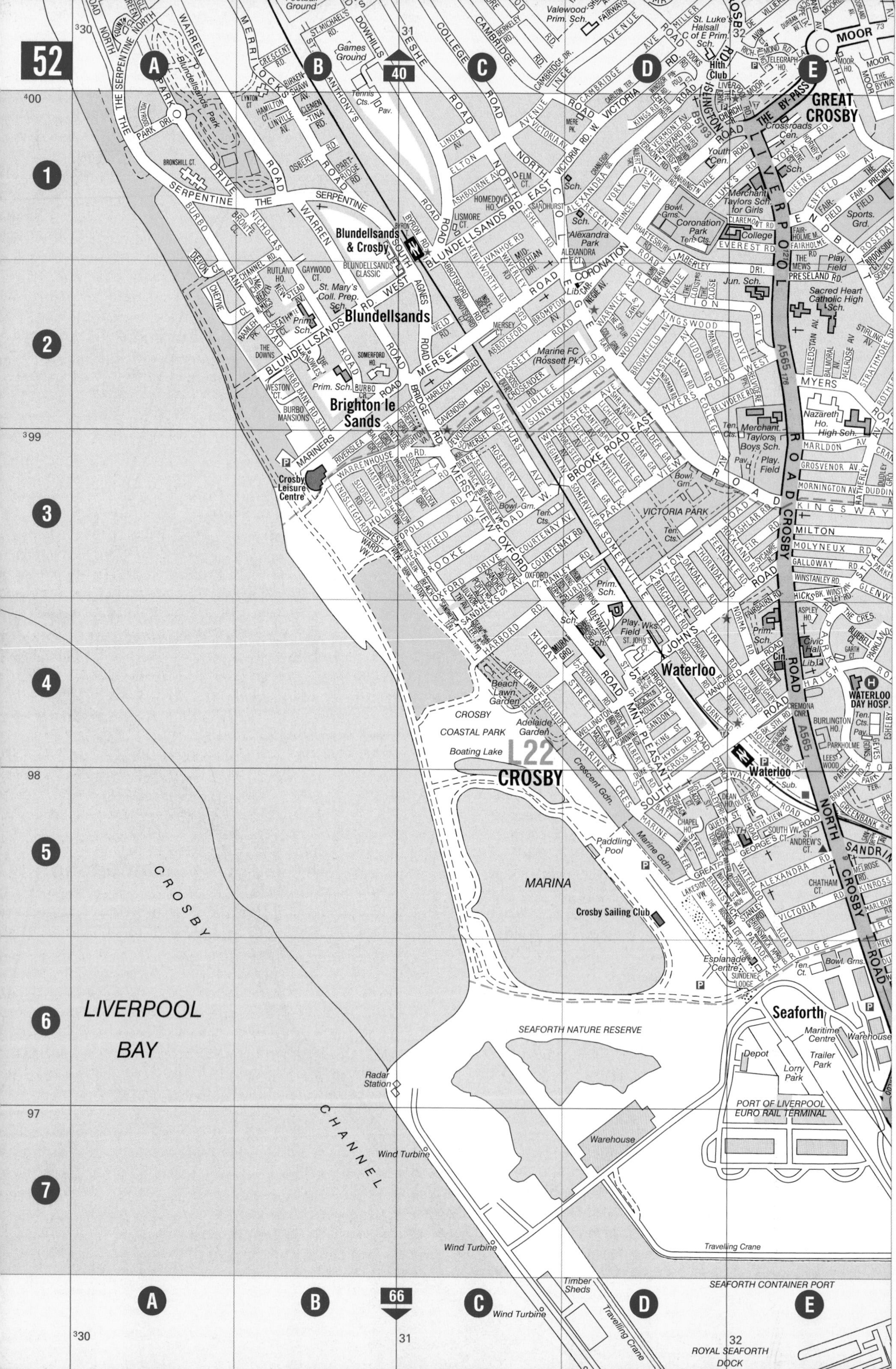
40
66
A
B
C
D
E
1
2
3
4
5
6
7
330
31
32
400
399
98
97
LIVERPOOL
BAY
CROSBY
CHANNEL
GREAT
CROSBY
Blundellsands
& Crosby
Blundellsands
Brighton le
Sands
Waterloo
L22
CROSBY
Seaforth
Crosby
Leisure
Centre
CROSBY
COASTAL PARK
Boating Lake
MARINA
Crosby Sailing Club
Paddling
Pool
Marine Gdn.
Crescent Gdn.
Beach
Lawn
Garden
Adelaide
Garden
Esplanade
Centre
SEAFORTH NATURE RESERVE
Radar
Station
Wind Turbine
Wind Turbine
Wind Turbine
Warehouse
Timber
Sheds
Travelling Crane
Travelling Crane
SEAFORTH CONTAINER PORT
ROYAL SEAFORTH
DOCK
PORT OF LIVERPOOL
EURO RAIL TERMINAL
Depot
Lorry
Park
Trailer
Park
Maritime
Centre
Warehouse
Games
Ground
Tennis
Cts.
Pav.
Blundellsands Park
THE SERPENTINE
SERPENTINE
THE WARREN
BLUNDELLSANDS RD. WEST
BLUNDELLSANDS RD. EAST
ST. MARY'S
Coll. Prep.
Sch.
Prim. Sch.
Marine FC
(Rossett Pk.)
VICTORIA PARK
Alexandra
Park
Coronation
Park
Ten. Cts.
Merchant
Taylors Sch.
for Girls
Merchant
Taylors
Boys Sch.
Sacred Heart
Catholic High
Sch.
Nazareth
Ho.
High Sch.
Sports.
Grd.
Play.
Field
Jun. Sch.
Youth
Cen.
Crossroads
Cen.
Hlth.
Club
St. Luke's
Halsall
of E Prim.
Sch.
Valewood
Prim. Sch.
Civic
Hall
Lib.
WATERLOO
DAY HOSP.
Bowl. Grns.
A565
B5193
LIVERPOOL ROAD
CROSBY ROAD
CROSBY ROAD NORTH
THE BY-PASS
MOOR
COLLEGE ROAD
COLLEGE ROAD NORTH
CAMBRIDGE ROAD
VICTORIA RD.
CORONATION ROAD
BROOKE ROAD EAST
SOMERVILLE
ST. JOHN'S ROAD
MERSEY ROAD
MERSEY VIEW
OXFORD ROAD
MARINERS
SOUTH ROAD
MNT PLEASANT
MARINE CRES.
Waterloo
MYERS ROAD WEST
KINGSWAY
MILTON
MOLYNEUX RD
GALLOWAY
HAIGH
ALEXANDRA RD.
VICTORIA RD.
CAMBRIDGE

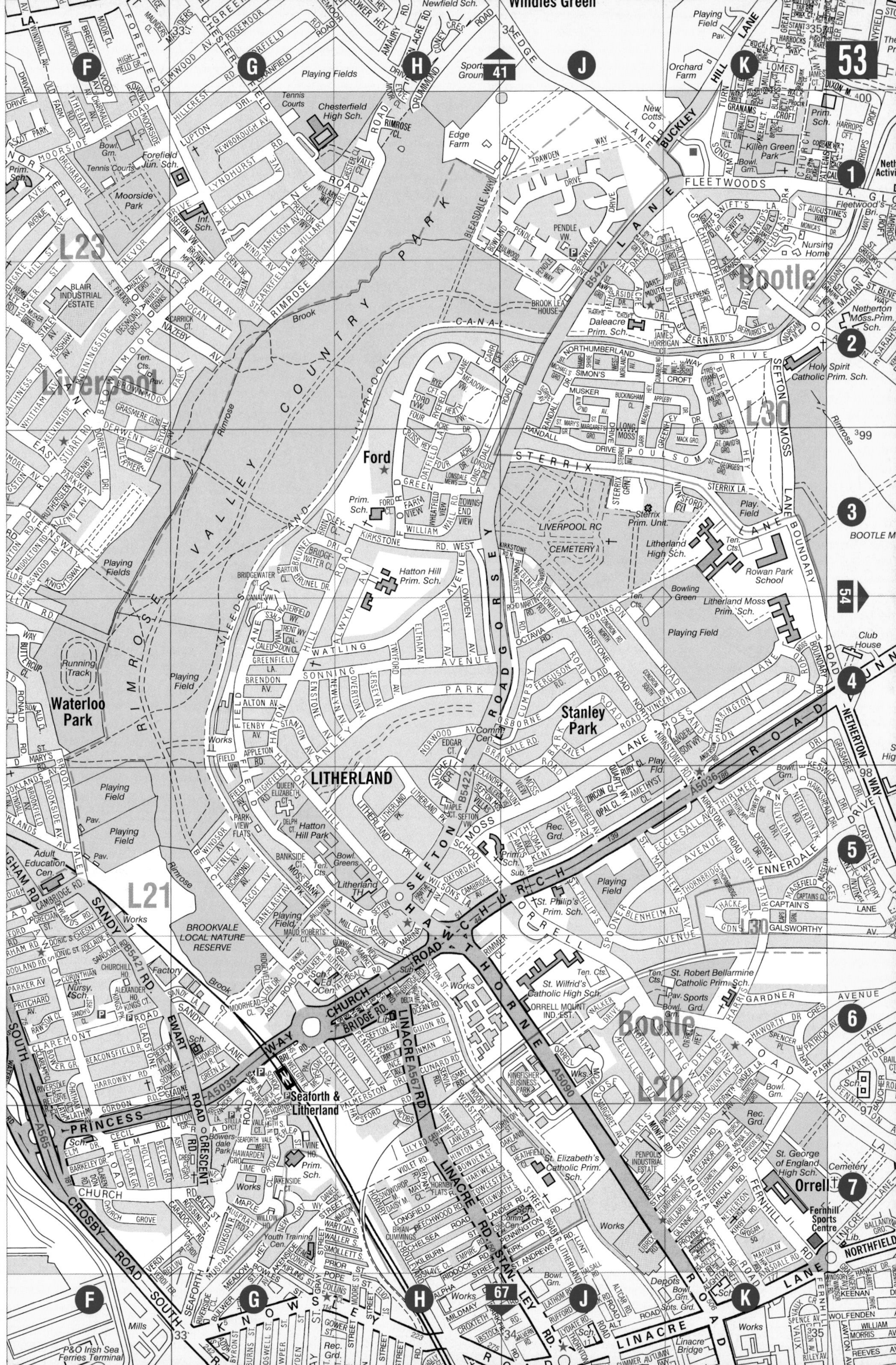

53
Windles Green
F
G
H
J
K
1
2
3
4
5
6
7
41
54
67
L23
L30
L21
L20
Liverpool
Bootle
Ford
LITHERLAND
Orrell
Stanley Park
Waterloo Park
RIMROSE VALLEY COUNTRY PARK
LEEDS AND LIVERPOOL CANAL
Chesterfield High Sch.
Edge Farm
Orchard Farm
Killen Green Park
Moorside Park
BLAIR INDUSTRIAL ESTATE
Daleacre Prim. Sch.
Holy Spirit Catholic Prim. Sch.
LIVERPOOL RC CEMETERY
Litherland High Sch.
Rowan Park School
Litherland Moss Prim. Sch.
Hatton Hill Prim. Sch.
Hatton Hill Park
BROOKVALE LOCAL NATURE RESERVE
Running Track
Playing Fields
Playing Field
Adult Education Cen.
St. Philip's Prim. Sch.
St. Wilfrid's Catholic High Sch.
St. Robert Bellarmine Catholic Prim. Sch.
ORRELL MOUNT IND. EST.
KINGFISHER BUSINESS PARK
St. Elizabeth's Catholic Prim. Sch.
PENPOLL INDUSTRIAL ESTATE
St. George of England High Sch.
Fernhill Sports Centre
Seaforth & Litherland
Youth Training Cen.
Bowersdale Park
Linacre Bridge
P&O Irish Sea Ferries Terminal
Mills
Works
FLEETWOODS LA.
STERRIX LA.
KIRKSTONE RD. WEST
SEFTON MOSS LANE
NETHERTON WAY
CHURCH ROAD
HAWTHORNE ROAD
LINACRE RD.
LINACRE LANE
CROSBY ROAD SOUTH
PRINCESS WAY
SOUTH RD.
KNOWSLEY RD.
ORRELL RD.
GORSEY LANE
BUCKLEY HILL LANE
EDGE LANE
WATTS LA.
NORTHFIELD
A5036
A5090
A567
A565
B5422
B5421

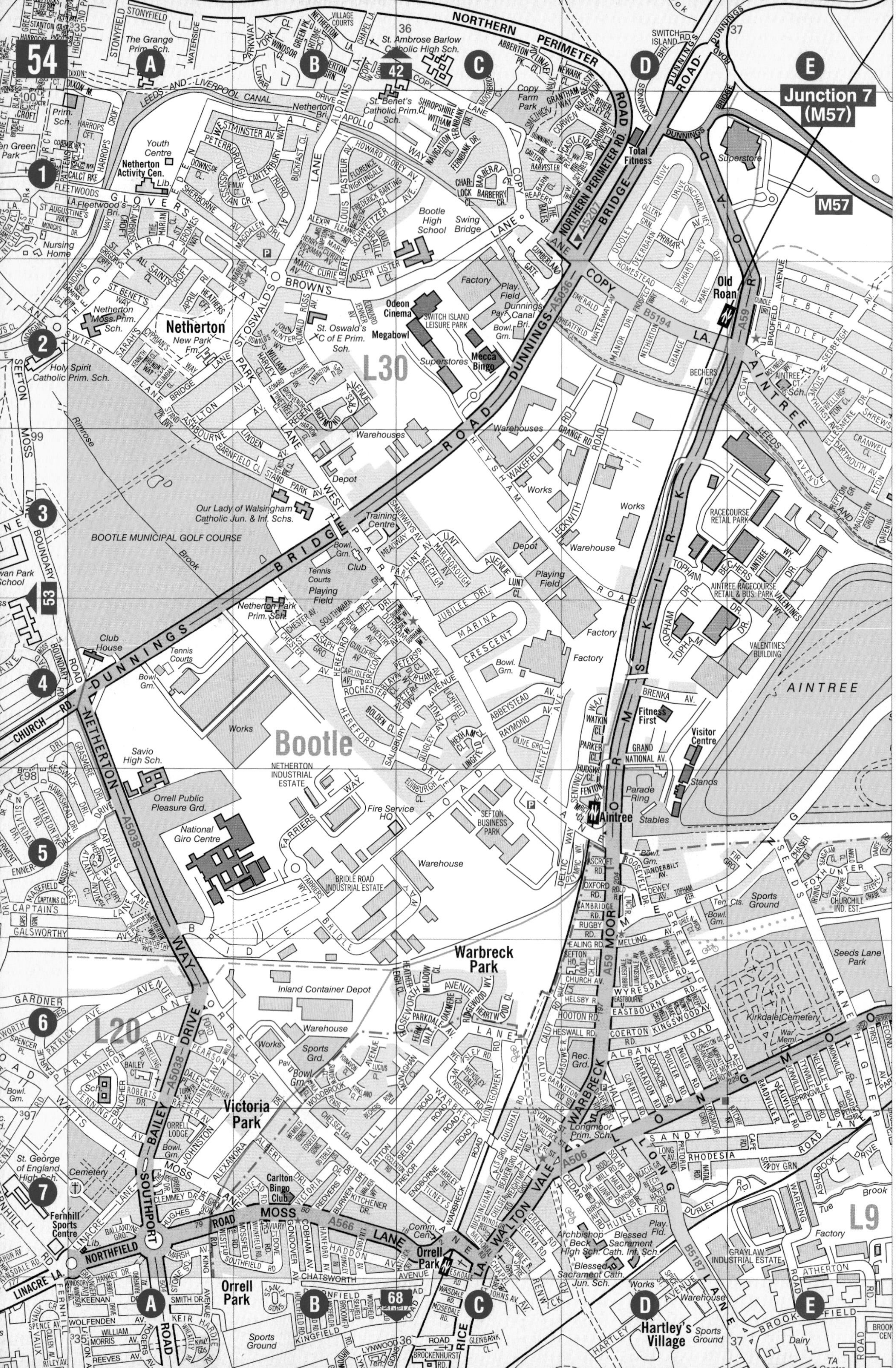

54
Junction 7 (M57)
M57
NORTHERN PERIMETER ROAD
LEEDS AND LIVERPOOL CANAL
The Grange Prim. Sch.
St. Ambrose Barlow Catholic High Sch.
St. Benet's Catholic Prim. Sch.
Copy Farm Park
Total Fitness
Superstore
Youth Centre
Netherton Activity Cen.
Nursing Home
Bootle High School
Swing Bridge
Old Roan
Netherton Moss Prim. Sch.
Netherton
New Park Fm.
Holy Spirit Catholic Prim. Sch.
St. Oswald's C of E Prim. Sch.
Odeon Cinema
Megabowl
SWITCH ISLAND LEISURE PARK
Superstores
Mecca Bingo
L30
Warehouses
Depot
Works
Our Lady of Walsingham Catholic Jun. & Inf. Schs.
BOOTLE MUNICIPAL GOLF COURSE
Training Centre
Tennis Courts
Playing Field
Club
RACECOURSE RETAIL PARK
AINTREE RACECOURSE RETAIL & BUS. PARK
VALENTINES BUILDING
AINTREE
Netherton Park Prim. Sch.
Club House
DUNNINGS BRIDGE ROAD
Factory
Fitness First
Visitor Centre
Stands
Parade Ring
Stables
Aintree
Bootle
NETHERTON INDUSTRIAL ESTATE
Savio High Sch.
Orrell Public Pleasure Grd.
National Giro Centre
Fire Service HQ
SEFTON BUSINESS PARK
BRIDLE ROAD INDUSTRIAL ESTATE
Warehouse
Sports Ground
CHURCHILL IND. EST.
Seeds Lane Park
Warbreck Park
Inland Container Depot
Kirkdale Cemetery
L20
Victoria Park
Sports Grd.
Rec. Grd.
Longmoor Prim. Sch.
St. George of England High Sch.
Cemetery
Carlton Bingo Club
Fernhill Sports Centre
Orrell Park
Comm. Cen.
Archbishop Beck High Sch.
Blessed Sacrament Cath. Inf. Sch.
Blessed Sacrament Cath. Jun. Sch.
Play. Fld.
GRAYLAW INDUSTRIAL ESTATE
L9
Hartley's Village
Dairy
TA Centre
A5036
A59
A5038
A566
A506
B5194
B5187
A5207
42
53
68

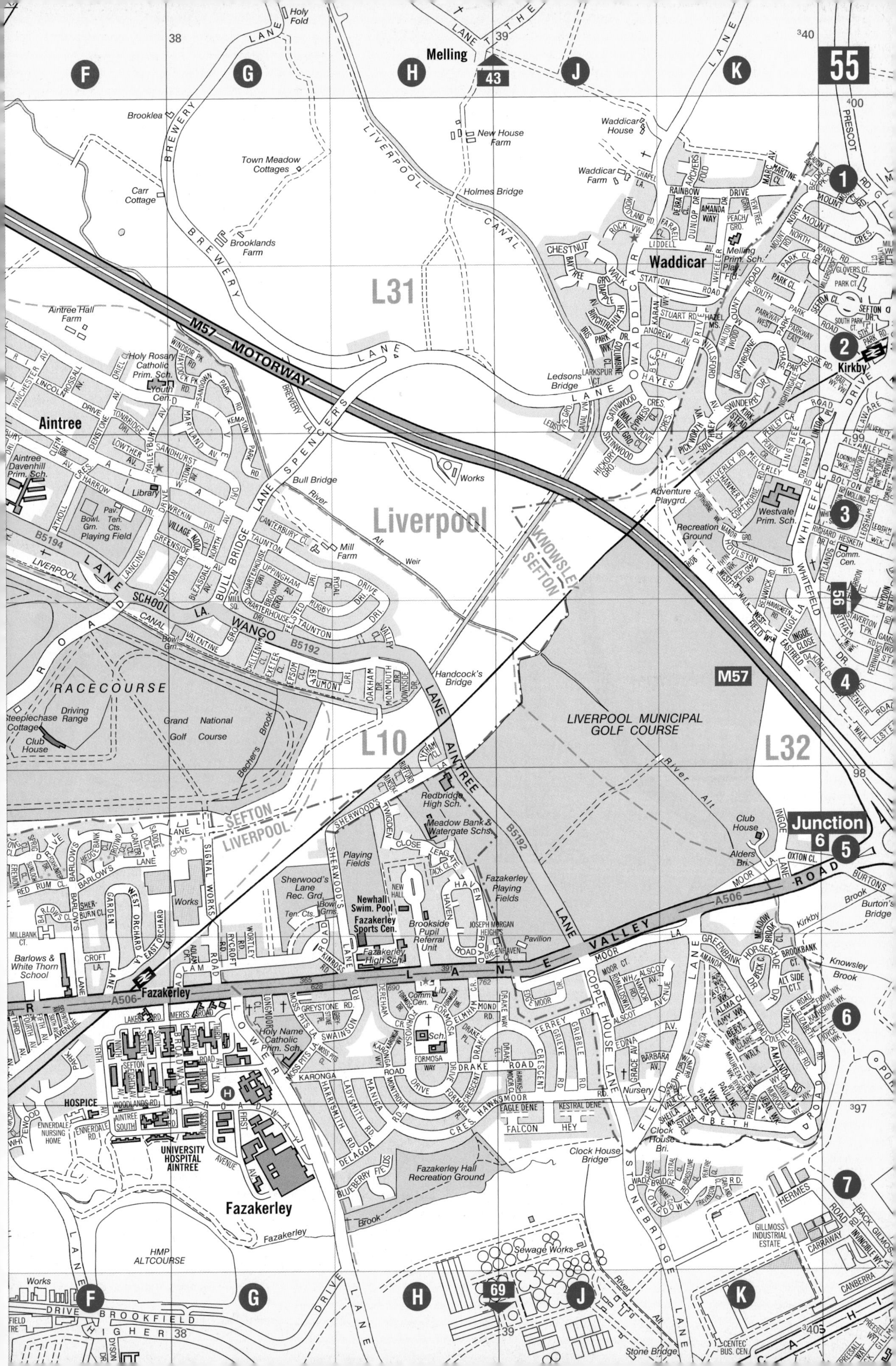
Melling
Waddicar
Kirkby
Aintree
Liverpool
L31
L10
L32
Fazakerley
M57 MOTORWAY
RACECOURSE
Grand National Golf Course
LIVERPOOL MUNICIPAL GOLF COURSE
Junction 6
UNIVERSITY HOSPITAL AINTREE
HMP ALTCOURSE
GILLMOSS INDUSTRIAL ESTATE
Fazakerley Hall Recreation Ground
Sewage Works
KNOWSLEY
SEFTON
LIVERPOOL
43
56
69

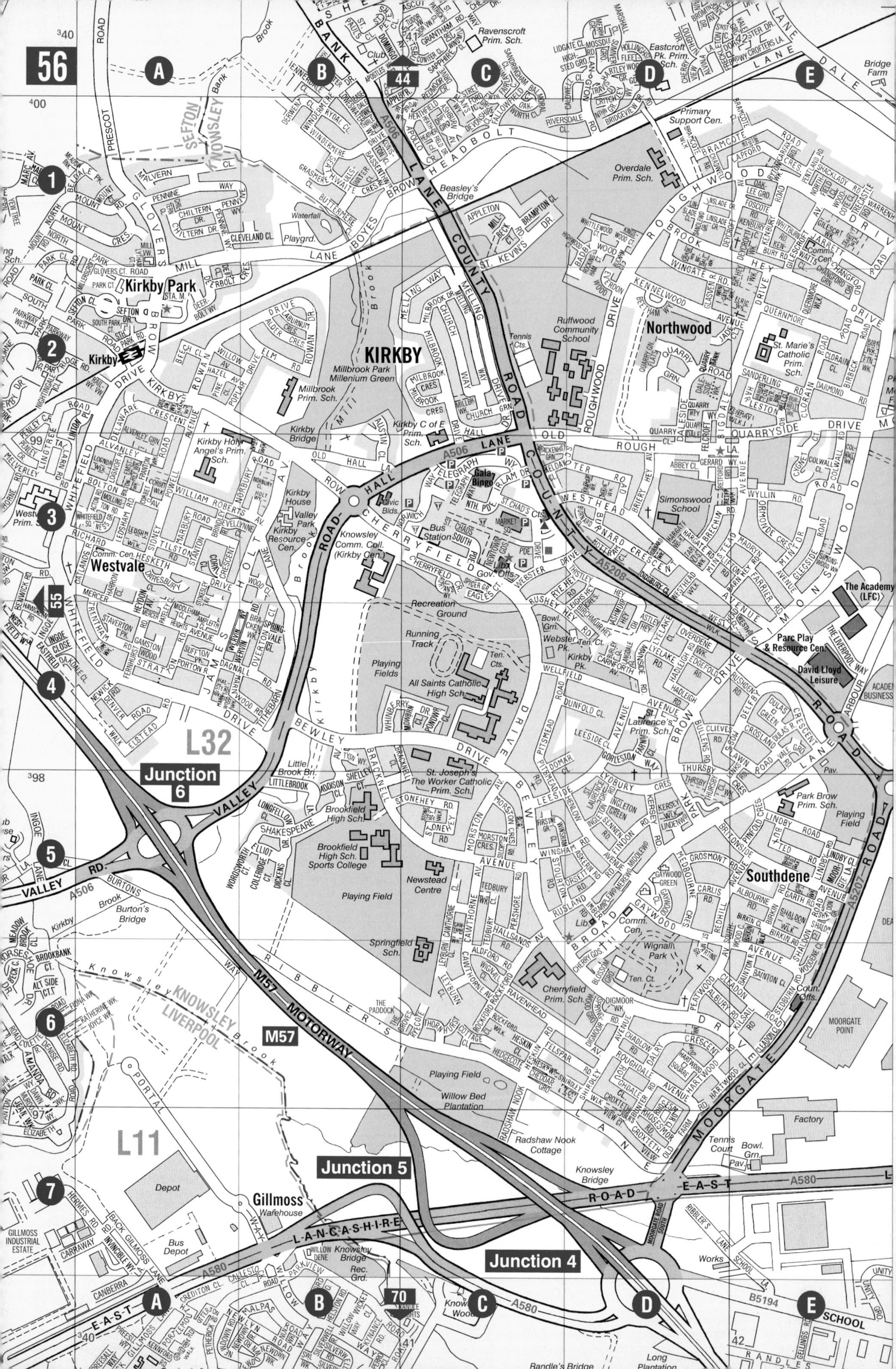
KIRKBY
Kirkby Park
Westvale
Northwood
Southdene
L32
L11
Junction 6
Junction 5
Junction 4
M57 MOTORWAY
Ruffwood Community School
St. Marie's Catholic Prim. Sch.
Simonswood School
All Saints Catholic High Sch.
Brookfield High Sch. Sports College
Knowsley Comm. Coll. (Kirkby Cen.)
Millbrook Prim. Sch.
Overdale Prim. Sch.
Recreation Ground
Playing Fields
Gillmoss
Moorgate Point
Factory
Depot
Bus Depot
The Academy (LFC)
David Lloyd Leisure
Parc Play & Resource Cen.
Willow Bed Plantation
Radshaw Nook Cottage
Knowsley Bridge
Gillmoss Industrial Estate

SIMONSWOOD MOSS

1

2

3

WEST LANCASHIRE
KNOWSLEY

58

Liverpool

4

5

6

7

L33

Playing Field

Ay. Field
oss Lane
arm

NORTH PERIMETER LANE
The Cott.
Woodward's
Cotts.
Southead
Keeper's
House
Bullens
Farm
Eccleston
House
Spencer's
House Farm

NORTH MERSEY
BUSINESS CENTRE
Knowsley Ind.
Pk. Rail Terminal
DEPOT
WOODWARD ROAD
Acorn Venture
Urban Farm
Works

MOSS END WAY

ROAD

BOUNDARY
Top House
Farm

ASHCROFT ROAD
MARL ROAD
HAMMOND ROAD
BRADMAN ROAD
WELL ROAD
DRAW
MOSS

LA
ROAD
NEWSTET ROAD
Courtyard Works
LODGE WORKS
KNOWSLEY INDUSTRIAL PARK
MANOR COMPLEX
KIRKBY
BIRCHILL
BANK
CRANSTON RD
STOCKPIT ROAD

Kirkby Moss

ARBUR LA.

ACORN BUS. CEN.
GLADESWOOD RD.
CHARLEYWOOD
LEES
YARDLEY CENTRE
VENTURE WORKS
WEBBER
YARDLEY
CAPITOL TRADING PARK
ROAD
Playing
Field
CHARLEY
WOOD

MY PARK

GORES ROAD
CUSSON ROAD
Knowsley
Enterprise
Workshops
DELENCY
DIXON RD.
BECKETT CL.
ROAD
ACORNFIELD ROAD

Sandy
Brow

98

ON PARK

A5208
SOUTH
HORNHOUSE
WEB COMPLEX
ADMIN
CENTRO PARK
GALE ROAD
BUSINESS RESOURCE CENTRE
Acornfield Plantation
Local Nature
Reserve

Sandy Brow
Cottage

RED
LANE

CUT
Private

New Cut
House

Works

Warehouse
SENATOR POINT
BOUNDARY ROAD
SPINNEY CL.
SPINNEY VW.
ROAD
Cooper's
Farm
MOLLY'S
LANE
Electricity
Sub Station

Sandy Lane
Farm

SANDY BROW
CUT
LANE

Cooper's Moss
Farm

NEW
LANE

Knowsley Brook

Tokenspire
Park

ABERCROMBIE ROAD
OWEN ROAD
FARADAY
Briton
Plantation

Sports
Ground

Tennis
Courts
Sports
Ground
Works

COOPER'S LANE

Works
HEWITTS LANE
Moss Side
New Road
Farm
Moss
Cottages

LANCASHIRE ROAD EAST

A580 ROAD 97

LANCASHIRE ROAD

AINSWORTH GRO
Quarry
Farm
KNOWSLEY
BUSINESS PARK
RYN
VILLIERS ROAD
VILLIERS CT.
KITLING ROAD
OVERBROOK LANE
LOCKTON RD LA.
NORTHROPE
KITLING RD
KCT

Prescot
L34

Tincle Peg
Cottages
Tincle Peg
Farm
ORMSKIRK

KNOWSLEY ROAD
71
B5202
CANROW
CANROW
Canrow
Cottage
Canr
LANE
Cottages

Moss
Plantation

Scamper
Plantation

Potato Pie
(Hunting Lo

WALK

43

44

³45

⁴00

99

³98

⁴97

³45

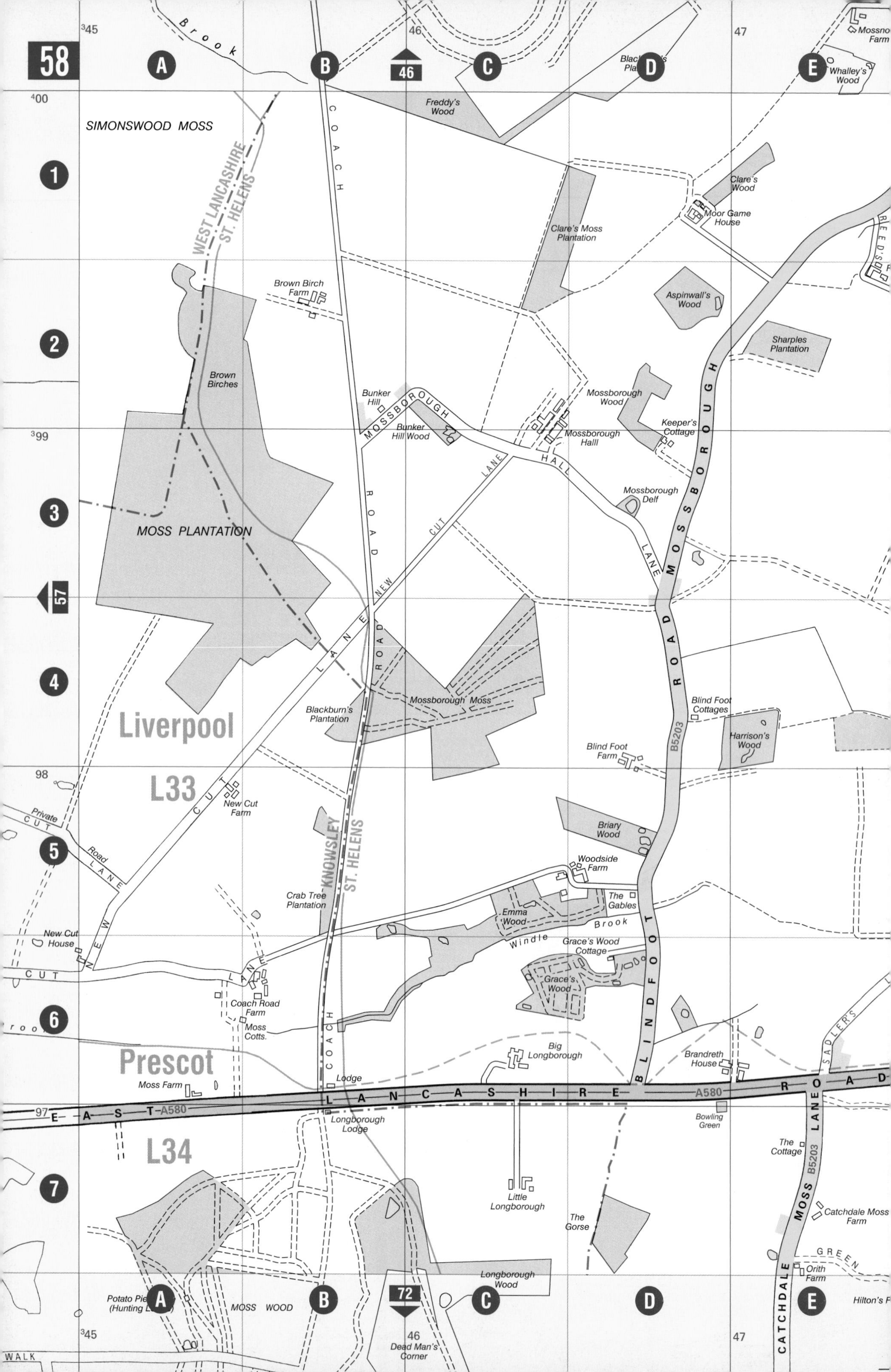
Brook
46
Freddy's Wood
SIMONSWOOD MOSS
WEST LANCASHIRE
ST. HELENS
COACH
Clare's Moss Plantation
Clare's Wood
Moor Game House
Brown Birch Farm
Aspinwall's Wood
Sharples Plantation
Brown Birches
Bunker Hill
MOSSBOROUGH
Bunker Hill Wood
Mossborough Wood
Keeper's Cottage
Mossborough Halll
HALL
LANE
Mossborough Delf
MOSS PLANTATION
ROAD
CUT
NEW
57
LANE
MOSSBOROUGH
ROAD
Mossborough Moss
Blackburn's Plantation
Blind Foot Cottages
Harrison's Wood
Liverpool
Blind Foot Farm
B5203
L33
New Cut Farm
Private Road
CUT LANE
Briary Wood
KNOWSLEY
ST. HELENS
Woodside Farm
Crab Tree Plantation
The Gables
Emma Wood
Brook
Windle
New Cut House
Grace's Wood Cottage
Grace's Wood
BLINDFOOT
Coach Road Farm
Moss Cotts.
Prescot
Big Longborough
Brandreth House
SADLER'S
Lodge
Moss Farm
EAST LANCASHIRE ROAD
A580
Longborough Lodge
Bowling Green
The Cottage
L34
MOSS LANE
B5203
Little Longborough
Catchdale Moss Farm
The Gorse
GREEN
Orith Farm
Longborough Wood
72
MOSS WOOD
Hilton's F
46
Dead Man's Corner
CATCHDALE
WALK
47
Mossno Farm
Whalley's Wood
REED'S

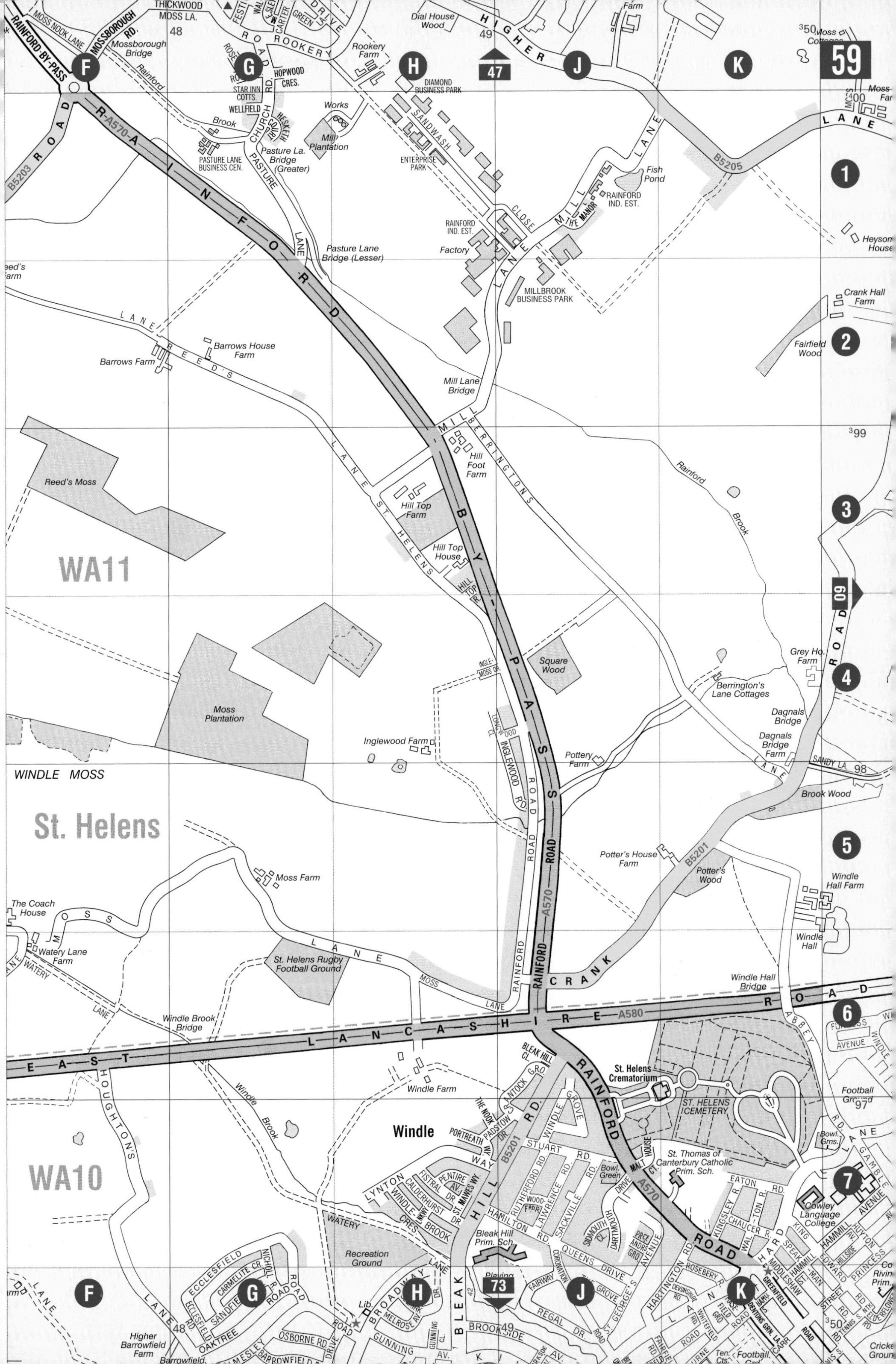
RAINFORD-BY-PASS
MOSS NOOK LANE
MOSSBOROUGH RD.
Mossborough Bridge
THICKWOOD MOSS LA.
48
ROOKERY
Rookery Farm
Dial House Wood
HIGHER
49
47
Farm
Moss Cottages
STAR INN COTTS.
WELLFIELD
HOPWOOD CRES.
Rainford
Brook
CHURCH RD.
Works
Mill Plantation
DIAMOND BUSINESS PARK
SANDWASH
ENTERPRISE PARK
PASTURE LANE BUSINESS CEN.
Pasture La. Bridge (Greater)
PASTURE LANE
Pasture Lane Bridge (Lesser)
B5203 ROAD
A570
RAINFORD
LANE
B5205
Fish Pond
RAINFORD IND. EST.
THE MANOR
MILL LANE
CLOSE
Factory
MILLBROOK BUSINESS PARK
Heyson House
Crank Hall Farm
Fairfield Wood
Reed's Farm
REED'S LANE
Barrows House Farm
Barrows Farm
Mill Lane Bridge
MILL
BERRINGTONS
Hill Foot Farm
399
Reed's Moss
ST. HELENS LANE
Hill Top Farm
Hill Top House
HILL TOP RD.
BY-PASS
Rainford Brook
WA11
60
ROAD
INGLEMOSS DR.
Square Wood
Grey Ho. Farm
Berrington's Lane Cottages
Dagnals Bridge
Dagnals Bridge Farm
Moss Plantation
Inglewood Farm
LONGWOOD CL.
INGLEWOOD RD.
Pottery Farm
SANDY LA.
98
Brook Wood
WINDLE MOSS
St. Helens
A570 ROAD
Potter's House Farm
B5201
Potter's Wood
Windle Hall Farm
Moss Farm
The Coach House
MOSS LANE
Watery Lane Farm
WATERY LANE
St. Helens Rugby Football Ground
RAINFORD
CRANK
Windle Hall
Windle Hall Bridge
MOSS LANE
Windle Brook Bridge
EAST LANCASHIRE ROAD
A580
ABBEY RD.
FURNESS AVENUE
WINDLE
Windle Farm
BLEAK HILL CL.
QUANTOCK GRO.
RAINFORD
St. Helens Crematorium
ST. HELENS CEMETERY
Football Ground
97
Windle Brook
HOUGHTON'S LANE
THE NOOK
PADSTOW
Windle
PORTREATH WAY
B5201 RD.
WINDLE GROVE
STUART RD.
Bowl. Gms.
St. Thomas of Canterbury Catholic Prim. Sch.
WA10
LYNTON WAY
FISTRAL DR.
PENTIRE AV.
ST. MAWES WY.
CALDERHURST DR.
WINDLE CRES.
BROOK
RUTHERFORD RD.
WOODFORD
LAWRENCE RD.
SACKVILLE RD.
Bowl. Green
MALT HOUSE CT.
SIDMOUTH CL.
DARTMOUTH DRIVE
EATON RD.
KINGSLEY RD.
CHAUCER R.
WALTON R.
GAMBLE AVENUE
Cowley Language College
WATERY LANE
Recreation Ground
HAMILTON RD.
Bleak Hill Prim. Sch.
QUEENS DRIVE
CORONATION
PRINCE ANDREWS GRO.
AVENUE
ROAD
HARD LANE
KING
SPEAKMAN
HAMMILL ST.
HUXTON
HILLSIDE
EDWARD
PRINCESS
Rivington Prim. Sch.
ECCLESFIELD
CARMELITE CR.
NICHOLL R.
ECCLESFIELD RD.
SANDFIELD
OAKTREE
ROAD
BROADWAY
MELROSE AV.
Lib.
GUNNING CL.
BLEAK HILL
Playing
73
FAIRWAY
GROVE
ST. GEORGE'S RD.
REGAL DR.
HARTINGTON RD.
ROSEBERY
DEVONSHIRE RD.
LANE
WHITEFIELD
GREENFIELD
MIDDLESHAW
DENTONS GRN. LA.
CARR
Football Grd.
Ten. Cts.
Higher Barrowfield Farm
Barrowfield
48
OSBORNE RD.
BARROWFIELD
GUNNING AV.
BROOKSIDE
49
350
Cricket Ground
F
G
H
J
K
1
2
3
4
5
6
7

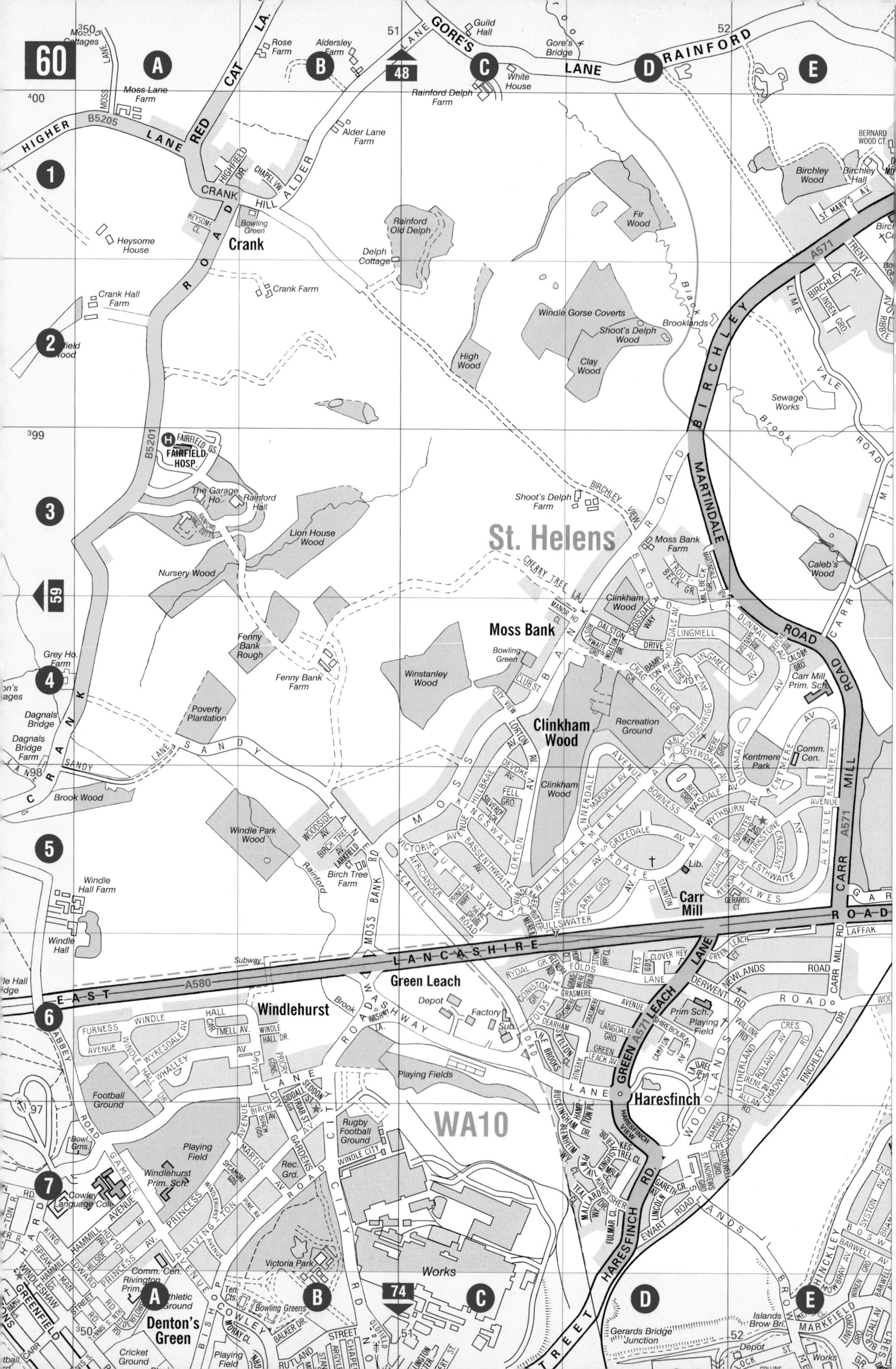

48
59
74
A
B
C
D
E
1
2
3
4
5
6
7
350
51
52
400
399
398
397
Moss Cottages
Moss Lane Farm
Rose Farm
Aldersley Farm
Guild Hall
Gore's Bridge
GORE'S LANE
RAINFORD
White House
Rainford Delph Farm
Alder Lane Farm
HIGHER LANE
B5205
RED CAT LA.
HIGHFIELD DR.
CHAPEL VW.
CRANK HILL
ALDER
HEYSOME CL.
Bowling Green
Heysome House
Crank
Crank Hall Farm
Crank Farm
Rainford Old Delph
Delph Cottage
Fir Wood
Birchley Wood
Birchley Hall
BERNARD WOOD CT.
ST. MARY'S AV.
A571
TRENT
BIRCHLEY AV.
LINDEN GRO.
LIME
RIBBLE
VALE
Brook
Black Brook
Brooklands
Windle Gorse Coverts
Shoot's Delph Wood
Clay Wood
High Wood
Sewage Works
BIRCHLEY ROAD
MARTINDALE ROAD
CARR MILL ROAD
B5201
FAIRFIELD GS.
FAIRFIELD HOSP.
The Garage Ho.
Rainford Hall
RAINFORD HALL COTTS.
Lion House Wood
Nursery Wood
Shoot's Delph Farm
BIRCHLEY VIEW
St. Helens
Moss Bank Farm
CHERRY TREE LA.
Caleb's Wood
Clinkham Wood
Moss Bank
Fenny Bank Rough
Fenny Bank Farm
Winstanley Wood
Grey Ho. Farm
Dagnals Bridge
Dagnals Bridge Farm
Poverty Plantation
Bowling Green
CLUB ST.
CITY VIEW
Clinkham Wood
Recreation Ground
Carr Mill Prim. Sch.
Kentmere Park
Comm. Cen.
SANDY LANE
CRANK ROAD
Brook Wood
Windle Park Wood
WOODSIDE AV.
BIRCH TREE AV.
LARKFIELD CT.
Birch Tree Farm
Rainford Brook
MOSS BANK RD.
VICTORIA AVENUE
AFRICANDER ROAD
SCAFELL
QUEENSWAY
KINGSWAY
BASSENTHWAITE AV.
LORTON AV.
WINDERMERE
ULLSWATER
THIRLMERE
TARN GRO.
ESKDALE AV.
GRIZEDALE AV.
BOWNESS AV.
WASDALE AV.
WYTHBURN AV.
KENDAL DR.
ESTHWAITE
HAWES CRESCENT
KENTMERE AVENUE
Lib.
Carr Mill
GERARDS CT.
Windle Hall Farm
Windle Hall
Subway
EAST LANCASHIRE ROAD
A580
Green Leach
Depot
Factory
Sub.
GREEN LEACH LANE
A571
NEWLANDS ROAD
DERWENT RD.
CARR MILL RD.
Prim. Sch.
Playing Field
FINCHLEY DR.
Windlehurst
FURNESS AVENUE
WINDLE HALL DR.
WYRESDALE AV.
WHALLEY AV.
CARTMELL AV.
WASHWAY LA.
Brook
Playing Fields
Haresfinch
WOODLANDS
LITHERLAND RD.
ROLAND AV.
CHADWICK RD.
GREEN LANE
BUCKINGHAM DR.
HARESFINCH VIEW
ABBEY ROAD
Football Ground
Playing Field
Windlehurst Prim. Sch.
CITY LANE
CITY ROAD
WA10
Rugby Football Ground
Rec. Grd.
WINDLE CITY
HARESFINCH RD.
EWART ROAD
Bowl Grns.
Cowley Language Coll.
GAMBLE AVENUE
PRINCESS AV.
Victoria Park
Works
Comm. Cen.
Rivington Prim.
Athletic Ground
Denton's Green
Bowling Greens
BISHOP
COWLEY
Cricket Ground
Playing Field
GREENFIELD
WINDLESHAW
Gerards Bridge Junction
Islands Brow Bri.
Depot
Works
HINCKLEY
MARKFIELD

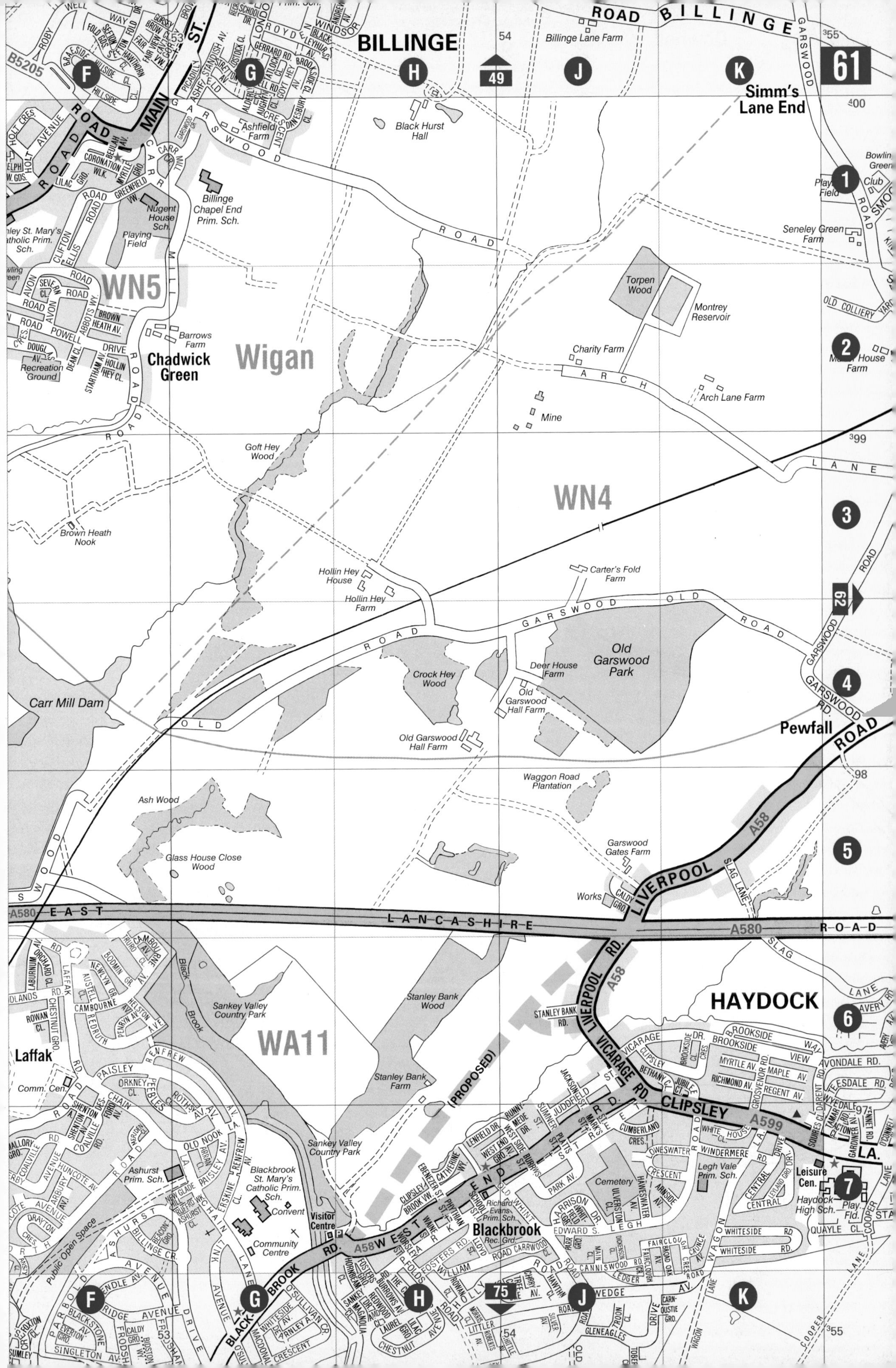
61
BILLINGE
ROAD BILLINGE
Billinge Lane Farm
Black Hurst Hall
Simm's Lane End
Ashfield Farm
Billinge Chapel End Prim. Sch.
Nugent House Sch.
Playing Field
WN5
Barrows Farm
Chadwick Green
Wigan
Recreation Ground
Torpen Wood
Montrey Reservoir
Charity Farm
Arch Lane Farm
Mine
Seneley Green Farm
Goft Hey Wood
Brown Heath Nook
WN4
Hollin Hey House
Hollin Hey Farm
Carter's Fold Farm
GARSWOOD OLD ROAD
Crock Hey Wood
Deer House Farm
Old Garswood Park
Old Garswood Hall Farm
Carr Mill Dam
Pewfall
Waggon Road Plantation
Ash Wood
Glass House Close Wood
Garswood Gates Farm
Works
LIVERPOOL ROAD
A58
A580 EAST LANCASHIRE ROAD
HAYDOCK
Sankey Valley Country Park
Stanley Bank Wood
Stanley Bank Farm
WA11
(PROPOSED)
Laffak
Comm. Cen.
Ashurst Prim. Sch.
Blackbrook St. Mary's Catholic Prim. Sch.
Convent
Community Centre
Visitor Centre
Public Open Space
Richard Evans Prim. Sch.
Blackbrook
Cemetery
Legh Vale Prim. Sch.
Leisure Cen.
Haydock High Sch.
CLIPSLEY LA.
A599
WEST END RD.
BLACKBROOK RD.
49
62
75
F G H J K
1 2 3 4 5 6 7

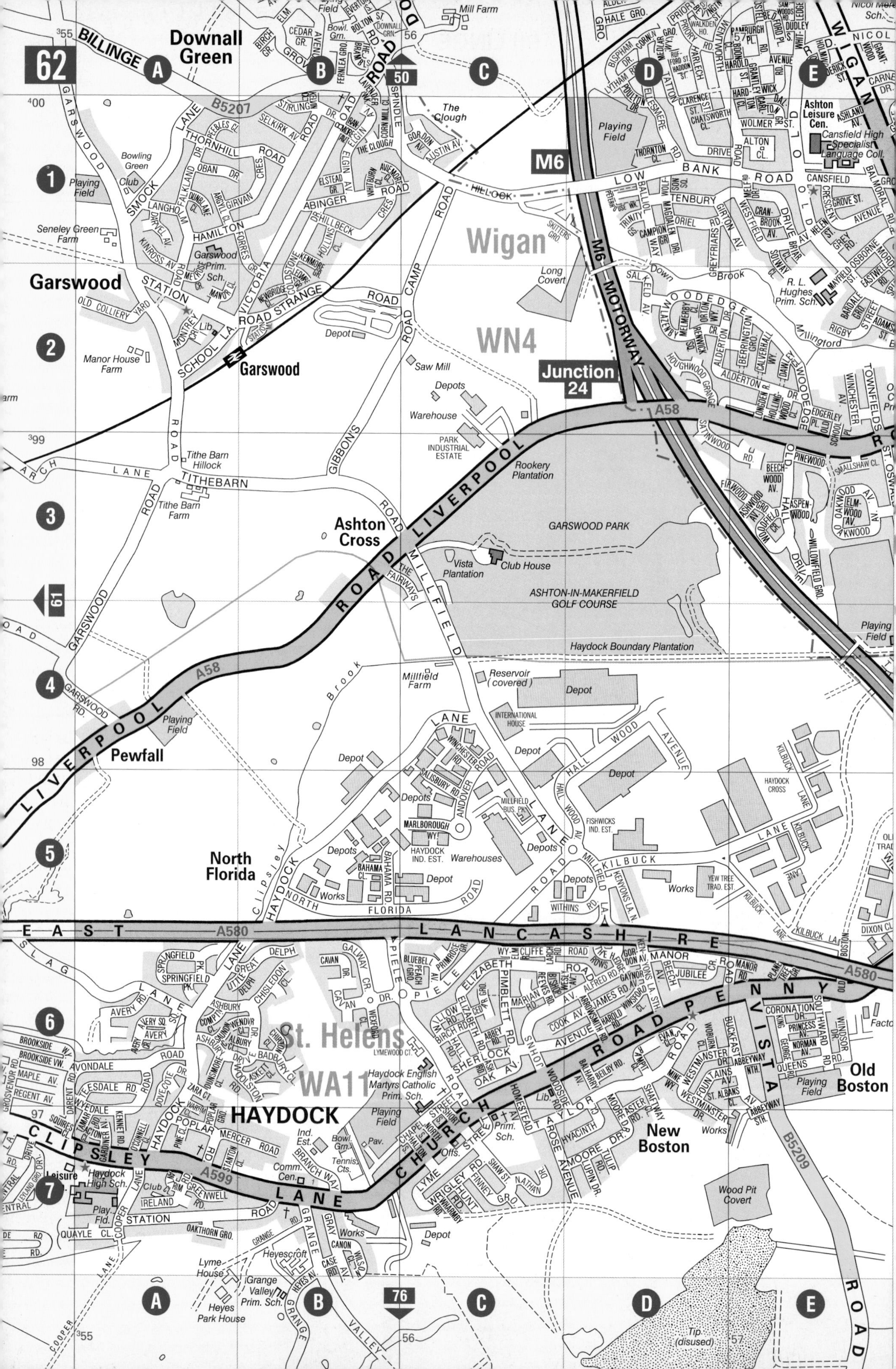
Downall Green
Garswood
Wigan
WN4
Junction 24
M6
M6 MOTORWAY
Ashton Cross
GARSWOOD PARK
ASHTON-IN-MAKERFIELD GOLF COURSE
Haydock Boundary Plantation
Pewfall
North Florida
St. Helens
WA11
HAYDOCK
New Boston
Old Boston
EAST LANCASHIRE ROAD A580
LIVERPOOL ROAD A58
CLIPSLEY LANE A599
PENNY ROAD
CHURCH ROAD
Ashton Leisure Cen.
Cansfield High Specialist Language Coll.
R. L. Hughes Prim. Sch.
Garswood Prim. Sch.
Haydock English Martyrs Catholic Prim. Sch.
Haydock High Sch.
Grange Valley Prim. Sch.
Wood Pit Covert
Tip (disused)
Rookery Plantation
Vista Plantation
Club House
Tithe Barn Farm
Manor House Farm
Seneley Green Farm
Mill Farm
The Clough
Long Covert
Millfield Farm
Reservoir (covered)
PARK INDUSTRIAL ESTATE
HAYDOCK IND. EST.
FISHWICKS IND. EST.
YEW TREE TRAD. EST.
HAYDOCK CROSS
INTERNATIONAL HOUSE
Heyes Park House
Lyme House
Heyescroft
50
61
76

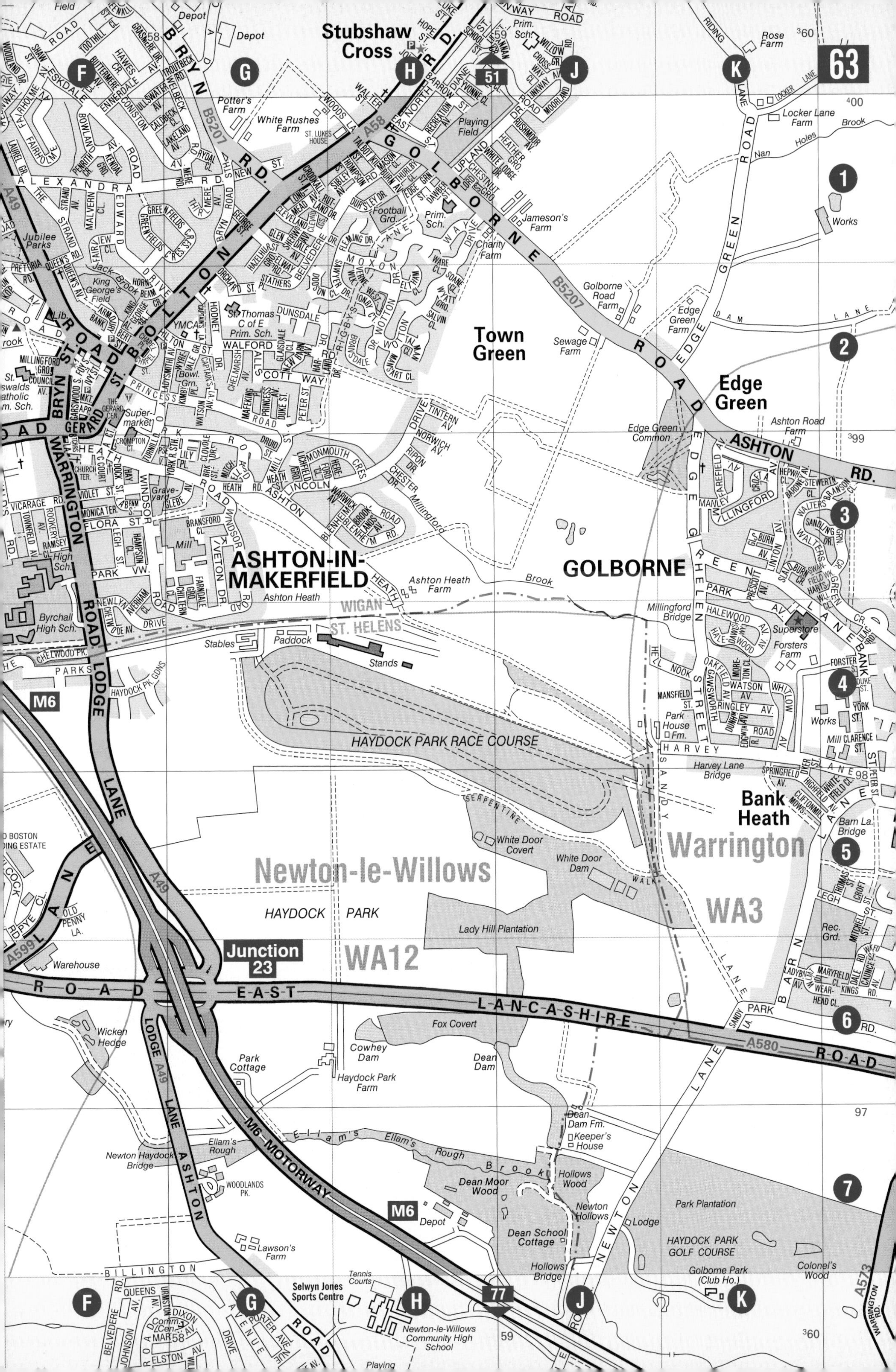
Stubshaw Cross
Town Green
Edge Green
ASHTON-IN-MAKERFIELD
GOLBORNE
Bank Heath
Warrington
WA3
Newton-le-Willows
WA12
HAYDOCK PARK
HAYDOCK PARK RACE COURSE
Junction 23
M6
M6 MOTORWAY
A49
A58
A580
A573
A599
B5207
BOLTON ROAD
BRYN ROAD
GOLBORNE ROAD
ASHTON RD.
EDGE GREEN LANE
EDGE GREEN ROAD
WARRINGTON ROAD
LODGE LANE
ASHTON LANE
EAST LANCASHIRE ROAD
NEWTON LANE
SANDY LANE
BARN LANE
PARK RD.
ALEXANDRA RD.
HEATH RD.
ASHTON HEATH
Ashton Heath
Ashton Heath Farm
WIGAN
ST. HELENS
Stables
Paddock
Stands
Jubilee Parks
King George's Field
Byrchall High Sch.
High Sch.
Football Grd.
Playing Field
Potter's Farm
White Rushes Farm
Jameson's Farm
Charity Farm
Golborne Road Farm
Sewage Farm
Edge Green Farm
Edge Green Common
Ashton Road Farm
Rose Farm
Locker Lane Farm
Works
Superstore
Forsters Farm
Millingford Bridge
Park House Fm.
Harvey Lane Bridge
Barn La. Bridge
Rec. Grd.
White Door Covert
White Door Dam
Lady Hill Plantation
Fox Covert
Cowhey Dam
Dean Dam
Dean Dam Fm.
Keeper's House
Park Cottage
Haydock Park Farm
Ellam's Rough
Newton Haydock Bridge
Dean Moor Wood
Hollows Wood
Newton Hollows
Dean School Cottage
Hollows Bridge
Lodge
Park Plantation
HAYDOCK PARK GOLF COURSE
Golborne Park (Club Ho.)
Colonel's Wood
Wicken Hedge
Warehouse
Lawson's Farm
Depot
Selwyn Jones Sports Centre
Tennis Courts
Newton-le-Willows Community High School
BILLINGTON
F G H J K
1 2 3 4 5 6 7
400 399 98 97 360 58 59

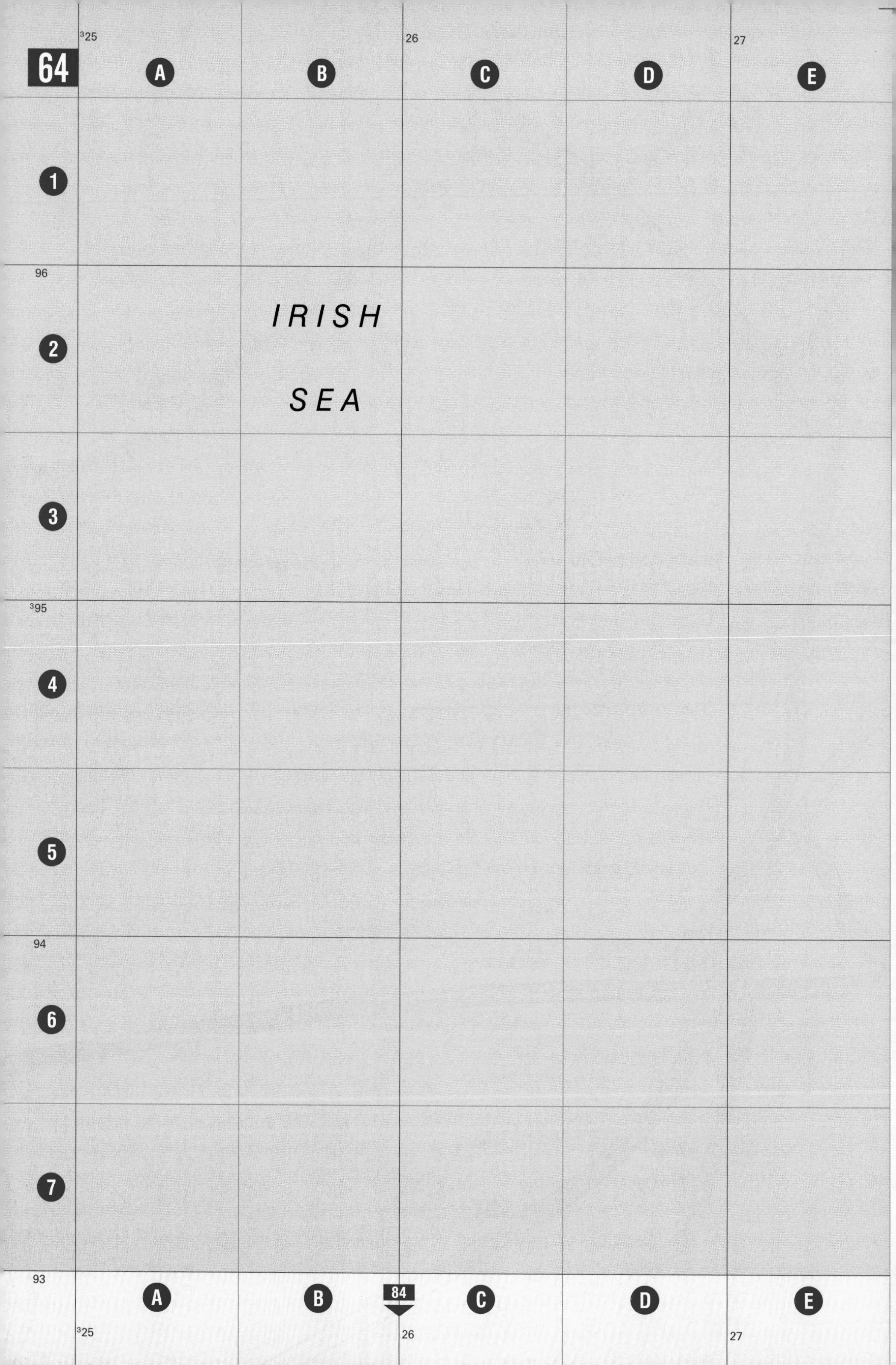

A B C D E

1

2

3

4

5

6

7

IRISH

SEA

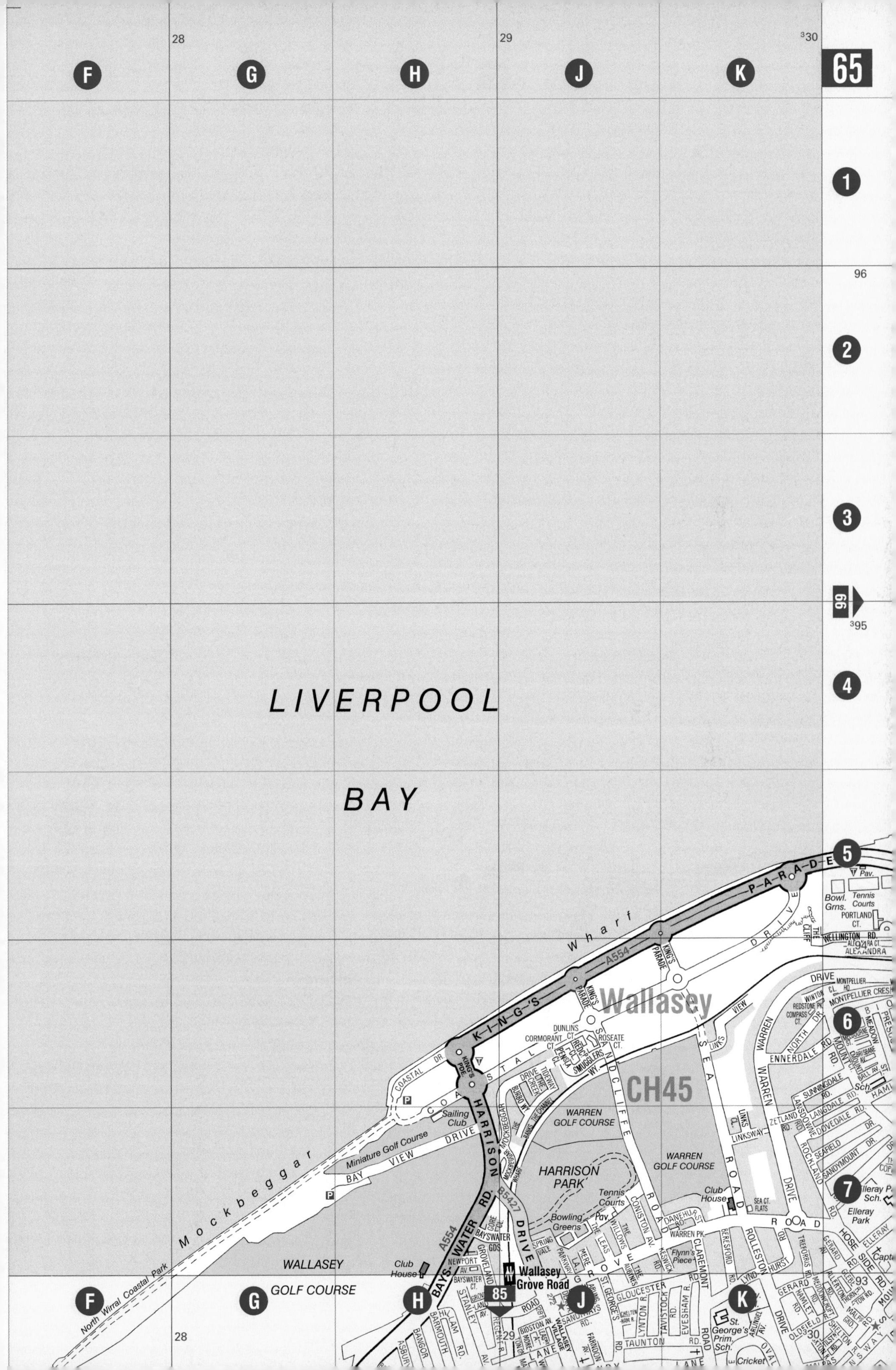

28 29 ³30

1

96

2

3

66 ▶
³95

4

LIVERPOOL

BAY

5

P-A-R-A-D-E
Wharf
A554
KING'S PARADE
Bowl. Tennis
Grns. Courts
PORTLAND
CT.
WELLINGTON RD.
ALEXANDRA
THE CLIFF
DRIVE
Montpellier
CL. HD
WINTON
Montpellier Cres.
REDSTONE PK
COMPASS CT.
Wallasey
DUNLINS
CORMORANT
CT.
ROSEATE
CT.
SMUGGLERS
WD.
LINKS
VIEW
WARREN
NORTH DRIVE
ENNERDALE RD.
PRESTON
MEADOW RD.
6
SEA
SUNNINGDALE
RD.
LANGDALE RD.
DOVEDALE DR.
SEAFIELD
ROCHALLO
CH45
WARREN
GOLF COURSE
LINKS
ROAD
LINKSWAY
ZETLAND RD.
WARREN
GOLF COURSE
SANDYMOUNT DR.
Sailing
Club
HARRISON
DRIVE
Club
House
SEA CT.
FLATS
7
Elleray P.
Sch.
Miniature Golf Course
BAY VIEW DRIVE
HARRISON PARK
Tennis
Courts
WARREN PK.
Elleray
Park
Mockbeggar
Bowling
Greens
Pav.
THE WILLOWS
CONISTON AV.
DANEHU
BERESFORD
ROLLESTON
ROAD
HOSE
TREFORES
CAPT.
North Wirral Coastal Park
P
NEWPORT
AV.
BAYSWATER
CT.
GROVELAND
DRIVE
Flynn's
Piece
GERARD
93

WALLASEY
GOLF COURSE
Club
House
A554
BAYSWATER RD.
A5427
WILLIAM RD.
STANLEY
BANGOR
ASBURY
85
W **Wallasey
Grove Road**
★
WALLASEY
VILLAGE
BIDSTON AV.
SPRING
VALE
ST. GEORGE'S
MERE
GROVE
GROVE
GLOUCESTER
EVESHAM RD.
LYNTON RD.
TAUNTON
St.
George's
Prim. Sch.
OVAL
N.S.W.Y.
30
28 29 Cricket

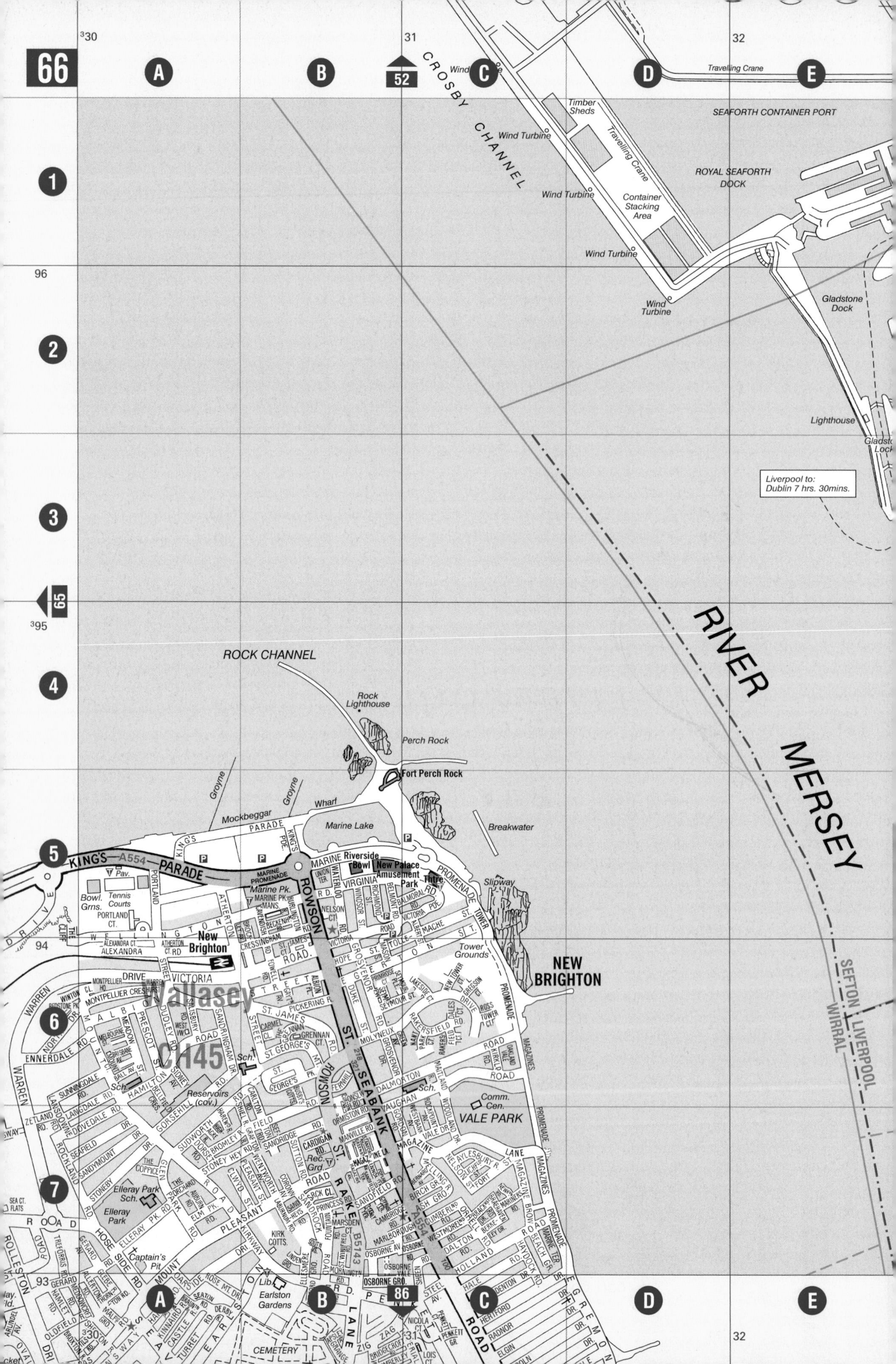

CROSBY CHANNEL

Wind Turbine
Wind Turbine
Wind Turbine
Wind Turbine
Wind Turbine

SEAFORTH CONTAINER PORT

Travelling Crane

Timber Sheds

Travelling Crane

Container Stacking Area

ROYAL SEAFORTH DOCK

Gladstone Dock

Lighthouse

Gladstone Lock

Liverpool to:
Dublin 7 hrs. 30mins.

RIVER MERSEY

ROCK CHANNEL

Rock Lighthouse

Perch Rock

Fort Perch Rock

Breakwater

Slipway

Wharf

Marine Lake

Groyne

Mockbeggar

PARADE

KINGS

KINGS PARADE A554

Bowl. Grns.

Tennis Courts

PORTLAND CT.

MARINE PROMENADE

Pav.

Marine Pk.

MARINE PK. MANS

New Brighton

Alexandra Ct.

ALEXANDRA

Montpellier Cres.

Montpellier Ho.

Victoria

Wallasey
CH45

Reservoirs (cov.)

Ennerdale Rd.

Warren

Sunningdale Rd.

Langdale Rd.

Zetland Rd.

Dovedale Rd.

Seafield Rd.

Sandymount

Rockland Rd.

THE COPPICE

Elleray Park Sch.

Elleray Park

SEA CT. FLATS

Captain's Pit

St. James

St. George's

St. Pickering Rd.

Marine Riverside Bowl

New Palace Amusement Park

PROMENADE

NEW BRIGHTON

Tower Grounds

VALE PARK

Comm. Cen.

MAGAZINE LANE

PROMENADE

MAGAZINES

SEFTON LIVERPOOL WIRRAL

Earlston Gardens

CEMETERY

OSBORNE GRO.

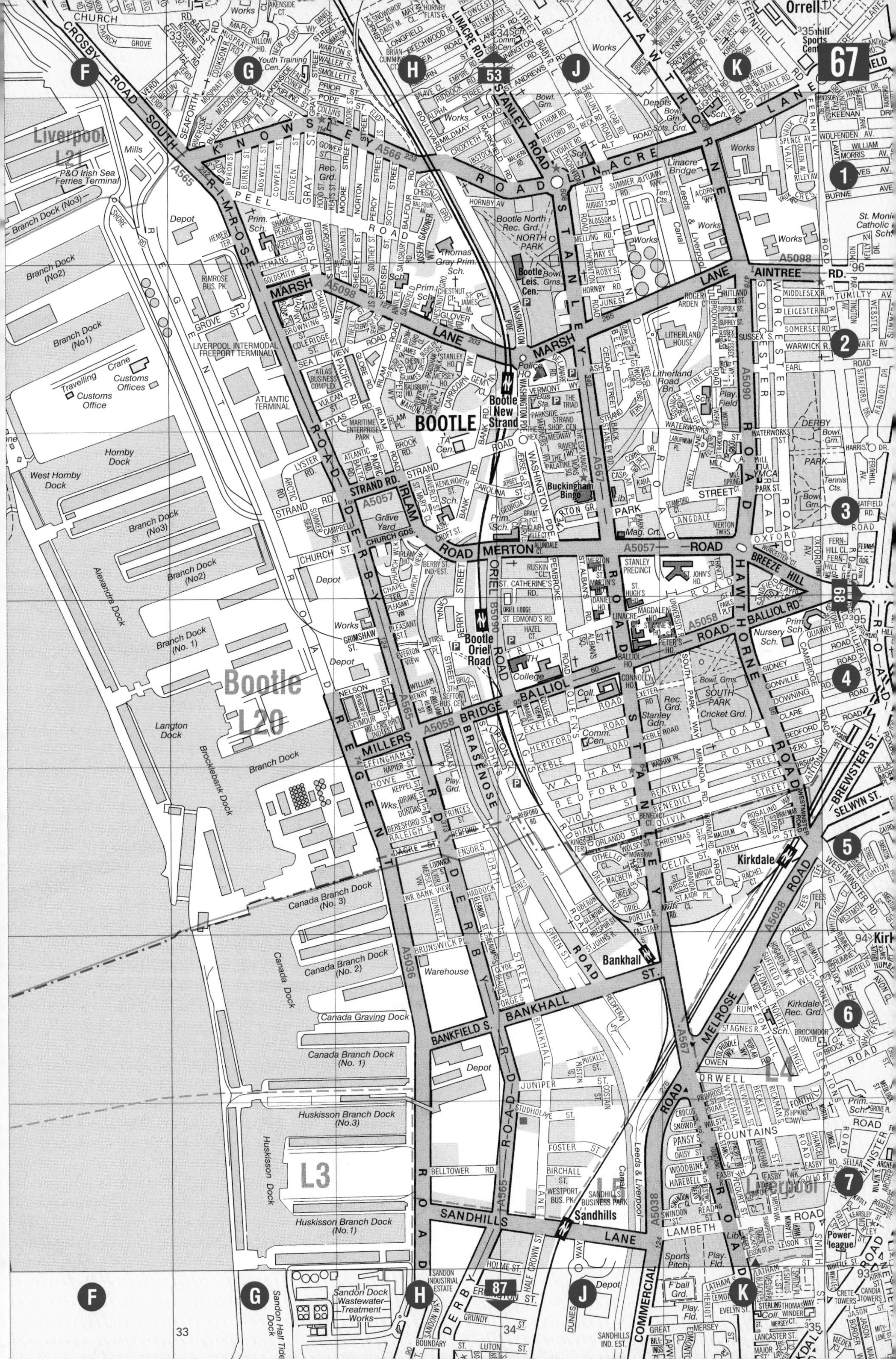
53
BOOTLE
Bootle L20
Liverpool L21
L3
L4
L5
Bootle New Strand
Bootle Oriel Road
Bankhall
Sandhills
Kirkdale
Liverpool
P&O Irish Sea Ferries Terminal
Liverpool Intermodal Freeport Terminal
Atlantic Terminal
Alexandra Dock
Hornby Dock
West Hornby Dock
Langton Dock
Brocklebank Dock
Canada Dock
Canada Graving Dock
Huskisson Dock
Sandon Dock Wastewater Treatment Works
Sandon Half Tide Dock
Sandon Industrial Estate
Sandhills Ind. Est.
Westport Bus. Pk.
Sandhills Business Park
Rimrose Bus. Pk.
Atlas Business Complex
Maritime Enterprise Park
South Park Cricket Grd.
Kirkdale Rec. Grd.
Bootle North Rec. Grd.
North Park
Bootle Leis. Cen.
Buckingham Bingo
Power-league
Leeds & Liverpool Canal
Crosby Road South
Knowsley Road
Linacre Road
Stanley Road
Hawthorne Road
Derby Road
Regent Road
Rimrose Road
Marsh Lane
Merton Road
Strand Rd.
Balliol Road
Bridge Road
Millers Bridge
Bankhall St.
Bankhall Lane
Sandhills Lane
Commercial Road
Melrose Road
Westminster Road
Kirkdale Road
Aintree Rd.
Linacre Lane
Breeze Hill
Oriel Road
Irlam Road
Knowsley Road
Washington Pde.
A565
A566
A567
A5098
A5057
A5058
A5090
A5036
A5038
B5090
F
G
H
J
K
1
2
3
4
5
6
7
33
34
35
68
87

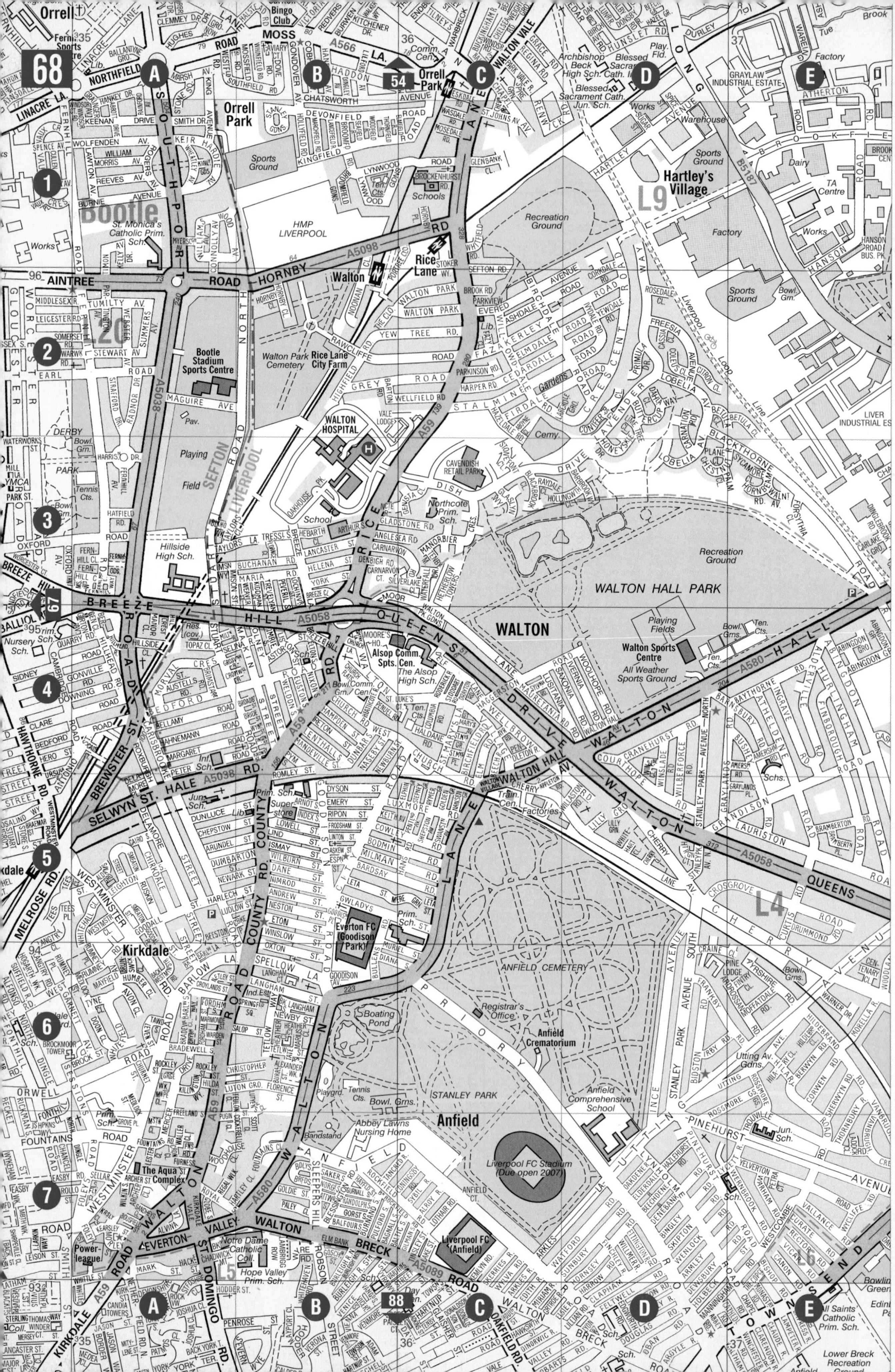
Orrell
Orrell Park
Bootle
Aintree
Walton
Kirkdale
Anfield
Hartley's Village
Rice Lane
Walton Vale
HMP LIVERPOOL
Sports Ground
Recreation Ground
Walton Park Cemetery
Rice Lane City Farm
Bootle Stadium Sports Centre
Playing Field
Hillside High Sch.
WALTON HOSPITAL
CAVENDISH RETAIL PARK
Northcote Prim. Sch.
WALTON HALL PARK
Walton Sports Centre
All Weather Sports Ground
Alsop Comm. Spts. Cen.
The Alsop High Sch.
Everton FC (Goodison Park)
ANFIELD CEMETERY
Anfield Crematorium
Registrar's Office
STANLEY PARK
Boating Pond
Abbey Lawns Nursing Home
Anfield Comprehensive School
Liverpool FC Stadium (Due open 2007)
Liverpool FC (Anfield)
The Aqua Complex
Power-league
Notre Dame Catholic Coll.
Hope Valley Prim. Sch.
All Saints' Catholic Prim. Sch.
Lower Breck Recreation Ground
GRAYLAW INDUSTRIAL ESTATE
LIVER INDUSTRIAL ESTATE
Archbishop Beck High Sch.
Blessed Sacrament Cath. Jun. Sch.
St. Monica's Catholic Prim. Sch.
A5038
A5098
A59
A580
A5058
A566
A5089
B5187
L9
L20
L4
L5
L6
54
67
88
A
B
C
D
E
1
2
3
4
5
6
7

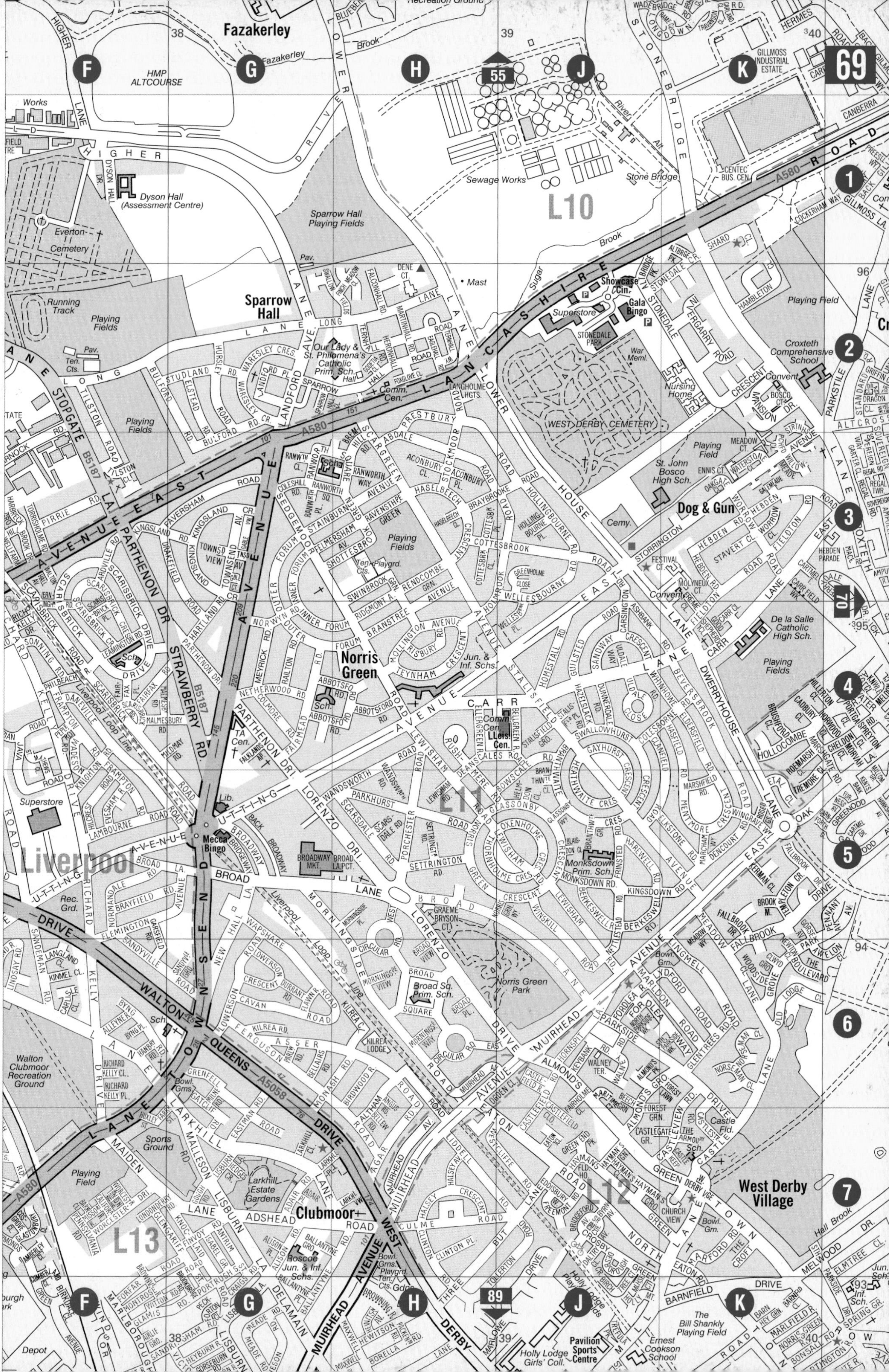
Fazakerley
HMP ALTCOURSE
Works
Dyson Hall (Assessment Centre)
Everton Cemetery
Running Track
Playing Fields
Sparrow Hall Playing Fields
Sparrow Hall
Sewage Works
Stone Bridge
L10
GILLMOSS INDUSTRIAL ESTATE
CENTEC BUS. CEN.
Showcase Cin.
Gala Bingo
Superstore
STONEDALE PARK
War Meml.
WEST DERBY CEMETERY
Nursing Home
Croxteth Comprehensive School
Convent
Our Lady & St. Philomena's Catholic Prim. Sch.
Comm. Cen.
Mast
Playing Field
St. John Bosco High Sch.
Dog & Gun
Cemy.
De la Salle Catholic High Sch.
Norris Green
Jun. & Inf. Schs.
Comm. Cen.
L. Leis. Cen.
L11
Monksdown Prim. Sch.
TA Cen.
Lib.
Mecca Bingo
Liverpool
Superstore
BROADWAY MKT.
BROAD LA. PCT.
Rec. Grd.
Broad Sq. Prim. Sch.
Norris Green Park
Walton Clubmoor Recreation Ground
Sports Ground
Playing Field
Larkhill Estate Gardens
Clubmoor
L13
Roscoe Jun. & Inf. Schs.
L12
West Derby Village
Castle Fld.
The Armoury
The Bill Shankly Playing Field
Pavilion Sports Centre
Ernest Cookson School
Holly Lodge Girls' Coll.
Depot
A580 EAST LANCASHIRE ROAD
QUEENS DRIVE
WALTON HALL AVENUE
UTTING AVENUE
MUIRHEAD AVENUE
CARR LANE
LOWER HOUSE LANE
LONG LANE
STONEBRIDGE LANE
DWERRYHOUSE LANE
BROAD LANE
EAST LANCASHIRE ROAD
55
70
89
F G H J K
1 2 3 4 5 6 7
38 39 340 96 395 94 93

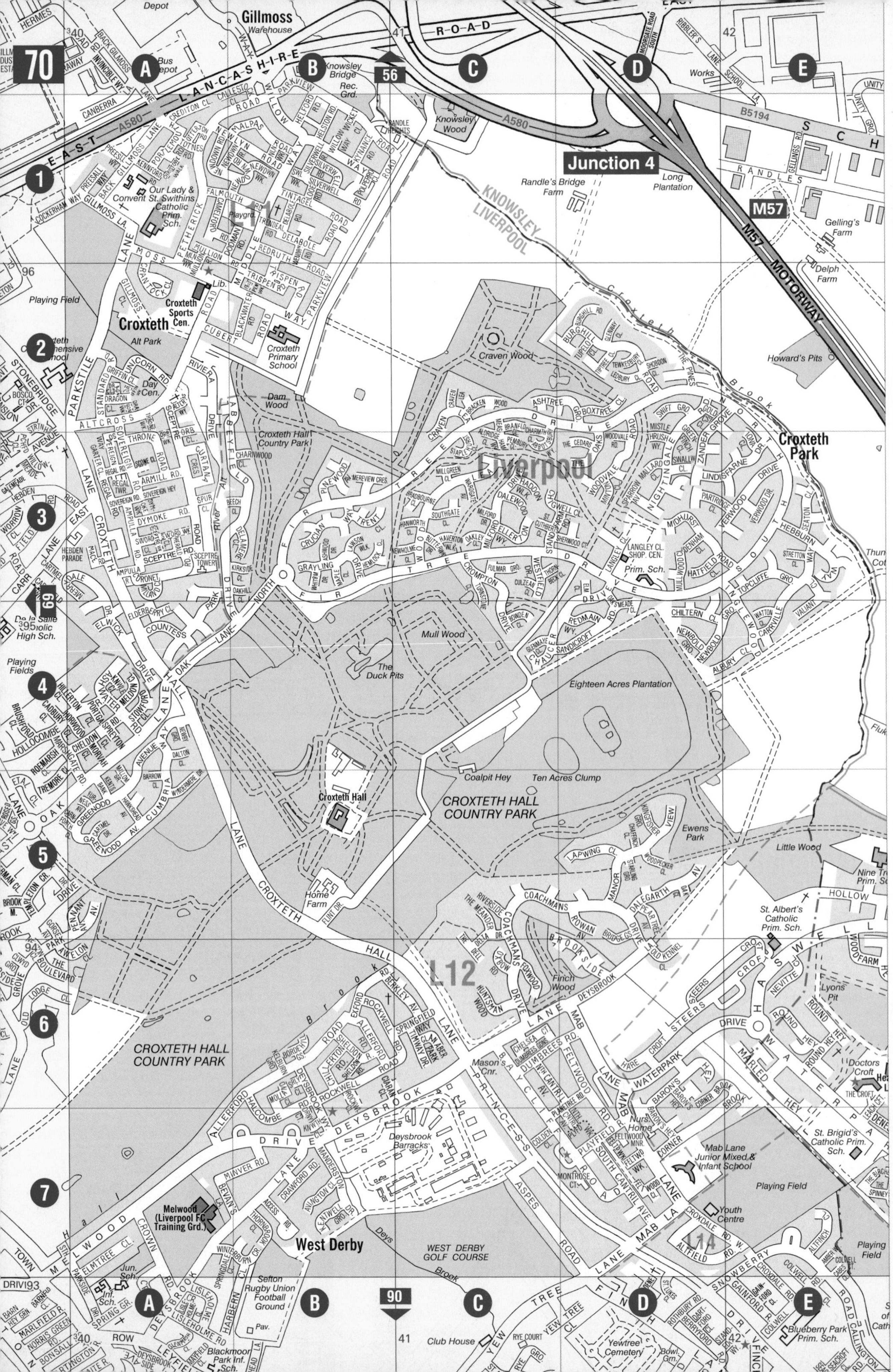

Depot
Gillmoss
Warehouse
Bus Depot
EAST LANCASHIRE ROAD
A580
Knowsley Bridge
Rec. Grd.
56
Knowsley Wood
RANDLE HEIGHTS
Junction 4
Randle's Bridge Farm
Long Plantation
KNOWSLEY
LIVERPOOL
M57
M57 MOTORWAY
B5194
Works
Gelling's Farm
Delph Farm
Howard's Pits
Our Lady & St. Swithins Catholic Prim. Sch.
Convent
L11
Playgrd.
Lib.
Croxteth Sports Cen.
Croxteth
Alt Park
Playing Field
Croxteth Primary School
Day Cen.
Dam Wood
Croxteth Hall Country Park
Craven Wood
Croxteth Brook
Croxteth Park
Liverpool
LANGLEY CL. SHOP. CEN.
Prim. Sch.
Mull Wood
The Duck Pits
Eighteen Acres Plantation
Coalpit Hey
Ten Acres Clump
Croxteth Hall
CROXTETH HALL COUNTRY PARK
Ewens Park
Little Wood
Home Farm
St. Albert's Catholic Prim. Sch.
L12
Finch Wood
Lyons Pit
Doctors Croft
Mason's Cnr.
Deysbrook Barracks
Nurs. Home
Mab Lane Junior Mixed & Infant School
St. Brigid's Catholic Prim. Sch.
Playing Field
Youth Centre
L14
Melwood (Liverpool FC Training Grd.)
West Derby
WEST DERBY GOLF COURSE
Deys Brook
Sefton Rugby Union Football Ground
Pav.
Jun. Sch.
Inf. Sch.
Blackmoor Park Inf. Sch.
Club House
Yewtree Cemetery
Bowl. Grn.
Blueberry Park Prim. Sch.
De La Salle Catholic High Sch.
Playing Fields
CROXTETH HALL COUNTRY PARK
69
90
A B C D E
1 2 3 4 5 6 7

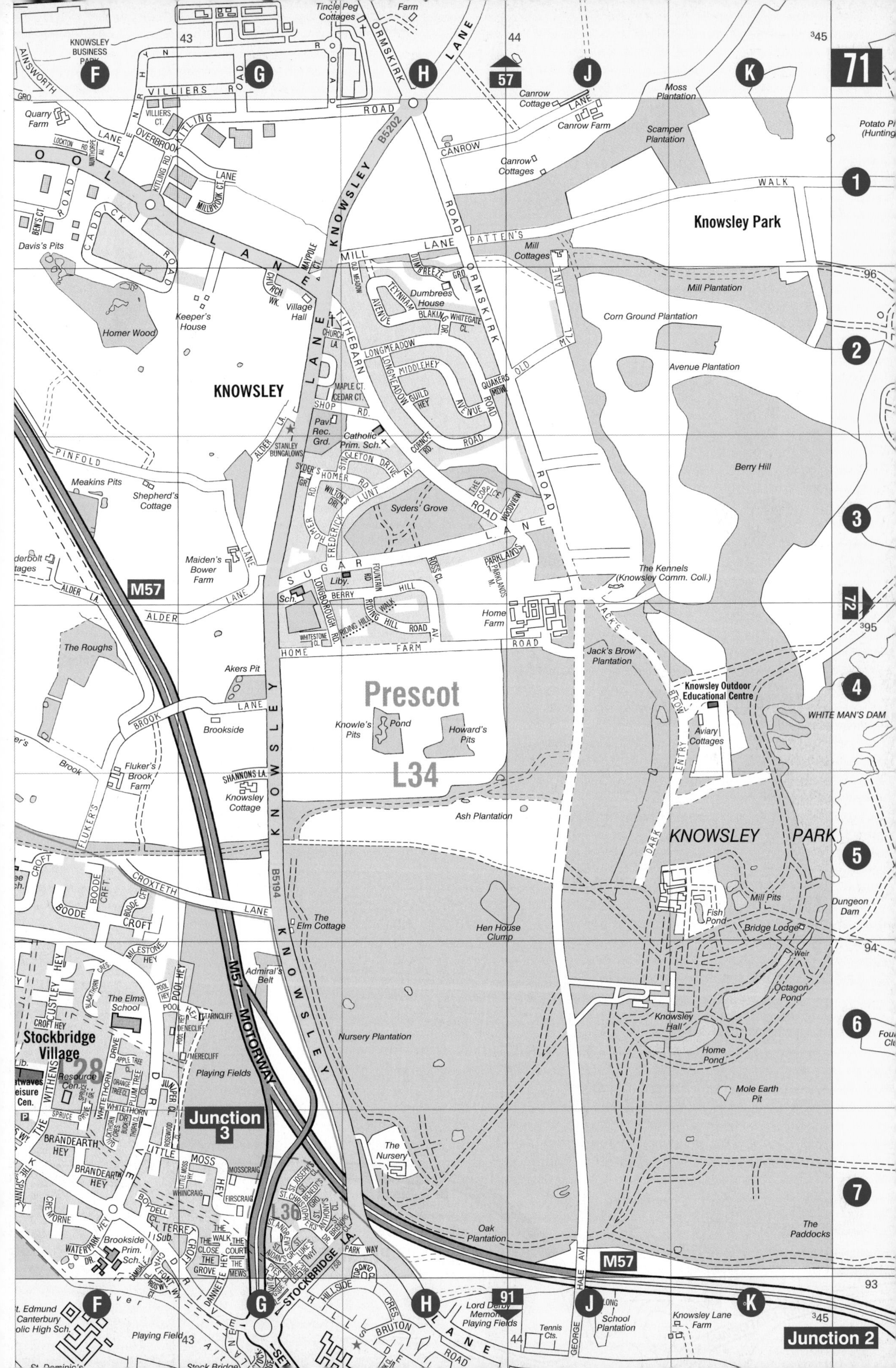

Knowsley Park
KNOWSLEY
Prescot
L34
KNOWSLEY PARK
Stockbridge Village
L28
L36
Junction 3
Junction 2
M57
M57 MOTORWAY
KNOWSLEY BUSINESS PARK
Quarry Farm
Davis's Pits
Homer Wood
Keeper's House
Village Hall
Meakins Pits
Shepherd's Cottage
Maiden's Bower Farm
The Roughs
Akers Pit
Brookside
Fluker's Brook Farm
Knowsley Cottage
Canrow Cottage
Canrow Farm
Canrow Cottages
Moss Plantation
Scamper Plantation
Mill Cottages
Mill Plantation
Corn Ground Plantation
Avenue Plantation
Berry Hill
Dumbrees House
Syders' Grove
The Kennels (Knowsley Comm. Coll.)
Home Farm
Jack's Brow Plantation
Knowsley Outdoor Educational Centre
Aviary Cottages
WHITE MAN'S DAM
Knowle's Pits
Pond
Howard's Pits
Ash Plantation
Hen House Clump
Mill Pits
Fish Pond
Bridge Lodge
Dungeon Dam
Weir
Octagon Pond
Knowsley Hall
Home Pond
Mole Earth Pit
Nursery Plantation
The Elm Cottage
Admiral's Belt
The Nursery
Oak Plantation
The Paddocks
The Elms School
Playing Fields
Resource Cen.
Brookside Prim. Sch.
Lord Derby Memorial Playing Fields
Tennis Cts.
School Plantation
Knowsley Lane Farm
Catholic Prim. Sch.
Pav. Rec. Grd.
Liby.
Sch.
Tincle Peg Cottages
Farm
Potato Pit (Hunting)
KNOWSLEY LANE
ORMSKIRK ROAD
CANROW LANE
PATTEN'S WALK
MILL LANE
TITHEBARN ROAD
SUGAR LANE
HOME FARM ROAD
ALDER LANE
BROOK LANE
CROXTETH LANE
PINFOLD
HALE AV.
STOCKBRIDGE LA.
OVERBROOK LANE
KITLING ROAD
VILLIERS ROAD
CADDICK ROAD
B5202
B5194
43
44
345
96
95
94
93
57
72
91
F
G
H
J
K
1
2
3
4
5
6
7

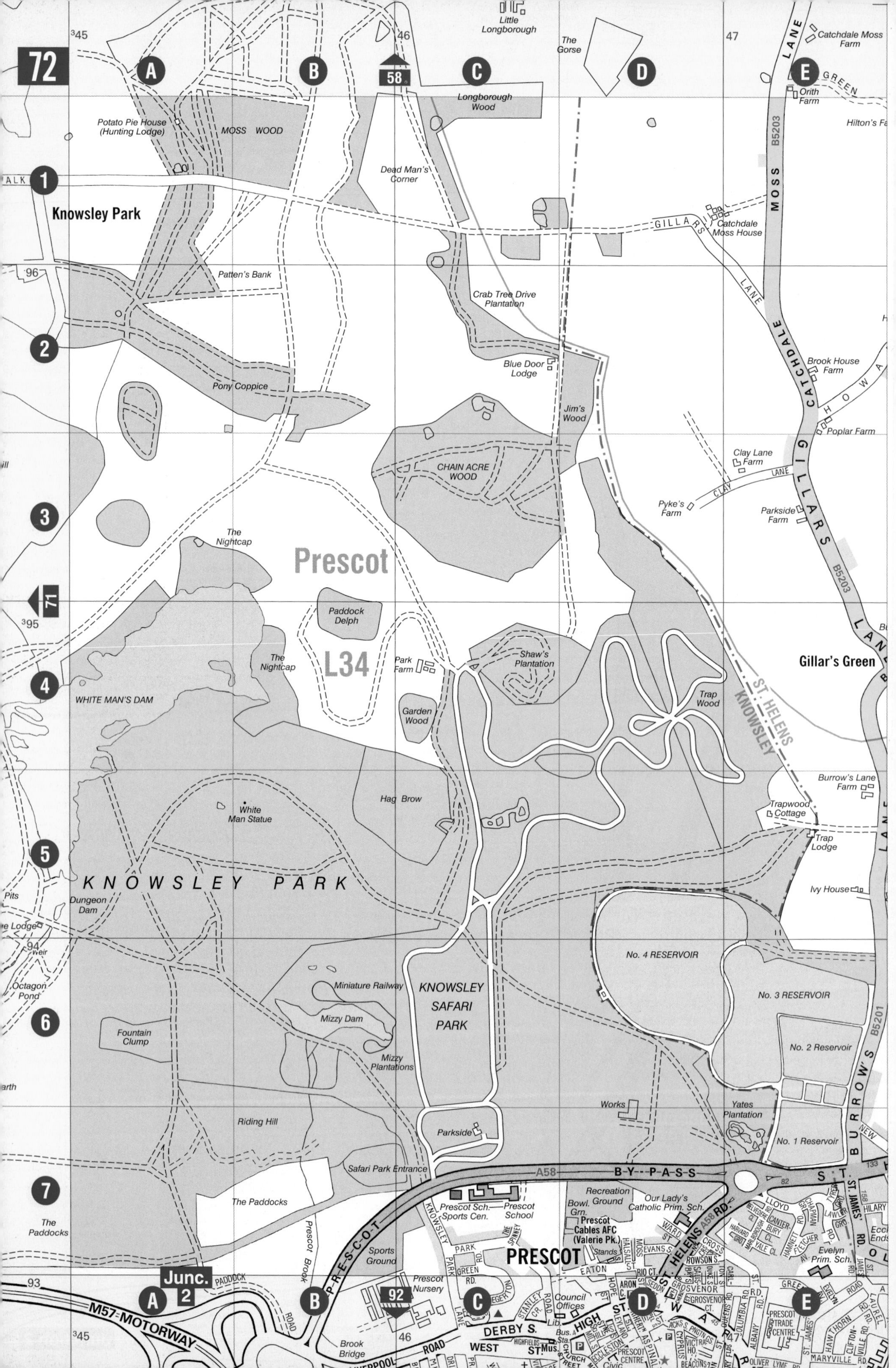

Little Longborough
The Gorse
Catchdale Moss Farm
Orith Farm
Longborough Wood
Potato Pie House (Hunting Lodge)
MOSS WOOD
Hilton's Fa
Dead Man's Corner
Knowsley Park
GILLARS LANE
Catchdale Moss House
MOSS LANE
B5203
Patten's Bank
Crab Tree Drive Plantation
CATCHDALE
Blue Door Lodge
Brook House Farm
Pony Coppice
Jim's Wood
Poplar Farm
GILLARS
Clay Lane Farm
CLAY LANE
CHAIN ACRE WOOD
Pyke's Farm
Parkside Farm
The Nightcap
Prescot
Paddock Delph
L34
Park Farm
Shaw's Plantation
Gillar's Green
The Nightcap
WHITE MAN'S DAM
Garden Wood
Trap Wood
ST. HELENS
KNOWSLEY
Hag Brow
White Man Statue
Burrow's Lane Farm
Trapwood Cottage
Trap Lodge
KNOWSLEY PARK
Ivy House
Dungeon Dam
Pits
Lodge
Weir
Octagon Pond
No. 4 RESERVOIR
No. 3 RESERVOIR
Miniature Railway
KNOWSLEY SAFARI PARK
Mizzy Dam
Fountain Clump
Mizzy Plantations
No. 2 Reservoir
B5201
BURROW'S LANE
Works
Riding Hill
Yates Plantation
Parkside
No. 1 Reservoir
Safari Park Entrance
A58 BY-PASS
ST. HELENS RD.
The Paddocks
Recreation Ground
Our Lady's Catholic Prim. Sch.
Prescot Sch. Sports Cen.
Prescot School
Bowl. Grn.
Prescot Cables AFC (Valerie Pk.)
The Paddocks
Prescot Brook
PRESCOT ROAD
Sports Ground
PRESCOT
Evelyn Prim. Sch.
Junc. 2
PADDOCK
Prescot Nursery
Council Offices
M57 MOTORWAY
ROAD
DERBY S.
HIGH ST.
Brook Bridge
LIVERPOOL ROAD
WEST ST
PRESCOT TRADE CENTRE
PRESCOT CENTRE
MARYVILLE
OLIVER LYME

58
71
92

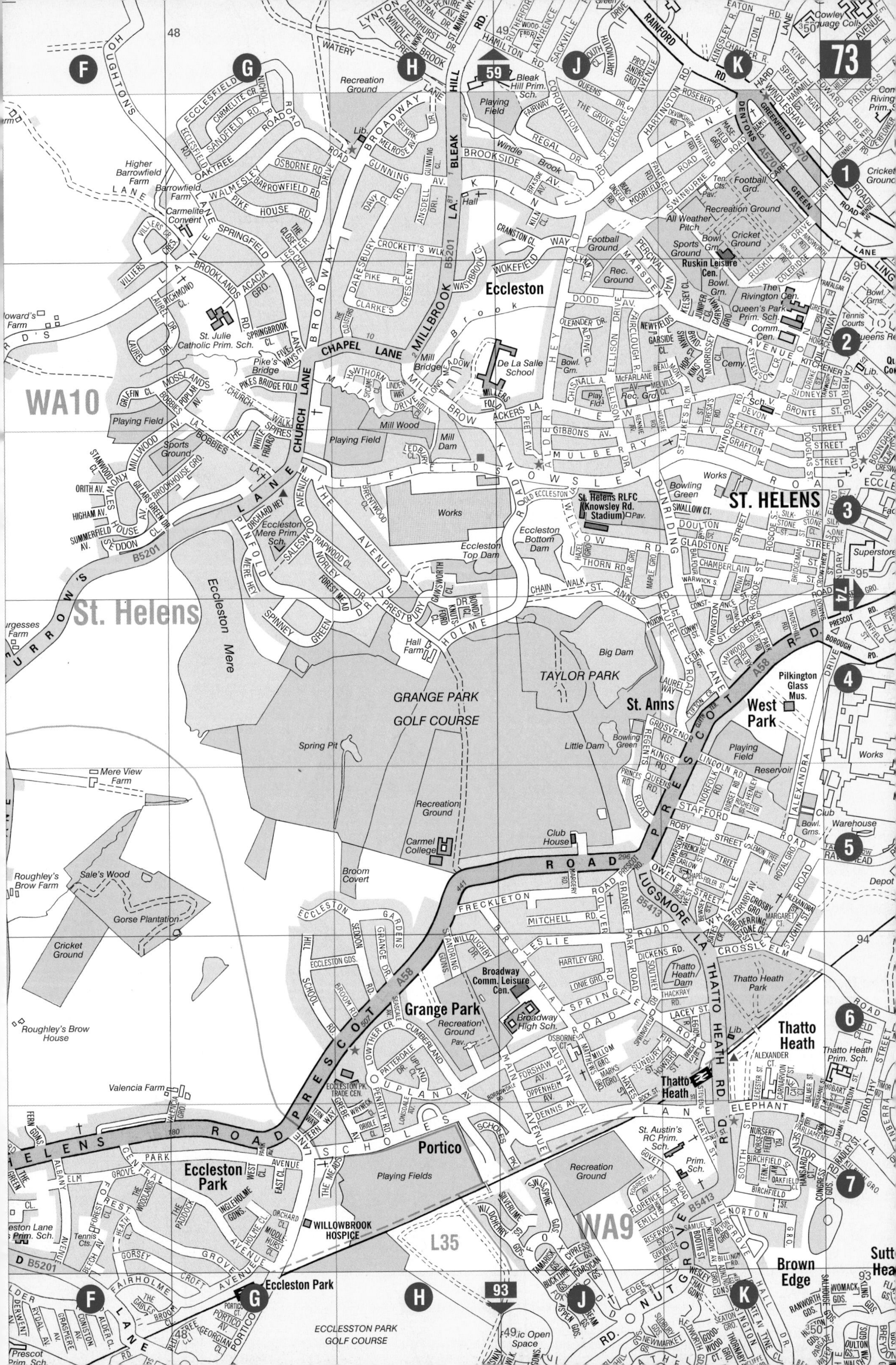
Eccleston
ST. HELENS
St. Helens
WA10
WA9
L35
TAYLOR PARK
GRANGE PARK GOLF COURSE
Eccleston Mere
St. Anns
West Park
Grange Park
Thatto Heath
Eccleston Park
Portico
Brown Edge
De La Salle School
St. Helens RLFC (Knowsley Rd. Stadium)
Pilkington Glass Mus.
Ruskin Leisure Cen.
Broadway Comm. Leisure Cen.
Broadway High Sch.
Carmel College
Willowbrook Hospice
Eccleston Mere Prim. Sch.
St. Julie Catholic Prim. Sch.
Bleak Hill Prim. Sch.
Thatto Heath Prim. Sch.
St. Austin's RC Prim. Sch.
Queen's Park Prim. Sch.
The Rivington Cen.
Thatto Heath Park
Big Dam
Little Dam
Eccleston Top Dam
Eccleston Bottom Dam
Mill Wood
Mill Dam
Spring Pit
Broom Covert
Sale's Wood
Gorse Plantation
Roughley's Brow Farm
Roughley's Brow House
Valencia Farm
Mere View Farm
Higher Barrowfield Farm
Barrowfield Farm
Carmelite Convent
Hall Farm
Eccleston Pk. Trade Cen.
Eccleston Park Golf Course
PRESCOT ROAD
A58
B5201
B5413
A570
CHURCH LANE
MILLBROOK LANE
CHAPEL LANE
KNOWSLEY ROAD
BROADWAY
BLEAK HILL RD.
DUNRIDING LANE
THATTO HEATH RD.
LUGSMORE LA.
ELEPHANT LANE
SCHOLES LANE
RAINFORD RD.
WINDLESHAW
GREENFIELD
WINDLE BROOK
F
G
H
J
K
1
2
3
4
5
6
7
59
74
93
48
49
50
94
95
96

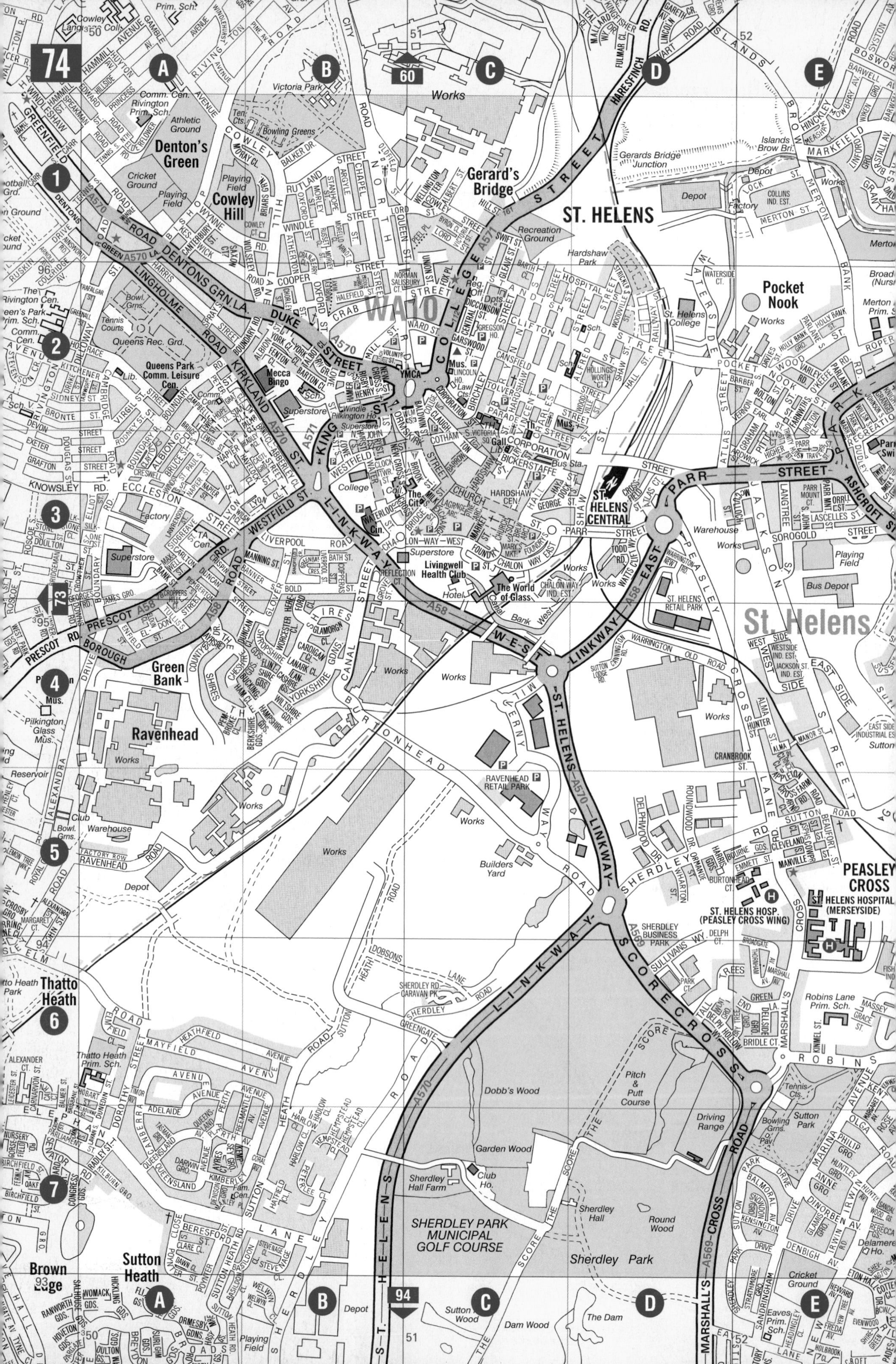
ST. HELENS
St. Helens
WA10
Denton's Green
Cowley Hill
Gerard's Bridge
Pocket Nook
Green Bank
Ravenhead
Thatto Heath
Sutton Heath
Peasley Cross
Brown Edge
Victoria Park
Athletic Ground
Cricket Ground
Playing Field
Queens Rec. Grd.
Queens Park Comm. Leisure Cen.
Mecca Bingo
Superstore
YMCA
College
Mus.
ST. HELENS CENTRAL
St. Helens College
Recreation Ground
Hardshaw Park
Gerards Bridge Junction
Islands Brow Bri.
Collins Ind. Est.
Depot
Works
Warehouse
Bus Depot
ST. HELENS RETAIL PARK
RAVENHEAD RETAIL PARK
Builders Yard
Livingwell Health Club
The World of Glass
Hotel
Pilkington Glass Mus.
Reservoir
Sherdley Business Park
ST. HELENS HOSP. (PEASLEY CROSS WING)
ST. HELENS HOSPITAL (MERSEYSIDE)
Robins Lane Prim. Sch.
Sutton Park
Pitch & Putt Course
Driving Range
Dobb's Wood
Garden Wood
Sherdley Hall Farm
Club Ho.
SHERDLEY PARK MUNICIPAL GOLF COURSE
Sherdley Hall
Round Wood
Sherdley Park
The Dam
Dam Wood
Sutton Wood
Thatto Heath Prim. Sch.
Eaves Prim. Sch.
DUKE STREET
COLLEGE STREET
HARESFINCH RD.
LINKWAY
LINKWAY WEST
LINKWAY EAST
ST. HELENS LINKWAY
SCORECROSS ROAD
MARSHALL'S CROSS ROAD
PARR STREET
KING ST.
WESTFIELD ST.
PRESCOT RD.
BOROUGH ROAD
KIRKLAND ST.
DENTONS GRN. LA.
LINGHOLME ROAD
BURTONHEAD ROAD
PEASLEY CROSS LANE
SUTTON LANE
SUTTON HEATH ROAD
ROBINS LANE
A570
A571
A58
A569
60
73
94
A B C D E
1 2 3 4 5 6 7
50 51 52
93 94 95 96

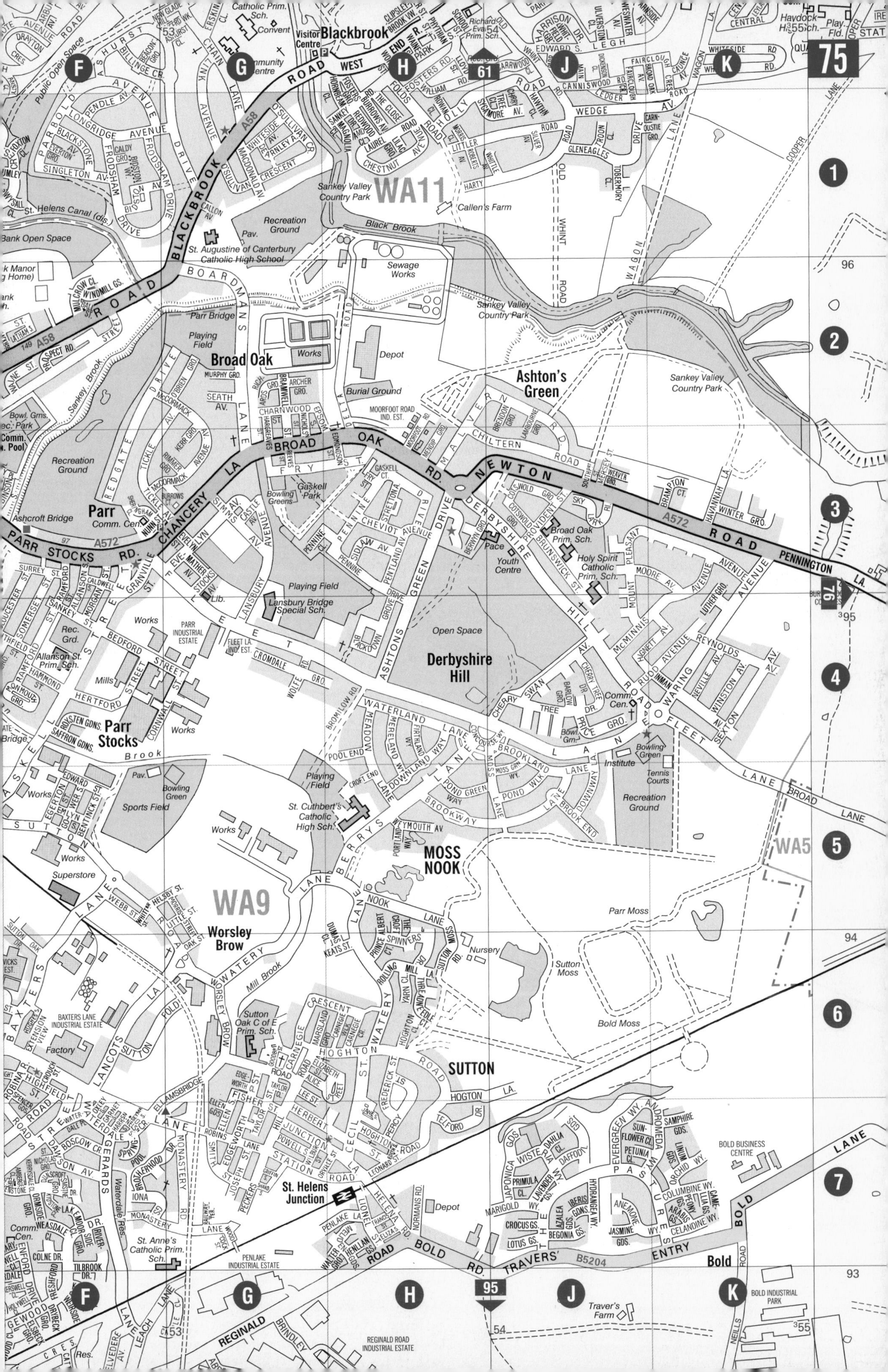
Blackbrook
Visitor Centre
Catholic Prim. Sch.
Convent
Community Centre
WEST END ROAD
BLACKBROOK ROAD
A58
Richard Evans Prim. Sch.
Rec. Grd.
61
WA11
Sankey Valley Country Park
Callen's Farm
Recreation Ground
Pav.
St. Augustine of Canterbury Catholic High School
Black Brook
Sewage Works
St. Helens Canal (dis.)
Bank Open Space
Parr Bridge
Playing Field
Broad Oak
Works
Depot
Burial Ground
Ashton's Green
MOORFOOT ROAD IND. EST.
BROAD OAK RD.
NEWTON ROAD
A572
PENNINGTON LA.
76
Recreation Ground
Parr
Comm. Cen.
Ashcroft Bridge
PARR STOCKS RD.
CHANCERY LA
Bowling Greens
Gaskell Park
Pace Youth Centre
Broad Oak Prim. Sch.
Holy Spirit Catholic Prim. Sch.
Playing Field
Lansbury Bridge Special Sch.
Lib.
PARR INDUSTRIAL ESTATE
FLEET LA. IND. EST.
Open Space
Derbyshire Hill
Rec. Grd.
Allanson St. Prim. Sch.
Mills
Parr Stocks
Brook
Comm. Cen.
Bowl. Grn.
Bowling Green
Institute
Tennis Courts
Recreation Ground
FLEET LANE
BROAD LANE
Playing Field
St. Cuthbert's Catholic High Sch.
Pav.
Bowling Green
Sports Field
Works
Superstore
MOSS NOOK
WA5
WA9
Parr Moss
Worsley Brow
Nursery
Sutton Moss
Mill Brook
BAXTERS LANE INDUSTRIAL ESTATE
Factory
Sutton Oak C of E Prim. Sch.
Bold Moss
SUTTON
St. Helens Junction
Depot
BOLD BUSINESS CENTRE
BOLD LANE
Comm. Cen.
St. Anne's Catholic Prim. Sch.
PENLAKE INDUSTRIAL ESTATE
BOLD RD.
TRAVERS' ENTRY
B5204
Bold
BOLD INDUSTRIAL PARK
95
Traver's Farm
REGINALD ROAD INDUSTRIAL ESTATE
F
G
H
J
K
1
2
3
4
5
6
7
96
95
94
93
53
54
55

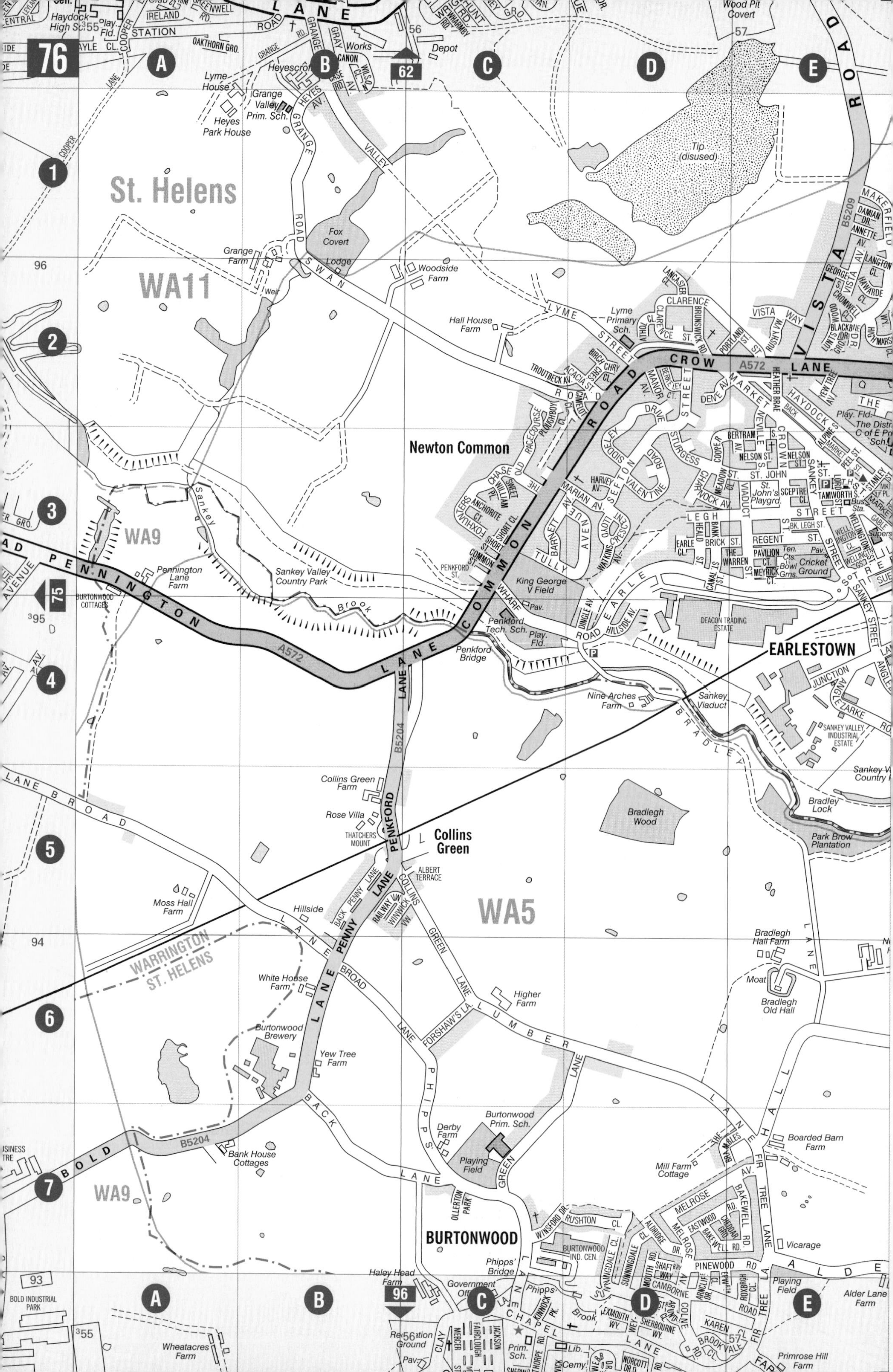
St. Helens
WA11
WA9
WA5
Newton Common
EARLESTOWN
Collins Green
BURTONWOOD
Tip (disused)
Fox Covert
Sankey Valley Country Park
King George V Field
Bradlegh Wood
Park Brow Plantation
Bradlegh Old Hall
Burtonwood Brewery
Burtonwood Prim. Sch.
DEACON TRADING ESTATE
SANKEY VALLEY INDUSTRIAL ESTATE
BOLD INDUSTRIAL PARK
WARRINGTON
ST. HELENS
PENNINGTON LANE
CROW LANE
COMMON ROAD
PENKFORD LANE
PENNY LANE
BROAD LANE
LUMBER LANE
HALL LANE
BOLD ROAD
CHAPEL LANE
ALDER LANE
VISTA ROAD
SWAN ROAD
Sankey Viaduct
Nine Arches Farm
Penkford Bridge
Phipps' Bridge
Wood Pit Covert
Heyes Park House
Grange Farm
Woodside Farm
Hall House Farm
Pennington Lane Farm
Collins Green Farm
Rose Villa
Moss Hall Farm
White House Farm
Yew Tree Farm
Bank House Cottages
Higher Farm
Derby Farm
Bradlegh Hall Farm
Boarded Barn Farm
Mill Farm Cottage
Haley Head Farm
Wheatacres Farm
Alder Lane Farm
Primrose Hill Farm
62
75
96

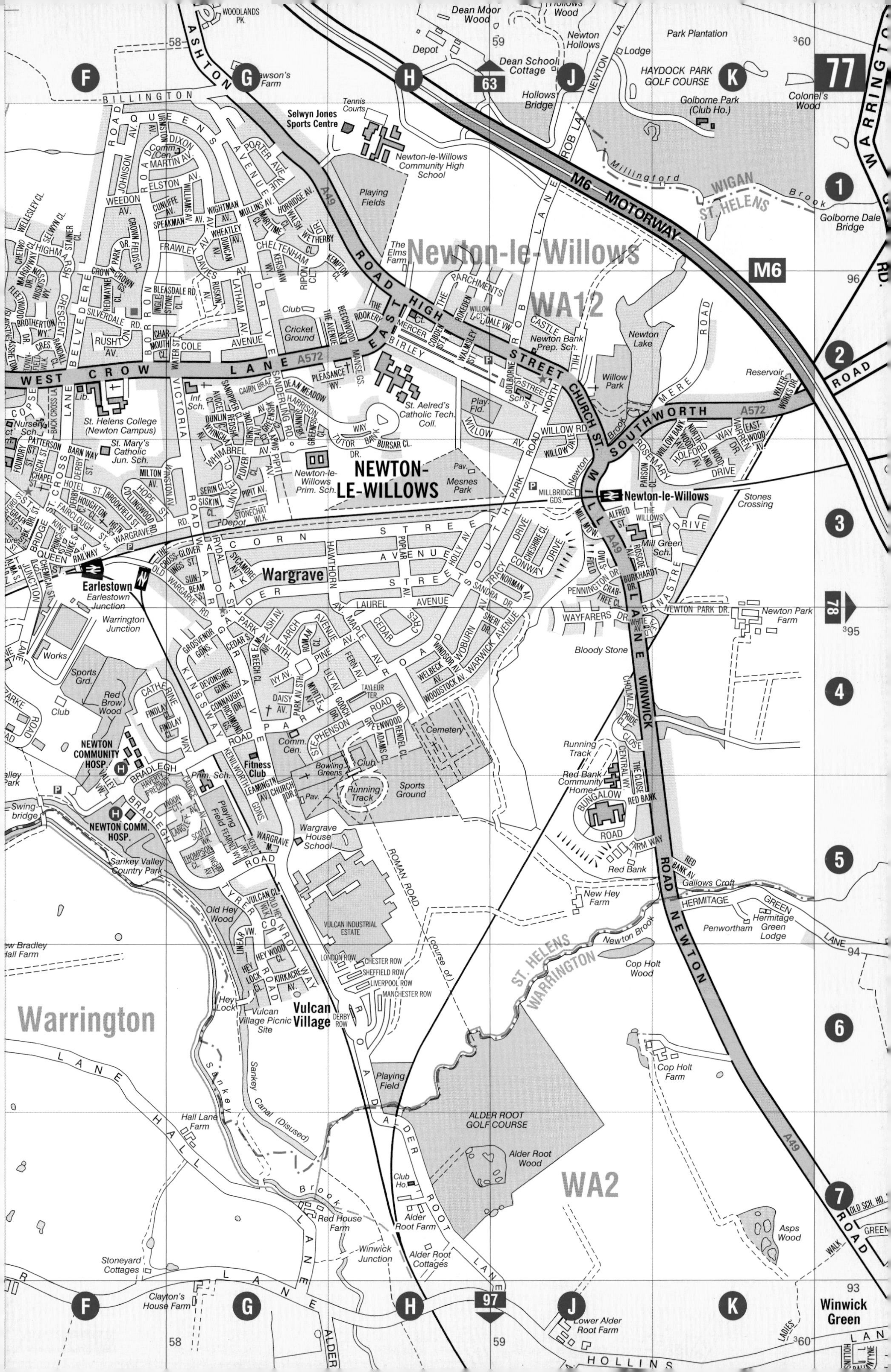
77
Newton-le-Willows
WA12
NEWTON-LE-WILLOWS
Wargrave
Earlestown
Earlestown Junction
Warrington Junction
Warrington
Vulcan Village
WA2
Winwick Green
M6 MOTORWAY
M6
63
97
78
WIGAN
ST. HELENS
WARRINGTON
Dean Moor Wood
Newton Hollows
Dean School Cottage
Hollows Bridge
Depot
Lodge
Park Plantation
HAYDOCK PARK GOLF COURSE
Golborne Park (Club Ho.)
Colonel's Wood
Millingford Brook
Golborne Dale Bridge
Selwyn Jones Sports Centre
Tennis Courts
Newton-le-Willows Community High School
Playing Fields
The Elms Farm
Newton Lake
Willow Park
Newton Bank Prep. Sch.
Reservoir
St. Aelred's Catholic Tech. Coll.
Mesnes Park
Newton-le-Willows Prim. Sch.
St. Helens College (Newton Campus)
St. Mary's Catholic Jun. Sch.
Cricket Ground
Newton-le-Willows
Stones Crossing
Mill Green Sch.
Newton Park Farm
Bloody Stone
Running Track
Red Bank Community Home
Red Bank
Gallows Croft
New Hey Farm
Hermitage Green Lodge
Penwortham
Newton Brook
Cop Holt Wood
Cop Holt Farm
Cemetery
Sports Ground
Bowling Greens
Fitness Club
Wargrave House School
VULCAN INDUSTRIAL ESTATE
Roman Road (course of)
NEWTON COMMUNITY HOSP.
NEWTON COMM. HOSP.
Sankey Valley Country Park
Swing-bridge
Old Hey Wood
Red Brow Wood
Sports Grd.
Works
Hey Lock
Vulcan Village Picnic Site
Sankey Canal (Disused)
Sankey Brook
Playing Field
ALDER ROOT GOLF COURSE
Alder Root Wood
Club Ho.
Alder Root Farm
Alder Root Cottages
Winwick Junction
Red House Farm
Hall Lane Farm
Stoneyard Cottages
Clayton's House Farm
Lower Alder Root Farm
Asps Wood
New Bradley Hall Farm
WEST CROW LANE
EAST LANCASHIRE ROAD
HIGH STREET
SOUTHWORTH ROAD
WINWICK LANE
NEWTON ROAD
CHURCH ST.
MILL LANE
ALDER ROOT LANE
HALL LANE
ALDER LANE
HOLLINS LANE
HERMITAGE GREEN LANE
CORN STREET
ALDER STREET
PARK ROAD
KINGSWAY
BRADLEGH ROAD
TYRER ROAD
CONROY WAY
A49
A572
F G H J K
1 2 3 4 5 6 7
58 59 360 96 95 94 93

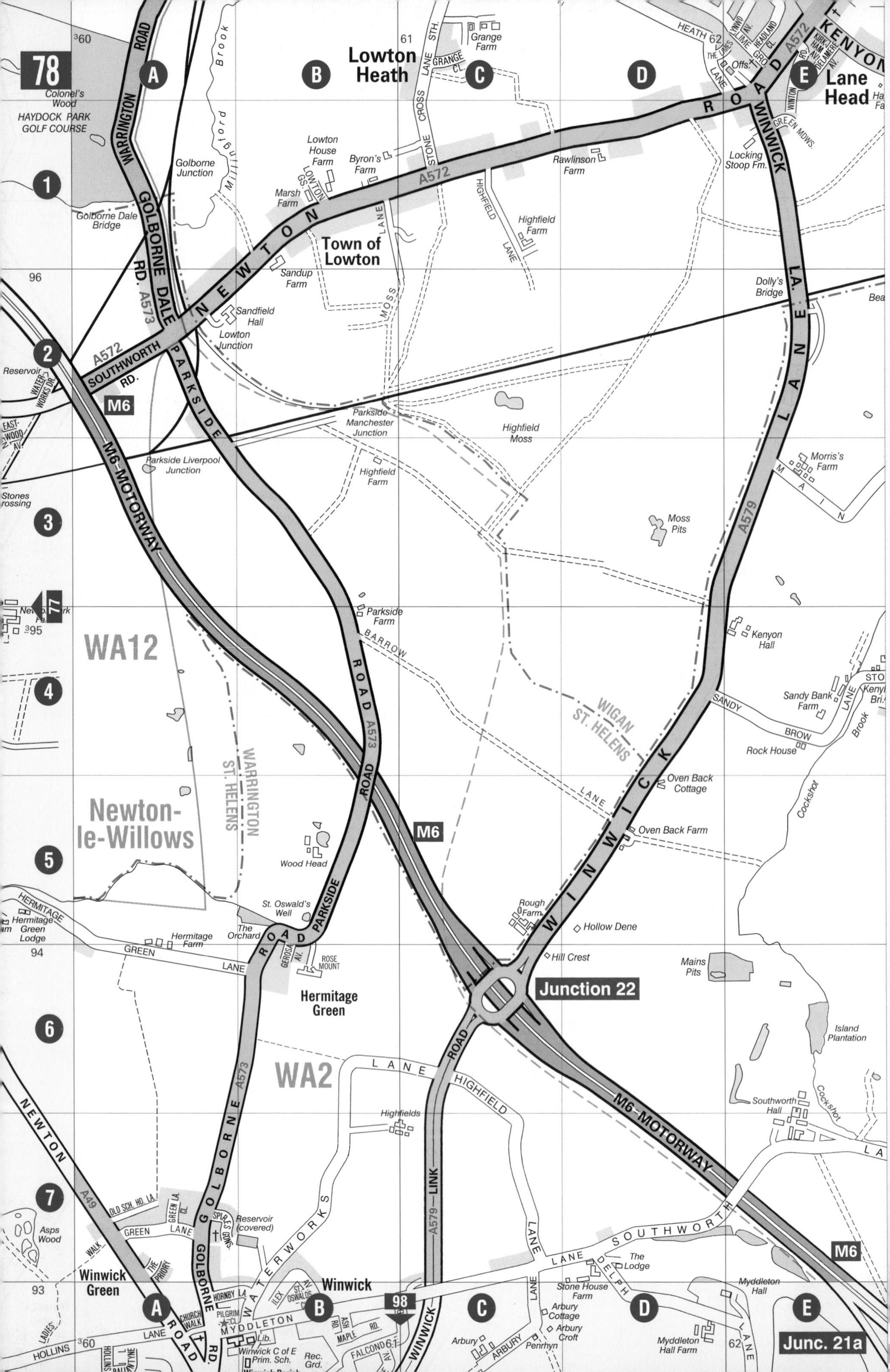
Lowton Heath
Town of Lowton
Lane Head
Haydock Park Golf Course
Colonel's Wood
Golborne Junction
Golborne Dale Bridge
Lowton House Farm
Byron's Farm
Grange Farm
Marsh Farm
Rawlinson Farm
Highfield Farm
Sandup Farm
Sandfield Hall
Lowton Junction
Locking Stoop Fm.
Dolly's Bridge
Parkside Manchester Junction
Parkside Liverpool Junction
Highfield Moss
Morris's Farm
Moss Pits
Parkside Farm
Kenyon Hall
Sandy Bank Farm
Rock House
Oven Back Cottage
Oven Back Farm
WA12
Newton-le-Willows
Wood Head
St. Oswald's Well
The Orchard
Hermitage Farm
Hermitage Green Lodge
Hermitage Green
Rough Farm
Hollow Dene
Hill Crest
Junction 22
Mains Pits
Island Plantation
WA2
Highfields
Southworth Hall
Reservoir (covered)
Asps Wood
Winwick Green
Winwick
The Lodge
Stone House Farm
Arbury Cottage
Arbury Croft
Penrhyn
Arbury
Myddleton Hall
Myddleton Hall Farm
Winwick C of E Prim. Sch.
Rec. Grd.
Junc. 21a
M6
M6 MOTORWAY
A572
A573
A579
A49
NEWTON ROAD
WINWICK ROAD
GOLBORNE DALE RD.
SOUTHWORTH RD.
PARKSIDE ROAD
WINWICK LANE
WINWICK LA.
LINK ROAD
HIGHFIELD LANE
GOLBORNE RD.
WATERWORKS
SOUTHWORTH LANE
DELPH LANE
MYDDLETON LANE
HERMITAGE GREEN LANE
SANDY BROW
BARROW LANE
MOSS LANE
WARRINGTON ST. HELENS
WIGAN ST. HELENS
Reservoir
Stones Crossing
77
98

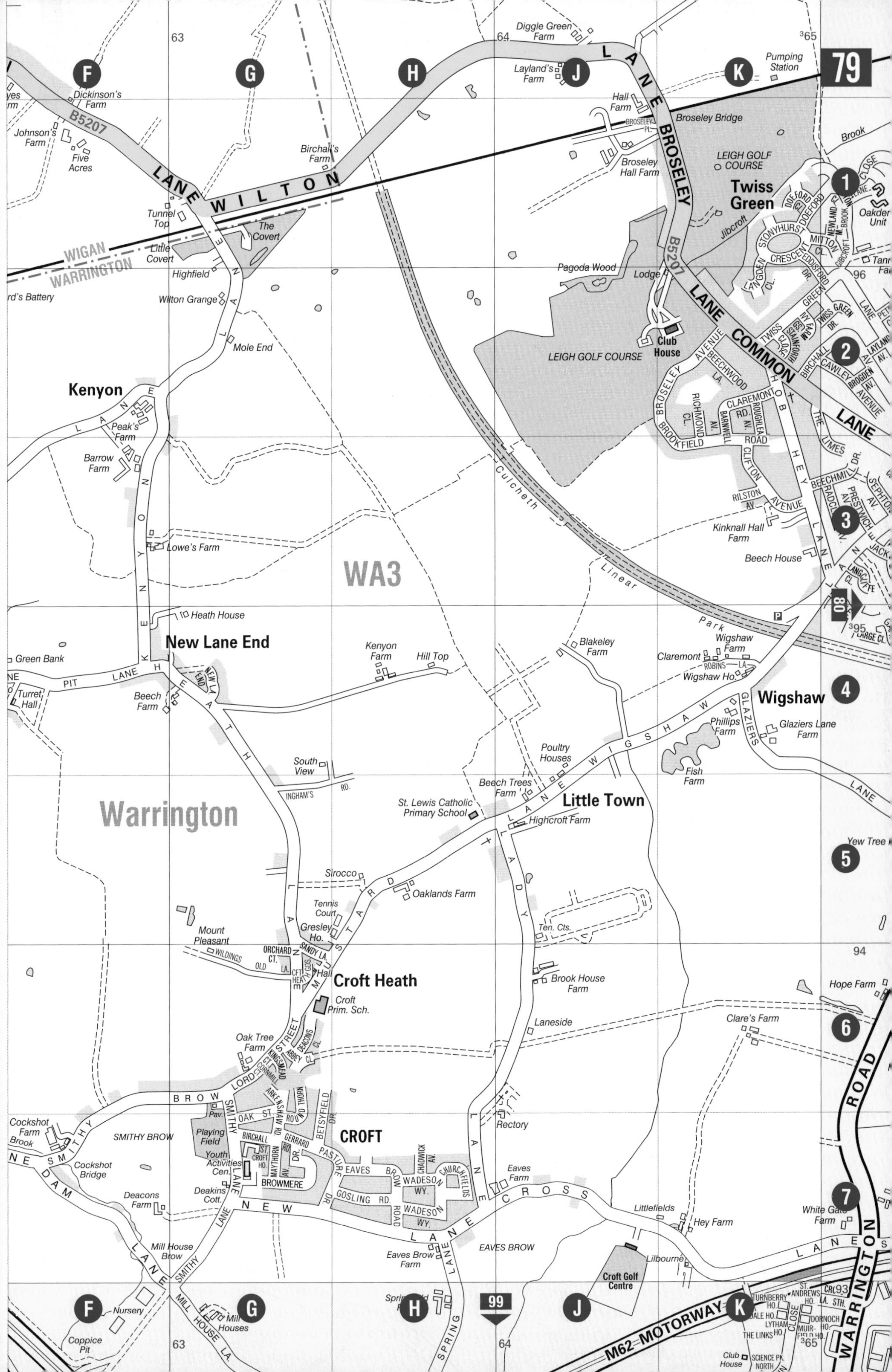
Diggle Green Farm
Layland's Farm
Pumping Station
Dickinson's Farm
B5207
Johnson's Farm
Five Acres
Birchall's Farm
WILTON LANE
BROSELEY LANE
Hall Farm
Broseley Bridge
Broseley Hall Farm
LEIGH GOLF COURSE
Twiss Green
Tunnel Top
The Covert
Little Covert
WIGAN
WARRINGTON
Highfield
Wilton Grange
Pagoda Wood
Lodge
COMMON LANE
Mole End
Club House
LEIGH GOLF COURSE
Kenyon
Peak's Farm
Barrow Farm
Culcheth
Lowe's Farm
WA3
Linear Park
Kinknall Hall Farm
Beech House
Heath House
New Lane End
Green Bank
Kenyon Farm
Hill Top
Blakeley Farm
Claremont
Wigshaw Farm
Wigshaw Ho.
Wigshaw
PIT LANE
Turret Hall
Beech Farm
KENYON LANE
HEATH LANE
South View
INGHAM'S RD.
WIGSHAW LANE
Phillips Farm
Glaziers Lane Farm
Fish Farm
Poultry Houses
Beech Trees Farm
Little Town
St. Lewis Catholic Primary School
Highcroft Farm
Warrington
Yew Tree
Sirocco
Oaklands Farm
Tennis Court
Gresley Ho.
Mount Pleasant
Ten. Cts.
Croft Heath
Croft Prim. Sch.
Brook House Farm
Laneside
Hope Farm
Clare's Farm
Oak Tree Farm
LADY LANE
MUSTARD LANE
Cockshot Farm
Cockshot Brook
SMITHY BROW
Playing Field
Youth Activities Cen.
CROFT
Rectory
Cockshot Bridge
Deacons Farm
Deakins Cott.
BROWMERE
Eaves Farm
NEW LANE
CROSS LANE
Littlefields
Hey Farm
White Gate Farm
Mill House Brow
Eaves Brow Farm
EAVES BROW
Lilbourne
Croft Golf Centre
Nursery
Coppice Pit
Mill Houses
MILL HOUSE LA.
SPRING LANE
M62 MOTORWAY
WARRINGTON ROAD
Club House
99
80

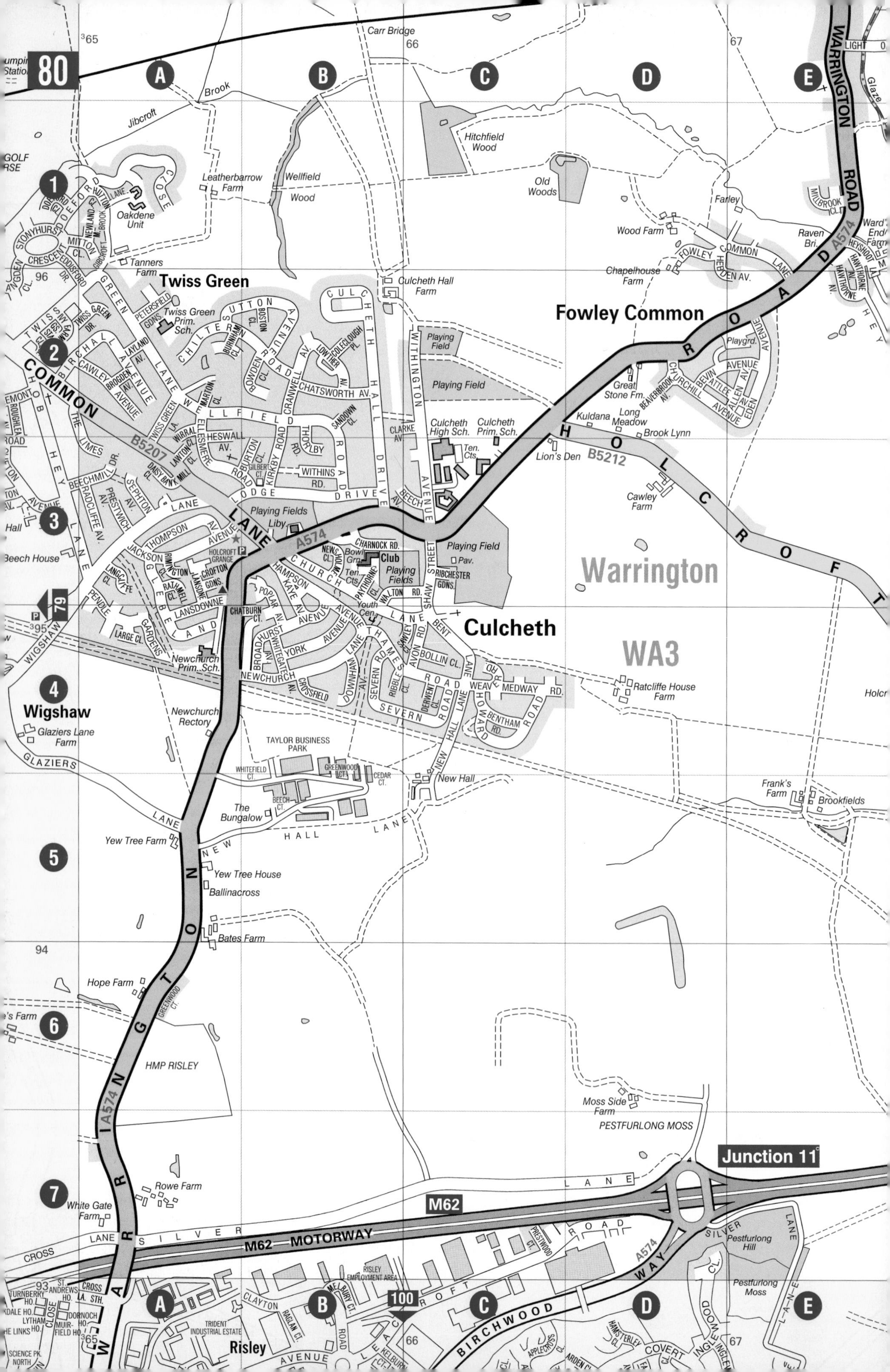
Twiss Green
Fowley Common
Culcheth
Warrington
WA3
Wigshaw
Risley
Junction 11
M62 MOTORWAY
WARRINGTON ROAD
HOLCROFT LANE
COMMON LANE
Carr Bridge
Hitchfield Wood
Old Woods
Wellfield Wood
Leatherbarrow Farm
Oakdene Unit
Tanners Farm
Culcheth Hall Farm
Wood Farm
Chapelhouse Farm
Culcheth High Sch.
Culcheth Prim. Sch.
Lion's Den
Cawley Farm
Ratcliffe House Farm
TAYLOR BUSINESS PARK
New Hall
The Bungalow
Yew Tree Farm
Yew Tree House
Ballinacross
Bates Farm
Hope Farm
HMP RISLEY
Rowe Farm
White Gate Farm
Moss Side Farm
PESTFURLONG MOSS
Pestfurlong Hill
Glaziers Lane Farm
Newchurch Rectory
Newchurch Prim. Sch.
Frank's Farm
Brookfields
TRIDENT INDUSTRIAL ESTATE
RISLEY EMPLOYMENT AREA
BIRCHWOOD WAY
79
100

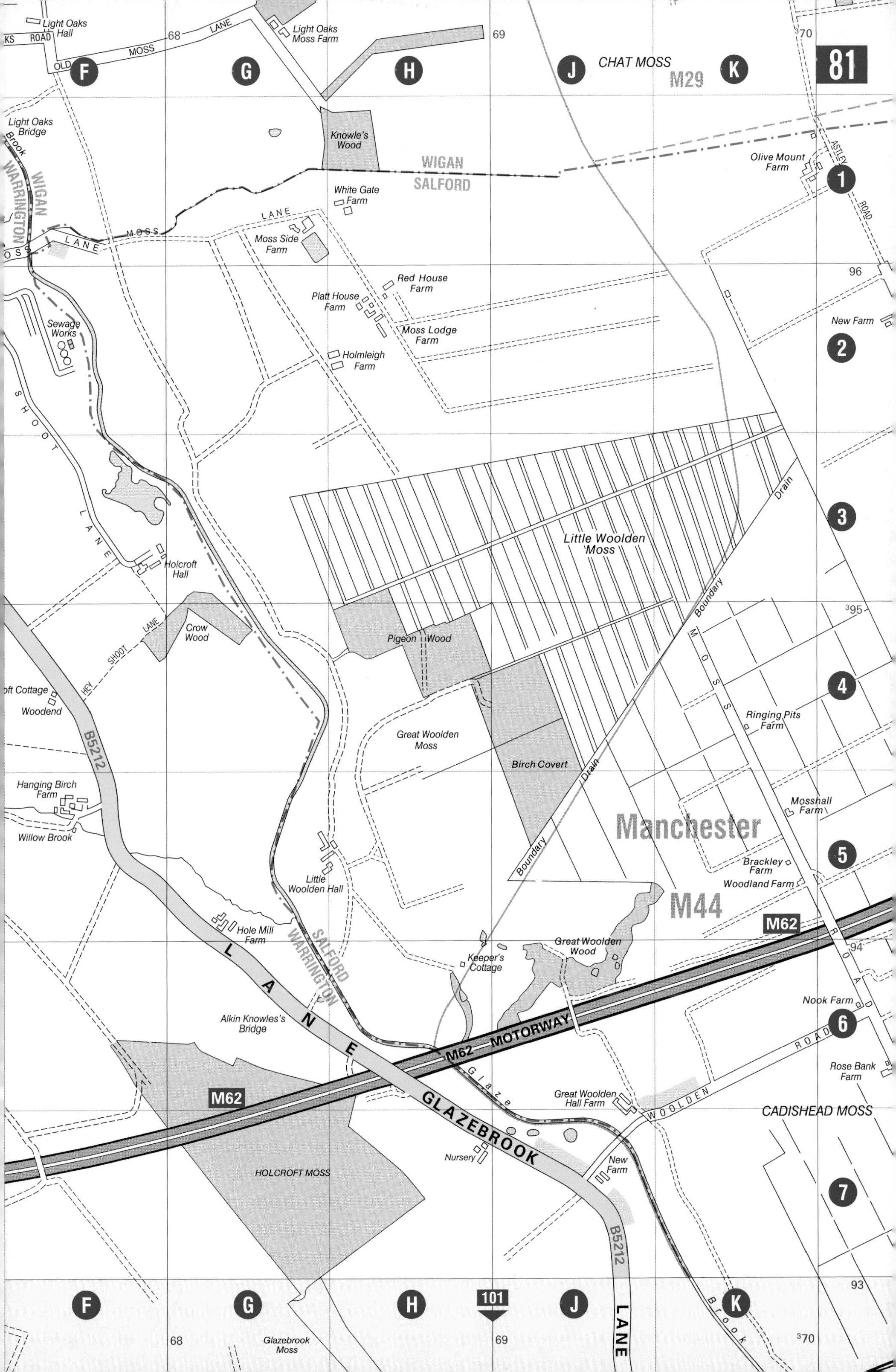

Light Oaks Hall

KS ROAD

OLD

MOSS LANE

68

LANE

Light Oaks Moss Farm

69

70

M29

Light Oaks Bridge

Knowle's Wood

WIGAN SALFORD

Olive Mount Farm

ASTLEY ROAD

Brook

WARRINGTON

MOSS

White Gate Farm

1

Sewage Works

MOSS LANE

SHOOT LANE

LANE

Moss Side Farm

Red House Farm

Platt House Farm

Moss Lodge Farm

Holmleigh Farm

96

New Farm

2

Little Woolden Moss

Drain

3

³95

Holcroft Hall

Crow Wood

Pigeon Wood

Boundary

MOSS

Ringing Pits Farm

4

oft Cottage

Woodend

HEY SHOOT LANE

B5212

Great Woolden Moss

Birch Covert

Drain

Mosshall Farm

Hanging Birch Farm

Willow Brook

Little Woolden Hall

Manchester

Boundary

Brackley Farm

Woodland Farm

5

M44

Hole Mill Farm

WARRINGTON

SALFORD

LANE

Keeper's Cottage

Great Woolden Wood

M62

94

ROAD

Nook Farm

6

Alkin Knowles's Bridge

Glaze

M62 — MOTORWAY

Great Woolden Hall Farm

WOOLDEN

Rose Bank Farm

M62

GLAZEBROOK

Nursery

New Farm

CADISHEAD MOSS

HOLCROFT MOSS

7

Brook

ROAD

93

68

Glazebrook Moss

69

³70

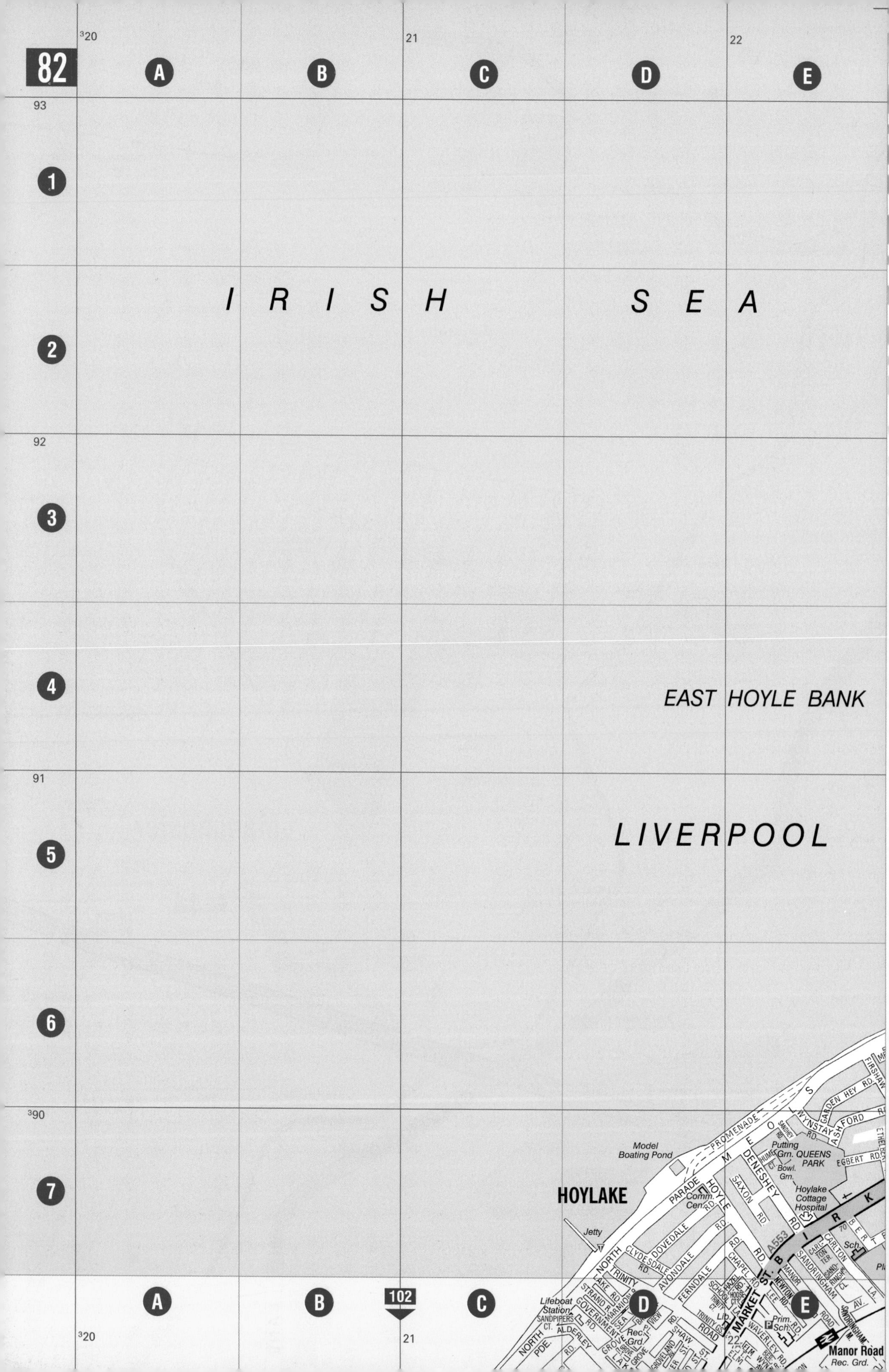

³20

21

22

93

1

I R I S H   S E A

2

92

3

4

EAST HOYLE BANK

91

LIVERPOOL

5

6

³90

Model
Boating Pond

PROMENADE

Putting
Grn. QUEENS
PARK

7

HOYLAKE

Comm.
Cen.

Hoylake
Cottage
Hospital

Jetty

NORTH CLYDESDALE RD.

DOVEDALE

AVONDALE

RD.

A553

³20

21

Lifeboat
Station
SANDPIPERS
CT.

NORTH
PDE.

STRAND RD.

GOVERNMENT

TRINITY

RD.

GROVE

CHAPEL

FERNDALE

RD.

MARKET ST.

TRINITY ROAD

WAVERLEY RD.

SANDRINGHAM

CARLTON
TER.

Prim.
Sch.

Manor Road
Rec. Grd.

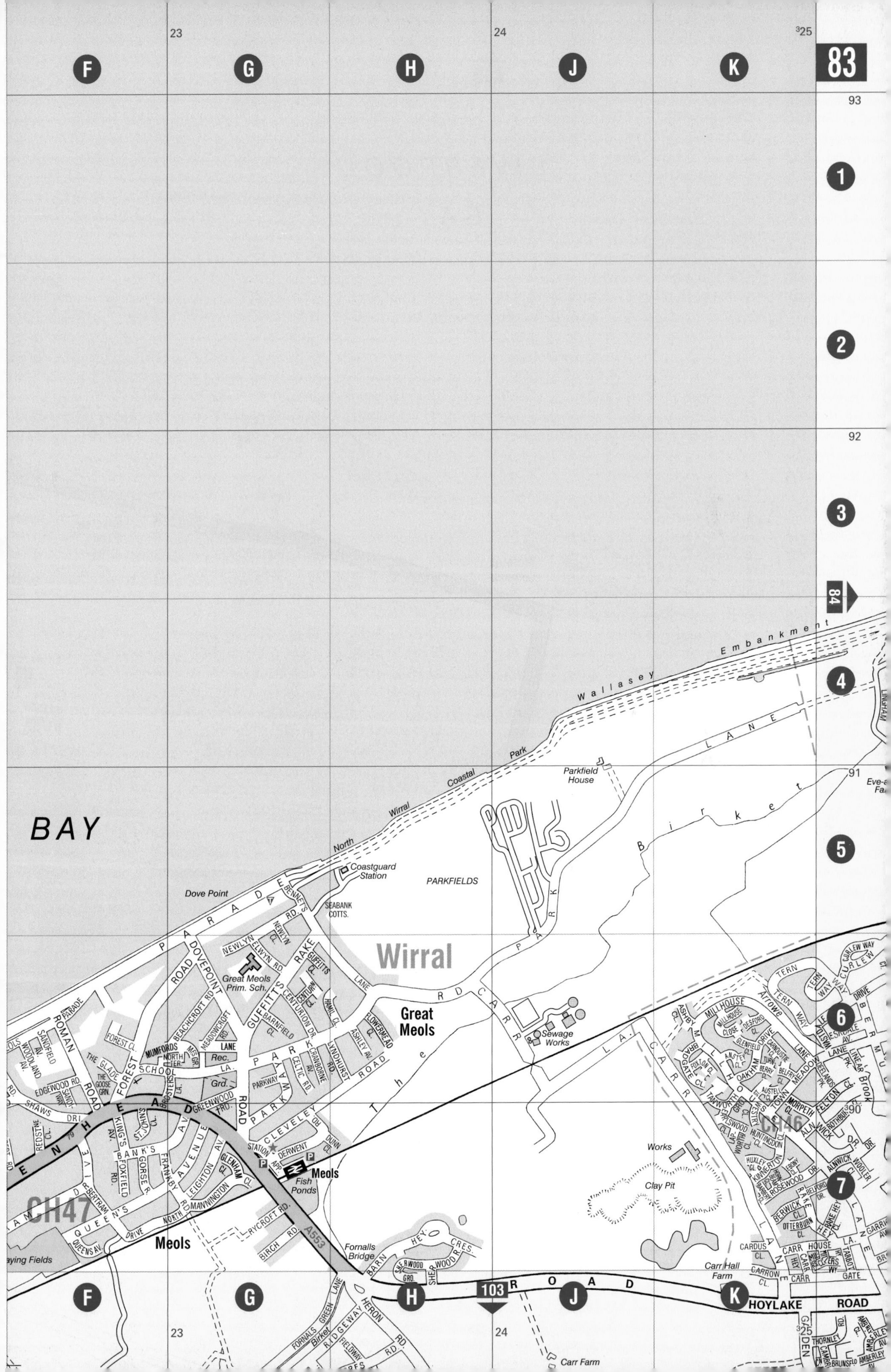

BAY
Wallasey Embankment
North Wirral Coastal Park
Dove Point
Coastguard Station
PARKFIELDS
Parkfield House
Birket
Wirral
Great Meols
Meols
Sewage Works
Works
Clay Pit
Fish Ponds
Fornalls Bridge
Carr Hall Farm
Carr Farm
CH47
CH46
PARADE
ROMAN ROAD
DOVEPOINT ROAD
FOREST ROAD
SCHOOL LANE
MUMFORDS LANE
GUFFITTS RAKE
PARK LANE
PARKWAY
CARR LANE
CARR ROAD
HOYLAKE ROAD
BIRKENHEAD ROAD
A553
Great Meols Prim. Sch.
Rec. Grd.
Playing Fields

84
103

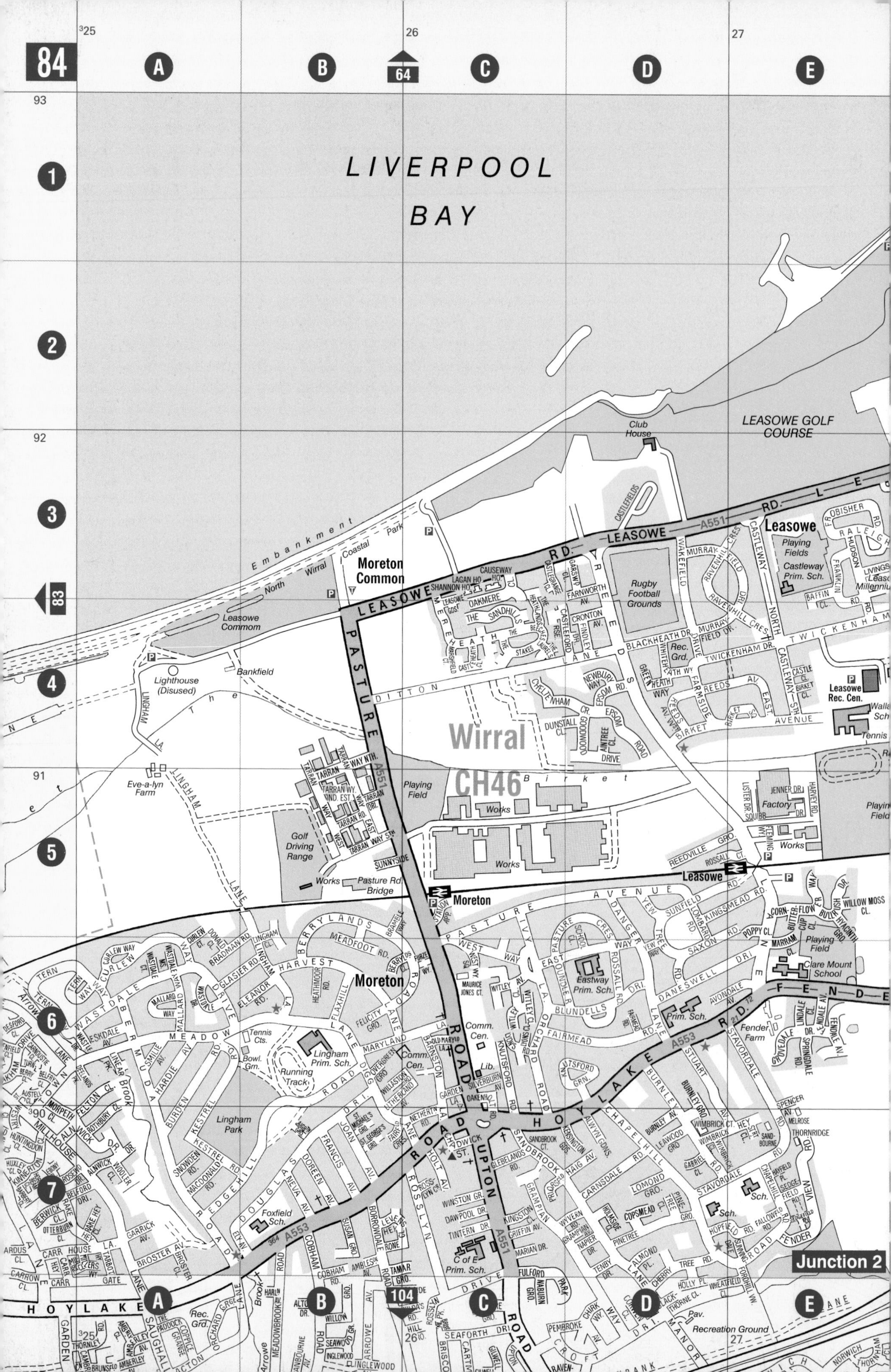

LIVERPOOL
BAY
64
83
104
Junction 2
LEASOWE GOLF COURSE
Club House
Moreton Common
Leasowe Commom
Lighthouse (Disused)
Bankfield
Eve-a-lyn Farm
North Wirral Coastal Park
Embankment
Wirral
CH46
Leasowe
Moreton
Playing Fields
Castleway Prim. Sch.
Leasowe Rec. Cen.
Rugby Football Grounds
Golf Driving Range
Playing Field
Works
Factory
Pasture Rd Bridge
Lingham Park
Lingham Prim. Sch.
Running Track
Eastway Prim. Sch.
Clare Mount School
Fender Farm
Foxfield Sch.
C of E Prim. Sch.
Recreation Ground
LEASOWE RD.
PASTURE ROAD
HOYLAKE RD.
UPTON ROAD
FENDER LANE
PASTURE AVENUE
BIRKET AVENUE
TWICKENHAM DR.

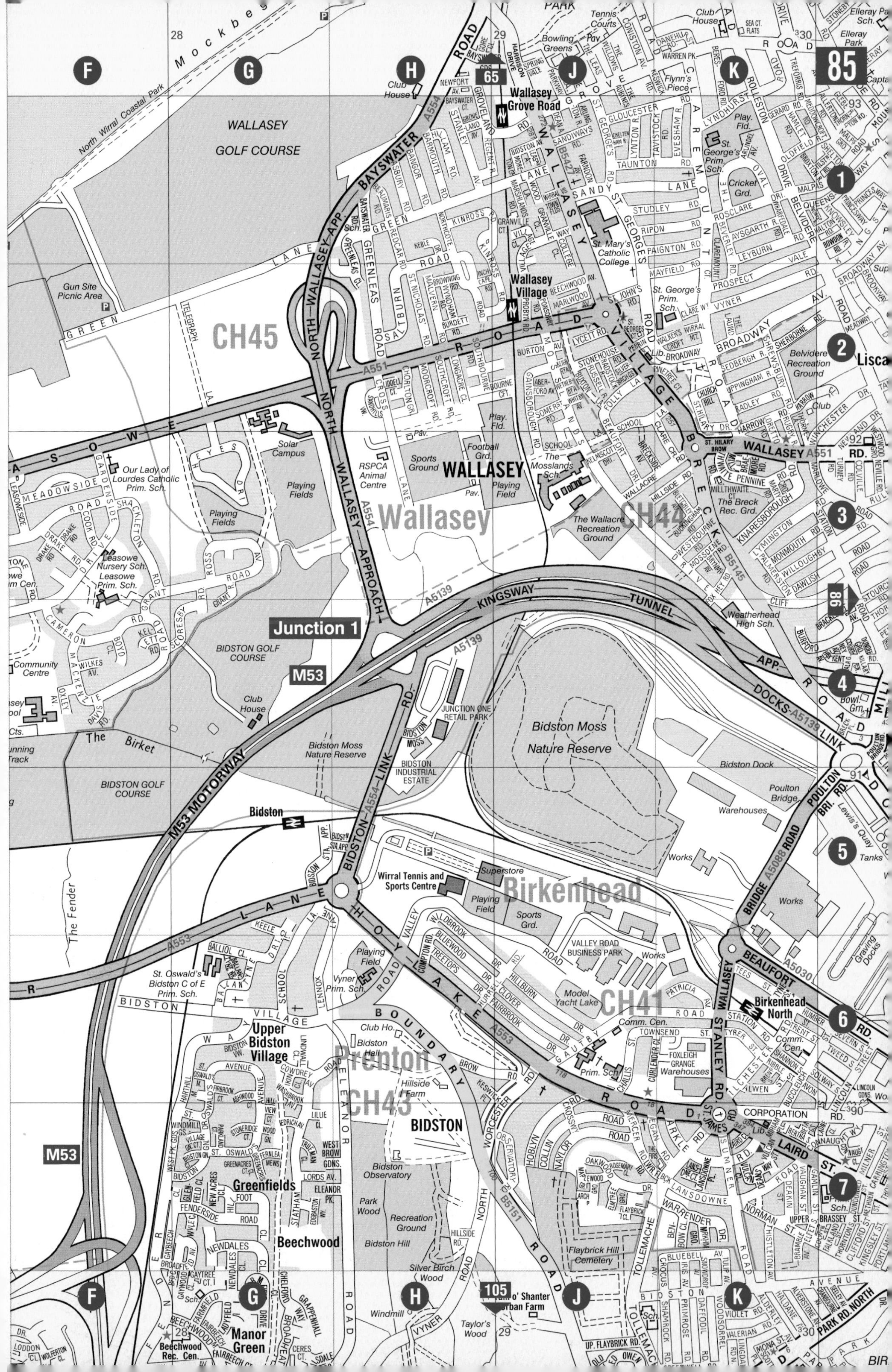
F
G
H
J
K
28
29
30
65
86
105
1
2
3
4
5
6
7
North Wirral Coastal Park
Mockbeggar
WALLASEY GOLF COURSE
Gun Site Picnic Area
Club House
Wallasey Grove Road
Wallasey Village
WALLASEY
Wallasey
CH45
CH44
CH41
CH43
LEASOWE ROAD
NORTH WALLASEY APPROACH
BAYSWATER ROAD
Solar Campus
Playing Fields
Our Lady of Lourdes Catholic Prim. Sch.
Leasowe Nursery Sch.
Leasowe Prim. Sch.
Community Centre
RSPCA Animal Centre
Sports Ground
Football Grd.
Playing Field
The Mosslands Sch.
The Wallacre Recreation Ground
St. Mary's Catholic College
St. George's Prim. Sch.
Cricket Grd.
Belvidere Recreation Ground
The Breck Rec. Grd.
Weatherhead High Sch.
Junction 1
M53
M53 MOTORWAY
KINGSWAY TUNNEL APP.
A5139
A551
A554
A553
A5088
A5030
B5145
B5151
BIDSTON GOLF COURSE
The Birket
JUNCTION ONE RETAIL PARK
BIDSTON INDUSTRIAL ESTATE
Bidston Moss Nature Reserve
Bidston Dock
Poulton Bridge
Warehouses
Works
Bidston
Wirral Tennis and Sports Centre
Superstore
Birkenhead
VALLEY ROAD BUSINESS PARK
Model Yacht Lake
Birkenhead North
St. Oswald's Bidston C of E Prim. Sch.
Vyner Prim. Sch.
Upper Bidston Village
Prenton
BIDSTON
Bidston Hill
Bidston Observatory
Park Wood
Recreation Ground
Silver Birch Wood
Windmill
Taylor's Wood
Tam o' Shanter Urban Farm
Flaybrick Hill Cemetery
Greenfields
Beechwood
Manor Green
Beechwood Rec. Cen.
The Fender
HOYLAKE ROAD
BIDSTON LINK RD.
BOUNDARY ROAD
STANLEY RD.
CORPORATION RD.
LAIRD ST.
DOCKS LINK
POULTON BRIDGE ROAD
Graving Docks
Lewis's Quay
Tanks
Liscard

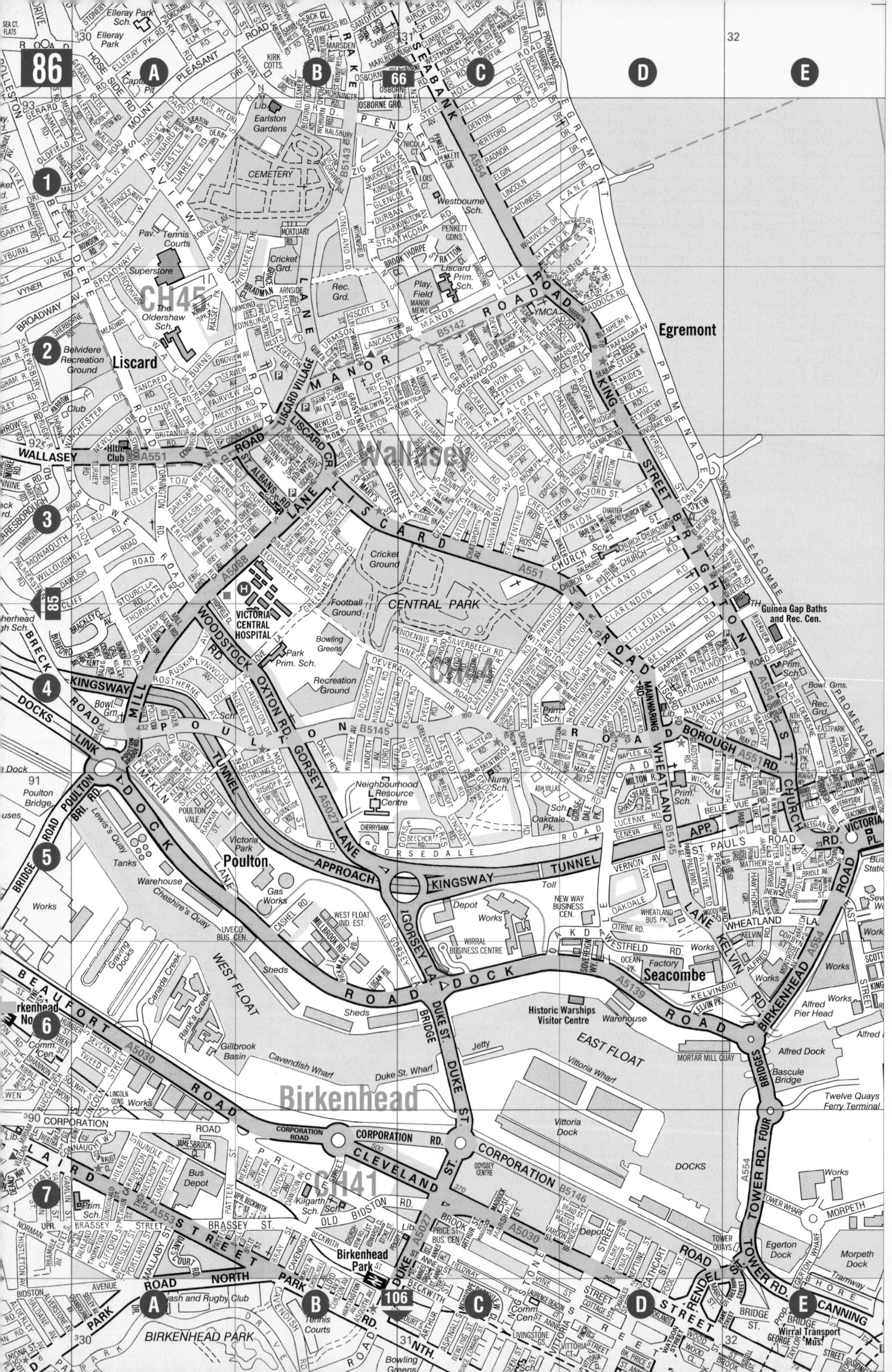

86
A
B
C
D
E
1
2
3
4
5
6
7
66
85
106
30
31
32
93
92
91
90
Elleray Park Sch.
Elleray Park
Captains Pit
Earlston Gardens
Lib.
CEMETERY
Westbourne Sch.
Penkett Gdns.
Mortuary Rd.
Pav.
Tennis Courts
Superstore
Cricket Grd.
Rec. Grd.
Play. Field
Liscard Prim. Sch.
Manor Mews
YMCA
CH45
The Oldershaw Sch.
Liscard
Belvidere Recreation Ground
Club
Egremont
Hlth. Club
Wallasey
St. Albans Sch.
Cricket Ground
Football Ground
CENTRAL PARK
Victoria Central Hospital
Bowling Greens
Park Prim. Sch.
Recreation Ground
CH44
Guinea Gap Baths and Rec. Cen.
Prim. Sch.
Bowl. Grns.
Rec. Grd.
Bowl. Grn.
Neighbourhood Resource Centre
Nursy. Sch.
Oakdale Pk.
Sch.
Lib.
Prim. Sch.
St. Paul's
Victoria Park
Poulton
Poulton Bridge
Lewis's Quay
Tanks
Warehouse
Works
Cheshire's Quay
Gas Works
West Float Ind. Est.
Uveco Bus. Cen.
Depot
Works
Wirral Business Centre
New Way Business Cen.
Toll
Wheatland Bus. Pk.
Ocean Pk.
Factory
Seacombe
Works
Alfred Pier Head
Alfred Dock
Graving Docks
Canada Creek
Rank's Creek
Sheds
WEST FLOAT
Gillbrook Basin
Cavendish Wharf
Duke St. Wharf
Jetty
Historic Warships Visitor Centre
Warehouse
EAST FLOAT
Vittoria Wharf
Mortar Mill Quay
Bascule Bridge
Twelve Quays Ferry Terminal
Vittoria Dock
DOCKS
Birkenhead
Comm. Cen.
Lincoln Gdns.
Works
Bus Depot
Kilgarth Sch.
Odyssey Centre
CH41
Prim. Sch.
Birkenhead Park
Tower Quays
Egerton Dock
Morpeth Dock
Works
Tower Wharf
Tramway
Wirral Transport Mus.
Rugby Club
Tennis Courts
BIRKENHEAD PARK
Bowling Greens
Comm. Cen.
Bus Station
SEABANK ROAD
A554
KING STREET
BRIGHTON STREET
EGREMONT PROMENADE
PROMENADE
SEACOMBE PROMENADE
MANOR ROAD
B5142
LISCARD ROAD
LISCARD VILLAGE
LISCARD LANE
A551
WALLASEY ROAD
MILL LANE
A5088
POULTON ROAD
B5145
KINGSWAY
DOCKS LINK
BRECK ROAD
POULTON BRIDGE ROAD
BRIDGE ROAD
DOCK ROAD
A5139
TUNNEL APPROACH
KINGSWAY TUNNEL APPROACH
GORSEY LANE
A5027
WOODSTOCK RD.
OXTON RD.
CHURCH ROAD
WHEATLAND LANE
MAINWARING RD.
BOROUGH RD.
CHURCH ST.
BIRKENHEAD ROAD
KELVIN RD.
KELVINSIDE
TOWER RD.
FOUR BRIDGES
BEAUFORT ROAD
A5030
CORPORATION ROAD
CLEVELAND ST.
DUKE ST.
B5146
LAIRD STREET
A553
PARK ROAD NORTH
CANNING ST.
RENDEL ST.
CATHCART ST.
VICTORIA PL.

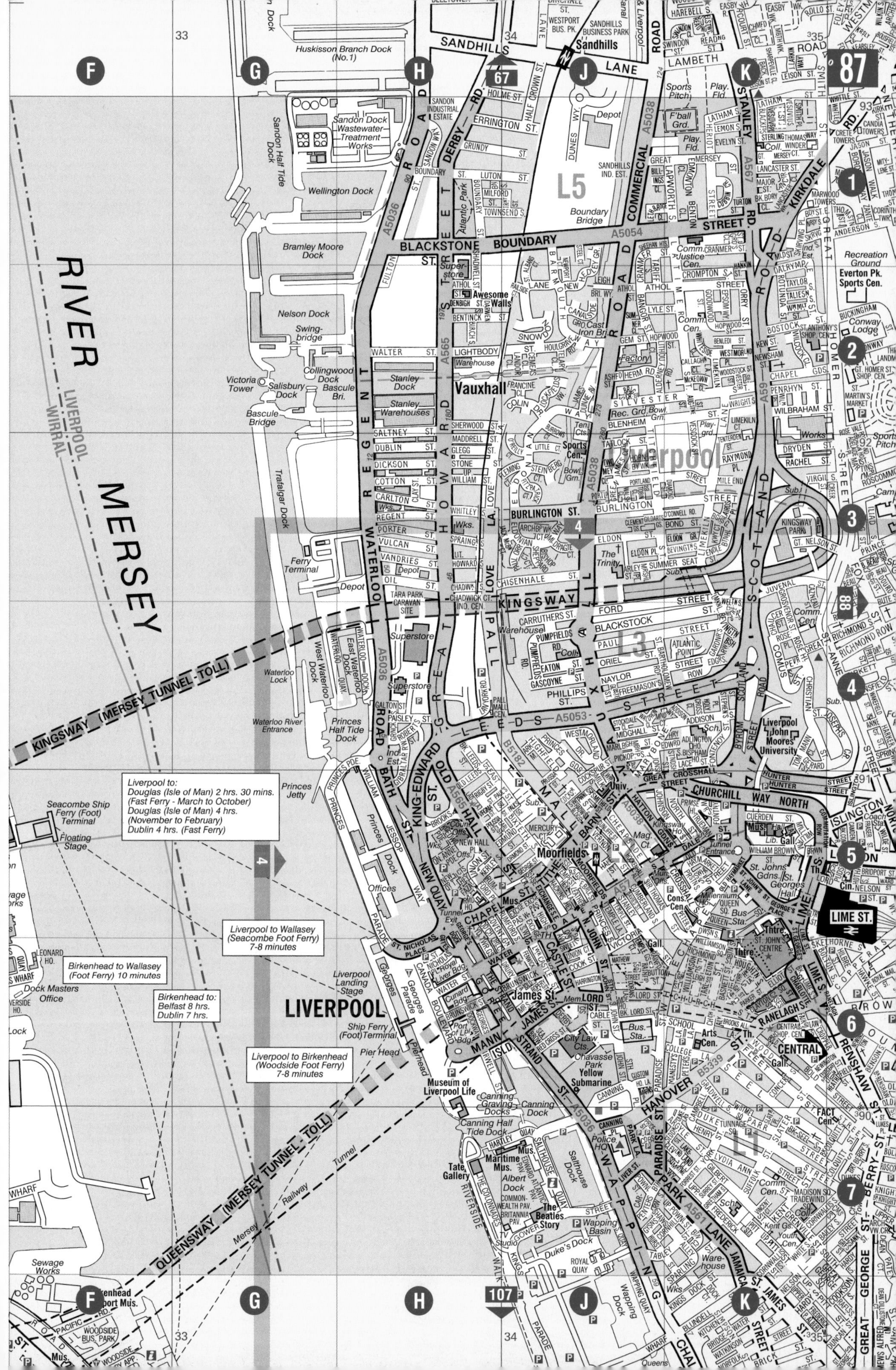

RIVER

MERSEY

LIVERPOOL

Liverpool to:
Douglas (Isle of Man) 2 hrs. 30 mins.
(Fast Ferry - March to October)
Douglas (Isle of Man) 4 hrs.
(November to February)
Dublin 4 hrs. (Fast Ferry)

Liverpool to Wallasey
(Seacombe Foot Ferry)
7-8 minutes

Birkenhead to Wallasey (Foot Ferry) 10 minutes

Birkenhead to:
Belfast 8 hrs.
Dublin 7 hrs.

Liverpool to Birkenhead
(Woodside Foot Ferry)
7-8 minutes

KINGSWAY (MERSEY TUNNEL-TOLL)

QUEENSWAY (MERSEY TUNNEL-TOLL)

LIME ST.

CENTRAL

Vauxhall

KINGSWAY

BURLINGTON ST.

BLACKSTONE BOUNDARY

SANDHILLS

Sandhills

Moorfields

James St.

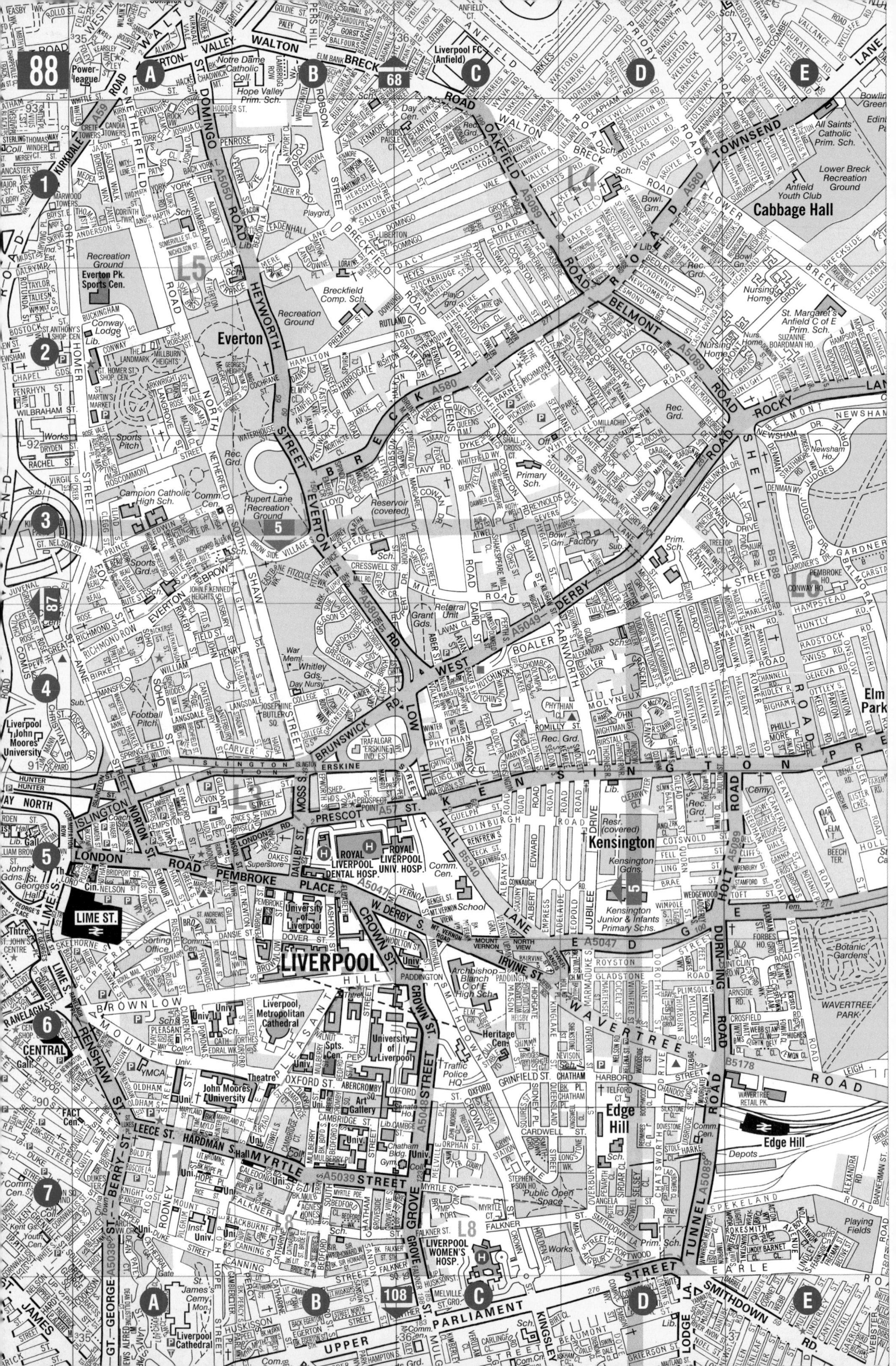
A
B
C
D
E
1
2
3
4
5
6
7
68
108
87
5
Power-league
Notre Dame Catholic Coll.
Hope Valley Prim. Sch.
Liverpool FC (Anfield)
All Saints' Catholic Prim. Sch.
Lower Breck Recreation Ground
Anfield Youth Club
Cabbage Hall
Recreation Ground
Everton Pk. Sports Cen.
Everton
Breckfield Comp. Sch.
Conway Lodge
St. Margaret's Anfield C of E Prim. Sch.
Campion Catholic High Sch.
Rupert Lane Recreation Ground
Reservoir (covered)
Primary Sch.
Sports Pitch
Sports Grd.
Football Pitch
War Meml.
Whitley Gds.
Trafalgar Ind. Est.
Liverpool John Moores University
Elm Park
Kensington
Kensington Gdns.
Kensington Junior & Infants Primary Schs.
ROYAL LIVERPOOL UNIV. HOSP.
ROYAL LIVERPOOL DENTAL HOSP.
University of Liverpool
LIVERPOOL
LIME ST.
CENTRAL
Liverpool Metropolitan Cathedral
Archbishop Blanch C of E High Sch.
Heritage Cen.
Traffic Police HQ
John Moores University
Art Gallery
University of Liverpool
Botanic Gardens
WAVERTREE PARK
WAVERTREE RETAIL PK.
Edge Hill
Depots
Playing Fields
LIVERPOOL WOMEN'S HOSP.
St. James's Cemy. Mon.
Liverpool Cathedral
Public Open Space
Works
EVERTON
BRECK
A580
HEYWORTH
A5050
WALTON
BRECK ROAD
OAKFIELD
A5089
BELMONT ROAD
ROCKY LANE
DERBY
A5049
WEST DERBY
ISLINGTON
KENSINGTON
PRESCOT ST.
A57
LONDON ROAD
PEMBROKE PLACE
A5047
BROWNLOW HILL
MOUNT PLEASANT
MYRTLE STREET
A5039
HARDMAN ST.
LEECE ST.
CROWN ST.
GROVE STREET
A5048
UPPER PARLIAMENT STREET
SMITHDOWN RD.
EARLE
TUNNEL ROAD
DURNING ROAD
A5089
WAVERTREE
EDGE LANE
LODGE LA.
GT. GEORGE ST.
BERRY ST.
A5038
RENSHAW ST.
LIME ST.
HOMER STREET
NORTH STREET
SHEIL ROAD
B5188
B5340
B5178

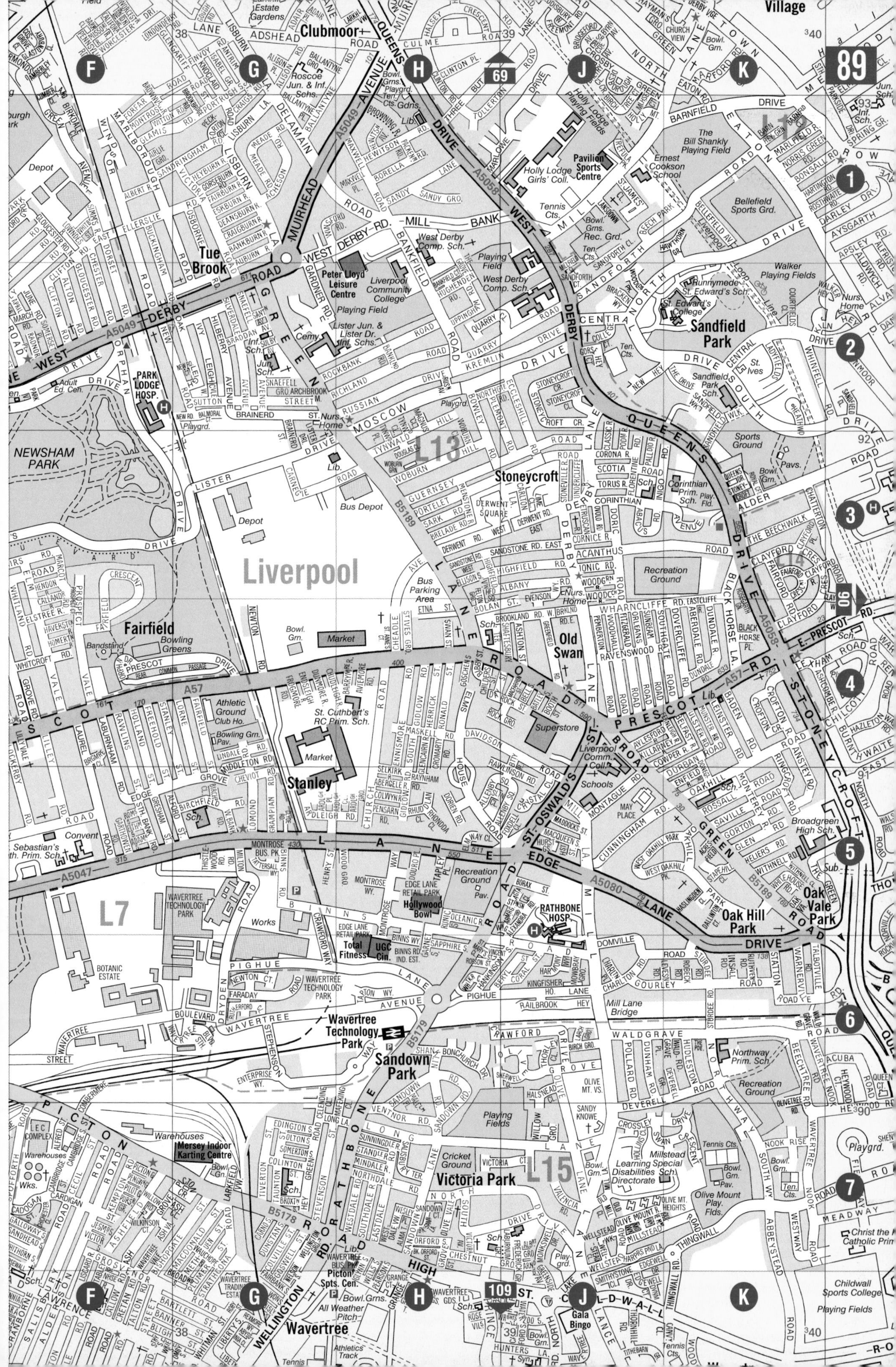
Clubmoor
Tue Brook
Stoneycroft
Liverpool
Fairfield
Old Swan
Stanley
Sandfield Park
Oak Hill Park
Oak Vale Park
Sandown Park
Victoria Park
Wavertree
Wavertree Technology Park
Newsham Park
L13
L14
L7
L15
L12
69
90
109
F
G
H
J
K
1
2
3
4
5
6
7
Holly Lodge Girls' Coll.
Pavilion Sports Centre
Ernest Cookson School
The Bill Shankly Playing Field
Bellefield Sports Grd.
Walker Playing Fields
St. Edward's College
Runnymede St. Edward's Sch.
Peter Lloyd Leisure Centre
Liverpool Community College
West Derby Comp. Sch.
Park Lodge Hosp.
Bus Depot
Depot
Market
Superstore
Recreation Ground
Corinthian Prim. Sch.
St. Cuthbert's RC Prim. Sch.
Liverpool Comm. Coll.
Broadgreen High Sch.
Rathbone Hosp.
Hollywood Bowl
Edge Lane Retail Park
Total Fitness
UGC Cin.
Wavertree Technology Park
Botanic Estate
Works
Mersey Indoor Karting Centre
Warehouses
Northway Prim. Sch.
Millstead Special Sch.
Learning Disabilities Directorate
Olive Mount Play. Flds.
Childwall Sports College
Playing Fields
Picton Spts. Cen.
All Weather Pitch
Gala Bingo
Christ the King Catholic Prim.
Mill Lane Bridge
A5049
A5058
A57
A5047
A5080
B5189
B5179
B5178
QUEENS DRIVE
WEST DERBY ROAD
PRESCOT ROAD
EDGE LANE
PICTON ROAD
ROATHBONE ROAD
STONEYCROFT
CHILDWALL
HIGH ST.
MUIRHEAD AVENUE
GREEN LANE
OAKHILL PARK
BLACK HORSE LA.
LISTER DRIVE
TUEBROOK

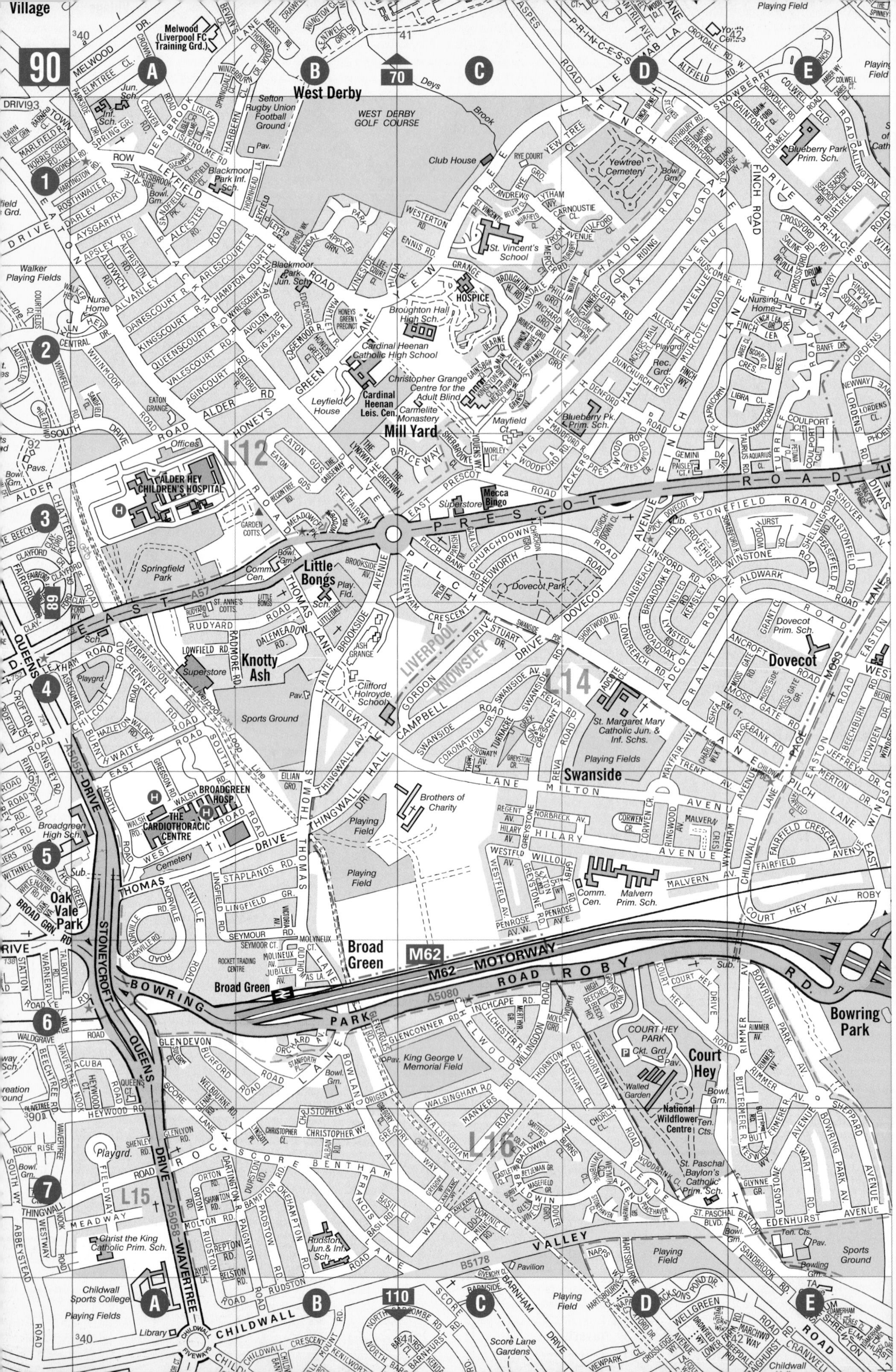

West Derby
West Derby Golf Course
Melwood (Liverpool FC Training Grd.)
Sefton Rugby Union Football Ground
Club House
Yewtree Cemetery
Blueberry Park Prim. Sch.
St. Vincent's School
Blackmoor Park Inf. Sch.
Blackmoor Park Jun. Sch.
Walker Playing Fields
Hospice
Broughton Hall High Sch.
Cardinal Heenan Catholic High School
Christopher Grange Centre for the Adult Blind
Cardinal Heenan Leis. Cen.
Leyfield House
Carmelite Monastery
Mill Yard
Blueberry Pk. Prim. Sch.
Alder Hey Children's Hospital
L12
Springfield Park
Superstore
Mecca Bingo
Little Bongs
Knotty Ash
Dovecot Park
Dovecot Prim. Sch.
Dovecot
Sports Ground
Clifford Holroyde School
L14
St. Margaret Mary Catholic Jun. & Inf. Schs.
Playing Fields
Swanside
Broadgreen Hosp
The Cardiothoracic Centre
Brothers of Charity
Playing Field
Broadgreen High Sch.
Oak Vale Park
Malvern Prim. Sch.
Broad Green
M62 Motorway
Bowring Park
King George V Memorial Field
Court Hey Park
Court Hey
National Wildflower Centre
St. Paschal Baylon's Catholic Prim. Sch.
L16
L15
Christ the King Catholic Prim. Sch.
Rudston Jun.& Inf. Sch.
Childwall Sports College
Playing Fields
Score Lane Gardens
Prescot Road
East Prescot Road
Queens Drive
Stoneycroft
Thomas Lane
Roby Road
Bowring Park Road
Childwall Valley Road
Rocky Lane
Finch Lane
Princess Drive
Liverpool Loop Line
A57
A5058
A5080
B5178
70
110

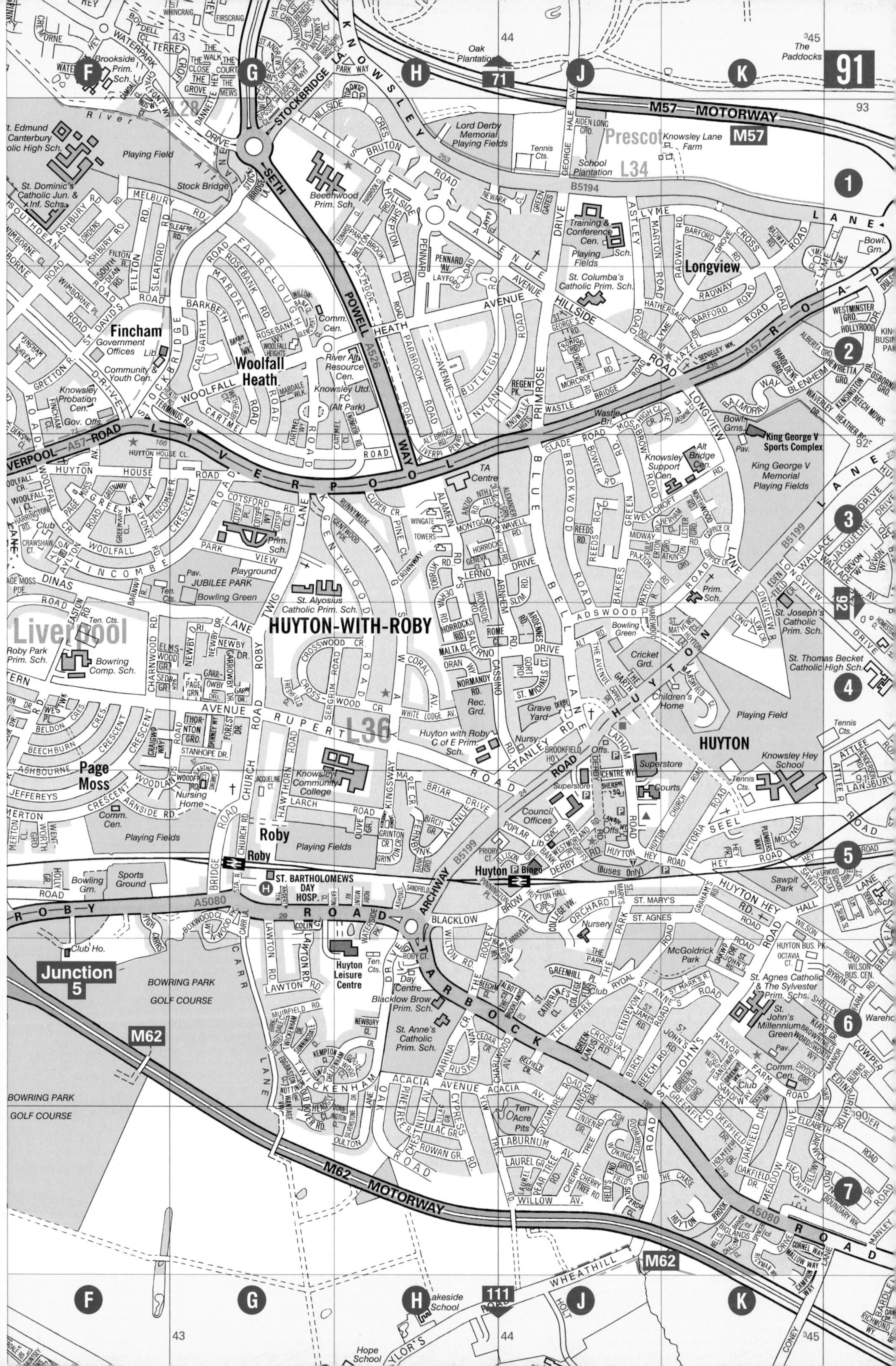
F
G
H
J
K
43
44
345
Oak Plantation
71
The Paddocks
M57 MOTORWAY
M57
93
KNOWSLEY LANE
STOCKBRIDGE LA.
Lord Derby Memorial Playing Fields
Prescot
L34
Knowsley Lane Farm
School Plantation
B5194
Tennis Cts.
WATERPARK
Brookside Prim. Sch.
River Alt
L28
St. Edmund Canterbury Catholic High Sch.
Playing Field
Stock Bridge
St. Dominic's Catholic Jun. & Inf. Schs.
SETH POWELL WAY
A526
Beechwood Prim. Sch.
HILLSIDE AVENUE
Training & Conference Cen.
Playing Fields
St. Columba's Catholic Prim. Sch.
Longview
LYME CROSS
BARFORD
RADWAY
HATHERSAGE
Bowl. Grn.
1
2
3
4
5
6
7
Fincham
Government Offices
Lib.
Community & Youth Cen.
Knowsley Probation Cen.
Gov. Offs.
Woolfall Heath
Comm. Cen.
River Alt Resource Cen.
Knowsley Utd. FC (Alt Park)
HEATH
PARBROOK
BUTLEIGH
PRIMROSE
A57
LIVERPOOL ROAD
Wastle Bri.
WASTLE BRIDGE
HAZEL ROAD
LONGVIEW
Bowl. Grns.
King George V Sports Complex
King George V Memorial Playing Fields
TA Centre
Alt Bridge Cen.
Knowsley Support Cen.
B5199
WINGATE TOWERS
HUYTON HOUSE
WOOLFALL CRESCENT
GREENWAY
LINCOMBE
Club
Prim. Sch.
Playground
JUBILEE PARK
Bowling Green
Pav.
Ten. Cts.
Liverpool
St. Aloysius Catholic Prim. Sch.
HUYTON-WITH-ROBY
BLUEBELL LANE
Bowling Green
Cricket Grd.
Prim. Sch.
St. Joseph's Catholic Prim. Sch.
St. Thomas Becket Catholic High Sch.
92
Roby Park Prim. Sch.
Bowring Comp. Sch.
Rec. Grd.
Grave Yard
Children's Home
Playing Field
HUYTON
Tennis Cts.
Knowsley Hey School
RUPERT ROAD
L36
Huyton with Roby C of E Prim. Sch.
Nursy.
STANLEY ROAD
Superstore
Offs.
Courts
Page Moss
Nursing Home
Knowsley Community College
Council Offices
Lib.
Comm. Cen.
Playing Fields
Roby
Playing Fields
ARCHWAY
HUYTON HEY
Roby
Huyton
Bingo
(Buses Only)
Sawpit Park
Bowling Grn.
Sports Ground
ST. BARTHOLOMEWS DAY HOSP.
A5080
ROBY ROAD
Club Ho.
Junction 5
BOWRING PARK GOLF COURSE
Huyton Leisure Centre
Ten. Cts.
Day Centre
Blacklow Brow Prim. Sch.
TARBOCK ROAD
Nursery
McGoldrick Park
Club
St. Agnes Catholic & The Sylvester Prim. Schs.
St. John's Millennium Green
Pav.
Comm. Cen.
Club
M62
St. Anne's Catholic Prim. Sch.
Ten Acre Pits
ACACIA AVENUE
M62 MOTORWAY
A5080
M62
WHEATHILL
111
Lakeside School
Hope School
COPPER
Wareho

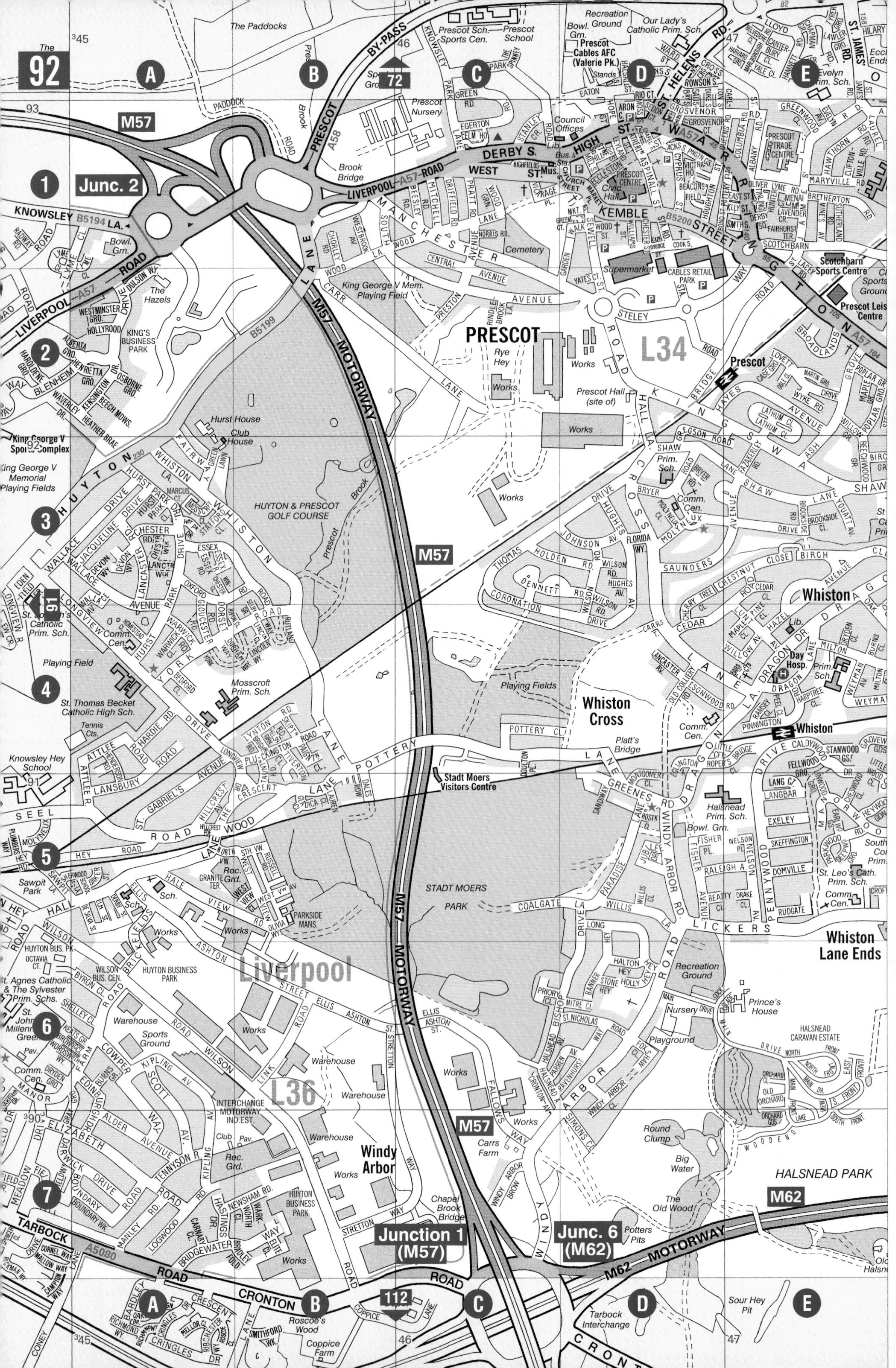

92
The Paddocks
M57
Junc. 2
KNOWSLEY LA.
B5194
LIVERPOOL A57 ROAD
PRESCOT BY-PASS
A58
Prescot Sch. Sports Cen.
Prescot School
72
Prescot Nursery
Brook Bridge
DERBY S.
WEST ST.
HIGH ST.
Council Offices
Recreation Ground
Our Lady's Catholic Prim. Sch.
Prescot Cables AFC (Valerie Pk.)
ST. HELENS RD.
WARRINGTON RD.
PRESCOT TRADE CENTRE
PRESCOT CENTRE
Civic Hall
KEMBLE STREET
B5200
Supermarket
CABLES RETAIL PARK
Scotchbarn Sports Centre
Prescot Leisure Centre
Cemetery
MANCHESTER RD.
King George V Mem. Playing Field
CARR AVENUE
STELEY WAY
PRESCOT
L34
Rye Hey
Works
Prescot Hall (site of)
Prescot
KINGSWAY
The Hazels
KING'S BUSINESS PARK
B5199
King George V Sports Complex
King George V Memorial Playing Fields
Hurst House
Club House
HUYTON LA.
HUYTON & PRESCOT GOLF COURSE
Prescot Brook
M57 MOTORWAY
Shaw Prim. Sch.
Comm. Cen.
MOLYNEUX DR.
SAUNDERS AV.
Whiston
Lib.
Day Hosp.
Prim. Sch.
St. Thomas Becket Catholic High Sch.
Mosscroft Prim. Sch.
Playing Field
Knowsley Hey School
Playing Fields
Whiston Cross
Whiston
POTTERY LANE
Platt's Bridge
Stadt Moers Visitors Centre
Halsnead Prim. Sch.
Bowl. Grn.
St. Leo's Cath. Prim. Sch.
Whiston Lane Ends
SEEL ROAD
HEY ROAD
Sawpit Park
STADT MOERS PARK
COALGATE LA.
LICKERS LA.
Recreation Ground
Prince's House
HALSNEAD CARAVAN ESTATE
Liverpool
HUYTON BUSINESS PARK
ELLIS ASHTON STREET
Warehouse
Sports Ground
St. Agnes Catholic & The Sylvester Prim. Schs.
L36
INTERCHANGE MOTORWAY IND. EST.
Windy Arbor
Carrs Farm
Round Clump
Big Water
The Old Wood
HALSNEAD PARK
M62
Junction 1 (M57)
Junc. 6 (M62)
Potters Pits
M62 MOTORWAY
TARBOCK A5080 ROAD
CRONTON ROAD
112
Roscoe's Wood
Coppice Farm
Tarbock Interchange
Sour Hey Pit
Chapel Brook Bridge
A B C D E
1 2 3 4 5 6 7
91

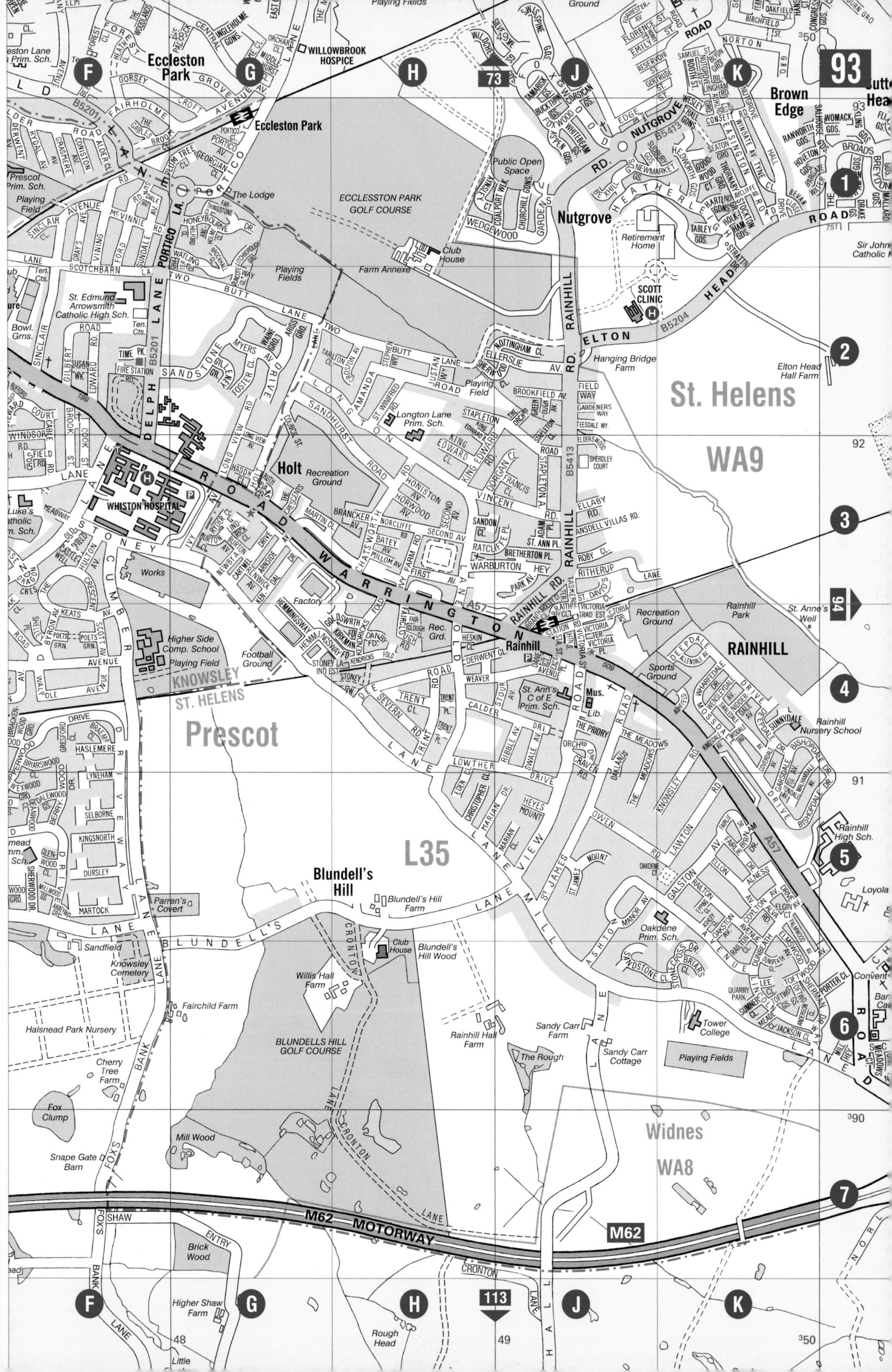

93
Eccleston Park
Willowbrook Hospice
73
Brown Edge
Nutgrove
Eccleston Park Golf Course
Public Open Space
The Lodge
Playing Fields
Farm Annexe
Club House
Retirement Home
Scott Clinic
St. Edmund Arrowsmith Catholic High Sch.
Elton Head Hall Farm
Hanging Bridge Farm
St. Helens
WA9
Longton Lane Prim. Sch.
Holt
Recreation Ground
Whiston Hospital
Warrington Road
Rainhill
Rainhill Park
RAINHILL
St. Anne's Well
94
Higher Side Comp. School
Football Ground
Knowsley
St. Helens
Prescot
St. Ann's C of E Prim. Sch.
Mus.
Lib.
Rainhill Nursery School
Rainhill High Sch.
Loyola
L35
Blundell's Hill
Blundell's Hill Farm
Blundell's Hill Wood
Parren's Covert
Sandfield
Knowsley Cemetery
Fairchild Farm
Halsnead Park Nursery
Willis Hall Farm
Blundells Hill Golf Course
Rainhill Hall Farm
Sandy Carr Farm
Sandy Carr Cottage
The Rough
Oakdene Prim. Sch.
Tower College
Playing Fields
Cherry Tree Farm
Fox Clump
Mill Wood
Snape Gate Barn
Widnes
WA8
M62 Motorway
M62
Brick Wood
Higher Shaw Farm
Rough Head
113
48
49
350
390

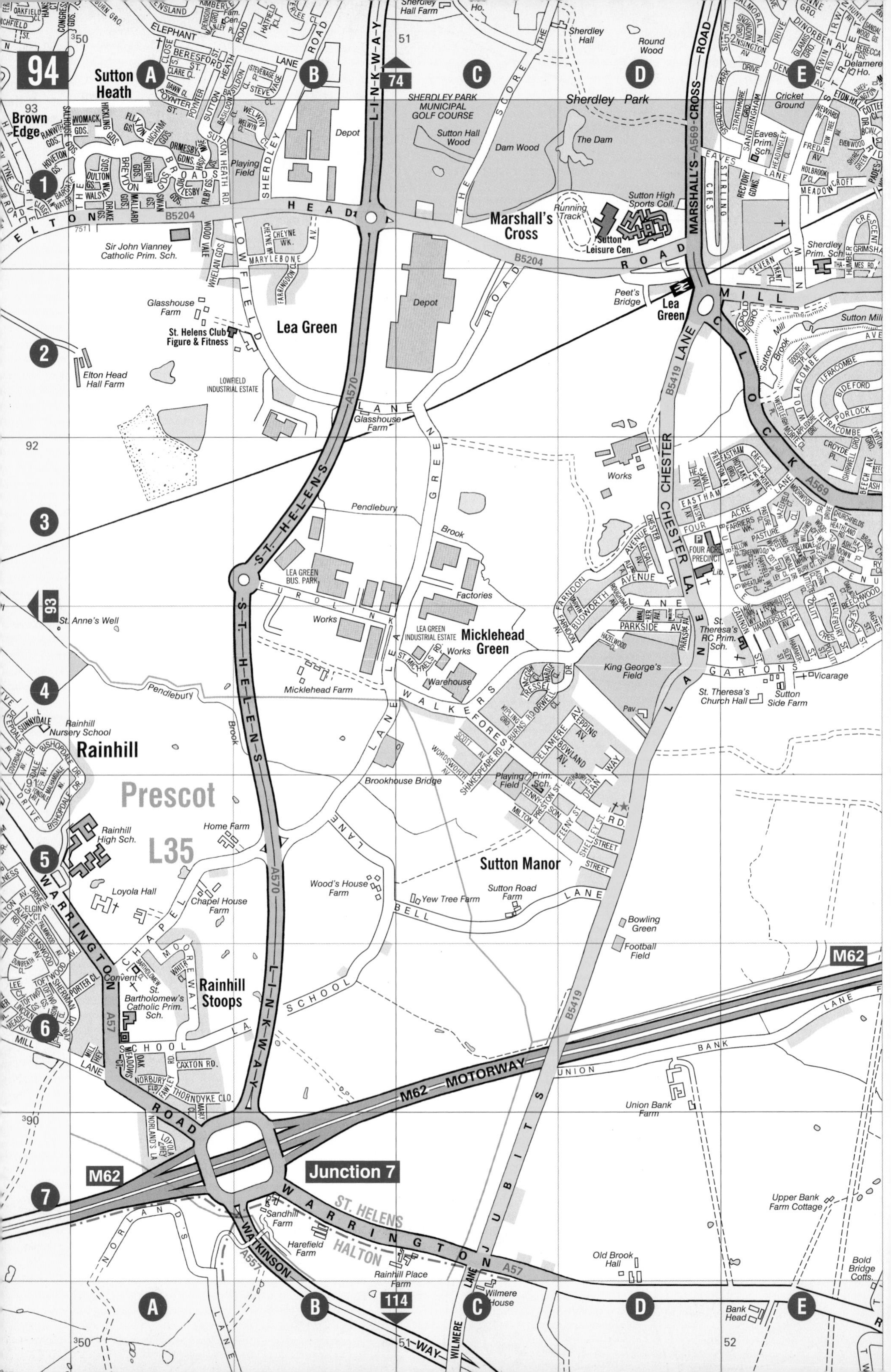
Sutton Heath
Brown Edge
Sherdley Hall Farm
Sherdley Hall
Round Wood
74
Sherdley Park
SHERDLEY PARK MUNICIPAL GOLF COURSE
Depot
Sutton Hall Wood
Dam Wood
The Dam
Cricket Ground
Eaves Prim. Sch.
Delamere Ho.
Playing Field
Sutton High Sports Coll.
Running Track
Sutton Leisure Cen.
Marshall's Cross
ELTON HEAD ROAD
B5204
MARSHALL'S CROSS ROAD
A569
Sir John Vianney Catholic Prim. Sch.
Sherdley Prim. Sch.
Glasshouse Farm
St. Helens Club Figure & Fitness
Lea Green
Peet's Bridge
Elton Head Hall Farm
LOWFIELD INDUSTRIAL ESTATE
Glasshouse Farm
Sutton Mill
CLOCK LANE
CHESTER LANE
B5419
Works
A570
ST. HELENS LINKWAY
Pendlebury Brook
LEA GREEN BUS. PARK
FOUR ACRE PRECINCT
Lib.
Factories
93
St. Anne's Well
Works
LEA GREEN INDUSTRIAL ESTATE
Works
Micklehead Green
St. Theresa's RC Prim. Sch.
King George's Field
Warehouse
Micklehead Farm
Vicarage
St. Theresa's Church Hall
Sutton Side Farm
Rainhill Nursery School
Rainhill
Pav.
Prescot
Brookhouse Bridge
Playing Field
Prim. Sch.
L35
Rainhill High Sch.
Home Farm
Sutton Manor
Loyola Hall
Chapel House Farm
Wood's House Farm
Yew Tree Farm
Sutton Road Farm
Bowling Green
Football Field
Convent
St. Bartholomew's Catholic Prim. Sch.
Rainhill Stoops
M62
M62 MOTORWAY
Union Bank Farm
Junction 7
WARRINGTON ROAD
A57
Sandhill Farm
Harefield Farm
ST. HELENS
HALTON
Upper Bank Farm Cottage
Old Brook Hall
Bold Bridge Cotts.
Rainhill Place Farm
Wilmere House
114
Bank Head
JUBITS LANE
WATKINSON WAY
A557
WILMERE LANE

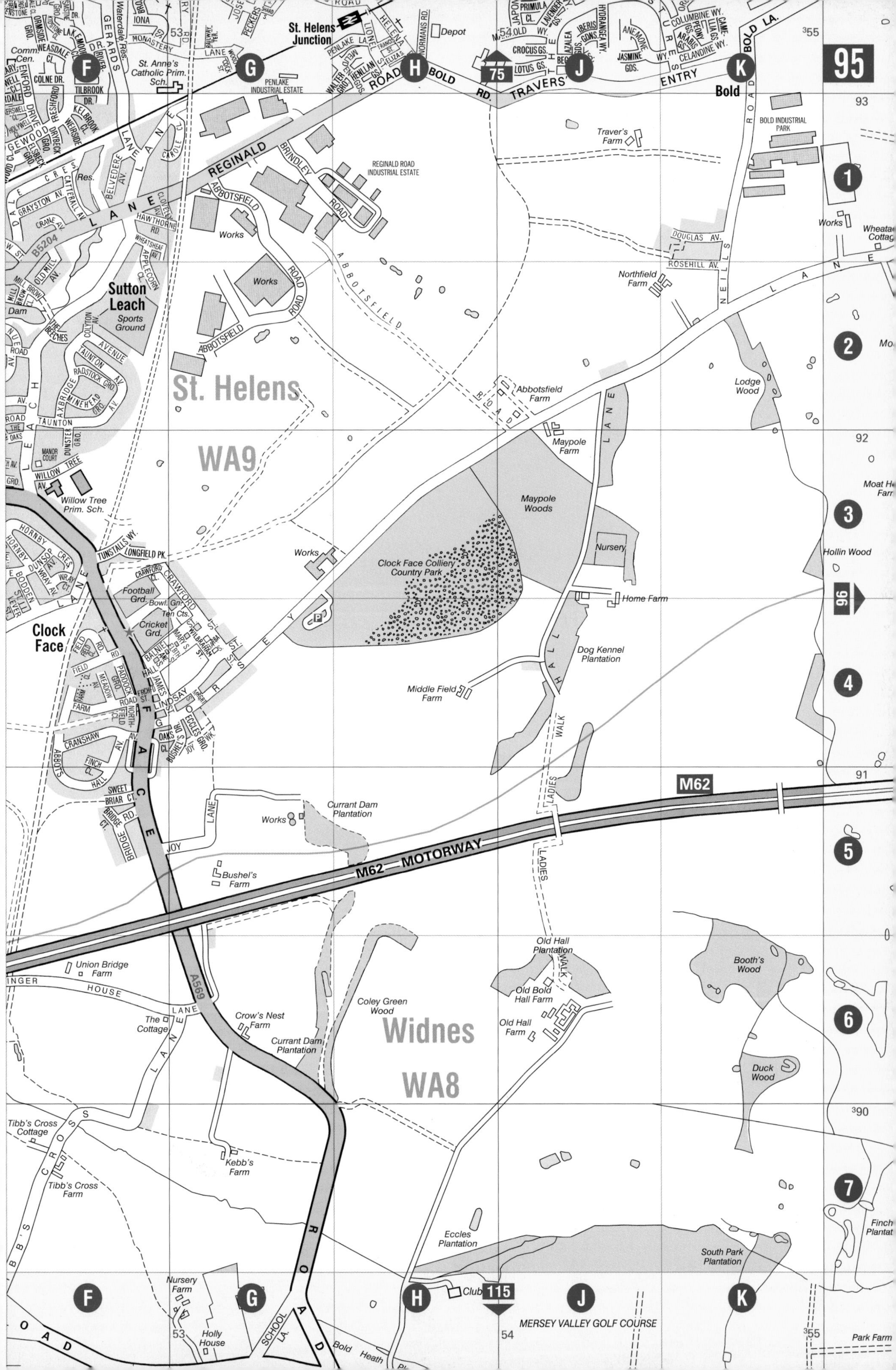
St. Helens Junction
St. Anne's Catholic Prim. Sch.
Penlake Industrial Estate
Reginald Road Industrial Estate
Bold Industrial Park
Bold
Traver's Farm
Northfield Farm
Works
Sutton Leach
Sports Ground
St. Helens
WA9
Abbotsfield Farm
Maypole Farm
Maypole Woods
Lodge Wood
Hollin Wood
Moat House Farm
Willow Tree Prim. Sch.
Clock Face Colliery Country Park
Nursery
Home Farm
Dog Kennel Plantation
Middle Field Farm
Clock Face
Football Grd.
Cricket Grd.
Currant Dam Plantation
Bushel's Farm
M62 MOTORWAY
M62
A569
Union Bridge Farm
The Cottage
Crow's Nest Farm
Coley Green Wood
Widnes
WA8
Old Hall Plantation
Old Bold Hall Farm
Old Hall Farm
Booth's Wood
Duck Wood
Tibb's Cross Cottage
Tibb's Cross Farm
Kebb's Farm
Eccles Plantation
South Park Plantation
Finch Plantation
Nursery Farm
Holly House
Club
MERSEY VALLEY GOLF COURSE
Park Farm
75
96
115
F
G
H
J
K
1
2
3
4
5
6
7

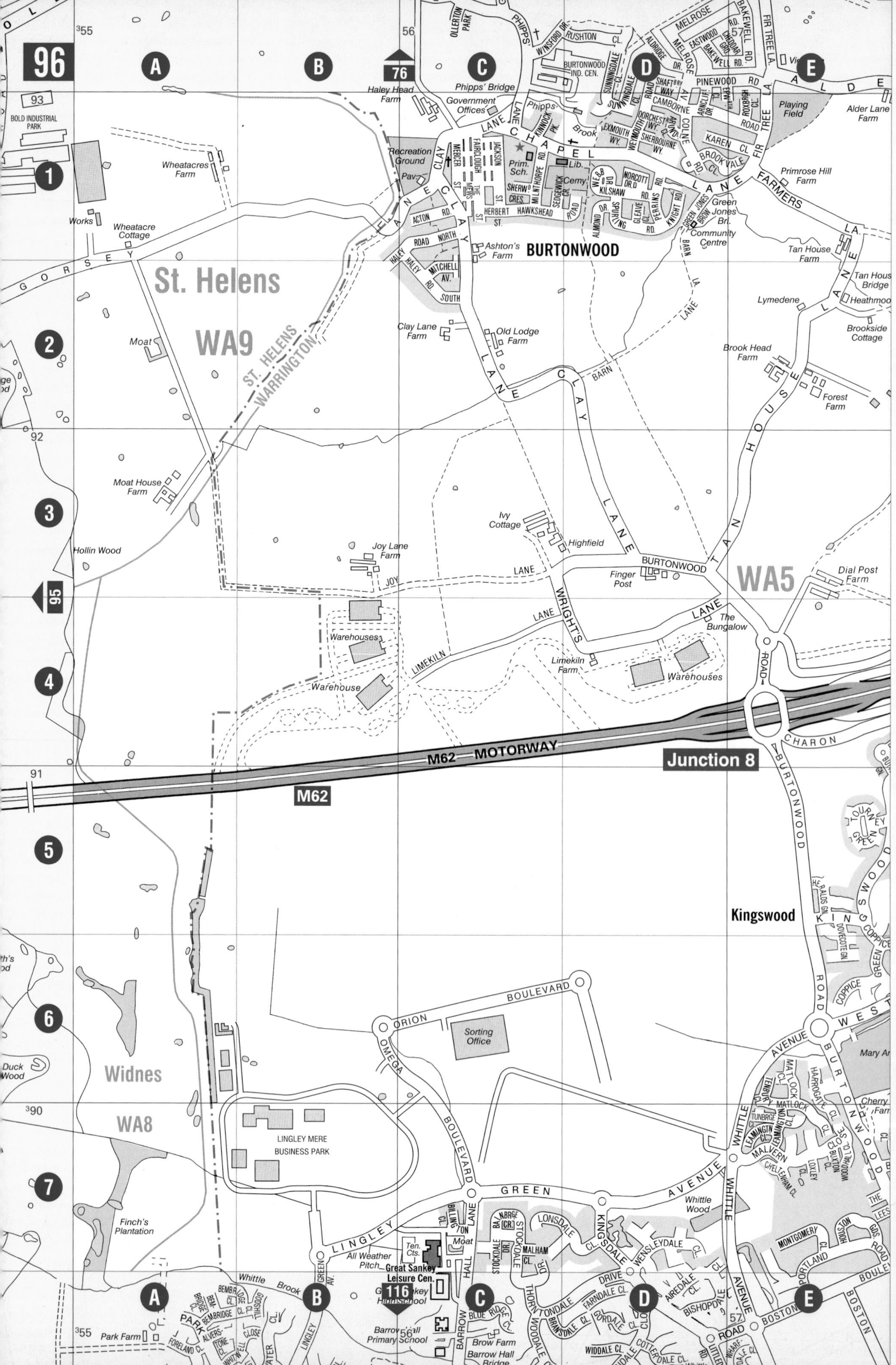
BURTONWOOD
St. Helens
WA9
WA5
Widnes
WA8
Kingswood
Junction 8
M62 MOTORWAY
M62
ST. HELENS
WARRINGTON
BOLD INDUSTRIAL PARK
Wheatacres Farm
Works
Wheatacre Cottage
Moat
Moat House Farm
Hollin Wood
Haley Head Farm
Government Offices
Phipps' Bridge
Recreation Ground
Pav.
Prim. Sch.
Lib.
Cemy.
BURTONWOOD IND. CEN.
Ashton's Farm
Clay Lane Farm
Old Lodge Farm
Green Jones Bri.
Community Centre
Playing Field
Alder Lane Farm
Primrose Hill Farm
Tan House Farm
Tan House Bridge
Heathmoor
Lymedene
Brookside Cottage
Brook Head Farm
Forest Farm
Ivy Cottage
Highfield
Joy Lane Farm
Finger Post
Dial Post Farm
The Bungalow
Warehouses
Warehouse
Limekiln Farm
Sorting Office
LINGLEY MERE BUSINESS PARK
Finch's Plantation
Duck Wood
Whittle Wood
All Weather Pitch
Ten. Cts.
Moat
Great Sankey Leisure Cen.
Great Sankey High School
Barrow Hall Primary School
Brow Farm
Barrow Hall Bridge
Park Farm
Mary Ann
Cherry Farm
Whittle Brook
GORSEY LANE
CLAY LANE
CHAPEL LANE
JOY LANE
LIMEKILN LANE
WRIGHTS LANE
BURTONWOOD ROAD
TAN HOUSE LANE
FARMERS LANE
ALDER LANE
BARN LANE
CHARON WAY
ORION BOULEVARD
OMEGA BOULEVARD
LINGLEY GREEN AVENUE
WHITTLE AVENUE
WEST AVENUE
BOSTON BOULEVARD
BARROW HALL LANE

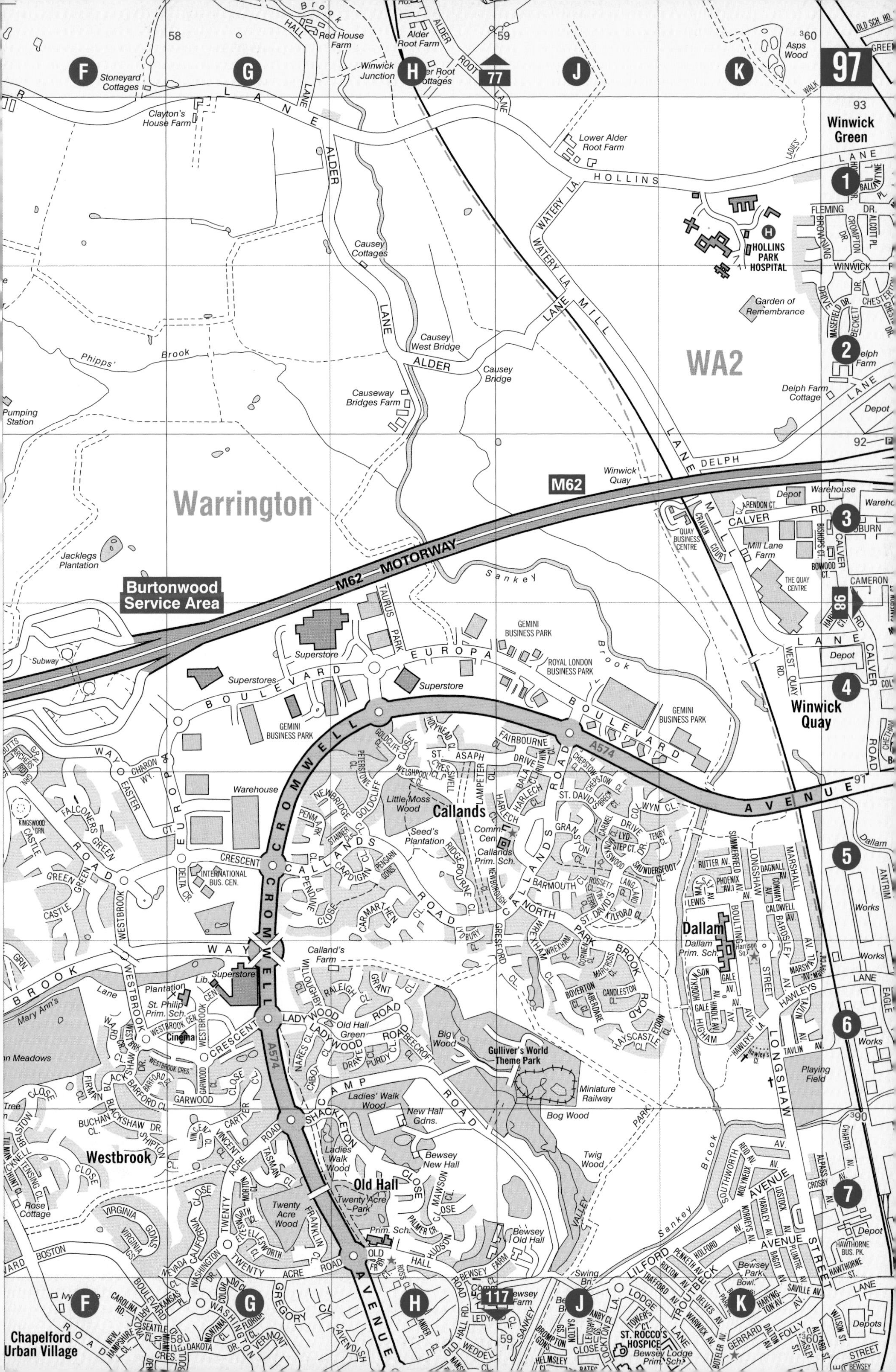

WA2

Warrington

Burtonwood
Service Area

M62 MOTORWAY

Winwick Green

Hollins Park Hospital

Winwick Quay

Callands

Dallam

Westbrook

Old Hall

Gulliver's World Theme Park

Chapelford Urban Village

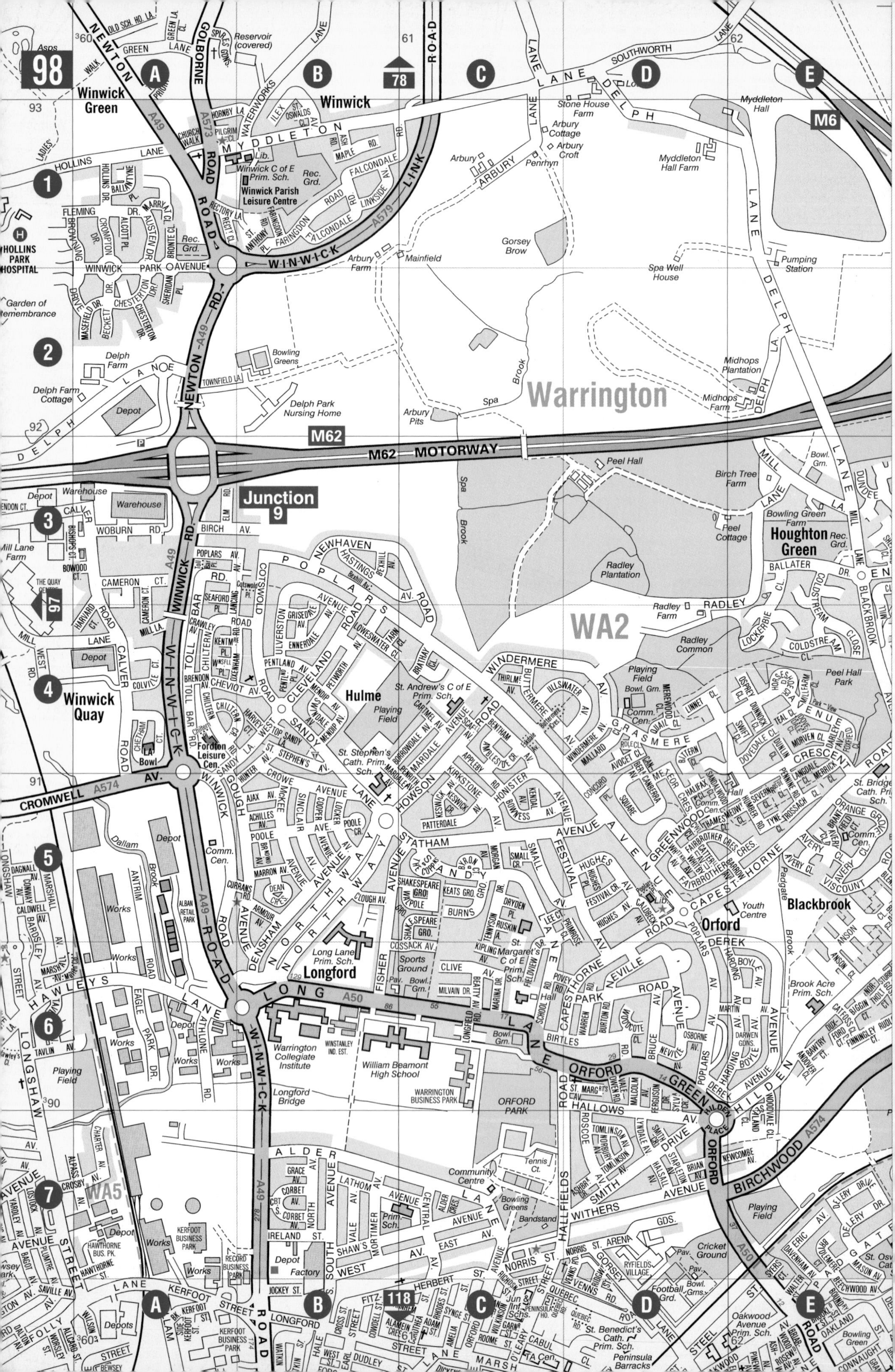

Winwick Green
Winwick
Warrington
WA2
WA5
Junction 9
M62 MOTORWAY
M62
M6
78
97
118
Hulme
Longford
Orford
Houghton Green
Blackbrook
Winwick Quay
HOLLINS PARK HOSPITAL
Garden of Remembrance
Winwick C of E Prim. Sch.
Winwick Parish Leisure Centre
Myddleton Hall
Myddleton Hall Farm
Stone House Farm
Arbury Cottage
Arbury Croft
Penrhyn
Gorsey Brow
Mainfield
Arbury Farm
Spa Well House
Pumping Station
Midhops Plantation
Midhops Farm
Delph Farm
Delph Farm Cottage
Delph Park Nursing Home
Bowling Greens
Arbury Pits
Peel Hall
Birch Tree Farm
Bowling Green Farm
Peel Cottage
Radley Plantation
Radley Farm
Radley Common
Peel Hall Park
St. Andrew's C of E Prim. Sch.
St. Stephen's Cath. Prim. Sch.
Fordton Leisure Cen.
Long Lane Prim. Sch.
Sports Ground
St. Margaret's C of E Prim. Sch.
Youth Centre
Brook Acre Prim. Sch.
Warrington Collegiate Institute
William Beamont High School
Warrington Business Park
Orford Park
Longford Bridge
Community Centre
Bowling Greens
Bandstand
Cricket Ground
Football Grd.
Ryfields Village
Kerfoot Business Park
Hawthorne Bus. Pk.
Record Business Park
Winstanley Ind. Est.
Alban Retail Park
St. Benedict's Cath. Prim. Sch.
Oakwood Avenue Prim. Sch.
Peninsula Barracks
Playing Field
WINWICK ROAD
NEWTON ROAD
GOLBORNE ROAD
WINWICK LINK
CROMWELL AV.
LONG LANE
ORFORD GREEN
BIRCHWOOD WAY
POPLARS AVENUE
WINDERMERE AV.
GRASMERE AVENUE
HOWSON LANE
NORTHWAY
SANDY LANE
MYDDLETON LANE
SOUTHWORTH LANE
DELPH LANE
ARBURY LANE
HOLLINS LANE
ALDER LANE
WITHERS AVENUE
A49
A50
A573
A574
A579

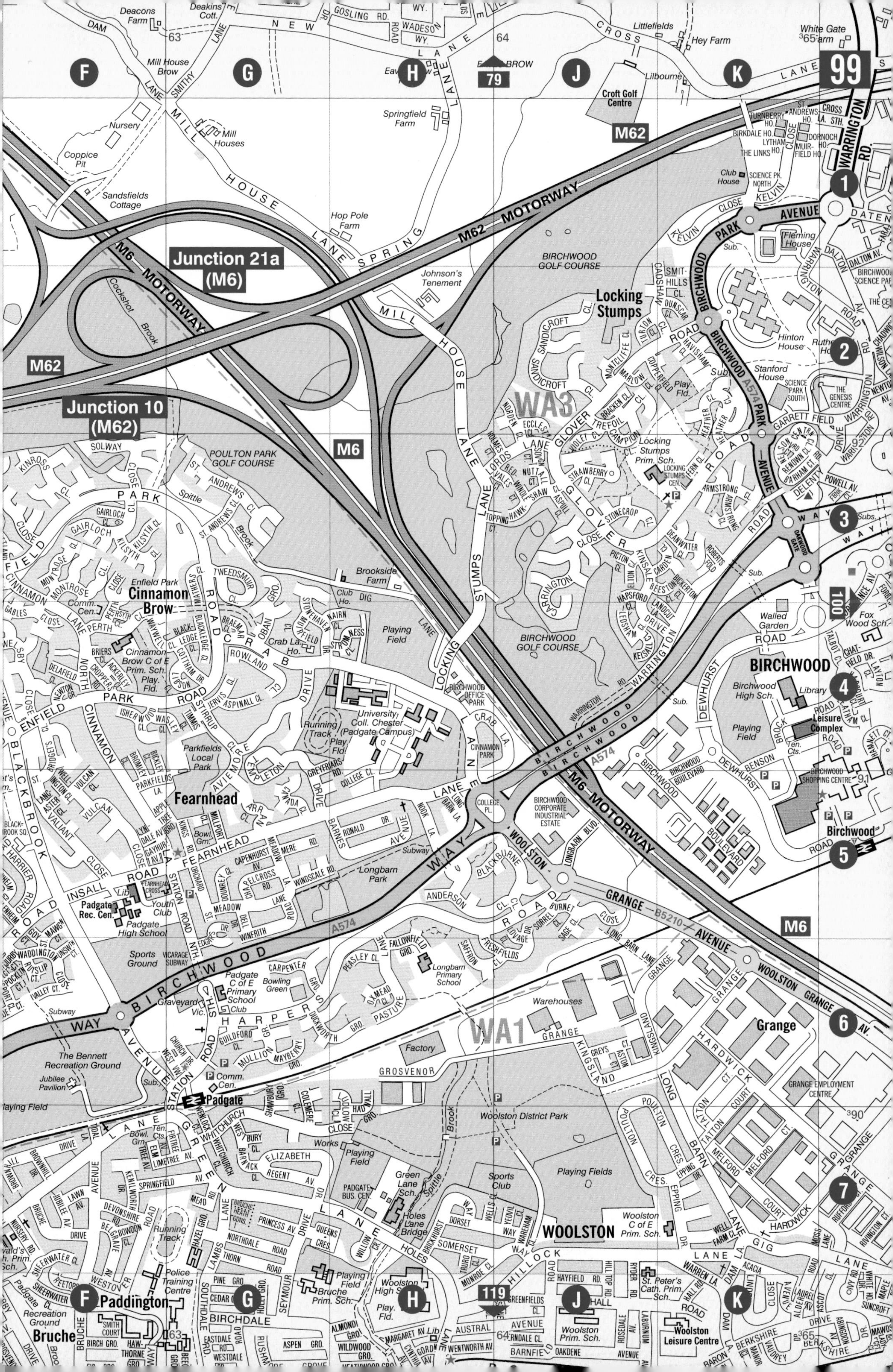
F
G
H
J
K
79
100
119
1
2
3
4
5
6
7
63
64
65
90
91
M62
M6
M62 MOTORWAY
M6 MOTORWAY
Junction 21a (M6)
Junction 10 (M62)
WA3
WA1
Locking Stumps
Cinnamon Brow
Fearnhead
BIRCHWOOD
Grange
WOOLSTON
Paddington
Bruche
Deacons Farm
Deakins Cott.
Mill House Brow
Nursery
Coppice Pit
Mill Houses
Sandsfields Cottage
Springfield Farm
Hop Pole Farm
Johnson's Tenement
Croft Golf Centre
Littlefields
Hey Farm
White Gate Farm
Lilbourne
BIRCHWOOD GOLF COURSE
POULTON PARK GOLF COURSE
Brookside Farm
Club Ho.
Playing Field
Crab La. Ho.
University Coll. Chester (Padgate Campus)
Running Track
BIRCHWOOD OFFICE PARK
CINNAMON PARK
Parkfields Local Park
Enfield Park
Cinnamon Brow C of E Prim. Sch.
Locking Stumps Prim. Sch.
Fleming House
Hinton House
Stanford House
SCIENCE PARK SOUTH
THE GENESIS CENTRE
Birchwood High Sch.
Library
Leisure Complex
BIRCHWOOD SHOPPING CENTRE
Birchwood
Walled Garden
Fox Wood Sch.
BIRCHWOOD CORPORATE INDUSTRIAL ESTATE
Longbarn Park
Longbarn Primary School
Padgate Rec. Cen.
Padgate High School
Youth Club
Sports Ground
Padgate C of E Primary School
Bowling Green
Warehouses
Factory
The Bennett Recreation Ground
Jubilee Pavilion
Padgate
Woolston District Park
GRANGE EMPLOYMENT CENTRE
Playing Fields
Sports Club
Green Lane Sch.
PADGATE BUS. CEN.
Holes Lane Bridge
Woolston C of E Prim. Sch.
Police Training Centre
Bruche Prim. Sch.
Woolston High Sch.
St. Peter's Cath. Prim. Sch.
Woolston Prim. Sch.
Woolston Leisure Centre
Padgate Recreation Ground
WARRINGTON RD.
BIRCHWOOD PARK AVENUE
BIRCHWOOD WAY
A574
B5210
GRANGE AVENUE
WOOLSTON GRANGE AV.
MILL HOUSE LANE
SPRING LANE
LOCKING STUMPS LANE
CRAB LANE
GLOVER ROAD
ENFIELD PARK ROAD
CINNAMON LANE
BLACKBROOK AVENUE
FEARNHEAD LANE
INSALL ROAD
HARPERS ROAD
GROSVENOR GRO.
HOLES LANE
GREEN LANE
HILLOCK LANE
HARDWICK GRANGE
LONG BARN LANE
DEWHURST ROAD
BIRCHWOOD BOULEVARD
NEW LANE
CROSS LANE
DAM LANE
GIG LANE
BIRCHDALE ROAD

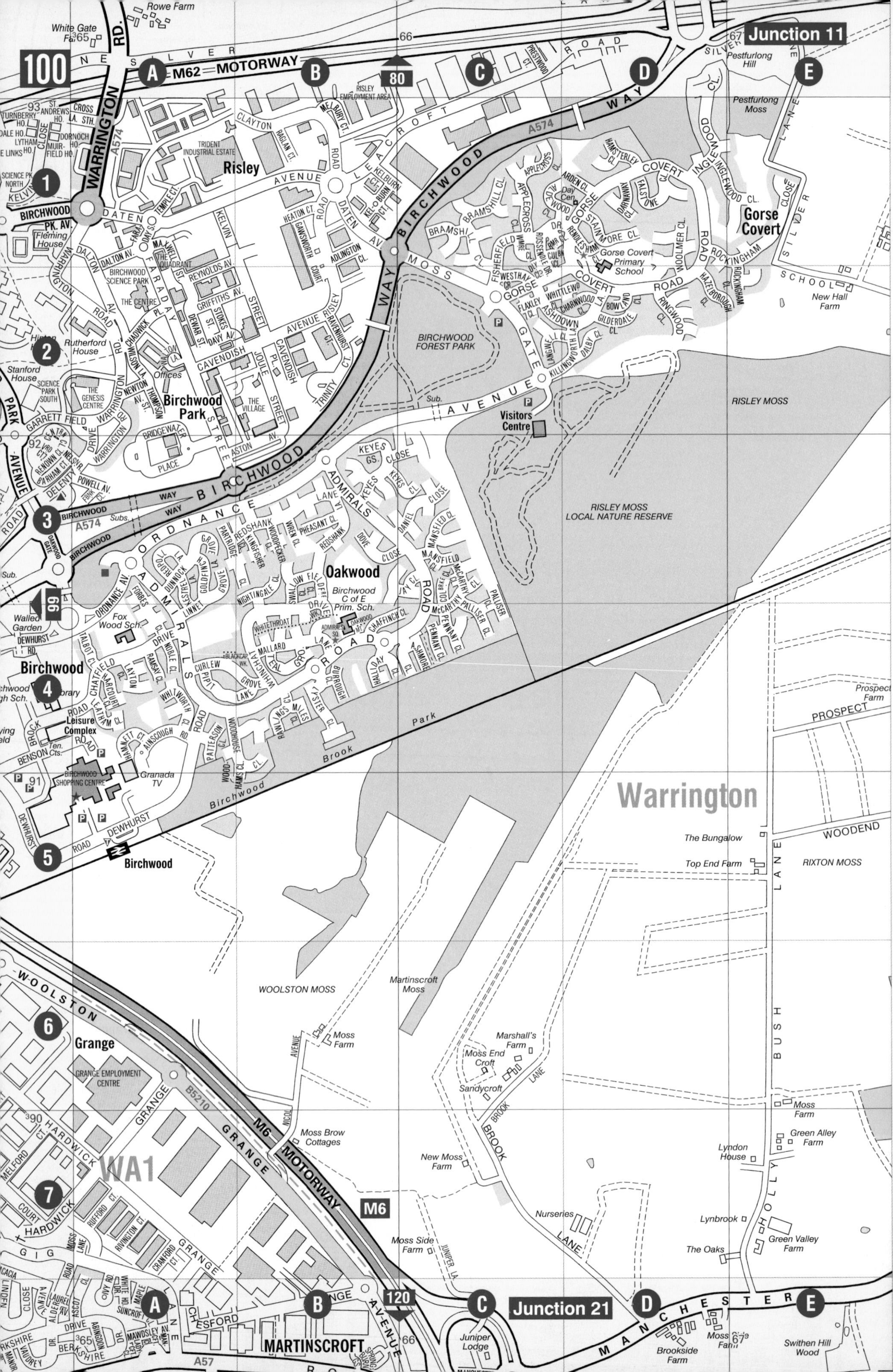
100
Junction 11
Junction 21
M62 MOTORWAY
M6 MOTORWAY
80
99
120
Rowe Farm
White Gate Fa.
SILVER ROAD
WARRINGTON RD.
A574
BIRCHWOOD WAY
Risley
TRIDENT INDUSTRIAL ESTATE
RISLEY EMPLOYMENT AREA
CLAYTON
LEACROFT
Pestfurlong Hill
Pestfurlong Moss
Gorse Covert
Gorse Covert Primary School
GORSE COVERT ROAD
SILVER LANE
SCHOOL LANE
New Hall Farm
BIRCHWOOD FOREST PARK
MOSS GATE
RISLEY MOSS
Visitors Centre
RISLEY MOSS LOCAL NATURE RESERVE
BIRCHWOOD SCIENCE PARK
Birchwood Park
Rutherford House
Stanford House
Fleming House
THE GENESIS CENTRE
THE VILLAGE
BRIDGEWATER PLACE
ORDNANCE AVENUE
ADMIRALS ROAD
Oakwood
Birchwood C of E Prim. Sch.
Fox Wood Sch.
Walled Garden
Birchwood
Leisure Complex
BIRCHWOOD SHOPPING CENTRE
Granada TV
DEWHURST ROAD
Birchwood
Birchwood Brook Park
Warrington
Prospect Farm
PROSPECT
WOODEND
The Bungalow
Top End Farm
RIXTON MOSS
WOOLSTON MOSS
Martinscroft Moss
Moss Farm
Marshall's Farm
Moss End Croft
Sandycroft
BROOK LANE
Moss Brow Cottages
New Moss Farm
Nurseries
Moss Side Farm
JUNIPER LA.
BUSH LANE
HOLLY
Moss Farm
Green Alley Farm
Lyndon House
Lynbrook
Green Valley Farm
The Oaks
WOOLSTON
Grange
GRANGE EMPLOYMENT CENTRE
WA1
B5210
GRANGE AVENUE
HARDWICK
GIG LANE
MARTINSCROFT
A57
MANCHESTER ROAD
Juniper Lodge
Brookside Farm
Moss Farm
Swithen Hill Wood

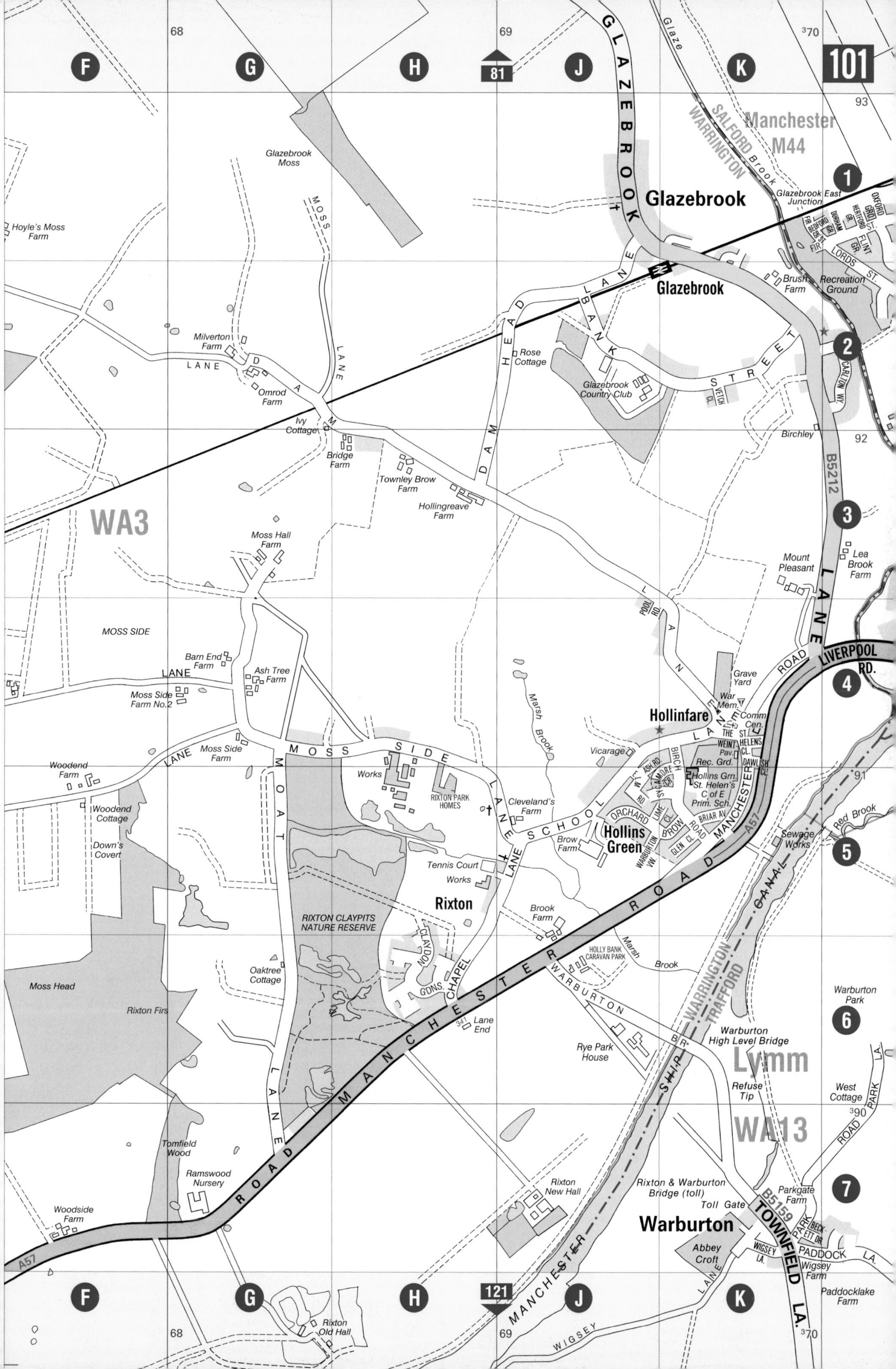
Glazebrook Moss
Hoyle's Moss Farm
Milverton Farm
Omrod Farm
Ivy Cottage
Bridge Farm
Townley Brow Farm
Hollingreave Farm
Rose Cottage
Glazebrook Country Club
Glazebrook
Glazebrook East Junction
Brush Farm
Recreation Ground
Manchester M44
WA3
Moss Hall Farm
MOSS SIDE
Barn End Farm
Ash Tree Farm
Moss Side Farm No.2
Moss Side Farm
Woodend Farm
Woodend Cottage
Down's Covert
Birchley
Mount Pleasant
Lea Brook Farm
Grave Yard
War Mem.
Hollinfare
Vicarage
Marsh Brook
Cleveland's Farm
RIXTON PARK HOMES
Works
Tennis Court
Rixton
RIXTON CLAYPITS NATURE RESERVE
Hollins Green
Hollins Grn. St. Helen's C of E Prim. Sch.
Rec. Grd.
Brow Farm
Brook Farm
HOLLY BANK CARAVAN PARK
Oaktree Cottage
Moss Head
Rixton Firs
Lane End
Rye Park House
Sewage Works
Red Brook
Warburton Park
Warburton High Level Bridge
Lymm
Refuse Tip
WA13
West Cottage
Tomfield Wood
Ramswood Nursery
Woodside Farm
Rixton New Hall
Rixton & Warburton Bridge (toll)
Toll Gate
Parkgate Farm
Warburton
Abbey Croft
Wigsey Farm
Paddocklake Farm
Rixton Old Hall
MANCHESTER ROAD
LIVERPOOL RD.
MOSS SIDE LANE
MOAT LANE
DAM HEAD LANE
BANK STREET
SCHOOL LANE
CHAPEL LANE
WARBURTON BR.
TOWNFIELD LA.
MANCHESTER SHIP CANAL
WARRINGTON TRAFFORD
GLAZEBROOK LANE
B5212
B5159
A57
81
121

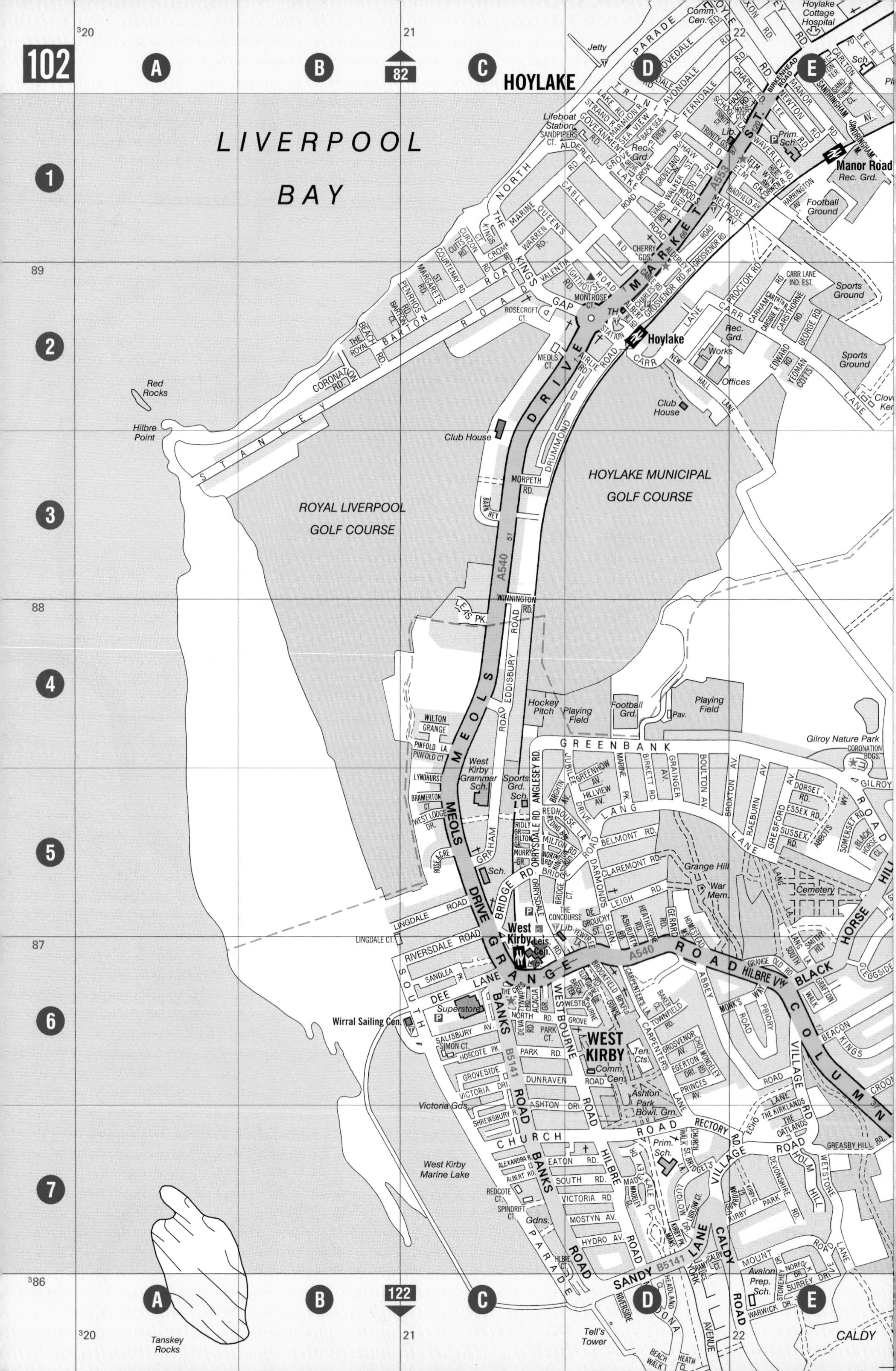

102
82
122
HOYLAKE
LIVERPOOL BAY
Red Rocks
Hilbre Point
Tanskey Rocks
ROYAL LIVERPOOL GOLF COURSE
HOYLAKE MUNICIPAL GOLF COURSE
West Kirby Marine Lake
WEST KIRBY
CALDY
Manor Road
Hoylake
West Kirby
Hoylake Cottage Hospital
Lifeboat Station
Jetty
Club House
Sports Ground
Football Ground
Playing Field
Hockey Pitch
Gilroy Nature Park
Cemetery
Grange Hill
War Mem.
Superstore
Wirral Sailing Cen.
Victoria Gds.
Ashton Park Bowl. Grn.
Tell's Tower
West Kirby Grammar Sch.
Avalon Prep. Sch.
MEOLS DRIVE
MARKET ST.
GRANGE ROAD
BANKS ROAD
STANLEY ROAD
GREENBANK
COLUMN ROAD
SANDY LANE
A540
A553
B5141

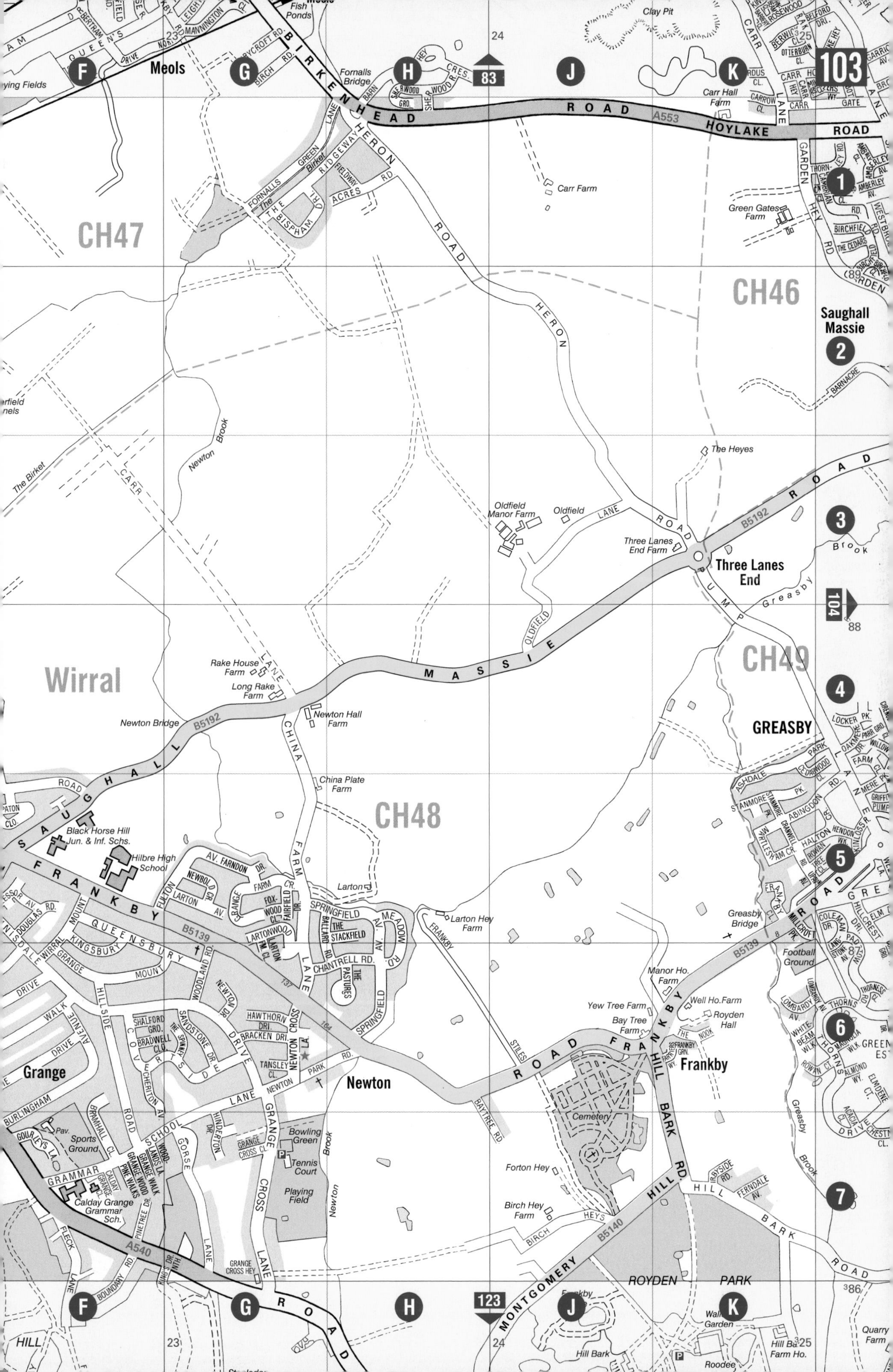
Meols
CH47
CH46
CH48
CH49
Wirral
Saughall Massie
Three Lanes End
GREASBY
Frankby
Newton
Grange
BIRKENHEAD ROAD
A553
HOYLAKE ROAD
HERON ROAD
SAUGHALL MASSIE ROAD
B5192
FRANKBY ROAD
B5139
A540
B5140
MONTGOMERY HILL
BARK HILL RD.
HILL BARK ROAD
PUMP LANE
CHINA FARM LANE
CARR LANE
GRANGE CROSS LANE
SCHOOL LANE
Carr Farm
Green Gates Farm
Carr Hall Farm
Clay Pit
Fish Ponds
Fornalls Bridge
Oldfield Manor Farm
Oldfield
Three Lanes End Farm
The Heyes
Rake House Farm
Long Rake Farm
Newton Hall Farm
Newton Bridge
China Plate Farm
Larton
Larton Hey Farm
Black Horse Hill Jun. & Inf. Schs.
Hilbre High School
Greasby Bridge
Football Ground
Manor Ho. Farm
Yew Tree Farm
Well Ho.Farm
Royden Hall
Bay Tree Farm
Cemetery
Forton Hey
Birch Hey Farm
Bowling Green
Tennis Court
Playing Field
Sports Ground
Calday Grange Grammar Sch.
ROYDEN PARK
Quarry Farm
Hill Bark
Roodee
Hill Bark Farm Ho.
Newton Brook
Greasby Brook
The Birket
83
104
123

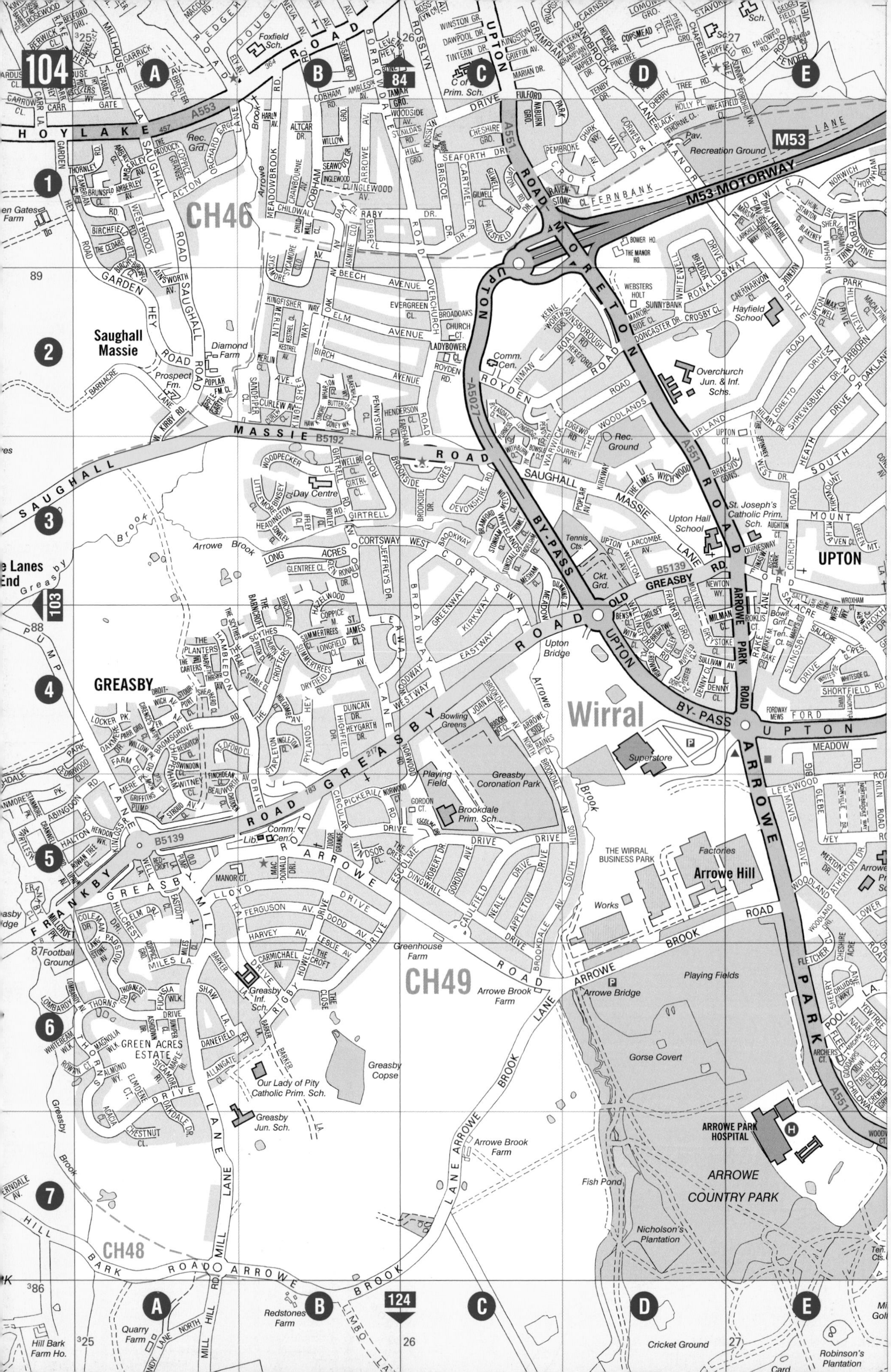

A
B
C
D
E
1
2
3
4
5
6
7
25
26
27
89
88
87
86
84
103
124
CH46
CH49
CH48
HOYLAKE
A553
M53
M53-MOTORWAY
Recreation Ground
Saughall Massie
Diamond Farm
Prospect Fm.
SAUGHALL
MASSIE
B5192
ROAD
Day Centre
Arrowe Brook
GREASBY
B5139
Greasby Coronation Park
Playing Field
Brookdale Prim. Sch.
Bowling Greens
Comm. Cen.
Lib.
Wirral
Superstore
UPTON
BY-PASS
A551
A5027
Upton Bridge
Overchurch Jun. & Inf. Schs.
Hayfield School
Upton Hall School
St. Joseph's Catholic Prim. Sch.
Rec. Ground
Tennis Cts.
Ckt. Grd.
THE WIRRAL BUSINESS PARK
Factories
Arrowe Hill
Works
Playing Fields
Arrowe Bridge
Arrowe Brook Farm
Greenhouse Farm
Greasby Copse
Greasby Inf. Sch.
Our Lady of Pity Catholic Prim. Sch.
Greasby Jun. Sch.
GREEN ACRES ESTATE
Football Ground
Gorse Covert
Fish Pond
Nicholson's Plantation
ARROWE PARK HOSPITAL
ARROWE COUNTRY PARK
Redstones Farm
Quarry Farm
Hill Bark Farm Ho.
Cricket Ground
Robinson's Plantation
Foxfield Sch.
C of E Prim. Sch.
Arrowe Park
Greasby Brook
HILL BARK ROAD
ARROWE BROOK ROAD
MILL HILL LANE
FRANKBY ROAD

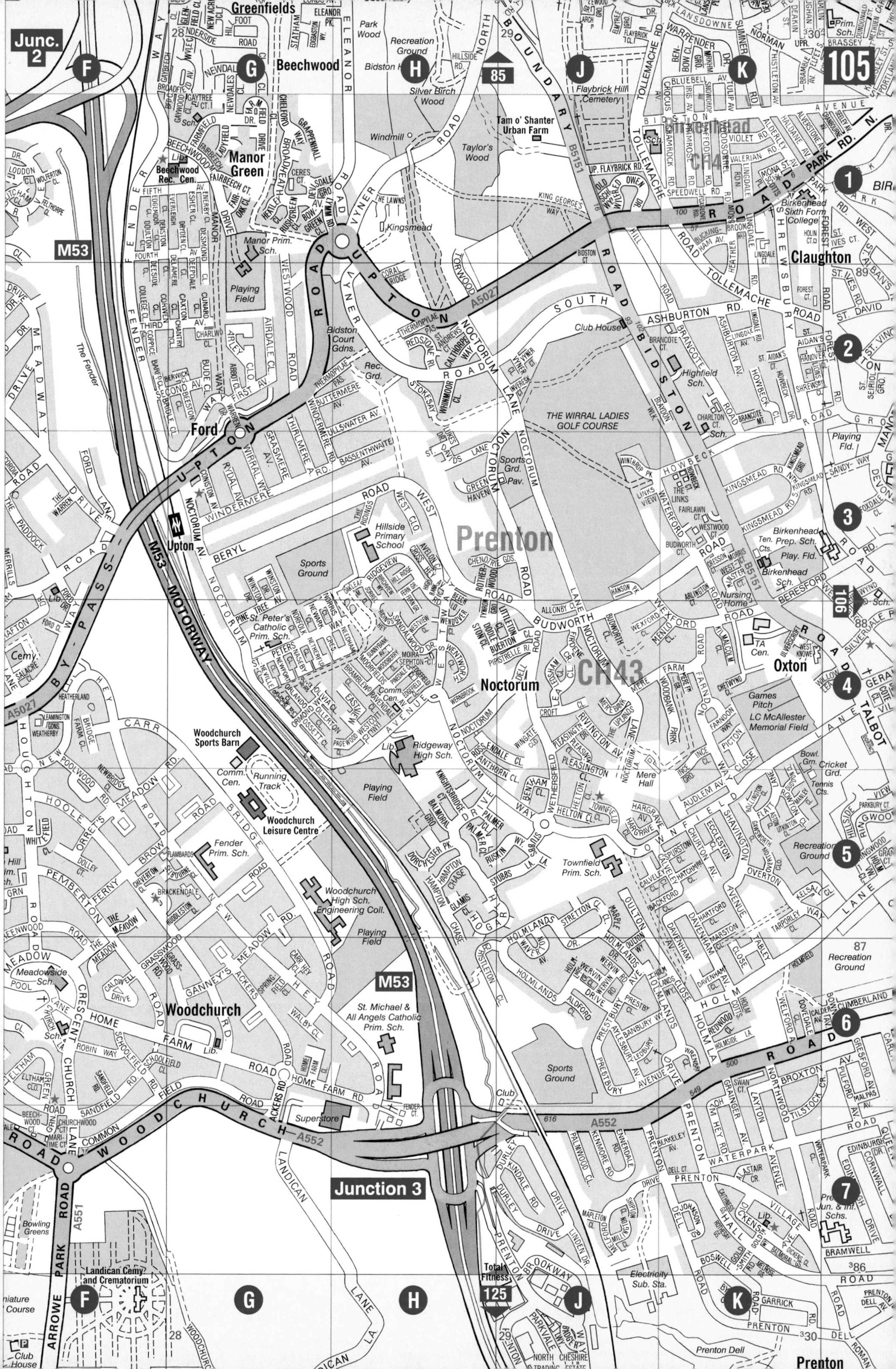
105
Junc. 2
Greenfields
Beechwood
Park Wood
Recreation Ground
Silver Birch Wood
85
Flaybrick Hill Cemetery
Tam o' Shanter Urban Farm
Taylor's Wood
Windmill
Manor Green
Beechwood Rec. Cen.
Manor Prim. Sch.
Playing Field
Kingsmead
Bidston Court Gdns.
Rec. Grd.
Birkenhead
CH41
Birkenhead Sixth Form College
Claughton
M53
The Fender
Ford
Upton
UPTON BY-PASS
A5027
M53 MOTORWAY
Club House
THE WIRRAL LADIES GOLF COURSE
Highfield Sch.
Charlton Ct. Sch.
Sports Grd. Pav.
Hillside Primary School
Sports Ground
Prenton
Birkenhead Ten. Prep. Sch.
Play. Fld.
Birkenhead Sch.
106
Nursing Home
TA Cen.
Oxton
Games Pitch
LC McAllester Memorial Field
St. Peter's Catholic Prim. Sch.
Noctorum
CH43
Comm. Cen.
Ridgeway High Sch.
Lib.
Cemy.
Woodchurch Sports Barn
Running Track
Woodchurch Leisure Centre
Playing Field
Mere Hall
Bowl. Grn.
Cricket Grd.
Tennis Cts.
Fender Prim. Sch.
Townfield Prim. Sch.
Recreation Ground
Woodchurch High Sch. Engineering Coll.
Meadowside Sch.
87
Woodchurch
St. Michael & All Angels Catholic Prim. Sch.
Sports Ground
Superstore
Club
A552
Junction 3
A551
Bowling Greens
Landican Cemy. and Crematorium
Total Fitness
125
Electricity Sub. Sta.
Prenton Jun. & Inf. Schs.
86
Club House
Prenton Dell
Prenton
NORTH CHESHIRE TRADING ESTATE
F
G
H
J
K
1
2
3
4
5
6
7
28
29
30
88
89

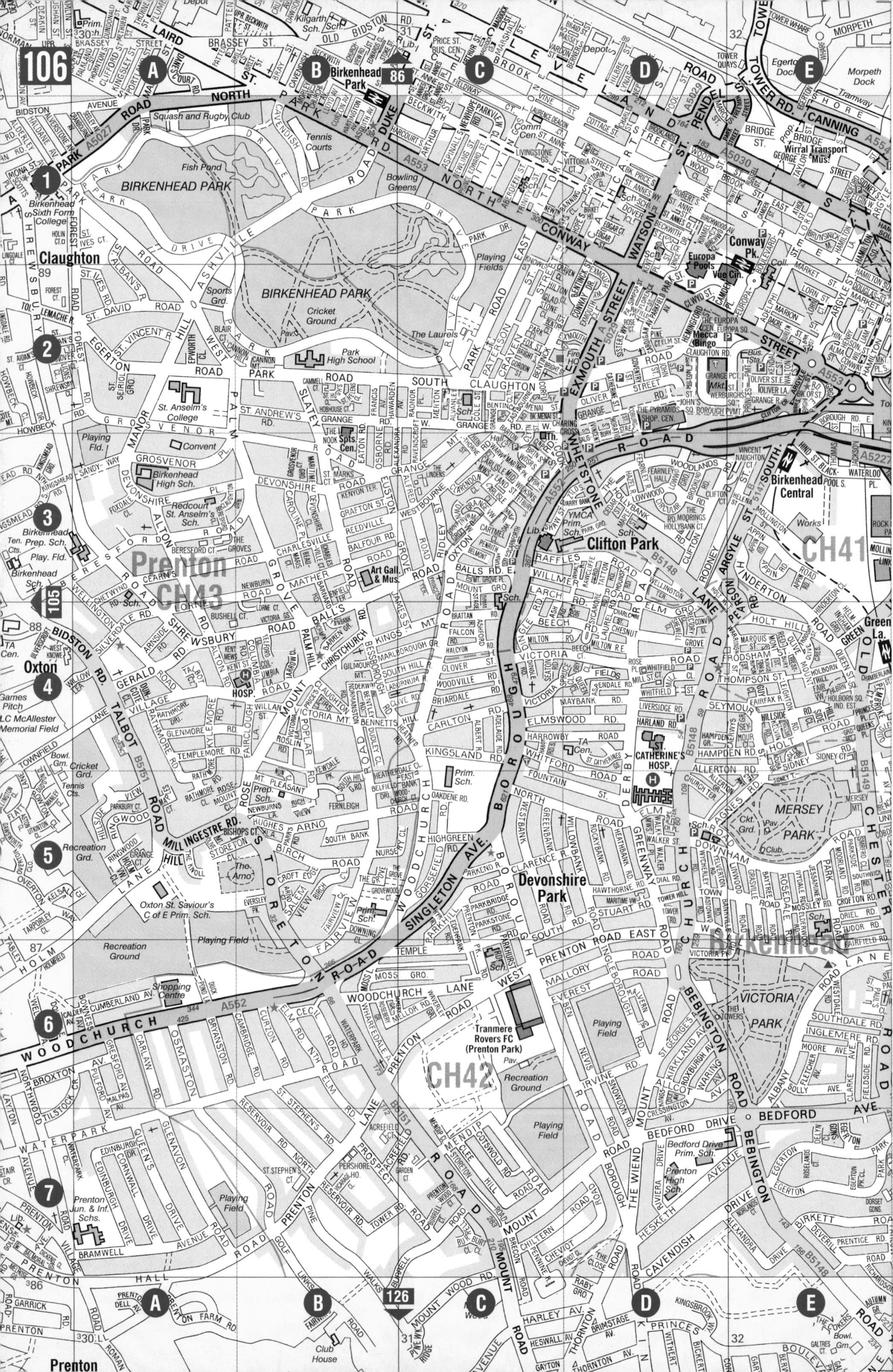

106
A
B
C
D
E
1
2
3
4
5
6
7
86
105
126
Birkenhead Park
BIRKENHEAD PARK
Fish Pond
Squash and Rugby Club
Tennis Courts
Bowling Greens
Sports Grd.
Cricket Ground
Pav.
The Laurels
Park High School
Playing Fields
Birkenhead Sixth Form College
Claughton
St. Anselm's College
Convent
Playing Fld.
Birkenhead High Sch.
Redcourt St. Anselm's Sch.
Birkenhead Ten. Prep. Sch.
Play. Fld.
Birkenhead Sch.
Prenton
CH43
Oxton
Games Pitch
LC McAllester Memorial Field
Cricket Grd.
Tennis Cts.
Bowl. Grn.
Recreation Grd.
Oxton St. Saviour's C of E Prim. Sch.
Recreation Ground
Playing Field
Shopping Centre
The Arno
Prep. Sch.
Spts. Cen.
Art Gall. & Mus.
Hosp.
Prim. Sch.
Clifton Park
YMCA Prim. Sch.
Lib.
Mecca Bingo
Grange Pct. Mkt.
The Pyramids Shop. Cen.
Europa Pools
Vue Cin.
Conway Pk.
Bus Sta.
Birkenhead Central
Works
CH41
Wirral Transport Mus.
Egerton Dock
Morpeth Dock
Tower Quays
St. Catherine's Hosp.
TA Cen.
Devonshire Park
Tranmere Rovers FC (Prenton Park)
CH42
Recreation Ground
Playing Field
MERSEY PARK
Ckt. Grd.
Club
VICTORIA PARK
The Towers
Bedford Drive Prim. Sch.
Prenton High Sch.
Prenton Jun. & Inf. Schs.
Club House
Bowl. Grn.
Prenton
Birkenhead
PARK ROAD NORTH
A5027
DUKE ST.
A553
CONWAY ST.
EXMOUTH STREET
A5029
BOROUGH ROAD
A552
WOODCHURCH ROAD
SINGLETON AVE.
TALBOT ROAD
B5151
STORETON ROAD
BIDSTON RD.
SHREWSBURY ROAD
GROSVENOR RD.
CLAUGHTON RD.
ARGYLE ST.
CHESTER STREET
B5149
CHURCH ROAD
BEBINGTON ROAD
B5148
BEDFORD AVE.
BEDFORD DRIVE
CAVENDISH DRIVE
MOUNT ROAD
PRENTON ROAD WEST
PRENTON ROAD EAST
WOODCHURCH LANE
CANNING ST.
A5030
A554
A5227
HOLM LANE
PRENTON HALL ROAD
PRINCES WAY

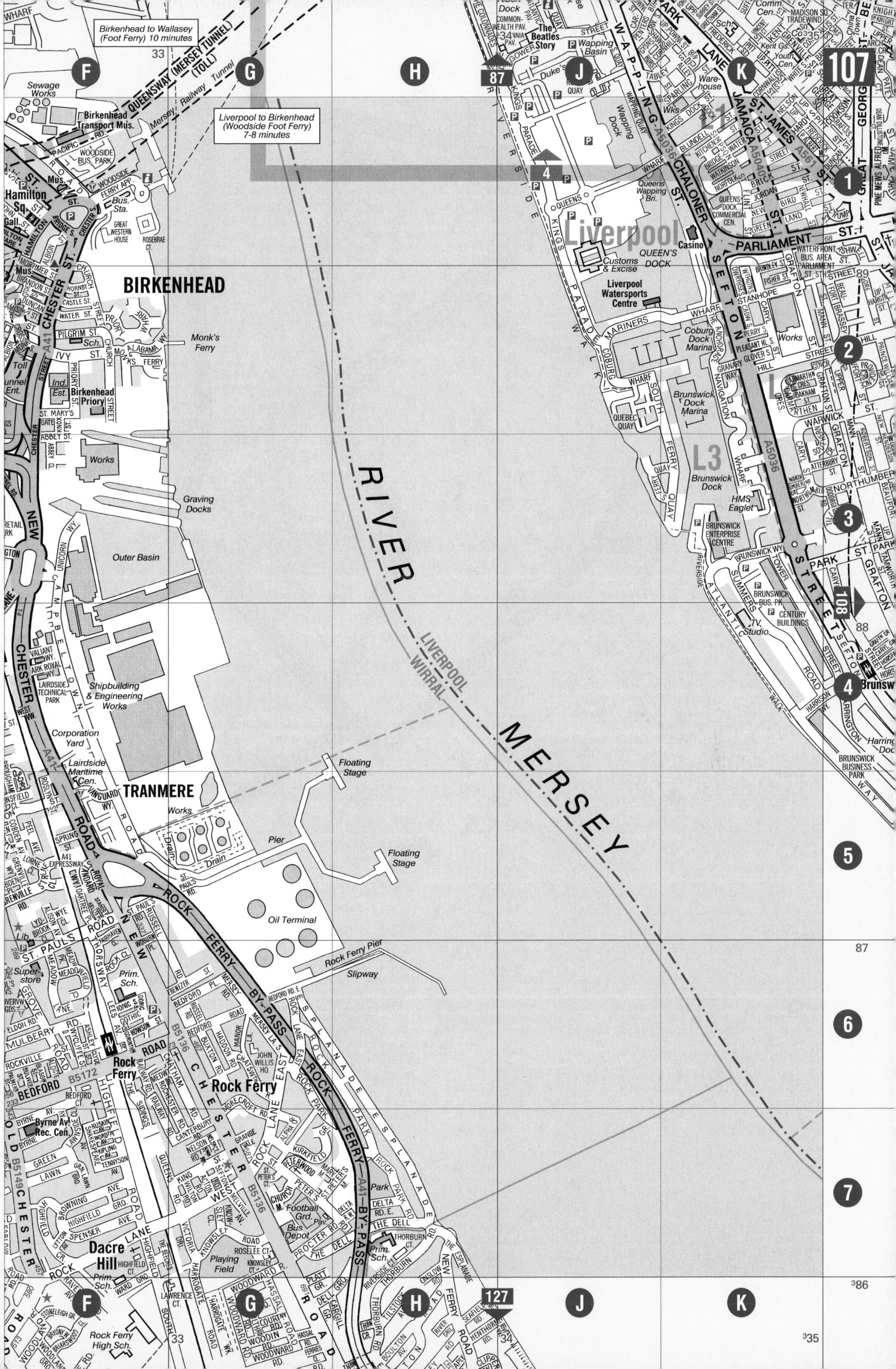
107
Birkenhead to Wallasey (Foot Ferry) 10 minutes
QUEENSWAY (MERSEY TUNNEL) (TOLL)
Mersey Railway Tunnel
Liverpool to Birkenhead (Woodside Foot Ferry) 7-8 minutes
Sewage Works
Birkenhead Transport Mus.
WOODSIDE BUS. PARK
Bus Sta.
GREAT WESTERN HOUSE
Hamilton Sq.
BIRKENHEAD
Monk's Ferry
Birkenhead Priory
Works
Graving Docks
Outer Basin
Shipbuilding & Engineering Works
LAIRDSIDE TECHNICAL PARK
Corporation Yard
Lairdside Maritime Cen.
TRANMERE
Floating Stage
Pier
Oil Terminal
Rock Ferry Pier
Slipway
ROCK FERRY BY-PASS
Rock Ferry
Dacre Hill
Playing Field
Football Grd.
Bus Depot
Byrne Av. Rec. Cen.
Rock Ferry High Sch.
RIVER MERSEY
LIVERPOOL
WIRRAL
The Beatles Story
Wapping Basin
Wapping Dock
Queens Wapping Bri.
Liverpool
QUEEN'S DOCK
Casino
Customs & Excise
Liverpool Watersports Centre
Coburg Dock Marina
Brunswick Dock Marina
Brunswick Dock
HMS Eaglet
BRUNSWICK ENTERPRISE CENTRE
BRUNSWICK BUS. PK.
CENTURY BUILDINGS
TV Studio
BRUNSWICK BUSINESS PARK
PARLIAMENT ST.
SEFTON STREET
CHALONER ST.
WAPPING
JAMAICA ST.
ST. JAMES ST.
KINGS PARADE
RIVERSIDE WALK
87
4
108
127
F G H J K
1 2 3 4 5 6 7
L3

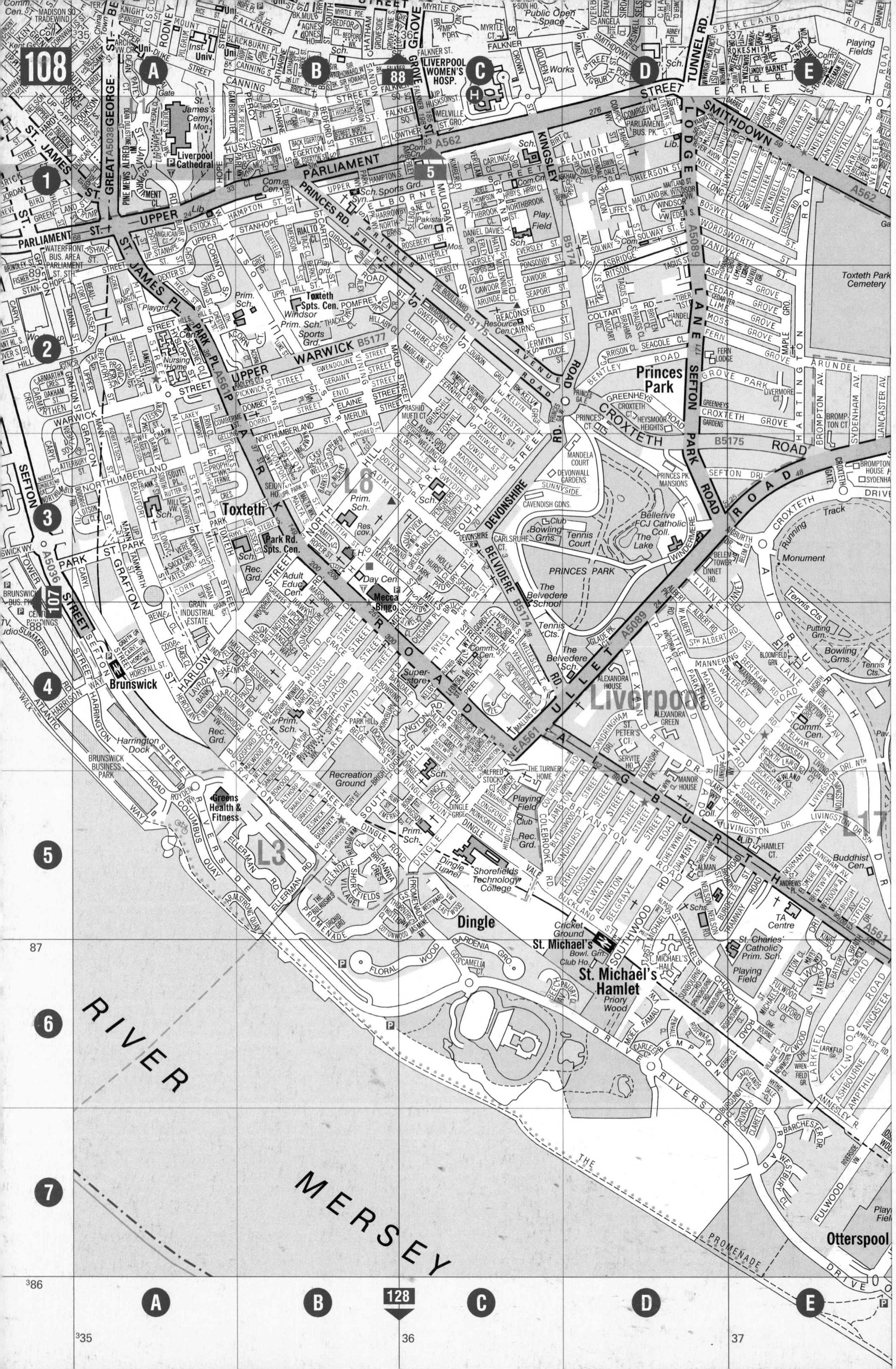

108
A
B
C
D
E
1
2
3
4
5
6
7
88
5
107
128
L8
L3
L17
Liverpool Cathedral
St. James's Cemy
LIVERPOOL WOMEN'S HOSP.
Toxteth
Toxteth Spts. Cen.
Windsor Prim. Sch.
Park Rd. Spts. Cen.
Mecca Bingo
Day Cen.
Adult Educ. Cen.
Brunswick
Harrington Dock
BRUNSWICK BUSINESS PARK
Greens Health & Fitness
Recreation Ground
Dingle
Dingle Tunnel
Shorefields Technology College
St. Michael's
St. Michael's Hamlet
Priory Wood
Princes Park
PRINCES PARK
Bellerive FCJ Catholic Coll.
The Lake
The Belvedere School
Liverpool
Toxteth Park Cemetery
Monument
Running Track
Otterspool
St. Charles' Catholic Prim. Sch.
TA Centre
Buddhist Cen.
Playing Fields
RIVER MERSEY
PARLIAMENT ST.
UPPER PARLIAMENT ST.
PRINCES RD.
PRINCES AVENUE
UPPER WARWICK ST.
PARK RD.
ULLET RD.
AIGBURTH RD.
CROXTETH ROAD
SMITHDOWN RD.
LODGE LANE
SEFTON PARK ROAD
DEVONSHIRE RD.
BELVIDERE RD.
GREAT GEORGE ST.
ST. JAMES PL.
SEFTON STREET
RIVERSIDE DRIVE
OTTERSPOOL PROMENADE
A562
A561
A5089
B5175
B5174
B5177
A5036
A5038
87
86
35
36
37

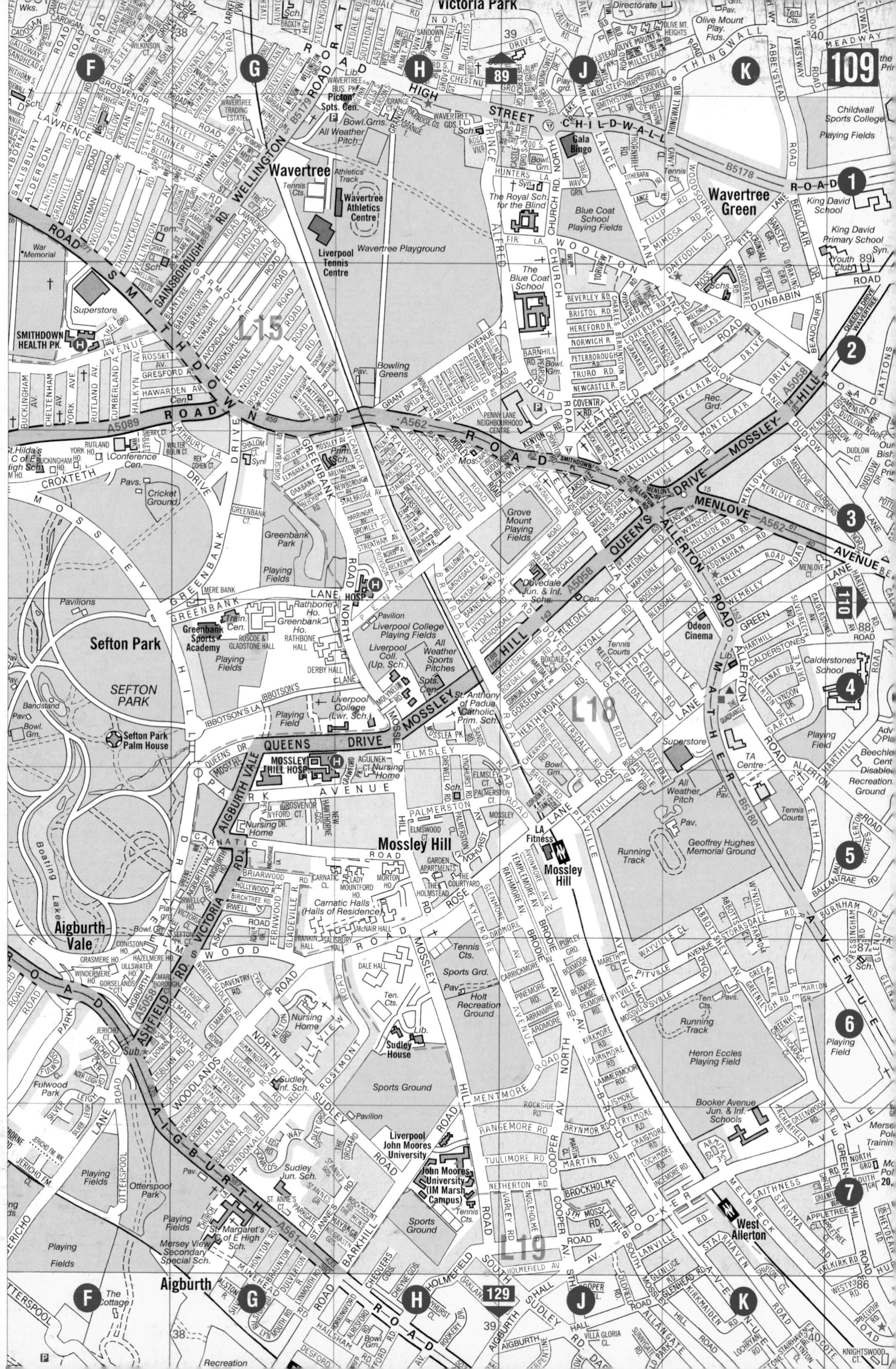
Victoria Park
Olive Mount Play. Flds.
F
G
H
J
K
89
39
Wavertree
Wavertree Athletics Centre
Liverpool Tennis Centre
Wavertree Playground
Athletics Track
All Weather Pitch
Picton Spts. Cen.
HIGH STREET
CHILDWALL ROAD
B5178
Childwall Sports College Playing Fields
Gala Bingo
The Royal Sch. for the Blind
Blue Coat School Playing Fields
Wavertree Green
King David School
King David Primary School
Youth Club
WOOLTON ROAD
The Blue Coat School
SMITHDOWN ROAD
A5089
Superstore
SMITHDOWN HEALTH PK.
WELLINGTON RD.
B5179
L15
Bowling Greens
Penny Lane Neighbourhood Centre
A562
Rec. Grd.
QUEEN'S DRIVE
MOSSLEY HILL
A5058
MENLOVE AVENUE
Conference Cen.
Cricket Ground
Grove Mount Playing Fields
Dovedale Jun. & Inf. Schs.
Greenbank Park
Playing Fields
Sefton Park
SEFTON PARK
Pavilions
Bandstand
Sefton Park Palm House
Boating Lake
Greenbank Sports Academy
Train. Cen.
Rathbone Ho.
Greenbank Ho.
Liverpool College Playing Fields
All Weather Sports Pitches
Liverpool Coll. (Up. Sch.)
Liverpool College (Lwr. Sch.)
St. Anthony of Padua Catholic Prim. Sch.
L18
Odeon Cinema
Tennis Courts
Calderstones School
110
Superstore
All Weather Pitch
TA Centre
Beechley Cent Disabled Recreation Ground
Playing Field
MOSSLEY HILL HOSP.
Nursing Home
QUEENS DRIVE
AIGBURTH VALE
PARK AVENUE
Mossley Hill
Carnatic Halls (Halls of Residence)
Garden Apartments
LA Fitness
Mossley Hill
Running Track
Geoffrey Hughes Memorial Ground
B5180
Aigburth Vale
ASHFIELD RD.
VICTORIA RD.
Tennis Cts.
Sports Grd.
Holt Recreation Ground
Sudley House
Sudley Inf. Sch.
Sudley Jun. Sch.
Sports Ground
Liverpool John Moores University
John Moores University (IM Marsh Campus)
Running Track
Heron Eccles Playing Field
Booker Avenue Jun. & Inf. Schools
Fulwood Park
Playing Fields
Otterspool Park
St. Margaret's C of E High Sch.
Mersey View Secondary Special Sch.
AIGBURTH ROAD
A561
Sports Ground
L19
West Allerton
Aigburth
The Cottage
129
Recreation
1
2
3
4
5
6
7

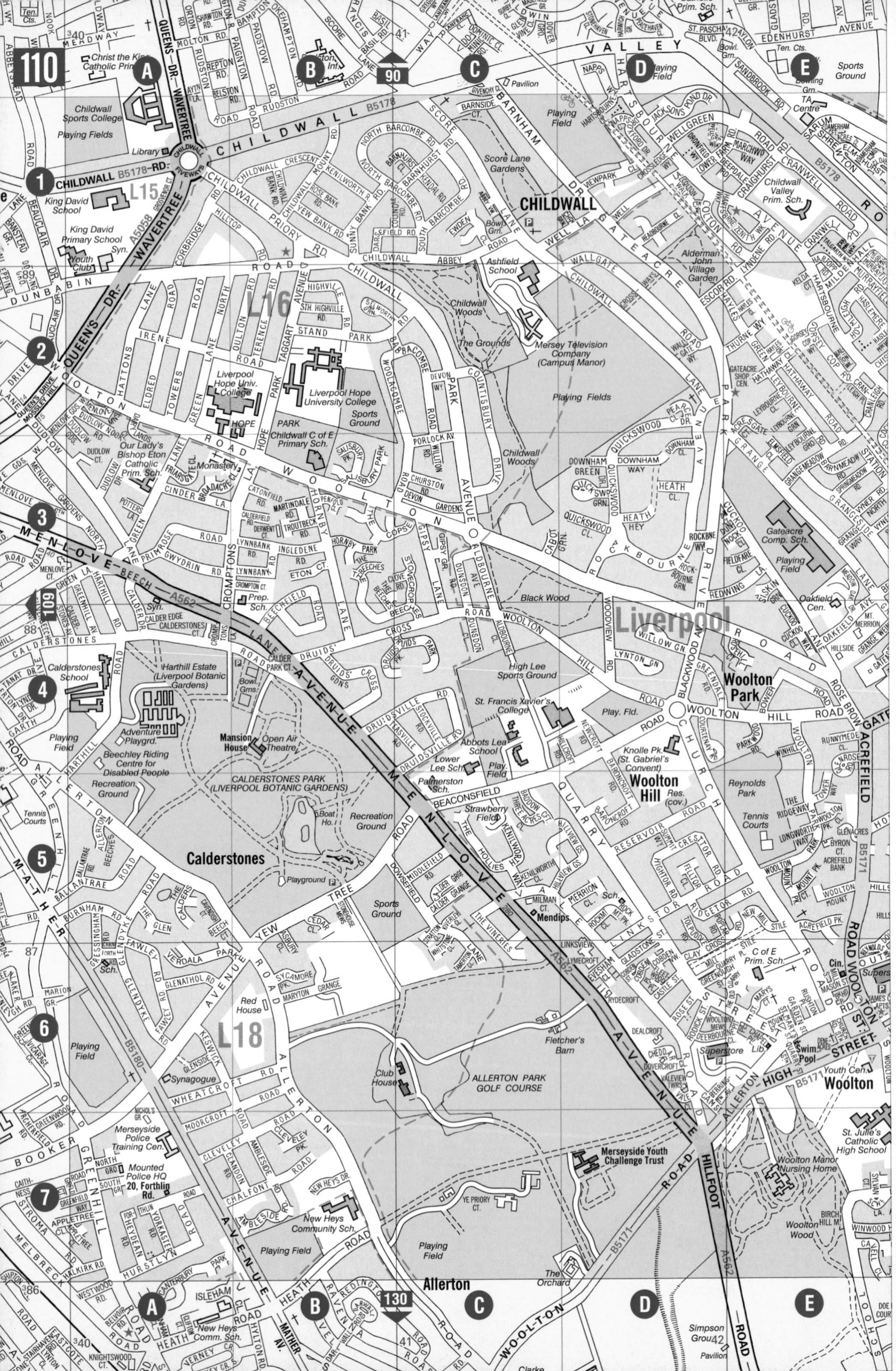

CHILDWALL
Liverpool
Woolton Park
Woolton Hill
Woolton
Calderstones
Allerton
L15
L16
L18
CALDERSTONES PARK (LIVERPOOL BOTANIC GARDENS)
ALLERTON PARK GOLF COURSE
Liverpool Hope University College
Childwall Sports College
King David School
Calderstones School
Gateacre Comp. Sch.
Merseyside Police Training Cen.
New Heys Community Sch.
Merseyside Youth Challenge Trust
Woolton Manor Nursing Home
St. Julie's Catholic High School
Mersey Television Company (Campus Manor)
Childwall Woods
Black Wood
High Lee Sports Ground
Reynolds Park
Mansion House
Open Air Theatre
MENLOVE AVENUE
QUEENS DR.
WOOLTON ROAD
CHILDWALL ABBEY ROAD
CHILDWALL VALLEY ROAD
HILLFOOT ROAD
ALLERTON ROAD
MATHER AVENUE
90
109
130

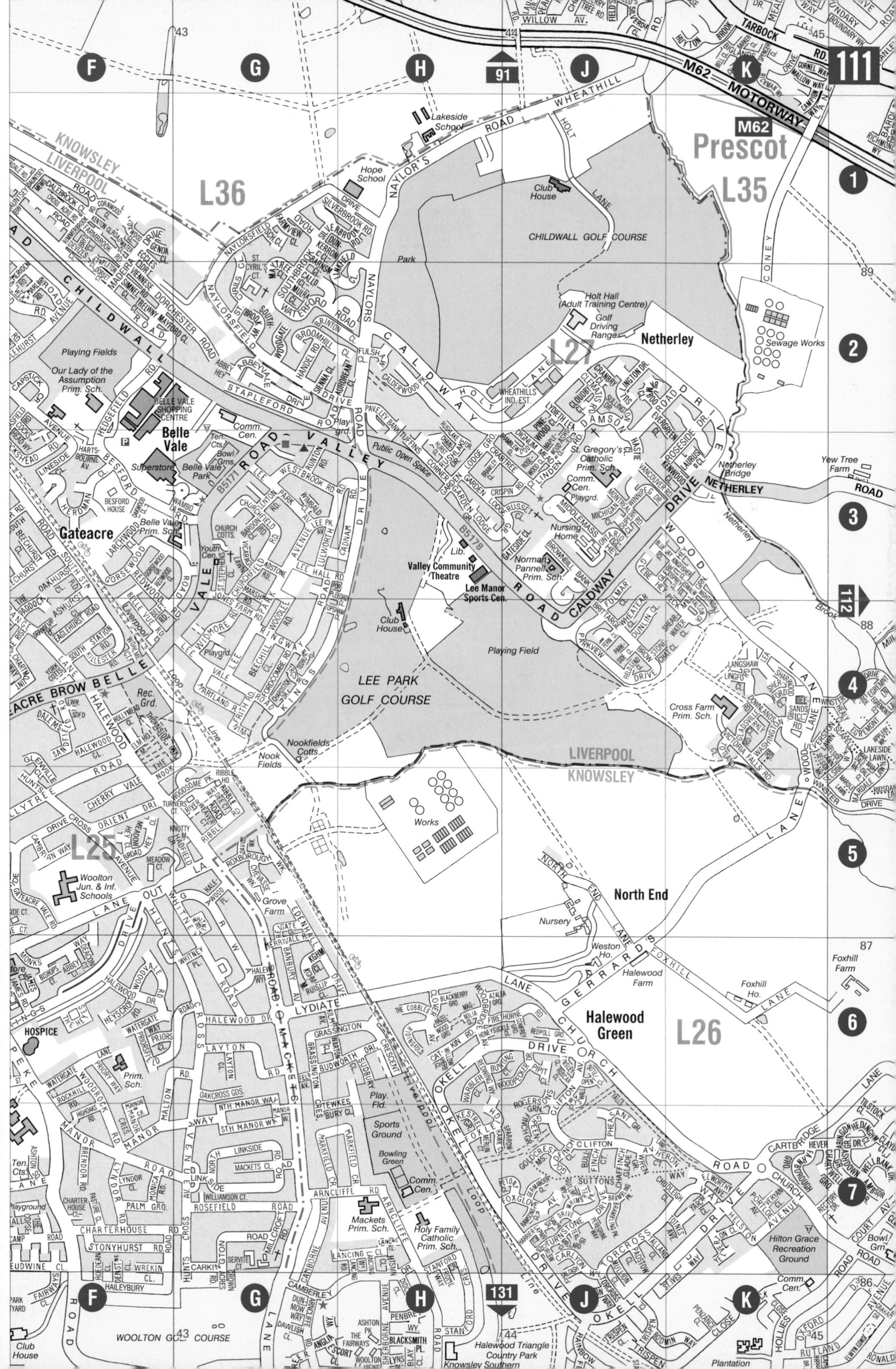
F
G
H
J
K
91
M62 MOTORWAY
M62
TARBOCK RD.
Prescot
L35
L36
L27
L25
L26
KNOWSLEY
LIVERPOOL
Lakeside School
Hope School
NAYLOR'S ROAD
WHEATHILL
HOLT LANE
Club House
CHILDWALL GOLF COURSE
Park
Holt Hall (Adult Training Centre)
Golf Driving Range
Netherley
Sewage Works
CALDWAY DRIVE
CHILDWALL ROAD
Playing Fields
Our Lady of the Assumption Prim. Sch.
BELLE VALE SHOPPING CENTRE
Belle Vale
Superstore
Belle Vale Park
Comm. Cen.
Public Open Space
WHEATHILLS IND. EST.
St. Gregory's Catholic Prim. Sch.
Netherley Bridge
NETHERLEY ROAD
Yew Tree Farm
Gateacre
BESFORD HOUSE
Belle Vale Prim. Sch.
Youth Cen.
Lib.
Valley Community Theatre
Lee Manor Sports Cen.
Norman Pannell Prim. Sch.
Nursing Home
B5171
B5178
VALLEY ROAD
CALDWAY ROAD
112
Brook
Club House
Playing Field
LEE PARK GOLF COURSE
Cross Farm Prim. Sch.
Rec. Grd.
Nookfields Cotts.
Nook Fields
Works
NORTH END LANE
North End
Nursery
Weston Ho.
Halewood Farm
FOXHILL LANE
Foxhill Ho.
Foxhill Farm
Halewood Green
GERRARD LANE
CHURCH ROAD
Woolton Jun. & Inf. Schools
Grove Farm
HOSPICE
Prim. Sch.
Play. Fld.
Sports Ground
Bowling Green
Comm. Cen.
Mackets Prim. Sch.
Holy Family Catholic Prim. Sch.
Hilton Grace Recreation Ground
Bowl. Grn.
Comm. Cen.
Playground
Ten. Cts.
131
WOOLTON GOLF COURSE
Club House
Halewood Triangle Country Park
Knowsley Southern
Plantation
1
2
3
4
5
6
7
43
44
45
89
88
87
86

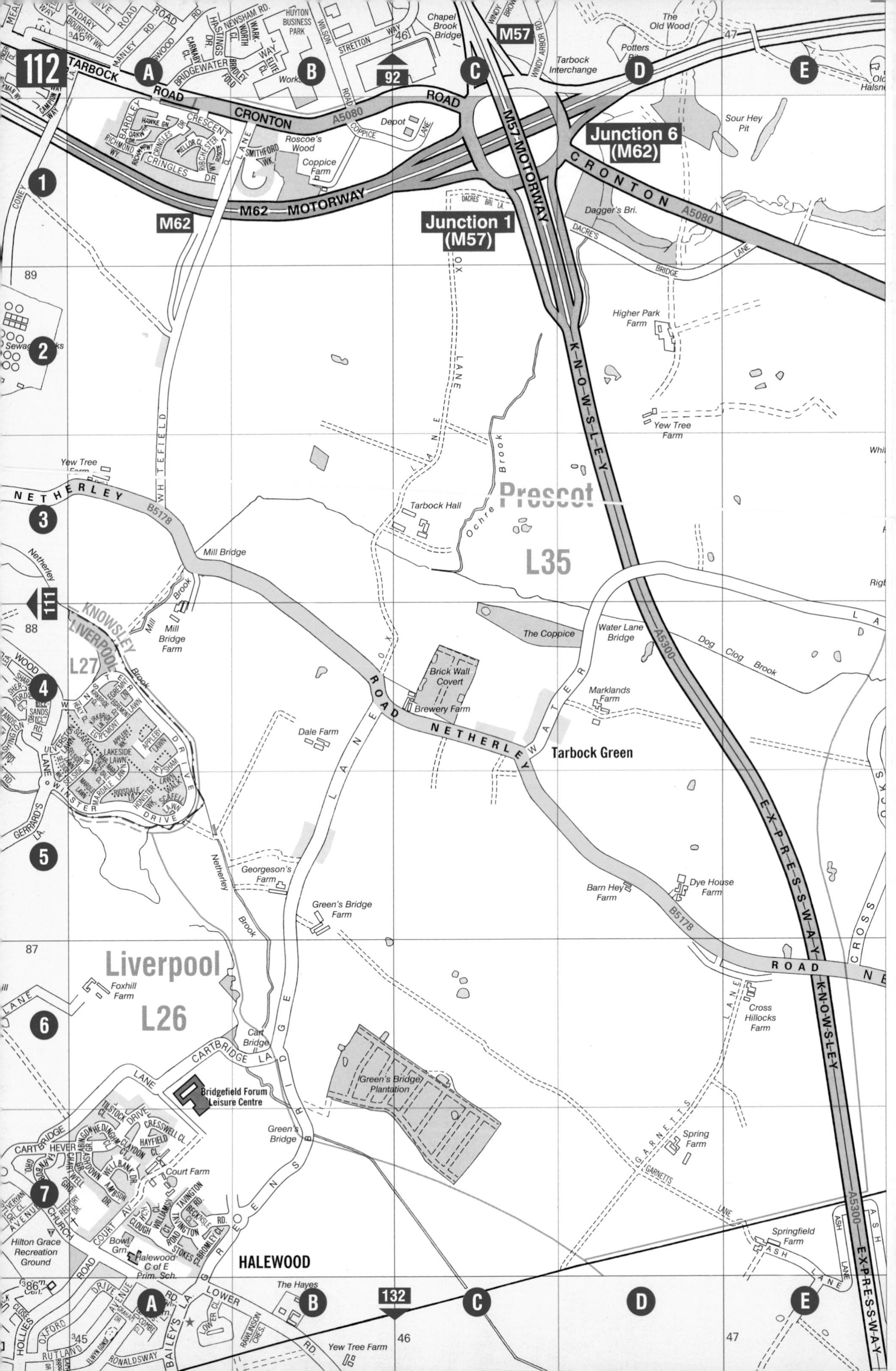
TARBOCK ROAD
CRONTON ROAD
A5080
M57
92
Chapel Brook Bridge
Tarbock Interchange
The Old Wood
Potters Pit
Huyton Business Park
Works
Depot
Roscoe's Wood
Coppice Farm
Junction 6 (M62)
Junction 1 (M57)
M62 MOTORWAY
M57 MOTORWAY
Sour Hey Pit
Dagger's Bri.
DACRES BRIDGE LANE
Higher Park Farm
Yew Tree Farm
Sewage Works
WHITEFIELD LANE
OX LANE
Ochre Brook
Tarbock Hall
Prescot
L35
NETHERLEY ROAD
B5178
Mill Bridge
Mill Bridge Farm
Netherley Brook
KNOWSLEY
LIVERPOOL
L27
111
The Coppice
Water Lane Bridge
Dog Clog Brook
Brick Wall Covert
Brewery Farm
Marklands Farm
Dale Farm
Tarbock Green
WATER LANE
KNOWSLEY EXPRESSWAY
A5300
Georgeson's Farm
Green's Bridge Farm
Barn Hey Farm
Dye House Farm
Cross Hillocks Farm
Liverpool
L26
Foxhill Farm
Cart Bridge
CARTBRIDGE LA.
Bridgefield Forum Leisure Centre
Green's Bridge Plantation
Green's Bridge
GREENS BRIDGE LANE
Spring Farm
GARNETTS LANE
Springfield Farm
ASH LANE
Court Farm
Hilton Grace Recreation Ground
Halewood C of E Prim. Sch.
HALEWOOD
The Hayes
132
Yew Tree Farm
LOWER ROAD
BAILEY'S LA.
A B C D E
1 2 3 4 5 6 7
89 88 87 86
345 46 47

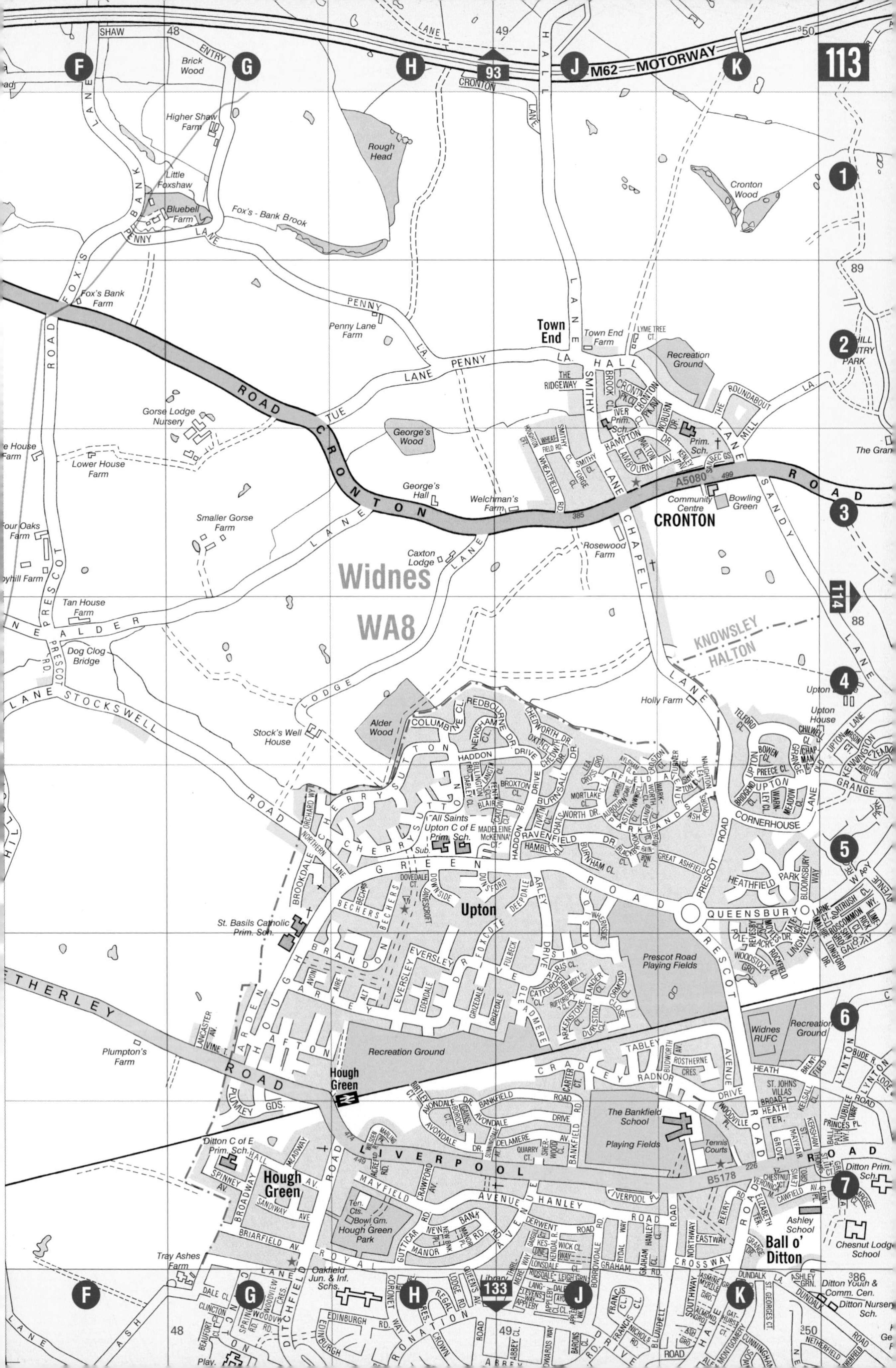
M62 MOTORWAY
93
Brick Wood
Higher Shaw Farm
Little Foxshaw
Bluebell Farm
Fox's - Bank Brook
Rough Head
Cronton Wood
Fox's Bank Farm
Penny Lane Farm
Town End
Town End Farm
Recreation Ground
Gorse Lodge Nursery
George's Wood
Lower House Farm
George's Hall
Welchman's Farm
Smaller Gorse Farm
Community Centre
Bowling Green
CRONTON
Caxton Lodge
Rosewood Farm
Widnes
WA8
Tan House Farm
Dog Clog Bridge
KNOWSLEY
HALTON
Holly Farm
Alder Wood
Stock's Well House
Upton House
All Saints Upton C of E Prim. Sch.
Upton
St. Basils Catholic Prim. Sch.
Prescot Road Playing Fields
Plumpton's Farm
Recreation Ground
Hough Green
Widnes RUFC
The Bankfield School
Playing Fields
Tennis Courts
Ditton C of E Prim. Sch.
Hough Green
Hough Green Park
Ashley School
Ball o' Ditton
Chesnut Lodge School
Tray Ashes Farm
Oakfield Jun. & Inf. Schs.
Library
133
Ditton Youth & Comm. Cen.
Ditton Nursery Sch.
Ditton Prim. Sch.
114
CRONTON ROAD
PRESCOT ROAD
LIVERPOOL ROAD
HOUGH GREEN ROAD
QUEENSBURY WAY
A5080
B5178

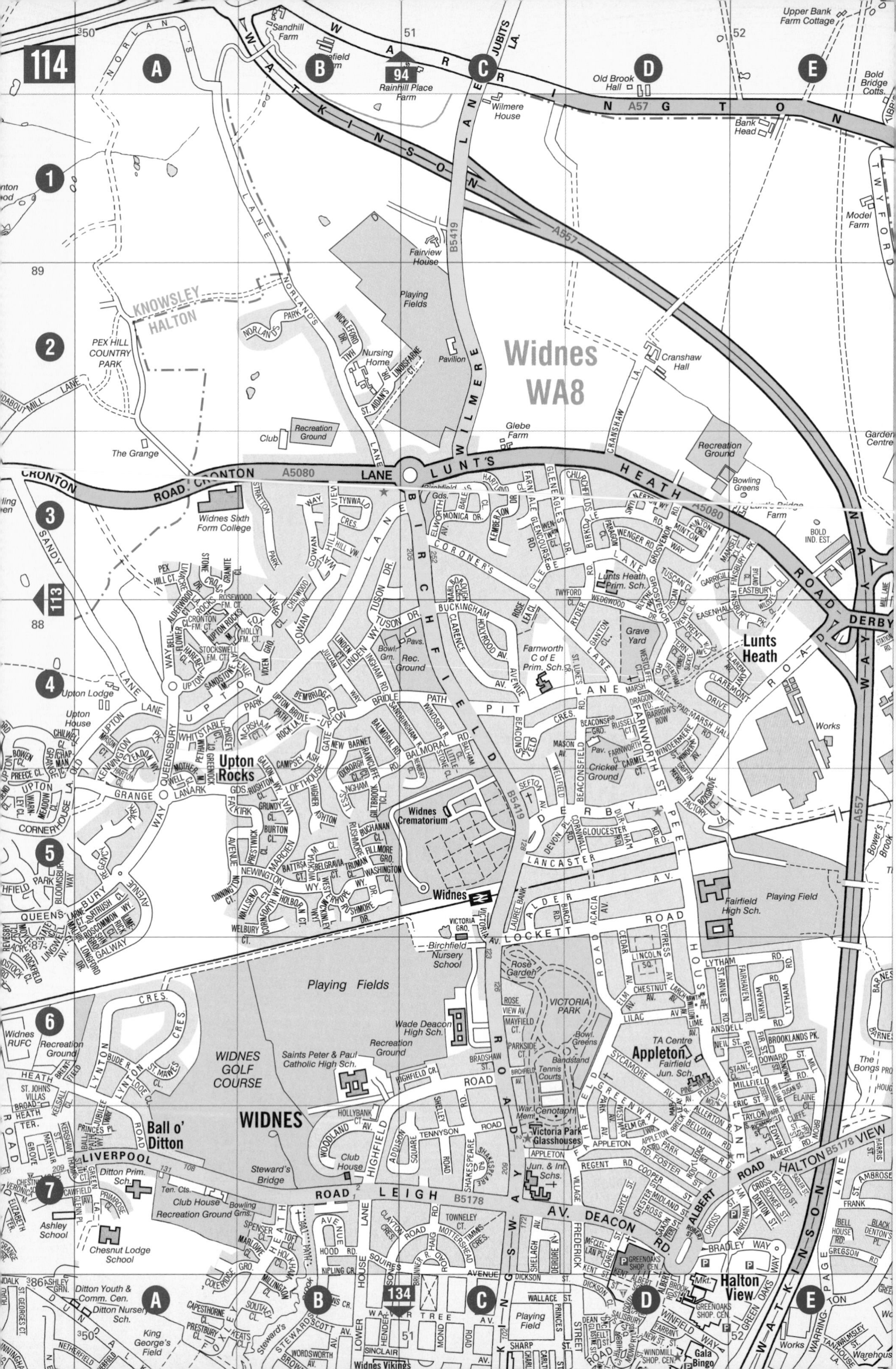
114
A
B
C
D
E
1
2
3
4
5
6
7
350
51
52
89
88
87
86
94
113
134
Widnes
WA8
WIDNES
Upton Rocks
Ball o' Ditton
Appleton
Lunts Heath
Halton View
KNOWSLEY
HALTON
Sandhill Farm
Rainhill Place Farm
Wilmere House
Old Brook Hall
Upper Bank Farm Cottage
Bold Bridge Cotts.
Bank Head
Model Farm
Fairview House
Playing Fields
Nursing Home
Pavilion
Cranshaw Hall
PEX HILL COUNTRY PARK
Club
Recreation Ground
The Grange
Glebe Farm
Garden Centre
Bowling Greens
Lunt's Bridge Farm
BOLD IND. EST.
Widnes Sixth Form College
Upton Lodge
Upton House
Lunts Heath Prim. Sch.
Grave Yard
Farnworth C of E Prim. Sch.
Cricket Ground
Works
Widnes Crematorium
Widnes
Fairfield High Sch.
Playing Field
Birchfield Nursery School
Rose Garden
VICTORIA PARK
Wade Deacon High Sch.
Saints Peter & Paul Catholic High Sch.
WIDNES GOLF COURSE
Widnes RUFC
TA Centre
Fairfield Jun. Sch.
Bandstand
Tennis Courts
Cenotaph
War. Mem.
Victoria Park Glasshouses
Jun. & Inf. Schs.
Club House
Steward's Bridge
Ditton Prim. Sch.
Ten. Cts.
Club House
Bowling Grns.
Recreation Ground
Ashley School
Chesnut Lodge School
GREENOAKS SHOP. CEN.
Mkt.
Ditton Youth & Comm. Cen.
Ditton Nursery Sch.
King George's Field
Widnes Vikings
Gala Bingo
WINDMILL SHOP. CEN.
Warehouse
The Bongs
Bower's Brook
A5080
A57
A557
B5419
B5178
WARRINGTON
WATKINSON WAY
CRONTON ROAD
CRONTON LANE
LUNT'S HEATH ROAD
DERBY ROAD
BIRCHFIELD ROAD
WILMERE LANE
NORLAND'S LANE
LIVERPOOL ROAD
LEIGH AV.
DEACON RD.
ALBERT ROAD
HALTON VIEW
KINGSWAY
FARNWORTH ST.
PEEL HOUSE LANE
LOCKETT ROAD
UPTON LANE
PIT LANE
CORONER'S LANE
GLEBE LANE
QUEENSBURY WAY
GRANGE WAY
APPLETON VILLAGE
GREENWAY
BRADLEY WAY
GREEN OAKS WAY

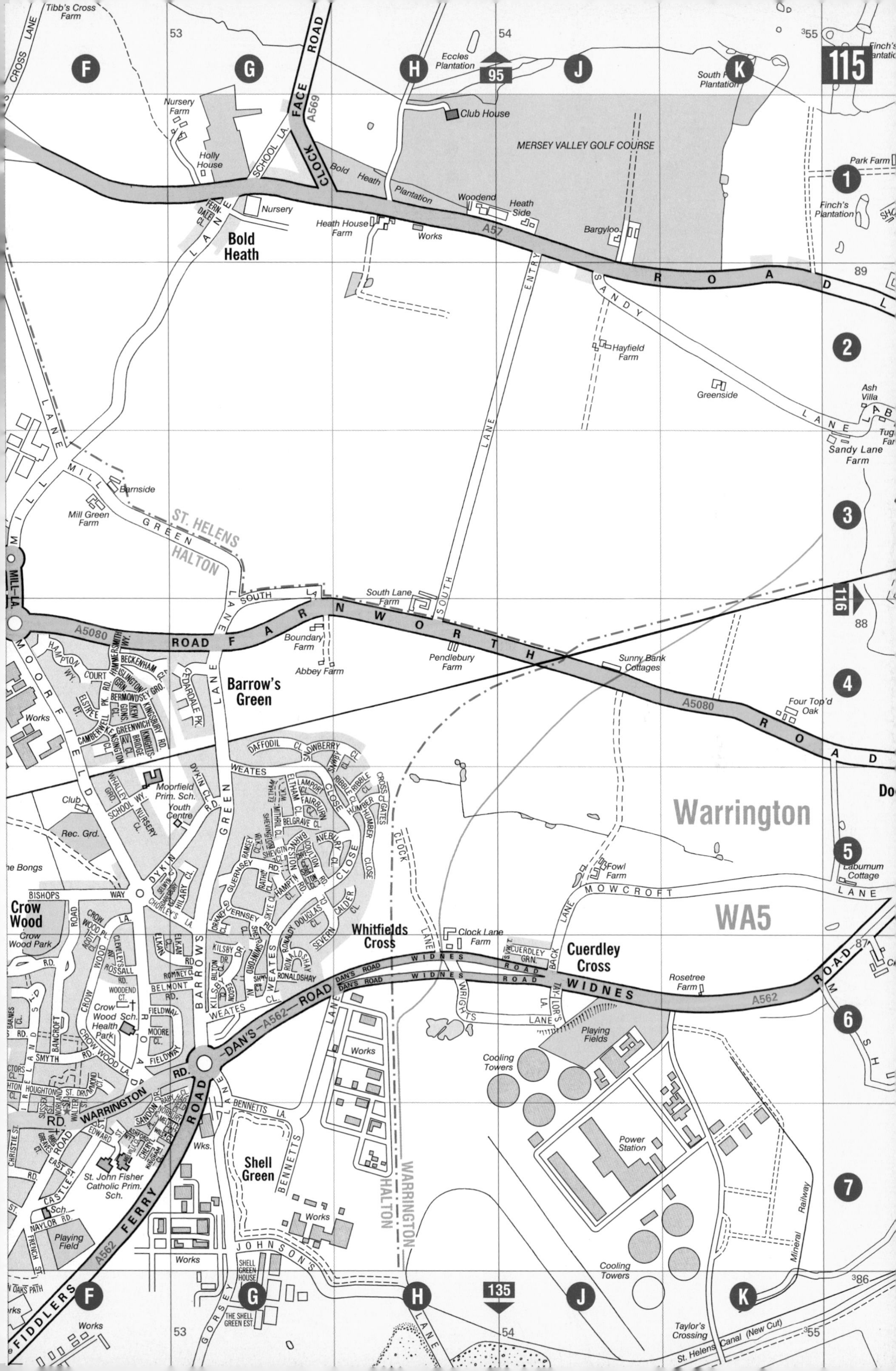
Tibb's Cross Farm
CROSS LANE
53
54
55
F
G
H
J
K
Eccles Plantation
95
South P Plantation
Finch's Plantation
FACE ROAD
A569
CLOCK
Nursery Farm
Holly House
SCHOOL LA.
Club House
MERSEY VALLEY GOLF COURSE
Park Farm
Bold Heath Plantation
Woodend
Heath Side
Finch's Plantation
Nursery
FERNDALE CL.
LANE
Bold Heath
Heath House Farm
Works
A57
Bargyloo
ROAD
89
ENTRY
SANDY
Hayfield Farm
Greenside
Ash Villa
LANE
Tug Far
Sandy Lane Farm
LANE
MILL
MILL
Barnside
Mill Green Farm
GREEN
ST. HELENS
HALTON
SOUTH
MILL-LA.
SOUTH
LA
LANE
South Lane Farm
SOUTH
116
88
A5080
ROAD
FARNWORTH
Boundary Farm
Pendlebury Farm
Sunny Bank Cottages
Abbey Farm
Barrow's Green
A5080
ROAD
Four Top'd Oak
MOORFIELD
HAMPTON WY.
COURT
HAMMERSMITH WY.
BECKENHAM CL.
ISLINGTON GRN.
BERMONDSEY GRO.
KEW CL.
KINGSBURY RD.
CEDARDALE PK.
ELSTREE CT.
CAMBERWELL PK. RD.
GREENWICH AV.
BRIDGE CL.
KNIGHTS
KENSINGTON CL.
Works
DAFFODIL CL.
SNOWBERRY CL.
WEATES
DYKIN CL.
ELTHAM
LAMPORT CL.
FAIRBURN CL.
RIBBLE CL.
CROSS GATES
HUMBER CL.
Dor
Warrington
Moorfield Prim. Sch.
Club
WHALLEY GRO.
SCHOOL WY.
NURSERY CL.
Youth Centre
Rec. Grd.
BELGRAVE CL.
AVEBURY CL.
CLOSE
HUMBER CLOSE
CLOCK
GUERNSEY
RAMSEY
HAMPTN
DYKIN
RD.
GREEN
The Bongs
HILARY CL.
Fowl Farm
Laburnum Cottage
5
MOWCROFT
LANE
BISHOPS
WAY
CHORLEY'S LA
SKYE CL.
DOUGLAS CL.
CALDER CL.
SEVERN
Crow Wood
Crow Wood Park
CROW WOOD PL.
LA.
CLEVELEYS AV.
ROSSALL RD.
ELKAN RD.
ELKAN CL.
ROMNEY CL.
BARROWS
KILSBY DR.
WEATES
RONALDSHAY
GUERNSEY CL.
ORKNEY CL.
Whitfields Cross
Clock Lane Farm
LANE
WIDNES
ROAD
CUERDLEY GRN.
BACK LANE
Cuerdley Cross
WA5
87
ROAD
ROAD
WIDNES
Rosetree Farm
A562
DAN'S ROAD
ROAD
BELMONT RD.
WOODEND CT.
Crow Wood Health Park
Sch.
FIELDWAY
MOORE CL.
FIELDWAY
BANCROFT
CROW WOOD LA.
SMYTH
WEATES CL.
DAN'S A562 ROAD
LANE
Works
WRIGHTS LANE
TAYLOR'S LA.
Playing Fields
Cooling Towers
6
RD.
WARRINGTON
HOUGHTON
ST. DRUMMOND
SUSSEX
NORLAND
WALTER
SANDON
ROAD
EDWARD
CHRISTIE ST.
EAST ST
CASTLE
St. John Fisher Catholic Prim. Sch.
Wks.
BENNETTS LA.
BENNETTS
Shell Green
Power Station
Railway
Mineral
7
WARRINGTON
HALTON
Sch.
NAYLOR RD.
Playing Field
FRENCH ST.
A562
FERRY
FIDDLERS
Works
Works
JOHNSON'S
SHELL GREEN HOUSE
Cooling Towers
86
OAKS PATH
F
G
H
135
J
K
Works
GORSEY
THE SHELL GREEN EST.
LANE
53
54
Taylor's Crossing
St. Helens Canal (New Cut)
55

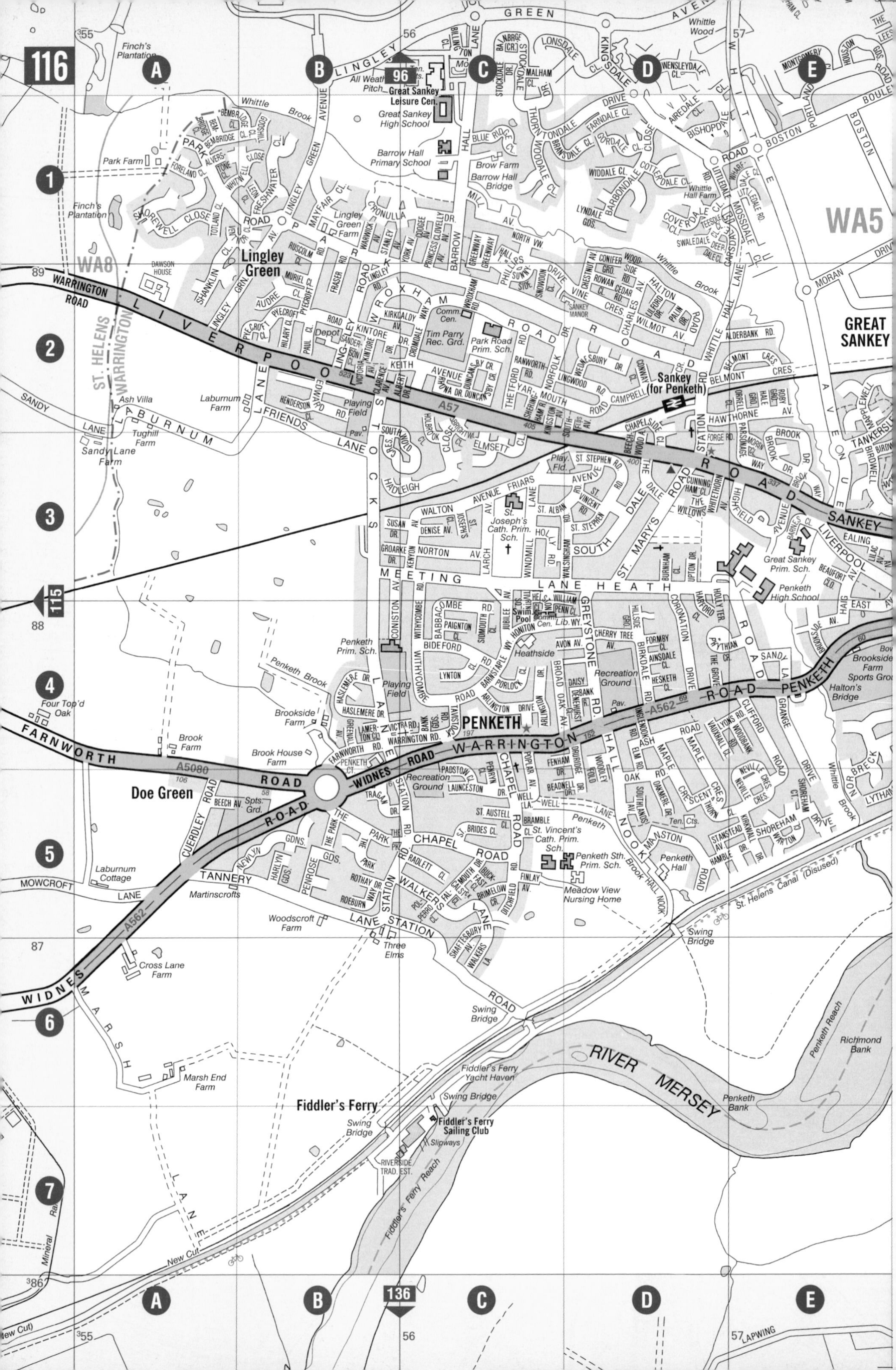
116
A
B
C
D
E
1
2
3
4
5
6
7
96
115
136
WA5
WA8
Lingley Green
GREAT SANKEY
PENKETH
Doe Green
Fiddler's Ferry
Great Sankey Leisure Cen.
Great Sankey High School
Barrow Hall Primary School
Park Road Prim. Sch.
Tim Parry Rec. Grd.
Sankey (for Penketh)
St. Joseph's Cath. Prim. Sch.
Great Sankey Prim. Sch.
Penketh High School
Penketh Prim. Sch.
Heathside
Recreation Ground
St. Vincent's Cath. Prim. Sch.
Penketh Sth. Prim. Sch.
Meadow View Nursing Home
Penketh Hall
Fiddler's Ferry Yacht Haven
Fiddler's Ferry Sailing Club
RIVER MERSEY
St. Helens Canal (Disused)
Finch's Plantation
Park Farm
Whittle Brook
Penketh Brook
Brookside Farm
Brook Farm
Brook House Farm
Four Top'd Oak
Laburnum Farm
Ash Villa
Tughill Farm
Sandy Lane Farm
Laburnum Cottage
Martinscrofts
Woodscroft Farm
Three Elms
Cross Lane Farm
Marsh End Farm
Swing Bridge
Riverside Trad. Est.
Penketh Reach
Richmond Bank
Penketh Bank
Fiddler's Ferry Reach
New Cut
WARRINGTON ROAD
LIVERPOOL ROAD
FARNWORTH ROAD
WIDNES ROAD
MEETING LANE
STOCKS LANE
LINGLEY GREEN AVENUE
BOSTON BOULEVARD
A57
A562
A5080
ST. HELENS
WARRINGTON

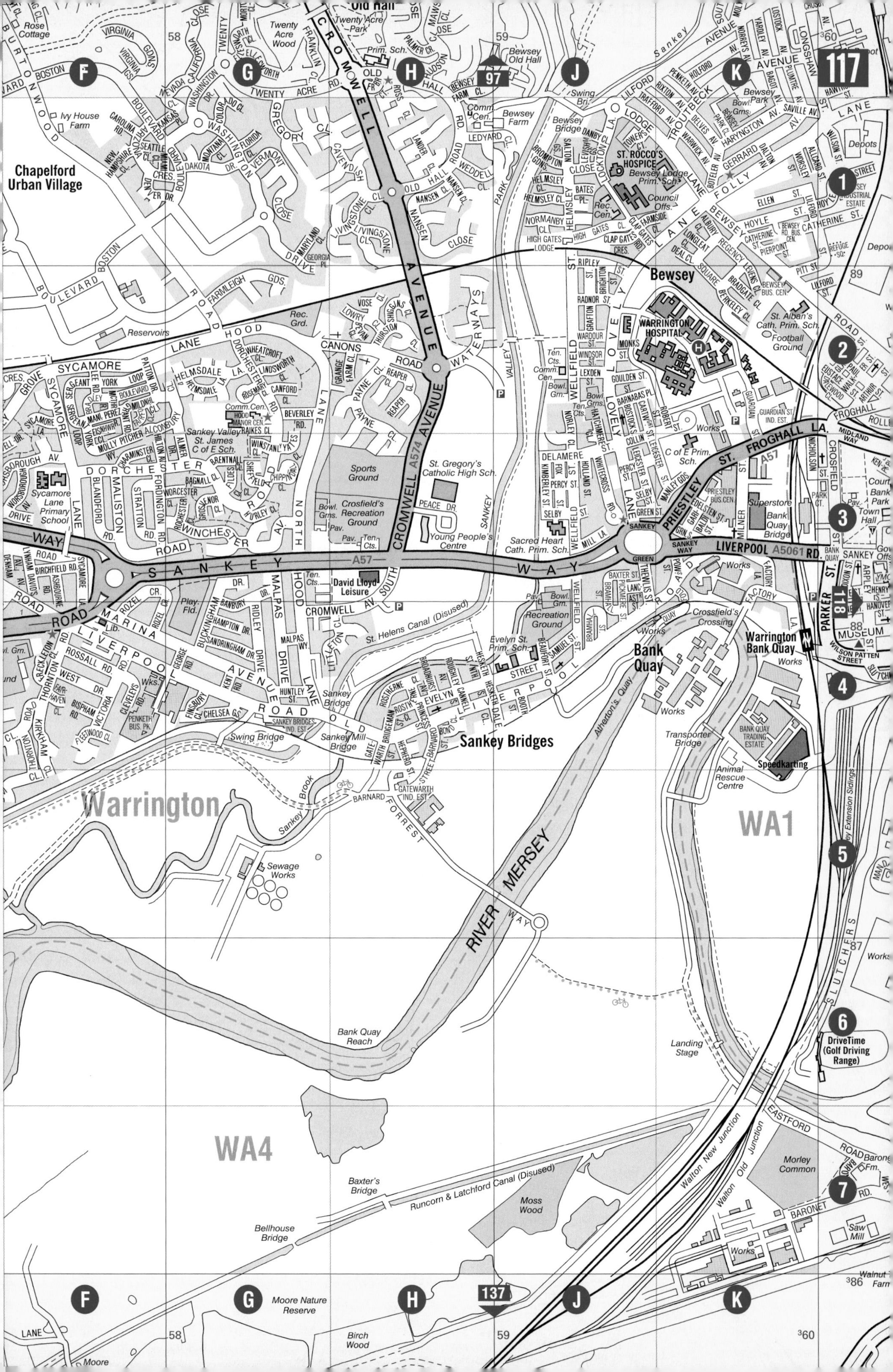
Chapelford
Urban Village
Warrington
Bewsey
Bank
Quay
Sankey Bridges
WA1
WA4
RIVER MERSEY
CROMWELL AVENUE
A574
SANKEY WAY
A57
LIVERPOOL RD.
A5061
FROGHALL LA.
PRIESTLEY ST.
LIVERPOOL AVENUE
OLD ROAD
BOULEVARD
SYCAMORE LANE
DORCHESTER
HOOD LANE
LOVELY LANE
FOLLY LANE
LODGE LANE
TROUTBECK AVENUE
TWENTY ACRE RD.
OLD HALL RD.
PARKER ST.
SLUTCHERS LANE
EASTFORD ROAD
BARONET RD.
FORREST WAY
Twenty Acre
Wood
Rose
Cottage
Ivy House
Farm
Bewsey
Old Hall
Bewsey
Farm
Bewsey
Park
ST. ROCCO'S
HOSPICE
Bewsey Lodge
Prim. Sch.
Council
Offs.
WARRINGTON
HOSPITAL
St. Alban's
Cath. Prim. Sch.
Football
Ground
Sports
Ground
St. Gregory's
Catholic High Sch.
Crosfield's
Recreation
Ground
Young People's
Centre
David Lloyd
Leisure
Sycamore
Lane
Primary
School
Sankey Valley
St. James
C of E Sch.
Sacred Heart
Cath. Prim. Sch.
Evelyn St.
Prim. Sch.
Recreation
Ground
C of E Prim.
Sch.
Superstore
Bank
Quay
Bridge
Warrington
Bank Quay
Town
Hall
MUSEUM
Works
BANK QUAY
TRADING
ESTATE
Speedkarting
Transporter
Bridge
Animal
Rescue
Centre
Crossfield's
Crossing
St. Helens Canal (Disused)
Atherton's Quay
Sewage
Works
Bank Quay
Reach
Landing
Stage
DriveTime
(Golf Driving
Range)
Morley
Common
Walton New Junction
Walton Old Junction
Runcorn & Latchford Canal (Disused)
Moss
Wood
Baxter's
Bridge
Bellhouse
Bridge
Moore Nature
Reserve
Birch
Wood
Saw
Mill
Swing Bridge
Sankey Mill
Bridge
Sankey
Bridge
Sankey Brook
Reservoirs
97
118
137
F
G
H
J
K
1
2
3
4
5
6
7
58
59
360
86
87
88
89

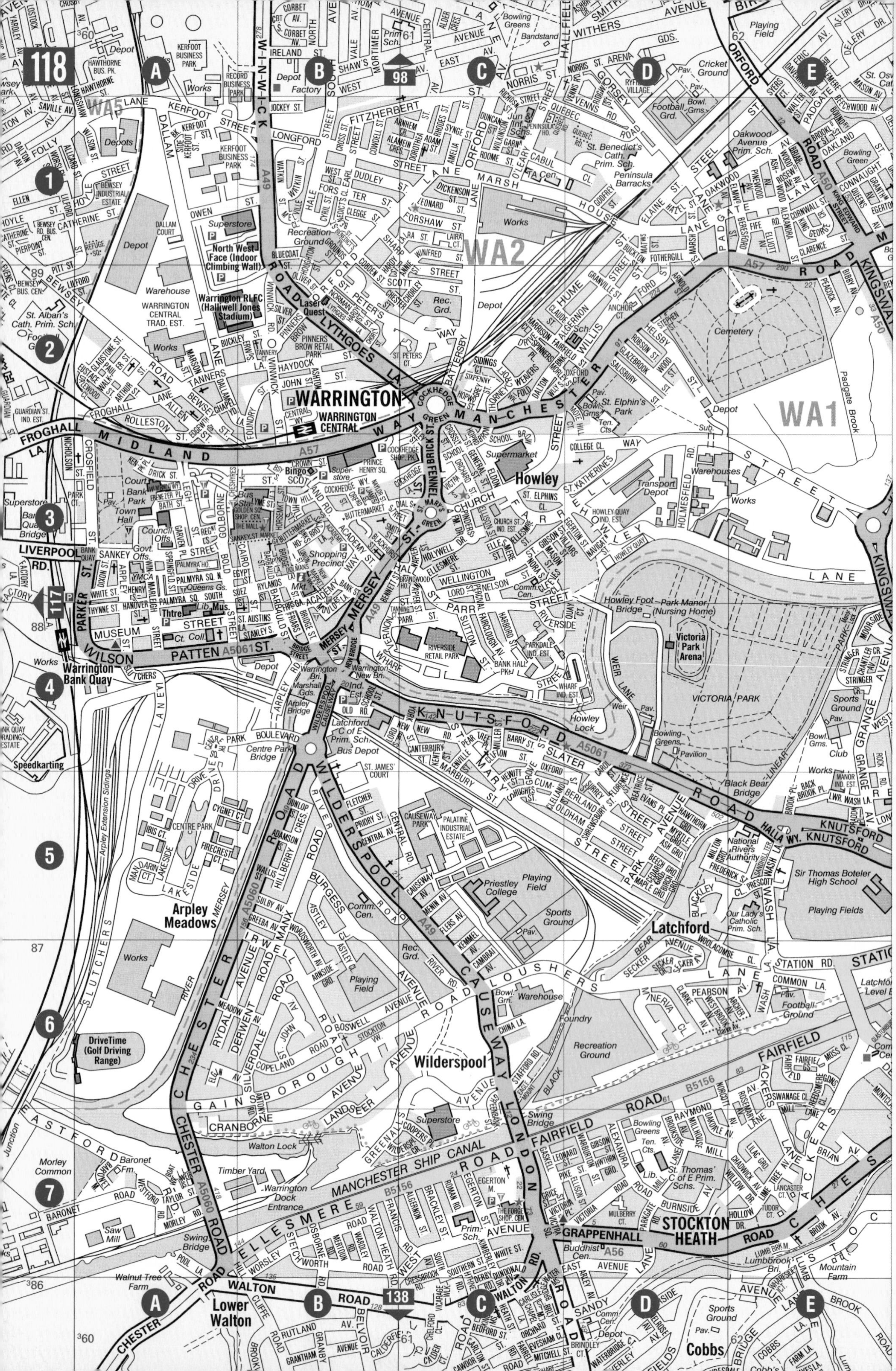

118
A
B
C
D
E
1
2
3
4
5
6
7
98
117
138
WA5
WA2
WA1
WARRINGTON
WARRINGTON CENTRAL
Howley
Latchford
Arpley Meadows
Wilderspool
STOCKTON HEATH
Lower Walton
Cobbs
Warrington Bank Quay
Kerfoot Business Park
Hawthorne Bus. Pk.
Record Business Park
Bewsey Industrial Estate
Dallam Court
Superstore
North West Face (Indoor Climbing Wall)
Warrington RLFC (Halliwell Jones Stadium)
Warrington Central Trad. Est.
Laser Quest
Pinners Brow Retail Park
Recreation Ground
Rec. Grd.
St. Alban's Cath. Prim. Sch.
St. Benedict's Cath. Prim. Sch.
Peninsula Barracks
Oakwood Avenue Prim. Sch.
Football Grd.
Cricket Ground
Ryfields Village
Bowling Greens
Bandstand
Playing Field
Cemetery
Padgate Brook
St. Elphin's Park
Transport Depot
Warehouses
Works
Supermarket
Cockhedge Shop. Pk.
Prince Henry Sq.
Town Hall
Bank Park
Council Offs.
Govt. Offs.
Queens Gs.
Lib. Mus.
Thtre
Museum
Ct. Coll.
Bus Sta. Golden Sq. Shop. Cen. The Mall
Shopping Precinct
Mkt.
Riverside Retail Park
Parkdale Ind. Est.
Bank Hall Pk.
Wharf Ind. Est.
Howley Quay Ind. Est.
Howley Foot Bridge
Park Manor (Nursing Home)
Victoria Park Arena
Victoria Park
Howley Lock
Weir
Pavilion
Black Bear Bridge
National Rivers Authority
Sir Thomas Boteler High School
Playing Fields
Our Lady's Catholic Prim. Sch.
Sports Ground
Warrington Bri.
Warrington New Bri.
Marshall Gds.
Arpley Bridge
Latchford C of E Prim. Sch.
Bus Depot
Centre Park Bridge
Centre Park
Arpley Extension Sidings
St. James' Court
Causeway Park
Palatine Industrial Estate
Priestley College
Comm. Cen.
Speedkarting
DriveTime (Golf Driving Range)
Morley Common
Baronet Fm.
Timber Yard
Warrington Dock Entrance
Saw Mill
Swing Bridge
Walton Lock
Walnut Tree Farm
Superstore
Foundry
Recreation Ground
Latchford Level Br.
Football Ground
St. Thomas' C of E Prim. Schs.
The Forge Shop. Cen.
Egerton M.
Prim. Sch.
Buddhist Cen.
Lumbbrook Bri.
Mountain Farm
Sports Ground
MANCHESTER SHIP CANAL
MIDLAND WAY
MANCHESTER ROAD
KNUTSFORD ROAD
CHESTER ROAD
WILDERSPOOL CAUSEWAY
LONDON ROAD
ELLESMERE ROAD
FAIRFIELD ROAD
GAINSBOROUGH ROAD
LOUSHERS LANE
WINWICK ROAD
LYTHGOES LANE
ORFORD LANE
PADGATE LANE
KINGSWAY
A49
A50
A57
A56
A5060
A5061
B5156

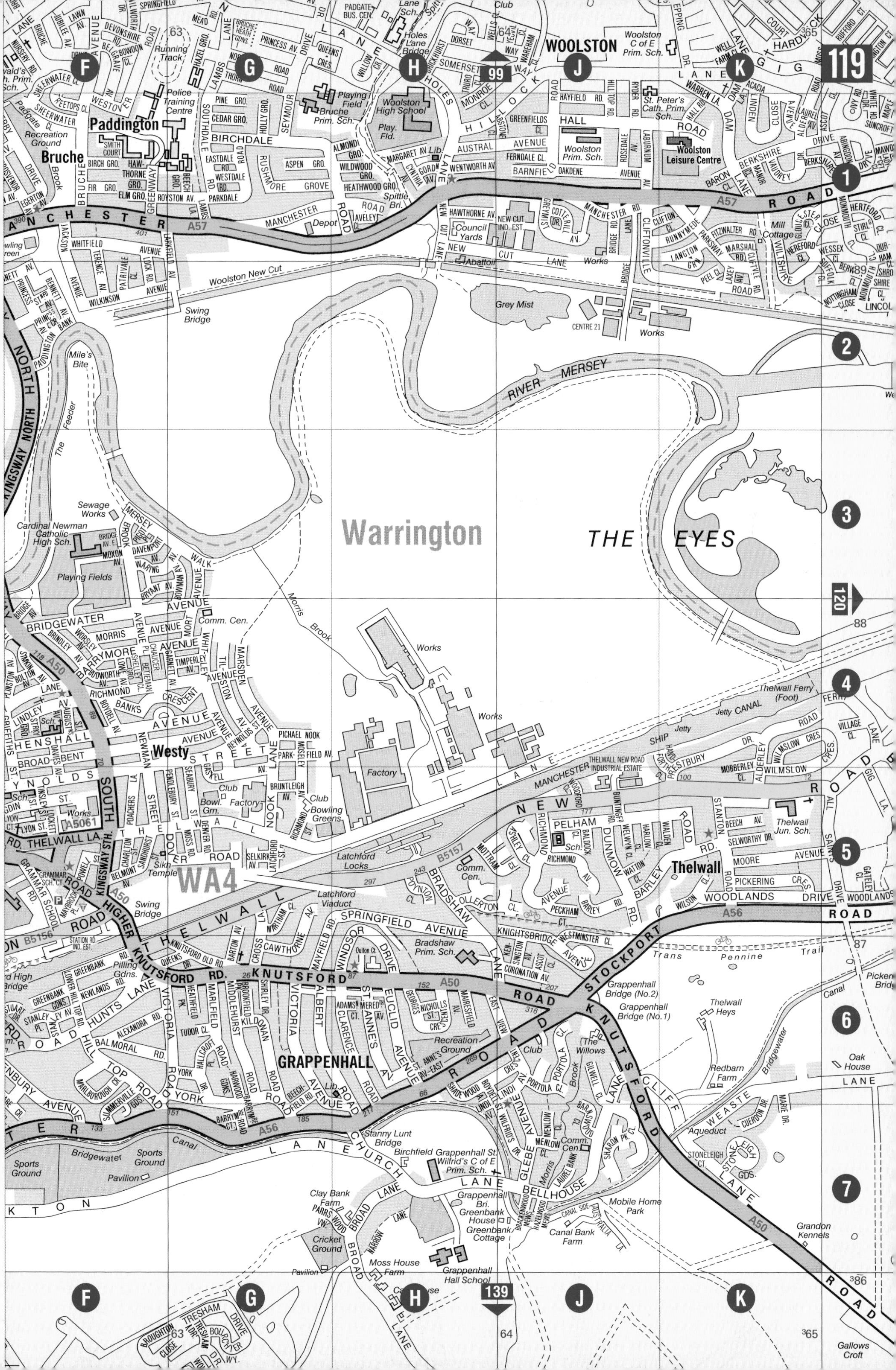
Woolston
Paddington
Bruche
Warrington
THE EYES
Westy
Thelwall
GRAPPENHALL
WA4
River Mersey
Manchester Ship Canal
Woolston New Cut
Manchester Road
A57
A50
A56
B5157
Knutsford Road
Stockport Road
Kingsway North
Kingsway South
Thelwall New Road
Woolston Leisure Centre
Woolston High School
Police Training Centre
Cardinal Newman Catholic High Sch.
Latchford Locks
Latchford Viaduct
Thelwall Ferry (Foot)
Trans Pennine Trail
Bridgewater Canal
Grappenhall Hall School
Thelwall Jun. Sch.
Bradshaw Prim. Sch.
Grappenhall St. Wilfrid's C of E Prim. Sch.
Factory
Works
Grey Mist
Centre 21
Sports Ground
Cricket Ground
Gallows Croft
Grandon Kennels
Mobile Home Park
99
120
139

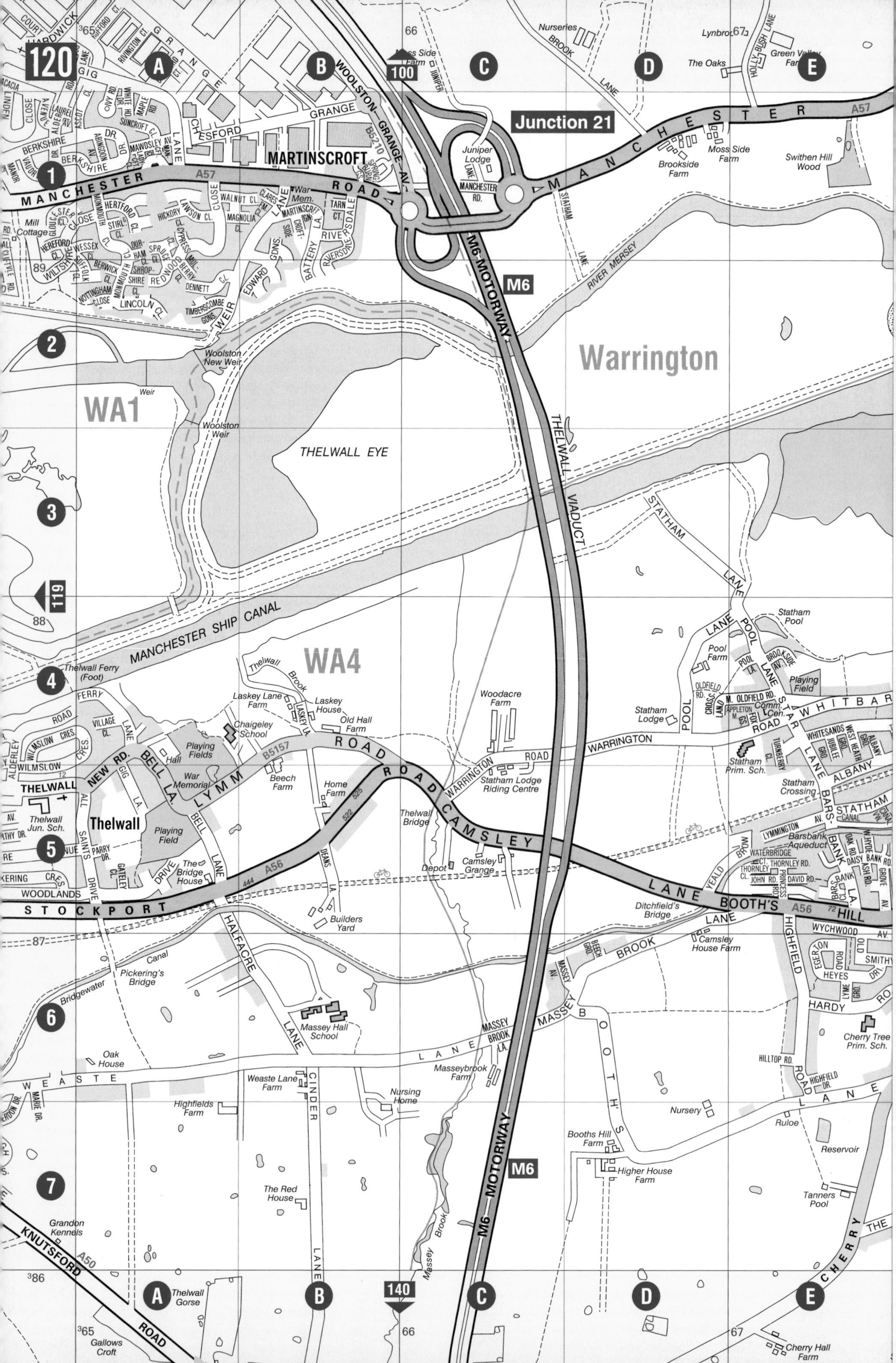

Junction 21
MARTINSCROFT
MANCHESTER ROAD
A57
WOOLSTON GRANGE AV.
M6 MOTORWAY
M6
Warrington
WA1
WA4
THELWALL EYE
Woolston New Weir
Woolston Weir
River Mersey
THELWALL VIADUCT
MANCHESTER SHIP CANAL
Thelwall Ferry (Foot)
Thelwall
Chaigeley School
Playing Fields
War Memorial
Beech Farm
LYMM ROAD
B5157
CAMSLEY LANE
STOCKPORT ROAD
A56
BOOTH'S HILL
Statham Pool
Pool Farm
Statham Lodge
Statham Prim. Sch.
Statham Crossing
Woodacre Farm
Statham Lodge Riding Centre
Thelwall Bridge
Camsley Grange
Depot
Builders Yard
Bridgewater Canal
Pickering's Bridge
Massey Hall School
MASSEY BROOK LANE
WEASTE LANE
Oak House
Weaste Lane Farm
Highfields Farm
Masseybrook Farm
Nursing Home
Booths Hill Farm
Higher House Farm
Nursery
Ruloe
Reservoir
Tanners Pool
Cherry Tree Prim. Sch.
The Red House
Grandon Kennels
KNUTSFORD ROAD
A50
Thelwall Gorse
Gallows Croft
Cherry Hall Farm
Moss Side Farm
Brookside Farm
Swithen Hill Wood
Green Valley Farm
The Oaks
Juniper Lodge
Thelwall Jun. Sch.
Ditchfield's Bridge
Camsley House Farm
Barsbank Aqueduct
100
119
140

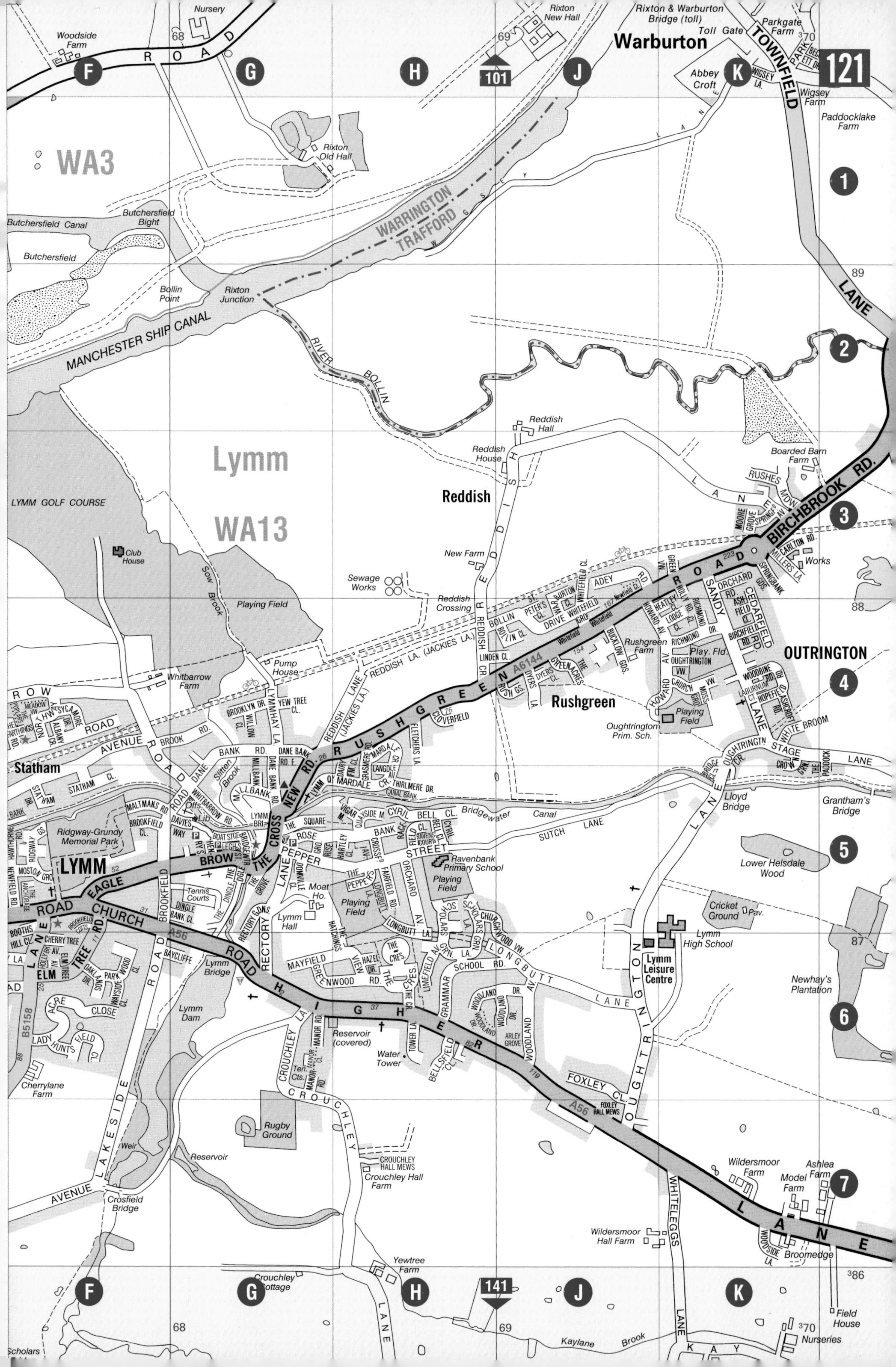
Nursery
Woodside Farm
ROAD
Rixton New Hall
Rixton & Warburton Bridge (toll)
Toll Gate
Warburton
Parkgate Farm
TOWNFIELD
Abbey Croft
WIGSEY LA.
Wigsey Farm
Paddocklake Farm
101
WA3
Rixton Old Hall
WARRINGTON
TRAFFORD
WIGSEY LANE
Butchersfield Canal
Butchersfield Bight
Butchersfield
Bollin Point
Rixton Junction
MANCHESTER SHIP CANAL
RIVER BOLLIN
LANE
Reddish Hall
Reddish House
Boarded Barn Farm
Lymm
LYMM GOLF COURSE
Reddish
WA13
BIRCHBROOK RD.
Club House
New Farm
Sewage Works
Reddish Crossing
Works
Playing Field
Sow Brook
OUTRINGTON
Pump House
Whitbarrow Farm
REDDISH LA. (JACKIES LA.)
RUSHGREEN ROAD
A6144
Rushgreen Farm
Rushgreen
Oughtrington Prim. Sch.
Play. Fld.
Playing Field
WHITE BROOM
STAGE LANE
Statham
AVENUE
BROOK RD.
NEW RD.
THE CROSS
Lloyd Bridge
Grantham's Bridge
Bridgewater Canal
SUTCH LANE
Ridgway-Grundy Memorial Park
LYMM
EAGLE BROW
PEPPER STREET
Ravenbank Primary School
Playing Field
Lower Helsdale Wood
Moat Ho.
Lymm Hall
Playing Field
Cricket Ground
Pav.
Lymm High School
Lymm Leisure Centre
CHURCH ROAD
A56
Lymm Bridge
HIGHER LANE
Lymm Dam
LONGBUTT LANE
OUGHTRINGTON LANE
Newhay's Plantation
Reservoir (covered)
Water Tower
FOXLEY CL.
FOXLEY HALL MEWS
Cherrylane Farm
CROUCHLEY LANE
Rugby Ground
Weir
Reservoir
LAKESIDE ROAD
CROUCHLEY HALL MEWS
Crouchley Hall Farm
Wildersmoor Farm
Ashlea Farm
Model Farm
WHITELEGGS LANE
AVENUE
Crosfield Bridge
Wildersmoor Hall Farm
Broomedge
Yewtree Farm
Crouchley Cottage
141
Field House
Nurseries
Kaylane Brook
KAY LANE
Scholars
F G H J K
1 2 3 4 5 6 7
68 69 370 386
89 88 87

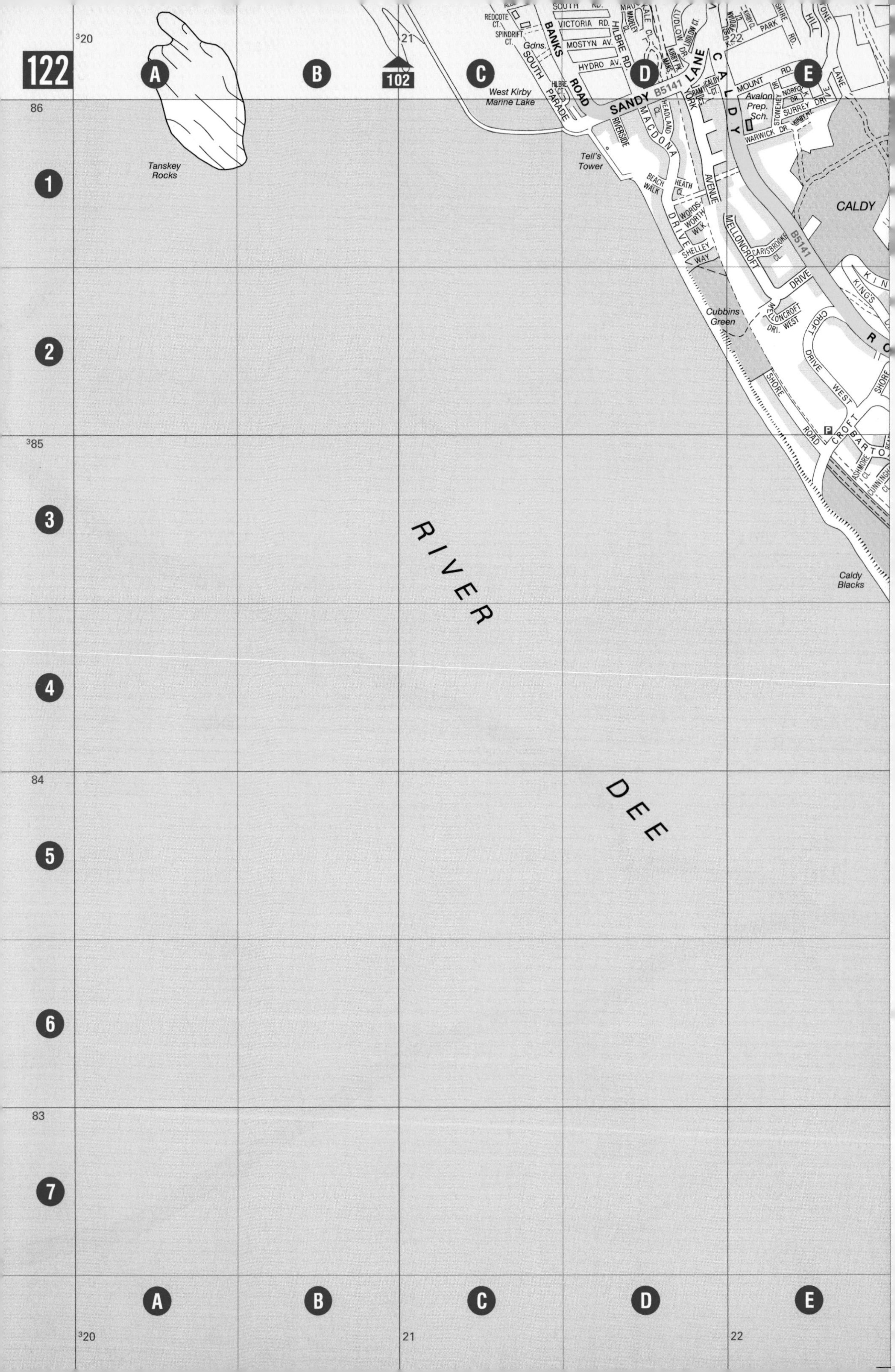

Tanskey Rocks
West Kirby Marine Lake
Tell's Tower
Cubbins Green
CALDY
Caldy Blacks
RIVER
DEE
Avalon Prep. Sch.
SANDY LANE
B5141
BANKS ROAD
SOUTH PARADE
VICTORIA RD.
MOSTYN AV.
HYDRO AV.
HILBRE RD.
RIVERSIDE
MACDONA
HEADLAND CL.
BEACH WALK
HEATH CL.
DRIVE
WORDSWORTH WLK.
SHELLEY WAY
AVENUE
YORK
CALDY
MELLONCROFT
CARISBROOKE CL.
DRIVE
MELLONCROFT DRI. WEST
CROFT DRIVE WEST
SHORE ROAD
MOUNT RD.
SURREY DR.
WARWICK DR.
STONEHEY
PARK
LANE
HILL
REDCOTE CT.
SPINDRIFT CT.
Gdns.
LUDLOW DR.
LUDLOW CT.

102

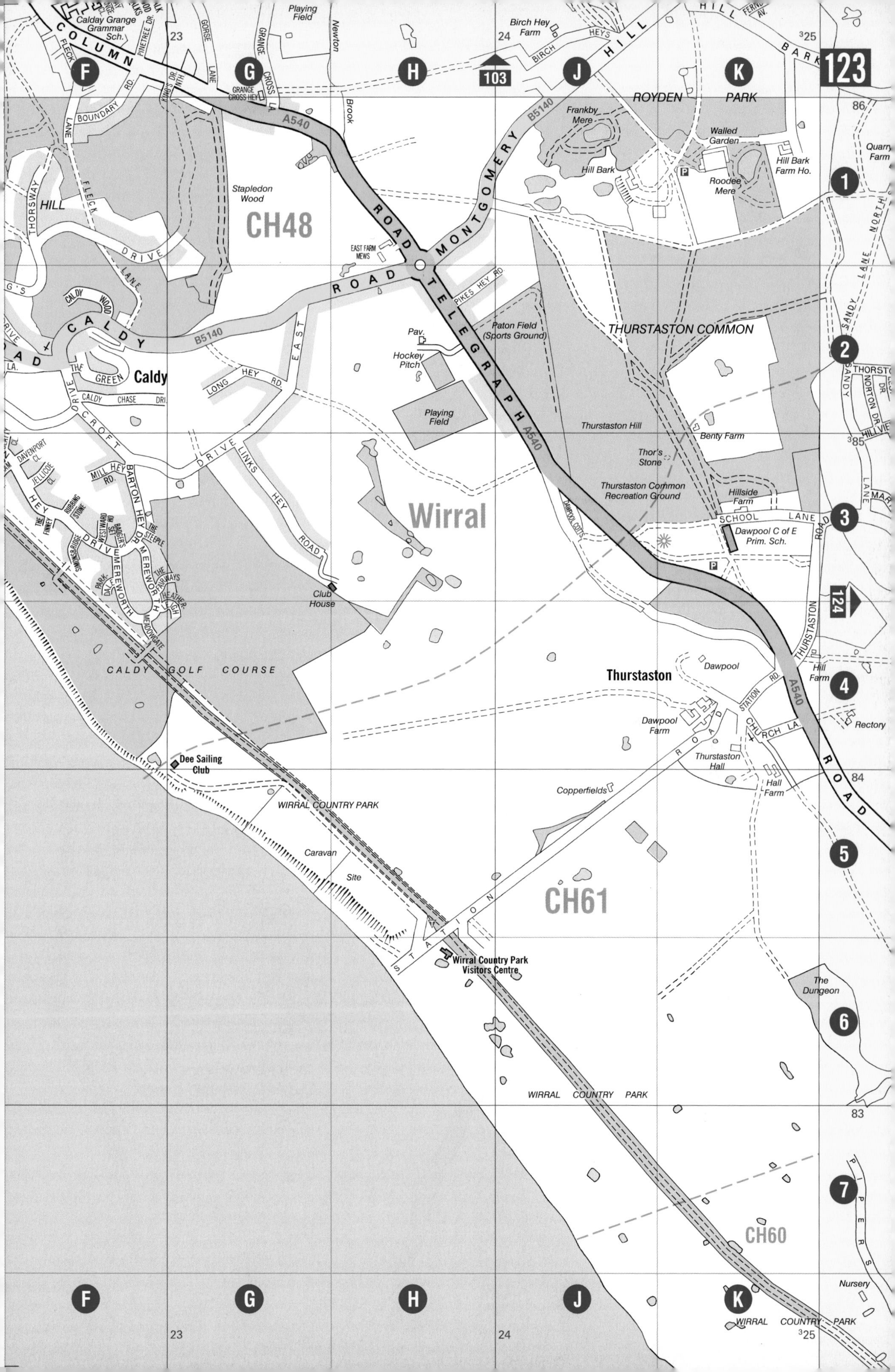
Calday Grange Grammar Sch.
Playing Field
Newton
Birch Hey Farm
BIRCH HEYS
HILL BARK
103
COLUMN
FLECK
PINETREE DR.
GORSE LANE
GRANGE
GRANGE CROSS HEY
CROSS LA.
BOUNDARY RD.
A540
Brook
MONTGOMERY
B5140
Frankby Mere
ROYDEN PARK
Walled Garden
Hill Bark
Roodee Mere
Hill Bark Farm Ho.
Quarry Farm
THORSWAY
HILL
FLECK LANE
DRIVE
Stapledon Wood
CH48
EAST FARM MEWS
ROAD
TELEGRAPH
PIKES HEY RD.
CALDY WOOD
CALDY ROAD
B5140
EAST
Pav.
Hockey Pitch
Paton Field (Sports Ground)
THURSTASTON COMMON
SANDY LANE
NORTH
THE GREEN
Caldy
CALDY CHASE DRI.
LONG HEY RD.
Playing Field
THORSTONE
NORTON DR.
HILLVIEW
DAVENPORT CL.
JELLICOE CL.
MILL HEY RD.
CROFT DRIVE
LINKS HEY ROAD
Thurstaston Hill
Benty Farm
Thor's Stone
Wirral
Thurstaston Common Recreation Ground
Hillside Farm
SCHOOL LANE
Dawpool C of E Prim. Sch.
DAWPOOL COTTS.
BARTON HEY DR.
THE STEEPLE
RUBBING STONE
WESTWARD HO
BADGERS SET
THE FINNEY
SIMONSBRIDGE
PARK DALE
MEREWORTH
THE FAIRWAYS
HEATHER LEIGH
MEADOWGATE
Club House
124
THURSTASTON ROAD
CALDY GOLF COURSE
Thurstaston
Dawpool
Hill Farm
Rectory
STATION RD.
Dawpool Farm
CHURCH LA.
Dee Sailing Club
Thurstaston Hall
Copperfields
Hall Farm
WIRRAL COUNTRY PARK
Caravan Site
CH61
STATION ROAD
Wirral Country Park Visitors Centre
The Dungeon
WIRRAL COUNTRY PARK
PIPERS
CH60
Nursery
WIRRAL COUNTRY PARK
F G H J K
1 2 3 4 5 6 7
23 24 325
86 385 84 83

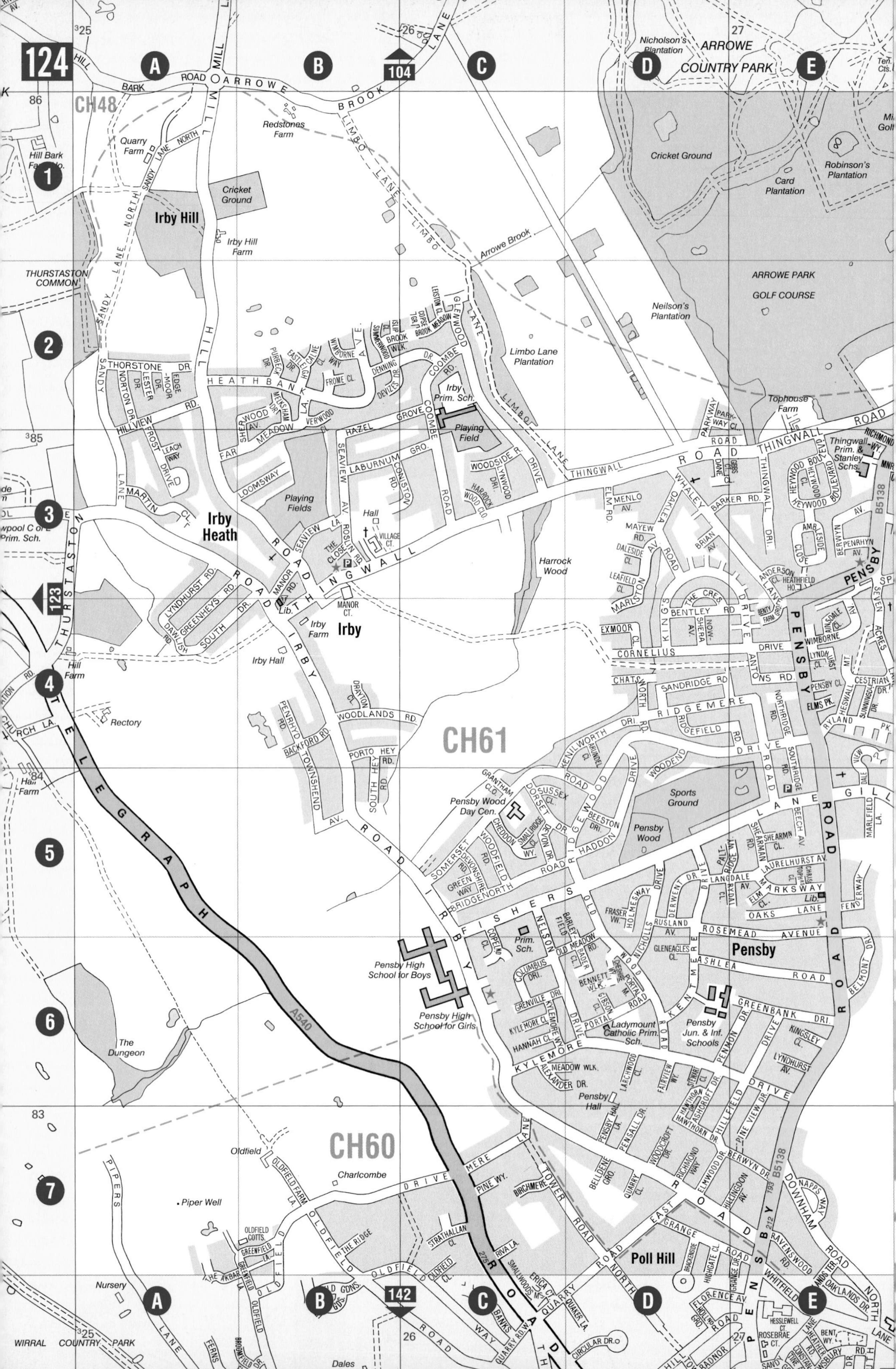

Irby Hill
Irby Heath
Irby
Pensby
Poll Hill
CH48
CH61
CH60
ARROWE COUNTRY PARK
ARROWE PARK GOLF COURSE
Cricket Ground
Robinson's Plantation
Card Plantation
Nicholson's Plantation
Neilson's Plantation
Limbo Lane Plantation
Harrock Wood
Tophouse Farm
Redstones Farm
Quarry Farm
Irby Hill Farm
Thurstaston Common
Irby Farm
Irby Hall
Hill Farm
Rectory
The Dungeon
Oldfield
Charlcombe
Piper Well
Nursery
Wirral Country Park
Pensby High School for Boys
Pensby High School for Girls
Ladymount Catholic Prim. Sch.
Pensby Jun. & Inf. Schools
Pensby Wood Day Cen.
Sports Ground
Pensby Wood
Pensby Hall
Thingwall Prim. & Stanley Schs.
Irby Prim. Sch.
Playing Field
Playing Fields
Arrowe Brook
TELEGRAPH ROAD
A540
THINGWALL ROAD
PENSBY ROAD
B5138
IRBY ROAD
ARROWE BROOK LANE
104
123
142

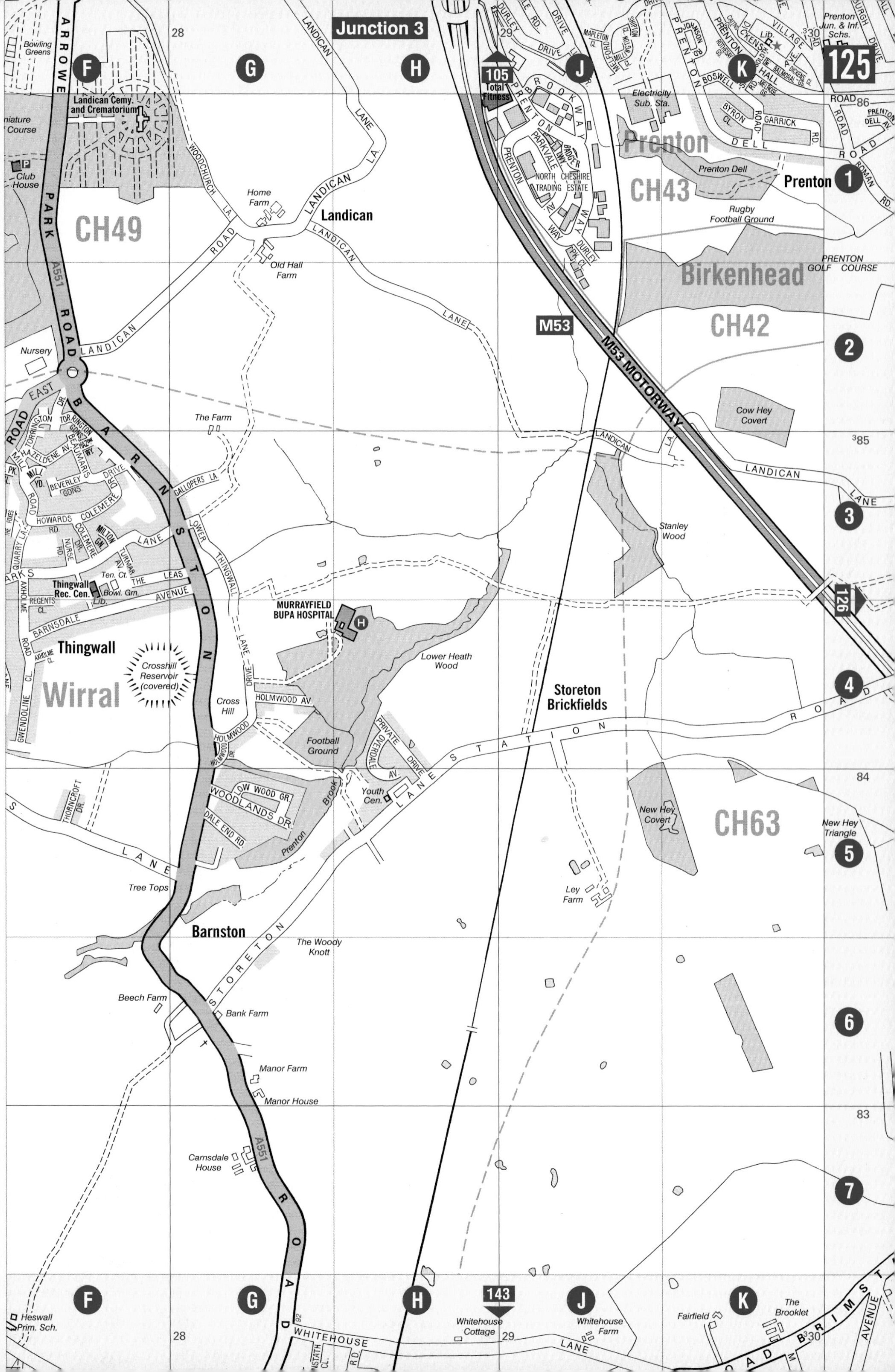

Junction 3
Landican Cemy. and Crematorium
Bowling Greens
Club House
CH49
Landican
Home Farm
Old Hall Farm
Nursery
The Farm
Thingwall
Thingwall Rec. Cen.
Wirral
Crosshill Reservoir (covered)
MURRAYFIELD BUPA HOSPITAL
Lower Heath Wood
Cross Hill
Football Ground
Youth Cen.
Tree Tops
Barnston
The Woody Knott
Beech Farm
Bank Farm
Manor Farm
Manor House
Carnsdale House
Heswall Prim. Sch.
Whitehouse Cottage
Whitehouse Farm
Fairfield
The Brooklet
Storeton Brickfields
Stanley Wood
New Hey Covert
New Hey Triangle
Ley Farm
CH63
Cow Hey Covert
M53 MOTORWAY
M53
CH42
Birkenhead
PRENTON GOLF COURSE
Rugby Football Ground
Prenton Dell
Prenton
CH43
Electricity Sub. Sta.
NORTH CHESHIRE TRADING ESTATE
Total Fitness
Prenton Jun. & Inf. Schs.
105
126
143
ARROWE PARK ROAD
A551
BARNSTON ROAD
STORETON LANE
STATION ROAD
LANDICAN LANE
WHITEHOUSE LANE

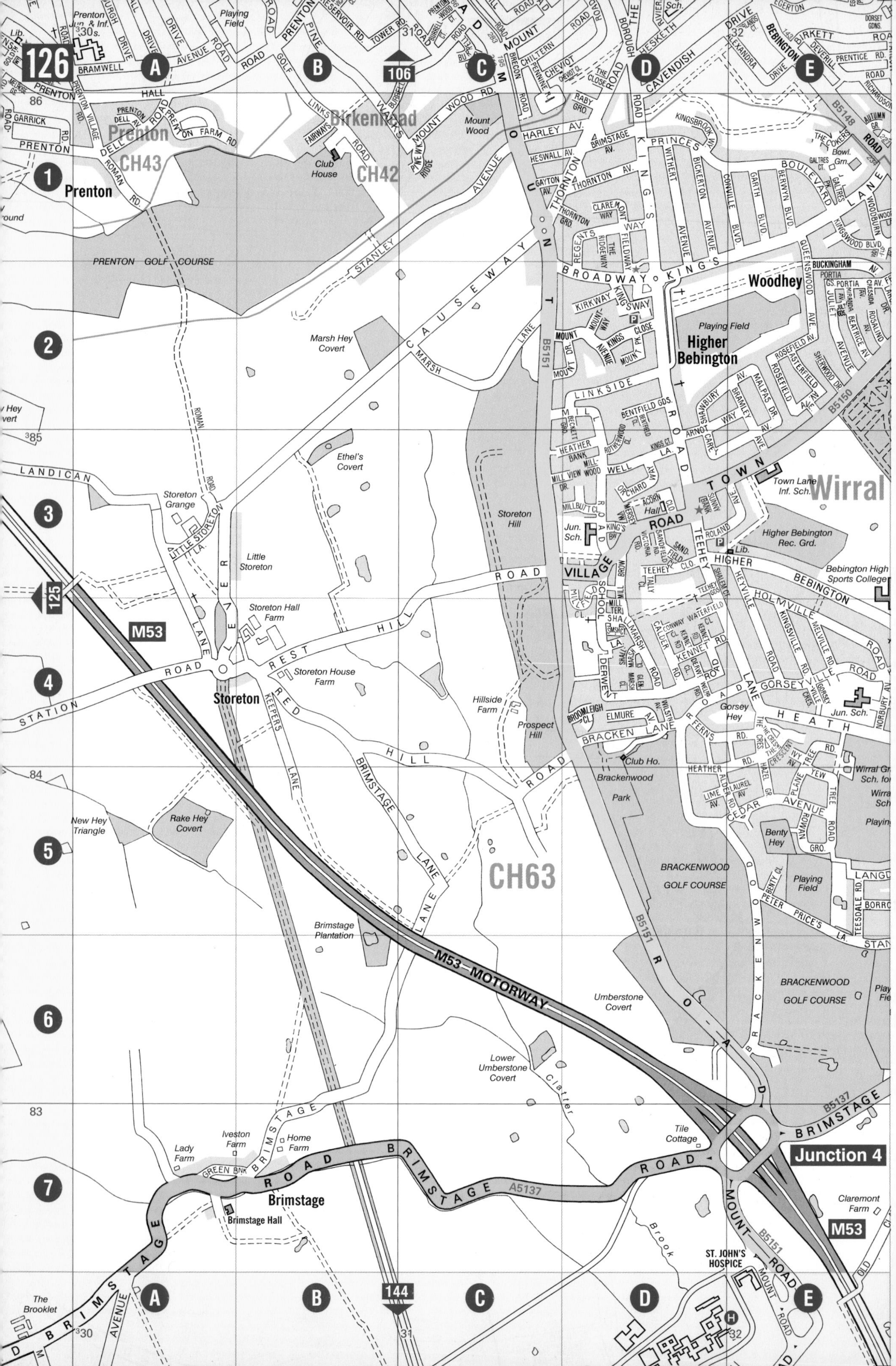

106
125
144
A
B
C
D
E
1
2
3
4
5
6
7
86
385
84
83
30
31
32
Prenton
Birkenhead
CH43
CH42
CH63
Prenton Jun. & Inf. Sch.
Lib.
Playing Field
BRAMWELL AVENUE
HALL ROAD
PRENTON HALL ROAD
PRENTON VILLAGE RD.
GARRICK RD.
PRENTON DELL AV.
DELL ROAD
PRENTON FARM RD
ROMAN RD.
PRENTON GOLF COURSE
Club House
LINKS
FAIRWAYS
WALKS
PINE WK.
MOUNT WOOD RD.
MOUNT WOOD RIDGE
Mount Wood
RESERVOIR RD.
TOWER RD.
BURRELL RD.
STANLEY AVENUE
CAUSEWAY
MARSH LANE
Marsh Hey Covert
Ethel's Covert
LANDICAN LANE
Storeton Grange
LITTLE STORETON LA.
Little Storeton
LEVER LANE
Storeton Hall Farm
REST HILL ROAD
Storeton House Farm
STATION ROAD
Storeton
RED HILL ROAD
KEEPERS LANE
BRIMSTAGE LANE
M53
M53 MOTORWAY
New Hey Triangle
Rake Hey Covert
Brimstage Plantation
Storeton Hill
Hillside Farm
Prospect Hill
Umberstone Covert
Lower Umberstone Covert
Clatter Brook
Tile Cottage
Iveston Farm
Home Farm
Lady Farm
GREEN BNK
Brimstage
Brimstage Hall
BRIMSTAGE ROAD
A5137
The Brooklet
AVENUE
MOUNT ROAD
B5151
HARLEY AV.
HESWALL AV.
GAYTON AV.
THORNTON AV.
THORNTON GRO.
BRIMSTAGE AV.
KING'S ROAD
PRINCES
WITHERT AVENUE
BICKERTON AVENUE
CONVILLE BLVD.
GARTH BLVD.
BERWYN BLVD.
BOULEVARD
KINGSWOOD BLVD.
KINGSBROOK WY.
CLAREMONT WAY
REGENTS WAY
THE RIDGEWAY
FIELDWAY
BROADWAY
KIRKWAY
KINGSWAY
MOUNT DR.
MOUNT AVENUE
KINGS CLOSE
Woodhey
Playing Field
Higher Bebington
LINKSIDE
MILL BECKETT GRO.
HEATHER BANK
MILL VIEW DR.
BENTFIELD GDS.
ROTHERWOOD CL.
KINGS CT.
WELL LA.
ORCHARD WAY
ACORN CLO.
Hall
MILLBUTT CL.
Jun. Sch.
KING'S RD.
VILLAGE ROAD
VICTORIA RD.
SANDFIELD
TEEHEY LANE
TEEHEY CLO.
TALLY
SCHOOL LANE
SHALLMARSH ROAD
CONWAY
WATERFIELD CL.
CALDER RD.
KENNET RD.
DERWENT ROAD
GLEN MARSH
SHRUBBERY AV.
BRAMLEY WAY
MALPAS DR.
ARNOT WAY
CAREY AVE.
ROSEFIELD AV.
ASTERFIELD AV.
SHERWOOD DR.
QUEENSWOOD AVE.
BUCKINGHAM AV.
PORTIA
JULIET AV.
ROSALIND AV.
BEATRICE AV.
TOWN LANE
Town Lane Inf. Sch.
Wirral
Higher Bebington Rec. Grd.
Lib.
HIGHER BEBINGTON ROAD
Bebington High Sports College
HEYVILLE
HOLMVILLE
KINGSVILLE RD.
MELVILLE RD.
GORSEY LANE
GORSEYVILLE
Jun. Sch.
HEATH ROAD
Gorsey Hey
BROOMLEIGH CL.
ELMURE AV.
BRACKEN LANE
FERNS RD.
Club Ho.
Brackenwood Park
HEATHER RD.
THE CRESCENT
IVY AV.
TREE RD.
YEW TREE
LIME AV.
LAUREL AV.
CEDAR AVENUE
ROWAN GRO.
Benty Hey
BRACKENWOOD GOLF COURSE
BRACKENWOOD ROAD
BENTY CL.
PETER PRICE'S LA.
Playing Field
TEESDALE RD.
Wirral Gr. Sch.
B5150
B5148
B5137
BRIMSTAGE ROAD
Junction 4
Claremont Farm
ST. JOHN'S HOSPICE
BEBINGTON DRIVE
BIRKETT
DEVERILL
PRENTICE RD.
EGERTON
DORSET GDNS.
RICHARDSON
CAVENDISH DRIVE
ALEXANDRA
HESKETH
THE BOROUGH ROAD
CHILTERN
CHEVIOT
RABY GRO.
THE CLOSE
Bowl. Grn.
AUTUMN GR.
THE COKERS

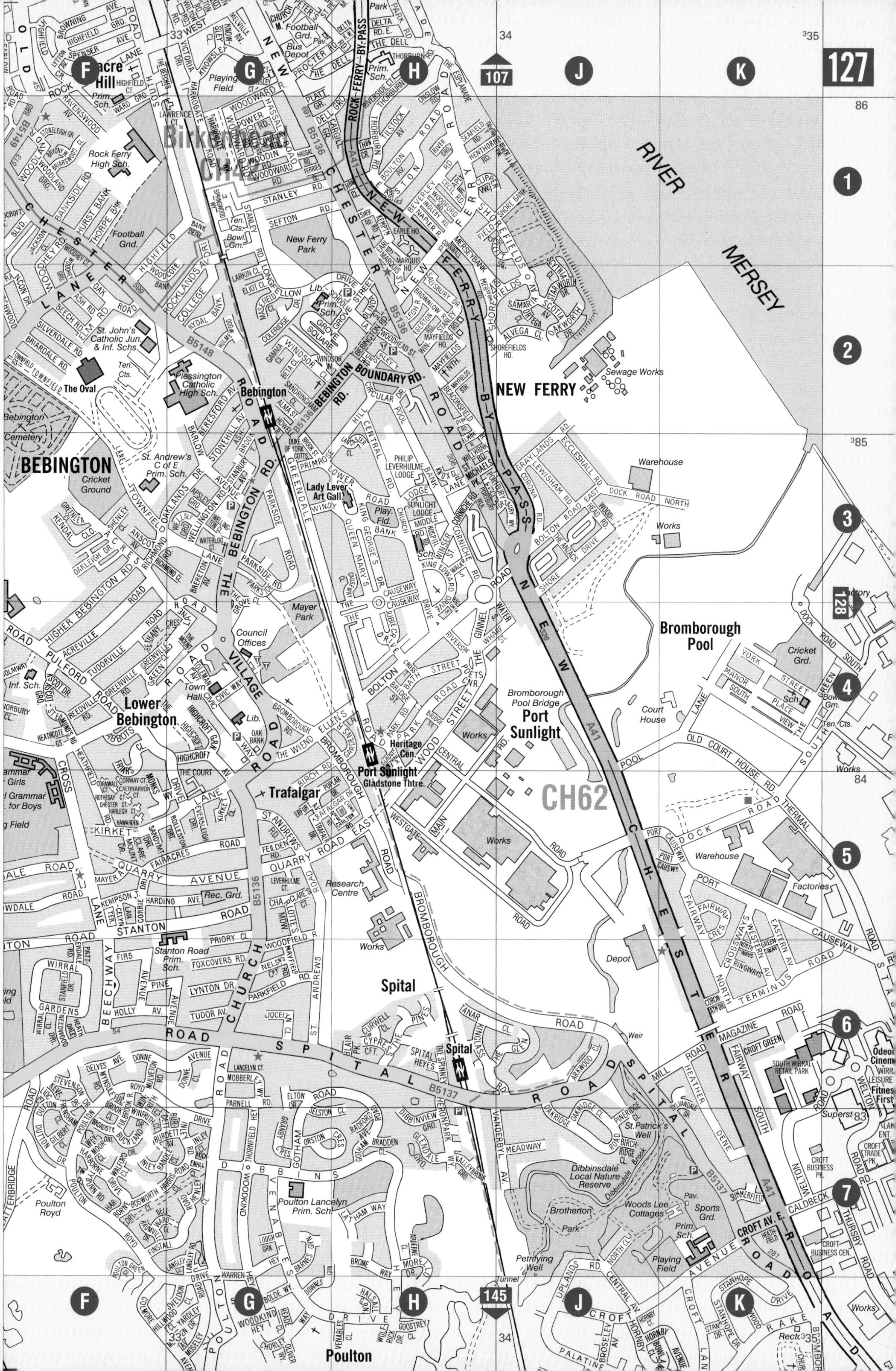

F
G
H
J
K
107
128
145
1
2
3
4
5
6
7
34
335
86
385
84
83
RIVER MERSEY
NEW FERRY
Sewage Works
BEBINGTON
Bebington
Lower Bebington
Port Sunlight
Spital
Poulton
Trafalgar
Bromborough Pool
CH62
Bebington Cemetery
Cricket Ground
The Oval
Rock Ferry High Sch.
Football Gnd.
New Ferry Park
St. John's Catholic Jun. & Inf. Schs.
Plessington Catholic High Sch.
St. Andrew's C of E Prim. Sch.
Lady Lever Art Gall.
Philip Leverhulme Lodge
Sunlight Lodge
Mayer Park
Council Offices
Town Hall
Heritage Cen.
Gladstone Thtre.
Bromborough Pool Bridge
Works
Warehouse
Court House
Cricket Grd.
Research Centre
Depot
Factories
Stanton Road Prim. Sch.
Poulton Lancelyn Prim. Sch.
Dibbinsdale Local Nature Reserve
Brotherton Park
Woods Lee Cottages
St. Patrick's Well
Petrifying Well
Sports Grd.
Playing Field
Poulton Royd
South Wirral Retail Park
Croft Business Pk.
Croft Business Cen.
CHESTER NEW ROAD
ROCK FERRY BY-PASS
NEW FERRY BY-PASS
NEW CHESTER ROAD
SPITAL ROAD
BROMBOROUGH ROAD
THE VILLAGE
CHURCH ROAD
BEBINGTON RD.
A41
B5137
B5136
B5148

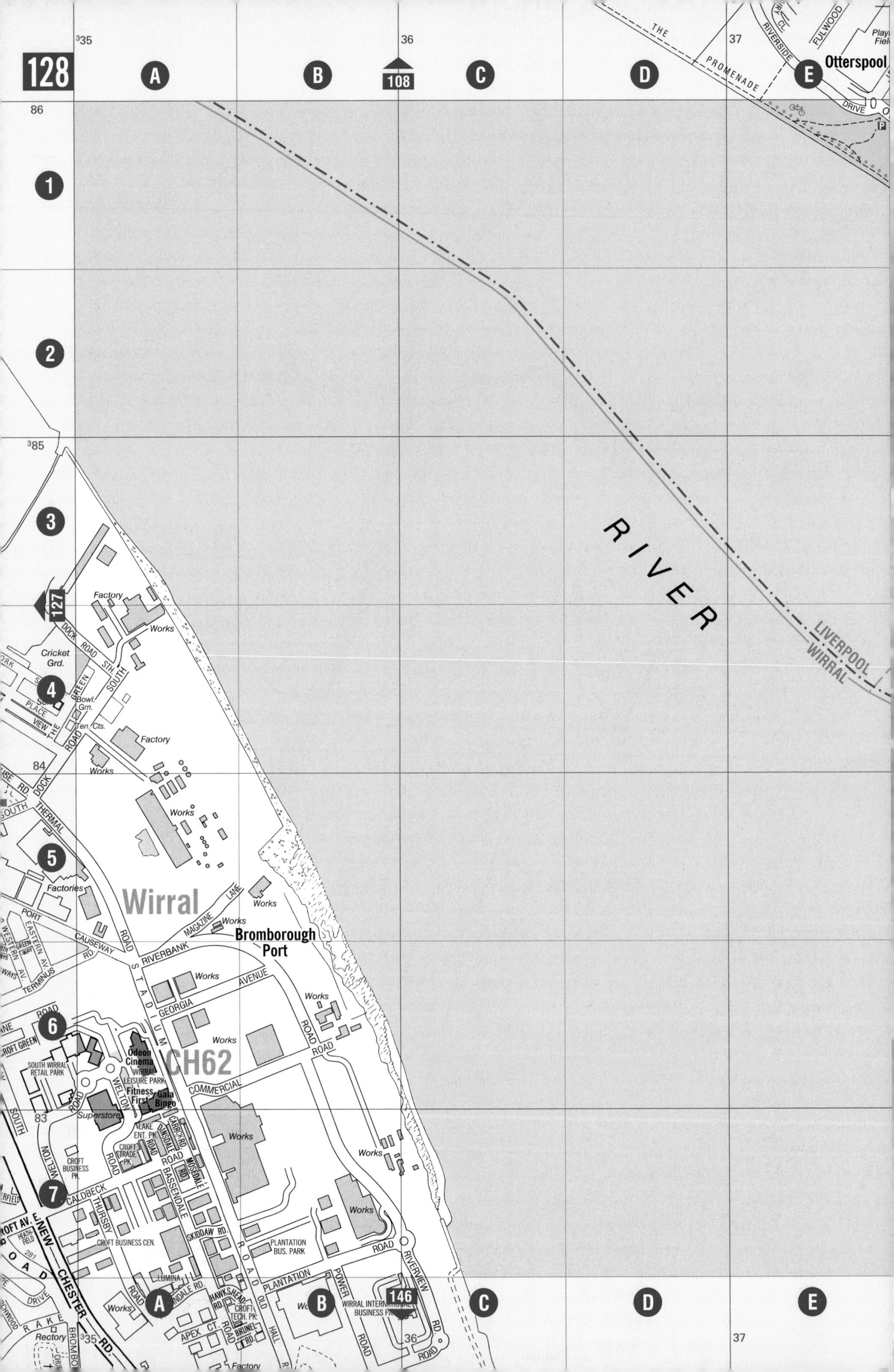

A **B** 108 **C** **D** **E** Otterspool

THE PROMENADE

1

2

385

3

127

Factory

Works

Cricket Grd.

4

Bowl. Grn.

Ten. Cts.

Factory

Works

84

Works

5

Factories

Wirral

Works

Works

Bromborough Port

Works

Works

Works

CH62

Odeon Cinema
WIRRAL LEISURE PARK
Fitness First Gala Bingo

SOUTH WIRRAL RETAIL PARK

6

Superstore

Works

83

Croft Business Pk.

Works

Works

7

Croft Business Cen.

PLANTATION BUS. PARK

LUMINA

A **B** 146 **C** **D** **E**

CROFT TECH. PK.

Wirral International Business Park

NEW CHESTER RD.

Rectory

R I V E R

LIVERPOOL WIRRAL

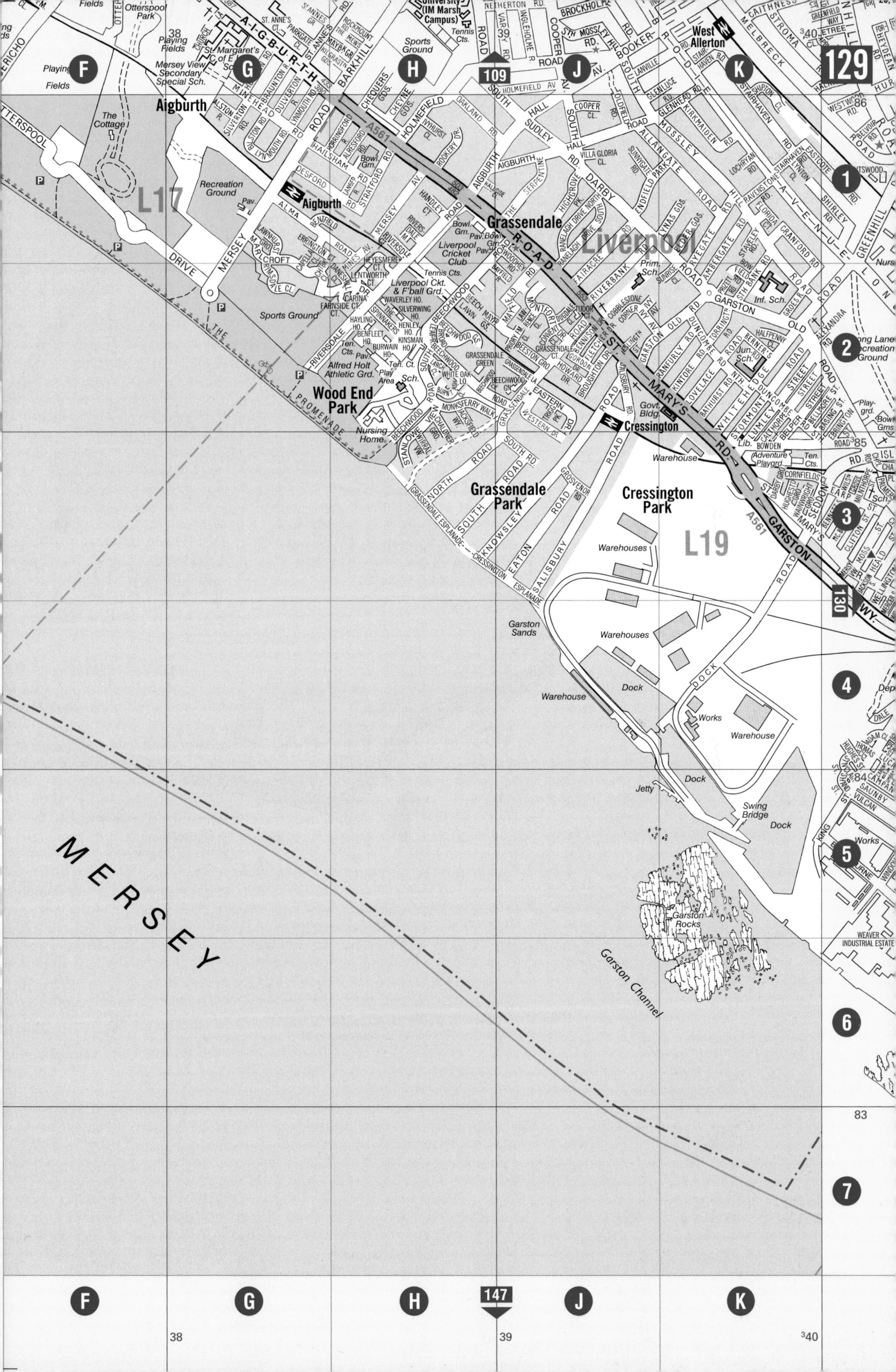
Aigburth
Grassendale
Liverpool
L17
L19
Wood End Park
Grassendale Park
Cressington Park
Cressington
West Allerton
Recreation Ground
Sports Ground
Liverpool Cricket Club
Alfred Holt Athletic Grd.
Garston Sands
Garston Rocks
Garston Channel
Warehouses
Dock
Swing Bridge
Jetty
MERSEY
AIGBURTH ROAD
ST. MARY'S RD.
A561
WEAVER INDUSTRIAL ESTATE

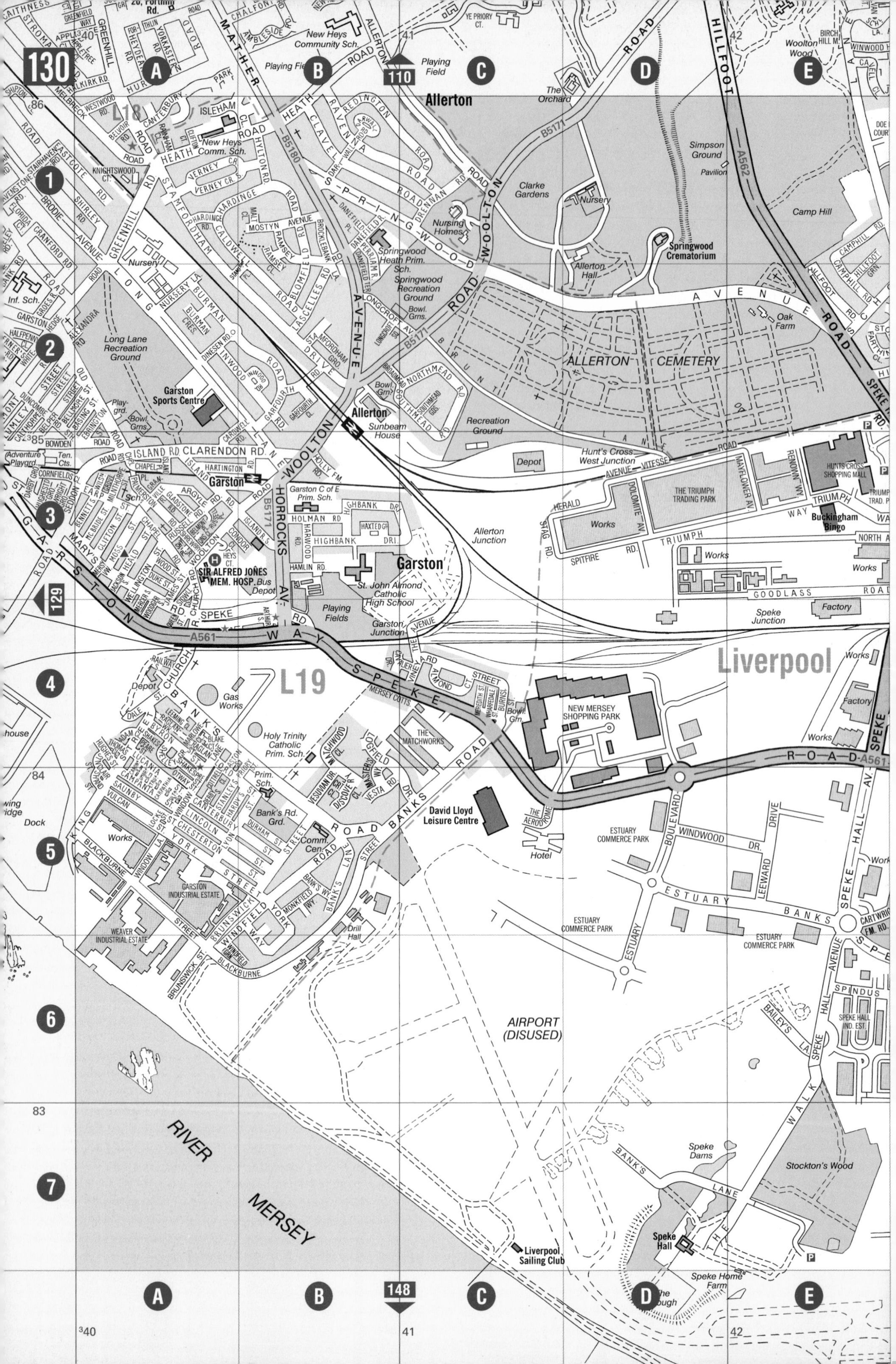

130
110
129
148
A
B
C
D
E
1
2
3
4
5
6
7
40
41
42
86
85
84
83
L18
L19
Allerton
Garston
Liverpool
MATHER AVENUE
ALLERTON ROAD
WOOLTON ROAD
HILLFOOT ROAD
SPRINGWOOD AVENUE
GARSTON WAY
SPEKE ROAD
HORROCKS AV.
HEATH ROAD
GREENHILL RD
LONG LANE
ISLAND RD
CLARENDON RD.
BANKS ROAD
ESTUARY BANKS
ESTUARY BOULEVARD
SPEKE HALL AV.
THE WALK
BANK'S LANE
TRIUMPH WAY
GOODLASS ROAD
HUNTS CROSS AVENUE
VITESSE ROAD
A561
A562
B5171
B5180
New Heys Community Sch.
New Heys Comm. Sch.
Playing Field
The Orchard
Simpson Ground
Pavilion
Clarke Gardens
Nursery
Nursing Homes
Springwood Crematorium
Allerton Hall
Springwood Heath Prim. Sch.
Springwood Recreation Ground
Camp Hill
Oak Farm
ALLERTON CEMETERY
Long Lane Recreation Ground
Garston Sports Centre
Sunbeam House
Recreation Ground
Depot
Hunt's Cross West Junction
HUNTS CROSS SHOPPING MALL
THE TRIUMPH TRADING PARK
Buckingham Bingo
Works
Allerton Junction
Garston C of E Prim. Sch.
St. John Almond Catholic High School
Playing Fields
Garston Junction
Speke Junction
Factory
SIR ALFRED JONES MEM. HOSP.
Bus Depot
Gas Works
Holy Trinity Catholic Prim. Sch.
THE MATCHWORKS
NEW MERSEY SHOPPING PARK
David Lloyd Leisure Centre
Hotel
ESTUARY COMMERCE PARK
GARSTON INDUSTRIAL ESTATE
WEAVER INDUSTRIAL ESTATE
Bank's Rd. Grd.
Comm. Cen.
Drill Hall
AIRPORT (DISUSED)
SPEKE HALL IND. EST.
RIVER MERSEY
Speke Dams
Stockton's Wood
Speke Hall
Speke Home Farm
Liverpool Sailing Club
Dock

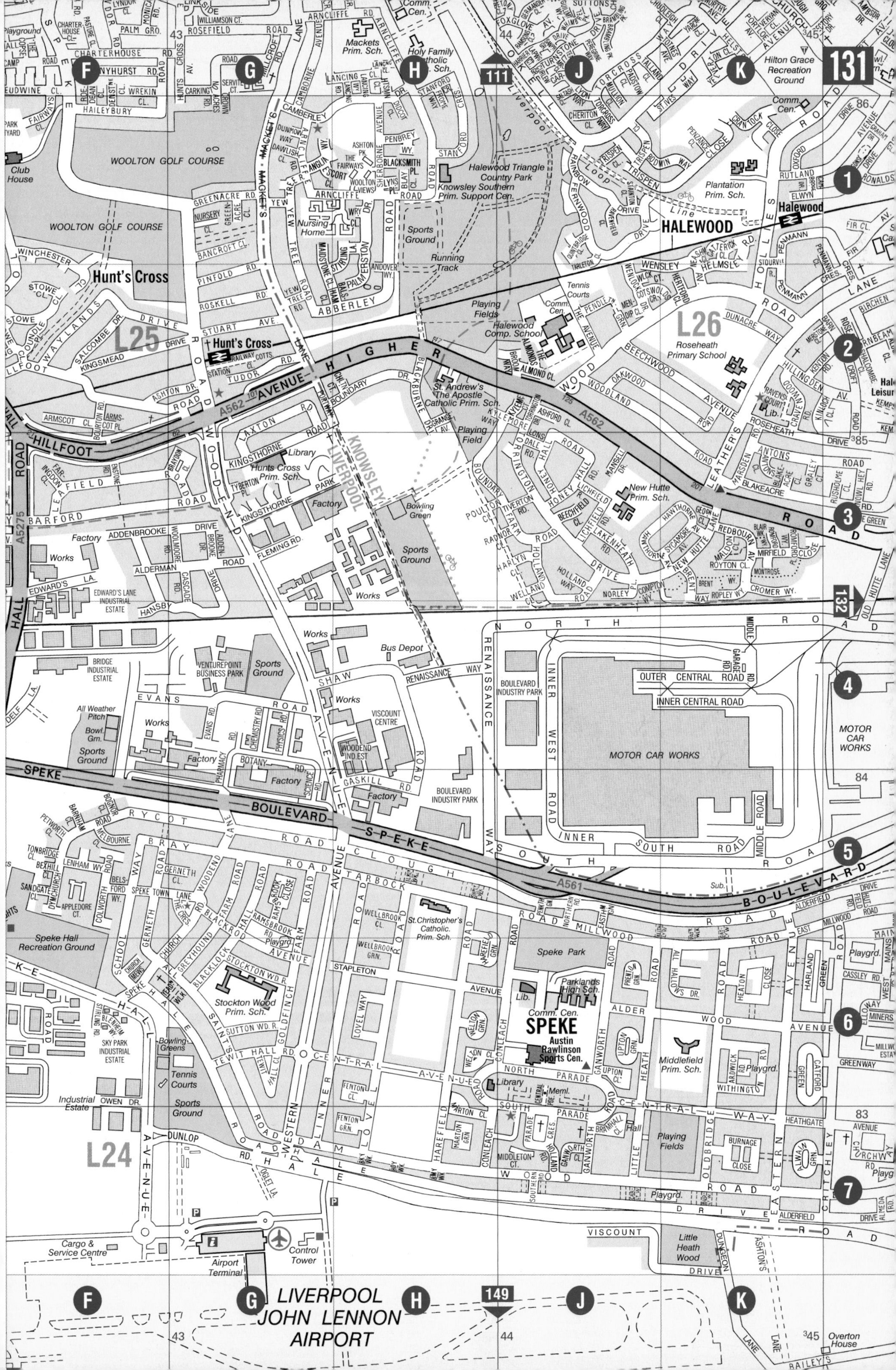
F
G
H
J
K
43
44
345
111
132
149
1
2
3
4
5
6
7
WOOLTON GOLF COURSE
Club House
Hunt's Cross
L25
L26
L24
HALEWOOD
Halewood
SPEKE
Mackets Prim. Sch.
Holy Family Catholic Sch.
Hilton Grace Recreation Ground
Halewood Triangle Country Park
Knowsley Southern Prim. Support Cen.
Plantation Prim. Sch.
Nursing Home
Sports Ground
Running Track
Playing Fields
Halewood Comp. School
Roseheath Primary School
St. Andrew's The Apostle Catholic Prim. Sch.
Playing Field
Library
Hunts Cross Prim. Sch.
New Hutte Prim. Sch.
Factory
Works
Bowling Green
EDWARD'S LANE INDUSTRIAL ESTATE
BRIDGE INDUSTRIAL ESTATE
VENTUREPOINT BUSINESS PARK
Bus Depot
BOULEVARD INDUSTRY PARK
MOTOR CAR WORKS
VISCOUNT CENTRE
WOODEND IND. EST
All Weather Pitch
Bowl. Gm.
St.Christopher's Catholic Prim. Sch.
Speke Park
Parklands High Sch.
Comm. Cen.
Lib.
Austin Rawlinson Sports Cen.
Middlefield Prim. Sch.
Speke Hall Recreation Ground
Stockton Wood Prim. Sch.
SKY PARK INDUSTRIAL ESTATE
Industrial Estate
Bowling Greens
Tennis Courts
Playgrd.
Little Heath Wood
Cargo & Service Centre
Airport Terminal
Control Tower
LIVERPOOL JOHN LENNON AIRPORT
Overton House
HIGHER AVENUE
A562
A561
A5275
HILLFOOT ROAD
SPEKE BOULEVARD
NORTH ROAD
SOUTH ROAD
RENAISSANCE WAY
INNER WEST ROAD
OUTER CENTRAL ROAD
INNER CENTRAL ROAD
INNER SOUTH ROAD
MIDDLE ROAD
WOODEND AVENUE
KNOWSLEY LIVERPOOL
MACKET'S LANE
HALE ROAD
WESTERN AVENUE
CENTRAL AVENUE
CENTRAL WAY
EASTERN AVENUE
DUNLOP ROAD
VISCOUNT DRIVE
DUNGEON LANE
ALDERFIELD DRIVE
MILLWOOD ROAD
CLOUGH ROAD
TARBOCK ROAD
STAPLETON AVENUE
LEATHERS LANE
ROSEHEATH DRIVE
BEECHWOOD AVENUE
WOODLAND
BLACKBURNE DRIVE
BOUNDARY DRIVE
HOLLAND WAY
LAKENHEATH DRIVE
CROMER WY.
OLD HUTTE LANE
WAYLANDS DRIVE
KINGSMEAD DRIVE
STUART AVE.
ROSKELL RD.
PINFOLD RD.
BANCROFT CL.
GREENACRE RD.
YEW TREE RD.
ARNCLIFFE RD.
ABBERLEY
CHARTERHOUSE ROAD
HAILEYBURY
ROSEFIELD ROAD
PALM GRO.
HUNTS CROSS AV.
EVANS ROAD
ALDERMAN ROAD
ADDENBROOKE DRIVE
BARFORD ROAD
EDWARD'S LA.
FLEMING RD.
KINGSTHORNE PARK
SHAW
GASKILL RD.
BOTANY RD.
RYCOT ROAD
BRAY ROAD
SPEKE TOWN LANE
BLACKROD AVENUE
GREYHOUND FARM ROAD
STOCKTON WD.R.
TEWIT HALL RD.
SPEKE HALL AVENUE
SPEKE CHURCH RD.
SAINTS RD.
GOLDFINCH FARM RD.
NORTH PARADE
SOUTH PARADE
ALDER WOOD AVENUE
OLDBRIDGE
HEATHGATE AVENUE
CRITCHLEY
GREENWAY
Liverpool Loop Line
TRISPEN CL.
BODMIN WAY
PENZANCE CLOSE
RUTLAND AVENUE
WENSLEY AV.
HELMSLEY RD.
DUNACRE WAY
HOLLIES ROAD
PENMANN CRES.
FIR CL.
RONALDS

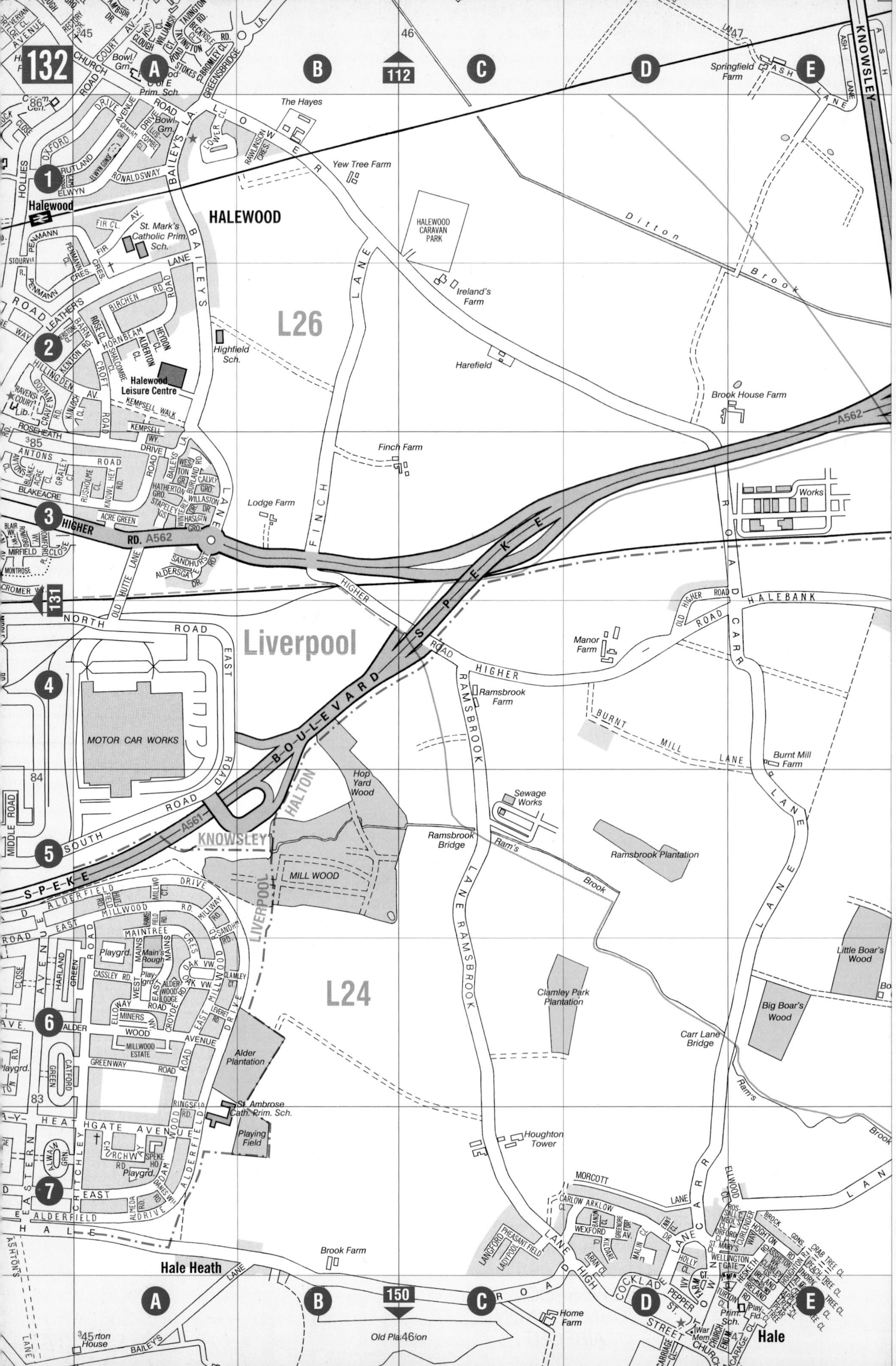
HALEWOOD
Halewood
L26
Liverpool
L24
KNOWSLEY
HALTON
LIVERPOOL
The Hayes
Yew Tree Farm
HALEWOOD CARAVAN PARK
Ireland's Farm
Harefield
Highfield Sch.
Halewood Leisure Centre
St. Mark's Catholic Prim. Sch.
Finch Farm
Lodge Farm
Brook House Farm
Springfield Farm
Works
Manor Farm
Ramsbrook Farm
Burnt Mill Farm
MOTOR CAR WORKS
Hop Yard Wood
MILL WOOD
Sewage Works
Ramsbrook Bridge
Ramsbrook Plantation
Little Boar's Wood
Big Boar's Wood
Clamley Park Plantation
Carr Lane Bridge
Alder Plantation
St Ambrose Cath. Prim. Sch.
Playing Field
Houghton Tower
Brook Farm
Hale Heath
Home Farm
Hale
Old Plantation
HIGHER RD. A562
SPEKE BOULEVARD
A561
SPEKE ROAD
HALEBANK
CARR LANE
RAMSBROOK LANE
FINCH LANE
BAILEYS LANE
LOWER ROAD
HIGH STREET
Ditton Brook
Ram's Brook
112
131
150

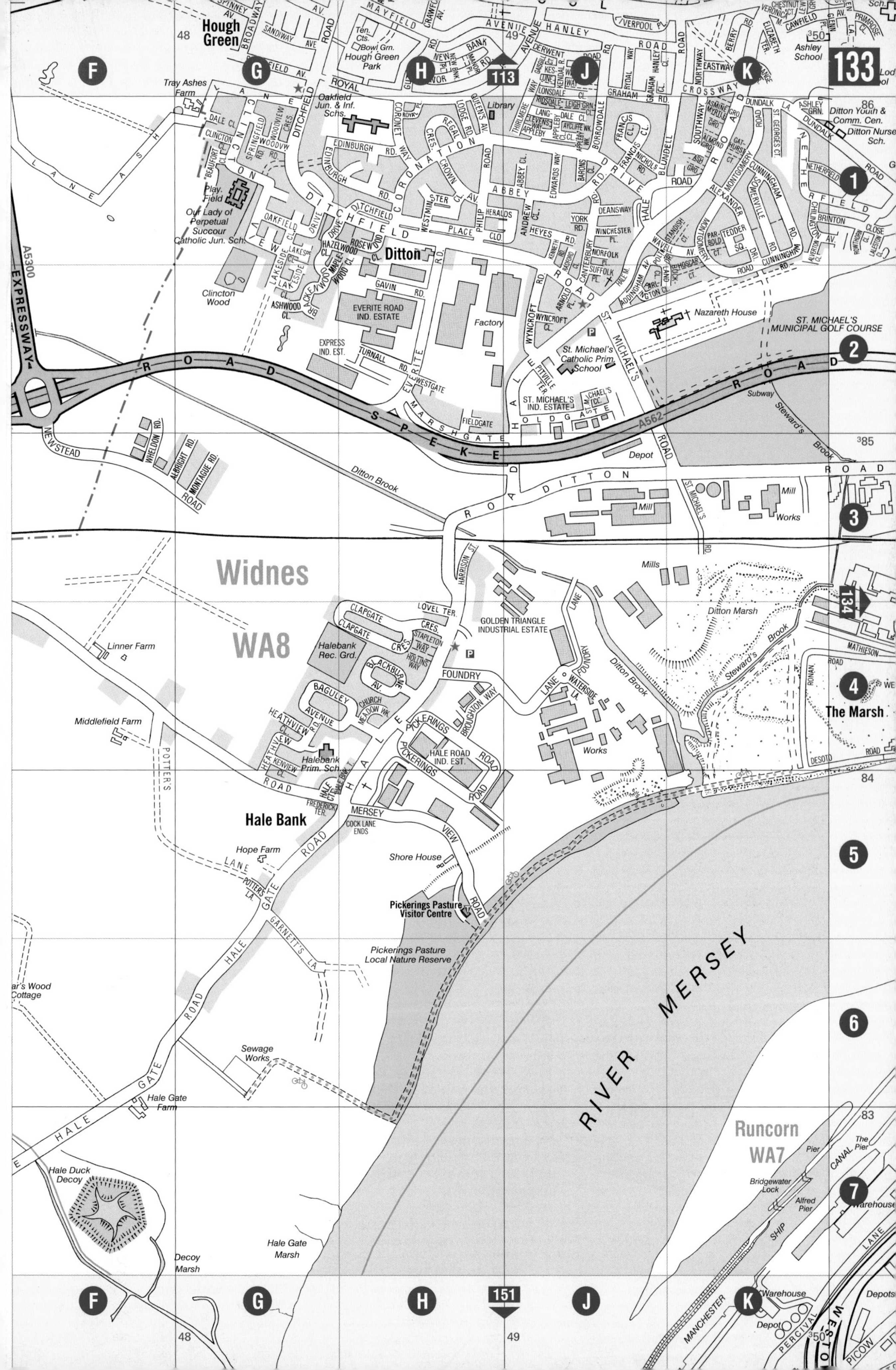
Hough Green
Ditton
Widnes
WA8
Hale Bank
Runcorn
WA7
RIVER MERSEY
SPEKE ROAD
A562
A5300
EXPRESSWAY
Everite Road Ind. Estate
Express Ind. Est.
Golden Triangle Industrial Estate
Hale Road Ind. Est.
St. Michael's Ind. Estate
St. Michael's Municipal Golf Course
Nazareth House
Oakfield Jun. & Inf. Schs.
Our Lady of Perpetual Succour Catholic Jun. Sch.
St. Michael's Catholic Prim. School
Halebank Prim. Sch.
Halebank Rec. Grd.
Hough Green Park
Ashley School
Ditton Youth & Comm. Cen.
Ditton Nurse Sch.
Library
Factory
Depot
Mill
Mills
Works
Ditton Marsh
The Marsh
Ditton Brook
Steward's Brook
Clincton Wood
Tray Ashes Farm
Linner Farm
Middlefield Farm
Hope Farm
Hale Gate Farm
Shore House
Pickerings Pasture Visitor Centre
Pickerings Pasture Local Nature Reserve
Sewage Works
Hale Duck Decoy
Decoy Marsh
Hale Gate Marsh
Bridgewater Lock
Alfred Pier
The Pier
Pier
Warehouse
Depots
Subway
Play. Field
113
134
151
F G H J K
1 2 3 4 5 6 7
48
49
350
386
385
84
83

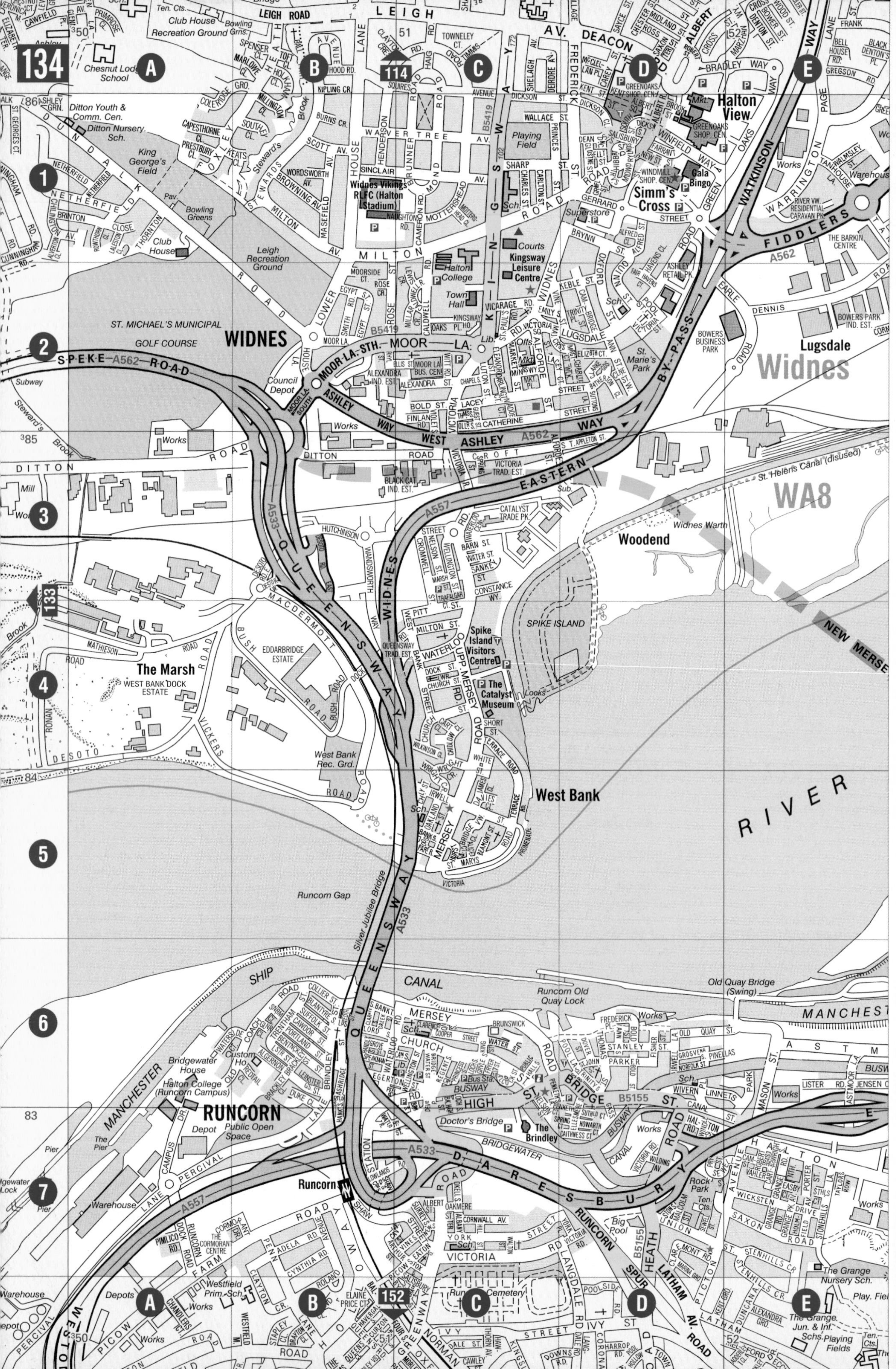

WIDNES
Widnes
RUNCORN
WA8
RIVER
Runcorn Gap
Silver Jubilee Bridge
QUEENSWAY
A533
SPEKE ROAD
A562
WEST ASHLEY WAY
EASTERN
WIDNES WAY
A557
DARESBURY
RUNCORN SPUR ROAD
FIDDLERS
WATKINSON WAY
B5155
B5419
LEIGH ROAD
DITTON ROAD
MILTON AV.
MOOR LA.
MOOR LA. STH.
SHIP CANAL
MANCHESTER
BRIDGE ST.
HIGH ST.
VICTORIA RD.
HEATH RD.
NEW MERSEY
Chesnut Lodge School
Ditton Youth & Comm. Cen.
Ditton Nursery Sch.
King George's Field
Leigh Recreation Ground
ST. MICHAEL'S MUNICIPAL GOLF COURSE
Bowling Greens
Club House
Widnes Vikings RLFC (Halton Stadium)
Halton College
Town Hall
Kingsway Leisure Centre
Courts
Playing Field
Halton View
Simm's Cross
Gala Bingo
GREENOAKS SHOP. CEN.
WINDMILL SHOP. CEN.
ASHLEY RETAIL PK.
St. Marie's Park
Lugsdale
BOWERS BUSINESS PARK
BOWERS PARK IND. EST.
THE BARKIN CENTRE
RIVER VW. RESIDENTIAL CARAVAN PK.
Council Depot
Works
BLACK CAT IND. EST.
VICTORIA TRAD. EST.
CATALYST TRADE PK.
St. Helens Canal (disused)
Widnes Warth
Woodend
SPIKE ISLAND
Spike Island Visitors Centre
The Catalyst Museum
Locks
West Bank
West Bank Rec. Grd.
EDDARBRIDGE ESTATE
The Marsh
WEST BANK DOCK ESTATE
QUEENSWAY TRAD. EST.
Old Quay Bridge (Swing)
Runcorn Old Quay Lock
Bridgewater House
Halton College (Runcorn Campus)
Public Open Space
Depot
The Pier
Pier
Warehouse
Runcorn
Doctor's Bridge
The Brindley
Bus Sta.
Big Pool
Rock Park
THE CORMORANT CENTRE
Westfield Prim. Sch.
Runcorn Cemetery
The Grange Nursery Sch.
The Grange Jun. & Inf. Schs.
Playing Fields
114
133
152
A
B
C
D
E
1
2
3
4
5
6
7

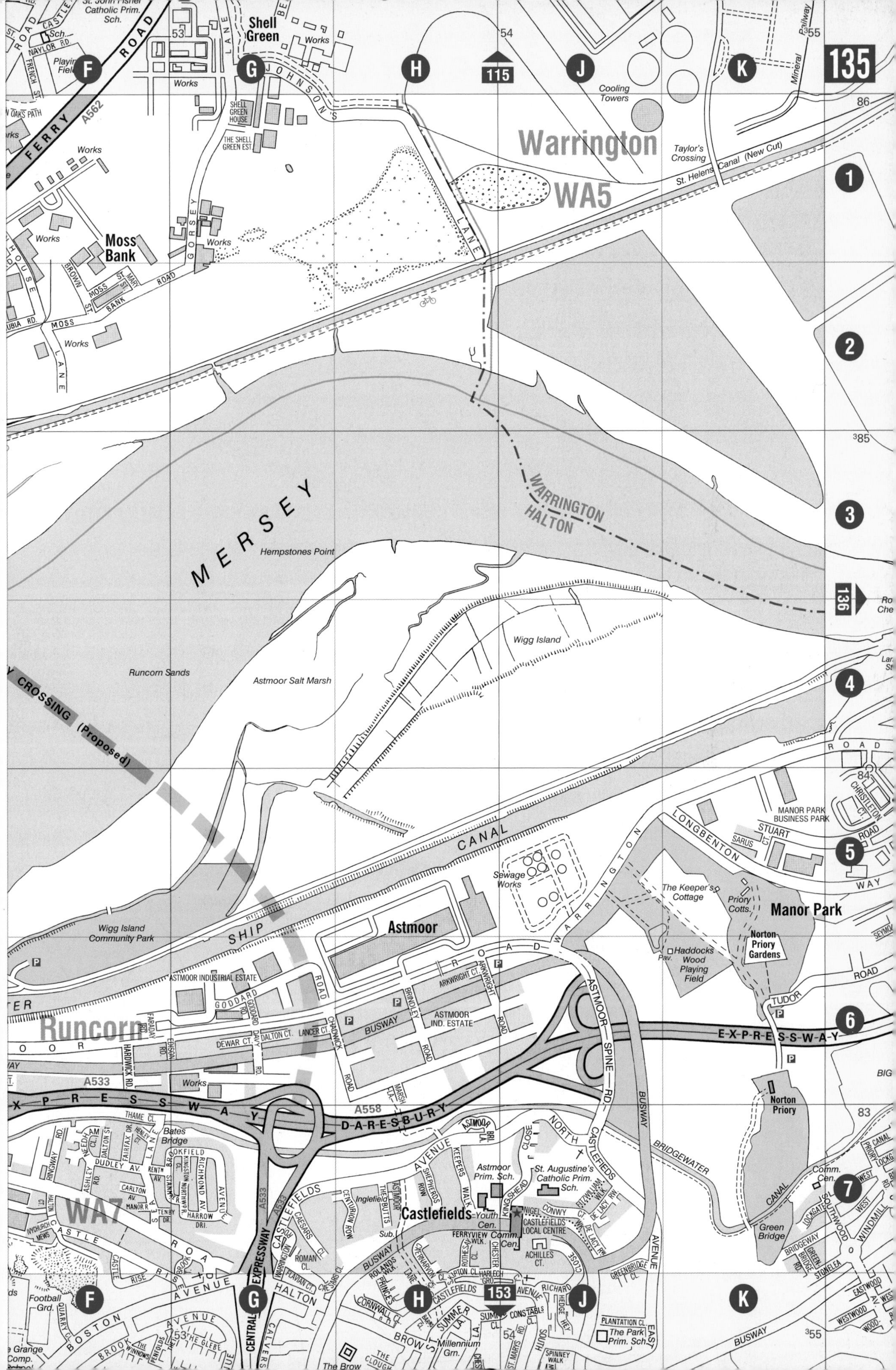

Shell Green
Works
Warrington
WA5
Cooling Towers
Taylor's Crossing
St. Helens Canal (New Cut)
Moss Bank
MERSEY
WARRINGTON
HALTON
Hempstones Point
Wigg Island
Runcorn Sands
Astmoor Salt Marsh
CROSSING (Proposed)
SHIP CANAL
Sewage Works
Astmoor
ASTMOOR INDUSTRIAL ESTATE
ASTMOOR IND. ESTATE
Wigg Island Community Park
Runcorn
MANOR PARK BUSINESS PARK
The Keeper's Cottage
Priory Cotts.
Manor Park
Norton Priory Gardens
Haddocks Wood Playing Field
Norton Priory
EXPRESSWAY
DARESBURY
A558
A533
A562
WA7
Castlefields
Astmoor Prim. Sch.
St. Augustine's Catholic Prim. Sch.
Youth Cen.
Comm. Cen.
CASTLEFIELDS LOCAL CENTRE
Bates Bridge
Green Bridge
BRIDGEWATER CANAL
Football Grd.
The Park Prim. Sch.
Millennium Grn.
The Brow
115
136
153

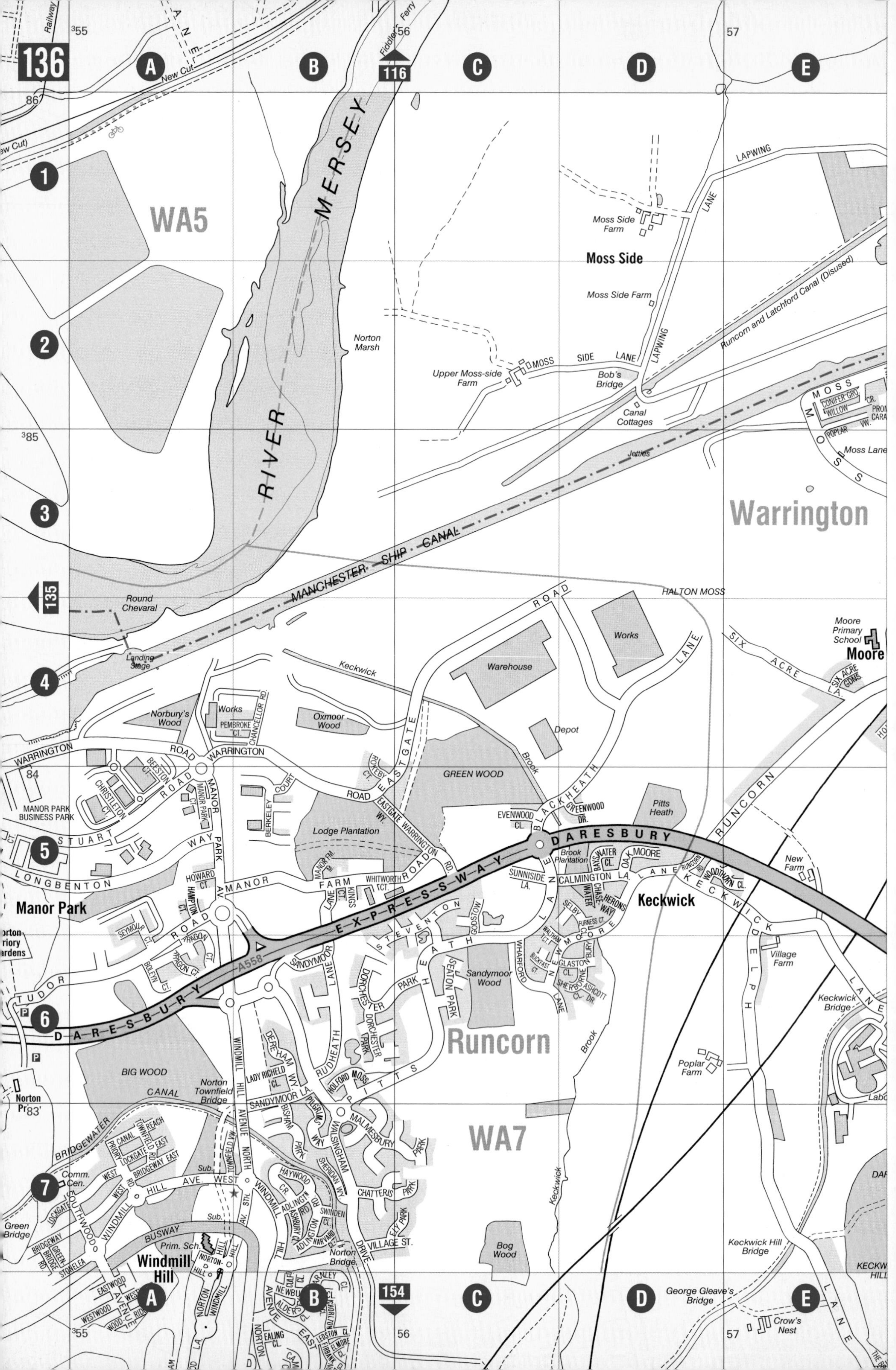
A
B
C
D
E
116
1
2
3
4
5
6
7
135
154
WA5
RIVER MERSEY
New Cut
Fiddler's Ferry
Norton Marsh
Moss Side Farm
Moss Side
Upper Moss-side Farm
Bob's Bridge
Canal Cottages
LAPWING LANE
MOSS SIDE LANE
Runcorn and Latchford Canal (Disused)
Jetties
Warrington
MANCHESTER SHIP CANAL
Round Chevaral
Landing Stage
HALTON MOSS
Moore Primary School
Moore
SIX ACRE LA.
Keckwick
Warehouse
Works
Depot
Norbury's Wood
Oxmoor Wood
GREEN WOOD
Lodge Plantation
Pitts Heath
Brook Plantation
MANOR PARK BUSINESS PARK
WARRINGTON ROAD
STUART WAY
LONGBENTON
Manor Park
MANOR PARK AV.
MANOR ROAD
EASTGATE ROAD
DARESBURY EXPRESSWAY
A558
Keckwick
KECKWICK LANE
New Farm
Village Farm
Keckwick Bridge
DELPH LANE
RUNCORN ROAD
Sandymoor Wood
Runcorn
Poplar Farm
BIG WOOD
Norton Townfield Bridge
BRIDGEWATER CANAL
WA7
Comm. Cen.
Green Bridge
Windmill Hill
Prim. Sch.
Norton Bridge
Bog Wood
Keckwick Hill Bridge
George Gleave's Bridge
Crow's Nest
55
56
57
85
84
83
86

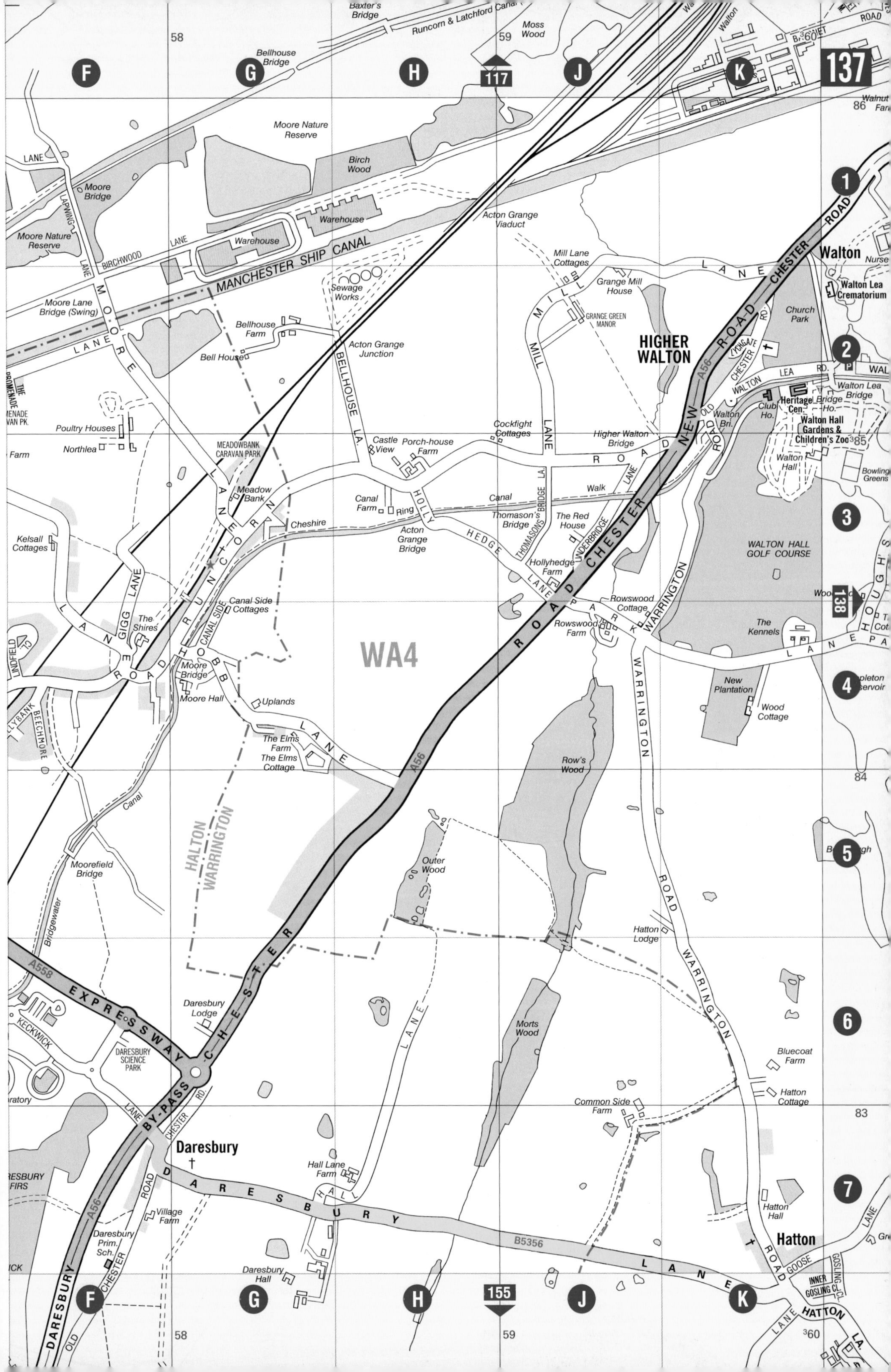
Baxter's Bridge
Runcorn & Latchford Canal
Moss Wood
Bellhouse Bridge
Moore Nature Reserve
Birch Wood
Moore Bridge
Warehouse
Warehouse
Acton Grange Viaduct
MANCHESTER SHIP CANAL
Moore Lane Bridge (Swing)
Sewage Works
Bellhouse Farm
Bell House
Acton Grange Junction
Mill Lane Cottages
Grange Mill House
GRANGE GREEN MANOR
HIGHER WALTON
Walton
Walton Lea Crematorium
Church Park
Walton Lea Bridge
Heritage Cen.
Club Ho.
Walton Bri.
Walton Hall Gardens & Children's Zoo
Walton Hall
Bowling Greens
Poultry Houses
Northlea
MEADOWBANK CARAVAN PARK
Castle View
Porch-house Farm
Cockfight Cottages
Higher Walton Bridge
Meadow Bank
Canal Farm
Ring
Canal
Thomason's Bridge
The Red House
Acton Grange Bridge
Cheshire
Kelsall Cottages
Hollyhedge Farm
WALTON HALL GOLF COURSE
Canal Side Cottages
Rowswood Cottage
Rowswood Farm
The Shires
The Kennels
WA4
Moore Bridge
Moore Hall
Uplands
New Plantation
Wood Cottage
The Elms Farm
The Elms Cottage
Row's Wood
HALTON
WARRINGTON
Canal
Moorefield Bridge
Outer Wood
Bridgewater
Hatton Lodge
Daresbury Lodge
Morts Wood
DARESBURY SCIENCE PARK
Bluecoat Farm
Hatton Cottage
Common Side Farm
Daresbury
Hall Lane Farm
Village Farm
Daresbury Prim. Sch.
Daresbury Hall
Hatton Hall
Hatton
B5356
A56
A558
EXPRESSWAY
CHESTER BY-PASS
DARESBURY LANE
NEW CHESTER ROAD
WARRINGTON ROAD
HOLLY HEDGE LANE
BELLHOUSE LA.
MILL LANE
MOORE LANE
RUNCORN ROAD
HOBB LANE
GIGG LANE
PARK LANE
HALL LANE
GOOSE LANE
HATTON LANE
INNER GOSLING CL.
117
138
155
58
59
360
86
85
84
83
F G H J K
1 2 3 4 5 6 7

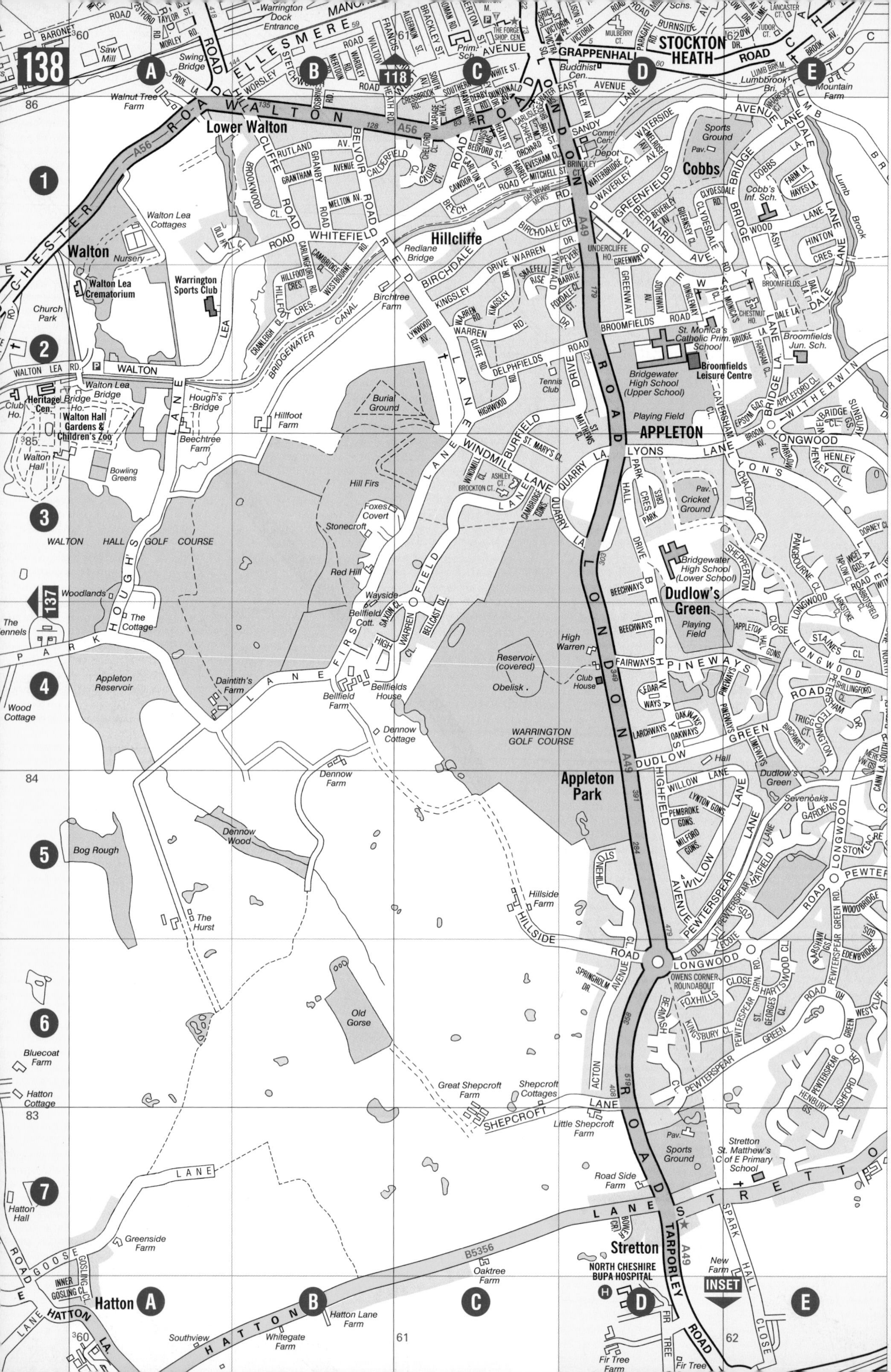
Lower Walton
Walton
Walton Lea Crematorium
Warrington Sports Club
Hillcliffe
Cobbs
APPLETON
Dudlow's Green
Appleton Park
STOCKTON HEATH
Stretton
NORTH CHESHIRE BUPA HOSPITAL
Hatton
Walton Hall Gardens & Children's Zoo
Heritage Cen.
Bridgewater High School (Upper School)
Bridgewater High School (Lower School)
Broomfields Leisure Centre
St. Monica's Catholic Prim. School
WALTON HALL GOLF COURSE
WARRINGTON GOLF COURSE
Appleton Reservoir
Bog Rough
Old Gorse
Dennow Wood
Hill Firs
Burial Ground
Reservoir (covered)
Obelisk
Sports Ground
Playing Field
Cricket Ground
A56
A49
B5356
CHESTER ROAD
LONDON ROAD
TARPORLEY ROAD
HATTON LANE
STRETTON LANE
BRIDGEWATER CANAL
INSET
118
137
A B C D E
1 2 3 4 5 6 7
60 61 62
83 84 85 86

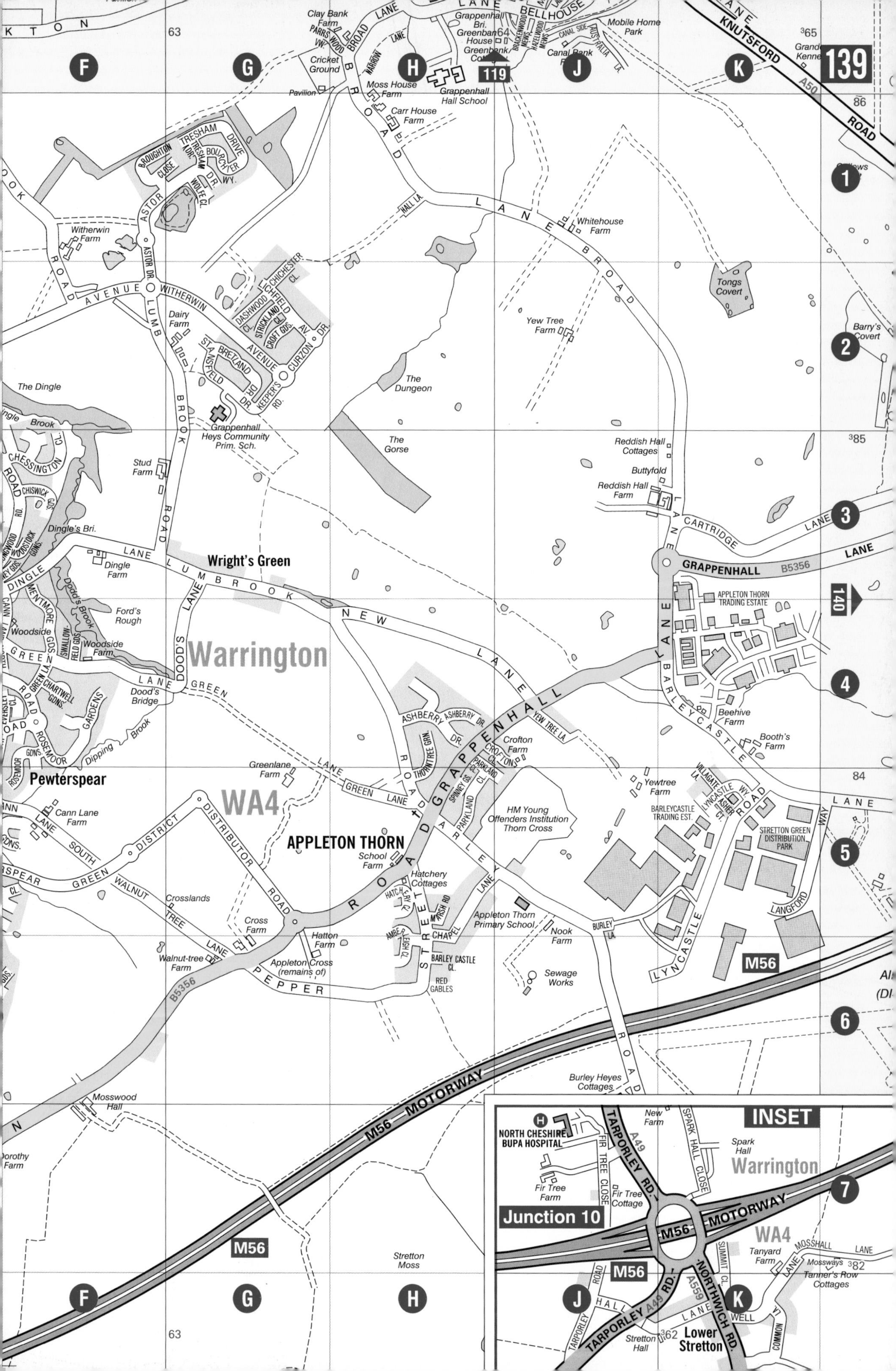
Warrington
Wright's Green
APPLETON THORN
Pewterspear
WA4
M56 MOTORWAY
GRAPPENHALL LANE
BROAD LANE
LUMB BROOK ROAD
NEW LANE
BARLEYCASTLE LANE
KNUTSFORD ROAD
A50
B5356
Grappenhall Hall School
Grappenhall Heys Community Prim. Sch.
HM Young Offenders Institution Thorn Cross
Appleton Thorn Primary School
APPLETON THORN TRADING ESTATE
BARLEYCASTLE TRADING EST.
STRETTON GREEN DISTRIBUTION PARK
Stretton Moss
INSET
Junction 10
NORTH CHESHIRE BUPA HOSPITAL
Lower Stretton
119
140

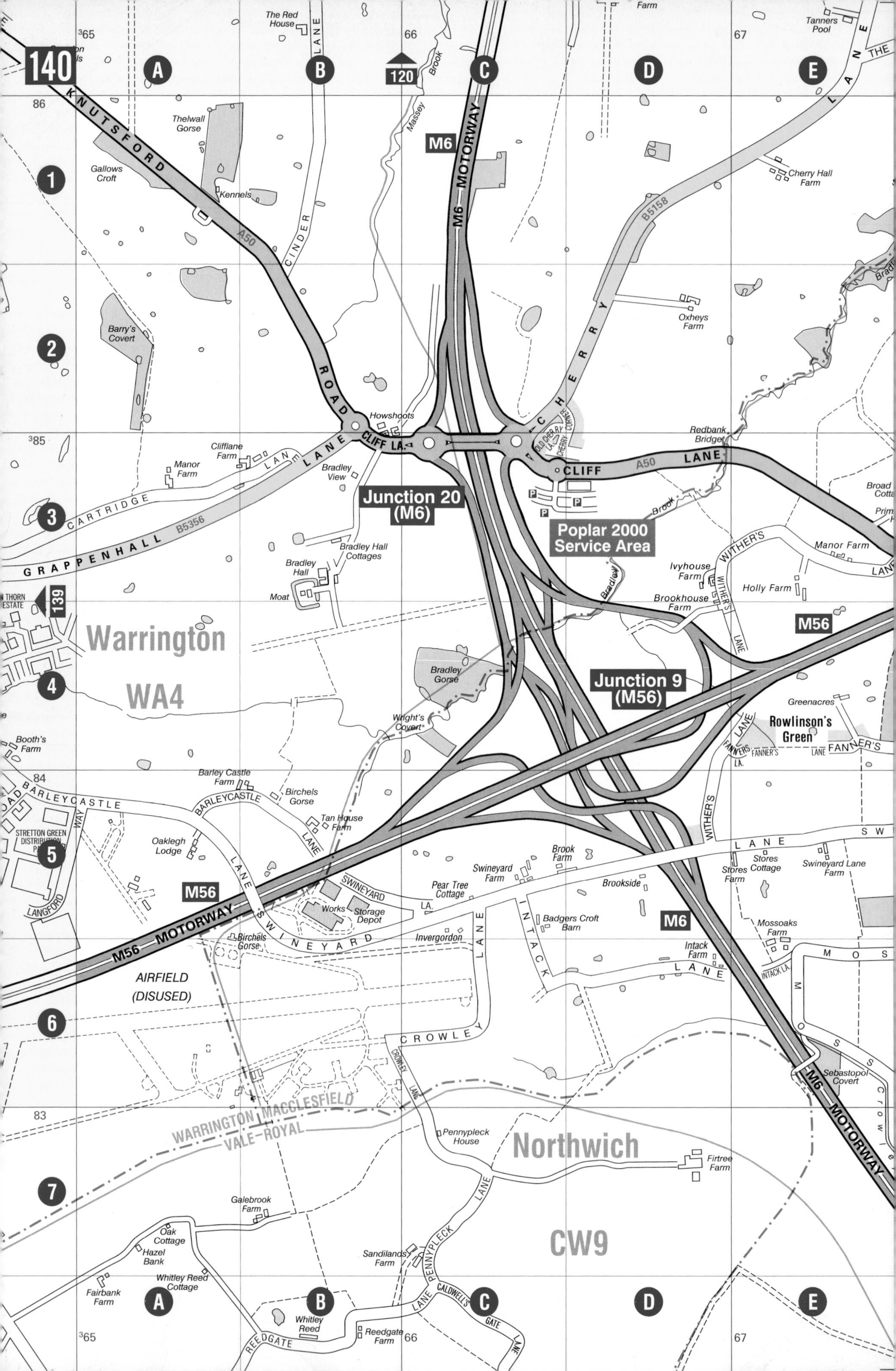

120
139
A
B
C
D
E
1
2
3
4
5
6
7
365
66
67
86
385
84
83
The Red House
Tanners Pool
Thelwall Gorse
Gallows Croft
Kennels
KNUTSFORD ROAD
A50
CINDER LANE
Massey Brook
M6
M6 MOTORWAY
B5158
Cherry Hall Farm
Barry's Covert
Oxheys Farm
CHERRY LANE
Howshoots
CLIFF LA.
CLIFF LANE
Redbank Bridge
Cliflane Farm
Manor Farm
Bradley View
Junction 20 (M6)
Poplar 2000 Service Area
CARTRIDGE LANE
GRAPPENHALL LANE
B5356
Bradley Hall Cottages
Bradley Hall
Moat
Ivyhouse Farm
WITHER'S LANE
Manor Farm
Holly Farm
Brookhouse Farm
Broad
Warrington
WA4
M56
Bradley Gorse
Junction 9 (M56)
Wright's Covert
Greenacres
Rowlinson's Green
FANNER'S LANE
Booth's Farm
Barley Castle Farm
Birchels Gorse
BARLEYCASTLE LANE
Tan House Farm
Oaklegh Lodge
STRETTON GREEN DISTRIBUTION
Brook Farm
Swineyard Farm
Pear Tree Cottage
Brookside
Stores Farm
Stores Cottage
Swineyard Lane Farm
M56 MOTORWAY
SWINEYARD LA.
Works
Storage Depot
LANGFORD
Badgers Croft Barn
Birchels Gorse
Invergordon
Mossoaks Farm
INTACK LANE
Intack Farm
INTACK LA.
MOSS LANE
AIRFIELD (DISUSED)
CROWLEY LANE
Sebastopol Covert
M6 MOTORWAY
WARRINGTON MACCLESFIELD
WARRINGTON VALE ROYAL
Pennypleck House
Northwich
Firtree Farm
Galebrook Farm
Oak Cottage
Hazel Bank
CW9
Sandilands Farm
PENNYPLECK LANE
Whitley Reed Cottage
Fairbank Farm
CALDWELL'S GATE LANE
Whitley Reed
REEDGATE
Reedgate Farm

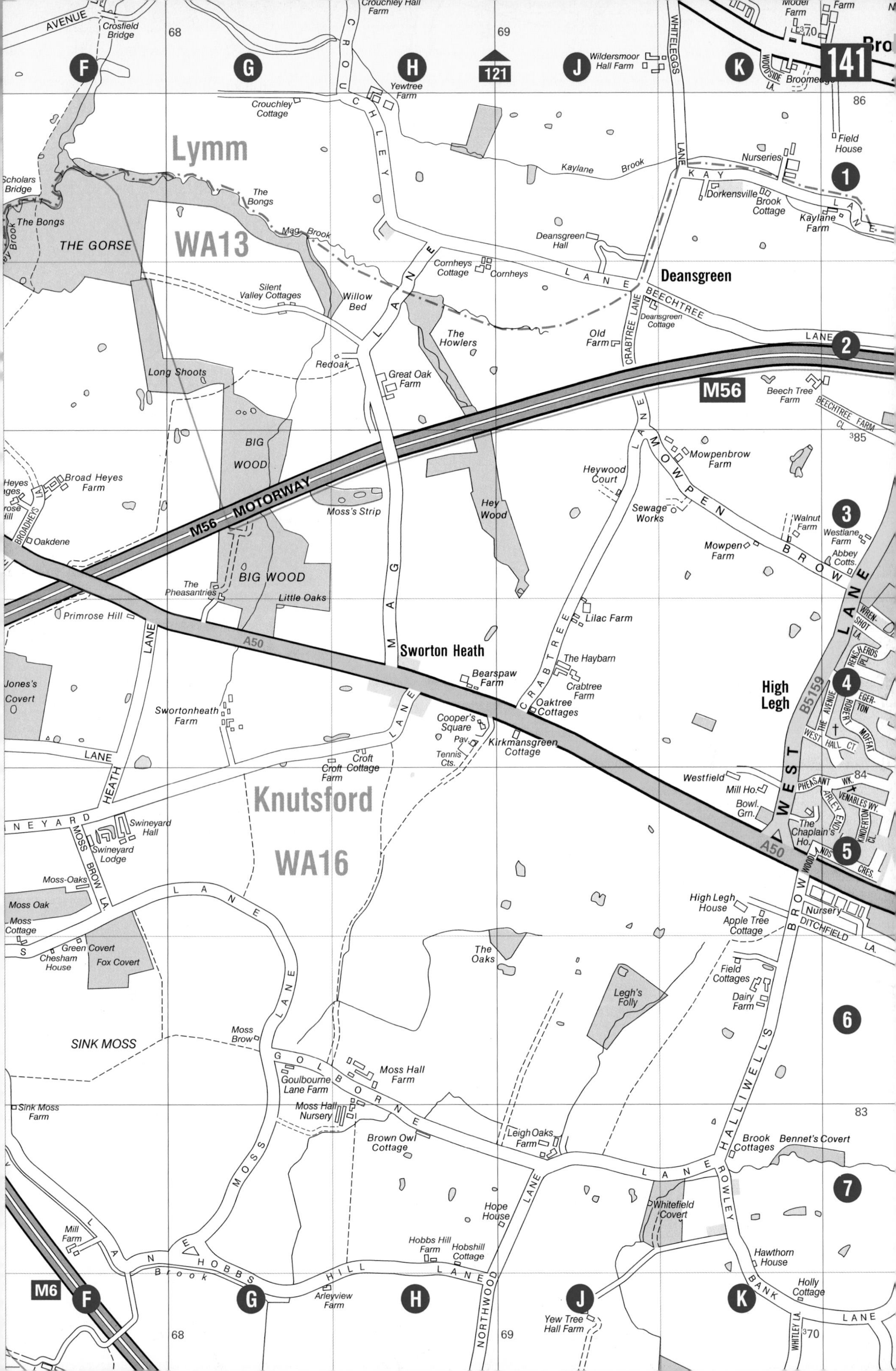
Lymm
WA13
Knutsford
WA16
Deansgreen
Sworton Heath
High Legh
M56 MOTORWAY
M56
A50
B5159
M6
THE GORSE
BIG WOOD
SINK MOSS
Crosfield Bridge
Crouchley Hall Farm
Yewtree Farm
Crouchley Cottage
Wildersmoor Hall Farm
Model Farm
Broomedge
Field House
Nurseries
Dorkensville
Brook Cottage
Kaylane Farm
Kaylane Brook
Deansgreen Hall
Cornheys Cottage
Cornheys
The Bongs
Mag Brook
Scholars Bridge
Silent Valley Cottages
Willow Bed
The Howlers
Old Farm
Deansgreen Cottage
Redoak
Great Oak Farm
Long Shoots
Beech Tree Farm
Mowpenbrow Farm
Heywood Court
Broad Heyes Farm
Moss's Strip
Hey Wood
Sewage Works
Walnut Farm
Westlane Farm
Abbey Cotts.
Mowpen Farm
Oakdene
The Pheasantries
Little Oaks
Primrose Hill
Lilac Farm
The Haybarn
Crabtree Farm
Oaktree Cottages
Bearspaw Farm
Jones's Covert
Swortonheath Farm
Cooper's Square
Kirkmansgreen Cottage
Croft Cottage
Croft Farm
Westfield
Mill Ho.
Bowl. Grn.
The Chaplain's Ho.
Swineyard Hall
Swineyard Lodge
Moss-Oaks
Moss Oak
Moss Cottage
Green Covert
Chesham House
Fox Covert
High Legh House
Apple Tree Cottage
Nursery
The Oaks
Field Cottages
Dairy Farm
Legh's Folly
Moss Brow
Moss Hall Farm
Goulbourne Lane Farm
Moss Hall Nursery
Sink Moss Farm
Brown Owl Cottage
Leigh Oaks Farm
Brook Cottages
Bennet's Covert
Whitefield Covert
Hope House
Mill Farm
Hobbs Hill Farm
Hobshill Cottage
Hawthorn House
Arleyview Farm
Holly Cottage
Yew Tree Hall Farm
CROUCHLEY LANE
WHITELEGGS LANE
KAY LANE
WOODSIDE LA.
BEECHTREE LANE
CRABTREE LANE
BEECHTREE FARM CL.
MOWPEN BROW
MAG LANE
LANE
WEST LANE
WRENSHOT LA.
SHEPHERDS PL.
THE AVENUE
ROBERT
EGERTON
MOFFAT
WEST HALL CT.
PHEASANT WK.
VENABLES WY.
ARLEY END
KINDERTON CL.
WOODLANDS CRES.
BROW
DITCHFIELD LA.
HEATH LANE
SWINEYARD
MOSS BROW LA.
GOLBORNE LANE
MOSS LANE
HALLIWELL'S BROW
ROWLEY BANK LANE
NORTHWOOD LANE
HOBBS HILL LANE
Brook
WHITLEY LA.
BROADHEYS LA.
AVENUE
Pav.
Tennis Cts.
F
G
H
J
K
1
2
3
4
5
6
7
68
69
370
86
385
84
83
121

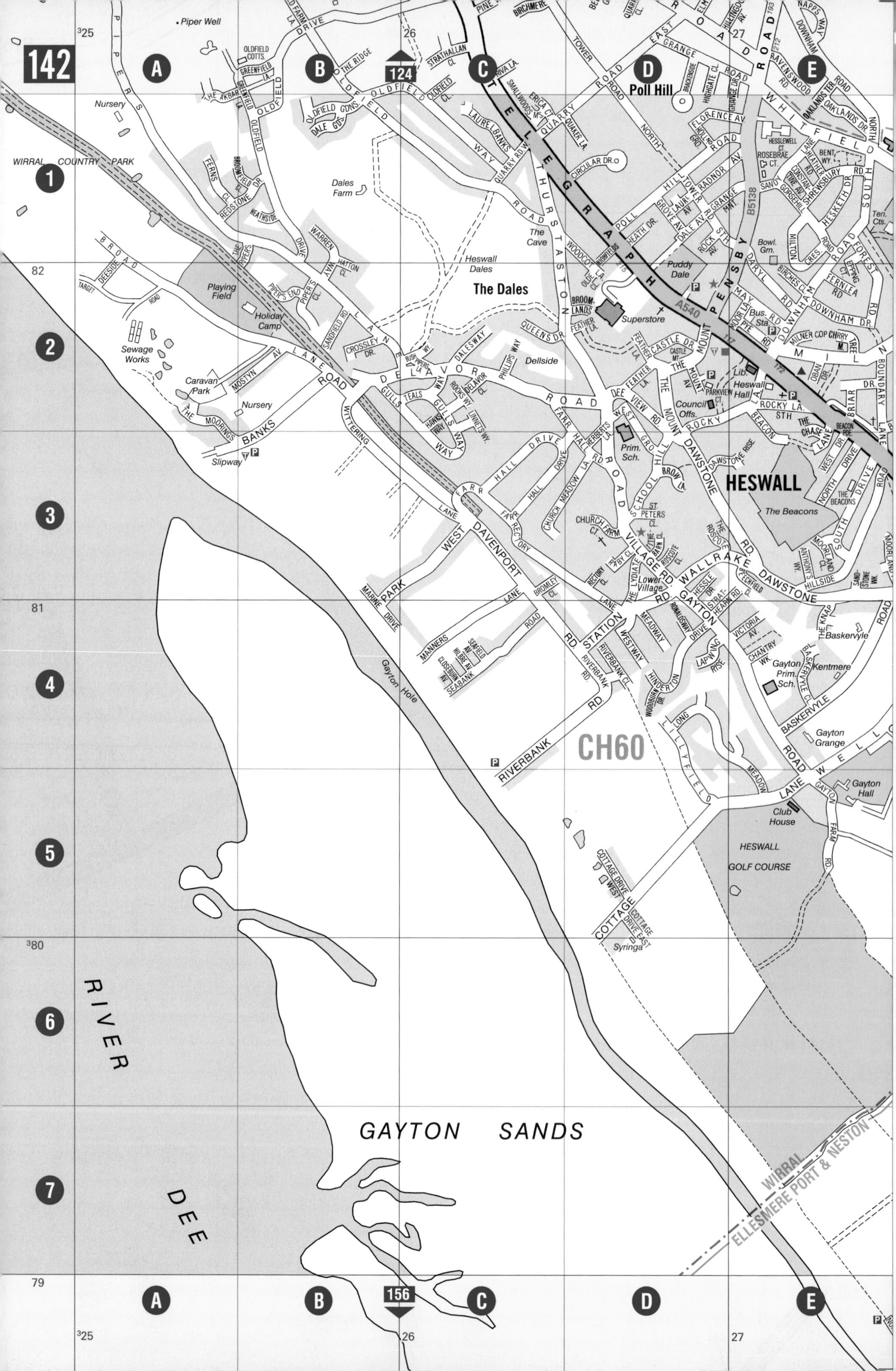

124
156
A
B
C
D
E
1
2
3
4
5
6
7
325
26
27
82
81
380
79
Piper Well
Nursery
WIRRAL COUNTRY PARK
Dales Farm
The Cave
Heswall Dales
The Dales
Poll Hill
Puddy Dale
Superstore
Dellside
Playing Field
Holiday Camp
Sewage Works
Caravan Park
Nursery
Slipway
Prim. Sch.
Lower Village
Council Offs.
Lib.
Heswall Hall
Bus. Sta.
HESWALL
The Beacons
Baskervyle
Kentmere
Gayton Prim. Sch.
Gayton Grange
Gayton Hall
Club House
HESWALL GOLF COURSE
Syringa
CH60
Gayton Hole
GAYTON SANDS
RIVER
DEE
WIRRAL
ELLESMERE PORT & NESTON
TELEGRAPH ROAD
A540
B5138
PENSBY ROAD
WHITFIELD
POLL HILL ROAD
QUARRY ROAD EAST
THURSTASTON ROAD
OLDFIELD DRIVE
OLDFIELD LANE
PIPERS LANE
BROAD LANE
BANKS ROAD
DELAVOR ROAD
FARR HALL DRIVE
FARR HALL ROAD
WEST GROVE
SCHOOL HILL
THE MOUNT
DAWSTONE ROAD
WALLRAKE
VILLAGE RD.
STATION RD.
DAVENPORT ROAD
WEST
PARK WEST
MARINE DRIVE
RIVERBANK RD.
GAYTON ROAD
GAYTON LANE
WELL LANE
COTTAGE LANE
LONG HEY
MEADOW
ROCKY LANE
BEACON LANE
MILNER ROAD
DOWNHAM RD.
BOUNDARY LANE
FOREST RD.

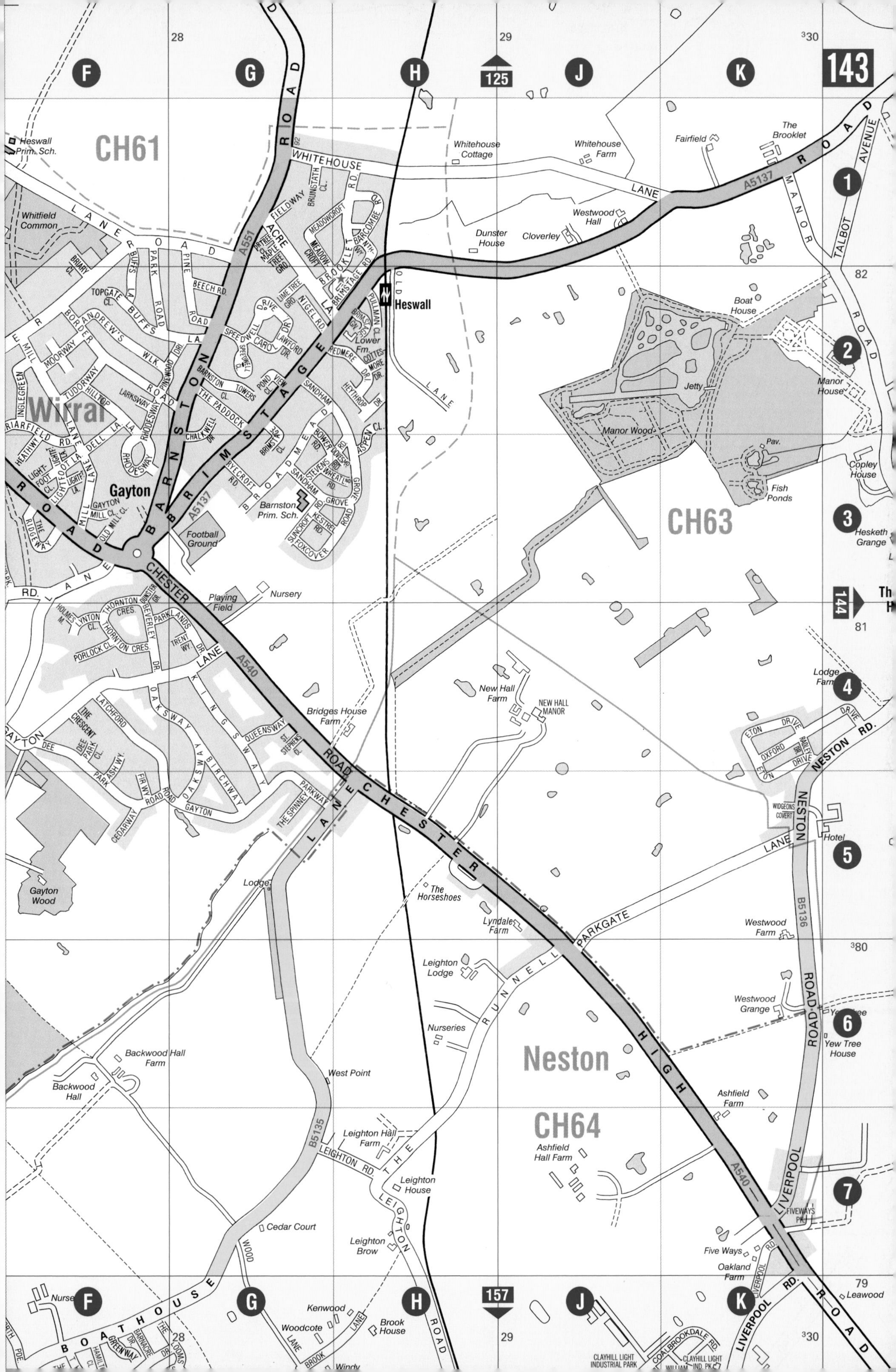
CH61
CH63
CH64
Wirral
Gayton
Neston
Heswall
Heswall Prim. Sch.
Whitfield Common
Barnston Prim. Sch.
Football Ground
Playing Field
Nursery
Bridges House Farm
Whitehouse Cottage
Whitehouse Farm
Fairfield
The Brooklet
Westwood Hall
Dunster House
Cloverley
Boat House
Manor House
Manor Wood
Jetty
Copley House
Fish Ponds
Hesketh Grange
Lodge Farm
New Hall Farm
NEW HALL MANOR
Widgeons Covert
Hotel
Westwood Farm
Westwood Grange
Yew Tree House
Ashfield Farm
Ashfield Hall Farm
Five Ways
Oakland Farm
Leawood
Lodge
The Horseshoes
Lyndales Farm
Leighton Lodge
Nurseries
West Point
Leighton Hall Farm
Leighton House
Cedar Court
Leighton Brow
Kenwood
Woodcote
Brook House
Backwood Hall Farm
Backwood Hall
Gayton Wood
Lower Fm.
CLAYHILL LIGHT INDUSTRIAL PARK
A540
A551
A5137
B5135
B5136
125
144
157
28
29
330
82
81
380
79

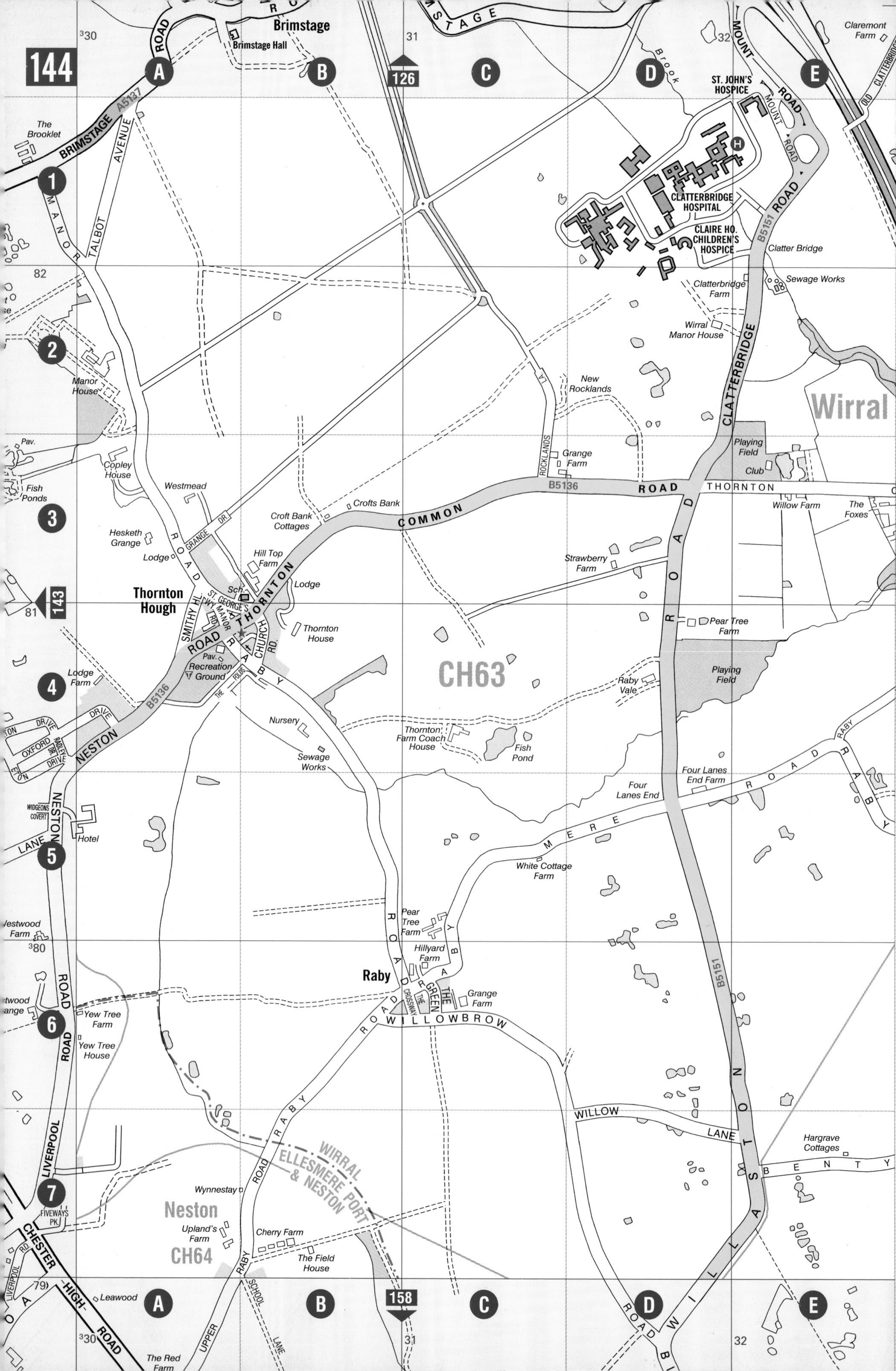
Brimstage
Brimstage Hall
BRIMSTAGE ROAD
A5137
The Brooklet
MANOR ROAD
TALBOT AVENUE
Manor House
Pav.
Fish Ponds
Copley House
Westmead
Hesketh Grange
Lodge
GRANGE DR.
Thornton Hough
SMITHY HL.
ST. GEORGE'S WY.
MANOR RD.
CHURCH RD.
Sch.
Hill Top Farm
Lodge
Thornton House
Pav.
Recreation Ground
Lodge Farm
B5136
NESTON ROAD
OXFORD DR.
RADLEY DR.
ETON DRIVE
THORNTON ROAD
RABY ROAD
Croft Bank Cottages
Crofts Bank
COMMON ROAD
B5136
Nursery
Sewage Works
Thornton Farm Coach House
Fish Pond
CH63
WIDGEONS COVERT
Hotel
NESTON LANE
Westwood Farm
Westwood Grange
Yew Tree Farm
Yew Tree House
LIVERPOOL ROAD
FIVEWAYS PK.
CHESTER HIGH ROAD
LIVERPOOL RD.
Leawood
The Red Farm
Neston
CH64
Upland's Farm
Wynnestay
Cherry Farm
The Field House
RABY ROAD
SCHOOL LANE
UPPER RABY ROAD
WIRRAL
ELLESMERE PORT & NESTON
Raby
Pear Tree Farm
Hillyard Farm
Grange Farm
THE GREEN
THE CROSSWAY
RABY ROAD
WILLOWBROW
WILLOW LANE
MERE ROAD
White Cottage Farm
Four Lanes End
Four Lanes End Farm
Raby Vale
Playing Field
Pear Tree Farm
Strawberry Farm
ROAD
Grange Farm
ROCKLANDS
New Rocklands
LA.
THORNTON ROAD
Playing Field
Club
Willow Farm
The Foxes
Wirral
CLATTERBRIDGE ROAD
B5151
Wirral Manor House
Clatterbridge Farm
Sewage Works
Clatter Bridge
CLAIRE HO. CHILDREN'S HOSPICE
CLATTERBRIDGE HOSPITAL
ST. JOHN'S HOSPICE
MOUNT ROAD
Brook
Claremont Farm
OLD CLATTERBRIDGE RD.
BRIMSTAGE RD.
B5151
RABY ROAD
Hargrave Cottages
BENTY
WILLASTON ROAD
ROAD
A B C D E
1 2 3 4 5 6 7
126
143
158
330 31 32
82 81 80 79

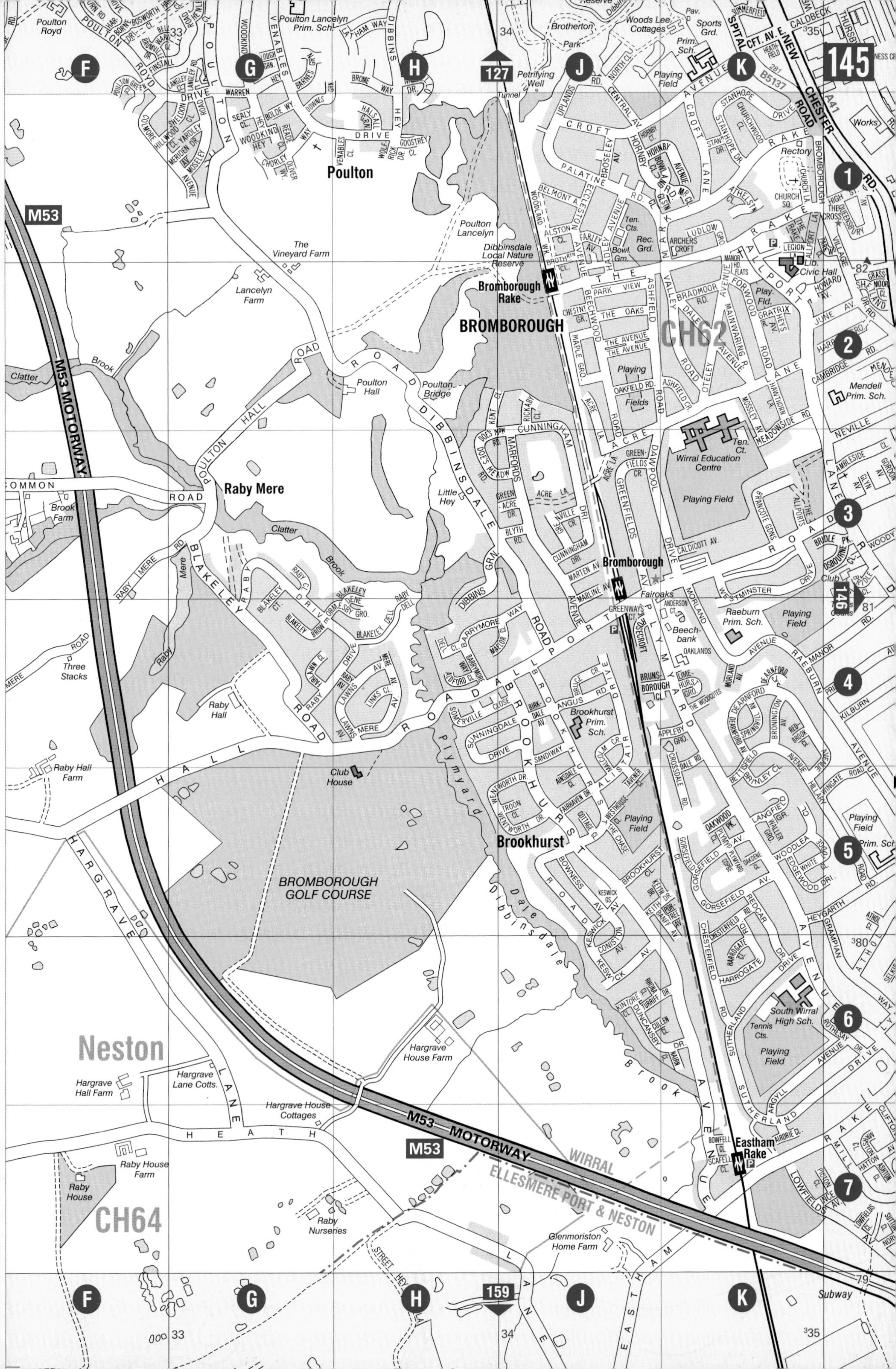

Poulton
BROMBOROUGH
Bromborough Rake
Bromborough
Brookhurst
Raby Mere
Neston
CH62
CH64
Eastham Rake
BROMBOROUGH GOLF COURSE
M53 MOTORWAY
Poulton Lancelyn
Dibbinsdale Local Nature Reserve
The Vineyard Farm
Lancelyn Farm
Poulton Hall
Poulton Bridge
Little Hey
Three Stacks
Raby Hall
Raby Hall Farm
Brook Farm
Club House
Wirral Education Centre
Playing Field
Raeburn Prim. Sch.
Mendell Prim. Sch.
Brookhurst Prim. Sch.
South Wirral High Sch.
Hargrave House Farm
Hargrave Hall Farm
Hargrave Lane Cotts.
Hargrave House Cottages
Raby House Farm
Raby House
Raby Nurseries
Glenmoriston Home Farm
WIRRAL
ELLESMERE PORT & NESTON
Petrifying Well
Brotherton Park
Woods Lee Cottages
Sports Grd.
Poulton Royd
Poulton Lancelyn Prim. Sch.
Civic Hall
Rectory
Subway
Works
127
146
159

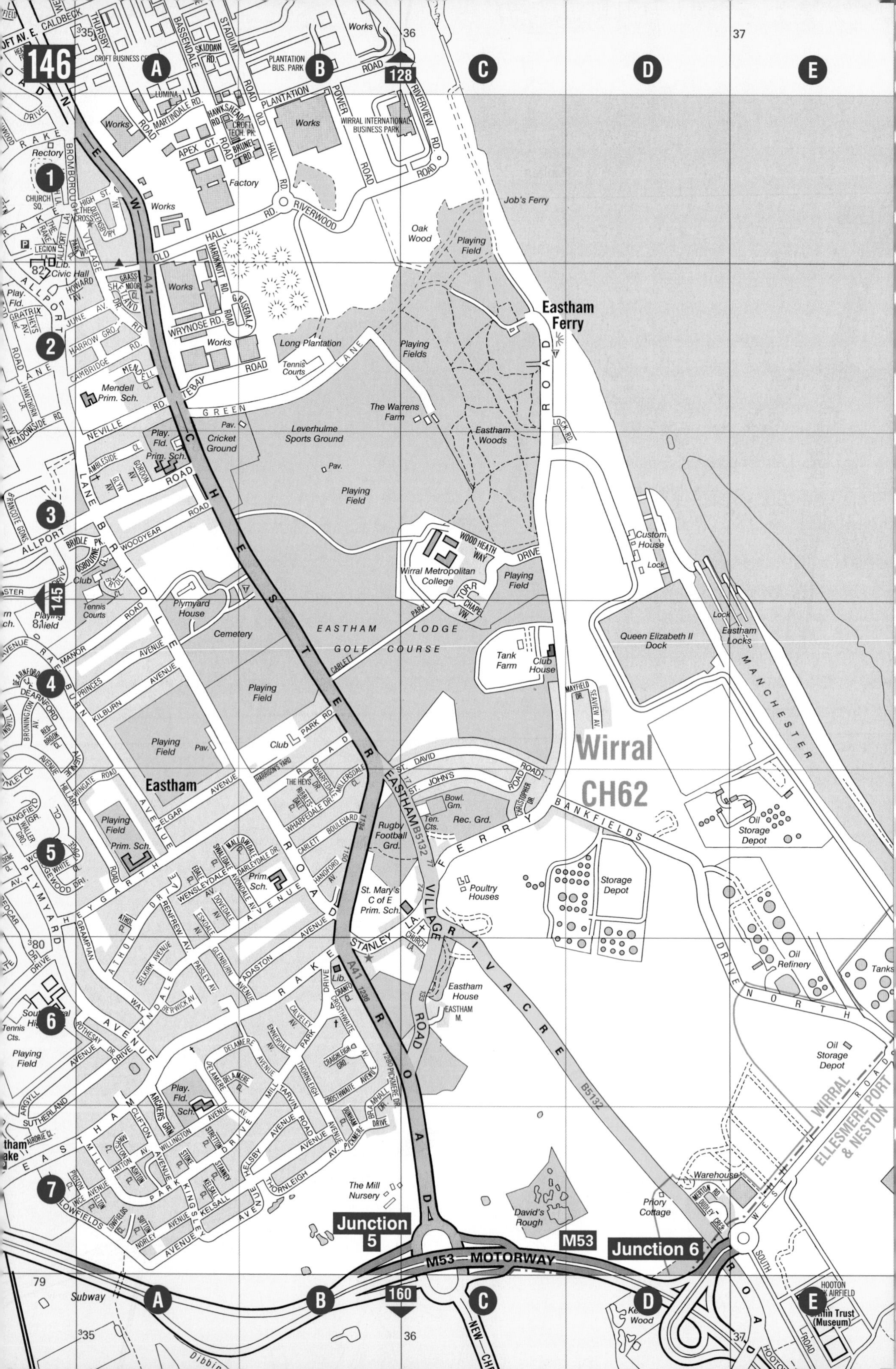

146
A
B
C
D
E
1
2
3
4
5
6
7
36
37
35
79
80
81
82
128
145
160
Works
Plantation Bus. Park
Croft Business Ce
Wirral International Business Park
Factory
Job's Ferry
Oak Wood
Playing Field
Eastham Ferry
Long Plantation
Tennis Courts
Playing Fields
The Warrens Farm
Eastham Woods
Leverhulme Sports Ground
Cricket Ground
Mendell Prim. Sch.
Prim. Sch.
Custom House
Lock
Wirral Metropolitan College
Plymyard House
Cemetery
EASTHAM LODGE GOLF COURSE
Tank Farm
Club House
Queen Elizabeth II Dock
Eastham Locks
MANCHESTER
Wirral
CH62
Eastham
Rugby Football Grd.
Rec. Grd.
Bowl. Grn.
St. Mary's C of E Prim. Sch.
Poultry Houses
Storage Depot
Oil Storage Depot
Oil Refinery
Tanks
Eastham House
The Mill Nursery
David's Rough
Priory Cottage
Warehouse
Junction 5
Junction 6
M53
M53 MOTORWAY
Subway
Hooton Airfield
Trust (Museum)
WIRRAL
ELLESMERE PORT & NESTON
A41
B5132
CHESTER ROAD
RIVACRE ROAD
FERRY ROAD
BANKFIELDS DRIVE
NORTH ROAD
EASTHAM RAKE
EASTHAM VILLAGE ROAD
PLANTATION ROAD
RIVERWOOD RD.
OLD HALL RD.
POWER ROAD
RIVERVIEW RD.
WOOD HEATH WAY
NEVILLE RD.
ALLPORT ROAD
BRIDLE ROAD
PLYMYARD AVENUE
HEYGARTH ROAD
STANLEY LA.
CHURCH LA.
MILL PARK DRIVE
LOWFIELDS AVENUE
KINGSLEY ROAD

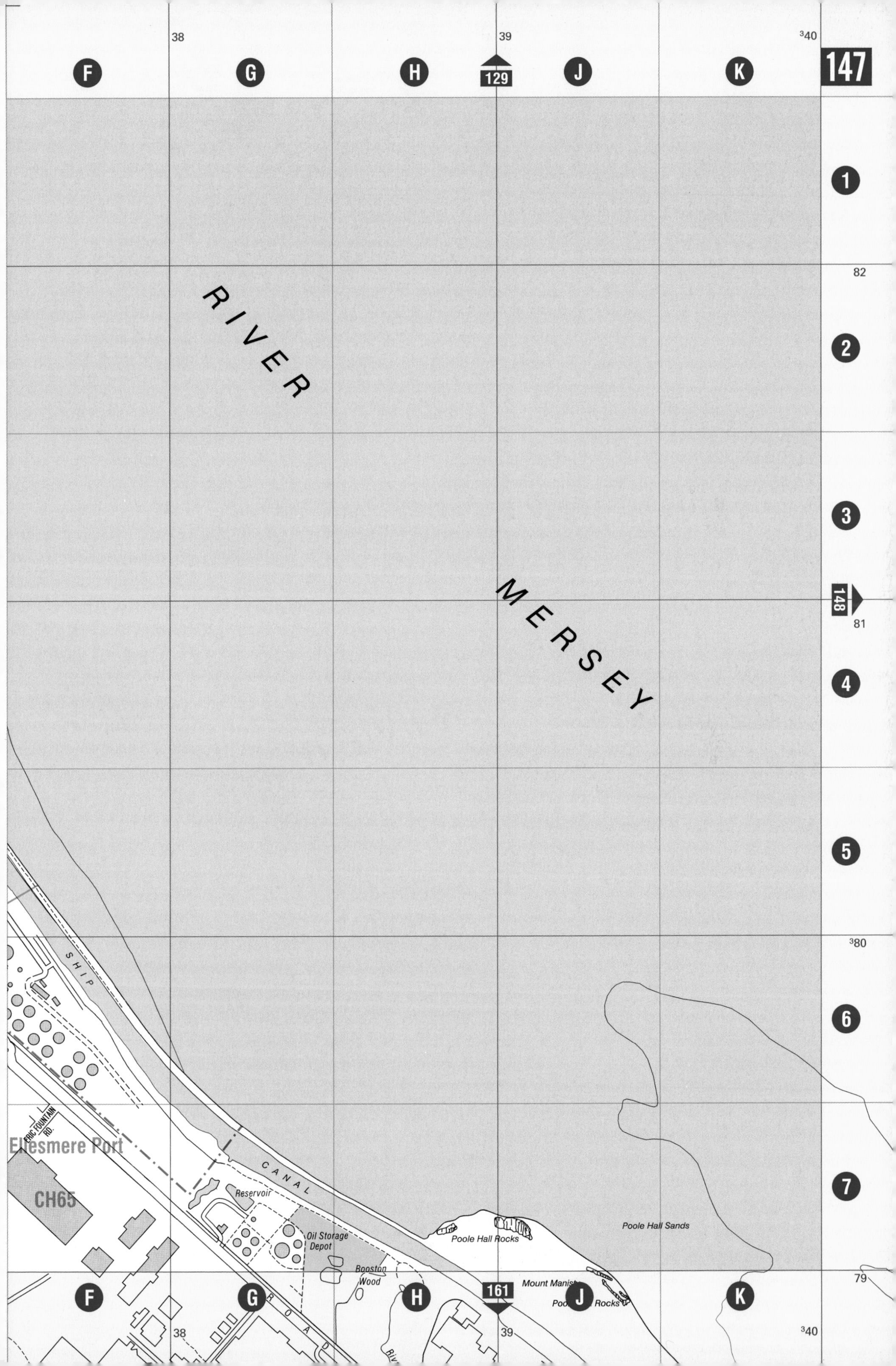

R I V E R

M E R S E Y

82

81   148

³80

SHIP

Ellesmere Port

CH65

CANAL

Reservoir

Oil Storage
Depot

Booston
Wood

Poole Hall Rocks

Poole Hall Sands

Mount Manis...
Poo... ...Rocks

ERIC FOUNTAIN RD.

161

79

1
2
3
4
5
6
7

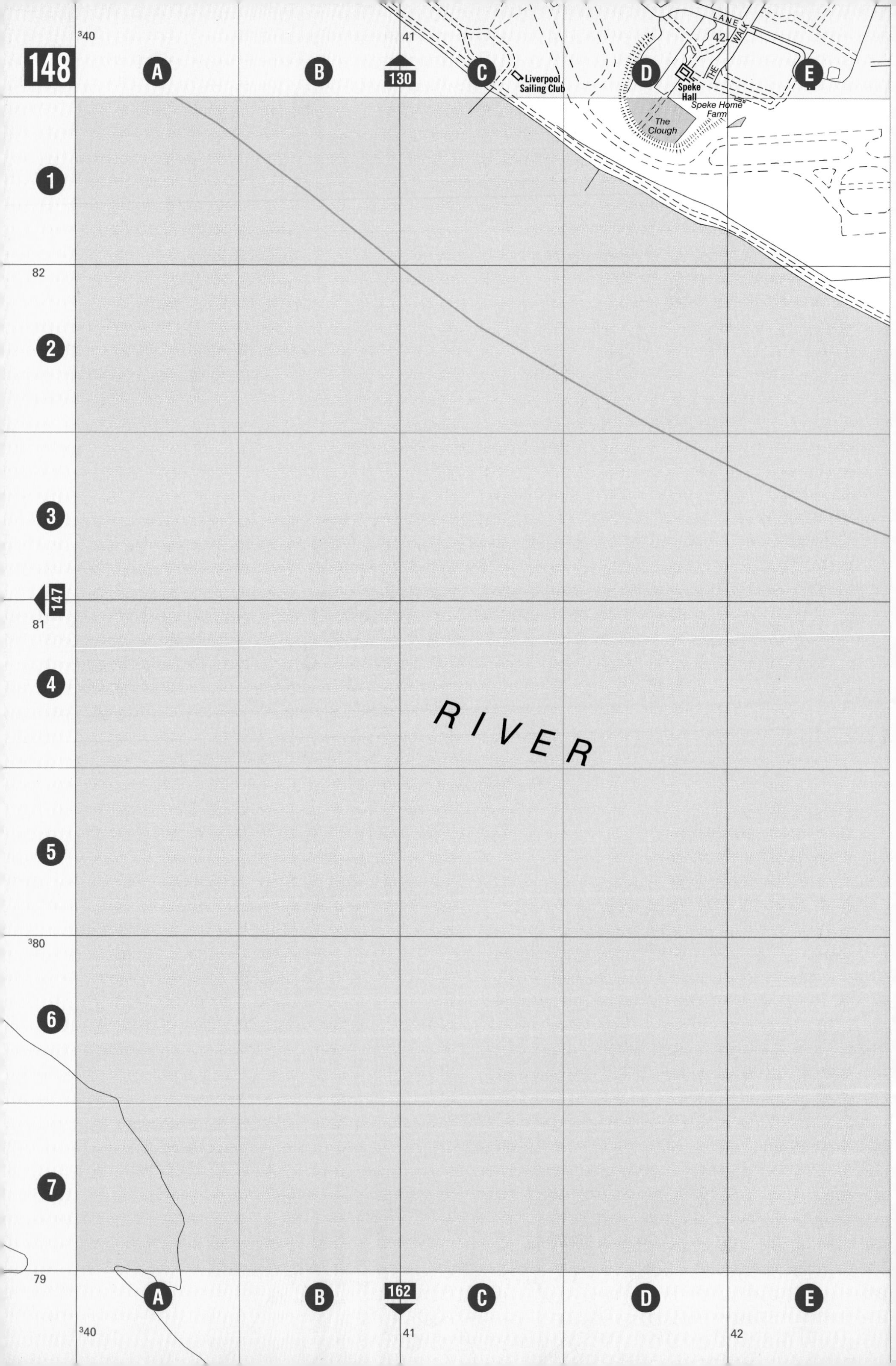

³40

41

42

A

B

130

C

Liverpool
Sailing Club

D

Speke
Hall

Speke Home
Farm

The Clough

E

THE LANE WALK

1

82

2

3

147

81

4

R I V E R

5

³80

6

7

79

A

B

162

C

D

E

³40

41

42

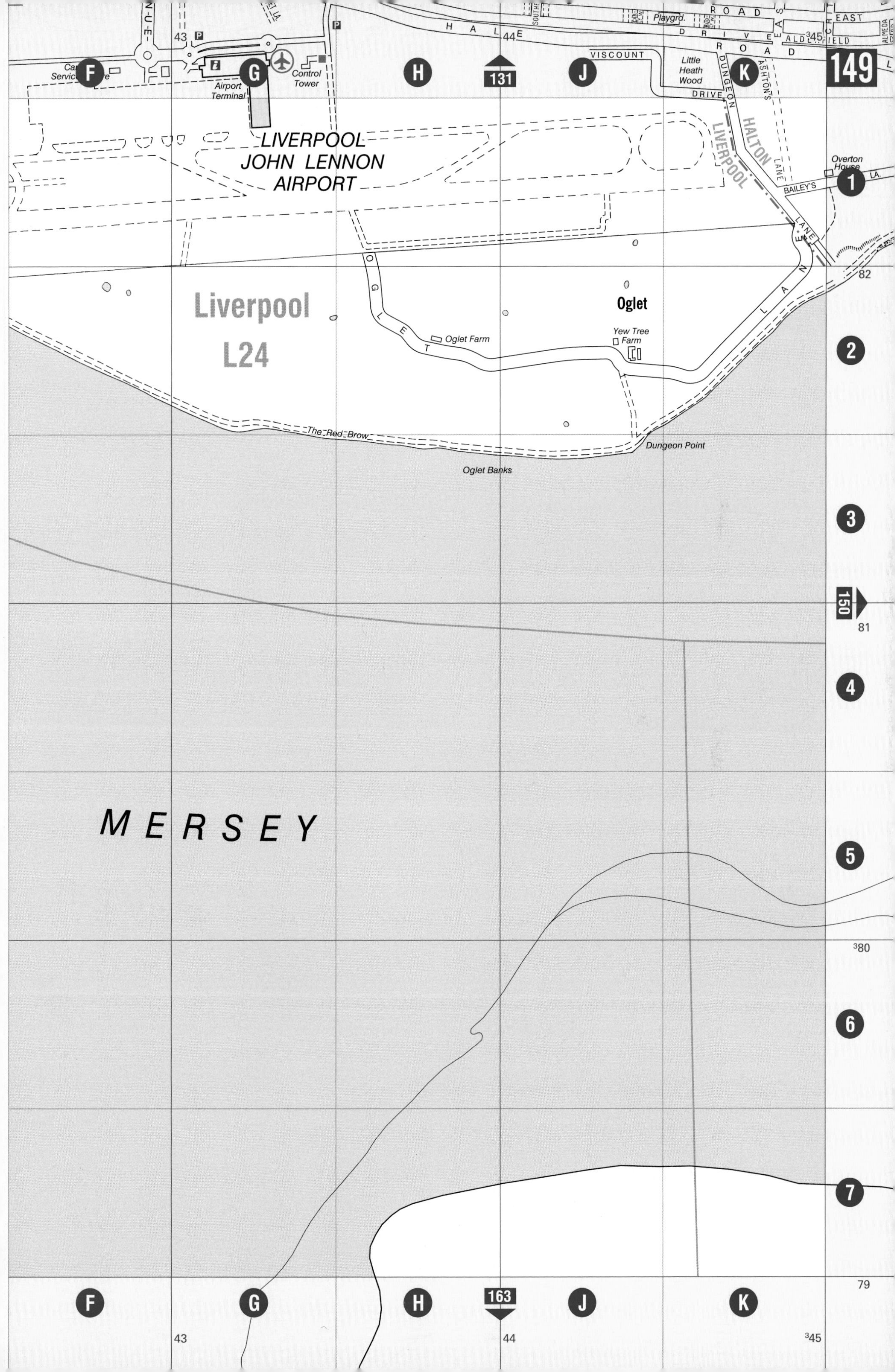

F

G
Airport
Terminal

**LIVERPOOL
JOHN LENNON
AIRPORT**

**Liverpool
L24**

Control
Tower

H

131

J
VISCOUNT

Little
Heath
Wood

K

DRIVE

Overton
House

BAILEY'S

1

82

Oglet Farm

Oglet

Yew Tree
Farm

2

The Red Brow

Dungeon Point

3

Oglet Banks

150
81

4

M E R S E Y

5

380

6

7

79

F

G

H

163

J

K

43

44

345

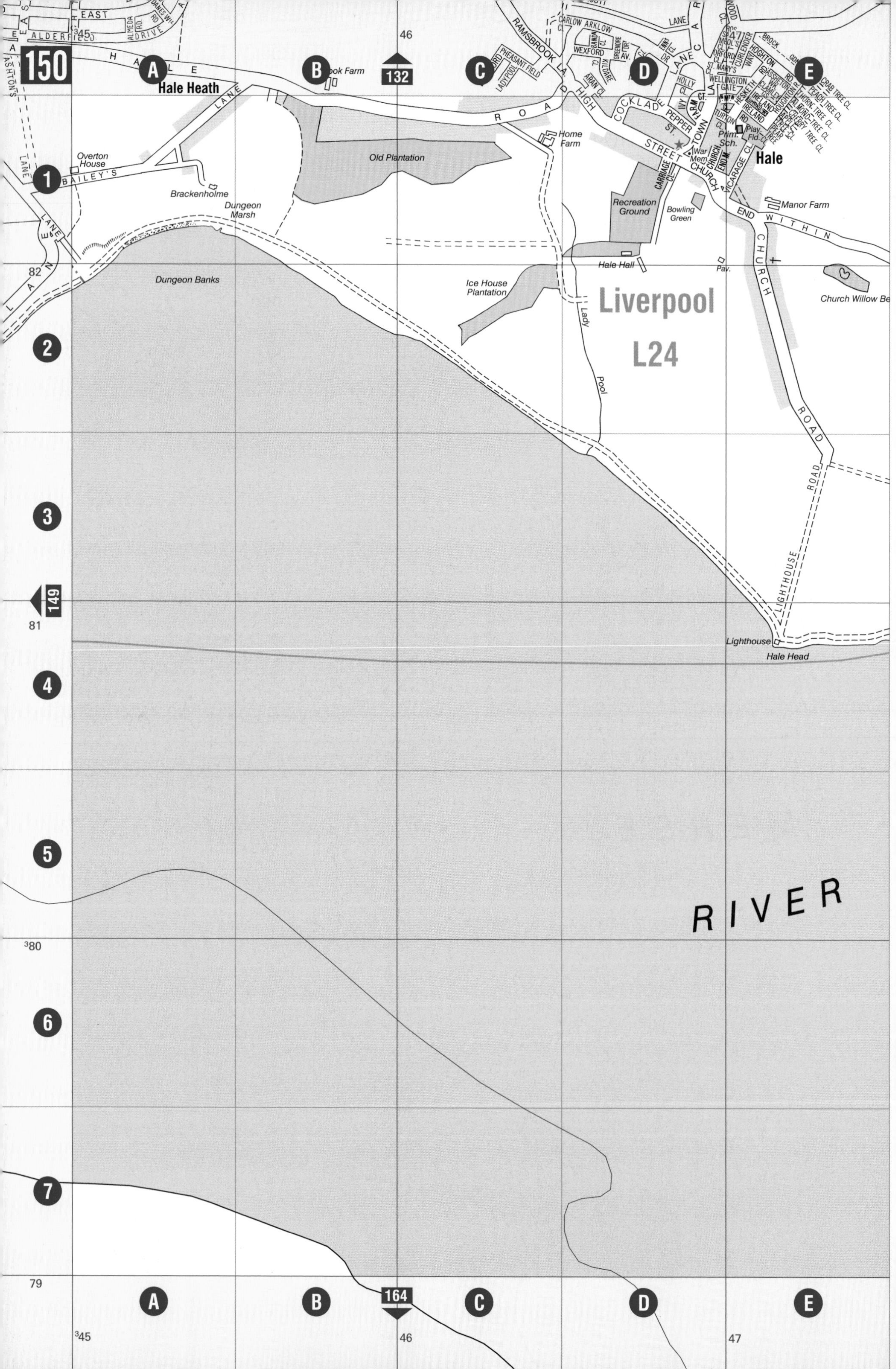

150

A   **Hale Heath**   B   132   C   D   E

Liverpool
L24

Overton House
Brackenholme
Dungeon Marsh
Dungeon Banks

Old Plantation
Home Farm

Ice House
Plantation

Recreation
Ground
Bowling
Green
Hale Hall
Pav.

Hale
Manor Farm
Church Willow Be

Lighthouse
Hale Head

R I V E R

149

A   B   164   C   D   E

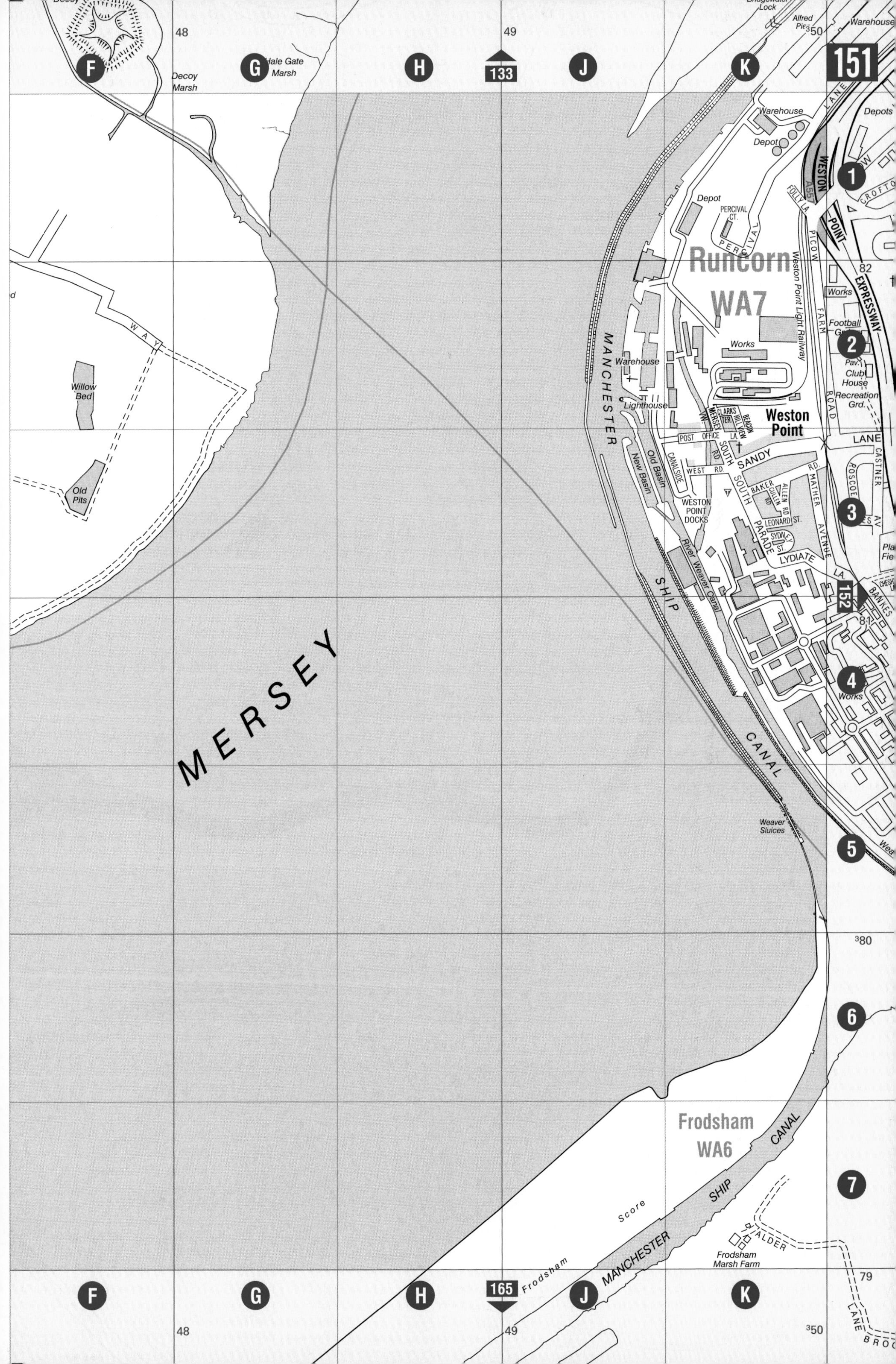

Runcorn
WA7
Weston Point
Frodsham
WA6
MERSEY
MANCHESTER SHIP CANAL
Hale Gate Marsh
Decoy Marsh
Willow Bed
Old Pits
WAY
Warehouse
Depot
Depots
PERCIVAL CT.
Works
Weston Point Light Railway
WESTON POINT EXPRESSWAY
FOLLY LA.
PICOW FARM ROAD
Football Gd.
Pav.
Club House
Recreation Grd.
Lighthouse
Old Basin
New Basin
CANALSIDE
POST OFFICE LA.
WEST RD.
SOUTH RD.
SANDY LANE
SOUTH PARADE
MATHER AVENUE
ROSCOE
CASTNER AV.
BAKER
LEONARD ST.
SYDNEY ST.
LYDIATE LA.
BANKES
WESTON POINT DOCKS
River Weaver Canal
Weaver Sluices
Frodsham Score
Frodsham Marsh Farm
ALDER LANE
133
152
165
48
49
350
380
82
81
79

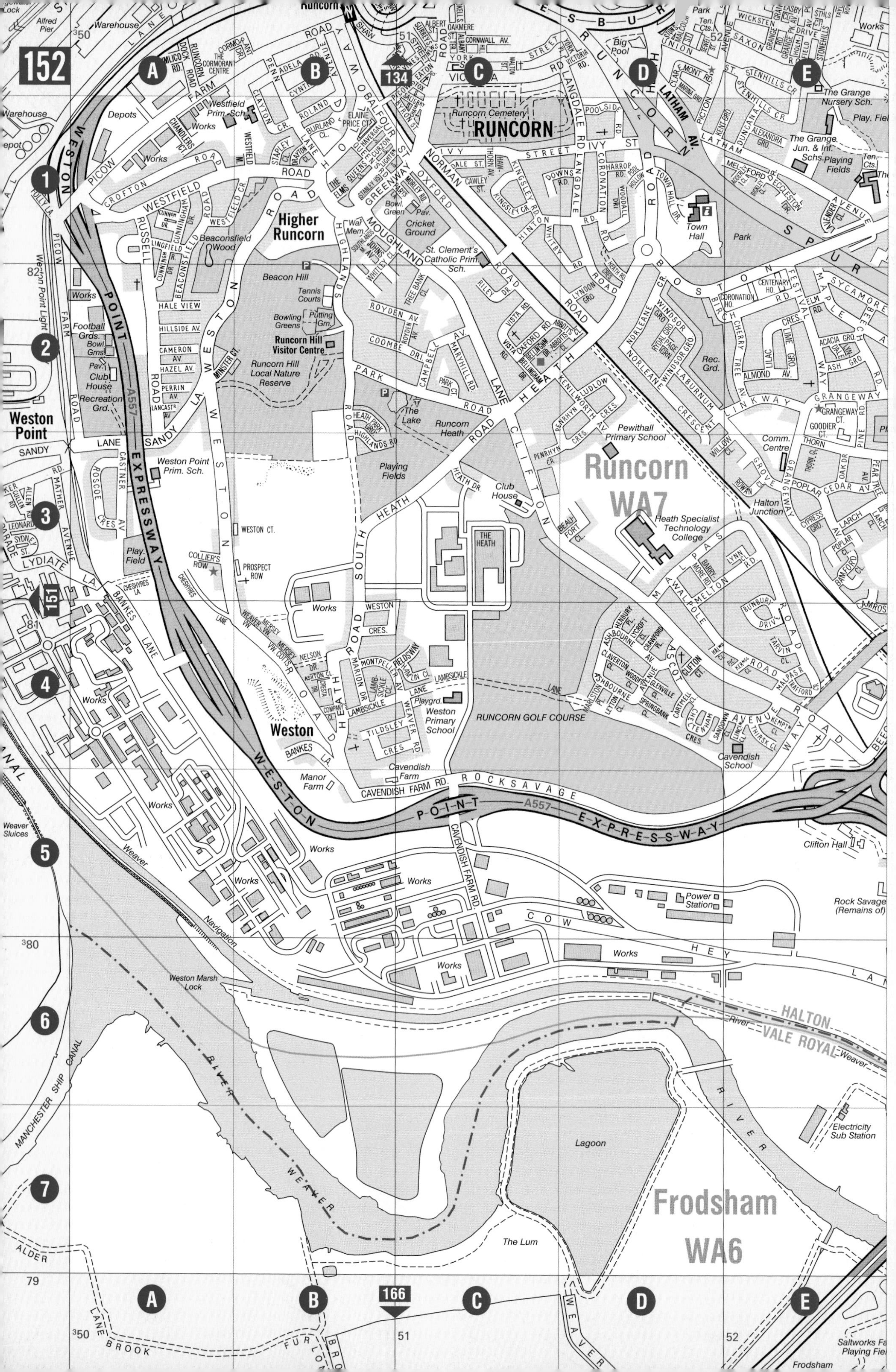
RUNCORN
Higher Runcorn
Runcorn WA7
Weston Point
Weston
Frodsham WA6
Runcorn Cemetery
Westfield Prim. Sch.
Beaconsfield Wood
Beacon Hill
Tennis Courts
Bowling Greens
Putting Grn.
Runcorn Hill Visitor Centre
Runcorn Hill Local Nature Reserve
War Mem.
Bowl. Green
Pav.
Cricket Ground
St. Clement's Catholic Prim. Sch.
The Lake
Runcorn Heath
Playing Fields
Club House
Pewithall Primary School
Heath Specialist Technology College
Town Hall
Park
Rec. Grd.
Comm. Centre
Halton Junction
Cavendish School
Weston Point Prim. Sch.
Football Grds.
Club House
Recreation Grd.
Play. Field
Weston Primary School
Playgrd.
Cavendish Farm
Manor Farm
RUNCORN GOLF COURSE
Power Station
Works
Depots
Warehouse
Alfred Pier
Weaver Sluices
Weston Marsh Lock
Lagoon
The Lum
Electricity Sub Station
Rock Savage (Remains of)
Clifton Hall
The Grange Nursery Sch.
The Grange Jun. & Inf. Schs.
Playing Fields
Saltworks Fa Playing Fie
WESTON POINT EXPRESSWAY
A557
ROCKSAVAGE
COW HEY LANE
CAVENDISH FARM RD.
HEATH ROAD
SOUTH HEATH ROAD
WESTON ROAD
PARK ROAD
CLIFTON LANE
MALPAS ROAD
WALPOLE
BOSTON AVENUE
SPUR
LATHAM AV.
LINKWAY
GRANGEWAY
IVY STREET
LANGDALE RD
NORMAN ROAD
MOUGHLAND LANE
HIGHLANDS RD
GREENWAY
PICOW FARM ROAD
WESTFIELD ROAD
BANKES LANE
SANDY LANE
MANCHESTER SHIP CANAL
RIVER WEAVER
Weaver Navigation
HALTON
VALE ROYAL
ALDER LANE
BROOK FURLONG
A B C D E
1 2 3 4 5 6 7
350
51
52
82
81
380
79
134
151
166

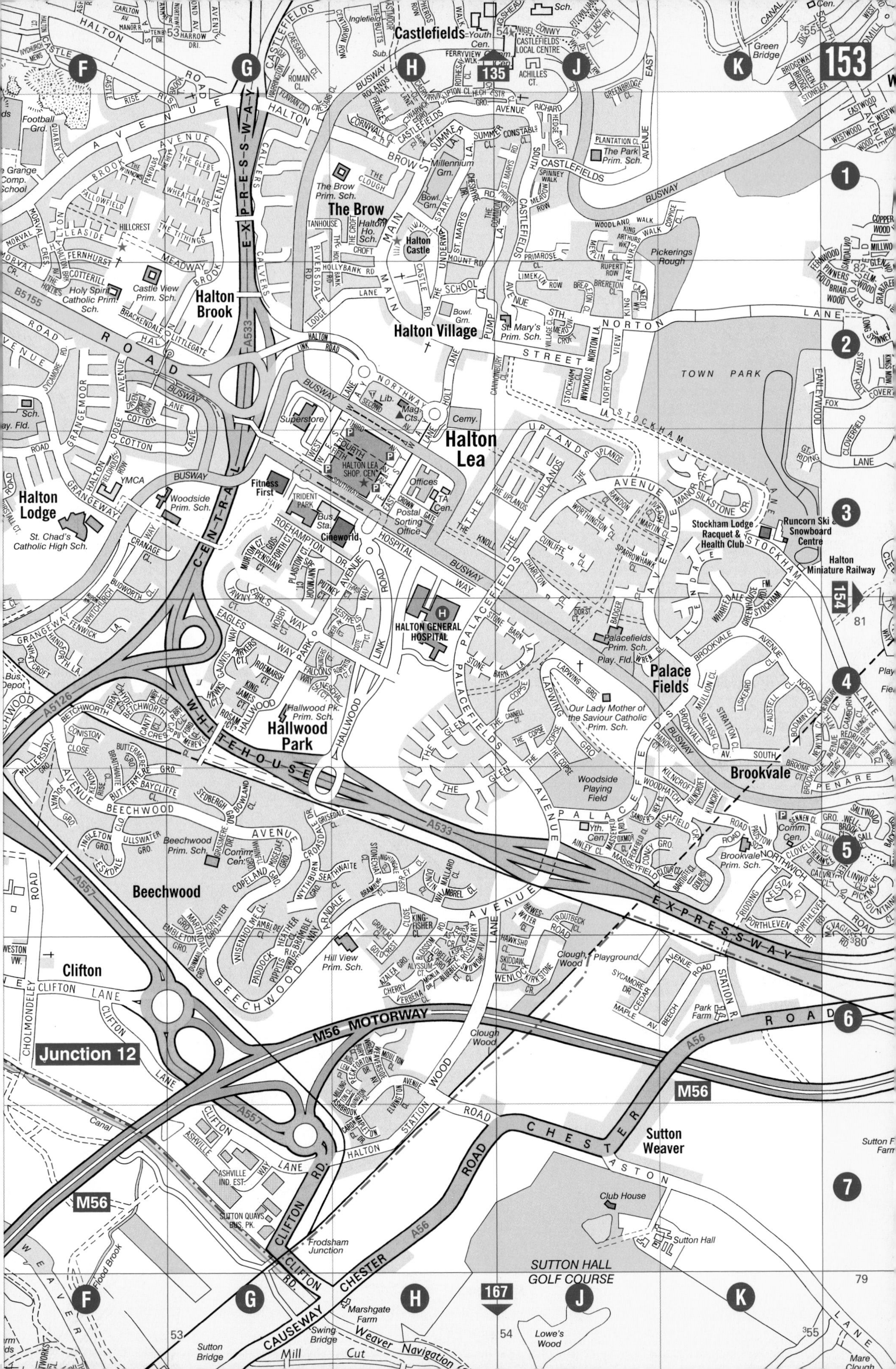

153
Castlefields
Castlefields Local Centre
The Park Prim. Sch.
The Brow
The Brow Prim. Sch.
Halton Castle
Halton Village
St. Mary's Prim. Sch.
Pickerings Rough
Town Park
Halton Brook
Castle View Prim. Sch.
Holy Spirit Catholic Prim. Sch.
Football Grd.
Halton Lea
Halton Lea Shop. Cen.
Superstore
Fitness First
Cineworld
Bus Sta.
Postal Sorting Office
Halton General Hospital
Halton Lodge
St. Chad's Catholic High Sch.
Woodside Prim. Sch.
YMCA
Runcorn Ski & Snowboard Centre
Stockham Lodge Racquet & Health Club
Halton Miniature Railway
154
Palacefields Prim. Sch.
Palace Fields
Our Lady Mother of the Saviour Catholic Prim. Sch.
Woodside Playing Field
Brookvale
Brookvale Prim. Sch.
Hallwood Pk. Prim. Sch.
Hallwood Park
Beechwood
Beechwood Prim. Sch.
Hill View Prim. Sch.
Clifton
Junction 12
M56 Motorway
Clough Wood
Sutton Weaver
Park Farm
Ashville Ind. Est.
Sutton Quays Bus. Pk.
Frodsham Junction
Club House
Sutton Hall
Sutton Hall Golf Course
Marshgate Farm
Swing Bridge
Weaver Navigation
Mill Cut
Sutton Bridge
Lowe's Wood
167
Expressway
Central Expressway
Whitehouse Expressway
A533
A5126
A557
A56
B5155
M56
Chester Road
Halton Road
Palacefields Avenue
Stockham Lane
Norton Lane
Beechwood Avenue
Clifton Lane
F G H J K
1 2 3 4 5 6 7
53 54 55
79 80 81

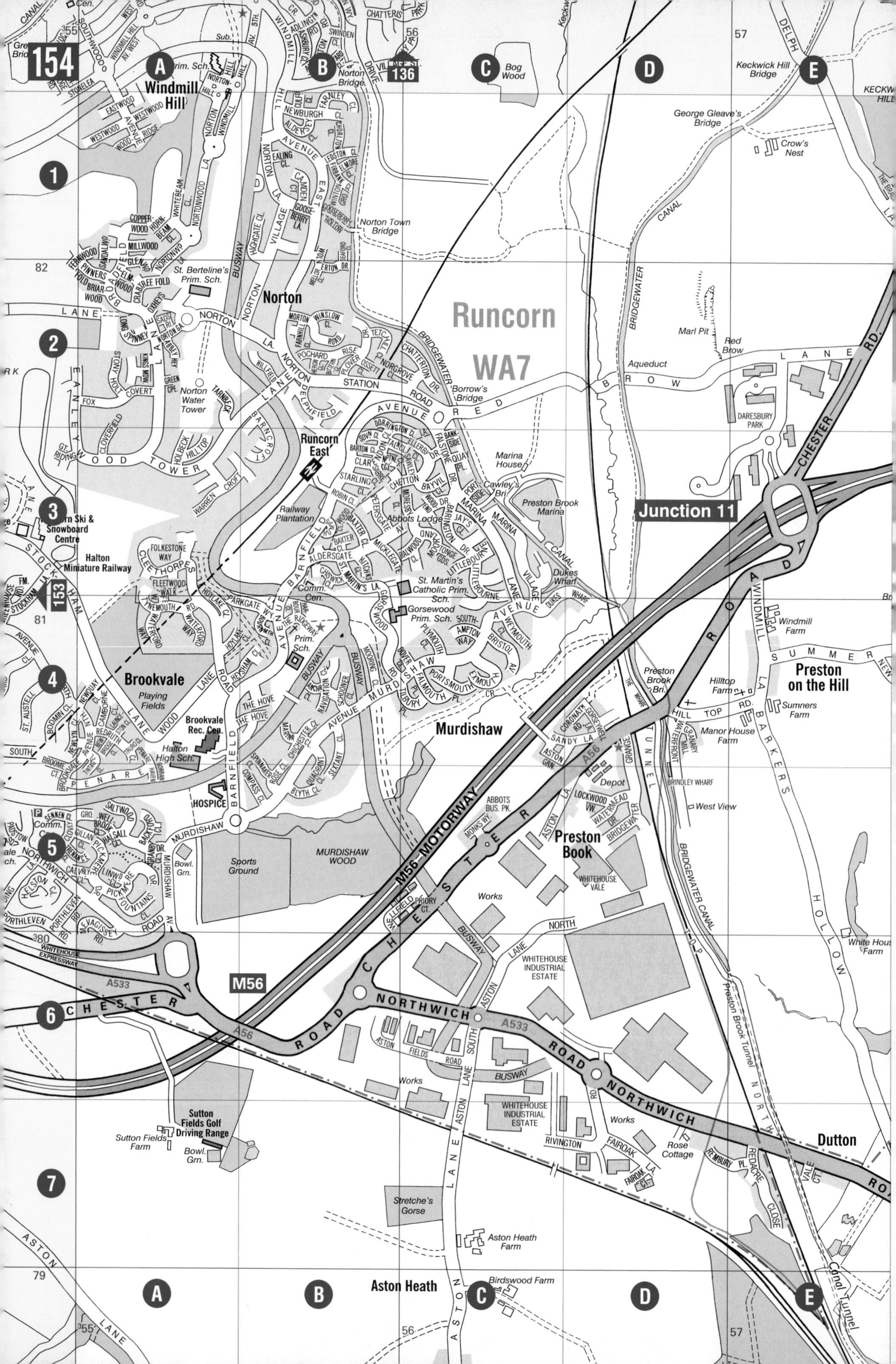

154
Windmill Hill
Norton
Runcorn
WA7
Runcorn East
Brookvale
Playing Fields
Murdishaw
Preston Book
Preston on the Hill
Dutton
Aston Heath
Junction 11
M56
M56 MOTORWAY
CHESTER ROAD
NORTHWICH ROAD
BRIDGEWATER CANAL
Bog Wood
Norton Bridge
Keckwick Hill Bridge
George Gleave's Bridge
Crow's Nest
Norton Town Bridge
St. Berteline's Prim. Sch.
Norton Water Tower
Borrow's Bridge
Aqueduct
Marl Pit
Red Brow
DARESBURY PARK
Marina House
Cawley's Bri.
Preston Brook Marina
Railway Plantation
Abbots Lodge
St. Martin's Catholic Prim. Sch.
Gorsewood Prim. Sch.
Comm. Cen.
Prim. Sch.
Dukes Wharf
Windmill Farm
Hilltop Farm
Sumners Farm
Manor House Farm
Preston Brook Bri.
BRINDLEY WHARF
West View
Halton Miniature Railway
Snowboard Centre
Brookvale Rec. Cen.
Halton High Sch.
HOSPICE
Sports Ground
MURDISHAW WOOD
Bowl. Grn.
ABBOTS BUS. PK.
Depot
WHITEHOUSE VALE
Works
WHITEHOUSE INDUSTRIAL ESTATE
White House Farm
Preston Brook Tunnel
Sutton Fields Golf Driving Range
Sutton Fields Farm
Stretche's Gorse
Aston Heath Farm
Birdswood Farm
Rose Cottage
Canal Tunnel
WHITEHOUSE EXPRESSWAY
A533
A56
153
136

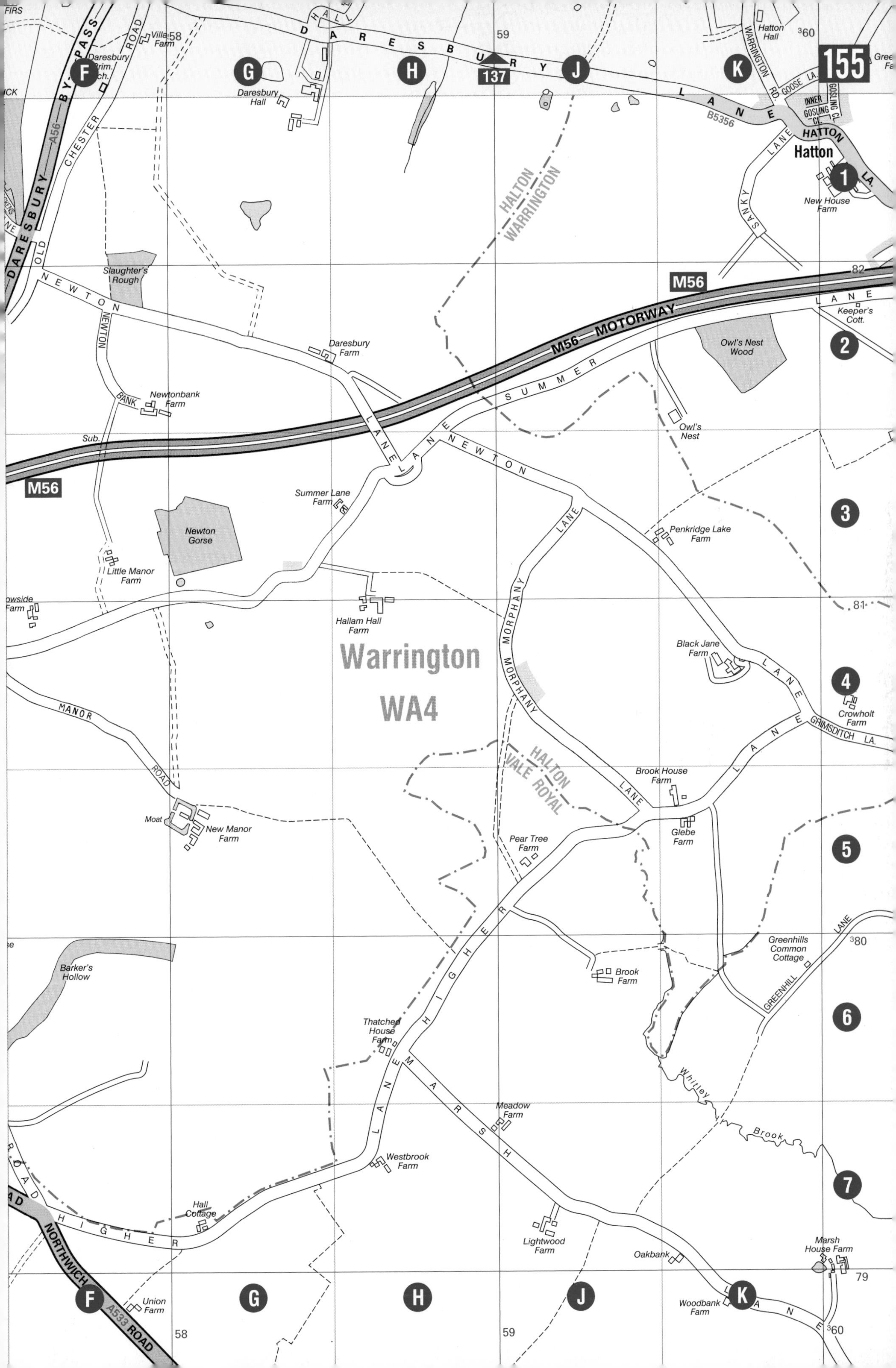
DARESBURY LANE
B5356
137
Daresbury Hall
Hatton
Hatton Hall
New House Farm
HALTON
WARRINGTON
M56 MOTORWAY
M56
NEWTON LANE
Slaughter's Rough
Daresbury Farm
Newtonbank Farm
Owl's Nest Wood
Keeper's Cott.
Owl's Nest
SUMMER LANE
Summer Lane Farm
Newton Gorse
Little Manor Farm
Penkridge Lake Farm
Hallam Hall Farm
Warrington
WA4
MORPHANY LANE
Black Jane Farm
Crowholt Farm
GRIMSDITCH LA.
MANOR ROAD
HALTON
VALE ROYAL
Brook House Farm
Glebe Farm
Moat
New Manor Farm
Pear Tree Farm
Greenhills Common Cottage
GREENHILL LANE
Brook Farm
Barker's Hollow
Thatched House Farm
HIGHER LANE
MARSH LANE
Whitley Brook
Meadow Farm
Westbrook Farm
Hall Cottage
Lightwood Farm
Oakbank
Marsh House Farm
Woodbank Farm
NORTHWICH ROAD
A533
Union Farm
DARESBURY BY-PASS
A56
CHESTER ROAD
Villa Farm
Daresbury Prim. Sch.
WARRINGTON RD.
GOOSE LA.
INNER GOSLING CL.
GOSLING CL.
HATTON LA.
SANKY LANE
Sub.
F G H J K
1 2 3 4 5 6 7
58 59 360
82 81 380 79

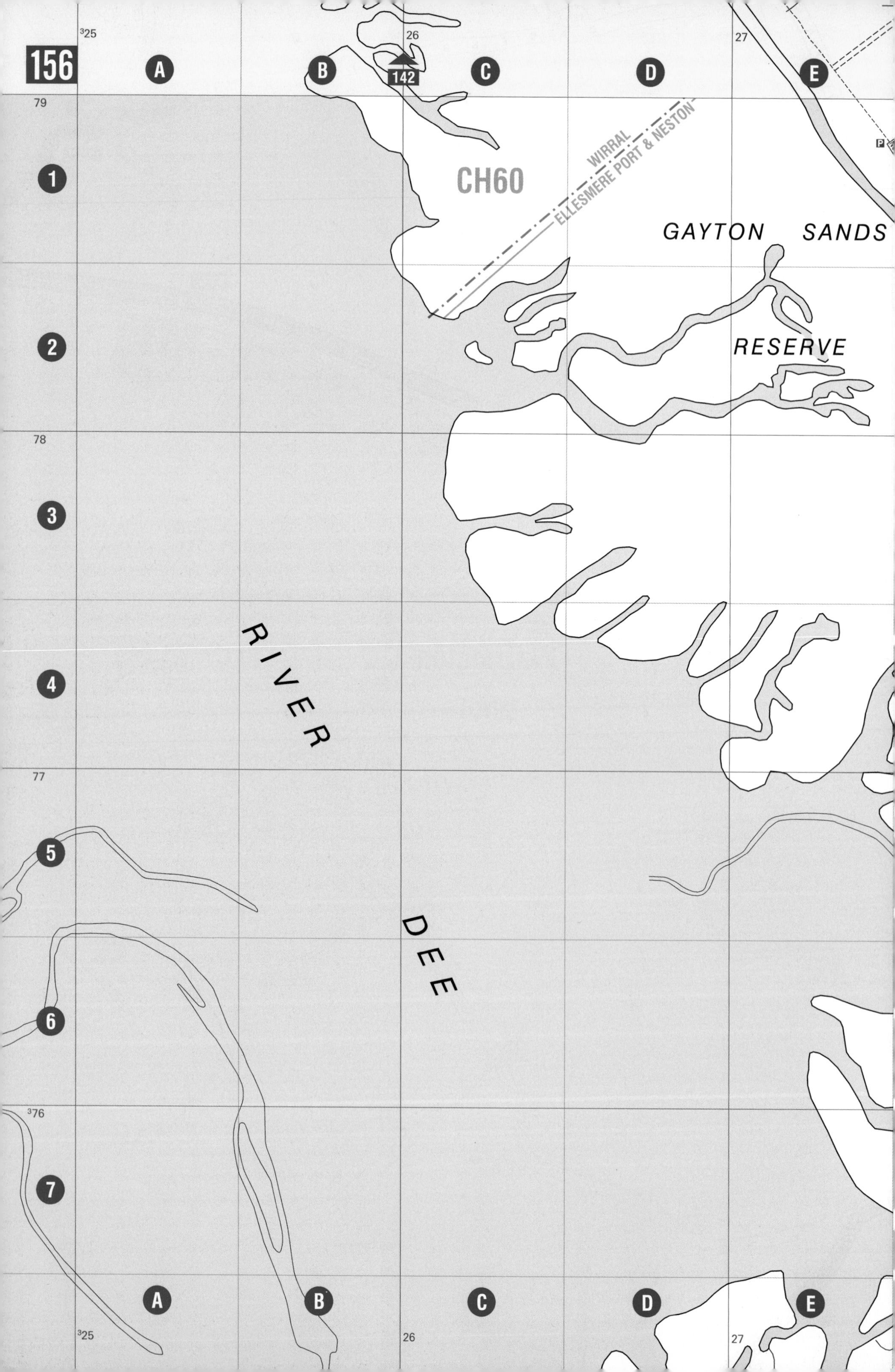

CH60

WIRRAL
ELLESMERE PORT & NESTON

GAYTON SANDS

RESERVE

RIVER

DEE

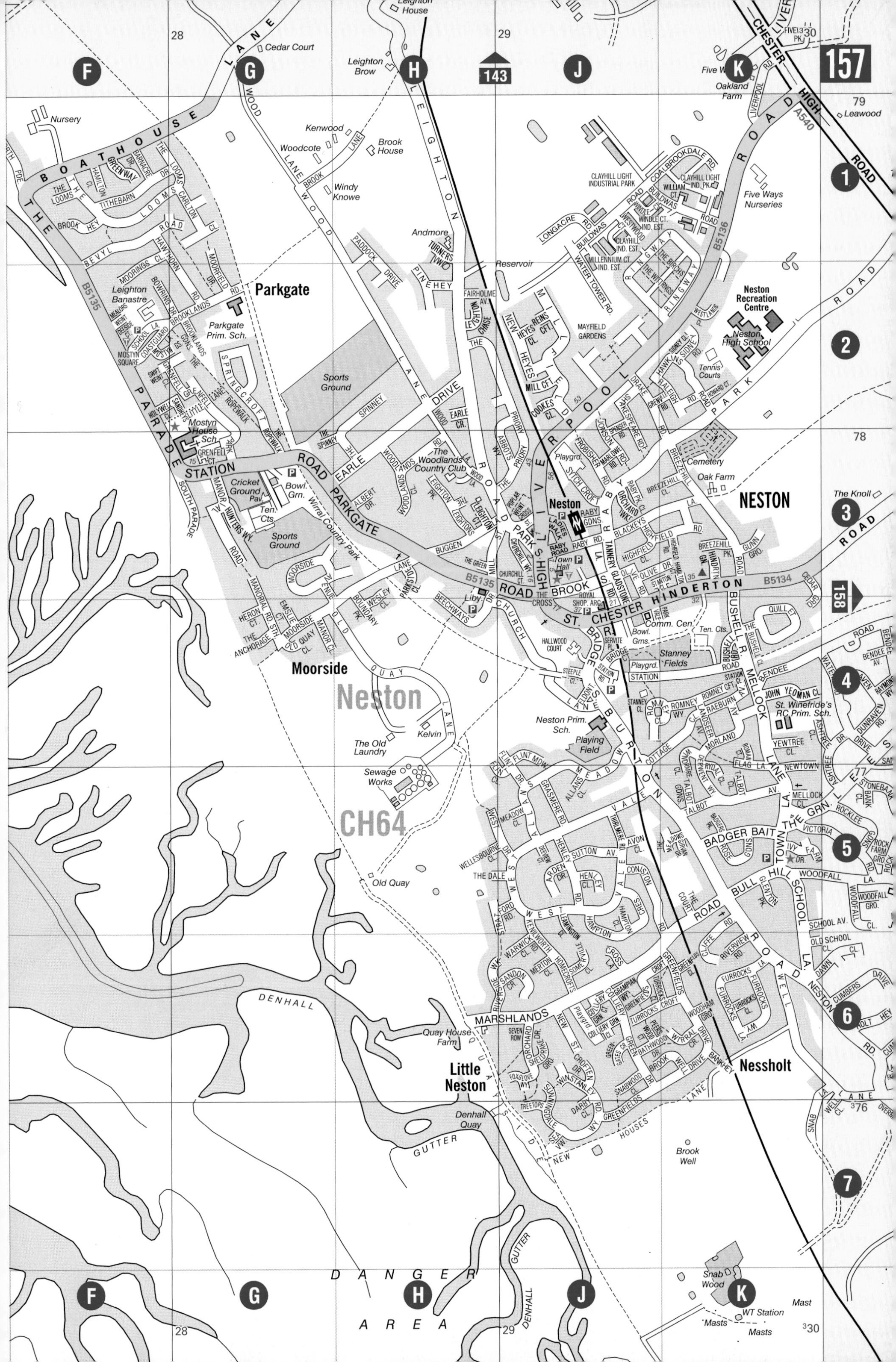

Leighton House
Cedar Court
Leighton Brow
143
Five Ways
Oakland Farm
Leawood
Nursery
BOATHOUSE LANE
WOOD LANE
Kenwood
Woodcote
Brook House
Windy Knowe
Andmore
LEIGHTON ROAD
CHESTER HIGH ROAD
A540
CLAYHILL LIGHT INDUSTRIAL PARK
CLAYHILL LIGHT IND. PK.
Five Ways Nurseries
MILLENNIUM CT. IND. EST.
WATER TOWER RD.
RINGWAY
B5136
Reservoir
Parkgate
Parkgate Prim. Sch.
Leighton Banastre
MOSTYN SQUARE
THE PARADE
B5135
Neston Recreation Centre
Neston High School
Tennis Courts
MAYFIELD GARDENS
Sports Ground
LIVERPOOL ROAD
PARK ROAD
Mostyn House Sch.
STATION ROAD
PARKGATE ROAD
Cricket Ground
Bowl. Grn.
Ten. Cts.
Sports Ground
Wirral Country Park
The Woodlands Country Club
Cemetery
Oak Farm
The Knoll
NESTON
Neston
Town Hall
Liby.
CHESTER HINDERTON ROAD
B5134
158
BROOK ST.
Comm. Cen.
Bowl. Grns.
Stanney Fields
Moorside
Neston
HALLWOOD COURT
St. Winefride's RC Prim. Sch.
Neston Prim. Sch.
Playing Field
Kelvin
The Old Laundry
Sewage Works
CH64
BADGER BAIT
TOWN LANE
BULL HILL
Old Quay
THE DALE
DENHALL
MARSHLANDS
Quay House Farm
Little Neston
Denhall Quay
GUTTER
Nessholt
NEW HOUSES LANE
Brook Well
Snab Wood
WT Station
Mast
Masts
DANGER AREA
F
G
H
J
K
1
2
3
4
5
6
7
28
29
330
79
78
376

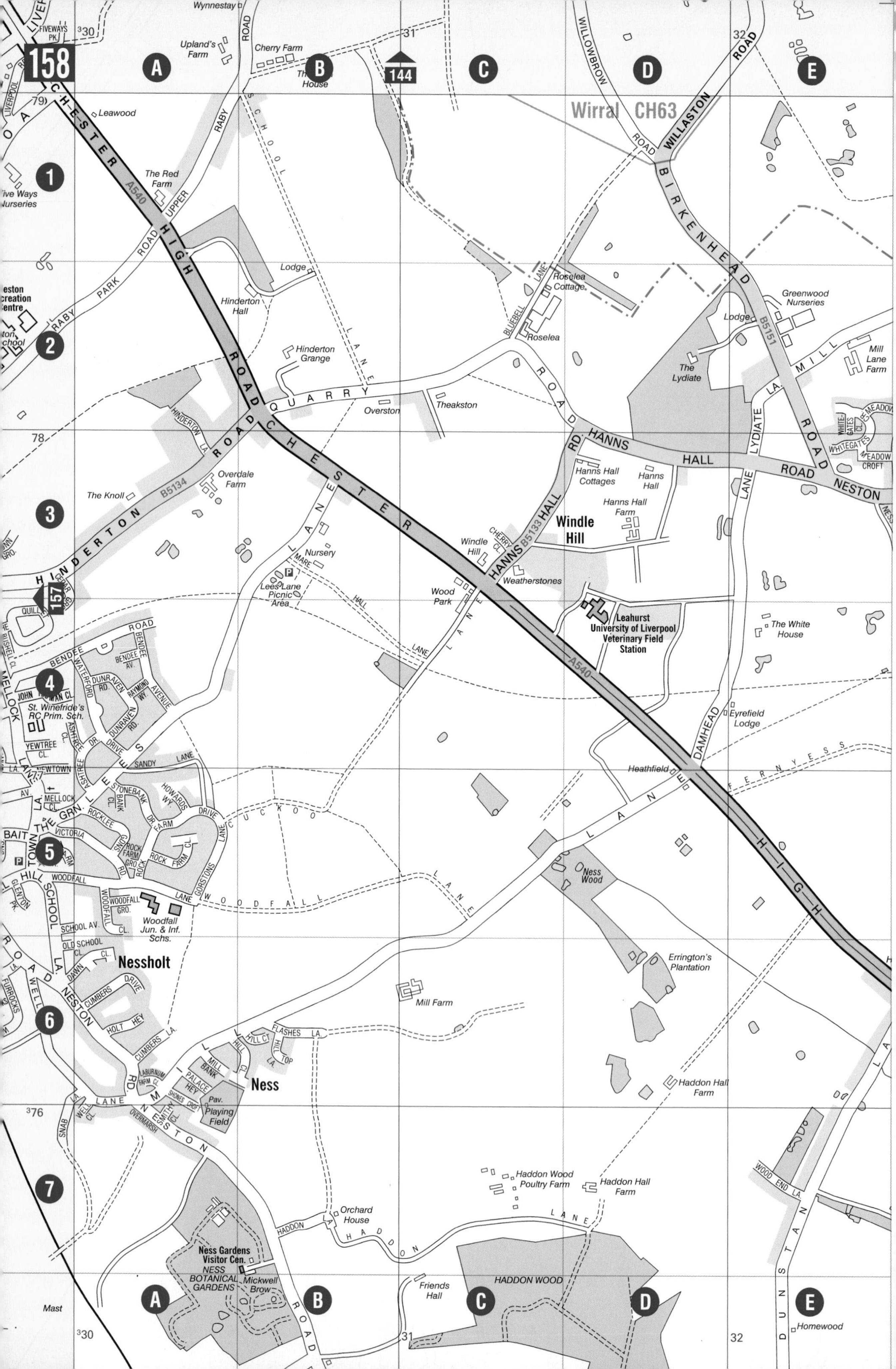
Wirral CH63
CHESTER HIGH ROAD
A540
HINDERTON ROAD
B5134
QUARRY ROAD
HANNS HALL ROAD
B5133
BIRKENHEAD ROAD
B5151
WILLASTON ROAD
NESTON ROAD
LYDIATE LANE
DAMHEAD LANE
FERNYESS LANE
CUCKOO LANE
WOODFALL LANE
SCHOOL LANE
UPPER RABY ROAD
RABY PARK ROAD
LEES LANE
HADDON LANE
NESTON ROAD
DUNSTAN LANE
WOOD END LA.
MILL LANE
FLASHES LA.
HILL TOP LA.
SANDY LANE
Windle Hill
Nessholt
Ness
Leahurst University of Liverpool Veterinary Field Station
Ness Gardens Visitor Cen.
NESS BOTANICAL GARDENS
HADDON WOOD
Ness Wood
Errington's Plantation
Mill Farm
Haddon Hall Farm
Haddon Wood Poultry Farm
Orchard House
Friends Hall
Mickwell Brow
Woodfall Jun. & Inf. Schs.
St. Winefride's RC Prim. Sch.
Lees Lane Picnic Area
Nursery
Wood Park
Windle Hill
Weatherstones
Hanns Hall Farm
Hanns Hall Cottages
Hanns Hall
Overston
Theakston
Hinderton Grange
Hinderton Hall
Lodge
The Red Farm
Upland's Farm
Cherry Farm
Wynnestay
Leawood
The Knoll
Overdale Farm
Roselea
Roselea Cottage
The Lydiate
Greenwood Nurseries
Mill Lane Farm
The White House
Eyrefield Lodge
Heathfield
Homewood
Mast
Pav.
Playing Field
144
157
A B C D E
1 2 3 4 5 6 7
30 31 32
79 78 376

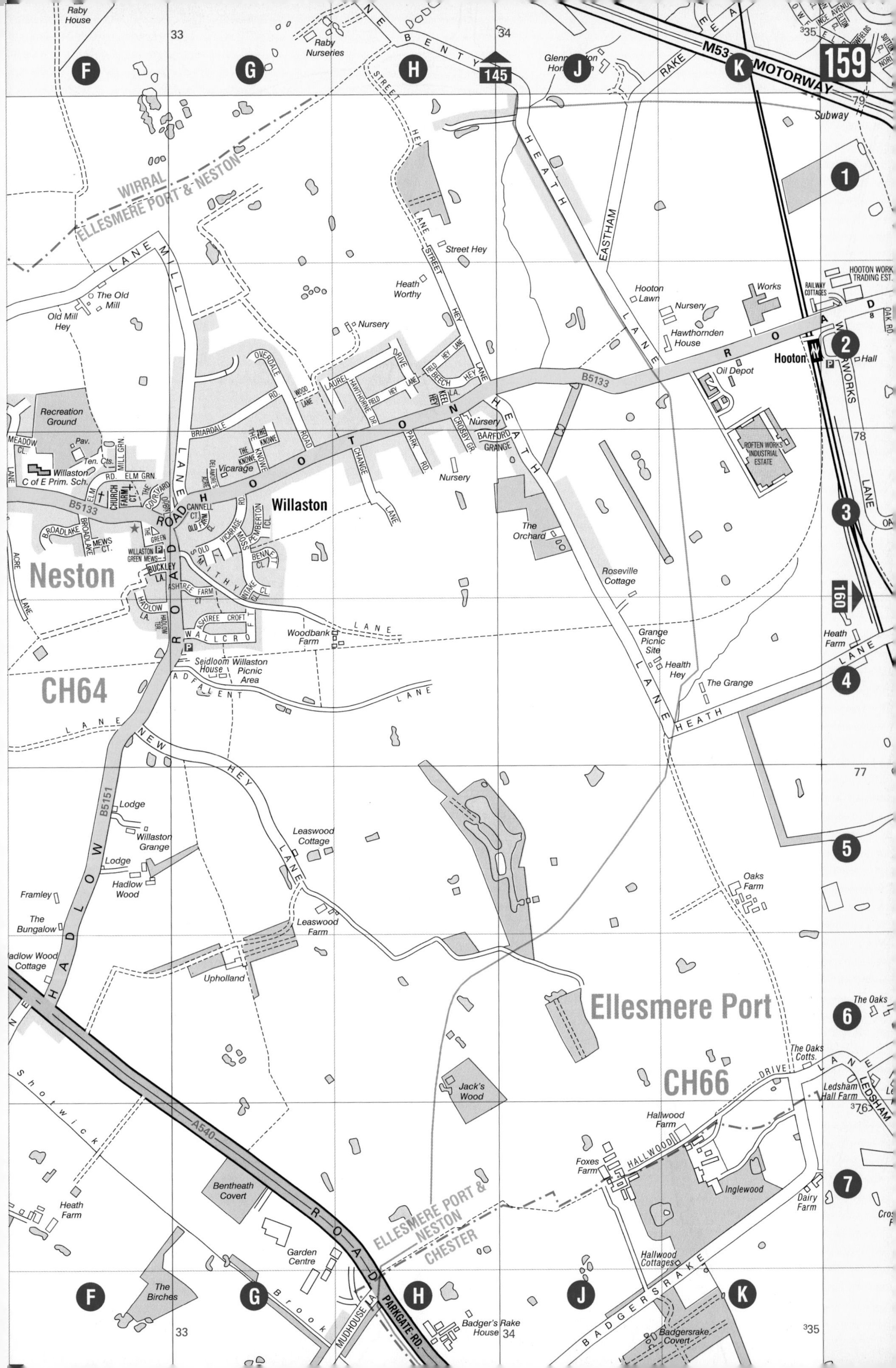
Willaston
Neston
CH64
Ellesmere Port
CH66
Hooton
M53 MOTORWAY
B5133
B5151
A540
HOOTON ROAD
HADLOW ROAD
PARKGATE RD.
BENTY HEATH LANE
HEATH LANE
EASTHAM RAKE
STREET HEY LANE
MILL LANE
NEW HEY LANE
BADGERSRAKE
HALLWOOD DRIVE
LEDSHAM LANE
Shotwick Brook
WIRRAL
ELLESMERE PORT & NESTON
CHESTER
Raby House
Raby Nurseries
Street Hey
Heath Worthy
Nursery
The Old Mill
Old Mill Hey
Recreation Ground
Pav.
Willaston C of E Prim. Sch.
Vicarage
The Orchard
Roseville Cottage
Grange Picnic Site
Health Hey
The Grange
Hooton Lawn
Hawthornden House
Works
Oil Depot
ROFTEN WORKS INDUSTRIAL ESTATE
HOOTON WORKS TRADING EST.
RAILWAY COTTAGES
Hall
Subway
Heath Farm
Woodbank Farm
Seidloom House
Willaston Picnic Area
Lodge
Willaston Grange
Hadlow Wood
Framley
The Bungalow
Hadlow Wood Cottage
Leaswood Cottage
Leaswood Farm
Upholland
Jack's Wood
Bentheath Covert
Garden Centre
The Birches
Badger's Rake House
Badgersrake Covert
Hallwood Cottages
Hallwood Farm
Foxes Farm
Inglewood
Dairy Farm
Oaks Farm
The Oaks
The Oaks Cotts.
Ledsham Hall Farm
145
160
33
34
35
76
77
78
79
F
G
H
J
K
1
2
3
4
5
6
7

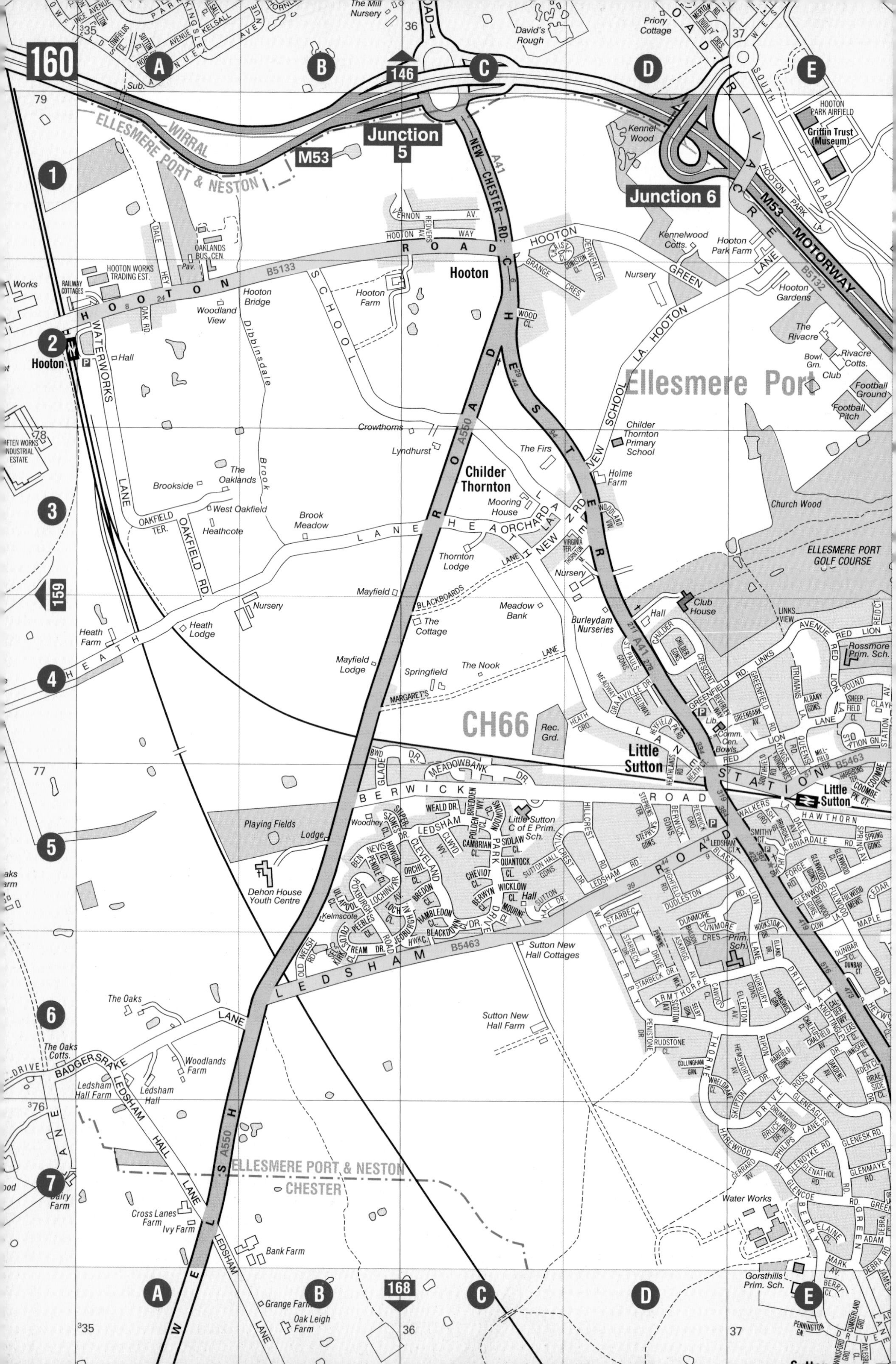
Junction 5
M53
Junction 6
M53 MOTORWAY
146
159
168
ELLESMERE PORT & NESTON
CHESTER
WIRRAL
Hooton
Ellesmere Port
Childer Thornton
Little Sutton
CH66
HOOTON ROAD
B5133
NEW CHESTER RD.
A41
A550
WELSH ROAD
LEDSHAM ROAD
B5463
BERWICK ROAD
STATION RD.
HOOTON GREEN
SCHOOL LA. HOOTON
WATERWORKS LANE
OAKFIELD RD.
HEATH LANE
BADGERS RAKE LANE
LEDSHAM HALL LANE
HOOTON WORKS TRADING EST.
OAKLANDS BUS CEN.
Hooton Bridge
Hooton Farm
Woodland View
Dibbinsdale Brook
Brookside
The Oaklands
West Oakfield
Heathcote
Brook Meadow
Heath Lodge
Heath Farm
Nursery
Kennel Wood
Kennelwood Cotts.
Hooton Park Farm
Hooton Gardens
The Rivacre
Rivacre Cotts.
Bowl. Grn.
Club
Football Ground
Football Pitch
HOOTON PARK AIRFIELD
Griffin Trust (Museum)
Childer Thornton Primary School
Holme Farm
The Firs
Crowthorns
Lyndhurst
Mooring House
Thornton Lodge
Mayfield
Meadow Bank
The Cottage
Burleydam Nurseries
Mayfield Lodge
Springfield
The Nook
Rec. Grd.
Club House
Church Wood
ELLESMERE PORT GOLF COURSE
Rossmore Prim. Sch.
Comm. Cen.
Lib.
Bowls.
Playing Fields
Lodge
Dehon House Youth Centre
Little Sutton C of E Prim. Sch.
Sutton New Hall Cottages
Sutton New Hall Farm
Prim. Sch.
The Oaks
The Oaks Cotts.
Woodlands Farm
Ledsham Hall Farm
Ledsham Hall
Dairy Farm
Cross Lanes Farm
Ivy Farm
Bank Farm
Grange Farm
Oak Leigh Farm
Water Works
Gorsthills Prim. Sch.
The Mill Nursery
David's Rough
Priory Cottage
Works
Hall

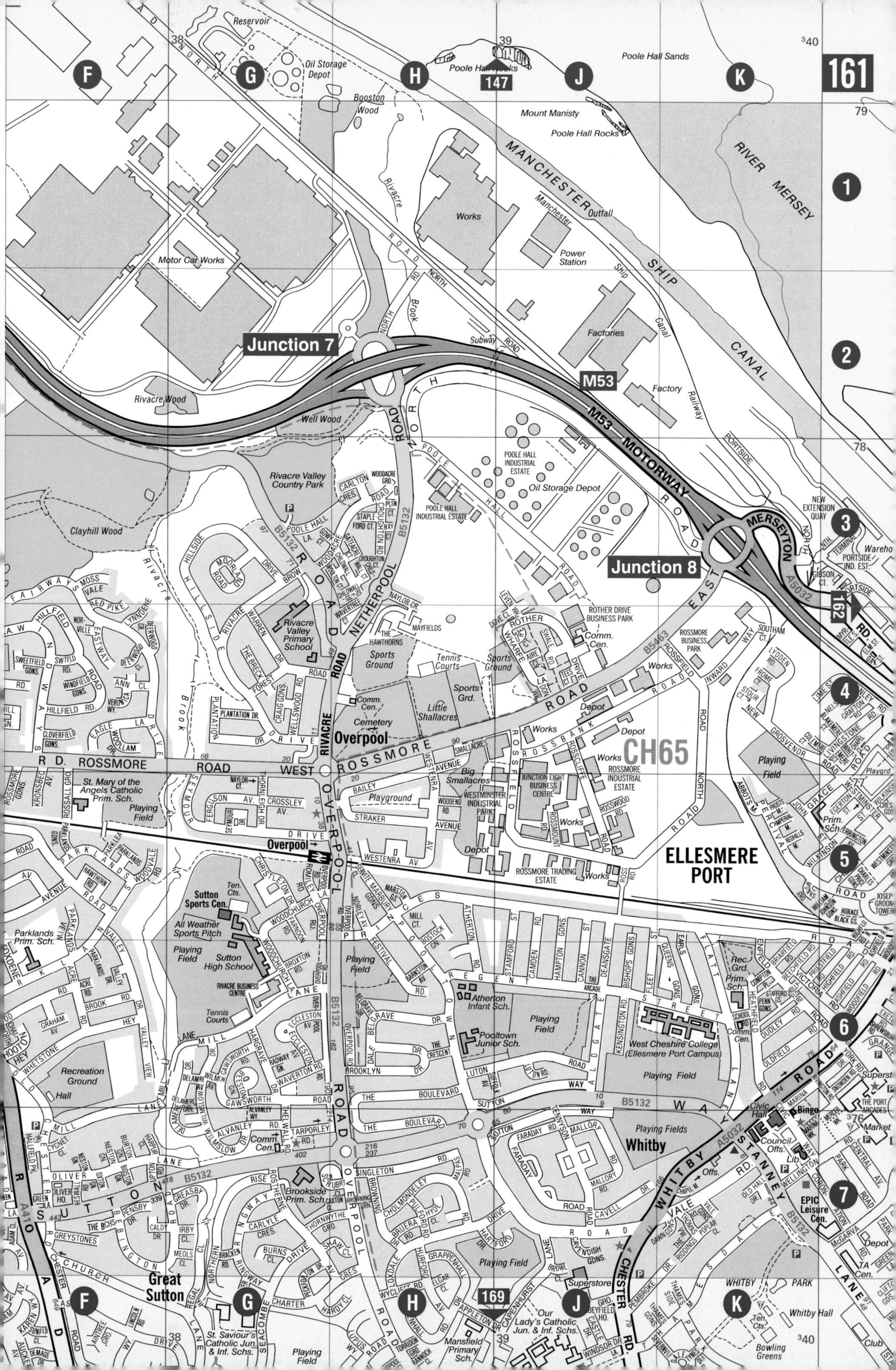
Reservoir
Oil Storage Depot
Booston Wood
Poole Hall Rocks
147
Poole Hall Sands
Mount Manisty
Poole Hall Rocks
RIVER MERSEY
MANCHESTER SHIP CANAL
Manchester Outfall
Works
Power Station
Motor Car Works
Rivacre
NORTH ROAD
Brook
Factories
Factory
Railway
Junction 7
M53
Subway
Rivacre Wood
Well Wood
M53 MOTORWAY
POOLE HALL INDUSTRIAL ESTATE
Oil Storage Depot
POOLE HALL ROAD
PORTSIDE
NEW EXTENSION QUAY
MERSEYTON
A5032
Junction 8
PORTSIDE IND. EST.
GIBSON CT.
162
Rivacre Valley Country Park
Clayhill Wood
POOLE HALL
B5132
NETHERPOOL ROAD
ROTHER DRIVE BUSINESS PARK
Comm. Cen.
ROSSMORE BUSINESS PARK
SOUTHAM CT.
Rivacre Valley Primary School
MAYFIELDS
THE HAWTHORNS
Sports Ground
Tennis Courts
Sports Ground
Sports Grd.
Little Shallacres
B5463
EAST ROAD
Works
Depot
Cemetery
Comm. Cen.
Overpool
RIVACRE ROAD
ROSSMORE ROAD
WEST
ROSSBANK
CH65
ROSSMORE INDUSTRIAL ESTATE
Playing Field
GROSVENOR
St. Mary of the Angels Catholic Prim. Sch.
Playing Field
Playground
Big Smallacres
WESTMINSTER INDUSTRIAL PARK
JUNCTION EIGHT BUSINESS CENTRE
Works
Depot
ROSSMORE TRADING ESTATE
ELLESMERE PORT
Prim. Sch.
Overpool
OVERPOOL ROAD
Sutton Sports Cen.
All Weather Sports Pitch
Playing Field
Sutton High School
Parklands Prim. Sch.
RIVACRE BUSINESS CENTRE
Tennis Courts
Playing Field
Atherton Infant Sch.
Playing Field
Pooltown Junior Sch.
West Cheshire College (Ellesmere Port Campus)
Rec. Grd.
Prim. Sch.
Comm. Cen.
Recreation Ground
Hall
Playing Field
B5132
SUTTON WAY
Playing Fields
Whitby
Civic Hall
Bingo
Council Offs.
Lib.
Superstore
THE PORT ARCADES
Market
WHITBY ROAD
A5032
STANNEY LANE
EPIC Leisure Cen.
Comm. Cen.
Brookside Prim. Sch.
SUTTON LANE
B5132
Playing Field
Superstore
CHESTER RD.
Depot
TA Cen.
Great Sutton
A410
169
WHITBY PARK
Whitby Hall
Our Lady's Catholic Jun. & Inf. Schs.
St. Saviour's Catholic Jun. & Inf. Schs.
Playing Field
Mansfield Primary Sch.
Bowling Greens
Club
F
G
H
J
K
1
2
3
4
5
6
7
38
39
340
79
78
77
76

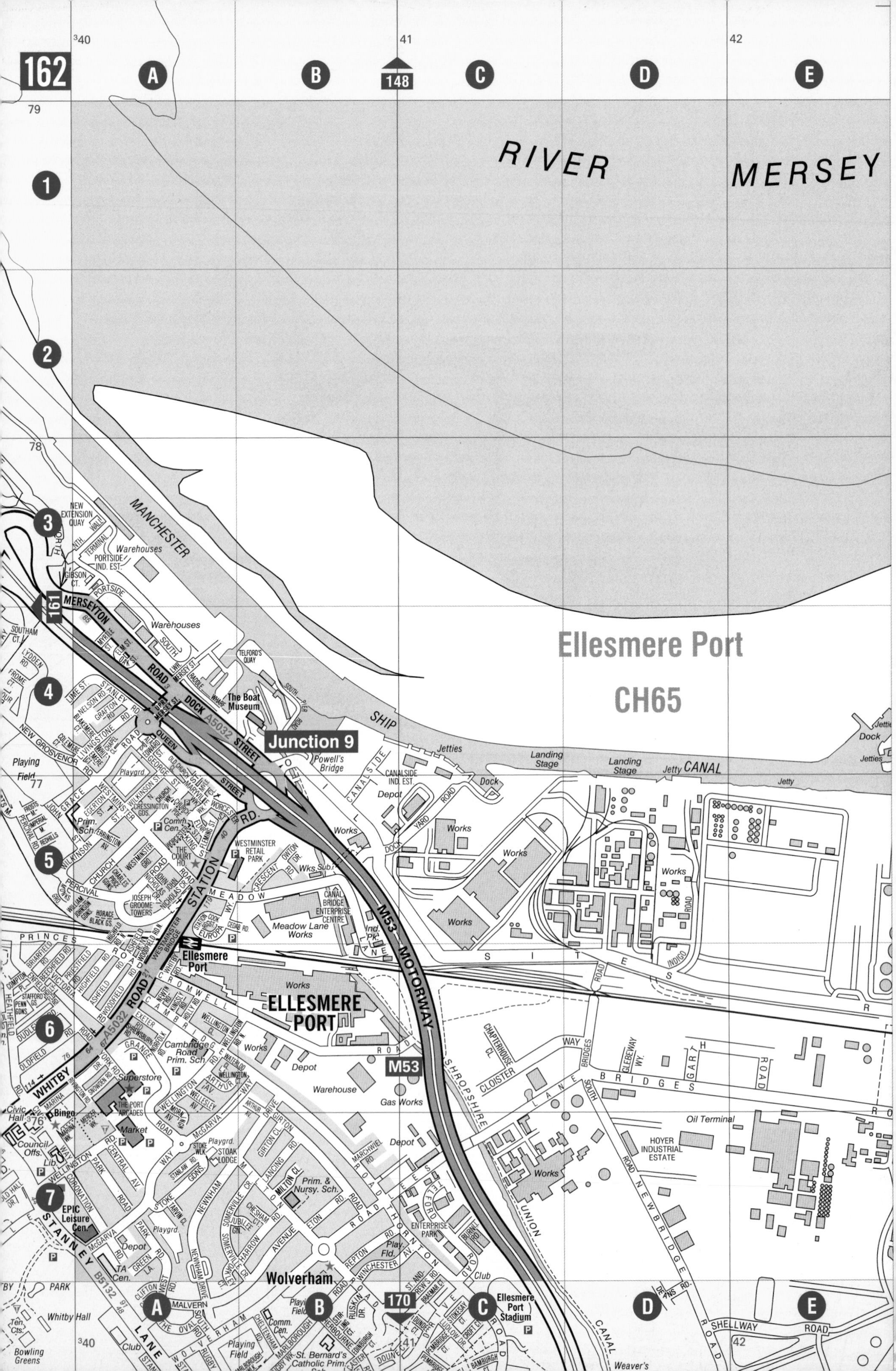

RIVER MERSEY
Ellesmere Port
CH65
MANCHESTER SHIP CANAL
Junction 9
The Boat Museum
ELLESMERE PORT
Ellesmere Port
M53 MOTORWAY
Warehouses
Works
Depot
Gas Works
Oil Terminal
HOYER INDUSTRIAL ESTATE
Wolverham
Ellesmere Port Stadium
EPIC Leisure Cen.
Whitby Hall
Civic Hall
Council Offs.
Market
Superstore
Landing Stage
Jetties
Dock
Powell's Bridge
Meadow Lane Works
CANAL BRIDGE ENTERPRISE CENTRE
WESTMINSTER RETAIL PARK
ENTERPRISE PARK
Cambridge Road Prim. Sch.
Prim. & Nursy. Sch.
St. Bernard's Catholic Prim.
SHROPSHIRE UNION CANAL

148 161 170

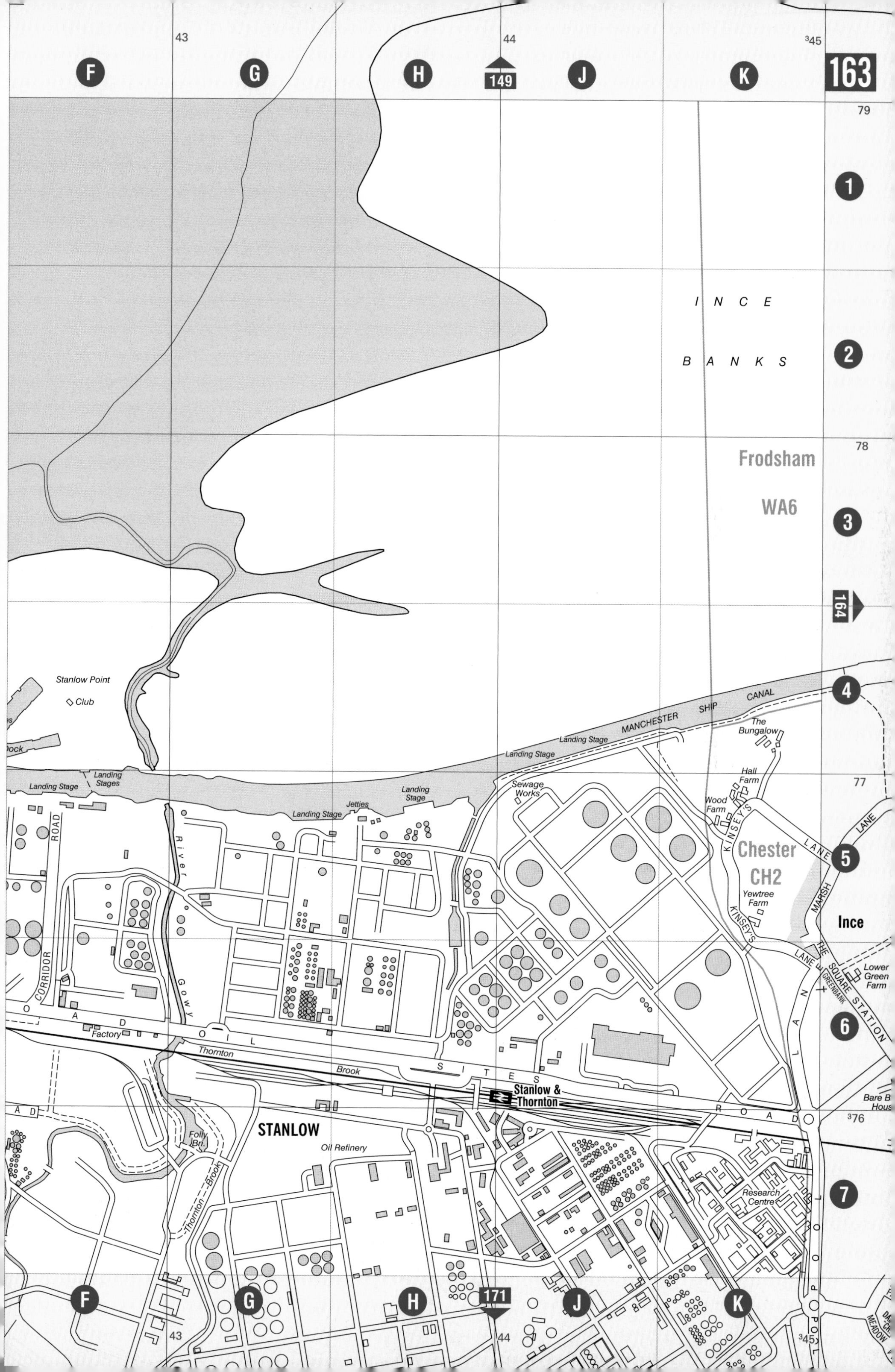

43   44   345

79

1

I N C E

B A N K S

2

Frodsham   78

WA6

3

164

Stanlow Point   MANCHESTER   SHIP   CANAL   **4**

◊ Club   The Bungalow

Landing Stage   Landing Stage

Dock   Landing Stage   Hall Farm   77

Landing   Wood Farm

Stages   Landing Stage   Sewage   **Chester**   Kinsey's Lane   MARSH LANE   **5**

Landing Stage   Landing Stage   Jetties   Works   **CH2**   Yewtree Farm   **Ince**

ROAD   River Gowy   Kinsey's Lane   GREENBANK   Lower Green Farm

CORRIDOR   THE SQUARE   STATION   **6**

ROAD   Factory   OIL   Thornton   S I T E S   Bare B Hous

376

Thornton   Brook   ROAD

Folly Br.   **Stanlow & Thornton**

ROAD   **STANLOW**   Oil Refinery

Research   **7**

Centre

43   44   345

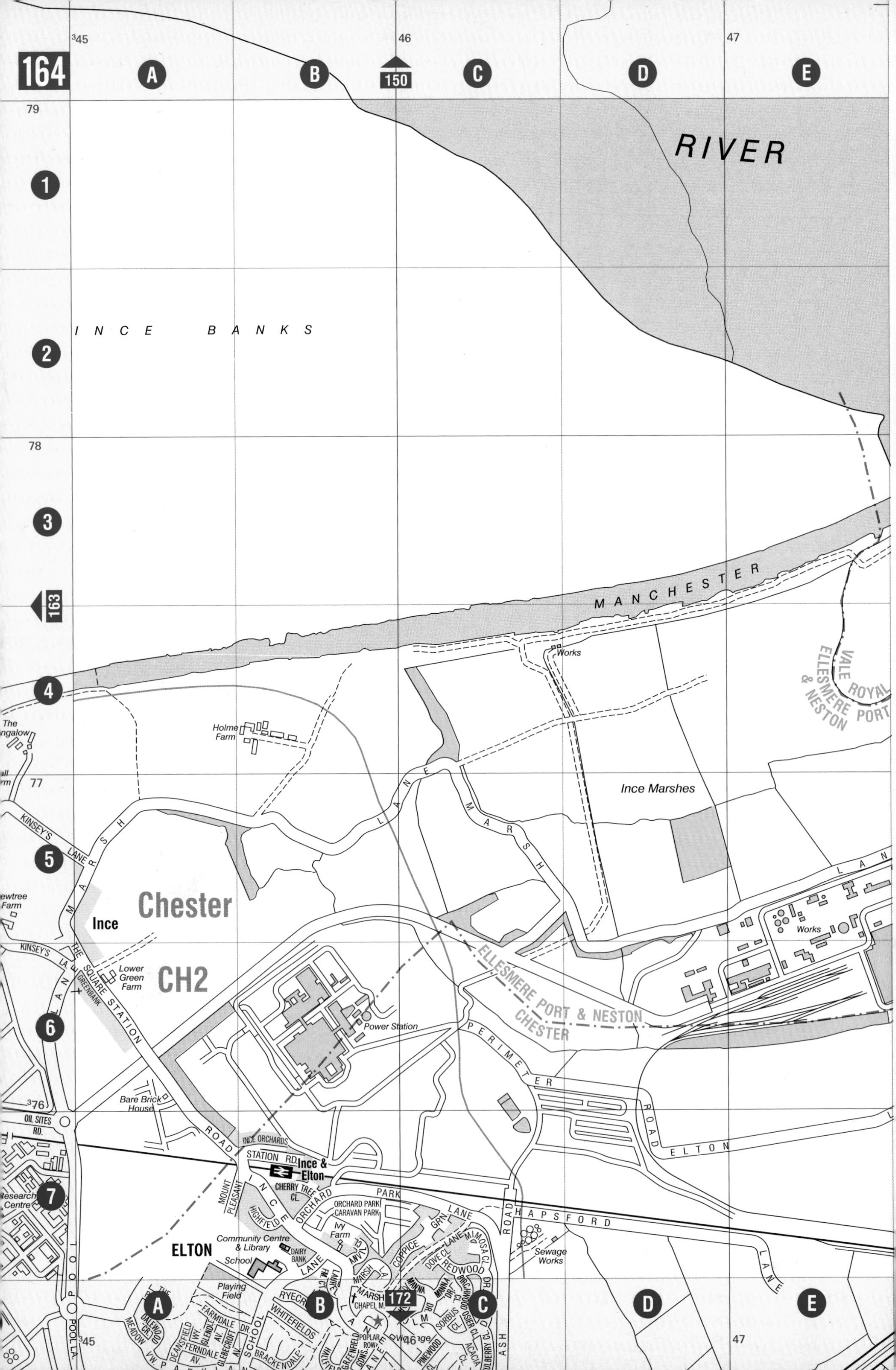

345
46
47
A
B
C
D
E
150
79
1
2
3
4
5
6
7
78
77
376
163
172
RIVER
MANCHESTER
INCE BANKS
Holme Farm
Works
Ince Marshes
VALE ROYAL
ELLESMERE PORT & NESTON
MARSH LANE
KINSEY'S LANE
Chester
Ince
CH2
Lower Green Farm
THE SQUARE
STATION
GREENBANK
Power Station
ELLESMERE PORT & NESTON
CHESTER
PERIMETER ROAD
ELTON
Bare Brick House
OIL SITES RD.
ROAD
INCE ORCHARDS
STATION RD.
Ince & Elton
CHERRY TREE CL.
MOUNT PLEASANT
INCE
ORCHARD
PARK
HIGHFIELD
ORCHARD PARK CARAVAN PARK
Ivy Farm
HAPSFORD
LANE
Community Centre & Library
ELTON
School
DAIRY BANK
Playing Field
Sewage Works
Research Centre
POOL LA.
MARSH
COPPICE
GRN.
DOVE CL.
REDWOOD
MIMOSA CL.
CHAPEL M.
POPLAR ROW
Vicarage
WHITEFIELDS
FARMDALE DR.
DEANSFIELD
FERNDALE AV.
GLEBECROFT AV.
BRACKENDALE
SCHOOL
PINEWOOD
SORBUS CL.
OSIER CL.
ACACIA
MULBERRY CL.
ASH
The Bungalow
Newtree Farm

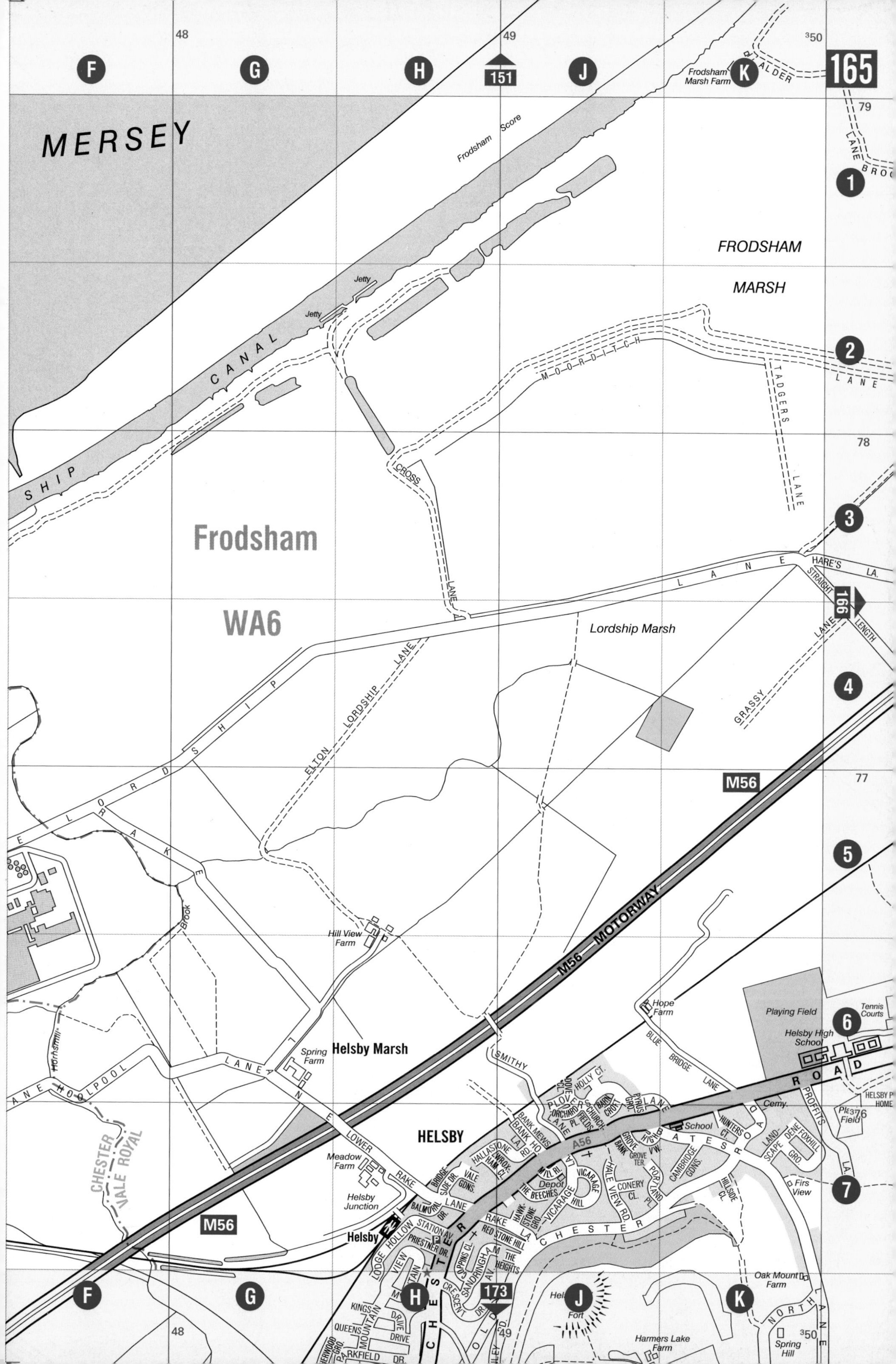
MERSEY
SHIP CANAL
Frodsham Score
Frodsham Marsh Farm
FRODSHAM MARSH
Frodsham
WA6
Lordship Marsh
Hill View Farm
Spring Farm
Helsby Marsh
HELSBY
Meadow Farm
Helsby Junction
Helsby
M56 MOTORWAY
M56
Hope Farm
Playing Field
Tennis Courts
Helsby High School
School
Cemy.
Depot
Firs View
Oak Mount Farm
Harmers Lake Farm
Spring Hill
Fort
MOORDITCH LANE
TADGERS LANE
CROSS LANE
LORDSHIP LANE
ELTON LORDSHIP LANE
GRASSY LANE
HARE'S LA.
STRAIGHT LENGTH
RAKE LANE
HOOLPOOL LANE
LOWER RAKE LANE
CHESTER VALE ROYAL
SMITHY LANE
BLUE BRIDGE LANE
CHESTER ROAD
BATES ROAD
PROFFITS LA.
NORTH LANE
ALDER LANE
Brook
Hornsmill
151
166
173
F G H J K
1 2 3 4 5 6 7
48 49 350
79 78 77 376

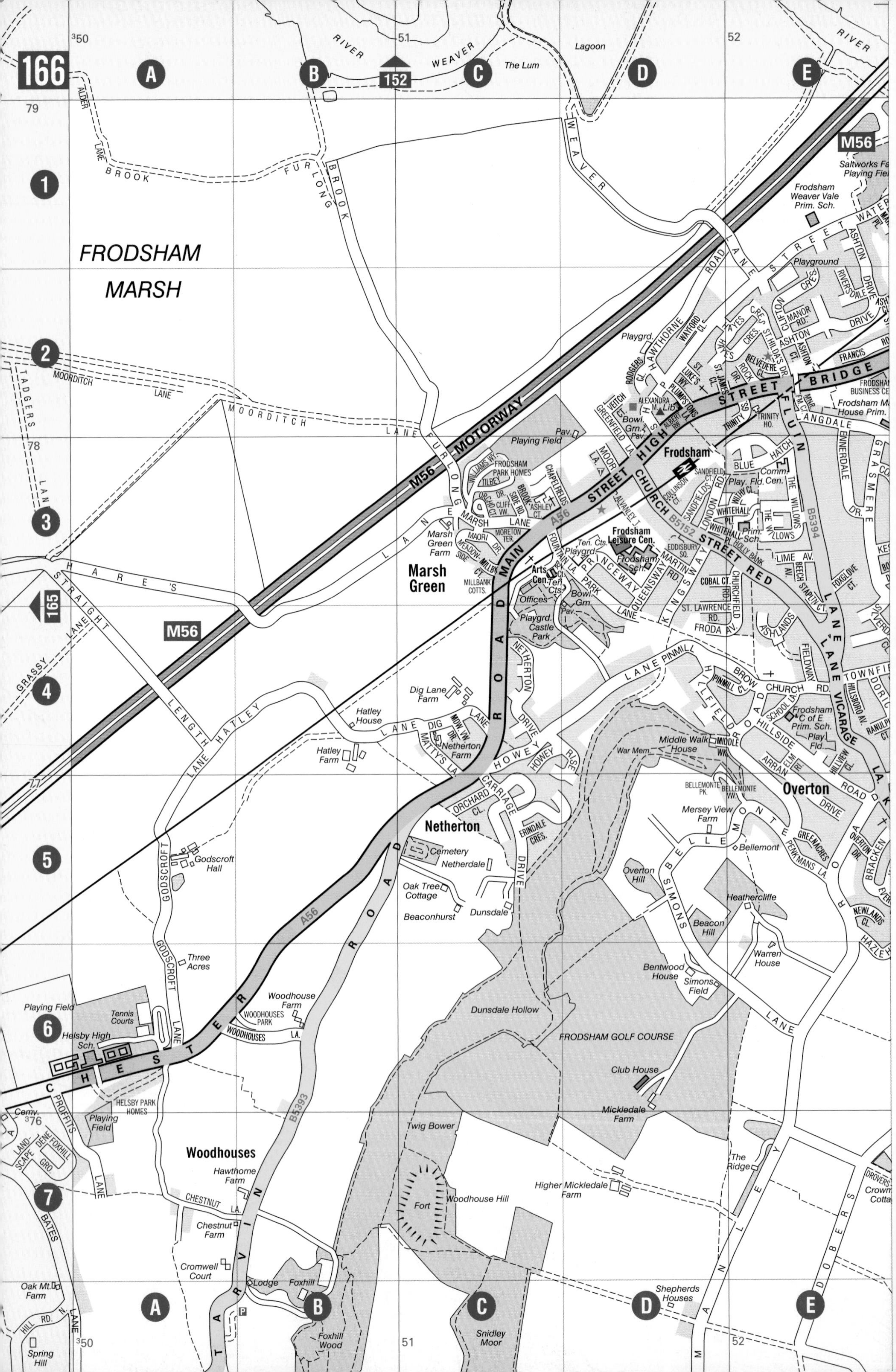

FRODSHAM MARSH
RIVER WEAVER
152
165
M56
M56 MOTORWAY
The Lum
Lagoon
ALDER LANE BROOK
FURLONG BROOK
MOORDITCH LANE
TADGERS LANE
HARE'S LANE
STRAIGHT LENGTH
GRASSY LANE
HATLEY LANE
Saltworks Farm Playing Field
Frodsham Weaver Vale Prim. Sch.
Playground
Playgrd.
Playing Field
FRODSHAM PARK HOMES
MARSH LANE
Marsh Green Farm
Marsh Green
Frodsham
Frodsham Leisure Cen.
Frodsham Sch.
Arts Cen.
Offices
Playgrd. Castle Park
MAIN STREET
HIGH STREET
CHURCH STREET
BRIDGE STREET
MAIN ROAD
A56
B5152
B5394
FLUIN LANE
VICARAGE LANE
Frodsham Business Centre
Frodsham Manor House Prim.
LANGDALE
ENNERDALE
GRASMERE
Comm. Cen.
Play. Fld.
Prim. Sch.
Dig Lane Farm
Hatley House
Hatley Farm
Netherton Farm
Netherton
Cemetery
Netherdale
Oak Tree Cottage
Beaconhurst
Dunsdale
Godscroft Hall
GODSCROFT LANE
Three Acres
Playing Field
Tennis Courts
Helsby High Sch.
CHESTER ROAD
WOODHOUSES LA.
Woodhouse Farm
HELSBY PARK HOMES
Woodhouses
Hawthorne Farm
CHESTNUT LA.
Chestnut Farm
Cromwell Court
Oak Mt. Farm
Spring Hill
Lodge
Foxhill
Foxhill Wood
TARVIN ROAD
B5393
Twig Bower
Fort
Woodhouse Hill
Snidley Moor
Dunsdale Hollow
FRODSHAM GOLF COURSE
Club House
Mickledale Farm
Higher Mickledale Farm
Shepherds Houses
MANLEY LANE
DOBERS LANE
The Ridge
Overton
Middle Walk House
War Mem.
Frodsham C of E Prim. Sch.
Mersey View Farm
Bellemont
Overton Hill
Beacon Hill
Heathercliffe
Warren House
Bentwood House
Simons Field
SIMONS LANE
BELLEMONTE ROAD
HILLSIDE
PINMILL LANE
CHURCH RD.
Crowmere Cottage

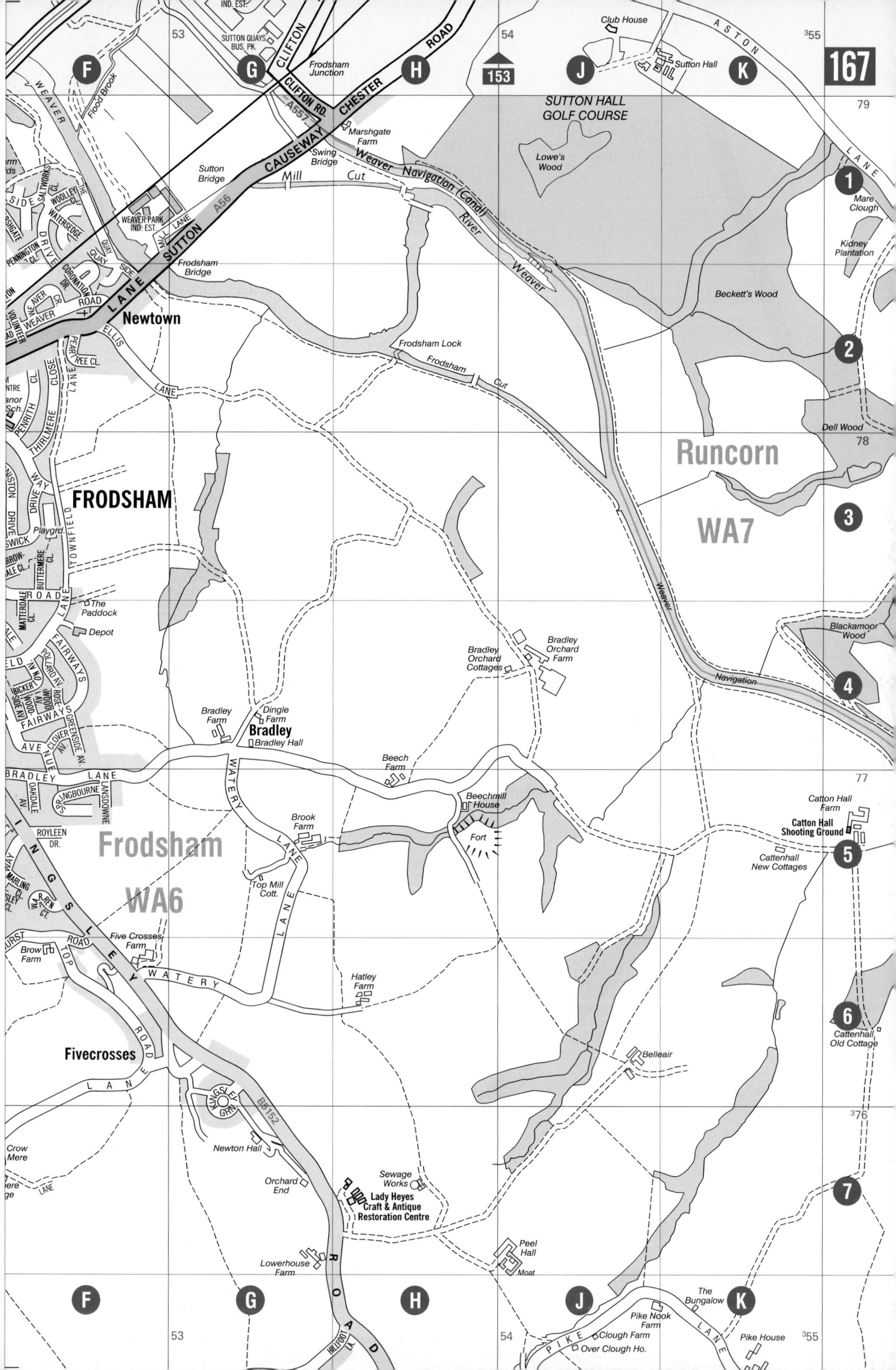

SUTTON HALL GOLF COURSE
Club House
Sutton Hall
Lowe's Wood
Frodsham Junction
Marshgate Farm
Swing Bridge
Sutton Bridge
Weaver Navigation (Canal)
Mill Cut
River Weaver
Frodsham Bridge
Frodsham Lock
Frodsham Cut
Newtown
FRODSHAM
Mare Clough
Kidney Plantation
Beckett's Wood
Dell Wood
Runcorn
WA7
Blackamoor Wood
Bradley Orchard Farm
Bradley Orchard Cottages
Bradley Farm
Dingle Farm
Bradley
Bradley Hall
Beech Farm
Beechmill House
Fort
Brook Farm
Top Mill Cott.
Catton Hall Farm
Catton Hall Shooting Ground
Cattenhall New Cottages
Cattenhall Old Cottage
Frodsham
WA6
Five Crosses Farm
Brow Farm
Hatley Farm
Fivecrosses
Belleair
Newton Hall
Orchard End
Sewage Works
Lady Heyes Craft & Antique Restoration Centre
Peel Hall
Moat
Lowerhouse Farm
Crow Mere
The Bungalow
Pike Nook Farm
Clough Farm
Over Clough Ho.
Pike House
WEAVER PARK IND. EST.
SUTTON QUAYS BUS. PK.
Playgrd.
The Paddock
Depot
CHESTER ROAD
CAUSEWAY
SUTTON LANE
CLIFTON RD.
A557
A56
B5152
KINGSLEY ROAD
WATERY LANE
BRADLEY LANE
PIKE LANE
ASTON LANE
ELLIS LANE
TOWNFIELD LANE
153

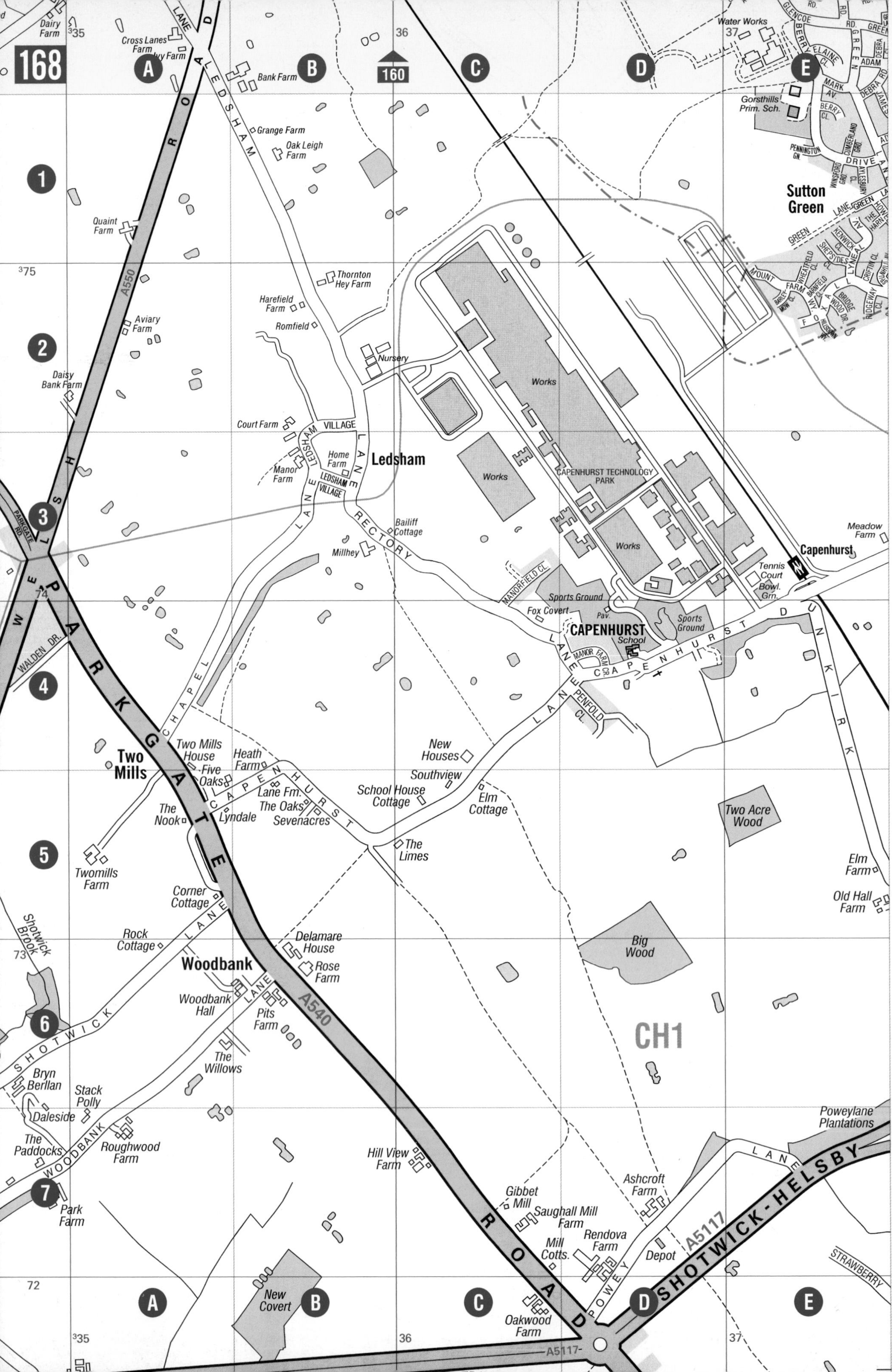

Sutton Green

Gorsthills Prim. Sch.

Water Works

Dairy Farm

Cross Lanes Farm
Ivy Farm

Bank Farm

160

Grange Farm

Oak Leigh Farm

Quaint Farm

Aviary Farm

Thornton Hey Farm

Harefield Farm

Romfield

Nursery

Daisy Bank Farm

Court Farm

LEDSHAM VILLAGE

Home Farm

Manor Farm

LEDSHAM VILLAGE

Ledsham

Works

Works

CAPENHURST TECHNOLOGY PARK

Works

Meadow Farm

Capenhurst

Bailiff Cottage

Millhey

RECTORY

Manorfield Cl.

Fox Covert

Sports Ground

Pav.

Tennis Court
Bowl. Grn.

Sports Ground

Walden Dr.

CAPENHURST
School

MANOR FARM DR.

CAPENHURST

DUNKIRK

Two Mills House
Five Oaks

Heath Farm

New Houses

Southview

Two Mills

The Nook

Lyndale

Lane Fm.
The Oaks
Sevenacres

School House Cottage

Elm Cottage

Two Acre Wood

Penfold Cl.

Twomills Farm

Corner Cottage

The Limes

Elm Farm

Old Hall Farm

Shotwick Brook

Rock Cottage

Delamare House

Rose Farm

Big Wood

CH1

Woodbank

Woodbank Hall

Pits Farm

The Willows

A540

Poweylane Plantations

Bryn Berllan

Stack Polly

Daleside

The Paddocks

Roughwood Farm

Hill View Farm

Ashcroft Farm

SHOTWICK-HELSBY

LANE

Park Farm

Gibbet Mill

Saughall Mill Farm

Mill Cotts.

Rendova Farm

Depot

POWEY

A5117

New Covert

Oakwood Farm

A5117

ROAD

STRAWBERRY

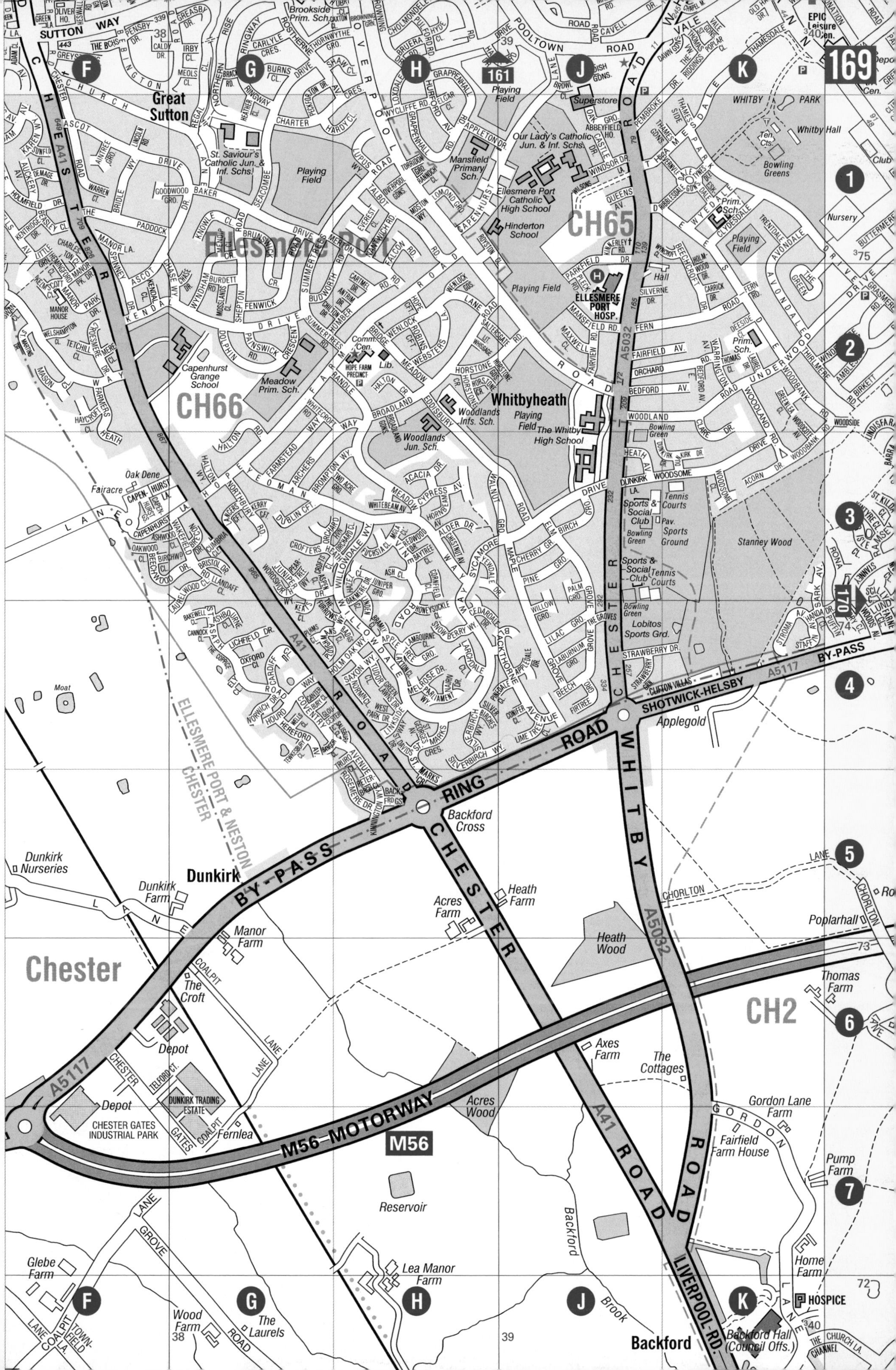
Great Sutton
Ellesmere Port
CH65
CH66
CH2
Whitbyheath
Chester
Dunkirk
Backford
Backford Cross
SUTTON WAY
CHESTER ROAD
POOLTOWN ROAD
OVERPOOL ROAD
WHITBY ROAD
SHOTWICK-HELSBY BY-PASS
RING ROAD
BY-PASS
M56 MOTORWAY
A41 ROAD
LIVERPOOL RD.
St. Saviour's Catholic Jun. & Inf. Schs.
Capenhurst Grange School
Meadow Prim. Sch.
Mansfield Primary Sch.
Our Lady's Catholic Jun. & Inf. Schs.
Ellesmere Port Catholic High School
Hinderton School
ELLESMERE PORT HOSP.
Woodlands Infs. Sch.
Woodlands Jun. Sch.
The Whitby High School
Whitby Hall
WHITBY PARK
Stanney Wood
Heath Wood
Acres Wood
Reservoir
Lobitos Sports Grd.
Sports & Social Club
Tennis Courts
Applegold
Dunkirk Nurseries
Dunkirk Farm
Manor Farm
Acres Farm
Heath Farm
Axes Farm
The Cottages
Gordon Lane Farm
Fairfield Farm House
Pump Farm
Home Farm
HOSPICE
Backford Hall (Council Offs.)
Thomas Farm
Poplarhall
Lea Manor Farm
Glebe Farm
Wood Farm
The Laurels
Fernlea
The Croft
Depot
CHESTER GATES INDUSTRIAL PARK
DUNKIRK TRADING ESTATE
ELLESMERE PORT & NESTON
CHESTER
Oak Dene
Fairacre
Moat
EPIC Leisure Cen.
Superstore
Playing Field
Nursery
Bowling Greens
161
170

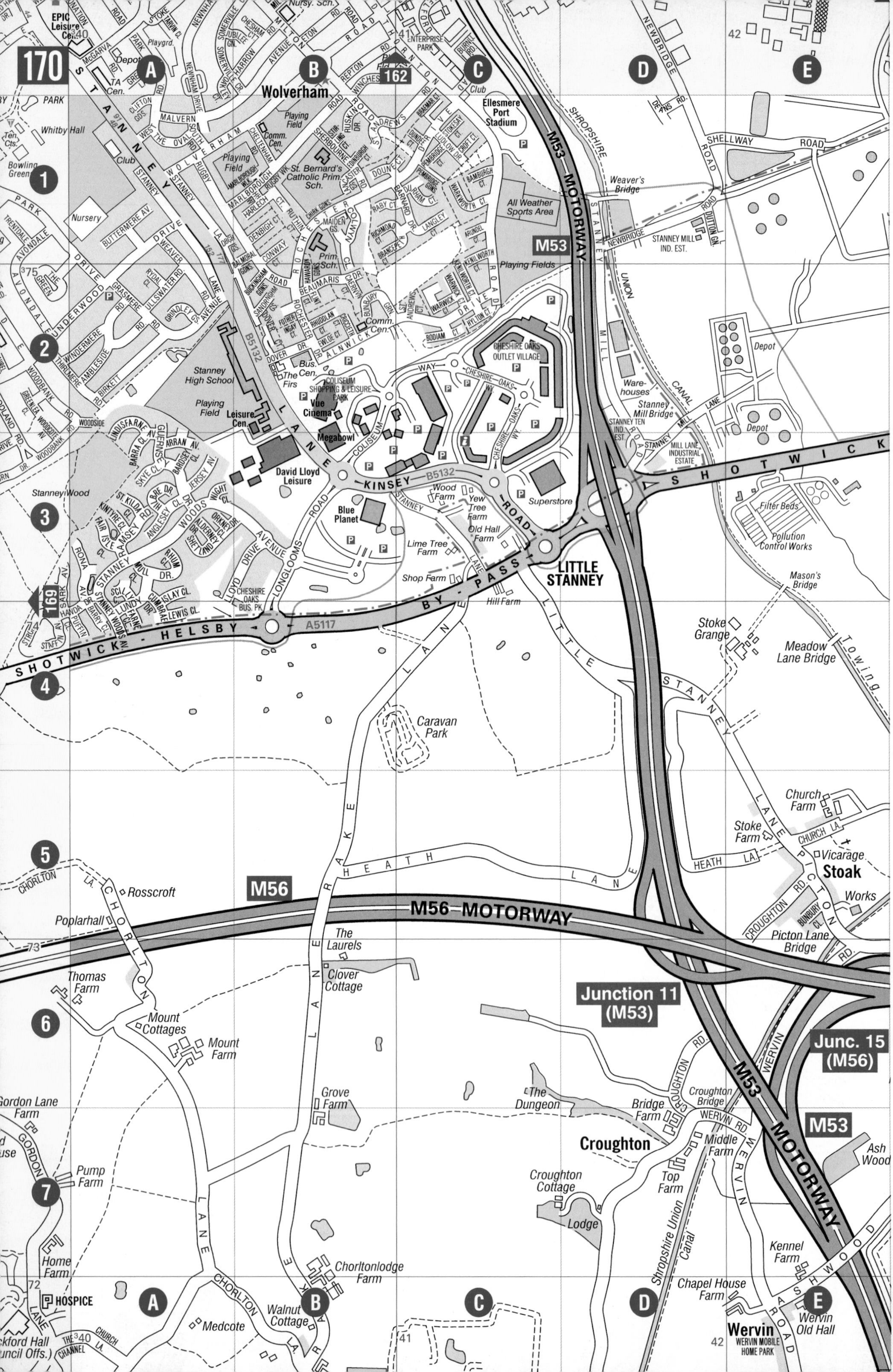
Wolverham
Ellesmere Port Stadium
St. Bernard's Catholic Prim. Sch.
All Weather Sports Area
Playing Fields
CHESHIRE OAKS OUTLET VILLAGE
COLISEUM SHOPPING & LEISURE PARK
Vue Cinema
Megabowl
David Lloyd Leisure
Blue Planet
Superstore
Stanney High School
Stanney Wood
LITTLE STANNEY
M53 MOTORWAY
M56 MOTORWAY
Junction 11 (M53)
Junc. 15 (M56)
Stoak
Croughton
Wervin
Caravan Park
Pollution Control Works
Mason's Bridge
Meadow Lane Bridge
Stoke Grange
Church Farm
Stoke Farm
Vicarage
Picton Lane Bridge
Thomas Farm
Mount Cottages
Mount Farm
Grove Farm
The Laurels
Clover Cottage
Chorltonlodge Farm
Walnut Cottage
Medcote
HOSPICE
Home Farm
Pump Farm
Gordon Lane Farm
Croughton Cottage
Lodge
The Dungeon
Bridge Farm
Middle Farm
Top Farm
Kennel Farm
Chapel House Farm
Wervin Old Hall
WERVIN MOBILE HOME PARK
Ash Wood
Shropshire Union Canal
Poplarhall
Rosscroft
Hill Farm
Shop Farm
Lime Tree Farm
Wood Farm
Yew Tree Farm
Old Hall Farm
Stanney Mill Bridge
STANNEY MILL IND. EST.
MILL LANE INDUSTRIAL ESTATE
Weaver's Bridge
Depot
Whitby Hall
Nursery
EPIC Leisure Cen.

162
169

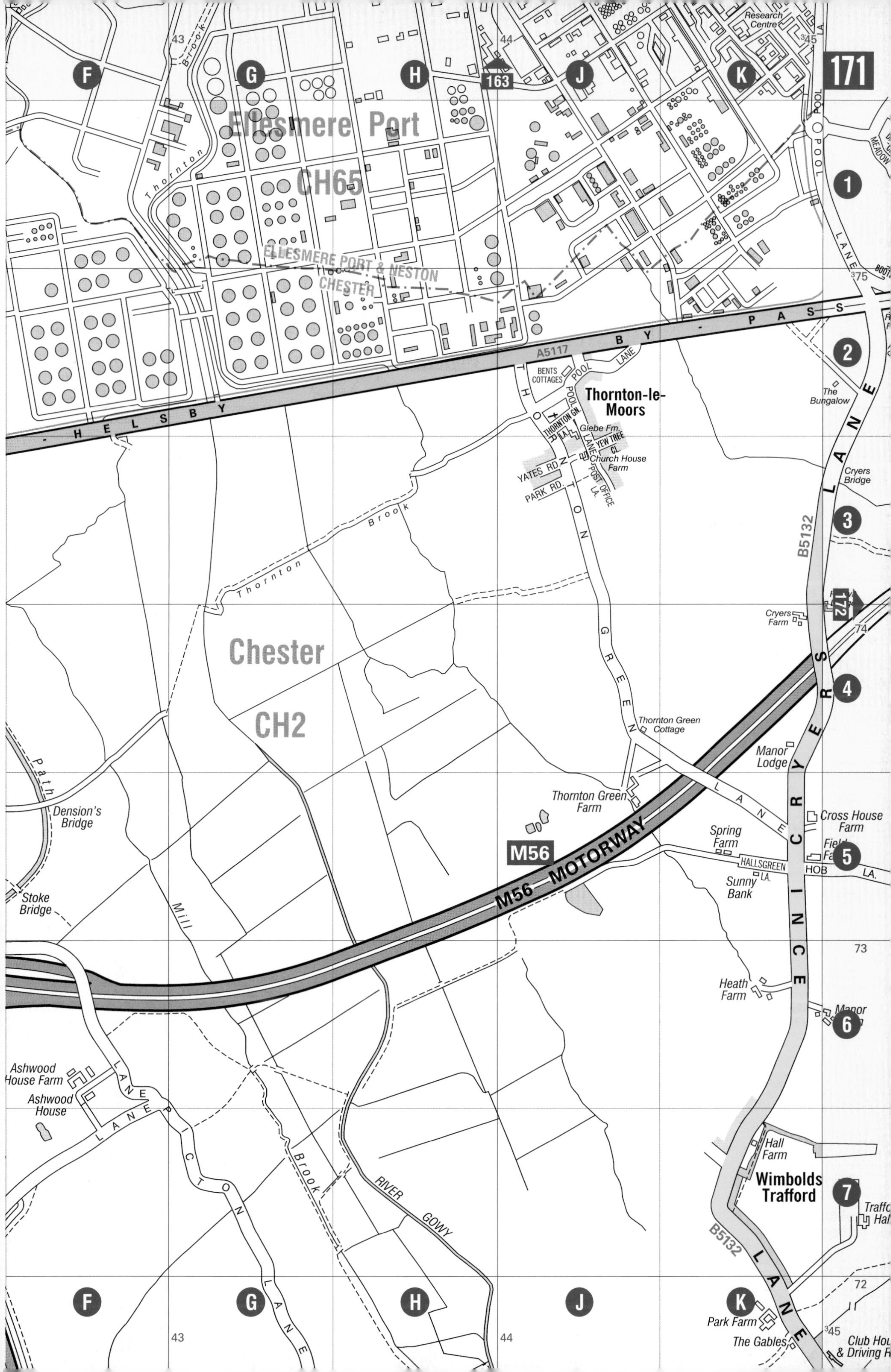

F G H J K

1
2
3
4
5
6
7

Ellesmere Port
CH65

ELLESMERE PORT & NESTON
CHESTER

163

Thornton

Brook

HELSBY

Chester

CH2

Thornton

Brook

Mill

Path

Dension's
Bridge

Stoke
Bridge

Ashwood
House Farm

Ashwood
House

LANE

PICTON

Brook

RIVER GOWY

A5117   BY - PASS

POOL LANE

BENTS
COTTAGES

THORNTON GN.
LA.

YATES RD.

PARK RD.

POST OFFICE
LA.

THORNTON

Thornton-le-
Moors

Glebe Fm.

YEW TREE
CL.
Church House
Farm

GREEN

Thornton Green
Cottage

Thornton Green
Farm

M56   M56 - MOTORWAY

LANE

Spring
Farm

HALLSGREEN
LA.

Sunny
Bank

Heath
Farm

The
Bungalow

Cryers
Bridge

B5132

172
74

Cryers
Farm

Manor
Lodge

LANE

Cross House
Farm

Field
Fa

HOB

LA.

73

Manor

Hall
Farm

Wimbolds
Trafford

B5132

LANE

Park Farm

The Gables

Club Hou
& Driving R

Traffo
Hal

PRINCE   CRYERS   LANE

POOL   LANE

Research
Centre
345

MEADOW

375

BOOTL

F G H J K

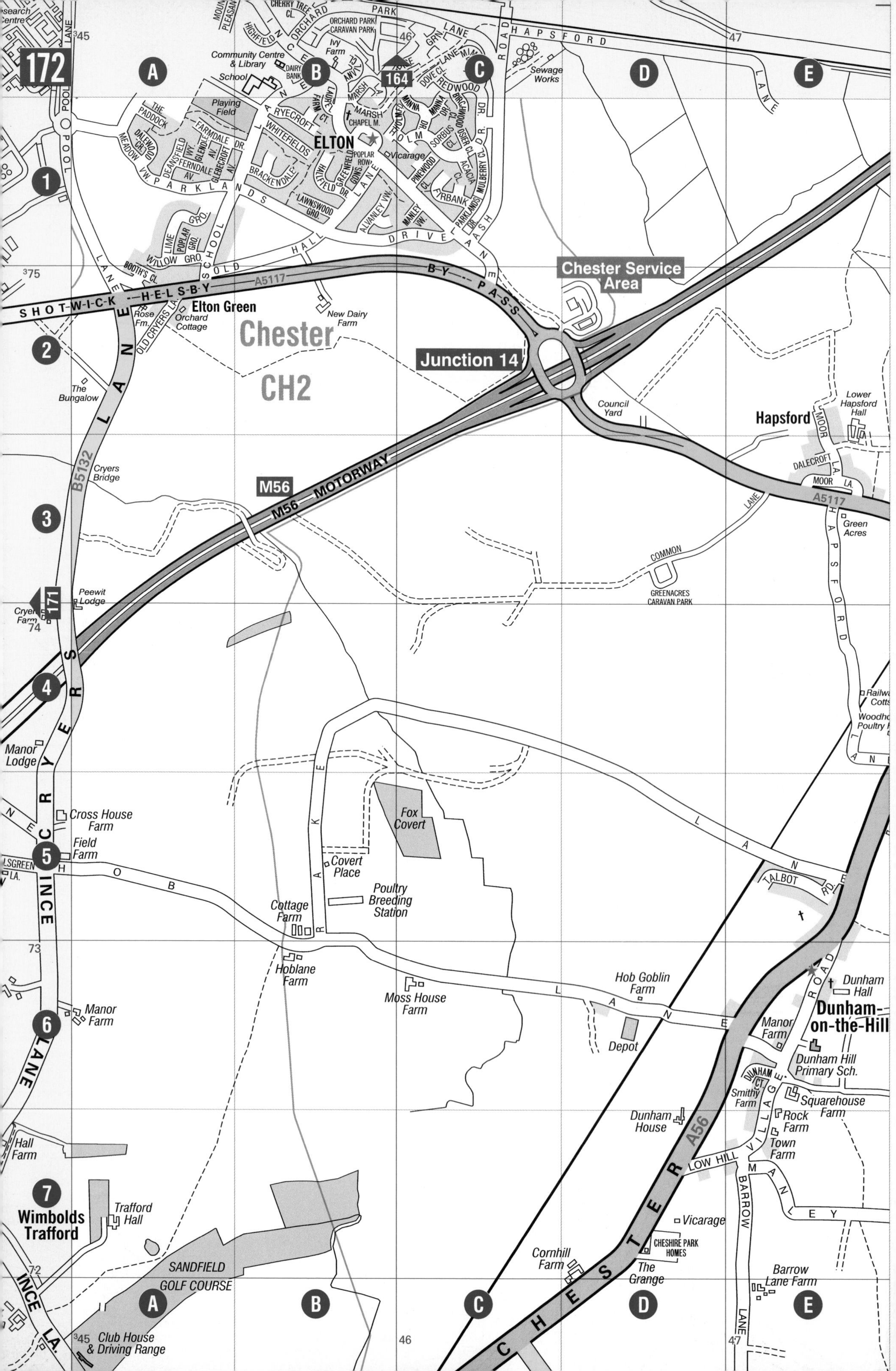

A   **B**   **C**   **D**   **E**

search
centre

MOUNT
PLEASAN

CHERRY TREE
CL.

ORCHARD
PARK

HAPSFORD

Community Centre
& Library

ORCHARD PARK
CARAVAN PARK

Road

HAPSFORD

164

Sewage
Works

Chester Service
Area

School

Playing
Field

THE
PADDOCK

Ivy
Farm

MARSH
CHAPEL M.

Vicarage

ELTON

THE
PADDOCK

PARKLAND

BOOTH'S CL.

WILLOW GRO.

POPLAR GRO.

LIME GRO.

A5117

ELTON-BY-PASS

Chester
CH2

Junction 14

1

375

SHOT·WICK

HELSBY

Rose
Fm.

Old Cryers La.

Orchard
Cottage

Elton Green

New Dairy
Farm

2

The
Bungalow

B5132

Cryers
Bridge

Council
Yard

Hapsford

Lower
Hapsford
Hall

DALECROFT

MOOR LA.

MOOR
LA.

A5117

3

M56   **M56 — MOTORWAY**

COMMON

Green
Acres

171

Peewit
Lodge

74

Cryers
Farm

GREENACRES
CARAVAN PARK

4

Manor
Lodge

LANE

HAPSFORD

Railway
Cotts

Woodhou
Poultry F

Cross House
Farm

Field
Farm

LSGREEN
LA.

Fox
Covert

Covert
Place

Poultry
Breeding
Station

TALBOT

Road

†

5

73

HOB

KE

R

Cottage
Farm

Hoblane
Farm

Moss House
Farm

LANE

Hob Goblin
Farm

Dunham
Hall

†

**Dunham-
on-the-Hill**

Manor
Farm

Dunham Hill
Primary Sch.

6

PRINCE

LANE

Manor
Farm

Depot

DUNHAM
CT.

Smithy
Farm

Rock
Farm

Squarehouse
Farm

Town
Farm

Hall
Farm

Dunham
House

VILLAGE

A56

LOW HILL

MANLEY

7

**Wimbolds
Trafford**

INCE LA.

Trafford
Hall

SANDFIELD
GOLF COURSE

Cornhill
Farm

CHESTER

The
Grange

Vicarage

CHESHIRE PARK
HOMES

Road

BARROW

Barrow
Lane Farm

LANE

345

Club House
& Driving Range

46

47

A   **B**   **C**   **D**   **E**

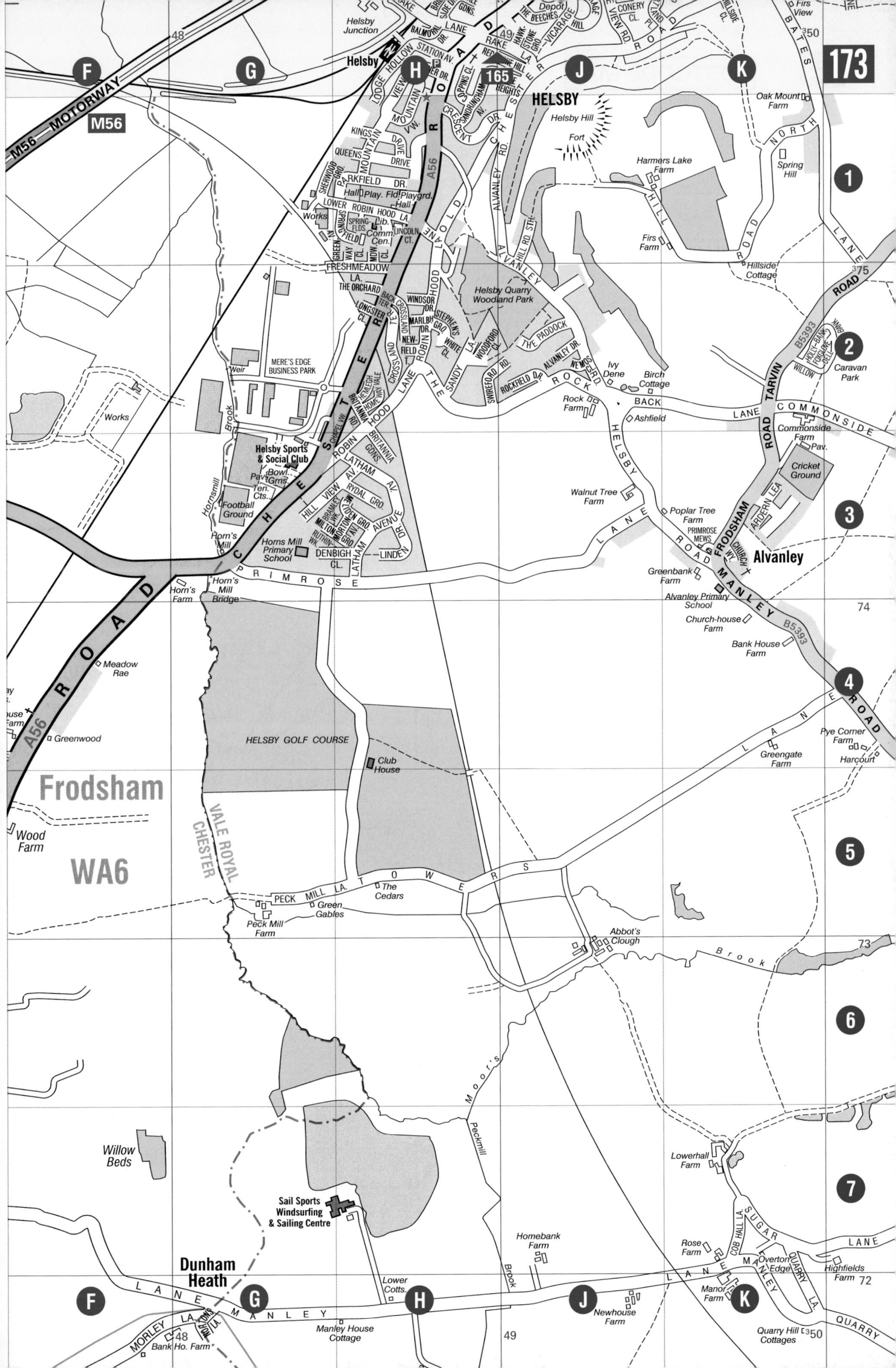

M56 MOTORWAY
M56
Helsby Junction
Helsby
HELSBY
Helsby Hill
Fort
165
CHESTER ROAD
A56
Harmers Lake Farm
Firs Farm
Oak Mount Farm
Spring Hill
Hillside Cottage
Helsby Quarry Woodland Park
MERE'S EDGE BUSINESS PARK
Weir
Works
Helsby Sports & Social Club
Football Ground
Horns Mill Primary School
Horn's Mill
Horn's Farm
Horn's Mill Bridge
PRIMROSE LANE
ROCK LANE
BACK LANE
COMMONSIDE
Commonside Farm
Cricket Ground
Ivy Dene
Birch Cottage
Rock Farm
Ashfield
Walnut Tree Farm
Poplar Tree Farm
PRIMROSE MEWS
Greenbank Farm
Alvanley
Alvanley Primary School
Church-house Farm
Bank House Farm
MANLEY ROAD
B5393
TARVIN ROAD
FRODSHAM ROAD
Caravan Park
Meadow Rae
Greenwood
Frodsham
WA6
Wood Farm
HELSBY GOLF COURSE
Club House
VALE ROYAL
CHESTER
PECK MILL LA.
TOWERS LANE
The Cedars
Green Gables
Peck Mill Farm
Abbot's Clough
Brook
Greengate Farm
Pye Corner Farm
Harcourt
Moor's Brook
Peckmill Brook
Willow Beds
Sail Sports Windsurfing & Sailing Centre
Dunham Heath
Lower Cotts.
Manley House Cottage
Bank Ho. Farm
MORLEY LA.
Homebank Farm
Newhouse Farm
Lowerhall Farm
Rose Farm
Manor Farm
Overton Edge
Highfields Farm
SUGAR LANE
QUARRY LA.
Quarry Hill Cottages
F G H J K
1 2 3 4 5 6 7
48 49 50
72 73 74 75

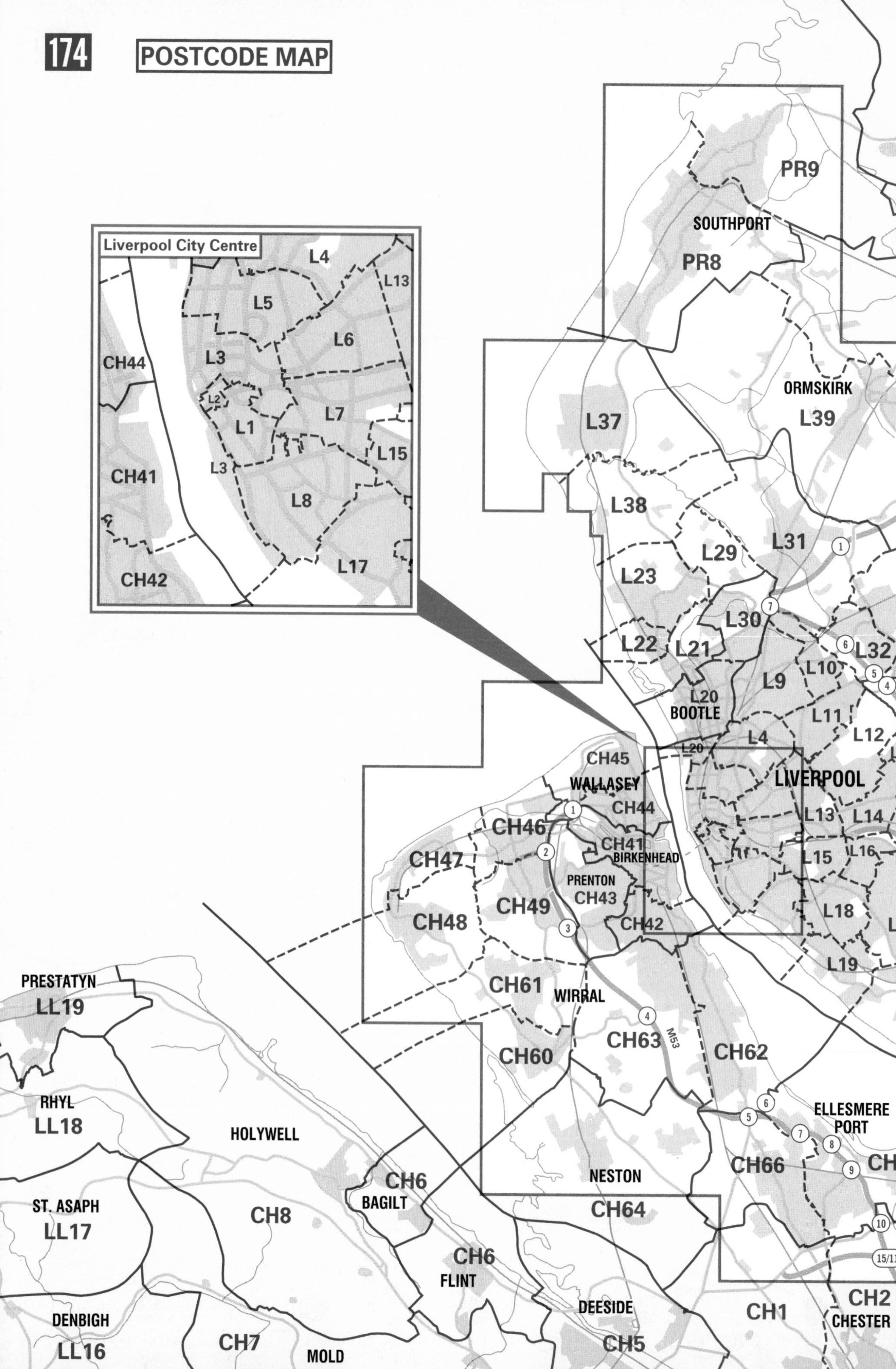

Liverpool City Centre

L4
L13
L5
L6
CH44
L3
L2
L7
L1
L15
L3
CH41
L8
CH42
L17

PR9
SOUTHPORT
PR8
ORMSKIRK
L39
L37
L38
L29
L23
L31
L30
L22
L21
L9
L10
L32
L20
BOOTLE
L20
L11
L12
CH45
WALLASEY
L4
LIVERPOOL
CH46
CH44
L13
L14
CH47
CH41
BIRKENHEAD
L15
L16
PRENTON
CH49
CH43
L18
CH48
CH42
L19
CH61
WIRRAL
CH63
CH60
M53
CH62
ELLESMERE
PORT
CH66
CH
PRESTATYN
LL19
RHYL
LL18
HOLYWELL
NESTON
CH6
BAGILT
CH64
ST. ASAPH
LL17
CH8
CH6
FLINT
CH2
CHESTER
DENBIGH
DEESIDE
CH1
LL16
CH7
MOLD
CH5

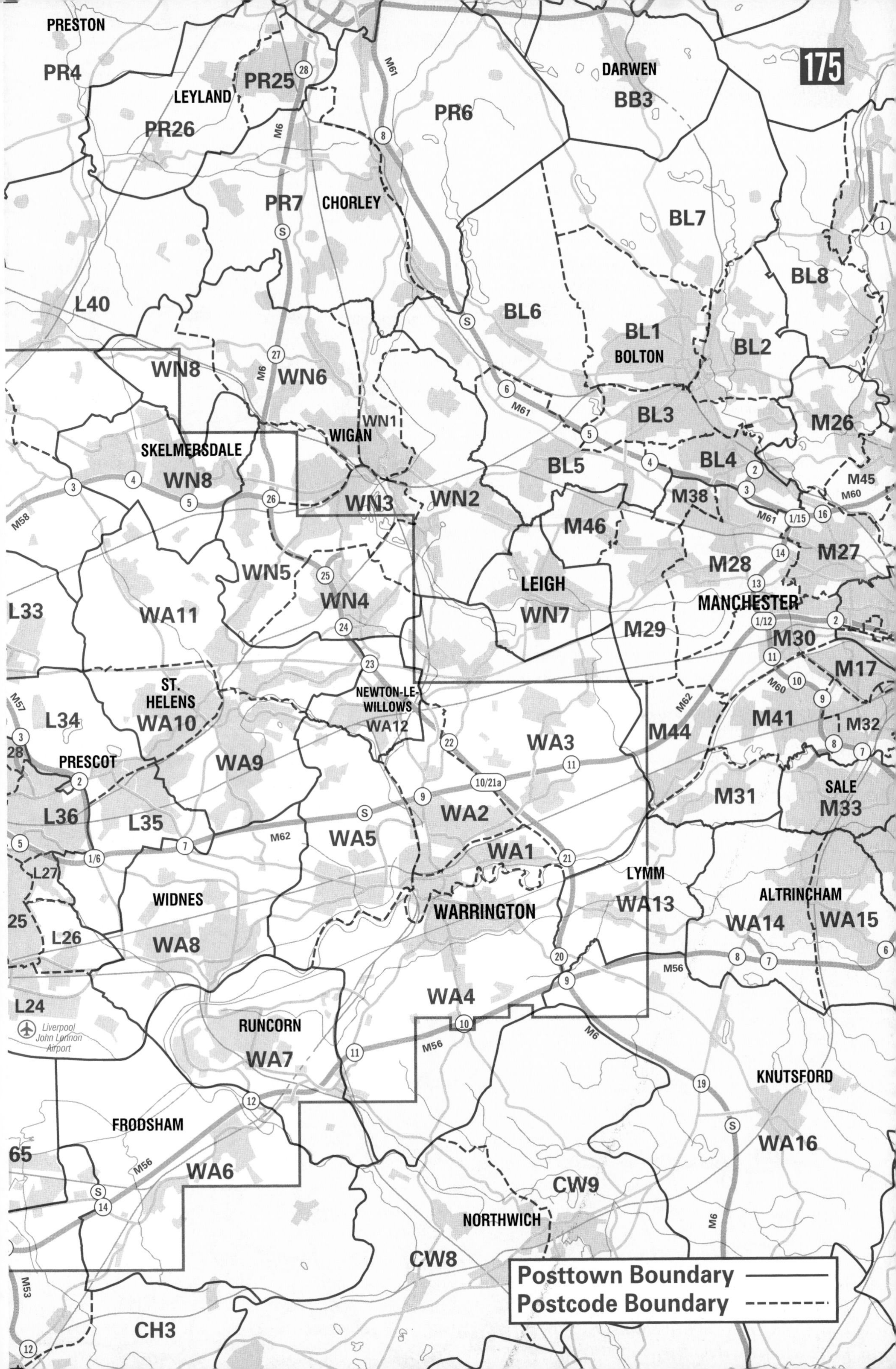

PRESTON

PR4

LEYLAND

PR26

PR25

28

PR6

DARWEN

BB3

PR7 CHORLEY

BL7

BL8

L40

BL6

BL1
BOLTON

BL2

M26

WN8

WN6

6

BL3

M45
M60

WIGAN

WN1

5

BL5

4

BL4

M38

3

2

16

SKELMERSDALE

27

M6

WN8

26

WN3 WN2

5

M46

M28

13

1/15

14

M27

WN5

25

WN4

LEIGH

WN7

MANCHESTER

1/12

M30

11

2

M17

L33

WA11

24

M29

10

9

M32

23

M44

M41

M31

M62

8

7

ST.
HELENS
WA10

NEWTON-LE-
WILLOWS
WA12

22

WA3

11

SALE
M33

L34

WA9

9

10/21a

WA2

L36

L35

S

WA5

WA1

21

LYMM

WA13

ALTRINCHAM
WA14

WA15

WIDNES

M62

7

WARRINGTON

20

8 7

6

25

L26

WA8

9

L24
Liverpool
John Lennon
Airport

WA4

10

M56

KNUTSFORD

19

RUNCORN

WA7

11

S

WA16

FRODSHAM

12

65

WA6

CW9

S
14

NORTHWICH

CH3

CW8

Posttown Boundary ——
Postcode Boundary - - -

12

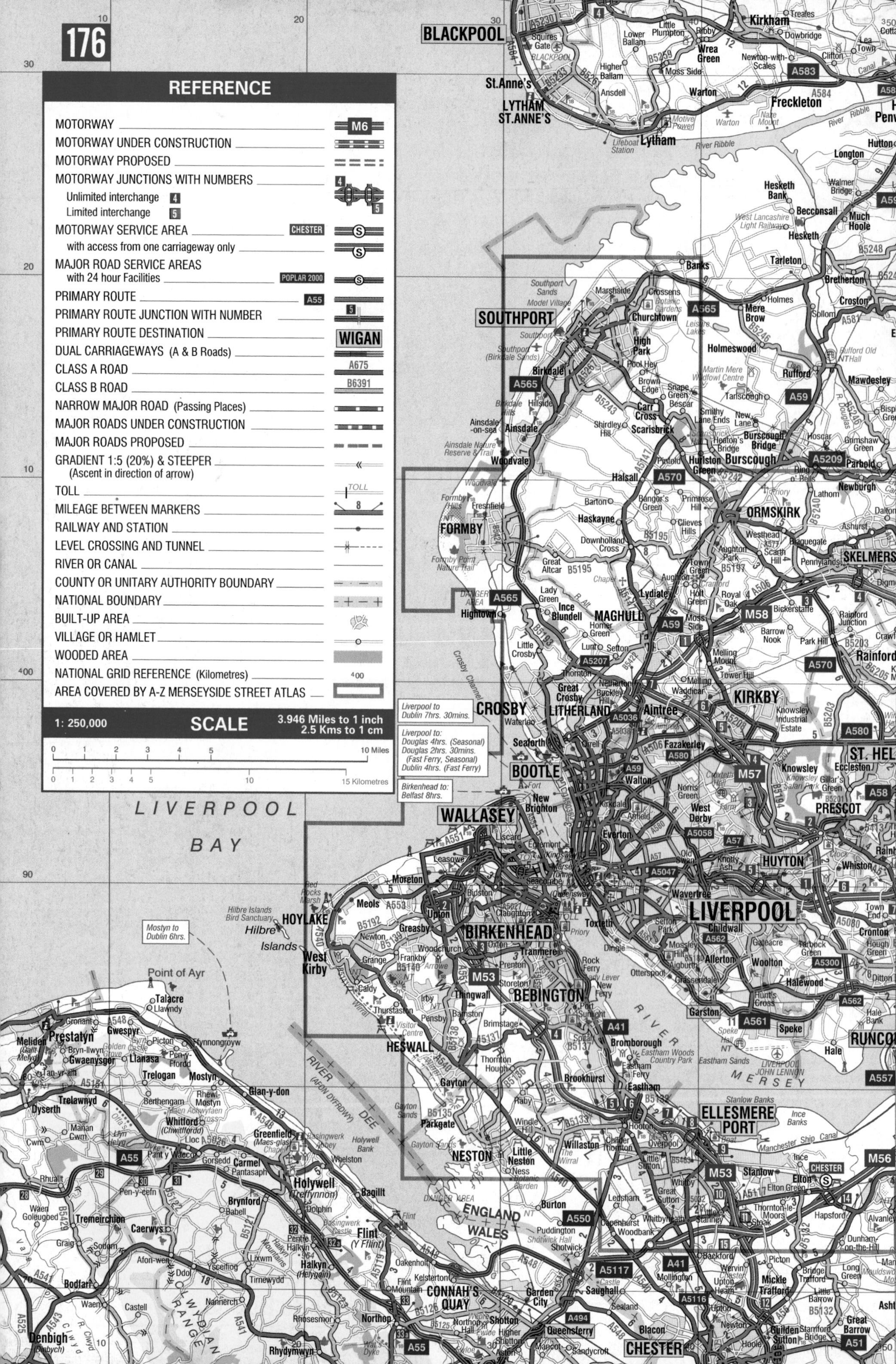
176
REFERENCE
MOTORWAY
M6
MOTORWAY UNDER CONSTRUCTION
MOTORWAY PROPOSED
MOTORWAY JUNCTIONS WITH NUMBERS
Unlimited interchange 4
Limited interchange 5
MOTORWAY SERVICE AREA
CHESTER
with access from one carriageway only
MAJOR ROAD SERVICE AREAS with 24 hour Facilities
POPLAR 2000
PRIMARY ROUTE
A55
PRIMARY ROUTE JUNCTION WITH NUMBER
PRIMARY ROUTE DESTINATION
WIGAN
DUAL CARRIAGEWAYS (A & B Roads)
CLASS A ROAD
A675
CLASS B ROAD
B6391
NARROW MAJOR ROAD (Passing Places)
MAJOR ROADS UNDER CONSTRUCTION
MAJOR ROADS PROPOSED
GRADIENT 1:5 (20%) & STEEPER (Ascent in direction of arrow)
TOLL
MILEAGE BETWEEN MARKERS
RAILWAY AND STATION
LEVEL CROSSING AND TUNNEL
RIVER OR CANAL
COUNTY OR UNITARY AUTHORITY BOUNDARY
NATIONAL BOUNDARY
BUILT-UP AREA
VILLAGE OR HAMLET
WOODED AREA
NATIONAL GRID REFERENCE (Kilometres)
400
AREA COVERED BY A-Z MERSEYSIDE STREET ATLAS
1: 250,000
SCALE
3.946 Miles to 1 inch
2.5 Kms to 1 cm
0 1 2 3 4 5 10 Miles
0 1 2 3 4 5 10 15 Kilometres
Liverpool to Dublin 7hrs. 30mins.
Liverpool to: Douglas 4hrs. (Seasonal) Douglas 2hrs. 30mins. (Fast Ferry, Seasonal) Dublin 4hrs. (Fast Ferry)
Birkenhead to: Belfast 8hrs.
Mostyn to Dublin 6hrs.
LIVERPOOL BAY
BLACKPOOL
LYTHAM ST.ANNE'S
Lytham
Kirkham
Freckleton
River Ribble
SOUTHPORT
FORMBY
ORMSKIRK
MAGHULL
CROSBY
LITHERLAND
BOOTLE
KIRKBY
WALLASEY
BIRKENHEAD
LIVERPOOL
HUYTON
PRESCOT
BEBINGTON
HOYLAKE
West Kirby
Hilbre Islands
HESWALL
NESTON
ELLESMERE PORT
RIVER MERSEY
RIVER DEE
Point of Ayr
Prestatyn
Holywell
Flint
CONNAH'S QUAY
CHESTER
Denbigh
ENGLAND
WALES
CLWYDIAN RANGE
M53
M56
M57
M58
A55
A41
A59
A565
A570
A580
A550

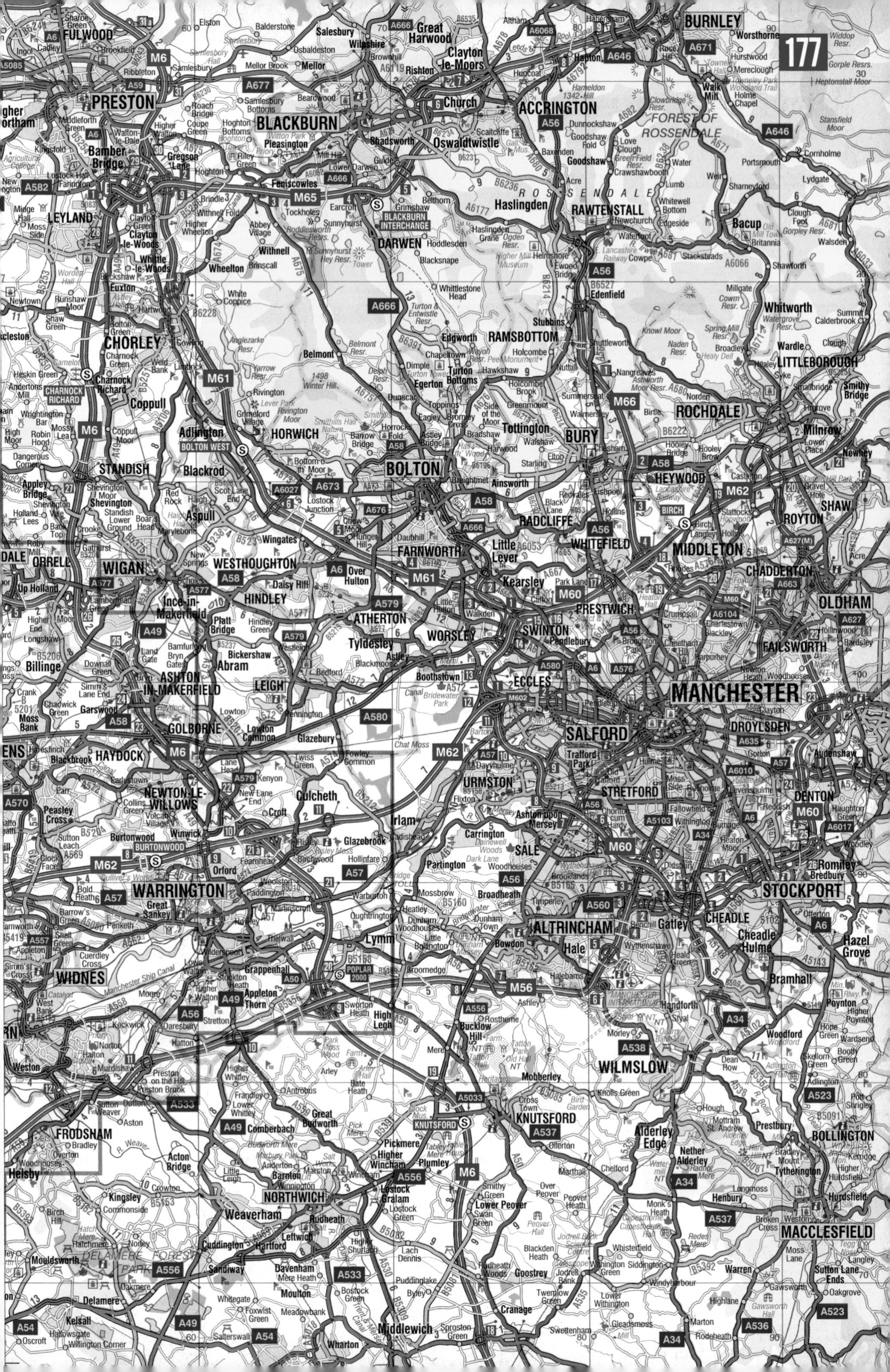
FULWOOD
PRESTON
BLACKBURN
Great Harwood
Clayton-le-Moors
Church
ACCRINGTON
Oswaldtwistle
BURNLEY
Worsthorne
Hapton
FOREST OF ROSSENDALE
Bamber Bridge
LEYLAND
Feniscowles
BLACKBURN INTERCHANGE
DARWEN
Haslingden
RAWTENSTALL
Bacup
Whitworth
LITTLEBOROUGH
Edenfield
RAMSBOTTOM
CHORLEY
Coppull
CHARNOCK RICHARD
Adlington
BOLTON WEST
HORWICH
Tottington
BURY
ROCHDALE
Milnrow
STANDISH
Blackrod
BOLTON
Ainsworth
HEYWOOD
ROYTON
SHAW
Aspull
Wingates
WESTHOUGHTON
FARNWORTH
RADCLIFFE
WHITEFIELD
MIDDLETON
CHADDERTON
OLDHAM
ORRELL
WIGAN
HINDLEY
Little Lever
Kearsley
PRESTWICH
Ince-in-Makerfield
ATHERTON
Tyldesley
WORSLEY
SWINTON
Pendlebury
FAILSWORTH
Abram
ASHTON-IN-MAKERFIELD
LEIGH
Boothstown
ECCLES
MANCHESTER
Billinge
GOLBORNE
Glazebury
SALFORD
DROYLSDEN
HAYDOCK
Lowton Common
Trafford Park
Audenshaw
NEWTON-LE-WILLOWS
Culcheth
URMSTON
STRETFORD
DENTON
Irlam
Glazebrook
Carrington
SALE
BURTONWOOD
WARRINGTON
Partington
STOCKPORT
Great Sankey
Altrincham
CHEADLE
Cheadle Hulme
Lymm
Hale
Gatley
Hazel Grove
WIDNES
Grappenhall
POPLAR 2000
Bramhall
Appleton Thorn
High Legh
Poynton
Runcorn
Weston
Halton
Daresbury
WILMSLOW
Mobberley
FRODSHAM
Great Budworth
KNUTSFORD
Alderley Edge
Prestbury
BOLLINGTON
Helsby
Acton Bridge
Comberbach
NORTHWICH
Lostock Gralam
Lower Peover
Henbury
MACCLESFIELD
Kingsley
Weaverham
Rudheath
Cuddington
Hartford
Mouldsworth
DELAMERE FOREST PARK
Sandiway
Davenham
Goostrey
Delamere
Moulton
Cranage
Kelsall
Middlewich
Wharton
M6
M61
M65
M66
M62
M60
M602
M56
A666
A56
A58
A580
A57
A49
A556
A533
A54
A34
A523
A537
A538
A5033
A560
A6
A646
A671
A677
A673
A676
A579
A577
A5103
A635
A6010
A6017
A627
A663
A6104
A576
A582
A570
A552
A50
A559
A570
A536

INDEX

Including Streets, Places & Areas, Industrial Estates, Selected Flats & Walkways,
Stations and Selected Places of Interest.

HOW TO USE THIS INDEX

1. Each street name is followed by its Postcode District and then by its Locality abbreviation(s) and then by its map reference; e.g. **Abacus Rd.** L13: Liv . . . .3J **89** is in the L13 Postcode District and the Liverpool Locality and is to be found in square 3J on page **89**. The page number is shown in bold type.
2. A strict alphabetical order is followed in which Av., Rd., St., etc. (though abbreviated) are read in full and as part of the street name; e.g. **Abbey St.** appears after **Abbeystead Rd.** but before **Abbeyvale Dr.**
3. Streets and a selection of flats and walkways too small to be shown on the maps, appear in the index with the thoroughfare to which it is connected shown in brackets; e.g. **Alexander Way** *L8: Liv . . . .4B **108** (off Park Hill Rd.)*
4. Addresses that are in more than one part are referred to as not continuous.
5. Places and areas are shown in the index in **BLUE TYPE** and the map reference is to the actual map square in which the town centre or area is located and not to the place name shown on the map; e.g. **AIGBURTH VALE** **6F 109**
6. An example of a selected place of interest is **Aintree Racecourse** **4E 54**
7. An example of a station is **Aigburth Station (Rail)** . . . .**1G 129**. Included are Rail **(Rail)** and Park and Ride **(Park and Ride)**
8. Map references shown in brackets; e.g. **Aber St.** L6: Liv . . . .4C **88** (2M **5**) refer to entries that also appear on the large scale pages **4-5**.

GENERAL ABBREVIATIONS

All. : Alley
App. : Approach
Arc. : Arcade
Av. : Avenue
Bk. : Back
Blvd. : Boulevard
Bri. : Bridge
B'way. : Broadway
Bldg. : Building
Bldgs. : Buildings
Bus. : Business
Cvn. : Caravan
C'way. : Causeway
Cen. : Centre
Chu. : Church
Cl. : Close
Comn. : Common
Cnr. : Corner
Cott. : Cottage
Cotts. : Cottages
Ct. : Court
Cres. : Crescent
Cft. : Croft
Dr. : Drive
E. : East
Ent. : Enterprise
Est. : Estate
Fld. : Field
Flds. : Fields
Gdn. : Garden
Gdns. : Gardens
Gth. : Garth
Ga. : Gate
Gt. : Great
Grn. : Green
Gro. : Grove
Hgts. : Heights
Ho. : House
Ho's. : Houses
Ind. : Industrial
Info. : Information
Intl. : International
Junc. : Junction
La. : Lane
Lit. : Little
Lwr. : Lower
Mnr. : Manor
Mans. : Mansions
Mkt. : Market
Mdw. : Meadow
Mdws. : Meadows
M. : Mews
Mt. : Mount
Mus. : Museum
Nth. : North
Pde. : Parade
Pk. : Park
Pas. : Passage
Pav. : Pavilion
Pl. : Place
Pct. : Precinct
Prom. : Promenade
Ri. : Rise
Rd. : Road
Rdbt. : Roundabout
Shop. : Shopping
Sth. : South
Sq. : Square
Sta. : Station
St. : Street
Ter. : Terrace
Twr. : Tower
Trad. : Trading
Up. : Upper
Va. : Vale
Vw. : View
Vs. : Villas
Vis. : Visitors
Wlk. : Walk
W. : West
Yd. : Yard

LOCALITY ABBREVIATIONS

Aig : **Aigburth**
Ains : **Ainsdale**
Ain : **Aintree**
Aller : **Allerton**
Alv : **Alvanley**
Ant : **Antrobus**
App : **Appleton**
App T : **Appleton Thorn**
Ash M : **Ashton-in-Makerfield**
Ast : **Astmoor**
Aston : **Aston**
Augh : **Aughton**
Back : **Backford**
Bam : **Bamfurlong**
Banks : **Banks**
Barn : **Barnston**
Bart : **Barton**
Beb : **Bebington**
Beech : **Beechwood**
Bic : **Bickerstaffe**
Bid : **Bidston**
Bil : **Billinge**
Bchwd : **Birchwood**
B'dale : **Birkdale**
Birk : **Birkenhead**
Blun : **Blundellsands**
Bold : **Bold**
Bold H : **Bold Heath**
Boot : **Bootle**
Brim : **Brimstage**
B Grn : **Broad Green**
Brom : **Bromborough**
Brook : **Brookvale**
Burs : **Burscough**
Burt : **Burton**
B'wood : **Burtonwood**
Cad : **Cadishead**
Caldy : **Caldy**
Call : **Callands**
Cap : **Capenhurst**
Cas : **Castlefields**
Chil T : **Childer Thornton**
Child : **Childwall**
Chor B : **Chorlton-by-Backford**
Chu : **Churchtown**
C'ton : **Claughton**
Clftn : **Clifton**
Clock F : **Clock Face**
C Grn : **Collins Green**
Crank : **Crank**
Croft : **Croft**
Cron : **Cronton**
C'by : **Crosby**
Cros : **Crossens**
C'ton : **Croughton**
Crox : **Croxteth**
Cuerd : **Cuerdley**
Cul : **Culcheth**
Dalt : **Dalton**
Dares : **Daresbury**
Down : **Downholland**
Dun H : **Dunham-on-the-Hill**
Dunk : **Dunkirk**
Dutt : **Dutton**
East : **Eastham**
Eccl : **Eccleston**
Ecc P : **Eccleston Park**
Ell P : **Ellesmere Port**
Elt : **Elton**
Faz : **Fazakerley**
Fearn : **Fearnhead**
Ford : **Ford**
Form : **Formby**
Frank : **Frankby**
Frod : **Frodsham**
Gars : **Garston**
Gars : **Garswood**
Gate : **Gateacre**
G'brk : **Glazebrook**
G'bury : **Glazebury**
Golb : **Golborne**
Grap : **Grappenhall**
Gras : **Grassendale**
Grea : **Greasby**
Gt Alt : **Great Altcar**
Gt San : **Great Sankey**
Gt Sut : **Great Sutton**
Hale : **Hale**
Hale B : **Hale Bank**
Halew : **Halewood**
Hals : **Halsall**
Halt : **Halton**
Hap : **Hapsford**
Has : **Haskayne**
Hatt : **Hatton**
Hay : **Haydock**
Hel : **Helsby**
Hes : **Heswall**
High B : **Higher Bebington**
H Walt : **Higher Walton**
H Legh : **High Legh**
High : **Hightown**
Hoot : **Hooton**
Hou G : **Houghton Green**
Hoy : **Hoylake**
Hunts X : **Hunts Cross**
Huy : **Huyton**
Ince : **Ince**
Ince B : **Ince Blundell**
Ince M : **Ince-in-Makerfield**
Irby : **Irby**
Irlam : **Irlam**
K'ley : **Kingsley**
Kings M : **Kings Moss**
K'by : **Kirkby**
Kirk : **Kirkdale**
K Ash : **Knotty Ash**
Know : **Knowsley**
Know I : **Knowsley Industrial Park**
Know P : **Knowsley Park**
Latch : **Latchford**
Lath : **Lathom**
Lea B : **Lea-by-Backford**
Leas : **Leasowe**
Led : **Ledsham**
Lith : **Litherland**
Lit B : **Little Barrow**
Lit C : **Little Crosby**
Lit N : **Little Neston**
Lit Stan : **Little Stanney**
Lit Sut : **Little Sutton**
Liv : **Liverpool**
Lwr S : **Lower Stretton**
Lwr Wh : **Lower Whitley**
Low : **Lowton**
Lyd : **Lydiate**
Lymm : **Lymm**
Mag : **Maghull**
Manl : **Manley**
Mnr P : **Manor Park**
Marsh : **Marshside**
Mell : **Melling**
Meols : **Meols**
Mick T : **Mickle Trafford**
Moll : **Mollington**
Moore : **Moore**
More : **Moreton**
Moss H : **Mossley Hill**
Mos : **Moston**
Murd : **Murdishaw**
Ness : **Ness**
Nest : **Neston**
N'ley : **Netherley**
N'ton : **Netherton**
New B : **New Brighton**
Newb : **Newburgh**
New F : **New Ferry**
Newt : **Newton**
New W : **Newton-le-Willows**
Noct : **Noctorum**
N Grn. : **Norris Green**
Nort : **Norton**
Old H : **Old Hall**
Orm : **Ormskirk**
Orr : **Orrell**
O'ton : **Oxton**
P'ton : **Paddington**
P'gate : **Padgate**
Pal F : **Palace Fields**
Parb : **Parbold**
Park : **Parkgate**
Penk : **Penketh**
Pens : **Pensby**
Pict : **Picton**
Platt B : **Platt Bridge**
Port S : **Port Sunlight**
Pren : **Prenton**
Prsct : **Prescot**
Pres B : **Preston Brook**
Pres H : **Preston on the Hill**
Raby : **Raby**
Raby M : **Raby Mere**
R'ford : **Rainford**
R'hill : **Rainhill**
Ris : **Risley**
Rix : **Rixton**
Roby : **Roby**
Roby M : **Roby Mill**
R Ferr : **Rock Ferry**
Run : **Runcorn**
Scar : **Scarisbrick**
Sea : **Seaforth**
Seft : **Sefton**
Sim : **Simonswood**
Skel : **Skelmersdale**
South : **Southport**
Speke : **Speke**
Spit : **Spital**
St. H : **St. Helens**
Stoak : **Stoak**
Stock V : **Stockbridge Village**
S Hth : **Stockton Heath**
Store : **Storeton**
S'ton : **Stretton**
Sut L : **Sutton Leach**
Sut M : **Sutton Manor**
Sut W : **Sutton Weaver**
Tar G : **Tarbock Green**
Thel : **Thelwall**
Thing : **Thingwall**
Thorn : **Thornton**
Thorn H : **Thornton Hough**
Thor M : **Thornton-le-Moors**
Thurs : **Thurstaston**
Tran : **Tranmere**
Uph : **Upholland**
Upton : **Upton**
Wall : **Wallasey**
Walt : **Walton**
Warb : **Warburton**
Warr : **Warrington**
Water : **Waterloo**
W'tree : **Wavertree**
Wer : **Wervin**
W Der : **West Derby**
W Kir : **West Kirby**
W'brk : **Westbrook**
Westh : **Westhead**
West : **Weston**
West P : **Weston Point**
Westy : **Westy**
Whis : **Whiston**
Whit : **Whitby**
Wid : **Widnes**
Wigan : **Wigan**
Will : **Willaston**
Wim T : **Wimbolds Trafford**
Windle : **Windle**
Wind H : **Windmill Hill**
Wins : **Winstanley**
Win : **Winwick**
W'bnk : **Woodbank**
W'chu : **Woodchurch**
W'ston : **Woolston**
Wltn : **Woolton**

20, Forthlin Road (Childhood Home of Paul McCartney) 7A 110

A

A41 Expressway CH42: Tran 5F **107**
Abacus Rd. L13: Liv 3J **89**
Abberley Cl. WA10: St. H 3B **74**
Abberley Rd. L25: Hunts X 2G **131**
Abberley Way WN3: Wigan 7K **39**
Abberton Pk. L30: N'ton 7C **42**
Abbey Cl. CH41: Birk 3F **107**
L33: K'by 3D **56**
L37: Form 1B **30**
WA3: Croft 6G **79**
WA8: Wid 1J **133**
WN8: Uph 4E **38**
Abbey Ct. L25: Wltn 6F **111**
Abbey Dr. WN5: Orr 5G **39**
Abbeyfield Dr. L12: Crox 2B **70**
Abbeyfield Ho. CH65: Whit 1J **169**
Abbey Gdns. PR8: B'dale 4G **11**
Abbey Hey WA7: Nort 2A **154**
Abbey La. L40: Burs, Lath 1G **25**
Abbey La. Ind. Est. L40: Burs 1G **25**
Abbey Rd. CH48: W Kir 6D **102**
L6: Liv 1D **88**
WA8: Wid 1J **133**
WA10: St. H 6K **59**
WA11: Hay 6C **62**
Abbeystead WN8: Skel 4H **37**
Abbeystead Av. L30: N'ton 4C **54**
Abbeystead Rd. L15: W'tree 7K **89**
Abbey St. CH41: Birk 3F **107**
Abbeyvale Dr. L25: Gate 2G **111**
Abbey Vw. L16: Child 1C **110**
Abbeyway Nth. WA11: Hay 6E **62**
Abbeyway Sth. WA11: Hay 6E **62**
Abbeywood WN8: Skel 5J **37**
Abbeywood Gro. L35: Whis 5F **93**
Abbot Cl. CH43: Bid 2G **105**
Abbotsbury Way L12: Crox 3C **70**
Abbots Bus. Pk. WA7: Pres B 5C **154**
Abbots Cl. L37: Form 2A **30**
Abbots Dr. CH63: Beb 4F **127**
Abbotsfield Cl. WA4: App 3E **138**
Abbotsfield Rd. WA9: St. H . . . .1G **95** (not continuous)
Abbotsford L39: Orm 5D **24**
Abbotsford Ct. L23: Blun 2C **52**
Abbotsford Gdns. L23: C'by 2C **52**

Abbotsford Rd.—All Saints Ct.

Abbotsford Rd. L11: N Grn. 4G 69
L23: Blun 2C 52
Abbotsford St. CH44: Wall 5E 86
Abbots Hall Av.
WA9: Clock F 4F 95
Abbots M. CH65: Ell P 5K 161
Abbots Way CH48: W Kir 5E 102
CH64: Nest 3J 157
L37: Form 2A 30
WN5: Bil 2F 61
Abbott Dr. L20: Boot 1A 68
Abbotts Cl. L18: Moss H 5K 109
WA7: Run 2C 152
Abbottshey Av. L18: Moss H 5K 109
Abdale Rd. L11: N Grn. 3H 69
Abercrombie Rd.
L33: Know I 6F 57
Abercromby Sq. L7: Liv 6B 88 (8L 5)
(not continuous)
Aberdale Rd. L13: Liv 4K 89
Aberdare Cl. WA5: Call 6J 97
Aberdeen St. CH41: Birk 1C 106
Aberford Av. CH45: Wall 2J 85
Abergele Rd. L13: Liv 5H 89
Aber St. L6: Liv 4C 88 (2M 5)
Abingdon Av. WA1: W'ston 1A 120
Abingdon Dr. WN2: Platt B 3K 51
Abingdon Gro. L4: Walt 4E 68
L26: Halew 7A 112
Abingdon Rd. CH49: Grea 5K 103
L4: Walt 4E 68
Abinger Rd. WN4: Gars 1B 62
Abington Dr. PR9: Banks 2J 9
Abington Wlk. WA7: Brook 5A 154
Abney Cl. L7: Liv 7D 88 (9P 5)
Aboyne Cl. L9: Walt 2C 68
Abrams Fold PR9: Banks 2H 9
Abrams Grn. PR9: Banks 2H 9
Abram St. L5: Liv 2A 88
Abstone Cl. WA1: W'ston 1J 119
Abyssinia Cl. L15: W'tree 1G 109
Acacia Av. L36: Huy 6H 91
WA1: W'ston 7K 99
WA8: Wid 5D 114
Acacia Cl. CH2: Elt 1C 172
CH49: Grea 7A 104
Acacia Dr. CH66: Gt Sut 3H 169
Acacia Gro. CH44: Wall 5E 86
CH48: W Kir 6C 102
L9: Ain 7D 54
WA7: Run 2E 152
WA10: Eccl 2G 73
Acacia St. WA12: New W 2D 76
Academy Bus. Pk.
L33: Know I 4E 56
Academy, The (LFC) 3E 56
Academy Pl. WA1: Warr 3B 118
Academy St. WA1: Warr 3B 118
Academy Way WA1: Warr 3B 118
Acanthus Rd. L13: Liv 3J 89
Access Rd. L12: W Der 7B 70
Acer Leigh L17: Aig 6F 109
Acheson Rd. L13: Liv 1G 89
Achilles Av. WA2: Warr 5B 98
Achilles Ct. WA7: Cas 7J 135
Ackerley Cl. WA2: Fearn 4F 99
Ackers Hall Av. L14: K Ash 3D 90
Ackers Hall Cl. L14: K Ash 2D 90
Ackers La. L23: Lit C 5C 40
WA4: S Hth 6E 118
WA10: St. H 2J 73
Ackers Rd. CH49: W'chu 6G 103
WA4: S Hth 7E 118
Ackers St. L34: Prsct 1D 92
Ackhurst La. WN5: Orr 1J 39
Acland Rd. CH44: Wall 3B 86
Aconbury Cl. L11: N Grn. 3H 69
Aconbury Pl. L11: N Grn. 3H 69
Acorn Bus. Cen. L33: Know I 4F 57
Acorn Cl. CH63: High B 3D 126
WA9: Clock F 3E 94
Acorn Ct. L8: Liv 2A 108
Acorn Dr. CH65: Whit 3K 169
Acornfield Cl. L33: Know I 5G 57
Acornfield Rd. L33: Know I 4H 57
Acorns, The L39: Augh 7A 24
Acorn St. WA12: New W 3G 77
Acorn Venture Urban Farm 1H 57
Acorn Way L20: Boot 1K 67
A Court WN4: Ash M 3J 63
Acrefield WN8: Newb 1G 27
Acrefield Bank L25: Wltn 5E 110
Acrefield Ct. CH42: Tran 7B 106
Acrefield Pk. L25: Wltn 5E 110
Acrefield Rd. CH42: Tran 7B 106
L25: Wltn 4E 110
WA8: Wid 7H 113
Acregate WN8: Skel 5J 37
Acre Grn. L26: Halew 3A 132
Acre Gro. PR8: B'dale 5F 11
Acre La. CH60: Hes 1G 143
CH62: Brom 3J 145
CH63: Brom 3J 145
Acre Rd. CH66: Gt Sut 6F 161
Acres Cl. L25: Gate 1E 110
Acresfield L13: Liv 5K 89
Acresgate Ct. L25: Gate 2E 110
Acres La. L31: Lyd 3A 32
L37: Gt Alt 3E 30
L39: Down 3A 32
Acres Rd. CH47: Meols 1H 103
CH63: Beb 3F 127
Acreville Rd. CH63: Beb 4F 127
Acton Av. WA4: App 6D 138
Acton Cl. WA11: Hay 7A 62
Acton Gro. L6: Liv 1E 88
Acton La. CH46: More 1A 104
Acton Rake L30: N'ton 7K 41
Acton Rd. CH42: R Ferr 7G 107
L32: K'by 3A 56
WA5: B'wood 1C 96
Acton Way L7: Liv 7E 88
Acuba Gro. CH42: Tran 4E 106
Acuba Rd. L15: W'tree 6A 90
Adair Pl. L13: Liv 7G 69
Adair Rd. L13: Liv 7G 69
Adam Av. CH66: Gt Sut 7E 160
(not continuous)
Adam Cl. CH66: Gt Sut 7F 161
L19: Gars 4A 130
Adams Cl. WA12: New W 4H 77
Adamson Ct. WA4: Grap 6H 119
Adamson St. L7: Liv 5F 89
WA4: Warr 5B 118
WN4: Ash M 2E 62
Adam St. L5: Liv 1B 88
WA2: Warr 1C 118
Adaston Av. CH62: East 6B 146
Adcote Cl. L14: B Grn 4D 90
Adcote Rd. L14: K Ash 4D 90
Addenbrooke Dr. L24: Speke 3F 131
Adderley Cl. WA7: Run 1E 152
Adderley St. L7: Liv 5D 88
Addingham Av. WA8: Wid 2J 133
Addingham Rd. L18: Moss H 3K 109
Addington St. CH44: Wall 4D 86
Addison Cl. L32: K'by 5B 56
Addison Sq. WA8: Wid 7B 114
Addison St. L3: Liv 4K 87 (3F 4)
L20: Boot 1G 67
Addison Way L3: Liv 4K 87 (3F 4)
Adelaide Av. WA9: St. H 7A 74
Adelaide Cl. WA8: Wid 2C 134
Adelaide Pl. L5: Liv 3A 88
Adelaide Rd. CH42: Tran 4C 106
L7: Liv 5C 88 (5P 5)
(not continuous)
L21: Sea 6F 53
Adelaide St. CH44: Wall 4B 86
Adelaide Ter. L22: Water 4C 52
Adela Rd. WA7: Run 7B 134
Adele Thompson Dr. L8: Liv 1C 108 (10N 5)
Adelphi St. CH41: Birk 2E 106
Adey Rd. WA13: Lymm 3J 121
Adfalent La. CH64: Will 4G 159
Adkins St. L5: Liv 1C 88
Adlam Cres. L9: Faz 6G 55
Adlam Rd. L9: Faz 6G 55
L10: Faz 6G 55
Adlington Ct. WA3: Ris 1B 100
Adlington Ho. L3: Liv 4K 87 (3F 4)
Adlington Rd. WA7: Wind H 7B 136
Adlington St. L3: Liv 3F 4
Admin Rd. L33: Know I 5G 57
Admiral Gro. L8: Liv 2C 108
Admirals Rd. WA3: Bchwd 3A 100
Admirals Sq. WA3: Bchwd 4B 100
Admiral St. L8: Liv 3B 108
Admiralty Cl. L40: Burs 1F 25
Adrian's Way L32: K'by 3C 56
Adshead Rd. L13: Liv 7G 69
Adstone Rd. L25: Gate 3G 111
Adswood Rd. L36: Huy 4J 91
Aerodrome, The L24: Speke 5C 130
Africander Rd. WA11: St. H 5C 60
Afton WA8: Wid 6G 113
Agar Rd. L11: N Grn. 7H 69
Agate St. L5: Liv 2C 88
Agincourt Rd. L12: W Der 2A 90
Agnes Gro. CH44: Wall 2C 86
Agnes Jones Ho. L8: Liv 7B 88 (9L 5)
Agnes Rd. CH42: Tran 5D 106
L23: Blun 2C 52
Agnes St. WA9: Clock F 4E 94
Agnes Way L7: Liv 6D 88
Agulnek Ct. L18: Moss H 4H 109
Aiden Long Gro. L34: Know P 1J 91
AIGBURTH 1G 129
Aigburth Dr. L17: Aig 3E 108
Aigburth Gro. CH46: More 7B 84
Aigburth Hall Av. L19: Aig 1H 129
Aigburth Hall Rd. L19: Aig 1J 129
Aigburth Ho. L17: Aig 5G 109
Aigburth Rd. L17: Aig 4D 108
L19: Aig 1H 129
Aigburth Station (Rail) 1G 129
Aigburth St. L7: Liv 7D 88 (9P 5)
AIGBURTH VALE 6F 109
Aigburth Va. L17: Aig 6F 109
(not continuous)
Ailsa Rd. CH45: Wall 2A 86
Aindow Ct. PR8: B'dale 5F 11
Ainley Cl. WA7: Brook 5J 153
Ainscough Rd. WA3: Bchwd 4A 100
AINSDALE 4C 14
Ainsdale Cl. CH61: Thing 4E 124
CH63: Brom 5J 145
L10: Faz 5H 55
WA5: Penk 4D 116
AINSDALE-ON-SEA 4A 14
Ainsdale Rd. L20: Boot 7K 53
Ainsdale Sand Dunes National
Nature Reserve 1J 19
Ainsdale Station (Rail) 4C 14
Ainsworth Av. CH46: More 2A 104
Ainsworth La. L34: Know 7F 57
Ainsworth Rd. WA10: St. H 1K 73
Ainsworth St. L3: Liv 6A 88 (6J 5)
AINTREE 3F 55
Aintree Cl. CH46: Leas 4D 84
Aintree Ct. L10: Ain 2E 54
Aintree Cres. PR8: South 4B 12
Aintree Gro. CH66: Gt Sut 1F 169
Aintree La. L10: Ain 2E 54
L10: Faz 4H 55
Aintree Racecourse 4E 54
Aintree Racecourse Retail & Bus. Pk.
L9: Ain 3D 54
Aintree Rd. L9: Ain 7F 55
L20: Boot 2K 67
Aintree Station (Rail) 5D 54
Aintree Vis. Cen. &
Grand National Experience 4D 54
Aintree Way L9: Ain 3E 54
Airdale Cl. CH43: Bid 2G 105
Airdale Rd. L15: W'tree 2G 109
Airdrie Cl. CH62: East 7K 145
Aire WA8: Wid 6H 113
Aire Cl. CH65: Ell P 4J 161
Airedale Cl. WA5: Gt San 1D 116
Airegate L31: Mag 2D 42
Airlie Gro. L13: Liv 1F 89
Airlie Rd. CH47: Hoy 2D 102
Airton Pl. WN3: Wigan 1F 51
Aisthorpe Gro. L31: Mag 5F 43
Ajax Av. WA2: Warr 5B 98
Akbar, The CH60: Hes 1A 142
AK Bus. Pk. PR9: South 2C 12
Akenside Ct. L20: Boot 7G 53
Akenside St. L20: Boot 7G 53
Alabama Way CH41: Birk 2F 107
Alamein Cres. WA2: Warr 1B 118
Alamein Rd. L36: Huy 3H 91
Alan's Way L33: K'by 1C 56
Alastair Cres. CH43: Pren 7K 105
Alban Retail Pk. WA2: Warr 5A 98
Alban Rd. L16: Child 7B 90
Albany Av. L34: Ecc P 7F 73
Albany Cres. WA13: Lymm 4F 121
Albany Gdns. CH66: Lit Sut 4E 160
Albany Gro. WA13: Lymm 4E 120
Albany Rd. CH42: R Ferr 6E 106
L7: Liv 5C 88 (5N 5)
L9: Ain 6D 54
L13: Liv 3J 89
L34: Prsct 1E 92
PR9: South 6J 7
WA13: Lymm 5E 120
Albany Ter. WA7: Run 7C 134
Albemarle Rd. CH44: Wall 4D 86
Alberta Gro. L34: Prsct 2K 91
Albert Ct. PR9: South 6K 7
Albert Dr. CH64: Nest 3H 157
L9: Walt 7B 54
WA5: Gt San 2B 116
Albert Edward Rd. L7: Liv 5C 88 (5N 5)
(not continuous)
Albert Gro. L15: W'tree 7J 89
L23: C'by 1D 52
Albert Pk. L17: Aig 3D 108
Albert Pl. PR9: South 7H 7
Albert Rd. CH42: Tran 4C 106
CH47: Hoy 2D 102
CH48: W Kir 7C 102
L13: Liv 1F 89
L22: Water 4D 52
L37: Form 3F 29
PR9: South 7J 7
WA4: Grap 6G 119
WA8: Wid 1D 134
Albert Row WA6: Frod 2D 166
Albert Schweitzer Av. L30: N'ton 2B 54
Albert Sq. WA8: Wid 1D 134
Albert St. CH45: New B 5C 66
L7: Liv 6C 88 (6N 5)
WA7: Run 7C 134
WA10: St. H 1C 74
WN4: Ash M 2F 63
Albert Ter. PR8: B'dale 3G 11
WA5: C Grn 5C 76
Albion Pl. CH45: New B 6B 66
Albion St. CH41: Birk 2F 107
(not continuous)
CH45: New B 6A 66
L5: Liv 1A 88
WA10: St. H 3A 74
(not continuous)
Albourne Rd. L32: K'by 5E 56
Albright Rd. WA8: Wid 3G 133
Albury Cl. L12: Crox 4D 70
WA5: Warr 1K 117
WA11: Hay 6A 62
Albury Rd. L32: K'by 6D 56
Alcester Rd. L12: W Der 5F 71
Alcock St. WA7: Run 6C 134
Alconbury Cl. WA5: Gt San 2F 117
Alcott Pl. WA2: Win 1A 98
Aldams Gro. L4: Kirk 5A 68
Aldbourne Av. L25: Wltn 3C 110
Aldbourne Cl. L25: Wltn 4C 110
Alder Av. L36: Huy 7A 92
WA8: Wid 5C 114
WN4: Ash M 7D 50
WN5: Bil 7F 49
Alderbank Rd. WA5: Gt San 2E 116
Alder Cl. L34: Prsct 1F 93
Alder Cres. L32: K'by 2B 56
WA2: Warr 7C 98
Alderdale Av. PR8: Ains 4A 14
Alder Dr. CH66: Gt Sut 3H 169
Alderfield Dr. L24: Speke 5K 131
Alder Gro. L22: Water 3D 52
Alder Hey Rd. WA10: St. H 3J 73
Alder La. L34: Know 3F 71
(not continuous)
L39: Bart 3E 20
WA2: Warr 7B 98
WA5: B'wood 7E 76
WA6: Frod 7K 151
WA8: Cron 4F 113
WA11: Crank 1B 60
WN8: Parb 1J 27
Alder Lee Cl. WN3: Wins 2B 50
Alderlee PR8: South 6C 12
Alderley WN8: Skel 5J 37
Alderley Av. CH41: Birk 1K 105
Alderley Cl. WN5: Bil 1G 61
Alderley Rd. CH44: Wall 4B 86
CH47: Hoy 1D 102
WA4: Thel 5K 119
Alderman Rd. L24: Speke 3F 131
Alderney Cl. CH65: Ell P 3A 170
Alderney Dr. WN3: Wigan 1E 50
Alderney Rd. L5: Liv 2J 87
Alder Rd. CH63: High B 5D 126
L12: W Der 3K 89
L34: Prsct 1F 93
WA1: W'ston 1K 119
Alder Root La. WA2: Win 7H 77
Aldersey Cl. WA7: Wind H 1B 154
Aldersgate CH42: R Ferr 6F 107
Aldersgate Av. WA7: Murd 3B 154
Aldersgate Dr. L26: Halew 3A 132
Aldersley St. L3: Liv 4K 87 (2G 4)
Alderson Cres. L37: Form 6K 19
Alderson Rd. L15: W'tree 1F 109
Alder St. WA12: New W 4G 77
Alderton Cl. L26: Halew 2A 132
Alderton Dr. WN4: Ash M 2D 62
Alderville Rd. L4: Walt 4E 68
Alder Wood Av. L24: Speke 6J 131
Alderwood Ct. WA8: Wid 4A 114
Alderwood Lodge L24: Speke 6A 132
Aldewood Cl. WA3: Bchwd 1C 100
Aldford Cl. CH43: O'ton 6J 105
CH63: Brom 4H 145
Aldford Rd. L32: K'by 6C 56
Aldgate CH65: Ell P 6J 161
Aldridge Cl. L12: Crox 3C 70
WN3: Wigan 1F 51
Aldridge Dr. WA5: B'wood 7D 76
Aldrins La. L30: N'ton 1B 54
Aldwark Rd. L14: K Ash 3E 90
Aldwych Rd. L12: W Der 1A 90
Aldykes L31: Mag 4G 43
Alexander Dr. CH61: Pens 6C 124
L31: Lyd 1F 43
WA8: Wid 1K 133
Alexander Fleming Av.
L30: N'ton 1B 54
Alexander Grn. L36: Huy 3J 91
Alexander Ho. L21: Sea 6F 53
L34: Prsct 7D 72
Alexander Wlk. L4: Walt 6B 68
Alexander Way *L8: Liv* *4B 108*
(off Park Hill Rd.)
Alexandra B'way. *PR9: South* *7K 7*
(off Alexandra Rd.)
Alexandra Cl. L6: Liv 4D 88 (2P 5)
WN8: Skel 2E 36
Alexandra Ct. CH45: New B 6A 66
L23: C'by 1D 52
PR9: South 7K 7
WA9: St. H 6K 73
Alexandra Dr. CH42: R Ferr 7E 106
L17: Aig 4D 108
L20: Boot 7A 54
WA10: St. H 5K 73
Alexandra Grn. L17: Aig 4D 108
Alexandra Gro. WA7: Run 1E 152
Alexandra Ho. L17: Aig 4D 108
Alexandra Ind. Est. WA8: Wid 2B 134
Alexandra M. L39: Orm 4C 24
PR9: South 7J 7
WA6: Frod 2D 166
Alexandra Mt. L21: Lith 5H 53
Alexandra Pk. L17: Aig 5D 108
Alexandra Rd. CH43: O'ton 3B 106
CH45: New B 6A 66
CH48: W Kir 7C 102
L7: Liv 7E 88
L13: Liv 5J 89
L19: Gars 2A 130
L22: Water 5E 52
L23: C'by 1D 52
L37: Form 3F 29
PR9: South 6J 7
WA4: Grap 6F 119
WA4: S Hth 7D 118
WN4: Ash M 1F 63
Alexandra St. CH65: Ell P 4A 162
WA1: Warr 1E 118
WA8: Wid 2C 134
WA10: St. H 5K 73
Alexandra Ter. L8: Liv 10L 5
Alexandra Vs. L21: Lith 5H 53
Alex Cl. L8: Liv 2B 108
Alfonso Rd. L4: Kirk 6K 67
Alford Av. WA9: Sut M 3D 94
Alforde St. WA8: Wid 3C 134
(Ashley Way)
WA8: Wid 2C 134
(Victoria Sq.)
Alford St. L7: Liv 5F 89
Alfred Cl. WA8: Wid 1D 134
Alfred M. L1: Liv 1A 108 (10H 5)
Alfred Pl. L8: Liv 4C 108
Alfred Rd. CH43: O'ton 3C 106
CH44: Wall 6E 86
WA11: Hay 6D 62
Alfred Stocks Ct. L8: Liv 5C 108
Alfred St. L15: W'tree 7F 89
WA8: Wid 1D 134
WA10: St. H 2D 74
WA11: R'ford 5F 47
WA12: New W 3J 77
Alfriston Rd. L12: W Der 1A 90
Algernon St. WA1: Warr 2D 118
WA4: S Hth 7C 118
WA7: Run 6B 134
WN3: Wigan 1E 50
Alice Ct. WA8: Wid 5C 134
Alice St. WA9: St. H 6G 75
Alicia Wlk. L10: Faz 6K 55
Alison Av. CH42: R Ferr 5F 107
Alison Pl. L13: Liv 7G 69
Alison Rd. L13: Liv 7G 69
Alistair Dr. CH63: Brom 5J 145
Allangate Cl. CH49: Grea 6A 104
Allangate Rd. L19: Gras 1J 129
Allan Rd. WA11: St. H 6E 60
Allans Cl. CH64: Nest 5J 157
Allans Mdw. CH64: Nest 5J 157
Allanson St. WA9: St. H 4F 75
Allcard St. WA5: Warr 1K 117
Allcot Av. CH42: Tran 6D 106
Allen Av. WA3: Cul 2E 80
Allenby Av. L23: C'by 3F 53
Allenby Sq. L13: Liv 5H 89
Allendale WA7: Pal F 4K 153
Allendale Av. L9: Ain 6D 54
L35: R'hill 4K 93
Allengate L23: C'by 7E 40
Allen Rd. WA7: West P 3K 151
Allen St. WA2: Warr 2A 118
Allerford Rd. L12: W Der 7A 70
ALLERTON 1B 130
Allerton Beeches
L18: Moss H 5A 110
Allerton Dr. L18: Moss H 4K 109
Allerton Gro. CH42: Tran 5D 106
Allerton Rd. CH42: Tran 4D 106
CH45: Wall 1A 86
L18: Aller, Moss H 3J 109
L25: Wltn 6E 110
PR9: South 6A 8
WA8: Wid 7D 114
Allerton Station (Rail) 2B 130
Allesley Rd. L14: K Ash 2D 90
Alleyne Rd. L4: Walt 6F 69
All Hallows Dr. L24: Speke 6K 131
Allington St. L17: Aig 5D 108
Allonby Cl. CH43: Noct 4J 105
Allport La. CH62: Brom 2K 145
(not continuous)
Allport Rd. CH62: Brom 4J 145
CH63: Brom 4J 145
Allports, The CH62: Brom 3K 145
All Saints Cl. L30: N'ton 2A 54
All Saints Ct. WA11: R'ford 7G 47

All Saints Dr.—Arvon St.

All Saints Dr. WA4: Thel 5A 120
All Saints Rd. L24: Speke 6G 131
Allscott Way WN4: Ash M 2G 63
Allysum Ct. WA7: Beech 6H 153
Alma Cl. L10: Faz 6K 55
WN8: Uph 4E 38
Alma Ct. PR8: Ains 2F 15
WN8: Uph 4E 38
Almacs Cl. L23: Blun 2B 52
Alma Grn. WN8: Uph 4D 38
Alma Gro. WN3: Wigan 2C 50
Alma Hill WN8: Uph 4D 38
Alman Ct. L17: Aig 5D 108
Alma Pde. WN8: Uph 4E 38
Alma Pl. WA9: St. H 4E 74
Alma Rd. L17: Aig 1G 129
PR8: B'dale 4G 11
WN8: Uph 4E 38
Alma St. CH41: Birk 2E 106
CH62: New F 2G 127
WA9: St. H 4E 74
WA12: New W 3F 77
Alma Ter. L15: W'tree 7H 89
Alma Wlk. WN8: Uph 4E 38
Almeda Rd. L24: Speke 7A 132
Almer Dr. WA5: Gt San 3G 117
Almond Av. L30: N'ton 2J 53
WA7: Run 2E 152
Almond Brow PR9: Banks 3J 9
Almond Cl. L26: Halew 2J 131
WA11: Hay 1H 75
Almond Ct. L19: Gars 4C 130
Almond Dr. WA5: B'wood 1D 96
Almond Gro. WA1: P'ton 1H 119
WA8: Wid 1K 133
Almond Pl. CH46: More 7D 84
Almonds, The L26: Halew 2J 131
Almond's Grn. L12: W Der 6J 69
Almond's Gro. L12: W Der 7J 69
Almond's Pk. L12: W Der 6J 69
Almonds Turn L30: N'ton 1K 53
Almond Tree Cl. L24: Hale 1E 150
Almond Way CH49: Grea 6A 104
Alness Dr. L35: R'hill 5K 93
Alnwick Dr. CH46: More 7K 83
CH65: Ell P 2B 170
Aloeswood Cl. L6: Liv 2D 88
Alpass Av. WA5: Warr 7K 97
Alpass Rd. L17: Aig 5D 108
Alpha Dr. CH42: R Ferr 7G 107
Alpha St. L21: Lith 1H 67
Alpine Cl. WA10: St. H 2J 73
Alpine St. WA12: New W 3E 76
Alresford Rd. L19: Aig 1H 129
Alroy Rd. L4: Walt 7C 68
Alscot Av. L10: Faz 6J 55
Alscot Cl. L31: Mag 4F 43
Alsop Community Sports Cen. 4B 68
Alston Cl. CH62: Brom 1J 145
Alston Ct. PR8: Ains 3E 14
Alstonfield Rd. L14: K Ash 3E 90
Alston Rd. L17: Aig 1G 129
Alt WA8: Wid 6H 113
Alt Av. L31: Mag 5E 42
Altbridge Pk. L11: Crox 2J 69
(not continuous)
Altbridge Rd. L36: Huy 3H 91
Altcar Av. L15: W'tree 1E 108
Altcar Dr. CH46: More 1B 104
Altcar La. L31: Lyd 6B 32
L37: Form 6C 20
(Downholland Moss La.)
L37: Form 2K 29
(Hoggs Hill La.)
L39: Down 2B 32
Altcar Rifle Range Est.
L38: High 6K 29
Altcar Rd. L20: Boot 1J 67
L37: Form 1A 30
Altcross Rd. L11: Crox 2A 70
Altcross Way L11: Crox 2A 70
Altfield Rd. L14: K Ash 7D 70
Altfinch Cl. L14: K Ash 7E 70
Altham Rd. L11: N Grn. 7H 69
PR8: South 6A 12
Althorpe Dr. PR8: South 5A 12
Althorp St. L8: Liv 5B 108
Altmoor Rd. L36: Huy 2H 91
Alton Av. L21: Lith 4G 53
Alton Cl. L38: High 7F 29
WN4: Ash M 1E 62
Alton Rd. CH43: O'ton 3A 106
L6: Liv 2F 89
Alt Rd. L20: Boot 1J 67
L36: Huy 4J 91
L37: Form 1A 30
L38: High 5F 29
(not continuous)
Altside Ct. L10: Faz 6K 55
Alt St. L8: Liv 1D 108
Altway L10: Ain 2E 54
Altway Ct. *L10: Ain* *2E 54*
(off Altway)
Altys La. L39: Orm 6D 24
Alundale Ct. L20: Boot 3J 67
Alundale Rd. L12: W Der 2C 90
ALVANLEY 3K 173
Alvanley Cl. WN5: Wigan 3K 39
Alvanley Dr. WA6: Hel 2J 173
Alvanley Grn. L32: K'by 2A 56
Alvanley Pl. CH43: O'ton 2C 106
Alvanley Rd. CH66: Gt Sut 7G 161
L12: W Der 2A 90
L32: K'by 3A 56
WA6: Hel 1H 173
Alvanley Ter. WA6: Frod 3D 166
Alvanley Vw. CH2: Elt 1B 172
Alvanley Way CH66: Gt Sut 7G 161
Alva Rd. L35: R'hill 5K 93
Alvega Cl. CH62: New F 2J 127
Alverstone Av. CH41: Birk 1K 105
Alverstone Cl. WA5: Gt San 1A 116
Alverstone Rd. CH44: Wall 4D 86
L18: Moss H 3H 109
Alverton Cl. WA8: Wid 1K 133
Alvina La. L4: Walt 7A 68
L33: K'by 7D 44
Alwain Grn. L24: Speke 7K 131
Alwen St. CH41: Birk 6K 85
Alwyn Av. L21: Lith 4H 53
Alwyn Cl. L17: Aig 5D 108
Alwyn Gdns. CH46: More 7D 84
Alwyn St. L17: Aig 5D 108
Amanda Rd. L10: Faz 6K 55
L35: R'hill 2H 93
Amanda Way L31: Mell 1K 55
Amaury Cl. L23: Thorn 7H 41
Amaury Rd. L23: Thorn 7H 41
Ambassador Dr. L26: Halew 7A 112
Ambergate WN8: Skel 4H 37
Ambergate Cl. WA9: St. H 7F 75
Ambergate Rd. L19: Gras 2K 129
Amberleigh Cl. WA4: App T 5H 139
Amberley Av. CH46: More 1A 104
Amberley Cl. CH46: More 1A 104
L6: Liv 7F 69
Amberley St. L8: Liv 1C 108 (10M 5)
Amber Way L14: K Ash 7E 70
Ambleside WN5: Wigan 4K 39
Ambleside Av. CH46: More 7B 84
Ambleside Cl. CH61: Thing 3E 124
CH62: Brom 3A 146
WA7: Beech 5G 153
Ambleside Cres. WA2: Warr 4C 98
Ambleside Pl. WA11: St. H 4D 60
Ambleside Rd. CH65: Ell P 2A 170
L18: Aller 7B 110
L31: Mag 2F 43
Amelia Cl. L6: Liv 4B 88 (3L 5)
WA8: Wid 4D 114
Amelia St. WA2: Warr 1C 118
Amersham WN8: Skel 4H 37
Amersham Rd. L4: Walt 4E 68
(not continuous)
Amery Gro. CH42: Tran 6B 106
Amesbury Dr. WN3: Wins 2A 50
Amethyst Cl. L6: Liv 3D 88
L21: Lith 5J 53
Amherst Rd. L17: Aig 6E 108
Amity St. L8: Liv 3B 108
Amos Av. L21: Lith 5J 53
Ampleforth Cl. L32: K'by 4A 56
Ampthill Rd. L17: Aig 6E 108
Ampulla Rd. L11: Crox 3A 70
Amy Wlk. L10: Faz 6K 55
Ancaster Rd. L17: Aig 6E 108
Ancholme Cl. L35: Whis 1G 93
Anchorage, The CH64: Park 4G 157
L3: Liv 2K 107
WA13: Lymm 5F 121
Anchorage La. L18: Moss H 5G 109
Anchor Cl. WA7: Murd 4B 154
Anchor Ct. PR8: B'dale 3F 11
WA1: Warr 2D 118
Anchorite Ct. WA12: New W 3C 76
Anchor St. PR9: South 1H 11
Ancient Mdws. L9: Ain 6D 54
Ancroft Rd. L14: K Ash 4E 90
Ancrum Rd. L33: K'by 6B 44
Anders Dr. L33: K'by 7D 44
Anderson Cl. CH61: Thing 3E 124
L35: R'hill 6K 93
WA2: P'gate 5H 99
Anderson Ct. CH62: Brom 4K 145
Anderson Rd. L21: Lith 4K 53
Anderson St. L5: Liv 1A 88
(not continuous)
Anderson Way L21: Lith 4K 53
Anderton Ter. L36: Roby 5G 91
Andover Cl. WA2: P'gate 6E 98
Andover Cres. WN3: Wins 2A 50
Andover Rd. WA11: Hay 5C 62
Andover Way L25: Hunts X 2H 131
Andreas Cl. PR8: B'dale 4H 11
Andrew Av. L31: Mell 2J 55
WN5: Bil 7H 49
Andrew Cl. WA8: Wid 1J 133
Andrew Ho. L8: Liv 10K 5
Andrews Cl. L37: Form 2J 29
Andrews La. L37: Form 1J 29
Andrew St. L4: Walt 5B 68
Andrew's Wlk. CH60: Hes 2F 143
Andrews Yort L37: Form 2J 29
Andromeda Way WA9: Bold 7J 75
Anemone Way WA9: Bold 7J 75
ANFIELD 7C 68
Anfield 7C 68
Anfield Ct. L4: Walt 7C 68
Anfield Crematorium L4: Walt 6C 68
Anfield Rd. L4: Walt 7B 68
Angela St. L7: Liv 7D 88 (9P 5)
Angers La. L31: Mell 6K 43
Anglesea Rd. L9: Walt 3B 68
Anglesea Way L8: Liv 4B 108
Anglesey Cl. CH65: Ell P 3A 170
Anglesey Rd. CH44: Wall 2B 86
CH48: W Kir 5C 102
Anglezark Cl. L7: Liv 5D 88
Anglezarke Rd. WA12: New W 4E 76
Anglia Way L25: Hunts X 1G 131
Anglican Ct. L8: Liv 1A 108
Anglo Cl. L9: Ain 5E 54
Angus Rd. CH63: Brom 4J 145
L11: N Grn. 6H 69
Annandale Cl. L33: K'by 6B 44
Annandale Gdns. WN8: Uph 4B 38
Annan Gro. WN4: Ash M 7J 51
Ann Cl. CH66: Lit Sut 4F 161
Ann Conway Ho. *L15: W'tree* *1F 109*
(off Garmoyle Cl.)
Anne Av. PR8: Ains 3E 14
Anne Gro. WA9: St. H 7E 74
Annesley Cres. WN3: Wigan 1D 50
Annesley Rd. CH44: Wall 4C 86
L17: Aig 6E 108
Anne St. WA9: Clock F 4F 95
Annette Av. WA12: New W 1E 76
Annie Rd. L20: Boot 7K 53
Annie St. WA2: Warr 2C 118
Ann St. WA7: Run 6D 134
WN8: Skel 3E 36
Ann St. W. WA8: Wid 2D 134
Anscot Av. CH63: Beb 3F 127
Ansdell Dr. WA10: Eccl 1H 73
Ansdell Gro. PR9: Chu 3C 8
Ansdell Rd. WA8: Wid 6D 114
Ansdell Vs. Rd. L35: R'hill 3J 93
Anson Cl. WA2: P'gate 5E 98
Anson St. L3: Liv 5A 88 (5K 5)
Anstey Cl. CH46: More 6K 83
Anstey Rd. L13: Liv 4K 89
Ansty Cl. WA11: St. H 7F 61
Anthony's Way CH60: Hes 3E 142
Anthorn Cl. CH43: Noct 4H 105
Anthorn Rd. WN3: Wigan 1C 50
Antler Ct. WN4: Ash M 6F 51
Antonio St. L20: Boot 5K 67
Antons Cl. L26: Halew 3K 131
Antons Rd. CH61: Pens 4E 124
L26: Halew 3K 131
Antony Rd. WA4: Warr 6B 118
Antrim Cl. WA11: Hay 7A 62
WN3: Wins 2A 50
Antrim Dr. CH66: Gt Sut 2H 169
Antrim Rd. WA2: Warr 5A 98
Antrim St. L13: Liv 7G 69
Anvil Cl. CH2: Elt 7B 164
L20: Boot 2H 67
WN5: Orr 6F 39
Anzacs, The CH62: Port S 3J 127
Anzio Rd. L36: Huy 3H 91
Apartments, The PR9: South 6H 7
Apex Ct. CH62: Brom 1A 146
Apollo Cres. L33: K'by 1C 56
Apollo Way L6: Liv 2D 88
L30: N'ton 1B 54
Apostles Way L33: K'by 7B 44
Appin Rd. CH41: Birk 3E 106
Appleby Cl. WA8: Wid 1J 133
Appleby Dr. L30: N'ton 2J 53
Appleby Grn. L12: W Der 1B 90
Appleby Gro. CH62: Brom 4K 145
Appleby Lawn L27: N'ley 4A 112
Appleby Rd. L33: K'by 1B 56
WA2: Warr 4C 98
WA8: Wid 1J 133
Appleby Wlk. L27: N'ley 4A 112
WA8: Wid 1J 133
Applecorn Cl. WA9: Sut L 1F 95
Apple Ct. *L6: Liv* *4D 88*
(off Coleridge St.)
Applecross Cl. WA3: Bchwd 1C 100
Appledale Dr. CH66: Whit 4J 169
Appledore Ct. L24: Speke 5F 131
Appledore Gro. WA9: Sut L 2E 94
Appleford Cl. WA4: App 2E 138
Apple Gth. CH46: More 2A 104
APPLETON
Warrington 2E 138
Widnes 6D 114
Appleton Dr. CH49: Grea 5C 104
CH65: Whit 1H 169
Appleton Hall Gdns. WA4: App 4E 138
Appleton M. WA13: Lymm 4E 120
APPLETON PARK 5D 138
Appleton Rd. L4: Walt 5C 68
L21: Lith 4G 53
L33: K'by 1C 56
WA8: Wid 7D 114
WA9: St. H 5E 74
WN8: Skel 1F 37
Appleton St. WA8: Wid 3D 134
APPLETON THORN 5H 139
Appleton Thorn Trad. Est.
WA4: App T 3K 139
Appleton Village WA8: Wid 7C 114
Apple Tree Cl. L24: Hale 1E 150
L28: Stock V 6F 71
Appletree Cl. L18: Aller 7K 109
Apple Tree Gro. CH66: Gt Sut 4H 169
Appletree Gro. WA2: Fearn 5F 99
April Gro. L6: Liv 2F 89
April Ri. L30: N'ton 2A 54
Apsley Av. CH45: Wall 1B 86
Apsley Brow L31: Mag 3D 42
Apsley Gro. CH63: Beb 3G 127
Apsley Rd. CH62: New F 1H 127
L12: W Der 1A 90
Aqua Complex, The 7A 68
Aquarius Cl. L14: K Ash 3E 90
Arabis Gdns. WA9: Bold 7K 75
Aragon Cl. L31: Lyd 1G 43
Aragon Ct. WA7: Mnr P 6A 136
Aran Cl. L24: Hale 7D 132
Arborn Dr. CH49: Upton 2E 104
Arbour La. L33: Know I 4E 56
Arbour St. PR8: South 2J 11
Arbury Av. WA11: St. H 7F 61
Arbury La. WA2: Win 1C 98
Arcade, The CH65: Ell P 6J 161
Arcadia Av. L31: Lyd 1F 43
Archbishop Warlock Ct.
L3: Liv 3J 87 (1D 4)
Archbrook M. L13: Liv 2G 89
Archer Av. WA4: Latch 6E 118
Archer Cl. L4: Kirk 7A 68
Archerfield Rd. L18: Aller 7K 109
Archer Gro. WA9: St. H 2G 75
Archers Ct. CH49: W'chu 6E 104
Archers Cft. CH62: Brom 1K 145
Archers Fold L31: Mell 1K 55
Archers Grn. CH62: East 6A 146
Archers Rd. WA5: W'brk 4F 97
Archer St. L4: Kirk 7A 68
Archers Way CH49: W'chu 6E 104
CH66: Gt Sut 3G 169
Arch La. WN4: Gars 2J 61
Arch Vw. Cres. L1: Liv 7A 88 (9H 5)
Archway Rd. L36: Huy 5H 91
Archway Wlk. WA12: New W 3J 77
Arctic Rd. L20: Boot 3G 67
Arden WA8: Wid 6G 113
Arden Cl. PR8: Ains 4A 14
WA3: Bchwd 1D 100
Arden Dr. CH64: Nest 5J 157
Ardennes Rd. L36: Huy 4J 91
Arderne Cl. CH63: Spit 7H 127
Ardern Lea WA6: Alv 3K 173
Ardleigh Av. PR8: South 5A 12
Ardleigh Cl. L13: Liv 5H 89
Ardleigh Gro. L13: Liv 5H 89
Ardleigh Pl. L13: Liv 5G 89
Ardleigh Rd. L13: Liv 5G 89
Ardmore Rd. L18: Moss H 6J 109
Ardrossan Rd. L4: Walt 6E 68
Ardville Rd. L11: N Grn. 3F 69
Ardwick Rd. L24: Speke 6K 131
Ardwick St. WA9: St. H 3E 74
Arena Gdns. WA2: Warr 7D 98
Argameols Cl. PR8: South 3B 12
Argameols Gro. L37: Form 5J 19
Argameols Rd. L37: Form 4J 19
Argo Rd. L22: Water 4D 52
Argos Pl. L20: Kirk 5K 67
Argos Rd. L20: Kirk 5K 67
Argyle Ct. PR9: South 5K 7
Argyle Lawn Tennis Club 5A 8
Argyle Pk. PR9: South 7K 7
Argyle Rd. L4: Walt 1D 88
L19: Gars 3A 130
PR9: South 6K 7
Argyle St. CH41: Birk 2E 106
L1: Liv 7K 87 (8F 4)
WA10: St. H 1B 74
Argyle St. Sth. CH41: Birk 3D 106
Argyll Av. CH62: East 6K 145
Argyll Cl. WN4: Gars 1A 62
Aries Cl. L14: K Ash 2E 90
Ariss Gro. L35: Whis 2G 93
Arizona Cres. WA5: Gt San 1F 117
Arkenshaw Rd. WA3: Croft 6G 79
Arkenstone Cl. WA8: Wid 6J 113
Arkle Rd. CH41: Birk 7K 85
CH43: Bid 7K 85
Arkles La. L4: Walt 7C 68
Arkles Rd. L4: Walt 1C 88
Arklow Dr. L24: Hale 7D 132
Ark Royal Way CH41: Tran 4F 107
Arkwood Cl. CH62: Spit 6J 127
Arkwright Ct. WA7: Ast 6H 135
Arkwright Rd. WA7: Ast 6H 135
Arkwright St. L5: Liv 2A 88
Arlescourt Rd. L12: W Der 2A 90
Arley Av. WA4: S Hth 7D 118
Arley Cl. CH43: Bid 2G 105
Arley Dr. WA8: Wid 6G 113
Arley End WA16: H Legh 5K 141
Arley Gro. WA13: Lymm 6J 121
Arley Rd. WA4: App T 5H 139
Arley St. L3: Liv 3J 87 (1E 4)
WN3: Ince M 1J 51
Arlington Av. L18: Moss H 3G 109
Arlington Cl. PR8: Ains 4A 14
Arlington Ct. CH43: O'ton 3K 105
Arlington Dr. WA5: Penk 4C 116
Arlington Rd. CH45: Wall 1J 85
Armill Rd. L11: Crox 3A 70
Armitage Gdns. L18: Aller 7K 109
Armley Rd. L4: Walt 7D 68
Armour Av. WA2: Warr 5B 98
Armour Gro. L13: Liv 5J 89
Armour Ho. L1: Liv 6E 4
Armoury, The L12: W Der 7K 69
Armoury Bank WN4: Ash M 2F 63
Armscot Cl. L25: Hunts X 2F 131
Armscot Pl. L25: Hunts X 2F 131
Armstrong Cl. WA3: Bchwd 3K 99
Armstrong Quay L3: Liv 5A 108
Armthorpe Dr. CH66: Lit Sut 6D 160
Arncliffe Dr. WA5: B'wood 1D 96
Arncliffe Rd.
L25: Hunts X, Wltn 1G 131
Arndale WA7: Beech 5G 153
Arnhem Cres. WA2: Warr 1C 118
Arnhem Rd. L36: Huy 3J 91
Arnian Ct. L39: Augh 3A 34
Arnian Rd. WA11: R'ford 5F 47
Arnian Way WA11: R'ford 5F 47
Arno Ct. CH43: O'ton 5B 106
Arnold Av. WA10: St. H 1K 73
Arnold Cl. WA9: St. H 5E 74
Arnold Cres. L8: Liv 2B 108
Arnold Gro. L15: W'tree 7J 89
Arnold Pl. WA8: Wid 2J 133
Arnold St. CH45: Wall 2B 86
WA1: Warr 2D 118
Arno Rd. CH43: O'ton 5B 106
Arnot Cl. WA10: St. H 1B 74
Arnot St. L4: Walt 5B 68
Arnot Way CH63: High B 3D 126
Arnside L21: Lith 5K 53
Arnside Av. L35: R'hill 3G 93
WA11: Hay 7K 61
Arnside Gro. WA4: Warr 6B 118
Arnside Rd. CH43: O'ton 4A 106
CH45: Wall 2B 86
L7: Liv 6E 88
L36: Huy 5F 91
PR9: South 1J 11
WN5: Orr 3K 39
Arnside Ter. PR9: South 1J 11
Aron Ct. L34: Prsct 1D 92
ARPLEY MEADOWS 5B 118
Arpley Rd. WA1: Warr 4B 118
Arpley St. WA1: Warr 3A 118
Arrad St. L7: Liv 7B 88 (8K 5)
Arran Av. CH65: Ell P 3A 170
Arran Cl. WA2: Fearn 5G 99
WA11: St. H 7G 61
Arran Dr. WA6: Frod 4E 166
Arranmore Rd. L18: Moss H 6J 109
Arrowe Av. CH46: More 1B 104
Arrowe Brook La. CH49: Grea 7B 104
Arrowe Brook Rd. CH49: W'chu 6D 104
Arrowe Country Pk. 7D 104
Arrowe Ct. *CH49: W'chu* *6E 104*
(off Childwall Grn.)
ARROWE HILL 5D 104
Arrowe Pk. Rd.
CH49: Upton, W'chu 3E 104
Arrowe Rd. CH49: Grea 5B 104
Arrowe Side CH49: Grea 4C 104
Arrowe Vw. CH49: Upton 3E 104
Arrowsmith Rd. WA11: Hay 6D 62
Arthur Av. CH65: Ell P 6A 162
Arthur St. CH41: Birk 1C 106
(not continuous)
L9: Walt 3B 68
L19: Gars 4B 130
WA2: Warr 2A 118
WA7: Run 7B 134
Arundel Av. CH45: Wall 1K 85
L17: Liv 2E 108
Arundel Cl. CH61: Pens 4D 124
L8: Liv 2C 108
Arundel Ct. CH65: Ell P 1C 170
Arundell Cl. WA5: B'wood 1D 96
Arundel Rd. PR8: B'dale 1F 15
Arundel St. L4: Walt 5A 68
Arvon St. L20: Boot 7K 53

Asbridge St.—Back La.

Asbridge St. L8: Liv 1D 108
Asbury Cl. L18: Aller 5B 110
Asbury Rd. CH45: Wall 1H 85
Ascot Av. L21: Lith 5G 53
WA7: Run 4D 152
Ascot Cl. PR8: B'dale 3E 10
WA1: W'ston 1A 120
WA4: Grap 6J 119
Ascot Dr. CH63: Beb 4F 127
CH66: Gt Sut 1F 169
L33: K'by 7C 44
Ascot Gro. CH63: Beb 4F 127
Ascot Pk. L23: C'by 1F 53
Ascroft Rd. L9: Ain 5D 54
Ash Av. WA12: New W 4G 77
Ashbank Rd. L11: N Grn. 4J 69
Ashberry Dr. WA4: App T 4H 139
Ashbourne Av. L23: Blun 1C 52
L30: N'ton 2A 54
WA7: Run 4D 152
Ashbourne Cl. CH66: Gt Sut 4G 169
Ashbourne Cres. L36: Huy 5F 91
Ashbourne Rd. L17: Aig 6E 108
WA5: Gt San 3F 117
Ashbrook Av. WA7: Sut W 7H 153
Ashbrook Cres. WA2: Warr 7D 98
Ashbrook Dr. L9: Ain 7E 54
Ashbrook Ter. CH63: Beb 3G 127
Ash Brow WN8: Newb 1G 27
Ashburn Av. L33: K'by 1C 56
Ashburton Av. CH43: C'ton 2K 105
Ashburton Rd. CH43: C'ton 2K 105
CH44: Wall 3B 86
CH48: W Kir 5D 102
Ashbury Cl. WA7: Wind H 7B 136
Ashbury Dr. WA11: Hay 6A 62
Ashbury Rd. L14: K Ash 1F 91
Ashby Cl. CH46: More 6K 83
Ashby Rd. WN3: Wigan 1F 51
Ash Cl. CH66: Gt Sut 3H 169
L15: W'tree 7G 89
L39: Orm 5B 24
Ashcombe Rd. L14: K Ash 4K 89
Ash Cres. L36: Huy 7J 91
Ashcroft Av. L39: Orm 4D 24
Ashcroft Dr. CH61: Hes 7D 124
Ashcroft Rd. L33: Know I 2F 57
L37: Form 2K 29
WA13: Lymm 4K 121
Ashcroft St. L20: Boot 3H 67
WA9: St. H 3E 74
Ashdale L36: Huy 5H 91
Ashdale Cl. L37: Form 1G 29
Ashdale Pk. CH49: Grea 5K 103
Ashdale Rd. L9: Walt 2C 68
L18: Moss H 3J 109
L22: Water 3D 52
WN3: Wigan 2E 50
Ashdown Cl. PR8: South 4A 12
Ashdown Cres. WA9: Clock F 3E 94
Ashdown Dr. CH49: Grea 6A 104
Ashdown Gro. L26: Halew 7A 112
Ashdown La. WA3: Bchwd 2C 100
Asher Ct. WA4: App T 5K 139
Ashfarm Ct. L14: K Ash 4D 90
Ashfield L15: W'tree 7F 89
L35: R'hill 4K 93
Ashfield Cl. WA13: Lymm 4K 121
Ashfield Cres. CH62: Brom 2K 145
WN5: Bil 7G 49
Ashfield Ho. CH64: Nest 3J 157
Ashfield Rd. CH62: Brom 2J 145
CH65: Ell P 6A 162
L17: Aig 6F 109
Ashfield Rd. Nth. CH65: Ell P 6A 162
Ashfield St. L5: Liv 2J 87
Ashford Cl. L26: Halew 2J 131
Ashford Dr. WA4: App 6E 138
Ashford Rd. CH41: Birk 4C 106
CH47: Meols 7E 82
Ashford Way WA8: Wid 7F 115
Ash Grange L14: K Ash 4B 90
Ash Gro. CH45: New B 7C 66
CH66: Lit Sut 5E 160
L15: W'tree 7F 89
L21: Sea 7G 53
L35: Prsct 3E 92
L37: Form 2G 29
WA4: Warr 5D 118
WA7: Run 2E 152
WA8: Wid 1K 133
WA9: Clock F 3E 94
WA11: R'ford 6F 47
WN5: Orr 5H 39
WN8: Skel 2D 36
Ash Gro. Cres. WN5: Bil 6F 49
Ashington Cl. WN5: Wigan 2K 39
Ashland Av. WN4: Ash M 1E 62
Ashlands WA6: Frod 4E 166
Ash La. WA4: App 1E 138
WA8: Wid 7E 112
Ashlar Gro. L17: Aig 5G 109
Ashlar Rd. L17: Aig 5G 109
L22: Water 3E 52
Ashlea Rd. CH61: Pens 6D 124
Ashleigh Rd. L31: Mag 5H 43
Ashley Av. CH47: Meols 6H 83
Ashley Cl. L33: K'by 7C 44
L35: R'hill 5K 93
WA4: Grap 5J 119
Ashley Ct. WA4: App 3C 138
WA6: Frod 3C 166
Ashley Grn. WA8: Wid 1K 133
Ashley Retail Pk. WA8: Wid 2D 134
Ashley Rd. PR9: South 1J 11
WA7: Run 7F 135
WN8: Skel 7H 27
Ashley St. CH42: R Ferr 6F 107
Ashley Way WA8: Wid 3C 134
Ashley Way W. WA8: Wid 2B 134
Ashmead Rd. WN8: Skel 6G 27
Ashmore Cl. CH48: Caldy 3E 122
WA3: Bchwd 4C 100
Ashmuir Hey L32: K'by 4D 56
Ashover Av. L14: K Ash 3E 90
Ash Priors WA8: Wid 5K 113
Ashridge St. WA7: Run 6B 134
Ashridge Way WN5: Orr 2K 39
Ash Rd. CH2: Elt 1C 172
CH42: Tran 4C 106
Ash Rd. CH63: High B 2F 127
L21: Lith 6G 53
WA2: Win 1B 98
WA3: Rix 5J 101
WA5: Penk 4D 116
WA11: Hay 6C 62
WA13: Lymm 5E 120
Ash St. L20: Boot 2J 67
PR8: South 3J 11
Ashton Av. L35: R'hill 6J 93
Ashton Cl. CH62: East 7A 146
WA6: Frod 2E 166
WA7: West 4B 152
Ashton Ct. WA6: Frod 2E 166
ASHTON CROSS 3B 62
Ashton Dr. CH48: W Kir 6C 102
L25: Hunts X 2F 131
WA6: Frod 1E 166
Ashton Grange Ind. Est.
WN4: Ash M 6F 51
Ashton Heath WN4: Ash M
3G 63
Ashton Leisure Cen. 1E 62
ASHTON-IN-MAKERFIELD 3F 63
Ashton Pk. L25: Hunts X 1H 131
Ashton Pl. PR8: South 2H 11
Ashton Rd. PR8: B'dale 7F 11
WA3: Golb 3K 63
WA12: New W 7G 63
WN5: Bil 4K 49
ASHTON'S GREEN 3H 75
Ashtons Grn. Dr. WA9: St. H
4H 75
Ashton's La. L24: Hale 7K 131
L37: Form 2G 29
Ashton Sq. L25: Wltn 7F 111
Ashton St. L3: Liv 5B 88 (5L 5)
L13: Liv 4J 89
WA2: Warr 2B 118
Ashtree Cl. CH64: Lit N 4K 157
Ashtree Cft. CH64: Will 4G 159
Ashtree Dr. CH64: Lit N 5A 158
Ashtree Farm Ct.
CH64: Will 3G 159
Ashtree Gro. L12: Crox 2C 70
ASHURST 6H 27
Ashurst Cl. L25: Gate 4F 111
WA11: St. H 7G 61
WN8: Skel 6G 27
Ashurst Ct. L37: Form 1J 29
Ashurst Dr. WA11: St. H 7F 61
Ashurst Gdns. WN8: Skel 6H 27
Ashurst Rd. WN8: Skel 7H 27
Ash Va. L15: W'tree 7F 89
Ash Vs. CH44: Wall 5C 86
Ashville Ind. Est. WA7: Sut W 7G 153
Ashville Rd. CH41: Birk 2A 106
CH43: C'ton 2A 106
CH44: Wall 4C 86
Ashville Way WA7: Sut W 7G 153
Ashwall St. WN8: Skel 3D 36
Ashwater Rd. L12: W Der 4A 70
Ash Way CH60: Hes 4F 143
Ashwell St. L8: Liv 1A 108
Ashwood WN8: Skel 7J 27
Ashwood Av. WA1: Warr 1E 118
WN4: Ash M 3E 62
Ashwood Cl. CH66: Gt Sut 3F 169
L27: N'ley 3J 111
Ashwood Cl. L33: K'by 7C 44
WA8: Wid 2G 133
Ashwood Ct. CH43: Bid 6G 85
Ashwood Dr. L12: Crox 3B 70
Ashwood Gro. CH2: Wer 7E 170
Askern Rd. L32: K'by 5D 56
Askett Cl. WA11: Hay 6B 62
Askew Cl. CH44: Wall 3D 86
Askew St. L4: Walt 5B 68
Askham Cl. L8: Liv 1D 108 (10P 5)
Askrigg Av. CH66: Lit Sut 6D 160
Asland Gdns. PR9: Cros 3E 8
Asmall Cl. L39: Orm 4B 24
Asmall La. L39: Hals 2F 23
L39: Orm, Scar 2K 23
L40: Hals, Scar 2K 23
Aspen Cl. CH60: Hes 3H 143
CH66: Gt Sut 3G 169
L33: K'by 6D 44
Aspendale Rd. CH42: Tran 4D 106
Aspen Gdns. WA9: St. H 1J 93
Aspen Gro. L8: Liv 2D 108
L37: Form 2G 29
WA1: P'ton 1G 119
Aspen Way WN8: Skel 1E 36
Aspenwood WN4: Ash M 3E 62
Aspes Rd. L12: W Der 7C 70
Aspinall Cl. WA2: Fearn 4G 99
Aspinall Cres. L37: Gt Alt 2F 31
Aspinall St. CH41: Birk 1C 106
L34: Prsct 1D 92
Aspley Ho. L22: Water 4E 52
Aspull Cl. WA3: Bchwd 3J 99
Asquith Av. CH41: Birk 1B 106
Asser Rd. L11: N Grn. 6G 69
Assheton Cl. WA12: New W 2F 77
Assheton Wlk. L24: Hale 7E 132
Assissian Cres. L30: N'ton 1A 54
Aster Ct. L31: Lyd 1E 42
Aster Cres. WA7: Beech 5H 153
Aster Dr. L33: K'by 7B 44
Asterfield Av. CH63: High B 2E 126
Aster Rd. WA11: Hay 6D 62
Astley Cl. WA4: Warr 5B 118
WA8: Wid 5J 113
WA11: R'ford 5F 47
Astley Rd. L36: Huy 1J 91
M44: Irlam 1K 81
ASTMOOR 6H 135
Astmoor Bri. La. WA7: Cas 7H 135
Astmoor Ind. Est. WA7: Ast 6H 135
(Brindley Rd.)
WA7: Ast 6G 135
(Goddard Rd.)
Astmoor La. WA7: Ast 6E 134
WA7: Cas 7H 135
Astmoor Rd. WA7: Ast 6E 134
Astmoor Spine Rd. WA7: Ast 6J 135
Aston Av. WA3: Ris 3B 100
Aston Cl. CH43: O'ton 5K 105
Aston Ct. WA1: W'ston 6J 99
Aston Fields Rd. WA7: Pres B 6B 154
Aston Grn. WA7: Pres B 4C 154
ASTON HEATH 7B 154
Aston La.
WA7: Aston, Sut W 7K 153 & 7C 154
WA7: Pres B 5C 154
Aston La. Nth. WA7: Pres B 6C 154
Aston La. Sth. WA7: Pres B 7C 154
Aston St. L19: Gars 4A 130
Astonwood Rd. CH42: Tran 5D 106
Astor Dr. WA4: Grap 1F 139
Astor St. L4: Walt 4B 68
Atheldene Rd. L4: Walt 4E 68
Athelstan Cl. CH62: Brom 1K 145
Atherton Cl. L5: Liv 2A 88
Atherton Ct. CH45: New B 6A 66
Atherton Dr. CH49: W'chu 5E 104
Atherton Rake L30: N'ton 1K 53
Atherton Rd. CH65: Ell P 5H 161
L9: Ain 7E 54
Atherton St. CH45: New B 5A 66
L34: Prsct 1D 92
WA10: St. H 1B 74
Athlone Rd. WA2: Warr 6A 98
Athol Cl. CH62: East 5A 146
WA12: New W 2D 76
Athol Dr. CH62: East 6A 146
Athole Gro. PR9: South 1B 12
Atholl Cres. L10: Ain 3F 55
Atholl Gro. WN3: Wigan 1E 50
Athol St. CH41: Birk 1E 106
L5: Liv 2H 87
(Gt. Howard St.)
L5: Liv 2J 87
(Vauxhall Rd., not continuous)
Atkinson Art Gallery (within Library)
1H 11
Atkinson Gro. L36: Huy 3K 91
Atlanta Ct. L33: K'by 5B 44
Atlantic Pav. L3: Liv 7J 87 (9D 4)
Atlantic Point L3: Liv 4K 87 (2F 4)
Atlantic Rd. L20: Boot 3H 67
Atlantic Terminal L20: Boot 2G 67
Atlantic Way L3: Liv 3K 107
L30: Boot 5A 54
Atlas Bus. Complex L20: Boot 2G 67
Atlas Ct. WA9: St. H 3D 74
Atlas Rd. L20: Boot 2H 67
Atlas St. WA9: St. H 3D 74
Atterbury Cl. WA8: Wid 6J 113
Atterbury St. L8: Liv 3K 107
Attlee Av. WA3: Cul 2D 80
Attlee Rd. L36: Huy 4A 92
Attwood St. L4: Walt 7B 68
Atwell St. L6: Liv 3C 88 (1N 5)
Atworth Ter. *CH64: Will 3F 159*
(off Neston Rd.)
Aubourn Cl. WA8: Wid 5J 113
Aubrey Ct. L6: Liv 3C 88 (1N 5)
Aubrey St. L6: Liv 3B 88 (1L 5)
Auburn Rd. CH45: Wall 7A 66
L13: Liv 1G 89
Aubynes, The CH45: Wall 7J 65
Auckery Av. CH66: Gt Sut 1F 169
Auckland Rd. L18: Moss H 3J 109
Audlem Av. CH43: O'ton 5K 105
Audlem Cl. WA7: Sut W 6H 153
Audley St. L3: Liv 5A 88 (4J 5)
Audre Cl. WA5: Gt San 2B 116
Audrey Wlk. L10: Faz 6K 55
AUGHTON 4J 33
Aughton Cl. WN5: Bil 1G 61
Aughton Ct. CH49: Upton 3E 104
Aughton M. PR8: B'dale 3G 11
AUGHTON PARK 1B 34
Aughton Pk. Dr. L39: Augh 1B 34
Aughton Park Station (Rail) 1B 34
Aughton Rd. L20: Boot 1K 67
PR8: B'dale 2F 11
Aughton St. L39: Orm 6B 24
(not continuous)
Augusta Cl. L13: Liv 5J 89
August Rd. L6: Liv 2E 88
August St. L20: Boot 1J 67
Aukland Gro. WA9: St. H 1K 93
Aurorean Cl. L27: N'ley 2H 111
Austell Cl. WA11: St. H 6F 61
Austen Dr. WA2: Win 1A 98
Austin Av. WA10: St. H 6J 73
WN4: Gars 1C 62
Austin Cl. L32: K'by 2B 56
Austin Rawlinson Sports Cen. 6J 131
Austin St. CH44: Wall 5A 86
Austral Av. WA1: W'ston 1H 119
Australia La. WA4: Grap 7J 119
Autumn Gro. CH42: R Ferr 1E 126
Autumn Way L20: Boot 1J 67
WA9: Clock F 4E 94
Avalon Ter. L20: Boot 2H 67
Avebury Cl. WA8: Wid 5G 115
Aveley Cl. WA1: P'ton 1H 119
Aveling Dr. PR9: Banks 1J 9
Avelon Cl. CH43: Noct 3H 105
L31: Lyd 6D 32
Avenham Cl. PR9: Banks 2K 9
Avenue, The CH62: Brom 2J 145
L19: Gars 4C 130
L26: Halew 2J 131
L36: Huy 4J 91
L39: Orm 4B 24
(Halsall La.)
L39: Orm 4C 24
(Southport Rd.)
PR9: Banks 2H 9
PR9: South 3G 13
WA10: Eccl 3G 73
WA11: R'ford 6F 47
WA12: New W 2H 77
WA13: Lymm 7E 120
WA16: H Legh 4K 141
WN5: Bil 1F 49
Averham Cl. WN4: Ash M 4F 63
Avery Cl. WA2: Warr 5E 98
Avery Cres. WA11: Hay 6A 62
Avery Rd. WA11: Hay 6A 62
Avery Sq. WA11: Hay 6A 62
Aviary Ct. L9: Walt 7B 54
Aviemore Cl. WN4: Gars 1B 62
Aviemore Dr. WA2: Fearn 5G 99
Aviemore Rd. L13: Liv 4H 89
Avington Cl. L12: W Der 7B 70
Avis Wlk. L10: Faz 6K 55
Avocet Cl. WA2: Warr 4D 98
WA12: New W 2G 77
Avolon Rd. L12: W Der 2B 90
Avon WA8: Wid 6G 113
Avon Av. WA5: Penk 4C 116
Avon Cl. CH64: Nest 5J 157
L4: Kirk 6A 68
L33: K'by 6D 44
Avon Ct. L23: C'by 7E 40
Avondale CH65: Whit 1K 169
Avondale Av. CH46: More 6D 84
CH62: East 5A 146
L31: Mag 4E 42
Avondale Dr. WA8: Wid 7H 113
Avondale Rd. CH47: Hoy 1D 102
L15: W'tree 2G 109
PR9: South 7H 7
WA11: Hay 6A 62
Avondale Rd. Nth. PR9: South 6J 7
Avonmore Av. L18: Moss H 5J 109
Avon Rd. WA3: Cul 4C 80
WN4: Ash M 7J 51
WN5: Bil 2F 61
Avon St. CH41: Birk 6K 85
L6: Liv 2D 88
Awelon Cl. L12: W Der 6K 69
Awesome Walls Climbing Cen. 2H 87
Axbridge Av. WA9: Sut L 2F 95
Axholme Cl. CH61: Thing 4F 125
Axholme Rd. CH61: Thing 3F 125
Ayala Cl. L9: Walt 6B 54
Aycliffe Rd. WA9: St. H 1K 93
Aycliffe Wlk. WA8: Wid 1J 133
Aylesbury Av. CH43: O'ton 6J 105
Aylesbury Cl. CH66: Gt Sut 1E 168
Aylesbury Rd. CH45: New B 7C 66
Aylesford Rd. L13: Liv 4J 89
Aylsham Cl. WA8: Wid 4J 113
Aylsham Dr. CH49: Upton 1E 104
Aylton Rd. L36: Huy 3F 91
Aylward Pl. L20: Boot 2H 67
Aynsley Ct. WA9: St. H 1H 93
Ayr Cl. PR8: South 4B 12
Ayr Rd. L4: Walt 4C 68
Ayrshire Gdns. WA10: St. H 4A 74
Ayrshire Rd. L4: Walt 6E 68
Aysgarth Av. L12: W Der 1A 90
Aysgarth Rd. CH45: Wall 1K 85
Ayton La. L16: Child 7A 90
Azalea Gro. L26: Halew 6H 111
WA7: Beech 6H 153

B

Babbacombe Rd. L16: Child 2C 110
WA5: Penk 4C 116
Bk. Barlow La. L4: Kirk 6A 68
Bk. Bath St. PR9: South 7H 7
Bk. Beau St. L5: Liv 3A 88 (1H 5)
Bk. Bedford St. L7: Liv 7B 88 (8L 5)
(not continuous)
Bk. Belmont Rd. L6: Liv 2D 88
Bk. Berry St. L1: Liv 7A 88 (8H 5)
Bk. Blackfield Ter. L4: Kirk 7K 67
Bk. Bold St. L1: Liv 6A 88 (7G 4)
Bk. Botanic Rd. PR9: Chu 5D 8
Bk. Boundary Cl. L5: Kirk 1K 87
Back Bri. Rd. *L23: Blun 2C 52*
(off Riverslea Rd.)
Back Bri. St. WA12: New W 3F 77
Bk. Bridport St. L3: Liv 5H 5
Back B'way. L11: N Grn. 5G 69
Bk. Brook Pl. WA4: Westy 5E 118
Back Brow WN8: Uph 4E 38
Bk. Canning St. L8: Liv 7A 88 (9K 5)
Bk. Catharine St. L8: Liv 7B 88 (9K 5)
Bk. Chadwick Mt. L5: Liv 7A 68
Bk. Chatham Pl. L7: Liv 6D 88 (8P 5)
Bk. Colquitt St. L1: Liv 7K 87 (8H 5)
Bk. Commutation Row
L3: Liv 5A 88 (4H 5)
Bk. Compton Rd. PR8: B'dale 5H 11
Bk. Crossland Ter. WA6: Hel 2H 173
Bk. Cross La. WA12: New W 2F 77
Bk. Dovecot Pl. L14: K Ash 3D 90
Bk. Eastford Rd. *WA4: Warr 7A 118*
(off Eastford Rd.)
Bk. Egerton St. Nth.
L8: Liv 1B 108 (10L 5)
Bk. Egerton St. Sth.
L8: Liv 1B 108 (10L 5)
Bk. Falkner St. Sth.
L8: Liv 7B 88 (9M 5)
BACKFORD 7K 169
Backford Cl. CH43: O'ton 5J 105
WA7: Brook 5A 154
Backford Gdns. CH1: Back 5H 169
Backford Rd. CH61: Irby 4B 124
Bk. Forest Rd. PR8: South 2K 11
(not continuous)
Bk. Gillmoss La. L11: Crox
7A 56
Bk. Granton Rd. L5: Liv 1C 88
Bk. Guilford St. L6: Liv 3B 88 (1L 5)
Bk. Hadfield Pl. *L25: Wltn 6E 110*
(off Church Rd.)
Bk. High St. *L25: Wltn 6E 110*
(off High St.)
WA7: Run 6C 134
Bk. Holland Pl. L7: Liv 6D 88 (6P 5)
Bk. Hope Pl. L1: Liv 7A 88 (8J 5)
Bk. Huskisson St.
L8: Liv 1B 108 (10K 5)
Bk. Irvine St. L7: Liv 6C 88 (6N 5)
Bk. Kelvin Gro. L8: Liv 2C 108
Bk. Kerfoot St. WA2: Warr 1A 118
Bk. Knight St. L1: Liv 7A 88 (9H 5)
Back La. L23: Lit C 4E 40
L39: Augh 4G 33
L39: Bic 1E 44
L39: Down 7K 21
(not continuous)
WA5: C Grn 7B 76
WA5: Cuerd 6J 115
WA6: Alv 2J 173
WA11: Crank 7B 48
WN8: Newb 1E 26

Beach Gro.—Bertha St.

Beach Gro. CH45: Wall 7C 66
Beach Lawn L22: Water 4C 52
Beach M. PR8: B'dale 2F 11
Beach Priory Gdns. PR8: South 2F 11
Beach Rd. CH47: Hoy 2B 102
L21: Lith 5G 53
(not continuous)
PR8: B'dale 2F 11
Beach Wlk. CH48: W Kir 1D 122
Beacon Ct. CH60: Hes 2E 142
Beacon Country Pk. 2B 38
Beacon Dr. CH48: W Kir 6E 102
Beacon Gro. WA11: St. H 7F 61
Beacon Hgts. WN8: Uph 3C 38
Beacon Hill Vw. WA7: West P 2K 151
Beacon Ho. L5: Liv 3A 88
Beacon La. CH60: Hes 2E 142
L5: Liv 1B 88
WN8: Dalt 4G 27 & 1A 38
Beacon Pde. CH60: Hes 2E 142
Beacon Rd. WN5: Bil 5F 49
Beacons, The CH60: Hes 3E 142
L37: Form 7K 19
(off School La.)
Beaconsfield L34: Prsct 1D 92
Beaconsfield Cl. CH42: Tran 5E 106
Beaconsfield Ct. L39: Orm 5D 24
Beaconsfield Cres. WA8: Wid 4C 114
Beaconsfield Gro. WA8: Wid 4D 114
Beaconsfield Rd. CH62: New F 2H 127
L21: Sea 6F 53
L25: Wltn 5C 110
PR9: South 2B 12
WA7: Run 2A 152
WA8: Wid 5D 114
WA10: St. H 1J 73
Beaconsfield St. L8: Liv 2C 108
Beaconsfield Ter. *L19: Gars 3K 129*
(off St Mary's Rd.)
Beacon Vw. Dr. WN8: Uph 4D 38
Beadnell Dr. WA5: Penk 5C 116
Beaford Cl. WN5: Wigan 6K 39
Beal Dr. WN2: Platt B 2K 51
Beames Cl. L7: Liv 6E 88
Beamish Cl. WA4: App 6D 138
Beamont St. WA8: Wid 5C 134
Bearncroft WN8: Skel 5J 37
Beasley Cl. CH66: Gt Sut 1F 169
Beatles Story, The 7J 87 (9D 4)
Beatrice Av. CH63: High B 2E 126
Beatrice St. L20: Boot 5K 67
WA4: Warr 5D 118
Beattock Cl. L33: K'by 6B 44
Beatty Av. WA2: Warr 6C 98
Beatty Cl. CH48: Caldy 3E 122
L35: Whis 5D 92
Beatty Rd. L13: Liv 4J 89
PR8: South 3A 12
Beauclair Dr. L15: W'tree 1K 109
Beaufort L37: Form 1A 30
Beaufort Cl. L39: Augh 2J 33
WA5: Gt San 3E 116
WA7: Run 3D 152
WA8: Wid 1G 133
Beaufort Dr. CH44: Wall 2J 85
Beaufort Rd. CH41: Birk 6K 85
Beaufort St. L8: Liv 2A 108
(Hill St.)
L8: Liv 3A 108
(Northumberland St.)
L8: Liv 2A 108
(Stanhope St.)
WA5: Warr 4J 117
WA9: St. H 5E 74
Beau La. L3: Liv 3A 88 (2H 5)
Beaumaris Ct. CH43: O'ton 3B 106
Beaumaris Dr. CH61: Thing 3F 125
CH65: Ell P 2B 170
Beaumaris Rd. CH45: Wall 1H 85
Beaumaris St. L20: Kirk 6H 67
(not continuous)
Beaumont Av. WA10: St. H 2J 73
Beaumont Cres. L39: Augh 1B 34
Beaumont Dr. L10: Ain 4G 55
Beaumont Gro. WN5: Orr 3K 39
Beaumont St. L8: Liv 1D 108 (10P 5)
Beau St. L3: Liv 3A 88 (1H 5)
Beauworth Av. CH49: Grea 5A 104
Beaverbrook Av. WA3: Cul 2D 80
Beaver Ct. WN4: Ash M 6G 51
Beaver Gro. L9: Ain 7C 54
Beavers La. WN8: Skel 5K 37
Beavers Way WN8: Skel 5K 37
BEBINGTON 5F 127
Bebington Rd. CH42: Tran 6D 106
CH62: New F 2G 127
CH63: Beb 3G 127
CH66: Gt Sut 7F 161
Bebington Station (Rail) 2G 127
Bebles Rd. L39: Orm 7A 24
Bechers WA8: Wid 5H 113
Bechers Ct. L30: N'ton 2D 54
Bechers Dr. L9: Ain 3E 54
Bechers Row L9: Walt 7B 54
Beck Cl. L10: Faz 6K 55
Beckenham Av. L18: Moss H 3H 109
Beckenham Cl. WA8: Wid 4F 115
Beckenham Rd. CH45: New B 5B 66
Becket St. L4: Kirk 6K 67
Beckett Cl. L33: Know I 5G 57
Beckett Dr. WA2: Win 2A 98
WA13: Warb 7K 101
Beckett Gro. CH63: High B 2D 126
Beck Gro. WA11: St. H 5D 60
Beckinsale Cl. L26: Halew 7A 112
Beck Rd. L20: Boot 1J 67
Beckwith St. CH41: Birk 7B 86
L1: Liv 7J 87 (9F 4)
Beckwith St. E. CH41: Birk 1D 106
Becky St. L6: Liv 2D 88
Becontree Rd. L12: W Der 3B 90
Bective St. L7: Liv 7E 88
Bedale Wlk. L33: K'by 1D 56
Bedburn Dr. L36: Huy 4E 90
Bede Cl. L33: K'by 6C 44
Bedford Av. CH42: R Ferr 7E 106
CH65: Whit 2J 169
L31: Mell 6G 43
Bedford Av. E. CH65: Whit 2K 169
Bedford Cl. L7: Liv 7B 88 (9L 5)
L36: Huy 4A 92
Bedford Ct. CH42: R Ferr 6F 107
PR8: B'dale 6G 11
Bedford Dr. CH42: R Ferr 7D 106
Bedford Gro. M44: Cad 1K 101
Bedford Pl. CH42: R Ferr 6G 107
L20: Boot 5H 67
L21: Sea 6F 53
WN4: Ash M 7E 50
Bedford Rd. CH42: R Ferr 6F 107
CH45: Wall 1B 86
L20: Boot 5J 67
PR8: B'dale 6G 11
Bedford Rd. E.
CH42: R Ferr 6G 107
Bedford St. WA4: S Hth 1C 138
WA9: St. H 4F 75
Bedford St. Nth. L7: Liv 6B 88 (7L 5)
Bedford St. Sth. L7: Liv 7B 88 (10L 5)
(not continuous)
Bedford Wlk. L7: Liv 7B 88 (9L 5)
Beecham Cl. L36: Huy 6H 91
Beech Av. CH49: Upton 2B 104
CH61: Pens 5E 124
L17: Aig 6C 108
L23: C'by 6G 41
L31: Mell 2J 55
L34: Ecc P 7F 73
WA3: Cul 3C 80
WA4: Thel 5K 119
WA5: Penk 5A 116
WA6: Frod 3E 166
WA9: Clock F 3E 94
WA11: Hay 6D 62
WN8: Parb 1J 27
Beechbank Rd. L18: Moss H 3G 109
Beechburn Cres. L36: Huy 4F 91
Beechburn Rd. L36: Huy 4E 90
Beech Cl. L12: Crox 3B 70
L32: K'by 2A 56
WA12: New W 4G 77
WN8: Skel 2E 36
Beech Ct. CH42: Tran 4D 106
L18: Moss H 5A 110
PR9: South 7K 7
WA3: Ris 5B 80
Beechcroft L31: Mag 3E 42
Beechcroft Dr. CH65: Whit 1K 169
Beechcroft Rd. CH44: Wall 5C 86
Beechdale Rd. L18: Moss H 4J 109
Beechdene Rd. L4: Walt 7D 68
Beech Dr. L37: Form 6H 19
Beeches, The CH42: R Ferr 7F 107
CH46: Leas 4C 84
CH66: Gt Sut 7F 161
L18: Moss H 3B 110
WA6: Hel 7J 165
Beechfield L31: Mag 3G 43
Beechfield Cl. CH60: Hes 3E 142
L26: Halew 3J 131
Beechfield Gdns.
PR8: South 2F 11
Beechfield M. PR9: South 1H 11
Beechfield Rd. CH65: Ell P 6K 161
L18: Moss H 4B 110
WA4: Grap 6G 119
Beech Gdns. WA11: R'ford 5E 46
Beech Grn. L12: W Der 6J 69
Beech Gro. CH66: Whit 4J 169
L9: Ain 7D 54
L21: Sea 7F 53
L30: N'ton 3C 54
PR9: South 1A 12
WA1: P'ton 1G 119
WA4: Warr 5D 118
WA13: Lymm 6D 120
Beech Hey La. CH64: Will 2H 159
Beechill Cl. L25: Gate 4G 111
Beech La. L18: Moss H 3A 110
Beech Lawn L19: Gras 2H 129
Beech Lodge CH43: Noct 3H 105
Beech Mdw. L39: Orm 6E 24
Beech Mdws. L34: Prsct 2A 92
Beechmill Dr. WA3: Cul 3K 79
Beechmore WA4: Moore 4F 137
Beech Mt. L7: Liv 5E 88
Beech Pk. L12: W Der 1J 89
L23: C'by 6F 41
Beech Rd. CH42: Tran 4C 106
CH60: Hes 2G 143
CH63: High B 2F 127
L4: Walt 4C 68
L36: Huy 6J 91
L39: Augh 5J 33
WA4: S Hth 1C 138
WA7: Run 2E 152
WA7: Sut W 6K 153
Beech St. L7: Liv 5E 88
L20: Boot 2J 67
WA10: St. H 6K 73
WN4: Ash M 6E 50
Beech Ter. L7: Liv 5E 88
WA8: Wid 5C 134
Beechtree Farm Cl.
WA16: H Legh 2K 141
Beech Tree Ho's. WN2: Bam 6J 51
Beechtree La. WA13: Lymm 2K 141
Beechtree Rd. L15: W'tree 6K 89
Beechtrees WN8: Skel 4J 37
Beechurst Cl. L25: Gate 3F 111
Beechurst Rd. L25: Gate 3F 111
Beech Wlk. WN3: Wins 2A 50
Beechwalk, The L14: K Ash 3K 89
Beechway CH63: Beb 6F 127
L31: Mag 2K 43
Beechway Av. L31: Mag 2K 43
Beechways WA4: App 3D 138
Beechways Dr. CH64: Nest 4H 157
BEECHWOOD
Prenton 7G 85
Runcorn 5G 153
Beechwood WN8: Skel 7J 27
Beechwood Av. CH45: Wall 2J 85
L26: Halew 2J 131
WA1: P'gate 1E 118
WA5: Gt San 3D 116
WA7: Beech 4E 152
WA12: New W 2H 77
WN4: Ash M 3E 62
Beechwood Cl. L19: Gras 2H 129
WA9: Clock F 3E 94
Beechwood Ct. CH49: W'chu 7F 105
L31: Mag 3G 43
WN8: Skel 5K 37
Beechwood Cres. WN5: Orr 5G 39
Beechwood Dr. CH43: Bid 1G 105
CH66: Gt Sut 3F 169
L37: Form 2G 29
L39: Orm 5B 24
Beechwood Gdns. L19: Gras 2H 129
Beechwood Grn. L19: Gras 2J 129
Beechwood Gro. L35: Prsct 3E 92
Beechwood La. WA3: Cul 2K 79
Beechwood Recreation Cen. 1F 105
Beechwood Rd. CH62: Brom 2J 145
L19: Gras 2H 129
L21: Lith 7H 53
Beechwood Rd. Sth. L19: Gras 3H 129
Beecroft Cl. WA5: Old H 6H 97
Beeford Dr. WN5: Orr 6G 39
Beesands Cl. L27: N'ley 4K 111
Beesley Rd. L34: Prsct 1C 92
Beeston Cl. CH43: Bid 2G 105
WA3: Bchwd 3K 99
Beeston Ct. WA7: Mnr P 5A 136
Beeston Dr. CH61: Pens 5D 124
L30: N'ton 7D 42
Beeston Grn. CH66: Gt Sut 6G 161
Beeston Gro. L19: Gras 2J 129
Beeston St. L4: Kirk 5A 68
Beetham Plaza L2: Liv 6D 4
Beetham Way L33: K'by 2D 56
Begonia Gdns. WA9: Bold 7J 75
Beilby Rd. WA11: Hay 6D 62
Beldale Pk. L32: K'by 1K 55
Beldon Cres. L36: Huy 4F 91
Belem Cl. L17: Aig 3E 108
Belem Twr. L17: Aig 3D 108
Belfast Rd. L13: Liv 4K 89
Belfield WN8: Skel 5K 37
Belfield Cres. L36: Huy 6J 91
Belfield Dr. CH43: O'ton 5B 106
Belford Dr. CH46: More 7K 83
Belfort Rd. L25: Gate 4F 111
Belfry Cl. CH46: More 6K 83
L12: W Der 1C 90
Belgrave Av. CH44: Wall 3C 86
WA1: P'gate 7F 99
Belgrave Cl. WA8: Wid 5G 115
WN3: Wins 1B 50
Belgrave Dr. CH65: Ell P 6H 161
Belgrave Pl. PR8: B'dale 5F 11
Belgrave Rd. L17: Aig 5D 108
L21: Sea 6F 53
PR8: B'dale 5F 11
Belgrave St. CH44: Wall 2B 86
Belgravia Ct. WA8: Wid 5B 114
Belhaven Rd. L18: Moss H 3H 109
BELL, THE 3K 39
Bellair Av. L23: C'by 1G 53
Bellairs Rd. L11: N Grn. 6G 69
Bellamy Rd. L4: Walt 4A 68
Bellcast Cl. WA4: App 4C 138
Bell Cl. L36: Huy 7K 91
Belldene Gro. CH61: Hes 7D 124
Bellefield Av. L12: W Der 1K 89
Bellemonte Pk. WA6: Frod 5D 166
Bellemonte Rd. WA6: Frod 5D 166
Bellemonte Vw. WA6: Frod 5E 166
BELLE VALE 2F 111
Belle Va. Rd. L25: Gate 4F 111
Belle Va. Shop. Cen. L25: Gate 2F 111
Belle Vue Rd. CH44: Wall 5D 86
L25: Gate 4F 111
Bellew Rd. L11: N Grn. 7H 69
Bellfield Cres. CH45: New B 6A 66
Bellflower Cl. WA8: Wid 4A 114
Bellgreen Rd. L11: N Grn. 4J 69
Bellhouse La. WA4: Grap 7J 119
WA4: H Walt 2H 137
Bell Ho. Rd. WA8: Wid 7E 114
Bellingham Dr. WA7: Run 2C 152
Bellini Cl. L21: Sea 7F 53
Bellis Av. PR9: Chu 5B 8
Bellis Gro. L33: K'by 7B 44
Bell La. L35: R'hill 5C 94
WA4: Thel 5A 120
WA9: Sut M 5C 94
WN5: Orr 3K 39
Bellmore St. L19: Gars 2K 129
Bell Rd. CH44: Wall 4D 86
Bell's Cl. L31: Lyd 7D 32
Bellsfield Cl. WA13: Lymm 6H 121
Bells La. L31: Lyd 1C 42
Bell St. L13: Liv 4J 89
Belltower Rd. L20: Kirk 7H 67
Bellward Cl. CH63: Spit 7F 127
Belmont CH41: Birk 3C 106
Belmont Av. CH62: Brom 1J 145
WA4: Westy 5F 119
WN5: Bil 1F 49
Belmont Cres. WA5: Gt San 2D 116
Belmont Dr. CH61: Pens 6E 124
L6: Liv 2E 88
Belmont Gro. CH43: O'ton 3C 106
L6: Liv 2D 88
Belmont Pl. L19: Gars 3A 130
Belmont Rd. CH45: New B 5B 66
CH48: W Kir 5D 102
L6: Liv 2D 88
WA8: Wid 6F 115
Belmont St. PR8: South 2G 11
WA10: St. H 3K 73
WN5: Wigan 5K 39
Belmont Vw. *L6: Liv 2E 88*
(off Bk. Belmont Rd.)
Beloe St. L8: Liv 4B 108
Belper St. L19: Gars 3K 129
Belsford Way L24: Speke 5F 131
Belston Rd. L16: Child 7A 90
Belton Rd. L36: Huy 1H 91
(not continuous)
Belvedere Av. WA9: Sut L 1F 95
Belvedere Cl. L34: Prsct 7E 72
WA6: Frod 2E 166
Belvedere Ct. *CH49: W'chu 7F 105*
(off Childwall Grn.)
Belvedere Dr. L37: Form 2K 29
Belvedere Pk. L39: Augh 4A 34
Belvedere Rd. PR8: Ains 4C 14
WA12: New W 2F 77
WN4: Ash M 2G 63
Belvidere Pk. L23: C'by 2E 52
Belvidere Rd. CH45: Wall 1K 85
L8: Liv 3C 108
L23: C'by 2D 52
Belvoir Rd. L18: Aller 1A 130
WA4: Walt 1B 138
WA8: Wid 7D 114
Bembridge Cl. WA5: Gt San 1A 116
WA8: Wid 4B 114
Bembridge Ct. WN3: Wins 2C 50
Bempton Rd. L17: Aig 6D 108
Benbow Cl. CH43: Bid 7K 85
Benbow St. L20: Boot 4H 67
Bendee Av. CH64: Lit N 4A 158
Bendee Rd. CH64: Lit N 4K 157
Benedict Ct. L20: Boot 5J 67
Benedict St. L20: Boot 5K 67
Benfleet Ho. L19: Aig 2H 129
Bengarth Rd. PR9: South 7B 8
Bengel St. L7: Liv 5C 88 (5M 5)
Benjamin Fold WN4: Ash M 7F 51
Ben La. L39: Bic 3K 45
Ben La. Ct. L39: Bic 2B 46
Benledi St. L5: Liv 2K 87
Benmore Rd. L18: Moss H 6J 109
Bennet's La. CH47: Meols 5G 83
Bennett Av. WA1: Warr 2E 118
Bennett Cl. CH64: Will 3G 159
Bennett Dr. WN5: Orr 7F 39
Bennetts Hill CH43: O'ton 4B 106
Bennetts La. WA8: Wid 7G 115
Bennett St. L19: Gars 3A 130
WA1: Warr 3B 118
Bennett Wlk. CH61: Pens 6D 124
Ben Nevis Dr. CH66: Lit Sut 5B 160
Ben Nevis Rd. CH42: Tran 6D 106
Bennison Dr. L19: Gras 2J 129
Ben's Ct. L34: Know 1F 71
Benson Cl. CH49: Upton 4D 104
Benson Rd. WA3: Bchwd 4K 99
Benson St. L1: Liv 6A 88 (7H 5)
Bentfield L17: Aig 1G 129
Bentfield Cl. CH63: High B 2D 126
Bentfield Gdns. CH63: High B 2D 126
Bentham Av. WA2: Warr 4C 98
Bentham Cl. CH43: Noct 5J 105
Bentham Dr. L16: Child 7B 90
Bentham Rd. WA3: Cul 4C 80
Bentham St. PR8: South 3H 11
Bentham's Way PR8: South 6H 11
Bentinck Cl. CH41: Birk 2C 106
Bentinck Pl. CH41: Birk 2C 106
Bentinck St. CH41: Birk 2C 106
(not continuous)
L5: Liv 2H 87
WA7: Run 6B 134
WA9: St. H 5F 75
WN3: Wigan 1C 50
Bent La. WA3: Cul 4C 80
Bentley Rd. CH43: O'ton 4B 106
CH61: Pens 4D 124
L8: Liv 2D 108
Bentley St. WA9: Clock F 3E 94
Benton Cl. L5: Liv 1K 87
Bents Cotts. CH2: Thor M 2J 171
Bent Way CH60: Hes 1E 142
Benty Cl. CH63: High B 5E 126
Benty Farm Gro. CH61: Pens 4E 124
Benty Heath La. CH64: Will 7E 144
CH66: Hoot 7E 144
Benwick Rd. L32: K'by 3K 55
Berbice Rd. L18: Moss H 2J 109
Beresford Av. CH63: Beb 2G 127
Beresford Cl. CH43: O'ton 3A 106
Beresford Ct. CH43: O'ton 3A 106
Beresford Dr. PR9: Chu 6B 8
Beresford Gdns. PR9: Chu 5B 8
Beresford Rd. CH43: O'ton 3K 105
CH45: Wall 7K 65
L8: Liv 4B 108
Beresford St. L5: Liv 3A 88 (1J 5)
L20: Boot 5H 67
WA1: Warr 1E 118
WA9: St. H 7A 74
Berey's Bldgs. L3: Liv 5D 4
Bergen Cl. L20: Boot 4A 68
Berkeley Av. CH43: Pren 7K 105
WN3: Wins 2B 50
Berkeley Cl. WA5: Warr 2K 117
Berkeley Ct. *CH49: W'chu 7E 104*
(off Childwall Grn.)
WA7: Mnr P 5B 136
WA12: New W 2D 76
Berkeley Dr. CH45: New B 7C 66
Berkeley Rd. L23: C'by 7C 40
Berkeswell Rd. L11: N Grn. 5J 69
Berkley Av. L12: W Der 6B 70
Berkley Cl. L8: Liv 2B 108
Berkley St. L8: Liv 1B 108 (10K 5)
Berkshire Dr. WA1: W'ston 1K 119
Berkshire Gdns. WA10: St. H 4B 74
Bermondsey Gro. WA8: Wid 4F 115
Bermuda Rd. CH46: More 6A 84
Bernard Av. CH45: New B 7C 66
WA4: App 1D 138
Bernard Wood Ct. WN5: Bil 1E 60
Berner's Rd. L19: Gras 2K 129
Berner St. CH41: Birk 7D 86
Berrington Av. L25: Wltn 6D 110
Berrington Gro. WN4: Ash M 2E 62
Berringtons La. WA11: R'ford 3H 59
Berry Cl. CH66: Gt Sut 1E 168
WN8: Skel 1F 37
Berry Dr. CH66: Gt Sut 7E 160
Berryford Rd. L14: K Ash 1D 90
Berry Hill Av. L34: Know 3G 71
Berrylands Cl. CH46: More 6B 84
Berrylands Rd. CH46: More 5B 84
Berry Rd. WA8: Wid 7K 113
Berrys La. WA9: St. H 5H 75
Berry St. L1: Liv 7A 88 (9H 5)
L20: Boot 4H 67
WN8: Skel 1F 37
Berry St. Ind. Est. L20: Boot 3H 67
Berrywood Dr. L35: Whis 5F 93
Bertha Gdns. CH41: Birk 7K 85
Bertha St. CH41: Birk 7K 85

Bertram Dr.—Blyth Hey

Bertram Dr. CH47: Meols 7E 82
Bertram Dr. Nth. CH47: Meols 7F 83
Bertram Rd. L17: Aig 4E 108
Bertram St. WA12: New W 3E 76
Berwick Av. CH62: East 6A 146
PR8: Ains 3C 14
Berwick Cl. CH43: Bid 2G 105
CH46: More 7K 83
L6: Liv 3D 88
WA1: W'ston 2A 120
Berwick Dr. L23: C'by 7C 40
Berwick Gdns. CH66: Lit Sut 5D 160
Berwick Gro. CH66: Lit Sut 5D 160
Berwick Rd. CH66: Lit Sut 5B 160
Berwick St. L6: Liv 3D 88
Berwyn Av. CH47: Hoy 1E 102
CH61: Thing 3E 124
Berwyn Blvd. CH63: High B 1E 126
Berwyn Cl. CH66: Lit Sut 5C 160
Berwyn Ct. PR8: South 4K 11
Berwyn Dr. CH61: Hes 7E 124
Berwyn Gro. WA9: St. H 3H 75
Berwyn Rd. CH44: Wall 2C 86
L4: Walt 6E 68
Beryl Rd. CH43: Noct 3G 105
Beryl St. L13: Liv 6J 89
Beryl Wlk. L10: Faz 6K 55
BESCAR 2J 17
Bescar Brow La. L40: Scar 2G 17
Bescar La. L40: Scar 7K 13
Bescar Lane Station (Rail) 7K 13
Besford Ho. L25: Gate 3F 111
Besford Rd. L25: Gate 3F 111
Bessborough Rd. CH43: O'ton 4B 106
Bessbrook Rd. L17: Aig 6F 109
Bessemer St. L8: Liv 4B 108
Beta Cl. CH62: New F 2G 127
Betchworth Cres. WA7: Beech 4F 153
Bethany Cl. WA11: Hay 6J 61
Bethany Cres. CH63: Beb 4F 127
Bethel Gro. L15: Liv 2F 109
Betjeman Cl. WA4: Westy 4F 119
Betjeman Gro. L16: Child 7C 90
Betony Cl. L26: Halew 7J 111
Betsyfield Dr. WA3: Croft 7G 79
Bettisfield Av. CH62: Brom 5K 145
Betula Cl. L9: Walt 2D 68
Beulah Av. WN5: Bil 1F 61
Bevan Cl. WA5: Gt San 2H 117
WA9: St. H 1K 93
Bevan's La. L12: W Der 7A 70
Beverley Av. WA4: App 1D 138
WN5: Bil 3G 49
Beverley Cl. PR9: Cros 2E 8
Beverley Dr. CH60: Hes 4F 143
Beverley Gdns. CH61: Thing 3F 125
Beverley Rd. CH45: Wall 1K 85
CH62: New F 1H 127
L15: W'tree 2J 109
WA5: Gt San 2G 117
WN5: Wigan 3K 39
Beverley Way CH66: Lit Sut 4D 160
Beversbrook Rd. L11: N Grn. 4K 69
Bevin Av. WA3: Cul 2D 80
Bevington Bush L3: Liv 4K 87 (2F 4)
Bevington Hill L3: Liv 3K 87 (1F 4)
Bevington St. L3: Liv 3K 87 (1F 4)
WN4: Ash M 7D 50
Bevyl Rd. CH64: Park 1F 157
Bewcastle Dr. L40: Westh 7F 25
Bewey Cl. L8: Liv 4A 108
Bewley Dr. L32: K'by 4B 56
Bewsey Bus. Cen. WA5: Warr 2K 117
Bewsey Farm Cl. WA5: Old H 7H 97
Bewsey Ind. Est. WA5: Warr 1A 118
Bewsey Pk. Cl. WA5: Warr 1K 117
Bewsey Rd. WA2: Warr 1K 117
WA5: Warr 1K 117
Bewsey Rd. Bus. Cen.
WA5: Warr 1K 117
Bewsey St. WA2: Warr 2A 118
(not continuous)
WA10: St. H 5K 73
Bexhill Av. WA2: Warr 3B 98
(not continuous)
Bexhill Cl. L24: Speke 5F 131
Bexhill Gdns. WA9: St. H 1J 93
Bianca St. L20: Boot 5J 67
Bibby Av. WA1: Warr 2E 118
Bibby Rd. PR9: Chu 5C 8
Bibbys La. L20: Boot 1G 67
Bibby St. L13: Liv 4H 89
BICKERSTAFFE 6K 35
Bickerstaffe St. L3: Liv 4A 88 (2J 5)
WA10: St. H 3C 74
Bickerton Av. CH63: High B 1D 126
WA6: Frod 4F 167
Bickerton Cl. WA3: Bchwd 3K 99
Bickerton Rd. PR8: B'dale 4F 11
Bickerton St. L17: Aig 5E 108
Bickley Cl. WA2: Fearn 4F 99
WA7: Run 1E 152
Bicknell Cl. WA5: Gt San 7F 97
Bidder St. L3: Liv 4A 88 (2J 5)
Bideford Av. WA9: Sut L 2E 94
Bideford Rd. WA5: Penk 4C 116
BIDSTON 7H 85
Bidston Av. CH41: Birk 1K 105
CH45: Wall 1J 85
WA11: St. H 1F 75
Bidston Ct. CH43: Noct 1J 105
Bidston Grn. CH66: Gt Sut 7F 161
Bidston Grn. Ct. CH43: Bid 7G 85
Bidston Grn. Dr. CH43: Bid 7G 85
Bidston Ind. Est. CH44: Wall 4H 85
Bidston Link Rd. CH43: Bid 5H 85
Bidston Moss CH44: Wall 4H 85
Bidston Moss Nature Reserve 4J 85
Bidston Rd. CH43: C'ton, O'ton 2J 105
L4: Walt 6D 68
Bidston Sta. App. CH43: Bid 5G 85
Bidston Station (Rail) 5G 85
Bidston Vw. CH43: Bid 6G 85
Bidston Village Rd.
CH43: Bid 6F 85
Bidston Way WA11: St. H 1F 75
Bigdale Dr. L33: K'by 2D 56
Biggin Ct. WA2: P'gate 6E 98
Bigham Rd. L6: Liv 4E 88
Biglands Dr. L36: Huy 7K 91
Big Mdw. Rd. CH49: W'chu 4E 104
BILLINGE 7G 49
Billinge Cres. WA11: St. H 7F 61
Billinge La. L39: Bic 6C 34
Billinge Rd. WN3: Wigan 1A 50
WN4: Gars 7A 50
WN5: Bil 7K 49
Billingham Rd. WA9: St. H 7K 73
Billings Cl. L5: Kirk 1J 87
Billington Av. WA12: New W 7F 63
Billington Cl. WA5: Gt San 7C 96
Billington Rd. WA8: Wid 5H 113
Bill's La. L37: Form 2K 29
Bilston Rd. L17: Aig 1G 129
Bilton Cl. WA8: Wid 6G 115
Bingley Rd. L4: Walt 7D 68
Binns Rd. L7: Liv 5G 89
L13: Liv 5G 89
Binns Rd. Ind. Est. L13: Liv 6H 89
Binns Way L13: Liv 6H 89
Binsey Cl. CH49: Upton 3B 104
Birbeck Rd. L33: K'by 2E 56
Birbeck Wlk. L33: K'by 2E 56
Birchall Av. WA3: Cul 2K 79
Birchall St. L20: Kirk 7J 67
WA3: Croft 7G 79
Birch Av. CH49: Upton 2B 104
L9: Ain 7D 54
WA2: Win 3A 98
WA10: St. H 7B 60
Birch Brook Rd. WA13: Lymm 3K 121
Birch Cl. CH43: O'ton 5B 106
L31: Mag 3H 43
L35: Whis 3E 92
Birch Ct. *L8: Liv* 4C 108
(off Weller Way)
Birch Cres. WA12: New W 2D 76
Birchdale Cl. CH49: Grea 3B 104
Birchdale Cres. WA4: App 1C 138
Birchdale Rd. L9: Walt 2C 68
L22: Water 3D 52
WA1: P'ton 1G 119
WA4: App 2C 138
Birchen Rd. L26: Halew 2A 132
Birches, The CH44: Wall 5E 86
CH64: Nest 1K 157
L28: Stock V 7E 70
L37: Form 5J 19
Birches Cl. CH60: Hes 2E 142
Birchfield CH46: More 1A 104
Birchfield Av. WA8: Wid 6C 114
Birchfield Cl. CH46: More 1A 104
L7: Liv 5G 89
Birchfield Rd. L4: Walt 4C 68
L7: Liv 5G 89
WA5: Gt San 3F 117
WA8: Wid 3C 114
WA13: Lymm 4K 121
Birchfield St. L3: Liv 4A 88 (3J 5)
WA9: St. H 7K 73
Birchfield Way L31: Lyd 6D 32
Birch Gdns. WA10: St. H 7B 60
BIRCH GREEN 1J 37
Birch Grn. L37: Form 5H 19
Birch Grn. Rd. WN8: Skel 7H 27
Birch Gro. CH45: New B 7C 66
CH66: Whit 3J 169
L15: W'tree 6J 89
L35: Prsct 3E 92
L36: Huy 5H 91
WA1: P'ton 1F 119
WA4: Warr 5D 118
WN4: Gars 7A 50
Birch Heys CH48: Frank 7J 103
Birch Hill M. L25: Wltn 7E 110
Birchill Rd. L33: Know I 3G 57
Birchley Av. WN5: Bil 2E 60
Birchley Rd. WN5: Bil 2D 60
Birchley St. WA10: St. H 2C 74
Birchley Vw. WA11: St. H 3D 60
Birchmere CH60: Hes 7C 124
Birchmuir Hey L32: K'by 4D 56
Birchridge Cl. CH62: Spit 7J 127
Birch Rd. CH43: O'ton 5B 106
CH47: Meols 7G 83
CH63: Beb 5G 127
L36: Huy 6J 91
WA3: Rix 4K 101
WA7: Run 2D 152
WA8: Wid 5D 114
WA11: Hay 6C 62
Birch St. L5: Liv 2H 87
PR8: South 4H 11
WN8: Skel 2E 36
Birch Tree Av. WA11: St. H 5B 60
Birch Tree Ct. L12: W Der 1J 89
Birchtree Dr. L31: Mell 2J 55
Birchtree Rd. L17: Aig 5G 109
Birchview Way CH43: Noct 3H 105
Birchway CH60: Hes 5G 143
Birchways WA4: App 4E 138
Birchwood Av. CH41: Birk 1D 106
Birchwood Blvd. WA3: Bchwd 4J 99
Birchwood Cl. CH2: Elt 1C 172
CH41: Birk 1D 106
CH66: Gt Sut 3F 169
WN3: Wins 2B 50
Birchwood Corporate Ind. Est.
WA2: Bchwd 5J 99
Birchwood La. WA4: Moore 1F 137
Birchwood Leisure & Tennis Complex 4A 100
Birchwood Office Pk.
WA2: Fearn 4H 99
BIRCHWOOD PARK 2A 100
Birchwood Pk. Av.
WA3: Bchwd, Ris 2K 99
Birchwood Science Pk.
WA3: Ris 2A 100
Birchwood Shop. Cen.
WA3: Bchwd 5K 99
Birchwood Station (Rail) 5A 100
Birchwood Way L33: K'by 7E 44
WA2: P'gate 7E 98
WA3: Bchwd 4J 99
Birdcage Cotts. *WA11: Hay* 6C 62
(off Church Rd.)
Bird i' th' Hand Cotts. L39: Orm 4C 24
Bird St. L7: Liv 1E 108
Birdwell Dr. WA5: Gt San 3E 116
Birdwood Rd. L11: N Grn. 6H 69
BIRKDALE 4F 11
Birkdale Av. CH63: Brom 4J 145
Birkdale Cl. L6: Liv 1F 89
L36: Roby 6G 91
Birkdale Cop PR8: South 6K 11
Birkdale Hill Nature Reserve 2A 14
Birkdale Ho. WA3: Ris 1K 99
Birkdale Rd. WA5: Penk 4D 116
WA8: Wid 3D 114
Birkdale Station (Rail) 4F 11
Birkdale Trad. Est. PR8: B'dale 6G 11
BIRKENHEAD 2F 107
Birkenhead Central Station (Rail) 3E 106
Birkenhead North Station (Rail) 6K 85
Birkenhead Park Station (Rail) 7B 86
Birkenhead Priory 2F 107
Birkenhead Rd. CH44: Wall 6E 86
CH47: Hoy, Meols 7E 82
CH64: Will 1D 158
Birkenhead Transport Mus. 1F 107
Birkenshaw Av. L23: Blun 7B 40
Birket Av. CH46: Leas 4D 84
Birket Cl. CH46: Leas 4E 84
Birket Ho. CH41: Birk 1D 106
Birket Sq. CH46: Leas 4E 84
Birkett Av. CH65: Ell P 2A 170
Birkett Rd. CH42: R Ferr 7E 106
CH48: W Kir 4D 102
Birkett St. L3: Liv 4A 88 (2H 5)
Birkey La. L37: Form 1K 29
Birkin Cl. L32: K'by 5E 56
Birkin Rd. L32: K'by 5E 56
Birkin Wlk. L32: K'by 5E 56
Birkrig WN8: Skel 5K 37
Birkside Cl. WN3: Wigan 3E 50
Birley Ct. L8: Liv 1B 108 (10K 5)
PR8: South 3H 11
Birley St. WA12: New W 2H 77
Birleywood WN8: Skel 5K 37
Birnam Dr. L35: R'hill 5K 93
Birnam Rd. CH44: Wall 4D 86
Birstall Av. WA11: St. H 1E 74
Birstall Ct. WA7: Run 3F 153
Birstall Rd. L6: Liv 4D 88 (3P 5)
Birt Cl. L8: Liv 1C 108 (10P 5)
Birtles Rd. WA2: Warr 6C 98
Birtley Ct. WA8: Wid 6H 113
Bisham Pk. WA7: Nort 7B 136
Bishopdale Cl. WA5: Gt San 1D 116
Bishopdale Dr. L35: R'hill 4K 93
Bishop Dr. L35: Whis 6C 92
Bishopgate St. L15: W'tree 7F 89
Bishop Reeves Rd. WA11: Hay 6C 62
Bishop Rd. CH44: Wall 5B 86
L6: Liv 7E 68
WA10: St. H 1A 74
Bishops Ct. CH43: O'ton 5A 106
L25: Wltn 6F 111
WA2: Win 3K 97
Bishops Gdns. CH65: Ell P 6J 161
Bishop Sheppard Ct.
L3: Liv 3J 87 (1D 4)
Bishops Way WA8: Wid 5F 115
Bisley St. CH45: Wall 2B 86
L15: W'tree 1G 109
Bispham Ct. WN5: Bil 2F 49
Bispham Dr. CH47: Meols 1G 103
WN4: Ash M 7D 50
Bispham Hall Bus. Pk. WN5: Bil 2E 48
Bispham Ho. L3: Liv 4K 87 (3F 4)
Bispham Rd. PR9: South 1B 12
WA5: Gt San 4F 117
Bittern Cl. WA2: Warr 4D 98
WA7: Nort 2B 154
Bixteth St. L3: Liv 5J 87 (4D 4)
Blackacre La. L39: Orm 2C 24
L40: Burs 2C 24
Black-a-Moor La. L39: Down 7B 22
Blackberry Gro. L26: Halew 6H 111
Blackboards La. CH66: Chil T 4C 160
BLACKBROOK
St Helens 7H 61
Warrington 6F 99
Blackbrook Av. WA2: Warr 3E 98
Blackbrook Cl. L9: Walt 3C 68
WA8: Wid 5J 113
Blackbrook Rd. WA11: St. H 1G 75
Blackbrook Sq. WA2: Warr 5F 99
Blackburne Av. WA8: Hale B 4H 133
Blackburne Cl. WA2: P'gate 5H 99
Blackburne Dr. L25: Hunts X 2H 131
WA12: New W 2E 76
Blackburne Pl. L8: Liv 7B 88 (9K 5)
Blackburne St. L19: Gars 5A 130
Blackburne Ter. L8: Liv 7B 88 (9K 5)
Blackcap Wlk. WA3: Bchwd 4A 100
Blackcar La. L29: Thorn 1G 41
Black Cat Ind. Est. WA8: Wid 3B 134
Black Denton's Pl. WA8: Wid 7E 114
Blackdown Cl. CH66: Lit Sut 6C 160
Blackdown Gro. WA9: St. H 4H 75
Blackeys La. CH64: Nest 3J 157
Blackfield St. L5: Kirk 1K 87
Blackheath Dr. CH46: Leas 4D 84
Blackheath La. WA7: Mnr P 5C 136
Black Horse Cl. CH48: W Kir 5E 102
Black Horse Hill CH48: W Kir 6E 102
Black Horse La. L13: Liv 3K 89
Black Horse Pl. L13: Liv 4K 89
Blackhorse St. WA9: St. H 2F 75
Blackhouse Wlk. L9: Walt 3A 68
Blackhurst Rd. L31: Lyd 6E 32
Blackhurst St. WA1: Warr 3B 118
Blackledge Cl. WA2: Fearn 4G 99
WN5: Orr 6G 39
Blackley Cl. WA4: Latch 5D 118
Blackley Gro. *L33: K'by* 7D 44
(off Carl's Way)
Blackleyhurst Av. WN5: Bil 7G 49
Black Lion La. CH66: Lit Sut 5D 160
Blacklock Hall Rd. L24: Speke 6G 131
Blacklow Brow L36: Huy 5H 91
Blackmoor Dr. L12: W Der 1A 90
Black Moss La. L39: Augh, Orm 6D 24
L39: Orm 7B 24
L40: Scar 2F 17
Blackpool St. CH41: Birk 3E 106
Blackrod Av. L24: Speke 5G 131
Blackshaw Dr. WA5: W'brk 6F 97
Blacksmith Pl. L25: Hunts X 1H 131
Blackstock Ct. L30: N'ton 1K 53
Blackstock St. L3: Liv 4J 87 (2E 4)
Blackstone Av. WA11: St. H 1F 75
Blackstone St. L5: Liv 1H 87
Blackthorn Cres. L28: Stock V 6F 71
Blackthorne Av. CH66: Whit 4J 169
Blackthorne Cl. CH46: More 1D 104
Blackthorne Rd. L9: Walt 2D 68
Blackwater Rd. L11: Crox 2B 70
Blackwood Av. L25: Wltn 4D 110
BLAGUEGATE 2C 36
Blaguegate La. WN8: Skel 1A 36
Blair Ct. CH43: C'ton 2A 106
Blair Dr. WA8: Wid 5H 113
Blairgowrie Gdns. L39: Orm 6E 24
Blair Gro. PR9: South 1B 12
Blair Ind. Est. L23: C'by 2F 53
Blair Pk. CH63: Spit 6H 127
Blair St. L8: Liv 1A 108 (10J 5)
Blair Wlk. L26: Halew 3K 131
Blaisdon Cl. L11: N Grn. 5J 69
Blakeacre Cl. L26: Halew 3K 131
Blakeacre Rd. L26: Halew 3K 131
Blake Ct. L19: Gars 4A 130
Blakefield Rd. L23: Thorn 6J 41
Blakehall WN8: Skel 4K 37
Blakeley Brow CH63: Raby M 4G 145
Blakeley Ct. CH63: Raby M 4G 145
Blakeley Dell CH63: Raby M 4H 145
Blakeley Dene CH63: Raby M 3H 145
Blakeley Rd. CH63: Raby M 3G 145
Blakemere Ct. CH65: Ell P 4A 162
Blakenhall Way CH49: Upton 2B 104
Blaking Dr. L34: Know 2H 71
Blandford Cl. PR8: B'dale 3F 11
Blandford Rd. WA5: Gt San 3F 117
Blantyre Rd. L15: W'tree 2F 109
Blantyre St. WA7: Run 6B 134
Blay Cl. L25: Hunts X 1H 131
Blaydon Cl. L30: N'ton 4B 54
Blaydon Gro. WA9: St. H 7K 73
Blaydon Pk. WN8: Skel 4K 37
Blaydon Wlk. CH43: C'ton 2J 105
Bleak Hill Cl. WA10: Windle 6J 59
Bleak Hill Rd.
WA10: Eccl, Windle 1H 73
Bleaklow Cl. WN3: Wigan 2F 51
Bleasdale Av. L10: Ain 3G 55
Bleasdale Cl. CH49: Upton 2C 104
L39: Augh 4B 34
Bleasdale Rd. L18: Moss H 4J 109
WA12: New W 2F 77
Bleasdale Way L21: Ford 1H 53
Blenheim Av. L21: Lith 5J 53
Blenheim Cl. WA2: P'gate 5E 98
Blenheim Dr. L34: Prsct 2K 91
Blenheim Rd. CH44: Wall 2D 86
L18: Moss H 3H 109
PR8: Ains 3B 14
WN4: Ash M 3H 63
Blenheim St. L5: Liv 2J 87
Blenheim Way L24: Speke 6F 131
WA11: St. H 7D 60
Blessington Rd. L4: Walt 7B 68
Bletchley Av. CH44: Wall 3K 85
Bligh St. L15: W'tree 1F 109
Blindfoot Rd. WA10: R'ford 6D 58
WA11: R'ford 6D 58
Blindman's La. L39: Orm 3A 24
Blisworth St. L21: Lith 7H 53
Blomfield Rd. L19: Aller 2B 130
Bloomfield Grn. L17: Aig 4E 108
Bloomsbury Way WA8: Wid 5K 113
Blossom Gro. L32: K'by 6D 56
Blossom St. L20: Boot 1J 67
BLOWICK 2B 12
Blucher St. L22: Water 4C 52
Bluebell Av. CH41: Birk 7K 85
WA11: Hay 6C 62
Bluebell Cl. L22: Water 4E 52
Bluebell Ct. WA7: Beech 6H 153
Blue Bell La. L36: Huy 3J 91
Bluebell La. CH64: Nest 2C 158
Blueberry Flds. L10: Faz 7H 55
Blue Bri. La. WA6: Hel 6J 165
Bluecoat Arts Cen. 6K 87 (7F 4)
Bluecoat Chambers L1: Liv 7F 4
Bluecoat Display Cen. 6K 87 (7F 4)
Bluecoat St. WA2: Warr 1B 118
Bluefields St. L8: Liv 1B 108
Blue Hatch WA6: Frod 3E 166
Blue Jay Cl. L27: N'ley 3J 111
Blue Planet 3B 170
Blue Ridge Cl. WA5: Gt San 1C 116
Bluestone La. L31: Mag 3G 43
Bluewood Dr. CH41: Birk 6H 85
Blundell Av. L37: Form 6F 19
L38: High 6F 29
PR8: B'dale 6F 11
Blundell Cres. PR8: B'dale 6F 11
Blundell Dr. PR8: B'dale 6F 11
Blundell Gro. L38: High 6F 29
Blundell La. PR9: Chu 4E 8
Blundell Links Ct. PR8: Ains 5C 14
Blundell Rd. L38: High 6F 29
WA8: Wid 1J 133
BLUNDELLSANDS 1C 52
Blundellsands & Crosby Station (Rail) 1C 52
Blundellsands Classic
L23: Blun 2B 52
Blundellsands Ct. *L23: Blun* 2B 52
(off Blundellsands Rd. W.)
Blundellsands Rd. E. L23: Blun 1C 52
Blundellsands Rd. W. L23: Blun 2B 52
Blundellsands Sailing Club 7F 29
Blundells Ct. WN3: Wigan 1B 50
Blundells Dr. CH46: More 6D 84
BLUNDELL'S HILL 5H 93
Blundell's La. L35: R'hill 6G 93
Blundell St. L1: Liv 1K 107 (10F 4)
Blyth Cl. WA7: Murd 5B 154
Blythe Av. WA8: Wid 4D 114
Blythe La. L40: Lath 2H 25
Blythe M. PR8: B'dale 1G 15
Blythewood WN8: Skel 4J 37
Blyth Hey L30: N'ton 1K 53

Blyth Rd.—Brickmakers Arms Yd.

Blyth Rd. CH63: Brom 3J **145**
Blythswood St. L17: Aig 5C **108**
Boaler St. L6: Liv 4C **88** (2N **5**)
Boaler St. Ind. Est.
L6: Liv 3D **88** (2P **5**)
Boardmans La. WA9: St. H 2G **75**
WA11: St. H 2G **75**
Boathouse La. CH64: Park 1F **157**
Boat Mus., The 4B **162**
Boat Stage WA13: Lymm 5G **121**
Boat Wlk. WA4: Warr 7A **118**
Bobbies La. WA10: Eccl 2F **73**
Bobbiners La. PR9: Banks 4J **9**
Bob Paisley Ct. L5: Liv 1B **88**
Bodden St. WA9: Clock F 3F **95**
Bodiam Ct. CH65: Ell P 2C **170**
Bodley St. L4: Walt 7B **68**
Bodmin Av. PR9: Marsh 2D **8**
Bodmin Cl. WA7: Brook 4K **153**
Bodmin Gro. WA11: St. H 6F **61**
Bodmin Rd. L4: Walt 5B **68**
Bodmin Way L26: Halew 1J **131**
Bognor Cl. L24: Speke 5F **131**
Bolan St. L13: Liv 4H **89**
Bold Bus. Cen. WA9: Bold 7K **75**
Bolden Cl. L30: N'ton 4B **54**
Bolde Way CH63: Spit 1G **145**
BOLD HEATH 1G **115**
Bold Ind. Est. WA8: Wid 3E **114**
Bold Ind. Pk. WA9: Bold 1K **95**
Bold La. L39: Augh 4J **33**
WA5: C Grn 7K **75**
WA9: Bold 7K **75**
Bold Pl. L1: Liv 7A **88** (8H **5**)
Bold Rd. WA9: St. H 7H **75**
Bold St. L1: Liv 6K **87** (7G **4**)
PR9: South 7H **7**
WA1: Warr 3A **118**
WA7: Run 6D **134**
(not continuous)
WA8: Wid 2C **134**
WA10: St. H 3B **74**
Boleyn, The L31: Lyd 1G **43**
Boleyn Ct. WA7: Mnr P 6A **136**
Bollin Cl. WA3: Cul 4C **80**
WA13: Lymm 4J **121**
Bollin Dr. WA13: Lymm 4J **121**
Bollington Cl. CH43: O'ton 5K **105**
Bolton Av. L32: K'by 3A **56**
WA4: Westy 4F **119**
Bolton Cl. L37: Form 1A **30**
WA9: St. H 2E **74**
Bolton Rd. CH62: Port S 4H **127**
PR8: B'dale 4G **11**
WN2: Bam 2F **63**
WN4: Ash M 2F **63**
Bolton Rd. E. CH62: Port S 3J **127**
Bolton St. L3: Liv 6K **87** (6H **5**)
WA9: St. H 2E **74**
(not continuous)
WN4: Gars 7B **50**
Bolton Wlk. L32: K'by 3A **56**
Bombay Rd. WN5: Wigan 3K **39**
Bonchurch Dr. L15: W'tree 6H **89**
Bond Cl. WA5: Warr 4H **117**
Bond's La. PR9: Banks 1J **9**
Bond St. L3: Liv 3K **87** (1F **4**)
L34: Prsct 1D **92**
Bonnington Av. L23: C'by 7C **40**
Bonsall Rd. L12: W Der 1K **89**
Boode Cft. L28: Stock V 5F **71**
Booker Av. L18: Moss H, Aller 7J **109**
Booth's Brow Rd. WN4: Ash M 6B **50**
Booth's Cl. CH2: Elt 2A **172**
Booths Hill Cl. WA13: Lymm 6F **121**
Booth's Hill Rd. WA13: Lymm 5E **120**
Booth's La. L39: Augh 5H **23**
WA13: Lymm 6D **120**
Booth St. L13: Liv 4J **89**
PR9: South 7H **7**
WA5: Warr 4J **117**
WA9: St. H 7K **73**
Boothwood Cl. L7: Liv 7D **88** (7P **5**)
BOOTLE 3J **67**
Bootle Leisure Cen. 2J **67**
Bootle New Strand Station (Rail) 2J **67**
Bootle Oriel Road Station (Rail) 4H **67**
Bor Av. WN3: Wigan 1F **51**
Borax St. L13: Liv 5J **89**
Bordehill Gdns. L12: W Der 6B **70**
Border Rd. CH60: Hes 2F **143**
Border Way L5: Liv 1A **88**
Borella Rd. L13: Liv 1H **89**
Borough Pavement CH41: Birk 2D **106**
Borough Pl. CH41: Birk 2E **106**
Borough Rd. CH41: Birk 5C **106**
CH42: Tran 5C **106**
CH44: Wall 4D **86**
WA10: St. H 4A **74**
Borough Rd. E. CH41: Birk 2E **106**
CH44: Wall 5E **86**
Borough Way CH44: Wall 5E **86**
Borron Rd. WA12: New W 2F **77**
Borron Rd. Ind. Est.
WA12: New W 2F **77**
Borrowdale L37: Form 5K **19**
Borrowdale Av. WA2: Warr 4C **98**
Borrowdale Cl. WA6: Frod 3F **167**
Borrowdale Rd. CH46: More 7B **84**
CH63: Beb 5E **126**
L15: W'tree 2G **109**
WA8: Wid 1J **133**
WA10: St. H 6J **73**
WN5: Wigan 4K **39**
Bosco Ct. L11: Crox 2K **69**
Boscow Cres. WA9: St. H 7F **75**
Bosnia St. L8: Liv 5C **108**
Bossom Ct. L22: Water 5D **52**
Bostock Grn. CH65: Ell P 5H **161**
Bostock St. L5: Liv 2K **87**
WA5: Warr 2J **117**
Boston Av. WA7: Run 2D **152**
Boston Blvd. WA5: Gt San 1E **116**
Boston Cl. WA3: Cul 2B **80**
Boswell Av. WA4: Warr 6B **118**
Boswell Pl. WN3: Wigan 1D **50**
Boswell Rd. CH43: Pren 7K **105**
Boswell St. L8: Liv 1D **108**
L20: Boot 1G **67**
Bosworth Cl. CH63: Spit 7F **127**
Bosworth Dr. PR8: Ains 5B **14**
Bosworth Rd. WA11: St. H 7E **60**
Botanic Est. L7: Liv 6F **89**
Botanic Gardens 5D **8**
Botanic Gardens Mus. 5D **8**
Botanic Gro. L7: Liv 6E **88**
Botanic Pl. L7: Liv 5E **88**
Botanic Rd. L7: Liv 5E **88**
PR9: Chu 6C **8**
Botany Rd. L24: Speke 4G **131**
Boteler Av. WA5: Warr 1K **117**
Botley Cl. CH49: Upton 3B **104**
Bouchier Way WA4: Grap 1G **139**
Boulevard L6: Liv 3E **88**
Boulevard, The CH65: Gt Sut 6H **161**
L8: Liv 2C **108**
L12: W Der 6K **69**
Boulevard Industry Pk.
L24: Halew 4J **131**
(not continuous)
Boulting Av. WA5: Warr 5K **97**
Boulton Av. CH48: W Kir 4D **102**
CH62: New F 1H **127**
Boundary Dr. L23: C'by 6D **40**
L25: Hunts X 2H **131**
Boundary Farm Rd. L26: Halew 3H **131**
Boundary La. CH60: Hes 2E **142**
L6: Liv 3C **88** (1P **5**)
L33: Know 3J **57**
Boundary Pk. CH64: Park 4H **157**
Boundary Rd. CH43: Bid 6H **85**
CH48: W Kir 1F **123**
CH62: Port S 2H **127**
L21: Lith 3K **53**
(not continuous)
L36: Huy 7A **92**
WA10: St. H 3A **74**
Boundary St. L5: Liv 1H **87**
PR8: South 4H **11**
WA1: Warr 1E **118**
Boundary St. E. L5: Liv 1K **87**
Boundary Wlk. L36: Huy 7A **92**
Bourne Gdns. WA9: St. H 5E **74**
Bournemouth Cl. WA7: Murd 4B **154**
Bourne St. L6: Liv 4D **88** (2P **5**)
Bourton Rd. L25: Hunts X 2F **131**
Bousfield St. L4: Walt 7A **68**
Boverton Cl. WA5: Call 6J **97**
Bowden Cl. L12: Crox 4C **70**
WA3: Cul 2B **80**
Bowden Rd. L19: Gars 3K **129**
Bowden St. L21: Lith 7H **53**
Bowdon Cl. WA1: P'gate 7F **99**
WA10: Eccl 4H **73**
Bowdon Rd. CH45: Wall 1A **86**
Bowen Cl. WA8: Wid 4K **113**
Bower Cres. WA4: S'ton 7D **138**
Bower Gro. L21: Sea 6F **53**
Bower Ho. CH49: Upton 1D **104**
Bower Rd. CH60: Hes 3G **143**
L25: Wltn 4E **110**
L36: Huy 3J **91**
Bowers Bus. Pk. WA8: Wid 2D **134**
Bowers Pk. Ind. Est. WA8: Wid 2E **134**
Bower St. WA8: Wid 7E **114**
Bowfell Cl. CH62: East 7K **145**
Bowfield Rd. L19: Gras 2K **129**
Bowgreen Cl. CH43: Bid 1G **105**
BOWKER'S GREEN 6B **34**
Bowker's Grn. La.
L39: Augh, Bic 6B **34**
Bowland Av. L16: Child 6B **90**
WA9: Sut M 4D **94**
WN4: Ash M 1F **63**
Bowland Cl. CH62: Brom 1J **145**
WA3: Bchwd 2D **100**
WA7: Beech 5G **153**
Bowland Ct. *PR9: South 7J 7*
(off Gordon St.)
Bowland Dr. L21: Ford 1H **53**
Bowles St. L20: Boot 7G **53**
Bowley Rd. L13: Liv 2H **89**
Bowling Grn. Cl. PR8: South 3B **12**
Bowman Av. WA4: Westy 3G **119**
Bowness Av. CH43: Pren 6A **106**
CH63: Brom 5J **145**
PR8: Ains 6C **14**
WA2: Warr 5C **98**
WA11: St. H 5D **60**
Bowood Ct. WA2: Win 3A **98**
Bowood St. L8: Liv 5B **108**
Bowring Dr. CH64: Park 2F **157**
BOWRING PARK 6E **90**
Bowring Pk. Av. L16: Child 5E **90**
Bowring Pk. Rd. L14: B Grn 6A **90**
Bowring St. L8: Liv 4B **108**
Bowscale Cl. CH49: Upton 3C **104**
Bowscale Rd. L11: N Grn. 5J **69**
Boxdale Ct. L18: Moss H 4J **109**
Boxdale Rd. L18: Moss H 4J **109**
Boxgrove Cl. WA8: Wid 5D **114**
Boxmoor Rd. L18: Moss H 6J **109**
Boxtree Cl. L12: Crox 2D **70**
Boxwood Cl. L36: Roby 5G **91**
Boycott St. L5: Liv 1C **88**
Boyd Cl. CH46: Leas 4F **85**
Boydell Av. WA4: Grap 6H **119**
WA4: Westy 4F **119**
Boydell Cl. L28: Stock V 7F **71**
Boyer Av. L31: Mag 5F **43**
Boyes Brow L33: K'by 1B **56**
Boyle Av. WA2: Warr 6E **98**
Boyton Ct. L7: Liv 7E **88**
Brabant Rd. L17: Aig 7G **109**
Braby Rd. L21: Lith 7J **53**
Bracebridge Dr. PR8: South 6B **12**
Bracewell Cl. WA9: St. H 5E **94**
Bracken Cl. WA3: Bchwd 2J **99**
Bracken Ct. WA9: Clock F 3E **94**
Brackendale CH2: Elt 1B **172**
CH49: W'chu 5G **105**
WA7: Run 2F **153**
Brackendale Av. L9: Ain 6D **54**
Bracken Dr. CH48: W Kir 6G **103**
Brackenhurst Dr. CH45: New B 7C **66**
Brackenhurst Grn. L33: K'by 3C **56**
Bracken La. CH63: High B 4D **126**
Bracken Rd. CH66: Gt Sut 7G **161**
Brackens, The WA4: Dares 1E **154**
Brackenside CH60: Hes 7D **124**
Bracken Wlk. L32: K'by 4B **56**
Bracken Way L12: W Der 2J **89**
WA6: Frod 5E **166**
Brackenway L37: Form 4A **20**
Bracken Wood L12: Crox 2C **70**
Brackenwood Dr. WA8: Wid 2G **133**
Brackenwood Gro. L35: Whis 4F **93**
Brackenwood M. WA4: Grap 7J **119**
Brackenwood Rd. CH63: High B 6E **126**
Brackley Cl. CH44: Wall 4A **86**
WA7: Run 6B **134**
Brackley St. WA4: S Hth 7C **118**
WA7: Run 6B **134**
Bracknell Av. L32: K'by 4B **56**
Bracknell Cl. L32: K'by 4B **56**
Bracknel Way L39: Augh 2J **33**
Bradbourne Cl. L12: Crox 3C **70**
Bradda Cl. CH49: Upton 1D **104**
Braddan Av. L13: Liv 2G **89**
Bradden Cl. CH63: Spit 7H **127**
Brade St. PR9: Cros 3E **8**
Bradewell Cl. L4: Kirk 6A **68**
Bradewell St. L4: Kirk 6A **68**
Bradfield Av. L10: Ain 2E **54**
Bradfield St. L7: Liv 5E **88**
Bradgate Cl. CH46: More 6K **83**
WA5: Warr 2K **117**
Bradkirk Ct. L30: N'ton 7K **41**
Bradlegh Rd. WA12: New W 5F **77**
BRADLEY 4G **167**
Bradley Blvd. WA5: Gt San 2F **117**
Bradley Fold L36: Huy 7B **92**
Bradley La. WA5: B'wood 4D **76**
WA6: Frod 5F **167**
Bradley Pl. *PR8: South 1H 11*
(off Eastbank St.)
Bradley Rd. L21: Lith 4H **53**
Bradley St. PR9: South 7J **7**
Bradley Way WA8: Wid 7D **114**
Bradman Cl. CH45: Wall 2B **86**
Bradman Rd. CH46: More 6A **84**
L33: Know I 2G **57**
Bradmoor Rd. CH62: Brom 2K **145**
Bradshaw Cl. WA10: St. H 2K **73**
Bradshaw La. WA4: Grap 5H **119**
WN8: Parb 1J **27**
Bradshaw's La. PR8: Ains 3D **14**
Bradshaw St. WA8: Wid 6C **114**
WN5: Orr 5J **39**
Bradshaw Wlk. L20: Boot 2H **67**
Bradstone Cl. L10: Faz 7K **55**
Bradville Rd. L9: Ain 6E **54**
Bradwall Cl. CH65: Whit 7J **161**
Bradwell Cl. CH48: W Kir 6F **103**
Braehaven Rd. CH45: New B 7C **66**
Braemar Av. PR9: Chu 5B **8**
(not continuous)
Braemar Cl. L35: Whis 4F **93**
WA2: Fearn 4G **99**
Braemar Ct. CH65: Ell P 1C **170**
Braemar St. L20: Kirk 5K **67**
Braemore Cl. WN3: Wins 2A **50**
Braemore Rd. CH44: Wall 3K **85**
Braeside Cl. CH66: Gt Sut 6E **160**
Braeside Cres. WN5: Bil 7F **49**
Braeside Gdns. CH49: Upton 3D **104**
Brae St. L7: Liv 5D **88**
Brahms Cl. L8: Liv 2D **108**
Braid St. CH41: Birk 2F **107**
Brainerd St. L13: Liv 2G **89**
Braithwaite Cl. L35: R'hill 4J **93**
WA7: Beech 4F **153**
Bramberton Pl. L4: Walt 5E **68**
Bramberton Rd. L4: Walt 5E **68**
Bramble Av. CH41: Birk 7K **85**
Bramble Cl. WA5: Penk 5C **116**
Brambles, The WN4: Gars 7B **50**
Bramble Way CH46: More 5B **84**
WA7: Beech 6G **153**
WN8: Parb 1J **27**
Bramblewood Cl. CH43: Noct 4H **105**
Brambling Cl. WA7: Beech 5H **153**
Brambling Pk. L26: Halew 7J **111**
Bramcote Av. WA11: St. H 7E **60**
Bramcote Cl. L33: K'by 1E **56**
Bramcote Rd. L33: K'by 1D **56**
Bramcote Wlk. L33: K'by 1D **56**
Bramerton Ct. CH48: W Kir 5C **102**
Bramford Cl. CH49: Upton 3C **104**
Bramhall Cl. CH48: W Kir 7F **103**
L24: Speke 7J **131**
Bramhall Dr. CH62: East 7B **146**
Bramhall Rd. L22: Water 5E **52**
WN8: Skel 1F **37**
Bramhall St. WA5: Warr 3J **117**
(not continuous)
Bramley Av. CH63: High B 2E **126**
Bramley Cl. CH66: Gt Sut 4H **169**
L27: N'ley 3H **111**
Bramley M. WA4: S Hth 1C **138**
Bramleys, The L31: Mag 5E **42**
Bramley Wlk. L24: Speke 7H **131**
WA6: Hel 3G **173**
Bramley Way L32: K'by 2A **56**
Brampton Cl. L33: K'by 1C **56**
WN2: Platt B 3K **51**
Brampton Ct. WA9: St. H 3K **75**
Brampton Dr. L8: Liv 7C **88** (9M **5**)
Bramshill Cl. WA3: Bchwd 1C **100**
Bramwell Av. CH43: Pren 7A **106**
Bramwell St. WA9: St. H 2G **75**
Brancepeth Ct. CH65: Ell P 1B **170**
Branch Way WA11: Hay 7B **62**
Brancker Av. L35: R'hill 3H **93**
Brancote Ct. CH43: C'ton 2J **105**
Brancote Gdns. CH62: Brom 3K **145**
Brancote Mt. CH43: C'ton 2K **105**
Brancote Rd. CH43: C'ton 2K **105**
Brandearth Hey L28: Stock V 7F **71**
Brandearth Ho. L28: Stock V 7F **71**
Brandon WA8: Wid 6G **113**
Brandon Cl. WN8: Uph 4C **38**
Brandon St. CH41: Birk 2F **107**
Brandreth Cl. L35: R'hill 4J **93**
Brandwood Av. WA2: Warr 5B **98**
Brandwood Ho. WA1: Warr 3C **118**
Branfield Cl. L12: Crox 2C **70**
Bransdale Cl. WA5: Gt San 1C **116**
Bransdale Dr. WN4: Ash M 2H **63**
Bransfield Cl. WN3: Wigan 1E **50**
Bransford Cl. WN4: Ash M 3G **63**
Branson Cl. WA3: Golb 3K **63**
Branstree Av. L11: N Grn. 4H **69**
Bran St. L8: Liv 3A **108**
Brant Fld. Ct. WA2: Warr 5E **98**
Branthwaite Cl. L11: N Grn. 5J **69**
Branthwaite Cres. L11: N Grn. 4J **69**
Branthwaite Gro. L11: N Grn. 5J **69**
Brasenose Rd. L20: Boot 4H **67**
Brassey St. CH41: Birk 7A **86**
L8: Liv 2A **108**
Brathay Cl. WA2: Warr 4C **98**
Brattan Rd. CH41: Birk 4C **106**
Bratton Cl. WN3: Wins 3A **50**
Braunton Rd. CH45: Wall 1A **86**
L17: Aig 7G **109**
Braybrooke Rd. L11: N Grn. 3H **69**
Bray Cl. WA7: Beech 4F **153**
Braydon Cl. L25: Hunts X 3G **131**
Brayfield Rd. L4: Walt 5F **69**
Bray Rd. L24: Speke 5F **131**
Bray St. CH41: Birk 7B **86**
Brechin Rd. L33: K'by 3D **56**
Breck, The CH66: Ell P 4G **161**
Breckfield Pl. L5: Liv 2B **88**
Breckfield Rd. Nth. L5: Liv 1B **88**
Breckfield Rd. Sth. L6: Liv 2C **88**
Breck Pl. CH44: Wall 4A **86**
Breck Rd. CH44: Wall 3K **85**
L5: Liv 3B **88** (1L **5**)
WA8: Wid 7D **114**
Breckside Av. CH44: Wall 3J **85**
Breckside Pk. L6: Liv 1E **88**
Brecon Av. L30: N'ton 4B **54**
Brecon Ct. WA5: Call 5J **97**
Brecon Dr. CH66: Gt Sut 3G **169**
Brecon Rd. CH42: Tran 7C **106**
Brecon St. L6: Liv 3D **88** (1P **5**)
Brecon Wlk. L30: N'ton 4C **54**
Bredon Cl. CH66: Lit Sut 5C **160**
Bredon Ct. L37: Form 6J **19**
Breeze Cl. L9: Walt 3B **68**
Breeze Hill L9: Walt 4B **68**
L20: Boot 3K **67**
Breezehill Cl. CH64: Nest 3J **157**
Breezehill Pk. CH64: Nest 3K **157**
Breezehill Rd. CH64: Nest 3K **157**
Breeze La. L9: Walt 3B **68**
Breeze Rd. PR8: B'dale 6E **10**
Brelade Rd. L13: Liv 3H **89**
Bremhill Rd. L11: N Grn. 3H **69**
Bremner Cl. L7: Liv 6E **88**
Brenda Cres. L23: Thorn 5G **41**
Brendale Av. L31: Mag 4E **42**
Brendan's Way L30: N'ton 2A **54**
Brendon Av. L21: Lith 4G **53**
WA2: Warr 4A **98**
Brendon Gro. WA9: St. H 2J **75**
Brendor Rd. L25: Wltn 7F **111**
Brenig St. CH41: Birk 6K **85**
Brenka Av. L9: Ain 2E **54**
Brentfield WA8: Wid 6K **113**
Brentnall Cl. WA5: Gt San 3G **117**
Brent Way L26: Halew 3K **131**
(not continuous)
Brentwood Av. L17: Aig 5E **108**
L23: C'by 7F **41**
Brentwood Cl. L38: High 7F **29**
WA10: Eccl 3H **73**
Brentwood Ct. *CH49: W'chu 6E 104*
(off Childwall Grn.)
PR9: South 7K **7**
Brentwood Gro. L33: K'by 6C **44**
Brentwood St. CH44: Wall 4C **86**
Brereton Av. CH63: Beb 3G **127**
L15: W'tree 1J **109**
Brereton Cl. WA7: Cas 2J **153**
(not continuous)
Bretherton Pl. L35: R'hill 3J **93**
Bretherton Rd. L34: Prsct 1E **92**
Bretland Dr. WA4: Grap 2G **139**
Bretlands Rd. L23: Thorn 6H **41**
Brett Cl. L33: K'by 7B **44**
Bretton Fold PR8: South 3B **12**
Brett St. CH41: Birk 7B **86**
Brewery La. L31: Mell 1G **55**
(not continuous)
L37: Form 4K **19**
Brewster St. L4: Boot 5A **68**
L20: Walt 5A **68**
Breydon Gdns. WA9: St. H 1A **94**
Brian Av. CH61: Irby 3D **124**
WA2: Warr 7D **98**
WA4: S Hth 7E **118**
Brian Cummings Ct. L21: Lith 7H **53**
Briar Av. WA3: Rix 5K **101**
Briar Cl. WN4: Ash M 1E **62**
Briardale Gdns. CH66: Lit Sut 5E **160**
Briardale Rd. CH42: Tran 4C **106**
CH44: Wall 5E **86**
CH63: High B 2F **127**
CH64: Will 3G **159**
CH66: Lit Sut 5E **160**
L18: Moss H 3H **109**
Briar Dr. CH60: Hes 2E **142**
L36: Huy 5H **91**
Briarfield Av. WA8: Wid 7G **113**
Briarfield Rd. CH60: Hes 2F **143**
CH65: Ell P 6K **161**
Briar Rd. PR8: Ains 5D **14**
Briars, The PR8: B'dale 7F **11**
Briars Cl. L35: R'hill 6K **93**
Briars Grn. WA10: St. H 1B **74**
WN8: Skel 6H **27**
Briars La. L31: Mag 3G **43**
Briar St. L4: Kirk 7K **67**
Briarswood Cl. CH42: R Ferr 1F **127**
L35: Whis 4F **93**
Briarwood L23: Blun 6B **40**
WA7: Nort 2A **154**
Briarwood Av. WA1: Warr 1E **118**
Briarwood Rd. L17: Aig 5G **109**
Briary Cl. CH60: Hes 1F **143**
Briary Cft. L38: High 6F **29**
Brickcroft WN5: Wigan 5K **39**
Brickfields L36: Huy 6A **92**
Brickhurst Way WA1: W'ston 7H **99**
Brickmakers Arms Yd. *L39: Orm 4B 24*
(off Asmall La.)

Brick St.—Broxton Cl.

Brick St. L1: Liv 1K **107** (10G **4**)
WA1: Warr 3C **118**
WA12: New W 3D **76**
Brickwall Grn. L29: Seft 5B **42**
Brickwall La. L29: Seft 7K **41**
Bride St. L4: Walt 4B **68**
Bridge Av. L39: Orm 5C **24**
WA4: Westy 4F **119**
Bridge Av. E. WA4: Westy 3F **119**
Bridge Cl. WA13: Lymm 5K **121**
Bridge Ct. CH48: W Kir 5C **102**
CH64: Nest 4J **157**
L30: N'ton 1K **53**
WA9: Clock F 5F **95**
Bridge Cft. L21: Ford 2J **53**
Bridgecroft Rd. CH45: Wall 1B **86**
Bri. Farm Cl. CH49: W'chu 4F **105**
Bri. Farm Dr. L31: Mag 2H **43**
Bridgefield Cl. L25: Gate 1F **111**
Bridgefield Forum Leisure Cen. 6A **112**
Bridgeford Av. L12: W Der 7J **69**
Bridge Gdns. L12: W Der 5D **70**
Bridge Gro. PR8: South 2H **11**
Bridgehall Dr. WN8: Uph 4D **38**
Bridge Ho. L39: Orm 6C **24**
Bridge Ind. Est. L24: Speke 4F **131**
Bridge La. L30: N'ton 2A **54**
WA1: W'ston 2J **119**
WA4: App 1E **138**
WA6: Frod 2E **166**
Bridgeman St. WA5: Warr 4H **117**
WA10: St. H 3K **73**
(not continuous)
Bridge Mdw. CH66: Gt Sut 2H **169**
Bridgemere Cl. L7: Liv 4F **89**
Bridgemere Ho. *L17: Aig* *6F 109*
(off Mossley Hill Dr.)
Bridgend Cl. WA8: Wid 5K **113**
Bridgend Dr. PR8: Ains 5B **14**
Bridgenorth Rd. CH61: Pens 5C **124**
Bridge Rd. CH48: W Kir 5C **102**
L7: Liv 7E **88**
L18: Moss H 5J **109**
L21: Lith 6G **53**
L23: Blun 2C **52**
L31: Mag 5F **43**
L34: Prsct 2D **92**
L36: Roby 5G **91**
WA1: W'ston 1J **119**
WA9: Clock F 5F **95**
Bridgeside Dr. WA6: Hel 7H **165**
Bridges La. L29: Seft 5B **42**
Bridges Rd. CH65: Ell P 6D **162**
Bridge St. CH41: Birk 1E **106**
(not continuous)
CH62: Port S 4H **127**
(not continuous)
CH64: Nest 4J **157**
L20: Boot 4H **67**
L39: Orm 6C **24**
PR8: South 2H **11**
WA1: Warr 3B **118**
WA7: Run 6D **134**
WA10: St. H 3C **74**
WA12: New W 3F **77**
Bridge Vw. Cl. WA8: Wid 5C **134**
Bridgeview Dr. L33: K'by 1D **56**
Bridge Wlk. *WA7: Pal F* *3H 153*
(off Halton Lea Shop. Cen.)
Bridgewater Av. WA4: Westy 4F **119**
Bridgewater Cl. L21: Lith 3G **53**
Bridgewater Ct. L21: Lith 3G **53**
Bri. Water Grange WA7: Pres B 5D **154**
Bridgewater M. WA4: S Hth 1C **138**
Bridgewater Pl. WA3: Ris 2A **100**
Bridgewater St. L1: Liv 1K **107** (10F **4**)
WA7: Run 6C **134**
WA13: Lymm 5G **121**
Bridgewater Way L36: Huy 7A **92**
Bridgeway L11: N Grn. 5G **69**
Bridgeway E. WA7: Wind H 7A **136**
Bridgeway W. WA7: Wind H 7K **135**
Bridgewills La. PR9: Cros 2E **8**
Bri. Wood Dr. CH66: Gt Sut 2E **168**
Bridle Av. CH44: Wall 5E **86**
Bridle Cl. CH43: Bid 2F **105**
CH62: Brom 3A **146**
Bridle Ct. WA9: St. H 6E **74**
Bridlemere Ct. WA1: P'gate 7E **98**
Bridle Pk. CH62: Brom 3K **145**
Bridle Rd. CH44: Wall 5E **86**
CH62: Brom 3A **146**
L30: N'ton 5A **54**
Bridle Rd. Ind. Est. L30: N'ton 5B **54**
Bridle Way CH66: Gt Sut 1F **169**
L30: N'ton 5B **54**
L33: K'by 6C **44**
Bridport St. L3: Liv 5A **88** (5H **5**)
Briedden Way CH66: Lit Sut 5C **160**
Brierfield WN8: Skel 5K **37**
Brierfield Rd. L15: W'tree 2H **109**
Brierley Cl. L30: N'ton 1D **54**
Briers Cl. WA2: Fearn 4F **99**
Briery Hey Av. L33: K'by 3D **56**
Brighouse Cl. L39: Orm 5B **24**
Brightgate Cl. L7: Liv 7D **88** (8P **5**)
BRIGHTON LE SANDS 2B **52**
Brighton Rd. L22: Water 4D **52**
L36: Huy 4B **92**
PR8: B'dale 5G **11**
Brighton St. CH44: Wall 3D **86**
WA5: Warr 2J **117**
Brighton Va. L22: Water 3C **52**
Brightstone Cl. PR9: Banks 2K **9**
Bright St. CH41: Birk 2C **106**
(not continuous)
L6: Liv 4B **88** (2M **5**)
PR9: South 1B **12**
Bright Ter. L8: Liv 5B **108**
Brightwell Cl. CH49: Upton 4D **104**
WA5: Gt San 2C **116**
Brill St. CH41: Birk 7B **86**
Brimelow Cres. WA5: Penk 5C **116**
BRIMSTAGE 7B **126**
Brimstage Av. CH63: High B 1D **126**
Brimstage Cl. CH60: Hes 3G **143**
Brimstage Grn. CH60: Hes 2H **143**
Brimstage Hall 7A **126**
Brimstage La.
CH63: Brim, Store 5B **126**
Brimstage Rd. CH60: Hes 3G **143**
CH63: Beb, High B, Brim 3G **143**
L4: Walt 4A **68**
Brimstage St. CH41: Birk 3C **106**
Brindley, The 7C **134**
Brindley Av. WA4: Westy 4F **119**
Brindley Cl. L21: Lith 3G **53**
Brindley Ct. WA4: S Hth 1D **138**
Brindley Rd. L32: K'by 3A **56**
WA7: Ast 6H **135**
WA9: St. H 1G **95**
Brindley St. L8: Liv 2K **107**
WA7: Run 6B **134**
Brindley Wharf
WA4: Dutt, Pres H 5D **154**
Brinklow Cl. PR8: Ains 4A **14**
Brinley Cl. CH62: Brom 5K **145**
Brinton Cl. L27: N'ley 2G **111**
WA8: Wid 1K **133**
Brisbane Av. CH45: New B 6A **66**
Brisbane St. WA9: St. H 7K **73**
Briscoe Av. CH46: More 1C **104**
Briscoe Dr. CH46: More 1C **104**
Bristol Av. CH44: Wall 3C **86**
WA7: Murd 4C **154**
Bristol Dr. CH66: Gt Sut 3G **169**
Bristol Rd. L15: W'tree 2J **109**
Bristow Cl. WA5: Gt San 7F **97**
Britannia Av. L15: W'tree 1E **108**
Britannia Cres. L8: Liv 5B **108**
Britannia Gdns. WA6: Hel 3H **173**
Britannia Pav. L3: Liv 7J **87** (9D **4**)
Britannia Rd. CH45: Wall 2A **86**
WA6: Hel 2H **173**
WN5: Wigan 3K **39**
British Lawnmower Mus. 3H **11**
Britonside Av. L32: K'by 5D **56**
Brittarge Brow L27: N'ley 4J **111**
Britten Cl. L8: Liv 2D **108**
Broadacre WN8: Uph 5C **38**
Broadacre Cl. L18: Moss H 3A **110**
Broadbelt St. L4: Walt 4B **68**
Broadbent Av. WA4: Westy 4F **119**
Broadbent Ho. *L31: Mag* *5F 43*
(off Boyer Av.)
Broadfield WA7: Nort 2A **154**
Broadfield Av. CH43: Bid 7F **85**
Broadfield Cl. CH43: Bid 1G **105**
Broadgate Av. WA9: St. H 6E **74**
BROAD GREEN 6B **90**
Broad Grn. Rd. L13: Liv 4J **89**
Broad Green Station (Rail) 6B **90**
Broadheath Av. CH43: Bid 1G **105**
Broadheath Ter. WA8: Wid 7K **113**
Broad Hey L30: N'ton 2K **53**
Broad Hey Cl. L25: Wltn 5F **111**
Broadheys La. WA13: H Legh 3F **141**
Broadhurst Av. WA3: Cul 4B **80**
WA5: Warr 4H **117**
Broadhurst St. L17: Aig 5D **108**
Broadlake CH64: Will 3F **159**
Broadland Gdns. CH66: Gt Sut 2H **169**
Broadland Rd. CH66: Gt Sut 2H **169**
Broadlands L35: Prsct 2E **92**
PR8: B'dale 5E **10**
Broad La. CH60: Hes 1A **142**
L4: Walt 5F **69**
L29: Thorn 3J **41**
L32: K'by 5D **56**
L37: Form 3B **20**
L37: Gt Alt 1E **30**
L39: Augh 1D **32**
L39: Bart 3B **20**
WA4: Grap 7H **119**
WA5: C Grn 5A **76**
WA11: St. H 3D **60**
Broad La. Pct. L11: N Grn. 5H **69**
Broadleaf Rd. L19: Gras 2H **129**
Broadmead CH60: Hes 3G **143**
L19: Aller 2B **130**
WN8: Parb 1J **27**
BROAD OAK 2G **75**
Broad Oak Av. WA5: Penk 4C **116**
WA11: Hay 7K **61**
Broad Oak Rd. WA9: St. H 3G **75**
Broadoak Rd. L14: K Ash 4D **90**
L31: Mag 3G **43**
Broadoaks CH49: Upton 2C **104**
Broad Pl. L11: N Grn. 6H **69**
Broads, The WA9: St. H 1A **94**
Broad Sq. L11: N Grn. 6H **69**
Broadstone Dr. CH63: Spit 7F **127**
Broad Vw. L11: N Grn. 6H **69**
Broadway CH45: Wall 2K **85**
CH49: Grea 3C **104**
CH63: High B 2D **126**
L9: Ain 6G **55**
L11: N Grn. 5G **69**
WA8: Wid 7G **113**
WA10: Eccl 2G **73**
WA10: St. H 6J **73**
Broadway Av. CH45: Wall 2K **85**
Broadway Cl. PR8: Ains 4B **14**
Broadway Community Leisure Cen. 6H **73**
Broadway Mkt. L11: N Grn. 5G **69**
Broadwood Av. L31: Mag 5E **42**
Broadwood St. L15: W'tree 1G **109**
Brock Av. L31: Mag 2G **43**
Brockenhurst Rd. L9: Walt 1C **68**
Brock Gdns. L24: Hale 7E **132**
Brock Hall Cl. WA9: Clock F 3E **94**
Brockhall Cl. L35: Whis 1G **93**
Brockholme Rd. L18: Moss H 7J **109**
Brocklebank La. L19: Aller 1B **130**
Brocklebank Rd. PR9: South 6A **8**
Brockley Av. CH45: New B 5B **66**
Brockmoor Twr. L4: Kirk 6K **67**
Brock Pl. WN2: Platt B 2K **51**
Brock Rd. WA3: Bchwd 4K **99**
Brock St. L4: Kirk 6A **68**
Brockton Ct. WA4: App 3C **138**
Brocstedes Av. WN4: Ash M 6C **50**
Brocstedes Rd. WN4: Ash M 4B **50**
(not continuous)
Brodie Av. L18: Moss H 5J **109**
L19: Aig, Aller 6J **109**
Brogden Av. WA3: Cul 2A **80**
BROMBOROUGH 2J **145**
BROMBOROUGH POOL 4K **127**
BROMBOROUGH PORT 6B **128**
Bromborough Rake Station (Rail) 2J **145**
Bromborough Rd. CH63: Beb 4G **127**
Bromborough Station (Rail) 3J **145**
Bromborough Village Rd.
CH62: Brom 1K **145**
Brome Way CH63: Spit 7H **127**
Bromilow Rd. WA9: St. H 4H **75**
WN8: Skel 2C **36**
Bromley Av. L18: Moss H 3H **109**
Bromley Cl. CH60: Hes 3C **142**
L26: Halew 7A **112**
WA2: Fearn 4F **99**
Bromley Rd. CH45: New B 7A **66**
Brompton Av. CH44: Wall 3C **86**
L17: Liv 2E **108**
L23: C'by 2C **52**
L33: K'by 7D **44**
Brompton Ct. L17: Liv 2E **108**
Brompton Gdns. WA5: Warr 1J **117**
Brompton Ho. L17: Aig 3E **108**
Brompton Rd. PR8: South 1A **12**
Brompton Way CH66: Gt Sut 3G **169**
Bromsgrove Rd. CH49: Grea 4A **104**
Bromyard Cl. L20: Boot 2H **67**
Bronington Av. CH62: Brom 4K **145**
Bronshill Ct. L23: Blun 1A **52**
Bronte Cl. L23: Blun 1B **52**
WA2: Win 1A **98**
Bronte St. L3: Liv 5A **88** (5J **5**)
WA10: St. H 2K **73**
Brook Av. WA4: S Hth 7E **118**
WA4: Westy 3F **119**
Brookbank Ct. L10: Faz 6K **55**
Brookbridge Rd. L13: Liv 1G **89**
Brook Cl. CH44: Wall 2C **86**
WA8: Cron 2J **113**
Brookdale PR8: Ains 6D **14**
Brookdale Av. Nth. CH49: Grea 4C **104**
Brookdale Av. Sth. CH49: Grea 4C **104**
Brookdale Cl. CH49: Grea 4C **104**
Brookdale Rd. L15: W'tree 2G **109**
Brook Dr. WA5: Gt San 3E **116**
Brooke Cl. PR9: South 1D **12**
Brook End WA9: St. H 5J **75**
Brooke Rd. E. L22: Water 3D **52**
Brooke Rd. W. L22: Water 3C **52**
Brook Farm Cl. L39: Orm 6C **24**
Brookfield WN8: Parb 1J **27**
Brookfield Av. L22: Water 5F **53**
L23: C'by 2D **52**
L35: R'hill 2J **93**
WA7: Run 7F **135**
Brookfield Cen. L9: Ain 1E **68**
Brookfield Cl. WA13: Lymm 5F **121**
Brookfield Cotts. WA13: Lymm 5F **121**
Brookfield Dr. L9: Ain 1E **68**
Brookfield Gdns. CH48: W Kir 6D **102**
Brookfield Ho. L36: Huy 4J **91**
Brookfield La. L39: Augh 7J **33**
Brookfield Pk. WA4: Grap 6G **119**
Brookfield Rd. CH48: W Kir 6D **102**
WA3: Cul 2K **79**
WA13: Lymm 5F **121**
WN8: Uph 4D **38**
BROOKFIELDS GREEN 6J **33**
Brookfield St. WA12: New W 3F **77**
Brook Furlong WA6: Frod 1A **166**
Brook Hey CH64: Park 1F **157**
Brook Hey Dr. L33: K'by 1D **56**
Brook Hey Wlk. L33: K'by 2E **56**
Brookhill Cl. L20: Boot 3K **67**
Brookhill Rd. L20: Boot 2K **67**
Brook Ho. PR8: South 3J **11**
Brookhouse Gro. WA10: Eccl 3F **73**
Brookhouse Rd. L39: Orm 4B **24**
BROOKHURST 5J **145**
Brookhurst Av. CH62: East 4J **145**
CH63: Brom, East 4J **145**
Brookhurst Cl. CH63: Brom 5J **145**
Brookhurst Rd. CH63: Brom 4J **145**
Brookland La. WA9: St. H 4J **75**
Brookland Rd. CH41: Birk 3D **106**
Brookland Rd. E. L13: Liv 4J **89**
Brookland Rd. W. L13: Liv 4J **89**
Brooklands CH41: Birk 1D **106**
L39: Orm 4E **24**
Brooklands, The L36: Huy 6J **91**
Brooklands Av. L22: Water 5E **52**
WN4: Ash M 3H **63**
Brooklands Dr. L31: Mag 4F **43**
WN5: Orr 6F **39**
Brooklands Gdns. CH64: Park 2G **157**
Brooklands Pk. WA8: Wid 6E **114**
Brooklands Rd. CH64: Park 2G **157**
WA10: Eccl 2G **73**
WN8: Uph 4E **38**
Brookland St. WA1: Warr 1E **118**
Brook La. CH64: Park 1G **157**
L39: Orm 6C **24**
WA3: Rix 7C **100**
WA11: Kings M 5B **48**
WN5: Orr 6J **39**
Brook Lea Ho. L21: Ford 2J **53**
Brooklet Rd. CH60: Hes 2G **143**
Brooklyn Dr. CH65: Gt Sut 6H **161**
WA13: Lymm 4G **121**
Brooklyn Pk. & Country Club
PR9: Banks 3H **9**
Brook Mdw. CH61: Irby 2C **124**
Brook Pk. L31: Mag 5E **42**
Brook Pl. WA4: Latch 5E **118**
Brook Rd. CH66: Gt Sut 6F **161**
L9: Walt 2C **68**
L20: Boot 3H **67**
L23: Thorn 6G **41**
L31: Mag 4G **43**
WA13: Lymm 4G **121**
Brooks, The WA11: St. H 6C **60**
Brooks All. L1: Liv 6K **87** (7F **4**)
Brookside L12: W Der 6D **70**
L31: Mag 3G **43**
Brookside Av. L14: K Ash 4B **90**
L22: Water 5F **53**
WA4: S Hth 7D **118**
WA5: Gt San 4E **116**
WA10: Eccl 1H **73**
WA11: R'ford 5E **46**
Brookside Av. WA13: Lymm 4E **120**
WN4: Ash M 4D **50**
Brookside Cl. L35: Prsct 3E **92**
WA11: Hay 6K **61**
WN5: Bil 7G **49**
Brookside Ct. L23: C'by 1E **52**
Brookside Cres. CH49: Upton 3B **104**
Brookside Dr. CH49: Upton 3C **104**
Brookside Rd. L35: Prsct 3E **92**
PR8: South 7J **11**
WA6: Frod 3C **166**
Brookside Vw. WA11: Hay 6K **61**
Brookside Way WA11: Hay 6K **61**
Brooks Rd. L37: Form 1H **29**
Brook St. CH41: Birk 7C **86**
CH62: Port S 3G **127**
CH64: Nest 3J **157**
L3: Liv 5H **87** (4C **4**)
L35: Whis 2F **93**
PR9: Cros 3F **9**
WA7: Run 6C **134**
WA8: Wid 1D **134**
WA10: St. H 3C **74**
WN3: Wigan 1D **50**
WN4: Ash M 3G **63**
WN5: Orr 5K **39**
Brook St. E. CH41: Birk 1E **106**
Brooks Way L37: Form 1H **29**
Brook Ter. CH48: W Kir 6D **102**
WA7: Run 7G **135**
Brookthorpe Cl. CH45: Wall 1B **86**
BROOKVALE 5A **154**
Brook Va. L22: Water 5F **53**
Brookvale Av. Nth. WA7: Brook 4K **153**
Brookvale Av. Sth. WA7: Brook 4K **153**
Brookvale Cl. WA5: B'wood 1D **96**
Brookvale Local Nature Reserve 5G **53**
Brookvale Recreation Cen. 4A **154**
Brook Wlk. CH61: Irby 2B **124**
Brook Way WA5: Gt San 3E **116**
Brookway CH43: Pren 7J **105**
CH45: Wall 2A **86**
CH49: Grea 3C **104**
Brookway La. WA9: St. H 5H **75**
Brook Well CH64: Lit N 6J **157**
Brookwood Cl. WA4: Walt 1B **138**
Brookwood Rd. L36: Huy 3J **91**
Broom Av. WA4: App 3E **138**
Broom Cl. L34: Ecc P 1F **93**
Broome Cl. PR8: B'dale 5H **11**
Broome Ct. WA7: Brook 4K **153**
BROOMEDGE 7K **121**
Broome Rd. PR8: B'dale 5H **11**
Broomfield Cl. CH60: Hes 1B **142**
Broomfield Gdns. L9: Walt 1B **68**
Broomfield Rd. L9: Walt 1B **68**
(not continuous)
Broomfields WA4: App 2E **138**
Broomfields Leisure Cen. 2D **138**
Broomfields Rd. WA4: App 2D **138**
Broom Hill CH43: C'ton 1K **105**
Broomhill Cl. L27: N'ley 2G **111**
Broomlands CH60: Hes 2D **142**
Broomleigh Cl. CH63: High B 4D **126**
Broom Rd. WA10: St. H 6H **73**
Brooms Gro. L10: Ain 3G **55**
Broom Way L26: Halew 2J **131**
Broseley Av. CH62: Brom 1J **145**
WA3: Cul 2K **79**
Broseley La. WA3: Cul 1K **79**
Broseley Pl. WA3: Cul 1J **79**
Broster Av. CH46: More 7A **84**
Broster Cl. CH46: More 7A **84**
Brosters La. CH47: Meols 6G **83**
Brotherhood Dr. WA9: St. H 7F **75**
Brotherton Cl. CH62: Brom 1J **145**
Brotherton Rd. CH44: Wall 5E **86**
Brotherton Way WA12: New W 2F **77**
Brougham Av. CH41: Tran 4F **107**
Brougham Rd. CH44: Wall 4D **86**
Brougham Ter. L6: Liv 4C **88** (2M **5**)
Broughton Av. CH48: W Kir 5C **102**
PR8: South 4K **11**
Broughton Cl. WA4: Grap 1F **139**
Broughton Dr. L19: Gras 2J **129**
Broughton Hall Rd. L12: W Der 2C **90**
Broughton Rd. CH44: Wall 4B **86**
Broughton Way WA8: Hale B 4H **133**
BROW, THE 1H **153**
Brow La. CH60: Hes 3D **142**
Browmere Dr. WA3: Croft 7G **79**
Brownbill Bank L27: N'ley 3J **111**
BROWN EDGE
St Helens 7K **73**
Southport 6C **12**
Brown Edge Cl. PR8: South 6C **12**
Brownheath Av. WN5: Bil 2F **61**
Brownhill Dr. WA1: P'gate 7F **99**
Browning Av. CH42: R Ferr 7F **107**
WA8: Wid 1B **134**
WN3: Wigan 1D **50**
Browning Cl. L36: Huy 6K **91**
Browning Dr. CH65: Gt Sut 7H **161**
WA2: Win 1K **97**
Browning Grn. CH65: Gt Sut 7H **161**
Browning Rd. CH45: Wall 2H **85**
L13: Liv 1H **89**
L22: Water 3D **52**
Browning St. L20: Boot 2G **67**
BROWNLOW 3F **49**
Brownlow Arc. WA10: St. H 3C **74**
Brownlow Hill L3: Liv 6A **88** (6H **5**)
Brownlow La. WN5: Bil 3E **48**
Brownlow Rd. CH62: New F 2H **127**
Brownlow St. L3: Liv 6B **88** (6K **5**)
Brownmoor Cl. L23: C'by 1G **53**
Brownmoor La. L23: C'by 2F **53**
Brownmoor Pk. L23: C'by 2F **53**
Brown's La. L30: N'ton 2B **54**
Brown St. WA8: Wid 2F **135**
Brownville Rd. L13: Liv 7F **69**
Brow Rd. CH43: Bid 6H **85**
Brows Cl. L37: Form 1J **29**
Brow Side L5: Liv 3B **88** (1K **5**)
Brows La. L37: Form 1J **29**
Broxholme Way L31: Mag 5F **43**
Broxton Av. CH43: Pren 6K **105**
CH48: W Kir 5E **102**
WN5: Orr 4H **39**
Broxton Cl. WA8: Wid 5J **113**

Broxton Rd.—Cambridge Cl.

Broxton Rd. CH45: Wall 1K 85
CH66: Ell P 6G 161
Broxton St. L15: W'tree 7G 89
Bruce Av. WA2: Warr 6D 98
Bruce Cres. CH63: Brom 4J 145
Bruce Dr. CH66: Gt Sut 7E 160
Bruce St. L8: Liv 4C 108
WA10: St. H 2A 74
BRUCHE 1E 118
Bruche Av WA1: P'ton, P'gate 1F 119
Bruche Dr. WA1: P'gate 7F 99
Bruche Heath Gdns. WA1: P'gate 7G 99
Bruera Rd. CH65: Gt Sut 7H 161
Brunel Dr. L21: Lith 3G 53
Brunel M. L5: Liv 2C 88
Brunel Rd. CH62: Brom 1B 146
Brunner Rd. WA8: Wid 1C 134
Brunsborough Cl. CH62: Brom 4J 145
Brunsfield Cl. CH46: More 1A 104
Brunstath Cl. CH60: Hes 1G 143
Brunswick WA7: Run 6C 134
Brunswick Bus. Pk. L3: Liv 3K 107
(not continuous)
Brunswick Cl. L4: Kirk 6A 68
Brunswick Ct. CH41: Birk 1E 106
Brunswick Cres. CH66: Gt Sut 1G 169
Brunswick Ent. Cen. L3: Liv 3K 107
Brunswick M. CH41: Birk 1E 106
L22: Water 5E 52
Brunswick Pde. L22: Water 5D 52
Brunswick Pl. L20: Kirk 6H 67
Brunswick Rd. L6: Liv 4B 88 (3L 5)
WA12: New W 2D 76
Brunswick Station (Rail) 4A 108
Brunswick St. L2: Liv 6J 87 (6D 4)
L3: Liv 6H 87 (7C 4)
L19: Gars 6A 130
WA9: St. H 3J 75
Brunswick Way L3: Liv 3K 107
Brunt La. L19: Aller 2C 130
Bruntleigh Av. WA4: Westy 5G 119
Brushford Cl. L12: W Der 4K 69
Bruton Rd. L36: Huy 1H 91
(not continuous)
Bryanston Rd. CH42: Tran 6A 106
L17: Aig 5D 108
Bryant Av. WA4: Westy 3F 119
Bryant Rd. L21: Lith 7H 53
Bryceway, The L12: W Der 3B 90
Brydges St. L7: Liv 6C 88 (7N 5)
Bryer Rd. L35: Prsct 3D 92
BRYN 7E 50
Bryn Bank CH44: Wall 3C 86
BRYN GATES 5J 51
Bryn Gates La. WN2: Bam 4G 51
Brynmor Rd. L18: Moss H 7J 109
Brynmoss Av. CH44: Wall 3K 85
Brynn St. WA8: Wid 1D 134
WA10: St. H 2C 74
Bryn Rd. WN4: Ash M 6E 50
Bryn Rd. Sth. WN4: Ash M 1G 63
Bryn Station (Rail) 7E 50
Bryn St. WN2: Bam 5K 51
WN4: Ash M 2F 63
Bryony Cl. WN5: Orr 6F 39
Bryony Way CH42: R Ferr 1F 127
Brythen St. L1: Liv 6K 87 (6G 4)
Buccleuch St. CH41: Birk 6K 85
Buchanan Cl. WA8: Wid 5B 114
Buchanan Rd. CH44: Wall 4D 86
L9: Walt 3B 68
Buchan Cl. WA5: W'brk 7F 97
Buckfast Av. WA11: Hay 6E 62
Buckfast Cl. L30: N'ton 1B 54
WA5: Penk 5C 116
Buckfast Ct. WA7: Nort 6C 136
Buckfast Dr. L37: Form 1B 30
Buckingham Av. CH43: C'ton 1K 105
CH63: High B 2E 126
L17: Liv 2F 109
WA8: Wid 4C 114
Buckingham Bingo
Bootle 3J 67
Hunt's Cross 3E 130
Huyton 5J 91
Buckingham Cl. L30: N'ton 2J 53
Buckingham Ct. L33: K'by 1D 56
Buckingham Dr. WA5: Gt San 4G 117
WA11: St. H 6C 60
Buckingham Gdns. CH65: Ell P 2B 170
Buckingham Gro. L37: Form 2J 29
Buckingham Ho. L17: Aig 3F 109
Buckingham Rd. CH44: Wall 3K 85
L9: Walt 7C 54
L13: Liv 1F 89
L31: Mag 3E 42
Buckingham St. L5: Liv 2A 88
Buckland Cl. WA8: Wid 2J 133
Buckland Dr. CH63: Spit 7F 127
WN5: Wigan 2K 39
Buckland St. L17: Aig 5D 108
Buckley Hill La. L29: Seft 1K 53
Buckley La. CH64: Will 3F 159
Buckley St. WA2: Warr 2A 118
Buckley Wlk. L24: Speke 7H 131
Buckley Way L30: N'ton 7K 41
Bucklow Gdns. WA13: Lymm 4J 121
Buckthorn Cl. L28: Stock V 7F 71
Buckthorn Gdns. WA9: St. H 1J 93
Buckton St. WA1: Warr 1D 118
Bude Cl. CH43: Bid 2G 105
Bude Rd. WA8: Wid 6A 114
Budworth Av. WA4: Westy 4F 119
WA8: Wid 6K 113
WA9: Sut M 4D 94
Budworth Cl. CH43: O'ton 4J 105
WA7: Run 3F 153
Budworth Ct. CH43: O'ton 3K 105
Budworth Dr. L25: Wltn 6G 111
Budworth Rd. CH66: Gt Sut 2G 169
Buer Av. WN3: Wigan 1D 50
Buerton Cl. CH43: Noct 4J 105
Buffs La. CH60: Hes 1F 143
Buggen La. CH64: Nest 3H 157
Buildwas Rd. CH64: Nest 1J 157
Bulford Rd. L9: Faz 2F 69
Bulkeley Rd. CH44: Wall 4D 86
Bull Bri. La. L10: Ain 3G 55
Bull Cop L37: Form 7A 20
Bullens La. L40: Scar 2F 17
Bullens Rd. L4: Walt 6B 68
L32: K'by 4D 56
Bullfinch Ct. L26: Halew 7J 111
Bull Hill CH64: Lit N 5K 157
Bull La. L9: Ain 6C 54
L9: Walt 7B 54
Bullrush Dr. CH46: More 5E 84
Bulrushes, The L17: Aig 5B 108
Bulwer St. CH42: R Ferr 6F 107
L5: Liv 2C 88
L20: Boot 1G 67
Bunbury Cl. CH2: Stoak 5E 170
Bunbury Dr. WA7: Run 4E 152
Bunbury Grn. CH65: Ell P 2B 170
Bundoran Rd. L17: Aig 6F 109
Bungalow Rd. WA12: New W 5J 77
Bungalows, The *CH63: Thorn H* *4B 144*
(off Raby Rd.)
WN4: Ash M 5D 50
Bunter Rd. L32: K'by 6D 56
Bunting Ct. L26: Halew 6H 111
Buntingford Rd. WA4: Thel 5J 119
Burbo Bank Rd. L23: Blun 1A 52
Burbo Bank Rd. Nth. L23: Blun 7A 40
Burbo Bank Rd. Sth. L23: Blun 2B 52
Burbo Cres. L23: Blun 2B 52
Burbo Mans. L23: Blun 2B 52
Burbo Way CH45: Wall 6J 65
Burden Rd. CH46: More 7A 84
Burdett Av. CH63: Spit 7F 127
Burdett Cl. CH63: Spit 7G 127
Burdett Rd. CH45: Wall 2H 85
CH66: Gt Sut 2G 169
L22: Water 3D 52
Burdett St. L17: Aig 5D 108
Burfield Dr. WA4: App 3C 138
Burford Av. CH44: Wall 4K 85
Burford Rd. L16: Child 6A 90
Burgess Av. WA4: Warr 5B 118
Burgess Gdns. L31: Mag 2E 42
Burgess' La. L37: Gt Alt 2F 31
Burgess St. L3: Liv 5A 88 (4J 5)
Burghill Rd. L12: Crox 2D 70
Burgundy Cl. L17: Aig 6E 108
Burkhardt Dr. WA12: New W 3J 77
Burland Cl. WA7: Run 1B 152
Burland Rd. L26: Halew 3A 132
Burleigh M. L5: Liv 7B 68
Burleigh Rd. Nth. L5: Liv 7B 68
Burleigh Rd. Sth. L5: Liv 1B 88
Burley Cl. L32: K'by 4D 56
Burley Cres. WN3: Wins 2A 50
Burley La. WA4: App T 5J 139
Burlingham Av. CH48: W Kir 7F 103
Burlington Av. L37: Form 7B 20
Burlington Ho. L22: Water 4E 52
Burlington Rd. CH45: New B 5B 66
PR8: B'dale 5F 11
Burlington St. CH41: Birk 2E 106
L3: Liv 3J 87 (1D 4)
Burman Cres. L19: Gars 2A 130
Burman Rd. L19: Gars 2A 130
Burnage Av. WA9: Clock F 3E 94
Burnage Cl. L24: Speke 7K 131
Burnand St. L4: Walt 7B 68
Burnard Cl. L33: K'by 3D 56
Burnard Cres. L33: K'by 3D 56
Burnard Wlk. L33: K'by 3D 56
Burnell Cl. WA10: St. H 2B 74
Burnell Rd. CH65: Ell P 7C 162
Burnet Cl. WA2: P'gate 5J 99
Burnham Cl. WA3: Cul 2A 80
WA5: Penk 3D 116
WA8: Wid 5J 113
Burnham Rd. L18: Moss H 5A 110
Burnie Av. L20: Boot 1A 68
Burnley Av. CH46: More 7D 84
PR8: Ains 4D 14
Burnley Cl. L6: Liv 3C 88 (1N 5)
Burnley Gro. CH46: More 6D 84
Burnley Rd. CH46: More 6D 84
PR8: Ains 4C 14
Burnsall Dr. WA8: Wid 5J 113
Burnsall St. L19: Gars 4C 130
Burns Av. CH45: Wall 2A 86
Burns Cl. CH66: Gt Sut 7G 161
L16: Child 7D 90
L35: Whis 4E 92
WN3: Wigan 1E 50
WN4: Ash M 6D 50
WN5: Bil 3F 49
Burns Cres. WA8: Wid 1B 134
Burns Gro. L36: Huy 6A 92
WA2: Warr 5C 98
Burnside WN8: Parb 1H 27
Burnside Av. CH44: Wall 5B 86
WA4: S Hth 7D 118
Burnside Rd. CH44: Wall 5B 86
Burns Rd. WA9: Sut M 4C 94
Burns St. L20: Boot 1G 67
Burnt Ash Cl. L19: Gras 2H 129
Burnthwaite Rd. L14: K Ash 4A 90
Burnt Mill La. WA8: Hale B 4D 132
Burnvale WN3: Wins 2B 50
Burrell Cl. CH42: Tran 7C 106
Burrell Ct. CH42: Tran 7C 106
Burrell Dr. CH46: More 1B 104
Burrell Rd. CH42: Tran 1B 126
Burrell St. L4: Walt 6B 68
Burrough Cl. WA3: Bchwd 4B 100
Burroughs Gdns. L3: Liv 3K 87 (1F 4)
Burrow's Av. WA11: Hay 1H 75
Burrows Ct. L3: Liv 2J 87
WA9: St. H 3G 75
Burrows La. WA10: Eccl 4F 73
L34: Ecc P 7E 72
Burrows St. WA11: Hay 7J 61
Bursar Cl. WA12: New W 3H 77
Burscough Rd. L39: Orm 4D 24
Burscough St. L39: Orm 5C 24
Burton Av. CH45: Wall 2J 85
L35: R'hill 3G 93
Burton Cl. L1: Liv 7K 87 (9F 4)
L35: R'hill 3G 93
WA3: Cul 3B 80
WA8: Wid 5B 114
Burton Grn. CH66: Gt Sut 7F 161
Burtonhead Ct. WA9: St. H 5D 74
Burtonhead Rd. WA9: St. H 4B 74
WA10: St. H 4B 74
Burton Rd. CH64: Lit N 4J 157
WA2: Warr 6D 98
Burton St. L5: Kirk 1H 87
Burtons Way L32: K'by 5A 56
BURTONWOOD 1C 96
Burtonwood Ind. Cen.
WA5: B'wood 7D 76
Burtonwood Rd. WA5: B'wood 3D 96
Burtree Rd. L14: K Ash 1E 90
Burwain Ho. L19: Aig 2H 129
Burwell Av. L37: Form 2H 29
Burwell Cl. L33: K'by 2E 56
Burwell Wlk. L33: K'by 2E 56
Burwen Dr. L9: Walt 7B 54
Bury Rd. PR8: B'dale 5H 11
Busby's Cotts. CH45: New B 6B 66
Bushbys La. L37: Form 1G 29
Bushbys Pk. L37: Form 1G 29
Bushell Cl. CH64: Nest 4K 157
Bushell Ct. CH43: O'ton 4A 106
Bushell Rd. CH64: Nest 4K 157
Bushel's Dr. WA9: Clock F 4G 95
Bushey La. WA11: R'ford 2D 46
Bushey Rd. L4: Walt 4E 68
Bushley Cl. L20: Boot 2H 67
Bush Rd. WA8: Wid 4B 134
Bush Way CH60: Hes 2C 142
Bus. Resource Cen.
L33: Know I 5G 57
Butchers La. WN4: Ash M 3F 63
L39: Augh 6H 33
Bute St. L5: Liv 3A 88 (2H 5)
(not continuous)
Butleigh Rd. L36: Huy 2H 91
Butler Cres. L6: Liv 4D 88 (2P 5)
Butler St. L6: Liv 3D 88 (1P 5)
(not continuous)
Buttercup Cl. CH46: More 5E 84
L22: Water 4F 53
Buttercup Way L9: Walt 2D 68
Butterfield Gdns. L39: Augh 7B 24
Butterfield St. L4: Walt 7B 68
Buttermarket St. WA1: Warr 3B 118
(not continuous)
Buttermere Av. CH43: Noct 2G 105
CH65: Ell P 1A 170
WA2: Warr 4C 98
WA11: St. H 5C 60
WN4: Ash M 7F 51
Buttermere Cl. L31: Mag 3G 43
L33: K'by 1B 56
L37: Form 7H 19
WA6: Frod 3F 167
Buttermere Ct. *CH41: Birk* *3C 106*
(off Penrith St.)
Buttermere Cres. WA2: Warr 4C 98
WA11: R'ford 2F 47
Buttermere Gdns. L23: C'by 3F 53
Buttermere Gro. WA7: Beech 4F 153
Buttermere Rd. L16: Child 6E 90
WN5: Wigan 4K 39
Buttermere St. L8: Liv 1D 108 (10P 5)
Butterton Av. CH49: Upton 2B 104
Butterwick Dr. L12: Crox 3C 70
Button St. L2: Liv 6J 87 (6F 4)
Butts, The WA7: Cas 7H 135
Butts Grn. WA5: W'brk 4E 96
Butts La. PR8: South 3B 12
Buxted Rd. L32: K'by 5E 56
Buxted Wlk. L32: K'by 5E 56
Buxton Cl. WA5: Gt San 7E 96
Buxton La. CH44: Wall 2J 85
Buxton Rd. CH42: R Ferr 6G 107
Bye La. L39: Augh 7E 22
Byerley St. CH44: Wall 5D 86
Byfleet Cl. WN3: Wins 3A 50
Byland Cl. L37: Form 1B 30
WA8: Wid 3E 114
Byles St. L8: Liv 4C 108
Byng Pl. L4: Walt 6F 69
Byng Rd. L4: Walt 6F 69
Byng St. L20: Boot 4H 67
By-Pass, The L23: C'by 1E 52
Byrne Av. CH42: R Ferr 7F 107
Byrne Avenue Recreation Cen. 7F 107
Byrom St. L3: Liv 4K 87 (4G 4)
PR9: South 1B 12
Byron Av. L12: W Der 7J 69
L35: Whis 4F 93
Byron Cl. CH43: Pren 1K 125
L36: Huy 6A 92
L37: Form 6K 19
WA10: St. H 1C 74
WN5: Orr 4H 39
Byron Ct. L25: Wltn 5E 110
WA2: Warr 5C 98
Byron Rd. L23: Blun 1C 52
L31: Lyd 1F 43
Byron St. L19: Gars 4A 130
L20: Boot 1G 67
WA7: Run 1C 152
Byron Ter. L23: Blun 1C 52
Byton Wlk. L33: K'by 1E 56
Bywater Way L10: Faz 6K 55
Byway, The L23: C'by 7E 40

C

CABBAGE HALL 1D 88
Cabes Cl. L14: K Ash 7E 70
Cabin La. L39: Hals 5J 15
PR9: South 4G 9
Cablehouse L2: Liv 4E 4
Cable Rd. CH47: Hoy 1D 102
L35: Whis 2F 93
Cables Retail Pk. L34: Prsct 2D 92
Cable St. L1: Liv 6J 87 (7E 4)
L37: Form 6A 20
PR9: South 1H 11
Cabot Cl. WA5: Old H 6G 97
Cabot Grn. L25: Wltn 3C 110
Cabul Cl. WA2: Warr 1C 118
Cadbury Cl. L12: W Der 4K 69
Caddick Rd. L34: Know 1F 71
Cadmus Wlk. L6: Liv 3B 88 (1L 5)
Cadnam Rd. L25: Gate 3H 111
Cadogan Dr. WN3: Wins 2B 50
Cadogan St. L15: W'tree 7F 89
Cadshaw Cl. WA3: Bchwd 2K 99
Cadwell Rd. L31: Lyd 6D 32
Caecars Cl. WA7: Cas 1G 153
Caernarvon Cl. CH49: Upton 2E 104
WA7: Cas 7H 135
Caernarvon Ct. CH63: Beb 5F 127
CH65: Ell P 2B 170
Caerwys Gro. CH42: Tran 4E 106
Caesars Cl. WA7: Cas 7G 135
Caird St. L6: Liv 4C 88 (2N 5)
Cairn Brae WA12: New W 2G 77
Cairn Ct. WA9: St. H 6K 73
Cairnmore Rd. L18: Moss H 6J 109
Cairns St. L8: Liv 2C 108
Cairo St. L4: Kirk 5A 68
WA1: Warr 3B 118
WA10: St. H 5K 73
Caister Cl. WN8: Skel 3K 37
Caithness Ct. WA7: Run 7D 134
Caithness Dr. CH45: Wall 1C 86
L23: C'by 2F 53
Caithness Gdns. CH43: Pren 7K 105
Caithness Rd. L18: Aller 7K 109
Calcott Rake L30: N'ton 1A 54
(not continuous)
Calday Grange Cl. CH48: W Kir 7F 103
Caldbeck Av. WA2: Warr 5D 98
Caldbeck Cl. WN4: Ash M 1F 63
Caldbeck Gro. WA11: St. H 4E 60
Caldbeck Rd. CH62: Brom 7K 127
Calder Av. CH43: Pren 6K 105
L39: Orm 7B 24
Calder Bank WN5: Orr 5J 39
Calder Cl. L33: K'by 6D 44
WA8: Wid 5H 115
Calder Dr. L18: Moss H 3A 110
L31: Mag 2G 43
L35: R'hill 4H 93
WN2: Platt B 2K 51
Calder Edge L18: Moss H 4A 110
Calderfield Cl. WA4: S Hth 1B 138
Calderfield Rd. L18: Moss H 3B 110
Calder Grange L18: Aller 5C 110
Calderhurst Dr. WA10: Windle 7H 59
Calder Pk. Ct. L18: Moss H 4B 110
Calder Rd. CH63: High B 4D 126
L5: Liv 1B 88
Calders, The L18: Moss H 5A 110
Calderstone Pk.
(Liverpool Botanic Gardens) 5B 110
CALDERSTONES 5A 110
Calderstones Av. L18: Moss H 3C 109
Calderstones Ct. L18: Moss H 4A 110
Calderstones Rd.
L18: Moss H 4K 109
Calder Way CH66: Gt Sut 6E 160
Calderwood Pk. L27: N'ley 2H 111
Caldicott Av. CH62: Brom 3K 145
Caldon Cl. L21: Lith 4G 53
Caldway Dr. L27: N'ley 2H 111
Caldwell Av. WA5: Warr 5K 97
Caldwell Cl. L33: K'by 1D 56
Caldwell Dr. CH49: W'chu 6F 105
Caldwell Rd. L19: Aller 1A 130
WA8: Wid 2C 134
Caldwell's Ga. La. CW9: Ant 7C 140
Caldwell St. WA9: St. H 3F 75
CALDY 2F 123
Caldy Chase Dr. CH48: Caldy 2F 123
Caldy Ct. CH48: W Kir 7D 102
Caldy Dr. CH66: Gt Sut 7F 161
Caldy Gro. WA11: Hay 5J 61
WA11: St. H 1F 75
Caldy Rd. CH45: Wall 2B 86
CH48: Caldy, W Kir 7D 102
L9: Ain 6C 54
Caldy Wood CH48: Caldy 2F 123
Caldywood Dr. L35: Whis 4E 92
Caledonian Cres. L21: Lith 4G 53
Caledonia St. L7: Liv 7B 88 (8K 5)
Calgarth Rd. L36: Huy 2G 91
California Cl. WA5: Gt San 7G 97
California Rd. L13: Liv 7F 69
Callaghan Cl. L5: Liv 2K 87
Callander Rd. L6: Liv 4F 89
CALLANDS 5H 97
Callands Rd. WA5: Call 5G 97
Callard Cl. L27: N'ley 2G 111
Callestock Cl. L11: Crox 1A 70
Callington Cl. L14: K Ash 1E 90
Callon Av. WA11: St. H 1G 75
Callow Rd. L15: W'tree 1F 109
Calmet Cl. L5: Liv 1A 88
Calmington La. WA7: Nort 5D 136
Calne Cl. CH61: Irby 2B 124
Calstock Cl. WA5: Penk 5C 116
Calthorpe St. L19: Gars 3K 129
Calthorpe Way CH43: Noct 2H 105
Calton Cl. WN3: Wigan 1B 50
Calvados Cl. L17: Aig 7E 108
Calveley Av. CH62: East 6B 146
Calveley Cl. CH43: O'ton 5K 105
Calveley Gro. L26: Halew 3A 132
Calverhall Way WN4: Ash M 2E 62
Calverley Cl. WA7: Brook 5K 153
Calver Rd. WA2: Win 3K 97
Calvers WA7: Halt 1G 153
Camberley Cl. PR8: B'dale 3E 10
Camberley Dr. L25: Hunts X 1G 131
Camberwell Pk. Rd.
WA8: Wid 4F 115
Camborne Av. L25: Wltn 7G 111
Camborne Cl. WA7: Brook 4A 154
Camborne Rd. WA5: B'wood 1D 96
Cambourne Av. WA11: St. H 6F 61
Cambrai Av. WA4: Warr 6C 118
Cambrian Cl. CH46: More 1A 104
CH66: Lit Sut 5C 160
Cambrian Ct. PR9: South 7K 7
Cambrian Cres. WN3: Wins 2A 50
Cambrian Rd. CH46: More 1A 104
Cambrian Way L25: Wltn 5F 111
Cambria St. Nth. L6: Liv 4D 88 (2P 5)
Cambria St. Sth. L6: Liv 4D 88 (2P 5)
Cambridge Arc. PR8: South 1H 11
Cambridge Av. L21: Lith 5H 53
L23: C'by 7D 40
PR9: Chu 5B 8
Cambridge Cl. WA4: S Hth 1B 138

Cambridge Ct.—Causeway La.

Cambridge Ct. CH65: Ell P . . . 6A 162
L7: Liv . . . 6B 88 (7K 5)
(not continuous)
PR9: Chu . . . 5B 8
Cambridge Dr. L23: C'by . . . 7C 40
L26: Halew . . . 1K 131
Cambridge Gdns. PR9: Chu . . . 5B 8
WA4: App . . . 3C 138
WA6: Hel . . . 7K 165
Cambridge Rd. CH42: Tran . . . 6B 106
CH45: New B . . . 7B 66
CH62: Brom . . . 2A 146
CH65: Ell P . . . 6A 162
L9: Ain . . . 5D 54
L20: Boot . . . 4K 67
L21: Sea . . . 5F 53
L22: Water . . . 6E 52
L23: C'by . . . 7C 40
L37: Form . . . 2G 29
(not continuous)
PR9: Chu, South . . . 6A 8
WA10: St. H . . . 2A 74
WN5: Orr . . . 3H 39
WN8: Skel . . . 2E 36
Cambridge St. L7: Liv . . . 7B 88
(not continuous)
L15: W'tree . . . 7F 89
(not continuous)
L34: Prsct . . . 1D 92
WA7: Run . . . 7E 134
WA8: Wid . . . 2D 134
Cambridge Walks *PR8: South* . . . *1H 11*
(off Eastbank St.)
Camdale Cl. L28: Stock V . . . 7F 71
Camden Ct. WA7: Nort . . . 1B 154
Camden Pl. CH41: Birk . . . 2D 106
Camden Rd. CH65: Ell P . . . 6J 161
Camden St. CH41: Birk . . . 1E 106
L3: Liv . . . 5A 88 (4H 5)
Camelford Rd. L11: Crox . . . 1A 70
Camelia Ct. L17: Aig . . . 6C 108
Camellia Gdns. WA9: Bold . . . 7K 75
Camelot Cl. WA12: New W . . . 2D 76
Camelot Ter. *L20: Boot* . . . *2H 67*
(off Tennyson St.)
Camelot Way WA7: Cas . . . 2J 153
Cameo Cl. L6: Liv . . . 3D 88
Cameron Av. WA7: Run . . . 2A 152
Cameron Ct. WA2: Win . . . 3A 98
Cameron Rd. CH46: Leas . . . 4F 85
WA8: Wid . . . 1C 134
Cameron St. L7: Liv . . . 5E 88
Cammell Ct. CH43: C'ton . . . 2B 106
Campania St. L19: Gars . . . 5A 130
Campbell Av. WA7: Run . . . 2C 152
Campbell Cres. L33: K'by . . . 6B 44
WA5: Gt San . . . 2D 116
Campbell Dr. L14: B Grn . . . 4C 90
Campbell Sq. L1: Liv . . . 8F 4
Campbell St. L1: Liv . . . 7K 87 (8F 4)
L20: Boot . . . 3G 67
WA10: St. H . . . 2A 74
Campbeltown Rd. CH41: Tran . . . 3F 107
Camperdown St. CH41: Birk . . . 2F 107
Camphill Rd. L25: Wltn . . . 1E 130
Campion Cl. WA3: Bchwd . . . 3J 99
WA11: St. H . . . 6D 60
Campion Gro. WN4: Ash M . . . 1D 62
Campion Way L36: Huy . . . 1K 111
Camp Rd. L25: Wltn . . . 7F 111
WA5: Old H . . . 6G 97
WN4: Gars . . . 2C 62
Campsey Ash WA8: Wid . . . 4B 114
Camrose Cl. WA7: Run . . . 4E 152
Camsley La. WA13: Lymm . . . 5C 120
Cam St. L25: Wltn . . . 6D 110
Canada Blvd. L3: Liv . . . 6H 87 (6C 4)
Canada Cl. WA2: Fearn . . . 5G 99
Canal Bank L31: Lyd . . . 4E 32
WA13: Lymm . . . 5H 121
(Mardale Cres.)
WA13: Lymm . . . 5E 120
(Statham Av.)
Canal Bank Cotts. L31: Lyd . . . 4E 32
Canal Bri. Ent. Cen.
CH65: Ell P . . . 5B 162
Canal Reach WA7: Wind H . . . 7A 136
Canal Side WA4: Grap . . . 7J 119
WA4: Moore . . . 4G 137
Canalside CH65: Ell P . . . 5B 162
WA7: West P . . . 3K 151
Canalside Gro. L5: Liv . . . 2J 87
Canalside Ind. Est. CH65: Ell P . . . 4B 162
Canal St. L20: Boot . . . 4H 67
WA7: Run . . . 6D 134
WA10: St. H . . . 4B 74
WA12: New W . . . 3D 76
Canal Vw. L31: Mell . . . 2J 55
WA13: Lymm . . . 5E 120
Canal Vw. Ct. L21: Lith . . . 3G 53
Canberra Av. WA2: Warr . . . 4D 98
WA9: St. H . . . 7A 74
Canberra La. L11: Crox . . . 1A 70
Canberra Rd. WN5: Wigan . . . 3K 39
Canberra Sq. WA2: Warr . . . 5D 98
Candia Towers L5: Liv . . . 1A 88
Candleston Cl. WA5: Call . . . 6J 97
Canford Cl. WA5: Gt San . . . 2G 117
Cannell Ct. CH64: Will . . . 3G 159
WA7: Pal F . . . 4J 153
Cannell St. WA5: Warr . . . 4H 117
Canning Pl. L1: Liv . . . 6J 87 (8E 4)
Canning Rd. PR9: South . . . 1C 12
Canning St. CH41: Birk . . . 1E 106
L8: Liv . . . 7B 88 (9K 5)
L22: Water . . . 4D 52
Cannington Rd. WA9: St. H . . . 4D 74
Canniswood Rd. WA11: Hay . . . 7J 61
Cann La. Nth. WA4: App . . . 4F 139
Cann La. Sth. WA4: App . . . 5E 138
Cannock Cl. CH66: Gt Sut . . . 4G 169
Cannock Grn. L31: Mag . . . 3D 42
Cannonbury Cl. WA7: Halt . . . 2J 153
Cannon Hill CH43: C'ton . . . 2B 106
Cannon Mt. CH43: C'ton . . . 2B 106
Cannon St. CH65: Ell P . . . 6J 161
WA9: Clock F . . . 4E 94
Canon Rd. L6: Liv . . . 7E 68
Canons Rd. WA5: Gt San . . . 2H 117
Canon St. WA7: Run . . . 6C 134
Canon Wilson Cl. WA11: Hay . . . 7B 62
Canova Cl. *L27: N'ley* . . . *4K 111*
(off Victoria Falls Rd.)
Canrow La. L34: Know . . . 1H 71
Cansfield Gro. WN4: Ash M . . . 1E 62
Cansfield St. WA10: St. H . . . 2C 74
Canterbury Av. L22: Water . . . 2D 52
Canterbury Cl. CH66: Gt Sut . . . 4G 169
L10: Ain . . . 3G 55
L34: Prsct . . . 7E 72
L37: Form . . . 4K 19
PR8: B'dale . . . 4F 11
Canterbury Pk. L18: Aller . . . 1A 130
Canterbury Rd. CH42: R Ferr . . . 7G 107
CH44: Wall . . . 4C 86
WA8: Wid . . . 2J 133
Canterbury St. L3: Liv . . . 4A 88 (3J 5)
L19: Gars . . . 5A 130
WA4: Warr . . . 4C 118
WA10: St. H . . . 1A 74
Canterbury Way L3: Liv . . . 4A 88 (3K 5)
L30: N'ton . . . 1B 54
Canter Cl. L9: Ain . . . 5F 55
Cantley Cl. WA7: Beech . . . 4F 153
Cantlow Fold PR8: Ains . . . 5A 14
Cantsfield St. L7: Liv . . . 1E 108
Canvey Cl. L15: W'tree . . . 1K 109
Capella Cl. L17: Aig . . . 1G 129
CAPENHURST . . . 4D 168
Capenhurst Av. WA2: Fearn . . . 5G 99
Capenhurst Gdns.
CH66: Gt Sut . . . 3F 169
Capenhurst La. CH1: Cap . . . 5A 168
CH65: Whit . . . 1H 169
CH66: Gt Sut . . . 3F 169
Capenhurst Station (Rail) . . . 3E 168
Capenhurst Technology Pk.
CH1: Cap . . . 3D 168
Cape Rd. L9: Ain . . . 7E 54
Capesthorne Cl. WA8: Wid . . . 1A 134
Capesthorne Rd. WA2: Warr . . . 6D 98
Capilano Pk. L39: Augh . . . 3A 34
Capital Ga. L3: Liv . . . 4K 5
Capitol Trad. Pk. L33: Know I . . . 4G 57
Caplin Cl. L33: K'by . . . 6C 44
Capper Gro. L36: Huy . . . 4J 91
Capricorn Cres. L14: K Ash . . . 2D 90
Capricorn Way L20: Boot . . . 2H 67
Capstick Cres. L25: Gate . . . 2F 111
Captains Cl. L30: Boot . . . 5K 53
Captains Grn. L30: Boot . . . 5K 53
Captains La. L30: Boot . . . 5A 54
WN4: Ash M . . . 2G 63
(not continuous)
Caradoc Rd. L21: Sea . . . 7G 53
Caraway Cl. L23: Thorn . . . 7H 41
Caraway Gro. WA10: St. H . . . 2K 73
Carbis Cl. L10: Faz . . . 7J 55
Carden Cl. L4: Kirk . . . 7A 68
WA3: Bchwd . . . 3K 99
Cardeston Cl. WA7: Sut W . . . 7H 153
Cardiff Cl. CH66: Gt Sut . . . 4G 169
Cardiff St. WN8: Skel . . . 2D 36
Cardigan Av. CH41: Birk . . . 2D 106
Cardigan Cl. WA5: Call . . . 5H 97
WA10: St. H . . . 4B 74
Cardigan Rd. CH45: New B . . . 7B 66
PR8: B'dale . . . 7F 11
Cardigan St. L15: W'tree . . . 7F 89
Cardigan Way L6: Liv . . . 3D 88
L30: N'ton . . . 1D 54
Cardinal Heenan Leisure Cen. . . . 2B 90
Cardus Cl. CH46: More . . . 7K 83
Cardwell Rd. L19: Gars . . . 3A 130
Cardwell St. L7: Liv . . . 7C 88 (8N 5)
Carey Av. CH63: High B . . . 3D 126
Carey Cl. WN3: Wins . . . 2B 50
Carey St. WA8: Wid . . . 7D 114
Carfax Rd. L33: K'by . . . 1E 56
Carfield WN8: Skel . . . 5A 38
Cargill Gro. CH42: R Ferr . . . 1H 127
Carham Rd. CH47: Hoy . . . 2E 102
Carina Ct. L19: Aig . . . 2H 129
Carisbrooke Cl. CH48: Caldy . . . 1E 122
Carisbrooke Dr. PR9: Chu . . . 6B 8
Carisbrooke Pl. L4: Kirk . . . 5B 68
Carisbrooke Rd. L20: Boot . . . 4A 68
Carkington Rd. L25: Wltn . . . 7G 111
Carlake Gro. L9: Ain . . . 3E 68
Carland Cl. L10: Faz . . . 7K 55
Carlaw Rd. CH42: Tran . . . 6A 106
Carleen Cl. L17: Aig . . . 6D 108
Carlett Blvd. CH62: East . . . 5B 146
Carlett Pk. CH62: East . . . 4B 146
Carley Wlk. L24: Speke . . . 7J 131
Carlile Way L33: K'by . . . 6D 44
Carlingford Cl.
L8: Liv . . . 1C 108 (10N 5)
Carlingford Rd. WA4: S Hth . . . 1B 138
Carlisle Av. L30: N'ton . . . 4B 54
Carlisle Cl. CH43: O'ton . . . 3C 106
L4: Walt . . . 6F 69
Carlisle M. CH43: O'ton . . . 3C 106
Carlisle Rd. PR8: B'dale . . . 6G 11
Carlisle St. WA4: S Hth . . . 1C 138
Carlis Rd. L32: K'by . . . 5D 56
Carlow Cl. L24: Hale . . . 7D 132
Carlow St. WA10: St. H . . . 5K 73
Carlsruhe Ct. L8: Liv . . . 3C 108
Carl's Way L33: K'by . . . 6E 44
Carlton Av. L18: Moss H . . . 3J 109
WA7: Run . . . 7F 135
WN8: Uph . . . 4C 38
Carlton Bingo Club . . . 7B 54
Carlton Cl. CH64: Park . . . 1G 157
WN4: Ash M . . . 1E 62
Carlton Cres. CH66: Ell P . . . 3H 161
Carlton La. CH47: Meols . . . 7E 82
L13: Liv . . . 3J 89
Carlton Mt. CH42: Tran . . . 5E 106
Carlton Rd. CH42: Tran . . . 4C 106
CH45: New B . . . 6B 66
CH63: Beb . . . 5H 127
PR8: Ains . . . 3C 14
WA13: Lymm . . . 3K 121
Carlton St. L3: Liv . . . 3H 87 (1B 4)
L34: Prsct . . . 7E 72
WA4: S Hth . . . 1C 138
WA8: Wid . . . 1C 134
WA10: St. H . . . 3A 74
Carlton Ter. CH47: Meols . . . 7E 82
L23: C'by . . . 1D 52
Carlton Way WA3: G'brk . . . 2K 101
Carlyle Cres. CH66: Gt Sut . . . 7G 161
Carlyon Way L26: Halew . . . 7J 111
Carmarthen Cl. WA5: Call . . . 5H 97
Carmarthen Cres. L8: Liv . . . 2K 107
Carmel Cl. CH45: New B . . . 6B 66
L39: Augh . . . 1B 34
WA5: Call . . . 5J 97
Carmel Ct. WA8: Wid . . . 4D 114
Carmelite Cres. WA10: Eccl . . . 1G 73
Carmichael Av. CH49: Grea . . . 6B 104
Carnaby Cl. L36: Huy . . . 7A 92
Carnarvon Ct. L9: Walt . . . 3B 68
Carnarvon Rd. L9: Walt . . . 3B 68
PR8: B'dale . . . 7F 11
Carnarvon St. WA9: St. H . . . 7K 73
Carnatic Cl. L18: Moss H . . . 5G 109
Carnatic Rd. L18: Moss H . . . 5G 109
Carnation Rd. L9: Walt . . . 2D 68
Carneghie Ct. PR8: B'dale . . . 4F 11
Carnegie Av. L23: C'by . . . 2D 52
Carnegie Cres. WA9: St. H . . . 6G 75
Carnegie Dr. WN4: Ash M . . . 7E 50
Carnegie Rd. L13: Liv . . . 3G 89
Carnegie Wlk. WA9: St. H . . . 6H 75
Carnforth Av. L32: K'by . . . 4D 56
Carnforth Cl. CH41: Birk . . . 3C 106
L12: W Der . . . 5K 69
Carnforth Rd. L18: Moss H . . . 6A 110
Carno St. L15: W'tree . . . 7G 89
Carnoustie Cl. CH46: More . . . 6K 83
L12: W Der . . . 1D 90
PR8: B'dale . . . 4F 11
Carnoustie Gro. WA11: Hay . . . 1K 75
Carnoustie Ho. *WA3: Ris* . . . *1K 99*
(off Kelvin Clo.)
Carnsdale Rd. CH46: More . . . 7D 84
Carol Dr. CH60: Hes . . . 2G 143
Carole Cl. WA9: Sut L . . . 1G 95
Carolina Rd. WA5: Gt San . . . 1F 117
Carolina St. L20: Boot . . . 3H 67
Caroline Pl. CH43: O'ton . . . 3B 106
Caroline St. WA8: Wid . . . 2D 134
Carol St. WA4: Warr . . . 4D 118
Caronia St. L19: Gars . . . 5A 130
Carpathia St. L19: Gars . . . 5A 130
Carpenter Gro. WA2: P'gate . . . 6G 99
Carpenter's La. CH48: W Kir . . . 6D 102
Carpenters Row L1: Liv . . . 7J 87 (9E 4)
Carraway Rd. L11: Crox . . . 7K 55
Carr Bri. Rd. CH49: W'chu . . . 4F 105
Carr Cl. L11: N Grn. . . . 4K 69
Carr Cft. L21: Ford . . . 2H 53
CARR CROSS . . . 1F 17
Carrfield Av. L23: C'by . . . 2G 53
Carr Fld. Wlk. L11: N Grn. . . . 3K 69
Carr Ga. CH46: More . . . 1K 103
Carr Hey CH46: More . . . 7K 83
Carr Hey Cl. CH49: W'chu . . . 6G 105
Carr Ho. La. CH46: More . . . 1K 103
L38: Ince B . . . 7E 30
CARR HOUSES . . . 7F 31
Carriage Cl. L24: Hale . . . 1D 150
Carriage Dr. WA6: Frod . . . 5C 166
Carrick Ct. L23: C'by . . . 2G 53
Carrick Dr. CH65: Whit . . . 2K 169
Carrickmore Av. L18: Moss H . . . 6J 109
Carrington Cl. WA3: Bchwd . . . 4J 99
Carrington Rd. CH45: Wall . . . 1B 86
Carrington St. CH41: Birk . . . 7A 86
Carr La. CH46: More . . . 6K 83
CH47: Hoy . . . 2D 102
CH47: Meols . . . 6J 83
CH47: W Kir . . . 3F 103
CH48: W Kir . . . 3F 103
L11: N Grn. . . . 4H 69
L24: Hale . . . 7D 132
L31: Lyd . . . 6B 32
L34: Prsct . . . 2B 92
L36: Roby . . . 5G 91
PR8: Ains . . . 2F 15
(not continuous)
WA8: Hale B . . . 4E 132
WN3: Wigan . . . 1E 50
Carr La. E. L11: N Grn. . . . 4K 69
Carr La. Ind. Est. CH47: Hoy . . . 2E 102
Carr Mdw. Hey L30: N'ton . . . 3J 53
CARR MILL . . . 5D 60
Carr Mill Cres. WN5: Bil . . . 1G 61
Carr Mill Rd. WA11: St. H . . . 6E 60
WN5: Bil . . . 1F 61
(not continuous)
Carr Moss La. L39: Hals . . . 5G 15
Carrock Rd. CH62: Brom . . . 7A 128
Carroll Cres. L39: Orm . . . 3D 24
Carrow Cl. CH46: More . . . 1K 103
Carr Rd. L20: Boot . . . 6K 53
Carr's Cres. L37: Form . . . 2J 29
Carr's Cres. W. L37: Form . . . 2H 29
Carr Side La. L29: Thorn . . . 1G 41
Carrs Ter. L35: Whis . . . 4D 92
Carr St. WA10: St. H . . . 1H 73
Carruthers St. L3: Liv . . . 4J 87 (2D 4)
Carrville Way L12: Crox . . . 4E 70
Carrwood Cl. WA11: Hay . . . 7J 61
Carrwood Pk. PR8: South . . . 5H 11
Carsdale Rd. L18: Moss H . . . 3J 109
Carsgoe Rd. CH47: Hoy . . . 2E 102
Carsington Rd. L11: N Grn. . . . 4J 69
Carstairs Rd. L6: Liv . . . 3E 88
Carsthorne Rd. CH47: Hoy . . . 2E 102
Cartbridge La. L26: Halew . . . 7K 111
Carter Av. WA11: R'ford . . . 7G 47
Carters, The CH49: Grea . . . 4A 104
L30: N'ton . . . 1C 54
Carter St. L8: Liv . . . 1B 108 (10L 5)
Carterton Rd. CH47: Hoy . . . 2E 102
Cartier Cl. WA5: Old H . . . 7G 97
Cartmel Av. L31: Mag . . . 2G 43
WA2: Warr . . . 4C 98
Cartmel Cl. CH41: Birk . . . 3C 106
PR8: South . . . 5B 12
Cartmel Dr. CH46: More . . . 1C 104
CH66: Gt Sut . . . 2H 169
L12: W Der . . . 5A 70
L35: R'hill . . . 3G 93
L37: Form . . . 1B 30
Cartmell Av. WA10: St. H . . . 6A 60
Cartmell Cl. WA7: Run . . . 4D 152
Cartmel Rd. L36: Huy . . . 2G 91
Cartmel Ter. L11: N Grn. . . . 3K 69
Cartmel Way L36: Huy . . . 3G 91
Cartridge La. WA4: Grap . . . 3K 139
Cartwright Cl. WA11: R'ford . . . 6F 47
Cartwright Ct. WA11: R'ford . . . 5F 47
Cartwrights Farm Rd.
L24: Speke . . . 5E 130
Cartwright St. WA5: Warr . . . 2J 117
WA7: Run . . . 7E 134
Carver St. L3: Liv . . . 4B 88 (3K 5)
Caryl Gro. L8: Liv . . . 4A 108
Caryl St. L8: Liv . . . 3A 108
(Park St.)
L8: Liv . . . 2K 107
(Stanhope St.)
L8: Liv . . . 3K 107
(Warwick St.)
Cascade Rd. L24: Speke . . . 3G 131
Case Gro. L35: Prsct . . . 2E 92
Case Rd. WA11: Hay . . . 7B 62
Cases St. L1: Liv . . . 6K 87 (6G 4)
Cashel Rd. CH41: Birk . . . 5B 86
Caspian Pl. L20: Boot . . . 3J 67
Caspian Rd. L4: Walt . . . 4E 68
Cassia Cl. L9: Walt . . . 2D 68
Cassino Rd. L36: Huy . . . 4H 91
Cassio St. L20: Boot . . . 4A 68
Cassley Rd. L24: Speke . . . 6A 132
Cassville Rd. L18: Moss H . . . 2J 109
Castell Gro. WA10: St. H . . . 3B 74
Castle Av. WA9: St. H . . . 3G 75
Castle Cl. CH46: Leas . . . 4E 84
Castle Dr. CH60: Hes . . . 2D 142
CH65: Whit . . . 1J 169
L37: Form . . . 2K 29
Castlefield Cl. L12: W Der . . . 7J 69
Castlefield Rd. L12: W Der . . . 7J 69
CASTLEFIELDS . . . 7J 135
Castlefields CH46: Leas . . . 3D 84
Castlefields Av. E. WA7: Cas . . . 1J 153
Castlefields Av. Nth.
WA7: Cas . . . 7G 135
Castlefields Av. Sth.
WA7: Cas . . . 1H 153
Castleford Ri. CH46: Leas . . . 4C 84
Castleford St. L15: W'tree . . . 1J 109
Castlegate Gro. L12: W Der . . . 7J 69
Castlegrange Cl. CH46: Leas . . . 3C 84
Castle Grn. WA5: W'brk . . . 5F 97
Castleheath Cl. CH46: Leas . . . 4C 84
Castlehey WN8: Skel . . . 5A 38
Castle Hill L2: Liv . . . 6D 4
WA12: New W . . . 2J 77
Castle Keep L12: W Der . . . 7K 69
Castle La. L12: W Der . . . 7K 69
L40: Lath, Westh . . . 4H 25
Castlemere Cl. WN3: Wins . . . 3B 50
Castle Mt. CH60: Hes . . . 2D 142
Castle Pk. . . . 4C 166
Castle Pk. Arts Cen. . . . 3C 166
Castle Ri. WA7: Run . . . 7F 135
Castle Rd. CH45: Wall . . . 1A 86
WA7: Halt . . . 2H 153
Castlesite Rd. L12: W Der . . . 7K 69
Castle St. CH41: Birk . . . 2F 107
L2: Liv . . . 6J 87 (6D 4)
L25: Wltn . . . 6D 110
PR9: South . . . 7H 7
WA8: Wid . . . 7F 115
Castleton Dr. L30: N'ton . . . 1D 54
Castleton Way WN3: Wins . . . 2A 50
Castletown Cl. L16: Child . . . 7C 90
Castleview Rd. L12: W Der . . . 7K 69
Castle Wlk. PR8: South . . . 2G 11
Castleway Nth. CH46: Leas . . . 3E 84
Castleway Sth. CH46: Leas . . . 4E 84
Castlewell L35: Whis . . . 3F 93
Castlewood Rd. L6: Liv . . . 2D 88
Castner Av. WA7: West P . . . 3A 152
Castor St. L6: Liv . . . 2D 88
Catalyst Mus., The . . . 4C 134
Catalyst Trade Pk. WA8: Wid . . . 3C 134
Catchdale Moss La.
WA10: Eccl . . . 2E 72
Catford Cl. WA8: Wid . . . 6J 113
Catford Grn. L24: Speke . . . 6K 131
Catfoss Cl. WA2: P'gate . . . 6E 98
Catharine's La. L39: Bic . . . 1D 34
Catharine St. L8: Liv . . . 1B 108 (10K 5)
Cathcart St. CH41: Birk . . . 1D 106
Cathedral Cl. L1: Liv . . . 1A 108 (10J 5)
Cathedral Ct. L8: Liv . . . 9K 5
Cathedral Ga. L1: Liv . . . 7A 88 (9J 5)
Cathedral Rd. L6: Liv . . . 1E 88
Cathedral Wlk. L3: Liv . . . 6A 88 (7J 5)
Catherine Ct. *L21: Lith* . . . *7H 53*
(off Linacre Rd.)
Catherine St. CH41: Birk . . . 2D 106
L21: Lith . . . 7H 53
WA5: Warr . . . 1K 117
(not continuous)
WA8: Wid . . . 2C 134
Catherine Way WA11: Hay . . . 7H 61
WA12: New W . . . 4F 77
Catkin Rd. L26: Halew . . . 6H 111
Caton Cl. PR9: Marsh . . . 3B 8
Catonfield Rd. L18: Moss H . . . 3B 110
Cat Tail La. PR8: South . . . 7G 13
Cattan Grn. L37: Form . . . 7B 20
Catterall Av. WA2: Warr . . . 5D 98
WA9: Sut L . . . 1F 95
Catterick Cl. L26: Halew . . . 1K 131
Catterick Fold PR8: South . . . 5B 12
Catton Hall Shooting Ground . . . 5K 167
Caulfield Dr. CH49: Grea . . . 5C 104
Caunce Av. PR9: Banks . . . 1J 9
WA3: Golb . . . 6K 63
WA11: Hay . . . 7K 61
WA12: New W . . . 5G 77
Caunce's Rd. PR9: South . . . 4K 13
Causeway, The CH62: Port S . . . 4H 127
(not continuous)
L12: W Der . . . 3B 90
PR9: Cros . . . 2E 8
Causeway Av. WA4: Warr . . . 5C 118
Causeway Cl. CH62: Port S . . . 3H 127
Causeway Ho. CH46: Leas . . . 3C 84
Causeway La. L37: Gt Alt . . . 2G 31

Chester New Rd. WA4: H Walt 3J 137
Chester Rd. CH1: Back 5H 169
CH60: Hes 3F 143
CH64: Nest 4J 157
CH65: Whit 7J 161
CH66: Chil T, Gt Sut, Hoot, Lit Sut 2C 160
CH66: Whit 4J 169
L6: Liv 2F 89
L36: Huy 3A 92
PR9: South 7B 8
WA4: Dares 7G 137
(Daresbury La., not continuous)
WA4: Dares 3E 154
(Red Brow La.)
WA4: H Walt, Walt, Warr 6A 118
WA4: S Hth 7E 118
WA6: Dun H 7C 172
WA6: Frod, Hel 3G 173
WA7: Sut W, Pres B 1H 167
Chester Row WA12: New W 6H 77
Chester St. CH41: Birk 3F 107
CH44: Wall 4A 86
Chester St. L8: Liv 1A 108
L34: Prsct 1D 92
WA2: Warr 2B 118
WA8: Wid 7D 114
Chesterton Dr. WA2: Win 2A 98
Chesterton St. L19: Gars 5A 130
Chester Wlk. L36: Huy 3A 92
Chestnut Av. CH66: Gt Sut 3H 169
L23: C'by 6F 41
L36: Huy 7H 91
WA5: Gt San 2D 116
WA8: Wid 6D 114
WA11: Hay 1H 75
Chestnut Cl. CH49: Grea 7A 104
L35: Whis 3E 92
L39: Hals 1E 22
Chestnut Ct. L20: Boot 2H 67
L39: Orm 4D 24
PR9: South 7J 7
WA8: Wid 7K 113
Chestnut Grange L39: Orm 7B 24
Chestnut Gro. CH42: Tran 4D 106
CH62: Brom 2J 145
L15: W'tree 7H 89
L20: Boot 1H 67
(not continuous)
WA11: St. H 6F 61
WN4: Ash M 1H 63
Chestnut Ho. L20: Boot 2H 67
WA4: App 2E 138
Chestnut La. WA6: Frod 7A 166
Chestnut Rd. L9: Walt 3D 68
Chestnut St. PR8: South 4J 11
Chestnut Wlk. L31: Mell 1J 55
Chestnut Way L37: Form 2G 29
Cheswood Cl. L35: Whis 5E 92
Cheswood Ct. *CH49: W'chu 7E 104*
(off Childwall Grn.)
Chetham Ct. WA2: Win 4A 98
Chetton Dr. WA7: Murd 3B 154
Chetwode Av. WN4: Ash M 4F 63
Chetwood Av. L23: C'by 7F 41
Chetwood Cl. WA12: New W 1F 77
Chetwood Dr. WA8: Wid 3B 114
Chetwynd Cl. CH43: O'ton 4K 105
Chetwynd Rd. CH43: O'ton 3A 106
Chetwynd St. L17: Aig 5D 108
Chevasse Wlk. L25: Wltn 5G 111
Cheverton Cl. CH49: W'chu 5F 105
Chevin Rd. L9: Walt 1C 68
Cheviot Av. WA2: Warr 4A 98
WA9: St. H 3H 75
Cheviot Cl. CH42: Tran 7D 106
CH66: Lit Sut 5C 160
WN3: Wins 2A 50
Cheviot Rd. CH42: Tran 7C 106
L7: Liv 5G 89
Cheviot Way L33: K'by 6D 44
Cheyne Cl. L23: Blun 2A 52
Cheyne Gdns. L19: Aig 1H 129
Cheyne Wlk. WA9: St. H 1B 94
Chichester Cl. L15: W'tree 7F 89
WA4: Grap 2G 139
WA7: Murd 4B 154
Chidden Cl. CH49: Grea 5A 104
Chidlow Cl. WA8: Wid 4C 134
Chigwell Cl. L12: Crox 3C 70
Chilcott Rd. L14: K Ash 4A 90
Childer Cres. CH66: Lit Sut 4D 160
Childer Gdns. CH66: Lit Sut 4D 160
Childers St. L13: Liv 4H 89
CHILDER THORNTON 3C 160
CHILDWALL 1C 110
Childwall Abbey Rd. L16: Child 1B 110
Childwall Av. CH46: More 1B 104
L15: W'tree 1E 108
Childwall Bank Rd. L16: Child 1B 110
Childwall Cl. CH46: More 1B 104
Childwall Ct. CH66: Ell P 3H 161
Childwall Cres. L16: Child 1B 110
Childwall Fiveways L15: W'tree 1A 110
Childwall Gdns. CH66: Ell P 3H 161
Childwall Grn. CH49: W'chu 6E 104
Childwall La. L14: B Grn 5E 90
L25: Child 2D 110
Childwall Mt. Rd. L16: Child 1B 110
Childwall Pk. Av. L16: Child 2B 110
Childwall Priory Rd. L16: Child 1A 110
Childwall Rd. CH66: Ell P 3H 161
L15: W'tree 1J 109
Childwall Valley Rd. L16: Child 1B 110
L25: Gate 1B 110
L27: N'ley 2F 111
Chilham St. WN5: Orr 5J 39
Chilhem Cl. L8: Liv 4B 108
Chilington Av. WA8: Wid 1K 133
Chillerton Rd. L12: W Der 6B 70
Chillingham St. L8: Liv 4C 108
Chiltern Cl. L12: Crox 4D 70
L32: K'by 1A 56
WN4: Ash M 3G 63
Chiltern Cres. WA2: Warr 4A 98
Chiltern Dr. L32: K'by 1A 56
WN3: Wins 1A 50
Chiltern Pl. WA2: Warr 4A 98
Chiltern Rd. CH42: Tran 7C 106
PR8: Ains 3A 14
Chiltern Rd. WA2: Warr 4A 98
WA3: Cul 2A 80
WA9: St. H 3H 75
Chilton Cl. L31: Mag 3F 43
Chilton Ct. L31: Mag 3F 43
Chilton Dr. CH66: Gt Sut 2G 169
Chilton M. L31: Mag 3F 43
Chilwell Cl. WA8: Wid 4K 113
Chimes Rd. WN4: Ash M 6D 50
China Farm La. CH48: W Kir 4G 103
China La. WA4: Warr 6C 118
Chindit Cl. L37: Form 1H 29
Chippenham Av. CH49: Grea 4A 104
Chippindall Cl. WA5: Gt San 3G 117
Chipping Av. PR8: Ains 4A 14
Chirkdale St. L4: Kirk 5A 68
Chirk Gdns. CH65: Ell P 1B 170
Chirk Way CH46: More 1D 104
Chirton Cl. WA11: Hay 6B 62
Chisenhale St. L3: Liv 3J 87 (1D 4)
Chisledon Cl. WA11: Hay 6B 62
Chislehurst Av. L25: Gate 2E 110
Chislet Ct. WA8: Wid 4A 114
Chisnall Av. WA10: St. H 2J 73
Chiswell St. L7: Liv 5E 88
Chiswick Cl. WA7: Murd 3B 154
Chiswick Gdns. WA4: App 3F 139
Cholmley Cl. WA12: New W 4J 77
Cholmondeley Rd. CH48: W Kir 6D 102
CH65: Gt Sut 7H 161
WA7: Clftn 6F 153
Cholmondeley St. WA8: Wid 5C 134
Cholsey Cl. CH49: Upton 4D 104
Chorley Cl. PR9: Banks 2G 9
Chorley Rd. L34: Prsct 1B 92
Chorley's La. WA8: Wid 5F 115
Chorley St. WA2: Warr 2C 118
(Chester St.)
WA2: Warr 2B 118
(Norman St.)
WA10: St. H 2B 74
Chorley Way CH63: Spit 1G 145
Chorlton Cl. L16: Child 7D 90
WA7: Wind H 1B 154
Chorlton Gro. CH45: Wall 2H 85
Chorlton La. CH2: Chor B 5K 169
Christchurch Rd. CH43: O'ton 4B 106
Christian St. L3: Liv 4K 87 (3G 4)
Christie Cl. CH66: Hoot 1C 160
Christie St. WA8: Wid 7F 115
Christleton Cl. CH43: O'ton 6H 105
Christleton Ct. WA7: Mnr P 5A 136
Christleton Dr. CH66: Ell P 5G 161
Christmas St. L20: Kirk 5K 67
Christopher Cl. L16: Child 7B 90
L35: R'hill 5H 93
Christopher Dr. CH62: East 5C 146
Christophers Cl. CH61: Pens 5E 124
Christopher St. L4: Walt 6B 68
Christopher Taylor Ho.
L31: Mag 5F 43
Christopher Way L16: Child 7B 90
Christowe Wlk. L11: Crox 1A 70
Chrisward Cl. L7: Liv 6E 88
Chromolyte Ind. Est. PR8: South 3H 11
Chudleigh Cl. L26: Halew 7J 111
Chudleigh Rd. L13: Liv 4G 89
Chung Hok Ho. L1: Liv 10H 5
Church All. L1: Liv 6K 87 (7F 4)
Church Av. L9: Ain 6D 54
Church Cl. CH44: Wall 3D 86
L37: Form 7A 20
PR9: South 7C 8
Church Cl. Ct. L37: Form 7A 20
Church Cotts. L25: Gate 3G 111
Church Ct. CH49: Upton 2C 104
Church Cres. CH44: Wall 5E 86
Churchdown Cl. L14: K Ash 3D 90
Churchdown Gro. L14: K Ash 3C 90
Churchdown Rd. L14: K Ash 3C 90
Church Dr. CH62: Port S 3H 127
WA2: P'gate 6G 99
WA12: New W 5G 77
WN5: Orr 6F 39
Church End L24: Hale 1D 150
Church End M. L24: Hale 1D 150
Church Farm Ct. CH60: Hes 3D 142
CH64: Will 3F 159
Churchfield Ct. *L25: Gate 4G 111*
(off Jones Farm Rd.)
Churchfield Rd. L25: Gate 3G 111
WA6: Frod 3E 166
Church Flds. L39: Orm 5C 24
L40: Scar 2H 17
Churchfields PR8: B'dale 5F 11
WA3: Croft 7H 79
WA6: Hel 7J 165
WA8: Wid 3D 114
WA9: Clock F 3E 94
Church Flats L4: Walt 4B 68
Church Gdns. CH44: Wall 3D 86
L20: Boot 3H 67
Churchgate PR9: Chu 6B 8
(not continuous)
Churchgate M. PR9: Chu 6C 8
Church Grn. L16: Child 1D 110
L32: K'by 2C 56
L37: Form 1G 29
WA13: Warb 7K 101
WN8: Skel 2F 37
Church Gro. L21: Sea 7F 53
Church Hill CH45: Wall 2K 85
Church Hill Rd. L39: Orm 4B 24
Churchill Av. CH41: Birk 1B 106
PR9: Chu 5B 8
WA3: Cul 2D 80
Churchill Ct. CH64: Nest 3J 157
Churchill Gdns. WA9: St. H 1J 93
Churchill Gro. CH44: Wall 2C 86
Churchill Ho. L21: Sea 6F 53
Churchill Ind. Est. L9: Ain 5E 54
Churchill Mans. *WA7: Run 6C 134*
(off Cooper St.)
Churchill Way CH64: Nest 3J 157
Churchill Way Nth. L3: Liv 5K 87 (4F 4)
Churchlands *CH44: Wall 5E 86*
(off Bridle Rd.)
Church La. CH2: Stoak 5E 170
CH44: Wall 3D 86
(not continuous)
Church La. CH49: W'chu 6F 105
CH61: Thurs 4K 123
CH62: Brom 1K 145
CH62: East 5C 146
CH64: Nest 4J 157
CH66: Gt Sut 7F 161
L4: Walt 4B 68
L17: Aig 7G 109
L31: Lyd 3B 32
L34: Know 2G 71
L39: Augh 4J 33
WA3: Cul 3B 80
WA4: Grap 7H 119
WA10: Eccl 3G 73
Churchmeadow Cl. CH44: Wall 3D 86
Church Mdw. La. CH60: Hes 3C 142
Church Mdw. Wlk.
WA8: Hale B 4H 133
Church M. CH42: R Ferr 7G 107
L24: Speke 6F 131
Church Mt. L7: Liv 6D 88 (6P 5)
Church Pde. CH65: Ell P 5A 162
Church Path L37: Form 5K 19
Church Pl. CH42: Tran 5D 106
Church Rd. CH42: Tran 5D 106
CH44: Wall 5E 86
CH48: W Kir 7C 102
CH49: Upton 3E 104
CH63: Beb 6G 127
CH63: Thorn H 4B 144
L4: Walt 4C 68
L13: Liv 5H 89
L15: W'tree 1J 109
L19: Gars 4A 130
L20: Boot 7K 53
L21: Lith 6H 53
L21: Sea 7F 53
L22: Water 4D 52
L23: C'by 1E 52
L24: Hale 1E 150
L25: Wltn 4D 110
L26: Halew 6J 111
L31: Mag 5F 43
L37: Form 6A 20
L39: Bic 5J 35
PR9: Banks 1J 9
WA6: Frod 4E 166
WA11: Hay 7C 62
WA11: R'ford 6F 47
WA13: Lymm 5F 121
WN8: Skel 2F 37
Church Rd. Nth. L15: W'tree 1J 109
Church Rd. Roby L36: Roby 5G 91
Church Rd. Sth. L25: Wltn 6E 110
Church Rd. W. L4: Walt 4B 68
Church Sq. CH62: Brom 1K 145
WA10: St. H 3C 74
Church St. CH41: Birk 2F 107
(not continuous)
CH44: Wall 3D 86
CH65: Ell P 5A 162
L1: Liv 6K 87 (6F 4)
L20: Boot 3G 67
L34: Prsct 1D 92
L39: Orm 5C 24
PR9: South 1J 11
WA1: Warr 3C 118
WA6: Frod 3D 166
WA7: Run 6C 134
WA8: Wid 4C 134
WA10: St. H 3C 74
WA12: New W 2J 77
WN5: Orr 6F 39
WN5: Wigan 5K 39
WN8: Uph 4E 38
Church St. Ind. Est.
WA1: Warr 3C 118
Church Ter. CH42: Tran 5D 106
WN4: Ash M 3F 63
CHURCHTOWN 6C 8
Churchtown Ct. PR9: Chu 5C 8
Churchtown Gdns. PR9: Chu 4C 8
Church Vw. L12: W Der 7K 69
L20: Boot 3H 67
L39: Augh 4J 33
WA13: Lymm 4K 121
Church Vw. Ct. *L39: Orm 5C 24*
(off Burscough St.)
Churchview Rd. CH41: Birk 7B 86
Church Wlk. CH48: W Kir 7D 102
CH65: Ell P 5A 162
L20: Boot 3H 67
L34: Know 2G 71
WA2: Win 1A 98
WA10: Eccl 2G 73
Church Walks L39: Orm 5C 24
Churchward Ct. *L25: Wltn 6E 110*
(off Garden St.)
Church Way L30: N'ton 1K 53
L32: K'by 2C 56
L37: Form 1G 29
WA6: Alv 3K 173
Churchway Rd. L24: Speke 7A 132
Churchwood Cl. CH62: Brom 1K 145
Churchwood Ct. CH49: W'chu 7F 105
Churchwood Vw. WA13: Lymm 5H 121
Churnet St. L4: Kirk 6A 68
Churn Way CH49: Grea 4B 104
Churston Rd. L16: Child 3C 110
Churton Av. CH43: O'ton 5K 105
Churton Ct. L6: Liv 4B 88 (2M 5)
Ciaran Cl. L12: W Der 6B 70
Cicely St. L7: Liv 6D 88 (6P 5)
Cinder La. L18: Moss H 3A 110
L20: Boot 6K 53
WA4: Thel 6B 120
Cineworld
Runcorn 3H 153
St Helens 3B 74
CINNAMON BROW 4F 99
Cinnamon Brow WN8: Uph 5E 38
Cinnamon La. WA2: Fearn 4F 99
Cinnamon La. Nth. WA2: Fearn 3F 99
Cinnamon Pk. WA2: Fearn 4H 99
Circular Dr. CH49: Grea 5B 104
CH60: Hes 1D 142
CH62: Port S 2H 127
Circular Rd. CH41: Birk 3D 106
Circular Rd. E. L11: N Grn. 6H 69
Circular Rd. W. L11: N Grn. 6H 69
Cirencester Av. CH49: Grea 4A 104
Cirrus Dr. L39: Augh 2J 33
Citrine Rd. CH44: Wall 5D 86
Citron Cl. L9: Walt 2D 68
City Gdns. WA10: St. H 6B 60
City Rd. L4: Walt 5B 68
WA10: St. H 7B 60
WN5: Wigan 3K 39
City Vw. WA11: St. H 4C 60
Civic Way CH63: Beb 4G 127
CH65: Ell P 7K 161
L36: Huy 5J 91
Clairville PR8: B'dale 3F 11
Clairville Cl. L20: Boot 3J 67
Clairville Ct. L20: Boot 3J 67
Clairville Way L13: Liv 2G 89
Clamley Ct. L24: Speke 6A 132
Clamley Gdns. L24: Hale 7E 132
Clandon Rd. L18: Aller 7A 110
Clanfield Av. WA8: Wid 5J 113
Clanfield Rd. L11: N Grn. 4J 69
Clanwood Cl. WN3: Wins 2C 50
Clapgate Cres. WA8: Hale B 4H 133
Clap Ga. La. WN3: Wigan 1C 50
Clap Gates Cres. WA5: Warr 1J 117
Clap Gates Rd. WA5: Warr 1J 117
Clapham Rd. L4: Walt 1D 88
Clare Cl. WA9: St. H 7A 74
Clare Cres. CH44: Wall 2K 85
Clare Dr. CH65: Whit 2K 169
Claremont Av. L31: Mag 4D 42
PR8: B'dale 4G 11
WA8: Wid 4E 114
Claremont Cl. L21: Sea 6F 53
Claremont Ct. CH45: Wall 1K 85
Claremont Dr. L39: Augh 7B 24
WA8: Wid 4D 114
Claremont Rd. CH48: W Kir 5D 102
L15: W'tree 2G 109
L21: Sea 6F 53
L23: C'by 1E 52
PR8: B'dale 4G 11
WA3: Cul 2K 79
WA7: Run 7D 134
WN5: Bil 7G 49
Claremont Way CH63: High B 1D 126
Claremount Dr. CH63: Beb 5F 127
Claremount Rd. CH45: Wall 7K 65
Clarence Av. WA5: Gt San 2B 116
WA8: Wid 4C 114
Clarence Cl. WA9: St. H 4E 74
Clarence Rd. CH42: Tran 5C 106
CH44: Wall 5D 86
PR8: B'dale 4G 11
WA4: Grap 6H 119
Clarence St. L3: Liv 6A 88 (6J 5)
WA1: Warr 1E 118
WA3: Golb 4K 63
WA7: Run 6B 134
WA12: New W 2D 76
WN4: Ash M 1D 62
Clarence Ter. WA7: Run 6C 134
Clarendon Cl. CH43: O'ton 3C 106
WA7: Murd 3B 154
Clarendon Ct. WA2: Win 3K 97
Clarendon Gro. L31: Lyd 6E 32
Clarendon Rd. CH44: Wall 4D 86
L6: Liv 1E 88
L19: Gars 3A 130
L21: Sea 7F 53
Clare Rd. L20: Boot 4K 67
Clares Farm Cl. WA1: W'ston 1B 120
Claret Cl. L17: Aig 7E 108
Clare Wlk. L10: Faz 6K 55
Clare Way CH45: Wall 2K 85
Claribel St. L8: Liv 2C 108
Clarke Av. CH42: R Ferr 6E 106
WA3: Cul 2B 80
WA4: Latch 6D 118
(not continuous)
Clarke Gardens 1C 130
Clarke Gdns. WA8: Wid 2D 134
Clarke's Cres. WA10: Eccl 2H 73
Clarks Ter. WA7: West P 2K 151
Classic Rd. L13: Liv 3J 89
Clatterbridge Rd. CH63: Spit 2D 144
Claude Rd. L6: Liv 1E 88
Claude St. WA1: Warr 2C 118
CLAUGHTON 1K 105
Claughton Cl. L7: Liv 6E 88
Claughton Dr. CH44: Wall 4B 86
Claughton Firs CH43: O'ton 4B 106
Claughton Grn. CH43: O'ton 3A 106
Claughton Pl. CH41: Birk 2C 106
Claughton Rd. CH41: Birk 2C 106
Claughton St. WA10: St. H 2C 74
Clavell Rd. L19: Aller 1B 130
Claverton Cl. WA7: Run 4D 152
Claybridge Cl. WN5: Wigan 2K 39
Clay Brow Rd. WN8: Skel 5A 38
Clay Cross Rd. L25: Wltn 6D 110
Claydon Ct. L26: Halew 7A 112
Claydon Gdns. WA3: Rix 6H 101
Clayfield Cl. L20: Boot 3K 67
Clayford Cres. L14: K Ash 3K 89
Clayford Pl. L14: K Ash 3K 89
Clayford Rd. L14: K Ash 3K 89
Clayford Way L14: K Ash 3A 90
Clayhill Grn. CH66: Lit Sut 4E 160
Clayhill Ind. Est. CH64: Nest 1J 157
Clayhill Light Ind. Pk.
CH64: Nest 1K 157
Clay La. WA5: B'wood 1C 96
WA10: Eccl 3D 72
Claypole Cl. L7: Liv 7E 88
Clay St. L3: Liv 3H 87 (1C 4)
Clayton Cl. WA10: St. H 3A 74
Clayton Cres. WA7: Run 1B 152
WA8: Wid 7B 114
Clayton La. CH44: Wall 5A 86
Clayton M. WN8: Skel 2D 36
Clayton Pl. CH41: Birk 3C 106
Clayton Rd. WA3: Ris 1B 100
Clayton Sq. L1: Liv 6K 87 (6G 4)
Clayton Sq. Shop. Cen. L1: Liv 6G 4
Clayton St. CH41: Birk 3C 106
WN8: Skel 2D 36
Cleadon Cl. L32: K'by 6E 56
Cleadon Rd. L32: K'by 6D 56
Cleadon Way WA8: Wid 4A 114

Clearwater Cl.—Cooper La.

Clearwater Cl. L7: Liv .5D **88** (4P **5**)
Cleary St. L20: Boot .2H **67**
Clee Hill Rd. CH42: Tran .7C **106**
Cleethorpes Rd. WA7: Murd .3A **154**
Cleeves Cl. WA1: Warr .3C **118**
Clegge St. WA2: Warr .1B **118**
Clegg St. L5: Liv .3A **88** (1H **5**)
WN8: Skel .2D **36**
Clelland St. WA4: Warr .5C **118**
Clematis Rd. L27: N'ley .2J **111**
Clement Gdns. L3: Liv .3J **87** (1E **4**)
Clementina Rd. L23: Blun .1B **52**
Clements Way L33: K'by .7B **44**
Clemmey Dr. L20: Boot .7A **54**
Clenger's Brow PR9: Chu .5B **8**
Clent Av. L31: Lyd, Mag .1E **42**
Clent Gdns. L31: Lyd .1E **42**
Clent Rd. L31: Mag .1E **42**
Cleopas St. L8: Liv .4B **108**
Clevedon Dr. WN3: Wigan .1A **50**
Cleveland Av. WN3: Wins .2A **50**
Cleveland Bldgs. L1: Liv .7J **87** (8F **4**)
Cleveland Cl. L32: K'by .1A **56**
Cleveland Dr. CH66: Lit Sut .5C **160**
WN4: Ash M .1G **63**
Cleveland Gdns. WN4: Ash M .1G **63**
Cleveland Rd. WA2: Warr .4B **98**
Cleveland Sq. L1: Liv .7K **87** (8F **4**)
Cleveland St. CH41: Birk .7B **86**
WA9: St. H .5E **74**
Cleveley Pk. L18: Aller .7B **110**
Cleveley Rd. CH47: Meols .7G **83**
L18: Aller .7A **110**
Cleveleys Av. PR9: Chu .3C **8**
WA8: Wid .6F **115**
Cleveleys Rd. PR9: Chu .4C **8**
WA5: Gt San .4F **117**
Cleves, The L31: Lyd .1G **43**
Cleve Way L37: Form .1B **30**
CLIEVES HILLS .7J **23**
Clieves Hills L39: Hals .4G **23**
Clieves Hills La. L39: Augh .1G **33**
Clieves Rd. L32: K'by .4D **56**
Clifden Ct. L37: Form .7K **19**
Cliff, The CH45: New B .5K **65**
Cliff Dr. CH44: Wall .2D **86**
Cliffe Rd. CH64: Lit N .6K **157**
WA4: App .2C **138**
Cliffe St. WA8: Wid .7E **114**
Cliff La. WA4: Grap .3B **140**
(Grappenhall La.)
WA4: Grap .6J **119**
(Knutsford Rd.)
WA13: Lymm .3D **140**
Clifford Rd. CH44: Wall .4B **86**
PR8: B'dale .7G **11**
WA5: Penk .4E **116**
Clifford St. CH41: Birk .7A **86**
L3: Liv .5A **88** (4J **5**)
Cliff Rd. CH44: Wall .4K **85**
PR9: South .5K **7**
Cliff St. L7: Liv .5E **88**
Cliff Vw. WA6: Frod .3C **166**
CLIFTON .6F **153**
Clifton Av. CH62: East .7A **146**
L26: Halew .7J **111**
WA3: Cul .3K **79**
Clifton Cl. WA1: W'ston .1K **119**
WA7: Run .4D **152**
Clifton Ct. CH41: Birk .3D **106**
L19: Aller .1A **130**
Clifton Cres. CH41: Birk .2E **106**
WA6: Frod .2E **166**
WA10: St. H .4K **73**
Clifton Dr. L10: Ain .3F **55**
Clifton Gdns. CH65: Ell P .1A **170**
Clifton Ga. CH41: Birk .3D **106**
Clifton Gro. CH44: Wall .3C **86**
L5: Liv .3A **88** (1J **5**)
Clifton La. WA7: Clftn .6F **153**
(not continuous)
Cliftonmill Mdws. WA3: Golb .5K **63**
CLIFTON PARK .3D **106**
Clifton Rd. CH41: Birk .3D **106**
L6: Liv .2F **89**
L37: Form .5A **20**
PR8: South .2B **12**
WA7: Run .3C **152**
WA7: Sut W .7G **153**
WN4: Ash M .6D **50**
WN5: Bil .1F **61**
Clifton Rd. E. L6: Liv .2F **89**
Clifton St. L19: Gars .3A **130**
WA4: Warr .4C **118**
WA10: St. H .2C **74**
Clifton Ter. WA10: St. H .4K **73**
Clifton Vs. CH1: Back .4J **169**
Cliftonville Rd. L34: Prsct .1E **92**
WA1: W'ston .1J **119**
Clincton Cl. WA8: Wid .1G **133**
Clincton Vw. WA8: Wid .1G **133**
CLINKHAM WOOD .4C **60**
Clinning Rd. PR8: B'dale .6G **11**
Clinton Pl. L12: W Der .7H **69**
Clinton Rd. L12: W Der .7H **69**
Clint Rd. L7: Liv .6E **88**
Clint Rd. W. L7: Liv .6E **88**
Clint Way L7: Liv .6E **88**
Clipper Vw. CH62: New F .1H **127**
Clipsley Brook Vw. WA11: Hay .7H **61**
Clipsley Cres. WA11: Hay .6J **61**
Clipsley La. WA11: Hay .7K **61**
Clive Av. WA2: Warr .6C **98**
Clive Lodge PR8: B'dale .6F **11**
Clive Rd. CH43: O'ton .4B **106**
PR8: B'dale .6F **11**
CLOCK FACE .4F **95**
Clock Face Colliery Country Pk. .3H **95**
Clock Face Rd. WA8: Bold H .2E **94**
WA9: Clock F .2E **94**
Clock La. WA8: Wid .5H **115**
Clock Tower St. WA10: St. H .3B **74**
Cloister Grn. L37: Form .1B **30**
Cloisters, The L23: C'by .2D **52**
L37: Form .7K **19**
WA10: Eccl .2H **73**
Cloister Way CH65: Ell P .6C **162**
Clorain Cl. L33: K'by .2E **56**
Clorain Rd. L33: K'by .2E **56**
Close, The CH49: Grea .6B **104**
CH61: Irby .3B **124**
CH63: High B .7D **106**
L9: Walt .2B **68**
L23: C'by .2D **52**
L28: Stock V .7G **71**
L38: Ince B .1E **40**
PR9: Banks .2J **9**
WA10: Eccl .1G **73**
WA11: Hay .1H **75**
WA12: New W .5J **77**
Closeburn Av. CH60: Hes .4C **142**
Close St. WA9: St. H .7A **74**
Cloudberry Cl. L27: N'ley .2J **111**
Clough, The WA7: Halt .1H **153**
WN4: Gars .1B **62**
Clough Av. WA2: Warr .5B **98**
Clough Gro. WN4: Ash M .7D **50**
Clough Rd. L24: Speke .5H **131**
L26: Halew .7A **112**
Clovelly Av. WA5: Gt San .1C **116**
WA9: Sut L .1F **95**
Clovelly Dr. PR8: B'dale .1E **14**
WN8: Newb .1G **27**
Clovelly Gro. WA7: Brook .5K **153**
Clovelly Rd. L4: Walt .1D **88**
Clover Av. L26: Halew .6H **111**
WA6: Frod .4F **167**
Clover Ct. WA7: Brook .5K **153**
Cloverdale Dr. WN4: Ash M .3G **63**
Cloverdale Rd. L25: Gate .1E **110**
Clover Dr. CH41: Birk .6J **85**
Cloverfield WA7: Nort .3A **154**
WA13: Lymm .4H **121**
Cloverfield Gdns.
CH66: Lit Sut .4F **161**
Clover Hey WA11: St. H .6D **60**
CLUBMOOR .7G **69**
Club St. WA11: St. H .4C **60**
Clucas Gdns. L39: Orm .4C **24**
Clwyd Gro. L12: W Der .6K **69**
Clwyd St. CH41: Birk .2D **106**
CH45: New B .7A **66**
Clwyd Way CH66: Lit Sut .5C **160**
Clyde Rd. L7: Liv .5G **89**
Clydesdale CH65: Whit .1K **169**
Clydesdale Rd. CH44: Wall .2D **86**
CH47: Hoy .7D **82**
WA4: App .1D **138**
Clyde St. CH42: R Ferr .6F **107**
L20: Kirk .6J **67**
Clyffes Farm Cl. L40: Scar .2J **17**
Coach Ho. Ct. L29: Seft .6A **42**
Coachmans Dr. L12: W Der .5C **70**
Coach Rd. L33: Know .6B **58**
L39: Bic .2K **45**
WA11: R'ford, Bic .1B **58**
Coalbrookdale Rd. CH64: Nest .1J **157**
Coalgate La. L35: Whis .5C **92**
Coal Pit La. L39: Bic .7C **36**
Coalpit La.
CH1: Dunk, Lea B, Moll .7F **169**
(not continuous)
Coalport Wlk. WA9: St. H .1J **93**
Coal St. L1: Liv .5A **88** (5H **5**)
Coalville Rd. WA11: St. H .7F **61**
Coastal Dr. CH45: Wall .6H **65**
Coastal Rd. PR8: Ains, B'dale .3A **14**
Coastguard La. CH64: Park .2F **157**
Coastline M. PR9: Chu .3C **8**
Cobal Ct. WA6: Frod .3D **166**
Cobb Av. L21: Lith .7H **53**
Cobbles, The L26: Halew .6H **111**
Cobblestone Cnr. L19: Gras .2J **129**
COBBS .1D **138**
Cobbs Brow La. L40: Lath .5F **27**
WN8: Newb .2G **27**
Cobbs Clough Rd. L40: Lath .5F **27**
Cobbs La. WA4: App .1E **138**
Cobden Av. CH42: Tran .5F **107**
Cobden Ct. CH42: Tran .5E **106**
Cobden Pl. CH42: Tran .5F **107**
L25: Wltn .6D **110**
Cobden Rd. PR9: South .2B **12**
Cobden St. L6: Liv .4B **88** (2L **5**)
L25: Wltn .6D **110**
WA2: Warr .2B **118**
WA12: New W .2H **77**
Cobden Vw. L25: Wltn .6D **110**
Cob Hall La. WA6: Manl .7K **173**
Cobham Av. L9: Walt .7B **54**
Cobham Rd. CH46: More .1B **104**
Cobham Wlk. L30: N'ton .1K **53**
Cob Moor Av. WN5: Bil .3F **49**
Cob Moor Rd. WN5: Bil .3F **49**
Coburg St. CH41: Birk .2D **106**
Coburg Wharf L3: Liv .2J **107**
Cochrane St. L5: Liv .2B **88**
Cockburn St. L8: Liv .4B **108**
Cockerell Cl. L4: Walt .7B **68**
Cockerham Way L11: Crox .1K **69**
Cock Glade L35: Whis .6D **92**
Cockhedge Grn. WA1: Warr .2C **118**
Cockhedge La. WA1: Warr .3C **118**
Cockhedge Shopping Pk.
WA1: Warr .3B **118**
Cockhedge Way WA1: Warr .3B **118**
Cocklade La. L24: Hale .1D **150**
Cock La. Ends WA8: Hale B .5H **133**
Cockle Dick's La. PR9: Chu .5A **8**
Cocksfield Rd. L25: Gate .2F **111**
Cockshead Rd. L25: Gate .3F **111**
Cockshead Way L25: Gate .2F **111**
Cockspur St. L3: Liv .5J **87** (4E **4**)
Cockspur St. W. L3: Liv .5J **87** (4D **4**)
Coerton Rd. L9: Ain .6D **54**
Coffin La. WN2: Bam .6H **51**
Cokers, The CH42: High B .1E **126**
Colbern Cl. L31: Mag .3G **43**
Colburn Cl. WN3: Wigan .2E **50**
Colby Cl. L16: Child .7C **90**
Colby Rd. WN3: Wigan .1F **51**
Colchester Rd. PR8: South .6B **12**
Colden Cl. L12: W Der .7C **70**
Coldstone Dr. WN4: Gars .2B **62**
Coldstream Cl. WA2: Warr .3E **98**
Coldstream Dr. CH66: Lit Sut .6B **160**
Cole Av. WA12: New W .2G **77**
Colebrooke Cl. WA3: Bchwd .3C **100**
Colebrooke Rd. L17: Aig .5C **108**
Coleclough Pl. WA3: Cul .2B **80**
Cole Cres. L39: Augh .3A **34**
Coleman Dr. CH49: Grea .5A **104**
Colemere Cl. WA1: P'gate .6G **99**
Colemere Ct. CH65: Ell P .4K **161**
Colemere Dr. CH61: Thing .3F **125**
Coleridge Av. WA10: St. H .2K **73**
WN5: Orr .5J **39**
Coleridge Ct. L32: K'by .5B **56**
Coleridge Dr. CH62: New F .2G **127**
Coleridge Gro. WA8: Wid .1A **134**
Coleridge Pl. WN3: Wigan .1D **50**
Coleridge Rd. WN5: Bil .3F **49**
Coleridge St. L6: Liv .4D **88**
L20: Boot .2G **67**
Colerne Way WN3: Wins .2B **50**
Colesborne Rd. L11: N Grn. .4J **69**
Coles Cres. L23: Thorn .6H **41**
Coleshill Ri. WN3: Wins .2A **50**
Coleshill Rd. L11: N Grn. .3G **69**
Cole St. CH43: O'ton .2C **106**
Colette Rd. L10: Faz .6K **55**
Coleus Cl. L9: Walt .2D **68**
Colin Cl. L36: Roby .5G **91**
Colindale Rd. L16: Child .1C **110**
Colin Dr. L3: Liv .2J **87**
Colinmander Gdns. L39: Orm .7A **24**
Colinton WN8: Skel .4A **38**
Colinton St. L15: W'tree .7G **89**
Coliseum Shop. & Leisure Pk.
CH65: Ell P .2B **170**
Coliseum Way CH65: Ell P .3B **170**
College Av. L23: C'by .2D **52**
L37: Form .5J **19**
College Cl. CH43: Bid .2F **105**
CH45: Wall .1J **85**
L37: Form .6H **19**
PR8: B'dale .5G **11**
WA1: Warr .3D **118**
WA2: Fearn .5H **99**
College Ct. L12: W Der .2J **89**
College Dr. CH63: Beb .2G **127**
College Farm WN8: Roby M .2C **38**
College Flds. L36: Huy .6J **91**
College Grn. Flats L23: C'by .2D **52**
College La. L1: Liv .6K **87** (7F **4**)
College Path L37: Form .5H **19**
College Pl. WA2: P'gate .5H **99**
College Rd. L23: C'by .1C **52**
WN8: Uph .2D **38**
College Rd. Nth. L23: Blun .7C **40**
College St. WA10: St. H .2C **74**
(not continuous)
College St. Nth. L6: Liv .4B **88** (3K **5**)
College St. Sth. L6: Liv .4B **88** (3L **5**)
College Vw. L20: Boot .4J **67**
L36: Huy .5J **91**
Collier's Row WA7: West .3A **152**
Collier St. WA7: Run .6B **134**
Colliery Grn. Cl. CH64: Lit N .6J **157**
Colliery Grn. Ct. CH64: Lit N .6J **157**
Colliery Grn. Dr. CH64: Lit N .6J **157**
Collingham Grn. CH66: Lit Sut .6D **160**
Collingwood Rd. CH63: Beb .5H **127**
WA12: New W .3F **77**
Collin Rd. CH43: Bid .7J **85**
Collins Cl. L20: Boot .1G **67**
COLLINS GREEN .5B **76**
Collins Grn. La. WA5: C Grn .5C **76**
Collins Ind. Est. WA9: St. H .1E **74**
Collinson Ct. WA6: Frod .3D **166**
Collin St. WA5: Warr .3J **117**
Collisdene Rd. WN5: Orr .5F **39**
Colmoor Cl. L33: K'by .6D **44**
Colmore Av. CH63: Spit .1F **145**
Colmore Rd. L11: N Grn. .4G **69**
Colne Dr. WA9: St. H .7F **75**
Colne Rd. WA5: B'wood .1D **96**
Colonnades, The L3: Liv .7H **87** (9D **4**)
Colorado Cl. WA5: Gt San .1G **117**
Colquitt St. L1: Liv .7A **88** (8H **5**)
Coltart Rd. L8: Liv .2D **108**
Colton Rd. L25: Gate .1D **110**
Colton Wlk. L25: Gate .1D **110**
Columban Cl. L30: N'ton .2A **54**
Columbia La. CH43: O'ton .4B **106**
Columbia Rd. CH43: O'ton .4B **106**
L4: Walt .4C **68**
L34: Prsct .1E **92**
Columbine Cl. L31: Mell .2J **55**
WA8: Wid .4H **113**
Columbine Way WA9: Bold .7K **75**
Columbus Dr. CH61: Pens .6C **124**
Columbus Quay L3: Liv .5A **108**
Columbus St. *WN4: Ash M .7D 50*
(off Priory Rd.)
Columbus Way L21: Lith .6H **53**
Column Rd. CH48: Caldy, W Kir .6E **102**
Colville Ct. WA2: Win .4A **98**
Colville Rd. CH44: Wall .3A **86**
Colville St. L15: W'tree .7G **89**
Colwall Cl. L33: K'by .3E **56**
Colwall Rd. L33: K'by .3E **56**
Colwall Wlk. L33: K'by .3E **56**
Colwell Cl. L14: K Ash .7E **70**
Colwell Ct. L14: K Ash .7E **70**
Colwell Rd. L14: K Ash .1E **90**
Colworth Rd. L24: Speke .5F **131**
Colwyn Cl. CH65: Ell P .1B **170**
WA5: Call .5J **97**
Colwyn Rd. L13: Liv .5H **89**
Colwyn St. CH41: Birk .7A **86**
Colyton Av. WA9: Sut L .2F **95**
Combermere St. L8: Liv .2A **108**
L15: W'tree .7F **89**
Comely Av. CH44: Wall .3C **86**
Comely Bank Rd. CH44: Wall .3D **86**
Comer Gdns. L31: Lyd .1E **42**
Comfrey Gro. L26: Halew .6J **111**
Commerce Way L8: Liv .1D **108** (10P **5**)
Commercial Rd. CH62: Brom .6A **128**
L5: Kirk .1J **87**
Common, The WA7: Halt .1J **153**
Common Fld. Rd. CH49: W'chu .7F **105**
Common La. PR9: Banks .5K **9**
WA3: Cul .2K **79**
WA4: Latch .6E **118**
WA6: Hap .3D **172**
Common Rd. WA12: New W .4C **76**
Commonside WA6: Alv .2K **173**
Common St. WA9: St. H .7K **73**
WA12: New W .3C **76**
Commonwealth Pav.
L3: Liv .7J **87** (9D **4**)
Commutation Row L1: Liv .5K **87** (4H **5**)
Company's Cl. WA7: West .4B **152**
Compass Cl. WA7: Murd .5B **154**
Compass Ct. CH45: Wall .6K **65**
Compton Cl. WA11: Hay .6A **62**
Compton Pl. CH65: Ell P .6K **161**
Compton Rd. CH41: Birk .6H **85**
L6: Liv .3C **88** (1N **5**)
PR8: B'dale .5H **11**
Compton Wlk. L20: Boot .2H **67**
Compton Way L26: Halew .3J **131**
Comus St. L3: Liv .4K **87** (2G **4**)
Concert Sq. L1: Liv .7G **4**
Concert St. L1: Liv .6K **87** (7G **4**)
Concorde Av. WN3: Wigan .1F **51**
Concordia Av. CH49: Upton .3E **104**
Concord Pl. WA2: Warr .5D **98**
Concourse, The CH48: W Kir .5C **102**
Concourse Shop. Cen., The
WN8: Skel .2H **37**
Concourse Way WA9: St. H .4H **75**
Condor Cl. L19: Gars .3A **130**
Condron Rd. Nth. L21: Lith .4J **53**
Condron Rd. Sth. L21: Lith .4J **53**
Conery Cl. WA6: Hel .7J **165**
Coney Cres. L23: Thorn .7H **41**
Coney Gro. WA7: Brook .5J **153**
Coney La. L35: Tar G .1K **111**
L36: Huy .1K **111**
Coney Wlk. CH49: Upton .2B **104**
Congress Gdns. WA9: St. H .7K **73**
Conifer Cl. CH66: Whit .4J **169**
L9: Walt .2D **68**
L33: K'by .7C **44**
Conifer Ct. L37: Form .1K **29**
Conifer Gro. WA4: Moore .2E **136**
WA5: Gt San .1D **116**
Conifers, The L31: Mag .1E **42**
Coningsby Dr. CH45: Wall .3A **86**
Coningsby Rd. L4: Walt .7C **68**
Coniston Av. CH43: Noct .3G **105**
CH45: Wall .7J **65**
CH63: East .6J **145**
L34: Prsct .1F **93**
WA5: Penk .4B **116**
WN4: Ash M .1F **63**
WN5: Orr .4H **39**
Coniston Cl. CH66: Hoot .2D **160**
L9: Ain .6D **54**
L33: K'by .1B **56**
WA7: Beech .4F **153**
Coniston Ct. PR8: Ains .6C **14**
Coniston Dr. WA6: Frod .3E **166**
Coniston Gro. WA11: St. H .6C **60**
Coniston Ho. L17: Aig .6F **109**
Coniston Rd. CH61: Irby .3B **124**
CH64: Nest .5J **157**
L31: Mag .2F **43**
L37: Form .1H **29**
Coniston St. L5: Liv .1C **88**
Coniston Way WA11: R'ford .2F **47**
Conleach Rd. L24: Speke .7H **131**
Connaught Av. WA1: Warr .1E **118**
Connaught Cl. CH41: Birk .7A **86**
Connaught Dr. WA12: New W .4G **77**
Connaught Rd. L7: Liv .5C **88** (5N **5**)
Connaught Way CH41: Birk .7K **85**
Connolly Av. L20: Boot .1A **68**
Connolly Ho. L20: Boot .4J **67**
Conroy Way WA12: New W .5G **77**
Conservation Cen. .5K **87** (5F **4**)
Consett Rd. WA9: St. H .1K **93**
Constables Cl. WA7: Cas .1J **153**
Constance St. L3: Liv .5B **88** (4K **5**)
WA10: St. H .4K **73**
Constance Way WA8: Wid .3C **134**
Constantia St. WN3: Ince M .1K **51**
Constantine Av. CH60: Hes .1E **142**
Convent Cl. CH42: Tran .4D **106**
L19: Gras .2J **129**
L39: Augh .1C **34**
Conville Blvd. CH63: High B .1D **126**
Conway Av. WA5: Warr .5K **97**
Conway Cl. CH63: High B .4D **126**
L33: K'by .7B **44**
WA5: Gt San .2D **116**
Conway Ct. CH63: Beb .5F **127**
CH65: Ell P .1B **170**
WA7: Cas .7J **135**
Conway Cres. WN5: Bil .6G **49**
Conway Dr. CH41: Birk .2D **106**
WA12: New W .3J **77**
WN5: Bil .7H **49**
Conway Ho. L6: Liv .3E **88**
Conway Park Station (Rail) .1E **106**
Conway Rd. WN4: Ash M .7J **51**
Conway St. CH41: Birk .1C **106**
(not continuous)
L5: Liv .2A **88**
WA10: St. H .4K **73**
Conwy Dr. L6: Liv .2D **88** (1P **5**)
Conyers Av. PR8: B'dale .5F **11**
Coogee Av. WA5: Gt San .1C **116**
Cook Av. WA11: Hay .6C **62**
Cookes Cl. CH64: Nest .2J **157**
Cooke St. WN4: Ash M .6D **50**
Cook Rd. CH46: Leas .3F **85**
Cookson Rd. L21: Sea .7G **53**
Cookson St. L1: Liv .1A **108** (10H **5**)
Cooks Rd. L23: C'by .7D **40**
Cook St. CH41: Birk .3C **106**
CH65: Ell P .5A **162**
L2: Liv .6J **87** (7D **4**)
L34: Prsct .1D **92**
L35: Whis .3F **93**
Coombe Dr. WA7: Run .2B **152**
Coombe Pk. CH66: Lit Sut .5E **160**
Coombe Pk. Ct. CH66: Lit Sut .5E **160**
Coombe Rd. CH61: Irby .2C **124**
Cooperage Cl. L8: Liv .4A **108**
Cooper Av. WA2: Warr .5B **98**
WA12: New W .3D **76**
Cooper Av. Nth. L18: Moss H .7J **109**
Cooper Av. Sth. L19: Aig .7J **109**
Cooper Cl. L19: Aig .1J **129**
Cooper La. WA11: Hay .1K **75**

Cromwell Av.—Darley Cl.

Cromwell Av. WA2: Warr 5G **97**
WA5: Gt San, Old H, W'brk 5G **97**
Cromwell Av. Sth. WA5: Gt San 4G **117**
Cromwell Cl. L39: Augh 1A **34**
WA12: New W 2E **76**
Cromwell Ct. *WA1: Warr 3A 118*
(off Arpley St.)
Cromwell Rd. CH65: Ell P 6A **162**
L4: Walt 4A **68**
Cromwell St. WA8: Wid 3C **134**
Crondall Gro. L15: W'tree 1K **109**
CRONTON 3J **113**
Cronton Av. CH46: Leas 4D **84**
L35: Whis 6C **92**
Cronton Farm Ct. WA8: Wid 4A **114**
Cronton La. L35: R'hill 5H **93**
WA8: Cron 7H **93**
WA8: Wid 3A **114**
Cronton Pk. Av. WA8: Cron 2J **113**
Cronton Pk. Cl. WA8: Cron 2J **113**
Cronton Rd. L15: W'tree 3J **109**
L35: Tar G 1B **112**
WA8: Cron 3H **113**
Cronulla Dr. WA5: Gt San 1B **116**
Crookall St. WN4: Ash M 1G **63**
Crookhurst Av. WN5: Bil 6F **49**
Croome Dr. CH48: W Kir 6E **102**
Croppers Hill Ct.
WA10: St. H 3A **74**
Croppers La. L39: Bic 2D **34**
Croppers Rd. WA2: Fearn 4F **99**
Cropper St. L1: Liv 6K **87** (7H **5**)
Cropton Rd. L37: Form 7K **19**
CROSBY 4C **52**
Crosby Av. WA5: Warr 7K **97**
Crosby Cl. CH49: Upton 2D **104**
Crosby Coastal Pk. 4C **52** & 6F **29**
Crosby Grn. L12: W Der 7J **69**
Crosby Gro. CH64: Will 2H **159**
WA10: St. H 5K **73**
Crosby Leisure Cen. 3B **52**
Crosby Rd. PR8: B'dale 5F **11**
Crosby Rd. Nth. L22: Water 3E **52**
Crosby Rd. Sth. L21: Sea 7F **53**
L22: Water 5E **52**
Crosby Sailing Club 5D **52**
Crosender Rd. L23: C'by 2C **52**
Crosfield Cl. L7: Liv 6E **88**
Crosfield Rd. CH44: Wall 4C **86**
L7: Liv 6E **88**
L35: Prsct 3F **93**
Crosfield St. WA1: Warr 3A **118**
Crosfield Wlk. L7: Liv 6E **88**
Crosgrove Rd. L4: Walt 5D **68**
Crosland Rd. L32: K'by 4E **56**
Cross, The CH62: Brom 1A **146**
CH64: Nest 4J **157**
L38: Ince B 1E **40**
WA13: Lymm 5G **121**
Cross Acre Rd. L25: Gate 1F **111**
Cross Barn La. L38: Ince B 2E **40**
Crossdale Rd. CH62: Brom 4K **145**
L23: C'by 2C **52**
Crossdale Way WA11: St. H 4D **60**
CROSSENS 3F **9**
Crossens Way PR9: Cros 1E **8**
Cross Farm Rd. WA9: St. H 5E **74**
Crossfield Av. WA3: Cul 4B **80**
WA13: Lymm 5H **121**
Crossfield Rd. WN8: Skel 3J **37**
Crossfield St. WA9: St. H 3D **74**
Crossford Cl. WN3: Wigan 1B **50**
Crossford Rd. L14: K Ash 1E **90**
Cross Gates WA8: Wid 5H **115**
Cross Grn. L37: Form 1A **30**
Cross Grn. Cl. L37: Form 1A **30**
Crosshall Brow L39: Orm 6F **25**
L40: Westh 6F **25**
Crosshall St. L1: Liv 5K **87** (5F **4**)
Cross Hey L21: Ford 3H **53**
L31: Mag 5G **43**
Cross Hey Av. CH43: Noct 3H **105**
Cross Hillocks La. WA8: Wid 6E **112**
Crossings, The WA12: New W 3F **77**
Crossland M. WA13: Lymm 4D **120**
Crossland Ter. WA6: Hel 2H **173**
Cross La. CH45: Wall 2H **85**
CH63: Beb 5F **127**
CH64: Lit N 6J **157**
L35: Prsct, Whis 3D **92**
L39: Hals 7D **16**
WA3: Croft 7J **79**
WA4: Grap 6G **119**
WA6: Frod 3H **165**
WA12: New W 3F **77**
WN5: Bil 1F **49**
Cross La. Sth. WA3: Ris 1A **100**
Crossledge Way L25: Gate 1D **110**
Crossley Av. CH66: Ell P 5G **161**
Crossley Dr. CH60: Hes 2B **142**
L15: W'tree 7J **89**
Crossley Rd. WA10: St. H 6K **73**
Crossley St. WA1: Warr 2C **118**
Cross Mdw. Ct. *WA9: St. H 5E 74*
(off Appleton Rd.)
Cross Pit La. WA11: R'ford 6F **47**
Cross St. CH41: Birk 2F **107**
CH62: Port S 4H **127**
CH64: Nest 3J **157**
L22: Water 4D **52**
L34: Prsct 7D **72**
PR8: South 2H **11**
WA2: Warr 1B **118**
WA7: Run 6C **134**
WA8: Wid 7D **114**
(not continuous)
WA10: St. H 3B **74**
WN3: Ince M 1J **51**
WN5: Orr 5K **39**
WN5: Wigan 5K **39**
Crossvale Rd. L36: Huy 6J **91**
Crossway CH43: Bid 7J **85**
WA8: Wid 7K **113**
Crossway, The CH63: Raby 6C **144**
Crossway Cl. WN4: Ash M 7J **51**
Crossways CH62: Brom 6K **127**
L25: Gate 2D **110**
Crosswood Cres. L36: Huy 4G **91**
Crosthwaite Av. CH62: East 6B **146**
Croston Av. L35: R'hill 2H **93**
Croston Cl. WA8: Wid 5J **113**
Croston's Brow PR9: Chu 4B **8**
Crotfft Av. WA3: Golb 3K **63**
Crouchley Hall M.
WA13: Lymm 7H **121**
Crouchley La. WA13: Lymm 6G **121**
Crouch St. L5: Liv 1C **88**
WA9: St. H 6F **75**
CROUGHTON 7D **170**
Croughton Ct. CH66: Ell P 3H **161**
Croughton Rd.
CH2: C'ton, Stoak 6D **170**
(not continuous)
CH66: Ell P 3H **161**
Crowe Av. WA2: Warr 5B **98**
Crowland Cl. PR9: South 2C **12**
Crowland St. PR9: South 3B **12**
Crowland St. Ind. Est.
PR9: South 2C **12**
Crowland Way L37: Form 1B **30**
Crow La. WN8: Dalt 1B **38**
Crow La. E. WA12: New W 2F **77**
Crow La. W. WA12: New W 2D **76**
Crowley La. WA16: H Legh 6C **140**
Crowmarsh Cl.
CH49: Upton 4D **104**
Crown Acres Rd. L25: Wltn 1G **131**
Crown Av. WA8: Wid 1H **133**
Crown Cl. L37: Form 1A **30**
Crown Flds. Cl. WA12: New W 1F **77**
Crown Gdns. WA12: New W 2F **77**
Crown Ga. WA7: Pal F 3H **153**
Crown Grn. WA13: Lymm 4K **121**
Crown Pk. Dr. WA12: New W 1F **77**
Crown Rd. L12: W Der 7A **70**
Crown Sta. Pl.
L7: Liv 7C **88** (8N **5**)
Crown St. L7: Liv 5B **88** (5L **5**)
L8: Liv 7C **88**
WA1: Warr 3B **118**
WA9: St. H 7K **73**
WA12: New W 3E **76**
Crownway L36: Huy 3H **91**
Crow St. L8: Liv 2K **107**
Crowther Dr. WN3: Wins 3C **50**
Crowther St. WA10: St. H 3K **73**
CROW WOOD 6F **115**
Crow Wood La. WA8: Wid 6F **115**
Crow Wood Pl. WA8: Wid 5F **115**
Croxdale Rd. L14: K Ash 7E **70**
Croxdale Rd. W. L14: K Ash 7D **70**
Croxeth Gro. L17: Aig 3E **108**
CROXTETH 2A **70**
Croxteth Av. CH44: Wall 3B **86**
L21: Lith 6G **53**
Croxteth Cl. L31: Mag 1G **43**
Croxteth Ct. L8: Liv 2D **108**
Croxteth Dr. L17: Aig 3E **108**
WA11: R'ford 5F **47**
Croxteth Gro. L8: Liv 2D **108**
Croxteth Hall 5B **70**
Croxteth Hall Country Pk. 5C **70**
Croxteth Hall La. L11: Crox 3A **70**
L12: Crox, W Der 5B **70**
Croxteth La. L34: Know 5F **71**
CROXTETH PARK 3D **70**
Croxteth Rd. L8: Liv 2D **108**
L20: Boot 1H **67**
Croxteth Sports Cen. 2A **70**
Croxteth Vw. L32: K'by 6D **56**
(not continuous)
Croxton Ct. PR9: South 6A **8**
Croyde Cl. PR9: Marsh 2D **8**
Croyde Pl. WA9: Sut L 3E **94**
Croyde Rd. L24: Speke 6A **132**
Croydon Av. L18: Moss H 3H **109**
Croylands St. L4: Kirk 6A **68**
Crucian Way L12: Crox 3B **70**
Crummock Dr. WN3: Wigan 1D **50**
Crump St. L1: Liv 1A **108** (10H **5**)
Crutchley Av. CH41: Birk 7B **86**
Cryers La. CH2: Thor M 5K **171**
Crystal Cl. L13: Liv 5J **89**
WN2: Platt B 1K **51**
Cubbin Cres. L5: Kirk 1K **87**
Cubert Rd. L11: Crox 2A **70**
Cuckoo Cl. L25: Gate 4E **110**
Cuckoo La. CH64: Lit N, Nest 5B **158**
L25: Gate 3E **110**
Cuckoo Way L25: Gate 4E **110**
Cuerden St. L3: Liv 5K **87** (4G **4**)
Cuerdley Grn. WA5: Cuerd 6J **115**
Cuerdley Rd. WA5: Penk 5A **116**
Cuerdon Dr. WA4: Thel 7K **119**
Culbin Cl. WA3: Bchwd 1C **100**
CULCHETH 4C **80**
Culcheth Hall Dr. WA3: Cul 2B **80**
Culcross Av. WN3: Wigan 1A **50**
Culford Cl. WA7: Wind H 1B **154**
Cullen Av. L20: Boot 1K **67**
Cullen Cl. CH63: East 6J **145**
Cullen Dr. L21: Lith 6G **53**
Cullen Rd. WA7: West P 3K **151**
Cullen St. L8: Liv 1E **108**
Culme Rd. L12: W Der 7H **69**
Culshaw Way L40: Scar 2H **17**
Culzean Cl. L12: Crox 3C **70**
Cumberbatch Pl. WN3: Ince M 1K **51**
Cumberland Av. CH43: Pren 6A **106**
L17: Liv 2F **109**
L30: N'ton 2J **53**
WA10: St. H 6H **73**
Cumberland Cl. L6: Liv 1F **89**
Cumberland Cres. WA11: Hay 7J **61**
Cumberland Ga. L30: N'ton 1C **54**
Cumberland Gro. CH66: Gt Sut 1E **168**
Cumberland Rd. CH45: New B 7C **66**
PR8: South 3K **11**
Cumberland St. L1: Liv 5J **87** (5E **4**)
WA4: Warr 5C **118**
Cumber La. L35: Whis 3F **93**
Cumbers Dr. CH64: Ness 6A **158**
Cumbers La. CH64: Ness 6A **158**
Cumbrae Dr. CH65: Ell P 4A **170**
Cumbria Cl. CH66: Gt Sut 3G **169**
Cumbria Way L12: W Der 5A **70**
Cummings St. L1: Liv 7A **88** (9H **5**)
Cummins Av. L37: Form 5J **19**
Cumpsty Rd. L21: Lith 4J **53**
Cunard Av. CH44: Wall 2D **86**
Cunard Cl. CH43: Bid 2G **105**
Cunard Rd. L21: Lith 6H **53**
Cunliffe Av. WA12: New W 1F **77**
Cunliffe Cl. WA7: Pal F 3J **153**
Cunliffe St. L2: Liv 5J **87** (4E **4**)
Cunningham Cl. CH48: Caldy 3E **122**
WA5: Gt San 3D **116**
Cunningham Dr. CH63: Brom 2J **145**
WA7: Run 2A **152**
Cunningham Rd. L13: Liv 5J **89**
WA8: Wid 1K **133**
Cunscough La. L31: Mag 2B **44**
Cuper Cres. L36: Huy 3H **91**
Curate Rd. L6: Liv 7E **68**
Curlender Cl. CH41: Birk 6J **85**
Curlender Way L24: Hale 7E **132**
Curlew Av. CH49: Upton 2B **104**
Curlew Cl. CH49: Upton 2B **104**
Curlew Ct. CH46: More 6A **84**
Curlew Gro. L26: Halew 7J **111**
WA3: Bchwd 4A **100**
Curlew Way CH46: More 6A **84**
Currans Rd. WA2: Warr 5B **98**
Curran Way L33: K'by 6B **44**
Curtana Cres. L11: Crox 3A **70**
Curtis Rd. L4: Walt 5E **68**
Curwell Cl. CH63: Spit 6H **127**
Curzon Av. CH41: Birk 1B **106**
CH45: New B 6B **66**
Curzon Dr. WA4: Grap 2G **139**
Curzon Rd. CH42: Tran 6B **106**
CH47: Hoy 1C **102**
L22: Water 4E **52**
PR8: South 3K **11**
Curzon St. WA7: Run 1B **152**
Cusson Rd. L33: Know I 4F **57**
Custley Hey L28: Stock V 6F **71**
Custom Ho. La. L1: Liv 6J **87** (7E **4**)
Cut La. L33: Know 6J **57**
L39: Hals 2H **23**
Cygnet Cl. CH66: Gt Sut 7F **161**
L39: Augh 1A **34**
Cygnet Ct. L33: K'by 3E **56**
WA1: Warr 5A **118**
Cynthia Av. WA1: W'ston 1H **119**
Cynthia Rd. WA7: Run 7B **134**
Cypress Av. CH66: Gt Sut 3H **169**
WA8: Wid 5D **114**
Cypress Cl. L31: Mell 2J **55**
WA1: W'ston 1A **120**
Cypress Cft. CH63: Spit 6H **127**
Cypress Gdns. WA9: St. H 7J **73**
Cypress Gro. WA7: Run 3E **152**
Cypress Rd. L36: Huy 7H **91**
PR8: South 2A **12**
Cyprian's Way L30: N'ton 2A **54**
Cyprus Gro. L8: Liv 4C **108**
Cyprus St. L34: Prsct 1D **92**
Cyprus Ter. CH45: New B 7B **66**
Cyril Bell Cl. WA13: Lymm 5H **121**
Cyril Gro. L17: Aig 6G **109**
Cyril St. WA2: Warr 1B **118**

D

DACRE HILL 1F **127**
Dacres Bri. La. L35: Tar G 1C **112**
(not continuous)
Dacre St. CH41: Birk 2E **106**
L20: Boot 5H **67**
Dacy Rd. L5: Liv 1C **88**
Daffodil Cl. WA8: Wid 4G **115**
Daffodil Gdns. WA9: Bold 7J **75**
Daffodil Rd. CH41: Birk 1K **105**
L15: W'tree 1K **109**
Dagnall Av. WA5: Warr 5K **97**
Dagnall Rd. L32: K'by 4A **56**
Dahlia Cl. L9: Walt 2D **68**
WA9: Bold 7J **75**
Dailton Rd. WN8: Uph 4C **38**
Dairy Bank CH2: Elt 7B **164**
Dairy Farm Cl. WA13: Lymm 5H **121**
Dairy Farm Rd. WA11: Bic 6B **46**
WA11: R'ford 6B **46**
Dairy Lands Cl. L18: Moss H 2A **110**
Daisy Av. WA12: New W 4G **77**
Daisy Bank Mill Cl. WA3: Cul 3A **80**
Daisy Bank Rd. WA5: Penk 4D **116**
WA13: Lymm 5E **120**
Daisy Cl. PR9: Banks 3J **9**
Daisy Gro. L7: Liv 6D **88** (6P **5**)
Daisy M. L21: Lith 7H **53**
Daisy Mt. L31: Mag 4G **43**
Daisy St. L5: Kirk 7K **67**
Daisy Wlk. *PR8: South 1A 12*
(off Beacham Rd.)
Daisy Way PR8: South 6J **11**
Dakin Wlk. L33: K'by 3D **56**
Dakota Dr. WA5: Gt San 1G **117**
Dalby Cl. WA3: Bchwd 2D **100**
WA11: St. H 1E **74**
Dale, The CH64: Nest 5H **157**
WA5: Gt San, Penk 3D **116**
Dale Acre Dr. L30: N'ton 2J **53**
Dale Av. CH60: Hes 1D **142**
CH62: Brom 2K **145**
CH66: Lit Sut 5E **160**
Dalebrook Cl. L25: Gate 1F **111**
Dale Cl. L31: Mag 2E **42**
WA5: Warr 4J **117**
WA8: Wid 1G **133**
Dale Cres. WA9: Sut L 1F **95**
Dalecrest WN5: Bil 3F **49**
Dalecroft WA6: Hap 3E **172**
Dale Dr. CH65: Gt Sut 6H **161**
Dale End Rd. CH61: Barn 5G **125**
Dale Gdns. CH60: Hes 1B **142**
CH65: Whit 1K **169**
Dalegarth Av. L12: W Der 5D **70**
Dale Hall L18: Moss H 6H **109**
Dalehead Pl. WA11: St. H 4D **60**
Dale Hey CH44: Wall 4B **86**
CH66: Hoot 1A **160**
Dalehurst Cl. CH44: Wall 3D **86**
Dale La. L33: K'by 7E **44**
WA4: App 1E **138**
(not continuous)
Dalemeadow Rd. L14: K Ash 4B **90**
Dale M. L25: Gate 4F **111**
Dale Rd. CH62: Brom 4K **145**
WA3: Golb 6K **63**
DALES, THE 2C **142**
Daleside Av. WN4: Ash M 4E **50**
Daleside Cl. CH61: Irby 3D **124**
Daleside Rd. L33: K'by 2D **56**
Daleside Wlk. L33: K'by 2D **56**
Dales Row L36: Huy 5B **92**
Dale St. L2: Liv 5J **87** (6D **4**)
L3: Liv 5K **87** (5F **4**)
L19: Gars 4A **130**
WA7: Run 1C **152**
WN3: Ince M 1K **51**
Dales Wlk. L37: Form 4A **20**
Dalesway CH60: Hes 2C **142**
Dale Vw. WA12: New W 2J **77**
Dale Vw. Cl. CH61: Pens 5E **124**
Dalewood L12: Crox 3C **70**
Dalewood Cl. WA2: Warr 2A **118**
Dalewood Cres. CH2: Elt 1A **172**
Dalewood Gdns. L35: Whis 5F **93**
Daley Pl. L20: Boot 6A **54**
Daley Rd. L21: Lith 4J **53**
Dallam Ct. WA2: Warr 1A **118**
Dallam La. WA2: Warr 1A **118**
Dallas Gro. L9: Ain 7C **54**
Dallinton Ct. L13: Liv 5K **89**
Dalmeny St. L17: Aig 5D **108**
Dalmorton Rd. CH45: New B 6B **66**
Dalry Cres. L32: K'by 6D **56**
Dalrymple St. L5: Liv 2K **87**
Dalry Wlk. L32: K'by 6D **56**
Dalston Dr. WA11: St. H 4D **60**
Dalston Gro. WN3: Wins 1B **50**
DALTON 5K **27**
Dalton Av. WA3: Ris 1A **100**
WA5: Warr 1K **117**
Dalton Bank WA1: Warr 2C **118**
Dalton Cl. L12: W Der 4A **70**
WN5: Orr 4K **39**
Dalton Ct. WA7: Ast 6G **135**
Dalton Dr. WN3: Wins 1C **50**
Dalton Gro. WN4: Ash M 1E **62**
Dalton Rd. CH45: New B 7C **66**
Dalton St. WA7: Run 7F **135**
Daltry Cl. L12: W Der 7J **69**
Dalwood Cl. WA7: Murd 3C **154**
Damerham Cft. L25: Gate 1E **110**
Damerham M. L25: Gate 1E **110**
Damfield La. L31: Mag 3E **42**
Dam Head La.
WA3: G'brk, Rix 3H **101**
Damhead La. CH64: Will 4D **158**
Damian Dr. WA12: New W 1E **76**
Dam La. L40: Scar 3K **17**
WA1: W'ston 1K **119**
WA3: Ash M 2K **63**
WA3: Croft 7F **79**
WA3: Rix 2G **101**
WN4: Ash M 2K **63**
Damson Rd. L27: N'ley 2J **111**
Dam Wood La. L40: Scar 4K **17**
Dam Wood Rd. L24: Speke 7G **131**
Danbers WN8: Uph 5B **38**
Danby Cl. L5: Liv 2B **88**
WA5: Warr 1J **117**
WA7: Beech 4F **153**
Danby Fold L35: R'hill 4H **93**
Dane Bank Rd. WA13: Lymm 5G **121**
Dane Bank Rd. E.
WA13: Lymm 4G **121**
Dane Cl. CH61: Irby 3D **124**
Dane Ct. L35: R'hill 4J **93**
Danefield Pl. L19: Aller 1B **130**
Danefield Rd. CH49: Grea 6A **104**
L19: Aller 1B **130**
Danefield Ter. L19: Aller 1B **130**
Danehurst Rd. CH45: Wall 7K **65**
L9: Ain 6D **54**
Danesbury Cl. WN5: Bil 1G **61**
Danescourt Rd. CH41: Birk 7A **86**
L12: W Der 2A **90**
Danescroft WA8: Wid 5H **113**
Daneshill Cl. L17: Aig 2H **129**
Dane St. L4: Walt 5B **68**
Daneswell Dr. CH46: More 6D **84**
Danes Well Rd. L24: Speke 7A **132**
Daneville Rd. L4: Walt 4F **69**
Daneway PR8: Ains 3B **14**
Danger La. CH46: More 5D **84**
Daniel Cl. L20: Boot 7G **53**
WA3: Bchwd 3C **100**
Daniel Davies Dr. L8: Liv 1C **108**
Daniel Ho. L20: Boot 4J **67**
Daniels La. WN8: Skel 4J **37**
Dannette Hey L28: Stock V 1G **91**
Dansie St. L3: Liv 5A **88** (6K **5**)
Dan's Rd. WA8: Wid 6G **115**
Dante Cl. L9: Ain 5E **54**
Danube St. L8: Liv 1D **108**
Dapple Heath Av. L31: Mell 2J **55**
Darby Cl. CH64: Lit N 7J **157**
Darby Gro. L19: Gars 3K **129**
Darby Rd. L19: Gras 1J **129**
D'Arcy Cotts. *CH63: Thorn H 4B 144*
(off Raby Rd.)
Darent Rd. WA11: Hay 6K **61**
DARESBURY 6F **137**
Daresbury Av. PR8: Ains 4A **14**
Daresbury By-Pass
WA4: Dares 1F **155**
Daresbury Cl. L32: K'by 3A **56**
Daresbury Ct. WA8: Wid 5F **115**
Daresbury Expressway
WA4: Moore, Dares 5D **136**
WA7: Run, Ast, Wind H, Nort 7C **134**
Daresbury La.
WA4: Dares, Hatt 7G **137**
Daresbury Pk. WA4: Dares 2E **154**
Daresbury Rd. CH44: Wall 3A **86**
WA10: Eccl 2H **73**
Daresbury Science Pk.
WA4: Dares 6F **137**
Darfield WN8: Uph 4B **38**
Dark Entry L34: Know P 5J **71**
Dark La. L31: Mag 3F **43**
L40: Lath 4F **25**
Darley Av. WA2: Warr 4E **98**
Darley Cl. WA8: Wid 5H **113**

Darleydale Dr.—Dickson St.

Darleydale Dr. CH62: East 5B 146
Darley Dr. L12: W Der 1A 90
Darley Rd. WN3: Wigan 1F 51
Darlington Cl. CH44: Wall 3D 86
Darlington Ct. WA8: Wid 2C 134
Darlington St. CH44: Wall 3D 86
Darmond Rd. L33: K'by 2E 56
Darmond's Grn. CH48: W Kir 5D 102
Darmonds Grn. Av. L6: Liv 7E 68
Darnaway Cl. WA3: Bchwd 1D 100
Darnhall St. WN3: Ince M 1K 51
Darnley St. L8: Liv 3A 108
Darran Av. WN3: Wigan 1D 50
Darrel Dr. L7: Liv 1E 108
Darsefield Rd. L16: Child 1B 110
Dartford Cl. L14: K Ash 1D 90
Dartington Rd. L16: Child 7A 90
WN2: Platt B 1K 51
Dartmouth Av. L10: Ain 3E 54
Dartmouth Dr. L30: N'ton 1J 53
WA10: Windle 7J 59
Darvel Av. WN4: Gars 1A 62
Darwall Rd. L19: Aller 1B 130
Darwen Dr. WN2: Platt B 2K 51
Darwen Gdns. WA2: Warr 6E 98
Darwen St. L5: Liv 2H 87
Darwick Dr. L36: Huy 7K 91
Darwin Ct. PR9: South 6A 8
Darwin Gro. WA9: St. H 7A 74
Daryl Rd. CH60: Hes 1E 142
Dashwood Cl. WA4: Grap 2G 139
Daten Av. WA3: Ris 1A 100
Daulby St. L3: Liv 5B 88 (5K 5)
Dauntsey Brow L25: Gate 1F 111
Dauntsey M. L25: Gate 1F 111
Davenham Av. CH43: O'ton 5K 105
WA1: P'gate 7E 98
Davenham Cl. CH43: O'ton 6K 105
Davenham Ct. L15: W'tree 1J 109
Davenham Rd. L37: Form 6K 19
Davenhill Pk. L10: Ain 3E 54
Davenport Av. WA4: Westy 3F 119
Davenport Cl. CH48: Caldy 3F 123
Davenport Gro. L33: K'by 1C 56
Davenport Rd. CH60: Hes 3C 142
Davenport Row WA7: Run 2F 153
Daventree Rd. CH45: Wall 2B 86
Daventry Rd. L17: Aig 6G 109
David Lloyd Leisure
Cheshire Oaks 3B 170
Knowsley 4E 56
Liverpool 5C 130
Warrington 3H 117
David Rd. WA13: Lymm 5E 120
David's Av. WA5: Gt San 3F 117
Davidson Rd. L13: Liv 4H 89
David St. L8: Liv 4B 108
Davids Wlk. L25: Wltn 5G 111
Davies Av. WA4: Westy 4F 119
WA12: New W 1G 77
Davies Cl. WA8: Wid 5C 134
Davies St. L1: Liv 5J 87 (5E 4)
L20: Boot 2K 67
WA9: St. H 2E 74
Davies Way WA13: Lymm 5G 121
Davis Rd. CH46: Leas 4F 85
Davy Av. WA3: Ris 2A 100
Davy Cl. WA10: Eccl 1H 73
Davy Rd. WA7: Ast 6G 135
Davy St. L5: Liv 1C 88
Dawber Cl. L6: Liv 3C 88 (1N 5)
Dawber St. WN4: Ash M 1H 63
Dawley Cl. WN4: Ash M 2E 62
Dawlish Cl. L25: Hunts X 1G 131
WA3: Rix 4K 101
Dawlish Dr. PR9: Marsh 2C 8
Dawlish Rd. CH44: Wall 3K 85
CH61: Irby 4A 124
Dawlish Way WA3: Golb 4K 63
Dawn Cl. CH64: Ness 6A 158
WA9: St. H 7A 74
Dawn Gdns. CH65: Whit 7K 161
Dawn Wlk. L10: Faz 6K 55
Dawpool Cotts. CH48: Caldy 3J 123
Dawpool Dr. CH46: More 7C 84
CH62: Brom 3J 145
Dawson Av. CH41: Birk 7B 86
PR9: Cros 2E 8
WA9: St. H 7F 75
Dawson Gdns. L31: Mag 2E 42
Dawson Ho. WA5: Gt San 2A 116
Dawson Rd. L39: Orm 3D 24
Dawson St. L1: Liv 5K 87 (6F 4)
Dawson Way L1: Liv 6G 4
Dawstone Ri. CH60: Hes 3D 142
Dawstone Rd. CH60: Hes 3D 142
Daybrook WN8: Uph 4B 38
Dayfield WN8: Uph 4C 38
Days Mdw. CH49: Grea 5A 104
Day St. L13: Liv 4H 89
Deacon Cl. L22: Water 5D 52
Deacon Ct. L22: Water 5D 52
L25: Wltn 6F 111
Deacon Pk. L33: Know I 5E 56
Deacon Rd. WA8: Wid 7D 114
Deacons Cl. WA3: Croft 6G 79
Deacon Trad. Est. WA12: New W 4D 76
Deakin St. CH41: Birk 7K 85
Deal Cl. WA5: Warr 1K 117
Dealcroft L25: Wltn 6D 110
Dean Av. CH45: Wall 1J 85
Dean Cl. WA8: Wid 1D 134
WN5: Bil 2F 61
WN8: Uph 4E 38
Dean Ct. WN5: Orr 2K 39
Dean Cres. WA2: Warr 5B 98
WN5: Orr 3K 39
Dean Dillistone Ct.
L1: Liv 1A 108 (10H 5)
Deane Rd. L7: Liv 5E 88
Dean Ho. L22: Water 5D 52
Dean Mdw. WA12: New W 2G 77
Dean Patey Ct. L1: Liv 7A 88 (9J 5)
Deansburn Rd. L13: Liv 1G 89
Deanscales Rd. L11: N Grn. 4H 69
Deans Ct. L37: Form 5K 19
Deansfield Way CH2: Elt 1A 172
Deansgate CH65: Ell P 6J 161
Deansgate La. L37: Form 5B 20
Deansgate La. Nth. L37: Form 4A 20
DEANSGREEN 2K 141
Deans La. WA4: Thel 5B 120
Deans Rd. CH65: Ell P 1D 170
Dean St. L22: Water 5D 52
WA8: Wid 1D 134
Deans Way CH41: Birk 7K 85
Deansway WA8: Wid 1J 133
Deanwater Cl. WA3: Bchwd 3K 99
Dean Way WA9: Sut M 5D 94
Dean Wood Av. WN5: Orr 3G 39
Deanwood Cl. L35: Whis 5F 93
Dearden Way WN8: Uph 4C 38
Dearham Av. WA11: St. H 6C 60
Dearne Cl. L12: W Der 2C 90
Dearnford Av. CH62: Brom 4K 145
Dearnford Cl. CH62: Brom 4K 145
Dearnley Av. WA11: St. H 1G 75
Deauville Rd. L9: Ain 6E 54
Debra Cl. CH66: Gt Sut 7E 160
L31: Mell 1K 55
Debra Rd. CH66: Gt Sut 7E 160
Dee Cl. L33: K'by 6D 44
Dee Ct. L25: Gate 5G 111
Dee Ho. *L25: Gate 5G 111*
(off Woodsome Pk.)
Deelands Pk. CH46: More 6A 84
Dee La. CH48: W Kir 6C 102
Deeley Cl. L7: Liv 6E 88
Dee Pk. Cl. CH60: Hes 4F 143
Dee Pk. Rd. CH60: Hes 4F 143
Deepdale WA8: Wid 5J 113
Deepdale Av. L20: Boot 1G 67
WA11: St. H 4E 60
Deepdale Cl. CH43: Bid 2G 105
WA5: Gt San 1D 116
Deepdale Dr. L35: R'hill 4K 93
Deepdale Rd. L25: Gate 1E 110
Deepfield Dr. L36: Huy 7K 91
Deepfield Rd. L15: W'tree 2H 109
Deepwood Gro. L35: Whis 5E 92
Deerbarn Dr. L30: N'ton 1D 54
Deerbolt Cl. L32: K'by 2A 56
Deerbolt Cres. L32: K'by 2A 56
Deerbolt Way L32: K'by 2A 56
Deerbourne Cl. L25: Wltn 6D 110
Dee Rd. L35: R'hill 4H 93
Deer Pk. Ct. WA7: Pal F 4H 153
Deerwood Cl. CH66: Lit Sut 4F 161
Deerwood Cres.
CH66: Lit Sut 4F 161
Deeside CH60: Hes 2A 142
CH65: Whit 1K 169
Deeside Cl. CH43: Bid 2F 105
CH65: Whit 2K 169
Deeside Ct. CH64: Park 2F 157
Deeview Ct. CH64: Nest 5J 157
Dee Vw. Rd. CH60: Hes 2D 142
De Grouchy St. CH48: W Kir 5D 102
De-Haviland Way WN8: Skel 3A 38
Deighton Cl. WN5: Orr 6G 39
Deirdre Av. WA8: Wid 7C 114
Dekker Rd. L33: K'by 6C 44
Delabole Rd. L11: Crox 1B 70
De Lacy Row WA7: Cas 7J 135
Delafield Cl. WA2: Fearn 4F 99
Delagoa Rd. L10: Faz 7H 55
Delamain Rd. L13: Liv 1G 89
Delamere Av. CH62: East 6A 146
CH66: Gt Sut 6G 161
WA3: Low 1E 78
WA8: Wid 7J 113
WA9: Sut M 4C 94
Delamere Cl. CH43: Bid 2G 105
CH62: East 6A 146
L12: Crox 3B 70
Delamere Dr. CH66: Gt Sut 7G 161
Delamere Grn. CH66: Gt Sut 6G 161
Delamere Gro. CH44: Wall 5E 86
Delamere Rd. PR8: Ains 4B 14
WN8: Skel 1F 37
Delamere St. WA5: Warr 3J 117
Delamere Way WN8: Uph 4C 38
Delamore Pl. L4: Kirk 5A 68
Delamore's Acre CH64: Will 3G 159
Delamore St. L4: Kirk 5A 68
Delavor Cl. CH60: Hes 2C 142
Delavor Rd. CH60: Hes 2C 142
Delaware Cres. L32: K'by 2A 56
Delaware Rd. L20: Boot 2J 67
Delenty Dr. WA3: Ris 3K 99
Delery Dr. WA1: P'gate 7E 98
Delfby Cres. L32: K'by 4E 56
Delf Ho. WN8: Skel 2J 37
Delf La. L4: Walt 4C 68
L24: Speke 4F 131
L39: Has, Down 5C 22
Dell, The CH42: R Ferr 7G 107
L12: W Der 6C 70
WN8: Uph 4D 38
Dell Cl. CH63: Brom 4H 145
Dell Ct. CH43: Pren 7K 105
Dell Dr. WA2: Fearn 5G 99
Dellfield La. L31: Mag 3G 43
Dell Gro. CH42: R Ferr 1G 127
Dell La. CH60: Hes 3F 143
Dellside Cl. WN4: Ash M 6B 50
Dellside Gro. WA9: St. H 6E 74
Dell St. L7: Liv 5E 88
Delph Cl. L39: Augh 2A 34
Delph Comn. Rd. L39: Augh 2K 33
Delph Ct. L21: Lith 5G 53
WA9: St. H 5D 74
Delphfield WA7: Nort 2B 154
Delphfields Rd. WA4: App 2C 138
Delph Hollow Way WA9: St. H 6D 74
Delph La. L35: Whis 2F 93
L37: Form 7G 19
L39: Augh 2A 34
WA2: Hou G 7D 78
WA2: Win 3K 97
WA4: Dares 6E 136
Delph Mdw. Gdns. WN5: Bil 1F 61
Delph Pk. Av. L39: Augh 2K 33
Delph Rd. L23: Lit C 4D 40
Delphside Cl. WN5: Orr 6F 39
Delphside Rd. WN5: Orr 6F 39
Delph Top L39: Orm 4E 24
Delphwood Dr. WA9: St. H 5D 74
Delta Cres. WA5: W'brk 5G 97
Delta Dr. L12: W Der 6C 70
Delta Rd. L21: Lith 6H 53
WA9: St. H 2H 75
Delta Rd. E. CH42: R Ferr 7H 107
Delta Rd. W. CH42: R Ferr 7H 107
Deltic Way L30: N'ton 5D 54
L33: Know I 5F 57
Delves Av. CH63: Spit 6F 127
WA5: Warr 1K 117
Delyn Cl. CH42: R Ferr 7E 106
Demage Dr. CH66: Gt Sut 1F 169
Demesne St. CH44: Wall 4E 86
Denbigh Av. PR9: Chu 4B 8
WA9: St. H 7E 74
Denbigh Cl. WA6: Hel 3G 173
Denbigh Ct. CH65: Ell P 1B 170
Denbigh Gdns. CH65: Ell P 1A 170
Denbigh Rd. CH44: Wall 4C 86
L9: Walt 3B 68
Denbigh St. L5: Liv 2H 87
Denbury Av. WA4: S Hth 6F 119
Dencourt Rd. L11: N Grn. 5K 69
Deneacres L25: Wltn 6E 110
Dene Av. WA12: New W 2D 76
Denebank Rd. L4: Walt 7D 68
Denecliff L28: Stock V 6G 71
Dene Ct. L9: Faz 2H 69
Denefield Ho. *PR8: South 2H 11*
(off Portland St.)
Denehurst Cl. WA5: Penk 4D 116
Deneshey Rd. CH47: Meols 7E 82
Denes Way L28: Stock V 7E 70
Denford Cl. WN3: Wigan 1D 50
Denford Rd. L14: K Ash 2D 90
Denham Av. WA5: Gt San 3F 117
Denham Cl. L12: Crox 3D 70
Denham Dr. WN3: Wigan 1E 50
Denholme WN8: Uph 4B 38
Denise Av. WA5: Penk 3C 116
Denise Rd. L10: Faz 6K 55
Denison Gro. WA9: St. H 7A 74
Denman Dr. L6: Liv 3E 88
Denman Gro. CH44: Wall 5E 86
Denman St. L6: Liv 4D 88
Denman Way L6: Liv 3E 88
Denmark Rd. PR9: Chu 5C 8
Denmark St. L22: Water 4D 52
Dennett Cl. L31: Mag 5F 43
WA1: W'ston 2A 120
Dennett Rd. L35: Prsct 3C 92
Denning Dr. CH61: Irby 2B 124
Dennis Av. WA10: St. H 7J 73
Dennis Rd. WA8: Wid 2E 134
Denny Cl. CH49: Upton 4D 104
Densham Av. WA2: Warr 6B 98
Denshaw WN8: Uph 4B 38
Denston Cl. CH43: Bid 1F 105
Denstone Av. L10: Ain 3F 55
Denstone Cl. L14: K Ash 3F 91
L25: Wltn 1F 131
Dentdale Dr. L5: Liv 3A 88 (1J 5)
Denton Dr. CH45: Wall 1C 86
Denton Gro. L6: Liv 2E 88
WN5: Orr 3K 39
DENTON'S GREEN 1A 74
Dentons Grn. La.
WA10: St. H 1K 73
Denton St. L8: Liv 4B 108
WA8: Wid 7E 114
Dentwood St. L8: Liv 4C 108
Denver Dr. WA5: Gt San 1F 117
Denver Rd. L32: K'by 4A 56
WA4: Westy 5G 119
Denwall Ho. CH64: Nest 3J 157
Depot Rd. L33: Know I 1H 57
Derby Bldgs. L7: Liv 6C 88 (6P 5)
Derby Cl. WA12: New W 3F 77
Derby Ct. L37: Form 5J 19
Derby Dr. WA1: Warr 1E 118
WA11: R'ford 6G 47
Derby Gro. L31: Mag 6F 43
Derby Hall L17: Aig 4G 109
Derby Hill Cres. L39: Orm 5E 24
Derby Hill Rd. L39: Orm 5E 24
Derby Ho. L39: Orm 5D 24
Derby La. L13: Liv 3J 89
Derby Rd. CH42: Tran 5D 106
CH45: Wall 1A 86
L5: Kirk 1H 87
L20: Boot 3H 67
L36: Huy 4J 91
L37: Form 5J 19
PR9: South 1J 11
WA4: S Hth 1C 138
WA8: Wid 5C 114
WN8: Skel 3C 36
Derby Row WA12: New W 6H 77
DERBYSHIRE HILL 4H 75
Derbyshire Hill Rd. WA9: St. H 3H 75
Derbyshire Rd. WN3: Wins 3B 50
Derby Sq. L2: Liv 6J 87 (7D 4)
L34: Prsct 1E 92
Derby St. L19: Gars 5A 130
L34: Prsct 1C 92
L36: Huy 5A 92
L39: Orm 5D 24
WA12: New W 3F 77
WN3: Ince M 1K 51
Derby St. W. L39: Orm 5C 24
Derby Ter. L36: Huy 4J 91
Dereham Av. CH49: Upton 1E 104
Dereham Cres. L10: Faz 6H 55
Dereham Way WA7: Nort 6B 136
WN3: Wins 1B 50
Derek Av. WA2: Warr 6D 98
Derna Rd. L36: Huy 3H 91
Derringstone Cl. WA10: St. H 5K 73
Derrylea L9: Ain 6E 54
Derwent Av. L34: Prsct 1F 93
L37: Form 1H 29
PR9: Chu 6B 8
Derwent Cl. CH63: High B 4D 126
L31: Mag 2H 43
L33: K'by 1B 56
L35: R'hill 4H 93
WA3: Cul 4C 80
Derwent Ct. L18: Moss H 3B 110
Derwent Dr. CH45: Wall 1A 86
CH61: Pens 5D 124
CH66: Hoot 1D 160
L21: Lith 5K 53
Derwent Rd. CH43: O'ton 4B 106
CH47: Meols 7G 83
CH63: High B 4D 126
L23: C'by 2F 53
WA4: Warr 6B 118
WA8: Wid 7J 113
WA11: St. H 6D 60
WN4: Ash M 7J 51
WN5: Orr 3H 39
Derwent Rd. E. L13: Liv 3J 89
Derwent Rd. W. L13: Liv 3H 89
Derwent Sq. L13: Liv 3H 89
Derwent Way CH64: Lit N 4K 157
Desborough Cres.
L12: W Der 7J 69
Desford Av. WA11: St. H 7F 61
Desford Cl. CH46: More 6K 83
Desford Rd. L19: Aig 1G 129
De Silva St. L36: Huy 5A 92
Desmond Cl. CH43: Bid 1G 105
Desmond Gro. L23: C'by 2F 53
Desoto Rd. WA8: Wid 4K 133
Desoto Rd. E. WA8: Wid 3B 134
(not continuous)
Desoto Rd. W. WA8: Wid 3B 134
Deva Cl. L33: K'by 5C 44
Deva Rd. CH48: W Kir 6C 102
Deveraux Dr. CH44: Wall 4B 86
Deverell Gro. L15: W'tree 6K 89
Deverell Rd. L15: W'tree 7J 89
Deverill Rd. CH42: R Ferr 7E 106
Devilla Cl. L14: K Ash 1E 90
De Villiers Av. L23: C'by 7E 40
Devisdale Gro. CH43: Bid 1G 105
Devizes Cl. L25: Gate 1F 111
Devizes Dr. CH61: Irby 2B 124
Devoke Av. WA11: St. H 4C 60
Devon Av. CH45: Wall 2C 86
WN8: Uph 5D 38
Devon Cl. L23: Blun 2A 52
Devon Ct. L5: Liv 2C 88
Devondale Rd. L18: Moss H 3J 109
Devon Dr. CH61: Pens 5C 124
Devon Farm Way L37: Form 7B 20
Devonfield Rd. L9: Walt 1B 68
Devon Gdns. CH42: R Ferr 7E 106
L16: Child 3C 110
Devon Pl. WA8: Wid 5C 114
Devonport St. L8: Liv 3B 108
Devonshire Cl. CH43: O'ton 3B 106
L33: K'by 1C 56
Devonshire Gdns. WA12: New W 4G 77
DEVONSHIRE PARK 5C 106
Devonshire Pl. CH43: O'ton 3A 106
L5: Liv 1A 88
WA7: Run 6C 134
Devonshire Rd. CH43: O'ton 3B 106
CH44: Wall 3B 86
CH48: W Kir 7E 102
CH49: Upton 3C 104
CH61: Pens 5C 124
L8: Liv 3C 108
L22: Water 3C 52
PR9: South 7C 8
WA1: P'gate 7F 99
WA10: St. H 1K 73
Devonshire Rd. W. L8: Liv 3C 108
Devon St. L3: Liv 5A 88 (4J 5)
WA10: St. H 2K 73
Devonwall Gdns. L8: Liv 3D 108
Devon Way L16: Child 2C 110
L36: Huy 3A 92
(not continuous)
Dewar Ct. WA7: Ast 6G 135
Dewar St. WA3: Ris 2A 100
Dewberry Cl. CH42: Tran 4D 106
Dewberry Flds. WN8: Uph 4D 38
Dewey Av. L9: Ain 5D 54
Dewhurst Rd. WA3: Bchwd 4K 99
Dewlands Rd. L21: Sea 5F 53
Dewsbury Rd. L4: Walt 1D 88
Dexter St. L8: Liv 2A 108
Dexter Way WN8: Uph 5D 38
Deycroft Av. L33: K'by 1D 56
Deycroft Wlk. L33: K'by 1E 56
Deyes Ct. L31: Mag 3G 43
Deyes End L31: Mag 3F 43
Deyes La. L31: Mag 3F 43
Deyes Lane Swimming Pool 3F 43
Deysbrook La. L12: W Der 1A 90
(not continuous)
Deysbrook Side L12: W Der 1A 90
Deysbrook Way L12: W Der 6B 70
Dial Rd. CH42: Tran 5D 106
Dial St. L7: Liv 5E 88
WA1: Warr 3C 118
Diamond Bus. Pk. WA11: R'ford 7H 47
Diamond St. L5: Liv 3K 87 (1F 4)
Diana Rd. L20: Boot 6K 53
Diana St. L4: Walt 6B 68
Diane Ho. L8: Liv 10K 5
Diane Rd. WN4: Ash M 7H 51
Dibbinsdale Local Nature Reserve
7J 127
Dibbinsdale Rd. CH63: Brom 2H 145
Dibbins Grn. CH63: Brom 4H 145
Dibbins Hey CH63: Spit 7G 127
Dibbinview Gro. CH63: Spit 7H 127
Dibb La. L23: Lit C 5C 40
Dicconson's La. L39: Hals 7E 22
Dicconson St. WA10: St. H 2C 74
Dicconson Way L39: Orm 6E 24
Dickens Av. CH43: Pren 7K 105
Dickens Cl. CH43: Pren 7K 105
L32: K'by 5B 56
Dickenson St. L1: Liv 9F 4
WA2: Warr 1C 118
Dickens Pl. WN3: Wigan 1D 50
Dickens Rd. WA10: St. H 6J 73
Dickens St. L8: Liv 2B 108
Dicket's La. WN8: Skel 7K 25
Dickinson Cl. L37: Form 1K 29
WA11: Hay 7J 61
Dickinson Ct. PR8: B'dale 6G 11
Dickinson Rd. L37: Form 1K 29
Dick's La. L40: Westh 6J 25
Dickson Cl. WA8: Wid 1D 134
Dickson St. L3: Liv 3H 87 (1B 4)
WA8: Wid 1C 134
(not continuous)

Didcot Cl.—Durham Ct.

Didcot Cl. L25: Hunts X . . . 1H **131**
Didsbury Cl. L33: K'by . . . 3D **56**
Digg La. CH46: More . . . 6B **84**
Dig La. WA2: Fearn . . . 3H **99**
WA6: Frod . . . 4C **166**
DIGMOOR . . . 5K **37**
Digmoor Dr. WN8: Skel . . . 4H **37**
Digmoor Rd. L32: K'by . . . 6D **56**
WN8: Skel . . . 4J **37**
Digmoor Wlk. L32: K'by . . . 6D **56**
Dignum Mead L27: N'ley . . . 3J **111**
Dilloway St. WA10: St. H . . . 2K **73**
Dinas La. L36: Huy . . . 3E **90**
Dinas La. Pde. L14: K Ash . . . 3E **90**
Dinesen Rd. L19: Gars . . . 2A **130**
DINGLE . . . 5C **108**
Dingle, The WA13: Lymm . . . 5G **121**
Dingle Av. WA12: New W . . . 4D **76**
WN8: Uph . . . 3D **38**
Dingle Bank Cl.
WA13: Lymm . . . 5G **121**
Dinglebrook Rd. L9: Ain . . . 3E **68**
Dingle Brow L8: Liv . . . 5C **108**
Dingle Cl. L39: Augh . . . 2A **34**
Dingle Grange L8: Liv . . . 5C **108**
Dingle Gro. L8: Liv . . . 4C **108**
Dingle La. L8: Liv . . . 5C **108**
WA4: App . . . 3F **139**
Dingle Mt. L8: Liv . . . 5C **108**
Dingle Rd. CH42: Tran . . . 4C **106**
L8: Liv . . . 5B **108**
WN8: Uph . . . 4D **38**
Dingle Ter. L8: Liv . . . 4C **108**
Dingle Va. L8: Liv . . . 5C **108**
Dingleway WA4: App . . . 1D **138**
Dingley Av. L9: Walt . . . 7B **54**
Dingwall Dr. CH49: Grea . . . 5C **104**
Dinmore Rd. CH44: Wall . . . 3B **86**
Dinnington Ct. WA8: Wid . . . 5A **114**
Dinorben Av. WA9: St. H . . . 7E **74**
Dinorwic Rd. L4: Walt . . . 1C **88**
PR8: B'dale . . . 5G **11**
Dinsdale Rd. CH62: Brom . . . 7A **128**
Discovery Cl. L19: Gars . . . 5B **130**
Ditchfield L37: Form . . . 1A **30**
Ditchfield La. WA16: H Legh . . . 5K **141**
Ditchfield Pl. WA8: Wid . . . 1H **133**
Ditchfield Rd. WA5: Penk . . . 5C **116**
WA8: Wid . . . 1G **133**
DITTON . . . 1J **133**
Ditton La. CH46: Leas . . . 4B **84**
Ditton Rd. WA8: Wid . . . 3J **133**
(not continuous)
Dixon Av. WA12: New W . . . 1G **77**
Dixon Cl. WA11: Hay . . . 5E **62**
Dixon M. L30: N'ton . . . 7A **42**
Dixon Rd. L33: Know I . . . 5F **57**
Dixon St. WA1: Warr . . . 3A **118**
Dobbs Dr. L37: Form . . . 6A **20**
Dobers La. WA6: Frod . . . 7E **166**
Dobsons La. WA9: St. H . . . 6B **74**
Dobson St. L6: Liv . . . 3B **88** (1M **5**)
Dobson Wlk. L6: Liv . . . 3C **88** (1M **5**)
Dock Rd. CH41: Birk . . . 5A **86**
L19: Gars . . . 4K **129**
WA8: Wid . . . 4B **134**
Dock Rd. Nth. CH62: Port S . . . 3J **127**
Dock Rd. Sth. CH62: Brom . . . 5K **127**
Docks Link CH44: Wall . . . 4K **85**
Dock St. CH65: Ell P . . . 4A **162**
WA8: Wid . . . 4C **134**
Dock Yd. Rd. CH65: Ell P . . . 5B **162**
Doctor's La. L37: Gt Alt . . . 2E **30**
Dodd Av. CH49: Grea . . . 5B **104**
WA10: St. H . . . 2J **73**
Doddridge Rd. L8: Liv . . . 3A **108**
Dodds La. L31: Mag . . . 2E **42**
Dodleston Cl. CH43: Noct . . . 4H **105**
Dodman Rd. L11: Crox . . . 1B **70**
Dodson Cl. WN4: Ash M . . . 2G **63**
Dodworth Av. PR8: South . . . 3A **12**
Doeford Cl. WA3: Cul . . . 1K **79**
DOE GREEN . . . 5B **116**
Doe Mdw. WN8: Newb . . . 1G **27**
(not continuous)
Doe Pk. Courtyard L25: Wltn . . . 1E **130**
Doe's Mdw. Rd. CH63: Brom . . . 3H **145**
DOG & GUN . . . 3J **69**
Dolly's La. PR9: South . . . 7F **9**
Dolmans La. WA1: Warr . . . 3B **118**
Dolomite Av. L24: Speke . . . 3D **130**
Dolphin Cres. CH66: Gt Sut . . . 2G **169**
Domar Cl. L32: K'by . . . 4C **56**
Dombey Pl. L8: Liv . . . 2B **108**
Dombey St. L8: Liv . . . 2B **108**
Domingo Dr. L33: K'by . . . 7B **44**
Dominic Cl. L16: Child . . . 7C **90**
Dominic Rd. L16: Child . . . 7C **90**
Dominion St. L6: Liv . . . 2E **88**
Domville L35: Whis . . . 5E **92**
Domville Cl. WA13: Lymm . . . 5G **121**
Domville Dr. CH49: W'chu . . . 5E **104**
Domville Rd. L13: Liv . . . 6J **89**
Donaldson Ct. L5: Liv . . . 1C **88**
Donaldson St. L5: Liv . . . 1C **88**
Donalds Way L17: Aig . . . 7G **109**
Doncaster Dr. CH49: Upton . . . 2D **104**
Donegal Rd. L13: Liv . . . 4K **89**
Donne Av. CH63: Spit . . . 6F **127**
Donne Cl. CH63: Spit . . . 6G **127**
Donnington Cl. L36: Roby . . . 7H **91**
Donnington Lodge PR8: South . . . 2F **11**
Donsby Rd. L9: Ain . . . 7D **54**
Don Wlk. CH65: Ell P . . . 4J **161**
Dood's La. WA4: App . . . 4G **139**
Dooley Dr. L30: N'ton . . . 1D **54**
Doon Cl. L4: Kirk . . . 6A **68**
Dorans La. L2: Liv . . . 6J **87** (6E **4**)
Dorbett Dr. L23: C'by . . . 3F **53**
Dorchester Cl. CH49: Upton . . . 4D **104**
Dorchester Dr. L33: K'by . . . 7D **44**
Dorchester Pk. CH43: Noct . . . 5H **105**
WA7: Nort . . . 6B **136**
Dorchester Rd. L25: Gate . . . 2F **111**
WA5: Gt San . . . 3F **117**
WN8: Uph . . . 4C **38**
Dorchester Way WA5: B'wood . . . 1D **96**
Doreen Av. CH46: More . . . 7B **84**
Dorgan Cl. L35: R'hill . . . 3H **93**
Doric Av. WA6: Frod . . . 4E **166**
Doric Grn. WN5: Bil . . . 1F **49**
Doric Rd. L13: Liv . . . 3J **89**
Doric St. CH42: R Ferr . . . 6F **107**
L21: Sea . . . 6F **53**
Dorien Rd. L13: Liv . . . 5H **89**
Dorin Ct. CH43: O'ton . . . 4A **106**
Dorking Gro. L15: W'tree . . . 2K **109**
Dorney Cl. WA4: App . . . 3E **138**
Dorney Ct. L12: W Der . . . 7B **70**
Dornoch Ho. WA3: Ris . . . 1K **99**
Dorothea St. WA2: Warr . . . 1C **118**
Dorothy St. L7: Liv . . . 6D **88** (6P **5**)
WA9: St. H . . . 7A **74**
Dorothy Wlk. WN2: Bam . . . 4K **51**
Dorrington Cl. WA7: Murd . . . 2B **154**
Dorrit St. L8: Liv . . . 2B **108**
Dorset Av. L15: W'tree . . . 1E **108**
PR8: Ains . . . 7C **14**
Dorset Cl. L20: Boot . . . 3K **67**
Dorset Ct. L25: Gate . . . 2F **111**
WA7: Pal F . . . 4J **153**
Dorset Dr. CH61: Pens . . . 5C **124**
Dorset Gdns. CH42: R Ferr . . . 7E **106**
Dorset Rd. CH45: New B . . . 7A **66**
CH48: W Kir . . . 5E **102**
L6: Liv . . . 1F **89**
L36: Huy . . . 4A **92**
WA10: St. H . . . 5K **73**
Dorset Way WA1: W'ston . . . 7H **99**
Douglas Arc. *CH41: Birk* . . . *2E 106*
(off Douglas St.)
Douglas Av. WA9: Bold . . . 1K **95**
WN5: Bil . . . 2F **61**
WN8: Uph . . . 4D **38**
Douglas Cl. L13: Liv . . . 3H **89**
WA8: Wid . . . 5G **115**
Douglas Dr. CH46: More . . . 7B **84**
L31: Mag . . . 2H **43**
L39: Orm . . . 3B **24**
WN5: Orr . . . 4H **39**
Douglas Pl. L20: Boot . . . 4H **67**
Douglas Rd. CH48: W Kir . . . 5F **103**
L4: Walt . . . 1D **88**
PR9: Cros . . . 3E **8**
Douglas St. CH41: Birk . . . 2E **106**
WA10: St. H . . . 3K **73**
Douglas Way L33: K'by . . . 6D **44**
WN2: Platt B . . . 2K **51**
Doulton Cl. CH43: Bid . . . 1F **105**
WN2: Platt B . . . 1K **51**
Doulton Pl. L35: Whis . . . 4C **92**
Doulton St. WA10: St. H . . . 3K **73**
Doune Ct. CH65: Ell P . . . 1B **170**
Dounrey Cl. WA2: Fearn . . . 5G **99**
Douro Pl. L13: Liv . . . 5H **89**
Douro St. L5: Liv . . . 3A **88** (1H **5**)
Dove Cl. CH2: Elt . . . 7C **164**
CH66: Ell P . . . 4J **161**
WA3: Bchwd . . . 3B **100**
WA6: Hel . . . 6J **165**
DOVECOT . . . 3D **90**
Dovecot Av. L14: K Ash . . . 4D **90**
Dovecote Dr. WA11: Hay . . . 6A **62**
Dovecote Grn. WA5: W'brk . . . 5E **96**
Dovecot Pl. *L14: K Ash* . . . *3D 90*
(off Dovecot Av.)
Dove Ct. L25: Wltn . . . 5E **110**
Dovedale Av. CH62: East . . . 5A **146**
L31: Mag . . . 2E **42**
Dovedale Cl. CH43: Pren . . . 6K **105**
WA2: Warr . . . 4E **98**
(not continuous)
Dovedale Ct. WA8: Wid . . . 5H **113**
Dovedale Cres. WN4: Ash M . . . 4E **50**
Dovedale Rd. CH45: Wall . . . 7A **66**
CH47: Hoy . . . 7D **82**
L18: Moss H . . . 3H **109**
WN4: Ash M . . . 5D **50**
Dovepoint Rd. CH47: Meols . . . 6G **83**
Dovercliffe Rd. L13: Liv . . . 4K **89**
Dover Cl. CH41: Birk . . . 1D **106**
WA7: Murd . . . 4C **154**
Dover Ct. CH65: Ell P . . . 2B **170**
Dovercroft L25: Wltn . . . 6D **110**
Dover Dr. CH65: Ell P . . . 2B **170**
Dover Gro. L16: Child . . . 7C **90**
Dove Rd. L9: Walt . . . 7B **54**
Dover Rd. L31: Mag . . . 6E **42**
PR8: B'dale . . . 6E **10**
WA4: Westy . . . 5G **119**
Dover St. L3: Liv . . . 5B **88** (6K **5**)
WA7: Run . . . 6D **134**
Dovesmead Rd. CH60: Hes . . . 3H **143**
Dovestone Cl. L7: Liv . . . 7D **88** (8P **5**)
Dove St. L8: Liv . . . 1D **108** (10P **5**)
Dovey St. L8: Liv . . . 3B **108**
Doward St. WA8: Wid . . . 6E **114**
Dower St. WN2: Platt B . . . 1K **51**
Dowhills Dr. L23: Blun . . . 7B **40**
Dowhills Pk. L23: Blun . . . 6B **40**
Dowhills Rd. L23: Blun . . . 6B **40**
DOWNALL GREEN . . . 7B **50**
Downall Grn. WN4: Gars . . . 7B **50**
Downall Grn. Rd. WN4: Ash M . . . 7C **50**
Downbrook Way *WN4: Ash M* . . . *7H 51*
(off North St.)
Downes Grn. CH63: Spit . . . 1G **145**
Downham Av. WA3: Cul . . . 4B **80**
Downham Cl. L25: Wltn . . . 3D **110**
Downham Dr. CH60: Hes . . . 2E **142**
Downham Grn. L25: Wltn . . . 3D **110**
Downham Rd. CH42: Tran . . . 5D **106**
Downham Rd. Nth. CH61: Hes . . . 7E **124**
Downham Rd. Sth. CH60: Hes . . . 2E **142**
Downham Wlk. WN5: Bil . . . 3F **49**
Downham Way L25: Wltn . . . 3D **110**
DOWNHOLLAND . . . 1A **32**
DOWNHOLLAND CROSS . . . 7D **22**
Downholland Moss La.
L37: Form . . . 6B **20**
Downing Cl. CH43: O'ton . . . 5B **106**
WN2: Platt B . . . 2K **51**
Downing Rd. L20: Boot . . . 4K **67**
Downing St. L5: Liv . . . 2B **88**
Downlands Rd. L27: N'ley . . . 4K **111**
Downland Way WA9: St. H . . . 5H **75**
Downs, The L23: Blun . . . 2B **52**
WN3: Wigan . . . 7K **39**
Downside WA8: Wid . . . 5H **113**
Downside Cl. L30: N'ton . . . 1A **54**
Downside Dr. L10: Ain . . . 4H **55**
Downs Rd. WA7: Run . . . 1C **152**
WA10: St. H . . . 4K **73**
Downway La. WA9: St. H . . . 5J **75**
Dowsefield La. L18: Aller . . . 5C **110**
Dragon Cl. L11: Crox . . . 2A **70**
WN8: Skel . . . 3A **38**
Dragon Cres. L35: Whis . . . 3F **93**
Dragon Dr. L35: Whis . . . 4E **92**
Dragon La. L35: Whis . . . 5D **92**
Dragons Health Club . . . 5H **7**
Dragon Wlk. L11: Crox . . . 2A **70**
Dragon Yd. WA8: Wid . . . 4D **114**
Drake Cl. L10: Faz . . . 6J **55**
L35: Whis . . . 5E **92**
L39: Augh . . . 1A **34**
WA5: Old H . . . 6H **97**
Drake Cres. L10: Faz . . . 6H **55**
Drakefield Rd. L11: N Grn. . . . 3F **69**
Drake Gdns. WA9: St. H . . . 1A **94**
Drake Pl. L10: Faz . . . 6H **55**
Drake Rd. CH46: Leas . . . 3F **85**
CH64: Nest . . . 2J **157**
L10: Faz . . . 6H **55**
Drake St. L20: Boot . . . 5H **67**
WA10: St. H . . . 2K **73**
Drake Way L10: Faz . . . 6J **55**
Draw Well Rd. L33: Know I . . . 3H **57**
Draycott St. L8: Liv . . . 5B **108**
Drayton Cl. CH61: Irby . . . 4B **124**
WA7: Run . . . 1B **152**
Drayton Cres. WA11: St. H . . . 7F **61**
Drayton Rd. CH44: Wall . . . 4C **86**
L4: Walt . . . 4C **68**
Drennan Rd. L19: Aller . . . 1C **130**
Drewell Rd. L18: Moss H . . . 4H **109**
Drewitt Cres. PR9: Cros . . . 3F **9**
Driffield Rd. L34: Prsct . . . 1C **92**
Drinkwater Gdns. L3: Liv . . . 4A **88** (2H **5**)
Drive, The L12: W Der . . . 2K **89**
DriveTime (Golf Driving Range)
. . . 6A **118**
Driveway L35: Whis . . . 5F **93**
Droitwich Av. CH49: Grea . . . 4A **104**
Dromore Av. L18: Moss H . . . 5H **109**
Dronfield Way L25: Gate . . . 1D **110**
Drovers La. WA6: Frod . . . 7E **166**
Droxford Dr. L25: Gate . . . 1D **110**
Druids' Cross Gdns.
L18: Moss H . . . 4B **110**
Druids' Cross Rd.
L18: Moss H . . . 4B **110**
Druids Pk. L18: Moss H . . . 4C **110**
Druid St. WN4: Ash M . . . 3G **63**
Druidsville Rd. L18: Moss H . . . 4B **110**
Druids Way CH49: W'chu . . . 6E **104**
Drum Cl. L14: K Ash . . . 2E **90**
DRUMMERSDALE . . . 2K **17**
Drummersdale La. L40: Scar . . . 7K **13**
Drummer's La. WN4: Ash M . . . 5B **50**
Drummond Av. CH66: Gt Sut . . . 7E **160**
Drummond Ct. WA8: Wid . . . 6F **115**
Drummond Rd. CH47: Hoy . . . 3C **102**
L4: Walt . . . 5E **68**
L23: Thorn . . . 1H **53**
Drummoyne Ct. L23: Blun . . . 7A **40**
Druridge Dr. WA5: Penk . . . 4D **116**
Drury La. L2: Liv . . . 6J **87** (6D **4**)
Drybeck Gro. WA9: St. H . . . 1F **95**
Dryburgh Way L4: Kirk . . . 6A **68**
Dryden Av. WN4: Ash M . . . 5D **50**
Dryden Cl. CH43: Bid . . . 1G **105**
L35: Whis . . . 4E **92**
Dryden Gro. L36: Huy . . . 6K **91**
Dryden Pl. WA2: Warr . . . 5C **98**
Dryden Rd. L7: Liv . . . 6G **89**
Dryden St. L5: Liv . . . 3K **87**
L20: Boot . . . 1G **67**
Dryfield Cl. CH49: Grea . . . 4B **104**
Dublin Cft. CH66: Gt Sut . . . 3G **169**
Dublin St. L3: Liv . . . 3H **87**
Ducie St. L8: Liv . . . 2C **108**
Duckinfield St. L3: Liv . . . 6B **88** (6K **5**)
Duck Pond La. CH42: Tran . . . 6A **106**
Duckworth Gro. WA2: P'gate . . . 6G **99**
Duddingston Av. L18: Moss H . . . 3H **109**
L23: C'by . . . 3E **52**
Duddon Av. L31: Mag . . . 2H **43**
Duddon Cl. CH43: O'ton . . . 5K **105**
Dudleston Rd. CH66: Lit Sut . . . 5D **160**
Dudley Av. WA7: Run . . . 7F **135**
Dudley Cl. CH43: O'ton . . . 4B **106**
Dudley Cres. CH65: Hoot . . . 7D **146**
Dudley Gro. L23: C'by . . . 3E **52**
Dudley Pl. WA9: St. H . . . 3E **74**
Dudley Rd. CH45: New B . . . 6A **66**
CH65: Ell P . . . 6K **161**
L18: Moss H . . . 3H **109**
Dudley St. WA2: Warr . . . 1B **118**
WA9: St. H . . . 3E **74**
WN4: Ash M . . . 7E **50**
Dudlow Ct. L18: Moss H . . . 3A **110**
Dudlow Dr. L18: Moss H . . . 3A **110**
Dudlow Gdns. L18: Moss H . . . 2A **110**
Dudlow Grn. Rd. WA4: App . . . 4D **138**
Dudlow La. L18: Moss H . . . 2K **109**
Dudlow Nook Rd.
L18: Moss H . . . 2A **110**
DUDLOW'S GREEN . . . 3D **138**
Dugdale Cl. L19: Gras . . . 2J **129**
Duke Av. PR8: South . . . 4J **11**
Duke Cl. WA7: Run . . . 6B **134**
Duke of York Cotts.
CH62: New F . . . 3G **127**
Dukes Rd. L5: Liv . . . 1A **88**
Dukes Ter. L1: Liv . . . 7A **88** (8H **5**)
Duke St. CH41: Birk . . . 6C **86**
CH45: New B . . . 6B **66**
L1: Liv . . . 7K **87** (8F **4**)
L19: Gars . . . 3A **130**
L22: Water . . . 5D **52**
L34: Prsct . . . 7D **72**
L37: Form . . . 1J **29**
PR8: South . . . 2G **11**
(not continuous)
WA3: Golb . . . 4K **63**
WA10: St. H . . . 2B **74**
WA12: New W . . . 3F **77**
WN3: Wigan . . . 1D **50**
WN4: Ash M . . . 2G **63**
Duke St. Bri. CH41: Birk . . . 6C **86**
Duke St. La. L1: Liv . . . 7K **87** (8F **4**)
Dukes Way L37: Form . . . 1K **29**
Dukes Wharf WA7: Pres B . . . 4C **154**
Duke's Wood La. WN8: Skel . . . 1K **47**
Dulas Grn. L32: K'by . . . 4E **56**
Dulas Rd. L15: W'tree . . . 2K **109**
L32: K'by . . . 4E **56**
Dulson Way L34: Prsct . . . 2A **92**
Dulverton Rd. L17: Aig . . . 1G **129**
Dumbarton St. L4: Walt . . . 5A **68**
Dumbrees Gdns. L12: W Der . . . 6C **70**
Dumbrees Rd. L12: W Der . . . 6C **70**
Dumbreeze Gro. L34: Know . . . 1H **71**
Dumfries Way L33: K'by . . . 6B **44**
Dunacre Way L26: Halew . . . 2K **131**
Dunbabin Rd. L15: W'tree . . . 2K **109**
L16: Child . . . 2K **109**
Dunbar Cl. CH66: Lit Sut . . . 6E **160**
Dunbar Ct. CH66: Lit Sut . . . 6E **160**
Dunbar Cres. PR8: B'dale . . . 1F **15**
Dunbar Rd. PR8: B'dale . . . 6E **10**
Dunbar St. L4: Walt . . . 4B **68**
Dunbeath Av. L35: R'hill . . . 6K **93**
Dunbeath Cl. L35: R'hill . . . 6K **93**
Dunblane Cl. WN4: Gars . . . 1A **62**
Duncan Av. WA7: Run . . . 1E **152**
WA12: New W . . . 1G **77**
Duncan Cl. WA10: St. H . . . 4A **74**
Duncan Dr. CH49: Grea . . . 4B **104**
Duncansby Cres. WA5: Gt San . . . 2C **116**
Duncansby Dr. CH63: East . . . 6J **145**
Duncan St. CH41: Birk . . . 2F **107**
L1: Liv . . . 1A **108** (10H **5**)
WA2: Warr . . . 1C **118**
WA10: St. H . . . 3A **74**
Dunchurch Rd. L14: K Ash . . . 2D **90**
Duncombe Rd. Nth. L19: Gras . . . 2K **129**
Duncombe Rd. Sth. L19: Gars . . . 2K **129**
Duncote Cl. CH43: O'ton . . . 4A **106**
L35: Whis . . . 2G **93**
Dundale Rd. L13: Liv . . . 4K **89**
Dundalk La. WA8: Wid . . . 1K **133**
Dundalk Rd. WA8: Wid . . . 1K **133**
Dundas St. L20: Boot . . . 5H **67**
Dundee Cl. WA2: Fearn . . . 3E **98**
Dundee Ct. CH65: Ell P . . . 1C **170**
Dundee Gro. CH44: Wall . . . 4A **86**
Dundonald Av. WA4: S Hth . . . 7C **118**
Dundonald Rd. L17: Aig . . . 7G **109**
Dundonald St. CH41: Birk . . . 7A **86**
Dunedin St. WA9: St. H . . . 7A **74**
Dunes Dr. L37: Form . . . 6G **19**
Dunes Leisure Cen. . . . 1F **11**
Dunes Way L5: Kirk . . . 1J **87**
Dunfold Cl. L32: K'by . . . 4D **56**
Dungeon La. L24: Hale . . . 7K **131**
WN8: Dalt . . . 3J **27**
Dunham Av. WA3: Golb . . . 4K **63**
Dunham Cl. CH62: East . . . 7B **146**
Dunham Ct. WA6: Dun H . . . 6E **172**
DUNHAM HEATH . . . 7G **173**
DUNHAM-ON-THE-HILL . . . 6E **172**
Dunham Rd. L15: W'tree . . . 6J **89**
Dunkeld Cl. L6: Liv . . . 4C **88** (2N **5**)
Dunkeld St. L6: Liv . . . 4C **88** (2N **5**)
Dunkerron Cl. L27: N'ley . . . 1G **111**
DUNKIRK . . . 6G **169**
Dunkirk Cres. CH65: Whit . . . 3J **169**
Dunkirk Dr. CH65: Whit . . . 3K **169**
Dunkirk La. CH1: Dunk . . . 4E **168**
CH65: Whit . . . 3J **169**
Dunkirk Rd. PR8: B'dale . . . 6F **11**
Dunkirk Trad. Est. CH1: Dunk . . . 6G **169**
Dunley Cl. WA3: Bchwd . . . 1C **100**
Dunlin Av. WA12: New W . . . 2G **77**
Dunlin Cl. L27: N'ley . . . 4J **111**
WA2: Warr . . . 4E **98**
WA7: Beech . . . 5H **153**
Dunlin Ct. L25: Gate . . . 3E **110**
Dunlins Cl. CH45: Wall . . . 6J **65**
Dunlop Av. PR8: Ains . . . 7C **14**
Dunlop Dr. L31: Mell . . . 1K **55**
Dunlop Rd. L24: Speke . . . 7G **131**
Dunlop St. WA4: Warr . . . 5B **118**
Dunluce St. L4: Walt . . . 5A **68**
Dunmail Av. WA11: St. H . . . 4E **60**
Dunmail Gro. WA7: Beech . . . 6G **153**
Dunmore Cres. CH66: Lit Sut . . . 5D **160**
Dunmore Rd. CH66: Lit Sut . . . 5D **160**
L13: Liv . . . 4G **89**
Dunmow Rd. WA4: Thel . . . 5J **119**
Dunmow Way L25: Hunts X . . . 1G **131**
Dunnerdale Rd. L11: N Grn. . . . 4J **69**
Dunnett St. L20: Kirk . . . 5H **67**
Dunning Cl. CH49: Upton . . . 3C **104**
Dunnings Bri. Rd. L30: N'ton . . . 4A **54**
L31: Mag . . . 7D **42**
Dunnings Wlk. L30: N'ton . . . 1C **54**
Dunnock Cl. L25: Gate . . . 3E **110**
WA2: Warr . . . 4E **98**
Dunnock Gro. WA3: Bchwd . . . 3A **100**
Dunraven Rd. CH48: W Kir . . . 6C **102**
CH64: Lit N . . . 4A **158**
Dunriding La. WA10: St. H . . . 3K **73**
Dunscar Cl. WA3: Bchwd . . . 2K **99**
Dunscore Rd. WN3: Wins . . . 1C **50**
Dunscroft WA9: St. H . . . 7F **75**
Dunsdale Dr. WN4: Ash M . . . 2G **63**
Dunsdon Cl. L25: Wltn . . . 4C **110**
Dunsdon Rd. L25: Wltn . . . 3C **110**
Dunsford WA8: Wid . . . 5H **113**
Dunsmore Cl. WA11: Hay . . . 6A **62**
Dunsop Av. WA9: Clock F . . . 3F **95**
Dunstall Cl. CH46: Leas . . . 4C **84**
Dunstan La. CH64: Burt . . . 7E **158**
L7: Liv . . . 7E **88**
Dunstan St. L15: W'tree . . . 7G **89**
Dunster Cl. WN2: Platt B . . . 3K **51**
Dunster Gro. CH60: Hes . . . 3F **143**
WA9: Sut L . . . 3F **95**
Dunster Rd. PR8: B'dale . . . 1E **14**
Durants Cotts. L31: Mag . . . 5G **43**
Durban Av. L23: C'by . . . 2F **40**
Durban Rd. CH45: Wall . . . 1B **86**
L13: Liv . . . 5K **89**
Durden St. L7: Liv . . . 1E **108**
Durham Av. L30: N'ton . . . 4B **54**
Durham Cl. WA1: W'ston . . . 1A **120**
Durham Ct. CH65: Ell P . . . 1C **170**

Durham Gro.—Ellison Dr.

Durham Gro. M44: Cad 1K 101
Durham M. E. L30: N'ton 4C 54
Durham M. W. L30: N'ton 4B 54
Durham Rd. L21: Sea 6E 52
WA8: Wid 5D 114
Durham St. L19: Gars 5B 130
WN8: Skel 1D 36
Durham Way L30: N'ton 4C 54
L36: Huy 4A 92
Durley Dr. CH43: Pren 7J 105
Durley Pk. Cl. CH43: Pren 1J 125
Durley Rd. L9: Ain 7D 54
Durlston Cl. WA8: Wid 6J 113
Durning Rd. L7: Liv 6D 88
Durrant Rd. L11: N Grn. 6G 69
Dursley L35: Whis 5F 93
Dursley Dr. WN4: Ash M 1H 63
Durston Rd. L16: Child 7B 90
DUTTON 7E 154
Dutton Dr. CH63: Spit 7F 127
Dutton Grn. CH2: Lit Stan 1D 170
Duxbury Cl. L31: Mag 1G 43
WA11: R'ford 5G 47
Duxford Ct. WA2: P'gate 6E 98
Dwerryhouse La. L11: N Grn. 4K 69
Dwerryhouse St. L8: Liv 2K 107
Dyers Cl. WA13: Lymm 4J 121
Dyers La. L39: Orm 6C 24
WA13: Lymm 4J 121
Dyer St. WA3: Golb 4K 63
Dyke St. L6: Liv 3C 88
Dykin Cl. WA8: Wid 5G 115
Dykin Rd. WA8: Wid 5F 115
Dymchurch Rd. L24: Speke 5F 131
Dymoke Rd. L11: Crox 3A 70
Dymoke Wlk. L11: Crox 3A 70
Dyson Hall Dr. L9: Faz 1F 69
Dyson St. L4: Walt 5B 68

E

Eager La. L31: Lyd 3D 32
Eagle Brow WA13: Lymm 5F 121
Eagle Cres. WA11: R'ford 6G 47
Eagle Dene L10: Faz 7J 55
Eaglehall Rd. L9: Faz 2H 69
Eaglehurst Rd. L25: Gate 4F 111
Eagle La. CH66: Lit Sut 4F 161
Eagle Mt. WA4: Warr 6C 118
Eagle Pk. Dr. WA2: Warr 6A 98
Eagles Ct. L32: K'by 3C 56
Eaglesfield Cl. WA9: St. H 7F 75
Eagles Way WA7: Pal F 4G 153
Ealing Cl. WA7: Nort 1B 154
Ealing Rd. L9: Ain 6D 54
WA5: Gt San 3E 116
Eamont Av. PR9: Marsh 2D 8
Eanleywood La. WA7: Nort 2K 153
Eardisley Rd. L18: Moss H 2J 109
Earhart Cl. WN8: Skel 3A 38
Earle Cl. WA12: New W 3D 76
Earle Cres. CH64: Nest 2H 157
Earle Dr. CH64: Park 3H 157
Earle Ho. CH62: New F 1H 127
Earle Rd. L7: Liv 7E 88
WA8: Wid 2E 134
EARLESTOWN 3E 76
Earlestown Station (Rail) 3F 77
Earle St. L3: Liv 5J 87 (4C 4)
(not continuous)
WA12: New W 4D 76
Earl Rd. L20: Boot 2K 67
Earl's Cl. L23: C'by 2D 52
Earlsfield Rd. L15: W'tree 2H 109
Earls Gdns. CH65: Ell P 6K 161
Earlston Rd. CH45: Wall 1A 86
Earl St. CH62: New F 1H 127
WA2: Warr 1B 118
WA9: St. H 2E 74
Earls Way WA7: Pal F 3G 153
Earlswood WN8: Skel 2A 38
Earlswood Cl. CH46: More 7K 83
Earlwood Gdns. L35: Whis 5E 92
Earp St. L19: Gars 3A 130
Easby Cl. L37: Form 1A 30
WA7: Run 7E 134
Easby Rd. L4: Kirk 7K 67
(not continuous)
Easby Wlk. L4: Kirk 7K 67
Easedale Dr. PR8: Ains 5B 14
Easedale Wlk. L33: K'by 1B 56
Easenhall Cl. WA8: Wid 4D 114
Easington Rd. WA9: St. H 1K 93
E. Albert Rd. L17: Aig 4D 108
East Av. WA2: Warr 7C 98
WA4: S Hth 7D 118
WA5: Gt San 4E 116
East Bank CH42: Tran 5C 106
Eastbank Ho. PR8: South 2H 11
Eastbank St. PR8: South 1H 11
Eastbank St. Sq. PR8: South 1H 11
Eastbourne M. L9: Ain 6D 54
Eastbourne Rd. CH41: Birk 2C 106
L9: Ain 6D 54
L22: Water 3B 52
PR8: B'dale 5G 11
Eastbourne Wlk. L6: Liv 3B 88 (1K 5)
E. Brook St. L5: Liv 1C 88
Eastbury Cl. WA8: Wid 3E 114
Eastcliffe Rd. L13: Liv 4K 89
East Cl. L34: Ecc P 7G 73
Eastcote Rd. L19: Aller 1K 129
Eastcott Cl. CH49: Grea 5A 104
Eastcroft Rd. CH44: Wall 4C 86
Eastdale Rd. L15: W'tree 7H 89
WA1: P'ton 1G 119
E. Dam Wood Rd. L24: Speke 7A 132
Eastdene WN8: Parb 1H 27
Easter Ct. WA5: W'brk 5F 97
Eastern Av. CH62: Brom 5K 127
L24: Speke 7K 131
Eastern Dr. L19: Gras 2J 129
E. Farm M. CH48: Caldy 1H 123
Eastfield Dr. L17: Aig 5E 108
Eastfield Wlk. L32: K'by 4K 55
Eastford Rd. WA4: Warr 7K 117
East Front L35: Whis 6E 92
Eastgate Way WA7: Mnr P 5B 136
EAST GILLIBRANDS 3G 37
EASTHAM 5A 146
Eastham Cl. L16: Child 6D 90
Eastham Cres. WA9: Clock F 3D 94
EASTHAM FERRY 2C 146
Eastham Grn. L24: Speke 5J 131
Eastham M. CH62: East 6C 146
Eastham Rake CH62: East 7K 145
CH66: East, Hoot 1J 159
Eastham Rake Station (Rail) 7K 145
Eastham Village Rd.
CH62: East 5B 146
Eastlake Av. L5: Liv 2B 88
E. Lancashire Rd. L11: N Grn. 3G 69
L32: K'by 3G 69
L33: Know I 7D 56
L34: Know 7H 57
WA3: Golb 6G 63
WA10: Eccl, St. H, R'ford 6F 59
WA11: Hay 5F 61
WA12: New W 6G 63
East La. L29: Thorn 2H 41
WA7: Pal F 3H 153
Eastleigh WN8: Skel 2K 37
Eastleigh Dr. CH61: Irby 2B 124
East Mains L24: Speke 6A 132
Eastman Rd. L13: Liv 7G 69
East Mead L39: Augh 2K 33
East Meade L31: Mag 2E 42
E. Millwood Rd. L24: Speke 5K 131
East Mt. WN5: Orr 5H 39
Easton Cl. WN3: Wigan 2E 50
Easton Rd. CH62: New F 1H 127
L36: Huy 4E 90
E. Orchard La. L9: Ain 6F 55
Eastpark Ct. CH44: Wall 4E 86
EAST PIMBO 7B 38
E. Prescot Rd. L14: K Ash 4A 90
East Rd. L14: B Grn 5A 90
L24: Halew 4A 132
L31: Mag 3H 43
East Side WA9: St. H 4E 74
E. Side Ind. Est. WA9: St. H 4E 74
East St. CH41: Birk 5E 86
L3: Liv 5H 87 (4D 4)
L22: Water 4D 52
L34: Prsct 1E 92
PR9: South 1K 11
WA8: Wid 7F 115
WN4: Ash M 1H 63
East Vw. WA4: Grap 6H 119
Eastview Cl. CH43: Noct 4H 105
East Way CH46: More 6C 84
Eastway CH49: Grea 4C 104
CH66: Lit Sut 4F 161
L31: Mag 2F 43
(not continuous)
WA7: Pal F 3H 153
WA8: Wid 7K 113
Eastwell Rd. WN4: Ash M 2E 62
Eastwood L17: Aig 5C 108
WA7: Wind H 1A 154
Eastwood Av. WA12: New W 2K 77
Eastwood Rd. WA5: B'wood 7D 76
Eaton Av. CH44: Wall 3C 86
L20: Boot 7K 53
L21: Lith 6H 53
Eaton Cl. L12: W Der 7J 69
L36: Roby 5G 91
Eaton Gdns. L12: W Der 3B 90
Eaton Grange L12: W Der 2A 90
Eaton Rd. CH43: O'ton 3B 106
CH48: W Kir 7C 102
L12: W Der 7K 69
(not continuous)
L19: Gras 3J 129
L31: Mag 6F 43
WA10: St. H 7K 59
Eaton Rd. Nth. L12: W Der 7H 69
Eaton St. CH44: Wall 2B 86
L3: Liv 4J 87 (2D 4)
L34: Prsct 7D 72
WA7: Run 7C 134
Eaves Brow Rd. WA3: Croft 7H 79
Eavesdale WN8: Skel 3A 38
Eaves La. WA9: St. H 1D 94
Ebenezer Howard Rd.
L21: Ford 3J 53
Ebenezer Pl. WA1: Warr 3A 118
Ebenezer Rd. L7: Liv 5E 88
Ebenezer St. CH42: R Ferr 6G 107
WA11: Hay 7H 61
Eberle St. L2: Liv 5J 87 (5E 4)
Ebony Cl. CH46: More 7K 83
Ebony Way L33: K'by 7C 44
Ebor La. L5: Liv 3A 88 (1H 5)
Ebrington St. L19: Gars 2A 130
Ecclesall Av. L21: Lith 5K 53
Eccles Dr. L25: Gate 1F 111
Ecclesfield Rd. WA10: Eccl 1G 73
Eccles Gro. WA9: Clock F 4G 95
Eccleshall Rd. CH62: Port S 3J 127
Eccleshill Rd. L13: Liv 2J 89
Eccles Rd. L37: Form 2H 29
WN5: Orr 2K 39
ECCLESTON 1H 73
Eccleston Av. CH62: Brom 1J 145
CH66: Ell P 6G 161
Eccleston Cl. CH43: O'ton 5K 105
WA3: Bchwd 2J 99
Eccleston Dr. WA7: Run 1E 152
Eccleston Gdns. WA10: St. H 5G 73
(not continuous)
ECCLESTON PARK 7G 73
Eccleston Park Station (Rail) 1G 93
Eccleston Pk. Trade Cen.
WA10: St. H 6H 73
Eccleston Rd. L9: Walt 7B 54
Eccleston St. L34: Prsct 1D 92
WA10: St. H 3A 74
Echo La. CH48: W Kir 7E 102
Edale Cl. CH62: East 5A 146
Edale Rd. L18: Moss H 4J 109
Eddarbridge Est. WA8: Wid 4B 134
Eddisbury Rd. CH44: Wall 2C 86
CH47: Hoy 4C 102
CH48: W Kir 4C 102
CH66: Whit 2H 169
Eddisbury Sq. WA6: Frod 3D 166
Eddisbury Way L12: W Der 7J 69
Eddisford Dr. WA3: Cul 1K 79
Eddleston St. WN4: Ash M 6D 50
Edelsten St. WA5: Warr 3K 117
Eden Av. PR9: Chu 4B 8
WA3: Cul 2E 80
WA11: R'ford 5E 46
Edenbridge Gdns. WA4: App 6E 138
Eden Cl. CH66: Gt Sut 6E 160
L33: K'by 6D 44
L35: R'hill 5H 93
Edendale WA8: Wid 6H 113
Eden Dr. Nth. L23: C'by 1G 53
Eden Dr. Sth. L23: C'by 2G 53
Edenfield Cl. PR8: South 5A 12
Edenfield Cres. L36: Huy 3K 91
Edenfield Rd. L15: W'tree 2H 109
Edenhall Dr. L25: Wltn 5G 111
Edenhurst WN8: Skel 3A 38
Edenhurst Av. CH44: Wall 2C 86
L16: Child 7E 90
Edenhurst Cl. L37: Form 1G 29
Edenhurst Ct. L36: Huy 3F 91
Edenhurst Dr. L37: Form 1G 29
Edenpark Rd. CH42: Tran 5C 106
Eden St. L8: Liv 1D 108
Eden Va. L30: N'ton 1A 54
Edgar Ct. CH41: Birk 1D 106
L21: Lith 4H 53
Edgars Dr. WA2: Fearn 6G 99
Edgar St. CH41: Birk 1D 106
L3: Liv 4K 87 (2F 4)
Edgbaston Cl. L36: Roby 6G 91
Edgbaston Way CH43: Bid 7G 85
Edgefield Cl. CH43: Noct 4H 105
Edgefold Rd. L32: K'by 4D 56
EDGE GREEN 3K 63
Edge Grn. La. WA3: Golb 3K 63
Edge Grn. Rd. WN4: Ash M 2K 63
Edge Grn. St. WN4: Ash M 1H 63
Edge Gro. L7: Liv 5F 89
Edge Hall Rd. WN5: Orr 7G 39
(not continuous)
EDGE HILL 6D 88 (7P 5)
Edgehill Rd. CH46: More 7A 84
Edge Hill Station (Rail) 7E 88
Edge La. L7: Liv 6D 88 (6P 5)
L13: Liv 5D 88
L23: Thorn 6G 41
Edge La. Dr. L13: Liv 5J 89
Edge La. Retail Pk. L13: Liv 5H 89
(not continuous)
Edgeley Gdns. L9: Walt 7B 54
Edgemoor Cl. CH43: Bid 1F 105
L12: W Der 2B 90
L23: Thorn 7H 41
Edgemoor Dr. CH61: Irby 2A 124
L10: Faz 6J 55
L23: Thorn 6G 41
Edgemoor Rd. L12: W Der 2B 90
Edgerley Pl. WN4: Ash M 2E 62
Edge St. WA9: St. H 1J 93
Edgeware Gro. WN3: Wins 1B 50
Edgeway Rd. WN3: Wigan 3E 50
Edgewell Dr. L15: W'tree 7J 89
Edgewood Dr. CH62: Brom 5K 145
Edgewood Rd. CH47: Meols 6F 83
CH49: Upton 2D 104
Edgeworth Cl. WA9: St. H 6G 75
Edgeworth Rd. WA3: Golb 4K 63
Edgeworth St. WA2: Warr 2A 118
WA9: St. H 7G 75
Edgley Dr. L39: Orm 5E 24
Edgworth Rd. L4: Walt 1D 88
Edinburgh Cl. L30: N'ton 5C 54
Edinburgh Ct. CH65: Ell P 1B 170
Edinburgh Dr. CH43: Pren 7A 106
L36: Huy 6A 92
Edinburgh Rd. CH45: Wall 2B 86
L7: Liv 5C 88 (4N 5)
L37: Form 2J 29
WA8: Wid 1G 133
Edington St. L15: W'tree 7G 89
Edison Rd. WA7: Ast 6F 135
Edith Rd. CH44: Wall 4D 86
L4: Walt 1C 88
L20: Boot 7K 53
Edith St. WA7: Run 6B 134
WA9: St. H 7H 75
Edmondson St. WA9: St. H 3H 75
Edmonton Cl. L5: Kirk 1K 87
Edmund St. L3: Liv 5J 87 (5D 4)
Edna Av. L10: Faz 6J 55
Edrich Av. CH43: Bid 7G 85
Edward Dr. WN4: Ash M 1F 63
Edward Gdns. WA1: W'ston 2B 120
Edward Jenner Av. L30: N'ton 2B 54
Edward Pav. L3: Liv 7J 87 (8D 4)
Edward Rd. CH47: Hoy 2E 102
L35: Whis 2F 93
WA5: Gt San 2B 116
Edward's La. L24: Speke 3F 131
Edward's La. Ind. Est.
L24: Speke 3F 131
Edward St. CH65: Ell P 4A 162
L3: Liv 6A 88 (6J 5)
WA8: Wid 7F 115
WA9: St. H 5F 75
WA11: Hay 7J 61
Edwards Way WA8: Wid 1J 133
Edwin St. WA8: Wid 7E 114
Effingham St. L20: Boot 4H 67
Egan Rd. CH43: Bid 7J 85
Egbert Rd. CH47: Meols 7E 82
Egdon Cl. WA8: Wid 6G 115
Egerton WA16: H Legh 4K 141
WN8: Skel 3K 37
Egerton Av. WA1: Warr 1E 118
(not continuous)
Egerton Dr. CH48: W Kir 6D 102
Egerton Gdns. CH42: R Ferr 7E 106
Egerton Gro. CH45: Wall 2B 86
Egerton M. WA4: S Hth 7C 118
Egerton Pk. CH42: R Ferr 7E 106
Egerton Pk. Cl. CH42: R Ferr 7E 106
Egerton Rd. CH43: C'ton 2A 106
CH62: New F 2H 127
L15: W'tree 1F 109
L34: Prsct 7C 72
WA13: Lymm 6E 120
Egerton St. CH45: New B 6B 66
CH65: Ell P 5A 162
Egerton St. L8: Liv 1B 108 (10L 5)
WA1: Warr 3D 118
WA4: S Hth 7C 118
WA7: Run 6B 134
WA9: St. H 5F 75
Egerton Wharf CH41: Birk 1E 106
Eglington Av. L35: Whis 4D 92
EGREMONT 2D 86
Egremont Cl. L27: N'ley 4A 112
Egremont Lawn L27: N'ley 4A 112
(not continuous)
Egremont Prom. CH44: Wall 1D 86
CH45: Wall 1D 86
Egypt St. WA1: Warr 3B 118
WA8: Wid 2B 134
Eight Acre La. L37: Form 4A 20
(not continuous)
Eighth Av. L9: Ain 6F 55
Eilian Gro. L14: K Ash 5B 90
Eisenhower Cl. WA5: Gt San 2F 117
Elaine Cl. CH66: Gt Sut 7E 160
WA8: Wid 6E 114
WN4: Ash M 7H 51
Elaine Norris Sports Cen. 3J 87 (1D 4)
Elaine Price Ct. WA7: Run 1B 152
Elaine St. L8: Liv 2B 108
WA1: Warr 1D 118
Elbow La. L37: Form 7K 19
Elderberry Cl. L11: Crox 4A 70
Elderdale Rd. L4: Walt 7D 68
Elderflower Rd. WA10: St. H 1A 74
Elder Gdns. L19: Gras 1K 129
Elder Gro. CH48: W Kir 6D 102
Eldersfield Rd. L11: N Grn. 4K 69
Elderswood L35: R'hill 3J 93
Elderwood Rd. CH42: Tran 5E 106
Eldon Cl. WA10: St. H 4A 74
Eldon Gdns. WN4: Ash M 6E 50
Eldon Gro. L3: Liv 3K 87 (1F 4)
Eldonian Way L3: Liv 3J 87 (1D 4)
Eldon Pl. L3: Liv 3J 87 (1E 4)
Eldon Rd. CH42: R Ferr 6F 107
CH44: Wall 3B 86
Eldons Cft. PR8: Ains 4D 14
Eldon St. L3: Liv 3J 87 (1E 4)
WA1: Warr 3C 118
WA10: St. H 4A 74
Eldon Ter. CH64: Nest 4J 157
Eldred Rd. L16: Child 2A 110
Eleanor Pk. CH43: Bid 7G 85
Eleanor Rd. CH43: Bid 6H 85
CH46: More 6B 84
L20: Boot 7K 53
Eleanor St. CH65: Ell P 5A 162
L20: Kirk 5H 67
WA8: Wid 2C 134
Elephant La. WA9: St. H 7K 73
Elfet St. CH41: Birk 7K 85
Elgar Av. CH62: East 5A 146
Elgar Cl. CH65: Gt Sut 1H 169
Elgar Rd. L14: K Ash 2D 90
Elgin Av. WA4: Warr 6A 118
WN4: Gars 1B 62
Elgin Ct. L35: R'hill 5K 93
Elgin Dr. CH45: Wall 1C 86
Elgin Way CH41: Birk 1E 106
Eliot Cl. CH62: New F 2G 127
Eliot St. L20: Boot 1H 67
Elizabethan Dr. WN3: Ince M 1J 51
Elizabethan Wlk. WN2: Platt B 1K 51
Elizabeth Av. PR8: Ains 3E 14
Elizabeth Ct. WA8: Wid 2D 134
Elizabeth Dr. WA1: P'gate 7G 99
Elizabeth Rd. L10: Faz 6K 55
L20: Boot 7K 53
L36: Huy 7K 91
WA11: Hay 6C 62
Elizabeth St. L3: Liv 5B 88 (5L 5)
WA9: Clock F 4G 95
WA9: St. H 6G 75
Elizabeth Ter. WA8: Wid 7K 113
Eliza St. WA9: St. H 7H 75
Elkan Cl. WA8: Wid 6G 115
Elkan Rd. WA8: Wid 6F 115
Elkstone Cl. WN3: Wins 2A 50
Elkstone Rd. L11: N Grn. 5K 69
Ellaby Rd. L35: R'hill 3J 93
Ellamsbridge Rd.
WA9: St. H 7F 75
Elland Dr. CH66: Lit Sut 6E 160
Ellel Gro. L6: Liv 2E 88
Ellen Gdns. WA9: St. H 7G 75
Ellens Cl. L6: Liv 5C 88 (4M 5)
Ellen's La. CH63: Beb 4G 127
Ellen St. WA5: Warr 1K 117
WA9: St. H 7G 75
Elleray Dr. L8: Liv 4B 108
Elleray Pk. Rd. CH45: Wall 7A 66
Ellerbrook Way L39: Orm 4C 24
Ellerby Cl. WA7: Murd 3C 154
Ellergreen Rd. L11: N Grn. 4H 69
Ellerman Rd. L3: Liv 5A 108
Ellerslie Av. L35: R'hill 2H 93
Ellerslie Rd. L13: Liv 1F 89
Ellerton Av. CH66: Lit Sut 6E 160
Ellerton Cl. WA8: Wid 5J 113
Ellerton Way L12: Crox 3C 70
Ellesmere Dr. L10: Ain 3E 54
Ellesmere Gro. CH45: Wall 1B 86
ELLESMERE PORT 6A 162
Ellesmere Port Stadium 1C 170
Ellesmere Port Station (Rail)
6A 162
Ellesmere Rd. WA3: Cul 2A 80
WA4: S Hth, Walt 7B 118
WN4: Ash M 7D 50
Ellesmere St. WA1: Warr 3C 118
(not continuous)
WA7: Run 7D 134
Ellesworth Cl. WA5: Old H 7G 97
Elliot Dr. L32: K'by 5B 56
Elliot St. L1: Liv 6K 87 (6G 4)
WA8: Wid 1D 134
WA10: St. H 3A 74
Elliott Av. WA1: Warr 1E 118
Ellis Ashton St. L35: Whis 6C 92
L36: Huy 5A 92
(not continuous)
Ellis La. WA6: Frod 2F 167
Ellison Dr. WA10: St. H 2J 73

F

Fairfield Dr. CH48: W Kir 5G 103
L39: Orm 3C 24
Fairfield Gdns. WA4: S Hth 6E 118
WA11: Crank 3A 60
Fairfield Rd. CH42: Tran 6E 106
PR8: Ains 4C 14
WA4: S Hth 7C 118
WA8: Wid 7D 114
WA10: St. H 1J 73
WA13: Lymm 5H 121
Fairfield St. L7: Liv 4G 89
WA1: Warr 2C 118
Fairford Cl. WA5: Gt San 2F 117
Fairford Cres. L14: K Ash 3K 89
Fairford Rd. L14: K Ash 3K 89
Fairhaven L33: K'by 7C 44
WN8: Skel 7H 27
Fairhaven Cl. CH42: R Ferr 6F 107
WA5: Gt San 4F 117
Fairhaven Dr. CH63: Brom 5J 145
Fairhaven Ho. *L19: Aig* 2H 129
(off Spinnakers, The)
Fairhaven Rd. PR9: Chu 3D 8
WA8: Wid 6E 114
Fair Havens Ct. WA8: Wid 2D 134
Fairholme Av. CH64: Nest 2H 157
L34: Ecc P 1F 93
WN4: Ash M 1F 63
Fairholme Cl. L12: W Der 6J 69
Fairholme M. L23: C'by 1E 52
Fairholme Rd. L23: C'by 1E 52
Fairhurst Ter. L34: Prsct 1E 92
Fair Isle Cl. CH65: Ell P 3A 170
Fairlawn Cl. CH63: Raby M 4G 145
Fairlawn Ct. CH43: O'ton 3K 105
Fairlawne Cl. L33: K'by 7C 44
Fairlie WN8: Skel 7J 27
Fairlie Cres. L20: Boot 6K 53
Fairlie Dr. L35: R'hill 5K 93
Fairmead Rd. CH46: More 6C 84
L11: N Grn. 4G 69
Fairoak Cl. CH43: Bid 1G 105
Fairoak Ct. WA7: Pres B 7D 154
Fairoak La. WA7: Pres B 7D 154
Fairstead WN8: Skel 7J 27
Fairthorn Wlk. L33: K'by 2E 56
Fair Vw. CH41: Tran 4E 106
WN5: Bil 7F 49
Fair Vw. Av. WN5: Bil 7F 49
Fairview Av. CH45: Wall 2A 86
Fairview Cl. CH43: O'ton 5B 106
WN4: Ash M 1F 63
Fairview Rd. CH43: O'ton 6B 106
CH65: Whit 2J 169
Fairview Way CH61: Pens 6D 124
Fairway L36: Huy 3A 92
PR9: South 5J 7
WA10: Windle 1J 73
Fairway, The L12: K Ash 3B 90
Fairway Cres. CH62: Brom 5K 127
Fairway Nth. CH62: Brom 5K 127
Fairways CH42: Tran 1B 126
L23: C'by 7D 40
WA4: App 4D 138
WA6: Frod 4F 167
Fairways, The CH48: Caldy 3F 123
L25: Hunts X 1H 131
WN4: Ash M 3B 62
WN8: Skel 7K 27
Fairways Cl. L25: Wltn 1F 131
Fairways Ct. L37: Form 5G 19
Fairways Dr. CH66: Lit Sut 3F 161
Fairway Sth. CH62: Brom 6K 127
Falcon Cres. L27: N'ley 4K 111
Falcondale Rd. WA2: Win 1B 98
Falconers Grn. WA5: W'brk 5F 97
Falconer St. L20: Boot 7G 53
Falcongate Ind. Est.
CH44: Wall 6C 86
(off Old Gorsey La.)
Falconhall Rd. L9: Faz 2H 69
Falcon Hey L10: Faz 7J 55
Falcon Rd. CH41: Birk 4C 106
CH66: Gt Sut 1H 169
Falcons Way WA7: Pal F 4G 153
Falkirk Av. WA8: Wid 5A 114
Falkirk Gro. WN5: Wigan 3K 39
Falkland WN8: Skel 7J 27
Falkland Dr. WN4: Gars 1A 62
Falkland Rd. CH44: Wall 3D 86
PR8: South 4K 11
Falklands App. L11: N Grn. 4G 69
Falkland St. CH41: Birk 7A 86
L3: Liv 5B 88 (4K 5)
(not continuous)
Falkner Sq. L8: Liv 7B 88 (9M 5)
Falkner St. L8: Liv 7B 88 (9K 5)
(not continuous)
Falkner Ter. L8: Liv 10M 5
Fallbrook Dr. L12: W Der 6K 69
(not continuous)
Fallow Cl. WA9: Clock F 3E 94
Fallowfield L33: K'by 1C 56
WA7: Run 1F 153
Fallowfield Gro. WA2: P'gate 6H 99
Fallowfield Rd. CH46: More 7E 84
L15: W'tree 2H 109
Fallows Way L35: Whis 6C 92
Falls La. L26: Halew 6J 111
Falmouth Dr. WA5: Penk 5C 116
Falmouth Pl. WA7: Murd 4C 154
Falmouth Rd. L11: Crox 1A 70
Falstaff St. L20: Kirk 5J 67
Falstone Cl. WA3: Bchwd 1D 100
WN3: Wins 2C 50
Falstone Dr. WA7: Murd 3C 154
Fanner's La. WA16: H Legh 4E 140
(not continuous)
Faraday Rd. CH65: Whit 7J 161
L13: W'tree 6G 89
L33: Know I 6F 57
WA7: Ast 6F 135
Faraday St. L5: Liv 2C 88
WA3: Ris 1A 100
Fardon Cl. WN3: Wigan 1D 50
Farefield Av. WA3: Golb 3K 63
Fareham Cl. CH49: Upton 2C 104
Fareham Dr. PR9: Banks 2J 9
Fareham Rd. L7: Liv 5E 88
Faringdon Cl. L25: Hunts X 3F 131
Faringdon Rd. WA2: Win 1B 98
Farley Av. CH62: Brom 1J 145
Farlow Rd. CH42: R Ferr 7F 107
Farmbrook Rd. L25: Gate 1F 111
Farm Cl. CH49: Grea 4A 104
PR9: Chu 7C 8
WA9: Clock F 4F 95
Farm Ct. CH2: Elt 1B 172
Farmdale Cl. L18: Moss H 5K 109
Farmdale Dr. CH2: Elt 1A 172
L31: Mag 3G 43
Far Mdw. La. CH61: Irby 3A 124
Farmer Pl. L20: Boot 6A 54
Farmers Heath CH66: Gt Sut 2F 169
Farmers La. WA5: B'wood 1E 96
Farmer Ted's Farm Pk. 2B 32
Farmfield Dr. CH43: Bid 1G 105
Farm La. WA4: App 1E 138
Farmleigh Gdns.
WA5: Gt San 2G 117
Farm Mdw. Rd. WN5: Orr 6G 39
FAR MOOR 7F 39
Far Moss Rd. L23: Blun 6B 40
Farm Rd. WA9: Clock F 4F 95
Farmside CH46: Leas 4D 84
Farmside Cl. WA5: Warr 1J 117
Farmstead Way CH66: Gt Sut 3G 169
Farm Vw. L21: Ford 3H 53
Farmview Cl. L27: N'ley 1G 111
Farm Way WA12: New W 5J 77
Farnborough Gro. L26: Halew 7K 111
Farnborough Rd. PR8: B'dale 1F 15
Farndale WA8: Wid 3C 114
Farndale Cl. WA5: Gt San 1D 116
Farndale Gro. WN4: Ash M 3G 63
Farndon Av. CH45: Wall 1J 85
WA9: Sut M 3D 94
Farndon Dr. CH48: W Kir 5G 103
Farndon Rd. CH66: Ell P 5G 161
Farndon Way CH43: O'ton 4K 105
Farne Cl. CH65: Ell P 4A 170
Farnham Cl. L32: K'by 4D 56
WA4: App 2E 138
Farnhill Cl. WA7: Nort 2B 154
Farnley Cl. WA7: Wind H 1B 154
Farnside Ct. L17: Aig 2G 129
Farnworth Av. CH46: Leas 3D 84
Farnworth Cl. WA8: Wid 4D 114
Farnworth Gro. L33: K'by 7C 44
Farnworth Rd. WA5: Penk 4B 116
WA8: Wid 4G 115
Farnworth St. L6: Liv 4D 88 (2P 5)
WA8: Wid 4D 114
WA9: St. H 2E 74
Farrant St. WA8: Wid 1D 134
Farrar St. L13: Liv 7F 69
Farrell Cl. L31: Mell 1K 55
Farrell Rd. WA4: S Hth 1C 138
Farrell St. WA1: Warr 3C 118
Farr Hall Dr. CH60: Hes 3C 142
Farr Hall Rd. CH60: Hes 2C 142
Farrier Rd. L33: K'by 3E 56
Farriers Wlk. WA9: Clock F 3E 94
Farriers Way CH48: Frank 6K 103
L30: N'ton 5B 54
Farringdon Cl. WA9: St. H 2B 94
Farrington Dr. L39: Orm 4C 24
Farthing Cl. L25: Hunts X 2E 130
Farthings, The WA13: Lymm 4F 121
Farthingstone Cl. L35: Whis 1G 93
Fatherside Dr. L30: N'ton 2J 53
Faulkner Cl. PR8: Ains 4C 14
Faulkner Gdns. PR8: Ains 3C 14
Faversham Rd. L11: N Grn. 3G 69
Fawcett WN8: Skel 7H 27
Fawcett Rd. L31: Lyd 1F 43
Fawley Rd. L18: Moss H 6A 110
L35: R'hill 6A 94
FAZAKERLEY 6H 55
Fazakerley Bri. *L3: Liv* 5C 4
(off Fazakerley St.)
Fazakerley Cl. L9: Walt 2C 68
Fazakerley Rd. L9: Walt 2C 68
L35: Prsct 3E 92
Fazakerley Sports Cen. 5H 55
Fazakerley Station (Rail) 6F 55
Fazakerley St. L3: Liv 5H 87 (5C 4)
FEARNHEAD 5G 99
Fearnhead Cross WA2: P'gate 5F 99
Fearnhead La. WA2: Fearn 5G 99
Fearnley Hall CH41: Birk 3D 106
Fearnley Rd. CH41: Birk 3D 106
Fearnley Way WA12: New W 5G 77
Fearnside St. L7: Liv 7E 88
Feather La. CH60: Hes 2D 142
(not continuous)
Feeny St. WA9: Sut M 5D 94
Feilden Rd. CH63: Beb 5G 127
Felcroft Way L33: K'by 3D 56
Felicity Gro. CH46: More 6B 84
Fell Gro. WA11: St. H 5C 60
Fell St. CH44: Wall 5E 86
L7: Liv 5D 88
Felltor Cl. L25: Wltn 5D 110
Fell Vw. PR9: Cros 1F 9
Fellwood Gro. L35: Whis 4E 92
Felmersham Av. L11: N Grn. 3G 69
Felspar Rd. L32: K'by 6C 56
Felstead WN8: Skel 1H 37
Felsted Av. L25: Wltn 6G 111
Felsted Dr. L10: Ain 4G 55
Felthorpe Cl. CH49: Upton 1F 105
Felton Cl. CH46: More 7A 84
Felton Gro. L13: Liv 3H 89
Feltons WN8: Skel 1H 37
Feltree Ho. CH43: Bid 1G 105
Feltwell Rd. L4: Walt 1D 88
Feltwood Cl. L12: W Der 7D 70
Feltwood Mnr. L12: W Der 7D 70
Feltwood Rd. L12: W Der 6D 70
Feltwood Wlk. L12: W Der 7D 70
Fendale Av. CH46: More 6E 84
Fender Ct. CH49: W'chu 7H 105
Fender La. CH43: Bid 6F 85
CH46: More 6E 84
Fenderside Rd. CH43: Bid 7G 85
Fender Vw. Rd. CH46: More 7E 84
Fender Way CH43: Bid 1F 105
Fenderway CH61: Pens 5E 124
Fenham Dr. WA5: Penk 4C 116
Fennel St. WA1: Warr 3C 118
Fenney Ct. WN8: Skel 2J 37
Fenton Cl. L24: Speke 6H 131
L30: N'ton 5D 54
WA8: Wid 5H 113
WA10: St. H 2B 74
Fenton Grn. L24: Speke 7H 131
Fenwick La. WA7: Run 4F 153
Fenwick Rd. CH66: Gt Sut 2G 169
Fenwick St. L2: Liv 6J 87 (6D 4)
Ferguson Av. CH49: Grea 5B 104
CH66: Ell P 5G 161
Ferguson Dr. WA2: Warr 6D 98
Ferguson Rd. L11: N Grn. 6G 69
L21: Lith 4J 53
Fern Av. WA12: New W 4H 77
Fern Bank L31: Mag 3F 43
WA11: R'ford 5E 46
Fernbank Av. L36: Huy 5H 91
Fernbank Cl. WA3: Ris 3A 100
Fernbank Dr. L30: N'ton 1C 54
Fernbank La. CH49: Upton 1D 104
Fern Cl. L27: N'ley 4J 111
WA3: Bchwd 3K 99
WN8: Skel 2E 36
Ferndale WN8: Skel 1H 37
Ferndale Av. CH2: Elt 1A 172
CH44: Wall 3C 86
CH48: Frank 7K 103
Ferndale Cl. L9: Walt 6C 54
WA1: W'ston 1J 119
WA8: Bold H 1G 115
Ferndale Rd. CH47: Hoy 1D 102
L15: W'tree 2G 109
L22: Water 3D 52
Fern End PR9: Banks 3J 9
Fern Gdns. L34: Ecc P 7F 73
Fern Gro. CH43: Noct 3H 105
L8: Liv 2D 108
L20: Boot 2J 67
Fern Hey L23: Thorn 7H 41
Fernhill CH45: New B 6B 66
Fernhill Av. L20: Boot 3A 68
Fernhill Cl. L20: Boot 3A 68
(not continuous)
Fernhill Dr. L8: Liv 2C 108
Fernhill Gdns. L20: Boot 3A 68
Fernhill M. E. L20: Boot 3A 68
Fernhill M. W. L20: Boot 3A 68
Fernhill Rd. L20: Boot 7K 53
Fernhill Sports Cen. 7K 53
Fernhill Wlk. WA9: Clock F 3E 94
Fernhill Way L20: Boot 3A 68
Fernhurst WA7: Run 1F 153
Fernhurst Ga. L39: Augh 1K 33
Fernhurst Rd. L32: K'by 4A 56
Fernie Cres. L8: Liv 3A 108
Fernlea Av. WA9: St. H 7K 73
Fernlea Gro. WN4: Gars 7B 50
Fernlea M. CH43: Bid 7G 85
Fernlea Rd. CH60: Hes 2E 142
Fernleigh CH43: O'ton 5B 106
Fernleigh Rd. L13: Liv 4K 89
Fernley Rd. PR8: South 3G 11
Fern Lodge L8: Liv 2D 108
Fern Rd. CH65: Whit 2J 169
Ferns Cl. CH60: Hes 1A 142
Fernside Gro. WN3: Wins 3B 50
Ferns Rd. CH63: High B 4D 126
Fernwood WA7: Nort 2K 153
Fernwood Dr. L26: Halew 1J 131
Fernwood Rd. L17: Aig 5G 109
Ferny Brow Rd. CH49: W'chu 5F 105
Fernyess La. CH64: Will 5E 158
Ferny Knoll Rd. WA11: R'ford 1E 46
Ferrer St. WN4: Ash M 6D 50
Ferrey Rd. L10: Faz 6J 55
Ferries Cl. CH42: R Ferr 1G 127
Ferry La. WA4: Thel 4A 120
Ferry Rd. CH62: East 5C 146
Ferryside CH44: Wall 5E 86
Ferry Side La. PR9: Cros 2E 8
Ferry Vw. Rd. CH44: Wall 5E 86
Ferryview Wlk. WA7: Cas 7H 135
Festival Av. WA2: Warr 5C 98
Festival Ct. L11: N Grn. 3J 69
Festival Cres. WA2: Warr 5D 98
Festival Rd. CH65: Ell P 6H 161
WA11: R'ford 7G 47
Festival Way WA7: Run 2E 152
Ffrancon Dr. CH63: High B 2F 127
FIDDLER'S FERRY
Southport 1F 9
Warrington 7B 116
Fiddlers Ferry Rd. WA8: Wid 1E 134
Fiddler's Ferry Sailing Club 7C 116
Fidler St. WA10: St. H 5K 73
Field Av. L21: Lith 5G 53
Field Cl. CH62: New F 1H 127
WA9: Clock F 4F 95
Fieldfare Cl. L25: Gate 3E 110
WA3: Bchwd 3B 100
Fieldgate WA8: Wid 2H 133
Field Hey La. CH64: Will 2H 159
(not continuous)
Field Ho. L12: W Der 7J 69
Fieldhouse Row WA7: Run 3F 153
Fieldings, The L31: Lyd 7D 32
Fielding St. L6: Liv 4C 88 (3N 5)
Fieldlands PR8: South 6C 12
Field La. L10: Faz 7J 55
L21: Lith 4G 53
WA4: App 3C 138
Field Rd. CH45: New B 7B 66
WA9: Clock F 4F 95
Field's End L36: Huy 7J 91
Fieldsend Cl. L27: N'ley 4J 111
Fieldside Rd. CH42: R Ferr 6E 106
Field St. L3: Liv 4A 88 (2J 5)
(not continuous)
Field St. WN3: Ince M 1K 51
WN8: Skel 1D 36
Fieldsway WA7: West 4C 152
Fieldton Rd. L11: N Grn. 4K 69
Field Vw. L21: Lith 4G 53
Fieldview WN8: Uph 4C 38
Fieldview Dr. WA2: Warr 6C 98
Field Wlk. L23: Thorn 7H 41
L39: Orm 5F 25
Field Way L35: R'hill 2J 93
Fieldway CH45: Wall 2A 86
CH47: Meols 1H 103
CH60: Hes 1G 143
CH63: High B 1D 126
CH66: Lit Sut 4D 160
L15: W'tree 7A 90
L31: Mag 5F 43
L36: Huy 7K 91
WA6: Frod 4E 166
WA8: Wid 6F 115
Fieldway Ct. CH41: Birk 7C 86
Fife Rd. WA1: Warr 1E 118
Fifth Av. CH43: Bid 1F 105
L9: Ain 6G 55
(Meres Rd.)
L9: Ain 6F 55
(Park Av.)
WA7: Pal F 3H 153
Filbert Cl. L33: K'by 6D 44
Filby Gdns. WA9: St. H 1A 94
Fildes Cl. WA5: Gt San 3G 117
Fillmore Gro. WA8: Wid 5B 114
Filton Rd. L14: K Ash 2F 91
Finborough Rd. L4: Walt 4E 68
FINCHAM 2F 91
Fincham Cl. L14: K Ash 2F 91
Fincham Grn. L14: K Ash 2F 91
Fincham Rd. L14: K Ash 2E 90
Fincham Sq. L14: K Ash 2E 90
Finch Av. WA11: R'ford 7G 47
Finch Cl. WA9: Clock F 4F 95
Finch Ct. CH41: Birk 1D 106
Finchdean Cl. CH49: Grea 5A 104
Finch Dene L14: K Ash 1D 90
Finch La. L14: K Ash 1D 90
L26: Halew 3B 132
Finch Lea Dr. L14: K Ash 2E 90
Finchley Dr. WA11: St. H 6E 60
Finchley Rd. L4: Walt 7D 68
Finch Mdw. Cl. L9: Faz 2H 69
Finch Pl. L3: Liv 5B 88 (4K 5)
Finch Rd. L14: K Ash 1E 90
Finch Way L14: K Ash 2D 90
Findlay Cl. WA12: New W 4F 77
(not continuous)
Findley Dr. CH46: Leas 4D 84
Findon WN8: Skel 1J 37
Findon Rd. L32: K'by 5D 56
Fine Jane's Way
PR9: Chu 7D 8
Fingall Rd. L15: W'tree 2J 109
Finger Ho. La. WA8: Bold H 6F 95
Fingland Rd. L15: W'tree 1G 109
Finlan Rd. WA8: Wid 2C 134
Finlay Av. WA5: Penk 5C 116
Finlay Ct. L30: N'ton 1B 54
Finlay St. L6: Liv 4E 88
Finney, The CH48: Caldy 3F 123
Finney Gro. WA11: Hay 7C 62
Finningley Ct. WA2: P'gate 6E 98
Finsbury Cl. WA5: Gt San 4G 117
Finsbury Pk. WA8: Wid 3E 114
Finstall Rd. CH63: Spit 7F 127
Finvoy Rd. L13: Liv 7G 69
Fiona Wlk. L10: Faz 6A 56
Fir Av. L26: Halew 1A 132
Firbank CH2: Elt 1C 172
Firbank Cl. WA7: Wind H 1B 154
Firbank Rd. WN3: Wigan 1F 51
Firbeck WN8: Skel 2H 37
Firbrook Ct. CH43: Bid 6G 85
Fir Cl. L26: Halew 1A 132
Fir Cotes L31: Mag 3G 43
Firdale Rd. L9: Walt 2C 68
Firdene Cres. CH43: Noct 4J 105
Firecrest Ct. WA1: Warr 5A 118
Fire Sta. Rd. L35: Whis 2A 92
Firethorne Rd. L26: Halew 6H 111
Fir Gro. L9: Ain 5E 54
WA1: P'ton 1F 119
Fir La. L15: W'tree 1J 109
Firman Cl. WA5: W'brk 6F 97
Fir Rd. L22: Water 3E 52
Firs, The CH43: Bid 7J 85
Firs Av. CH63: Beb 6F 127
Firs Cl. L37: Form 5H 19
Firscraig L28: Stock V 7G 71
Firs Cres. L37: Form 5H 19
Firshaw Rd. CH47: Meols 6E 82
Firs La. L39: Augh 7G 23
WA4: App 4B 138
Firs Link L37: Form 6H 19
First Av. CH43: Bid 2G 105
L9: Ain 7G 55
(Lower La.)
L9: Ain 6E 54
(Park Av.)
L23: C'by 1D 52
L35: R'hill 3H 93
Firstone Gro. L32: K'by 5C 56
Fir St. M44: Cad 1K 101
PR8: South 2A 12
WA8: Wid 6E 114
WA10: St. H 6K 73
First St. WN2: Bam 5J 51
Firswood Rd. WN8: Skel 1B 36
Firthland Way WA9: St. H 4H 75
Firtree Av. WA1: P'gate 7G 99
Fir Tree Cl. WA4: S'ton 7J 139
WA11: Kings M 5B 48
WN8: Skel 4K 37
Fir Tree Cres. WN3: Ince M 1K 51
Fir Tree Dr. WN3: Ince M 1K 51
Fir Tree Dr. Nth. L12: Crox 3B 70
Fir Tree Dr. Sth. L12: Crox 3B 70
Firtree Gro. CH66: Whit 4J 169
Fir Tree La. L39: Augh, Hals 6H 23
WA5: B'wood 7E 76
Fir Tree St. WN3: Ince M 1K 51
Fir Way CH60: Hes 5F 143
Firwood WN8: Skel 7K 27
Firwood Gro. WN4: Ash M 3D 62
Fisher Av. L35: Whis 5D 92
WA2: Warr 6B 98
Fisher Dr. PR9: South 1B 12
WN5: Orr 5G 39
Fisherfield Dr. WA3: Bchwd 2C 100
Fishermans Cl. L37: Form 4J 19
Fisherman's Path L37: Form 2G 19
Fisher Pl. L35: Whis 5D 92

Fishers La.—Galbraith Cl.

Fishers La. CH61: Pens 5C 124
Fisher St. L8: Liv 2K 107
WA7: Run 6D 134
WA9: St. H 6G 75
Fishguard Cl. L6: Liv 3B 88 (1L 5)
Fishwicks Ind. Est. WA9: St. H 6E 74
WA11: Hay 5D 62
Fistral Cl. L10: Faz 7K 55
Fistral Dr. WA10: Windle 7H 59
Fitness First
Bootle 4D 54
Bromborough 6A 128
Runcorn 3G 153
Fitzclarence Wlk. L6: Liv 3B 88 (1K 5)
Fitzclarence Way L6: Liv 3B 88 (1L 5)
Fitzgerald Rd. L13: Liv 4J 89
Fitzherbert St. WA2: Warr 1B 118
Fitzpatrick Ct. L3: Liv 3J 87 (1D 4)
Fitzroy Way L6: Liv 4C 88 (3M 5)
Fitzwalter Rd. WA1: W'ston 1K 119
Fitzwilliam Wlk. WA7: Cas 7J 135
FIVECROSSES 6F 167
Fiveways WA10: Eccl 2G 73
Fiveways Pk. CH64: Nest 7K 143
Flag La. CH64: Lit N 4K 157
Flail Cl. CH49: Grea 4B 104
Flambards CH49: W'chu 5G 105
Flamstead WN8: Skel 2J 37
Flander Cl. WA8: Wid 6J 113
Flashes La. CH64: Ness 6B 158
Flatfield Way L31: Mag 3G 43
Flatman's La. L39: Down 2A 32
Flatt La. CH43: O'ton 5K 105
CH65: Ell P 6K 161
Flavian Ct. WA7: Cas 1G 153
Flawn Rd. L11: N Grn. 6G 69
Flaxfield Rd. L37: Form 7A 20
Flaxhill CH46: More 6B 84
Flax La. L40: Lath 1K 25
Flaxley Cl. WA3: Bchwd 2C 100
Flaxman St. L7: Liv 5E 88
Flaxton WN8: Skel 2J 37
Flaybrick Cl. CH43: Bid 7J 85
Fleck La. CH48: Caldy, W Kir 7F 103
Fleet Cft. Rd. CH49: W'chu 6E 104
Fleet La. WA9: St. H 3G 75
Fleet La. Ind. Est. WA9: St. H 4G 75
Fleet St. CH65: Ell P 6J 161
L1: Liv 6K 87 (7G 4)
WN5: Wigan 5K 39
Fleetwood Cl. PR9: Chu 4B 8
WA5: Gt San 4F 117
Fleetwood Ct. PR9: South 6J 7
Fleetwood Cres. PR9: Banks 1J 9
Fleetwood Dr. PR9: Banks 1J 9
WA12: New W 2F 77
Fleetwood Gdns. L33: K'by 7D 44
(not continuous)
Fleetwood Pl. L25: Wltn 6D 110
Fleetwood Rd. PR9: South 6J 7
(not continuous)
Fleetwoods La. L30: N'ton 1K 53
Fleetwood Wlk. WA7: Murd 3A 154
Fleming Ct. L3: Liv 3J 87 (1D 4)
Fleming Dr. WA2: Win 1A 98
WN4: Ash M 1H 63
Fleming Ind. Est. *WA1: Warr 3C 118*
(off Fennel St.)
Fleming Rd. L24: Speke 3G 131
Fleming St. CH65: Ell P 5A 162
Flemington Av. L4: Walt 5F 69
Fleming Way CH46: Leas 5E 84
Flers Av. WA4: Warr 5C 118
Fletcher Av. CH42: R Ferr 6E 106
L34: Prsct 7E 72
Fletcher Cl. CH49: W'chu 6E 104
Fletcher Dr. L19: Gras 2J 129
Fletchers La. WA13: Lymm 4H 121
Fletcher St. WA4: Warr 5B 118
Flimby WN8: Skel 2K 37
Flint Cl. CH64: Nest 5J 157
Flint Ct. CH65: Ell P 2B 170
Flint Dr. CH64: Nest 4J 157
L12: Crox 5B 70
Flint Gro. M44: Cad 1K 101
Flint Mdw. CH64: Nest 4J 157
Flintshire Gdns. WA10: St. H 4B 74
Flint St. L1: Liv 1K 107 (10G 4)
Flixton Gdns. WA9: St. H 1A 94
Floodgates Rd. L38: High 6K 29
Floral Pavilion Theatre 5C 66
Floral Wood L17: Aig 6B 108
Flora St. WN4: Ash M 3F 63
Flordon WN8: Skel 2K 37
Florence Av. CH60: Hes 1D 142
Florence Cl. L9: Walt 3B 68
Florence Nightingale Cl.
L30: N'ton 1B 54
Florence Rd. CH44: Wall 4E 86
Florence St. CH41: Birk 2D 106
L4: Walt 6B 68
WA4: Warr 5D 118
WA9: St. H 7J 73
Florentine Rd. L13: Liv 3J 89
Florida Cl. WA5: Gt San 1G 117
Florida Ct. L19: Gras 1K 129
Florida Way L35: Prsct 3D 92
Flowermead Cl. CH47: Meols 6H 83
Fluin La. WA6: Frod 2E 166
Fluker's Brook La. L34: Know 5F 71
Foinavon Cl. L9: Walt 6B 54
Folds, The CH63: Thorn H 4A 144
Folds La. WA11: St. H 6C 60
Folds Rd. WA11: Hay 7H 61
Foley Cl. L4: Kirk 7A 68
Foley St. L4: Kirk 7A 68
(not continuous)
Folkestone Rd. PR8: South 5A 12
Folkestone Way WA7: Murd 3A 154
Folly La. CH44: Wall 2J 85
WA5: Warr 1K 117
WA7: Run 1K 151
Fontenoy St. L3: Liv 5K 87 (3F 4)
Fonthill Cl. L4: Kirk 7K 67
Fonthill Rd. L4: Kirk 6K 67
Forbes Cl. WA3: Bchwd 3A 100
Forbes Ho. L7: Liv 5E 88
FORD
Bootle 3H 53
Prenton 3G 105
Ford Av. L33: K'by 6C 44
Ford Cl. CH49: Upton 4F 105
L20: Boot 6A 54
L21: Ford 3H 53
Fordcombe Rd. L25: Gate 4G 111
Ford Dr. CH49: Upton 3F 105
Fordham Cl. PR8: South 5A 12
Fordham St. L4: Kirk 6A 68
Fordhill Vw. CH46: More 7E 84
Fordington Rd. WA5: Gt San 3F 117
Ford La. CH49: Upton 3F 105
L21: Ford 3H 53
Fordlea Rd. L12: W Der 6J 69
Fordlea Way L12: W Der 6J 69
Ford Rd. CH49: Upton 3E 104
L35: Prsct 1F 93
Ford St. L3: Liv 4J 87 (2E 4)
WA1: Warr 2D 118
Fordton Leisure Cen. 4A 98
Ford Vw. L21: Ford 2H 53
Ford Way CH49: Upton 4E 104
Fordway M. CH49: Upton 4E 104
Forefield La. L23: C'by 7F 41
Foreland Cl. WA5: Gt San 1A 116
Forest Cl. CH47: Meols 6F 83
L34: Ecc P 7F 73
Forest Ct. CH43: C'ton 2K 105
Forest Dr. L36: Huy 4G 91
WN8: Skel 7J 27
Forest Grn. L12: W Der 6J 69
Forest Gro. L34: Ecc P 7F 73
Forest Lawn L12: W Der 6K 69
Forest Mead WA10: Eccl 3G 73
Forest Rd. CH43: C'ton 1A 106
CH47: Meols 6F 83
CH60: Hes 1E 142
CH66: Ell P 4G 161
PR8: South 2K 11
WA9: Sut M 4C 94
Forest Wlk. *WA7: Pal F 3H 153*
(off Halton Lea Shop. Cen.)
Forfar Rd. L13: Liv 1F 89
Forge Cl. L40: Westh 6J 25
WA8: Cron 3J 113
Forge Cotts. L17: Aig 4E 108
Forge Rd. CH66: Lit Sut 5E 160
WA5: Gt San 3D 116
Forge Shop. Cen., The
WA9: S Hth 7C 118
Forge St. L20: Kirk 6J 67
FORMBY 1J 29
Formby Av. WA10: St. H 5K 73
Formby Bri. L37: Form 1H 29
Formby Bus. Pk. L37: Form 1C 30
Formby By-Pass
L37: Ains, Form, Ince B 3B 20
Formby Cl. WA5: Penk 4D 116
Formby Flds. L37: Form 1A 30
Formby Gdns. L37: Form 6K 19
Formby Golf Course 4G 19
Formby La. L37: Form 1B 30
L39: Augh 1F 33
Formby M. L37: Form 6K 19
Formby Point Cvn. Pk. L37: Form 2F 29
Formby Point Nature Reserve 2E 28
Formby Red Squirrel Reserve 5F 19
Formby Station (Rail) 1J 29
Formby St. L37: Form 1J 29
Formosa Dr. L10: Faz 6H 55
Formosa Rd. L10: Faz 6H 55
Formosa Way L10: Faz 6H 55
Fornalls Grn. La. CH47: Meols 1G 103
Forres Gro. WN4: Gars 1B 62
Forrester Av. WA9: St. H 7J 73
Forrest St. L1: Liv 7K 87 (9F 4)
Forrest Way WA5: Warr 5H 117
Forshaw Av. WA10: St. H 6J 73
Forshaw's La. WA5: C Grn 6C 76
Forshaw St. WA2: Warr 1C 118
FORSTERS GREEN 7K 27
Forsters Grn. Rd. WN8: Skel 7K 27
Forster St. WA2: Warr 1B 118
WA3: Golb 4K 63
Forsythia Cl. L9: Walt 3E 68
Forthlin Rd. L18: Aller 7A 110
(not continuous)
Forth St. L20: Kirk 5H 67
Forton Lodge Flats *L23: Blun 1C 52*
(off Blundellsands Rd. E.)
Forton Rd. WN3: Wigan 2D 50
Fort Perch Rock 5C 66
Fort St. CH45: New B 7C 66
Forum Ct. PR8: South 1G 11
Forwood Rd. CH62: Brom 2K 145
Foscote Rd. L33: K'by 1E 56
Foster Cl. L35: Whis 2G 93
Foster Rd. L37: Form 1H 29
Fosters Cl. PR9: Chu 7D 8
Fosters Gro. WA11: Hay 7H 61
Fosters Rd. WA11: Hay 7H 61
Foster St. L20: Kirk 7J 67
WA8: Wid 7D 114
Fotherby Pl. WN3: Wigan 1E 50
Fothergill St. WA1: Warr 1D 118
Fotheringay Ct. CH65: Ell P 2B 170
Foul La. PR8: South 4C 12
PR9: South 3C 12
Foundry La. WA8: Hale B 4H 133
WN3: Wigan 1B 50
Foundry St. WA2: Warr 2B 118
WA10: St. H 3C 74
(not continuous)
WA12: New W 3F 77
Fountain Ct. L23: Blun 7A 40
Fountain La. WA6: Frod 3C 166
Fountain Rd. CH45: New B 7B 66
L34: Know 3H 71
Fountains, The L39: Orm 4C 24
Fountains Av. WA11: Hay 6D 62
Fountains Cl. L4: Walt 7B 68
WA7: Brook 5A 154
Fountains Ct. L5: Kirk 7K 67
Fountains Rd. L4: Kirk 7K 67
(not continuous)
Fountain St. CH42: Tran 5C 106
WA9: St. H 1J 93
Fountains Way L37: Form 1A 30
Four Acre Dr. L21: Ford 2H 53
Four Acre La. WA9: Clock F 3D 94
Four Acre Pct. WA9: Clock F 3D 94
Fouracres L31: Mag 5D 42
Four Bridges CH41: Birk 7E 86
FOUR LANE ENDS 4A 36
Fourmarts Rd. WN5: Wigan 1K 39
Fourth Av. CH43: Bid 1F 105
L9: Ain 6G 55
(Lower La.)
L9: Ain 6F 55
(Park Av.)
WA7: Pal F 3H 153
Fourth St. WN2: Bam 5K 51
Fowell Rd. CH45: New B 6B 66
Fowler Cl. L7: Liv 6E 88
Fowler St. L5: Liv 2C 88
FOWLEY COMMON 2D 80
Fowley Comn. La. WA3: Cul 1D 80
Foxall Way CH66: Gt Sut 2E 168
Fox Bank Cl. WA8: Wid 4B 114
Foxcote WA8: Wid 6H 113
Foxcover Rd. CH60: Hes 3G 143
Foxcovers Rd. CH63: Beb 6G 127
Fox Covert WA7: Nort 2A 154
Foxdale Cl. CH43: O'ton 3A 106
PR8: South 5A 12
Foxdale Ct. WA4: App 2D 138
Foxdale Rd. L15: W'tree 2G 109
Foxdell Cl. L13: Liv 5J 89
Foxdene CH66: Lit Sut 6F 161
Foxdene Gro. WN3: Wins 2C 50
Foxes, The CH61: Thing 3F 125
Foxfield Cl. WA2: Warr 4E 98
Foxfield Rd. CH47: Meols 7F 83
Foxfold WN8: Skel 7K 27
Fox Gdns. WA13: Lymm 4E 120
Foxglove Av. L26: Halew 7J 111
Foxglove Cl. L9: Faz 2H 69
Foxglove Ct. WA6: Frod 3E 166
Foxglove Dell WA6: Alv 2K 173
Foxglove Rd. CH41: Birk 1K 105
Foxglove Way CH64: Lit N 6J 157
Fox Hey Rd. CH44: Wall 3K 85
Foxhill Cl. L8: Liv 2C 108
L37: Form 7G 19
Foxhill Gro. WA6: Hel 7K 165
Foxhill La. L26: Halew 6J 111
Foxhills Cl. WA4: App 6D 138
Foxhouse La. L31: Mag 4G 43
Foxhunter Dr. L9: Ain 5E 54
Foxhunters Chase WA12: New W 3C 76
Foxleigh L26: Halew 7H 111
Foxleigh Grange CH41: Birk 6K 85
Foxley Cl. WA13: Lymm 6J 121
Foxley Hall M. WA13: Lymm 7J 121
Foxley Heath WA8: Wid 1A 134
Fox Pl. WA10: St. H 2C 74
Fox's Bank La. L35: Whis 2F 113
Foxshaw Cl. L35: Whis 6D 92
Fox St. CH41: Birk 2C 106
L3: Liv 3A 88 (1H 5)
WA5: Warr 3J 117
WA7: Run 7C 134
Foxton Cl. CH46: More 6K 83
WA11: St. H 1F 75
Foxwood L12: W Der 6C 70
WA9: St. H 7J 73
Foxwood Cl. CH48: W Kir 5G 103
WN5: Orr 6G 39
Foy St. WN4: Ash M 2F 63
Frailey Cl. PR8: Ains 5C 14
Frampton Rd. L4: Walt 4F 69
Franceys St. L3: Liv 6A 88 (6J 5)
Francine Cl. L3: Liv 2J 87
Francis Av. CH43: C'ton 2B 106
CH46: More 7B 84
Francis Cl. L35: R'hill 3J 93
WA8: Wid 1J 133
Francis Rd. WA4: S Hth 7B 118
WA6: Frod 2E 166
Francis St. WA9: St. H 7H 75
Francis Way L16: Child 7B 90
FRANKBY 6K 103
Frankby Av. CH44: Wall 3A 86
Frankby Cl. CH49: Grea 5K 103
Frankby Grn. CH48: Frank 6K 103
Frankby Gro. CH49: Upton 3D 104
Frankby Rd. CH47: Meols 7F 83
CH48: Frank, W Kir 5F 103
CH49: Grea 6J 103
L4: Walt 6D 68
Frankby Stiles CH48: Frank 5H 103
Franklin Cl. WA5: Old H 7G 97
Franklin Gro. L33: K'by 6C 44
Franklin Pl. L6: Liv 2D 88
Franklin Rd. CH46: Leas 3E 84
Frank St. L8: Liv 3A 108
WA8: Wid 7E 114
Franton Wlk. L32: K'by 3A 56
Fraser Rd. WA5: Gt San 2B 116
Fraser St. L3: Liv 5A 88 (4H 5)
Frawley Av. WA12: New W 1G 77
Freckleton Cl. WA5: Gt San 4F 117
Freckleton Dr. L33: K'by 7D 44
Freckleton Rd. PR9: Marsh 3B 8
WA10: St. H 5H 73
Freda Av. WA9: St. H 1E 94
Frederick Banting Cl. L30: N'ton 1B 54
Frederick Gro. L15: W'tree 7J 89
Frederick Lunt Av. L34: Know 3G 71
Frederick St. L1: Liv 8E 4
WA4: Latch 5D 118
WA8: Wid 7D 114
WA9: St. H 6H 75
WN4: Ash M 7E 50
Frederick Ter. WA8: Hale B 5G 133
Fredric Pl. WA7: Run 6D 134
Freedom Cl. L7: Liv 7C 88 (8M 5)
Freehold St. L7: Liv 4F 89
Freeland St. L4: Kirk 7A 68
Freeman St. CH41: Birk 1E 106
L7: Liv 7E 88
Freemantle Av. WA9: St. H 7A 74
Freemason's Row L3: Liv 4J 87 (3E 4)
(not continuous)
Freemont Rd. L12: W Der 7J 69
Freeport Gro. L9: Ain 6D 54
Freesia Av. L9: Walt 2D 68
Freme Cl. L11: N Grn. 3K 69
Frenchfield St. WA9: Clock F 4F 95
French St. WA8: Wid 7F 115
WA10: St. H 5K 73
Frensham Cl. CH63: Spit 7F 127
FRESHFIELD 5J 19
Freshfield Cvn. Pk.
L37: Form 4F 19
Freshfield Cl. L36: Huy 4G 91
Freshfield Ct. L37: Form 6J 19
Freshfield Rd. L15: W'tree 2H 109
L37: Form 5J 19
WN3: Wigan 1C 50
Freshfields Dr. WA2: P'gate 6H 99
Freshfield Station (Rail) 5J 19
Freshford WA9: St. H 1F 95
Fresh Mdw. La. WA6: Hel 2H 173
Freshwater Cl. WA5: Gt San 1B 116
Friars Av. WA5: Gt San 3C 116
Friars Cl. CH63: Beb 4F 127
Friars Ga. WA1: Warr 4B 118
Friarsgate Cl. L18: Moss H 3A 110
Friars La. WA1: Warr 4B 118
Friar St. WA10: St. H 7B 60
Friars Wlk. L37: Form 1B 30
Friends La. WA5: Gt San 2B 116
Frinsted Rd. L11: N Grn. 5J 69
Frobisher Ct. WA5: Old H 7H 97
Frobisher Rd. CH46: Leas 3E 84
CH64: Nest 3J 157
Froda Av. WA6: Frod 4D 166
FRODSHAM 3D 166
Frodsham Bus. Cen. WA6: Frod 2E 166
Frodsham Dr. WA11: St. H 1F 75
Frodsham Leisure Cen. 3D 166
Frodsham Pk. Homes
WA6: Frod 3C 166
Frodsham Rd. WA6: Alv 3K 173
Frodsham Station (Rail) 3D 166
Frodsham St. CH41: Tran 4E 106
(not continuous)
L4: Walt 5B 68
Froghall La. WA1: Warr 3K 117
WA2: Warr 2A 118
Frogmore Rd. L13: Liv 4G 89
Frome Cl. CH61: Irby 2B 124
Frome Ct. CH65: Ell P 4K 161
Frome Way L25: Hunts X 1H 131
Frontfield Ct. *WA9: St. H 4E 74*
(off Appleton Rd.)
Frost Dr. CH61: Irby 3A 124
Frosts M. CH65: Ell P 5K 161
Frost St. L7: Liv 5E 88
Fryer St. WA7: Run 6C 134
Fry St. WA9: St. H 3G 75
(not continuous)
Fuchsia Cl. CH66: Gt Sut 3H 169
Fuchsia Wlk. CH49: Grea 6A 104
Fulbeck WA8: Wid 6J 113
Fulbeck Av. WN3: Wigan 2D 50
Fulbrook Cl. CH63: Spit 6F 127
Fulbrook Rd. CH63: Spit 7F 127
Fulford Cl. L12: W Der 1D 90
Fulford Pk. CH46: More 7C 84
Fullerton Gro. L36: Huy 3J 91
Fulmar Cl. L27: N'ley 3J 111
WA11: St. H 7D 60
Fulmar Gro. L12: Crox 3C 70
Fulshaw Cl. L27: N'ley 2H 111
Fulton Av. CH48: W Kir 5G 103
Fulton St. L5: Liv 2H 87
Fulwood Av. PR8: South 4K 11
Fulwood Cl. L17: Aig 6F 109
Fulwood Dr. L17: Aig 6E 108
Fulwood Gdns. CH66: Lit Sut 5E 160
Fulwood M. CH66: Lit Sut 5E 160
Fulwood Pk. L17: Aig 7E 108
Fulwood Rd. CH66: Lit Sut 5E 160
L17: Aig 6E 108
Fulwood Way L21: Ford 1J 53
Funchal Av. L37: Form 2H 29
Furlong Cl. L9: Ain 5E 54
WN2: Bam 5K 51
Furness Av. L12: W Der 5A 70
L37: Form 7K 19
L39: Orm 6C 24
WA10: St. H 6A 60
Furness Cl. CH49: Upton 2C 104
PR8: Ains 6B 14
Furness Ct. WA7: Nort 5D 136
Furness St. L4: Walt 7A 68
Furrocks Cl. CH64: Ness 6K 157
Furrocks La. CH64: Ness 6K 157
Furrocks Way CH64: Ness 6K 157
Furrows, The CH66: Gt Sut 4G 169
Furze Way CH46: More 6C 84
FX Leisure 4F 39
Fylde Rd. PR9: Chu 3B 8
Fylde Rd. Ind. Est. PR9: Marsh 3C 8

G

Gable Ct. L11: N Grn. 3G 69
Gable M. L37: Form 2A 30
Gables, The L31: Mag 5G 43
L34: Ecc P 1F 93
Gables Cl. WA2: Fearn 4F 99
Gable St. WA12: New W 3E 76
Gableside Av. L11: N Grn. 3G 69
Gable Vw. L11: N Grn. 3G 69
Gabriel Cl. CH46: More 7D 84
Gainford Cl. L14: K Ash 1E 90
WA8: Wid 5J 113
Gainford Rd. L14: K Ash 1E 90
Gainsborough Av. L31: Mag 4D 42
Gainsborough Cl. L12: W Der 2C 90
WN3: Wins 1B 50
Gainsborough Ct. WA8: Wid 7H 113
Gainsborough Rd. CH45: Wall 2J 85
CH49: Upton 2D 104
L15: W'tree 2F 109
PR8: B'dale 5E 10
WA4: Warr 6A 118
Gairloch Cl. WA2: Fearn 3F 99
Gaisgill Ct. WA8: Wid 7J 113
Gala Bingo
Bromborough 6A 128
Croxteth 2J 69
Kirkby 3C 56
Warrington 3B 118
Wavertree 1J 109
Widnes 1D 134
Gala Cl. L14: K Ash 3C 90
Galbraith Cl. L17: Aig 6C 108

Gale Av.—Godshill Cl.

Gale Av. WA5: Warr 6K 97
Galemeade L11: N Grn. 3K 69
Gale Rd. L21: Lith 4J 53
L33: Know I 5G 57
Galion Way WA8: Wid 4B 114
Gallagher Ind. Est. CH41: Birk 6B 86
Galleries, The L37: Form 7K 19
Gallopers La. CH61: Thing 3G 125
Galloway Dr. WN8: Uph 5D 38
Galloway Rd. L22: Water 3E 52
Galloway St. L7: Liv 7F 89
Galston Av. L35: R'hill 5K 93
Galston Cl. L33: K'by 6B 44
Galsworthy Av. L30: Boot 5K 53
Galsworthy Pl. L30: Boot 5A 54
Galsworthy Wlk. L30: Boot 6A 54
Galton St. L3: Liv 4H 87 (3B 4)
Galtres Ct. CH63: High B 1E 126
Galtres Pk. CH63: High B 1E 126
Galway Av. WA8: Wid 6A 114
Galway Cres. WA11: Hay 6B 62
Gambier Ter. L1: Liv 1A 108 (10K 5)
Gamble Av. WA10: St. H 7A 60
Gamlin St. CH41: Birk 7K 85
Gamston Wood L32: K'by 4A 56
Ganney's Mdw. Rd.
CH49: W'chu 6G 105
Gannock St. L7: Liv 5E 88
Gantley Av. WN5: Bil 7F 39
Gantley Cres. WN5: Bil 1F 49
Gantley Rd. WN5: Bil 7F 39
Ganton Cl. PR8: South 5A 12
WA8: Wid 4D 114
Ganworth Cl. L24: Speke 7J 131
Ganworth Rd. L24: Speke 7J 131
Garage Rd. L24: Halew 4K 131
Garden Apartments
L18: Moss H 5H 109
Garden Cotts. L12: W Der 3B 90
L39: Orm 5B 24
Garden Ct. CH42: Tran 7C 106
Gardeners Vw. L33: K'by 6D 44
Gardeners Way L35: R'hill 2J 93
Garden Hey Rd. CH46: More 1K 103
CH47: Meols 7E 82
Gardenia Gro. L17: Aig 6C 108
Garden La. CH46: More 6C 84
L5: Liv 3A 88 (1K 5)
L9: Ain 5F 55
Garden Lodge Gro. L27: N'ley 3H 111
Gardenside CH46: Leas 3F 85
Gardenside St. L6: Liv 4B 88 (2L 5)
Gardens Rd. CH63: Beb 4H 127
Garden St. L25: Wltn 6E 110
Garden Wlk. L34: Prsct 2D 92
Gardiner Av. WA11: Hay 7A 62
Gardiners Pl. WN8: Skel 3E 36
Gardner Av. L20: Boot 6K 53
Gardner Rd. L13: Liv 2G 89
L37: Form 7A 20
Gardner's Dr. L6: Liv 3E 88
Gardner's Row L3: Liv 4K 87 (2F 4)
Gareth Av. WA11: St. H 7D 60
Garfield Ter. CH49: Upton 3E 104
Garfourth Cl. L19: Gars 2B 130
Garfourth Rd. L19: Gars 2B 130
Garibaldi St. WA5: Warr 3K 117
Garmoyle Cl. L15: W'tree 1F 109
Garmoyle Rd. L15: W'tree 1G 109
Garner St. WA2: Warr 1C 118
Garnet St. L13: Liv 6H 89
WA9: St. H 7F 75
Garnett Av. L4: Kirk 6K 67
WA4: Westy 4G 119
Garnett Grn. L39: Orm 6B 24
Garnett Pl. WN8: Skel 4G 37
Garnetts La. L35: Tar G 7D 112
WA8: Hale B 5G 133
Garnge Wood CH48: W Kir 7F 103
Garrett Fld. WA3: Ris 2K 99
Garrick Av. CH46: More 7A 84
Garrick Pde. PR8: South 1G 11
Garrick Rd. CH43: Pren 1K 125
Garrick St. L7: Liv 1E 108
Garrigill Cl. WA8: Wid 3D 114
Garrison Cl. L8: Liv 2D 108
Garrowby Dr. L36: Huy 4G 91
Garsdale Av. L35: R'hill 5K 93
Garsdale Cl. WA5: Gt San 1D 116
Garsfield Rd. L4: Walt 5F 69
Garside Gro. WN3: Wigan 2C 50
Garstang Rd. PR9: Marsh 3B 8
GARSTON 3B 130
Garston Ind. Est. L19: Gars 5A 130
Garston Old Rd. L19: Gras 2J 129
Garston Sports Cen. 2A 130
Garston Station (Rail) 3B 130
Garston Way L19: Gars 3K 129
GARSWOOD 2A 62
Garswood Av. WA11: R'ford 5G 47
Garswood Cl. CH46: Leas 3D 84
L31: Mag 1G 43
Garswood Cres. WN5: Bil 1G 61
Garswood Old Rd. WA11: St. H 5E 60
WN4: Gars 4J 61
Garswood Rd. WA11: Hay 4A 62
WN4: Gars 7K 49
WN5: Bil 1G 61
Garswood Station (Rail) 2B 62
Garswood St. L8: Liv 5B 108
WA10: St. H 2C 74
WN4: Ash M 2F 63
Garter Cl. L11: Crox 3A 70
Garth, The L36: Huy 4J 91
Garth Blvd. CH63: High B 1E 126
Garth Ct. L22: Water 4E 52
Garthdale Rd. L18: Moss H 4J 109
Garth Dr. L18: Moss H 4K 109
Garthowen Rd. L7: Liv 5F 89
Garth Rd. CH65: Ell P 6D 162
L32: K'by 5E 56
Garth Wlk. L32: K'by 5E 56
Gartons La. WA9: Clock F, Sut M 4E 94
Garven Pl. WA1: Warr 3A 118
Garway L25: Wltn 5G 111
Garwood Cl. WA5: W'brk 6G 97
Gascoyne St. L3: Liv 4J 87 (3D 4)
Gaskell Av. WA4: Westy 5G 119
Gaskell Ct. WA9: St. H 3H 75
Gaskell Rake L30: N'ton 7K 41
Gaskell's Brow WN4: Ash M 7C 50
Gaskell St. WA4: S Hth 7C 118
WA9: St. H 5E 74
Gaskill Rd. L24: Speke 5H 131
Gas St. WA7: Run 7D 134
Gatclif Rd. L13: Liv 6G 69
GATEACRE 3F 111
Gateacre Brow L25: Gate 4E 110
Gateacre Ct. CH66: Ell P 3H 161
Gateacre Pk. Dr. L25: Gate 1D 110
Gateacre Ri. L25: Gate 4E 110
Gateacre Shop. Cen. L25: Gate 2E 110
Gateacre Va. Rd. L25: Wltn 5F 111
Gategill Gro. WN5: Bil 1F 49
Gateley Cl. WA4: Thel 5A 120
Gateside Cl. L27: N'ley 3J 111
Gates La. L29: Thorn 4H 41
Gatewarth Ind. Est. WA5: Warr 5H 117
Gatewarth St. WA5: Warr 4H 117
GATHURST 1H 39
Gathurst Ct. WA8: Wid 1K 133
Gathurst Rd. WN5: Orr 4G 39
Gathurst Station (Rail) 1J 39
Gatley Dr. L31: Mag 5G 43
Gatley Wlk. L24: Speke 5K 131
Gaunts Way WA7: Pal F 4G 153
Gautby Rd. CH41: Birk 6J 85
Gavin Rd. WA8: Wid 2H 133
Gaw Hill La. L39: Augh 7J 23
Gaw Hill Vw. L39: Augh 7K 23
Gawsworth Cl. CH43: O'ton 5K 105
WA10: Eccl 3H 73
Gawsworth Ct. WA3: Ris 1B 100
Gawsworth Rd. CH66: Gt Sut 6G 161
WA3: Golb 4K 63
Gaybeech Cl. CH43: Bid 7F 85
Gayhurst Av. WA2: Fearn 5F 99
Gayhurst Cres. L11: N Grn. 4J 69
Gaynor Av. WA11: Hay 6D 62
GAYTON 3F 143
Gayton Av. CH45: New B 6B 66
CH63: High B 1C 126
Gayton Ct. WN3: Wins 1B 50
Gayton Farm Rd. CH60: Hes 5E 142
Gayton La. CH60: Hes 4F 143
Gayton Mill Cl. CH60: Hes 3F 143
Gayton Parkway CH60: Hes 5G 143
Gayton Rd. CH60: Hes 4D 142
Gaytree Ct. CH43: Bid 1G 105
Gaywood Av. L32: K'by 5D 56
Gaywood Cl. CH43: Bid 1G 105
L32: K'by 5D 56
Gaywood Ct. L23: Blun 2B 52
Gaywood Grn. L32: K'by 5D 56
Gellings Rd. L34: Know 1E 70
Gelling St. L8: Liv 3A 108
Gemini Bus. Pk. WA5: W'brk 4G 97
(Europa Blvd.)
WA5: W'brk 4J 97
(Royal London Bus. Pk., not continuous)
Gemini Cl. L20: Boot 2H 67
Gemini Dr. L14: K Ash 3D 90
Gem St. L5: Liv 2J 87
General St. WA1: Warr 3C 118
Genesis Cen., The WA3: Ris 2A 100
Geneva Cl. L36: Huy 3H 91
Geneva Rd. CH44: Wall 5D 86
L6: Liv 4E 88
Genoa Cl. L25: Gate 1F 111
Gentwood Pde. L36: Huy 3H 91
Gentwood Rd. L36: Huy 3G 91
George Dr. PR8: Ains 4E 14
George Hale Av. L34: Know P 1J 91
George Harrison Cl.
L6: Liv 4D 88 (3P 5)
George Moore Ct. L23: Thorn 6J 41
George Rd. CH47: Hoy 2E 102
WA5: Gt San 4G 117
Georges Cres. WA4: Grap 6H 119
George's Dock Gates
L3: Liv 5H 87 (6C 4)
Georges Dockway L3: Liv 6H 87 (7D 4)
George's La. PR9: Banks 1J 9
George's Rd. L6: Liv 2D 88
George's Ter. WN5: Orr 6F 39
George St. CH41: Birk 1E 106
CH65: Ell P 4A 162
L3: Liv 5J 87 (5D 4)
WA10: St. H 3C 74
WA12: New W 2E 76
WN4: Ash M 1G 63
Georgia Av. CH62: Brom 6A 128
L33: K'by 6B 44
Georgia Cl. L20: Boot 3J 67
Georgian Cl. L26: Halew 3K 131
L35: Ecc P 1G 93
Georgian Pl. L37: Form 2J 29
Georgia Pl. WA5: Gt San 1G 117
Geraint St. L8: Liv 2B 108
Gerald Rd. CH43: O'ton 4A 106
Gerard Av. CH45: Wall 7A 66
Gerard Cen., The WN4: Ash M 2F 63
Gerard Rd. CH45: Wall 1K 85
CH48: W Kir 5D 102
GERARD'S BRIDGE 1C 74
Gerards Ct. WA11: St. H 5E 60
Gerards La. WA9: St. H, Sut L 7F 75
Gerard St. L3: Liv 4K 87 (4G 4)
WN4: Ash M 2F 63
Gerard Way L33: K'by 3D 56
Germander Cl. L26: Halew 7J 111
Gerneth Cl. L24: Speke 5G 131
Gerneth Rd. L24: Speke 5F 131
Gerosa Av. WA2: Win 6B 78
Gerrard Av. CH66: Gt Sut 7E 160
WA5: Warr 1K 117
Gerrard Pl. WN8: Skel 4F 37
Gerrard Rd. WA3: Croft 7G 79
WN5: Bil 7G 49
Gerrard's La. L26: Halew 6J 111
Gerrard St. WA8: Wid 1D 134
Gertrude Rd. L4: Walt 1C 88
Gertrude St. CH41: Birk 2F 107
WA9: St. H 7J 73
Geves Gdns. L22: Water 4E 52
Ghyll Gro. WA11: St. H 4D 60
Gibbons Av. WA10: St. H 3J 73
Gibbon's Rd. WN4: Gars 3B 62
Gibbs Ct. CH61: Irby 3E 124
Gibcroft Brook La. WA3: Cul 1A 80
Gibraltar Row L3: Liv 5H 87 (4C 4)
Gibson Cl. CH61: Pens 6D 124
L33: K'by 7B 44
Gibson Ct. CH65: Ell P 3A 162
Gibson Rd. L8: Liv 1B 108
Gibson St. WA1: Warr 3C 118
WA4: S Hth 7D 118
Giddygate La. L31: Mag, Mell 3K 43
Gidlow Rd. L13: Liv 4H 89
Gidlow Rd. Sth. L13: Liv 5H 89
Gigg La. WA4: Moore 4F 137
Gig La. WA1: W'ston 7K 99
WA4: Thel 5A 120
Gilbert Cl. CH63: Spit 7F 127
WA3: Cul 3B 80
Gilbert Rd. L35: Whis 2F 93
Gilbert St. L1: Liv 7K 87 (8F 4)
Gildarts Gdns. L3: Liv 3J 87 (1E 4)
Gildart St. L3: Liv 5A 88 (4K 5)
Gilderdale Cl. WA3: Bchwd 2D 100
Gilead St. L7: Liv 5D 88
Gilescroft Av. L33: K'by 1E 56
Gilescroft Wlk. L33: K'by 1E 56
Gillan Cl. WA7: Brook 5A 154
GILLAR'S GREEN 4E 72
Gillars Grn. Dr. WA10: Eccl 3F 73
Gillar's La. WA10: Eccl 1D 72
Gillbrook Sq. CH41: Birk 7K 85
(off Vaughan St., not continuous)
Gilleney Gro. L35: Whis 2G 93
Gillibrands Rd. WN8: Skel 3F 37
GILLMOSS 1B 70
Gillmoss Cl. L11: Crox 2A 70
Gillmoss Ind. Est. L10: Faz 7K 55
Gillmoss La. L11: Crox 1A 70
Gills La. CH61: Barn, Pens 5E 124
Gill St. L3: Liv 5A 88 (5K 5)
Gilman St. L4: Walt 7C 68
Gilmartin Gro. L6: Liv 4C 88 (3M 5)
Gilmour Mt. CH43: O'ton 4B 106
Gilpin Av. L31: Mag 2G 43
Gilpin Pl. WN2: Platt B 2K 51
Gilroy Rd. CH48: W Kir 5E 102
L6: Liv 4D 88
Giltbrook Cl. WA8: Wid 5B 114
Gilwell Av. CH46: More 1C 104
Gilwell Cl. CH46: More 1C 104
WA4: Grap 6J 119
Ginnel, The CH62: Port S 4H 127
Gipsy Gro. L18: Moss H 3C 110
Gipsy La. L18: Moss H 3C 110
Girton Av. L20: Boot 4A 68
WN4: Ash M 1D 62
Girton Cl. CH65: Ell P 7B 162
Girton Rd. CH65: Ell P 7B 162
Girtrell Cl. CH49: Upton 3B 104
Girtrell Rd. CH49: Upton 3B 104
Girvan Cres. WN4: Gars 1A 62
Girvan Dr. CH64: Lit N 5K 157
Gisburn Av. WA3: Golb 3K 63
Givenchy Cl. L16: Child 7C 90
Gladdenhey Dr. WN3: Wins 3B 50
Gladden Pl. WN8: Skel 3E 36
Glade, The CH47: Meols 6F 83
Glade Dr. CH66: Lit Sut 5B 160
Glade Pk. Cl. L8: Liv 4D 108
Glade Rd. L36: Huy 3J 91
Gladeswood Rd. L33: Know I 4F 57
Gladeville Rd. L17: Aig 5G 109
Gladica Cl. L36: Huy 5B 92
Gladstone Av. L16: Child 7E 90
L21: Sea 6G 53
Gladstone Cl. CH41: Birk 2C 106
Gladstone Ct. L8: Liv 10L 5
Gladstone Hall Rd.
CH62: Port S 4H 127
Gladstone Rd. CH44: Wall 4D 86
CH64: Nest 3J 157
L7: Liv 6D 88 (6P 5)
L9: Walt 3B 68
L19: Gars 3A 130
L21: Sea 6F 53
PR9: South 2B 12
Gladstone St. L3: Liv 4J 87 (3E 4)
L25: Wltn 6D 110
WA2: Warr 2A 118
WA8: Wid 1D 134
WA10: St. H 3K 73
Gladstone Ter. CH64: Will 3F 159
(off Neston Rd.)
Gladstone Theatre 5H 127
Gladstone Way WA12: New W 2F 77
Gladsville Rd. L27: N'ley 4K 111
Glaisdale Cl. WN4: Ash M 2G 63
Glaisdale Dr. PR8: South 5B 12
Glaisher St. L5: Liv 1C 88
Glamis Dr. PR9: Chu 4D 8
Glamis Gro. WA9: St. H 7E 74
Glamis Rd. L13: Liv 1F 89
Glamorgan Cl. WA10: St. H 4B 74
Glanaber Pk. L12: W Der 6C 70
Glasgow St. CH42: R Ferr 6F 107
Glasier Rd. CH46: More 6A 84
Glaslyn Way L9: Walt 3C 68
Glassonby Cres. L11: N Grn. 5J 69
Glassonby Way L11: N Grn. 5J 69
Glastonbury Cl. L6: Liv 7F 69
WA7: Nort 6D 136
Glastonbury M. WA4: S Hth 6E 118
Glasven Rd. L33: K'by 2D 56
GLAZEBROOK 2J 101
Glazebrook La. WA3: G'brk 7H 81
Glazebrook Station (Rail) 2J 101
Glazebrook St. WA1: Warr 2D 118
Glaziers La. WA3: Cul 4K 79
Gleadmere WA8: Wid 6J 113
Gleaner Cl. WA7: Run 6B 134
Gleaston Cl. CH62: Brom 1K 145
Gleave Cl. WA5: B'wood 1D 96
Gleave Cres. L6: Liv 3B 88 (1L 5)
Gleave St. WA10: St. H 2C 74
Glebe, The WA7: Run 1G 153
Glebe Av. WA4: Grap 7J 119
WN4: Ash M 3G 63
Glebe Cl. L31: Mag 3D 42
Glebecroft Av. CH2: Elt 1A 172
Glebe End L29: Seft 5A 42
Glebe Hey L27: N'ley 3J 111
Glebe Hey Rd. CH49: W'chu 5E 104
Glebeland WA3: Cul 3A 80
Glebelands Rd. CH46: More 7C 84
Glebe La. PR9: Banks 1J 9
WA8: Wid 3C 114
Glebe Pl. PR9: South 1H 11
Glebe Rd. CH45: Wall 1A 86
WN8: Skel 3G 37
Glebeway Way CH65: Ell P 6D 162
Gleggside CH48: W Kir 6E 102
Glegg St. L3: Liv 3H 87
Glegside Rd. L33: K'by 3E 56
Glemsford Cl. WN3: Wigan 1F 51
Glen, The CH63: Spit 6J 127
L18: Moss H 5A 110
WA7: Pal F 4H 153
Glenacres L25: Wltn 5E 110
Glenalmond Rd. CH44: Wall 3D 86
Glenathol Rd. CH66: Gt Sut 7E 160
L18: Moss H 6A 110
Glenavon Rd. CH43: Pren 7A 106
L16: Child 6A 90
Glenbank L22: Water 3C 52
Glenbank Cl. L9: Walt 1C 68
Glenburn Av. CH62: East 6A 146
Glenburn Rd. CH44: Wall 4D 86
WN8: Skel 6E 26
Glenby Av. L23: C'by 3F 53
Glencairn Rd. L13: Liv 4H 89
Glen Cl. WA3: Rix 5K 101
Glencoe Rd. CH45: Wall 1B 86
CH66: Gt Sut 7E 160
Glenconner Rd. L16: Child 6C 90
Glencourse Rd. WA8: Wid 3C 114
Glencoyne Dr. PR9: Marsh 1D 8
Glencroft Cl. L36: Huy 2G 91
Glendale Av. CH2: Elt 1A 172
WN4: Ash M 1G 63
Glendale Cl. L8: Liv 5B 108
Glendale Gro. CH63: Spit 7H 127
L33: K'by 7E 44
(off Dorchester Dri.)
Glendale Rd. WA11: St. H 6C 60
Glendale Way L37: Form 1K 29
Glendevon Rd. L16: Child 6A 90
L36: Huy 6J 91
Glendower Rd. L22: Water 4E 52
Glendower St. L20: Kirk 5J 67
Glendyke Rd. CH66: Gt Sut 7E 160
L18: Moss H 6A 110
Gleneagles Cl. CH61: Pens 6D 124
L33: K'by 6B 44
Gleneagles Dr. PR8: Ains 6B 14
WA8: Wid 3C 114
WA11: Hay 1J 75
Gleneagles Rd. CH66: Gt Sut 6E 160
L16: Child 6B 90
Glenesk Rd. CH66: Gt Sut 7E 160
Glenfield Cl. CH43: Bid 7G 85
CH46: More 6K 83
Glenfield Rd. L15: W'tree 2H 109
Glengariff St. L13: Liv 7F 69
Glenham Cl. CH47: Meols 7G 83
Glenhead Rd. L19: Aller 1K 129
Glenholm Rd. L31: Mag 5E 42
Glenista Cl. L9: Walt 3C 68
Glenluce Rd. L19: Aig 7J 109
Glenlyon Rd. L16: Child 7A 90
Glenmarsh Cl. CH63: High B 4D 126
L12: W Der 1A 90
Glenmarsh Way L37: Form 7B 20
Glenmaye Cl. L12: Crox 4C 70
Glenmaye Rd. CH66: Gt Sut 7E 160
Glenmore Av. L18: Moss H 5H 109
Glenmore Rd. CH43: O'ton 4A 106
Glenn Pl. WA8: Wid 7A 114
Glenpark Dr. PR9: Marsh 3D 8
Glen Pk. Rd. CH45: Wall 7A 66
Glen Rd. CH66: Gt Sut 6E 160
L13: Liv 5K 89
Glen Ronald Dr. CH49: Grea 3B 104
Glenrose Rd. L25: Wltn 4E 110
Glenrose Ter. PR8: B'dale 3G 11
Glenside L18: Aller 6A 110
Glenton Pk. CH64: Lit N 5K 157
Glentree Cl. CH49: Grea 3B 104
Glentrees Rd. L12: W Der 6K 69
Glentworth Cl. L31: Mag 4F 43
Glenville Cl. L25: Wltn 4F 111
WA7: Run 4D 152
Glen Vine Cl. L16: Child 7C 90
Glen Way L33: K'by 6D 44
Glenway Cl. L12: Crox 2D 70
Glenwood WA7: Nort 2A 154
Glenwood Cl. CH66: Lit Sut 5E 160
L35: Whis 5F 93
Glenwood Dr. CH61: Irby 2C 124
Glenwood Gdns. CH66: Lit Sut 5E 160
Glenwood Rd. CH66: Lit Sut 5E 160
Glenwyllin Rd. L22: Water 3E 52
Globe Rd. L20: Boot 2H 67
Globe St. L4: Walt 7A 68
Gloucester Cl. CH66: Gt Sut 4G 169
WA1: W'ston 1K 119
Gloucester Ct. L6: Liv 4C 88 (3N 5)
Gloucester Rd. CH45: Wall 1J 85
L6: Liv 2F 89
L20: Boot 2K 67
L36: Huy 4A 92
PR8: B'dale 3F 11
WA8: Wid 5D 114
Gloucester Rd. Nth. L6: Liv 1F 89
Gloucester St. L1: Liv 5K 87 (5H 5)
WA9: St. H 4F 75
Glover Pl. L20: Boot 2H 67
Glover Rd. WA3: Bchwd 3J 99
Glover's Brow L32: K'by 1A 56
Glover's La. L30: N'ton 1A 54
Glover St. CH42: Tran 4C 106
L8: Liv 2K 107
WA10: St. H 4B 74
WA12: New W 3G 77
Glyn Av. CH62: Brom 3A 146
Glynne Gro. L16: Child 7E 90
Glynne St. L20: Boot 7K 53
Glynn St. L15: W'tree 1H 109
Glyn Rd. CH44: Wall 2B 86
Goddard Rd. WA7: Ast 6G 135
Godetia Cl. L9: Walt 2H 69
Godfrey St. WA2: Warr 1D 118
Godscroft La. WA6: Frod 5A 166
Godshill Cl. WA5: Gt San 1B 116

Godstow—Greenburn Av.

Godstow WA7: Nort 5C 136
GOLBORNE 3K 63
Golborne Dale Rd. WA12: New W 1A 78
Golborne La. WA16: H Legh 6G 141
Golborne Rd. WA2: Win 7A 78
WN4: Ash M 1H 63
Golborne St. WA1: Warr 3A 118
WA12: New W 2J 77
Goldcliff Cl. WA5: Call 4H 97
Goldcrest Cl. L12: Crox 2D 70
WA7: Beech 6H 153
Goldcrest M. L26: Halew 7J 111
Golden Gro. L4: Walt 5C 68
Golden Sq. Shop. Cen.
WA1: Warr 3B 118
Golden Triangle Ind. Est.
WA8: Hale B 4H 133
Goldfinch Cl. L26: Halew 7J 111
Goldfinch Farm Rd. L24: Speke 6G 131
Goldfinch La. WA3: Bchwd 3A 100
Goldie St. L4: Walt 7B 68
Goldsmith Rd. CH43: Pren 7K 105
Goldsmith St. L6: Liv 4D 88 (2P 5)
L20: Boot 2G 67
Goldsmith Way CH43: Pren 7K 105
Goldsworth Fold L35: R'hill 4H 93
Golf Links Rd. CH42: Tran 7B 106
Gondover Av. L9: Walt 7B 54
Gonville Rd. L20: Boot 4K 67
Gooch Dr. WA12: New W 4H 77
Goodacre Rd. L9: Ain 6D 54
Goodakers Ct. CH49: W'chu 6E 104
(off Goodakers Mdw.)
Goodakers Mdw. CH49: W'chu 6E 104
Goodall Pl. L4: Kirk 5A 68
Goodall St. L4: Kirk 5A 68
Goodban St. WA9: St. H 6G 75
Goodier Ct. WA7: Run 2E 152
Goodison Av. L4: Walt 6B 68
Goodison Pk. 5B 68
Goodison Pl. L4: Walt 5B 68
Goodison Rd. L4: Walt 5B 68
Goodlass Rd. L24: Speke 3E 130
Goodleigh Pl. WA9: Sut L 2E 94
Good Shepherd Cl. L11: N Grn. 4K 69
Goodwood Cl. L36: Roby 6H 91
Goodwood Ct. WA9: St. H 1K 93
Goodwood Dr. CH46: Leas 4D 84
Goodwood Gro. CH66: Gt Sut 1F 169
Goodwood St. L5: Liv 2K 87
Gooseberry Hollow
WA7: Wind H 1B 154
Gooseberry La. WA7: Nort 1B 154
GOOSE GREEN 1C 50
Goose Grn., The CH47: Meols 6F 83
Goose La. WA4: Hatt 7K 137
Goostrey Cl. CH63: Spit 1H 145
Gordale Cl. L8: Liv 4C 108
WA5: Gt San 1D 116
Gordon Av. CH49: Grea 5C 104
CH62: Brom 3A 146
L22: Water 3C 52
L31: Mag 1E 42
PR9: South 6J 7
WA1: W'ston 1H 119
WA11: Hay 6D 62
WN4: Gars 1C 62
Gordon Ct. CH49: Grea 5C 104
Gordon Dr. L14: B Grn 4C 90
L19: Gras 2J 129
Gordon La. CH2: Back 7K 169
Gordon M. PR9: South 6J 7
Gordon Pl. L18: Moss H 5J 109
Gordon Rd. CH45: New B 7B 66
L21: Sea 7F 53
Gordonstoun Cres. WN5: Orr 4H 39
Gordon St. CH41: Birk 2C 106
L15: W'tree 1G 109
PR9: South 7H 7
Gordon Ter. CH64: Will 3F 159
(off Neston Rd.)
Gordon Way PR9: South 7J 7
(off Gordon St.)
Gore Dr. L39: Augh 7C 24
Goree L2: Liv 6H 87 (6C 4)
Gores La. L37: Form 5J 19
WA11: Crank 6B 48
Gores Rd. L33: Know I 4F 57
Gore St. L8: Liv 2A 108
WN5: Wigan 5K 39
Gorleston M. L32: K'by 5D 56
Gorleston Way L32: K'by 4D 56
Gorran Haven WA7: Brook 5A 154
Gorse Av. L12: W Der 5K 69
Gorsebank Rd. L18: Moss H 3G 109
Gorsebank St. CH44: Wall 4C 86
Gorseburn Rd. L13: Liv 1G 89
GORSE COVERT 1D 100
Gorse Covert Rd. WA3: Bchwd 2C 100
Gorse Cres. CH44: Wall 5C 86
Gorsedale Pk. CH44: Wall 5D 86
Gorsedale Rd. CH44: Wall 5B 86
L18: Moss H 4J 109
Gorsefield L37: Form 4A 20
WA9: St. H 7K 73
Gorsefield Av. CH62: Brom 5K 145
L23: Thorn 7H 41
Gorsefield Cl. CH62: Brom 5K 145
Gorsefield Rd. CH42: Tran 5C 106
Gorse Hey Ct. L13: W Der 2J 89
Gorsehill Rd. CH45: New B 7A 66
CH60: Hes 1E 142
Gorselands Ct. L17: Aig 6F 109
Gorse La. CH48: W Kir 7G 103
Gorse Rd. CH47: Meols 7F 83
Gorse Way L37: Form 6G 19
Gorsewood Cl. L25: Gate 3G 111
(off Gorsewood Rd.)
Gorsewood Gro. L25: Gate 3F 111
Gorsewood Rd. L25: Gate 3F 111
WA7: Murd 4B 154
Gorsey Av. L30: N'ton 2J 53
Gorsey Brow WN5: Bil 7F 49
Gorsey Brow Cl. WN5: Bil 7F 49
Gorsey Cop Rd. L25: Gate 2E 110
Gorsey Cop Way L25: Gate 2E 110
Gorsey Cft. L34: Ecc P 7F 73
Gorsey La. CH44: Wall 4B 86
L21: Ford 4H 53
L30: N'ton 4H 53
Gorsey La. L38: High 7G 29
L39: Bart 3H 21
PR9: Banks 1K 9
WA1: Warr 1D 118
WA2: Warr 7D 98
WA8: Wid 1G 135
WA9: Bold 4G 95
WA9: Clock F 4F 95
Gorsey Pl. WN8: Skel 4G 37
Gorseyville Cres.
CH63: High B 4E 126
Gorseyville Rd. CH63: High B 4E 126
Gorseywell La. WA7: Pres B 4D 154
Gorstons La. CH64: Lit N 5A 158
Gorst St. L4: Walt 7B 68
Gorsuch La. L40: Scar 6F 17
Gorton Rd. L13: Liv 5K 89
Gort Rd. L36: Huy 4J 91
Goschen St. L5: Liv 7B 68
L13: Liv 4H 89
Gosford St. L8: Liv 4B 108
Gosforth Ct. WA7: Pal F 3G 153
Gosforth Rd. PR9: South 7B 8
Gosling Cl. WA4: Hatt 7A 138
Gosling Rd. WA3: Croft 7H 79
Gosport Cl. WA2: P'gate 6E 98
Goswell St. L15: W'tree 7G 89
Gotham Rd. CH63: Spit 7G 127
Gothic St. CH42: R Ferr 6F 107
Gough Av. WA2: Warr 5A 98
Gough Rd. L13: Liv 7G 69
Goulden St. WA5: Warr 2J 117
Goulders Ct. WA7: Brook 5K 153
Gourley Rd. L13: Liv 6J 89
Gourleys La. CH48: W Kir 7F 103
Government Rd. CH47: Hoy 1D 102
Govett Rd. WA9: St. H 7J 73
Gower St. L3: Liv 7J 87 (9D 4)
L20: Boot 1G 67
WA9: St. H 5F 75
Gowrie Gro. L21: Lith 6H 53
Gowy Ct. CH66: Ell P 3G 161
Goyt Hey Av. WN5: Bil 7G 49
Graburn Rd. L37: Form 6K 19
Grace Av. L10: Faz 6J 55
WA2: Warr 7B 98
Grace Cl. CH45: Wall 2B 86
Grace Rd. CH65: Ell P 5K 161
L9: Walt 7C 54
Grace St. L8: Liv 4B 108
WA9: St. H 6E 74
Gradwell St. L1: Liv 6K 87 (7F 4)
Graeme Bryson Ct. L11: N Grn. 5H 69
Grafton Cres. L8: Liv 2K 107
Grafton Dr. CH49: Upton 4F 105
PR8: Ains 4A 14
Grafton Gro. L8: Liv 4A 108
Grafton Rd. CH45: New B 7B 66
CH65: Ell P 4A 162
Grafton St. CH43: O'ton 3B 106
L8: Liv 5B 108
(Beresford Rd.)
L8: Liv 2K 107
(Grafton Cres.)
L8: Liv 3A 108
(Park St.)
L8: Liv 2K 107
(Parliament St.)
WA5: Warr 2J 117
WA10: St. H 3K 73
WA12: New W 3F 77
Grafton Wlk. CH48: W Kir 6E 102
Graham Av. CH66: Gt Sut 6F 161
Graham Cl. WA8: Wid 7J 113
Graham Dr. L26: Halew 1A 132
Graham Rd. CH48: W Kir 5C 102
WA8: Wid 7J 113
Graham's Rd. L36: Huy 5K 91
Graham St. WA9: St. H 3E 74
Grainger Av. CH43: Pren 6K 105
CH48: W Kir 4D 102
L20: Boot 7A 54
Grain Ind. Est. L8: Liv 4A 108
Grain St. L8: Liv 4A 108
Graley Cl. L26: Halew 3K 131
Grammar School Ct.
WA4: Latch 5F 119
Grammar School La.
CH48: W Kir 7F 103
Grammar School Rd.
WA4: Latch 5F 119
WA13: Lymm 6H 121
Grampian Av. CH46: More 7D 84
Grampian Rd. L7: Liv 5G 89
Grampian Way CH46: More 7C 84
CH62: East 5A 146
CH64: Lit N 6J 157
Granams Cft. L30: N'ton 1K 53
Granard Rd. L15: W'tree 2J 109
Granary Mill WA4: Pres H 4D 154
Granary Way L3: Liv 2K 107
Granborne Chase L32: K'by 2K 55
GRANBY 7B 88 (9L 5)
Granby Cl. PR9: Chu 4B 8
WA7: Brook 5A 154
Granby Cres. CH63: Spit 7G 127
Granby Rd. WA4: Walt 1B 138
Granby St. L8: Liv 1C 108 (10N 5)
Grand Central L3: Liv 6H 5
Grandison Rd. L4: Walt 5D 68
Grand National Av. L9: Ain 4D 54
GRANGE
Warrington 6K 99
Wirral 6F 103
Grange, The CH44: Wall 3C 86
PR9: Chu 4E 8
Grange Av. CH45: Wall 1B 86
L12: W Der 2C 90
L25: Hunts X 2H 131
PR9: South 7A 8
WA4: Westy 4E 118
WN5: Orr 4K 39
Grange Av. Nth. L12: W Der 2C 90
Grange Cl. WA3: Low 1C 78
Grange Ct. CH43: O'ton 5A 106
L15: W'tree 1H 109
Grange Cres. CH66: Hoot 2C 160
Grange Cross Cl. CH48: W Kir 7G 103
Grange Cross Hey CH48: W Kir 7G 103
Grange Cross La. CH48: W Kir 7G 103
Grange Dr. CH60: Hes 1E 142
CH63: Thorn H 3A 144
WA5: Penk 4E 116
WA8: Wid 7K 113
WA10: St. H 6H 73
Grange Employment Cen.
WA1: W'ston 6A 100
Grange Farm Cl. WA5: Gt San 2H 117
Grange Farm Cres.
CH48: W Kir 5G 103
Grange Green Mnr.
WA4: H Walt 2J 137
Grangehurst Ct. L25: Gate 4F 111
Grange La. L25: Gate 3E 110
L37: Form 5J 19
Grangemeadow Rd. L25: Gate 3E 110
Grangemoor WA7: Run 3F 153
Grange Mt. CH43: O'ton 3C 106
CH48: W Kir 6F 103
CH60: Hes 1D 142
Grange Old Rd. CH48: W Kir 6E 102
GRANGE PARK 6H 73
Grange Pk. L31: Mag 5G 43
Grange Pk. Av. WA7: Run 7E 134
Grange Pk. Rd. WA10: St. H 5J 73
Grange Pl. CH41: Birk 2C 106
Grange Pct. CH41: Birk 2D 106
Grange Rd. CH41: Birk 2D 106
(not continuous)
CH48: W Kir 6C 102
CH60: Hes 7D 124
CH65: Ell P 6A 162
L30: N'ton 3D 54
L38: High 4J 29
PR9: South 1A 12
WA7: Run 7E 134
WA11: Hay 1B 76
(not continuous)
WN4: Ash M 6D 50
Grange Rd. E. CH41: Birk 2E 106
Grange Road Sports Cen. 2B 106
Grange Rd. W. CH41: Birk 2C 106
CH43: O'ton 2B 106
Grangeside L25: Gate 3E 110
Grange St. L6: Liv 2E 88
Grange Ter. L15: W'tree 1H 109
Grange Va. CH42: R Ferr 7G 107
Grange Valley WA11: Hay 7B 62
Grange Vw. CH43: O'ton 3C 106
Grange Wlk. CH48: W Kir 7F 103
Grange Way L25: Gate 3E 110
Grangeway WA7: Run 2E 152
Grangeway Ct. WA7: Run 2E 152
Grange Weint L25: Gate 4E 110
Grangewood L16: Child 6D 90
Granite Ter. L36: Huy 5A 92
Granston Cl. WA5: Call 5J 97
Granton Av. L15: W'tree 2H 109
Grant Cl. L14: K Ash 4E 90
WA5: Old H 6H 97
WA10: St. H 2A 74
Grant Ct. L20: Boot 3J 67
Grantham Av. WA1: Warr 1E 118
WA4: Walt 1B 138
Grantham Cl. CH61: Pens 5C 124
PR8: B'dale 7G 11
Grantham Cres. WA11: St. H 1E 74
Grantham Rd. L33: K'by 7C 44
PR8: B'dale 7G 11
Grantham St. L6: Liv 4D 88
Grantham Way L30: N'ton 1D 54
Grantley Rd. L15: W'tree 2J 109
Grantley St. WN4: Ash M 7E 50
Granton Cl. L37: Form 7J 19
Granton Rd. L5: Liv 1B 88
Grant Rd. CH46: Leas 3F 85
L14: K Ash 4D 90
WA5: Gt San 2F 117
WN3: Wigan 1E 50
Grantwood WN4: Ash M 7E 50
Granville Av. L31: Mag 2E 42
Granville Cl. CH45: Wall 1J 85
L39: Augh 2K 33
Granville Ct. CH45: Wall 1J 85
PR9: South 6K 7
Granville Dr. CH66: Lit Sut 4D 160
Granville Pk. L39: Augh 3K 33
Granville Pk. W. L39: Augh 3K 33
Granville Rd. L15: W'tree 1F 109
L19: Gars 3A 130
PR8: B'dale 5D 10
Granville St. WA1: Warr 2D 118
WA7: Run 6C 134
WA9: St. H 3F 75
GRAPPENHALL 6G 119
Grappenhall La.
WA4: App T, Grap 5H 139
Grappenhall Rd. CH65: Gt Sut 7H 161
WA4: S Hth 7D 118
Grappenhall Way CH43: Bid 1G 105
Grasmere Av. CH43: Noct 3G 105
L34: Prsct 1F 93
WA2: Warr 4D 98
WA11: St. H 6D 60
WN5: Orr 3H 39
WN8: Uph 4D 38
Grasmere Cl. L33: K'by 1B 56
WA11: St. H 6D 60
Grasmere Ct. CH41: Birk 3C 106
(off Penrith St.)
WA11: St. H 6C 60
Grasmere Dr. CH45: Wall 1A 86
L21: Lith 4A 54
WA7: Beech 5G 153
WN4: Ash M 7F 51
Grasmere Fold
WA11: St. H 6D 60
Grasmere Gdns. L23: C'by 2F 53
Grasmere Ho. L17: Aig 6F 109
Grasmere Rd. CH64: Nest 5J 157
CH65: Ell P 2A 170
L31: Mag 2F 43
L37: Form 7H 19
L38: High 5G 29
WA6: Frod 3E 166
WA13: Lymm 5H 121
WN5: Wigan 4K 39
Grasmere St. L5: Liv 1C 88
GRASSENDALE 1J 129
Grassendale Ct. L19: Gras 2J 129
Grassendale Esplanade
L19: Gras 3H 129
Grassendale Grn. L19: Gras 2H 129
Grassendale La. L19: Gras 2J 129
GRASSENDALE PARK 3H 129
Grassendale Rd. L19: Gras 2J 129
Grassington Cres. L25: Wltn 6G 111
Grassmoor Cl. CH62: Brom 2A 146
Grasswood Rd. CH49: W'chu 6F 105
Grassy La. WA6: Frod 4K 165
Grasville Rd. CH42: Tran 5E 106
Gratrix Rd. CH62: Brom 2K 145
Gratton Pl. WN8: Skel 3G 37
Gravel Cl. PR9: Banks 2H 9
Gravel La. PR9: Banks 2H 9
(not continuous)
Graveyard La. L39: Bic 4E 34
Gray Av. WA11: Hay 7B 62
Gray Gro. L36: Huy 7K 91
Graylag Cl. WA7: Beech 5H 153
Graylands Pl. L4: Walt 5E 68
Graylands Rd. CH62: Port S 3J 127
L4: Walt 5D 68
Graylaw Ind. Est. L9: Ain 7E 54
Grayling Dr. L12: Crox 3B 70
Gray's Av. L35: Prsct 1F 93
Graysons Rd. WA11: R'ford 4F 47
Grayson St. L1: Liv 7J 87 (9F 4)
Grayston Av. WA9: Sut L 1F 95
Gray St. L20: Boot 1G 67
GREASBY 5B 104
Greasby Dr. CH66: Gt Sut 7G 161
Greasby Hill Rd. CH48: W Kir 7E 102
Greasby Rd. CH44: Wall 3A 86
CH49: Grea 5A 104
Gt. Ashfield WA8: Wid 5K 113
Gt. Charlotte St. L1: Liv 6K 87 (6G 4)
(not continuous)
GREAT CROSBY 1E 52
Gt. Crosshall St. L3: Liv 5J 87 (4E 4)
Gt. Delph WA11: Hay 6B 62
Gt. George Pl. L1: Liv 1A 108 (10H 5)
Gt. George Sq. L1: Liv 7K 87 (10H 5)
Gt. George's Rd. L22: Water 5D 52
Gt. George St. L1: Liv 1A 108 (10H 5)
Great Hey L30: N'ton 7K 41
Gt. Homer St. L5: Liv 1K 87 (1H 5)
Gt. Homer St. Shop. Cen.
L5: Liv 2A 88
Gt. Howard St. L3: Liv 4H 87 (1C 4)
GREAT MEOLS 6G 83
Gt. Mersey St. L5: Kirk 1J 87
(not continuous)
Gt. Nelson St. L3: Liv 3K 87 (1G 4)
Gt. Newton St. L3: Liv 5B 88 (5K 5)
Gt. Orford St. L3: Liv 6B 88 (7K 5)
Gt. Richmond St. L3: Liv 4K 87 (2G 4)
Great Riding WA7: Nort 3K 153
GREAT SANKEY 2D 116
Great Sankey Leisure Cen. 7C 96
GREAT SUTTON 7F 161
Gt. Western Ho. CH41: Birk 1F 107
Greaves Cl. PR9: Banks 1J 9
Greaves Hall Av. PR9: Banks 2J 9
Greaves St. L8: Liv 3B 108
Grebe Av. WA10: St. H 7H 73
Grebe Cl. WN3: Wigan 7K 39
Grecian St. L21: Sea 5F 53
Grecian Ter. L5: Liv 1A 88
Gredington St. L8: Liv 4C 108
Greeba Av. WA4: Warr 5B 118
Greek St. L3: Liv 5A 88 (5J 5)
WA7: Run 6B 134
Green, The CH48: Caldy 2F 123
CH62: Brom 4K 127
CH63: Raby 6C 144
CH64: Lit N 5K 157
CH64: Nest 3H 157
CH64: Will 3F 159
CH65: Whit 2K 169
L13: Liv 5K 89
L23: C'by 1D 52
L34: Ecc P 7F 73
WN5: Wigan 4K 39
(not continuous)
Greenacre L40: Westh 6J 25
Greenacre Cl. L25: Hunts X 1G 131
Greenacre Dr. CH63: Brom 3J 145
Greenacre Rd. L25: Hunts X 1G 131
Greenacres WA6: Frod 5E 166
Greenacres, The
WA13: Lymm 4J 121
Greenacres Cvn. Pk.
WA6: Hap 3D 172
Greenacres Cl. CH43: Bid 7G 85
Greenacres Ct. CH43: Bid 7G 85
Green Acres Est. CH49: Grea 6A 104
Greenall Av. WA5: Penk 4B 116
Greenall Ct. L34: Prsct 1D 92
Greenalls Av. WA4: Warr 7B 118
Greenall St. WA10: St. H 2K 73
WN4: Ash M 7F 51
Green Av. CH45: New B 6B 66
GREEN BANK 4A 74
Green Bank CH63: Brim 7A 126
Greenbank CH2: Ince 6A 164
L22: Water 5E 52
L39: Augh 1A 34
Greenbank Av. CH45: New B 7B 66
CH66: Lit Sut 4E 160
L31: Mag 1E 42
WN5: Bil 1F 49
Greenbank Ct. L17: Aig 3G 109
Greenbank Cres.
WA10: St. H 3B 74
Greenbank Dr. CH61: Pens 6E 124
L10: Faz 6K 55
L17: Aig 3G 109
PR8: B'dale 6E 10
Greenbank Gdns. WA4: S Hth 6F 119
Greenbank La. L17: Aig 4G 109
Greenbank Rd. CH42: Tran 5C 106
CH48: W Kir 4D 102
L18: Moss H 3G 109
WA4: S Hth 6F 119
Greenbank Sports Academy 4G 109
Greenbank St. WA4: Warr 6C 118
Greenbridge Cl. WA7: Cas 7J 135
Greenbridge Rd. WA7: Wind H 7K 135
Greenburn Av. WA11: St. H 4E 60

A-Z Merseyside 201

Hale Vw. Rd.—Hasfield Rd.

Hale Vw. Rd. L36: Huy 5A **92**
WA6: Hel 7J **165**
HALEWOOD 2K **131**
Halewood Av. WA3: Golb 4K **63**
Halewood Caravan Pk.
L26: Halew 1C **132**
Halewood Cl. L25: Gate 4F **111**
Halewood Dr. L25: Wltn 6G **111**
(Hunts Cross Av.)
L25: Wltn 6F **111**
(Kings Dri.)
HALEWOOD GREEN 6J **111**
Halewood Leisure Cen. 2A **132**
Halewood Pl. L25: Wltn 5G **111**
Halewood Rd. L25: Gate, Wltn 4F **111**
Halewood Station (Rail) 1K **131**
Halewood Triangle Country Pk. 1H **131**
Halewood Way L25: Wltn 6G **111**
Haley Rd. Nth. WA5: B'wood 1B **96**
Haley Rd. Sth. WA5: B'wood 2C **96**
Halfacre La. WA4: Thel 5A **120**
Half Crown St. L5: Kirk 1J **87**
Halfpenny Cl. L19: Gras 2K **129**
Halfpenny La. WN8: Skel 2A **36**
Halidon Ct. L20: Boot 2G **67**
Halifax Cl. WA2: Warr 5D **98**
Halifax Cres. L23: Thorn 6H **41**
Halifax Rd. PR8: Ains 4C **14**
Halkirk Rd. L18: Aller 7A **110**
Halkyn Av. L17: Liv 2F **109**
Halkyn Dr. L5: Liv 2C **88**
Hallam Wlk. L7: Liv 6E **88**
Hallastone Rd. WA6: Hel 7H **165**
Hall Av. WA8: Wid 7G **113**
Halla Way WA4: Latch 5E **118**
Hallbridge Gdns. WN8: Uph 3D **38**
Hall Brow Cl. L39: Orm 6F **25**
Hallcroft WN8: Skel 1J **37**
Hallcroft Pl. WA4: Grap 6G **119**
Hall Dr. CH49: Grea 5B **104**
L32: K'by 2C **56**
WA4: App 3D **138**
Hallfield Dr. CH2: Elt 1B **172**
Hallfield Pk. CH66: Gt Sut 7F **161**
Hallfields Rd. WA2: Warr 7C **98**
HALL GREEN 4C **38**
Hall Grn. WN8: Uph 4D **38**
Hall Grn. Cl. WN8: Uph 4D **38**
Halliday Cl. WA3: Bchwd 4B **100**
Halliwell Jones Stadium 2A **118**
Halliwells Brow WA16: H Legh 7K **141**
Hall La. L7: Liv 5C **88** (4M **5**)
L9: Ain 6D **54**
L31: Lyd 4D **32**
L31: Mag 4E **42**
L32: K'by 3B **56**
L33: Sim 5D **44**
L34: Prsct 2D **92**
L35: R'hill 1J **113**
L36: Huy 5K **91**
L38: Ince B 7F **31**
L39: Bic 1J **45**
L40: Lath 5A **26**
WA4: Dares 7G **137**
WA4: Grap 1H **139**
WA4: Lwr S, S'ton 7J **139**
(not continuous)
WA5: B'wood 7E **76**
WA8: Cron 1J **113**
WA9: Bold 4J **95**
WN3: Wigan 7H **39**
WN5: Bil 7G **39**
WN5: Wigan 7H **39**
Hallmoor Cl. L39: Augh 1C **34**
Hall Nook WA5: Penk 4D **116**
Hallows Av. WA2: Warr 6D **98**
Hall Rd. L40: Scar 2J **17**
WA1: W'ston 1J **119**
WA11: Hay 6C **62**
Hall Rd. E. L23: Blun 6B **40**
Hall Road Station (Rail) 6A **40**
Hall Rd. W. L23: Blun 6A **40**
Hallsands Rd. L32: K'by 5C **56**
Hallsgreen La. CH2: Wim T 5K **171**
Hallside Cl. L19: Aig 1H **129**
Hall St. PR9: South 2J **11**
WA1: Warr 3C **118**
WA9: Clock F 4F **95**
WA10: St. H 3C **74**
WN2: Bam 5J **51**
Hall Ter. WA5: Gt San 1C **116**
Halltine Cl. L23: Blun 6A **40**
Hallville Rd. CH44: Wall 4C **86**
L18: Moss H 3J **109**
Hall Wood Av. WA11: Hay 4D **62**
Hallwood Cl. WA7: Run 4D **152**
Hallwood Ct. CH64: Nest 4J **157**
Hallwood Dr. CH66: Led 7J **159**
Hallwood Link Rd. WA7: Pal F 4H **153**
HALLWOOD PARK 4G **153**
Hallwood Pk. Av. WA7: Pal F 4G **153**
HALSALL 1D **22**
Halsall Av. WA2: Warr 7D **98**
Halsall Bldgs. PR9: South 1K **11**
Halsall Cl. L23: C'by 7E **40**
WA7: Brook 5A **154**
Halsall Ct. L39: Orm 4B **24**
Halsall Grn. CH63: Spit 1H **145**
Halsall Hall Dr. L39: Hals 1D **22**
Halsall La. L37: Form 6K **19**
L39: Hals 5F **23**
L39: Orm 4B **24**
Halsall Manor Ct. L39: Hals 1D **22**
Halsall Rd. L20: Boot 7J **53**
L39: Hals 1E **22**
PR8: B'dale 1F **15**
Halsall St. L34: Prsct 7D **72**
Halsbury Rd. CH45: Wall 1B **86**
L6: Liv 4E **88**
Halsey Av. L12: W Der 7H **69**
Halsey Cres. L12: W Der 7H **69**
Halsnead Av. L35: Whis 6C **92**
Halsnead Cvn. Est. L35: Whis 6E **92**
Halsnead Cl. L15: W'tree 6J **89**
Halstead Rd. CH44: Wall 4C **86**
L9: Walt 7B **54**
Halstead Wlk. L32: K'by 4A **56**
HALTON BROOK 2G **153**
Halton Brook Av. WA7: Run 1F **153**
Halton Brow WA7: Halt 1G **153**
Halton Castle 1H **153**
Halton Chase L40: Westh 6J **25**
Halton Ct. WA7: Run 7F **135**
Halton Cres. CH49: Grea 5K **103**
CH66: Gt Sut 2H **169**
Halton Hey L35: Whis 6D **92**
HALTON LEA 3H **153**
Halton Link Rd. WA7: Pal F 2G **153**
HALTON LODGE 2E **152**
Halton Lodge Av. WA7: Run 3F **153**
Halton Miniature Railway 3A **154**
Halton Rd. CH45: Wall 1A **86**
CH66: Gt Sut 3G **169**
L31: Lyd 1F **43**
WA5: Gt San 2D **116**
WA7: Run 7D **134**
Halton Stadium 1B **134**
Halton Sta. Rd. WA7: Sut W 7H **153**
Halton St. WA11: Hay 7C **62**
HALTON VIEW 7E **114**
Halton Vw. Rd. WA8: Wid 7E **114**
HALTON VILLAGE 2H **153**
Halton Wlk. L25: Gate 2E **110**
Halton Way CH66: Gt Sut 3G **169**
Halton Wood L32: K'by 2K **55**
Hambledon Cl. CH66: Lit Sut 5C **160**
Hambledon Dr. CH49: Grea 4A **104**
Hamble Dr. WA5: Penk 5D **116**
Hambleton Cl. L11: Crox 2K **69**
WA8: Wid 5J **113**
Hamblett Cres. WA11: St. H 7D **60**
Hamer St. WA10: St. H 2B **74**
Hamer St. Sth. WA10: St. H 3B **74**
Hamil Cl. CH47: Meols 6G **83**
Hamilton Cl. CH64: Park 1F **157**
Hamilton Ct. CH64: Nest 3K **157**
L23: Blun 1B **52**
Hamilton La. CH41: Birk 1E **106**
Hamilton Rd. CH45: New B 6A **66**
L5: Liv 2B **88**
WA10: Windle 7J **59**
WN4: Gars 1A **62**
Hamilton Sq. CH41: Birk 1E **106**
Hamilton Square Station (Rail) 1F **107**
Hamilton St. CH41: Birk 2E **106**
(not continuous)
Hamlet Ct. L17: Aig 5E **108**
Hamlet Rd. CH45: Wall 1K **85**
Hamlin Cl. WA7: West 4C **152**
Hamlin Rd. L19: Gars 3B **130**
Hammersley Av. WA9: Clock F 4E **94**
Hammersley St. WA9: Clock F 4E **94**
Hammersmith Way WA8: Wid 4F **115**
Hammill St. WA10: St. H 1K **73**
(not continuous)
Hammond Rd. L33: Know I 2G **57**
Hammond St. WA9: St. H 4F **75**
Hamnett Ct. WA3: Bchwd 4A **100**
Hamnett Rd. L34: Prsct 7E **72**
Hampden Gro. CH42: Tran 4D **106**
Hampden Rd. CH42: Tran 4D **106**
Hampden St. L4: Walt 4B **68**
Hampshire Av. L30: N'ton 2J **53**
Hampshire Gdns. WA10: St. H 4B **74**
Hampson Av. WA3: Cul 3B **80**
Hampson Cl. WN4: Ash M 3F **63**
Hampson St. L6: Liv 2E **88**
Hampstead Rd. CH44: Wall 4C **86**
L6: Liv 4E **88**
Hampton Chase CH43: Noct 5H **105**
Hampton Cl. CH64: Nest 5J **157**
WA8: Wid 5G **115**
Hampton Ct. WA7: Mnr P 5A **136**
Hampton Ct. Rd. L12: W Der 2A **90**
Hampton Court Way WA8: Wid 4F **115**
Hampton Cres. CH64: Nest 5J **157**
Hampton Dr. WA5: Gt San 4G **117**
WA8: Cron 3J **113**
Hampton Gdns. CH65: Ell P 6J **161**
Hampton Pl. WA11: St. H 7D **60**
Hampton Rd. L37: Form 2J **29**
PR8: South 4H **11**
Hampton St. L8: Liv 1B **108** (10K **5**)
Hamsterley Cl. WA3: Bchwd 1D **100**
Hanbury Rd. L4: Walt 6F **69**
Hancock Ct. WA4: Warr 4C **118**
Handa Dr. CH65: Ell P 4K **169**
Handel Ct. L8: Liv 2D **108**
Handel Rd. L27: N'ley 2G **111**
Handfield Pl. L5: Liv 2C **88**
Handfield Rd. L22: Water 4D **52**
Handfield St. L5: Liv 2C **88**
Handford Av. CH62: East 5B **146**
Handforth Cl. WA4: Thel 4K **119**
Handforth La. WA7: Run 4F **153**
Handley Ct. L19: Aig 1H **129**
Handley St. WA7: Run 6B **134**
Hands St. L21: Lith 7H **53**
Handsworth Wlk. PR8: South 5B **12**
Hanford Av. L9: Walt 7B **54**
Hankey Dr. L20: Boot 1A **68**
Hankey St. WA7: Run 7B **134**
Hankinson St. L13: Liv 6H **89**
Hankin St. L5: Liv 1K **87**
Hanley Cl. WA8: Wid 7J **113**
Hanley Rd. WA8: Wid 7J **113**
Hanlon Av. L20: Boot 7K **53**
Hanmer Rd. L32: K'by 3K **55**
Hannah Cl. CH61: Pens 6C **124**
Hannan Rd. L6: Liv 4D **88**
Hanns Hall Rd.
CH64: Nest, Will 3C **158**
Hanover Cl. CH43: C'ton 2K **105**
Hanover Cl. WA7: Brook 4K **153**
Hanover St. L1: Liv 6J **87** (8F **4**)
WA1: Warr 4A **118**
Hansard Ct. WA9: St. H 7K **73**
Hansby Cl. WN8: Skel 3A **38**
Hansby Dr. L24: Speke 4F **131**
Hanson Pk. CH43: O'ton 3J **105**
Hanson Rd. L9: Ain 1E **68**
Hanson Rd. Bus. Pk. L9: Ain 1E **68**
Hans Rd. L4: Walt 5C **68**
Hanstock Cl. WN5: Orr 6G **39**
Hants La. L39: Orm 4C **24**
Hanwell St. L6: Liv 1D **88**
Hanworth Cl. L12: Crox 3C **70**
HAPSFORD 3E **172**
Hapsford Cl. WA3: Bchwd 3J **99**
Hapsford La. WA6: Hel 7C **164**
(Ash Rd.)
WA6: Hel 3E **172**
(Moor La.)
Hapsford Rd. L21: Lith 7H **53**
Hapton St. L5: Liv 1A **88**
Harbern Cl. L12: W Der 1A **90**
Harbord Rd. L22: Water 4C **52**
Harbord St. L7: Liv 6D **88** (7P **5**)
WA1: Warr 4C **118**
Harbord Ter. L22: Water 4C **52**
Harborne Dr. CH63: Spit 7F **127**
Harbour Cl. WA7: Murd 4B **154**
Harbreck Gro. L9: Ain 3F **69**
Harbury Av. PR8: Ains 5A **14**
Harcourt Av. CH44: Wall 4E **86**
Harcourt Cl. WA3: Bchwd 4A **100**
Harcourt St. CH41: Birk 1C **106**
L4: Kirk 7K **67**
Hardacre St. L39: Orm 4D **24**
Hardie Av. CH46: More 6A **84**
Hardie Cl. WA9: Sut M 4C **94**
Hardie Rd. L36: Huy 4A **92**
Harding Av. CH63: Beb 5F **127**
WA2: Warr 6E **98**
Harding Cl. L5: Liv 2C **88**
Hardinge Rd. L19: Aller 1A **130**
Hardknott Rd. CH62: Brom 1A **146**
Hard La. WA10: St. H 7K **59**
Hardman St. L1: Liv 7A **88** (8J **5**)
Hardrow Cl. WN3: Wigan 2F **51**
Hardshaw Cen. WA10: St. H 3C **74**
Hardshaw St. WA10: St. H 3C **74**
Hardwick Grange
WA1: W'ston 6K **99**
Hardwick Rd. WA7: Ast 6F **135**
WN4: Ash M 7E **50**
Hardy Cl. CH66: Gt Sut 1H **169**
Hardy Rd. WA13: Lymm 6E **120**
Hardy St. L1: Liv 1K **107** (10G **4**)
(not continuous)
L19: Gars 5A **130**
WA2: Warr 2B **118**
(not continuous)
Harebell Cl. L37: Form 2K **29**
WA8: Wid 4A **114**
Harebell St. L5: Kirk 7K **67**
Hare Cft. L28: Stock V 6D **70**
Harefield Grn. L24: Speke 6H **131**
Harefield Rd. L24: Speke 7H **131**
HARESFINCH 7D **60**
Haresfinch Cl. L26: Halew 7A **112**
Haresfinch Rd. WA11: St. H 7D **60**
Haresfinch Vw. WA11: St. H 7D **60**
Hares La. PR8: South 7E **12**
WA6: Frod 3A **166**
Harewell Rd. L11: N Grn. 5J **69**
Harewood Av. CH66: Gt Sut 7D **160**
PR8: Ains 3C **14**
Harewood Cl. L36: Huy 4J **91**
Harewood Rd. CH45: New B 7A **66**
Harewood St. L6: Liv 3C **88** (1N **5**)
Harfield Gdns. CH66: Lit Sut 6E **160**
Harford Cl. WA5: Penk 4D **116**
Hargate Rd. L33: K'by 3D **56**
Hargate Wlk. L33: K'by 3D **56**
Hargrave Av. CH43: O'ton 5J **105**
Hargrave Cl. CH43: O'ton 5J **105**
Hargrave Dr. CH66: Gt Sut 6G **161**
Hargrave La. CH64: Will 5F **145**
Hargreaves Ct. WA8: Wid 7F **115**
Hargreaves Ho. *WA8: Wid* *7F 115*
(off Hargreaves Ct.)
Hargreaves Rd. L17: Aig 5E **108**
Hargreaves St. PR8: South 2J **11**
WA9: St. H 2G **75**
Harington Cl. L37: Form 7H **19**
Harington Grn. L37: Form 7G **19**
Harington Rd. L37: Form 5G **19**
Harker St. L3: Liv 4A **88** (3H **5**)
Harke St. L7: Liv 7D **88**
Harland Dr. WN4: Ash M 2G **63**
Harland Grn. L24: Speke 6K **131**
Harland Rd. CH42: Tran 4D **106**
Harlech Cl. WA5: Call 5J **97**
Harlech Ct. CH63: Beb 5F **127**
CH65: Ell P 1B **170**
Harlech Gro. WA7: Cas 1H **153**
Harlech Rd. L23: Blun 2C **52**
Harlech St. CH44: Wall 5E **86**
L4: Kirk, Walt 5A **68**
WN4: Ash M 7D **50**
Harlech Way CH65: Ell P 1B **170**
Harleston Rd. L33: K'by 2E **56**
Harleston Wlk. L33: K'by 2E **56**
Harley Av. CH63: High B 1C **126**
Harley St. L9: Walt 7C **54**
Harlian Av. CH46: More 1B **104**
Harlow Cl. WA4: Thel 5J **119**
WA9: St. H 7B **74**
Harlow St. L8: Liv 4A **108**
Harlyn Cl. L26: Halew 3J **131**
Harlyn Gdns. WA5: Penk 5B **116**
Harmony Way L13: Liv 6J **89**
Harn, The CH66: Gt Sut 1E **168**
Harold Av. WN4: Ash M 7E **50**
Haroldene Gro. L34: Prsct 2K **91**
Harold Rd. WA11: Hay 6D **62**
Harper Rd. L9: Walt 2C **68**
Harpers Pond La. L15: W'tree 7J **89**
Harpers Rd. WA2: P'gate 6G **99**
Harper St. L6: Liv 5C **88** (4M **5**)
Harps Cft. L30: N'ton 2J **53**
Harptree Cl. L35: Whis 4E **92**
Harpur Cl. CH66: Gt Sut 7F **161**
Harradon Rd. L9: Ain 6D **54**
Harridge La. L40: Scar 2H **23**
Harrier Dr. L26: Halew 7J **111**
WN8: Skel 3A **38**
Harrier Rd. WA2: P'gate 5F **99**
Harringay Av. L18: Moss H 3H **109**
Harrington Av. CH47: Hoy 1E **102**
Harrington Rd. L3: Liv 4A **108**
L21: Lith 4K **53**
L23: C'by 1D **52**
L36: Huy 3F **91**
Harrington St. L2: Liv 6J **87** (6E **4**)
Harrington Vw. CH44: Wall 2D **86**
Harris Cl. CH63: Spit 7G **127**
Harris Dr. L20: Boot 7J **53**
L30: Boot 6K **53**
Harris Gdns. WA9: St. H 5D **74**
Harrismith Rd. L10: Faz 6G **55**
Harrison Cl. WA1: Warr 2C **118**
Harrison Dr. CH45: Wall 7H **65**
L20: Boot 3A **68**
WA11: Hay 7J **61**
WA11: R'ford 4F **47**
Harrison Hey L36: Huy 6J **91**
Harrison Sq. WA5: Warr 6K **97**
Harrisons Ter. CH66: Lit Sut 5E **160**
Harrison St. WA8: Hale B 3H **133**
WA9: St. H 7F **75**
Harrison's Yd. CH62: East 5B **146**
Harrison Way L3: Liv 4K **107**
WA12: New W 2G **77**
Harris St. WA8: Wid 7E **114**
WA10: St. H 2A **74**
Harrocks Cl. L30: N'ton 7K **41**
Harrock Wood Cl. CH61: Irby 3C **124**
Harrod Dr. PR8: B'dale 5E **10**
Harrogate Cl. CH62: East 6K **145**
WA5: Gt San 6E **96**
Harrogate Dr. L5: Liv 2B **88**
Harrogate Rd. CH42: R Ferr 7G **107**
CH62: East 6K **145**
Harrogate Wlk. CH42: R Ferr 1G **127**
Harrogate Way PR9: Cros 1E **8**
Harron Cl. L32: K'by 3A **56**
Harrop Rd. WA7: Run 1D **152**
Harrops Cft. L30: N'ton 1A **54**
Harrowby Cl. L8: Liv 1C **108** (10N **5**)
Harrowby Rd. CH42: Tran 4C **106**
CH44: Wall 3D **86**
L21: Sea 6F **53**
Harrowby Rd. Sth. CH42: Tran 4C **106**
Harrowby St. L8: Liv 1C **108** (10N **5**)
(Granby St.)
L8: Liv 1B **108** (10M **5**)
(Park Way)
Harrow Cl. CH44: Wall 2K **85**
L30: N'ton 2B **54**
WA4: App 3E **138**
WN5: Orr 3H **39**
Harrow Dr. L10: Ain 3F **55**
WA7: Run 7G **135**
Harrow Gro. CH62: Brom 2A **146**
Harrow Rd. CH44: Wall 2K **85**
CH65: Ell P 7B **162**
L4: Walt 1D **88**
Harsnips WN8: Skel 1J **37**
Harswell Cl. WN5: Orr 6G **39**
Hartdale Rd. L18: Moss H 4J **109**
L23: Thorn 6G **41**
Hartford Cl. CH43: O'ton 5K **105**
Hartford Dr. CH65: Whit 7H **161**
Harthill Av. L18: Moss H 4K **109**
Harthill M. CH43: Bid 6G **85**
Harthill Rd. L18: Moss H 3A **110**
Hartington Av. CH41: Birk 1B **106**
Hartington Rd. CH44: Wall 3B **86**
L8: Liv 2E **108**
L12: W Der 1K **89**
L19: Gars 3A **130**
WA10: St. H 1J **73**
Hartington Ter. *L19: Gars* *3K 129*
(off St Mary's Rd.)
Hartismere Rd. CH44: Wall 4D **86**
Hartland WN8: Skel 1J **37**
Hartland Av. PR9: Marsh 2D **8**
Hartland Cl. WA8: Wid 3C **114**
Hartland Gdns. WA9: St. H 1K **93**
Hartland Rd. L11: N Grn. 4G **69**
Hartley Av. L9: Ain 1D **68**
Hartley Cl. L4: Walt 7B **68**
WA13: Lymm 5H **121**
Hartley Cres. PR8: B'dale 6F **11**
Hartley Gro. L33: K'by 7D **44**
WA10: St. H 6J **73**
WN5: Orr 4K **39**
Hartley Quay L3: Liv 7H **87** (8D **4**)
Hartley Rd. PR8: B'dale 6F **11**
Hartley St. WN5: Wigan 5K **39**
HARTLEY'S VILLAGE 7D **54**
Hartnup St. L5: Liv 1B **88**
(not continuous)
Harton Cl. WA8: Wid 5A **114**
Hartopp Rd. L25: Gate 1E **110**
Hartopp Wlk. *L25: Gate* *1E 110*
(off Hartopp Rd.)
Hartsbourne Av. L25: Gate 7D **90**
(not continuous)
Hartsbourne Cl. L25: Gate 1D **110**
Hartsbourne Wlk. L25: Gate 1E **110**
Hartshead WN8: Skel 1J **37**
Hart's La. WN8: Uph 3B **38**
Hart St. L3: Liv 5A **88** (5J **5**)
PR8: South 2K **11**
Hartswell Cl. WA3: Golb 3K **63**
Hartswood Cl. WA4: App 6E **138**
Hartwell St. L21: Lith 7H **53**
Hartwood Cl. L32: K'by 6D **56**
Hartwood Rd. L32: K'by 6D **56**
PR9: South 1K **11**
Hartwood Sq. L32: K'by 6D **56**
Harty Rd. WA11: Hay 1H **75**
Harvard Cl. WA7: Wind H 7B **136**
Harvard Ct. WA2: Win 4A **98**
Harvard Gro. L34: Prsct 7E **72**
Harvester Way CH49: Grea 4A **104**
L30: N'ton 1C **54**
Harvest La. CH46: More 6B **84**
Harvest Way WA9: Clock F 3E **94**
Harvey Av. CH49: Grea 5B **104**
WA12: New W 3D **76**
Harvey Ct. WA2: Warr 4B **98**
Harvey La. WA3: Golb 4K **63**
Harvey Rd. CH45: Wall 1A **86**
CH46: Leas 5E **84**
Harvington Dr. PR8: Ains 4A **14**
Harwich Gro. L16: Child 7D **90**
Harwood Gdns. WA4: Grap 6G **119**
Harwood Rd. L19: Gars 3B **130**
Haryngton Av. WA5: Warr 1K **117**
HASAKAYNE 5B **22**
Haselbeech Cl. L11: N Grn. 3H **69**
Haselbeech Cres. L11: N Grn. 3H **69**
Haseldine St. WN4: Ash M 6D **50**
Hasfield Rd. L11: N Grn. 4K **69**

Haslam Dr.—Herons Way

Haslam Dr. L39: Orm . . . 3B 24
Haslemere L35: Whis . . . 4F 93
Haslemere Dr. WA5: Penk . . . 4B 116
Haslemere Ind. Est. WN4: Ash M . . . 4E 50
Haslemere Rd. L25: Gate . . . 2E 110
Haslemere Way L25: Gate . . . 2E 110
Haslingden Cl. L13: Liv . . . 5K 89
Haslington Gro. L26: Halew . . . 3A 132
Hassal Rd. CH42: R Ferr . . . 1G 127
Hassnes Cl. WN3: Wigan . . . 2F 51
Hastie Cl. L27: N'ley . . . 3J 111
Hastings Av. WA2: Warr . . . 3B 98
Hastings Dr. L36: Huy . . . 7A 92
Hastings Rd. L22: Water . . . 3B 52
PR8: B'dale . . . 6E 10
Haswell Dr. L28: Stock V . . . 6E 70
Hatchery Cl. WA4: App T . . . 5H 139
Hatchings, The WA13: Lymm . . . 6H 121
Hatchmere Cl. CH43: O'ton . . . 5K 105
WA5: Warr . . . 2J 117
Hatfield Cl. L12: Crox . . . 3D 70
WA9: St. H . . . 7B 74
Hatfield Gdns. L36: Huy . . . 6K 91
WA4: App . . . 5E 138
Hatfield Rd. L20: Boot . . . 3A 68
PR8: Ains . . . 3C 14
Hathaway L31: Mag . . . 5D 42
Hathaway Cl. L25: Gate . . . 2E 110
Hathaway Rd. L25: Gate . . . 2E 110
Hatherley Av. L23: C'by . . . 3E 52
Hatherley Cl. L8: Liv . . . 1C 108
(not continuous)
Hatherley St. CH44: Wall . . . 5E 86
L8: Liv . . . 1C 108
Hathersage Rd. L36: Huy . . . 2J 91
Hatherton Gro. L26: Halew . . . 3A 132
Hatley La. WA6: Frod . . . 4A 166
Hatters Row WA1: Warr . . . 3B 118
(off Horsemarket St.)
HATTON . . . 7A 138
Hatton Av. CH62: East . . . 7A 146
Hatton Cl. CH60: Hes . . . 2B 142
Hatton Gdn. L3: Liv . . . 5J 87 (4E 4)
Hatton Garden Ind. Est. L3: Liv . . . 4F 4
Hatton Hill Rd. L21: Lith . . . 4G 53
Hatton La. WA4: Hatt, S'ton . . . 7A 138
Hattons La. L16: Child . . . 2A 110
Hauxwell Gro. WA11: St. H . . . 7D 60
Havannah La. WA9: St. H . . . 3K 75
Havelock Cl. WA10: St. H . . . 3B 74
Haven Brow L39: Augh . . . 3A 34
Haven Rd. L10: Faz . . . 5H 55
Haven Wlk. L31: Lyd . . . 7E 32
Havercroft Cl. WN3: Wigan . . . 1C 50
Havergal St. WA7: Run . . . 1B 152
Haverstock Rd. L6: Liv . . . 4F 89
Haverton Wlk. L12: Crox . . . 3C 70
Haverty Pct. WA12: New W . . . 5F 77
Havisham Cl. WA3: Bchwd . . . 2K 99
Hawarde Cl. WA12: New W . . . 2E 76
Hawarden Av. CH43: O'ton . . . 2B 106
CH44: Wall . . . 3C 86
L17: Liv . . . 2F 109
Hawarden Ct. CH63: Beb . . . 5F 127
Hawarden Gdns. CH65: Ell P . . . 2B 170
Hawarden Gro. L21: Sea . . . 7G 53
Hawdon Ct. L7: Liv . . . 7E 88
Hawes Av. WA11: St. H . . . 5E 60
Hawes Cres. WN4: Ash M . . . 7F 51
Hawesside St. PR9: South . . . 1J 11
Haweswater Av. WA11: Hay . . . 7J 61
Haweswater Cl. L33: K'by . . . 7B 44
WA7: Beech . . . 5J 153
Haweswater Gro. L31: Mag . . . 2H 43
Hawgreen Rd. L32: K'by . . . 4K 55
Hawick Cl. CH66: Lit Sut . . . 6C 160
L33: K'by . . . 6B 44
Hawke Grn. L35: Tar G . . . 1A 112
Hawker Dr. WN8: Skel . . . 3A 38
Hawke St. L3: Liv . . . 6A 88 (6H 5)
Hawkesworth St. L4: Walt . . . 1C 88
Hawkhurst Cl. L8: Liv . . . 4B 108
Hawkins Rd. CH64: Nest . . . 2K 157
Hawkins St. L6: Liv . . . 4D 88
HAWKLEY . . . 2F 51
Hawkley Av. WN3: Wigan . . . 2D 50
Hawkley Brook Ct. WN3: Wigan . . . 2D 50
Hawkscloulgh WN8: Skel . . . 1J 37
Hawks Ct. WA7: Pal F . . . 4G 153
Hawkshaw Cl. WA3: Bchwd . . . 3J 99
Hawkshead Av. L12: W Der . . . 5A 70
Hawkshead Cl. L31: Mag . . . 2G 43
WA7: Beech . . . 6J 153
Hawkshead Dr. L21: Lith . . . 5K 53
Hawkshead Rd. CH62: Brom . . . 1A 146
WA5: B'wood . . . 1C 96
Hawkshead St. PR8: South . . . 1K 11
PR9: South . . . 7J 7
Hawksmoor Cl. L10: Faz . . . 6J 55
Hawksmoor Rd. L10: Faz . . . 7H 55
Hawksmore Cl. CH49: Upton . . . 2B 104
Hawkstone Gro. WA6: Hel . . . 7J 165
Hawkstone Wlk. L8: Liv . . . 4C 108
(off Gordale Cl.)
Hawks Way CH60: Hes . . . 2C 142
Hawksworth Cl. L37: Form . . . 4A 20
Hawksworth Dr. L37: Form . . . 4A 20
Hawley Brook Trad. Est.
WN3: Wigan . . . 2C 50
Hawley's Cl. WA5: Warr . . . 6K 97
Hawleys La. WA2: Warr . . . 6A 98
WA5: Warr . . . 6K 97
Haworth Dr. L20: Boot . . . 6K 53
Hawthorn Av. WA7: Run . . . 1C 152
WA8: Wid . . . 6D 114
WA12: New W . . . 3H 77
WN4: Gars . . . 7A 50
WN5: Orr . . . 5H 39
Hawthorn Cl. WA11: Hay . . . 1J 75
WN5: Bil . . . 7F 49
Hawthorn Cres. WN8: Skel . . . 2E 36
Hawthorn Dr. CH48: W Kir . . . 6G 103
CH61: Hes . . . 7D 124
WA10: Eccl . . . 2H 73
Hawthorne Av. L26: Halew . . . 3J 131
WA1: W'ston . . . 1H 119
WA3: Cul . . . 1E 80
WA5: Gt San . . . 2D 116
Hawthorne Bus. Pk.
WA5: Warr . . . 7A 98
Hawthorne Ct. L21: Lith . . . 5H 53
Hawthorne Cres. L37: Form . . . 1A 30
Hawthorne Dr. CH64: Will . . . 2H 159
Hawthorne Gro. CH44: Wall . . . 5E 86
PR9: South . . . 1B 12
WA1: P'ton . . . 1F 119
Hawthorne Rd. CH42: Tran . . . 5D 106
L20: Boot . . . 3K 67
L21: Lith . . . 5H 53
WA4: S Hth . . . 1C 138
WA6: Frod . . . 2D 166
WA9: Sut L . . . 1F 95
WA13: Lymm . . . 5F 121
Hawthorne St. WA5: Warr . . . 7A 98
Hawthorn Gro. L7: Liv . . . 6D 88 (6P 5)
L12: W Der . . . 1K 89
WA4: S Hth . . . 7D 118
WA4: Warr . . . 5D 118
Hawthorn La. CH62: Brom . . . 2K 145
Hawthorn Rd. CH64: Park . . . 1F 157
CH66: Lit Sut . . . 5E 160
L34: Prsct . . . 1E 92
L36: Roby . . . 5G 91
Hawthorns, The CH66: Ell P . . . 4H 161
WN8: Newb . . . 1G 27
Haxted Gdns. L19: Gars . . . 3B 130
Haycroft Cl. CH66: Gt Sut . . . 2F 169
Haydn Rd. L14: K Ash . . . 1D 90
HAYDOCK . . . 7A 62
Haydock Community Leisure Cen. . . . 7K 61
Haydock Cross WA11: Hay . . . 5E 62
Haydock Ind. Est. WA11: Hay . . . 5C 62
Haydock La. WA11: Hay . . . 7A 62
(not continuous)
Haydock Pk. Gdns.
WA12: New W . . . 4F 63
Haydock Park Race Course . . . 4H 63
Haydock Pk. Rd. L10: Ain . . . 2G 55
Haydock Rd. CH45: Wall . . . 7C 66
Haydock St. WA2: Warr . . . 2B 118
WA10: St. H . . . 3C 74
WA12: New W . . . 2E 76
WN4: Ash M . . . 3F 63
Hayes Av. L35: Prsct . . . 2E 92
Hayes Cres. WA6: Frod . . . 2E 166
Hayes Dr. L31: Mell . . . 2J 55
Hayes La. WA4: App . . . 1E 138
Hayes St. WA10: St. H . . . 6J 73
Hayfell Rd. WN3: Wigan . . . 3E 50
Hayfield Cl. L26: Halew . . . 7A 112
Hayfield Pl. CH46: More . . . 7E 84
Hayfield Rd. L39: Orm . . . 3C 24
WA1: W'ston . . . 1J 119
Hayfield St. L4: Walt . . . 7B 68
Hayfield Way WA9: Clock F . . . 3E 94
Haylemere Ct. PR8: B'dale . . . 3E 10
(off Oxford Rd.)
Hayles Cl. L25: Gate . . . 2E 110
Hayles Grn. L25: Gate . . . 2E 110
Hayles Gro. L25: Gate . . . 2E 110
Hayling Ho. L19: Aig . . . 2H 129
Haylock Cl. L8: Liv . . . 4B 108
Hayman's Cl. L12: W Der . . . 7J 69
Haymans Grn. L31: Mag . . . 3G 43
L12: W Der . . . 7J 69
Hayman's Gro. L12: W Der . . . 7J 69
Hayscastle Cl. WA5: Call . . . 6J 97
Hayward Ct. L37: Form . . . 6A 20
Haywood Cres. WA7: Wind H . . . 7B 136
Haywood Gdns. WA10: St. H . . . 4K 73
Hazel Av. L32: K'by . . . 2A 56
L35: Whis . . . 4E 92
WA7: Run . . . 2A 152
Hazelbank Gdns. L37: Form . . . 5J 19
Hazelborough Cl. WA3: Bchwd . . . 2D 100
Hazel Cl. CH66: Gt Sut . . . 3H 169
Hazel Ct. L8: Liv . . . 4C 108
(off Byles St.)
L20: Boot . . . 4J 67
Hazeldale Rd. L9: Walt . . . 2C 68
Hazeldene Av. CH45: Wall . . . 2A 86
CH61: Thing . . . 3F 125
Hazeldene Way CH61: Thing . . . 3F 125
Hazel Dr. WA13: Lymm . . . 6H 121
Hazelfield Ct. WA9: Clock F . . . 3E 94
Hazel Gro. CH61: Irby . . . 2B 124
CH63: High B . . . 5E 126
L9: Ain . . . 7D 54
L23: C'by . . . 2F 53
PR8: South . . . 1A 12
WA1: P'ton . . . 7G 99
WA10: St. H . . . 3J 73
Hazelhurst Cl. L37: Form . . . 1G 29
Hazelhurst Gro. WN4: Ash M . . . 1G 63
Hazel La. WN8: Skel . . . 5H 27
Hazelmere Ho. L17: Aig . . . 6F 109
Hazel M. L31: Mell . . . 2K 55
Hazel Rd. CH41: Birk . . . 3D 106
CH47: Hoy . . . 1E 102
L36: Huy . . . 2K 91
Hazelslack Rd. L11: N Grn. . . . 4J 69
Hazel St. WA1: Warr . . . 1D 118
Hazelwood CH49: Grea . . . 3B 104
Hazelwood Cl. WA8: Wid . . . 1G 133
WA9: Sut M . . . 4D 94
Hazelwood Gro.
L26: Halew . . . 6H 111
Hazelwood M. WA4: Grap . . . 7J 119
Hazlehurst Rd. L4: Walt . . . 7D 68
WA6: Frod . . . 6E 166
Hazleton Rd. L14: K Ash . . . 4A 90
Headbolt La. L33: K'by . . . 1C 56
PR8: B'dale . . . 3G 15
(not continuous)
Headbourne Cl. L25: Gate . . . 1D 110
Headen Av. WN5: Wigan . . . 6K 39
Headingley Cl. L36: Roby . . . 7G 91
WA9: St. H . . . 1E 94
Headingly Av. WN8: Skel . . . 1C 36
Headington Rd. CH49: Upton . . . 3B 104
Headland Cl. CH48: W Kir . . . 1D 122
WA3: Low . . . 1E 78
Headley Cl. WA10: St. H . . . 3B 74
Head St. L8: Liv . . . 2A 108
Heald St. L19: Gars . . . 3A 130
WA12: New W . . . 3D 76
Healy Cl. L27: N'ley . . . 4A 112
Heanor Dr. PR8: South . . . 5B 12
Heap Ct. PR9: South . . . 7A 8
Hearne Rd. WA10: St. H . . . 2K 73
Hearts Health Club
Liverpool . . . 7D 40
Wallasey . . . 3A 86
Heartwood Cl. L9: Walt . . . 6C 54
Heath, The WA7: West . . . 3C 152
Heath Av. CH65: Whit . . . 3J 169
Heathbank Av. CH44: Wall . . . 4A 86
CH61: Irby . . . 2A 124
Heathbank Rd. CH42: Tran . . . 5D 106
Heath Cl. CH48: W Kir . . . 1D 122
L25: Wltn . . . 3D 110
L34: Ecc P . . . 7F 73
Heathcote Cl. L7: Liv . . . 7D 88
Heathcote Gdns. CH63: Beb . . . 4F 127
Heathcote Rd. L4: Walt . . . 4B 68
Heath Ct. CH66: Lit Sut . . . 5D 160
Heath Dale CH63: Beb . . . 6F 127
Heath Dr. CH49: Upton . . . 3E 104
CH60: Hes . . . 1D 142
WA7: West . . . 3C 152
Heather Bank CH63: High B . . . 3D 126
Heather Brae L34: Prsct . . . 2A 92
WA12: New W . . . 2E 76
Heather Brow CH43: C'ton . . . 1K 105
Heather Cl. CH66: Gt Sut . . . 1G 169
L4: Walt . . . 6B 68
L33: K'by . . . 1C 56
L37: Form . . . 5B 20
PR8: Ains . . . 7D 14
WA3: Bchwd . . . 2K 99
WA7: Beech . . . 5G 153
Heather Ct. L4: Walt . . . 6B 68
Heatherdale Cl. CH42: O'ton . . . 5B 106
Heatherdale Rd. L18: Moss H . . . 4J 109
Heather Dene CH62: Brom . . . 6K 127
Heatherdene Rd.
CH48: W Kir . . . 5D 102
Heatherfield Ct. CH42: Tran . . . 4C 106
Heathergreen Ct. L4: Walt . . . 5D 68
Heather Gro. WN4: Ash M . . . 1J 63
Heatherland CH49: W'chu . . . 4F 105
Heatherlea Cl. WN8: Uph . . . 4E 38
Heatherleigh CH48: Caldy . . . 3G 123
WA9: St. H . . . 1J 93
Heatherleigh Cl. L9: Walt . . . 6C 54
Heather Rd. CH60: Hes . . . 1E 142
CH63: High B . . . 5D 126
Heathers Cft. L30: N'ton . . . 2A 54
Heather Way L23: Thorn . . . 6J 41
Heatherways L37: Form . . . 5A 20
Heathey La. L39: Hals . . . 3C 16
PR8: Hals, South . . . 1C 16
Heathfield CH62: Brom . . . 7K 127
Heathfield Av. WA9: St. H . . . 6A 74
Heathfield Cl. L21: Lith . . . 7J 53
L37: Form . . . 4A 20
Heathfield Dr. L33: K'by . . . 1C 56
Heathfield Ho. CH61: Thing . . . 3E 124
Heathfield Pk. WA4: Grap . . . 6G 119
WA8: Wid . . . 5K 113
Heathfield Rd. CH43: O'ton . . . 4C 106
CH63: Beb . . . 4F 127
CH65: Ell P . . . 6K 161
L15: W'tree . . . 2J 109
L22: Water . . . 3C 52
L31: Mag . . . 5H 43
PR8: Ains . . . 3E 14
Heathfield St. L1: Liv . . . 6A 88 (7H 5)
Heathgate WN8: Skel . . . 1J 37
Heathgate Av. L24: Speke . . . 7K 131
Heath Gro. CH66: Lit Sut . . . 4D 160
Heath Hey L25: Wltn . . . 3D 110
Heathland WN8: Uph . . . 4D 38
Heathland Rd. WA9: Clock F . . . 3E 94
Heathlands, The
CH46: Leas . . . 4C 84
Heathlands Rd. CH66: Lit Sut . . . 5D 160
Heath La. CH2: Lit Stan . . . 5B 170
CH2: Stoak . . . 5D 170
CH64: Chil T, Lit Sut, Will . . . 2J 159
CH66: Chil T . . . 4K 159
WA3: Croft . . . 4G 79
WA3: Low . . . 1D 78
WA16: H Legh . . . 5F 141
Heathmoor Rd. CH46: More . . . 6B 84
Heath Pk. Gro. WA7: Run . . . 2B 152
Heath Rd. CH63: Beb, High B . . . 4E 126
L19: Aller . . . 1A 130
L36: Huy . . . 2F 91
WA5: Penk . . . 3D 116
WA7: Run, West . . . 3B 152
WA8: Wid . . . 6K 113
WN4: Ash M . . . 3F 63
Heath Rd. Cres. WA7: Run . . . 2D 152
Heath Rd. Sth. WA7: West . . . 4B 152
Heathside CH60: Hes . . . 1B 142
Heath St. WA4: S Hth . . . 1C 138
WA9: St. H . . . 7K 73
WN4: Ash M . . . 3G 63
Heath Vw. L21: Ford . . . 2H 53
Heathview Cl. WA8: Hale B . . . 4G 133
Heathview Rd. WA8: Hale B . . . 4G 133
Heathwaite Cres. L11: N Grn. . . . 5J 69
Heathway CH60: Hes . . . 3F 143
Heathwood L12: W Der . . . 2K 89
Heathwood Gro. WA1: P'ton . . . 1H 119
Heathy La. L39: Bart . . . 2G 21
HEATLEY . . . 2K 121
Heatley Cl. CH43: Bid . . . 1G 105
WA13: Lymm . . . 4K 121
Heaton Cl. L24: Speke . . . 6K 131
WN8: Uph . . . 4C 38
Heaton Ct. WA3: Ris . . . 1B 100
Heatwaves Leisure Cen. . . . 6F 71
Hebburn Way L12: Crox . . . 3E 70
Hebden Av. WA3: Cul . . . 1D 80
Hebden Pde. L11: N Grn. . . . 3A 70
Hebden Rd. L11: N Grn. . . . 3K 69
Hebdon Cl. WN4: Ash M . . . 7E 50
Hedgebank Cl. L9: Ain . . . 5F 55
Hedgecote L32: K'by . . . 6C 56
Hedgecroft L23: Thorn . . . 6J 41
Hedgefield Rd. L25: Gate . . . 2F 111
Hedge Hey WA7: Cas . . . 1J 153
Hedgerows, The WA11: Hay . . . 6D 62
Hedges Cres. L13: Liv . . . 7G 69
Hedingham Cl. L26: Halew . . . 7A 112
Hedworth Gdns. WA9: St. H . . . 1K 93
Heights, The WA6: Hel . . . 7J 165
Helena Rd. WA9: St. H . . . 7H 75
Helena St. CH41: Birk . . . 3E 106
L7: Liv . . . 6D 88 (7P 5)
L9: Walt . . . 3B 68
Helen Bank Dr. WA11: R'ford . . . 4F 47
Helen Ho. L8: Liv . . . 10K 5
Helen St. WA3: Golb . . . 3K 63
WN4: Ash M . . . 1E 62
Helford Cl. L35: Whis . . . 1G 93
Helford Rd. L11: Crox . . . 1B 70
Heliers Rd. L13: Liv . . . 5K 89
Hell Nook WA3: Golb . . . 4J 63
Helmdon Cl. L11: N Grn. . . . 5J 69
Helmingham Gro. CH41: Tran . . . 4E 106
Helmsdale WN8: Skel . . . 7J 27
Helmsdale La. WA5: Gt San . . . 2G 117
Helmsley Cl. WA5: Warr . . . 1J 117
Helmsley Rd. L26: Halew . . . 2K 131
HELSBY . . . 7J 165
Helsby Av. CH62: East . . . 7B 146
HELSBY MARSH . . . 6H 165
Helsby Pk. Homes WA6: Frod . . . 6A 166
Helsby Rd. L9: Ain . . . 6D 54
WA6: Alv . . . 3J 173
Helsby Sports & Social Club . . . 3G 173
Helsby Station (Rail) . . . 7H 165
Helsby St. L7: Liv . . . 6C 88 (7N 5)
WA1: Warr . . . 2D 118
WA9: St. H . . . 5F 75
Helsby Way WN3: Wins . . . 2A 50
Helston Av. L26: Halew . . . 7K 111
WA11: St. H . . . 6F 61
Helston Cl. PR9: Marsh . . . 2D 8
WA5: Penk . . . 3C 116
WA7: Brook . . . 5K 153
Helston Grn. L36: Huy . . . 4B 92
Helston Rd. L11: Crox . . . 1B 70
Helton Cl. CH43: Noct . . . 5J 105
Helvellyn Rd. WN5: Wigan . . . 5K 39
Hemans St. L20: Boot . . . 2G 67
Hemer Ter. L20: Boot . . . 1G 67
Hemingford Cl. CH66: Gt Sut . . . 1F 169
Hemingford St. CH41: Birk . . . 2D 106
Hemlegh Va. WA6: Hel . . . 2H 173
Hemlock Cl. L12: Crox . . . 3B 70
Hemmingsway L35: R'hill . . . 4G 93
Hempstead Cl. WA9: St. H . . . 7B 74
Hemsworth Av. CH66: Lit Sut . . . 6E 160
Henbury Gdns. WA4: App . . . 6E 138
Henbury Pl. WA7: Run . . . 4D 152
Henderson Cl. CH49: Upton . . . 2B 104
WA5: Gt San . . . 2B 116
Henderson Dr. WA11: R'ford . . . 4G 47
Henderson Rd. L36: Huy . . . 4A 92
WA8: Wid . . . 1B 134
Hendon Rd. L6: Liv . . . 3F 89
Hendon Wlk. CH49: Grea . . . 5A 104
Hengest Cl. L33: K'by . . . 6C 44
Henglers Cl. L6: Liv . . . 4B 88 (3M 5)
Henley Av. L21: Lith . . . 5G 53
Henley Cl. CH63: Spit . . . 7G 127
CH64: Nest . . . 5J 157
WA4: App . . . 3E 138
Henley Ct. WA7: Run . . . 7F 135
WA10: St. H . . . 5K 73
Henley Dr. PR9: South . . . 6B 8
Henley Ho. L19: Aig . . . 2H 129
Henley Rd. CH64: Nest . . . 5J 157
L18: Moss H . . . 3K 109
Henllan Gdns. WA9: St. H . . . 7H 75
Henlow Av. L32: K'by . . . 5D 56
Hennawood Cl. L6: Liv . . . 2D 88
Henrietta Gro. L34: Prsct . . . 2A 92
Henry Edward St. L3: Liv . . . 4K 87 (3F 4)
Henry Hickman Cl. L30: N'ton . . . 1B 54
Henry St. CH41: Birk . . . 2E 106
L1: Liv . . . 7K 87 (8F 4)
L13: Liv . . . 5G 89
WA1: Warr . . . 3A 118
WA8: Wid . . . 7E 114
WA10: St. H . . . 2B 74
WA13: Lymm . . . 5G 121
Henshall Av. WA4: Westy . . . 4F 119
Henthorne Rd. CH62: New F . . . 1H 127
Henthorne St. CH43: O'ton . . . 3C 106
Hepherd St. WA5: Warr . . . 4H 117
Hepworth Cl. WA3: Golb . . . 3K 63
Herald Av. L24: Speke . . . 3D 130
Herald Cl. L11: Crox . . . 3A 70
Heralds Cl. WA8: Wid . . . 1H 133
Heralds Grn. WA5: W'brk . . . 5E 96
Herbarth Cl. L9: Walt . . . 3B 68
Herberts La. CH60: Hes . . . 3D 142
Herbert St. WA5: B'wood . . . 1C 96
WA9: St. H . . . 7G 75
Herbert Taylor Cl. L6: Liv . . . 2E 88
Herculaneum Ct. L8: Liv . . . 5B 108
Herculaneum Rd. L8: Liv . . . 4A 108
Herdman Cl. L25: Gate . . . 3F 111
Hereford Av. CH49: Upton . . . 2D 104
CH66: Gt Sut . . . 4G 169
Hereford Cl. WA1: W'ston . . . 1K 119
WA10: St. H . . . 4B 74
WN4: Ash M . . . 3H 63
Hereford Dr. L30: N'ton . . . 4B 54
Hereford Gro. WN8: Uph . . . 5D 38
Hereford Rd. L15: W'tree . . . 2J 109
L21: Sea . . . 6E 52
PR9: South . . . 1B 12
Heriot St. L5: Kirk . . . 1K 87
Heritage Cen. . . . 2K 137
Hermes Cl. L30: Boot . . . 5A 54
Hermes Rd. L11: Crox . . . 7K 55
HERMITAGE GREEN . . . 6B 78
Hermitage Grn. La. WA2: Win . . . 5K 77
Hermitage Gro. L20: Boot . . . 6K 53
Herm Rd. L5: Liv . . . 2J 87
Heron Cl. WA7: Nort . . . 2B 154
Heron Ct. CH64: Park . . . 4G 157
L26: Halew . . . 7J 111
Herondale Rd. L18: Moss H . . . 4H 109
Heron Dr. WN3: Wins . . . 2C 50
Heron Gro. WA11: R'ford . . . 7H 47
Heronhall Rd. L9: Faz . . . 2H 69
Heronpark Way CH63: Spit . . . 7H 127
Heron Pl. WN5: Wigan . . . 3K 39
Heron Rd. CH47: Meols . . . 1H 103
CH48: W Kir . . . 2J 103
Herons Ct. L31: Lyd . . . 7D 32
Herons Way WA7: Nort . . . 5D 136

Hollies Rd.—Hyde's Brow

Hollies Rd. L26: Halew 2K 131
HOLLINFARE 4K 101
Hollingbourne Pl. L11: N Grn. 3J 69
Hollingbourne Rd. L11: N Grn. 3J 69
Hollinghurst Rd. L33: K'by 7D 44
Hollington Way WN3: Wins 2A 50
Hollingwood Cl. WN4: Ash M 2E 62
Hollingworth Cl. L9: Walt 3C 68
Hollin Hey Cl. WN5: Bil 2F 61
Hollinhey Cl. L30: N'ton 7C 42
Hollins Cl. L15: W'tree 7J 89
WN4: Gars 1B 62
Hollins Dr. WA2: Win 1A 98
HOLLINS GREEN 5J 101
Hollins La. WA2: Win 1J 97
Hollins Way WA8: Hale B 4H 133
Hollocombe Rd. L12: W Der 4K 69
Holloway WA7: Run 1B 152
Hollow Cft. L28: Stock V 5E 70
Hollow Dr. WA4: S Hth 7E 118
Holly Av. CH63: Beb 6F 127
WA12: New W 3H 77
Holly Bank WA6: Alv 2K 173
WA6: Frod 3E 166
WA13: Lymm 6F 121
Hollybank WA4: Moore 4E 136
Hollybank Cvn. Pk.
WA3: Rix 6J 101
Hollybank Ct. CH41: Birk 3D 106
WA8: Wid 7B 114
Holly Bank Gro. WA9: St. H 2E 74
Hollybank Rd. CH41: Birk 3D 106
L18: Moss H 3G 109
WA7: Halt 1H 153
Holly Bank St. WA9: St. H 2E 74
Hollybrook Rd. PR8: South 3G 11
Holly Bush La. WA3: Rix 7E 100
Holly Cl. L24: Hale 7D 132
L40: Westh 6J 25
WA10: Eccl 2H 73
WN8: Skel 2E 36
Holly Ct. L20: Boot 1H 67
WA6: Hel 6J 165
Holly Cres. WA11: R'ford 7G 47
Hollydale Rd. L18: Moss H 3J 109
Holly Farm Ct. WA8: Wid 4B 114
Holly Farm Rd. L19: Gars 3B 130
Hollyfield Rd. CH65: Ell P 6K 161
L9: Walt 1B 68
Holly Fold La. L39: Bic 1E 46
Holly Gro. CH42: Tran 4E 106
L21: Sea 7F 53
L36: Roby 5F 91
PR9: Banks 3J 9
WA1: P'ton 1G 119
Hollyhedge La.
WA4: H Walt 3H 137
Holly Hey L35: Whis 6D 92
Hollyhurst Cl. L8: Liv 3C 108
Holly La. L39: Augh 6K 23
L39: Bic 7D 36
Hollymead Cl. L25: Gate 4F 111
Holly Mt. L12: W Der 1J 89
Holly Pl. CH46: More 1D 104
Holly Rd. CH65: Ell P 6A 162
L7: Liv 5E 88
WA5: Penk 3C 116
WA11: Hay 1H 75
WA13: Lymm 3K 121
Hollyrood L34: Prsct 2A 92
Holly St. L20: Boot 2J 67
Holly Ter. WA5: Penk 3D 116
Hollytree Rd. L25: Wltn 5E 110
Hollywood Bowl 5H 89
Hollywood Rd. L17: Aig 5G 109
Holman Rd. L19: Gars 3B 130
Holm Cotts. CH43: O'ton 6K 105
Holmdale Av. PR9: Cros 3D 8
Holm Dr. CH2: Elt 1C 172
Holme Cl. L34: Ecc P 7G 73
Holmefield Av. L19: Aig 7J 109
Holmefield Rd. L19: Aig 1H 129
Holme Rd. WA10: St. H 4H 73
Holmes Ct. WA3: Bchwd 3J 99
Holmesfield Rd. WA1: Warr 3D 118
Holmes Ho. Av. WN3: Wins 1A 50
Holmes La. *L21: Lith 6G 53*
(off Seaforth Rd.)
Holmes St. L8: Liv 1E 108
Holme St. L5: Kirk 7H 67
Holmesway CH61: Pens 5D 124
Holmfield CH2: Elt 1C 172
CH43: O'ton 6K 105
Holmfield Av. WA7: Run 7E 134
Holmfield Dr. CH66: Gt Sut 1F 169
Holmfield Gro. L31: Mag 3E 42
L36: Huy 7K 91
Holmfield Pk. L37: Form 6J 19
Holm Hey Rd. CH43: Pren 6K 105
Holm Hill CH48: W Kir 7E 102
Holmlands Cres. CH43: O'ton 6J 105
Holmlands Dr. CH43: O'ton 6J 105
Holmlands Way CH43: O'ton 6K 105
Holm La. CH43: O'ton 6K 105
Holmleigh Rd. L25: Gate 2E 110
Holm Oak Way CH66: Gt Sut 4H 169
Holmrook Rd. L11: N Grn. 4H 69
Holmside Cl. CH46: More 7D 84
Holmside La. CH43: O'ton 6K 105
Holmstead, The
L18: Moss H 5H 109
Holm Vw. Cl. CH43: O'ton 5A 106
Holmville Rd. CH63: High B 3E 126
Holmway CH63: High B 4F 127
Holmwood Av. CH61: Thing 4G 125
Holmwood Cl. L37: Form 7H 19
WN4: Ash M 7E 50
Holmwood Dr. CH61: Thing 4G 125
CH65: Whit 1K 169
L37: Form 6H 19
Holmwood Gdns. L37: Form 6H 19
HOLT 3G 93
Holt Av. CH46: More 7C 84
WN5: Bil 1F 61
Holt Coppice L39: Augh 4J 33
Holt Cres. WN5: Bil 1F 61
HOLT GREEN 5K 33
Holt Hey CH64: Ness 6A 158
Holt Hill CH41: Birk 4E 106
Holt Hill Ter. CH42: Tran 3D 106
Holt La. L27: N'ley 2H 111
L35: R'hill 3G 93
WA7: Halt 2H 153
Holton Way WN3: Wins 3C 50
Holt Rd. CH41: Tran 4E 106
L7: Liv 5E 88
Holt St. WN5: Orr 6F 39
Holt Way L32: K'by 3B 56
Holy Cross Cl. L3: Liv 4K 87 (3F 4)
Holyhead Cl. WA5: Call 4H 97
Holyrood L23: Blun 1A 52
Holyrood Av. WA8: Wid 4C 114
Holywell Cl. CH64: Park 2F 157
WA9: St. H 1F 95
Holywell Dr. WA1: Warr 3C 118
Homechase Ho. PR8: B'dale 4F 11
Homecrofts CH64: Lit N 6J 157
Homedove Ho. L23: Blun 1C 52
Home Farm Cl. CH49: W'chu 6G 105
Home Farm Rd. CH49: W'chu 6F 105
L34: Know 4G 71
Homeport Ho. *PR9: South 7J 7*
(off Hoghton St.)
HOMER GREEN 3J 41
Homer Rd. L34: Know 3G 71
Homerton Rd. L6: Liv 4F 89
Homesands Ho. PR9: South 7K 7
Homestall Rd. L11: N Grn. 4J 69
Homestead Av. L30: N'ton 2D 54
WA11: Hay 6C 62
Homestead Cl. L36: Huy 4A 92
Homestead M. CH48: W Kir 5D 102
Homeway WA6: Hel 2H 173
Honeybourne Dr. L35: Whis 1G 93
Honey Hall Rd. L26: Halew 3J 131
Honeys Grn. Cl. L12: W Der 2B 90
Honey's Grn. La. L12: W Der 2B 90
Honeys Grn. Pct. L12: W Der 2B 90
Honey St. WA9: St. H 7J 73
Honeysuckle Cl.
CH66: Gt Sut 4H 169
L26: Halew 6H 111
WA8: Wid 4D 114
Honeysuckle Dr. L9: Walt 3D 68
Honister Av. WA2: Warr 5C 98
WA11: St. H 5E 60
Honister Cl. L27: N'ley 5A 112
Honister Gro. WA7: Beech 5G 153
Honister Rd. WN5: Wigan 5K 39
Honister Wlk. L27: N'ley 5A 112
Honiston Av. L35: R'hill 3H 93
Honiton Rd. L17: Aig 7G 109
Honiton Way WA5: Penk 4C 116
Hood La. WA5: Gt San 3G 117
Hood La. Nth. WA5: Gt San 2G 117
Hood Mnr. Cen. WA5: Gt San 2G 117
Hood Rd. WA8: Wid 7B 114
Hood St. CH44: Wall 4D 86
L20: Boot 1G 67
Hookstone Dr. CH66: Lit Sut 5E 160
Hoole La. PR9: Banks 1J 9
Hoole Rd. CH49: W'chu 5F 105
Hoolpool La. WA6: Elt 6F 165
Hoose Ct. CH47: Hoy 1E 102
HOOTON 2C 160
Hooton Grn. CH66: Hoot 1C 160
Hooton Hey CH66: Gt Sut 6F 161
Hooton La. CH66: Hoot 2D 160
Hooton Pk. Airfield
CH65: Hoot 1E 160
Hooton Pk. La. CH65: Hoot 1E 160
Hooton Rd. CH64: Will 3G 159
CH66: Hoot 3G 159
L9: Ain 6D 54
Hooton Station (Rail) 2K 159
Hooton Way CH66: Hoot 1B 160
Hooton Works Trad. Est.
CH66: Hoot 2A 160
Hope Cl. WA10: St. H 2A 74
Hope Cotts. *CH66: Chil T 3C 160*
(off New Rd.)
Hope Cft. CH66: Gt Sut 2H 169
Hope Farm Pct. CH66: Gt Sut 2H 169
Hope Farm Rd. CH66: Gt Sut 3G 169
Hopefield Rd. WA13: Lymm 4K 121
Hope Pk. L16: Child 3B 110
Hope Pl. L1: Liv 7A 88 (8J 5)
Hope Sq. PR9: South 1J 11
Hope St. CH41: Birk 1D 106
CH45: New B 6B 66
L1: Liv 1A 108 (9K 5)
L34: Prsct 1D 92
PR9: South 1J 11
WA12: New W 3F 77
WN3: Ince M 1J 51
WN4: Ash M 7H 51
Hope Ter. CH42: Tran 5D 106
Hope Way L8: Liv 7B 88 (9J 5)
Hopfield Rd. CH46: More 7D 84
Hopkins Cl. WA10: St. H 2K 73
Hopwood Cres.
WA11: R'ford 7G 47
Hopwood St. L5: Liv 2J 87
(not continuous)
WA1: Warr 2C 118
(not continuous)
Horace Black Gdns. CH65: Ell P 5A 162
Horace St. WA10: St. H 2K 73
Horatio St. CH41: Birk 2D 106
Horbury Gdns. CH66: Gt Sut 6E 160
Hornbeam Av. CH66: Gt Sut 3H 169
Hornbeam Cl. CH46: More 7K 83
WA7: Wind H 1A 154
WA11: Hay 7H 61
Hornbeam Cres. WN4: Ash M 2F 63
Hornbeam Rd. L9: Walt 3E 68
L26: Halew 2A 132
Hornby Av. CH62: Brom 1J 145
L20: Boot 1H 67
Hornby Blvd. L20: Boot 7H 53
L21: Lith 7H 53
Hornby Chase L31: Mag 5F 43
Hornby Cl. L9: Walt 2B 68
Hornby Ct. CH62: Brom 1J 145
Hornby Cres. WA9: Clock F 3F 95
Hornby Flats L21: Lith 7H 53
Hornby La. L18: Moss H 3B 110
WA2: Win 1A 98
Hornby Pk. L18: Moss H 3B 110
Hornby Pl. L9: Walt 1C 68
Hornby Rd. CH62: Brom 1J 145
L9: Walt 2B 68
L20: Boot 1H 67
(Knowsley Rd.)
L20: Boot 2J 67
(Stanley Rd.)
PR9: Marsh 2C 8
Hornby St. CH41: Birk 2F 107
L21: Sea 7G 53
L23: C'by 1E 52
Hornby Wlk. L5: Liv 3J 87 (1E 4)
Horne St. L6: Liv 3D 88 (1P 5)
Hornet Cl. L6: Liv 2C 88
Hornhouse La. L33: Know I 5F 57
Hornsey Gro. WN3: Wins 1B 50
Hornsey Rd. L4: Walt 7D 68
Hornspit La. L12: W Der 6J 69
Horridge Av. WA12: New W 1G 77
Horringford Rd. L19: Aig 1H 129
Horrocks Av. L19: Gars 3B 130
Horrocks Cl. L36: Huy 3H 91
Horrocks La. WA1: Warr 3B 118
Horrocks Rd. L36: Huy 4H 91
Horseman Pl. CH44: Wall 5E 86
Horsemarket St. WA1: Warr 3B 118
Horseshoe Cres. WA2: Warr 4E 98
Horseshoe Dr. L10: Faz 6K 55
Horsey Mere Gdns. WA9: St. H 1A 94
Horsfall Gro. L8: Liv 4A 108
Horsfall St. L8: Liv 4A 108
Horstone Cres. CH66: Gt Sut 2H 169
Horstone Gdns. CH66: Gt Sut 2J 169
Horstone Rd. CH66: Gt Sut 2H 169
Horton Cl. L33: K'by 6C 44
Horwood Av. L35: R'hill 3H 93
Horwood Cl. L12: W Der 4A 70
Hoscar Ct. WA8: Wid 2K 133
Hoscote Pk. CH48: W Kir 6C 102
Hose Side Rd. CH45: Wall 7A 66
Hospital Rd. CH62: Port S 3H 127
Hospital St. WA10: St. H 2C 74
Hospital Way WA7: Pal F 3H 153
Hosta Cl. L33: K'by 7B 44
Hostock Cl. L35: Whis 5D 92
Hotel St. WA12: New W 3F 77
Hotham St. L3: Liv 5A 88 (5H 5)
Hothfield Rd. CH44: Wall 4D 86
Hotspur St. L20: Kirk 5J 67
HOUGH GREEN 7G 113
Hough Grn. Rd. WA8: Wid 6G 113
Hough Green Station (Rail) 6H 113
Hough's La. WA4: H Walt 4A 138
Houghton Cl. WA8: Wid 6E 114
WA12: New W 3F 77
Houghton Cft. WA8: Cron 3J 113
HOUGHTON GREEN 3E 98
Houghton La. L1: Liv 6K 87 (6G 4)
Houghton Rd. CH49: W'chu 4F 105
L24: Hale 1E 150
Houghton's La. WA10: Eccl 6F 59
WN8: Skel 2J 37
(not continuous)
Houghtons Rd. WN8: Skel 7G 27
Houghton St. L1: Liv 6K 87 (6G 4)
L34: Prsct 1D 92
L35: R'hill 4J 93
WA2: Warr 2B 118
WA8: Wid 6F 115
WA12: New W 3F 77
Houghton Way L1: Liv 6G 4
Houghwood Grange
WN4: Ash M 2D 62
Hougoumont Av. L22: Water 4E 52
Hougoumont Gro. L22: Water 4E 52
Houlding St. L4: Walt 1C 88
Houlgrave Rd. L5: Liv 2J 87
Houlston Rd. L32: K'by 3K 55
Houlston Wlk. L32: K'by 3K 55
Houlton St. L7: Liv 5D 88
Hourd Way CH66: Gt Sut 4G 169
House La. WA8: Wid 2B 134
Houston Gdns. WA5: Gt San 7E 96
Hove, The WA7: Murd 4B 154
(not continuous)
Hoveton Gdns. WA9: St. H 1K 93
Howard Av. CH62: Brom 2K 145
WA13: Lymm 4J 121
Howard Cl. L21: Ford 3J 53
L31: Mag 3H 43
Howard Ct. CH64: Nest 2K 157
PR9: South 6K 7
WA7: Mnr P 5A 136
Howard Dr. L19: Gras 2J 129
Howard Florey Av. L30: N'ton 1B 54
Howard Rd. WA3: Cul 4C 80
Howard's La. WA10: Eccl 2E 72
WN5: Orr 4H 39
Howards Rd. CH61: Thing 3F 125
Howard St. WA10: St. H 6J 73
WN5: Wigan 6K 39
Howards Way CH64: Lit N 5A 158
Howarth Ct. WA7: Run 7D 134
Howbeck Cl. CH43: C'ton 2K 105
Howbeck Cl. CH43: O'ton 3K 105
Howbeck Dr. CH43: C'ton 2K 105
Howbeck Rd. CH43: O'ton 3K 105
Howden Dr. L36: Huy 4E 90
WN3: Wigan 1E 50
Howell Dr. CH49: Grea 6B 104
Howell Rd. CH62: New F 2G 127
Howells Av. CH66: Gt Sut 1E 168
Howells Cl. L31: Mag 2F 43
Howe St. L20: Boot 5H 67
Howey La. WA6: Frod 4C 166
Howey Ri. WA6: Frod 4C 166
Howgill Cl. CH66: Lit Sut 5B 160
HOWLEY 3C 118
Howley La. WA1: Warr 3D 118
Howley Quay WA1: Warr 3D 118
Howley Quay Ind. Est.
WA1: Warr 3D 118
Howson Rd. WA2: Warr 5C 98
Howson St. CH42: R Ferr 6F 107
Hoyer Ind. Est. CH65: Ell P 7D 162
HOYLAKE 1D 102
Hoylake Cl. WA7: Murd 3A 154
(not continuous)
Hoylake Gro. WA9: Clock F 3E 94
Hoylake Rd. CH41: Birk 5H 85
CH46: More 1K 103
Hoylake Station (Rail) 2D 102
Hoyle Rd. CH47: Hoy 7D 82
Hoyle St. WA5: Warr 1K 117
Huddleston Cl. CH49: W'chu 5G 105
Hudleston Rd. L15: W'tree 6K 89
Hudson Cl. WA5: Old H 7H 97
Hudson Rd. CH46: Leas 3E 84
L31: Mag 5F 43
Hudson St. WA9: St. H 3E 74
Hudswell Cl. L30: N'ton 4D 54
Hughenden Rd. L13: Liv 2H 89
Hughes Av. L35: Prsct 3D 92
WA2: Warr 5D 98
Hughes Cl. L7: Liv 6E 88
Hughes Dr. L20: Boot 7A 54
Hughes La. CH43: O'ton 5B 106
Hughes Pl. WA2: Warr 5D 98
Hughes St. L6: Liv 3C 88 (1N 5)
(not continuous)
L19: Gars 4A 130
WA4: Warr 5C 118
WA9: St. H 6F 75
Hughestead Gro. L19: Gars 3K 129
Hughson St. L8: Liv 3A 108
HULME 4B 98
Hulmes Bri. Bus. Cen. L39: Hals 7E 16
Hulme St. PR8: South 1G 11
Hulmewood CH63: Beb 2G 127
Hulton Av. L35: Whis 3F 93
Humber Cl. L4: Kirk 6A 68
WA8: Wid 5H 115
Humber Cres. WA9: Sut L 1E 94
Humber Rd. CH66: Gt Sut 2H 169
WA2: Warr 5E 98
Humber St. CH41: Birk 6K 85
Hume Ct. CH47: Meols 7E 82
Hume St. WA1: Warr 2D 118
Humphrey's Cl. WA7: Murd 3B 154
Humphreys Hey L23: Thorn 7H 41
Humphrey St. L20: Boot 7K 53
Huncote Av. WA11: St. H 7F 61
Hunslet Rd. L9: Ain 7D 54
Hunstanton Cl. CH49: Upton 1E 104
Hunt Cl. WA5: Gt San 7F 97
Hunter Av. WA2: Warr 5B 98
Hunter Ct. L34: Prsct 1E 92
Hunters Chase WN5: Bil 3G 49
Hunters Ct. WA6: Hel 7K 165
WA7: Pal F 4G 153
Hunters La. L15: W'tree 1J 109
Hunter St. L3: Liv 5K 87 (4G 4)
WA9: St. H 4E 74
Hunters Way CH64: Park 3G 157
Huntingdon Cl. CH46: More 7K 83
Huntingdon Gro. L31: Lyd 7E 32
Huntley Av. WA9: St. H 7E 74
Huntley Gro. WA9: St. H 7E 74
Huntley St. WA5: Gt San 4G 117
Huntly Rd. L6: Liv 4E 88
Hunt Rd. L31: Mag 2F 43
WA11: Hay 7C 62
Hunts Cotts. PR9: Chu 6C 8
HUNT'S CROSS 2F 131
Hunts Cross Av. L25: Wltn 5F 111
(not continuous)
Hunts Cross Shop. Mall
L24: Hunts X 3E 130
Hunt's Cross Station (Rail) 2G 131
Hunts Fld. Cl. WA13: Lymm 6F 121
Hunts La. WA4: S Hth 6F 119
Huntsman Cl. L25: Hunts X 7H 111
Huntsman Wood L12: W Der 6C 70
Hurford Av. CH65: Gt Sut 7H 161
Hurley Cl. WA5: Gt San 3G 117
Hurlingham Rd. L4: Walt 4E 68
HURLSTON 7K 17
Hurlston Av. WN8: Skel 3J 37
Hurlston Dr. L39: Orm 3C 24
HURLSTON GREEN 5K 17
Hurlston Hall Country Cvn. Pk.
L40: Scar 1A 24
Hurlston La. L40: Scar 1K 23
Hurrell Rd. CH41: Birk 6H 85
Hursley Rd. L9: Faz 2G 69
Hurst Bank CH42: R Ferr 1F 127
Hurst Gdns. L13: Liv 5J 89
Hurstlyn Rd. L18: Aller 7A 110
Hurst Pk. Cl. L36: Huy 3A 92
Hurst Pk. Dr. L36: Huy 3A 92
Hurst Rd. L31: Mag 5G 43
Hurst's La. L39: Bic 2E 44
Hurst St. L1: Liv 7J 87 (9F 4)
L13: Liv 5J 89
WA8: Wid 5C 134
Huskisson St. L8: Liv 1B 108 (10K 5)
Huskisson Way
WA12: New W 2F 77
Hutchinson St. L6: Liv 4C 88 (3N 5)
WA8: Wid 3B 134
Hutchinson Wlk. L6: Liv 4C 88 (3N 5)
Hutfield Rd. L24: Speke 5A 132
Hutton Cl. WA3: Cul 1A 80
Hutton Ct. WN8: Skel 2D 36
Hutton Rd. WN8: Skel 2D 36
Hutton Way L39: Orm 5C 24
Huxley Cl. CH46: More 7K 83
Huxley Ct. CH66: Ell P 3H 161
Huxley St. L13: Liv 7F 69
HUYTON 5J 91
Huyton Av. WA10: St. H 7A 60
Huyton Brook L36: Huy 7K 91
Huyton Bus. Pk. L36: Huy 6A 92
Huyton Chu. Rd. L36: Huy 5J 91
Huyton Hall Cres.
L36: Huy 5J 91
Huyton Hey Rd. L36: Huy 5J 91
Huyton Ho. Cl. L36: Huy 3F 91
Huyton Ho. Rd. L36: Huy 3F 91
Huyton La. L34: Prsct 4J 91
L36: Huy 4J 91
Huyton Leisure Cen. 6H 91
Huyton Station (Rail) 5J 91
HUYTON-WITH-ROBY 4G 91
Hyacinth Av. L33: K'by 7B 44
Hyacinth Cl. WA11: Hay 7D 62
Hyacinth Gro. CH46: More 5E 84
Hyde Cl. CH65: Gt Sut 7H 161
WA7: Beech 4F 153
Hyde Rd. L22: Water 4D 52
Hyde's Brow WA11: R'ford 4G 47

Kelsall Cl.—Kirkham Av.

Kelsall Cl. WA3: Bchwd 4J **99**
WA8: Wid 6K **113**
Kelsey Cl. WA10: St. H 2K **73**
Kelso Cl. L33: K'by 6B **44**
Kelso Rd. L6: Liv 4E **88**
Kelton Gro. L17: Aig 6G **109**
Kelvin Cl. WA3: Ris 1K **99**
WN4: Gars 1B **62**
Kelvin Ct. CH44: Wall 5E **86**
Kelvin Gro. L8: Liv 2C **108**
WN3: Wigan 2C **50**
(not continuous)
Kelvin Pk. CH41: Birk 6D **86**
Kelvin Rd. CH41: Tran 4E **106**
CH44: Wall 6E **86**
Kelvinside CH44: Wall 6D **86**
L23: C'by 3F **53**
Kelvin St. WA3: Ris 1A **100**
Kemberton Dr. WA8: Wid 3C **114**
Kemble St. L6: Liv 4D **88** (3P **5**)
L34: Prsct 1D **92**
Kemlyn Rd. L4: Walt 7C **68**
Kemmel Av. WA4: Warr 6C **118**
Kempsell Wlk. L26: Halew 2A **132**
Kempsell Way L26: Halew 2A **132**
Kempsey Gro. WA9: St. H 7A **74**
Kempson Ter. CH63: Beb 5F **127**
Kempston St. L3: Liv 5A **88** (4J **5**)
Kempton Cl. L36: Roby 6G **91**
WA7: Run 4E **152**
WA12: New W 1H **77**
Kempton Pk. Fold PR8: South 5B **12**
Kempton Pk. Rd. L10: Ain 2G **55**
Kempton Rd. CH62: New F 1H **127**
L15: W'tree 7F **89**
Kemsley Rd. L14: K Ash 4D **90**
Kenbury Cl. L33: K'by 1E **56**
Kenbury Rd. L33: K'by 1E **56**
Kendal Av. WA2: Warr 5C **98**
Kendal Cl. CH63: Beb 3F **127**
CH66: Gt Sut 2F **169**
WA11: R'ford 2F **47**
Kendal Dr. CH66: Gt Sut 2F **169**
L31: Mag 2F **43**
L35: R'hill 3G **93**
WA11: R'ford 2E **46**
WA11: St. H 5D **60**
Kendal Gro. WN4: Ash M 1F **63**
Kendal Pk. L12: W Der 1B **90**
Kendal Ri. WA7: Beech 5F **153**
Kendal Rd. CH44: Wall 5A **86**
L16: Child 1C **110**
WA8: Wid 7J **113**
Kendal St. CH41: Birk 2E **106**
Kendal Way PR8: Ains 6B **14**
Kendricks Fold L35: R'hill 4H **93**
Kendrick St. WA1: Warr 3A **118**
Kenford Dr. WN3: Wins 2C **50**
Kenilworth Av. WA7: Run 2D **152**
Kenilworth Cl. L25: Wltn 5C **110**
Kenilworth Ct. CH65: Ell P 1C **170**
(not continuous)
Kenilworth Dr. CH61: Pens 4D **124**
WA1: P'gate 7F **99**
Kenilworth Gdns. CH49: Upton 2C **104**
WA12: New W 4G **77**
Kenilworth Rd. CH44: Wall 4D **86**
CH64: Nest 5J **157**
L16: Child 1B **110**
L23: Blun 1C **52**
PR8: Ains 4B **14**
Kenilworth St. L20: Boot 3H **67**
Kenilworth Way L25: Wltn 5C **110**
Kenley Av. WA8: Cron 3K **113**
Kenmare Rd. L15: W'tree 2G **109**
Kenmay Wlk. L33: K'by 2E **56**
Kenmore Gro. WN4: Gars 1B **62**
Kenmore Rd. CH43: Pren 7J **105**
Kennelwood Av. L33: K'by 2D **56**
Kennessee Cl. L31: Mag 4G **43**
KENNESSE GREEN 4F **43**
Kenneth Cl. L30: N'ton 2A **54**
Kenneth Rd. WA8: Wid 1J **133**
Kennet Rd. CH63: High B 4D **126**
WA11: Hay 7A **62**
Kennford Rd. L11: Crox 1A **70**
Kennington Pk. WA8: Wid 5A **114**
KENSINGTON 5E **88**
Kensington L7: Liv 5C **88** (4M **5**)
Kensington Av. WA4: Grap 6J **119**
WA9: St. H 7E **74**
Kensington Cl. WA8: Wid 4F **115**
Kensington Ct. L37: Form 7A **20**
Kensington Dr. L34: Prsct 2A **92**
Kensington Gdns. CH46: More 7D **84**
Kensington Ind. Est. PR9: South 2J **11**
Kensington Rd. CH65: Ell P 6J **161**
L37: Form 2J **29**
PR9: South 1J **11**
Kensington St. L6: Liv 4C **88** (3N **5**)
Kent Av. L21: Lith 5J **53**
L37: Form 2A **30**
WN2: Platt B 2K **51**
Kent Cl. CH63: Brom 2H **145**
L20: Boot 2K **67**
Kent Gro. WA7: Run 1D **152**
Kentmere Av. WA11: St. H 5E **60**
Kentmere Dr. CH61: Pens 6D **124**
Kentmere Pl. WA2: Warr 4A **98**
Kent M. CH43: O'ton 4A **106**
Kenton Cl. L25: Gate 1F **111**
L37: Form 4K **19**
Kenton Rd. L26: Halew 2K **131**
Kent Pl. CH41: Birk 2D **106**
Kentridge Dr. CH66: Gt Sut 1F **169**
Kent Rd. CH44: Wall 4A **86**
L37: Form 2K **29**
PR8: B'dale 4G **11**
WA5: Gt San 4G **117**
WA9: St. H 6E **74**
Kents Bank L12: W Der 5A **70**
Kent St. CH43: O'ton 4A **106**
L1: Liv 7K **87** (9G **4**)
(not continuous)
WA4: Warr 4C **118**
WA8: Wid 7D **114**
Kent Way WA12: New W 5G **77**
Kentwell Gro. L12: W Der 7B **70**
Kenview Cl. WA8: Hale B 4G **133**
Kenway WA11: R'ford 6G **47**
Kenwick Cl. CH66: Gt Sut 1E **168**
Kenwood Cl. L27: N'ley 3K **111**
Kenworthy's Flats PR9: South 7H **7**
Kenwright Cres. WA9: St. H 6E **74**
Kenwyn Rd. CH45: Wall 2B **86**
KENYON 2F **79**
Kenyon Av. WA5: Penk 3C **116**
Kenyon Cl. L33: K'by 6D **44**
Kenyon Ct. *L8: Liv* *2B **108***
(off Park Rd.)
Kenyon La. WA3: Croft 3F **79**
WA3: Low 1E **78**
Kenyon Rd. L15: W'tree 3J **109**
Kenyons La. L31: Lyd, Mag 7F **33**
L37: Form 7A **20**
Kenyons La. Nth. WA11: Hay 5D **62**
Kenyons La. Sth. WA11: Hay 6D **62**
Kenyon's Lodge L31: Lyd 1G **43**
Kenyon Ter. CH43: O'ton 3B **106**
Kepler St. L21: Sea 7G **53**
Keppel St. L20: Boot 5H **67**
Kerfoot Bus. Pk. WA2: Warr 7A **98**
(Kerfoot St.)
WA2: Warr 1A **118**
(Side Kerfoot St.)
Kerfoots La. WN8: Skel 3C **36**
Kerfoot St. WA2: Warr 1A **118**
Kerman Cl. L12: W Der 5K **69**
Kerr Cl. L33: K'by 6C **44**
Kerr Gro. WA9: St. H 3G **75**
Kerris Cl. L17: Aig 6D **108**
Kerry Cft. CH66: Gt Sut 3G **169**
Kerry La. PR9: Banks 3J **9**
Kerrysdale Cl. WA9: St. H 7F **75**
Kersey Rd. L32: K'by 5D **56**
Kersey Wlk. L32: K'by 5D **56**
Kershaw Av. L23: C'by 2F **53**
Kershaw St. WA8: Wid 7K **113**
WN5: Orr 5K **39**
Kershaw Way WA12: New W 1G **77**
Kersiake Way L38: High 5F **29**
Kerswell Cl. WA9: St. H 1F **95**
Kerton Row PR8: B'dale 4F **11**
Keston Wlk. L26: Halew 3K **131**
Kestral Dene L10: Faz 7J **55**
Kestrel Av. CH49: Upton 2B **104**
Kestrel Cl. CH49: Upton 2B **104**
WA11: St. H 7D **60**
Kestrel Ct. PR9: South 1K **11**
Kestrel Dr. WN4: Ash M 6G **51**
Kestrel Gro. L26: Halew 7H **111**
Kestrel La. WA3: Bchwd 3A **100**
Kestrel M. WN8: Skel 6J **27**
Kestrel Pk. WN8: Skel 6J **27**
Kestrel Rd. CH46: More 7A **84**
CH60: Hes 3G **143**
Kestrels Way WA7: Pal F 4H **153**
Keswick Av. CH63: East 6J **145**
WA2: Warr 5C **98**
Keswick Cl. L31: Mag 2G **43**
PR8: Ains 6C **14**
WA8: Wid 7J **113**
Keswick Cres. WA2: Warr 5C **98**
Keswick Dr. L21: Lith 5K **53**
WA6: Frod 3E **166**
Keswick Gdns. CH63: Brom 5J **145**
Keswick Pl. CH43: Bid 6H **85**
Keswick Rd. CH45: Wall 7K **65**
L18: Aller 6A **110**
WA10: St. H 1A **74**
Keswick Way L16: Child 7E **90**
WA11: R'ford 2F **47**
Kettering Rd. PR8: Ains 4B **14**
Kevelioc Cl. CH63: Spit 6F **127**
Kew Gdns. Cl. WA8: Wid 4F **115**
Kew Ho. Dr. PR8: South 6C **12**
Kew Retail Pk. PR8: South 4C **12**
Kew Rd. L37: Form 2H **29**
PR8: B'dale 5G **11**
Kew St. L5: Liv 2K **87**
Keybank Rd. L12: W Der 6J **69**
Keyes Cl. WA3: Bchwd 3B **100**
Keyes Gdns. WA3: Bchwd 3B **100**
Kiddman St. L9: Walt 3B **68**
Kidstone Cl. WA9: St. H 7F **75**
Kielder Cl. WN4: Ash M 5D **50**
Kilbuck La. WA11: Hay 5D **62**
Kilburn Av. CH62: East 4A **146**
WN4: Ash M 1H **63**
Kilburn Gro. WA9: St. H 7A **74**
WN3: Wins 1B **50**
Kilburn Rd. WN5: Orr 6E **38**
Kilburn St. L21: Lith 7H **53**
Kildale Cl. L31: Mag 2E **42**
Kildare Cl. L24: Hale 7D **132**
Kildonan Rd. L17: Aig 6F **109**
WA4: Grap 6G **119**
Kilford Cl. WA5: Call 5J **97**
Kilgraston Gdns. L17: Aig 7G **109**
Killarney Gro. CH44: Wall 4A **86**
Killarney Rd. L13: Liv 4J **89**
Killester Rd. L25: Gate 4F **111**
Killington Cl. WN3: Wigan 2F **51**
Killington Way L4: Kirk 6A **68**
Killingworth La. WA3: Bchwd 2C **100**
Kilmalcolm Cl. CH43: O'ton 4K **105**
Kilmore Cl. L9: Ain 5E **54**
Kilmory Av. L25: Wltn 6G **111**
Kiln Cl. WA10: Eccl 1J **73**
Kilncroft WA7: Brook 5K **153**
(not continuous)
Kiln Hey L12: W Der 2K **89**
Kiln La. WA10: Eccl, Windle 1H **73**
WN8: Skel 1E **36**
Kiln Rd. CH49: W'chu 5E **104**
Kilnyard Rd. L23: C'by 1D **52**
Kilrea Cl. L11: N Grn. 6H **69**
Kilrea Lodge L11: N Grn. 6H **69**
Kilrea Rd. L11: N Grn. 6G **69**
Kilsail Rd. L32: K'by 6E **56**
Kilsby Dr. WA8: Wid 6G **115**
Kilshaw Rd. WA5: B'wood 1D **96**
Kilshaw St. L6: Liv 3C **88** (1N **5**)
(not continuous)
Kilsyth Cl. WA2: Fearn 3F **99**
Kimberley Av. L23: C'by 2D **52**
WA9: St. H 7A **74**
Kimberley Cl. L8: Liv 1C **108** (10M **5**)
Kimberley Dr. L23: C'by 1D **52**
WA4: S Hth 7C **118**
Kimberley Pl. WN4: Ash M 2G **63**
Kimberley Rd. CH45: Wall 1B **86**
Kimberley St. WA5: Warr 3J **117**
Kindale Rd. CH43: Pren 7J **105**
Kinder Gro. WN4: Ash M 6D **50**
Kinder St. L6: Liv 4B **88** (3L **5**)
Kinderton Cl. WA16: H Legh 5K **141**
King Arthurs Wlk. WA7: Cas 2J **153**
King Av. L20: Boot 7A **54**
King Edward Cl. L35: R'hill 3H **93**
King Edward Dr. CH62: Port S 3H **127**
King Edward Ind. Est. L3: Liv 4C **4**
King Edward Pde. L3: Liv 5H **87** (4C **4**)
King Edward Rd. L35: R'hill 3H **93**
WA10: St. H 7K **59**
King Edward St. L3: Liv 5H **87** (4C **4**)
WA1: Warr 1E **118**
Kingfield Rd. L9: Walt 1B **68**
Kingfisher Bus. Pk. L20: Boot 6J **53**
Kingfisher Cl. L27: N'ley 3K **111**
L33: K'by 5C **44**
WA3: Bchwd 3B **100**
WA7: Beech 5H **153**
Kingfisher Ct. PR9: South 7K **7**
WN4: Ash M 6F **51**
Kingfisher Ct. Ind. Est.
WN4: Ash M 6F **51**
Kingfisher Dr. WA11: St. H 7D **60**
Kingfisher Gro. L12: W Der 5D **70**
Kingfisher Ho. L13: Liv 6J **89**
Kingfisher Pk. WN8: Skel 6J **27**
Kingfisher Way CH49: Upton 2B **104**
King George Cl. WN4: Ash M 2F **63**
King George Cres. WA1: Warr 1E **118**
King George Dr. CH44: Wall 1C **86**
King George Rd. WA11: Hay 6E **62**
King George's Dr. CH62: Port S 3H **127**
King George V Sports Complex 3K **91**
King George's Way CH43: Bid 1J **105**
Kingham Cl. L25: Wltn 6G **111**
WA8: Wid 7F **115**
Kingham M. L25: Wltn 6G **111**
King James Ct. WA7: Pal F 4G **153**
Kinglake Rd. CH44: Wall 2D **86**
Kinglake St. L7: Liv 6C **88** (6P **5**)
Kinglass Rd. CH63: Spit 6H **127**
King's Av. CH47: Meols 7F **83**
Kingsbrook Way CH63: High B 1D **126**
King's Brow CH63: High B 3D **126**
Kingsbury CH48: W Kir 6F **103**
Kingsbury Cl. PR8: Ains 5B **14**
WA4: App 6D **138**
Kingsbury Ct. WN8: Skel 6J **27**
Kingsbury Rd. WA8: Wid 4F **115**
King's Bus. Pk. L34: Prsct 2A **92**
Kings Cl. CH63: High B 2D **126**
L17: Aig 5E **108**
L37: Form 1J **29**
Kings Ct. CH47: Hoy 1C **102**
CH63: High B 3D **126**
L21: Sea 6F **53**
WA7: Mnr P 5B **136**
Kingscourt Rd. L12: W Der 2A **90**
Kingsdale Av. CH42: Tran 6D **106**
L35: R'hill 4K **93**
Kingsdale Rd. L18: Moss H 3J **109**
WA5: Gt San 7D **96**
Kings Dock St. L1: Liv 1K **107** (10F **4**)
Kingsdown Rd. L11: N Grn. 5J **69**
Kingsdown St. CH41: Tran 4E **106**
Kings Dr. L25: Gate 4G **111**
L25: Wltn 6F **111**
WA6: Hel 1H **173**
CH48: Caldy 2E **122**
CH61: Pens 4D **124**
King's Dr. Nth. CH48: W Kir 7G **103**
Kingsfield Rd. L31: Mag 5E **42**
King's Gap, The CH47: Hoy 1C **102**
Kingshead Cl. WA7: Cas 7J **135**
Kingsheath Av. L14: K Ash 3C **90**
Kings Hey Dr. PR9: Chu 6B **8**
Kingsland Cres. L11: N Grn. 3G **69**
Kingsland Grange
WA1: W'ston 6J **99**
Kingsland Rd. CH42: Tran 4C **106**
L11: N Grn. 3F **69**
King's La. CH63: High B 2E **126**
Kingsley Av. CH62: East 7A **146**
WN3: Wigan 1D **50**
Kingsley Cl. CH61: Pens 6E **124**
L31: Lyd 6E **32**
Kingsley Cres. WA7: Run 1C **152**
Kingsley Dr. WA4: App 2C **138**
Kingsley Grn. WA6: Frod 6G **167**
Kingsley Rd. CH44: Wall 4B **86**
CH65: Ell P 6A **162**
L8: Liv 1C **108** (10P **5**)
WA6: Frod 5F **167**
WA7: Run 1C **152**
WA10: St. H 7K **59**
Kingsley St. CH41: Birk 7A **86**
Kingsmead Ct. WA3: Croft 6K **79**
Kingsmead Dr. L25: Hunts X 2F **131**
Kingsmead Gro. CH43: O'ton 3K **105**
Kings Mdw. PR8: Ains 6D **14**
WA7: Nort 2A **154**
Kingsmead Rd. CH43: O'ton 3K **105**
CH46: More 5D **84**
Kingsmead Rd. Nth.
CH43: O'ton 3K **105**
Kingsmead Rd. Sth.
CH43: O'ton 3K **105**
Kings M. CH66: Lit Sut 4E **160**
WA4: S Hth 1C **138**
KINGS MOSS 5B **48**
Kings Moss La. WA11: Kings M 5A **48**
Kings Mt. CH43: O'ton 4B **106**
Kingsnorth L35: Whis 5F **93**
Kings Pde. L3: Liv 7J **87** (9D **4**)
CH45: Wall, New B 6H **65**
Kings Pk. L21: Sea 6F **53**
Kings Rd. CH66: Lit Sut 4E **160**
L23: C'by 1D **52**
L37: Form 1J **29**
WA2: Fearn 5G **99**
WA3: Golb 6K **63**
WA10: St. H 4J **73**
WN4: Ash M 7E **50**
CH63: High B 1D **126**
L20: Boot 4J **67**
Kings Sq. CH41: Birk 2E **106**
Kings Ter. L20: Boot 5J **67**
Kingsthorne Pk. L25: Hunts X 3G **131**
Kingsthorne Rd. L25: Hunts X 3G **131**
Kingston Av. WA5: Gt San 2C **116**
Kingston Cl. CH46: More 7C **84**
L12: W Der 2C **90**
WA7: Run 7G **135**
WN3: Wigan 1F **51**
Kingston Cres. PR9: Cros 2E **8**
King St. CH42: R Ferr 7G **107**
CH44: Wall 2D **86**
CH65: Ell P 5A **162**
L19: Gars 5A **130**
L22: Water 4D **52**
PR8: South 2G **11**
WA7: Run 6C **134**
WA10: St. H 3B **74**
WA12: New W 3F **77**
Kingsville Rd. CH63: High B 4E **126**
Kings Wlk. CH42: R Ferr 7G **107**
CH48: W Kir 6E **102**
Kingsway CH44: Wall 4F **87** (2B **4**)
CH45: Wall 1A **86**
CH60: Hes 4G **143**
CH63: High B 2D **126**
L3: Liv 4J **87** (2D **4**)
L22: Water 3E **52**
L34: Prsct 2D **92**
L35: Prsct 2D **92**
L36: Huy, Roby 3H **91**
PR8: South 1G **11**
WA6: Frod 3D **166**
WA8: Wid 2C **134**
WA11: St. H 5C **60**
WA12: New W 4G **77**
Kingsway Ct. *L1: Liv* *1A **108***
(off Raffles St.)
L3: Liv 3K **87** (1F **4**)
Kingsway Ho. *WA4: Westy* *4F **119***
(off Kingsway Sth.)
WA8: Wid 2C **134**
Kingsway Leisure Cen. 1C **134**
Kingsway Nth. WA1: Warr 2E **118**
Kingsway Pde. L36: Huy 3G **91**
Kingsway Pk. L3: Liv 3K **87** (1G **4**)
Kingsway Sth. WA1: Warr 3E **118**
WA4: Westy 5F **119**
Kingsway Tunnel App.
CH44: Wall 3J **85**
Kingswell Cl. L7: Liv 7D **88** (8P **5**)
Kings Wharf CH41: Birk 6E **86**
KINGSWOOD 5F **97**
Kingswood Av. L9: Ain 6D **54**
L22: Water 3F **53**
Kingswood Blvd. CH63: High B 1E **126**
Kingswood Ct. L33: K'by 1D **56**
Kingswood Dr. L23: C'by 2D **52**
Kingswood Grn. WA5: W'brk 5F **97**
Kingswood Ho. PR8: B'dale 3F **11**
Kingswood Pk. PR8: B'dale 3F **11**
Kingswood Pk. M. PR8: B'dale 2F **11**
Kingswood Rd. CH44: Wall 2C **86**
WA5: W'brk 5E **96**
Kington Rd. CH48: W Kir 5C **102**
Kinlet Rd. WN3: Wigan 7K **39**
Kinley Gdns. L20: Boot 1A **68**
Kinloch Cl. L26: Halew 2K **131**
Kinloch Way L39: Orm 5B **24**
Kinloss Rd. CH49: Grea 5A **104**
Kinmel Cl. CH41: Birk 1D **106**
L4: Walt 6F **69**
Kinmel St. L8: Liv 3C **108**
WA9: St. H 6E **74**
Kinnaird Rd. CH45: Wall 1A **86**
Kinnaird St. L8: Liv 5C **108**
Kinnerley Rd. CH65: Whit 1J **169**
Kinnerton Cl. CH46: More 7K **83**
Kinnington Way CH1: Back 5H **169**
Kinniside Rd. WN3: Wigan 2E **50**
Kinnock Pk. WA5: B'wood 1C **96**
Kinross Av. WN4: Gars 1A **62**
Kinross Cl. WA2: Fearn 3F **99**
Kinross Rd. CH45: Wall 1H **85**
L10: Faz 6G **55**
L22: Water 5E **52**
Kinsale Dr. WA3: Bchwd 3J **99**
Kinsey Rd. CH65: Ell P 3B **170**
Kinsey's La. CH2: Ince 5K **163**
Kinsman Ho. L19: Gras 2H **129**
Kintbury St. WN2: Bam 5K **51**
Kintore Cl. CH63: East 6J **145**
Kintore Dr. WA5: Gt San 2B **116**
Kintore Rd. L19: Gras 2K **129**
Kintyre Cl. CH65: Ell P 3A **170**
Kipling Av. CH42: R Ferr 7F **107**
L36: Huy 6A **92**
WA2: Warr 6C **98**
WN3: Wigan 1E **50**
Kipling Cres. WA8: Wid 7B **114**
Kipling Gro. WA9: Sut M 4C **94**
Kipling St. L20: Boot 7G **53**
Kirby Cl. CH48: W Kir 7E **102**
Kirby Mt. CH48: W Kir 1E **122**
Kirby Pk. CH48: W Kir 7E **102**
Kirby Pk. Mans. CH48: W Kir 7D **102**
Kirby Rd. L20: Boot 7K **53**
Kirkacre Av. WA12: New W 6G **77**
Kirkbride Cl. L27: N'ley 4A **112**
Kirkbride Lawn L27: N'ley 4A **112**
Kirkbride Wlk. *L27: N'ley* *4A **112***
(off Kirkbride Clo.)
Kirkburn Cl. L8: Liv 4B **108**
KIRKBY 3C **56**
Kirkby Bank Rd. L33: Know I 3F **57**
KIRKBY PARK 2A **56**
Kirkby Rd. WA3: Cul 3B **80**
Kirkby Row L32: K'by 2A **56**
Kirkby Station (Rail) 2A **56**
Kirkcaldy Av. WA5: Gt San 2B **116**
Kirk Cotts. CH45: Wall 7B **66**
KIRKDALE 6A **68**
Kirkdale Gdns. WN8: Uph 4C **38**
Kirkdale Rd. L5: Kirk 1K **87**
Kirkdale Station (Rail) 5K **67**
Kirkdale Va. L4: Walt 7A **68**
Kirket Cl. CH63: Beb 5G **127**
Kirket La. CH63: Beb 5F **127**
Kirkfield Gro. CH42: R Ferr 7G **107**
Kirkham Av. WA3: Low 1E **78**

Laurelbanks—Lingdale Rd. Nth.

Laurelbanks CH60: Hes . . . 1C 142
Laurel Ct. L7: Liv . . . 4F 89
(off Laurel Rd.)
WA11: St. H . . . 6D 60
Laurel Dr. CH64: Will . . . 2H 159
CH65: Whit . . . 2K 169
WA10: Eccl . . . 2F 73
WN8: Skel . . . 1E 36
Laurel Farm Ct. CH2: Elt . . . 7B 164
Laurel Gro. L8: Liv . . . 2E 108
L22: Water . . . 3D 52
L36: Huy . . . 7J 91
PR8: South . . . 1A 12
WN4: Ash M . . . 1F 63
Laurelhurst Av. CH61: Pens . . . 5E 124
Laurel Rd. CH42: Tran . . . 4D 106
L7: Liv . . . 4F 89
L34: Prsct . . . 1E 92
WA10: St. H . . . 4K 73
WA11: Hay . . . 1H 75
Laurels, The CH46: Leas . . . 4C 84
Laurelwood Dr. CH66: Gt Sut . . . 4G 169
Laurence Deacon Ct.
CH41: Birk . . . 1C 106
Lauren Cl. L36: Huy . . . 5B 92
Lauriston Rd. L4: Walt . . . 5E 68
Laurus Cl. L27: N'ley . . . 3K 111
Lavan Cl. L6: Liv . . . 4C 88 (2M 5)
Lavan St. L6: Liv . . . 4C 88 (2N 5)
WA9: St. H . . . 7A 74
Lavender Cl. WA7: Run . . . 1E 152
Lavender Cres. L34: Prsct . . . 1E 92
Lavender Gdns. L23: Thorn . . . 6H 41
WA9: Bold . . . 7J 75
Lavender Wlk. WN4: Gars . . . 7B 50
Lavender Way L9: Walt . . . 2D 68
Lavrock Bank L8: Liv . . . 4A 108
Lawford Dr. CH60: Hes . . . 2G 143
Lawler Gro. L34: Prsct . . . 7E 72
Lawler St. L21: Lith . . . 7H 53
Lawn Av. WA1: P'gate . . . 7F 99
Lawnhurst Gro. L17: Aig . . . 1G 129
Lawns, The CH43: Bid . . . 1H 105
PR9: Chu . . . 5B 8
Lawns Av. CH63: Raby M . . . 4H 145
WN5: Orr . . . 6E 38
Lawnside Cl. CH42: R Ferr . . . 7F 107
Lawnswood Gro. CH2: Elt . . . 1B 172
Lawrence Cl. L19: Gras . . . 2J 129
Lawrence Ct. CH42: R Ferr . . . 1G 127
Lawrence Gro. L15: W'tree . . . 1G 109
Lawrence Rd. L15: W'tree . . . 1F 109
WA10: Windle . . . 7J 59
Lawrenson St. WA10: St. H . . . 3A 74
Lawson Cl. WA1: W'ston . . . 1A 120
Lawson St. PR9: South . . . 1C 12
Lawson Wlk. L12: Crox . . . 3B 70
Lawswood L37: Form . . . 5J 19
Lawton Av. L20: Boot . . . 1A 68
Lawton Cl. WA3: Cul . . . 3A 80
Lawton Rd. L22: Water . . . 3D 52
L35: R'hill . . . 5K 93
L36: Roby . . . 5G 91
Lawton St. L1: Liv . . . 6K 87 (7H 5)
Laxey Av. WA1: W'ston . . . 2K 119
Laxey St. L8: Liv . . . 2A 108
Laxton Cl. CH66: Gt Sut . . . 4H 169
Laxton Rd. L25: Hunts X . . . 2G 131
Layford Cl. L36: Huy . . . 1H 91
Layford Rd. L36: Huy . . . 2H 91
Layland Av. WA3: Cul . . . 2A 80
Layton Av. CH43: Pren . . . 6K 105
Layton Cl. L25: Wltn . . . 6G 111
WA3: Bchwd . . . 4A 100
Layton Rd. L25: Wltn . . . 6G 111
Lazenby Cres. WN4: Ash M . . . 2D 62
Leach Cft. L28: Stock V . . . 7E 70
Leach La. WA9: Sut L . . . 3F 95
Leach St. WA10: St. H . . . 2B 74
Leach Way CH61: Irby . . . 3A 124
Lea Cl. CH43: Noct . . . 4J 105
Lea Cres. L39: Orm . . . 3C 24
Leacroft WN4: Ash M . . . 6D 50
Leacroft Rd. WA3: Ris . . . 1B 100
Lea Cross Gro. WA8: Wid . . . 5J 113
Leadenhall Cl. L5: Liv . . . 1B 88
Leader St. WN5: Wigan . . . 5K 39
Leafield Cl. CH61: Irby . . . 3D 124
Leafield Rd. L25: Hunts X . . . 3F 131
Leagate L10: Faz . . . 5H 55
Leagate Cl. WN3: Wigan . . . 1C 50
LEA GREEN . . . 2B 94
Lea Green Bus. Pk. WA9: St. H . . . 3B 94
Lea Green Ind. Est. WA9: St. H . . . 4C 94
Lea Grn. Rd. WA9: St. H . . . 4B 94
Lea Green Station (Rail) . . . 2D 94
Leahurst University of Liverpool
Veterinary Field Station . . . 4D 158
Leamington Av. PR8: Ains . . . 4D 14
WA12: New W . . . 5G 77
Leamington Cl. CH64: Nest . . . 5J 157
WA5: Gt San . . . 7E 96
Leamington Gdns.
CH49: W'chu . . . 4F 105
Leamington Rd. L11: N Grn. . . . 4F 69
PR8: Ains . . . 4C 14
Leander Rd. CH45: Wall . . . 2A 86
Lea Rd. CH44: Wall . . . 2C 86
Leas, The CH45: Wall . . . 7J 65
CH61: Thing . . . 3F 125
Leas Cl. CH66: Gt Sut . . . 6E 160
Leaside WA7: Run . . . 1F 153
LEASOWE . . . 3F 85
Leasowe Av. CH45: Wall . . . 1J 85
Leasowe Gdns. CH46: Leas . . . 4C 84
Leasowe Recreation Cen. . . . 4E 84
Leasowe Rd. CH44: Wall . . . 3E 84
CH45: Wall . . . 3E 84
CH46: Leas . . . 4B 84
L9: Ain . . . 6D 54
Leasoweside CH46: Leas . . . 3F 85
Leasowe Station (Rail) . . . 5D 84
Leas Pk. CH47: Hoy . . . 4C 102
Leatham Cl. WA3: Bchwd . . . 4A 100
Leatherbarrows La.
L31: Mag, Mell . . . 5H 43
Leather La. L2: Liv . . . 5J 87 (5E 4)
Leather's La. L26: Halew . . . 3K 131
Leathwood L31: Mag . . . 3G 43
Leaway CH49: Grea . . . 4B 104
Leawood Gro. CH46: More . . . 7D 84
LEC Complex L15: W'tree . . . 7F 89
Leckwith Rd. L30: N'ton . . . 3D 54
Leda Gro. L17: Aig . . . 4E 108
(off Hadassah Gro.)
Ledburn WN8: Skel . . . 7H 27
Ledbury Cl. CH43: O'ton . . . 6J 105
L12: Crox . . . 2D 70
WA10: Eccl . . . 3H 73
Ledger Rd. WA11: Hay . . . 1J 75
Ledmore Gro. WN4: Gars . . . 2B 62
LEDSHAM . . . 3B 168
Ledsham Cl. CH43: Noct . . . 4J 105
WA3: Bchwd . . . 4J 99
Ledsham Ct. CH66: Lit Sut . . . 5D 160
Ledsham Hall La. CH66: Led . . . 6A 160
Ledsham La. CH66: Led . . . 7A 160
Ledsham Pk. Dr. CH66: Lit Sut . . . 5C 160
Ledsham Rd. CH66: Lit Sut . . . 6B 160
L32: K'by . . . 3A 56
Ledsham Village CH66: Led . . . 3B 168
Ledsham Wlk. L32: K'by . . . 3A 56
Ledson Gro. L39: Augh . . . 4K 33
Ledson Pk. L33: K'by . . . 6D 44
Ledsons Gro. L31: Mell . . . 2J 55
Ledston Cl. WA7: Wind H . . . 1B 154
Ledyard Cl. WA5: Old H . . . 1H 117
Leece St. L1: Liv . . . 7A 88 (8J 5)
Lee Cl. L35: R'hill . . . 6K 93
Lee Ct. WA2: Warr . . . 5C 98
Leecourt Cl. L12: W Der . . . 2B 90
Leeds St. L3: Liv . . . 4H 87 (3C 4)
Lee Hall Rd. L25: Gate . . . 3G 111
Lee Manor Sports Cen. . . . 3H 111
Leeming Cl. L19: Gars . . . 4A 130
Lee Pk. Av. L25: Gate . . . 3G 111
Lee Rd. CH47: Hoy . . . 1E 102
WA5: Gt San . . . 2F 117
Lees, The WA5: Gt San . . . 7E 96
(not continuous)
Lees Av. CH42: R Ferr . . . 6F 107
Leeside Av. L32: K'by . . . 5C 56
Leeside Cl. L32: K'by . . . 4D 56
Lees La. CH64: Lit N, Nest . . . 5A 158
CH65: Ell P . . . 7B 162
WN8: Dalt . . . 2J 27
Lees Rd. L33: Know I . . . 4F 57
Lee St. WA9: St. H . . . 6G 75
Leeswood L22: Water . . . 4E 52
WN8: Skel . . . 7H 27
Leeswood Rd. CH49: W'chu . . . 5E 104
Lee Va. Rd. L25: Gate . . . 4G 111
Leeward Dr. L24: Speke . . . 5E 130
Legh Rd. CH62: New F . . . 2H 127
WA11: Hay . . . 7J 61
Legh St. WA1: Warr . . . 3A 118
WA3: Golb . . . 5K 63
WA12: New W . . . 3D 76
WA13: Lymm . . . 5G 121
WN4: Ash M . . . 3F 63
Legion La. CH62: Brom . . . 1K 145
Legion Rd. WA10: St. H . . . 6K 73
Leicester Av. L22: Water . . . 2D 52
Leicester Rd. L20: Boot . . . 2K 67
Leicester St. PR9: South . . . 6H 7
WA5: Warr . . . 3J 117
(not continuous)
WA9: St. H . . . 6K 73
Leigh Av. WA8: Wid . . . 7B 114
Leigh Bri. Way L5: Liv . . . 2J 87
Leigh Grn. Cl. WA8: Wid . . . 1J 133
Leigh Pl. L1: Liv . . . 6K 87 (6G 4)
Leigh Rd. CH48: W Kir . . . 5D 102
Leighs Hey Cres. L32: K'by . . . 4D 56
Leigh St. L1: Liv . . . 6K 87 (6F 4)
(not continuous)
L7: Liv . . . 6E 88
Leighton Av. CH47: Meols . . . 7G 83
L31: Mag . . . 2F 43
Leighton Chase CH64: Nest . . . 2H 157
Leighton Ct. CH64: Nest . . . 3H 157
Leighton Pk. CH64: Nest . . . 3H 157
Leighton Rd. CH41: Tran . . . 4E 106
CH64: Nest . . . 7G 143
Leightons, The CH64: Nest . . . 3H 157
Leighton St. L4: Kirk . . . 5A 68
Leinster Gdns. WA7: Run . . . 6B 134
Leinster Rd. L13: Liv . . . 4K 89
Leinster St. WA7: Run . . . 6B 134
Leison St. L4: Kirk . . . 7K 67
(not continuous)
Leiston Cl. CH61: Irby . . . 2C 124
Lemon Cl. L7: Liv . . . 6E 88
Lemon Gro. L8: Liv . . . 2E 108
Lemon St. L5: Kirk . . . 1K 87
Lemon Tree Wlk. WA10: St. H . . . 5K 73
Lendel Cl. L37: Form . . . 7J 19
Lenfield Dr. WA11: Hay . . . 7H 61
Lenham Way L24: Speke . . . 5F 131
Lennox Av. CH45: New B . . . 7B 66
Lennox La. CH43: Bid . . . 6G 85
Lenthall St. L4: Walt . . . 4B 68
Lenton Av. L37: Form . . . 6H 19
Lenton Rd. L25: Gate . . . 3G 111
Lentworth Ct. L19: Aig . . . 2H 129
Leo Casino . . . 1K 107
Leo Cl. L14: K Ash . . . 3D 90
Leominster Rd. CH44: Wall . . . 3B 86
Leonard Cheshire Dr. L30: N'ton . . . 2B 54
Leonard Ho. CH41: Birk . . . 6F 87
Leonards Cl. L36: Huy . . . 1H 91
Leonard St. WA2: Warr . . . 1C 118
WA4: S Hth . . . 7C 118
WA7: West P . . . 3K 151
WA9: St. H . . . 7H 75
Leon Cl. WA5: Gt San . . . 1B 116
Leonora St. L8: Liv . . . 4C 108
Leopold Gro. WA9: Sut L . . . 2E 94
Leopold Rd. L7: Liv . . . 5D 88 (5P 5)
(not continuous)
L22: Water . . . 3C 52
Leopold St. CH44: Wall . . . 4E 86
WN5: Wigan . . . 6K 39
(not continuous)
Lesley Rd. PR8: South . . . 1A 12
Leslie Av. CH49: Grea . . . 5B 104
Leslie Rd. WA10: St. H . . . 6J 73
Lesseps Rd. L8: Liv . . . 1E 108
Lessingham Rd. WA8: Wid . . . 5B 114
Lester Cl. L4: Kirk . . . 7A 68
Lester Dr. CH61: Irby . . . 2A 124
WA10: Eccl . . . 1G 73
Lester Gro. L36: Huy . . . 3K 91
Lestock St. L8: Liv . . . 1A 108
Leta St. L4: Walt . . . 5B 68
(not continuous)
Letchworth St. L6: Liv . . . 2D 88
Lethbridge Cl. L5: Kirk . . . 1J 87
Lethbridge Rd. PR8: South . . . 3K 11
Letitia St. L8: Liv . . . 3B 108
Letterstone Cl. L6: Liv . . . 3B 88 (1L 5)
Letterstone Wlk. L6: Liv . . . 3B 88 (1L 5)
Levens Cl. PR9: Banks . . . 2J 9
WA5: Warr . . . 2K 117
Levens Hey CH46: More . . . 7B 84
Leven St. L4: Kirk . . . 6A 68
Levens Way WA8: Wid . . . 1J 133
Leven Wlk. CH66: Ell P . . . 3J 161
Lever Av. CH44: Wall . . . 5E 86
Lever C'way.
CH63: High B, Store . . . 6A 126
Leveret Rd. L24: Speke . . . 6A 132
Leverhulme Ct. CH63: Beb . . . 5G 127
Lever St. WA9: Clock F . . . 4F 95
Lever Ter. CH42: Tran . . . 5E 106
Leveson Rd. L13: Liv . . . 6K 89
Levisham Gdns. WA5: Warr . . . 1J 117
Lewis Av. WA5: Warr . . . 5K 97
Lewis Cl. CH65: Ell P . . . 4A 170
Lewis Cres. WA8: Wid . . . 2C 134
Lewis Gro. WA8: Wid . . . 7K 113
Lewisham Rd. CH62: Port S . . . 3J 127
L11: N Grn. . . . 4H 69
Lewis St. WA10: St. H . . . 2A 74
Lewis Wlk. L33: K'by . . . 6C 44
Lexden St. WA5: Warr . . . 2J 117
Lexham Rd. L14: K Ash . . . 4K 89
Lexington Way L33: K'by . . . 5C 44
Lexton Dr. PR9: Chu . . . 4D 8
Leybourne Av. PR8: Ains . . . 2F 15
Leybourne Cl. L25: Gate . . . 2E 110
Leybourne Grn. L25: Gate . . . 2E 110
Leybourne Gro. L25: Gate . . . 3E 110
Leybourne Rd. L25: Gate . . . 2E 110
Leyburn Cl. L32: K'by . . . 6C 56
(not continuous)
Leyburn Rd. CH45: Wall . . . 1K 85
Ley Cl. WA9: Clock F . . . 3E 94
Leyfield Cl. L12: W Der . . . 1B 90
Leyfield Ct. L12: W Der . . . 1B 90
Leyfield Rd. L12: W Der . . . 1A 90
Leyfield Wlk. L12: W Der . . . 1B 90
Leyland Cl. PR9: Banks . . . 2G 9
LEYLAND GREEN . . . 7K 49
Leyland Grn. Rd. WN4: Gars . . . 7A 50
Leyland Gro. WA11: Hay . . . 7K 61
Leyland Mans. PR9: South . . . 7K 7
Leyland Rd. PR9: South . . . 6J 7
WA11: R'ford . . . 6F 47
Leyland St. L34: Prsct . . . 1D 92
Leyland Way L39: Orm . . . 5D 24
Leyton Cl. WA7: Run . . . 4D 152
Liberton Ct. L5: Liv . . . 1B 88
Liberty St. L15: W'tree . . . 1G 109
Libra Cl. L14: K Ash . . . 2E 90
Library St. WA10: St. H . . . 3C 74
Librex Rd. L20: Boot . . . 7J 53
Libson Cl. WA2: Fearn . . . 4G 99
Lichfield Av. L22: Water . . . 2D 52
WA4: Grap . . . 2G 139
Lichfield Cl. L30: N'ton . . . 4C 54
Lichfield Dr. CH66: Gt Sut . . . 4G 169
Lichfield Gro. WN4: Ash M . . . 3G 63
Lichfield Rd. L15: W'tree . . . 2J 109
L26: Halew . . . 3J 131
Lichfield St. CH45: New B . . . 7C 66
Lickers La. L35: Whis . . . 5D 92
Liddell Av. L31: Mell . . . 1J 55
Liddell Ct. CH45: Wall . . . 2H 85
Liddell Rd. L12: W Der . . . 7H 69
Lidderdale Rd. L15: W'tree . . . 2G 109
Lidgate Cl. L33: K'by . . . 7D 44
WN3: Wins . . . 1B 50
Lifeboat Rd. L37: Form . . . 2E 28
Lifestyles Millennium . . . 5F 4
Liffey Ct. L3: Liv . . . 4K 5
Liffey St. L8: Liv . . . 1D 108 (10P 5)
Lifton Rd. L33: K'by . . . 3D 56
Lightbody St. L5: Liv . . . 2H 87
Lightburn St. WA7: Run . . . 1B 152
Lightfoot Cl. CH60: Hes . . . 3F 143
Lightfoot La. CH60: Hes . . . 3F 143
Lighthorne Dr. PR8: Ains . . . 5A 14
Lighthouse Rd. CH47: Hoy . . . 2D 102
L24: Hale . . . 4E 150
Light Oaks Rd. WA3: G'bury . . . 1E 80
Lightwood Dr. L7: Liv . . . 7E 88
Lightwood St. L7: Liv . . . 7E 88
Lilac Av. PR8: Ains . . . 7D 14
WA5: Gt San . . . 3E 116
WA8: Wid . . . 6D 114
WN4: Gars . . . 7B 50
Lilac Cres. WA7: Run . . . 2E 152
Lilac Gdns. WN3: Ince M . . . 1K 51
Lilac Gro. CH66: Whit . . . 4J 169
L36: Huy . . . 7H 91
WA4: S Hth . . . 7E 118
WA11: Hay . . . 1H 75
WN5: Bil . . . 1F 61
WN8: Skel . . . 2E 36
Lilac Rd. WA3: Golb . . . 4K 63
Lilford Av. L9: Walt . . . 7B 54
WA5: Warr . . . 7J 97
Lilford Dr. WA5: Gt San . . . 2D 116
Lilford St. WA5: Warr . . . 1K 117
(not continuous)
Lilley Rd. L7: Liv . . . 4F 89
Lillian Rd. L4: Walt . . . 1D 88
Lillie Cl. CH43: Bid . . . 7G 85
Lillyfield CH60: Hes . . . 4D 142
Lilly Grn. L4: Walt . . . 5D 68
Lilly Gro. L4: Walt . . . 5D 68
(not continuous)
Lilly Va. L7: Liv . . . 4F 89
Lily Av. WA12: New W . . . 4H 77
Lily Gro. L7: Liv . . . 6D 88 (6P 5)
Lily La. WN2: Bam, Platt B . . . 5K 51
Lily Pl. WN4: Ash M . . . 3G 63
Lily Rd. L21: Lith . . . 7H 53
Lily St. WN4: Ash M . . . 7J 51
Limbo La. CH49: Grea . . . 1B 124
CH61: Irby . . . 1C 124
Lime Av. CH63: High B . . . 5D 126
WA6: Frod . . . 3E 166
WA8: Wid . . . 6D 114
Lime Cl. L13: Liv . . . 3J 89
WA3: Rix . . . 5J 101
Lime Ct. WN8: Skel . . . 2E 36
Limedale Rd. L18: Moss H . . . 3J 109
Limefield Av. WA13: Lymm . . . 6H 121
Limefield Dr. WN8: Skel . . . 4A 38
Lime Gro. CH2: Elt . . . 1A 172
L8: Liv . . . 2D 108
L21: Sea . . . 7G 53
WA3: Low . . . 1E 78
WA7: Run . . . 2E 152
WA11: R'ford . . . 6F 47
WN8: Skel . . . 2D 36
Limehurst Gro. CH62: Brom . . . 4K 145
Limekiln Ct. L5: Liv . . . 2K 87
Limekiln La. CH44: Wall . . . 5A 86
L3: Liv . . . 3K 87
L5: Liv . . . 1F 4
WA5: B'wood . . . 4C 96
Limekiln Row WA7: Cas . . . 2J 153
Limerick Cl. WA8: Wid . . . 5A 114
Limes, The CH49: Upton . . . 3D 104
WA3: Cul . . . 2K 79
WA3: Low . . . 1D 78
Lime St. CH65: Ell P . . . 4K 161
L1: Liv . . . 5K 87 (5G 4)
PR8: South . . . 2A 12
Lime St. Chambers L1: Liv . . . 5H 5
Lime Street Staion (Rail)
. . . 5A 88 (5H 5)
Lime Tree Av. WA4: S Hth . . . 7E 118
Limetree Av. WA1: P'gate . . . 7F 99
Lime Tree Cl. CH66: Whit . . . 4J 169
L9: Walt . . . 2D 68
Lime Tree Gro. CH60: Hes . . . 2G 143
Lime Tree Way L37: Form . . . 1G 29
Lime Va. WN3: Ince M . . . 1K 51
Lime Va. Rd. WN5: Bil . . . 2E 60
Limeways WA4: App . . . 4E 138
Limont Rd. PR8: Ains . . . 4D 14
Linacre Ct. L20: Boot . . . 4J 67
Linacre La. L20: Boot . . . 1J 67
L38: Gt Alt . . . 3G 31
WA8: Wid . . . 3A 114
Linacre Rd. L21: Lith . . . 6H 53
Linaker Dr. L39: Hals . . . 2D 22
Linaker St. PR8: South . . . 3H 11
Lincoln Cl. L6: Liv . . . 3D 88
L36: Huy . . . 4B 92
WA1: W'ston . . . 2A 120
WA7: Run . . . 4E 152
Lincoln Ct. WA6: Hel . . . 1H 173
Lincoln Cres. WA11: St. H . . . 7D 60
Lincoln Dr. CH45: Wall . . . 1C 86
L10: Ain . . . 2F 55
WN4: Ash M . . . 3G 63
Lincoln Gdns. CH41: Birk . . . 6A 86
Lincoln Grn. L31: Mag . . . 4D 42
Lincoln Ho. WA10: St. H . . . 2C 74
Lincoln Rd. CH66: Gt Sut . . . 1F 169
PR8: B'dale . . . 7G 11
WA10: St. H . . . 4K 73
Lincoln Sq. WA8: Wid . . . 6D 114
Lincoln St. CH41: Birk . . . 6A 86
L19: Gars . . . 5A 130
Lincoln Way L35: R'hill . . . 6K 93
L36: Huy . . . 4B 92
Lincombe Rd. L36: Huy . . . 3F 91
Lindale Cl. CH46: More . . . 6E 84
Lindale Dr. WA9: Clock F . . . 3E 94
Lindale Rd. L7: Liv . . . 4G 89
Lindby Cl. L32: K'by . . . 5E 56
Lindby Rd. L32: K'by . . . 5E 56
Linden Av. L23: Blun . . . 1C 52
L30: N'ton . . . 3B 54
WN4: Ash M . . . 7D 50
WN5: Orr . . . 5G 39
Linden Cl. CH66: Gt Sut . . . 4H 169
WA1: W'ston . . . 1K 119
WA13: Lymm . . . 4H 121
Linden Ct. WA8: Wid . . . 4B 114
WN5: Orr . . . 5G 39
Linden Dr. CH43: Pren . . . 7J 105
L36: Huy . . . 6J 91
WA6: Hel . . . 3H 173
Linden Gro. CH45: Wall . . . 7B 66
WN5: Bil . . . 2E 60
WN5: Orr . . . 5G 39
(not continuous)
Linden Rd. L27: N'ley . . . 3J 111
Lindens WN8: Skel . . . 7H 27
Lindens, The CH43: O'ton . . . 3C 106
L31: Mag . . . 5E 42
Linden Wlk. WN5: Orr . . . 5G 39
Linden Way WA8: Wid . . . 4B 114
WA10: Eccl . . . 2H 73
Lindenwood L32: K'by . . . 5D 56
Lindeth Av. CH44: Wall . . . 4B 86
Lindfield Cl. L8: Liv . . . 4A 108
WA4: Moore . . . 4F 137
Lindholme WN8: Skel . . . 7J 27
Lindi Av. WA4: Grap . . . 7H 119
Lindisfarne Av. CH65: Ell P . . . 3A 170
Lindisfarne Ct. WA8: Wid . . . 2B 114
Lindisfarne Dr. L12: Crox . . . 3D 70
Lindley Av. WA4: Westy . . . 4F 119
WN5: Orr . . . 6E 38
Lindley Cl. L7: Liv . . . 7E 88
Lindley St. L7: Liv . . . 7E 88
Lindrick Cl. L35: R'hill . . . 3G 93
Lindsay Rd. L4: Walt . . . 6F 69
Lindsay St. WA9: Clock F . . . 4F 95
Lind St. L4: Walt . . . 5B 68
Lindsworth Cl. WA5: Gt San . . . 2G 117
Lindwall Cl. CH43: Bid . . . 6G 85
Linear Pk. CH46: More . . . 6A 84
Linear Vw. WA12: New W . . . 6G 77
Lineside Cl. L25: Gate . . . 3F 111
Linford Gro. WA11: St. H . . . 1E 74
Lingdale Av. CH43: C'ton . . . 2K 105
Lingdale Ct. CH43: C'ton . . . 1K 105
CH48: W Kir . . . 6B 102
Lingdale Rd. CH43: C'ton . . . 1K 105
CH48: W Kir . . . 5B 102
Lingdale Rd. Nth. CH41: Birk . . . 1K 105

Lingdales—Lwr. Mersey Vw.

Lingdales L37: Form 4B **20**
Lingfield Cl. L30: N'ton 4C **54**
L36: Roby 6G **91**
Lingfield Gro. L14: B Grn 5A **90**
Lingfield Rd. L14: B Grn 5A **90**
WA7: Run 1A **152**
Lingford Cl. L27: N'ley 4K **111**
Lingham Cl. CH46: More 6B **84**
Lingham La. CH46: More 4A **84**
(not continuous)
Lingholme Rd. WA10: St. H 2A **74**
LINGLEY GREEN 1B **116**
Lingley Grn. Av. WA5: Gt San 2A **116**
Lingley Mere Bus. Pk.
WA5: Gt San 7B **96**
Lingley Rd. WA5: Gt San 2B **116**
Lingmell Av. WA11: St. H 4D **60**
Lingmell Rd. L12: W Der 6K **69**
Lingmoor Cl. WN3: Wigan 3E **50**
Ling St. L7: Liv 5D **88**
Lingtree Rd. L32: K'by 3K **55**
Lingwell Av. WA8: Wid 6K **113**
Lingwood Rd. WA5: Gt San 2C **116**
Linhope Way L17: Aig 5D **108**
Link Av. L23: Thorn 7G **41**
WA11: St. H 7G **61**
Linkfield Cl. L27: N'ley 2G **111**
Link Rd. L36: Huy 6B **92**
Links, The CH43: O'ton 3K **105**
WA3: Ris 1K **99**
Links Av. CH66: Lit Sut 4E **160**
PR9: Chu 5A **8**
Links Cl. CH45: Wall 7K **65**
CH63: Raby M 4H **145**
Links Hey Rd. CH48: Caldy 3G **123**
Linkside CH63: High B 2D **126**
Linkside Av. WA2: Win 1B **98**
Linkside Ct. L23: Blun 7A **40**
Linkside Rd. L25: Wltn 7G **111**
Linkside Way CH66: Gt Sut 4H **169**
Links Rd. L32: K'by 4E **56**
Linkstor Rd. L25: Wltn 5D **110**
Links Vw. CH43: O'ton 3J **105**
CH45: Wall 6K **65**
CH66: Lit Sut 4E **160**
Linksview L25: Wltn 6D **110**
Linksway CH45: Wall 7K **65**
Linkway WA7: Run 2E **152**
WA10: Windle 7H **59**
Linkway Av. WN4: Ash M 7J **51**
Linkway E. WA9: St. H 4D **74**
Linkway W. WA9: St. H 3B **74**
WA10: St. H 3B **74**
Linner Rd. L24: Speke 7G **131**
Linnet Cl. L17: Aig 3E **108**
WA2: Warr 4D **98**
WA12: New W 3G **77**
Linnet Gro. WA3: Bchwd 4A **100**
Linnet Ho. L17: Aig 3D **108**
Linnet La. L17: Aig 3D **108**
Linnets Pk. WA7: Run 6D **134**
Linnets Way CH60: Hes 2C **142**
Linnet Way L33: K'by 5C **44**
Linslade Cl. L33: K'by 1D **56**
Linslade Cres. L33: K'by 1D **56**
Linton Av. WA3: Golb 3K **63**
Linton Pl. L32: K'by 3K **55**
Linton St. L4: Walt 5B **68**
Linum Gdns. WA9: Bold 7K **75**
Linville Av. L23: Blun 1B **52**
Linwood Cl. WA7: Brook 5A **154**
Linwood Gro. L35: Whis 5E **92**
Linwood Rd. CH42: Tran 5E **106**
Lionel St. WA9: St. H 7H **75**
Lions Cl. CH43: C'ton 2K **105**
Lipton Cl. L20: Boot 4H **67**
Lisburn La. L13: Liv 1G **89**
(Delamain Rd.)
L13: Liv 7G **69**
(Malleson Rd.)
Lisburn Rd. L17: Aig 6F **109**
LISCARD 2B **86**
Liscard Cres. CH44: Wall 2B **86**
Liscard Gro. CH44: Wall 3A **86**
Liscard Ho. CH44: Wall 3B **86**
Liscard Rd. CH44: Wall 3B **86**
L15: W'tree 1F **109**
Liscard Village CH45: Wall 2B **86**
Liscard Way CH44: Wall 3B **86**
Liskeard Cl. WA7: Brook 4K **153**
Lisleholme Cl. L12: W Der 1A **90**
Lisleholme Cres. L12: W Der 1A **90**
Lisleholme Rd. L12: W Der 1A **90**
Lismore Ct. L23: Blun 1C **52**
Lismore Pk. PR8: B'dale 4E **10**
Lismore Rd. L18: Moss H 6J **109**
Lister Cres. L7: Liv 5E **88**
Lister Dr. CH46: Leas 5E **84**
L13: Liv 3G **89**
Lister Rd. L7: Liv 4E **88**
WA7: Ast 6E **134**
Liston St. L4: Walt 4B **68**
Litcham Cl. CH49: Upton 1F **105**
Litchborough Gro. L35: Whis 1G **93**
LITHERLAND 5H **53**
Litherland Av. CH46: More 6B **84**
Litherland Cres. WA11: St. H 6E **60**
Litherland Ho. L20: Boot 2K **67**
Litherland Pk. L21: Lith 5H **53**
Litherland Rd. L20: Boot 7J **53**
Lithou Cl. L5: Liv 2J **87**
Little Acre L31: Mag 4G **43**
LITTLE ALTCAR 2A **30**
Lit. Barn Hey L30: N'ton 7K **41**
LITTLE BONGS 3B **90**
Lit. Bongs L14: K Ash 3B **90**
Littlebourne WA7: Murd 3C **154**
Lit. Brewery La. L37: Form 4K **19**
Littlebrook La. L32: K'by 5B **56**
Lit. Canning St. L8: Liv 1B **108** (10K **5**)
Lit. Catharine St.
L8: Liv 1B **108** (10K **5**)
Lit. Church St. WN5: Wigan 5K **39**
Littlecote Cl. WA9: Clock F 3E **94**
Littlecote Gdns. WA4: App 5D **138**
Little Ct. L35: Liv 3J **87** (1D **4**)
Little Cft. L35: Whis 4D **92**
LITTLE CROSBY 5D **40**
Lit. Crosby Rd. L23: C'by, Lit C 4D **40**
Littledale L14: K Ash 4B **90**
Littledale Rd. CH44: Wall 4D **86**
WA5: Gt San 1D **116**
Lit. Delph WA11: Hay 6A **62**
Littlegate WA7: Run 2G **153**
Little Grn. CH66: Gt Sut 1F **169**
Lit. Hardman St. L1: Liv 7A **88** (8J **5**)
Lit. Heath Rd. L24: Speke 7J **131**
Lit. Heyes St. L5: Liv 1C **88**
Lit. Hey La. L37: Form 6B **20**
Lit. Howard St. L3: Liv 3H **87** (1C **4**)
Lit. Huskisson St.
L8: Liv 1B **108** (10L **5**)
Little La. CH64: Park 2G **157**
PR9: Chu 5D **8**
Littlemore Cl. CH49: Upton 3B **104**
Lit. Moss Hey L28: Stock V 7F **71**
LITTLE NESTON 6J **157**
Lit. Parkfield Rd. L17: Aig 4D **108**
Littler Rd. WA11: Hay 1H **75**
Lit. St Bride St. L8: Liv 7B **88** (9K **5**)
LITTLE STANNEY 3C **170**
Lit. Stanney La.
CH2: Lit Stan, Stoak 4C **170**
Littlestone Cl. WA8: Wid 4C **114**
Lit. Storeton La. CH63: Store 3A **126**
Little St. WA9: St. H 5G **75**
LITTLE SUTTON 5E **160**
Little Sutton Station (Rail) 5E **160**
Little Theatre 1H **11**
Littleton Cl. CH43: Noct 4J **105**
WA5: Gt San 4H **117**
LITTLE TOWN 5J **79**
Lit. Whissage CH66: Gt Sut 2H **169**
Littlewood Cl. L35: Whis 4E **92**
Lit. Woolton St. L7: Liv 6B **88** (6M **5**)
Littondale Av. L35: R'hill 5K **93**
Liver Ind. Est. L9: Ain 2E **68**
Livermore Ct. L8: Liv 2E **108**
LIVERPOOL 5J **87** (4E **4**)
Liverpool Av. PR8: Ains 4D **14**
Liverpool Cathedral Church of Christ
1A **108** (10J **5**)
Liverpool College Sports Cen. 4H **109**
Liverpool Empire Theatre
5K **87** (5H **5**)
Liverpool FC 7C **68**
Liverpool Institute for Performing Arts
9J 5
(off Mount St.)
Liverpool Intermodal Freeport Terminal
L20: Boot 2G **67**
Liverpool John Moores University
4K **87** (3G **4**)
Liverpool Metropolitan Cathedral
6B **88** (6K **5**)
Liverpool Mus. 5K **87** (4G **4**)
Liverpool Parish Church 5H **87** (6C **4**)
Liverpool Pl. WA8: Wid 7J **113**
Liverpool Playhouse 6K **87** (6G **4**)
Liverpool Rd. CH2: Back, Mos 7K **169**
CH64: Nest 3J **157**
(not continuous)
L23: C'by 7D **40**
L31: Lyd 1E **42**
L34: Prsct 1B **92**
L36: Huy 3F **91**
L37: Form 1A **30**
L39: Augh 1K **33**
L39: Bic 1C **44**
PR8: Ains 7C **14**
PR8: B'dale 4G **11**
WA1: Warr 3K **117**
WA3: G'brk 4K **101**
WA5: Gt San 2A **116**
WA5: Warr 3K **117**
WA8: Wid 7H **113**
WA10: St. H 3B **74**
WA11: Hay 6J **61**
WN4: Ash M 3C **62**
WN8: Skel 3C **36**
(not continuous)
Liverpool Rd. Nth. L31: Mag 1E **42**
Liverpool Rd. Sth. L31: Mag 3E **42**
L40: Burs 1F **25**
Liverpool Row WA12: New W 6H **77**
Liverpool Sailing Club 7C **130**
Liverpool St. WA10: St. H 3B **74**
Liverpool Tennis Cen. 1G **109**
Liverpool Watersports Cen. 2J **107**
Liverpool Way, The L33: K'by 4E **56**
Livingstone Rd. CH42: Tran 4D **106**
Liver St. L1: Liv 7J **87** (9E **4**)
Livesleys La. L37: Gt Alt 1F **31**
Livingston Av. L17: Aig 4E **108**
Livingston Ct. L17: Aig 4E **108**
Livingston Dr. L17: Aig 5E **108**
Livingston Dr. Nth. L17: Aig 5E **108**
Livingston Dr. Sth. L17: Aig 5E **108**
Livingstone Cl. WA5: Old H 1H **117**
Livingstone Gdns. CH41: Birk 1C **106**
Livingstone Rd. CH46: Leas 3E **84**
CH65: Ell P 4A **162**
Livingstone St. CH41: Birk 1C **106**
WN4: Ash M 7E **50**
Livingwell Health Club
St Helens 3C **74**
Llandaff Cl. CH66: Gt Sut 3G **169**
Llanrwst Cl. L8: Liv 3A **108**
Lloyd Av. CH41: Birk 1B **106**
Lloyd Cl. L6: Liv 3B **88** (1L **5**)
Lloyd Cres. WA12: New W 3D **76**
Lloyd Dr. CH49: Grea 5A **104**
CH65: Ell P 3A **170**
Lloyd Rd. L34: Prsct 7E **72**
Lloyd St. WA11: Hay 7H **61**
Lobelia Av. L9: Walt 2D **68**
Lobelia Gro. WA7: Beech 6H **153**
Local Cen. WA7: Cas 7J **135**
Lochinvar St. L9: Walt 3B **68**
Lochinver Av. CH66: Lit Sut 5B **160**
Lochmore Rd. L18: Moss H 7J **109**
Lochryan Rd. L19: Aller 1K **129**
Loch St. WA7: Run 6C **134**
(not continuous)
WN5: Orr 5K **39**
Locker Av. WA2: Warr 5B **98**
Lockerbie Cl. WA2: Warr 4E **98**
Lockerbie Pl. WN3: Wins 2C **50**
Lockerby Rd. L7: Liv 4F **89**
Locker La. WN4: Ash M 7K **51**
Locker Pk. CH49: Grea 4A **104**
Locke St. L19: Gars 5A **130**
Lockett Rd. WA8: Wid 5C **114**
WN4: Ash M 6F **51**
Lockett St. WA4: Latch 5F **119**
Lockfields Vw. L3: Liv 2J **87**
Lockgate E. WA7: Wind H 7A **136**
Lockgate W. WA7: Wind H 7K **135**
LOCKING STUMPS 2J **99**
Locking Stumps Cen.
WA3: Bchwd 3K **99**
Locking Stumps La.
WA2: Bchwd, Fearn 4H **99**
WA3: Bchwd 4H **99**
Lockington Cl. L8: Liv 4B **108**
Lock Rd. CH62: East 2C **146**
WA1: P'ton 2F **119**
Lock St. WA9: St. H 1E **74**
Lockton La. WA5: Warr 1J **117**
Lockton Rd. L34: Know 1F **71**
Lockwood Vw. WA7: Pres B 5D **154**
Loddon Cl. CH49: Upton 1F **105**
Lodge Cl. WA13: Lymm 4K **121**
Lodge Dr. WA3: Cul 3B **80**
Lodge Hollow WA6: Hel 7H **165**
Lodge La. CH62: Port S 3H **127**
L8: Liv 1D **108**
WA5: Warr 1J **117**
WA7: Halt 2G **153**
WA8: Cron 4G **113**
WA12: New W 4F **63**
(not continuous)
Lodge Rd. WA8: Wid 1H **133**
WN5: Orr 7G **39**
Lodge Works L33: Know I 2G **57**
Lodwick St. L20: Kirk 5H **67**
Lofthouse Ga. WA8: Wid 5B **114**
Logan Rd. CH41: Birk 6B **86**
Logfield Dr. L19: Gars 4B **130**
Lognor Rd. L32: K'by 3A **56**
Lognor Wlk. L32: K'by 3A **56**
Logwood Rd. L36: Huy 7A **92**
Lois Ct. CH45: Wall 1C **86**
Lombard Rd. CH46: More 5D **84**
Lombardy Av. CH49: Grea 6K **103**
Lomond Gro. CH46: More 7D **84**
CH66: Gt Sut 1H **169**
Lomond Rd. L7: Liv 5G **89**
Londonderry Rd. L13: Liv 7F **69**
London Flds. WN5: Bil 7G **49**
London La. PR8: South 2J **15**
London Rd. L3: Liv 5A **88** (5H **5**)
(not continuous)
WA4: App, Thel, S Hth 7C **118**
WA6: Frod 3D **166**
London Row WA12: New W 6H **77**
London Sq. PR9: South 1H **11**
London St. PR9: South 1H **11**
Longacre PR9: Chu 4B **8**
Longacre Cl. CH45: Wall 2H **85**
Longacre Rd. CH64: Nest 1J **157**
Long Acres CH49: Grea 3B **104**
Long Av. L9: Ain 7D **54**
Longbarn Blvd. WA2: Bchwd 5J **99**
Long Barn La. WA1: W'ston 6K **99**
WA2: Fearn 5H **99**
WA2: P'gate 5J **99**
(not continuous)
Longbenton Way WA7: Mnr P 5K **135**
Longborough Rd. L34: Know 3G **71**
Longbutt La. WA13: Lymm 5H **121**
(not continuous)
Longcliffe Dr. PR8: Ains 5B **14**
Longcroft Av. L19: Aller 2B **130**
Longcroft Sq. L19: Aller 2B **130**
Longdale La. L29: Seft 5K **41**
Longden Rd. WN4: Ash M 2E **62**
Longdin St. WA4: Westy 5E **118**
Longdown Rd. L10: Faz 7J **55**
Longfellow Cl. L32: K'by 5B **56**
Longfellow Dr. CH62: New F 2G **127**
Longfellow St. L8: Liv 1D **108**
(not continuous)
L20: Boot 1G **67**
Longfield L37: Form 5B **20**
Longfield Av. L23: C'by 6E **40**
Longfield Cl. CH49: Grea 4B **104**
Longfield Pk. WA9: Clock F 3F **95**
Longfield Rd. L21: Lith 7H **53**
WA2: Warr 6C **98**
Longfield Wlk. L23: C'by 6E **40**
Longfold L31: Mag 3G **43**
LONGFORD 6B **98**
Longford Dr. WA8: Wid 6A **114**
Longford Rd. PR8: B'dale 6G **11**
Longford St. L8: Liv 5C **108**
WA2: Warr 1B **118**
Long Hey L35: Whis 5D **92**
Longhey WN8: Skel 6J **27**
Long Hey Rd. CH48: Caldy 2G **123**
Longland Rd. CH45: Wall 1B **86**
Long La. L9: Ain 7D **54**
L15: W'tree 7G **89**
L19: Gars 2A **130**
L29: Thorn 4G **41**
L37: Form 6J **19**
(not continuous)
L39: Augh, Bic 7A **24**
PR9: Banks 1K **9**
WA2: Warr 6B **98**
WN8: Uph 1A **48**
Longleat Cl. WA5: Warr 1K **117**
Longlooms Rd. CH65: Ell P 3B **170**
Longmead Av. WN4: Ash M 1G **63**
Long Mdw. CH60: Hes 4D **142**
WA10: Eccl 2H **73**
Longmeadow Rd. L34: Know 2H **71**
Long Meanygate PR9: South 7H **9**
Longmoor Cl. L10: Faz 6G **55**
Longmoor Gro. L9: Ain 7D **54**
Longmoor La. L9: Ain 7D **54**
L10: Faz 7D **54**
Long Moss L30: N'ton 3J **53**
Longreach Rd. L14: K Ash 3D **90**
Longridge Av. CH49: Upton 2C **104**
WA11: St. H 1F **75**
Longridge Wlk. L4: Kirk 6A **68**
Longshaw Av. WN5: Bil 3G **49**
LONGSHAW BOTTOM 3G **49**
Longshaw Cl. WN5: Bil 3G **49**
LONGSHAW COMMON 4G **49**
Longshaw Comn. WN5: Bil 3G **49**
(not continuous)
Longshaw Old Rd. WN5: Bil 3G **49**
Longshaw St. WA5: Warr 5K **97**
Long Spinney WA7: Nort 2A **154**
Longster Cl. WA6: Hel 2H **173**
Longstone Wlk. L7: Liv 7D **88** (8P **5**)
Longton Ct. PR9: South 7K **7**
Longton Dr. L37: Form 4A **20**
Longton La. L35: R'hill 2G **93**
LONGVIEW 2K **91**
Long Vw. Av. L35: R'hill 3G **93**
Longview Av. CH45: Wall 2A **86**
Longview Cres. L36: Huy 4K **91**
Longview Dr. L36: Huy 3K **91**
Longview La. L36: Huy 2K **91**
Long Vw. Rd. L35: R'hill 3G **93**
Longview Rd. L36: Huy 3K **91**
Longville St. L8: Liv 3A **108**
Longwood Cl. WA11: R'ford 4H **59**
Longwood Rd. WA4: App 3E **138**
Longworth Way L25: Wltn 5E **110**
Lonie Gro. WA10: St. H 6J **73**
Lonmore Cl. PR9: Banks 2J **9**
Lonsborough Rd. CH44: Wall 4C **86**
Lonsdale Av. CH45: Wall 1A **86**
L39: Orm 3D **24**
WA10: St. H 7H **73**
Lonsdale Cl. L21: Ford 3H **53**
WA5: Gt San 7C **96**
WA8: Wid 7J **113**
Lonsdale M. L21: Ford 3H **53**
Lonsdale Rd. L21: Ford 3H **53**
L26: Halew 3J **131**
L37: Form 7J **19**
PR8: South 4K **11**
Lonsdale Vs. CH45: Wall 1A **86**
Lonsdale Wlk. WN5: Orr 3K **39**
Looe Cl. WA8: Wid 6A **114**
Looe Rd. L11: Crox 1B **70**
Looms, The CH64: Park 1F **157**
Loomsway CH61: Irby 3B **124**
Loraine St. L5: Liv 1B **88**
Lordens Cl. L14: K Ash 2E **90**
Lordens Rd. L14: K Ash 2E **90**
Lord Nelson St. L1: Liv 5K **87** (5H **5**)
L3: Liv 5A **88** (5H **5**)
WA1: Warr 3C **118**
Lords Av. CH43: Bid 7G **85**
Lord Sefton Way L37: Gt Alt 1D **30**
Lords Fold WA11: R'ford 5E **46**
Lordsgate La. L40: Burs 1G **25**
Lordship La. WA6: Frod 5F **165**
Lords La. WA3: Bchwd 3J **99**
Lords St. M44: Cad 1K **101**
Lord St. CH41: Birk 1E **106**
L2: Liv 6J **87** (6E **4**)
L19: Gars 4A **130**
PR8: South 2G **11**
PR9: South 1H **11**
WA3: Croft 6G **79**
WA4: Warr 4B **118**
WA7: Run 6B **134**
WA10: St. H 1B **74**
(not continuous)
WA12: New W 3E **76**
WN4: Ash M 1H **63**
Lord St. W. PR8: South 2G **11**
Loreburn Rd. L15: W'tree 2J **109**
Lorenzo Dr. L11: N Grn. 5G **69**
Loretto Dr. CH49: Upton 2E **104**
Loretto Rd. CH44: Wall 2K **85**
Lorn Ct. CH41: Birk 2E **106**
Lorne Ct. CH43: O'ton 4B **106**
Lorne Rd. CH43: O'ton 4A **106**
L22: Water 4D **52**
Lorne St. L7: Liv 4G **89**
Lorn St. CH41: Birk 2E **106**
Lorton Av. WA11: St. H 4C **60**
Lorton St. L8: Liv 1D **108** (10P **5**)
Lostock Av. WA5: Warr 7K **97**
Lostock Cl. WN5: Bil 7G **49**
Lothair Rd. L4: Walt 7C **68**
Lothian St. L8: Liv 2C **108**
Lotus Gdns. WA9: Bold 7J **75**
Loudon Gro. L8: Liv 2C **108**
Lough Grn. CH63: Spit 7G **127**
Loughlin Dr. L33: K'by 7D **44**
Loughrigg Av. WA11: St. H 4D **60**
Louis Braille Cl. L30: N'ton 1B **54**
Louis Pasteur Av. L30: N'ton 1B **54**
Loushers La.
WA4: Latch, Warr 6C **118**
Lovage Cl. WA2: P'gate 5J **99**
Lovelace Rd. L19: Gras 2K **129**
Love La. CH44: Wall 4A **86**
L3: Liv 3H **87** (1C **4**)
Lovel Rd. L24: Speke 7H **131**
Lovel Ter. WA8: Hale B 4H **133**
Lovel Way L24: Speke 6H **131**
Lovely La. WA5: Warr 2J **117**
Loves Cotts. L39: Orm 4B **24**
Lovett Dr. L35: Prsct 2E **92**
Low Bank Rd. WN4: Ash M 1D **62**
Lowcroft WN8: Skel 7J **27**
Lowden Av. L21: Lith 3H **53**
Lowe Av. WA4: Westy 4F **119**
Lowell St. L4: Walt 5B **68**
Lwr. Alt Rd. L38: High 5F **29**
Lwr. Appleton Rd. WA8: Wid 7D **114**
Lwr. Bank Vw. L20: Kirk 5H **67**
LOWER BEBINGTON 4G **127**
Lwr. Breck Rd. L6: Liv 1D **88**
Lwr. Carr La. L38: Gt Alt 4H **31**
(not continuous)
Lwr. Castle St. L2: Liv 6J **87** (6D **4**)
Lwr. Church St. WA8: Wid 4C **134**
Lower Cl. L26: Halew 1A **132**
Lwr. Farm Rd. L25: Gate 1D **110**
Lwr. Flaybrick Rd. CH43: Bid 7J **85**
Lwr. Gill St. L3: Liv 5A **88** (5K **5**)
Lower Grn. CH49: W'chu 5E **104**
Lower Hey L23: Thorn 7H **41**
Lwr. Hill Top Rd. WA4: S Hth 6F **119**
Lwr. House La. L11: N Grn. 2H **69**
WA8: Wid 2B **134**
Lower La. L9: Faz 6G **55**
Lwr. Mersey St. CH65: Ell P 4A **162**
Lwr. Mersey Vw. L20: Kirk 5H **67**

A-Z Merseyside 211

Lwr. Milk St. L3: Liv 5J 87 (4E 4)
Lwr. Promenade PR8: South 1G 11
PR9: South 7H 7
Lwr. Rake La. WA6: Hel 7H 165
Lower Rd. CH62: Port S 3H 127
L26: Halew 1B 132
WA8: Hale B 1B 132
Lwr. Robin Hood La. WA6: Hel 1G 173
Lwr. Sandfield L25: Gate 4F 111
Lowerson Cres. L11: N Grn. 6G 69
Lowerson Rd. L11: N Grn. 6G 69
LOWER STRETTON 7K 139
Lwr. Thingwall La. CH61: Thing 3G 125
LOWER WALTON 1B 138
Lwr. Wash La. WA4: Westy 5E 118
Lowes Grn. L37: Form 7B 20
Lowe's La. WN8: Newb 2E 26
Lowe St. WA10: St. H 2B 74
Lowe St. Sth. WA10: St. H 3B 74
Loweswater Cl. WA2: Warr 4B 98
Loweswater Cres. WA11: Hay 7J 61
Loweswater Way L33: K'by 1B 56
Lowfield Ind. Est. WA9: St. H 2A 94
Lowfield La. WA9: St. H 1B 94
Lowfield Rd. L14: K Ash 4A 90
Lowfields Av. CH62: East 7K 145
Lowfields Cl. CH62: East 7A 146
Low Hill L6: Liv 4C 88 (3M 5)
WA6: Dun H 7D 172
Lowlands Rd. WA7: Run 7B 134
Lowndes Rd. L6: Liv 1F 89
Lowry Bank CH44: Wall 4E 86
Lowry Cl. L33: K'by 6C 44
WA5: Gt San 2H 117
Lowry Hill La. L40: Lath 1B 26
Lowther Av. L10: Ain 3F 55
L31: Mag 2G 43
WA3: Cul 2B 80
Lowther Cres. WA10: St. H 6H 73
Lowther Dr. L35: R'hill 4H 93
Lowther St. L8: Liv 1C 108 (10M 5)
Lowton Gdns. WA3: Low 1B 78
LOWTON HEATH 1B 78
Low Wood L38: High 5K 29
Low Wood Gro. CH61: Barn 5G 125
Lowwood Gro. CH41: Birk 3D 106
Lowwood Rd. CH41: Birk 3D 106
Low Wood St. L6: Liv 4C 88 (4M 5)
Loxdale Cl. L8: Liv 4B 108
Loxdale Dr. CH65: Gt Sut 1H 169
Loxley Cl. WA5: Gt San 7E 96
Loxley Rd. PR8: South 4K 11
Loxton Cres. WN3: Wigan 1F 51
Loxwood Cl. L25: Gate 1F 111
Loyola Hey L35: R'hill 7A 94
Lucania St. L19: Gars 4A 130
Lucan Rd. L17: Aig 6F 109
Lucerne Rd. CH44: Wall 5D 86
Lucerne St. L17: Aig 5E 108
Lucius Cl. L9: Walt 6B 54
Lucknow St. L17: Aig 4E 108
Ludlow WN8: Skel 6J 27
Ludlow Cl. WA1: P'gate 6H 99
Ludlow Ct. CH48: W Kir 7D 102
Ludlow Cres. WA7: Run 2D 152
Ludlow Dr. CH48: W Kir 7D 102
CH65: Ell P 1C 170
L39: Orm 3B 24
Ludlow Gro. CH62: Brom 1K 145
Ludlow St. L4: Walt 5A 68
Ludwig Rd. L4: Walt 1D 88
Lugard Rd. L17: Aig 6G 109
LUGSDALE 2E 134
Lugsdale Rd. WA8: Wid 2D 134
Lugsmore La. WA10: St. H 5J 73
Luke St. CH44: Wall 5E 86
L8: Liv 2B 108
WN4: Ash M 7H 51
Lulworth WN8: Skel 6H 27
Lulworth Av. L22: Water 3C 52
Lulworth Lodge PR8: B'dale 3F 11
Lulworth Rd. L25: Gate 3G 111
PR8: B'dale 4F 11
Lulworth Vw. PR8: B'dale 4E 10
Lumb Brook M. WA4: S Hth 7E 118
Lumb Brook Rd. WA4: App 1E 138
(not continuous)
Lumber La. WA5: B'wood 6C 76
Lumbrook Rd. WA4: App, App T 3G 139
Lumina CH62: Brom 7A 128
Lumley Rd. CH44: Wall 4D 86
Lumley St. L19: Gars 2K 129
Lumley Wlk. L24: Hale 1E 150
Lunar Dr. L30: N'ton 7B 42
Lunar Rd. L9: Ain 7D 54
Lunds Cl. L40: Westh 6J 25
Lundy Dr. CH65: Ell P 4A 170
Lune Av. L31: Mag 2G 43
Lune Rd. WN2: Platt B 2K 51
Lunesdale Av. L9: Ain 6D 54
Lune St. L23: C'by 1E 52
Luneway WA8: Wid 7J 113
Lunsford Rd. L14: K Ash 3D 90
LUNT 4K 41
Lunt Av. L30: N'ton 3C 54
L35: Whis 4E 92
Lunt La. L29: Seft 4K 41
Lunt Rd. L20: Boot 7J 53
L29: Seft, Thorn 3J 41
LUNTS HEATH 4D 114
Lunt's Heath Rd. WA8: Wid 3C 114
Lunt's La. L37: Form 2A 30
Lunts Wood Gro. WA12: New W 2E 76
Lupin Dr. WA11: Hay 7D 62
Lupton Dr. L23: C'by 1G 53
Lupus Way CH66: Gt Sut 1H 169
Luscombe Cl. L26: Halew 1A 132
Lusitania Rd. L4: Walt 4C 68
Luther Gro. WA9: St. H 4K 75
Luton Gro. L4: Walt 6A 68
Luton Rd. CH65: Ell P 6H 161
Luton St. L5: Kirk 1H 87
WA8: Wid 2C 134
Lutyens Cl. L4: Walt 6B 68
Luxmore Rd. L4: Walt 5C 68
Lycett Rd. CH44: Wall 2J 85
L4: Walt 7D 68
Lyceum Pl. L1: Liv 7G 4
Lyceum St. L1: Liv 7G 4
Lychgate WA4: H Walt 2K 137

Lycroft Cl. WA7: Run 4D 152
Lydbrook Cl. CH42: R Ferr 5F 107
Lydbury Cl. WA5: Call 5H 97
Lydbury Cres. L32: K'by 5D 56
Lydden Rd. CH65: Ell P 4K 161
Lydford Rd. L12: W Der 6K 69
Lydia Ann St. L1: Liv 7K 87 (8F 4)
LYDIATE 6D 32
Lydiate, The CH60: Hes 3D 142
Lydiate La. CH64: Will 3E 158
L23: Thorn 6H 41
L25: Wltn 6G 111
L26: Halew 6G 111
L29: Seft 6H 41
WA7: West P 3K 151
Lydiate Pk. L23: Thorn 6H 41
Lydiate Rd. L20: Boot 1J 67
Lydiate Sta. Rd. L31: Lyd 6J 31
Lydia Wlk. L10: Faz 6K 55
Lydieth Lea L27: N'ley 2J 111
Lydney Rd. L36: Huy 3F 91
Lydstep Ct. WA5: Call 5J 97
Lyelake Cl. L32: K'by 4D 56
Lyelake Rd. L32: K'by 4D 56
L39: Bic 3K 35
WN8: Skel 2K 35
Lyle St. L5: Liv 2J 87
Lyme Cl. L36: Huy 1K 91
Lymecroft L25: Wltn 6D 110
Lyme Cross Rd. L36: Huy 1J 91
Lyme Gro. L36: Huy 2K 91
WA13: Lymm 6E 120
Lyme St. WA1: Warr 3B 118
WA11: Hay 7C 62
WA12: New W 2C 76
Lyme Tree Ct. WA8: Cron 2J 113
Lymewood Ct. WA11: Hay 6B 62
Lymington Gro. L30: N'ton 2B 54
Lymington Rd. CH44: Wall 3K 85
LYMM 5F 121
Lymm Bri. WA13: Lymm 5G 121
Lymmhay La. WA13: Lymm 4G 121
Lymmington Av. WA13: Lymm 5E 120
Lymm Leisure Cen. 6J 121
Lymm Rd. CH43: Bid 1G 105
WA4: Thel 5A 120
Lynas Gdns. L19: Gras 1K 129
Lynas St. CH41: Birk 7D 86
Lynbridge Cl. WN5: Orr 6G 39
Lyncastle Rd. WA4: App T 6K 139
Lyncastle Way WA4: App T 5K 139
Lyncot Rd. L9: Ain 5D 54
Lyncroft Rd. CH44: Wall 5C 86
Lyndale WA7: Run 2E 152
WN8: Skel 6H 27
Lyndale Av. CH62: East 6A 146
WA2: Fearn 5F 99
WA2: Warr 7D 98
Lyndene Rd. L25: Gate 2E 110
Lyndhurst CH48: W Kir 5C 102
L31: Mag 3F 43
WN8: Skel 6H 27
Lyndhurst Av. CH61: Pens 6E 124
L18: Moss H 5H 109
Lyndhurst Cl. CH61: Thing 4E 124
Lyndhurst Rd. CH45: Wall 1K 85
CH47: Meols 6H 83
CH61: Irby 4A 124
L18: Moss H 4H 109
L23: C'by 1G 53
PR8: B'dale 6G 11
Lyndhurst Way L36: Huy 5J 91
Lyndon Dr. L18: Moss H 4K 109
Lyndon Gro. WA7: Run 2D 152
Lyndor Cl. L25: Wltn 7F 111
Lyndor Rd. L25: Wltn 7F 111
Lyneal Av. CH66: Gt Sut 2E 168
Lyneham L35: Whis 5F 93
Lynham Av. WA5: Gt San 3F 117
Lynholme Rd. L4: Walt 7D 68
Lynmouth Rd. L17: Aig 1G 129
Lynnbank CH43: O'ton 4B 106
Lynnbank Rd. L18: Moss H 3B 110
Lynn Cl. WA7: Run 3E 152
WA10: St. H 2J 73
Lynndene CH66: Lit Sut 4F 161
Lynscot Pl. L16: Child 7B 90
Lynsted Rd. L14: K Ash 4D 90
Lynton Cl. CH60: Hes 4F 143
L19: Aller 1K 129
WA5: Penk 4C 116
Lynton Ct. L23: Blun 1B 52
Lynton Cres. WA8: Wid 6A 114
Lynton Dr. CH63: Beb 6G 127
PR8: B'dale 7E 10
Lynton Gdns. WA4: App 5D 138
Lynton Grn. L25: Wltn 4D 110
Lynton Gro. WA9: Sut L 2E 94
Lynton Rd. CH45: Wall 1J 85
L36: Huy 4B 92
PR8: B'dale 1E 14
Lynton Way WA10: Windle 7H 59
Lynwood Av. CH44: Wall 4A 86
L39: Augh 7A 24
WA4: App 2C 138
Lynwood Cl. WN8: Skel 4K 37
Lynwood Dr. CH61: Irby 3C 124
Lynwood End L39: Augh 7A 24
Lynwood Gdns. L9: Walt 1B 68
Lynwood Rd. L9: Walt 1B 68
Lynxway, The L12: W Der 3B 90
Lyon Cl. WA10: St. H 3B 74
Lyon Ct. WA4: Latch 5F 119
Lyon Rd. L4: Walt 1D 88
Lyons Cl. CH46: More 6C 84
Lyons La. WA4: App 3D 138
Lyons Pl. L25: Hunts X 1H 131
Lyons Rd. CH46: More 6C 84
PR8: B'dale 3G 11
WA5: Penk 4D 116
Lyon St. L19: Gars 5A 130
WA4: Latch 5F 119
WA10: St. H 3A 74
WN4: Ash M 5D 50
Lyra Rd. L22: Water 4D 52
Lyster Cl. WA3: Bchwd 4B 100
Lyster Rd. L20: Boot 3G 67
Lytham Cl. L10: Faz 4H 55
L12: W Der 1C 90
WA5: Gt San 5E 116

Lytham Ct. L32: K'by 1A 56
Lytham Ho. WA3: Ris 1K 99
Lytham Rd. PR9: Chu 3C 8
WA8: Wid 6D 114
WN4: Ash M 7D 50
Lythgoes La. WA2: Warr 2B 118
(not continuous)
Lytles Cl. L37: Form 1A 30
Lyttelton Rd. L17: Aig 6G 109
Lytton Av. CH42: R Ferr 7F 107
Lytton Gro. L21: Sea 7G 53
Lytton St. L6: Liv 4B 88 (2L 5)

M

Mab La. L12: W Der 6D 70
MacAlpine Cl. CH49: Upton 2E 104
MacArthur Rd. WA5: Gt San 2F 117
Macauley Pl. WN3: Wigan 1D 50
Macbeth St. L20: Kirk 5J 67
McBride St. L19: Gars 3A 130
McCarthy Cl. WA3: Bchwd 3C 100
McClellan Pl. WA8: Wid 7D 114
McCormack Av. WA9: St. H 2G 75
McCulloch St. WA9: St. H 3E 74
Macdermott Rd. WA8: Wid 4B 134
MacDona Dr. CH48: W Kir 1D 122
Macdonald Av. WA11: St. H 1G 75
WN3: Wigan 1E 50
Macdonald Dr. CH49: Grea 5B 104
Macdonald Rd. CH46: More 7A 84
MacDonald St. L15: W'tree 7G 89
WN5: Orr 5K 39
Mace Rd. L11: Crox 3A 70
McFarlane Av. WA10: St. H 2J 73
Macfarren St. L13: Liv 4J 89
McGarva Way CH65: Ell P 7A 162
McGough Cl. WA9: Sut M 4C 94
McGregor St. L5: Liv 2A 88
McKee Av. WA2: Warr 5B 98
Mackenzie Av. WN3: Wigan 1E 50
MacKenzie Rd. CH46: Leas 4F 85
McKeown Cl. L5: Liv 2K 87
Mackets Cl. L25: Wltn 7G 111
Macket's La. L25: Wltn 6G 111
Mack Gro. L30: N'ton 3K 53
McKinley Way WA8: Wid 5B 114
McMinnis Av. WA9: St. H 4J 75
McNair Hall L18: Moss H 5H 109
MacQueen St. L13: Liv 5J 89
McVinnie Rd. L35: Prsct 1F 93
Maddock Rd. CH44: Wall 2D 86
Maddocks St. L13: Liv 5J 89
Maddock St. CH41: Birk 7C 86
Maddrell St. L3: Liv 3H 87
Madeira Dr. L25: Gate 2F 111
Madelaine St. L8: Liv 2C 108
Madeleine McKenna Ct.
WA8: Wid 5H 113
Madeley Cl. CH48: W Kir 7D 102
WN3: Wigan 1C 50
Madeley Dr. CH48: W Kir 7D 102
Madeley St. L6: Liv 3E 88
Madingley Ct. PR9: Chu 5B 8
Madison Sq. L1: Liv 7K 87 (9H 5)
Madryn Av. L33: K'by 3E 56
Madryn St. L8: Liv 3C 108
Maelor Cl. CH63: Brom 4J 145
Maesbrook Cl. PR9: Banks 2K 9
Mafeking Cl. L15: W'tree 7H 89
Mafeking Pl. WN4: Ash M 2G 63
Magazine Av. CH45: New B 7B 66
Magazine Brow CH45: New B 7C 66
Magazine La. CH45: New B 7B 66
CH62: Brom 5A 128
Magazine Rd. CH62: Brom 6K 127
Magazines Prom. CH45: New B 6C 66
Magazine Wlk. CH62: Brom 6K 127
Magdala St. L8: Liv 1D 108
Magdalen Dr. WN4: Ash M 1D 62
Magdalen Ho. L20: Boot 4J 67
Magdalen Sq. L30: N'ton 1B 54
Maggots Nook Rd. WA11: R'ford 3G 47
MAGHULL 2E 42
Maghull Hey Cop L38: Gt Alt 6G 31
Maghull La. L31: Mag 3K 43
Maghull Smallholdings Est.
L31: Mag 1J 43
Maghull Station (Rail) 5G 43
Mag La. WA13: Lymm 4H 141
WA16: H Legh, Lymm 4H 141
Magnolia Cl. CH66: Gt Sut 3H 169
L26: Halew 6H 111
WA1: W'ston 1A 120
WA11: Hay 1H 75
Magnolia Dr. WA7: Beech 6H 153
Magnolia Wlk. CH49: Grea 6A 104
Magnum St. L5: Liv 2B 88
Magnus Cl. L13: Liv 2H 89
Maguire Av. L20: Boot 2A 68
Mahon Av. L20: Boot 7K 53
Mahon Ct. L8: Liv 1B 108 (10K 5)
Maiden Cl. WN8: Skel 1C 36
Maiden Gdns. CH65: Ell P 1B 170
Maiden La. L13: Liv 7F 69
Maidford Rd. L14: K Ash 2C 90
Maidstone Cl. L25: Hunts X 1G 131
Maidstone Dr. L12: W Der 2D 90
Main Av. WA10: St. H 6J 73
Main Cl. WA11: Hay 7J 61
Main Dr. L35: Whis 6D 92
Main Front L35: Whis 6E 92
Main La. WA3: Croft 3E 78
Main Rd. CH62: Port S 5H 127
Mains Av. WN2: Bam 5K 51
Mainside Rd. L32: K'by 4D 56
Main St. WA6: Frod 3C 166
WA7: Halt 1H 153
WN5: Bil 1F 61
Maintree Cres. L24: Speke 5A 132
Mainwaring Rd. CH44: Wall 4D 86
CH62: Brom 2K 145
Mairesfield Av. WA4: Grap 6H 119
Mairscough La. L39: Down 3C 32
Maitland Cl. L8: Liv 1D 108 (10P 5)
Maitland Rd. CH45: New B 6C 66
Maitland St. L8: Liv 1D 108
Majestic M. WN5: Orr 6F 39
Major Cross St. WA8: Wid 2C 134

Major St. L5: Kirk 1K 87
WN5: Wigan 5K 39
Makerfield Dr. WA12: New W 1E 76
Makin St. L4: Walt 4B 68
Malahide Ct. WA8: Wid 5K 113
Malcolm Av. WA2: Warr 6D 98
Malcolm Cres. CH63: Brom 4J 145
Malcolm Gro. L20: Kirk 5K 67
Malcolm Pl. L15: W'tree 6H 89
Malcolm St. WA7: Run 7D 134
Malden Rd. L6: Liv 4D 88
Maldon Cl. L26: Halew 3K 131
Maldwyn Rd. CH44: Wall 2B 86
Maley Cl. L8: Liv 4C 108
Malham Av. WN3: Wigan 2E 50
Malham Cl. PR8: South 5A 12
WA5: Gt San 7C 96
Malhamdale Av. L35: R'hill 5K 93
Malika Pl. WN4: Ash M 6C 50
Malin Cl. L24: Hale 7D 132
Maliston Rd. WA5: Gt San 3F 117
Mall, The L5: Liv 2C 88
L39: Orm 5D 24
WA1: Warr 3B 118
Mallaby St. CH41: Birk 7A 86
Mallard Cl. L12: Crox 3D 70
L26: Halew 7J 111
L39: Augh 1A 34
WA2: Warr 4D 98
WA7: Beech 5H 153
Mallard Gdns. WA9: St. H 1A 94
Mallard Ho. L31: Lyd 7D 32
Mallard La. WA3: Bchwd 4B 100
Mallards, The PR9: Cros 4E 8
Mallard Way CH46: More 6A 84
WA11: St. H 7D 60
Mallee Av. PR9: Chu 4C 8
Mallee Cres. PR9: Chu 4C 8
Malleson Rd. L13: Liv 7G 69
Mallins Cl. L8: Liv 4C 108
Mallory Av. L31: Lyd 7D 32
Mallory Gro. WA11: St. H 7F 61
Mallory Rd. CH42: Tran 6C 106
CH65: Whit 7J 161
Mallowdale Cl. CH62: East 5A 146
Mallow Rd. L6: Liv 4E 88
Mallow Way L36: Huy 7K 91
Malmesbury Cl. CH49: Grea 4A 104
Malmesbury Pk. WA7: Nort 7B 136
Malmesbury Rd. L11: N Grn. 4F 69
Malpas Av. CH43: Pren 6A 106
Malpas Dr. CH63: High B 2E 126
WA5: Gt San 3G 117
Malpas Gro. CH45: Wall 1A 86
Malpas Rd. CH45: Wall 1K 85
CH65: Gt Sut 7H 161
L11: Crox 1B 70
WA7: Run 3D 152
Malpas Way WA5: Gt San 4G 117
Malta Cl. L36: Huy 4H 91
Malta St. L8: Liv 3B 108
Malta Wlk. L8: Liv 3B 108
Malt Ho. Ct. WA10: Windle 7J 59
Maltkiln La. L39: Augh 2B 34
Maltmans Rd.
WA13: Lymm 5F 121
Malton Cl. WA8: Cron 3J 113
Malton Rd. L25: Wltn 7F 111
Malt St. L7: Liv 7D 88 (9P 5)
Malvern Av. CH65: Ell P 1A 170
L14: B Grn 5D 90
Malvern Cl. L32: K'by 1A 56
WA5: Gt San 7E 96
WN3: Wins 1A 50
WN4: Ash M 1F 63
Malvern Ct. PR8: South 2G 11
Malvern Cres. L14: B Grn 5D 90
Malvern Gdns. PR8: South 2G 11
Malvern Gro. CH42: Tran 6D 106
L10: Ain 3E 54
Malvern Rd. CH45: Wall 2H 85
L6: Liv 4E 88
L20: Boot 1J 67
WA9: St. H 3H 75
Malwood St. L8: Liv 4B 108
Manchester Rd. L34: Prsct 1C 92
PR9: South 7J 7
WA1: P'ton, Warr, W'ston 2C 118
WA3: Rix, W'ston 1C 120
Manchester Row WA12: New W 6H 77
Mancroft Cl. WA1: W'ston 1A 120
Mandarin Ct. WA1: Warr 5A 118
Mandela Ct. L8: Liv 3D 108
Manderston Dr. L12: W Der 7B 70
Manderville Cl. WN3: Wins 2B 50
Mandeville Rd. PR8: Ains 4B 14
Mandeville St. L4: Walt 4B 68
Manesty's La. L1: Liv 6K 87 (7F 4)
Manfield WN8: Skel 7G 27
Manfred St. L6: Liv 5B 88 (4M 5)
Manica Cres. L10: Faz 6H 55
Manion Av. L31: Lyd 6D 32
Manion Cl. L31: Lyd 6D 32
Manley Av. WA3: Golb 3K 63
Manley Cl. CH43: O'ton 5K 105
Manley Gdns. WA5: Warr 3K 117
Manley La. WA6: Dun H 7E 172
WA6: Manl 7G 173
Manley Pl. WA9: St. H 7A 74
Manley Quarry WA6: Manl 7K 173
Manley Rd. L22: Water 3C 52
L36: Huy 7A 92
WA6: Alv, Manl 4K 173
WA6: Frod 7D 166
Manley Vw. CH2: Elt 1C 172
Manna Dr. CH2: Elt 1C 172
Mannering Ct. L17: Aig 4E 108
Mannering Rd. L17: Aig 4D 108
Manners La. CH60: Hes 4C 142
Manningham Rd. L4: Walt 1D 88
Manning Rd. PR8: South 2A 12
Manning St. WA10: St. H 3B 74
Mannington Cl. CH47: Meols 7G 83
Mann Island L3: Liv 6H 87 (7C 4)
Mann St. L8: Liv 2K 107
Manor Av. L23: C'by 7D 40
L35: R'hill 5J 93
L40: Burs 1H 25
WA12: New W 2D 76
Manorbier Cres. L9: Walt 3C 68

Manor Cl.—Mavis Dr.

Manor Cl. CH64: Park 4G **157**
L20: Boot 4A **68**
WA1: W'ston 1K **119**
WA13: Lymm 6G **121**
WN4: Gars 2A **62**
Manor Complex L33: Know I 3F **57**
Manor Ct. CH49: Grea 5A **104**
CH61: Irby 4B **124**
PR9: Chu 5C **8**
WA9: Sut L 3F **95**
Manor Cres. L25: Wltn 7F **111**
Manor Dr. CH49: Upton 1D **104**
L23: C'by 7D **40**
L30: N'ton 2D **54**
L40: Burs 1H **25**
Manor Farm Ct. WA6: Frod 2E **166**
Manor Farm Cres. CH1: Cap 4D **168**
Mnr. Farm M. WA7: Mnr P 5B **136**
Mnr. Farm Rd. L36: Huy 6K **91**
WA7: Mnr P 5B **136**
Manor Fell WA7: Pal F 3K **153**
Manorfield Cl. CH1: Cap 3C **168**
Manor Gdns. L40: Burs 1H **25**
MANOR GREEN 1G **105**
Manor Gro. L32: K'by 3K **55**
WN5: Orr 3K **39**
WN8: Skel 2F **37**
Manor Hill CH43: C'ton, O'ton 2A **106**
Manor Ho. CH66: Gt Sut 2F **169**
L17: Aig 5D **108**
Manor Ho., The CH49: Upton 1D **104**
Manor Ho. Cl. L31: Mag 3E **42**
WA11: St. H 4C **60**
Manor Ho. Dr. WN8: Skel 1A **48**
Manor Ho. Flats CH62: Brom 1K **145**
Manorial Rd. CH64: Park 3G **157**
Manorial Rd. Sth. CH64: Park 3G **157**
Manor Ind. Est. WA4: Westy 5E **118**
Manor La. CH42: R Ferr 6G **107**
CH45: Wall 2C **86**
CH66: Gt Sut 1F **169**
Manor Lock WA4: Warr 4E **118**
Manor Lodge L37: Form 6J **19**
Manor M. CH45: Wall 2C **86**
MANOR PARK 5A **136**
Manor Pk. Av. WA7: Mnr P 5A **136**
Manor Park Bus. Pk.
WA7: Mnr P 5K **135**
Manor Pk. Cl. CH61: Thing 3E **124**
Manor Pk. Ct. WA7: Mnr P 5A **136**
Manor Pk. Dr. CH66: Gt Sut 2F **169**
Manor Pl. CH62: Brom 4K **127**
WA8: Wid 7H **113**
Manor Rd. CH44: Wall 2B **86**
CH45: Wall 2B **86**
CH47: Hoy 7E **82**
CH61: Irby 3B **124**
CH62: East 4K **145**
CH63: Thorn H 1K **143**
L23: Blun, C'by 6C **40**
L25: Wltn 7F **111**
L40: Burs 1H **25**
PR9: Chu 5C **8**
WA6: Frod 2E **166**
WA7: Run 7F **135**
WA8: Wid 7H **113**
WA11: Hay 6D **62**
WA13: Lymm 6G **121**
(not continuous)
Manor Road Station (Rail) 1E **102**
Manorside Cl. CH49: Upton 2D **104**
Manor St. WA9: St. H 4E **74**
Manor Vw. L12: W Der 5D **70**
Manor Way CH43: Bid 1G **105**
L25: Wltn 7F **111**
Manorwood Dr. L35: Whis 5E **92**
Mansart Cl. WN4: Ash M 2H **63**
Manse Gdns. WA12: New W 2H **77**
Mansell Cl. WA8: Wid 3D **114**
Mansell Dr. L26: Halew 3J **131**
Mansell Rd. L6: Liv 4D **88**
Mansfield Cl. WA3: Bchwd 3C **100**
Mansfield Rd. CH65: Whit 2J **169**
Mansfield St. L3: Liv 4A **88** (3H **5**)
WA3: Golb 4K **63**
Mansion Dr. L11: Crox 2K **69**
Mansion House 4A **110**
Manston Rd. WA5: Penk 5D **116**
Manton Rd. L6: Liv 4E **88**
Manuel Perez Rd. WA5: Gt San 2F **117**
Manvers Rd. L16: Child 7C **90**
Manville Rd. CH45: New B 7B **66**
Manville St. WA9: St. H 5E **74**
Manx Jane's La. PR9: Chu 3C **8**
Manx Rd. WA4: Warr 5B **118**
Maori Dr. WA6: Frod 3C **166**
Maple Av. CH66: Lit Sut 5E **160**
WA7: Run 2E **152**
WA7: Sut W 6J **153**
WA8: Wid 7D **114**
WA11: Hay 6K **61**
WA12: New W 4H **77**
Maple Cl. L12: Crox 3B **70**
L21: Sea 7G **53**
L35: Whis 4E **92**
L37: Form 2G **29**
WN5: Bil 7F **49**
Maple Ct. L34: Know 2H **71**
Maple Cres. L36: Roby 5H **91**
WA5: Penk 4D **116**
Mapledale Rd. L18: Moss H 3J **109**
Maple Gro. CH62: Brom 2J **145**
CH66: Whit 3J **169**
L8: Liv 2E **108**
L35: Prsct 2E **92**
WA4: Warr 5D **118**
WA10: St. H 3J **73**
Maple Rd. WA1: W'ston 1A **120**
WA2: Win 1B **98**
Maples Ct. CH43: O'ton 5A **106**
Maple St. CH41: Birk 3D **106**
PR8: South 2A **12**
WN4: Ash M 6E **50**
Mapleton Cl. CH43: Pren 7J **105**
Mapleton Dr. WA7: Sut W 7H **153**
Maple Tree Gro. CH60: Hes 1G **143**
Maple Vw. WN8: Skel 5F **37**
Maplewood L32: K'by 5D **56**
PR9: Chu 5B **8**
WN8: Skel 6G **27**
Maplewood Cl. L27: N'ley 3J **111**
WA8: Wid 2G **133**
Maplewood Gro. CH43: Bid 7J **85**
Mapplewell Cres. WA5: Gt San 2E **116**
Marathon Cl. L6: Liv 3B **88** (1L **5**)
Marble Cl. L20: Boot 4J **67**
Marble Pl. Shop. Cen. PR8: South 1H **11**
Marbury Gdns. CH65: Ell P 5H **161**
Marbury Rd. L32: K'by 3A **56**
Marbury St. WA4: Warr 5C **118**
Marc Av. L31: Mell 1K **55**
Marcham Way L11: N Grn. 5K **69**
Marchbank Rd. WN8: Skel 2D **36**
Marchfield Rd. L9: Walt 1B **68**
March Rd. L6: Liv 2F **89**
Marchwiel Rd. CH65: Ell P 7B **162**
Marchwood Way L25: Gate 1E **110**
Marcien Way WA8: Wid 5B **114**
Marcot Rd. L6: Liv 3F **89**
Marcross Cl. WA5: Call 6J **97**
Marcus Ct. L36: Huy 3A **92**
Marcus St. CH41: Birk 1D **106**
Mardale Av. WA2: Warr 4B **98**
WA11: St. H 5D **60**
Mardale Cl. L27: N'ley 4A **112**
PR8: Ains 5B **14**
Mardale Cres. WA13: Lymm 4H **121**
Mardale Lawn L27: N'ley 5A **112**
Mardale Rd. L36: Huy 2G **91**
Mardale Wlk. L27: N'ley 4A **112**
L36: Huy 2G **91**
Mare Hall La. CH64: Nest 3B **158**
Mareth Cl. L18: Moss H 6J **109**
Marford Rd. L12: W Der 7K **69**
Marfords Av. CH63: Brom 3J **145**
Margaret Av. L20: Boot 7J **53**
WA1: W'ston 1H **119**
WA9: St. H 7E **74**
Margaret Ct. WA8: Wid 2D **134**
WA10: St. H 5K **73**
Margaret Rd. L4: Walt 4A **68**
L23: Blun 7A **40**
Margaret's La. CH66: Chil T 4B **160**
Margaret St. L6: Liv 3C **88** (1M **5**)
WA9: Clock F 4G **95**
Margery Rd. WA10: St. H 5J **73**
Marian Av. WA12: New W 3D **76**
Marian Cl. L35: R'hill 5J **93**
Marian Cl., The L30: N'ton 1A **54**
Marian Dr. CH46: More 7C **84**
L35: R'hill 5H **93**
Marian Rd. WA11: Hay 6C **62**
Marians Dr. L39: Orm 2C **24**
Marian Sq. L30: N'ton 2B **54**
Marian Way, The L30: N'ton 1A **54**
Maria Rd. L9: Walt 3B **68**
Marie Curie Av. L30: N'ton 1B **54**
(not continuous)
Marie Dr. WA4: Thel 6K **119**
Marigold Way WA9: Bold 7J **75**
Marina Av. L21: Lith 6H **53**
WA5: Gt San 4F **117**
WA9: St. H 7E **74**
Marina Cres. L30: N'ton 4C **54**
L36: Huy 6H **91**
Marina Dr. CH65: Ell P 6K **161**
(not continuous)
WA2: Warr 6C **98**
Marina Gro. WA7: Run 7D **134**
Marina La. WA7: Murd 3C **154**
Marina Rd. L37: Form 2K **29**
Marina Village WA7: Pres B 3C **154**
Marina Wlk. CH65: Ell P 7K **161**
Marine Cres. L22: Water 4D **52**
Marine Dr. CH60: Hes 3B **142**
PR8: South 1F **11**
PR9: Chu, Cros, Marsh, South 4J **7**
Marine Ga. Mans. PR9: South 7H **7**
Marine Pk. CH48: W Kir 4D **102**
Marine Pk. Mans. CH45: New B 5B **66**
Marine Prom. CH45: New B 5B **66**
Mariner Cl. WA7: Murd 4B **154**
Marine Rd. CH47: Hoy 1C **102**
Mariners Pde. L1: Liv 6J **87** (7E **4**)
Mariners Pk. *CH44: Wall* *2D 86*
(off Cunard Av.)
Mariners Rd. CH45: New B 7C **66**
L23: Blun 3B **52**
Mariners Way L20: Boot 2J **67**
Mariners Wharf L3: Liv 2J **107**
Marine Ter. CH45: Wall 7C **66**
L22: Water 5D **52**
Marine Way PR8: South 7G **7**
Marion Dr. WA7: West 4B **152**
Marion Gro. L18: Moss H 6K **109**
Marion Pl. WN2: Bam 4K **51**
Marion Rd. L20: Boot 7K **53**
Marion St. CH41: Birk 2E **106**
Maritime Cl. WA12: New W 1G **77**
Maritime Ct. CH49: W'chu 7F **105**
L12: W Der 6J **69**
L30: N'ton 7B **42**
PR8: South 1H **11**
Maritime Enterprise Pk. L20: Boot 2H **67**
Maritime Grange CH44: Wall 5E **86**
Maritime Gro. CH43: O'ton 3B **106**
Maritime Lodge *L5: Liv* *1B 88*
(off Towson St.)
Maritime Pk. CH43: O'ton 3C **106**
Maritime Pl. L3: Liv 4A **88** (3J **5**)
Maritime Vw. CH42: Tran 5D **106**
Maritime Way L1: Liv 7K **87** (8F **4**)
Marius Cl. L4: Walt 6B **68**
Mark Av. CH66: Gt Sut 7E **160**
Market App. WN4: Ash M 2F **63**
Market Ga. WA1: Warr 3B **118**
Market Hall *WA7: Run* *6C 134*
(off Alcock St.)
Market Pl. L34: Prsct 1D **92**
WA8: Wid 2C **134**
WA12: New W 3E **76**
Market Pl. Sth. CH41: Birk 2E **106**
Market Sq. L1: Liv 6G **4**
L32: K'by *3C 56*
Market St. CH41: Birk 2E **106**
CH47: Hoy 2D **102**
PR8: South 1G **11**
WA8: Wid 2C **134**
WA10: St. H 3C **74**
WA12: New W 2E **76**
Market Way L1: Liv 6G **4**
L39: Orm 5C **24**
Markfield Cres. L25: Wltn 7G **111**
WA11: St. H 1E **74**
Markfield Rd. L20: Boot 1H **67**
Markham Dr. PR8: South 6A **12**
Markham Gro. CH43: Bid 7K **85**
Mark Rake CH62: Brom 1K **145**
Mark Rd. L38: High 5F **29**
Mark St. CH44: Wall 5E **86**
L5: Liv 7A **68**
Marksway CH61: Pens 5E **124**
Marland WN8: Skel 6G **27**
Marlborough WN8: Skel 6G **27**
Marlborough Av. L30: N'ton 3C **54**
L31: Lyd 1F **43**
Marlborough Cl. L17: Aig 6F **109**
PR9: South 1J **11**
WN8: Skel 6G **27**
Marlborough Cres. WA4: S Hth 6F **119**
WA8: Wid 3C **114**
Marlborough Dr. WA6: Hel 2H **173**
Marlborough Gdns. PR9: South 7J **7**
WN8: Skel 6G **27**
Marlborough Gro. CH43: O'ton 4B **106**
Marlborough Pl. L3: Liv 4J **87** (3E **4**)
Marlborough Rd. CH45: New B 7B **66**
CH65: Ell P 1B **170**
L13: Liv 1F **89**
L22: Water 5E **52**
L23: C'by 2D **52**
L34: Prsct 7E **72**
PR9: South 1J **11**
Marlborough St. L3: Liv 4J **87** (3E **4**)
Marlborough Ter. *PR9: South* *1J 11*
(off Marlborough Rd.)
Marlborough Wlk. CH65: Ell P 1B **170**
Marlborough Way WA11: Hay 5C **62**
Marlbrook Rd. L25: Gate 2F **111**
Marlcroft Dr. L17: Aig 1G **129**
L19: Aig 2H **129**
Marldon Av. L23: C'by 3E **52**
Marldon Rd. L12: W Der 6J **69**
Marled Hey L28: Stock V 6E **70**
Marley Cl. L35: R'hill 6A **94**
Marlfield La. CH61: Pens 5E **124**
Marlfield Rd. L12: W Der 1K **89**
WA4: Grap 6G **119**
Marl Gro. WN5: Orr 7F **39**
Marline Av. CH63: Brom 3J **145**
Marling Cl. WA6: Frod 5F **167**
Marling Pk. WA8: Wid 7H **113**
Marlow Cl. WA3: Bchwd 2J **99**
Marlowe Cl. L19: Gars 4A **130**
WA8: Wid 7B **114**
Marlowe Dr. L12: W Der 1H **89**
Marlowe Rd. CH44: Wall 3A **86**
CH64: Nest 3J **157**
Marl Rd. L30: N'ton 2D **54**
L33: Know I 2G **57**
Marlsford St. L6: Liv 4E **88**
Marlston Av. CH61: Irby 4D **124**
Marlston Pl. WA7: Run 4D **152**
Marlwood Av. CH45: Wall 2J **85**
Marmaduke St. L7: Liv 6D **88** (6P **5**)
Marmion Av. L20: Boot 6A **54**
Marmion Rd. CH47: Hoy 1D **102**
L17: Aig 4D **108**
Marmonde St. L4: Kirk 6A **68**
Marnwood Rd. L32: K'by 4A **56**
Marnwood Wlk. L32: K'by 4A **56**
Marple Cl. CH43: O'ton 5J **105**
Marquis Ho. CH62: New F 1H **127**
Marquis St. CH41: Tran 4E **106**
CH62: New F 1H **127**
L3: Liv 5A **88** (5J **5**)
Marram Cl. CH46: More 6E **84**
Marrick Cl. WN3: Wigan 2E **50**
Marron Av. WA2: Warr 5B **98**
Marryat Cl. WA2: Win 1A **98**
Marsden Av. WA4: Westy 4G **119**
WA10: St. H 2J **73**
Marsden Cl. CH44: Wall 2D **86**
Marsden Ct. WA8: Wid 4A **114**
Marsden Rd. L26: Halew 3K **131**
PR9: South 1A **12**
Marsden St. L6: Liv 4C **88** (3M **5**)
WN3: Ince M 1K **51**
Marsden Way L6: Liv 4C **88** (3M **5**)
MARSH, THE 4A **134**
Marshall Av. WA5: Warr 5K **97**
WA9: St. H 6E **74**
Marshall Cl. L33: K'by 7D **44**
Marshall Pl. L3: Liv 3J **87** (1E **4**)
Marshall Rd. WA1: W'ston 1K **119**
Marshallsay L37: Form 1A **30**
Marshall's Cl. L31: Lyd 7E **32**
MARSHALL'S CROSS 1C **94**
Marshall's Cross Rd. WA9: St. H 1D **94**
Marshall St. CH41: Birk 7C **86**
Marsham Cl. CH49: Upton 1E **104**
Marsham Rd. L25: Gate 3G **111**
Marsh Av. L20: Boot 7A **54**
Marsh Brows L37: Form 1J **29**
Marshfield Cl. L36: Huy 4K **91**
Marshfield Ct. CH46: Leas 4C **84**
Marshfield Rd. L11: N Grn. 5K **69**
Marshgate WA8: Wid 2H **133**
Marshgate Pl. WA6: Frod 1E **166**
Marshgate Rd. L12: W Der 4K **69**
MARSH GREEN 3C **166**
Marsh Hall Pad WA8: Wid 4D **114**
Marsh Hall Rd. WA8: Wid 4D **114**
Marsh Ho. La. WA1: Warr 1C **118**
WA2: Warr 1C **118**
Marshside Sands Nature Reserve 2J **7**
Marshlands Rd. CH45: Wall 1J **85**
CH64: Lit N 6H **157**
Marsh La. CH2: Elt 7B **164**
CH2: Ince 5K **163**
CH63: High B 2C **126**
L20: Boot 2G **67**
L38: Ince B 5C **30**
L40: Scar 2B **24**
WA4: Dutt, Lwr Wh 6H **155**
WA5: Cuerd 6A **116**
WA6: Frod 3C **166**
WA6: Hel 5C **164**
WA7: Ast 6H **135**
Marsh Rd. WA4: App T 5H **139**
MARSHSIDE 4C **8**
Marshside Cl. L8: Liv 3B **108**
Marshside Rd. PR9: Chu 2A **8**
Marsh St. L20: Kirk 5K **67**
WA1: Warr 1D **118**
WA8: Wid 3C **134**
WA9: St. H 2E **74**
Marshway Dr. WA12: New W 2F **77**
Marsland Gro. WA9: St. H 6G **75**
Marson St. WA2: Warr 2A **118**
Marston Cl. CH43: O'ton 5K **105**
CH62: East 7A **146**
Marston Cres. L38: High 7G **29**
Marston Gdns. CH65: Ell P 5H **161**
Marten Av. CH63: Brom 3J **145**
Martensen St. L7: Liv 6D **88** (6P **5**)
Martham Cl. WA4: Grap 5G **119**
Martin Av. WA2: Warr 6E **98**
WA10: St. H 7B **60**
WA12: New W 1F **77**
Martin Cl. CH61: Irby 3A **124**
L18: Moss H 7J **109**
L35: R'hill 3G **93**
WA7: Pal F 3J **153**
Martindale Gro. WA7: Beech 5G **153**
Martindale Rd. CH62: Brom 1A **146**
L18: Moss H 3B **110**
WA11: St. H 3D **60**
Martine Cl. L31: Mell 1K **55**
Martin Gro. L35: Prsct 2E **92**
Martinhall Rd. L9: Faz 2H **69**
Martin Rd. L18: Moss H 7J **109**
WA6: Frod 3D **166**
MARTINSCROFT 1A **120**
Martinscroft Grn. WA1: W'ston 1B **120**
Martins La. WN8: Skel 4K **37**
CH44: Wall 3C **86**
Martland Av. L10: Ain 2G **55**
Martland Rd. L25: Gate 4G **111**
Martlesham Cres. CH49: Grea 5K **103**
Martlett Rd. L12: W Der 2B **90**
Martock L35: Whis 5F **93**
Marton Cl. L24: Speke 7H **131**
WA3: Cul 2A **80**
Marton Grn. L24: Speke 7H **131**
Marton Rd. L36: Huy 1J **91**
Marus Av. WN3: Wigan 1D **50**
Marus Bri. Retail Pk.
WN3: Wigan 2D **50**
Marvin St. L6: Liv 4C **88** (3N **5**)
Marwood Towers L5: Liv 1K **87**
Mary Av. PR8: Ains 3E **14**
Marybone L3: Liv 4J **87** (4E **4**)
Maryfield Cl. WA3: Golb 6K **63**
Maryhill Rd. WA7: Run 2C **152**
Maryland Cl. WA5: Gt San 1G **117**
Maryland Ho. *L20: Boot* *3J 67*
(off Georgia Cl.)
Maryland La. CH46: More 6B **84**
Maryland St. L1: Liv 7A **88** (8J **5**)
(not continuous)
Marylebone Av. WA9: St. H 1B **94**
Mary Rd. L20: Boot 7K **53**
Mary St. WA8: Wid 2F **135**
WA9: Clock F 4G **95**
Maryton Grange L18: Aller 6B **110**
Maryville Cl. CH65: Ell P 5A **162**
Maryville Rd. L34: Prsct 1E **92**
Marywell Cl. WA9: St. H 7F **75**
Marzhan Way WA8: Wid 7E **114**
Masefield Av. WA8: Wid 1B **134**
WN5: Orr 5J **39**
Masefield Cl. CH62: New F 2G **127**
Masefield Cres. L30: Boot 5K **53**
Masefield Dr. WA2: Win 2A **98**
Masefield Gro. L16: Child 7C **90**
WA10: St. H 1K **73**
Masefield Pl. L30: Boot 5K **53**
Masefield Rd. L23: Thorn 6J **41**
Maskell Rd. L13: Liv 4H **89**
Mason Av. WA1: P'gate 7E **98**
WA8: Wid 4C **114**
Mason Cl. CH66: Gt Sut 2F **169**
WN4: Ash M 1H **63**
Mason St. CH45: New B 6B **66**
L7: Liv 6C **88** (6N **5**)
L22: Water 4D **52**
L25: Wltn 6E **110**
WA1: Warr 3C **118**
WA7: Run 6E **134**
Massam's La. L37: Form 4J **19**
Massey Av. WA5: Warr 5K **97**
WA13: Lymm 6C **120**
Massey Brook La.
WA13: Lymm 6C **120**
Masseyfield Rd. WA7: Brook 5J **153**
Massey Pk. CH45: Wall 2A **86**
Massey St. CH41: Birk 7D **86**
WA9: St. H 6E **74**
Master's Way L19: Gars 5B **130**
Matchwood Cl. L19: Gars 4B **130**
Matchworks, The L19: Gars 4C **130**
Mather Av. L18: Moss H 4C **109**
L19: Aller 4K **109**
WA7: West P 3K **151**
WA9: St. H 3G **75**
Mather Ct. CH43: O'ton 3B **106**
Mather Rd. CH43: O'ton 3B **106**
Mathers Cl. WA2: Fearn 3G **99**
Mathew St. L2: Liv 6J **87** (6E **4**)
Mathew Street Gallery 6J **87** (6F **4**)
Mathieson Rd. WA8: Wid 4A **134**
Matlock Av. L9: Walt 7C **54**
PR8: South 4H **11**
Matlock Cl. PR8: South 4H **11**
WA5: Gt San 7E **96**
Matlock Cres. PR8: South 4H **11**
Matlock Rd. PR8: B'dale 5H **11**
Matterdale Cl. WA6: Frod 4F **167**
Matthew Cl. CH44: Wall 5E **86**
Matthews St. WA1: Warr 1D **118**
Matthew St. CH44: Wall 5E **86**
Matty's La. WA6: Frod 4C **166**
Maud Roberts Ct. L21: Lith 5G **53**
Maud St. L8: Liv 2B **108**
Maunders Ct. L23: C'by 7G **41**
Maureen Wlk. L10: Faz 6K **55**
Mauretania Rd. L4: Walt 4C **68**
Maurice Jones Ct. CH46: More 6C **84**
Mavis Dr. CH49: W'chu 6E **104**

Middlewood Cl.—Moorwood Cres.

Middlewood Cl. L39: Augh 4A 34
Middlewood Dr. L39: Augh 4A 34
Middlewood Rd. L39: Augh 3A 34
Midge Hall La. PR9: South 4K 13
Midghall St. L3: Liv 4J 87 (3E 4)
Midhurst Dr. PR8: Ains 5B 14
Midhurst Rd. L12: Crox 3D 70
Midland St. CH43: O'ton 3C 106
WA8: Wid 7D 114
Midland Ter. L22: Water 4D 52
Midland Way WA1: Warr 3A 118
Midlothian Dr. L23: Blun 1C 52
Midway Rd. L36: Huy 3J 91
Midwood St. WA8: Wid 1D 134
Milbrook Cres. L32: K'by 2C 56
Milbrook Dr. L32: K'by 2C 56
Milbrook Wlk. L32: K'by 2C 56
Mildenhall Cl. WA5: Gt San 2F 117
Mildenhall Rd. L25: Gate 2E 110
Mildenhall Way L25: Gate 1E 110
Mildmay Rd. L11: N Grn. 4G 69
L20: Boot 1H 67
Mile End L5: Liv 3K 87 (1F 4)
Miles Cl. CH49: Grea 6A 104
WA3: Bchwd 4B 100
Miles La. CH49: Grea 6A 104
Miles St. L8: Liv 3C 108
Milestone Hey L28: Stock V 6F 71
Milford Cl. L37: Form 2G 29
Milford Dr. L12: Crox 3C 70
Milford Gdns. WA4: App 5D 138
Milford St. L5: Kirk 1H 87
Milk St. WA10: St. H 3C 74
Millachip Ct. L6: Liv 2D 88
Milland Cl. L11: Crox 3A 70
Millar Cres. WA8: Wid 2C 134
Millar's Pace PR9: Marsh 2D 8
Mill Av. WA5: Gt San 1C 116
Mill Bank CH64: Ness 6A 158
L13: Liv 1H 89
Millbank WA13: Lymm 5G 121
Millbank Cotts. L31: Mag 1G 43
WA6: Frod 3C 166
Millbank Ct. L9: Ain 5F 55
WA6: Frod 3C 166
Millbank La. L31: Augh, Mag 1H 43
Mill Bank Rd. CH44: Wall 4A 86
Millbeck Cl. L33: K'by 1C 56
Millbeck Gro. WA11: St. H 3D 60
Millbridge Gdns. WA12: New W 3J 77
Millbrook PR8: South 4H 11
Millbrook Bus. Pk. WA11: R'ford 2J 59
Millbrook Cl. WA3: G'bury 1E 80
WN8: Skel 1E 36
Millbrook Ct. L34: Know 1G 71
Millbrook La. WA10: Eccl 2H 73
Millbrook Rd. CH41: Birk 5B 86
Mill Brow CH63: High B 3D 126
WA8: Wid 6E 114
WA9: Sut L 2F 95
WA10: Eccl 2H 73
Mill Brow Cl. WA9: Sut L 2F 95
Millburn Hgts. L5: Liv 2A 88
Millbutt Cl. CH63: High B 3D 126
Mill Cl. CH42: Tran 4D 106
L23: C'by 6E 40
WA2: Fearn 4E 98
Mill Ct. CH65: Ell P 5H 161
L30: N'ton 7K 41
Mill Cft. CH64: Nest 2J 157
Millcroft L23: C'by 7G 41
Millcroft Av. WN5: Orr 6F 39
Millcroft Pk. CH49: Grea 5K 103
Millcroft Rd. L25: Wltn 7G 111
Mill Dam Cl. L40: Burs 1G 25
Mill Dam La. L40: Burs 1G 25
Millenium Wlk. WA5: Gt San 1F 117
(off Arizona Cres. not continuous)
Millennium Ct. Ind. Est.
CH64: Nest 1J 157
Millennium Rd. L8: Liv 2C 108
Miller Av. L23: C'by 7D 40
Millers Bri. L20: Boot 4H 67
Millers Bri. Ind. Est. L20: Boot 4H 67
Millers Cl. CH46: More 7K 83
Millers Ct. L39: Orm 5D 24
Millerscroft L32: K'by 2A 56
Millersdale WA9: Clock F 3E 94
Millersdale Av. L9: Ain 6D 54
Millersdale Cl. CH62: East 5B 146
Millersdale Gro. WA7: Beech 4F 153
Millersdale Rd. L18: Moss H 4J 109
Millers Fold WA10: Eccl 2H 73
Millers La. WA13: Lymm 3K 121
WN2: Platt B 2K 51
Millers Nook WN8: Uph 4D 38
Miller St. WA4: Warr 4C 118
Millers Way CH46: More 7A 84
Millervale Ho. WN2: Platt B 3K 51
(off Miller's La.)
Mill Farm Cl. WA2: Warr 4E 98
Millfield CH64: Nest 2J 157
WN8: Parb 1J 27
Millfield Bus. Pk. WA11: Hay 5C 62
Millfield Cl. CH63: High B 4D 126
L13: W Der 2J 89
Millfield La. WA11: Hay 5D 62
WN4: Ash M 3C 62
Millfield Rd. WA8: Wid 6E 114
Millfields WA10: Eccl 3G 73
Millfield Ter. CH66: Lit Sut 4E 160
Mill Gdns. L39: Orm 5D 24
Mill Grn. CH64: Will 3F 159
Millgreen Cl. L12: Crox 3C 70
WN8: Uph 4C 38
Mill Grn. La. WA8: Wid 3F 115
Mill Gro. L21: Lith 5H 53
Mill Hey L35: R'hill 6A 94
Mill Hey Rd. CH48: Caldy 3F 123
Mill Hill CH43: O'ton 5A 106
Mill Hill Rd. CH61: Irby 1A 124
Millhouse Av. WA4: S Hth 7D 118
Millhouse Cl. CH46: More 6K 83
Millhouse Ct. L12: W Der 1J 89
Mill Ho. La. WA3: Bchwd, Croft 1G 99
Millhouse La. CH46: More 6K 83
Mill House Lodge PR8: Ains 4D 14
Mill Ho. Vw. WN8: Uph 4E 38
Millingford Av. WA3: Golb 3K 63
Millingford Gro. WN4: Ash M 2F 63
Millington Cl. CH43: Pren 7J 105
WA7: Sut W 6H 153
WA8: Wid 1B 134
Mill La. CH44: Wall 4A 86
CH49: Grea 5A 104
CH60: Hes 2F 143
CH64: Ness 6A 158
CH64: Will 2E 158
CH66: Ell P, Gt Sut 7F 161
L3: Liv 5K 87 (4G 4)
L12: W Der 1J 89
L13: Liv 5J 89
L15: W'tree 5J 89
L20: Boot 3K 67
L32: K'by 2A 56
L34: Know 1H 71
L35: R'hill 5J 93
L39: Augh 2H 33
PR9: Chu 6C 8
WA2: Hou G 3E 98
WA2: Win 4A 98
(Cameron Ct.)
WA2: Win 2J 97
(Watery La.)
WA4: H Walt 2J 137
WA4: S Hth 7D 118
(not continuous)
WA5: Warr 3J 117
WA6: Frod 1F 167
WA8: Cron 3K 113
WA8: Wid, Bold H 4E 114
WA9: Sut L 2E 94
WA11: R'ford 2H 59
WA12: New W 3J 77
WN8: Dalt, Uph 1B 38
WN8: Parb 1J 27
Mill La. Cres. PR9: Chu 6C 8
Mill La. Ind. Est. CH2: Lit Stan 3D 170
Mill Leat Cl. WN8: Parb 1J 27
Mill Leat M. WN8: Parb 1J 27
Mill Mdw. WA12: New W 3J 77
Millom Av. L35: R'hill 3H 93
Millom Gro. L12: W Der 5A 70
WA10: St. H 6J 73
Mill Pk. Dr. CH62: East 7A 146
Millport Cl. WA2: Fearn 5G 99
Mill Ri. WA6: Hel 7J 165
Mill Rd. CH61: Thing 3F 125
CH62: Brom 6K 127
CH63: High B 2D 126
L6: Liv 3B 88 (1L 5)
(not continuous)
PR8: Ains 4D 14
WN5: Orr 6F 39
Millrose Cl. WN8: Skel 1F 37
Mill Spring Ct. L20: Boot 3K 67
Mill Sq. L10: Ain 3G 55
Millstead Rd. L15: W'tree 7J 89
Millstead Wlk. L15: W'tree 7J 89
Mill Stile L25: Wltn 6D 110
Mill St. CH42: Tran 4D 106
CH64: Nest 3H 157
L8: Liv 2A 108
L25: Wltn 6E 110
L34: Prsct 1D 92
L39: Orm 6D 24
PR8: South 2J 11
WA10: St. H 2B 74
WN4: Ash M 3G 63
Mill Ter. CH63: High B 4D 126
Millthwaite Ct. CH44: Wall 3K 85
Millthwaite Rd. CH44: Wall 3K 85
Millvale St. L6: Liv 4D 88
Mill Vw. L8: Liv 3A 108
L32: K'by 1A 56
Mill Vw. Ct. L39: Bic 5H 35
Mill Vw. Dr. CH63: High B 3C 126
Millway Rd. L24: Speke 5A 132
Millwood CH63: High B 3D 126
WA7: Nort 1A 154
Millwood Av. WA10: Eccl 3F 73
Millwood Cl. WN4: Ash M 7E 50
Millwood Ct. L24: Speke 5A 132
Millwood Est. L24: Speke 6A 132
Millwood Gdns. L35: Whis 5F 93
Millwood Rd. L24: Speke 5J 131
MILL YARD 3B 90
Mill Yd. CH61: Thing 3F 125
Milman Cl. CH49: Upton 4D 104
L39: Orm 7B 24
Milman Ct. L25: Wltn 5C 110
Milman Rd. L4: Walt 5B 68
Milner Cop CH60: Hes 2E 142
Milne Rd. L13: Liv 6G 69
Milner Rd. CH60: Hes 2E 142
L17: Aig 7G 109
Milner St. CH41: Birk 7A 86
WA5: Warr 3K 117
Milnthorpe Cl. L4: Kirk 6A 68
Milnthorpe Rd. WA5: B'wood 1C 96
Milnthorpe St. L19: Gars 3A 130
Milroy St. L7: Liv 6D 88
Milton Av. L14: B Grn 5D 90
L35: Whis 4E 92
WA8: Wid 1B 134
WA12: New W 3F 77
Milton Cl. CH65: Ell P 7B 162
L35: Whis 4E 92
Milton Cres. CH60: Hes 1E 142
Milton Dr. L39: Orm 6E 24
Milton Grn. CH61: Thing 3F 125
Milton Gro. WA4: Latch 5D 118
WA6: Hel 3G 173
WN5: Bil 3F 49
WN5: Orr 5J 39
Milton Pavement CH41: Birk 2D 106
Milton Rd. CH42: Tran 4C 106
CH44: Wall 5D 86
CH48: W Kir 5C 102
CH65: Ell P 7B 162
L4: Walt 4A 68
L7: Liv 5G 89
L22: Water 3E 52
WA8: Wid 1B 134
Milton Rd. E. CH42: Tran 4D 106
Milton St. L20: Boot 2H 67
PR9: South 1B 12
WA8: Wid 4C 134
WA9: Sut M 5C 94
Milton Way L31: Mag 2D 42
Milvain Dr. WA2: Warr 6C 98
Milverny Way WA9: St. H 4C 74
Milverton St. L6: Liv 3E 88
Mimosa Cl. CH2: Elt 7C 164
Mimosa Rd. L15: W'tree 1J 109
Mindale Rd. L15: W'tree 7H 89
Minehead Gro. WA9: Sut L 2F 95
Minehead Rd. L17: Aig 7G 109
Miners Way L24: Speke 6A 132
WA8: Wid 2C 134
Minerva Cl. WA4: Latch 6D 118
Mines Av. L17: Aig 2H 129
L34: Prsct 1E 92
Mine Way WA11: Hay 6D 62
Minshull St. L7: Liv 6C 88 (6M 5)
Minstead Av. L33: K'by 3D 56
Minster Ct. L7: Liv 7C 88 (8M 5)
WA7: Run 2A 152
Minto Cl. L7: Liv 5D 88
Minton Cl. L12: Crox 3D 70
Minton Way WA8: Wid 3D 114
Mintor Rd. L33: K'by 3E 56
Minto St. L7: Liv 5D 88
Minver Rd. L12: W Der 7B 70
Miranda Av. CH63: High B 2E 126
Miranda Pl. L20: Kirk 5K 67
Miranda Rd. L20: Boot 4K 67
Mirfield Cl. L26: Halew 3K 131
Mirfield St. L6: Liv 4D 88
Miriam Pl. CH41: Birk 7K 85
Miriam Rd. L4: Walt 1C 88
Miskelly St. L20: Kirk 6J 67
Missouri Rd. L13: Liv 7F 69
Mistle Thrush Way L12: Crox 2D 70
Miston St. L20: Kirk 6J 67
Misty Cl. WA8: Wid 6J 113
Mitchell Av. WA5: B'wood 2C 96
Mitchell Cres. L21: Lith 5H 53
Mitchell Pl. L1: Liv 6H 5
Mitchell Rd. L34: Prsct 1C 92
WA10: St. H 5J 73
WN5: Bil 7G 49
Mitchell St. WA3: Golb 5K 63
WA4: S Hth 1C 138
WN4: Ash M 3G 63
Mithril Cl. WA8: Wid 5G 115
Mitre Cl. L35: Whis 6D 92
Mitten's La. L37: Form 6A 20
Mitton Cl. WA3: Cul 1K 79
Mitylene St. L5: Liv 1A 88
Moat La. WA3: Rix 5G 101
Mobberley Cl. WA4: Thel 5K 119
Mobberley Way CH63: Spit 6G 127
Mockbeggar Dr. CH45: Wall 7J 65
Mockbeggar Wharf CH45: Wall 7J 65
Model Railway Village 1G 11
Modred St. L8: Liv 3B 108
Moel Famau Vw. L17: Aig 6D 108
Moffatdale Rd. L4: Walt 6E 68
Moffatt Rd. L9: Ain 6D 54
Moira Sephton Ct. CH43: Noct 4H 105
Moira St. L6: Liv 5B 88 (4L 5)
Molesworth Gro. L16: Child 6C 90
Molineux Av. L14: B Grn 6B 90
Molland Cl. L12: W Der 6B 70
Mollington Av. L11: N Grn. 4H 69
Mollington Link CH41: Birk 3E 106
Mollington Rd. CH44: Wall 4C 86
L32: K'by 3A 56
Mollington St. CH41: Birk 3E 106
Molly Pitcher Way WA5: Gt San 3F 117
Molly's La. L33: Know 6H 57
Molton Rd. L16: Child 7A 90
Molyneux Av. WA5: Warr 7K 97
Molyneux Cl. CH49: Upton 3D 104
L35: Prsct 3D 92
L36: Huy 5K 91
Molyneux Ct. L11: N Grn. 3K 69
L14: B Grn 5B 90
Molyneux Dr. CH45: New B 6B 66
L35: Prsct 3D 92
Molyneux Rd. L6: Liv 4D 88 (3P 5)
L18: Moss H 4H 109
L22: Water 3E 52
L31: Mag 5H 43
L39: Augh 4A 34
Molyneux Way L10: Ain 2E 54
Monaghan Cl. L9: Walt 6C 54
Monash Cl. L33: K'by 6C 44
Monash Rd. L11: N Grn. 6G 69
Monastery La. WA9: St. H 7F 75
Monastery Rd. L6: Liv 1E 88
WA9: St. H 7G 75
Mona St. CH41: Birk 1K 105
L20: Boot 7K 53
WA10: St. H 3K 73
Mond Rd. L10: Faz 6H 55
WA8: Wid 1C 134
Monfa Rd. L20: Boot 7J 53
Monica Dr. WA8: Wid 3C 114
Monica Rd. L25: Wltn 7F 111
Monica Ter. WN4: Ash M 3F 63
Monkfield Way L19: Gars 5B 130
Monk Rd. CH44: Wall 3B 86
Monks Carr La. L38: Gt Alt 5G 31
Monks Cl. L37: Form 2A 30
Monksdown Rd. L11: N Grn. 5J 69
Monks Dr. L37: Form 2A 30
Monks Ferry CH41: Birk 2F 107
Monksferry Wlk. L19: Gras 2H 129
Monks Gro. CH65: Ell P 5K 161
Monks St. WA5: Warr 2J 117
Monk St. CH41: Birk 2F 107
L5: Liv 1B 88
Monks Way CH48: W Kir 6E 102
CH63: Beb 5F 127
L25: Wltn 6F 111
WA7: Pres B 5C 154
Monkswell Dr. L15: W'tree 7J 89
Monkswell St. L8: Liv 5C 108
Monkswood Cl. WA5: Call 5J 97
Monmouth Cl. WA1: W'ston 1A 120
Monmouth Cres. WN4: Ash M 3G 63
Monmouth Dr. L10: Ain 4H 55
Monmouth Gro. WA9: St. H 4F 75
Monmouth Rd. CH44: Wall 3K 85
Monro Cl. L8: Liv 4B 108
Monroe Cl. WA1: W'ston 1H 119
WN3: Wigan 1E 50
Monro St. L8: Liv 4B 108
Mons Sq. L20: Boot 3J 67
Montague Rd. L13: Liv 5J 89
WA8: Wid 3G 133
Montagu M. L37: Form 5J 19
Montagu Rd. L37: Form 4J 19
Montana Cl. WA5: Gt San 1G 117
Montclair Dr. L18: Moss H 2K 109
Montclare Cres. WA4: S Hth 6E 118
Montcliffe Cl. WA3: Bchwd 2J 99
Monterey Rd. L13: Liv 5K 89
Montfort Dr. L19: Gras 2J 129
Montgomery Av. PR9: South 2C 12
Montgomery Cl. L35: Whis 5D 92
WA5: Gt San 7E 96
Montgomery Hill
CH48: Caldy, Frank 1H 123
Montgomery Rd. L9: Walt 6C 54
L36: Huy 3H 91
WA8: Wid 1K 133
Montgomery Way L6: Liv 3D 88
Montpelier Av. WA7: West 4B 152
Montpelier Dr. L8: Liv 4B 108
Montpellier Cres. CH45: New B 6A 66
Montpellier Ho. CH45: New B 6A 66
Montreal Rd. L27: N'ley 3J 111
Montrey Cres. WN4: Gars 2A 62
Montrose Av. CH44: Wall 6E 86
WN5: Wigan 3K 39
Montrose Bus. Pk. L7: Liv 5G 89
Montrose Cl. WA2: Fearn 3F 99
Montrose Ct. CH47: Hoy 2D 102
L12: W Der 7D 70
Montrose Dr. PR9: Chu 6B 8
Montrose Pl. L26: Halew 3K 131
Montrose Rd. L13: Liv 1F 89
Montrose Way L13: Liv 5H 89
Montrovia Cres. L10: Faz 6H 55
Monument Pl. L3: Liv 5A 88 (5J 5)
Monville Rd. L9: Ain 6E 54
Moorbridge Cl. L30: N'ton 1C 54
Moor Cl. L23: C'by 7F 41
PR8: Ains 7C 14
Moor Coppice L23: C'by 7F 41
Moor Ct. L10: Faz 6J 55
Moorcroft Rd. CH45: Wall 2H 85
L18: Aller 7A 110
Moorditch La. WA6: Frod 2J 165
(not continuous)
Moor Dr. L23: C'by 7E 40
WN8: Skel 4K 37
MOORE 4F 137
Moore Av. CH42: R Ferr 6E 106
WA4: Thel 5K 119
WA9: St. H 3J 75
Moore Cl. WA8: Wid 6F 115
Moore Dr. WA11: Hay 6D 62
Moore Gro. WA13: Lymm 3K 121
Moore Nature Reserve 1G 137
Moore's Ho. L4: Walt 4B 68
Moore St. L20: Boot 1H 67
Mooreway L35: R'hill 6A 94
Moorfield L33: K'by 7D 44
Moorfield Cen. L33: K'by 6D 44
Moorfield Dr. CH64: Park 1G 157
Moorfield La. L40: Scar 6K 17
Moorfield Rd. L23: C'by 7G 41
WA8: Wid 4F 115
WA10: St. H 1J 73
Moorfields L2: Liv 5J 87 (5E 4)
Moorfields Av. CH43: Noct 4H 105
Moorfields Station (Rail) 5J 87 (5E 4)
Moorfoot Rd. WA9: St. H 3H 75
Moorfoot Rd. Ind. Est.
WA9: St. H 2H 75
Moorfoot Way L33: K'by 6B 44
Moorgate L39: Orm 6C 24
Moorgate Av. L23: C'by 2F 53
Moorgate La. L32: K'by 5E 56
Moorgate Point L33: Know I 6E 56
Moorgate Rd. L33: K'by 7D 56
Moorgate Rd. Sth. L34: Know 7D 56
Moorgate St. L7: Liv 6D 88
Moorhead Cl. L21: Lith 6G 53
Moorhey Rd. L31: Mag 6E 42
Moor Ho. L23: C'by 7E 40
Mooring Cl. WA7: Murd 4B 154
Moorings, The CH41: Birk 3D 106
CH60: Hes 2A 142
L31: Lyd 7D 32
Moorings Cl. CH64: Park 2F 157
Moorland Av. L23: C'by 7E 40
Moorland Cl. CH60: Hes 3E 142
Moorland Dr. WA7: Murd 3C 154
Moorland Pk. CH60: Hes 3E 142
Moorland Rd. CH42: Tran 5E 106
CH66: Ell P 3G 161
L31: Mag 6E 42
WN4: Ash M 1J 63
Moorlands Rd. L23: Thorn 6H 41
Moor La. CH60: Hes 2E 142
L4: Walt 3B 68
L10: Faz 5K 55
L23: C'by 7E 40
L23: C'by, Thorn 7E 40
L29: Seft 4K 41
L32: K'by 5K 55
L38: Ince B 7D 30
PR8: Ains 7C 14
WA6: Frod 3D 166
WA6: Hap 2E 172
WA8: Wid 2B 134
(not continuous)
Moor La. Bus. Cen. WA8: Wid 2C 134
Moor La. Sth. WA8: Wid 2B 134
MOOR PARK 6E 40
Moor Pl. L3: Liv 5A 88 (5J 5)
Moor Rd. WN5: Orr 6F 39
MOORSIDE 4G 157
Moorside WA4: Westy 4E 118
Moorside Av. CH64: Park 3G 157
Moorside Cl. L23: C'by 1F 53
Moorside Ct. WA8: Wid 2B 134
Moorside La. CH64: Park 4G 157
Moorside Rd. L23: C'by 1F 53
Moorside Wlk. WN5: Orr 3K 39
Moor St. L2: Liv 6J 87 (6D 4)
L39: Orm 5C 24
(not continuous)
Moorway CH60: Hes 2F 143
Moorwood Cres. WA9: Clock F 3E 94

Moran Dr.—Netherfield Rd. Sth.

Moran Dr. WA5: Gt San 2E 116
Morano Dr. WN2: Platt B 1K 51
Moray Cl. WA10: St. H 1A 74
Morcott La. L24: Hale 7D 132
Morcroft Rd. L36: Huy 2J 91
Morden Av. WN4: Ash M 1E 62
Morden St. L6: Liv 3E 88
Morecambe St. L6: Liv 2E 88
Morecroft Rd. CH42: R Ferr 6G 107
Morella Rd. L4: Walt 6E 68
Morello Cl. WA10: St. H 1B 74
Morello Dr. CH63: Spit 7H 127
Moresby Cl. WA7: Murd 3C 154
Moret Cl. L23: C'by 7G 41
MORETON 7C 84
Moreton Av. WA9: Clock F 3E 94
Moreton Cl. WA3: Golb 4K 63
MORETON COMMON 3B 84
Moreton Gro. CH45: Wall 1J 85
Moreton Rd. CH49: Upton 1D 104
Moreton Station (Rail) 5C 84
Moreton Ter. WA6: Frod 3C 166
Morgan Av. WA2: Warr 5C 98
Morgan M. L30: N'ton 2K 53
Morgan St. WA9: St. H 4F 75
Morland Av. CH62: Brom 4K 145
CH64: Lit N 4K 157
Morley Av. CH41: Birk 7B 86
Morley Ct. L14: K Ash 3C 90
Morley La. WA6: Hel 7F 173
Morley Rd. CH44: Wall 4A 86
PR9: South 6A 8
WA4: Warr 7A 118
WA7: Run 1C 152
Morley St. L4: Walt 7A 68
WA1: Warr 2C 118
Morley St. WA10: St. H 1B 74
(not continuous)
Morley Way WA10: St. H 2B 74
Morningside L23: C'by 2F 53
Morningside Pl. L11: N Grn. 5H 69
Morningside Rd. L11: N Grn. 5G 69
Morningside Vw. L11: N Grn. 6H 69
Morningside Way L11: N Grn. 6H 69
Mornington Av. CH65: Ell P 6A 162
L23: C'by 3E 52
Mornington Rd. CH45: New B 7B 66
PR9: South 1J 11
Mornington St. L8: Liv 3A 108
Morpeth Cl. CH46: More 7K 83
Morpeth Rd. CH47: Hoy 3C 102
Morpeth St. L8: Liv 1B 108 (10K 5)
Morpeth Wharf CH41: Birk 7E 86
Morphany La. WA4: Dares 4J 155
Morris Av. WA4: Westy 4F 119
Morris Cl. WA11: Hay 1H 75
Morris Ct. CH43: O'ton 3K 105
Morris Hey L39: Hals 6F 17
Morris La. L39: Hals 6F 17
Morrison Cl. WA5: Gt San 3E 116
Morris Rd. WN8: Uph 4C 38
Morrissey Cl. WA10: St. H 2K 73
Morris St. WA9: St. H 5G 75
Morston Av. L32: K'by 5C 56
Morston Cres. L32: K'by 5C 56
Morston Wlk. L32: K'by 5C 56
Mortar Mill Quay CH41: Birk 6D 86
Mort Av. WA4: Westy 4G 119
Mortimer Av. WA2: Warr 7B 98
Mortimer St. CH41: Birk 1F 107
Mortlake Cl. WA8: Wid 5J 113
Morton Av. WA6: Hel 3H 173
Morton Cl. WA5: Old H 7G 97
WN3: Wins 2A 50
Morton Ho. L18: Moss H 5H 109
Morton Rd. WA7: Nort 2B 154
Morton St. L8: Liv 3B 108
(not continuous)
Mortuary Rd. CH45: Wall 1B 86
Morvah Cl. L12: W Der 4A 70
Morval Cres. L4: Walt 4A 68
WA7: Run 1F 153
Morven Cl. WA2: Warr 4E 98
Morven Gro. PR8: South 1A 12
Morville Dr. WN3: Wigan 1F 51
Moscow Dr. L13: Liv 2H 89
Mosedale Av. WA11: St. H 4D 60
Mosedale Gro. WA7: Beech 5G 153
Mosedale Rd. CH62: Brom 7A 128
L9: Walt 1C 68
Moseley Av. CH45: Wall 3A 86
WA4: Westy 4G 119
Moseley Rd. CH63: Spit 1G 145
Moses St. L8: Liv 4B 108
Mosley St. PR8: South 4H 11
Moss Av. WN5: Bil 1F 49
MOSS BANK
St Helens 4C 60
Widnes 2F 135
Moss Bank L39: Augh 1B 34
WA11: R'ford 5E 46
Moss Bank Ct. L39: Augh 1B 34
(not continuous)
Moss Bank Pk. L21: Lith 5G 53
Moss Bank Rd. WA8: Wid 2F 135
WA11: St. H 5B 60
Mossborough Hall La.
WA11: R'ford 3B 58
Mossborough Rd.
WA11: R'ford 3D 58
Moss Bri. La. L40: Lath 1C 26
Moss Brow WA11: R'ford 6G 47
Moss Brow La. WA16: H Legh 5F 141
Mossbrow Rd. L36: Huy 2J 91
Moss Cl. CH64: Will 3G 159
WA4: S Hth 6E 118
Mosscraig L28: Stock V 7G 71
Mosscroft Cl. L36: Huy 3A 92
Mossdale Cl. WA5: Gt San 1E 116
Mossdale Dr. L35: R'hill 4K 93
Mossdale Rd. L33: K'by 7D 44
WN4: Ash M 4E 50
Moss Delph La. L39: Augh 1K 33
Mossdene Rd. CH44: Wall 3K 85
Moss End Way L33: Know I 2H 57
Mossfield Rd. L9: Walt 7B 54
Moss Gdns. PR8: South 6J 11
Moss Ga. WA3: Bchwd 1C 100
Moss Ga. Gro. L14: K Ash 4E 90
Moss Ga. Rd. L14: K Ash 4E 90
Mossgiel Av. PR8: Ains 5B 14
Moss Grn. L37: Form 7A 20
Moss Grn. Way WA9: St. H 5J 75
Moss Gro. CH42: Tran 6B 106
L8: Liv 2D 108
WA13: Lymm 4K 121
Mosshall La. WA4: Lwr S 7K 139
Mosshill Cl. L31: Mag 1E 42
Mosslands WA10: Eccl 2G 73
Mosslands Cl. CH66: Gt Sut 2G 169
Mosslands Dr. CH44: Wall 2J 85
CH45: Wall 2J 85
Moss La. CH42: Tran 6B 106
L9: Walt 7A 54
L20: Boot 7A 54
L21: Lith 5H 53
L23: Lit C 1C 40
L31: Lyd 6D 32
L31: Mag 2G 43
L33: K'by 2F 57
L33: Sim 4D 44
L38: High 6A 30
L39: Bic 2K 45
PR9: Banks 1K 9
PR9: Chu 7C 8
PR9: South 7F 9
WA1: W'ston 7K 99
WA3: G'bury 1F 81
(not continuous)
WA3: Low 2B 78
WA3: Rix 1G 101
WA4: Moore 2E 136
WA9: St. H 5J 75
WA11: Crank 1A 60
WA11: Windle 5F 59
WA16: H Legh 6E 140
WN2: Platt B 1K 51
WN8: Skel 5F 37
Moss La. Vw. WN8: Skel 5F 37
Mosslawn Rd. L32: K'by 4E 56
Mosslea Pk. L18: Moss H 4H 109
Mossley Av. CH62: Brom 2K 145
L18: Moss H 3G 109
Mossley Ct. L18: Moss H 5H 109
MOSSLEY HILL 5J 109
Mossley Hill Dr. L17: Aig 3F 109
(not continuous)
Mossley Hill Rd. L18: Moss H 6H 109
L19: Aig 6H 109
Mossley Rd. CH42: Tran 5E 106
Mossley Station (Rail) 5J 109
MOSS NOOK 5H 75
Moss Nook L39: Augh 1A 34
Moss Nook La. L31: Mag 4J 43
WA11: R'ford 6E 46
(not continuous)
Moss Pits Cl. L10: Faz 6G 55
Moss Pits La. L10: Faz 6G 55
L15: W'tree 2K 109
Moss Rd. M44: Cad 4K 81
PR8: South 6H 11
WA4: Westy 5G 119
WN5: Bil 1F 49
MOSS SIDE
Liverpool 2G 43
Warrington 2D 136
Moss Side L14: K Ash 4E 90
L37: Form 6B 20
Moss Side La. WA3: Rix 4G 101
WA4: Moore 2C 136
Moss St. L6: Liv 5B 88 (4L 5)
L19: Gars 3A 130
L34: Prsct 7D 72
WA8: Wid 2F 135
WN3: Ince M 1K 51
WN5: Wigan 5K 39
Moss Ter. WN5: Wigan 6K 39
Moss Va. CH66: Lit Sut 3F 161
Moss Vw. L21: Lith 5J 53
L31: Mag 3H 43
L39: Orm 6C 24
Mossville Cl. L18: Moss H 6J 109
Mossville Rd. L18: Moss H 6J 109
Moss Way L11: Crox 1A 70
Mossy Bank Rd. CH44: Wall 3D 86
Moston Gro. WA13: Lymm 5F 121
Moston Way CH66: Gt Sut 1H 169
Mostyn Av. CH48: W Kir 7D 102
CH60: Hes 2B 142
L10: Ain 2E 54
L19: Aller 1B 130
Mostyn Cl. L4: Kirk 7A 68
Mostyn Gdns. CH64: Park 2F 157
Mostyn Sq. CH64: Park 2F 157
Mostyn St. CH44: Wall 4B 86
Motherwell Cl. WA8: Wid 5A 114
Motherwell Cres. PR8: South 5B 12
Mottershead Cl. WA8: Wid 1C 134
Mottershead Rd. WA8: Wid 1C 134
Mottram Cl. L33: K'by 3D 56
WA4: Grap 5H 119
Moughland La. WA7: Run 1B 152
Moulders La. WA1: Warr 4B 118
Mould St. L5: Liv 1K 87
Moulton Cl. WA7: Sut W 6H 153
Mounsey Rd. CH42: Tran 3D 106
Mount, The CH44: Wall 3C 86
CH60: Hes 2D 142
CH63: Beb 4G 127
WN8: Skel 3H 37
Mountain Vw. WA6: Hel 1H 173
Mount Av. CH60: Hes 2D 142
CH63: High B 2D 126
L20: Boot 6K 53
Mount Ct. L32: K'by 1A 56
Mount Ct. CH45: New B 6A 66
Mount Cres. L32: K'by 1K 55
WN5: Orr 5H 39
Mount Dr. CH63: High B 2D 126
Mt. Farm Way CH66: Gt Sut 2E 168
Mountfield Ct. WN5: Orr 4H 39
Mount Gro. CH41: Birk 3C 106
Mount Gro. Pl. CH41: Birk 3C 106
Mt. Haven Cl. CH49: Upton 3E 104
Mount Ho. Cl. L37: Form 5B 20
Mount Ho. Rd. L37: Form 5B 20
Mount Merrion L25: Gate 4E 110
Mount Olive CH43: O'ton 5A 106
Mount Pk. CH63: High B 2D 126
L25: Wltn 5E 110
Mount Pk. Ct. L25: Wltn 5E 110
Mt. Pleasant CH2: Elt 7A 164
CH43: O'ton 5B 106
L3: Liv 6A 88 (7H 5)
L22: Water 4D 52
WA8: Wid 6D 114
Mt. Pleasant Av. WA9: St. H 4J 75
Mt. Pleasant Rd.
CH45: New B, Wall 1A 86
Mount Rd. CH42: Tran 7C 106
CH45: Wall 6A 66
CH48: W Kir 7E 102
CH49: Upton 3E 104
CH63: High B, Spit 7E 126
L32: K'by 2K 55
(not continuous)
WA7: Halt 1H 153
Mount St. L1: Liv 7A 88 (9J 5)
L22: Water 4D 52
L25: Wltn 6E 110
PR9: South 1K 11
WA8: Wid 6D 114
Mount Ter. PR9: South 1K 11
Mount Vernon L7: Liv 6C 88 (6N 5)
Mt. Vernon Grn. L7: Liv 5C 88 (5N 5)
Mt. Vernon Rd. L7: Liv 5C 88 (6M 5)
Mt. Vernon St. L7: Liv 5B 88 (5M 5)
Mt. Vernon Vw. L7: Liv 5C 88 (5M 5)
Mountview Cl. L8: Liv 3C 108
Mountway CH63: High B 2D 126
Mountwood WN8: Skel 6G 27
Mountwood Lodge
PR8: Ains 4C 14
Mt. Wood Rd. CH42: Tran 1C 126
Mourne Cl. CH66: Lit Sut 5C 160
Mowbray Av. WA11: St. H 1E 74
Mowbray Ct. L20: Kirk 5J 67
Mowbray Gro. L13: Liv 6J 89
Mowcroft La. WA5: Cuerd 5J 115
Mowpen Brow WA16: H Legh 3J 141
Moxon Av. WA4: Westy 3F 119
Moxon St. WA10: St. H 4J 73
Moxon Way WN4: Ash M 1H 63
Moyles Cl. WA8: Wid 5K 113
Moyles Ct. WA8: Wid 6K 113
(off Moyles Clo.)
Mozart Cl. L8: Liv 2D 108
Muirfield Cl. L12: W Der 1C 90
WA2: Fearn 4G 99
Muirfield Dr. PR8: Ains 5C 14
Muirfield Ho. WA3: Ris 1K 99
Muirfield Rd. L36: Roby 6G 91
Muirhead Av. L6: Liv 3E 88
L13: Liv, W Der 1G 89
Muirhead Av. E. L11: W Der 6J 69
Mulberry Av. WA10: St. H 3J 73
Mulberry Cl. CH2: Elt 1C 172
L33: K'by 6D 44
WA1: W'ston 2A 120
Mulberry Ct. L7: Liv 8L 5
WA4: S Hth 7D 118
Mulberry Gro. CH44: Wall 4D 86
Mulberry Pl. L7: Liv 7B 88 (8L 5)
Mulberry Rd. CH42: R Ferr 6F 107
Mulberry St. L7: Liv 7B 88 (8L 5)
(not continuous)
Mulcrow Cl. WA9: St. H 2F 75
Mulgrave St. L8: Liv 1C 108 (10M 5)
Mull Cl. CH65: Ell P 3A 170
Mullen Cl. WA5: Warr 6K 97
Mulliner St. L7: Liv 1E 108
Mullins Av. WA12: New W 1G 77
Mullion Cl. L26: Halew 7J 111
PR9: Marsh 2D 8
WA7: Brook 4K 153
Mullion Gro. WA2: P'gate 6G 99
Mullion Rd. L11: Crox 1A 70
Mullion Wlk. L11: Crox 1A 70
Mullrea Cl. L27: N'ley 2G 111
Mullwood Cl. L12: Crox 3D 70
Mulveton Rd. CH63: Spit 6F 127
Mumfords Gro.
CH47: Meols 6G 83
Mumfords La. CH47: Meols 6F 83
Muncaster Cl. CH62: Brom 1K 145
Muncaster Dr. WA11: R'ford 5G 47
Munro Av. WN5: Orr 5G 39
Munster Rd. L13: Liv 4K 89
Murat Gro. L22: Water 4C 52
Murat St. L22: Water 4C 52
Murcote Rd. L14: K Ash 2D 90
MURDISHAW 4B 154
Murdishaw Av.
WA7: Brook, Murd 5A 154
Murdock Way L10: Faz 6K 55
Muriel Cl. WA5: Gt San 2B 116
Muriel St. L4: Walt 6B 68
Murphy Gro. WA9: St. H 2G 75
Murrayfield Dr. CH46: Leas 3D 84
Murrayfield Rd. L25: Gate 2E 110
Murrayfield Wlk. L25: Gate 2E 110
Murray Gro. CH48: W Kir 5C 102
Mus. of Liverpool Life
6H 87 (8C 4)
Museum St. WA1: Warr 4A 118
Musker Dr. L30: N'ton 2J 53
Musker Gdns. L23: C'by 2F 53
Musker St. L23: C'by 2F 53
Muspratt Rd. L21: Sea 7G 53
Mustard La. WA3: Croft 6G 79
Muttocks Rake L30: N'ton 7K 41
Myddleton La. WA2: Win 1B 98
Myers Av. L35: Whis 2G 93
Myerscough Av. L20: Boot 1A 68
Myers Ct. L23: C'by 3F 53
(off Myers Rd. E.)
Myers Rd. E. L23: C'by 2E 52
Myers Rd. W. L23: C'by 2D 52
Mynsule Rd. CH63: Spit 6F 127
Myrtle Av. WA11: Hay 6K 61
WA12: New W 4G 77
WN4: Ash M 6D 50
Myrtle Ct. L8: Liv 7C 88 (9N 5)
Myrtle Gro. CH44: Wall 4D 86
L22: Water 3D 52
PR8: South 2A 12
WA4: Warr 5D 118
WA8: Wid 1K 133
WN5: Bil 1F 61
Myrtle Pde. L7: Liv 7B 88 (9L 5)
Myrtle St. CH65: Ell P 4A 162
L7: Liv 7B 88 (8K 5)
Mystic M. L39: Orm 5C 24
(off Burscough St.)

N

Naburn Dr. WN5: Orr 6G 39
Naburn Gro. CH46: More 1C 104
Nairn Av. WN8: Skel 5H 27
Nairn Cl. CH63: East 6K 145
WA2: Fearn 4H 99
Nansen Cl. WA5: Old H 1H 117
Nansen Gro. L4: Walt 5C 68
Nant Pk. Ct. CH45: New B 6C 66
Nantwich Cl. CH49: W'chu 6E 104
Nantwich Rd. CH66: Gt Sut 1H 169
Napier Cl. WA10: St. H 3A 74
Napier Dr. CH46: More 7D 84
Napier Rd. CH62: New F 1H 127
Napier St. L20: Boot 5H 67
WA1: Warr 3C 118
(not continuous)
WA10: St. H 3A 74
Napier Ter. PR8: B'dale 3G 11
Naples Rd. CH44: Wall 4D 86
Napps Cl. L25: Gate 1D 110
Napps Wlk. L25: Gate 1D 110
(off Napps Clo.)
Napps Way CH61: Hes 7E 124
L25: Gate 7D 90
Nares Cl. WA5: Old H 6G 97
Narrow Cft. Rd. L39: Augh 2K 33
Narrow La. L39: Augh 2K 33
L39: Hals 3F 23
WA4: Grap 7H 119
NARROW MOSS 2C 24
Narrow Moss La. L40: Scar 1B 24
Naseby Cl. CH43: Noct 4G 105
Naseby St. L4: Walt 4B 68
Natal Rd. L9: Ain 7D 54
Nathan Dr. WA11: Hay 7C 62
Nathan Gro. L32: K'by 1D 56
National Wildflower Cen. 7D 90
Naughton Lea WA8: Wid 5K 113
Naughton Rd. WA8: Wid 1C 134
Navenby Rd. WN3: Wigan 2E 50
Navigation Cl. L30: N'ton 1C 54
WA7: Murd 4B 154
Navigation St. WA1: Warr 3D 118
Navigation Wharf L3: Liv 2K 107
Naylor Ct. CH66: Ell P 5G 161
Naylor Cres. CH66: Ell P 3H 161
Naylor Rd. CH43: Bid 7J 85
WA8: Wid 7F 115
Naylorsfield Dr. L27: N'ley 1G 111
Naylor's Rd. L27: N'ley 1H 111
Naylor St. L3: Liv 4J 87 (3E 4)
WA1: Warr 3B 118
Nazeby Av. L23: C'by 2F 53
Neale Dr. CH49: Grea 5C 104
Neales Fold PR9: Cros 2F 9
Neasham Cl. L26: Halew 1K 131
Nedens Gro. L31: Lyd 1E 42
Nedens La. L31: Lyd 1E 42
Needham Cl. WA7: Run 7F 135
Needham Cres. CH43: Noct 4H 105
Needham Rd. L7: Liv 5E 88
Needham Way WN8: Skel 5H 27
Needwood Dr. CH63: Beb 6F 127
Neills Rd. WA9: Bold 2K 95
Neilson Rd. L17: Aig 5D 108
Neilson St. L17: Aig 5D 108
Neil St. WA8: Wid 6D 114
Nell's La. L39: Augh 6H 33
Nelson Av. L35: Whis 5E 92
Nelson Ct. CH42: R Ferr 7G 107
CH45: New B 5B 66
PR8: B'dale 4F 11
Nelson Dr. CH61: Pens 5C 124
WA7: West 4B 152
Nelson Memorial 5D 4
(off Exchange Pas. W.)
Nelson Pl. L35: Whis 5E 92
Nelson Rd. CH42: R Ferr 7G 107
CH65: Ell P 4A 162
L7: Liv 6D 88 (7P 5)
L21: Lith 6H 53
WA3: Ris 3K 99
Nelson's Cft. CH63: Beb 6G 127
Nelson St. CH45: New B 7C 66
L1: Liv 1K 107 (10G 4)
L15: W'tree 1G 109
L20: Boot 4H 67
PR8: South 2G 11
WA7: Run 6C 134
WA8: Wid 3C 134
WA9: St. H 7F 75
WA12: New W 3E 76
(not continuous)
Nelville Rd. L9: Ain 6E 54
Nemos Cl. WA6: Hel 2J 173
Neptune Cl. WA7: Murd 3B 154
Neptune St. CH41: Birk 7D 86
Neptune Theatre 6K 87 (7G 4)
NESS 6A 158
Ness Acre La. CH64: Will 3E 158
Ness Botanical Gdns. 7A 158
Ness Botanical Gdns. Vis. Cen.
7A 158
Ness Gro. L32: K'by 3A 56
NESSHOLT 6K 157
NESTON 3J 157
Neston Av. WA9: Clock F 3D 94
Neston Grn. CH66: Gt Sut 7F 161
(not continuous)
Neston Recreation Cen. 2K 157
Neston Rd. CH63: Thorn H 5K 143
CH64: Ness 6K 157
CH64: Nest 5K 143
CH64: Will 3E 158
Neston Station (Rail) 3J 157
Neston St. L4: Walt 5B 68
Netherby St. L8: Liv 5B 108
Netherfield WA8: Wid 1K 133
Netherfield Cl. CH43: Noct 4G 105
Netherfield Rd. Nth. L5: Liv 1A 88
Netherfield Rd. Sth.
L5: Liv 3A 88 (1J 5)

Netherley—Nth. Perimeter Rd.

NETHERLEY 3J 111
Netherley Rd. L27: N'ley 3K 111
L35: Tar G 3K 111
WA8: Wid 6E 112
Netherpool Rd. CH66: Ell P 4H 161
NETHERTON
Bootle 2B 54
Frodsham 4C 166
Netherton Activity Cen. 1A 54
Netherton Dr. WA6: Frod 4C 166
Netherton Grange L30: N'ton 2D 54
Netherton Grn. L30: N'ton 7B 42
Netherton Ind. Est. L30: N'ton 4B 54
Netherton La. L30: N'ton 7A 42
(not continuous)
Netherton Pk. Rd. L21: Lith 5K 53
Netherton Rd. CH46: More 7C 84
L18: Moss H 7H 109
L20: Boot 7K 53
Netherton Way L30: Boot, N'ton 4A 54
(not continuous)
Netherwood Rd. L11: N Grn. 4G 69
Netley St. L4: Kirk 6A 68
Nettlestead Rd. L11: N Grn. 6J 69
Neva Av. CH46: More 7B 84
Nevada Cl. WA5: Gt San 7G 97
Neverstitch Cl. WN8: Skel 1F 37
Neverstitch Rd. WN8: Skel 2C 36
Neville Av. WA2: Warr 6D 98
WA9: St. H 4K 75
Neville Cl. CH43: Noct 4G 105
Neville Cres. WA5: Penk 5E 116
Neville Rd. CH44: Wall 3A 86
CH62: Brom 3A 146
L22: Water 4E 52
Neville St. WA12: New W 2E 76
Nevill St. PR9: South 7H 7
Nevin St. L6: Liv 4C 88 (2M 5)
Nevison St. L7: Liv 6D 88 (7P 5)
Nevitte Cl. L28: Stock V 6E 70
New Acres WN8: Newb 1G 27
New Acres Cl. CH43: Bid 7G 85
New Albert Ter. WA7: Run 6D 134
(off Bold St.)
Newark Cl. CH43: Noct 4G 105
L30: N'ton 7D 42
L36: Huy 1H 91
Newark St. L4: Walt 5A 68
New Bank Pl. WA8: Wid 7H 113
New Bank Rd. WA8: Wid 7H 113
New Barn Av. WN4: Ash M 2G 63
New Barnet WA8: Wid 4B 114
New Bird St. L1: Liv 1K 107 (10G 4)
Newbold Cres. CH48: W Kir 5G 103
Newbold Gro. L12: Crox 4D 70
Newborough Av. L18: Moss H 3H 109
L23: C'by 1G 53
Newborough Cl. WA5: Call 5H 97
NEW BOSTON 6C 62
New Bri. WA1: Warr 4B 118
Newbridge Cl. CH49: W'chu 5F 105
WA5: Call 5G 97
WA7: Brook 4A 154
WN4: Gars 2B 62
Newbridge Rd. CH65: Ell P 7D 162
NEW BRIGHTON 5B 66
New Brighton Station (Rail) 6A 66
NEWBURGH 1G 27
Newburgh Cl. WA7: Wind H 1B 154
Newburn CH43: O'ton 3B 106
Newburn Cl. WN3: Wigan 1C 50
WN8: Skel 5H 27
Newburns La. CH43: O'ton 5B 106
Newburn St. L4: Walt 4B 68
Newbury Cl. L36: Roby 6H 91
WA8: Wid 4C 114
Newbury Rd. WN8: Skel 5H 27
Newbury Way CH46: Leas 4D 84
L12: W Der 2C 90
Newby Av. L35: R'hill 3G 93
Newby Cl. PR8: Ains 6B 14
Newby Dr. L36: Huy 4G 91
WN8: Skel 5H 27
Newby Gro. L12: W Der 4A 70
Newby Pl. WA11: St. H 5C 60
Newby Sq. WN5: Wigan 6K 39
Newby St. L4: Walt 6B 68
New Carr La. L31: Gt Alt 4A 32
L38: Gt Alt 4A 32
Newcastle Rd. L15: W'tree 2J 109
New C'way. L37: Gt Alt 3B 30
New Chester Rd.
CH41: Birk, Tran 3F 107
CH42: R Ferr 5F 107
CH62: Brom, Port S, East 4J 127
CH62: New F 5F 107
CH66: Hoot 1C 160
Newchurch La. WA3: Cul 4B 80
Newcombe Av. WA2: P'gate 7E 98
Newcombe St. L6: Liv 2D 88
New Ct. Way L39: Orm 5D 24
Newcroft Rd. L25: Wltn 4D 110
New Cross St. L34: Prsct 7D 72
WA10: St. H 2B 74
(Duke St.)
WA10: St. H 3B 74
(Westfield St.)
New Cut Cl. PR8: B'dale 1G 15
New Cut Ind. Est. WA1: W'ston 1J 119
New Cut La. L33: Know 6A 58
L39: Hals 1G 15
PR8: B'dale 1G 15
WA1: W'ston 1H 119
WA11: R'ford 3B 58
Newdales Cl. CH43: Bid 7G 85
Newdown Rd. L11: Crox 1A 70
Newdown Wlk. L11: Crox 1B 70
Newell Rd. CH44: Wall 2B 86
Newenham Cres. L14: K Ash 3C 90
New Extension Quay
CH65: Ell P 3A 162
NEW FERRY 2H 127
New Ferry By-Pass
CH62: New F, Port S 1H 127
New Ferry Rd. CH62: New F 2H 127
Newfield Cl. L23: Thorn 6J 41
Newfield Ct. WA13: Lymm 3J 121
Newfield Rd. WA13: Lymm 5F 121
Newfields WA10: St. H 2J 73
Newfield Ter. WA6: Hel 2H 173
New Fold WN5: Orr 7E 38
Newfort Way L20: Boot 7G 53
New Foul La. PR8: South 4C 12
NEWGATE 4C 38
Newgate Rd. WN8: Uph 4B 38
New Glade Hill WA11: St. H 7G 61
New Grey Rock Cl.
L6: Liv 3D 88 (1P 5)
New Grosvenor Rd. CH65: Ell P 4K 161
New Hall L10: Faz 5H 55
NEW HALL FARM 7E 12
New Hall La. CH47: Hoy 2D 102
L11: N Grn. 6G 69
WA3: Ris 5A 80
(not continuous)
New Hall Manor CH64: Nest 4J 143
New Hall Pl. L3: Liv 5H 87 (5C 4)
Newhall St. L1: Liv 1K 107 (10H 5)
Newhall Swimming Pool 5H 55
New Hampshire Cl.
WA5: Gt San 1F 117
Newhaven Rd. CH45: New B 7C 66
WA2: Warr 3B 98
New Hawthorne Gdns.
L18: Moss H 5G 109
New Hedley Gro. L5: Liv 2J 87
New Henderson St. L8: Liv 2A 108
New Hey L12: W Der 2J 89
New Heyes CH64: Nest 2J 157
New Hey La. CH64: Will 4F 159
New Hey Rd. CH49: W'chu 4F 105
New Heys Dr. L18: Aller 7B 110
Newholme Cl. L12: Crox 3C 70
Newhope Rd. CH41: Birk 1C 106
Newhouse Dr. WN3: Wins 3B 50
Newhouse Rd. L15: W'tree 1F 109
NEW HOUSES 3A 50
New Houses La. CH64: Lit N 7J 157
New Hutte La. L26: Halew 3K 131
Newick Rd. L32: K'by 4A 56
Newington L1: Liv 6K 87 (7H 5)
Newington Way WA8: Wid 5B 114
New Islington L3: Liv 4A 88 (4H 5)
Newland Cl. WA8: Wid 5J 113
Newland Ct. L17: Aig 5E 108
Newland Dr. CH44: Wall 3A 86
Newland M. WA3: Cul 1A 80
Newlands Cl. WA6: Frod 5E 166
Newlands Rd. CH63: Beb 5H 127
WA4: S Hth 6F 119
WA11: St. H 6E 60
New La. L39: Augh 1C 34
L39: Down 6J 21
(not continuous)
PR9: Cros 3E 8
WA3: Croft 7G 79
WA4: App T 4H 139
NEW LANE END 4G 79
New La. End WA3: Croft 4G 79
New La. Pace PR9: Banks 1K 9
Newling St. CH41: Birk 1C 106
Newlyn Av. L21: Lith 4G 53
L31: Mag 3G 43
Newlyn Cl. CH47: Meols 5G 83
WA7: Brook 4K 153
Newlyn Dr. WN4: Ash M 3F 63
WN8: Skel 4K 37
Newlyn Gdns. WA5: Penk 5B 116
Newlyn Gro. WA11: St. H 6F 61
Newlyn Rd. CH47: Meols 6G 83
L11: Crox 1A 70
Newlyn Wlk. L11: Crox 1B 70
New Mnr. Rd. WA4: Pres H 4E 154
Newman St. L4: Kirk 6K 67
WA4: Westy 4F 119
New Mkt. Cl. L21: Lith 6H 53
Newmarket Gdns. WA9: St. H 1J 93
New Mkt. Hall WA7: Run 6C 134
(off Church St.)
New Market Wlk. WA1: Warr 3B 118
New Mdw. La. L37: Gt Alt 3E 30
New Mersey Shop. Pk.
L24: Speke 4D 130
New Mill Stile L25: Wltn 5E 110
Newmoore La. WA7: Nort 6C 136
Newmorn Ct. L17: Aig 6E 108
Newnham Dr. CH65: Ell P 7A 162
New Palace Amusement Park 5B 66
Newport Av. CH45: Wall 7H 65
Newport Cl. CH43: Noct 4G 105
Newport Ct. L5: Liv 1J 87
New Quay L3: Liv 5H 87 (5C 4)
Newquay Cl. WA7: Brook 4A 154
New Quay Ter. L3: Liv 5H 87 (5C 4)
New Red Rock Vw.
L6: Liv 3D 88 (1P 5)
New Rd. CH66: Chil T 3C 160
L13: Liv 2F 89
L34: Ecc P 7E 72
L37: Form 5A 20
WA4: Warr 4C 118
(not continuous)
WA13: Lymm 5G 121
New Rd. Ct. L13: Liv 2G 89
New School La.
CH66: Chil T 3D 160
Newsham Cl. WA8: Wid 4H 113
Newsham Dr. L6: Liv 3E 88
(not continuous)
Newsham Rd. L36: Huy 7B 92
Newsham St. L5: Liv 2K 87
Newsholme Cl. WA3: Cul 3B 80
News La. WA11: R'ford 1E 46
Newstead Av. L23: Blun 2B 52
Newstead Dr. WN8: Skel 5H 27
Newstead Rd. L8: Liv 1D 108
WA8: Wid 3F 133
WN3: Wigan 1C 50
Newstet Rd. L33: Know I 3F 57
New St. CH44: Wall 5E 86
CH64: Lit N 6J 157
L39: Hals 3C 22
WA4: Warr 4C 118
WA7: Run 7C 134
WA8: Wid 1D 134
WA9: Sut L 2E 94
WN4: Ash M 1G 63
WN5: Wigan 6K 39
NEWTON 6G 103
Newton Av. WA3: Ris 2A 100
Newton Bank WA4: Dares 2F 155
Newton Cl. L12: W Der 6K 69
NEWTON COMMON 3C 76
Newton Ct. L13: W'tree 6G 89
Newton Cross La.
CH48: W Kir 6G 103
Newton Dr. CH48: W Kir 6G 103
WN8: Skel 5H 27
Newton Gro. WA2: Fearn 4F 99
Newton La. WA4: Dares 2F 155
WA4: Dares, Lwr Wh 3H 155
WA12: New W 7J 63
NEWTON-LE-WILLOWS 2H 77
Newton-le-Willows Station (Rail)
3J 77
Newton Pk. Dr. WA12: New W 4K 77
Newton Pk. Rd. CH48: W Kir 6G 103
Newton Rd. CH44: Wall 3A 86
CH47: Hoy 1E 102
CH65: Ell P 6A 162
L13: Liv 4G 89
WA2: Win 5K 77
WA3: Low 2A 78
WA9: St. H 3J 75
WN5: Bil 6G 49
Newton St. CH41: Birk 1C 106
PR9: South 1B 12
Newton Wlk. L20: Boot 2H 67
Newton Way CH49: Upton 3D 104
L3: Liv 6B 88 (6K 5)
New Tower Ct. CH45: New B 6C 66
NEWTOWN 2F 167
Newtown CH64: Lit N 5K 157
Newtown Gdns. L32: K'by 3C 56
New Vale PR9: Banks 3J 9
New Way L14: K Ash 2E 90
L39: Bic 2F 45
New Way Bus. Cen.
CH44: Wall 5D 86
Nicander Rd. L18: Moss H 3H 109
Nicholas Rd. L23: Blun 1B 52
WA8: Wid 1J 133
Nicholas St. L3: Liv 4K 87 (2F 4)
Nicholl Rd. WA10: Eccl 7G 59
Nicholls Dr. CH61: Pens 6D 124
Nicholls St. WA4: Grap 6H 119
Nichol's Gro. L18: Aller 6A 110
Nicholson St. L5: Liv 1A 88
WA1: Warr 3K 117
WA9: St. H 2G 75
Nickleby Cl. L8: Liv 3B 108
Nickleford Hall Dr. WA8: Wid 2B 114
Nicola Ct. CH45: Wall 1C 86
Nicol Av. WA3: W'ston 7B 100
Nicol Mere Dr. WN4: Ash M 6E 50
Nicol Rd. WN4: Ash M 7E 50
Nidderdale Av. L35: R'hill 4K 93
Nigel Rd. CH60: Hes 2G 143
Nigel Wlk. WA7: Cas 7J 135
Nightingale Cl. L27: N'ley 3K 111
L32: K'by 2K 55
WA3: Bchwd 3B 100
WA7: Beech 5H 153
Nightingale Rd. L12: Crox 3D 70
Nimrod St. L4: Walt 5B 68
Ninth Av. L9: Ain 6F 55
Nipe La. WN8: Skel 6G 37
Nithsdale Rd. L15: W'tree 2G 109
Nixons La. WN8: Skel 4K 37
PR8: Ains 2E 14
Nixon St. L4: Walt 4B 68
Noble Cl. WA3: Bchwd 4A 100
NOCTORUM 4H 105
Noctorum Av. CH43: Noct 3G 105
Noctorum Dell CH43: Noct 4H 105
Noctorum La.
CH43: Noct, O'ton 2H 105
Noctorum Rd. CH43: Noct 3H 105
Noctorum Way CH43: Noct 4H 105
Noel Ga. L39: Augh 2K 33
Noel St. L8: Liv 1D 108
Nolan St. PR8: South 3J 11
Nook, The CH43: O'ton 3B 106
CH48: Frank 6K 103
L25: Gate 5F 111
L39: Augh 3A 34
WA10: Windle 7H 59
Nook La. WA2: Fearn 5H 99
WA4: Westy 5G 119
WA9: St. H 5H 75
Nook Ri. L15: W'tree 7K 89
Noonan Cl. L9: Walt 2B 68
Noon Ct. WA12: New W 5G 77
Nora St. WA1: Warr 3C 118
Norbreck Av. L14: B Grn 5C 90
Norbreck Cl. WA5: Gt San 5E 116
Norburn Cres. L37: Form 1K 29
Norbury Av. CH63: High B 4E 126
L18: Moss H 3H 109
WA2: Warr 7D 98
WN5: Bil 6F 49
Norbury Cl. CH63: High B 4F 127
L32: K'by 3B 56
PR9: Cros 2E 8
WA8: Wid 7F 115
Norbury Fold L35: R'hill 6A 94
Norbury Rd. L32: K'by 3B 56
Norbury Wlk. L32: K'by 3B 56
Norcliffe Rd. L35: R'hill 3H 93
Norcott Av. WA4: S Hth 6D 118
Norcott Dr. WA5: B'wood 1D 96
Norden Cl. WA3: Bchwd 2J 99
Norfield L39: Orm 5D 24
Norfolk Cl. CH43: Noct 4G 105
L20: Boot 2K 67
WA5: Gt San 2C 116
Norfolk Gro. PR8: B'dale 7F 11
Norfolk Pl. L21: Sea 6G 53
WA8: Wid 1J 133
Norfolk Rd. CH65: Ell P 6A 162
L31: Mag 5E 42
PR8: B'dale 7F 11
WA10: St. H 5K 73
WN5: Bil 3G 49
Norfolk St. L1: Liv 1K 107 (10F 4)
WA7: Run 6D 134
Norgate St. L4: Walt 7B 68
Norgrove Cl. WA7: Murd 2B 154
Norlands Ct. CH42: R Ferr 7E 106
Norland's La. L35: R'hill 7A 94
WA8: Cron 7A 94
WA8: Wid 2B 114
Norlands Pk. WA8: Wid 2B 114
Norland St. WA8: Wid 7F 115
Norleane Cres. WA7: Run 2D 152
Norley Av. CH62: East 7A 146
CH65: Ell P 5H 161
Norley Cl. WA5: Warr 2J 117
Norley Dr. WA10: Eccl 3G 73
Norley Pl. L26: Halew 3J 131
Norley Rd. WN5: Wigan 4K 39
Norman Av. WA11: Hay 6E 62
WA12: New W 3J 77
Normanby Cl. WA5: Warr 1J 117
Normanby St. WN5: Wigan 5K 39
Norman Cl. CH66: Gt Sut 4H 169
Normandale Rd. L4: Walt 5F 69
Normandy Rd. L36: Huy 4H 91
Norman Hays L39: Orm 2D 24
Normanhurst L39: Orm 6E 24
Norman Rd. CH44: Wall 5E 86
L20: Boot 6J 53
L23: C'by 2D 52
WA7: Run 1C 152
Norman Salisbury Ct.
WA10: St. H 2B 74
Normans Rd. WA9: St. H 7H 75
Normanston Cl. CH43: O'ton 4B 106
Normanston Rd. CH43: O'ton 4B 106
Norman St. CH41: Birk 7K 85
L3: Liv 5B 88 (4K 5)
WA2: Warr 2B 118
Normanton Av. L17: Aig 5E 108
Norma Rd. L22: Water 4E 52
Normington Cl. L31: Lyd 7E 32
Norreys Av. WA5: Warr 7K 97
Norris Cl. CH43: Noct 4G 105
NORRIS GREEN 4H 69
Norris Grn. Cres. L11: N Grn. 5H 69
Norris Green Leisure Cen. 4J 69
Norris Grn. Rd. L12: W Der 1K 89
Norris Grn. Way L11: N Grn. 5J 69
Norris Ho. Dr. L39: Augh 3A 34
Norris Rd. L34: Prsct 1C 92
Norris St. WA2: Warr 7C 98
Norris Way L37: Form 7B 20
Norseman Cl. L12: W Der 6K 69
Northam Cl. PR9: Marsh 2C 8
NORTH ASHTON 6B 50
Nth. Atlantic Ct. L36: Huy 3H 91
North Av. L10: Ain 3G 55
L24: Speke 3E 130
WA2: Warr 7B 98
Nth. Barcombe Rd. L16: Child 1B 110
Northbrook Cl. L8: Liv 1C 108 (10N 5)
Northbrooke Way CH49: W'chu 5E 104
Northbrook Rd. CH44: Wall 4D 86
Northbrook St. L8: Liv 1C 108 (10N 5)
(Granby St.)
L8: Liv 1B 108
(Park Way)
Northbury Rd. CH66: Gt Sut 3G 169
Nth. Cantril Av. L12: W Der 6C 70
(not continuous)
Nth. Cheshire Trad. Est.
CH43: Pren 1J 125
North Cl. CH62: Brom 7J 127
Northcote Cl. L5: Liv 3B 88
Northcote Rd. CH45: Wall 1H 85
L9: Walt 3B 68
Northdale Rd. L15: W'tree 7H 89
WA1: P'ton 7G 99
Northdene WN8: Parb 1H 27
North Dingle L4: Kirk 6K 67
North Dr. CH45: Wall 6K 65
CH60: Hes 3E 142
L12: W Der 2J 89
L15: W'tree 7H 89
Nth. Dunes L38: High 5F 29
NORTH END
L26 5J 111
L38 5C 30
Nth. End La. L26: Halew 5J 111
L38: High 5A 30
Northern La. WA8: Wid 5G 113
Northern Perimeter Rd.
L30: N'ton 7A 42
Northern Ri. CH66: Gt Sut 7G 161
Northern Rd. L24: Speke 5J 131
Northern Rd., The L23: C'by 7E 40
Northfield WN8: Skel 6H 27
Northfield Cl. L33: K'by 1E 56
WA9: Clock F 4F 95
Northfield Rd. L9: Walt 7A 54
L20: Boot 7A 54
NORTH FLORIDA 5B 62
Nth. Florida Rd. WA11: Hay 5B 62
North Front L35: Whis 6E 92
Northgate Rd. L13: Liv 2H 89
North Gro. L18: Aller 7A 110
Nth. Hill St. L8: Liv 3B 108
Nth. John St. L2: Liv 5J 87 (5E 4)
WA10: St. H 3B 74
Northleach Dr. PR8: Ains 4A 14
Nth. Linkside Rd. L25: Wltn 7G 111
Nth. Manor Way L25: Wltn 7G 111
North Meade L31: Mag 2D 42
Northmead Rd. L19: Aller 2C 130
North Meols Community Leisure Cen.
2J 9
Nth. Mersey Bus. Cen.
L33: Know I 1G 57
NORTH MOOR 7G 17
Nth. Moor La. L39: Hals 7F 17
Nth. Moss La. L37: Form 4C 20
Nth. Mossley Hill Rd.
L18: Moss H 4H 109
North Mt. Rd. L32: K'by 1K 55
Northolt Ct. WA2: P'gate 6E 98
Northop Rd. CH45: Wall 1K 85
North Pde. CH47: Hoy 1C 102
CH64: Park 1E 156
L24: Speke 6J 131
L32: K'by 3C 56
North Pk. Brook Rd. WA5: Call 5J 97
North Pk. Ct. CH44: Wall 4E 86
North Pk. Rd. L32: K'by 1K 55
Nth. Parkside Wlk. L12: W Der 6J 69
Nth. Perimeter Rd. L33: Know I 1G 57

A-Z Merseyside 217

Orange Gro.—Parkdale Rd.

Orange Gro. L8: Liv 2D 108
WA2: Warr 5E 98
Orange Tree Cl. L28: Stock V 6F 71
Oran Way L36: Huy 4H 91
Orb Cl. L11: Crox 2A 70
Orb Wlk. L11: Crox 3A 70
Orchard, The CH45: Wall 7A 66
L17: Aig 7H 109
L35: R'hill 2J 93
L36: Huy 5J 91
L39: Orm 5B 24
WA6: Hel 2H 173
Orchard Av. L14: B Grn 6B 90
WA13: Lymm 5H 121
Orchard Brow WA3: Rix 5J 101
Orchard Cl. CH66: Gt Sut 3H 169
L34: Ecc P 7G 73
L35: Whis 6E 92
WA6: Frod 5C 166
WA11: St. H 6F 61
Orchard Ct. CH41: Tran 5F 107
L31: Mag 3G 43
Orchard Ct. WA3: Croft 6G 79
WA6: Frod 3C 166
WN5: Bil 1F 49
Orchard Dale L23: C'by 1F 53
Orchard Dene L35: R'hill 4J 93
Orchard Dr. CH64: Lit N 6J 157
Orchard Gdns. L35: Whis 7E 92
Orchard Grange CH46: More 1A 104
Orchard Haven CH66: Gt Sut 3G 169
Orchard Hey L30: N'ton 1D 54
L31: Mag 4G 43
WA10: Eccl 3G 73
Orchard La. CH66: Chil T 3C 160
PR8: Ains 5D 14
Orchard Pk. Cvn. Pk.
CH2: Elt 7B 164
Orchard Pk. La. CH2: Elt 7B 164
Orchard Pl. WA6: Hel 7J 165
Orchard Rd. CH46: More 6C 84
CH65: Whit 2J 169
WA13: Lymm 3K 121
Orchards, The PR8: Ains 5D 14
WN5: Orr 6G 39
Orchard St. WA1: Warr 3C 118
WA2: Fearn 5G 99
WA4: S Hth 1C 138
WN4: Ash M 2G 63
Orchard Vw. L39: Augh 2B 34
Orchard Wlk. CH64: Nest 3J 157
WA7: Pal F 3H 153
(off Halton Lea Shop. Cen.)
Orchard Way CH63: High B 3D 126
WA8: Wid 5G 113
Orchid Cl. WN8: Uph 5D 38
Orchid Gro. L17: Aig 5B 108
Orchid Way WA9: Bold 7K 75
Orchil Cl. CH66: Lit Sut 5C 160
Ordnance Av. WA3: Bchwd 4A 100
O'Reilly Ct. L3: Liv 3J 87 (1D 4)
ORFORD 5D 98
Orford Av. WA2: Warr 1C 118
Orford Cl. L24: Hale 7D 132
Orford Grn. WA2: Warr 6D 98
Orford La. WA2: Warr 2B 118
Orford Rd. WA1: Warr 7D 98
WA2: Warr 7D 98
Orford St. L15: W'tree 7H 89
WA1: Warr 3B 118
Oriel Cl. L2: Liv 6H 87 (6D 4)
L10: Ain 2F 55
Oriel Cres. L20: Kirk 5J 67
Oriel Dr. L10: Ain 2E 54
Oriel Lodge L20: Boot 4J 67
Oriel Rd. CH42: Tran 5E 106
L20: Boot 3H 67
L20: Kirk 5J 67
WN4: Ash M 1D 62
Oriel St. L3: Liv 4J 87 (2E 4)
Orient Dr. L25: Wltn 5F 111
Origen Rd. L16: Child 6B 90
Oriole Cl. WA10: St. H 7H 73
Orion Blvd. WA5: Gt San 6C 96
Orith Av. WA10: Eccl 3F 73
Orkney Cl. CH65: Ell P 3A 170
WA8: Wid 5G 115
WA11: St. H 6F 61
Orlando Cl. CH43: Noct 4G 105
Orlando St. L20: Boot 5J 67
Orleans Rd. L13: Liv 4J 89
Ormande St. WA9: St. H 5D 74
Orme Ho. L39: Orm 5E 24
Ormesby Gdns. WA9: St. H 1A 94
Ormesby Gro. CH63: Raby M 4H 145
Ormiston Rd. CH45: New B 7B 66
Ormond Av. L40: Westh 6J 25
Ormond Cl. WA8: Wid 6J 113
Ormonde Av. L31: Mag 5E 42
Ormonde Cres. L33: K'by 3E 56
Ormonde Dr. L31: Mag 4E 42
Ormond M. CH43: Noct 4G 105
Ormond St. CH45: Wall 2B 86
L3: Liv 5J 87 (5D 4)
Ormond Way CH43: Noct 4G 105
Ormsby St. L15: W'tree 1G 109
Ormside Gro. WA9: St. H 7F 75
ORMSKIRK 5C 24
Ormskirk Bus. Pk. L39: Orm 4D 24
Ormskirk Civic Hall 4C 24
Ormskirk Old Rd. L39: Bic 4K 35
Ormskirk Rd. L9: Ain 5D 54
L10: Ain, N'ton 5D 54
L30: N'ton 5D 54
L34: Know 7H 57
L39: Bic 2G 35
WN5: Wigan 5K 39
WN8: Skel 2C 36
(Blaguegate La.)
WN8: Skel 3H 37
(Spencers La.)
WN8: Uph 4B 38
Ormskirk Station (Rail) 5D 24
Ormskirk St. WA10: St. H 2B 74
Orms Way L37: Form 7J 19
Orphan Dr. L6: Liv 2F 89
(not continuous)
Orphan St. L7: Liv 7C 88 (8M 5)
Orpington St.
WN5: Wigan 5K 39
ORRELL
Bootle 7K 53
Wigan 6F 39
Orrell Cl. WA5: Gt San 2E 116
Orrell Gdns. WN5: Orr 5H 39
Orrell Hall Cl. WN5: Orr 3K 39
Orrell Hey L20: Boot 6K 53
Orrell Hill La. L38: Ince B 7C 30
Orrell La. L9: Walt 6A 54
L20: Boot 6A 54
Orrell Mt. L20: Boot 6J 53
Orrell Mt. Ind. Est.
L21: Lith 6J 53
ORRELL PARK 7C 54
Orrell Park Station (Rail) 7C 54
ORRELL POST 4G 39
Orrell Rd. CH45: New B 7C 66
L20: Boot 6J 53
L21: Lith 5J 53
WN5: Orr 4F 39
Orrell Station (Rail) 7G 39
Orrell St. WA9: St. H 3E 74
Orrel Rugby Union Football Ground
6G 39
Orret's Mdw. Rd. CH49: W'chu 5F 105
Orrysdale Rd. CH48: W Kir 5C 102
Orry St. L5: Liv 2K 87
Orsett Rd. L32: K'by 5D 56
Orston Cres. CH63: Spit 7G 127
Ortega Cl. CH62: New F 2J 127
Orthes St. L3: Liv 6B 88 (7K 5)
Orton Rd. L16: Child 7A 90
Orton Way WN4: Ash M 2D 62
Orville St. WA9: St. H 7G 75
Orwell Cl. L37: Form 2H 29
WA9: Sut M 4C 94
Orwell Rd. L4: Kirk 6K 67
Osbert Rd. L23: Blun 1B 52
Osborne Av. CH45: New B 7B 66
WA2: Warr 6D 98
Osborne Gro. CH45: New B 1B 86
L34: Prsct 2A 92
Osborne Rd. CH43: O'ton 3B 106
CH45: New B 7C 66
L13: Liv 1G 89
L21: Lith 4J 53
L37: Form 2J 29
PR8: Ains 3B 14
WA4: Walt 7B 118
WA10: Eccl 1G 73
WN4: Ash M 1E 62
Osborne Va. CH45: New B 7B 66
Osborne Wood L17: Aig 7E 108
Osbourne Cl. CH62: Brom 3A 146
Osbourne Ct. WA10: St. H 6J 73
Osier Cl. CH2: Elt 1C 172
Osmaston Rd. CH42: Tran 6A 106
Osprey Cl. L27: N'ley 3K 111
WA2: Warr 4E 98
WA7: Beech 5H 153
Osprey's, The WN3: Wigan 1A 50
Ossett Cl. CH43: Noct 4G 105
WA7: Nort 2B 154
Osterley Gdns. L9: Walt 7B 54
O'Sullivan Cres. WA11: St. H 1G 75
Oswald Cl. L33: K'by 6C 44
Oteley Av. CH62: Brom 2K 145
Othello Cl. L20: Kirk 5J 67
Otterburn Cl. CH46: More 7K 83
OTTERSPOOL 7E 108
Otterspool Dr. L17: Aig 1F 129
Otterspool Rd. L17: Aig 7F 109
Otterton Rd. L11: Crox 1A 70
Ottery Cl. PR9: Marsh 2C 8
Ottley St. L6: Liv 4E 88
Otway St. L19: Gars 5A 130
OUGHTRINGTON 4K 121
Oughtrington Cres.
WA13: Lymm 4K 121
Oughtrington La. WA13: Lymm 6J 121
Oughtrington Vw. WA13: Lymm 4K 121
Oulton Cl. CH43: O'ton 5J 105
L31: Lyd 7D 32
Oulton Ct. WA4: Grap 6H 119
Oulton Gdns. WA9: St. H 1A 94
Oulton La. L36: Roby 7H 91
Oulton Rd. L16: Child 2B 110
Oulton Way CH43: O'ton 6J 105
Oundle Dr. L10: Ain 2E 54
Oundle Pl. L25: Hunts X 2F 131
Oundle Rd. CH46: More 6C 84
Outer Central Rd. L24: Halew 4J 131
Outer Forum L11: N Grn. 4G 69
Out La. L25: Wltn 6E 110
Outlet La. L31: Bic, Mell 3B 44
Outlook, The L38: High 7K 29
Oval, The 2F 127
Oval, The CH45: Wall 1K 85
CH65: Ell P 1A 170
PR9: Banks 3J 9
Overbrook La. L34: Know 1F 71
Overbury St. L7: Liv 7D 88 (7P 5)
Overchurch Rd. CH49: Upton 2C 104
Overdale Av. CH61: Barn 4H 125
Overdale Rd. CH64: Will 2G 159
Overdene Wlk. L32: K'by 4D 56
Overgreen Gro. CH46: More 6B 84
Overhill Way WN3: Wins 1B 50
Overmarsh CH64: Ness 7A 158
OVERPOOL 5G 161
Overpool Gdns. CH66: Gt Sut 1H 169
Overpool Rd.
CH66: Ell P, Gt Sut, Whit 5G 161
(not continuous)
Overpool Station (Rail) 5G 161
OVERTON 4E 166
Overton Av. L21: Lith 4H 53
Overton Cl. CH43: O'ton 5K 105
L32: K'by 4B 56
Overton Dr. WA6: Frod 5E 166
Overton Rd. CH44: Wall 3B 86
Overton St. L7: Liv 6D 88 (7P 5)
Overton Way CH43: O'ton 5K 105
Ovington Cl. WA7: Sut W 6H 153
Ovington Dr. PR8: South 2A 12
Ovolo Rd. L13: Liv 3J 89
Owdale Rd. L9: Walt 2C 68
Owen Av. L39: Orm 4D 24
Owen Cl. WA10: St. H 5K 73
Owen Dr. L24: Speke 6F 131
Owen Rd. L4: Kirk 6K 67
L33: Know I 6G 57
L35: R'hill 5J 93
Owens Corner Rdbt.
WA4: App 6D 138
Owen's La. L39: Down 1K 31
Owen St. WA2: Warr 1A 118
WA10: St. H 5J 73
Owlsfield WA12: New W 3J 77
Oxborough Cl. WA8: Wid 5B 114
Oxbow Rd. L12: W Der 6C 70
Oxendale Cl. L8: Liv 1D 108 (10P 5)
Oxenham Rd. WA2: Warr 4A 98
Oxenholme Cres.
L11: N Grn. 5J 69
Oxford Av. L20: Boot 3K 67
L21: Lith 5H 53
Oxford Cl. CH66: Gt Sut 4G 169
L17: Aig 6E 108
Oxford Ct. L22: Water 3C 52
PR8: B'dale 4F 11
Oxford Dr. CH63: Thorn H 4K 143
L22: Water 3C 52
Oxford Dr. L26: Halew 1K 131
Oxford Gdns. PR8: B'dale 4E 10
Oxford Gro. M44: Cad 1K 101
Oxford Ho. *L20: Boot 3A 68*
(off Fernhill Rd.)
Oxford Rd. CH44: Wall 3C 86
L9: Ain 5D 54
L20: Boot 3K 67
L22: Water 3C 52
L36: Huy 3A 92
PR8: B'dale 3E 10
WA7: Run 1C 152
WN5: Orr 4H 39
WN8: Skel 2E 36
Oxford St. L7: Liv 6B 88 (7K 5)
(not continuous)
WA4: Warr 4C 118
WA8: Wid 2D 134
WA10: St. H 2B 74
(Cooper St.)
WA10: St. H 1B 74
(Rutland St.)
WA12: New W 3F 77
Oxford St. E. L7: Liv 6C 88 (7N 5)
Oxheys WA7: Nort 2A 154
Oxhouse Rd. WN5: Orr 7F 39
Ox La. L35: Tar G 1C 112
Oxley Av. CH46: Leas 4F 85
Oxley St. WA9: St. H 7F 75
Oxmead Cl. WA2: P'gate 6H 99
Oxmoor Cl. WA7: Brook 5J 153
OXTON 4K 105
Oxton Cl. L17: Aig 6E 108
L32: K'by 5K 55
WA8: Wid 4J 113
Oxton Grn. CH66: Gt Sut 7F 161
Oxton Rd. CH41: Birk 3C 106
CH43: O'ton 3C 106
CH44: Wall 4B 86
Oxton St. L4: Walt 6B 68

P

Pacific Rd. CH41: Birk 1F 107
L20: Boot 3H 67
(Atlantic Rd.)
L20: Boot 2H 67
(Sea Vw. Rd.)
Packenham Rd. L13: Liv 1H 89
Padbury St. L8: Liv 3C 108
PADDINGTON 7F 99
Paddington L7: Liv 6C 88 (6M 5)
(not continuous)
Paddington Bank WA1: Warr 2F 119
Paddock, The CH2: Elt 1A 172
CH46: More 1A 104
CH49: Upton 3F 105
CH60: Hes 2G 143
CH66: Gt Sut 1F 169
L25: Gate 4F 111
L32: K'by 6B 56
L34: Ecc P 7G 73
L37: Form 5A 20
L39: Augh 7A 24
PR8: Ains 5B 14
WA6: Hel 2J 173
WA13: Lymm 5K 121
WN4: Ash M 6D 50
(not continuous)
Paddock Cl. L23: Blun 6B 40
Paddock Dr. CH64: Park 1H 157
Paddock Gro. WA9: Clock F 4F 95
Paddock La. WA13: Warb 7K 101
Paddock Ri. WA7: Beech 6G 153
Paddock Rd. L34: Prsct 1A 92
WN8: Skel 6J 37
Padeswood Cl. WA9: St. H 1E 94
Padgate Bus. Cen. *WA1: P'gate 7H 99*
(off Green La.)
Padgate La. WA1: Warr 1D 118
Padgate Recreational Cen. 5F 99
Padgate Station (Rail) 6G 99
Padstow Cl. L26: Halew 7J 111
PR9: Marsh 2C 8
WA5: Penk 5C 116
Padstow Dr. WA10: Windle 7H 59
Padstow Rd. CH49: Grea 5A 104
L16: Child 7B 90
Padstow Sq. WA7: Brook 5K 153
Pagebank Rd. L14: K Ash 4E 90
Page Ct. L37: Form 7K 19
Pagefield Rd. L15: W'tree 2H 109
Page Grn. L36: Huy 4G 91
Page La. WA8: Wid 7E 114
PAGE MOSS 5F 91
Page Moss Av. L36: Huy 3F 91
Page Moss La. L14: K Ash 4E 90
Page Moss Pde. L36: Huy 3F 91
Page Wlk. L3: Liv 4A 88 (3J 5)
(not continuous)
Pagewood Cl. CH43: Noct 4H 105
Paignton Cl. L36: Huy 4B 92
WA5: Penk 4C 116
WN5: Bil 4G 49
Paignton Rd. CH45: Wall 1K 85
L16: Child 7B 90
Painswick Rd. CH66: Gt Sut 2G 169
Paisley Av. CH62: East 6A 146
WA11: St. H 6F 61
Paisley Ct. L14: K Ash 3D 90
Paisley St. L3: Liv 4H 87 (3B 4)
Palace Arc. *WN4: Ash M 2F 63*
(off Bryn St.)
PALACE FIELDS 4J 153
Palacefields Av. WA7: Pal F 4H 153
Palace Hey CH64: Ness 6A 158
Palace Rd. L9: Ain 7C 54
PR8: B'dale 3E 10
Palatine, The L20: Boot 3J 67
Palatine Arc. WA10: St. H 3C 74
Palatine Cl. WN3: Wigan 1C 50
Palatine Ind. Est. WA4: Warr 5C 118
Palatine Rd. CH44: Wall 5D 86
CH62: Brom 1J 145
PR8: B'dale 3F 11
Palermo Cl. CH44: Wall 5D 86
Paley Cl. L4: Walt 7B 68
Palin Dr. WA5: Gt San 2D 116
Palladio Rd. L13: Liv 3J 89
Palliser Cl. WA3: Bchwd 4C 100
Pall Mall L3: Liv 4H 87 (2D 4)
Pall Mall Cen. L3: Liv 4H 87 (3D 4)
Palm Av. WN4: Gars 7B 50
Palm Cl. L9: Walt 3E 68
Palm Ct. *L8: Liv 4C 108*
(off Weller Way)
WN8: Skel 1E 36
Palmer Cl. CH43: Noct 5H 105
WA10: St. H 2B 74
Palmer Cres. WA5: Old H 7H 97
Palmerston Av. L21: Lith 6G 53
Palmerston Cl. L18: Moss H 5H 109
Palmerston Ct. L18: Moss H 5H 109
Palmerston Dr. L21: Lith 6H 53
L25: Hunts X 2H 131
Palmerston Rd. CH44: Wall 3K 85
L18: Moss H 5H 109
L19: Gars 3A 130
PR9: South 2B 12
Palmerston St. CH42: R Ferr 6F 107
Palm Gro. CH43: O'ton 2A 106
CH66: Whit 3J 169
L25: Wltn 7F 111
PR8: South 2A 12
Palm Hill CH43: O'ton 4B 106
Palmwood Av. L35: R'hill 5K 93
Palmwood Cl. CH43: Pren 7J 105
Palmyra Ho. WA1: Warr 3A 118
Palmyra Sq. Nth. WA1: Warr 3A 118
Palmyra Sq. Sth. WA1: Warr 3A 118
Paltridge Way CH61: Pens 5D 124
Pamela Cl. L10: Faz 6K 55
Pampas Gro. L9: Walt 2D 68
Pangbourne Cl. WA4: App 3E 138
Pankhurst Rd. L21: Ford 3J 53
Pansy St. L5: Kirk 7K 67
Panton Way L10: Faz 7K 55
Parade, The CH64: Park 1F 157
L15: W'tree 6K 89
L26: Halew 2J 131
Parade Cres. L24: Speke 7J 131
Parade St. WA10: St. H 2C 74
Paradise Gdns. L15: W'tree 1H 109
Paradise La. L35: Whis 5D 92
L37: Form 4K 19
Paradise St. L1: Liv 7J 87 (7F 4)
Paragon Cl. WA8: Wid 3D 114
PARBOLD 1J 27
Parbold Av. WA11: St. H 1F 75
Parbold Ct. WA8: Wid 1K 133
Parbrook Cl. L36: Huy 1H 91
Parbrook Rd. L36: Huy 1H 91
Parchments, The WA12: New W 2H 77
Parc Play & Resource Cen. 4E 56
Paris Av. WN3: Wins 1A 50
Parish M. L14: K Ash 3C 90
Park, The L36: Huy 6J 91
WA5: Penk 5B 116
(not continuous)
Park and Ride
Esplanade, The 1F 11
Park Av. CH44: Wall 4D 86
L9: Ain 6E 54
L18: Moss H 5G 109
L23: C'by 7E 40
L31: Lyd 1F 43
L34: Ecc P 7F 73
L35: R'hill 3J 93
L37: Form 2K 29
L39: Orm 5C 24
PR9: South 6A 8
WA3: Golb 3K 63
WA4: Warr 5D 118
WA8: Wid 6D 114
WA11: Hay 7J 61
WN5: Bil 3G 49
Park Av. Nth. WA12: New W 4G 77
Park Av. Sth. WA12: New W 4G 77
Park Blvd. WA1: Warr 4A 118
Parkbourn L31: Mag 2J 43
Parkbourn Dr. L31: Mag 2J 43
Parkbourn Nth. L31: Mag 2J 43
Parkbourn Sq. L31: Mag 2J 43
Parkbridge Rd. CH42: Tran 5C 106
Pk. Brow Dr. L32: K'by 5D 56
Parkbury Ct. CH43: O'ton 5A 106
Park Cl. CH41: Birk 2C 106
L32: K'by 1K 55
(not continuous)
L37: Form 3J 29
Park Ct. CH48: W Kir 6C 102
L22: Water 5E 52
L32: K'by 2A 56
PR9: South 7K 7
WA1: Warr 3K 117
WA6: Frod 3C 166
WA7: Run 2C 152
WA9: St. H 6D 74
Park Cres. L39: Has 6B 22
PR9: South 6K 7
WA4: App 3D 138
Park Cres. Ct. PR9: South 6A 8
Parkdale CH48: Caldy 3F 123
Parkdale Av. L9: Walt 6C 54
Parkdale Ind. Est. WA1: Warr 4C 118
Parkdale Rd. WA1: P'ton 1G 119

Park Dr.—Peony Gdns.

Park Dr. CH41: Birk 1B 106
CH43: C'ton 1A 106
CH65: Whit 1K 169
L23: Blun 7A 40
L23: Thorn 5G 41
Parkend Rd. CH42: Tran 5C 106
Parker Av. L21: Sea 6F 53
Parker Cl. L30: N'ton 4D 54
Parker Cres. L39: Orm 3C 24
Parkers Ct. WA7: Pal F 4G 153
Parker St. L1: Liv 6K 87 (6G 4)
WA1: Warr 4A 118
WA7: Run 6D 134
Parkfield Av. CH41: Birk 2D 106
L30: N'ton 5C 54
WA4: Westy 4G 119
Parkfield Cl. L39: Orm 7A 24
Parkfield Dr. CH44: Wall 3B 86
CH65: Whit 2J 169
WA6: Hel 1H 173
Parkfield Gro. L31: Mag 3E 42
Parkfield Pl. CH41: Birk 2D 106
Parkfield Rd. CH63: Beb 6G 127
L17: Aig 4D 108
L22: Water 3E 52
Parkfields La. WA2: Fearn 5F 99
PARKGATE 2G 157
Parkgate Cl. L17: Aig 7G 109
Parkgate Ho. CH64: Park 1F 157
Parkgate La. CH64: Nest 5J 143
Parkgate Rd. CH1: W'bnk 4A 168
CH64: Nest 3H 157
CH66: Led 3A 168
WA4: S Hth 7D 118
Parkgate Way WA7: Murd 4A 154
Park Gro. CH41: Birk 3D 106
PARK HILL 2D 46
Pk. Hill Ct. L8: Liv 4B 108
Park Hill Rd. L8: Liv 4B 108
Parkhill Rd. CH42: Tran 5C 106
Parkholme L22: Water 4E 52
Parkhurst Rd. CH42: Tran 6C 106
L11: N Grn. 5H 69
Park Ind. Est. WN4: Ash M 3C 62
Parkinson Rd. L9: Walt 2C 68
Parkland Cl. L8: Liv 3B 108
WA4: App T 4H 139
Parkland Ct. CH43: Bid 7G 85
Parklands CH66: Lit Sut 6E 160
L34: Know 3H 71
PR9: South 7A 8
WA8: Wid 5J 113
WA11: R'ford 5F 47
WN8: Skel 1K 37
Parklands Ct. *CH49: W'chu 6E 104*
(off Childwall Grn.)
Parklands Dr. CH2: Elt 1A 172
CH60: Hes 4F 143
Parklands Gdns.
CH66: Lit Sut 5F 161
Parklands Vw. CH66: Lit Sut 5F 161
Parklands Way L22: Water 4E 52
Park La. CH47: Meols 6J 83
L1: Liv 7J 87 (8E 4)
L20: Boot 6A 54
L30: N'ton 3B 54
L31: Mag 1H 43
WA4: App, H Walt 4J 137
WA6: Frod 3D 166
WA13: Warb 6K 101
Park La. Dr. L31: Mag 2J 43
Park La. W. L30: N'ton 2B 54
Parklea CH66: Lit Sut 5F 161
Park Link L39: Augh 2K 33
Park Pl. L8: Liv 2A 108
L20: Boot 3J 67
WA1: Warr 3A 118
Park Pool L39: Orm 5C 24
Park Rd. CH2: Thor M 3J 171
CH42: Tran 5E 106
CH44: Wall 4C 86
CH47: Meols 6G 83
CH48: W Kir 6C 102
CH60: Hes 1F 143
CH62: East 4B 146
CH62: Port S 4H 127
CH64: Will 3H 159
CH65: Ell P 7A 162
(not continuous)
L8: Liv 3B 108
L22: Water 4E 52
L32: K'by 2K 55
(not continuous)
L34: Prsct 7C 72
L37: Form 2J 29
L39: Orm 5C 24
PR9: South 6K 7
WA2: Warr 6D 98
WA3: Golb 6K 63
WA5: Gt San 1A 116
WA7: Run 2B 152
WA8: Wid 7D 114
WA9: St. H 2E 74
WA11: St. H 2E 74
WA13: Warb 7K 101
(not continuous)
WN5: Bil 3G 49
WN5: Orr 5J 39
Park Rd. E. CH41: Birk 2C 106
Park Rd. Nth. CH41: Birk 1K 105
WA12: New W 3J 77
Park Rd. Sth. CH43: C'ton 2B 106
WA12: New W 4G 77
Park Road Sports Cen. 3B 108
Park Rd. W. CH43: C'ton 1K 105
PR9: South 6J 7
Parks, The WA12: New W 4F 63
Parkside CH44: Wall 4C 86
L20: Boot 2J 67
Parkside Av. WA9: Sut M 4D 94
WN4: Ash M 4D 50
WN8: Skel 3D 36
Parkside Cl. CH63: Beb 3G 127
CH64: Park 3H 157
L27: N'ley 4J 111
Parkside Ct. PR9: South 6K 7
WA8: Wid 6C 114
Parkside Cres. WN5: Orr 5H 39
Parkside Dr. L12: W Der 6J 69
Parkside Mans. L36: Huy 5B 92
Parkside Rd. CH42: Tran 5E 106
CH63: Beb 3G 127
WA2: Win 2A 78
Parkside St. L6: Liv 4B 88 (2L 5)
Parkstile La. L11: Crox 2A 70
Parkstone Rd. CH42: Tran 5C 106
Park St. CH41: Birk 2D 106
(not continuous)
CH44: Wall 3C 86
CH64: Nest 3J 157
L8: Liv 3K 107
L20: Boot 3J 67
WA9: St. H 2E 74
WA11: Hay 7H 61
Parksway WA1: W'ston 1K 119
Park Ter. L22: Water 5E 52
Park Va. CH64: Nest 4K 157
Parkvale Av. CH43: Pren 1J 125
Pk. Vale Rd. L9: Walt 7C 54
Park Vw. CH62: Brom 2J 145
L6: Liv 2F 89
L22: Water 3D 52
L23: Thorn 5H 41
L36: Huy 3G 91
WA2: Warr 4E 98
WN4: Ash M 3F 63
Parkview L9: Walt 2C 68
Parkview Cl. CH41: Birk 1C 106
Parkview Ct. CH60: Hes 2D 142
Parkview Dr. L27: N'ley 4J 111
Park Vw. Flats L21: Lith 5G 53
Parkview Rd. L11: Crox 7B 56
Pk. Wall Rd. L29: Thorn 3G 41
L38: Ince B, Thorn 1F 41
Park Way L8: Liv 1B 108 (10L 5)
(not continuous)
L36: Huy 7H 71
L37: Form 2K 29
Parkway CH45: Wall 7J 65
CH47: Meols 7G 83
CH61: Irby 2D 124
L23: C'by 3F 53
L30: N'ton 7B 42
Parkway Cl. CH61: Irby 2D 124
Parkway E. L32: K'by 2K 55
Parkway W. L32: K'by 2K 55
Park W. CH60: Hes 3B 142
Parkwood Cl. CH62: Brom 1K 145
WA13: Lymm 6F 121
Parkwood Rd. L25: Wltn 4E 110
L35: Whis 5E 92
Parlane St. WA9: St. H 2E 74
(not continuous)
Parle Ct. L6: Liv 2D 88
Parliament Bus. Pk.
L8: Liv 1D 108 (10P 5)
Parliament Cl. L1: Liv 1A 108 (10J 5)
Parliament Pl. L8: Liv 1B 108 (10K 5)
Parliament St. L8: Liv 1K 107
WA9: St. H 7K 73
WN8: Uph 3E 38
Parliament Way CH66: Gt Sut 4H 169
Parlington Cl. WA8: Wid 2J 133
Parlow Rd. L11: N Grn. 6G 69
Parnell Rd. CH63: Spit 6G 127
PARR 3F 75
Parr Community Swimming Pool 3E 74
Parren Av. L35: Whis 6C 92
Parr Gro. CH49: Grea 4A 104
WA11: Hay 7J 61
Parr Ind. Est. WA9: St. H 4G 75
Parr Mt. Ct. WA9: St. H 3E 74
Parr Mt. St. WA9: St. H 3E 74
Parrs Cnr. Trad. Est. *L20: Boot 2J 67*
(off Stanley Rd.)
Parrs La. L39: Augh 3B 34
Parr's Rd. CH43: O'ton 5B 106
PARR STOCKS 4F 75
Parr Stocks Rd. WA9: St. H 3F 75
Parr St. L1: Liv 7K 87 (8G 4)
WA1: Warr 4C 118
(not continuous)
WA8: Wid 7E 114
WA9: St. H 3D 74
WA10: St. H 3D 74
Parrs Wood Vw. WA4: Grap 7G 119
Parry Dr. WA4: Thel 5A 120
Parry's La. WA7: Run 1C 152
Parry St. CH44: Wall 5D 86
Parsonage Brow WN8: Uph 3B 38
Parsonage Cl. WN8: Uph 4C 38
Parsonage Rd. WA8: Wid 5C 134
WN8: Uph 4C 38
Parsonage Way WA5: Gt San 2E 116
Parson's Brow WA11: R'ford 6E 46
Parthenon Dr. L11: N Grn. 3F 69
Partington Av. L20: Boot 2A 68
Parton St. L6: Liv 4E 88
Partridge Cl. L12: Crox 3D 70
WA3: Bchwd 3A 100
Partridge Rd. L23: Blun 1B 52
L32: K'by 2K 55
Part St. PR8: South 3G 11
Passway WA11: St. H 5E 60
Pasture Av. CH46: More 5C 84
Pasture Cl. L25: Wltn 7F 111
WA9: Clock F 3E 94
WN4: Ash M 6C 50
Pasture Cres. CH46: More 6C 84
Pasture Dr. WA3: Croft 7G 79
Pasture La. L37: Form 4C 20
WA2: P'gate 6H 99
WA11: R'ford 1G 59
Pasture La. Bus. Cen.
WA11: R'ford 1G 59
Pasture Rd. CH46: More 4B 84
Pastures, The CH48: W Kir 6H 103
PR9: Cros 2F 9
WA9: Bold 7J 75
Pateley Cl. L32: K'by 4A 56
Pateley Wlk. L24: Speke 5K 131
Paterson St. CH41: Birk 2C 106
Patmos Cl. L5: Liv 1A 88
Paton Cl. CH48: W Kir 5F 103
Patricia Av. CH41: Birk 6K 85
Patricia Ct. WA10: St. H 2B 74
Patricia Gro. L20: Boot 7K 53
Patrick Av. L20: Boot 6K 53
Patrivale Cl. WA1: P'ton 2F 119
Patten La. WA1: Warr 3B 118
Pattens Cl. L30: N'ton 1K 53
Patten St. CH41: Birk 7A 86
Patten's Wlk. L34: Know P 1H 71
Patterdale Av. WA2: Warr 5C 98
Patterdale Cl. PR8: Ains 6B 14
Patterdale Cres. L31: Mag 2G 43
Patterdale Dr. WA10: St. H 6H 73
Patterdale Rd. CH63: Beb 6F 127
L15: W'tree 2G 109
WN4: Ash M 4E 50
Patterson Cl. WA3: Bchwd 4A 100
Patterson St. WA12: New W 3F 77
Patton Dr. WA5: Gt San 2F 117
Paul Cl. WA5: Gt San 2B 116
Pauldings La. L21: Lith 5G 53
Pauline Wlk. L10: Faz 6K 55
Paul McCartney Way L6: Liv 4D 88 (3P 5)
Paul Orr Ct. L3: Liv 3J 87 (1D 4)
Paulsfield Dr. CH46: More 1C 104
Paul's La. PR9: Chu 4B 8
Paul St. L3: Liv 4J 87 (2E 4)
WA2: Warr 2A 118
Paulton Cl. L8: Liv 4B 108
Paverley Bank L27: N'ley 2H 111
Pavilion Cl. L8: Liv 1D 108 (10P 5)
Pavilion Ct. WA12: New W 3E 76
Pavilion Sports Cen. 1J 89
Paxton Pl. WN8: Skel 7J 37
Paxton Rd. L36: Huy 3J 91
Payne Cl. WA5: Gt San 2H 117
Paythorne Cl. WA3: Cul 3B 80
Peace Dr. WA5: Gt San 3H 117
Peacehaven WN8: Skel 2E 36
Peacehaven Cl. L16: Child 7D 90
Peach Gro. L31: Mell 1K 55
WA11: Hay 6C 62
Peach St. L7: Liv 6B 88 (7L 5)
Peach Tree Cl. L24: Hale 7E 132
Peacock Av. WA1: Warr 2E 118
Peak Climbing Cen. 3D 36
Pearce Cl. L25: Wltn 2D 110
Pear Gro. L6: Liv 4D 88 (2P 5)
Pearl Way L6: Liv 3D 88 (1P 5)
Pearson Av. WA4: Latch 6D 118
Pearson Dr. L20: Boot 6A 54
Pearson Rd. CH42: Tran 4E 106
Pearson St. L15: W'tree 1H 109
Pear Tree Av. L12: W Der 5D 70
WA7: Run 3E 152
Pear Tree Cl. CH60: Hes 1G 143
L24: Hale 1E 150
Peartree Cl. WA6: Frod 2F 167
Pear Tree Pl. WA4: Warr 4C 118
Pear Tree Rd. L36: Huy 7J 91
Peartree Way CH66: Gt Sut 3G 169
Peasefield Rd. L14: K Ash 3E 90
Peasley Cl. WA2: P'gate 6H 99
PEASLEY CROSS 5E 74
Peasley Cross La. WA9: St. H 3D 74
Peatwood Av. L32: K'by 6D 56
Peckers Hill Rd. WA9: St. H 7G 75
Peckfield Cl. WA7: Brook 5J 153
Peckforton Cl. L13: Liv 1G 89
Peckforton Dr. CH66: Gt Sut 1G 169
WA7: Sut W 6H 153
Peckmill Grn. L27: N'ley 4K 111
Peck Mill La. WA6: Hel 5G 173
Pecksniff Cl. L8: Liv 3B 108
Peebles Av. WA11: St. H 6F 61
Peebles Cl. CH66: Lit Sut 5B 160
L33: K'by 6B 44
WN4: Gars 1A 62
Peel Av. CH42: Tran 5F 107
Peel Cl. L35: Whis 4E 92
WA1: W'ston 2K 119
Peel Cott. L31: Mag 2D 42
Peel Ho. La. WA8: Wid 5D 114
Peel Pl. L8: Liv 1B 108 (10K 5)
WA10: St. H 1C 74
Peel Rd. L20: Boot 1G 67
WN8: Skel 6K 37
Peel St. L8: Liv 4C 108
PR8: South 2B 12
WA7: Run 6B 134
WA12: New W 3E 76
Peel Wlk. L31: Mag 2D 42
Peers Wood Ct. CH64: Lit N 6J 157
Peet Av. L39: Orm 6B 24
WA10: St. H 2J 73
Peets La. PR9: Chu 6C 8
Peet St. L7: Liv 6D 88
Pelham Gro. L17: Aig 4E 108
Pelham Rd. CH44: Wall 4A 86
WA4: Thel 5J 119
Pemberton Bus. Cen.
WN5: Wigan 5K 39
Pemberton Cl. CH64: Will 3G 159
Pemberton Rd. CH49: W'chu 5F 105
L13: Liv 4J 89
WN3: Wins 3J 49
WN5: Wins 4J 49
Pemberton St. WA10: St. H 3A 74
Pembridge Ct. CH65: Ell P 1C 170
Pembridge Gdns. CH65: Ell P 1C 170
Pembroke Av. CH46: More 1C 104
Pembroke Cl. WA10: St. H 4A 74
Pembroke Ct. CH41: Tran 4E 106
WA7: Mnr P 4A 136
Pembroke Dr. CH65: Whit 1J 169
Pembroke Gdns. L3: Liv 5B 88 (5K 5)
WA4: App 5D 138
Pembroke Ho. L6: Liv 3E 88
Pembroke Pl. L3: Liv 5A 88 (5K 5)
Pembroke Rd. L20: Boot 3J 67
Pembroke St. L3: Liv 5B 88 (6K 5)
Pembury Cl. L12: Crox 3C 70
Penare WA7: Brook 5A 154
Penarth Cl. L7: Liv 7D 88 (9P 5)
Penbrey Way L25: Hunts X 1H 131
Pencombe Rd. L36: Huy 3F 91
Penda Dr. L33: K'by 6C 44
Pendennis Rd. CH44: Wall 4C 86
Pendennis St. L6: Liv 2D 88
Pendine Cl. L6: Liv 3E 88
WA5: Call 5G 97
Pendle Av. WA11: St. H 1F 75
Pendlebury St. WA4: Westy 5G 119
WA9: Clock F 3E 94
Pendle Cl. CH49: Upton 2C 104
CH66: Lit Sut 5B 160
Pendle Dr. L21: Ford 1J 53
L39: Orm 4E 24
Pendle Gdns. WA3: Cul 3A 80
Pendle Pl. WN8: Skel 7K 37
Pendleton Grn. L26: Halew 2J 131
(not continuous)
Pendleton Rd. L4: Walt 4C 68
Pendle Vw. L21: Ford 1J 53
Pendle Vs. L21: Ford 2J 53
Penfold L31: Mag 3G 43
Penfold Cl. CH1: Cap 4D 168
L18: Moss H 3B 110
Penfolds WA7: Run 1F 153
Pengwern Gro. L15: W'tree 7F 89
Pengwern St. L8: Liv 3C 108
Pengwern Ter. CH45: New B 7C 66
Penhale Cl. L17: Aig 6D 108
Peninsula Cl. CH45: Wall 6J 65
Peninsula Ho. WA2: Warr 1C 118
Penistone Dr. CH66: Lit Sut 6D 160
PENKETH 4C 116
Penketh Av. WA5: Warr 7K 97
Penketh Bus. Pk. WA5: Gt San 4F 117
Penketh Ct. WA5: Penk 4B 116
WA7: Run 6D 134
Penketh Grn. L24: Speke 5J 131
Penketh Parish Swimming Pool 4C 116
Penketh Pl. WN8: Skel 6H 37
Penketh Rd. WA5: Gt San, Penk 4E 116
Penketh's La. WA7: Run 6C 134
Penkett Ct. CH45: Wall 1C 86
Penkett Gdns. CH45: Wall 1C 86
Penkett Gro. CH45: Wall 1C 86
Penkett Rd. CH45: Wall 1B 86
Penkford La. WA5: C Grn 5B 76
Penkford St. WA12: New W 3C 76
Penkmans La. WA6: Frod 5E 166
Penlake Ind. Est. WA9: St. H 7G 75
Penlake La. WA9: St. H 7H 75
Penley Cres. L32: K'by 3K 55
Penlinken Dr. L6: Liv 3D 88
Penmann Cl. L26: Halew 1K 131
Penmann Cres. L26: Halew 1K 131
Penmark Cl. WA5: Call 5G 97
Penmon Dr. CH61: Pens 6D 124
Pennant Av. L12: W Der 5A 70
Pennant Cl. WA3: Bchwd 4C 100
Pennard Av. L36: Huy 1H 91
Penn Gdns. CH65: Ell P 6K 161
Pennine Av. WN3: Wins 1A 50
Pennine Cl. WA9: St. H 3G 75
Pennine Dr. WA9: St. H 3H 75
Pennine Pl. WN8: Skel 5H 37
Pennine Rd. CH42: Tran 7C 106
CH44: Wall 3K 85
WA2: Warr 5E 98
Pennine Wlk. CH66: Lit Sut 6D 160
Pennine Way L32: K'by 1A 56
Pennington Av. L20: Boot 6A 54
L39: Orm 4C 24
Pennington Cl. WA6: Frod 1F 167
Pennington Ct. L39: Orm 4C 24
(not continuous)
Pennington Dr. WA12: New W 3J 77
Pennington Gdns. L34: Prsct 1D 92
Pennington Grn. CH66: Gt Sut 1E 168
Pennington La. WA5: C Grn 3K 75
WA9: St. H 3K 75
Pennington Rd. L21: Lith 7J 53
Pennington St. L4: Walt 4B 68
Penn La. WA7: Run 7B 134
Pennsylvania Rd. L13: Liv 7F 69
Pennyford Dr. L18: Moss H 5G 109
PENNYLANDS 2D 36
Penny La. L18: Moss H 4H 109
WA5: C Grn 6B 76
WA8: Cron 1F 113
WA11: Hay 6D 62
Penny La. Neighbourhood Cen.
L15: W'tree 2H 109
Pennypleck La. CW9: Ant 7C 140
Pennystone Cl. CH49: Upton 2B 104
Pennywood Dr. L35: Whis 5E 92
Penpoll Ind. Est. L20: Boot 7J 53
Penrhos Rd. CH47: Hoy 2C 102
Penrhyd Rd. CH61: Irby 4B 124
Penrhyn Av. CH61: Thing 3E 124
L21: Lith 6H 53
Penrhyn Cres. WA7: Run 3C 152
Penrhyn Rd. L34: Know 1F 71
Penrhyn St. L5: Liv 2K 87
Penrith Av. PR8: Ains 6C 14
WA2: Warr 4C 98
Penrith Cl. WA6: Frod 2F 167
Penrith Cres. L31: Mag 2G 43
WN4: Ash M 1F 63
Penrith Rd. WA10: St. H 6H 73
Penrith St. CH41: Birk 3C 106
Penrose Av. E. L14: B Grn 5C 90
Penrose Av. W. L14: B Grn 5C 90
Penrose Gdns. WA5: Penk 5B 116
Penrose Pl. WN8: Skel 7A 38
Penrose St. L5: Liv 1A 88
Penryn Av. WA11: St. H 6F 61
Penryn Cl. WA5: Penk 5C 116
Pensall Dr. CH61: Hes 7D 124
Pensarn Gdns. WA5: Call 5H 97
Pensarn Rd. L13: Liv 5H 89
PENSBY 5E 124
Pensby Cl. CH61: Thing 4E 124
Pensby Dr. CH66: Gt Sut 7F 161
Pensby Hall La. CH61: Hes 7D 124
Pensby Rd. CH60: Hes 2D 142
CH61: Pens, Thing 4E 124
Pensby St. CH41: Birk 7B 86
Penshaw Av. WN3: Wigan 1F 51
Penshaw Ct. WA7: Pal F 3G 153
Pentire Av. WA10: Windle 7H 59
Pentire Cl. L10: Faz 7K 55
Pentland Av. L4: Walt 5C 68
WA2: Warr 4B 98
WA9: St. H 3H 75
Pentland Pl. WA2: Warr 4B 98
Pentland Rd. L33: K'by 1E 56
Penty Pl. PR8: South 2H 11
Penuel Rd. L4: Walt 4B 68
Penvalley Cres. L6: Liv 3E 88
Penwell Fold WN8: Skel 3A 38
Peony Gdns. WA9: Bold 7K 75

Portico La.—Queensway

Portico La. L34: Ecc P 1G 93
L35: Prsct, Ecc P 1F 93
Portland Av. L22: Water 3C 52
Portland Cl. WN2: Platt B 3K 51
Portland Ct. CH45: New B 5A 66
Portland Gdns. L5: Liv 3J 87 (1E 4)
Portland Ga. CH62: Port S 3J 127
Portland Pl. L5: Liv 3A 88 (1H 5)
WA6: Hel 7J 165
Portland Rd. WA5: Gt San 1E 116
Portland St. CH41: Birk 7A 86
CH45: New B 5A 66
L5: Liv 3J 87 (1E 4)
Portland St. PR8: South 2G 11
WA7: Run 6B 134
WA12: New W 2D 76
Portland Way WA9: St. H 5H 75
Portlemouth Rd. L11: Crox 1A 70
Portloe Av. L26: Halew 7K 111
Portman Rd. L15: W'tree 1F 109
Porto Hey Rd. CH61: Irby 4B 124
Portola Cl. WA4: Grap 6J 119
Porton Rd. L32: K'by 4A 56
Portreath Way WA10: Windle 7H 59
Portree Av. CH63: East 5K 145
Portree Cl. L9: Walt 2B 68
Portrush Cl. WA8: Wid 5A 114
Portrush St. L13: Liv 1G 89
Portside WA7: Pres B 3C 154
Portside Ind. Est.
CH65: Ell P 3A 162
Portside Nth. CH65: Ell P 3K 161
Portside Sth. CH65: Ell P 3A 162
Portsmouth Pl. WA7: Murd 4C 154
PORT SUNLIGHT 4H 127
Port Sunlight Heritage Cen. 4H 127
Port Sunlight Station (Rail) 4H 127
Portway L25: Hunts X 2G 131
Portwood Cl. L7: Liv 7D 88 (9P 5)
Post Office Av. PR9: South 1H 11
Post Office La. CH2: Thor M 3J 171
WA7: West P 3K 151
Potter Pl. WN8: Skel 6K 37
Potters La. L18: Moss H 3A 110
WA8: Hale B 4F 133
Pottery Cl. L35: Whis 4C 92
Pottery Flds. L34: Prsct 1E 92
Pottery La. L35: Whis 4B 92
L36: Huy 4B 92
Poulsom Dr. L30: N'ton 3J 53
Poulter Rd. L9: Ain 6D 54
POULTON
Wallasey 4B 86
Wirral 1G 145
Poulton Bri. Rd. CH41: Birk 5A 86
Poulton Cl. L26: Halew 3H 131
Poulton Ct. PR9: South 1B 12
Poulton Cres. WA1: W'ston 6J 99
Poulton Dr. WA8: Wid 1J 133
WN4: Ash M 7D 50
Poulton Grn. Cl. CH63: Spit 7F 127
Poulton Hall Rd. CH44: Wall 4A 86
CH63: Raby M 3G 145
Poulton Rd. CH44: Wall 4A 86
CH63: Spit 6G 127
PR9: South 1B 12
Poulton Royd Dr. CH63: Spit 7F 127
Poulton Va. CH44: Wall 5A 86
Pound Rd. CH66: Lit Sut 4E 160
Poverty La. L31: Mag 4G 43
Povey Rd. WA2: Warr 6C 98
Powder Works La. L31: Mag 1A 44
Powell Av. WA3: Ris 3A 100
Powell Dr. WN5: Bil 2F 61
Powell St. WA4: Latch 5F 119
WA9: St. H 7G 75
Powerhouse L8: Liv 10P 5
Powerleague Liverpool 7A 68
Power Rd. CH42: R Ferr 1G 127
CH62: Brom 1B 146
Powey La. CH1: Moll 7D 168
Powis St. L8: Liv 3C 108
Pownall Sq. L3: Liv 5J 87 (4E 4)
Pownall St. L1: Liv 7J 87 (8E 4)
Powys St. WA5: Warr 3K 117
Poynter St. WA9: St. H 7A 74
Poynton Cl. WA4: Grap 5H 119
Pratt Rd. L34: Prsct 1C 92
Precincts, The L23: C'by 1E 52
Preece Cl. WA8: Wid 5K 113
Preesall Cl. PR9: Marsh 2B 8
Preesall Way L11: Crox 1A 70
(not continuous)
Prefect Pl. WN5: Wigan 3K 39
Premier Bowl 7G 7
Premier St. L5: Liv 2B 88
Prentice Rd. CH42: R Ferr 7E 106
PRENTON 1K 125
Prenton Av. WA9: Clock F 3D 94
Prenton Dell Av. CH43: Pren 1A 126
Prenton Dell Rd. CH43: Pren 7J 105
Prenton Farm Rd. CH43: Pren 1A 126
Prenton Grn. L24: Speke 6J 131
Prenton Hall Rd. CH43: Pren 7K 105
Prenton La. CH42: Tran 7B 106
Prenton Pk. 6C 106
Prenton Pk. Rd. CH42: Tran 5C 106
Prenton Rd. E. CH42: Tran 6C 106
Prenton Rd. W. CH42: Tran 6B 106
Prenton Village Rd.
CH43: Pren 7K 105
Prenton Way CH43: Pren 7J 105
Prentonwood Ct. CH42: Tran 7C 106
PRESCOT 1D 92
Prescot By-Pass L34: Prsct 1B 92
Prescot Cables AFC 7D 72
Prescot Cen. L34: Prsct 1D 92
Prescot Dr. L6: Liv 4F 89
Prescot Grn. L39: Orm 7B 24
Prescot Leisure Cen. 2E 92
Prescot Mus. of Clock & Watchmaking
1C 92
Prescot Rd. L7: Liv 4E 88
L13: Liv 4E 88
L31: Mag, Mell 1A 56
L39: Augh, Orm 1B 34
WA8: Cron 4F 113
WA8: Wid 5K 113
WA10: St. H 6G 73
Prescot Station (Rail) 2E 92
Prescot St. CH45: New B 6A 66
L7: Liv 5B 88 (4L 5)
Prescott Av. WA3: Golb 3K 63
Prescott La. WN5: Orr 3K 39
Prescot Trade Cen. L34: Prsct 1E 92
Prescott Rd. WN8: Skel 6B 38
Prescott St. WA4: Latch 5E 118
Preseland Rd. L23: C'by 2E 52
Prestbury Av. CH43: O'ton 6J 105
PR8: Ains 4B 14
WN3: Wigan 1C 50
Prestbury Cl. CH43: O'ton 6J 105
WA8: Wid 1A 134
Prestbury Dr. WA4: Thel 4K 119
WA10: Eccl 4H 73
Prestbury Rd. L11: N Grn. 2H 69
Preston Av. L34: Prsct 2C 92
PRESTON BROOK 4D 154
Preston Gro. L6: Liv 2E 88
Preston New Rd. PR9: Chu 5C 8
PRESTON ON THE HILL 4E 154
Preston Rd. PR9: South 7A 8
Preston St. L1: Liv 5K 87 (5F 4)
WA9: Sut M 5C 94
Preston Way L23: C'by 1G 53
Prestwich Av. WA3: Cul 3A 80
Prestwick Cl. WA8: Wid 5B 114
Prestwick Dr. L23: Blun 6C 40
Prestwood Ct. WA3: Ris 7C 80
Prestwood Cres. L14: K Ash 3D 90
Prestwood Pl. WN8: Skel 7B 38
Prestwood Rd. L14: K Ash 3D 90
Pretoria Rd. L9: Ain 7D 54
WN4: Ash M 1F 63
Price Gro. WA9: St. H 4J 75
Price's La. CH43: O'ton 4B 106
Price St. CH41: Birk 7B 86
L1: Liv 7J 87 (8F 4)
Price St. Bus. Cen. CH41: Birk 7C 86
Pride Cl. WA12: New W 4J 77
Priestfield Rd. CH65: Ell P 6K 161
Priesthouse Cl. L37: Form 7A 20
Priesthouse La. L37: Form 7A 20
Priestley Bus. Cen. WA5: Warr 3K 117
Priestley St. WA5: Warr 3K 117
Priestner Dr. WA6: Hel 7H 165
Primary Av. L30: N'ton 1D 54
Primrose Cl. L37: Form 5B 20
PR9: Cros 1E 8
WA2: Warr 5D 98
WA7: Cas 1J 153
WA8: Wid 7A 114
Primrose Ct. CH45: New B 6B 66
Primrose Dr. L36: Huy 2J 91
Primrose Gro. CH44: Wall 5E 86
WA11: Hay 6C 62
PRIMROSE HILL 2H 23
Primrose Hill CH62: Port S 3G 127
L3: Liv 5K 87 (4F 4)
Primrose La. WA6: Alv, Hel 3G 173
Primrose M. WA6: Alv 3K 173
Primrose Pl. WN4: Ash M 3F 63
(off Violet St.)
Primrose Rd. CH41: Birk 1K 105
L18: Moss H 3A 110
Primrose St. L4: Kirk 6K 67
Primrose Vw. WN4: Ash M 3F 63
Primula Cl. WA9: Bold 7J 75
Primula Dr. L9: Walt 2D 68
Prince Albert Ct. WA9: St. H 6H 75
Prince Albert M.
L1: Liv 1K 107 (10H 5)
Prince Alfred Rd. L15: W'tree 1H 109
Prince Andrew's Gro.
WA10: Windle 7J 59
Prince Charles Gdns.
PR8: B'dale 3F 11
Prince Edward St. CH41: Birk 1C 106
Prince Edwin St. L5: Liv 3A 88 (1H 5)
Prince Henry Sq. WA1: Warr 3B 118
Princes Av. CH48: W Kir 6D 102
CH62: East 4A 146
L8: Liv 1B 108
L23: C'by 2E 52
Princes Blvd. CH63: High B 1D 126
Prince's Cl. WA7: Cas 1H 153
Princes Ct. L8: Liv 2D 108
Princes Gdns. L3: Liv 4J 87 (3D 4)
Princes Ga. E. L8: Liv 2D 108
Princes Ga. W. L8: Liv 2C 108
Princes Pde. L3: Liv 5G 87 (4B 4)
PRINCES PARK 2D 108
Princes Pk. Mans. L8: Liv 3D 108
Princes Pavement
CH41: Birk 2E 106
Princes Pl. CH41: Tran 4E 106
WA8: Wid 7A 114
Princes Rd. CH65: Ell P 5H 161
L8: Liv 1B 108 (10L 5)
WA10: St. H 5J 73
Princess Av. WA1: P'gate 7G 99
WA1: Warr 2F 119
WA5: Gt San 1C 116
WA10: St. H 1A 74
WA11: Hay 6E 62
WN4: Ash M 2G 63
Princess Ct. PR9: South 7K 7
Princess Cres. WA1: Warr 2F 119
Princess Dr. L12: W Der 6C 70
L14: K Ash 6C 70
Princess Rd. CH45: New B 7B 66
WA13: Lymm 5E 120
WN4: Ash M 2F 63
Princess St. WA5: Warr 4H 117
WA7: Run 6C 134
Princess Ter. CH43: O'ton 3C 106
Princes St. L2: Liv 5J 87 (5E 4)
L20: Boot 5H 67
PR8: South 2G 11
WA8: Wid 1C 134
WA12: New W 3F 77
Princess Way L21: Sea 7F 53
Prince St. L22: Water 5E 52
WN4: Ash M 7E 50
Princes Way WA11: St. H 5C 60
Princesway CH45: Wall 1A 86
Princeway WA6: Frod 3D 166
Prince William St. L8: Liv 2A 108
Priors Cl. L25: Wltn 6F 111
Priorsfield CH46: More 7C 84
Priorsfield Rd. L25: Wltn 6F 111
Prior St. L20: Boot 7G 53
Priorswood Pl. WN8: Skel 7B 38
Priory, The CH64: Nest 2H 157
L35: R'hill 4J 93
WA2: Win 7A 78
Priory Cl. CH63: Beb 6G 127
L17: Aig 6D 108
L35: Whis 6C 92
L37: Form 1B 30
WA7: Halt 1J 153
WN5: Wigan 6K 39
Priory Ct. L36: Huy 5H 91
PR8: South 2F 11
WA7: Pres B 5C 154
Priory Farm Cl. L19: Gras 2J 129
Priory Gdns. PR8: B'dale 4F 11
WA10: St. H 6B 60
Priory Grange PR8: B'dale 4G 11
Priory Gro. L39: Orm 6B 24
Priory M. CH41: Birk 2F 107
PR8: South 2F 11
Priory Nook WN8: Uph 4E 38
Priory Rd. CH44: Wall 4E 86
CH48: W Kir 6E 102
L4: Walt 6C 68
WA7: Wind H 7A 136
WN4: Ash M 7D 50
WN8: Uph 4E 38
Priory St. CH41: Birk 2F 107
L19: Gars 5B 130
WA4: Warr 5B 118
Priory Way L25: Wltn 6F 111
Priory Wharf CH41: Birk 2F 107
Pritchard Av. L21: Sea 6F 53
Pritt St. L3: Liv 4A 88 (2H 5)
Private Dr. CH61: Barn 4H 125
Prizett Rd. L19: Gras 2K 129
Probyn Rd. CH45: Wall 2J 85
Procter Rd. CH42: R Ferr 7G 107
Proctor Ct. L30: N'ton 1K 53
Proctor Rd. CH47: Hoy 2E 102
L37: Form 6G 19
Proctors Cl. WA8: Wid 6E 114
Proffits La. WA6: Hel 6K 165
Progress Pl. L1: Liv 5E 4
Promenade CH47: Meols 7D 82
PR8: Ains 3A 14
PR8: South 1G 11
PR9: South 6H 7
Promenade, The L17: Aig 7D 108
L19: Aig 2G 129
WA4: Moore 2F 137
Promenade Cvn. Pk. WA4: Moore 2E 136
Promenade Gdns. L17: Aig 5B 108
Prophet Wlk. L8: Liv 3A 108
Prospect Ct. L6: Liv 3F 89
Prospect La. WA3: Rix 4E 100
Prospect Pl. WN8: Skel 6B 38
Prospect Point L6: Liv 5B 88 (4L 5)
Prospect Rd. CH42: Tran 7B 106
WA9: St. H 2F 75
Prospect Row WA7: West 3B 152
Prospect St. L6: Liv 5B 88 (4M 5)
Prospect Va. CH45: Wall 2K 85
L6: Liv 3F 89
Prospect Way L30: N'ton 2D 54
Providence Cres. L8: Liv 2A 108
Provident St. WA9: St. H 3J 75
Province Pl. L20: Boot 7K 53
Province Rd. L20: Boot 7K 53
Prussia St. L3: Liv 5H 87 (4D 4)
(Old Hall St.)
L3: Liv 5J 87 (4D 4)
(Pall Mall)
Public Hall St. WA7: Run 6C 134
Pudsey St. L1: Liv 5A 88 (5H 5)
Puffin Cl. CH65: Ell P 4A 170
Pugin St. L4: Walt 7A 68
Pulford Av. CH43: Pren 6A 106
Pulford Cl. WA7: Beech 4G 153
Pulford Rd. CH63: Beb 4F 127
CH65: Gt Sut 7H 161
Pulford St. L4: Walt 7B 68
Pullman Cl. CH60: Hes 2H 143
Pumpfields Rd. L3: Liv 4J 87 (2D 4)
Pump La. CH49: Grea 3K 103
WA7: Halt 2H 153
Punnell's La. L31: Lyd 6B 32
Purbeck Dr. CH61: Irby 2B 124
Purdy Cl. WA5: Old H 6H 97
Purley Gro. L18: Moss H 6J 109
Purley Rd. L22: Water 3C 52
Purser Gro. L15: W'tree 7F 89
Putney Ct. WA7: Pal F 3G 153
Pye Cl. WA11: Hay 5F 63
Pyecroft Cl. WA5: Gt San 2B 116
Pyecroft Rd. WA5: Gt San 2B 116
Pye Rd. CH60: Hes 2E 142
Pyes Gdns. WA11: St. H 6D 60
Pyes La. L36: Huy 7G 71
Pye St. L15: W'tree 1H 109
PYGON'S HILL 4F 33
Pygons Hill La. L31: Lyd 4F 33
Pym St. L4: Walt 4B 68
Pyramids Shop. Cen., The
CH41: Birk 2D 106
Pyrus Gro. WA6: Hel 7J 165

Q

Quadrangle, The L18: Moss H 4K 109
Quadrant, The CH47: Hoy 2D 102
(off Station Rd.)
WA3: Ris 1A 100
Quadrant Cl. WA7: Murd 5B 154
Quail Cl. WA2: Warr 4D 98
Quaker La. CH60: Hes 1D 142
Quakers All. L2: Liv 5E 4
Quakers Mdw.
L34: Know 2H 71
Quantock Cl. CH66: Lit Sut 5C 160
WN3: Wins 2A 50
Quarry Av. CH63: Beb 5F 127
Quarry Bank CH41: Birk 3D 106
L33: K'by 2D 56
Quarrybank St. CH41: Birk 3C 106
Quarrybank Workshops
CH41: Birk 3C 106
Quarry Cl. CH61: Hes 7D 124
L13: Liv 2H 89
L33: K'by 2D 56
WA7: Run 1F 153
Quarry Ct. WA8: Wid 7J 113
Quarry Dale L33: K'by 2D 56
Quarry Dr. L39: Augh 3A 34
Quarry Grn. L33: K'by 2D 56
Quarry Grn. Flats
L33: K'by 2D 56
Quarry Hey L33: K'by 2D 56
Quarry La. CH61: Thing 3F 125
WA4: App 3D 138
WA6: Manl 7K 173
Quarry Mt. L39: Orm 4E 24
Quarry Pk. L35: R'hill 6K 93
Quarry Pl. L25: Wltn 6D 110
Quarry Rd. CH64: Nest 2B 158
L13: Liv 2H 89
L20: Boot 4K 67
L23: Thorn 6G 41
Quarry Rd. E. CH60: Hes 1C 142
CH63: Beb 5G 127
Quarry Rd. W. CH60: Hes 1C 142
Quarryside Dr. L33: K'by 2E 56
Quarry St. L25: Wltn 5D 110
Quarry St. Sth. L25: Wltn 6E 110
Quartz Way L21: Lith 5J 53
Quay, The WA6: Frod 1F 167
Quay Bus. Cen. WA2: Win 3K 97
Quay Cen., The WA2: Win 3K 97
Quay Fold WA5: Warr 4K 117
Quayle Cl. WA11: Hay 7K 61
Quay Pl. WA7: Murd 3C 154
Quay Side WA6: Frod 1F 167
Quayside CH64: Lit N 6H 157
Quayside M. WA13: Lymm 5H 121
Quebec Quay L3: Liv 2J 107
Quebec Rd. WA2: Warr 1C 118
Queen Anne Pde. L3: Liv 5H 87 (5C 4)
Queen Anne St. L3: Liv 4A 88 (3H 5)
PR8: South 1H 11
(off Market St.)
Queen Av. L2: Liv 5J 87 (6E 4)
Queen Av. Shop. Arc. L2: Liv 6D 4
Queen Elizabeth Ct. L21: Lith 5G 53
Queen Mary's Dr.
CH62: Port S 3H 127
Queens Av. CH65: Whit 1J 169
L37: Form 5J 19
WA1: Warr 1E 118
CH47: Meols 7F 83
WA8: Wid 1H 133
WN4: Ash M 2F 63
Queensbury CH48: W Kir 5F 103
Queensbury Av. CH62: Brom 1A 146
Queensbury St. L8: Liv 3B 108
Queensbury Way WA8: Wid 5K 113
Queens Cl. L19: Gars 3A 130
WA7: Run 1B 152
Queens Ct. L6: Liv 2C 88
L15: W'tree 6A 90
L39: Orm 6C 24
Queenscourt Rd. L12: W Der 2A 90
Queens Cres. WA1: P'gate 7G 99
Queens Cft. L37: Form 1H 29
Queensdale Rd. L18: Moss H 3J 109
Queens Dock Commercial Cen.
L1: Liv 1K 107 (10F 4)
Queens Dr. CH60: Hes 2C 142
WA4: Grap 6G 119
WA6: Hel 1H 173
WA12: New W 1F 77
CH43: Pren 7A 106
WA10: Windle 7J 59
Queens Dr. Mossley Hill
L18: Moss H 4G 109
Queens Dr. Stoneycroft
L12: W Der 3K 89
L13: Liv 2J 89
Queens Dr. Walton L4: Walt 4C 68
Queens Dr. Wavertree
L15: W'tree 6A 90
Queens Dr. W. Derby
L13: W Der 6G 69
Queens Gdns. CH65: Ell P 6K 161
Queens Grn. L39: Has 5B 22
Queen's Hotel Ct. PR9: South 7H 7
Queensland Av. WA9: St. H 7A 74
Queensland Pl. WA9: St. H 7A 74
Queensland St. L7: Liv 6C 88 (7P 5)
Queens M. L6: Liv 2C 88
Queens Pk. Community Leisure Cen.
2A 74
Queens Pl. CH41: Tran 4E 106
Queen Sq. L1: Liv 5K 87 (5F 4)
(not continuous)
Queens Rd. CH42: R Ferr 7F 107
CH44: Wall 3E 86
CH66: Lit Sut 4E 160
L6: Liv 2C 88 (1M 5)
L23: C'by 1E 52
L34: Prsct 1E 92
L37: Form 1H 29
WA10: St. H 5J 73
WA11: Hay 6E 62
WN5: Orr 6E 38
CH47: Hoy 1C 102
L20: Boot 4J 67
PR9: South 7J 7
WA7: Run 1B 152
WN4: Ash M 1F 63
Queen St. CH41: Tran 4E 106
CH45: Wall 2B 86
CH65: Ell P 4A 162
L19: Gars 4A 130
L22: Water 5D 52
L39: Orm 6C 24
WA7: Run 6C 134
WA10: St. H 1B 74
WA12: New W 3F 77
WN5: Orr 5J 39
Queens Wlk. L1: Liv 1A 108 (10J 5)
Queensway CH41: Birk 7G 87 (8A 4)
CH45: Wall 1A 86
CH60: Hes 4G 143
L3: Liv 7G 87 (8A 4)
L22: Water 3F 53
WA6: Frod 3D 166
WA7: Run 6B 134

Retford Wlk.—Rosam Ct.

Retford Wlk. L33: K'by 3D 56
Reva Rd. L14: B Grn 4C 90
Revesby Cl. WA8: Wid 6K 113
Rex Cohen Ct. L17: Aig 3G 109
Rexmore Rd. L18: Moss H 6J 109
Rexmore Way L15: W'tree 1G 109
Reynolds Av. WA3: Ris 2A 100
WA9: St. H 4K 75
Reynolds Cl. L6: Liv 3C 88 (1N 5)
Reynolds St. WA4: Westy 5E 118
Reynolds Way L25: Wltn 6E 110
Rhiwlas St. L8: Liv 3C 108
Rhodesia Rd. L9: Ain 7D 54
Rhodes St. WA2: Warr 1C 118
Rhodesway CH60: Hes 3F 143
Rhona Cl. CH63: East 6J 145
Rhona Dr. WA5: Gt San 2C 116
Rhosesmor Cl. L32: K'by 6D 56
Rhosesmor Rd. L32: K'by 7D 56
Rhuddlan Cl. L13: Liv 5H 89
Rhuddlan Ct. CH65: Ell P 2B 170
Rhum Cl. CH65: Ell P 3A 170
Rhyl St. L8: Liv 3A 108
WA8: Wid 2B 134
Rialto Cl. L8: Liv 1B 108
Rib, The L37: Form 5F 21
L39: Down 7J 21
Ribbesford Rd. WN3: Wigan 1A 50
Ribble Av. L31: Mag 2G 43
L35: R'hill 4J 93
PR9: Cros 3E 8
Ribble Cl. WA3: Cul 4B 80
WA8: Wid 5H 115
Ribble Cres. WN5: Bil 2E 60
Ribbledale Rd. L18: Moss H 4J 109
Ribble Ho. L25: Gate 5G 111
Ribble Rd. L25: Gate 5G 111
WN2: Platt B 2K 51
Ribbler's Ct. L32: K'by 7D 56
Ribbler's La. L32: K'by 6B 56
L34: Know 7D 56
Ribblesdale CH65: Whit 1K 169
Ribblesdale Av. L9: Ain 6D 54
Ribblesdale Cl. CH62: East 5B 146
Ribble St. CH41: Birk 6K 85
Ribchester Gdns. WA3: Cul 3C 80
Ribchester Way L35: Tar G 1A 112
Rice Hey Rd. CH44: Wall 2C 86
Rice La. CH44: Wall 2C 86
L9: Walt 3B 68
Rice Lane City Farm 2B 68
Rice Lane Station (Rail) 1C 68
Rice St. L1: Liv 7A 88 (9J 5)
Richard Allen Way L5: Liv 3A 88 (1J 5)
Richard Chubb Dr. CH44: Wall 1D 86
Richard Cl. WA7: Cas 1J 153
Richard Gro. L12: W Der 2C 90
Richard Hesketh Dr. L32: K'by 3A 56
Richard Kelly Cl. L4: Walt 6F 69
Richard Kelly Dr. L4: Walt 4F 69
Richard Kelly Pl. L4: Walt 6F 69
Richard Martin Rd. L21: Ford 4J 53
Richard Rd. L23: Blun 6A 40
Richards Gro. WA9: St. H 2G 75
Richardson Rd. CH42: R Ferr 7E 106
Richardson St. L7: Liv 1E 108
WA2: Warr 7C 98
Richland Rd. L13: Liv 2H 89
Richmond Av. L21: Lith 5G 53
WA4: Grap 5J 119
WA4: Westy 4F 119
WA7: Run 7G 135
WA11: Hay 6K 61
Richmond Cl. CH63: Beb 3F 127
L38: High 7F 29
WA3: Cul 2K 79
WA10: Eccl 2G 73
WA13: Lymm 4K 121
Richmond Ct. CH65: Ell P 1B 170
L5: Liv 2C 88
L21: Lith 6H 53
Richmond Cres. L30: N'ton 2B 54
Richmond Dr. WA13: Lymm 4K 121
Richmond Gdns. WA12: New W 4G 77
Richmond Gro. L31: Lyd 1G 43
Richmond Hill WN5: Wigan 5K 39
Richmond Ho. L3: Liv 5H 87 (5C 4)
Richmond Pde. L3: Liv 5C 4
Richmond Pk. L6: Liv 1D 88
Richmond Rd. CH63: Beb 3F 127
L23: C'by 7E 40
PR8: B'dale 6F 11
WN4: Ash M 7D 50
Richmond Row L3: Liv 4A 88 (2H 5)
Richmond St. CH45: New B 5B 66
L1: Liv 6K 87 (6F 4)
WA4: Westy 5G 119
WA8: Wid 7E 114
Richmond Ter. L6: Liv 2C 88
Richmond Way CH61: Hes 7D 124
CH61: Thing 3E 124
L35: Tar G 1A 112
Rich Vw. CH43: O'ton 5B 106
Rickaby Cl. CH63: Brom 2J 145
Rickerby Ct. PR9: South 7J 7
Rickman St. L4: Kirk 6K 67
Rickman Way L36: Huy 7K 91
Ridding La. WA7: Brook 5K 153
Riddings, The CH65: Whit 7K 161
Riddock Rd. L21: Lith 1H 67
Ridge, The CH60: Hes 7B 124
Ridgebourne Cl. WA5: Call 5H 97
Ridge Cl. PR9: Cros 2E 8
Ridgefield Rd. CH61: Pens 4D 124
Ridgemere Rd. CH61: Pens 4D 124
Ridgetor Rd. L25: Wltn 5D 110
Ridgeview Rd. CH43: Noct 3H 105
Ridgeway, The CH47: Meols 1G 103
CH60: Hes 3F 143
CH63: High B 1D 126
L25: Wltn 5E 110
WA7: Murd 4B 154
WA8: Cron 2J 113
Ridgeway Cl. CH66: Gt Sut 2E 168
Ridgeway Dr. L31: Lyd 7F 33
Ridgewell Cl. L21: Lith 6G 53
Ridgewood Dr. CH61: Pens 5D 124
WA9: St. H 1E 94
Ridgewood Way L9: Walt 6C 54
Ridgmont Av. L21: N Grn. 4H 69
Ridgway Gdns. WA13: Lymm 5F 121
Ridgway St. WA2: Warr 1D 118
Riding Cl. WA9: Clock F 3E 94
Ridingfold L26: Halew 6H 111
Riding Hill Rd. L34: Know 4H 71
Riding Hill Wlk. L34: Know 4H 71
Riding La. L39: Has 6K 21
WN4: Ash M 6J 51
Ridings, The CH43: Noct 3H 105
PR9: Chu 4C 8
Ridings Hey CH43: Noct 4H 105
Riding St. L3: Liv 5A 88 (5K 5)
PR8: South 2H 11
Ridley Dr. WA5: Gt San 4G 117
Ridley Gro. CH48: W Kir 5C 102
Ridley La. L31: Mag 3F 43
Ridley Rd. L6: Liv 4E 88
Ridley St. CH43: O'ton 3C 106
Ridsdale WA8: Wid 1J 133
Ridsdale Lawn L27: N'ley 5A 112
Riesling Dr. L33: K'by 7B 44
Rigby Dr. CH49: Grea 6B 104
Rigby Rd. L31: Mag 1D 42
Rigbys La. WN4: Ash M 2H 63
Rigby St. L3: Liv 5H 87 (4C 4)
WA10: St. H 2B 74
WN4: Ash M 2E 62
Rigby St. Sth. WA10: St. H 3B 74
Rigby's Yd. WN5: Wigan 5K 39
Riley Av. L20: Boot 1K 67
Riley Dr. WA7: Run 2C 152
Rilston Av. WA3: Cul 3K 79
Rimington Cl. WA3: Cul 3A 80
Rimmer Av. L16: Child 6E 90
Rimmerbrook Rd. L25: Gate 1F 111
Rimmer Cl. L21: Lith 6H 53
Rimmer Grn. PR8: South 7F 13
Rimmer Gro. WA9: St. H 3G 75
Rimmer's Av. L37: Form 4J 19
PR8: South 2H 11
Rimmer St. L3: Liv 5A 88 (4J 5)
Rimmington Rd. L17: Aig 6G 109
Rimrose Bus. Pk. L20: Boot 2G 67
Rimrose Rd. L20: Boot 1G 67
Rimrose Valley Country Pk. 2G 53
Rimrose Valley Rd. L23: C'by 2G 53
Rimsdale Cl. L17: Aig 2G 129
Rindlebrook La. L34: Prsct 2C 92
Ringcroft Rd. L13: Liv 4K 89
Ringley Av. WA3: Golb 4K 63
Ringo Starr Dr. L6: Liv 4D 88 (3P 5)
Ring Rd. CH1: Back 5H 169
Ringsfield Rd. L24: Speke 6K 131
Ringway CH64: Nest 2J 157
CH66: Gt Sut 7G 161
Ringway Rd. L25: Gate 1F 111
WA7: Run 7F 135
Ringways CH62: Brom 6K 127
Ringwood CH43: O'ton 5A 106
Ringwood Av. L14: B Grn 5D 90
Ringwood Cl. WA3: Bchwd 2D 100
Rio Ct. L34: Prsct 7D 72
Ripley Av. L21: Lith 4H 53
Ripley Cl. L31: Mag 3G 43
Ripley Dr. WN3: Wigan 7K 39
Ripley St. WA5: Warr 1J 117
Ripon Av. CH66: Lit Sut 6E 160
Ripon Cl. L30: N'ton 4B 54
L36: Huy 4A 92
PR8: South 5B 12
WA12: New W 2G 77
Ripon Dr. WN4: Ash M 3H 63
Ripon Rd. CH45: Wall 1J 85
Ripon Row WA7: Run 3F 153
Ripon St. CH41: Tran 4E 106
L4: Walt 5B 68
Risbury Rd. L11: N Grn. 4H 69
Rishton Cl. L5: Liv 2B 88
Rishton St. L5: Liv 2C 88
RISLEY 1A 100
Risley Employment Area WA3: Ris 7B 80
Risley Moss Local Nature Reserve 3D 100
Risley Moss Local Nature Reserve Vis. Cen. 2C 100
Risley Rd. WA3: Ris 2B 100
Ritchie Av. L9: Ain 7E 54
Ritherup La. L35: R'hill 3J 93
Ritson St. L8: Liv 2D 108
Rivacre Brow CH66: Ell P 4G 161
Rivacre Bus. Cen. CH66: Ell P 6G 161
Rivacre Rd. CH62: East 5C 146
CH66: Ell P 4G 161
Rivacre Valley Country Pk. 3G 161
Riva La. CH60: Hes 7C 124
Riveacre Rd. CH65: Hoot 7D 146
River Avon St. L8: Liv 1D 108
Riverbank Cl. CH60: Hes 4D 142
Riverbank Rd. CH60: Hes 4D 142
CH62: Brom 6A 128
L19: Gras 2J 129
River Cl. L37: Form 2B 30
River Gro. CH62: New F 1H 127
Rivermeade PR8: South 4K 11
Riverpark Gdns. *L8: Liv* *2A 108*
(off Hyslop St.)
River Rd. WA4: Warr 5B 118
(not continuous)
Riversdale WA1: W'ston 1B 120
WA6: Frod 2E 166
Riversdale Cl. L33: K'by 1C 56
Riversdale Ct. L19: Aig 1H 129
Riversdale M. L19: Aig 1H 129
Riversdale Rd. CH44: Wall 3D 86
CH48: W Kir 6C 102
L19: Aig 2G 129
L21: Sea 6F 53
WA7: Halt 1G 153
Riverside CH48: W Kir 1D 122
CH62: Port S 4H 127
L12: W Der 5C 70
L38: High 5F 29
Riverside Bowl 5B 66
Riverside Cl. L20: Boot 1G 67
WA1: Warr 4C 118
Riverside Ct. CH62: New F 1H 127
Riverside Dr. L3: Liv 5A 108
L17: Aig 6D 108
Riverside Gro. WA9: St. H 7F 75
Riverside Ho. CH41: Birk 6F 87
Riverside Retail Pk. WA1: Warr 4C 118
Riverside Trad. Est. WA5: Cuerd 7B 116
Riverside Vw. L17: Aig 7E 108
Riverside Wlk. CH64: Lit N 6H 157
L3: Liv 7H 87 (9C 4)
Riverslea Rd. L23: Blun 3B 52
Rivers St. WN5: Orr 5G 39
River Vw. CH62: New F 1J 127
L22: Water 3C 52
Riverview Gdns. CH42: R Ferr 6F 107
River Vw. Residential Cvn. Pk.
WA8: Wid 1E 134
Riverview Rd. CH44: Wall 4E 86
CH62: Brom 7C 128
CH64: Lit N 6K 157
Riverview Wlk. L8: Liv 4B 108
River Wlk. *WA7: Pal F* *3H 153*
(off Halton Lea Shop. Cen.)
River Way L25: Gate 5G 111
Riverwood Rd. CH62: Brom 1B 146
Riviera Dr. CH42: R Ferr 7D 106
L11: Crox 2A 70
Rivington Av. CH43: Noct 4J 105
WA10: St. H 7A 60
Rivington Cl. PR8: B'dale 5G 11
Rivington Ct. WA1: W'ston 7A 100
Rivington Dr. WN8: Uph 4E 38
Rivington Rd. CH44: Wall 4C 86
CH65: Ell P 6K 161
WA7: Pres B 7C 154
WA10: St. H 3K 73
Rivington St. WA10: St. H 4K 73
RIXTON 5H 101
Rixton Av. WA5: Warr 7K 97
Rixton Claypits Nature Reserve 5G 101
Rixton Pk. Homes WA3: Rix 5H 101
Roadwater Cl. L25: Gate 1F 111
Robarts Rd. L4: Walt 1C 88
ROBBINS BRIDGE 6G 33
Robeck Rd. L13: Liv 6K 89
Robert Dr. CH49: Grea 5C 104
Robert Gro. L12: W Der 2C 90
Robert Moffat WA16: H Legh 4K 141
Roberts Av. WA11: Hay 1H 75
Roberts Ct. WA7: Pal F 4H 153
Roberts Dr. L20: Boot 6A 54
Robertsfield Rd. WA3: Bchwd 3K 99
Robertson St. L8: Liv 3A 108
Roberts St. L3: Liv 4H 87 (3B 4)
Robert St. CH41: Birk 1D 106
WA5: Warr 2K 117
WA7: Run 7E 134
WA8: Wid 7D 114
Robina Rd. WA9: St. H 6F 75
Robin Cl. WA7: Murd 3B 154
Robin Hood La. WA6: Hel 3H 173
Robins Cft. CH66: Gt Sut 2H 169
Robins La. WA3: Cul 4K 79
WA9: St. H 6E 74
WA11: Kings M 3B 48
Robinson M. *CH41: Birk* *2F 107*
(off Gertrude St.)
Robinson Pl. WA9: St. H 3E 74
Robinson Rd. L21: Lith 4J 53
Robinson St. WA9: St. H 3F 75
Robin Way CH49: W'chu 6F 105
Rob La. WA12: New W 2J 77
(not continuous)
Robsart St. L5: Liv 2A 88
Robson St. L5: Liv 7B 68
L13: Liv 6H 89
WA1: Warr 2D 118
ROBY 5G 91
Roby Cl. L35: R'hill 3J 93
Roby Ct. L36: Roby 6H 91
Roby Gro. WA5: Gt San 2E 116
ROBY MILL 1D 38
Roby Mt. Av. L36: Roby 5H 91
Roby Rd. L14: B Grn 6D 90
L36: Roby 5F 91
(not continuous)
Roby Station (Rail) 5G 91
Roby St. L15: W'tree 1G 109
L20: Boot 2J 67
WA10: St. H 5K 73
Roby Well Way WN5: Bil 7F 49
Rocastle Cl. L6: Liv 4C 88 (3N 5)
Rochester Av. L30: N'ton 4B 54
Rochester Cl. WA5: Gt San 3G 117
Rochester Dr. CH65: Ell P 2B 170
Rochester Gdns. WA10: St. H 5K 73
Rochester Rd. CH42: R Ferr 6F 107
Roch Pl. WN2: Platt B 2K 51
Rock, The WA6: Hel 2H 173
Rock Av. CH60: Hes 1D 142
Rock Bank CH49: Upton 3E 104
Rockbank Rd. L13: Liv 2G 89
Rockbourne Av. L25: Wltn 3D 110
Rockbourne Grn. L25: Wltn 3D 110
Rockbourne Way L25: Wltn 3D 110
Rock Cl. CH42: R Ferr 6F 107
Rock Dr. WA6: Frod 2E 166
Rocket Trad. Cen. L14: B Grn 4A 90
Rock Farm Cl. CH64: Lit N 5A 158
Rock Farm Dr. CH64: Lit N 5A 158
Rock Farm Gro. CH64: Lit N 5A 158
ROCK FERRY 6F 107
Rock Ferry By-Pass
CH42: R Ferr 5G 107
Rock Ferry Station (Rail) 6F 107
Rockfield Cl. WA8: Wid 6K 113
Rockfield Dr. WA6: Hel 2J 173
Rockfield Gdns. L31: Mag 2E 42
Rockfield Rd. L4: Walt 7B 68
Rockford Av. L32: K'by 6C 56
Rockford Cl. L32: K'by 6C 56
Rockford Wlk. L32: K'by 6C 56
Rock Gro. L13: Liv 4H 89
Rockhill Rd. L25: Wltn 6F 111
Rockhouse St. L6: Liv 2E 88
Rockingham Cl. WA3: Bchwd 1D 100
Rockingham Ct. L33: K'by 1D 56
Rockland Rd. CH45: Wall 7K 65
L22: Water 3E 52
Rocklands Av. CH63: Beb 2G 127
Rocklands La. CH63: Thorn H 3C 144
Rock La. L31: Mell 6H 43
WA8: Wid 4B 114
Rock La. E. CH42: R Ferr 7G 107
(not continuous)
Rock La. W. CH42: R Ferr 7F 107
Rocklee Gdns. CH64: Lit N 5A 158
Rockley St. L4: Kirk 6A 68
(not continuous)
Rockmount Cl. L25: Wltn 5D 110
Rock Mt. Pk. L25: Wltn 5D 110
Rockmount Rd. L17: Aig 7H 109
Rock Pk. CH42: R Ferr 6G 107
(not continuous)
Rock Pk. Rd. CH42: R Ferr 7H 107
Rockpoint Av. CH45: New B 7C 66
Rock Retail Pk. CH41: Birk 3E 106
Rock Rd. WA4: Westy 4E 118
Rocksavage Way WA7: Run 5C 152
Rockside Rd. L18: Moss H 6J 109
Rock St. L13: Liv 4J 89
WA10: St. H 6J 73
Rock Vw. L5: Liv 1A 88
L31: Mell 1J 55
Rockville Rd. L14: B Grn 6A 90
Rockville St. CH42: R Ferr 6F 107
Rockwell Cl. L12: W Der 6B 70
Rockwell Rd. L12: W Der 6B 70
Rockybank Rd. CH42: Tran 5D 106
Rocky La. CH60: Hes 2D 142
L6: Liv 2E 88
L16: Child 7A 90
Rocky La. Sth. CH60: Hes 2E 142
Roderick Rd. L4: Walt 4C 68
Roderick St. L3: Liv 4A 88 (3J 5)
Rodgers Cl. WA6: Frod 2D 166
Rodick St. L25: Wltn 6D 110
Rodmell Rd. L9: Ain 7D 54
Rodney St. CH41: Birk 3D 106
L1: Liv 7A 88 (9J 5)
WA10: St. H 3A 74
Roe All. L1: Liv 6K 87 (7G 4)
Roeburn Wlk. WN2: Platt B 2K 51
Roeburn Way WA5: Penk 5B 116
Roedean Cl. L25: Wltn 7F 111
L31: Mag 2F 43
Roehampton Dr. L23: Blun 6C 40
WA7: Pal F 3G 153
Roe La. PR9: South 7A 8
PR9: South, Chu 7K 7
Roemarsh Cl. L12: W Der 4K 69
Roemarsh Ct. WA7: Pal F 4G 153
Roe Pk. M. PR9: South 7K 7
Roe St. L1: Liv 6G 4
Roften Works Ind. Est.
CH66: Hoot 3K 159
Roger Arden Ct. L20: Boot 2K 67
Rogers Av. L20: Boot 1A 68
Rogersons Grn. L26: Halew 6J 111
Rokeby Cl. L3: Liv 3A 88 (2J 5)
Rokeby Ct. WA7: Mnr P 4B 136
Rokeby St. L3: Liv 4A 88 (2J 5)
Rokeden WA12: New W 2H 77
Roker Av. CH44: Wall 4A 86
Rokesmith Av. L7: Liv 7E 88
Roklis Ct. CH49: Upton 4E 104
Roland Av. CH63: High B 3D 126
WA7: Run 1B 152
WA11: St. H 6E 60
Rolands Wlk. WA7: Cas 7H 135
Rolesby Gdns. WA9: St. H 1A 94
Roleton Cl. L30: N'ton 1D 54
Rolleston Dr. CH45: Wall 7K 65
CH63: Beb 5G 127
Rolleston St. WA2: Warr 2A 118
Rolling Mill La. WA9: St. H 6H 75
Rollo St. L4: Kirk 7K 67
Roman Cl. WA7: Cas 7G 135
WA12: New W 4G 77
WN3: Wigan 1D 50
Roman Ct. CH64: Lit N 4K 157
Roman Rd. CH43: Pren 1A 126
CH47: Meols 6F 83
CH63: Store 2A 126
WA4: S Hth 7C 118
WN4: Ash M 7E 50
Rome Cl. L36: Huy 4H 91
Romer Rd. L6: Liv 4E 88
Romford Way L26: Halew 3K 131
(not continuous)
Romiley Dr. WN8: Skel 1F 37
Romiley Rd. CH66: Ell P 5G 161
Romilly St. L6: Liv 4C 88 (3N 5)
Romley St. L4: Walt 4B 68
Romney Cl. CH64: Lit N 4J 157
WA8: Wid 6G 115
Romney Cft. CH64: Lit N 4K 157
Romney Way CH64: Lit N 4K 157
Romsey Av. L37: Form 1B 30
Romsey Gro. WN3: Wins 2B 50
Romulus St. L7: Liv 5F 89
Rona Av. CH65: Ell P 3A 170
Ronald Cl. L22: Water 4F 53
Ronald Dr. WA2: Fearn 5H 99
Ronald Rd. L22: Water 4F 53
Ronald Ross Av. L30: N'ton 2B 54
Ronaldshay WA8: Wid 6G 115
Ronald St. L13: Liv 4H 89
Ronaldsway CH49: Upton 2D 104
CH60: Hes 4D 142
L10: Faz 6J 55
L23: Thorn 6G 41
L26: Halew 1A 132
Ronan Cl. L20: Boot 2G 67
Ronan Rd. WA8: Wid 4K 133
Rone Cl. CH46: More 7B 84
Rookery, The WA12: New W 2H 77
Rookery Av. WN4: Ash M 3F 63
Rookery Dr. L19: Aig 1H 129
WA11: R'ford 6G 47
Rookery La. WA11: R'ford 7G 47
Rookery Rd. PR9: South 6A 8
Rookley Cl. L27: N'ley 4K 111
Rooks Way CH60: Hes 2C 142
Rooley, The L36: Huy 6H 91
Roome St. WA2: Warr 1C 118
Roosevelt Dr. L9: Ain 5D 54
Roper's Bri. Cl. L35: Whis 4D 92
Roper St. L8: Liv 3B 108
WA9: St. H 2E 74
Ropewalk, The CH64: Park 2G 157
Ropewalks Sq. L1: Liv 8H 5
Rosalind Av. CH63: High B 2E 126
Rosalind Way L20: Kirk 5K 67
Rosam Ct. WA7: Pal F 4G 153

Rosclare Dr.—Saddleback Cres.

Rosclare Dr. CH45: Wall 1K 85
Roscoe & Gladstone Hall
L17: Aig 4G 109
Roscoe Av. WA2: Warr 7D 98
WA12: New W 3J 77
Roscoe Cl. L35: Tar G 1A 112
Roscoe Cres. WA7: West P 3A 152
Roscoe La. L1: Liv 7A 88 (8H 5)
Roscoe Pl. L1: Liv 6A 88 (8H 5)
Roscoe St. L1: Liv 7A 88 (9J 5)
WA10: St. H 4K 73
Roscommon St. L5: Liv 3A 88 (1H 5)
(not continuous)
Roscommon Way WA8: Wid 5A 114
Roscote, The CH60: Hes 3D 142
Roscote Cl. CH60: Hes 3D 142
Roseacre CH48: W Kir 5C 102
Roseate Ct. CH45: Wall 6J 65
Rose Av. L20: Boot 6J 53
WA9: St. H 7E 74
WA11: Hay 7C 62
Rose Bank WA13: Lymm 5G 121
Rose Bank Rd. L16: Child 1B 110
Rosebank Rd. L36: Huy 1G 91
Rosebank Way L36: Huy 2G 91
Rosebay Cl. L37: Form 7A 20
Roseberry Rd. WN4: Ash M 7E 50
Rosebery Av. CH44: Wall 3C 86
L22: Water 3C 52
Rosebery Gro. CH42: Tran 6B 106
Rosebery Rd. WA10: St. H 1K 73
Rosebery St. L8: Liv 1C 108
PR9: South 2C 12
Rosebourne Cl. L17: Aig 6D 108
Rose Brae L18: Moss H 4J 109
Rosebrae Ct. CH41: Birk 1F 107
CH60: Hes 1E 142
Rose Brow L25: Wltn 4E 110
Rose Cl. L26: Halew 2A 132
WA7: Murd 5B 154
Rose Ct. CH41: Birk 2D 106
L15: W'tree 1G 109
Rose Cres. PR8: Ains 7C 14
WA8: Wid 2B 134
WN8: Skel 2E 36
Rosecroft CH62: Brom 4J 145
Rosecroft Cl. L39: Orm 4C 24
Rosecroft Ct. CH47: Hoy 2C 102
Rosedale Av. L23: C'by 1E 52
WA1: W'ston 1J 119
Rosedale Cl. L9: Walt 2D 68
Rosedale Rd. CH42: Tran 5E 106
L18: Moss H 3J 109
Rose Dr. WA11: R'ford 7G 47
Rosefield Av. CH63: High B 2E 126
Rosefield Rd. L25: Wltn 7G 111
Rose Gdns. CH64: Lit N 5K 157
Rosegarth Grn. L13: Liv 3K 89
Roseheath Dr. L26: Halew 2K 131
ROSE HILL 6D 50
Rose Hill L3: Liv 4K 87 (2G 4)
PR8: South 2K 11
Rose Hill Av. WN5: Wigan 5K 39
Rosehill Av. WA9: Bold 2K 95
Rosehill Bus. Pk.
PR9: South 2K 11
Rosehill Ct. L25: Wltn 4E 110
Rosehill Dr. L39: Augh 1A 34
Rosehill Vw. WN4: Ash M 5D 50
Roseland Cl. L31: Lyd 7D 32
Roselands Ct. CH42: R Ferr 7E 106
Rose La. L18: Moss H 5H 109
Rose Lea Cl. WA8: Wid 4C 114
Roselea Dr. PR9: Cros 3E 8
Roselee Ct. CH42: R Ferr 7G 107
Rosemary Av. WA4: S Hth 6E 118
WA7: Beech 6H 153
Rosemary Cl. CH43: Bid 7J 85
L7: Liv 7C 88 (8N 5)
WA5: Gt San 2G 117
Rosemary Dr. WA12: New W 3J 77
Rosemary La. L37: Form 7J 19
L39: Hals, Has 5C 22
Rosemead Av. CH61: Pens 5D 124
Rosemere Dr. CH1: Back 5H 169
Rosemont Rd. L17: Aig 6G 109
Rosemoor Dr. L23: C'by 7G 41
Rosemoor Gdns. WA4: App 4F 139
Rose Mt. CH43: O'ton 5B 106
WA2: Win 6B 78
Rosemount Cl. CH43: O'ton 5A 106
Rose Mt. Dr. CH45: Wall 1A 86
Rose Path L37: Form 1A 30
Rose Pl. CH42: Tran 4D 106
L3: Liv 4K 87 (2G 4)
(not continuous)
L39: Augh 1B 34
WA11: R'ford 7G 47
Roseside Dr. L27: N'ley 3K 111
Rose St. L1: Liv 5G 4
L25: Wltn 6D 110
WA8: Wid 2B 134
Rose Ter. L18: Moss H 4J 109
Rose Theatre 7E 24
Rose Va. L5: Liv 2A 88
(Gt. Homer St., not continuous)
L5: Liv 2A 88
(Netherfield Rd. N.)
Rose Vw. Av. WA8: Wid 6C 114
Rose Vs. L15: W'tree 1H 109
Rosewarne Cl. L17: Aig 6D 108
Rosewood PR9: Chu 5B 8
Rosewood Av. WA1: Warr 1E 118
WA6: Frod 4F 167
Rosewood Cl. L27: N'ley 3J 111
L28: Stock V 7F 71
WA8: Wid 1H 133
Rosewood Dr. CH46: More 7K 83
Rosewood Farm Ct. WA8: Wid 3A 114
Rosewood Gdns. L11: N Grn. 5K 69
Roseworth Av. L9: Walt 6C 54
Rosina Cl. WN4: Ash M 6D 50
Roskell Rd. L25: Hunts X 2G 131
Rosley Rd. WN3: Wigan 1F 51
Roslin Rd. CH43: O'ton 4B 106
CH61: Irby 3B 124
Roslyn St. CH42: Tran 5F 107
Rossall Av. L10: Ain 2F 55
Rossall Cl. L24: Hale 7E 132
Rossall Ct. CH46: Leas 5D 84
Rossall Gro. CH66: Lit Sut 5F 161
Rossall Rd. CH46: More 6D 84
L13: Liv 5K 89
WA5: Gt San 4F 117
WA8: Wid 6F 115
Ross Av. CH46: Leas 3G 85
Rossbank Rd. CH65: Ell P 4J 161
Rosscliffe Rd. CH65: Ell P 4J 161
Ross Cl. L34: Know 3H 71
WA5: Old H 7H 97
WN5: Bil 6G 49
Ross Dr. CH66: Gt Sut 6E 160
Rossendale Cl. CH43: Noct 4H 105
Rossendale Dr. WA3: Bchwd 1C 100
Rosset Cl. WN3: Wins 2B 50
Rossett Av. L17: Liv 2F 109
Rossett Cl. WA5: Call 5J 97
Rossett Rd. L23: C'by 2C 52
Rossett St. L6: Liv 2E 88
Rossfield Rd. CH65: Ell P 4J 161
Rossini St. L21: Sea 7G 53
Rosslyn Av. L31: Mag 4D 42
Rosslyn Cres. CH46: More 7C 84
Rosslyn Dr. CH46: More 7C 84
Rosslyn Pk. CH46: More 1C 104
Rosslyn St. L17: Aig 5D 108
Rossmore Bus. Pk. CH65: Ell P 4K 161
Rossmore Gdns. CH66: Lit Sut 5F 161
L4: Walt 6D 68
Rossmore Ind. Est. CH65: Ell P 4J 161
Rossmore Rd. E. CH65: Ell P 4H 161
Rossmore Rd. W.
CH66: Ell P, Lit Sut 4F 161
Rossmore Trad. Est.
CH65: Ell P 5J 161
Rossmount Rd. CH65: Ell P 5J 161
Ross Rd. CH65: Ell P 5J 161
Ross St. WA8: Wid 7D 114
Ross Tower Cl. CH45: New B 6C 66
Rosswood Rd. CH65: Ell P 5J 161
Rostherne Av. CH44: Wall 4A 86
CH66: Gt Sut 7G 161
Rostherne Cl. WA5: Warr 4H 117
Rostherne Cres. WA8: Wid 6K 113
Rosthwaite Cl. WN3: Wigan 2E 50
Rosthwaite Gro. WA11: St. H 4D 60
Rosthwaite Rd. L12: W Der 1K 89
Rostron Cres. L37: Form 2J 29
Roswell Ct. L28: Stock V 1F 91
Rosyth Cl. WA2: Fearn 4F 99
Rothay Dr. WA5: Penk 5B 116
Rothbury Cl. CH46: More 7A 84
WA7: Beech 4G 153
Rothbury Ct. WA9: Sut M 5D 94
Rothbury Rd. L14: K Ash 1D 90
Rother Dr. CH65: Ell P 4J 161
Rother Dr. Bus. Pk. CH65: Ell P 4J 161
Rotherham Cl. L36: Huy 3J 91
Rotherwood CH43: Noct 3H 105
Rotherwood Cl. CH63: High B 3D 126
Rothesay Cl. WA7: Cas 7H 135
WA11: St. H 6G 61
Rothesay Ct. CH63: Beb 5F 127
Rothesay Dr. CH62: East 6A 146
L23: C'by 2E 52
Rothesay Gdns. CH43: Pren 7K 105
Rothley Av. PR8: Ains 5A 14
Rothsay Cl. L5: Liv 3A 88 (1J 5)
Rothwell Cl. L39: Orm 5B 24
Rothwell Dr. L39: Augh 1K 33
PR8: Ains 4A 14
Rothwells La. L23: Thorn 5H 41
Rothwell St. L6: Liv 3C 88 (1N 5)
Rotten Row PR8: South 3E 10
Rotunda St. L5: Liv 2K 87
Roughdale Av. L32: K'by 6D 56
WA9: Sut M 3D 94
Roughdale Cl. L32: K'by 6D 56
Rough La. L39: Bart 1D 20
Roughlea Av. WA3: Cul 2K 79
Roughley Av. WA5: Warr 4H 117
Roughsedge Ho. L28: Stock V 6F 71
Roughwood Dr. L33: K'by 2D 56
Roundabout, The WA8: Cron 2K 113
Round Hey L28: Stock V 6E 70
Round Meade, The L31: Mag 2D 42
Round Thorn WA3: Croft 7G 79
Roundway, The L38: High 6F 29
Roundwood Dr. WA9: St. H 5D 74
Routledge St. WA8: Wid 7D 114
Rowan Av. L12: W Der 5D 70
Rowan Cl. WA5: Gt San 2D 116
WA7: Run 3E 152
WA11: Hay 1H 75
WA11: St. H 6F 61
Rowan Ct. CH49: Grea 6K 103
CH63: High B 3D 126
L17: Aig 6G 109
Rowan Dr. L32: K'by 2A 56
Rowan Gro. CH63: High B 5E 126
L36: Huy 7H 91
Rowan La. WN8: Skel 6H 27
Rowans, The L39: Augh 4J 33
Rowan Tree Cl. CH49: Grea 5A 104
Rowena Cl. L23: C'by 7F 41
Rowland Cl. WA2: Fearn 4G 99
Rowley Bank La.
WA16: H Legh 7K 141
Rowlings Way L32: K'by 5D 56
ROWLINSON'S GREEN 4E 140
Rowsley Gro. L9: Ain 6D 54
Rowson St. CH45: New B 5B 66
L34: Prsct 7D 72
Rowthorn Cl. WA8: Wid 1A 134
Rowton Cl. CH43: O'ton 5K 105
Roxborough Cl. WA5: B'wood 1E 96
Roxborough Wlk. L25: Wltn 5G 111
Roxburgh Av. CH42: Tran 6D 106
L17: Aig 5E 108
Roxburgh Rd. CH66: Lit Sut 5B 160
Roxburgh St. L20: Boot 4A 68
Royal, The CH47: Hoy 2B 102
Royal Av. WA8: Wid 7H 113
Royal Birkdale Golf Course 7C 10
Royal Cl. L37: Form 2A 30
Royal Court Theatre 5K 87 (5G 4)
Royal Cres. L37: Form 2A 30
Royal Cft. L12: W Der 3K 89
Royal Gro. WA10: St. H 5K 73
Royal Liverpool Golf Course 3B 102
Royal London Bus. Pk.
WA5: W'brk 4J 97
Royal Mail St. L3: Liv 6A 88 (6H 5)
ROYAL OAK 7D 34
Royal Pk. PR8: B'dale 4E 10
Royal Pl. WA8: Wid 1H 133
Royal Quay L3: Liv 7J 87 (9E 4)
Royal Shop. Arc. CH64: Nest 4J 157
Royal Standard Way
CH42: Tran 5F 107
Royal St. L4: Walt 7A 68
Royal Ter. PR8: South 1G 11
Royden Av. CH44: Wall 2D 86
WA7: Run 2B 152
WN3: Wigan 2E 50
Royden Cres. WN5: Bil 7G 49
Royden Rd. CH49: Upton 2C 104
WN5: Bil 7G 49
Royden Way L3: Liv 5A 108
Royleen Dr. WA6: Frod 5F 167
Roysten Gdns. WA9: St. H 4F 75
Royston Av. CH44: Wall 3D 86
WA1: P'ton 1F 119
Royston Cl. CH66: Gt Sut 1H 169
Royston St. L7: Liv 6D 88 (6P 5)
Royton Cl. L26: Halew 3K 131
Royton Rd. L22: Water 3F 53
Rozel Cres. WA5: Gt San 4F 117
Rubbing Stone CH48: Caldy 3F 123
Ruby St. L8: Liv 5B 108
(not continuous)
Rudd Av. WA9: St. H 4J 75
Ruddington Rd. PR8: South 5A 12
Rudd St. CH47: Hoy 1D 102
Rudgate L35: Whis 5E 92
Rudgrave M. CH44: Wall 2D 86
Rudgrave Pl. CH44: Wall 2D 86
Rudgrave Sq. CH44: Wall 2D 86
Rudheath La. WA7: Nort 6B 136
Rudley Wlk. L24: Speke 7K 131
Rudloe Ct. WA2: P'gate 6E 98
Rudstone Cl. CH66: Lit Sut 6D 160
Rudston Rd. L16: Child 7A 90
Rudyard Cl. L14: K Ash 4A 90
Rudyard Rd. L14: K Ash 4A 90
Ruff La. L39: Orm 6D 24
Rufford Av. L31: Mag 1G 43
Rufford Cl. L10: Faz 5H 55
L35: Prsct 2F 93
WA8: Wid 6J 113
Rufford Ct. WA1: W'ston 7A 100
Rufford Dr. PR9: Banks 2H 9
Rufford Rd. CH44: Wall 4B 86
L6: Liv 4E 88
L20: Boot 1J 67
PR9: Cros 4E 8
WA11: R'ford 5F 47
Rufford St. WN4: Ash M 7D 50
Rufford Wlk. WA11: St. H 7G 61
Rugby Dr. L10: Ain 4G 55
WN5: Orr 3H 39
Rugby Rd. CH44: Wall 2K 85
CH65: Ell P 1A 170
L9: Ain 5D 54
Rugby Wlk. CH65: Ell P 1B 170
Ruislip Cl. L25: Wltn 6G 111
Ruislip Ct. WA2: P'gate 6F 99
Rullerton Rd. CH44: Wall 3A 86
Rumford Pl. L3: Liv 5H 87 (5C 4)
Rumford St. L2: Liv 5J 87 (5D 4)
Rumney Pl. L4: Kirk 6K 67
(not continuous)
Rumney Rd. L4: Kirk 6A 68
Rumney Rd. W. L4: Kirk 6K 67
RUNCORN 6C 134
Runcorn Dock Rd. WA7: Run 7A 134
Runcorn East Station (Rail) 3B 154
Runcorn Hill Local Nature Reserve
2B 152
Runcorn Hill Local Nature Reserve
Vis. Cen. 2B 152
Runcorn Rd. WA4: Dares, H Walt, Moore
5D 136
Runcorn Ski & Snowboard Cen.
3K 153
Runcorn Spur Rd. WA7: Run 7D 134
Runcorn Station (Rail) 7B 134
Runcorn Swimming Pool
WA7: Run 6D 134
(off Bridge St.)
Rundle Rd. L17: Aig 6G 109
Rundle St. CH41: Birk 7A 86
Runic St. L13: Liv 5H 89
Runnel, The L39: Hals 7D 16
Runnell, The CH64: Nest 7H 143
Runnell's La. L23: Thorn 7J 41
Runnymead Wlk. *WA8: Wid* 6E 114
(off William St.)
Runnymede L36: Huy 3H 91
WA1: W'ston 1K 119
Runnymede Cl. L25: Wltn 4E 110
Runnymede Ct. *WA8: Wid* 7E 114
(off William St.)
Runnymede Dr. WA11: Hay 7J 61
Runnymede Gdns. *WA8: Wid* 7E 114
(off Cliffe St.)
Runton Rd. L25: Gate 3G 111
Rupert Dr. L6: Liv 4C 88 (1M 5)
Rupert Rd. L36: Huy 4G 91
Rupert Row WA7: Cas 2J 153
Ruscar Cl. L26: Halew 6J 111
Ruscolm Cl. WA5: Gt San 1B 116
Ruscombe Rd. L14: K Ash 2D 90
Rushden Rd. L32: K'by 4E 56
Rushes Mdw. WA13: Lymm 3K 121
Rushey Hey Rd. L32: K'by 3C 56
Rushfield Cres. WA7: Brook 5K 153
Rush Gdns. WA13: Lymm 4J 121
RUSHGREEN 4J 121
Rushgreen Cl. CH43: Bid 1G 105
Rushgreen Rd. WA13: Lymm 4H 121
Rushlake Dr. L27: N'ley 3H 111
Rushmere Rd. L11: N Grn. 4H 69
Rushmoor Av. WN4: Ash M 1J 63
Rushmore Dr. WA8: Wid 5B 114
Rushmore Gro. WA1: P'ton 1G 119
Rusholme Cl. L26: Halew 3A 132
Rushton Av. WA12: New W 2F 77
Rushton Cl. WA5: B'wood 7D 76
WA8: Wid 5B 114
Rushton Pl. L25: Wltn 6E 110
Rushton's Wlk. L30: N'ton 1K 53
Rushy Vw. WA12: New W 2E 76
Ruskin Av. CH42: R Ferr 7F 107
CH44: Wall 4A 86
WA2: Warr 5C 98
WA12: New W 2G 77
WN3: Wigan 1D 50
Ruskin Cl. L20: Boot 3J 67
Ruskin Dr. CH65: Ell P 1B 170
WA10: St. H 2K 73
Ruskin Leisure Cen. 2K 73
Ruskin St. L4: Kirk 5A 68
Ruskin Way CH43: Noct 5H 105
L36: Huy 6H 91
Rusland Av. CH61: Pens 5D 124
Rusland Rd. L32: K'by 5C 56
Russeldene Rd. WN3: Wigan 1C 50
Russell Av. PR9: South 1C 12
Russell Ct. PR9: Cros 3E 8
WA8: Wid 4D 114
Russell Pl. L3: Liv 6A 88 (6J 5)
L19: Gars 3A 130
Russell Rd. CH42: R Ferr 5F 107
(not continuous)
CH44: Wall 2J 85
L18: Moss H 3H 109
L19: Gars 3A 130
L36: Huy 5B 92
PR9: South 1C 12
WA7: Run 1A 152
Russell St. CH41: Birk 1E 106
L3: Liv 5A 88 (5J 5)
Russet Cl. L27: N'ley 3J 111
WA10: St. H 1B 74
Russian Av. L13: Liv 2H 89
Russian Dr. L13: Liv 2H 89
Rutherford Cl. L13: W'tree 6G 89
Rutherford Rd. L18: Moss H 2J 109
L31: Mag 5G 43
WA10: Windle 7J 59
Rutherglen Av. L23: C'by 3F 53
Ruth Evans Ct. L35: R'hill 3G 93
Ruthin Cl. WA5: Call 4J 97
Ruthin Ct. CH65: Ell P 1B 170
Ruthin Wlk. WA6: Hel 3G 173
Ruthven Ct. *L21: Lith* 6G 53
(off Ruthven Rd.)
Ruthven Rd. L13: Liv 6K 89
L21: Lith 6G 53
Rutland Av. L17: Liv 2F 109
L26: Halew 1K 131
WA4: Walt 1B 138
Rutland Cl. L5: Liv 2B 88
Rutland Cres. L39: Orm 3B 24
Rutland Dr. WN4: Ash M 1G 63
Rutland Ho. L17: Aig 3F 109
L23: Blun 2B 52
Rutland Rd. PR8: South 3K 11
Rutland St. L20: Boot 2K 67
WA7: Run 6B 134
WA10: St. H 1B 74
Rutland Way L36: Huy 4B 92
Rutter Av. WA5: Warr 5K 97
Rutter St. L8: Liv 3A 108
Ryburn Rd. L39: Orm 7B 24
Rycot Rd. L24: Speke 5F 131
Rycroft Rd. CH44: Wall 4C 86
CH47: Meols 7G 83
L10: Faz 6G 55
Rydal Av. CH43: Noct 3G 105
L23: C'by 3F 53
L34: Prsct 1F 93
L37: Form 7H 19
WA4: Warr 6A 118
WN5: Orr 4H 39
Rydal Bank CH44: Wall 3C 86
CH63: Beb 2G 127
Rydal Cl. CH61: Pens 5E 124
CH64: Lit N 5K 157
CH65: Ell P 2A 170
L10: Ain 3H 55
L33: K'by 1B 56
WN4: Ash M 1G 63
Rydal Gro. WA6: Hel 3H 173
WA7: Run 2D 152
WA11: St. H 6C 60
Rydal Rd. L36: Huy 6J 91
Rydal St. L5: Liv 1C 88
WA12: New W 3G 77
Rydal Wlk. WN5: Wigan 4K 39
Rydal Way WA8: Wid 7J 113
Rydecroft L25: Wltn 6D 110
Ryder Cl. L35: R'hill 3G 93
L39: Augh 1A 34
Ryder Cres. L39: Augh 2A 34
PR8: B'dale 1E 14
Ryder Rd. WA1: W'ston 7J 99
WA8: Wid 4D 114
Rydinge, The L37: Form 4A 20
Rye Cl. WA9: Clock F 3E 94
Ryecote L32: K'by 6C 56
Rye Ct. L12: W Der 1C 90
Rye Cft. L21: Ford 2H 53
Ryecroft CH2: Elt 1B 172
Ryecroft Rd. CH60: Hes 3G 143
Ryedale Cl. L8: Liv 1D 108 (10P 5)
Ryefield La. L21: Ford 2H 53
Ryegate Rd. L19: Gras 1K 129
Ryeground La. L37: Form 5A 20
Rye Gro. L12: W Der 1C 90
Rye Hey Rd. L32: K'by 3C 56
Rye Moss La. L37: Gt Alt 3G 31
Ryfields Village WA2: Warr 7D 98
Rylance Rd. WN3: Wins 3B 50
Ryland Pk. CH61: Thing 4E 124
Rylands Hey CH49: Grea 4B 104
Rylands St. WA1: Warr 3B 118
WA8: Wid 1D 134
Ryleys Gdns. L2: Liv 5J 87 (5E 4)
Rymer Gro. L4: Walt 5C 68
Rymers Grn. L37: Form 6J 19

S

Sabden Brook Dr. WN2: Platt B 2K 51
Sabre Cl. WA7: Murd 3B 154
Sackville Rd. WA10: Windle 7J 59
Saddleback Cres. WN5: Wigan 5K 39

Saddleback Rd.—Sandbrook Ct.

Saddleback Rd. WN5: Wigan 4K 39
Saddle Cl. L9: Ain 5F 55
Saddlers Ri. WA7: Nort 2A 154
Saddlestone Gro. L8: Liv 3A 108
Sadler's La. WA11: Windle 6E 58
Sadler St. WA8: Wid 7E 114
Saffron Cl. WA2: P'gate 6H 99
Saffron Gdns. WA9: St. H 4F 75
Saffron M. L23: Thorn 6H 41
Sagar Fold L39: Augh 3B 34
Sage Cl. WA2: P'gate 5J 99
Sail Sports Windsurfing & Sailing Cen. 7G 173
St Agnes Rd. L4: Kirk 6K 67
L36: Huy 5J 91
St Aidan's Cl. WN5: Bil 6G 49
St Aidan's Ct. CH43: C'ton 2K 105
St Aidan's Gro. L36: Huy 7G 71
St Aidans Ter. *L5: Kirk* 1K 87
(off Latham St.)
CH43: C'ton 2K 105
St Aidan's Way L30: N'ton 2A 54
St Alban Rd. WA5: Penk 3C 116
St Albans L6: Liv 2C 88
St Albans Cl. WA11: Hay 6D 62
St Albans Ct. L5: Liv 2J 87
St Albans Rd. CH43: C'ton 1A 106
CH44: Wall 3B 86
L20: Boot 3J 67
St Alban's Sq. L20: Boot 4J 67
St Alexander Cl. L20: Kirk 5K 67
St Ambrose Cft. L30: N'ton 1A 54
St Ambrose Gro. L4: Walt 1D 88
St Ambrose Rd. WA8: Wid 7E 114
St Ambrose Way L5: Liv 3A 88 (1J 5)
St Andrew Rd. L4: Walt 1D 88
St Andrews Av. L12: W Der 1C 90
St Andrews Cl. WA2: Fearn 3G 99
St Andrews Ct. CH43: Noct 2H 105
CH65: Ell P 2C 170
L22: Water 5E 52
PR8: South 2H 11
St Andrews Dr. L23: Blun 6B 40
L36: Huy 7G 71
St Andrews Gdns. L3: Liv 5A 88 (5J 5)
St Andrews Gro. WA11: St. H 7D 60
L30: N'ton 2J 53
St Andrews Ho. WA3: Ris 1K 99
St Andrews Pl. L17: Aig 5E 108
PR8: South 2H 11
St Andrews Rd. CH63: Beb 5G 127
L20: Boot 7J 53
CH43: O'ton 2B 106
CH65: Ell P 1B 170
L23: Blun 6B 40
St Andrew St. L3: Liv 6A 88 (6K 5)
St Andrews Vw. L33: K'by 6C 44
St Anne's Av. WA4: Grap 6H 119
St Anne's Av. E. WA4: Grap 6H 119
St Annes Cl. CH41: Birk 1D 106
L37: Form 4K 19
St Anne's Cotts. L14: K Ash 3A 90
St Annes Ct. L3: Liv 2H 5
L13: Liv 4H 89
L17: Aig 7G 109
St Annes Gdns. L17: Aig 7G 109
St Annes Gro. CH41: Birk 7C 86
L17: Aig 7G 109
St Anne's Ho. L20: Boot 4J 67
St Annes Path L37: Form 4K 19
St Annes Pl. CH41: Birk 7C 86
St Annes Rd. L37: Form 4K 19
WA8: Wid 6D 114
L17: Aig 7G 109
L36: Huy 6J 91
L39: Orm 6B 24
PR9: Chu 3B 8
St Annes Ter. CH41: Birk 1C 106
St Anne St. CH41: Birk 7C 86
(not continuous)
L3: Liv 4K 87 (2H 5)
St Annes Way CH41: Birk 1D 106
St Ann Pl. L35: R'hill 3J 93
ST ANNS 4K 73
St Ann's Rd. WA10: St. H 3J 73
St Anthony Pl. WA2: Win 1B 98
St Anthony's Cl. L36: Huy 7G 71
St Anthony's Gro. L30: N'ton 2K 53
St Anthony's Rd. L23: Blun 7B 40
St Anthony's Shop. Cen. L5: Liv 2K 87
St Asaph Dr. WA5: Call 4H 97
St Asaph Gro. L30: N'ton 4B 54
St Asaph Rd. CH66: Gt Sut 4G 169
St Augustine's Av. WA4: Westy 4F 119
St Augustine St. L5: Liv 2K 87
St Augustine's Way L30: N'ton 1K 53
St Austell Cl. CH46: More 6K 83
WA5: Penk 5C 116
WA7: Brook 4K 153
St Austells Rd. L4: Walt 4A 68
St Austins La. WA1: Warr 4B 118
St Barnabas Pl. WA5: Warr 2J 117
St Bartholomew Rd. L3: Liv 4J 87 (2F 4)
St Bartholomews Ct. L36: Huy 4G 91
St Bedes Cl. L39: Orm 7B 24
St Benedict's Cl. WA2: Warr 1B 118
St Benedict's Gro. L36: Huy 7G 71
St Benedict's Pl. WA2: Warr 1B 118
St Benet's Way L30: N'ton 2A 54
St Bernards Cl. L8: Liv 1C 108 (10P 5)
L30: N'ton 2K 53
St Bernard's Dr. L30: N'ton 2K 53
St Brendan's Cl. L36: Huy 7G 71
St Brides Cl. WA5: Penk 5C 116
St Bride's Rd. CH44: Wall 2D 86
St Bride St. L8: Liv 7B 88 (9L 5)
St Bridget's Cl. WA2: Fearn 4F 99
St Bridget's Gro. L30: N'ton 2K 53
St Bridget's La. CH48: W Kir 7D 102
St Brigids Cres. L5: Liv 2J 87
St Catherine's Cl. L36: Huy 6J 91
St Catherines Gdns. CH42: Tran 4D 106
St Catherine's Rd. L20: Boot 3J 67
St Chad's Dr. L32: K'by 3C 56
St Chads Pde. L32: K'by 3C 56
St Christopher's Dr. L36: Huy 7G 71
St Christophers Av. L30: N'ton 1K 53
St Clair Dr. PR9: Chu 6C 8
St Clare Rd. L15: W'tree 1G 109
St Clement's St. WN3: Ince M 1K 51
St Columbas Cl. CH44: Wall 2D 86
St Cuthberts Cl. L12: Crox 3C 70
PR9: Chu 5C 8
St Cuthbert's Rd. PR9: Chu 5C 8
St Cyrils Cl. L27: N'ley 2G 111
St Cyril's Ct. L27: N'ley 1G 111
St Damian's Cft. L30: N'ton 2A 54
St David Rd. CH43: C'ton 2A 106
CH62: East 4C 146
St David's Cl. L35: R'hill 3J 93
St Davids Dr. CH66: Gt Sut 4H 169
WA5: Call 5J 97
St David's Gro. L30: N'ton 3K 53
St Davids La. CH43: Noct 3H 105
St Davids Rd. L4: Walt 1D 88
L14: K Ash 2F 91
St Domingo Gro. L5: Liv 1B 88
St Domingo Rd. L5: Liv 7A 68
St Domingo Va. L5: Liv 1B 88
St Dunstan's Gro. L30: N'ton 2K 53
St Edmond's Rd. L20: Boot 4J 67
St Edmund's Rd. CH63: Beb 4F 127
St Edwards Cl. CH41: Birk 7B 86
St Elmo Rd. CH44: Wall 2D 86
St Elphins Cl. WA1: Warr 3C 118
St Gabriel's Av. L36: Huy 5A 92
St Georges Av. CH66: Gt Sut 4H 169
CH42: Tran 6D 106
WA10: Windle 1J 73
St Georges Cl. WA4: App 6E 138
St Georges Ct. CH45: Wall 2J 85
L31: Mag 4F 43
WA8: Wid 1K 133
St George's Gro. CH46: More 7B 84
L30: N'ton 3K 53
St George's Hgts. L5: Liv 2A 88
St George's Hill L5: Liv 2A 88
St George's Mt. CH45: New B 6B 66
St George's Pk. CH45: New B 6B 66
St George's Pl. L1: Liv 5K 87 (5G 4)
PR9: South 1H 11
St Georges Rd. WA10: St. H 4K 73
CH45: Wall 1J 85
L36: Huy 2J 91
L37: Form 6J 19
L38: High 5G 29
St George's Way CH63: Thorn H 3A 144
L1: Liv 6G 4
St Gerald's Cl. L5: Liv 1K 87
St Gregory's Cft. L30: N'ton 1A 54
ST HELENS 3C 74
St Helens Central Station (Rail) 3D 74
St Helens Cl. CH43: C'ton 2B 106
WA3: Rix 4K 101
St Helens Club Figure & Fitness 2A 94
St Helens Crematorium
WA10: Windle 6J 59
St Helens Junction Station (Rail) 7H 75
St Helens Linkway L35: R'hill 3B 94
WA9: St. H 4C 74
St Helens Martial Arts & Fitness Studio 2C 74
(off Tolver St.)
St Helens Mus. & Art Gallery 2C 74
St Helens Retail Pk. WA9: St. H 3D 74
St Helens RLFC 3J 73
St Helens Rd. L34: Prsct, Ecc P 7D 72
L39: Orm 5D 24
WA11: R'ford 3H 59
St Helens Theatre Royal 2C 74
St Hilary Brow CH44: Wall 3K 85
St Hilary Dr. CH45: Wall 2K 85
St Hilda's Dr. WA6: Frod 2E 166
St Hilda St. L4: Walt 6A 68
St Hugh's Cl. CH43: C'ton 2B 106
St Hugh's Ho. L20: Boot 3J 67
St Ives Ct. CH43: C'ton 1A 106
St Ives Gro. L13: Liv 4H 89
St Ives Rd. CH43: C'ton 2A 106
St Ives Way L26: Halew 1K 131
St James Cl. CH49: Grea 4B 104
L40: Westh 7G 25
WA6: Frod 2D 166
L12: W Der 1J 89
St James Ct. CH45: New B 6B 66
WA4: Warr 4B 118
St James Dr. L20: Boot 2H 67
St James M. L20: Boot 2H 67
St James Mt. L35: R'hill 5J 93
St James Pl. L8: Liv 1A 108
St James Rd. CH41: Birk 7K 85
CH45: New B 6B 66
L1: Liv 1A 108 (10J 5)
L35: R'hill 5J 93
L36: Huy 6J 91
WN5: Orr 7F 39
L34: Prsct 1E 92
St James St. L1: Liv 1K 107 (10G 4)
PR8: South 3H 11
St James Way L30: N'ton 1K 53
St Jerome's Way L30: N'ton 1A 54
St John Av. WA4: Warr 6B 118
St Johns Av. L9: Walt 1C 68
St Johns Brow WA7: Run 6D 134
St John's Cen. L1: Liv 6K 87 (6G 4)
St John's Cl. CH47: Meols 7F 83
St Johns Ct. PR8: Ains 5D 14
L22: Water 4D 52
WA1: Warr 1F 119
St John's Ho. L20: Boot 3K 67
St John's La. L1: Liv 5K 87 (5G 4)
St John's Pavement CH41: Birk 2D 106
St John's Pl. L22: Water 4D 52
St John's Rd. CH45: Wall 2J 85
St John's Rd. CH62: East 5C 146
L20: Boot 4H 67
L20: Kirk 6J 67
L22: Water 4D 52
L36: Huy 6K 91
PR8: B'dale 7F 11
St John's Sq. CH41: Birk 2D 106
L1: Liv 6G 4
St John's Ter. L20: Boot 4H 67
St John St. CH41: Birk 2D 106
WA7: Run 6D 134
WA10: St. H 6K 73
WA12: Newt W 3E 76
WN5: Wigan 5K 39
St Johns Vs. WA8: Wid 6K 113
St Johns Way L1: Liv 6K 87 (6G 4)
St Josephs Cl. WA9: St. H 5E 74
L36: Huy 7G 71
WA5: Penk 3C 116
St Josephs Cres. L3: Liv 4K 87 (3H 5)
St Jude's Cl. L36: Huy 7G 71
St Katherines Way WA1: Warr 3D 118
St Kevin's Dr. L33: K'by 1C 56
St Kilda Cl. CH65: Ell P 3A 170
St Kilda's Rd. CH46: More 1C 104
St Laurence Cl. CH41: Birk 1D 106
St Laurence Dr. CH41: Birk 1D 106
St Laurence Gro. L32: K'by 5D 56
St Lawrence Cl. L8: Liv 4C 108
St Lawrence Rd. WA6: Frod 4D 166
St Leonard's Cl. L30: N'ton 1K 53
St Lucia Rd. CH44: Wall 2D 86
St Lukes Chu. Rd. L37: Form 1G 29
(not continuous)
St Lukes Cl. L14: K Ash 1D 90
St Luke's Ct. L4: Walt 4C 68
St Luke's Cres. WA8: Wid 4D 114
St Lukes Dr. L37: Form 1G 29
WN5: Orr 7F 39
St Luke's Gro. L30: N'ton 1K 53
PR9: South 1A 12
St Lukes Ho. WN4: Ash M 1G 63
St Lukes Pl. L1: Liv 7A 88 (8H 5)
St Luke's Rd. L23: C'by 1D 52
PR9: South 2K 11
WA10: St. H 3K 73
St Luke's Way L36: Huy 7G 71
WA6: Frod 2D 166
St Margarets Av. WA2: Warr 6D 98
St Margaret's Gro. L30: N'ton 2J 53
St Margaret's Rd. CH47: Hoy 2C 102
St Marks Cres. CH66: Gt Sut 4H 169
St Mark's Gro. L30: N'ton 1J 53
St Mark's Rd. L36: Huy 6K 91
St Mark's St. WA11: Hay 7J 61
St Martins Dr. CH66: Gt Sut 2F 169
St Martins Gro. L32: K'by 6D 56
St Martin's Ho. L20: Boot 3J 67
St Martin's La. WA7: Murd 3B 154
St Martin's Mkt. L5: Liv 2A 88
St Martins M. L5: Liv 3A 88 (1H 5)
St Mary's Arc. *WA10: St. H* 3C 74
(off St Mary's Mkt.)
St Mary's Av. CH44: Wall 3B 86
L4: Walt 4C 68
WN5: Bil 1E 60
St Mary's Cl. L13: Liv 6H 89
L20: Boot 3H 67
L24: Hale 7D 132
WA4: App 3C 138
St Marys Ct. L25: Wltn 6E 110
CH49: Upton 4E 104
St Mary's Gdns. PR8: Ains 2F 15
St Mary's Ga. CH41: Birk 2F 107
St Mary's Grn. WA1: Warr 3C 118
St Mary's Gro. L4: Walt 4C 68
L30: N'ton 2J 53
St Mary's La. L4: Walt 4C 68
St Mary's Mkt. WA10: St. H 3C 74
St Mary's Pl. L4: Walt 4C 68
St Marys Rd. WA7: Halt 1H 153
WA8: Wid 5C 134
L19: Gars, Gras 2J 129
L22: Water 4F 53
L36: Huy 5J 91
WA5: Gt San, Penk 3D 116
St Mary's St. CH44: Wall 3B 86
L25: Wltn 6E 110
WA4: Warr 4C 118
St Mathews Cl. L4: Walt 4F 69
L36: Huy 4K 91
St Matthew's Av. L21: Lith 5J 53
St Matthews Cl. WA4: App 2D 138
St Matthews Gro. WA10: St. H 6J 73
St Mawes Cl. WA8: Wid 6A 114
St Mawes Way WA10: Windle 7H 59
St Mawgan Ct. WA2: P'gate 5F 99
St Michael Rd. L39: Augh 4H 33
St Michael's Chu. Rd. L17: Aig 5D 108
St Michaels Cl. L17: Aig 6E 108
PR9: Chu 4B 8
WA8: Wid 2J 133
St Michaels Ct. L36: Huy 4J 91
St Michaels Gro. L6: Liv 3D 88 (1P 5)
CH46: More 7B 84
L30: N'ton 2J 53
St Michael's Hall L17: Aig 6D 108
ST MICHAEL'S HAMLET 5D 108
St Michael's Ind. Est.
WA8: Wid 2J 133
St Michaels Pk. CH62: Port S 3H 127
L39: Augh 4J 33
St Michaels Rd. WA9: St. H 4C 94
L17: Aig 6D 108
L23: Blun, C'by 7B 40
WA8: Wid 2J 133
St Michael's Station (Rail) 6D 108
St Monica's Cl. WA4: App 2E 138
St Monica's Dr. L30: N'ton 1K 53
St Nicholas' Dr. L30: N'ton 1K 53
St Nicholas Gro. WA9: St. H 7F 75
St Nicholas Pl. L3: Liv 6H 87 (6B 4)
(not continuous)
St Nicholas Rd. L35: Whis 6D 92
CH45: Wall 2H 85
St Oswald's Av. CH43: Bid 7G 85
St Oswalds Cl. WA2: Win 1B 98
St Oswald's Ct. L30: N'ton 2B 54
St Oswald's La. L30: N'ton 2B 54
St Oswald's M. CH43: Bid 6G 85
St Oswald's Rd. WN4: Ash M 3E 62
St Oswald's St. L13: Liv 5J 89
St Paschal Baylon Blvd.
L16: Child 7D 90
St Patrick's Cl. L33: K'by 7C 44
St Patrick's Dr. L30: N'ton 1K 53
St Paul's Av. CH44: Wall 5E 86
WN3: Wigan 1D 50
St Pauls Cl. L33: K'by 7B 44
CH42: R Ferr 6E 106
St Pauls Gdns. CH66: Lit Sut 4D 160
St Pauls Mansion PR8: South 2G 11
St Paul's Pas. PR8: South 2G 11
St Pauls Pl. L20: Boot 4K 67
St Paul's Rd. CH42: R Ferr 6F 107
(not continuous)
CH44: Wall 5D 86
WA8: Wid 2C 134
St Paul's Sq. L3: Liv 5H 87 (4D 4)
PR8: South 2G 11
St Paul's St. PR8: South 2G 11
St Paul St. WA10: St. H 3A 74
St Paul's Vs. CH42: R Ferr 6E 106
St Peter's Av. L37: Form 6H 19
St Peters Cl. CH60: Hes 3D 142
L33: K'by 7B 44
L37: Form 6H 19
WA13: Lymm 4J 121
St Peters Ct. WA2: Warr 2C 118
CH42: R Ferr 7G 107
L17: Aig 4D 108
St Peter's Ho. L20: Boot 4K 67
St Peter's M. CH42: R Ferr 7G 107
St Peter's Rd. CH42: R Ferr 7G 107
L9: Ain 7E 54
PR8: B'dale 5G 11
St Peters Row L31: Mag 6F 43
St Peter's Sq. L1: Liv 8H 5
St Peter's Way CH43: Noct 4G 105
WA2: Warr 2B 118
St Philip's Av. L21: Lith 5J 53
St Richards Cl. L20: Kirk 5K 67
St Seiriol Gro. CH43: C'ton 2A 106
St Stephen Rd.
WA5: Gt San, Penk 3D 116
St Stephen's Av. WA2: Warr 4B 98
St Stephens Cl. CH60: Hes 4G 143
L25: Gate 3G 111
St Stephen's Ct. CH42: Tran 7B 106
St Stephen's Gro. L30: N'ton 2K 53
St Stephen's Pl. L3: Liv 4K 87 (3F 4)
St Stephen's Rd. CH42: Tran 6B 106
L38: High 5F 29
St Teresa's Rd. WA10: St. H 2K 73
St Thomas Ct. WA8: Wid 7K 113
St Thomas's Ct. WN8: Uph 5E 38
St Thomas's Dr. L30: N'ton 2K 53
St Thomas Vw. CH65: Whit 7K 161
St Vincent Rd. CH43: C'ton 2A 106
CH44: Wall 2D 86
WA5: Penk 3D 116
St Vincents Cl. L12: W Der 1C 90
St Vincent St. L3: Liv 5A 88 (5J 5)
St Vincent's Way PR8: B'dale 4G 11
St Vincent Way L3: Liv 5A 88 (5J 5)
St Werburghs Sq. CH41: Birk 2D 106
St Wilfrid's Dr. WA4: Grap 7J 119
St William Rd. L23: Thorn 7H 41
St William Way L23: Thorn 7H 41
St Winifred Rd. CH45: New B 7B 66
L35: R'hill 2H 93
St Wyburn Ct. PR8: B'dale 2F 11
Saker St. L4: Walt 7B 68
Salacre Cl. CH49: Upton 4F 105
Salacre Cres. CH49: Upton 4E 104
Salacre La. CH49: Upton 3E 104
Salacre Ter. CH49: Upton 3E 104
Salcombe Dr. L25: Hunts X 2F 131
PR9: Marsh 2C 8
Salem Vw. CH43: O'ton 5B 106
Salerno Dr. L36: Huy 3H 91
Salesbury Way WN3: Wigan 1E 50
Sales Wood Av. WA10: Eccl 3G 73
Salford Rd. PR8: Ains 4C 14
Salhouse Gdns. WA9: St. H 1K 93
Saline Cl. L14: K Ash 1E 90
Salisbury Av. CH48: W Kir 6C 102
L30: N'ton 4B 54
Salisbury Cl. CH66: Gt Sut 4H 169
Salisbury Dr. CH62: New F 2H 127
Salisbury Hall L18: Moss H 6G 109
Salisbury Ho. L20: Boot 2H 67
Salisbury Pk. L16: Child 3B 110
Salisbury Rd. CH45: New B 6A 66
L5: Liv 1B 88
L15: W'tree 1F 109
L19: Gras 2J 129
L20: Boot 1H 67
WA11: Hay 5C 62
WN4: Ash M 7E 50
Salisbury St. CH41: Birk 3D 106
L3: Liv 3A 88 (1J 5)
(not continuous)
L34: Prsct 7D 72
PR9: South 2C 12
WA1: Warr 2D 118
WA7: Run 1C 152
WA8: Wid 1D 134
Salisbury Ter. L15: W'tree 7H 89
Salkeld Av. WN4: Ash M 2D 62
Sallowfields WN5: Orr 6F 39
Sally's La. PR9: Chu 5C 8
Salop St. L4: Walt 6B 68
Saltash Cl. L26: Halew 7J 111
WA7: Brook 4K 153
Saltburn Rd. CH45: Wall 2H 85
Saltergate Rd. L8: Liv 4C 108
Saltersgate CH66: Gt Sut 2H 169
Salthouse Quay L3: Liv 7J 87 (8D 4)
Saltney St. L3: Liv 2H 87
Salton Gdns. WA5: Warr 1J 117
Saltpit La. L31: Mag 3G 43
Saltram Rd. WN3: Wigan 1A 50
Saltwood Dr. WA7: Brook 5A 154
Saltworks Cl. WA6: Frod 1F 167
Salvia Way L33: K'by 7B 44
Salvin Cl. WN4: Ash M 2H 63
Salwick Cl. PR9: Marsh 2B 8
Salwick Cl. WN3: Wigan 1C 50
Samaria Av. CH62: New F 2J 127
Sambourn Fold PR8: Ains 4A 14
Samphire Gdns. WA9: Bold 7K 75
Samuel St. WA5: Warr 4J 117
WA9: St. H 7K 73
Samwoods Ho. WN4: Ash M 7E 50
Sanbec Gdns. WA8: Cron 3K 113
Sandalwood WA7: Nort 1A 154
Sandalwood Cl. L6: Liv 2D 88
WA2: Warr 5D 98
Sandalwood Dr. CH43: Noct 4H 105
Sandalwood Gdns. WA9: St. H 7E 74
Sandbeck St. L8: Liv 5B 108
Sandbourne CH46: More 7E 84
Sandbrook Ct. CH46: More 7C 84

Sandbrook Gdns.—Sedgemoor Rd.

Sandbrook Gdns. WN5: Orr 6F 39
Sandbrook La. CH46: More 7C 84
Sandbrook Rd. L25: Gate 7E 90
PR8: Ains 6D 14
WN5: Orr 6E 38
Sandbrook Way PR8: Ains 6C 14
Sandcliffe Rd. CH45: Wall 6J 65
Sandeman Rd. L4: Walt 6F 69
Sanderling Rd. L33: K'by 2E 56
WA12: New W 2G 77
Sanders Hey Cl. WA7: Brook 5J 153
Sanderson Cl. WA5: Gt San 2B 116
Sandfield L36: Huy 5H 91
Sandfield Av. CH47: Meols 6F 83
Sandfield Cl. CH63: High B 3D 126
L12: W Der 2A 90
Sandfield Cotts. L39: Augh 1B 34
Sandfield Ct. WA6: Frod 3D 166
Sandfield Cres. WA10: St. H 3B 74
Sandfield Hey *L12: W Der* *1A 90*
(off Sandfield Pk. E.)
SANDFIELD PARK 2K 89
Sandfield Pk. CH60: Hes 2B 142
L39: Augh 1B 34
Sandfield Pk. E. L12: W Der 1A 90
Sandfield Pl. L20: Boot 2H 67
Sandfield Rd. CH45: New B 7B 66
CH49: W'chu 7F 105
CH63: High B 3D 126
L20: Boot 3K 67
L25: Gate 4F 111
WA10: Eccl 1G 73
Sandfields WA6: Frod 3D 166
Sandfield Ter. CH45: New B 7B 66
Sandfield Wlk. L12: W Der 3K 89
Sandford Dr. L31: Mag 2F 43
Sandford Rd. WN5: Orr 6E 38
Sandford St. CH41: Birk 1E 106
Sandforth Cl. L12: W Der 1J 89
Sandforth Ct. L12: W Der 2J 89
Sandforth Rd. L12: W Der 2J 89
Sandgate Cl. L24: Speke 5F 131
Sandham Gro. CH60: Hes 2G 143
Sandham Rd. L24: Speke 5A 132
Sandhead St. L7: Liv 7F 89
Sandhey Rd. CH47: Meols 7E 82
Sandheys CH64: Park 2G 157
Sandheys Av. L22: Water 4C 52
Sandheys Cl. L4: Walt 7A 68
Sandheys Dr. PR9: South 6B 8
Sandheys Gro. L22: Water 3C 52
Sandheys Rd. CH45: New B 7B 66
Sandheys Ter. L22: Water 4C 52
Sandhills L38: High 6F 29
Sandhills, The CH46: Leas 4C 84
Sandhills Bus. Pk. L5: Kirk 7J 67
Sandhills Ind. Est. L5: Kirk 1J 87
Sandhills La. L5: Kirk 7H 67
Sandhills Station (Rail) 7J 67
Sandhills Vw. CH45: Wall 2H 85
Sandhill Ter. WA4: Latch 5E 118
Sandhurst L23: Blun 1C 52
Sandhurst Cl. L21: Sea 6F 53
L37: Form 2G 29
Sandhurst Dr. L10: Ain 3F 55
Sandhurst Rd. L26: Halew 3A 132
L35: R'hill 2G 93
Sandhurst St. L17: Aig 5C 108
WA4: Westy 5F 119
Sandhurst Way L31: Lyd 6D 32
Sandicroft Cl. WA3: Bchwd 2J 99
Sandicroft Rd. L12: Crox 4D 70
Sandilands Gro. L38: High 6F 29
Sandino St. L8: Liv 2A 108
Sandiway CH47: Meols 6F 83
CH63: Brom 4J 145
L35: Whis 5D 92
L36: Huy 6K 91
Sandiway Av. WA8: Wid 7G 113
Sandiway Ct. PR9: South 7A 8
Sandiways L31: Mag 3G 43
Sandiways Av. L30: N'ton 3C 54
Sandiways Rd. CH45: Wall 1J 85
Sandlea Pk. CH48: W Kir 6C 102
Sandlewood Gro. L33: K'by 1D 56
Sandling Dr. WA3: Golb 3K 63
Sandon Cl. L35: R'hill 3H 93
Sandon Ct. *L22: Water* *4D 52*
(off Sandon St.)
Sandon Cres. CH64: Lit N 6J 157
Sandon Gro. WA11: R'ford 6G 47
Sandon Ind. Est. L5: Kirk 1H 87
Sandon Pl. WA8: Wid 7F 115
Sandon Prom. CH44: Wall 3D 86
Sandon Rd. CH44: Wall 3D 86
PR8: B'dale 7F 11
Sandon St. L8: Liv 7B 88 (9L 5)
L22: Water 4D 52
Sandon Way L5: Kirk 1H 87
Sandown Cl. WA3: Cul 2B 80
WA7: Run 4D 152
Sandown Ct. L15: W'tree 7H 89
PR9: South 7J 7
Sandown La. L15: W'tree 7H 89
SANDOWN PARK 6H 89
Sandown Pk. Rd. L10: Ain 2G 55
Sandown Rd. L15: W'tree 6H 89
L21: Sea 6F 53
Sandpiper Cl. CH49: Upton 2B 104
WA12: New W 2G 77
Sandpiper Gro. L26: Halew 7J 111
Sandpiper Rd. WN3: Wigan 7K 39
Sandpipers Ct. CH47: Hoy 1C 102
Sandra Dr. WA12: New W 3H 77
Sandridge Rd. CH45: New B 7B 66
CH61: Pens 4D 124
Sandringham Av. CH47: Meols 7E 82
L22: Water 5E 52
WA6: Hel 1H 173
Sandringham Cl. CH47: Meols 7E 82
CH62: New F 2G 127
L33: K'by 7C 44
Sandringham Ct. PR9: South 7J 7
Sandringham Dr. CH45: New B 6A 66
L17: Aig 4D 108
WA5: Gt San 4G 117
WA9: St. H 1E 94
Sandringham Gdns.
CH65: Ell P 2B 170
Sandringham M. CH47: Meols 1E 102
Sandringham Rd. L13: Liv 1F 89
L22: Water 5E 52
L31: Mag 4E 42
L37: Form 2J 29
PR8: Ains 4C 14
PR8: B'dale 5E 10
WA8: Wid 4B 114
Sandrock Rd. CH45: New B 7B 66
Sands Rd. L18: Moss H 4H 109
Sandstone CH45: Wall 2C 86
Sandstone Cl. L35: R'hill 6J 93
Sandstone Dr. CH48: W Kir 6G 103
L35: Whis 2G 93
Sandstone M. WA8: Wid 4A 114
Sandstone Rd. WN3: Wins 2B 50
Sandstone Rd. E. L13: Liv 3H 89
Sandstone Rd. W. L13: Liv 3H 89
Sandstone Wlk. CH60: Hes 3E 142
Sandwash Cl. WA11: R'ford 1H 59
Sandway Cres. L11: N Grn. 4J 69
Sandwith Cl. WN3: Wigan 2F 51
Sandy Brow La. L33: Know 6J 57
WA3: Croft 4D 78
Sandy Cl. WN8: Newb 1F 27
Sandy Grn. L9: Ain 7E 54
Sandy Gro. L13: Liv 1H 89
Sandy Ho. *L21: Sea* *6F 53*
(off Sandy Rd.)
Sandy Knowle L15: W'tree 7J 89
Sandy La. CH45: Wall 1J 85
CH48: W Kir 1D 122
CH60: Hes 1E 142
CH61: Irby 2A 124
CH64: Lit N 4A 158
L9: Ain 7D 54
L13: Liv 1H 89
L21: Sea 6G 53
(not continuous)
L31: Lyd 5D 32
L31: Mell 7J 43
L38: High 5G 29
L39: Augh 5K 33
L40: Lath 3G 25
WA2: Warr 4B 98
WA3: Croft 6G 79
WA3: Golb 5K 63
(not continuous)
WA4: S Hth 1D 138
WA5: Penk 4E 116
WA6: Hel 2H 173
WA7: Pres B 4C 154
WA7: West P 3K 151
WA8: Cron 3K 113
WA8: Wid 2J 115
WA11: St. H 4A 60
WA13: Lymm 3K 121
WN5: Orr 7F 39
WN8: Newb 1F 27
WN8: Skel 2D 36
Sandy La. Cen. WN8: Skel 2D 36
Sandy La. Nth. CH61: Irby 2A 124
Sandy La. W. WA2: Warr 4A 98
Sandy Moor La. WA7: Nort 7B 136
Sandymoor La. WA7: Nort 6B 136
Sandymount Dr. CH45: Wall 7A 66
CH63: Beb 5F 127
Sandy Rd. L21: Sea 5F 53
Sandyville Gro. L4: Walt 6G 69
Sandyville Rd. L4: Walt 6F 69
Sandy Way CH43: O'ton 3A 106
Sanfield Cl. L39: Orm 4C 24
Sangness Dr. PR8: South 5A 12
SANKEY BRIDGES 4H 117
Sankey Bridges Ind. Est.
WA5: Gt San 4G 117
Sankey (for Penketh) Station (Rail)
2D 116
Sankey Grn. WA5: Warr 3J 117
Sankey Mnr. WA5: Gt San 2D 116
Sankey Rd. L31: Mag 5F 43
WA11: Hay 1H 75
Sankey St. L1: Liv 7A 88 (9H 5)
WA1: Warr 3A 118
(not continuous)
WA8: Wid 3C 134
WA9: St. H 4F 75
WA12: New W 3E 76
Sankey Valley Country Pk.
6G 61
Sankey Valley Country Pk. Vis. Cen.
7G 61
Sankey Valley Ind. Est.
WA12: New W 4E 76
Sankey Way WA5: Gt San 3E 116
WA5: Warr 3K 117
Sanky La. WA4: Hatt 1K 155
Santon Av. L13: Liv 2G 89
Sanvino Av. PR8: Ains 4D 14
Sapphire Dr. L33: K'by 7C 44
Sapphire St. L13: Liv 6H 89
Sarah's Cft. L30: N'ton 2A 54
Sark Av. CH65: Ell P 3K 169
Sark Rd. L13: Liv 3H 89
Sartfield Cl. L16: Child 7C 90
Sarum Rd. L25: Gate 1E 110
Sarus Ct. WA7: Mnr P 5K 135
Satinwood Cres. L31: Mell 2J 55
Satinwood Rd. WN4: Ash M 2D 62
SAUGHALL MASSIE 2A 104
Saughall Massie La.
CH49: Upton 3D 104
Saughall Massie Rd.
CH48: W Kir 5F 103
CH49: Grea, Upton 5F 103
(not continuous)
Saughall Rd. CH46: More 1A 104
Saunby St. L19: Gars 5A 130
Saunders Av. L35: Prsct 3D 92
Saundersfoot Cl. WA5: Call 5J 97
Saunders St. PR9: South 6H 7
Saunderton Cl. WA11: Hay 6A 62
Saville Av. WA5: Warr 1K 117
Saville Rd. L13: Liv 5K 89
L31: Lyd 1E 42
Savon Hook L37: Form 2A 30
Savoylands Cl. L17: Aig 6E 108
Sawdon Av. PR8: South 4A 12
Sawley Cl. WA3: Cul 4C 80
WA7: Murd 3C 154
Sawpit La. L36: Huy 5K 91
Sawyer Dr. WN4: Ash M 2H 63
Saxby Rd. L14: K Ash 2E 90
Saxenholme PR8: B'dale 3F 11
Saxon Cl. L6: Liv 2D 88
WA4: App 4B 138
Saxon Ct. WA10: St. H 1A 74
Saxonia Rd. L4: Walt 4C 68
Saxon Lodge PR8: B'dale 3F 11
Saxon Rd. CH46: More 6D 84
CH47: Meols 7E 82
L23: C'by 2D 52
PR8: B'dale 3F 11
WA7: Run 7E 134
Saxon Ter. WA8: Wid 7D 114
Saxon Way CH66: Gt Sut 4H 169
L33: K'by 6C 44
Saxony Rd. L7: Liv 5C 88 (5N 5)
(not continuous)
Saxthorpe Cl. WN3: Wins 1B 50
Sayce St. WA8: Wid 7D 114
Scafell Av. WA2: Warr 4C 98
Scafell Cl. CH62: East 7K 145
Scafell Dr. WN5: Wigan 5K 39
Scafell Lawn L27: N'ley 5A 112
Scafell Rd. WA11: St. H 5C 60
Scafell Wlk. L27: N'ley 4A 112
(not continuous)
Scaffold La. L38: Ince B 5B 30
Scape La. L23: C'by 7E 40
Scargreen Av. L11: N Grn. 3H 69
SCARISBRICK 2F 17
Scarisbrick Av. L21: Lith 6H 53
PR8: South 1G 11
Scarisbrick Cl. L31: Mag 1G 43
Scarisbrick Ct. PR8: South 2J 11
Scarisbrick Cres. L11: N Grn. 3F 69
Scarisbrick Dr. L11: N Grn. 3F 69
Scarisbrick Ho. L39: Orm 5D 24
Scarisbrick New Rd. PR8: South 2J 11
Scarisbrick Pk. L40: Scar 3J 17
Scarisbrick Pl. L11: N Grn. 4F 69
Scarisbrick Rd. L11: N Grn. 3F 69
WA11: R'ford 5F 47
Scarisbrick St. L39: Orm 4C 24
PR9: South 1H 11
Scarsdale Rd. L11: N Grn. 5H 69
SCARTH HILL 1F 35
Scarth Hill La. L39: Augh, Westh 2C 34
L40: Westh 1F 35
Scarth Pk. WN8: Skel 4J 37
Sceptre Cl. WA12: New W 3E 76
Sceptre Rd. L11: Crox 2A 70
Sceptre Twr. L11: Crox 3A 70
Sceptre Wlk. L11: Crox 3A 70
Scholars Ct. *CH64: Nest* *3J 157*
(off Cross St.)
Scholars Grn. La.
WA13: Lymm 5H 121
Scholar St. L7: Liv 1E 108
Scholes La. WA10: St. H 7H 73
Scholes Pk. WA10: St. H 7H 73
Schomberg St. L6: Liv 4C 88 (2N 5)
School Av. CH64: Lit N 5K 157
L37: Form 7K 19
School Brow WA1: Warr 3C 118
WN5: Bil 7G 49
School Cl. CH46: More 5D 84
L27: N'ley 1G 111
L39: Augh 2K 33
PR8: B'dale 6H 11
School Dr. WN5: Bil 7G 49
Schoolfield Cl. CH49: W'chu 6F 105
Schoolfield Rd. CH49: W'chu 6F 105
School Hill CH60: Hes 3D 142
School Ho. Grn. L39: Orm 5D 24
School La. CH2: Elt 1A 172
CH43: Bid 6G 85
CH45: Wall 3J 85
(not continuous)
CH47: Hoy 1D 102
(not continuous)
CH47: Meols 6F 83
CH61: Thurs 3K 123
CH62: New F 2H 127
CH63: High B 3D 126
CH64: Lit N 5K 157
CH64: Nest 1B 158
CH64: Park 2F 157
CH66: Chil T 2B 168
L1: Liv 6K 87 (7F 4)
L10: Ain 3F 55
L21: Lith 5H 53
L21: Sea 6G 53
L25: Wltn 2E 130
L31: Mag 2J 43
L31: Mell 7J 43
L34: Know 7E 56
L35: R'hill 6A 94
(not continuous)
L36: Huy 5A 92
L37: Form 7K 19
L39: Down, Has 7B 22
L40: Westh 1H 35
WA3: Ris 2E 100
WA3: Rix 5J 101
WA6: Frod 4E 166
WA7: Halt 2H 153
WA8: Bold H 1G 115
WN4: Gars 2A 62
WN8: Roby M 1D 38
WN8: Skel 1D 36
WN8: Uph 4E 38
School Pl. CH41: Birk 1D 106
School Rd. CH65: Ell P 6K 161
L38: High 5F 29
WA2: Warr 6C 98
School St. WA4: Warr 4B 118
WA11: Hay 7H 61
WA12: New W 3F 77
WN4: Ash M 7H 51
School Way L24: Speke 6F 131
WA8: Wid 5F 115
Schooner Cl. WA7: Murd 4B 154
Schubert Cl. CH66: Gt Sut 7H 161
Schwartzman Dr.
PR9: Banks 1J 9
Science Pk. Nth. WA3: Ris 1K 99
Science Pk. Sth. WA3: Ris 2K 99
Science Rd. L24: Speke 5G 131
Scilly Cl. CH65: Ell P 3A 170
Scone Cl. L11: Crox 3A 70
Score, The WA9: St. H 1C 94
Scorecross WA9: St. H 6D 74
Score La. L16: Child 6A 90
Scoresby Rd. CH46: Leas 4G 85
Scorpio Cl. L14: K Ash 2E 90
Scorton St. L6: Liv 2E 88
Scotchbarn La. L34: Prsct 1E 92
L35: Prsct 1F 93
Scotchbarn Sports Cen. 1E 92
Scoter Rd. L33: K'by 3D 56
Scotia Av. CH62: New F 2J 127
Scotia Rd. L13: Liv 3J 89
Scotland Rd. L3: Liv 4K 87 (3G 4)
L5: Liv 3K 87 (1G 4)
WA1: Warr 3B 118
Scott Av. L35: Whis 4F 93
L36: Huy 6A 92
WA8: Wid 1B 134
WA9: Sut M 4C 94
Scott Cl. L4: Walt 7B 68
L31: Mag 3F 43
Scott Dr. L39: Orm 3D 24
Scotton Av. CH66: Lit Sut 6D 160
Scotts Pl. CH41: Birk 1K 105
Scotts Quays CH41: Birk 6E 86
Scott St. CH45: Wall 2B 86
L20: Boot 1H 67
PR9: South 1C 12
WA2: Warr 2B 118
Scott Wlk. WA12: New W 5G 77
Scythes, The CH49: Grea 4A 104
L30: N'ton 1D 54
Scythia Cl. CH62: New F 1J 127
Seabank Av. CH44: Wall 2C 86
Seabank Cotts. CH47: Meols 5H 83
Seabank Rd. CH44: Wall 6B 66
CH45: New B 6B 66
CH60: Hes 4C 142
PR9: South 7H 7
Sea Brow L1: Liv 6J 87 (7D 4)
Seabury St. WA4: Westy 5G 119
Seacole Cl. L8: Liv 2D 108
Seacombe Dr. CH66: Gt Sut 1G 169
Seacombe Prom. CH44: Wall 3E 86
(not continuous)
Seacombe Vw. CH44: Wall 5E 86
Sea Ct. Flats CH45: Wall 7K 65
Seacroft Cl. L14: K Ash 1E 90
Seacroft Cres. PR9: Marsh 2D 8
Seacroft Rd. L14: K Ash 1E 90
Seafield L37: Form 1A 30
Seafield Av. CH60: Hes 4C 142
L23: C'by 2E 52
Seafield Dr. CH45: Wall 7K 65
Seafield Rd. CH62: New F 1H 127
L9: Walt 1B 68
L20: Boot 2H 67
PR8: Ains 3C 14
Seaford Cl. WA7: Wind H 1B 154
Seaford Pl. WA2: Warr 3A 98
Seafore Cl. L31: Lyd 7D 32
SEAFORTH 7G 53
Seaforth & Litherland Station (Rail)
6G 53
Seaforth Dr. CH46: More 1C 104
Seaforth Nature Reserve
6C 52
Seaforth Rd. L21: Sea 1G 67
Seaforth Va. Nth. L21: Sea 6G 53
Seaforth Va. W. L21: Sea 7G 53
Seagram Cl. L9: Ain 5E 54
Sealand Av. L37: Form 1H 29
Sealand Cl. L37: Form 1H 29
WA2: P'gate 7E 98
Sea La. WA7: Run 7F 135
Sealy Cl. CH63: Spit 1G 145
Seaman Rd. L15: W'tree 1G 109
Seaport St. L8: Liv 2C 108
Sea Rd. CH45: Wall 6K 65
Seascale Av. WA10: St. H 6H 73
Seath Av. WA9: St. H 2G 75
Seathwaite Cl. L23: Blun 2B 52
WA7: Beech 5G 153
Seathwaite Cres. L33: K'by 1B 56
Seatoller Pl. WN5: Wigan 4K 39
Seaton Cl. L12: Crox 3E 70
Seaton Gro. WA9: St. H 1K 93
Seaton Pk. WA7: Nort 6C 136
Seaton Pl. WN8: Skel 7E 26
Seaton Rd. CH42: Tran 4C 106
CH45: Wall 1A 86
Seaton Way PR9: Marsh 2C 8
Seattle Cl. WA5: Gt San 1F 117
Sea Vw. CH47: Hoy 1D 102
CH64: Lit N 7J 157
Seaview Av. CH45: Wall 2A 86
CH61: Irby 3B 124
CH62: East 4D 146
Seaview La. CH61: Irby 3B 124
Sea Vw. Rd. L20: Boot 2G 67
Seaview Rd. CH45: Wall 1A 86
Seaview Ter. L22: Water 4C 52
Seawood Gro. CH46: More 1B 104
Secker Av. WA4: Latch 6D 118
Secker Cres. WA4: Latch 6D 118
Second Av. CH43: Bid 2F 105
L9: Ain 7G 55
(Lower La.)
L9: Ain 6E 54
(Park Av.)
L23: C'by 1D 52
L35: R'hill 3H 93
WA7: Pal F 2H 153
Sedbergh Av. L10: Ain 2E 54
Sedbergh Gro. WA7: Beech 5G 153
Sedbergh Rd. CH44: Wall 2K 85
Sedburgh Gro. L36: Huy 4F 91
Sedburn Rd. L32: K'by 6E 56
Seddon Cl. WA10: Eccl 3F 73
Seddon Ct. L34: Prsct 1D 92
Seddon Pl. WN8: Skel 7E 26
Seddon Rd. L19: Gars 3K 129
WA10: St. H 5H 73
Seddon St. L1: Liv 7K 87 (8F 4)
WA10: St. H 6B 60
Sedgefield Cl. CH46: More 7E 84
Sedgefield Rd. CH46: More 7E 84
Sedgeley Wlk. L36: Huy 2K 91
Sedgemoor Rd. L11: N Grn. 3G 69

Sedgewick Cres.—Silverdale Dr.

Sedgewick Cres. WA5: B'wood 1C **96**
Sedley St. L6: Liv 1D **88**
Sedum Gro. L33: K'by 7B **44**
Seeds La. L9: Ain 5E **54**
Seeley Av. CH41: Birk 1A **106**
Seel Rd. L36: Huy 5K **91**
Seel St. L1: Liv 6K **87** (7F **4**)
SEFTON 5B **42**
Sefton Av. L21: Lith 6H **53**
WA8: Wid 5C **114**
WN5: Orr 6F **39**
Sefton Bus. Pk. L30: N'ton 5C **54**
Sefton Cl. L32: K'by 2K **55**
WN5: Orr 6F **39**
Sefton Dr. L8: Liv 3D **108**
L10: Ain 3F **55**
L23: Thorn 5G **41**
L31: Mag 4D **42**
L32: K'by 2A **56**
Sefton Fold Dr. WN5: Bil 7F **49**
Sefton Fold Gdns. WN5: Bil 7F **49**
Sefton Gdns. L39: Augh 4B **34**
Sefton Gro. L17: Aig 4E **108**
Sefton Ho. L9: Ain 6D **54**
Sefton La. L31: Mag 4C **42**
Sefton La. Ind. Est. L31: Mag 4C **42**
Sefton Mill La. L29: Seft 5B **42**
Sefton Mills L29: Seft 5B **42**
Sefton Moss La. L30: N'ton 2K **53**
Sefton Moss Vs. L21: Lith 5H **53**
SEFTON PARK 4G **109**
Sefton Pk. Ct. L17: Aig 5G **109**
Sefton Park Palm House 4F **109**
Sefton Pk. Rd. L8: Liv 2D **108**
Sefton Rd. CH42: R Ferr 7G **107**
CH45: New B 7B **66**
CH62: New F 1G **127**
L9: Ain 6F **55**
L9: Walt 1C **68**
L20: Boot 1K **67**
L21: Lith 5H **53**
L37: Form 1J **29**
WN3: Wigan 1D **50**
WN4: Ash M 6D **50**
WN5: Orr 6F **39**
Sefton St. L8: Liv 2K **107**
L21: Lith 5H **53**
(not continuous)
PR8: South 4H **11**
WA12: New W 3D **76**
SEFTON TOWN 1K **53**
Sefton Vw. L21: Lith 5H **53**
L23: C'by 1G **53**
WN5: Orr 6F **39**
Segars La. PR8: Ains 4D **14**
Seiont Ho. L8: Liv 3B **108**
Selborne L35: Whis 5F **93**
Selborne Cl. L8: Liv 1C **108** (10M **5**)
Selborne St. L8: Liv 1B **108** (10L **5**)
Selbourne Cl. CH49: W'chu 5G **105**
Selby Cl. WA7: Nort 5D **136**
WA10: St. H 4K **73**
Selby Dr. L37: Form 1B **30**
Selby Grn. CH66: Lit Sut 6D **160**
Selby Gro. L36: Huy 4B **92**
Selby Pl. WN8: Skel 7D **26**
Selby Rd. L9: Walt 7C **54**
Selby St. CH45: Wall 2B **86**
WA5: Warr 3J **117**
(not continuous)
Seldon St. L6: Liv 4C **88** (3P **5**)
Selina Rd. L4: Walt 4A **68**
Selkirk Av. CH62: East 6A **146**
WA4: Westy 5G **119**
WN4: Gars 1B **62**
Selkirk Cl. CH66: Lit Sut 6B **160**
Selkirk Dr. WA10: Eccl 1H **73**
Selkirk Gro. WN5: Wigan 3K **39**
Selkirk Rd. L13: Liv 5H **89**
Sellar St. L4: Kirk 7A **68**
Selsdon Rd. L22: Water 3C **52**
Selsey Cl. L7: Liv 7D **88** (9P **5**)
Selside WN3: Wigan 2F **51**
Selside Lawn L27: N'ley 4A **112**
Selside Rd. L27: N'ley 5A **112**
Selside Wlk. L27: N'ley 4K **111**
Selston Cl. CH63: Spit 7G **127**
Selworthy Dr. WA4: Thel 5K **119**
Selworthy Grn. L16: Child 2B **110**
Selworthy Rd. PR8: B'dale 5D **10**
Selwyn Cl. WA8: Wid 5F **115**
WA12: New W 1F **77**
Selwyn Jones Sports Cen. 1G **77**
Selwyn St. L4: Kirk 5A **68**
Senator Point L33: Know I 5G **57**
Senator Rd. WA9: St. H 7K **73**
Seneschal Ct. WA7: Pal F 4G **153**
Sennen Cl. WA7: Brook 5K **153**
Sennen Rd. L32: K'by 5D **56**
Sentinel Way L30: N'ton 5D **54**
Sephton Av. WA3: Cul 3A **80**
Sephton Dr. L39: Orm 3D **24**
(not continuous)
September Rd. L6: Liv 2E **88**
Serenade Rd. L33: K'by 6D **44**
Sergeant York Loop
WA5: Gt San 2F **117**
Sergrim Rd. L36: Huy 4G **91**
Serin Cl. WA12: New W 3G **77**
Serpentine, The L19: Gras 1J **129**
L23: Blun 1A **52**
L39: Augh 3B **34**
Serpentine Nth., The L23: Blun 7A **40**
Serpentine Rd. CH44: Wall 2C **86**
Serpentine Sth., The L23: Blun 1B **52**
Serpentine Wlk. WA12: New W 5H **63**
Servia Rd. L21: Lith 6H **53**
Servite Cl. CH65: Ell P 5H **161**
L22: Water 3C **52**
Servite Ct. L25: Wltn 7G **111**
Servite Ho. L17: Aig 4D **108**
Servite Pl. CH64: Nest 4J **157**
Sessions Rd. L4: Kirk 6K **67**
Seth Powell Way L36: Huy 1G **91**
Settrington Rd. L11: N Grn. 5H **69**
Seven Acre Rd. L23: Thorn 7H **41**
Seven Acres La. CH61: Thing 4E **124**
Sevenoaks Av. PR8: Ains 4B **14**
Sevenoaks Cl. L5: Liv 2A **88**
Seven Row CH64: Lit N 6J **157**
Seventh Av. L9: Ain 6F **55**
(Lakes Rd.)
L9: Ain 6F **55**
(Park Av.)
Severn Cl. WA2: Warr 5E **98**
WA8: Wid 6G **115**
WA9: Sut L 1E **94**
WN5: Bil 2F **61**
Severn Rd. L33: K'by 6D **44**
L35: R'hill 4H **93**
WA3: Cul 4B **80**
WN4: Ash M 7J **51**
Severn St. CH41: Birk 6A **86**
L5: Liv 1B **88**
Severnvale CH65: Whit 1K **169**
Severs St. L6: Liv 3C **88** (1N **5**)
Sewell St. L34: Prsct 1D **92**
WA7: Run 7D **134**
Sextant Cl. WA7: Murd 5B **154**
Sexton Av. WA9: St. H 4K **75**
Sexton Way L14: B Grn 5C **90**
Seymoor Ct. L14: B Grn 6B **90**
Seymour Ct. CH42: Tran 4E **106**
WA7: Mnr P 5A **136**
Seymour Dr. CH66: Ell P 5G **161**
L31: Lyd 1G **43**
WA1: P'ton, P'gate 1G **119**
Seymour Pl. E. CH45: New B 6B **66**
Seymour Pl. W. CH45: New B 6B **66**
Seymour Rd. L14: B Grn 5B **90**
L21: Lith 6H **53**
Seymour St. CH42: Tran 4D **106**
CH45: New B 6B **66**
L3: Liv 5A **88** (5J **5**)
L20: Boot 4H **67**
WA9: St. H 7F **75**
Seymour Ter. L3: Liv 5J **5**
Shacklady Rd. L33: K'by 1E **56**
Shackleton Cl. WA5: Old H 7G **97**
Shackleton Rd. CH46: Leas 3F **85**
Shadewood Cres. WA4: Grap 6H **119**
Shadwell St. L5: Liv 1H **87**
Shaftesbury Av. PR8: B'dale 1G **15**
WA5: Penk 6C **116**
Shaftesbury Gro. PR8: B'dale 7G **11**
Shaftesbury Rd. L23: C'by 1D **52**
PR8: B'dale 1G **15**
Shaftesbury St. L8: Liv 2A **108**
Shaftesbury Ter. L13: Liv 4J **89**
Shaftesbury Way WA5: B'wood 7D **76**
Shaftsbury Av. L33: K'by 7C **44**
Shaftsbury Rd. WN5: Orr 3J **39**
Shaftway Cl. WA11: Hay 6D **62**
Shakespeare Av. CH42: R Ferr 7F **107**
L32: K'by 5B **56**
Shakespeare Cen., The
PR8: South 3H **11**
Shakespeare Cl. L6: Liv 3C **88** (1N **5**)
Shakespeare Gro. WA2: Warr 5C **98**
(not continuous)
Shakespeare Rd. CH44: Wall 5D **86**
CH64: Nest 2J **157**
WA8: Wid 7C **114**
WA9: Sut M 5C **94**
Shakespeare St. L19: Gars 4A **130**
(not continuous)
L20: Boot 1G **67**
PR8: South 3H **11**
Shalcombe Cl. L26: Halew 2A **132**
Shaldon Cl. L32: K'by 5E **56**
Shaldon Gro. L32: K'by 5E **56**
Shaldon Rd. L32: K'by 6E **56**
Shaldon Wlk. L32: K'by 5E **56**
Shalem Ct. CH63: High B 3D **126**
Shalford Gro. CH48: W Kir 6F **103**
Shallcross Ct. L6: Liv 3C **88**
Shallcross Pl. L6: Liv 3C **88**
Shallmarsh Cl. CH63: High B 4D **126**
Shallmarsh Ct. CH63: High B 4D **126**
Shallmarsh Rd. CH63: High B 4D **126**
Shalom Ct. L17: Aig 3G **109**
Shamrock Rd. CH41: Birk 1K **105**
Shand St. L19: Gars 5A **130**
Shanklin Cl. WA5: Gt San 2A **116**
Shanklin Rd. L15: W'tree 6H **89**
Shannon Gro. WA8: Wid 6A **114**
Shannon Ho. CH46: Leas 3C **84**
Shannons La. L34: Know 5G **71**
Shannon St. CH41: Birk 6K **85**
Shapgate WN5: Wigan 4K **39**
Shard Cl. L11: Crox 1K **69**
Shard St. WA9: St. H 7G **75**
Sharon Pk. Cl. WA4: Grap 7J **119**
Sharon Sq. WN2: Bam 4K **51**
Sharpeville Cl. L4: Kirk 7K **67**
Sharples Cres. L23: C'by 2F **53**
Sharp St. WA2: Warr 1B **118**
WA8: Wid 1C **134**
Sharrock St. PR8: South 1H **11**
Sharwood Rd. L27: N'ley 4K **111**
Shavington Av. CH43: O'ton 5K **105**
Shawbury Av. CH63: High B 2D **126**
Shawbury Gro. WA1: P'gate 7G **99**
Shaw Cl. CH66: Gt Sut 7H **161**
L39: Hals 3B **16**
Shaw Cres. L37: Form 6B **20**
Shawell Ct. WA8: Wid 6G **115**
Shaw Entry L35: Whis 7F **93**
Shaw Gdns. WA9: St. H 1A **94**
Shaw Hall Cvn. Pk. L40: Scar 5K **17**
Shaw Hill St. L1: Liv 5K **87** (5F **4**)
Shaw La. CH49: Grea 6A **104**
L35: Prsct, Whis 3D **92**
L39: Bart 4K **21**
Shaw Rd. L24: Speke 4G **131**
Shaws All. L1: Liv 7J **87** (9F **4**)
Shaw's Av. PR8: B'dale 7G **11**
WA2: Warr 7B **98**
Shaws Dr. CH47: Meols 7F **83**
Shaws Gth. L39: Hals 3B **16**
Shaw's Rd. PR8: B'dale 7G **11**
Shaw St. CH41: Birk 3C **106**
CH47: Hoy 1D **102**
L6: Liv 3B **88** (1K **5**)
WA3: Cul 3C **80**
WA7: Run 7B **134**
(not continuous)
WA10: St. H 3D **74**
WA11: Hay 7C **62**
WN4: Ash M 7F **51**
Shawton Rd. L16: Child 7A **90**
Shearman Cl. CH61: Pens 5E **124**
Shearman Rd. CH61: Pens 5E **124**
Shearwater Cl. L27: N'ley 4K **111**
Sheehan Hgts. L5: Liv 1J **87**
Sheen Rd. CH45: New B 1C **86**
Sheepfield Cl. CH66: Lit Sut 4E **160**
Sheerwater Cl. WA1: P'gate 7F **99**
Sheffield Cl. WA5: Gt San 3G **117**
Sheffield Row WA12: New W 6H **77**
Shefford Cres. WN3: Wins 2A **50**
Sheila Wlk. L10: Faz 7K **55**
Sheil Pl. L6: Liv 4E **88**
Sheil Rd. L6: Liv 3E **88**
Shelagh Av. WA8: Wid 7C **114**
Sheldon Cl. CH63: Spit 1G **145**
Sheldon Rd. L12: W Der 6B **70**
Sheldrake Gro. CH64: Lit N 6J **157**
Shelley Cl. L36: Huy 6K **91**
Shelley Ct. L32: K'by 5B **56**
Shelley Dr. L39: Orm 4B **24**
WN5: Orr 5J **39**
Shelley Gro. L19: Gars 4A **130**
PR8: South 1B **12**
WA4: Westy 4F **119**
Shelley Pl. L35: Whis 4F **93**
Shelley Rd. WA8: Wid 7C **114**
Shelley St. L20: Boot 2H **67**
(not continuous)
WA9: Sut M 5D **94**
Shelley Way CH48: W Kir 1D **122**
Shellfield Rd. PR9: Chu 4C **8**
SHELL GREEN 7F **115**
Shell Green Est. WA8: Wid 1G **135**
Shell Grn. Ho. WA8: Wid 1G **135**
Shellingford Rd. L14: K Ash 3E **90**
Shellway Rd. CH65: Ell P 1D **170**
Shelmore Dr. L8: Liv 4A **108**
Shelton Cl. L13: Liv 5H **89**
WA8: Wid 5G **115**
Shelton Dr. PR8: Ains 5A **14**
Shelton Rd. CH45: Wall 1A **86**
Shenley Cl. CH63: Beb 3F **127**
Shenley Rd. L15: W'tree 7A **90**
Shenley Way PR9: Cros 2F **9**
Shenstone St. L7: Liv 6D **88** (7P **5**)
Shenton Av. WA11: St. H 7F **61**
Shepcroft La. WA4: S'ton 7C **138**
Shepherd Cl. CH49: Grea 4A **104**
Shepherds Fold Cl. L8: Liv 2C **108**
Shepherd's La. L39: Hals 5F **23**
Shepherds Row WA7: Cas 7H **135**
Shepherd St. L6: Liv 5B **88** (4L **5**)
Sheppard Av. L16: Child 7E **90**
Shepperton Cl. WA4: App 3E **138**
Shepsides Cl. CH66: Gt Sut 1E **168**
Shepston Av. L4: Walt 5C **68**
Shepton Av. WN2: Platt B 3K **51**
Shepton Rd. CH66: Gt Sut 2G **169**
L36: Huy 1H **91**
Sheraton Cl. WN5: Orr 2K **39**
Sherborne Av. L25: Hunts X 1H **131**
L30: N'ton 1A **54**
Sherborne Cl. WA7: Nort 6D **136**
Sherborne Rd. CH44: Wall 2K **85**
WN5: Orr 3J **39**
Sherborne Sq. L36: Huy 5J **91**
Sherbourne Rd. CH65: Ell P 1B **170**
Sherbourne Way
WA5: B'wood 1D **96**
Sherbrooke Cl. L14: K Ash 3C **90**
Sherburn Cl. L9: Ain 5F **55**
Sherdley Bus. Pk. WA9: St. H 5D **74**
Sherdley Ct. L35: R'hill 3J **93**
Sherdley Pk. 7D **74**
Sherdley Pk. Dr. WA9: St. H 1E **94**
Sherdley Rd. WA9: St. H 1B **94**
(not continuous)
Sherdley Rd. Cvn. Pk.
WA9: St. H 6C **74**
Sherford Cl. L27: N'ley 4K **111**
Sheridan Pl. WA2: Win 2A **98**
Sheridan Way WA7: Nort 7B **136**
Sheri Dr. WA12: New W 4H **77**
Sheriff Cl. L5: Liv 3A **88** (1J **5**)
Sheringham Cl. CH49: Upton 1E **104**
WA9: St. H 3F **75**
Sheringham Rd. WA5: Gt San 2C **116**
Sherlock Av. WA11: Hay 6C **62**
Sherlock La. CH44: Wall 5A **86**
Sherman Dr. L35: R'hill 6K **93**
Sherrat St. WN8: Skel 2D **36**
Sherringham Rd. PR8: B'dale 6E **10**
Sherry Ct. L17: Aig 3F **109**
Sherry La. CH49: W'chu 6E **104**
Sherwell Cl. L15: W'tree 6J **89**
Sherwood Av. CH61: Irby 3B **124**
L23: C'by 7D **40**
L39: Augh 1A **34**
WN4: Ash M 1G **63**
Sherwood Cl. L35: R'hill 2H **93**
WA8: Wid 7J **113**
Sherwood Ct. L12: Crox 3D **70**
L36: Huy 5K **91**
Sherwood Cres. WA5: B'wood 1C **96**
Sherwood Dr. CH63: High B 2E **126**
L35: Whis 5F **93**
WN8: Skel 7K **27**
Sherwood Gro. CH47: Meols 7H **83**
WA6: Hel 1G **173**
Sherwood Ho. PR8: Ains 4C **14**
Sherwood Lodge PR8: B'dale 3F **11**
Sherwood Rd. CH44: Wall 4C **86**
CH47: Meols 1H **103**
L23: C'by 7C **40**
Sherwood Row L26: Halew 3J **131**
Sherwood's La. L10: Faz 5H **55**
Sherwood St. L3: Liv 2H **87**
Sherwyn Rd. L4: Walt 6E **68**
Shetland Cl. WA2: Fearn 3E **98**
WA8: Wid 5G **115**
Shetland Dr. CH62: Brom 2A **146**
CH65: Ell P 3A **170**
Shevington Cl. WA8: Wid 5G **115**
WA9: St. H 7E **74**
Shevington's La. L33: K'by 7B **44**
Shevington Wlk. WA8: Wid 5G **115**
Shewell Cl. CH42: Tran 4D **106**
Shiel Rd. CH45: New B 7B **66**
Shiggins Cl. WA5: Gt San 2H **117**
Shillingford Cl. WA4: App 4E **138**
Shimmin St. L7: Liv 6C **88** (7N **5**)
Shipley Wlk. L24: Speke 5H **131**
Ship St. WA6: Frod 2D **166**
Shipton Cl. CH43: Pren 7J **105**
L19: Aller 7K **109**
WA5: W'brk 7F **97**
WA8: Wid 5K **113**
Shirdley Av. L32: K'by 6D **56**
Shirdley Cres. PR8: Ains 6C **14**
SHIRDLEY HILL 3C **16**
Shirdley Wlk. L32: K'by 6D **56**
Shirebourne Av. WA11: St. H 6D **60**
Shireburn Rd. L37: Form 5G **19**
Shiregreen WA9: St. H 1E **94**
Shires, The WA10: St. H 4A **74**
Shirewell Rd. WN5: Orr 6G **39**
Shirley Dr. WA4: Grap 6G **119**
Shirley Rd. L19: Aller 1A **130**
Shirley St. CH44: Wall 4E **86**
Shirwell Gro. WA9: Sut L 3E **94**
Shobdon Cl. L12: Crox 2D **70**
Shones Cft. CH64: Ness 6A **158**
Shop La. L31: Mag 3E **42**
Shop Rd. L34: Know 2G **71**
Shore Bank CH62: New F 1J **127**
Shore Dr. CH62: Port S 3J **127**
Shorefields CH62: New F 1H **127**
Shorefields Ho. CH62: New F 2J **127**
Shorefields Village L8: Liv 5B **108**
Shoreham Dr. WA5: Penk 5E **116**
Shore La. CH48: Caldy 2E **122**
Shore Rd. CH41: Birk 1E **106**
CH48: Caldy 2E **122**
L20: Boot 1F **67**
PR8: Ains 3A **14**
Shore Road Pumping Station 1F **107**
Shorewell Cl. WA5: Gt San 1A **116**
Short Cl. WA12: New W 3C **76**
Short Cft. La. L37: Gt Alt 2D **30**
Shortfield Rd. CH49: Upton 4E **104**
Shortfield Way CH49: Upton 4E **104**
Short St. WA8: Wid 4C **134**
WA11: Hay 7C **62**
WA12: New W 3C **76**
WN5: Wigan 5K **39**
Shortwood Rd. L14: K Ash 4D **90**
Shorwell Cl. WA5: Gt San 1A **116**
Shottesbrook Grn. L11: N Grn. 3H **69**
Shotwick-Helsby By-Pass
CH1: Back 4K **169**
CH2: Elt, Lit Stan, Thor M 3E **170**
CH65: Whit 4K **169**
Shotwick La. CH1: W'bnk 6A **168**
Showcase Cinema
Croxteth 2J **69**
Shrewsbury Av. L10: Ain 2E **54**
L22: Water 2D **52**
Shrewsbury Cl. CH43: C'ton 2K **105**
Shrewsbury Dr. CH49: Upton 2E **104**
Shrewsbury Pl. L19: Gars 3A **130**
Shrewsbury Rd. CH43: C'ton 1K **105**
CH44: Wall 2K **85**
CH48: W Kir 7C **102**
CH60: Hes 1E **142**
CH65: Ell P 6A **162**
L19: Gars 3A **130**
Shrewsbury St. WA4: Warr 5D **118**
Shrewton Rd. L25: Gate 1E **110**
Shropshire Cl. L30: N'ton 1C **54**
WA1: W'ston 2A **120**
Shropshire Gdns. WA10: St. H 4B **74**
Sibford Rd. L12: W Der 2B **90**
Sibley Av. WN4: Ash M 1H **63**
Siddall St. WA10: St. H 6B **60**
Siddeley Dr. WA12: New W 3D **76**
Siddeley St. L17: Aig 5E **108**
Side Kerfoot St. WA2: Warr 1A **118**
Sidgreave St. WA10: St. H 3A **74**
Siding La. L33: Sim 6G **45**
WA11: R'ford 3C **46**
Sidings, The CH42: R Ferr 6F **107**
L7: Liv 8N **5**
Sidings Ct. WA1: Warr 2C **118**
Sidlaw Av. WA9: St. H 3H **75**
Sidlaw Cl. CH66: Lit Sut 5C **160**
Sidmouth Cl. WA5: Penk 4C **116**
WA10: Windle 7J **59**
Sidmouth Gro.
WN3: Wigan 1C **50**
Sidney Av. CH45: New B 6A **66**
Sidney Cl. CH64: Nest 2K **157**
Sidney Ct. CH42: Tran 4E **106**
Sidney Pl. L7: Liv 6C **88** (7N **5**)
Sidney Powell Av. L32: K'by 3A **56**
Sidney Rd. CH42: Tran 4E **106**
CH64: Nest 2K **157**
L20: Boot 4K **67**
PR9: South 7B **8**
Sidney St. CH41: Birk 1E **106**
WA10: St. H 2K **73**
Sidney Ter. CH42: Tran 5E **106**
Sidwell St. L19: Gars 4A **130**
Sienna Cl. L27: N'ley 2G **111**
Signal Works Rd. L9: Ain 5G **55**
Silcock's Funland 7G **7**
Silcroft Rd. L32: K'by 5C **56**
Silkhouse Ct. L3: Liv 5D **4**
Silkhouse La. L2: Liv 5J **87** (5D **4**)
Silkstone Cl. L7: Liv 7D **88** (8P **5**)
WA10: St. H 3K **73**
Silkstone Cres. WA7: Pal F 3K **153**
Silkstone St. WA10: St. H 3K **73**
(not continuous)
Silver Av. WA11: Hay 1J **75**
Silverbeech Av. L18: Moss H 4K **109**
Silverbeech Rd. CH44: Wall 4C **86**
Silver Birches CH66: Whit 4H **169**
Silverbirch Gdns. CH44: Wall 2J **85**
Silver Birch Gro. WN4: Ash M 7E **50**
Silver Birch Way L31: Lyd 6D **32**
Silverbirch Way CH66: Whit 4H **169**
Silverbrook Rd. L27: N'ley 1G **111**
Silverburn Av. CH46: More 6C **84**
Silverdale PR8: B'dale 4E **10**
Silverdale Av. L13: Liv 2G **89**
Silverdale Cl. L36: Huy 7J **91**
WA6: Frod 4E **166**
Silverdale Ct. PR8: South 4A **12**
Silverdale Dr. L21: Lith 5K **53**

Spital Station (Rail)—Stoneleigh Gdns.

Spital Station (Rail) 6H 127
Spitfire Rd. L24: Speke 3D 130
Spofforth Rd. L7: Liv 7F 89
Spooner Av. L21: Lith 5J 53
Sprainger St. L3: Liv 3H 87 (1C 4)
Sprakeling Pl. L20: Boot 6A 54
Spray St. WA10: St. H 2A 74
Spreyton Cl. L12: W Der 4A 70
Sprig Cl. L9: Ain 5F 55
Spring Av. CH66: Lit Sut 5E 160
Springbank Cl. WA7: Run 4D 152
Springbank Gdns.
WA13: Lymm 3K 121
Spring Bank Rd. L4: Walt 2D 88
Springbourne WA6: Frod 5F 167
Springbourne Rd. L17: Aig 6D 108
Springbrook Cl. WA10: Eccl 2G 73
Springburn Gdns. WA1: W'ston 1B 120
Spring Cl. L33: K'by 7D 44
PR8: B'dale 3G 11
Spring Ct. WA7: Run 7D 134
Springcroft CH64: Park 2G 157
Springdale Cl. L12: W Der 1A 90
Springdale Rd. CH46: More 6E 84
Springfield L3: Liv 4A 88 (3H 5)
(not continuous)
WA11: R'ford 2E 46
Springfield Av. CH48: W Kir 6H 103
L21: Lith 5J 53
WA1: P'gate 7F 99
WA3: Golb 5K 63
WA4: Grap 5H 119
WA6: Hel 1H 173
WA13: Lymm 3K 121
Springfield Cl. CH49: W'chu 6G 105
L37: Form 1G 29
WA10: St. H 6J 73
Springfield La. WA10: Eccl 1G 73
Springfield Pk. WA11: Hay 6A 62
Springfield Rd. L39: Augh 6H 33
WA8: Wid 1G 133
WA10: St. H 6J 73
Springfields WA6: Hel 1H 173
Springfield Sq. L4: Walt 6B 68
Springfield St. WA1: Warr 3A 118
Springfield Way L12: W Der 6C 70
Spring Gdns. CH66: Lit Sut 5E 160
L31: Mag 4G 43
Spring Gro. L12: W Der 1A 90
Springhill Av. CH62: Brom 4K 145
Springholm Dr. WA4: App 6D 138
Spring La. WA3: Croft 1H 99
Springmeadow Rd. L25: Gate 3E 110
Springpool WA9: St. H 7F 75
WN3: Wins 2K 49
Spring Rd. WN5: Orr 3H 39
Springs Cl. L20: Boot 2K 67
Springside Cl. L36: Huy 1G 91
Spring St. CH42: Tran 5F 107
WA8: Wid 3C 134
SPRINGVALE 4G 47
Spring Va. CH45: Wall 7J 65
Springvale Cl. L32: K'by 4B 56
SPRING VIEW 1K 51
Springville Rd. L9: Ain 6E 54
Springwell Rd. L20: Boot 6K 53
Springwood Av. L19: Aller 1B 130
L25: Wltn 1B 130
Springwood Ct. *L19: Aller* *1B 130*
(off Ramsey Rd.)
Springwood Crematorium
L25: Wltn 1D 130
Springwood Gro. L32: K'by 6D 56
Springwood Way CH62: New F 1G 127
Spruce Cl. CH42: Tran 4D 106
WA1: W'ston 1A 120
Spruce Gro. L28: Stock V 7F 71
Spruce Way L37: Form 7G 19
Sprucewood Cl. L6: Liv 2D 88
Spunhill Av. CH66: Gt Sut 2E 168
Spur, The L23: C'by 2D 52
Spur Cl. L11: Crox 3A 70
Spurgeon Cl. L5: Liv 2B 88
Spurling Rd. WA5: B'wood 1D 96
Spurriers La. L31: Mell 4A 44
Spurstow Cl. CH43: O'ton 5K 105
Spymers Cft. L37: Form 4A 20
Square, The CH2: Ince 6A 164
WA13: Lymm 5G 121
Square Ho. La. PR9: Banks 1K 9
Squibb Dr. CH46: Leas 5E 84
Squires Av. WA8: Wid 7B 114
Squires Cl. WA11: Hay 7K 61
Squires St. L7: Liv 7C 88 (7N 5)
Squirrel Grn. L37: Form 5G 19
Stable Cl. CH49: Grea 4B 104
Stables, The L23: C'by 7G 41
Stables Bus. Cen. *L13: Liv* *7G 69*
(off Larkhill La.)
Stables Ct. WA9: St. H 4E 74
Stackfield, The CH48: W Kir 5H 103
Stadium Rd. CH62: Brom 6A 128
Stadt Moers Pk. 5C 92
Stadt Moers Vis. Cen. 5C 92
Staffin Av. CH65: Ell P 4K 169
Stafford Cl. L36: Huy 3A 92
Stafford Gdns. CH65: Ell P 6K 161
Stafford Moreton Way
L31: Mag 3E 42
(not continuous)
Stafford Rd. PR8: B'dale 7G 11
WA4: Warr 6C 118
WA10: St. H 5K 73
Staffordshire Cl. L5: Liv 1A 88
Stafford St. L3: Liv 5A 88 (4J 5)
WN8: Skel 1D 36
Stage La. WA13: Lymm 4K 121
Stag Rd. L24: Speke 3C 130
Stainburn Av. L11: N Grn. 3G 69
Stainer Cl. L14: K Ash 2D 90
WA12: New W 1F 77
Staines Cl. WA4: App 4E 138
Stainforth Cl. WA3: Cul 2K 79
Stainmore Cl. WA3: Bchwd 1D 100
Stainton Cl. L26: Halew 1J 131
WA11: St. H 5D 60
Stairhaven Rd. L19: Aller 7K 109
Stakes, The CH46: Leas 4C 84
Stalbridge Av. L18: Moss H 3H 109
Staley Av. L23: C'by 2F 53
Staley St. L20: Boot 7J 53
Stalisfield Av. L11: N Grn. 4J 69
Stalisfield Gro. L11: N Grn. 4J 69
Stalisfield Pl. L11: N Grn. 4J 69
Stalmine Rd. L9: Walt 2C 68
Stamford Ct. L20: Boot 3K 67
WA13: Lymm 5G 121
Stamfordham Dr. L19: Aller 1A 130
Stamfordham Gro. L19: Aller 2B 130
Stamfordham Pl. L19: Aller 2A 130
Stamford Rd. PR8: B'dale 5H 11
WN8: Skel 1D 36
Stamford St. CH65: Ell P 6J 161
L7: Liv 5E 88
Stanbury Av. CH63: Beb 3G 127
Standale Rd. L15: W'tree 7H 89
Standard Pl. CH42: R Ferr 5F 107
Standard Rd. L11: Crox 2A 70
Standedge Way L14: K Ash 1D 90
Standen Cl. WA10: St. H 2A 74
Stand Farm Rd. L12: Crox 3C 70
Standhouse La. L39: Augh 1A 34
Standish Av. WN5: Bil 7G 49
Standish Ct. WA8: Wid 1K 133
Standish Dr. WA11: R'ford 5G 47
Standish St. L3: Liv 4K 87 (3F 4)
WA10: St. H 2C 74
Stand Pk. Av. L30: N'ton 3B 54
Stand Pk. Cl. L30: N'ton 3B 54
Stand Pk. Rd. L16: Child 2B 110
Stand Pk. Way L30: N'ton 2A 54
Standring Gdns. WA10: St. H 6H 73
Standside Pk. WN8: Skel 3D 36
Stanedge Gro. WN3: Wigan 2F 51
Stanfield Av. L5: Liv 2B 88
Stanfield Dr. CH63: Beb 6F 127
Stanford Av. CH45: New B 7B 66
Stanford Cres. L25: Hunts X 7H 111
Stangate L31: Mag 2D 42
Stanhope Dr. CH62: Brom 1K 145
L36: Huy 4G 91
Stanhope St. L8: Liv 2K 107
(not continuous)
WA10: St. H 1B 74
Stanier Way L7: Liv 6E 88
Staniforth Pl. L16: Child 6B 90
Stanlaw Abbey Bus. Cen.
CH65: Ell P 2B 170
Stanlawe Rd. L37: Form 4J 19
Stanlaw Rd. CH65: Ell P 7A 162
STANLEY
Liverpool 5G 89
Skelmersdale 7E 26
Stanley Av. CH45: Wall 1H 85
CH63: High B 1B 126
PR8: B'dale 5F 11
WA4: S Hth 6F 119
WA5: Gt San 1B 116
WA11: R'ford 5E 46
Stanley Bank Rd. WA11: Hay 6J 61
Stanley Bungalows
L34: Know 3G 71
Stanley Cl. CH44: Wall 5E 86
L4: Kirk 7K 67
WA8: Wid 6E 114
Stanley Ct. CH42: Tran 5F 107
Stanley Cres. L34: Prsct 1C 92
Stanley Gdns. L9: Walt 1B 68
STANLEY GATE 4J 35
Stanley Ho. L20: Boot 2H 67
Stanley Ind. Est. WN8: Skel 7E 26
Stanley La. CH62: East 6B 146
STANLEY PARK 4J 53
Stanley Pk. L21: Lith 4G 53
Stanley Pk. Av. Nth. L4: Walt 5D 68
(not continuous)
Stanley Pk. Av. Sth. L4: Walt 6D 68
Stanley Pl. WA4: S Hth 6F 119
Stanley Pct. L20: Boot 3J 67
Stanley Rd. CH41: Birk 6K 85
CH47: Hoy 3A 102
CH62: New F 1G 127
CH65: Ell P 4A 162
L5: Kirk 4J 67
L20: Boot, Kirk 7J 53
L22: Water 5E 52
L31: Mag 6E 42
L36: Huy 4J 91
L37: Form 4J 19
WN8: Uph 4D 38
Stanley St. CH44: Wall 5E 86
L1: Liv 5J 87 (5E 4)
L7: Liv 4F 89
L19: Gars 5A 130
L39: Orm 5D 24
PR9: South 1H 11
WA1: Warr 4B 118
WA7: Run 6D 134
WA12: New W 3E 76
Stanley Ter. CH45: New B 7B 66
L8: Liv 10L 5
L18: Moss H 5J 109
Stanley Theatre *L7: Liv* *6B 88*
(off Mt. Pleasant)
Stanley Vs. WA7: Run 1B 152
Stanley Way WN8: Skel 7E 26
STANLOW 7G 163
Stanlow & Thornton Station (Rail)
. . . . 6J 163
Stanlowe Vw. L19: Gras 3H 129
Stanmore Pk. CH49: Grea 5K 103
Stanmore Rd. L15: W'tree 2K 109
WA7: Run 7F 135
Stannanought Rd. WN8: Skel 7J 27
(not continuous)
Stanner Cl. WA5: Call 5H 97
Stanney Cl. CH62: East 7A 146
CH64: Nest 4J 157
Stanney La. CH65: Ell P 7K 161
(not continuous)
Stanney Mill Ind. Est.
CH2: Lit Stan 1D 170
Stanney Mill La. CH2: Lit Stan 3D 170
Stanney Mill Rd. CH2: Lit Stan 1D 170
Stanney Oaks Leisure Cen. 2B 170
Stanney Ten Ind. Est.
CH2: Lit Stan 2D 170
Stanney Woods Av. CH65: Ell P 3A 170
Stannyfield Cl. L23: Thorn 6H 41
Stannyfield Dr. L23: Thorn 6H 41
Stansfield Av. L31: Mag 3H 43
WA1: Warr 2F 119
Stansfield Dr. WA4: Grap 2G 139
Stanstead Av. WA5: Penk 5D 116
Stanton Av. L21: Lith 4G 53
Stanton Cl. CH64: Nest 3J 157
L30: N'ton 7K 41
WA11: Hay 7A 62
WN3: Wigan 1F 51
Stanton Ct. *CH64: Nest* *3J 157*
(off Hinderton Rd.)
Stanton Cres. L32: K'by 3A 56
Stanton Rd. CH63: Beb 6E 126
L18: Moss H 3H 109
WA4: Thel 5K 119
Stanwood Cl. WA10: Eccl 3F 73
Stanwood Gdns. L35: Whis 4E 92
Stapehill Cl. L13: Liv 5K 89
Stapeley Gdns. L26: Halew 3A 132
Staplands Rd. L14: B Grn 5B 90
Stapleford Ct. CH66: Ell P 3H 161
Stapleford Rd. L25: Gate 2G 111
Staplehurst Cl. L12: Crox 3C 70
Stapleton Av. CH49: Grea 4B 104
L24: Speke 6H 131
L35: R'hill 3J 93
WA2: Warr 7D 98
Stapleton Cl. L25: Gate 1F 111
L35: R'hill 3J 93
Stapleton Ct. WA6: Frod 3E 166
Stapleton Rd. L35: R'hill 2H 93
L37: Form 3H 29
Stapleton Way WA8: Hale B 4H 133
Stapley Cl. WA7: Run 1B 152
Starbeck Dr. CH66: Lit Sut 5D 160
Star Inn Cotts. WA11: R'ford 7G 47
Starkey Gro. WA4: Westy 4F 119
Star La. WA13: Lymm 4E 120
Starling Cl. WA7: Murd 3B 154
Starling Gro. L12: W Der 5D 70
Star St. L8: Liv 2A 108
Startham Av. WN5: Bil 2F 61
Starworth Dr. CH62: New F 2J 127
STATHAM 4F 121
Statham Av. WA2: Warr 5C 98
WA13: Lymm 5E 120
Statham Cl. WA13: Lymm 5F 121
Statham Dr. WA13: Lymm 5F 121
Statham La. WA3: Rix 1C 120
WA13: Lymm 3D 120
Statham Rd. CH43: Bid 7G 85
WN8: Skel 6D 26
Statham Way L39: Orm 6C 24
Station App. CH46: More 5C 84
CH47: Meols 7G 83
L39: Orm 5D 24
Station Av. CH66: Lit Sut 4E 160
WA6: Hel 7H 165
WN5: Orr 6F 39
Station Cl. CH64: Nest 4K 157
L25: Hunts X 2G 131
Station Grn. CH66: Lit Sut 4E 160
Station M. L32: K'by 2A 56
WN4: Gars 2B 62
Station Pas. L9: Walt 2B 68
Station Rd. CH2: Elt 7B 164
CH2: Ince 6A 164
CH41: Birk 6K 85
CH44: Wall 3A 86
CH47: Hoy 2D 102
CH60: Hes 4D 142
CH61: Barn 4H 125
CH61: Thurs 6H 123
CH63: Store 4K 125
CH64: Nest 4J 157
(not continuous)
CH64: Park 3G 157
CH65: Ell P 5A 162
(not continuous)
CH66: Lit Sut 5E 160
L25: Gate 3E 110
L31: Lyd 5C 32
L31: Mag 4G 43
L31: Mell 2J 55
L34: Prsct 1D 92
(not continuous)
L35: R'hill 4J 93
L36: Roby 5G 91
L39: Bart 3K 21
L39: Orm 4D 24
PR8: Ains 4C 14
PR9: Banks 2G 9
WA4: Latch 6E 118
WA5: Gt San 3D 116
WA5: Penk 5B 116
WA7: Run 7B 134
WA7: Sut W 6K 153
WA8: Wid 4E 114
WA9: St. H 7G 75
WA11: Hay 7A 62
WN4: Gars 2A 62
WN8: Parb 1J 27
Station Rd. Ind. Est.
WA4: Latch 6F 119
Station Rd. Nth. WA2: Fearn 5G 99
Station Rd. Sth. WA2: P'gate 6G 99
Station St. L35: R'hill 4J 93
Statton Rd. L13: Liv 6K 89
Staveley Rd. L19: Gras 1K 129
PR8: Ains 5D 14
WN8: Skel 7E 26
Stavert Cl. L11: N Grn. 3K 69
Staverton Pk. L32: K'by 4A 56
Stavordale Rd. CH46: More 6E 84
Steble St. L8: Liv 3B 108
Steel Av. CH45: Wall 1C 86
Steel Ct. L5: Liv 1J 87
Steel St. WA1: Warr 1D 118
Steeple, The CH48: Caldy 3F 123
Steeplechase Cl. L9: Ain 5E 54
Steeple Ct. CH64: Nest 4J 157
Steeple Vw. L33: K'by 7C 44
Steers Cft. L28: Stock V 6D 70
Steinberg Ct. L3: Liv 3J 87 (1D 4)
Steley Way L34: Prsct 2D 92
Stella Pct. L21: Sea 7G 53
Stenhills Cres. WA7: Run 7E 134
Stephens Gdns. CH66: Lit Sut 5D 160
Stephen's Gro. WA6: Hel 2H 173
Stephens La. L2: Liv 5J 87 (5E 4)
Stephenson Ct. *L7: Liv* *6E 88*
(off Crosfield Rd.)
Stephenson Ho. L7: Liv 7C 88 (8N 5)
Stephenson Rd. L13: Liv 5J 89
WA12: New W 4G 77
Stephenson Way L13: W'tree 6G 89
L37: Form 7B 20
Stephens Ter. CH66: Lit Sut 5D 160
Stephen St. WA1: Warr 2D 118
Stephen Way L35: R'hill 2H 93
Stepney Gro. L4: Walt 5C 68
Sterling Way L5: Kirk 1K 87
Sterndale Cl. L7: Liv 7D 88
Sterrix Av. L30: N'ton 3J 53
Sterrix Grn. L21: Lith 3J 53
Sterrix La. L21: Lith 3J 53
L30: N'ton 3K 53
Stetchworth Rd. WA4: Walt 7B 118
Steve Biko Cl. L8: Liv 1D 108
Stevenage Cl. WA9: St. H 7B 74
Stevenson Cres. WA10: St. H 2K 73
Stevenson Dr. CH63: Spit 6F 127
Stevenson St. L15: W'tree 7G 89
Stevens Rd. CH60: Hes 3G 143
Stevens St. WA9: St. H 6K 73
Steventon WA7: Nort 6B 136
Steward Ct. L35: Prsct 2F 93
Stewards Av. WA8: Wid 1B 134
Stewart Av. L20: Boot 2A 68
Stewart Cl. CH61: Pens 6D 124
Stewart Rd. WN3: Wigan 1E 50
Stewerton Cl. WA3: Golb 3K 63
Stile Hey L23: Thorn 7H 41
Stiles, The L39: Orm 5C 24
Stiles Rd. L33: K'by 6D 44
Stillington Rd. L8: Liv 4C 108
Stiperstones Cl. CH66: Lit Sut 5B 160
Stirling Av. L23: C'by 2E 52
Stirling Cl. WA1: W'ston 1A 120
Stirling Ct. CH65: Ell P 1B 170
PR9: Chu 5C 8
Stirling Cres. WA9: St. H 1E 94
Stirling Dr. WN4: Gars 1B 62
Stirling La. L25: Hunts X 2H 131
Stirling Rd. L24: Speke 6F 131
Stirling St. CH44: Wall 5B 86
Stirrup Cl. WA2: Fearn 4G 99
STOAK 5E 170
Stoak Lodge CH65: Ell P 7A 162
Stockbridge La. L36: Huy 2F 91
(not continuous)
Stockbridge Pl. L5: Liv 1C 88
Stockbridge St. L5: Liv 2C 88
STOCKBRIDGE VILLAGE 6E 70
Stockdale Cl. L3: Liv 4J 87 (3E 4)
Stockdale Dr. WA5: Gt San 7C 96
Stockham Cl. WA7: Halt 2J 153
Stockham La.
WA7: Brook, Halt, Pal F 2J 153
(not continuous)
Stockham Lodge Racquet & Health Club
. . . . 3K 153
Stockley Cres. L39: Bic 5J 35
Stockmoor Rd. L11: N Grn. 3H 69
Stockpit Rd. L33: Know I 3G 57
Stockport Rd. WA4: Grap, Thel 6J 119
Stocks Av. WA9: St. H 3G 75
Stocks La. WA5: Gt San, Penk 3B 116
Stockswell Farm Ct. WA8: Wid 4A 114
Stockswell Rd. WA8: Wid 4F 113
Stockton Cres. L33: K'by 6B 44
Stockton Gro. WA9: St. H 1K 93
STOCKTON HEATH 7D 118
Stockton La. WA4: Grap 7E 118
Stockton Vw. WA4: Warr 6B 118
Stockton Wood Rd.
L24: Speke 6G 131
Stockville Rd. L18: Moss H 4C 110
Stockwell Cl. WN3: Wins 1B 50
Stoddart Rd. L4: Walt 4C 68
Stoke Cl. CH62: East 7A 146
Stoke Gdns. CH65: Ell P 7A 162
Stoker Way L9: Walt 1C 68
Stokesay CH43: Noct 2H 105
Stokesay Ct. CH65: Ell P 1C 170
Stokes Cl. L26: Halew 7A 112
Stokesley Av. L32: K'by 3A 56
Stokes St. WA3: Ris 2A 100
Stoke St. CH41: Birk 7B 86
Stoke Wlk. CH65: Ell P 7A 162
Stoneacre Gdns. WA4: App 5E 138
Stonebank Dr. CH64: Lit N 5A 158
Stonebarn Dr. L31: Mag 1E 42
Stone Barn La. WA7: Pal F 4H 153
Stonebridge La. L10: Faz 7J 55
L11: Crox 1K 69
Stoneby Dr. CH45: Wall 7A 66
Stonechat Cl. L27: N'ley 4J 111
WA7: Beech 5H 153
Stonechat Wlk. WA12: New W 3G 77
Stonecrop L18: Moss H 3C 110
Stonecrop Cl. WA3: Bchwd 3J 99
WA7: Beech 5H 153
Stone Cross Dr. WA8: Wid 3A 114
Stonecross Dr. L35: R'hill 6K 93
Stone Cross La. WA3: Low 1C 78
Stonedale Cres. L11: Crox 2J 69
Stonedale Pk. L11: Crox 2J 69
Stonefield Rd. L14: K Ash 3D 90
Stonefont Cl. L9: Walt 3C 68
Stonegate Dr. L8: Liv 4B 108
Stonehaven WN3: Wins 2B 50
Stonehaven Cl. L16: Child 7D 90
Stonehaven Dr. WA2: Fearn 4G 99
Stone Hey L35: Whis 6D 92
Stonehey Dr. CH48: W Kir 1E 122
Stonehey Rd. L32: K'by 5C 56
Stone Hey Wlk. L32: K'by 5C 56
Stonehill Av. CH63: Beb 3G 127
L4: Walt 1D 88
Stonehill Cl. WA4: App 5D 138
Stonehills Ct. WA7: Run 7E 134
Stonehills La. WA7: Run 7E 134
Stonehill St. L4: Walt 1D 88
Stonehouse M. L18: Aller 5B 110
Stonehouse Rd. CH44: Wall 2J 85
Stonelea WA7: Wind H 1K 153
Stoneleigh Cl. PR8: Ains 5C 14
Stoneleigh Ct. WA4: Grap 7K 119
Stoneleigh Gdns. WA4: Grap 7K 119

Stoneleigh Gro.—Tan Ho. La.

Stoneleigh Gro. CH42: R Ferr 1F 127
Stonemasons Ct. *L25: Wltn* *5E 110*
(off Clay Cross Rd.)
Stone Pit La. WA3: Croft 4E 78
Stoneridge Ct. CH43: Bid 7G 85
Stone Sq. L20: Boot 1A 68
Stone St. L3: Liv 3H 87 (1C 4)
L34: Prsct 1D 92
Stonethwaite Cl. WN3: Wigan 2E 50
Stoneville Rd. L13: Liv 3J 89
Stoney Brow WN8: Roby M 1D 38
Stoneycroft Cl. L13: Liv 2J 89
Stoneycroft Cres. L13: Liv 2J 89
Stoney Hey Rd. CH45: New B 7A 66
Stoneyhurst Av. L10: Ain 2E 54
Stoney La. L35: R'hill, Whis 3F 93
Stoney La. Ind. Est. L35: R'hill 4G 93
Stoney Vw. L35: R'hill 4H 93
Stonham Cl. CH49: Upton 3C 104
Stonyfield L30: N'ton 7A 42
Stony Holt WA7: Nort 2A 154
Stonyhurst Cl. WA11: St. H 6D 60
Stonyhurst Cres. WA3: Cul 1K 79
Stonyhurst Rd. L25: Wltn 7F 111
Stopford St. L8: Liv 4B 108
Stopgate La. L9: Ain 2F 69
L33: Sim 6E 44
Store St. L20: Kirk 5K 67
STORETON 4A 126
STORETON BRICKFIELDS 4J 125
Storeton Cl. CH43: O'ton 5A 106
Storeton La. CH61: Barn 6G 125
Storeton Rd. CH42: Tran 6B 106
CH43: O'ton 5B 106
Storewood Cl. WN5: Orr 6G 39
Stormont Rd. L19: Gars 2K 129
Storrington Av. L11: N Grn. 3J 69
Storrington Heys L11: N Grn. 2K 69
Storrsdale Rd. L18: Moss H 5K 109
Stour Av. L35: R'hill 4J 93
Stourcliffe Rd. CH44: Wall 3A 86
Stour Ct. CH65: Ell P 4K 161
Stourport Cl. CH49: Grea 4A 104
Stourton Rd. L32: K'by 5C 56
PR8: Ains 5C 14
Stourton St. CH44: Wall 5C 86
Stourvale Rd. L26: Halew 1K 131
Stowe Av. L10: Ain 3G 55
Stowe Cl. L25: Hunts X 2E 130
Stowell St. L7: Liv 7B 88 (8K 5)
Stowford Cl. L12: W Der 4A 70
Strada Way L3: Liv 4B 88 (3K 5)
Stradbroke Rd. L15: W'tree 2J 109
Strafford Dr. L20: Boot 2A 68
Straight Length WA6: Frod 3K 165
Straker Av. CH65: Ell P 5H 161
Strand, The L2: Liv 6H 87 (6D 4)
WN4: Ash M 1F 63
Strand Av. WN4: Ash M 1F 63
Strand Rd. CH47: Hoy 1D 102
L20: Boot 3H 67
(not continuous)
Strand Shop. Cen. L20: Boot 2J 67
Strand St. L1: Liv 6J 87 (7D 4)
Strange Rd. WN4: Gars 2B 62
Stratford Cl. PR8: Ains 3A 14
Stratford Rd. CH64: Nest 5J 157
L19: Aig 1H 129
Strathallan Cl. CH60: Hes 7C 124
Strathcona Rd. CH45: Wall 1B 86
L15: W'tree 1G 109
Strathearn Rd. CH60: Hes 4D 142
Strathlorne Cl. CH42: Tran 5F 107
Strathmore Av. WN4: Ash M 7E 50
Strathmore Dr. L23: C'by 2E 52
Strathmore Gro. WA9: St. H 1E 94
Strathmore Rd. L6: Liv 3E 88
Stratton Cl. CH45: Wall 1C 86
L18: Aller 5C 110
WA7: Brook 4K 153
Stratton Dr. WA9: St. H 1K 93
WN2: Platt B 3K 51
Stratton Pk. WA8: Wid 3B 114
Stratton Rd. L32: K'by 2E 138
WA5: Gt San 3F 117
Stratton Wlk. L32: K'by 4A 56
Strauss Cl. L8: Liv 2D 108
Strawberry Cl. WA3: Bchwd 3J 99
Strawberry Dr. CH66: Whit 4J 169
Strawberry Fld. L25: Wltn 5C 110
Strawberry Grn. CH66: Whit 4J 169
Strawberry La. CH1: Moll 7E 168
Strawberry Rd. L11: N Grn. 4G 69
Streatham Av. L18: Moss H 3H 109
Street Hey La. CH64: Will 7H 145
St. Marks Ct. CH43: O'ton 3B 106
Stretford Cl. L33: K'by 7C 44
Stretton Av. CH44: Wall 3A 86
WA9: St. H 3H 75
WN5: Bil 7G 49
Stretton Cl. CH43: O'ton 5J 105
CH62: East 7A 146
L12: Crox 3E 70
Stretton Dr. PR9: South 7B 8
Stretton Grn. Distribution Pk. WA4: App T 5K 139
Stretton Rd. WA4: App T, S'ton 7D 138
Stretton Way L36: Huy 6B 92
Strickland Cl. WA4: Grap 2G 139
Strickland St. WA10: St. H 2D 74
Stringer Cres. WA4: Westy 4E 118
Stringhey Rd. CH44: Wall 2C 86
Stroma Av. CH65: Ell P 4K 169
Stroma Rd. L18: Aller 7K 109
Stromness Cl. WA2: Fearn 4H 99
Stroud Cl. CH49: Grea 5A 104
Stuart Av. CH46: More 6D 84
L25: Hunts X 2G 131
Stuart Cl. CH46: More 7E 84
WN2: Platt B 2K 51
Stuart Cres. WN5: Bil 7F 49
Stuart Dr. L14: B Grn 4C 90
WA4: S Hth 6F 119
Stuart Gro. L20: Kirk 5K 67
Stuart Rd. CH42: Tran 5D 106
L4: Walt 4A 68
L22: Water 3E 52
L23: C'by 3F 53
L31: Mell 2K 55
WA7: Mnr P 5K 135
WA10: Windle 7J 59
Stuart Rd. Nth. L20: Boot 3A 68
Stubbs La. CH43: Noct 5J 105
STUBSHAW CROSS 7H 51
Studholme St. L20: Kirk 7J 67
Studland Rd. L9: Faz 2G 69
Studley Rd. CH45: Wall 1J 85
Sturby Ct. WA2: P'gate 6E 98
Sturdee Rd. L13: Liv 6K 89
Sturgess Cl. L39: Orm 3D 24
Sturgess St. WA12: New W 3D 76
Sturton Av. WN3: Wigan 1C 50
Suburban Rd. L6: Liv 1E 88
Sudbury Cl. L25: Wltn 6H 111
WN3: Wigan 2F 51
Sudbury Gdns. WA9: St. H 1J 93
Sudbury Rd. L22: Water 3B 52
Sudell Av. L31: Mag 2H 43
Sudell La. L31: Lyd 5F 33
L39: Augh *5F 33*
Sudley Grange L17: Aig 7G 109
Sudworth Rd. CH45: New B 7A 66
Suez St. WA1: Warr 3B 118
WA12: New W 3E 76
Suffield Rd. L4: Kirk 6K 67
Suffolk Av. CH65: Ell P 6J 161
Suffolk Cl. WA1: W'ston 2A 120
Suffolk Pl. WA8: Wid 2J 133
Suffolk Rd. PR8: B'dale 1G 15
Suffolk St. L1: Liv 7K 87 (9G 4)
L20: Boot 2K 67
WA7: Run 6B 134
Suffton Pk. L32: K'by 4A 56
Sugar La. L34: Know 3G 71
WA6: Manl 7K 173
Sugar St. L9: Ain 1D 68
Sugnall St. L7: Liv 7B 88 (9K 5)
(not continuous)
Sulby Av. L13: Liv 2G 89
WA4: Warr 5B 118
Sulby Cl. PR8: B'dale 5F 11
Sulgrave Cl. L16: Child 6A 90
Sullington Dr. L27: N'ley 2J 111
Sullivan Av. CH49: Upton 4D 104
Sullivans Way WA9: St. H 6D 74
Sumley Cl. WA11: St. H 1F 75
Summer Cl. WA7: Halt 1H 153
Summerfield CH62: Brom 7K 127
Summerfield Av. WA5: Warr 5K 97
WA10: Eccl 3F 73
Summerford Cl. CH42: Tran 5E 106
Summerhill Dr. L31: Mag 5H 43
Summer La. WA4: Dares, Hatt 2J 155
WA4: Pres H 4E 154
WA7: Halt 1H 153
Summer Rd. L20: Boot 1J 67
Summersales Ind. Est.
WN3: Wigan 7K 39
Summers Av. L20: Boot 2A 68
Summer Seat L3: Liv 3J 87 (1F 4)
L20: Boot 3G 67
Summers Rd. L3: Liv 3K 107
Summer St. WN8: Skel 6F 27
Summertrees Av. CH49: Grea 4B 104
Summertrees Cl. CH49: Grea 4B 104
Summertrees Rd. CH66: Gt Sut 2G 169
Summerville Gdns. WA4: S Hth 7F 119
Summerwood CH61: Irby 2B 124
Summerwood La. L39: Hals 1E 22
Summit, The CH44: Wall 2C 86
Summit Cl. WA4: Lwr S 7K 139
Summit Way L25: Wltn 5D 110
Sumner Av. L39: Has 6B 22
Sumner Cl. L5: Liv 2J 87
L35: R'hill 6K 93
Sumner Gro. L33: K'by 7D 44
Sumner Rd. CH43: Bid 7K 85
L37: Form 1F 17
Sumner St. WA11: Hay 7J 61
Sunbeam Cl. WA7: Run 6B 134
Sunbeam Rd. L13: Liv 4J 89
Sunbeam St. WA12: New W 3G 77
Sunbourne Rd. L17: Aig 6D 108
Sunbury Dr. PR8: Ains 5B 14
Sunbury Gdns. WA4: App 2E 138
Sunbury Rd. CH44: Wall 4C 86
L4: Walt 7D 68
Sunbury St. WA10: St. H 6J 73
Suncourt PR8: South 2F 11
Suncroft Cl. WA1: W'ston 1A 120
Suncroft Rd. CH60: Hes 3G 143
Sundale Av. L35: Prsct 1F 93
Sundene Lodge L22: Water 6E 52
Sundew Cl. L9: Walt 6B 54
Sundridge St. L8: Liv 4C 108
Sunfield Cl. CH66: Gt Sut 1F 169
Sunfield Rd. CH46: More 5D 84
Sunfield Vw. PR9: Banks 3J 9
Sunflower Cl. WA9: Bold 7J 75
Sunflower Lodge CH62: Port S 3H 127
Sunlight St. L6: Liv 2E 88
Sunloch Cl. L9: Ain 5F 55
Sunningdale CH46: More 7E 84
Sunningdale Av. WA8: Wid 7H 113
Sunningdale Cl. L36: Roby 6G 91
WA5: B'wood 1D 96
Sunningdale Dr. CH61: Thing 4E 124
CH63: Brom 4H 145
L23: Blun 6C 40
Sunningdale Gdns.
L37: Form 7J 19
Sunningdale Rd. CH45: Wall 6K 65
L15: W'tree 7H 89
Sunningdale Way CH64: Lit N 6J 157
Sunniside La. WA7: Nort 5C 136
Sunny Bank CH63: High B 3D 126
Sunnybank CH49: Upton 2D 104
Sunnybank Av. CH43: Noct 4H 105
Sunnybank Cl. WA12: New W 2G 77
Sunny Bank Rd. L16: Child 1B 110
Sunnydale L35: R'hill 4K 93
Sunny Dr. WN5: Orr 5H 39
Sunnyfields L39: Orm 5E 24
WN3: Wins 2A 50
Sunnygate Rd. L19: Gras 1J 129
Sunnymede Dr. L31: Lyd 1F 43
Sunny Rd. PR9: Chu 5C 8
Sunnyside CH46: More 5B 84
CH65: Ell P *5A 162*
(off Church St.)
L8: Liv 3C 108
Sunnyside L39: Augh 4A 34
PR8: B'dale 5F 11
WA5: Gt San 2C 116
Sunnyside Ct. PR9: South 6J 7
Sunnyside Rd. L23: C'by 2C 52
WN4: Ash M 6D 50
Sunrise Cl. L19: Gras 2K 129
Sunsdale Rd. L18: Moss H 3J 109
Sunset Cl. L33: K'by 7D 44
Superior Cl. L27: N'ley 3J 111
Surby Cl. L16: Child 7C 90
Surlingham Gdns. WA9: St. H 1A 94
Surrey Av. CH49: Upton 3D 104
Surrey Cl. PR9: Cros 2E 8
Surrey Dr. CH48: W Kir 1E 122
Surrey St. CH44: Wall 4A 86
L1: Liv 7K 87 (9F 4)
L20: Boot 2K 67
WA4: Warr 5D 118
WA7: Run 7C 134
(not continuous)
WA9: St. H 3F 75
Susan Dr. WA5: Penk 3B 116
Susan Gro. CH46: More 7B 84
Susan St. WA8: Wid 6E 114
Susan Wlk. L35: Whis 2F 93
Sussex Cl. CH61: Pens 5C 124
L20: Boot 2K 67
Sussex Gro. WA9: St. H 4E 74
Sussex Rd. CH48: W Kir 5E 102
L31: Mag 5F 43
PR8: South 1J 11
PR9: South 1J 11
Sussex St. L20: Boot 2K 67
L22: Water 3C 52
WA8: Wid 7F 115
Sutch La. WA13: Lymm 5J 121
Sutcliffe St. L6: Liv 4D 88 (2P 5)
Sutherland Ct. WA7: Run 7D 134
Sutherland Dr. CH62: East 6K 145
Sutherland Rd. L34: Prsct 1E 92
WN3: Wigan 1E 50
SUTTON 7H 75
Sutton Av. CH64: Nest 5J 157
WA3: Cul 2A 80
Sutton C'way. WA6: Frod 1G 167
Sutton Cl. CH62: East 7A 146
Sutton Fields Golf Driving Range 7A 154
Sutton Fold WA9: St. H 6F 75
SUTTON GREEN 1E 168
Sutton Hall Dr. CH66: Lit Sut 5C 160
Sutton Hall Gdns. CH66: Lit Sut 5C 160
SUTTON HEATH 7B 74
Sutton Heath Rd. WA9: St. H 1A 94
SUTTON LEACH 2F 95
Sutton Leisure Cen. 1D 94
Sutton Lodge Rd. WA9: St. H 4D 74
SUTTON MANOR 5D 94
Sutton Moss Rd. WA9: St. H 6H 75
Sutton Oak Dr. WA9: St. H 5F 75
Sutton Pk. Dr. WA9: St. H 7E 74
Sutton Quays Bus. Pk.
WA7: Sut W 7G 153
Sutton Rd. CH45: New B 7B 66
L37: Form 2J 29
WA9: St. H 5E 74
Suttons La. WA8: Wid 2D 134
L37: Gt Alt 1E 30
Sutton Sports Cen. 5G 161
Sutton St. L13: Liv 2G 89
WA1: Warr 4C 118
WA7: Run 7D 134
Suttons Way L26: Halew 7J 111
Sutton Way
CH65: Gt Sut, Whit 6H 161
CH66: Gt Sut 7F 161
SUTTON WEAVER 7J 153
Sutton Wood Rd. L24: Speke 6G 131
Suzanne Boardman Ho.
L6: Liv 2E 88
Swainson Rd. L10: Faz 6G 55
Swale Av. L35: R'hill 4J 93
Swaledale Av. L35: R'hill 4K 93
Swaledale Cl. CH62: East 5A 146
WA5: Gt San 1D 116
Swalegate L31: Mag 2E 42
Swale Rd. CH65: Ell P 4J 161
Swallow Cl. L12: Crox 3D 70
L27: N'ley 3K 111
L33: K'by 5C 44
WA3: Bchwd 3B 100
Swallow Ct. WA10: St. H 3K 73
Swallowfield Gdns. WA4: App 4F 139
Swallow Flds. L9: Faz 2G 69
Swallowhurst Cres.
L11: N Grn. 4J 69
Swanage Cl. WA4: S Hth 6E 118
Swan All. *L39: Orm* *5C 24*
(off Burscough St.)
Swan Av. WA9: St. H 4J 75
Swan Cl. CH66: Gt Sut 2F 169
Swan Ct. CH43: Pren 6K 105
Swan Cres. L15: W'tree 7J 89
Swan Delph L39: Augh 1A 34
Swanfield Wlk. WA3: Golb 3K 63
Swan Hey L31: Mag 5G 43
Swan La. L39: Augh 5G 33
Swanpool La. L39: Augh 2A 34
Swan Rd. WA12: New W 2B 76
SWANSIDE 5D 90
Swanside Av. L14: B Grn 4C 90
Swanside Pde. L14: K Ash 4C 90
Swanside Rd. L14: B Grn 4C 90
Swanston Av. L4: Walt 5C 68
Swan St. L13: Liv 4H 89
Swan Wlk. L31: Mag 5G 43
Sweden Gro. L22: Water 4D 52
Sweet Briar Ct. WA9: Clock F 5F 95
Sweetfield Gdns. CH66: Lit Sut 4F 161
Sweetfield Rd. CH66: Lit Sut 4F 161
Sweeting St. L2: Liv 6J 87 (6D 4)
Sweet William Pl.
WA12: New W 3C 76
Swift Cl. WA2: Warr 4E 98
Swift Gro. L12: Crox 2D 70
Swift's Cl. L30: N'ton 1K 53
Swifts Fold WN8: Skel 3D 36
Swift's La. L30: N'ton 1K 53
Swift St. WA10: St. H 1C 74
Swift Weint CH64: Park 2F 157
Swinbrook Grn. L11: N Grn. 3H 69
Swinburne Cl. L16: Child 7D 90
Swinburne Rd. WA10: St. H 1K 73
Swinburn Gro. WN5: Bil 3F 49
Swindale Av. WA2: Warr 4B 98
Swindale Cl. L8: Liv 1D 108 (10P 5)
Swinden Cl. WA7: Wind H 7B 136
Swinderby Dr. L31: Mell 2K 55
Swindon Cl. CH49: Grea 4A 104
L5: Kirk 7K 67
Swindon St. L5: Kirk 7K 67
Swineyard La. WA16: H Legh 5B 140
Swinford Av. WA8: Wid 6G 115
Swireford Rd. WA6: Hel 2H 173
Swisspine Gdns. WA9: St. H 7J 73
Swiss Rd. L6: Liv 4E 88
Switch Island L30: N'ton 7D 42
Switch Island Leisure Pk.
L30: N'ton 2C 54
Sword Cl. L11: Crox 3A 70
Sword Wlk. L11: Crox 3A 70
SWORTON HEATH 4H 141
Swynnerton Way WA8: Wid 3D 114
Sybil Rd. L4: Walt 7C 68
Sycamore Av. CH49: Upton 1B 104
L23: C'by 6F 41
L26: Halew 3K 131
WA8: Wid 6D 114
WA11: Hay 1H 75
WA12: New W 3G 77
Sycamore Cl. CH49: Upton 1B 104
L9: Walt 3E 68
WA10: Eccl 2H 73
Sycamore Ct. *L8: Liv* *4C 108*
(off Weller Way)
Sycamore Cres. WA3: Rix 5J 101
(not continuous)
Sycamore Dr. CH66: Whit 3H 169
WA7: Sut W 6J 153
WA13: Lymm 4F 121
WN3: Wins 2K 49
WN8: Skel 1E 36
Sycamore Gdns. WA10: St. H 7A 60
Sycamore Gro. L37: Form 2G 29
Sycamore La. WA5: Gt San 2F 117
Sycamore Pk. L18: Aller 6B 110
Sycamore Ri. CH49: Grea 6A 104
Sycamore Rd. CH42: Tran 4D 106
L22: Water 3E 52
L36: Huy 7J 91
WA7: Run 2E 152
Sydenham Av. L17: Liv 2E 108
Sydenham Ho. L17: Aig 3E 108
Syder's Gro. L34: Know 3G 71
Sydney St. L9: Ain 7C 54
WA7: West P 3K 151
Syers Ct. WA1: Warr 7E 98
Sylvan Ct. L25: Wltn 7E 110
Sylvandale Gro. CH62: Brom 6K 127
Sylvania Rd. L4: Walt 4C 68
Sylvia Cl. L10: Faz 7K 55
Sylvia Cres. WA2: Warr 6D 98
Synge St. WA2: Warr 1C 118
Syren St. L20: Kirk 6J 67
Syston Av. WA11: St. H 7E 60
Sytch Croft CH64: Nest 3J 157

T

Tabby's Nook WN8: Newb 1G 27
Tabley Av. WA8: Wid 6J 113
Tabley Cl. CH43: O'ton 6K 105
Tabley Gdns. WA9: St. H 1K 93
Tabley Rd. L15: W'tree 1F 109
Tabley St. L1: Liv 7J 87 (10F 4)
Tace Cl. L8: Liv 1B 108
Tadgers La. WA6: Frod 2K 165
Tadlow Cl. L37: Form 2G 29
Taggart Av. L16: Child 2B 110
Tagus Cl. L8: Liv 2D 108
Tagus St. L8: Liv 1D 108
Tailor's La. L31: Mag 4G 43
Talaton Cl. PR9: Marsh 2C 8
Talbot Av. CH63: Brim 1A 144
CH64: Lit N 5K 157
Talbot Cl. CH64: Lit N 5K 157
WA3: Bchwd 4A 100
WA10: St. H 2B 74
Talbot Ct. CH43: O'ton 4A 106
L36: Huy 6J 91
Talbot Dr. PR8: South 2H 11
Talbot Gdns. CH64: Lit N 5K 157
Talbot Rd. CH43: O'ton 4A 106
CH66: Gt Sut 1H 169
WA6: Dun H 5E 172
Talbot St. PR8: South 3G 11
WN4: Ash M 1H 63
Talbotville Rd. L13: Liv 6K 89
Talgarth Way L25: Gate 1E 110
Taliesin St. L5: Liv 2K 87
Talisman Cl. WA7: Murd 3B 154
Talisman Way L20: Boot 2G 67
Talland Cl. L26: Halew 7J 111
Tallarn Rd. L32: K'by 3K 55
Tall Trees WA9: St. H 6D 74
Talman Cl. WN4: Ash M 2H 63
Talton Rd. L15: W'tree 1F 109
Tamar Cl. L6: Liv 3C 88
Tamar Gro. CH46: More 7B 84
Tamarisk Gdns. WA9: St. H 7J 73
Tamar Rd. WA11: Hay 7A 62
Tamerton Cl. L18: Aller 6C 110
Tamneys, The WN8: Skel 2F 37
Tam o'Shanter Urban Farm 1J 105
Tamworth St. L8: Liv 3A 108
WA10: St. H 2A 74
WA12: New W 3E 76
Tanar Cl. CH63: Spit 6H 127
Tanat Dr. L18: Moss H 4K 109
Tancaster WN8: Skel 2E 36
Tancred Rd. CH45: Wall 2A 86
L4: Walt 7B 68
Tanfields WN8: Skel 2F 37
TANHOUSE 2K 37
Tanhouse WA7: Halt 1G 153
Tan Ho. Dr. WN3: Wins 2A 50
Tan Ho. La. WA5: B'wood 3D 96
WN3: Wins 2A 50

A-Z Merseyside 231

Tanhouse La.—Tithebarn Rd.

Tanhouse La. WA8: Wid 1E 134
Tanhouse Rd. L23: Thorn 7H 41
WN8: Skel 3J 37
Tankersley Gro. WA5: Gt San 3E 116
Tanners La. WA2: Warr 2A 118
Tannery Ct. WA2: Warr 2B 118
Tannery La. CH64: Nest 3J 157
WA5: Penk 5A 116
Tanning Ct. WA1: Warr 4B 118
Tan Pit La. WN3: Wins 2B 50
Tansley Cl. CH48: W Kir 6G 103
Tanworth Gro. CH46: More 6K 83
Tapley Pl. L13: Liv 5H 89
Taplow Cl. WA4: App 3E 138
Taplow St. L6: Liv 1D 88
Tapton Way L13: W'tree 6H 89
Tara Pk. Cvn. Site L3: Liv 3H 87
TARBOCK GREEN 4C 112
Tarbock Rd. L24: Speke 5H 131
L36: Huy 6H 91
Tarbot Hey CH46: More 7A 84
Tarbrock Ct. L30: N'ton 7K 41
Target Rd. CH60: Hes 2A 142
Tariff St. L5: Liv 2J 87
Tarleton Cl. L26: Halew 2J 131
Tarleton Rd. PR9: South 7C 8
Tarleton St. L1: Liv 6K 87 (6F 4)
Tarlswood WN8: Skel 2F 37
Tarlton Cl. L35: R'hill 2G 93
Tarnbeck WA7: Nort 2A 154
Tarn Brow L39: Orm 7A 24
Tarncliff L28: Stock V 6G 71
Tarn Cl. WN4: Ash M 7F 51
Tarn Ct. WA1: W'ston 1B 120
Tarn Gro. WA11: St. H 5D 60
Tarnrigg Cl. WN3: Wigan 1C 50
Tarn Rd. L37: Form 7H 19
Tarnside Rd. WN5: Orr 5G 39
Tarporley Cl. CH43: O'ton 5K 105
Tarporley Rd. CH66: Gt Sut 7G 161
WA4: S'ton 7D 138
Tarragon Cl. L23: Thorn 7H 41
Tarran Dr. CH46: More 5B 84
Tarran Rd. CH46: More 5B 84
Tarrant Cl. WN3: Wins 2B 50
Tarran Way E. CH46: More 4B 84
Tarran Way Ind. Est.
CH46: More 5B 84
Tarran Way Nth. CH46: More 5B 84
Tarran Way Sth. CH46: More 5B 84
Tarran Way W. CH46: More 5B 84
Tarves Wlk. L33: K'by 3D 56
Tarvin Cl. CH65: Ell P 7A 162
PR9: Cros 2F 9
WA7: Run 4E 152
WA9: Sut M 3D 94
Tarvin Rd. CH62: East 6B 146
WA6: Alv, Frod 2K 173 & 7A 166
Tasker Ter. L35: R'hill 3J 93
Tasman Cl. WA5: Old H 7G 97
Tasman Gro. WA9: St. H 7A 74
Tate Cl. WA8: Wid 5K 113
Tate Gallery 7H 87 (8C 4)
Tate St. L4: Walt 6B 68
Tatham Gro. WN3: Wins 3B 50
Tatlock Cl. WN5: Bil 7G 49
Tatlock St. L5: Liv 3J 87
(not continuous)
Tattersall Pl. L20: Boot 4H 67
Tattersall Rd. L21: Lith 6H 53
Tattersall Way L7: Liv 5G 89
Tatton Ct. WA1: W'ston 7K 99
Tatton Dr. WN4: Ash M 7D 50
Tatton Rd. CH42: Tran 3D 106
L9: Walt 7B 54
Taunton Av. WA9: Sut L 2F 95
Taunton Dr. L10: Ain 3G 55
Taunton Rd. CH45: Wall 1J 85
L36: Huy 5B 92
Taunton St. L15: W'tree 7G 89
Taurus Pk. WA5: W'brk 3H 97
Taurus Rd. L14: K Ash 3E 90
Tavener Cl. CH63: Brom 5J 145
Tavington Rd. L26: Halew 7A 112
Tavistock Dr. PR8: Ains 3B 14
Tavistock Rd. CH45: Wall 1K 85
WA5: Penk 4C 116
Tavlin Av. WA5: Warr 6K 97
Tavy Rd. L6: Liv 3C 88 (1M 5)
TAWD BRIDGE 4J 37
Tawd Rd. WN8: Skel 3J 37
Tawd St. L4: Kirk 6A 68
TAWD VALLEY PARK 1F 37
Tawny Ct. WA7: Pal F 3G 153
Taylor Av. L39: Orm 5E 24
Taylor Bus. Pk. WA3: Ris 4B 80
Taylor Cl. WA9: St. H 6G 75
Taylor Rd. WA11: Hay 7C 62
Taylors Cl. L9: Walt 3A 68
Taylors La. L9: Walt 3A 68
WA5: Cuerd 6J 115
WN3: Ince M 1J 51
Taylors Row WA7: Run 7E 134
Taylor St. CH41: Birk 1E 106
L5: Liv 2K 87
WA4: Warr 7A 118
WA8: Wid 7E 114
WA9: St. H 7G 75
WN8: Skel 2C 36
Taylor St. Ind. Est. L5: Liv 1K 87
Teakwood Cl. L6: Liv 2C 88
Teal Cl. L39: Augh 1A 34
WA2: Warr 4E 98
WA11: St. H 7D 60
WN3: Wigan 7K 39
Teal Gro. L26: Halew 7J 111
WA3: Bchwd 4B 100
Teals Way CH60: Hes 2C 142
Tears La. WN8: Newb 2E 26
Teasville Rd. L18: Moss H 4C 110
Tebay Cl. L31: Mag 2H 43
Tebay Rd. CH62: East 2A 146
Teck St. L7: Liv 5C 88 (5N 5)
Tedburn Cl. L25: Gate 4G 111
Tedbury Cl. L32: K'by 5C 56
Tedbury Wlk. L32: K'by 5C 56
Tedder Av. PR9: South 1C 12
Tedder Sq. WA8: Wid 1K 133
Teddington Cl. WA4: App 4E 138
Teehey Cl. CH63: High B 3D 126
Teehey Gdns. CH63: High B 3D 126
Teehey La. CH63: High B 3D 126
Tees Cl. L4: Kirk 5K 67
Tees Ct. CH65: Ell P 4J 161
Teesdale Cl. WA5: Gt San 1D 116
Teesdale Rd. CH63: Beb 5E 126
WA11: Hay 6A 62
Teesdale Way L35: R'hill 2J 93
Tees Pl. L4: Kirk 5K 67
Tees St. CH41: Birk 6K 85
L4: Kirk 5K 67
Teign Cl. L6: Liv 3C 88 (1M 5)
Teilo St. L8: Liv 3B 108
Telary Cl. L5: Liv 2J 87
Telegraph Ho. L23: C'by 7E 40
Telegraph La. CH45: Wall 2G 85
Telegraph Rd. CH48: Caldy 2H 123
CH60: Hes 2H 123
CH61: Thurs 2H 123
Telegraph Way L32: K'by 3C 56
Telford Cl. CH43: O'ton 4B 106
WA8: Wid 4K 113
Telford Ct. CH1: Dunk 6F 169
L7: Liv 6D 88 (7P 5)
Telford Dr. WA9: St. H 7H 75
Telford Rd. CH65: Ell P 7C 162
Telford's Quay CH65: Ell P 4B 162
Tempest Hey L2: Liv 5J 87 (5D 4)
Temple Ct. L2: Liv 6J 87 (6E 4)
WA3: Ris 1A 100
Temple La. L2: Liv 5J 87 (5E 4)
Templemartin WN8: Skel 1F 37
Templemore Av. L18: Moss H 5J 109
Templemore Rd. CH43: O'ton 4A 106
Temple Rd. CH42: Tran 6C 106
Temple St. L2: Liv 5J 87 (5E 4)
Templeton Cres. L12: W Der 5K 69
Templeton Dr. WA2: Fearn 5G 99
Tenbury Cl. WA5: Gt San 6E 96
Tenbury Dr. WN4: Ash M 1D 62
Tenby WN8: Skel 1E 36
Tenby Av. L21: Lith 4G 53
Tenby Cl. WA5: Call 5J 97
Tenby Dr. CH46: More 5B 84
WA7: Run 7F 135
Tenby St. L5: Liv 1C 88
Tennis St. WA10: St. H 1K 73
Tennis St. Nth. WA10: St. H 1A 74
Tennyson Av. CH42: R Ferr 7F 107
Tennyson Dr. L39: Orm 4B 24
WA2: Warr 5C 98
WN5: Bil 3F 49
Tennyson Rd. CH65: Whit 7J 161
L36: Huy 7A 92
WA8: Wid 7C 114
Tennyson St. L20: Boot 1H 67
WA9: Sut M 5C 94
Tennyson Way L32: K'by 4B 56
Tensing Cl. WA5: Gt San 7F 97
Tensing Rd. L31: Mag 3F 43
Tenterden St. L5: Liv 3K 87
Tenth Av. L9: Ain 6F 55
Terence Av. WA1: P'ton 1F 119
Terence Rd. L16: Child 2B 110
Terminus Rd. CH62: Brom 6K 127
L36: Huy 2F 91
Tern Cl. L33: K'by 5C 44
WA8: Wid 4D 114
Ternhall Rd. L9: Faz 2H 69
Ternhall Way L9: Faz 2H 69
Tern Way CH46: More 6K 83
WA10: St. H 7G 73
Terrace Rd. WA8: Wid 4C 134
Terret Cft. L28: Stock V 7F 71
Tetbury St. CH41: Birk 3C 106
Tetchill Cl. CH66: Gt Sut 2F 169
WA7: Nort 2B 154
Tetlow St. L4: Walt 6B 68
Tetlow Way L4: Walt 6B 68
Teulon Cl. L4: Walt 6B 68
Teversham WN8: Skel 1F 37
Teviot WN8: Skel 1E 36
Tewit Hall Cl. L24: Speke 6G 131
Tewit Hall Rd. L24: Speke 6G 131
Tewkesbury WN8: Skel 1E 36
Tewkesbury Cl. CH66: Gt Sut 4G 169
L12: Crox 2D 70
L25: Wltn 7G 111
Teynham Av. L34: Know 2H 71
Teynham Cres. L11: N Grn. 4H 69
Thackeray Cl. L8: Liv 2B 108
Thackeray Gdns. L30: Boot 5K 53
Thackray Rd. WA10: St. H 6K 73
Thames Cl. WA2: Warr 5D 98
Thamesdale CH65: Whit 1J 169
Thames Dr. WN5: Orr 4H 39
Thames Gdns. CH65: Whit 1J 169
Thames Rd. WA3: Cul 4B 80
WA9: Sut L 1E 94
Thames Side CH65: Whit 1K 169
Thames St. L8: Liv 2D 108
Thanet WN8: Skel 1F 37
Thatcher's Mt. WA5: C Grn 5B 76
THATTO HEATH 6K 73
Thatto Heath Rd. WA9: St. H 6K 73
WA10: St. H 6K 73
Thatto Heath Station (Rail) 6K 73
Thealby Cl. WN8: Skel 1E 36
THELWALL 5K 119
Thelwall La. WA4: Latch, Westy 5F 119
Thelwall New Rd.
WA4: Grap, Thel 5G 119
Thelwall New Rd. Ind. Est.
WA4: Westy 4J 119
Thelwall Rd. CH66: Gt Sut 7G 161
Thermal Rd. CH62: Brom 5K 127
Thermopylae Ct. *CH43: Noct 2H 105*
(off Redstone Ri.)
Thermopylae Pas. CH43: Noct 2G 105
(not continuous)
Thetford Rd. WA5: Gt San 2C 116
Thewlis St. WA5: Warr 3J 117
Thickwood Moss La.
WA11: R'ford 7F 47
THINGWALL 4F 125
Thingwall Av. L14: K Ash 5B 90
Thingwall Dr. CH61: Irby 3E 124
Thingwall Hall Dr. L14: B Grn 5B 90
Thingwall La. L14: K Ash 4B 90
Thingwall Recreation Cen. 3F 125
Thingwall Rd. CH61: Irby 3B 124
L15: W'tree 1K 109
Thingwall Rd. E. CH61: Thing 3E 124
Third Av. CH43: Bid 2F 105
L9: Ain 6G 55
(Meres Rd.)
L9: Ain 6F 55
(Park Av.)
L23: C'by 1D 52
WA7: Pal F 2H 153
Third St. WN2: Bam 5K 51
Thirlmere Av. CH43: Noct 2G 105
L21: Lith 5K 53
L37: Form 1A 30
WA2: Warr 4C 98
WA11: St. H 5C 60
WN4: Ash M 1G 63
WN5: Orr 3H 39
WN8: Uph 4D 38
Thirlmere Cl. L31: Mag 2G 43
WA6: Frod 3F 167
Thirlmere Ct. L5: Liv 2C 88
Thirlmere Dr. CH45: Wall 2B 86
L21: Lith 5K 53
PR8: Ains 6B 14
WA13: Lymm 5H 121
Thirlmere Grn. L5: Liv 2C 88
Thirlmere Rd. CH64: Nest 5J 157
CH65: Whit 2K 169
L5: Liv 2C 88
L38: High 5G 29
WN5: Wigan 4K 39
Thirlmere Wlk. L33: K'by 1B 56
Thirlmere Way WA8: Wid 1J 133
Thirlstane St. L17: Aig 5D 108
Thirsk WN8: Skel 1F 37
Thirsk Cl. WA7: Run 4E 152
Thirty Acre La. L37: Form 5D 20
Thistledown Cl. L17: Aig 5B 108
Thistleton Av. CH41: Birk 7K 85
Thistleton M. PR9: South 7J 7
Thistlewood Rd. L7: Liv 5G 89
Thistley Hey Rd. L32: K'by 3D 56
Thomas Cl. CH65: Whit 2K 169
L19: Gars 4A 130
Thomas Ct. WA7: Pal F 3H 153
Thomas Dr. L14: B Grn 5A 90
L35: Prsct 3C 92
Thomas La. L14: B Grn, K Ash 5B 90
L14: K Ash 3B 90
Thomasons Bri. La. WA4: H Walt 3J 137
Thomas St. CH41: Birk 3E 106
WA3: Golb 5K 63
WA7: Run 6D 134
WA8: Wid 2C 134
Thomaston St. L5: Liv 1A 88
(not continuous)
Thomas Winder Ct. L5: Kirk 1K 87
Thompson Av. L39: Orm 5E 24
WA3: Cul 3A 80
Thompson Cl. WA12: New W 5G 77
Thompson St. CH41: Tran 4E 106
WA3: Ris 2A 100
WA10: St. H 5K 73
WN4: Ash M 1H 63
Thomson Rd. L21: Sea 6F 53
(not continuous)
Thomson St. L6: Liv 3D 88 (1P 5)
Thorburn Cl. CH62: New F 1H 127
Thorburn Ct. CH62: New F 7H 107
Thorburn Cres. CH62: New F 1H 127
Thorburn Rd. CH62: New F 1H 127
Thorburn St. L7: Liv 6D 88
Thoresby Cl. WN3: Wigan 1C 50
Thorlby Rd. WA3: Cul 2B 80
Thorley Cl. L15: W'tree 6J 89
Thornaby Gro. WA9: St. H 1K 93
Thornbeck Av. L38: High 7F 29
Thornbeck Cl. L12: Crox 3C 70
Thornbridge Av. L21: Lith 5K 53
Thornbrook Cl. L12: W Der 7B 70
Thornbury WN8: Skel 1F 37
Thornbury Rd. L4: Walt 7E 68
Thornby WN8: Skel 1F 37
Thorncliffe Rd. CH44: Wall 4A 86
Thorn Cl. WA5: Penk 5D 116
WA7: Run 3E 152
Thorncroft Dr. CH61: Barn 5F 125
Thorndale WN8: Skel 1F 37
Thorndale Rd. L22: Water 3D 52
Thorndyke Cl. L35: R'hill 6A 94
Thorne Dr. CH66: Lit Sut 6D 160
Thorne La. CH44: Wall 2K 85
Thornes Rd. L6: Liv 4D 88 (3P 5)
Thorness Cl. CH49: Grea 6A 104
Thorneycroft Dr. WA1: Warr 2C 118
Thorneycroft St. CH41: Birk 7A 86
Thornfield Hey CH63: Spit 7G 127
Thornfield Rd. L9: Walt 1B 68
L23: Thorn 6G 41
Thornham Av. WA9: St. H 6E 74
Thornham Cl. CH49: Upton 1E 104
Thornhead La. L12: W Der 1B 90
Thornhill L39: Augh 2K 33
Thornhill Cl. L39: Augh 3K 33
Thornhill Rd. L15: W'tree 1J 109
WN4: Gars 1A 62
Thornholme Cres. L11: N Grn. 5H 69
Thornhurst L32: K'by 6C 56
Thornleigh Av. CH62: East 6B 146
Thornleigh Dr. CH66: Ell P 5G 161
Thornley Cl. WA13: Lymm 5E 120
Thornley Rd. CH46: More 1A 104
WA13: Lymm 5E 120
Thornridge CH46: More 7E 84
Thorn Rd. WA1: P'ton 7G 99
WA7: Run 3E 152
WA10: St. H 3J 73
Thorns, The L31: Mag 2D 42
Thorns Dr. CH49: Grea 6A 104
Thornside Wlk. L25: Gate 4F 111
Thornton WA8: Wid 1A 134
WN8: Skel 1F 37
Thornton Av. CH63: High B 1D 126
L20: Boot 6K 53
Thornton Cl. WN4: Ash M 1D 62
Thornton Comn. Rd.
CH63: Raby M, Thorn H 4B 144
Thornton Crematorium
L23: Thorn 5J 41
Thornton Cres. CH60: Hes 4F 143
Thorntondale Dr. WA5: Gt San 1C 116
Thornton Grn. La. CH2: Thor M 2J 171
Thornton Gro. CH63: High B 1D 126
L36: Huy 4G 91
THORNTON HAUGH 4A 144
THORNTON-LE-MOORS 2J 171
Thornton M. CH66: Chil T 3D 160
Thornton Rd. CH45: Wall 1A 86
CH63: High B 1C 126
CH65: Ell P 7B 162
L16: Child 6C 90
L20: Boot 1J 67
PR9: South 1B 12
WA5: Gt San 4F 117
Thornton St. CH41: Birk 7A 86
L21: Lith 7H 53
Thorn Tree Cl. L24: Hale 1E 150
Thorntree Cl. L17: Aig 5B 108
Thorntree Grn. WA4: App T 5H 139
Thornwood WN8: Skel 1F 37
Thornwood Cl. L6: Liv 2D 88
Thornwythe Gro. CH66: Gt Sut 7G 161
Thornycroft Rd. L15: W'tree 1F 109
Thorpe WN8: Skel 1F 37
Thorpe Bank CH42: R Ferr 1F 127
Thorstone Dr. CH61: Irby 2A 124
Thorsway CH42: R Ferr 6F 107
CH48: Caldy 1F 123
Threadneedle Ct. WA9: St. H 6H 75
Three Acres Cl. L25: Wltn 5C 110
Three But La. L12: W Der 1H 89
THREE LANES END 3K 103
Three Pools PR9: Cros 4E 8
(not continuous)
Three Sisters Enterprise Pk., The
WN4: Ash M 6F 51
Three Sisters Rd. WN4: Ash M 6F 51
Three Tuns La. L37: Form 7K 19
Threlfalls Cl. *PR9: Chu 4B 8*
(off Threlfalls La.)
Threlfalls La. PR9: Chu 5B 8
Threlfall St. L8: Liv 4C 108
Thresher Av. CH49: Grea 4A 104
Threshers, The L30: N'ton 1D 54
Throne Rd. L11: Crox 3A 70
Throne Wlk. L11: Crox 2A 70
Thurcroft Dr. WN8: Skel 1E 36
Thurlby Cl. WN4: Ash M 1H 63
Thurne Way L25: Gate 2E 110
Thurnham St. L6: Liv 2E 88
Thursby Cl. L32: K'by 5D 56
PR8: Ains 6B 14
Thursby Cres. L32: K'by 4D 56
Thursby Ho. WN5: Wigan 4K 39
Thursby Rd. CH62: Brom 7A 128
Thursby Wlk. L32: K'by 5D 56
Thurstan St. WN3: Ince M 1J 51
THURSTASTON 4K 123
Thurstaston Rd. CH60: Hes 1C 142
CH61: Irby, Thurs 4K 123
Thurston WN8: Skel 1E 36
Thurston Av. WN3: Wigan 1F 51
Thurston Cl. WA5: Gt San 2H 117
Thurston Rd. L4: Walt 1D 88
Thurstwood L37: Form 5J 19
Thynne St. WA1: Warr 4A 118
Tibb's Cross La. WA8: Bold H 1E 114
Tichbourne Way L6: Liv 4B 88 (3L 5)
Tickle Av. WA9: St. H 3F 75
Tidal La. WA1: P'gate 7F 99
Tideswell Av. WN5: Orr 2J 39
Tideswell Cl. L7: Liv 7D 88 (9P 5)
Tideway CH45: Wall 6J 65
Tilbey Dr. WA6: Frod 3C 166
Tilbrook Dr. WA9: St. H 7F 75
Tilbury Pl. WA7: Murd 4C 154
Tilcroft WN8: Skel 1E 36
Tildsley Cres. WA7: West 4B 152
Tilley St. WA1: Warr 2C 118
Tillotson Cl. L8: Liv 3A 108
Tilman Cl. WA5: Gt San 7F 97
Tilney St. L9: Walt 7C 54
Tilstock Av. CH62: New F 1H 127
Tilstock Cl. L26: Halew 6A 112
Tilstock Cres. CH43: Pren 7K 105
Tilston Av. WA4: Westy 4G 119
Tilston Cl. L9: Faz 3F 69
Tilston Rd. CH45: Wall 1A 86
L9: Faz 2F 69
L32: K'by 3A 56
Timberscombe Gdns.
WA1: W'ston 2A 120
Time Pk. L35: Whis 2F 93
Timmis Cl. WA2: Fearn 4G 99
Timmis Cres. WA8: Wid 7C 114
Timms Cl. L37: Form 5K 19
Timms La. L37: Form 5J 19
Timon Av. L20: Boot 1A 68
Timor Av. WA9: St. H 6A 74
Timperley Av. WA4: Westy 4G 119
Timperley Ct. *WA8: Wid 1D 134*
(off Alfred Cl.)
Timpron St. L7: Liv 7D 88
Timway Dr. L12: W Der 6C 70
Tinas Way CH49: Upton 3E 104
Tinling Cl. L34: Prsct 1E 92
Tinsley Av. PR8: South 5A 12
Tinsley Cl. L26: Halew 6J 111
Tinsley's La. PR8: South 7B 12
Tinsley St. L4: Walt 7C 68
WA4: Westy 5F 119
Tintagel WN8: Skel 1D 36
Tintagel Cl. WA7: Brook 5A 154
Tintagel Rd. L11: Crox 1B 70
Tintern Av. WN4: Ash M 2H 63
Tintern Cl. WA5: Call 5J 97
Tintern Dr. CH46: More 7C 84
L37: Form 1B 30
Tiptree Cl. L12: Crox 2D 70
Titchfield St. L5: Liv 3J 87 (1F 4)
Tithebarn Cl. CH60: Hes 3D 142
Tithebarn Dr. CH64: Park 1F 157
Tithebarn Gro. L15: W'tree 1J 109
Tithe Barn La. L32: K'by 4B 56
Tithebarn La. L31: Mell 7H 43
Tithebarn Rd. L23: C'by 1F 53
L34: Know 2H 71
PR8: South 2K 11
WN4: Gars 3A 62

Tithebarn St.—Up Holland

Tithebarn St. L2: Liv 5J 87 (5D 4)
WN8: Uph 4D 38
Tithings, The WA7: Run 1G 153
Tiverton Av. CH44: Wall 3A 86
WN8: Skel 1E 36
Tiverton Cl. L36: Huy 4B 92
WA8: Wid 5J 113
Tiverton Rd. L26: Halew 3J 131
Tiverton Sq. WA5: Penk 3C 116
Tiverton St. L15: W'tree 7G 89
Tobermory Cl. WA11: Hay 1J 75
Tobin Cl. L5: Liv 3J 87 (1E 4)
Tobin St. CH44: Wall 3D 86
Tobruk Rd. L36: Huy 3H 91
Todd Rd. WA9: St. H 3D 74
Todd's La. PR9: Banks 1J 9
Toft Cl. WA8: Wid 7B 114
Toft St. L7: Liv 5E 88
Toftwood Av. L35: R'hill 6K 93
Toftwood Gdns. L35: R'hill 6K 93
(not continuous)
Tokenspire Pk. L33: Know I 6F 57
Toleman Av. CH63: Beb 4G 127
Toll Bar Pl. WA2: Warr 3A 98
Toll Bar Rd. WA2: Warr 4A 98
Tollemache Rd. CH41: Birk 1J 105
CH43: Bid 7K 85
Tollemache St. CH45: New B 6B 66
Tollerton Rd. L12: W Der 1H 89
Tollgate Rd. L40: Burs 1F 25
Tolpuddle Rd. L25: Wltn 5D 110
Tolpuddle Way L4: Kirk 6K 67
Tolver Ho. WA10: St. H 2C 74
Tolver Rd. WN4: Ash M 6E 50
Tolver St. WA10: St. H 2C 74
Tomlinson Av. WA2: Warr 7D 98
Tom Mann Cl. L3: Liv 4K 87 (4G 4)
Tommy Gent Way L31: Mag 4F 43
Tonbridge Cl. L24: Speke 5F 131
Tonbridge Dr. L10: Ain 2F 55
Tongbarn WN8: Skel 1E 36
TONTINE 6F 39
Tontine WN5: Orr 6E 38
Tontine Rd. WN8: Uph 5E 38
Toothill Cl. WN4: Ash M 7F 51
Top Acre Rd. WN8: Skel 4J 37
Topaz Cl. L4: Walt 4A 68
Topcliffe Gro. L12: Crox 3E 70
Topgate Cl. CH60: Hes 2F 143
Topham Dr. L9: Ain 3D 54
Topham Ter. L9: Ain 5D 54
Topping Ct. WA3: Bchwd 3J 99
Top Rd. WA6: Frod 6F 167
Top Sandy La. WA2: Warr 4B 98
Topsham Cl. L25: Gate 4G 111
Torcross Cl. PR9: Marsh 2C 8
Torcross Way L25: Gate 4G 111
L26: Halew 7J 111
Tordelow Cl. L6: Liv 3C 88 (1M 5)
Toronto Cl. L36: Huy 7H 71
Toronto St. CH44: Wall 4E 86
Torquay Dr. WN5: Bil 4G 49
Torr Dr. CH62: East 3C 146
Torridon Gro. CH66: Gt Sut 1H 169
Torrington Dr. CH61: Thing 3F 125
L26: Halew 2J 131
Torrington Gdns. CH61: Thing 2F 125
Torrington Rd. CH44: Wall 3A 86
L19: Gras 2K 129
Torrisholme Rd. L9: Ain 3F 69
Torr St. L5: Liv 1A 88
(not continuous)
Torus Rd. L13: Liv 3J 89
Torver Cl. WN3: Wigan 2E 50
Torview L15: W'tree 2J 109
Torwood CH43: Noct 2H 105
Total Fitness
Netherton 1D 54
Prenton 7H 105
Victoria Park 6H 89
Tothale Turn L27: N'ley 4K 111
Totland Cl. WA5: Gt San 1A 116
Totnes Av. L26: Halew 7K 111
Totnes Dr. PR9: Marsh 2C 8
Totnes Rd. L11: Crox 1A 70
Tourist Info. Cen.
Liverpool 7J 87 (9D 4)
Queen Sq. 5K 87 (6G 4)
Runcorn 6C 134
Warrington 3B 118
Runcorn (Town Hall) 1D 152
Southport 1H 11
Tourney Grn. WA5: W'brk 5E 96
Towcester St. L21: Lith 7H 53
Tower Bldgs. PR9: South 7J 7
Tower End L37: Form 5G 19
Tower Gdns. L3: Liv 6H 87 (6D 4)
TOWER HILL 7D 44
Tower Hill CH42: Tran 5D 106
L39: Orm 5E 24
Tower Hill Rd. WN8: Uph 6B 38
Towerlands St. L7: Liv 6C 88 (6P 5)
Tower La. WA7: Nort 3A 154
WA13: Lymm 6H 121
Tower Nook WN8: Uph 6C 38
Tower Prom. CH45: New B 5C 66
Tower Quays CH41: Birk 7E 86
Tower Rd. CH41: Birk 7E 86
CH42: Tran 7B 106
(Reservoir Rd.)
CH42: Tran 5D 106
(Stuart Rd.)
Tower Rd. Nth. CH60: Hes 7C 124
Tower Rd. Sth. CH60: Hes 1D 142
Towers, The CH42: Tran 6E 106
Towers Av. L31: Mag 2E 42
Towers Ct. WA5: Warr 1J 117
Towers La. WA6: Alv, Hel 5H 173
Towers Rd. L16: Child 2A 110
Tower St. L3: Liv 3K 107
Tower Way L25: Wltn 5E 110
Tower Wharf CH41: Birk 7E 86
Towneley Ct. WA8: Wid 7C 114
TOWN END 2J 113
Town End Cl. L39: Orm 6B 24
Townfield Av. WN4: Ash M 3F 63
Townfield Cl. CH43: O'ton 5J 105
Townfield Gdns. CH63: High B 2F 127
Townfield La. CH1: Moll 7F 169
CH43: O'ton 5J 105
Townfield La. CH63: Beb, High B 2F 127
WA6: Frod 4E 166
WA13: Warb 7K 101
Townfield Rd. CH48: W Kir 6D 102
WA2: Win 2A 98
WA7: Wind H 7A 136
Town Flds. CH45: Wall 1J 85
Townfields WN4: Ash M 2E 62
Townfield Vw. WA7: Wind H 7A 136
Townfield Wlk. WA12: New W 2F 77
Townfield Way CH44: Wall 3B 86
TOWN GREEN
Newton-le-Willows 2H 63
Ormskirk 4A 34
Town Grn. Ct. L39: Augh 3A 34
Town Grn. Gdns. L39: Augh 3A 34
Town Grn. La. L39: Augh 3A 34
Town Green Station (Rail) 4A 34
Town Hall Dr. WA7: Run 1D 152
Town Hill WA1: Warr 3B 118
Town La. CH63: High B 3D 126
CH64: Lit N 5K 157
L24: Hale 1D 150
PR8: South 4K 11
(not continuous)
Town La. (Kew) PR8: South 5K 11
Townley Ct. *CH47: Hoy* *1D 102*
(off Marmion Rd.)
Town Mdw. La. CH46: More 6K 83
TOWN OF LOWTON 1B 78
Town Rd. CH42: Tran 5D 106
Town Row L12: W Der 7K 69
Townsend Av. L11: N Grn. 3G 69
L13: Liv 6G 69
Townsend La. L6: Liv 1E 88
L13: Liv 7F 69
Townsend St. CH41: Birk 6J 85
L5: Kirk 1H 87
Townsend Vw. L11: N Grn. 3G 69
L21: Ford 3H 53
Townshend Av. CH61: Irby 4B 124
Town Sq. *WA7: Pal F* *3H 153*
(off Halton Lea Shop. Cen.)
Town Vw. CH43: O'ton 3C 106
Town Vw. M. CH43: O'ton 3C 106
Town Wlk. *WA7: Pal F* *3H 153*
(off Halton Lea Shop. Cen.)
Towson St. L5: Liv 1B 88
(not continuous)
TOXTETH 3A 108
Toxteth Gro. L8: Liv 4C 108
Toxteth Sports Cen. 2B 108
Toxteth St. L8: Liv 3A 108
Tracks La. WN5: Bil 1F 49
Tracy Dr. WA12: New W 3J 77
Tradewind Sq. L1: Liv 7K 87 (9G 4)
TRAFALGAR 5G 127
Trafalgar Av. CH44: Wall 2D 86
Trafalgar Ct. PR8: B'dale 5F 11
WA8: Wid 3C 134
Trafalgar Dr. CH63: Beb 5G 127
Trafalgar Rd. CH44: Wall 2C 86
PR8: B'dale 6E 10
Trafalgar St. WA10: St. H 2A 74
Trafalgar Way L6: Liv 4B 88 (3L 5)
Trafford Av. WA5: Warr 1J 117
Trafford Cres. WA7: Run 4E 152
Tragan Dr. WA5: Penk 5B 116
Tramway Rd. L17: Aig 5E 108
TRANMERE 5E 106
Tranmere Rovers FC 6C 106
Trap Hill L37: Form 1G 29
Trapwood Cl. WA10: Eccl 3G 73
Travanson Cl. L10: Faz 7K 55
Travers' Entry WA9: Bold 7J 75
Traverse St. WA9: St. H 3E 74
Travis Dr. L33: K'by 7D 44
Travis St. WA8: Wid 1D 134
Trawden Way L21: Ford 1J 53
Treborth St. L8: Liv 3C 108
Trecastle Rd. L33: K'by 1E 56
Treebank Cl. WA7: Run 2C 152
Treen Cl. PR9: Marsh 1D 8
Treesdale Cl. PR8: B'dale 4F 11
Treetop Ct. L6: Liv 3D 88
Treetops CH64: Lit N 7J 157
Treetops Cl. WA1: P'gate 1F 119
Treetops Dr. CH41: Birk 6H 85
Treetop Vs. PR9: Chu 3B 8
Tree Vw. Ct. L31: Mag 4G 43
Trefoil Cl. WA3: Bchwd 2J 99
Treforris Rd. CH45: Wall 7K 65
Trefula Pk. L12: W Der 1J 89
Trelawney Cl. L25: Gate 2F 111
Tremore Cl. L12: W Der 5K 69
Trenance Cl. WA7: Brook 5K 153
Trendeal Rd. L11: Crox 1B 70
Trent Av. L14: B Grn 4D 90
L31: Mag 2H 43
Trent Cl. L12: Crox 3B 70
L35: R'hill 4H 93
WA8: Wid 4D 114
WA9: Sut L 2E 94
Trentdale CH65: Whit 1K 169
Trentham Av. L18: Moss H 3H 109
Trentham Cl. WA8: Wid 4D 114
Trentham Rd. CH44: Wall 4C 86
L32: K'by 4A 56
Trentham St. WA7: Run 6B 134
Trentham Wlk. L32: K'by 4A 56
Trent Pl. L35: R'hill 4H 93
(not continuous)
Trent Rd. L35: R'hill 4H 93
WN4: Ash M 7J 51
WN5: Bil 1E 60
Trent St. CH41: Birk 6K 85
L5: Kirk 1J 87
Trent Way CH60: Hes 4G 143
L21: Lith 4G 53
Tresham Dr. WA4: Grap 1G 139
Tressel Dr. WA9: Sut M 4C 94
Tressell St. L9: Walt 3B 68
Trevelyan Dr. WN5: Bil 3F 49
Trevelyan St. L9: Walt 3B 68
Treviot Cl. L33: K'by 6B 44
Trevor Dr. L23: C'by 1F 53
Trevor Rd. L9: Walt 7C 54
PR8: Ains 5C 14
Triad, The L20: Boot 2J 67
Trident Ind. Est. WA3: Ris 1A 100
Trident Pk. WA7: Pal F 3G 153
Trimley Cl. CH49: Upton 3C 104
Tring Cl. CH49: Upton 1E 104
Trinity Ct. CH47: Hoy 1D 102
WA3: Ris 2B 100
Trinity Gdns. CH47: Hoy 1D 102
PR8: South 2G 11
WA6: Frod 2E 166
WN4: Ash M 1D 62
Trinity Gro. L23: Blun 2B 52
Trinity Ho. WA6: Frod 2E 166
Trinity La. CH41: Birk 1E 106
Trinity M. PR9: South 1J 11
Trinity Pl. L20: Boot 3K 67
WA8: Wid 2D 134
Trinity Rd. CH44: Wall 2B 86
CH47: Hoy 1D 102
L20: Boot 4J 67
Trinity St. CH41: Birk 1C 106
WA7: Run 6D 134
WA9: St. H 2E 74
Trinity Wlk. L3: Liv 4A 88 (3J 5)
Trispen Cl. L26: Halew 1J 131
Trispen Rd. L11: Crox 2B 70
Trispen Wlk. L11: Crox 2B 70
Tristram's Cft. L30: N'ton 2K 53
Triumph Trad. Pk. L24: Hunts X 3E 130
Triumph Trading Pk., The
L24: Speke 3D 130
Triumph Way
L24: Hunts X, Speke 3D 130
Troon Cl. CH63: Brom 5J 145
L12: W Der 1C 90
WA11: Hay 1J 75
Trossach Cl. WA2: Warr 5E 98
Trotwood Cl. L9: Ain 5F 55
Troutbeck Av. L31: Mag 2G 43
WA5: Warr 1K 117
WA12: New W 2C 76
Troutbeck Cl. CH49: W'chu 6E 104
WA7: Beech 5J 153
Troutbeck Gro. WA11: St. H 3D 60
Troutbeck Ri. WN5: Wigan 5K 39
Troutbeck Rd. L18: Moss H 3B 110
WN4: Ash M 7G 51
Trouville Rd. L4: Walt 7E 68
Trowbridge St. L3: Liv 6A 88 (6J 5)
Trueman Cl. CH43: Bid 7G 85
Trueman St. L3: Liv 5K 87 (4F 4)
Truman Cl. WA8: Wid 5B 114
Trumans La. CH66: Lit Sut 4E 160
Trundle Pie La. L39: Hals 3E 22
Truro Av. L30: N'ton 1B 54
PR9: Marsh 2D 8
Truro Cl. CH66: Gt Sut 4H 169
WA1: W'ston 7H 99
WA7: Brook 4A 154
WA11: St. H 6F 61
Truro Rd. L15: W'tree 2J 109
Tudor Av. CH44: Wall 5E 86
CH63: Beb 6G 127
Tudor Cl. CH66: Gt Sut 4H 169
L7: Liv 6B 88 (7L 5)
WA4: Grap 6G 119
WA11: R'ford 4E 46
Tudor Ct. L19: Gras 2J 129
WA4: S Hth 7E 118
Tudor Gdns. L38: High 5F 29
Tudor Grange CH49: Grea 5B 104
Tudor Gro. WN3: Wins 2C 50
Tudor Mans. PR8: South 2F 11
Tudor Rd. CH42: Tran 5E 106
L23: C'by 2D 52
L25: Hunts X 2G 131
PR8: Ains 3B 14
WA7: Mnr P 6K 135
Tudor St. Nth. L6: Liv 4D 88 (2P 5)
Tudor St. Sth. L6: Liv 4D 88 (2P 5)
Tudor Vw. L33: K'by 7C 44
(not continuous)
Tudorville Rd. CH63: Beb 4F 127
Tudorway CH60: Hes 2F 143
TUE BROOK 1G 89
Tue La. WA8: Cron 2H 113
Tuffins Cnr. L27: N'ley 3H 111
Tulip Av. CH41: Birk 7K 85
Tulip Rd. L15: W'tree 1J 109
WA11: Hay 7D 62
Tulketh St. PR8: South 1H 11
Tullimore Rd. L18: Moss H 7H 109
Tullis St. WA10: St. H 4A 74
Tulloch St. L6: Liv 4D 88 (2P 5)
Tully Av. WA12: New W 3C 76
Tumilty Av. L20: Boot 2A 68
Tunbridge Cl. WA5: Gt San 7E 96
Tunnage Sq. L1: Liv 7K 87 (8G 4)
Tunnel Rd. CH41: Birk 3E 106
L7: Liv 7D 88
Tunnel Top Nth.
WA7: Dutt, Pres B 4D 154
Tunstall Cl. CH49: Upton 3C 104
Tunstall St. L7: Liv 1E 108
Tunstalls Way WA9: Clock F 3F 95
Tupelo Cl. L12: Crox 2D 70
Tupman St. L8: Liv 3B 108
Turmar Av. CH61: Thing 3F 125
Turnacre L14: B Grn 4C 90
L37: Form 4B 20
Turnall Rd. WA8: Wid 2H 133
Turnberry WN8: Skel 1D 36
Turnberry Cl. CH46: More 6K 83
L12: W Der 1D 90
L36: Roby 6G 91
WA13: Lymm 4E 120
Turnberry Ho. WA3: Ris 1K 99
Turnberry Way PR9: Cros 2F 9
Turnbridge Rd. L31: Mag 1E 42
Turner Av. L20: Boot 6A 54
Turner Cl. L8: Liv 5C 108
WA8: Wid 5K 113
Turner Gro. L33: K'by 6C 44
Turner Home, The L8: Liv 4C 108
Turners Ct. L25: Gate 5F 111
Turner St. CH41: Birk 3C 106
Turners Vw. CH64: Nest 1H 157
Turney Rd. CH44: Wall 3A 86
Turnill Dr. WN4: Ash M 3F 63
Turning La. PR8: South 1C 16
Turnpike Rd. L39: Augh 2J 33
Turnstone Av. WA12: New W 2G 77
Turnstone Cl. L12: Crox 3C 70
Turnstone Dr. L26: Halew 7J 111
Turret Rd. CH45: Wall 1A 86
Turriff Dr. CH63: East 6J 145
Turriff Rd. L14: K Ash 3E 90
Turrocks Cl. CH64: Lit N 6J 157
Turrocks Cft. CH64: Lit N 6J 157
Turton Cl. L24: Hale 1D 150
WA3: Bchwd 2J 99
Turton St. L5: Kirk 1K 87
Tuscan Cl. WA8: Wid 3D 114
Tuson Dr. WA8: Wid 4B 114
Tutor Bank Dr. WA12: New W 3H 77
Tweed Cl. L6: Liv 3D 88
Tweedsmuir Cl. WA2: Fearn 3G 99
Tweed St. CH41: Birk 6A 86
Twenty Acre Rd. WA5: Old H 7G 97
Twickenham Dr. CH46: Leas 4D 84
L36: Roby 6G 91
Twickenham St. L6: Liv 1D 88
Twigden Cl. L10: Faz 5H 55
Twig La. L31: Mag 3G 43
L36: Huy 4G 91
TWISS GREEN 2A 80
Twiss Grn. Dr. WA3: Cul 2A 80
Twiss Grn. La. WA3: Cul 2K 79
Twistfield Cl. PR8: B'dale 3F 11
Two Acre Gro. CH66: Gt Sut 3H 169
Two Butt La. L35: Whis, R'hill 2G 93
Twomey Cl. L5: Liv 3J 87 (1E 4)
TWO MILLS 4A 168
Two Saints Pl. L39: Orm 5C 24
Twyford Av. L21: Lith 4H 53
Twyford Cl. L31: Mag 3G 43
WA8: Wid 3D 114
Twyford La. WA8: Wid 1E 114
Twyford Pl. WA9: St. H 3E 74
Twyford St. L6: Liv 1D 88
Tyberton Pl. L25: Hunts X 3G 131
Tyburn Cl. CH63: Spit 7F 127
Tyburn Rd. CH63: Spit 7F 127
Tyndall Av. L22: Water 5F 53
Tyne Cl. L4: Kirk 6A 68
WA2: Warr 5E 98
WA9: St. H 1K 93
Tynemouth Cl. L5: Liv 2C 88
Tynemouth Rd. WA7: Murd 4A 154
Tynesdale CH65: Whit 1K 169
Tyne St. CH41: Birk 6K 85
Tynron Gro. CH43: Noct 4H 105
Tynville Rd. L9: Ain 6E 54
Tynwald Cl. L13: Liv 2H 89
Tynwald Cres. WA8: Wid 3B 114
Tynwald Dr. WA4: App 1C 138
Tynwald Hill L13: Liv 3H 89
Tynwald Pl. L13: Liv 3H 89
Tynwald Rd. CH48: W Kir 6C 102
Tyrer Gro. L34: Prsct 7E 72
Tyrer Rd. L39: Orm 3D 24
WA12: New W 5G 77
Tyrers Av. L31: Lyd 6D 32
Tyrers Cl. L37: Form 1K 29
Tyrer St. CH41: Birk 6K 85
L1: Liv 6K 87 (6G 4)

U

UCI Cinema 6G 97
UGC Cinema 6H 89
Uldale Cl. L11: N Grn. 4J 69
PR8: Ains 6B 14
Uldale Way L11: N Grn. 4J 69
Ullapool Cl. CH66: Lit Sut 5B 160
Ullet Rd. L8: Liv 4D 108
L17: Aig 4D 108
Ullet Wlk. L17: Aig 3F 109
Ullswater Av. CH43: Noct 2H 105
WA2: Warr 4C 98
WA11: St. H 5C 60
WN4: Ash M 1F 63
WN5: Orr 4H 39
Ullswater Cl. L33: K'by 1B 56
Ullswater Gro. WA7: Beech 5F 153
Ullswater Ho. L17: Aig 6F 109
Ullswater Rd. CH65: Ell P 2A 170
Ullswater St. L5: Liv 1C 88
Ulster Rd. L13: Liv 4K 89
Ultonia St. L19: Gars 5A 130
Ulverscroft CH43: O'ton 4K 105
Ulverston Av. WA2: Warr 4B 98
Ulverston Cl. L31: Mag 2G 43
WA11: Hay 7J 61
Ulverston Lawn L27: N'ley 4K 111
Ulverston Rd. WN3: Wigan 1D 50
Umbria St. L19: Gars 5A 130
Underbridge La. WA4: H Walt 3J 137
Undercliffe Ho. WA4: App 1D 138
Undercliffe Rd. L13: Liv 3J 89
Underhill Rd. WA10: St. H 4K 73
Underley St. L7: Liv 1E 108
Underley Ter. CH62: New F 2H 127
Underway, The WA7: Halt 2H 153
Underwood Dr.
CH65: Ell P, Whit 2K 169
Unicorn Rd. L11: Crox 2A 70
Unicorn Way CH41: Tran 3F 107
Union Bank La. WA8: Bold H 6D 94
Union Ct. L2: Liv 6J 87 (6E 4)
Union St. CH42: Tran 5E 106
CH44: Wall 3D 86
L3: Liv 5H 87 (5C 4)
PR9: South 7J 7
WA1: Warr 3B 118
WA7: Run 7D 134
WA10: St. H 1C 74
Union Ter. CH45: New B 5B 66
Unit Rd. PR8: Ains 4D 14
Unity Gro. L34: Know 7E 56
Unity Theatre 8J 5
University of Liverpool 5L 5
University of Liverpool Art Gallery
6B 88 (8L 5)
University of Liverpool Sports Cen.
6B 88
University Rd. L20: Boot 4K 67
Unsworth Ct. WA2: P'gate 6F 99
Upavon Av. CH49: Grea 5K 103
Upchurch Cl. L8: Liv 4B 108
UP HOLLAND 4E 38

Upholland Rd.—Walker St.

Upholland Rd. WN5: Bil . . . 7F 39
Upholland Station (Rail) . . . 7B 38
Upland Cl. WA10: St. H . . . 6H 73
Upland Dr. WN4: Ash M . . . 1H 63
Upland Rd. CH49: Upton . . . 2D 104
WA10: St. H . . . 6H 73
Uplands, The CH43: O'ton . . . 4J 105
WA7: Pal F . . . 3H 153
Uplands Rd. CH62: Brom . . . 1J 145
Up. Aughton Rd.
PR8: B'dale . . . 3G 11
Up. Baker St. L6: Liv . . . 4C 88 (2N 5)
Up. Beau St. L5: Liv . . . 3A 88 (1H 5)
Up. Beckwith St. CH41: Birk . . . 7B 86
UPPER BIDSTON VILLAGE . . . 6G 85
Up. Brassey St. CH41: Birk . . . 7K 85
Up. Bute St. L5: Liv . . . 3A 88 (1J 5)
Up. Duke St. L1: Liv . . . 7A 88 (9H 5)
Up. Essex St. L8: Liv . . . 3B 108
Up. Flaybrick Rd. CH41: Birk . . . 1J 105
Up. Frederick St. L1: Liv . . . 7K 87 (9F 4)
(not continuous)
Up. Hampton St.
L8: Liv . . . 1B 108 (10L 5)
Up. Harrington St. L8: Liv . . . 2A 108
Up. Hill St. L8: Liv . . . 2A 108
(not continuous)
Up. Hope Pl. L7: Liv . . . 7B 88 (8K 5)
Up. Huskisson St.
L8: Liv . . . 1C 108 (10M 5)
Up. Mann St. L8: Liv . . . 2A 108
(not continuous)
Up. Mason St. L7: Liv . . . 6C 88 (6N 5)
Up. Mersey Rd. WA8: Wid . . . 4C 134
Up. Mersey St. CH65: Ell P . . . 4A 162
Up. Newington L1: Liv . . . 6A 88 (7H 5)
Up. Park St. L8: Liv . . . 3B 108
Up. Parliament St.
L8: Liv . . . 1A 108 (10J 5)
Up. Pitt St. L1: Liv . . . 7K 87 (9G 4)
Up. Pownall St. L1: Liv . . . 7K 87 (9F 4)
Up. Raby Rd. CH64: Nest . . . 1A 158
Up. Rice La. CH44: Wall . . . 2C 86
Up. Stanhope St.
L8: Liv . . . 1A 108 (10K 5)
(not continuous)
Up. Warwick St. L8: Liv . . . 2B 108
Up. William St. L3: Liv . . . 3H 87 (1C 4)
Uppingham WN8: Skel . . . 2D 36
Uppingham Av. L10: Ain . . . 3G 55
Uppingham Rd. CH44: Wall . . . 2K 85
L13: Liv . . . 2H 89
UPTON
Widnes . . . 5J 113
Wirral . . . 3E 104
Upton Av. PR8: Ains . . . 3B 14
Upton Barn L31: Mag . . . 2E 42
Upton Bridle Path WA8: Wid . . . 4B 114
(not continuous)
Upton By-Pass CH49: Upton . . . 2C 104
Upton Cl. CH49: Upton . . . 3D 104
L24: Speke . . . 6J 131
Upton Ct. CH49: Upton . . . 2E 104
Upton Dr. WA5: Penk . . . 3D 116
Upton Grange WA8: Wid . . . 5K 113
Upton Grn. L24: Speke . . . 6J 131
Upton La. WA8: Wid . . . 4A 114
Upton Pk. Dr. CH49: Upton . . . 2E 104
Upton Rd. CH41: Birk . . . 2H 105
CH43: Bid, C'ton, Noct . . . 3G 105
CH46: More . . . 7C 84
CH66: Gt Sut . . . 7F 161
UPTON ROCKS . . . 5B 114
Upton Rocks Av. WA8: Wid . . . 4A 114
Upton Rocks M. WA8: Wid . . . 4A 114
Upton Station (Rail) . . . 3G 105
Ure Ct. CH65: Ell P . . . 1J 161
Urmson Rd. CH45: Wall . . . 2B 86
Urmston Av. WA12: New W . . . 1F 77
Ursula St. L20: Boot . . . 5K 67
Utkinton Cl. CH43: O'ton . . . 5K 105
Utting Av. L4: Walt . . . 7D 68
Utting Av. E. L11: N Grn . . . 5G 69
UVECO Bus. Cen.
CH41: Birk . . . 5A 86
Uxbridge St. L7: Liv . . . 7D 88
(not continuous)

V

Vahler Ter. WA7: Run . . . 7E 134
Vale Av. WA2: Warr . . . 7B 98
Vale Cl. L25: Wltn . . . 6D 110
Vale Ct. WA4: Dutt . . . 7E 154
Vale Cres. PR8: Ains . . . 7C 14
Vale Dr. CH45: New B . . . 7C 66
Vale Gdns. CH65: Whit . . . 7K 161
WA6: Hel . . . 7H 165
Vale Gro. L32: K'by . . . 4E 56
Vale La. L40: Lath . . . 6D 26
(not continuous)
Vale Lodge L9: Walt . . . 2B 68
Valencia Gro. L34: Ecc P . . . 7F 73
Valencia Rd. L15: W'tree . . . 7J 89
Valentia Rd. CH47: Hoy . . . 2C 102
Valentine Gro. L10: Ain . . . 4G 55
Valentine Rd. WA12: New W . . . 3D 76
Valentines Bldg. L9: Ain . . . 4E 54
Valentines Way L9: Ain . . . 3E 54
Valeowen Rd. WA2: Warr . . . 6D 98
Valerian Rd. CH41: Birk . . . 1K 105
Valerie Cl. L10: Faz . . . 7K 55
Valerie Park . . . 7D 72
Vale Rd. CH65: Whit . . . 7K 161
L23: C'by . . . 1D 52
L25: Wltn . . . 5C 110
Valescourt Rd. L12: W Der . . . 2A 90
Valeview Towers L25: Wltn . . . 6D 110
Valiant Cl. L12: Crox . . . 4E 70
WA2: P'gate . . . 5F 99
Valiant Way CH41: Tran . . . 4F 107
Valkyrie Rd. CH45: Wall . . . 2A 86
Vallance Rd. L4: Walt . . . 7E 68
Valleybrook Gro. CH63: Spit . . . 7H 127
Valley Cl. L10: Ain . . . 4H 55
L23: C'by . . . 1H 53
Valley Community Theatre . . . 3H 111
Valley Ct. WA2: P'gate . . . 6F 99
Valley Dr. CH66: Gt Sut . . . 6F 161
Valley Rd. CH41: Birk . . . 5H 85
CH62: Brom . . . 2K 145
L4: Walt . . . 1C 88
L10: Faz . . . 5J 55
L32: K'by . . . 5J 55
Valley Rd. Bus. Pk. CH41: Birk . . . 6J 85
Valley Vw. CH66: Gt Sut . . . 6F 161
WA12: New W . . . 5F 77
Vanbrugh Cres. L4: Walt . . . 7E 68
Vanbrugh Gro. WN5: Orr . . . 2K 39
Vanbrugh Rd. L4: Walt . . . 6E 68
Vancouver Rd. L27: N'ley . . . 3J 111
Vanderbilt Av. L9: Ain . . . 5D 54
Vanderbyl Av. CH62: Spit . . . 3C 144
Vandries St. L3: Liv . . . 3H 87 (1B 4)
Vandyke St. L8: Liv . . . 1D 108
Vanguard Ct. WA3: Ris . . . 3K 99
Vanguard St. L5: Liv . . . 1B 88
Vanguard Way CH41: Tran . . . 5F 107
Vardon St. CH41: Birk . . . 7C 86
Varley Rd. L19: Aig . . . 7J 109
WA9: St. H . . . 2E 74
Varlian Cl. L40: Westh . . . 7G 25
Varthen St. L5: Liv . . . 7B 68
Vatt Way L7: Liv . . . 6E 88
Vaudrey Dr. WA1: W'ston . . . 1K 119
Vaughan Cl. L37: Form . . . 6H 19
Vaughan Rd. CH45: New B . . . 7B 66
PR8: B'dale . . . 4H 11
Vaughan St. CH41: Birk . . . 7K 85
Vaux Cres. L20: Boot . . . 1K 67
VAUXHALL . . . 2J 87
Vauxhall Cl. WA5: Penk . . . 4D 116
Vauxhall Rd. L3: Liv . . . 4J 87 (2E 4)
L5: Liv . . . 3J 87 (2E 4)
Vaux Pl. L20: Boot . . . 1K 67
Venables Cl. CH63: Spit . . . 1H 145
Venables Dr. CH63: Spit . . . 7G 127
Venables Way WA16: H Legh . . . 5K 141
Venice St. L5: Liv . . . 1B 88
Venmore St. L5: Liv . . . 1B 88
(not continuous)
Venns Rd. WA2: Warr . . . 7D 98
Ventnor Cl. WA5: Gt San . . . 1A 116
Ventnor Rd. L15: W'tree . . . 7H 89
Venture Ct. *CH41: Birk* . . . *3E 106*
(off Clifton Rd.)
Venturepoint Bus. Pk.
L24: Speke . . . 4G 131
Venture Works L33: Know I . . . 4G 57
Verbena Cl. WA7: Beech . . . 6H 153
Verdala Pk. L18: Moss H . . . 6A 110
Verdi Av. L21: Sea . . . 7G 53
Verdi St. L21: Sea . . . 7F 53
Verdi Ter. L21: Sea . . . 7F 53
Vere St. L8: Liv . . . 3A 108
(not continuous)
Vermont Av. L23: C'by . . . 1D 52
Vermont Cl. L33: K'by . . . 5B 44
WA5: Gt San . . . 1G 117
Vermont Rd. L23: C'by . . . 1D 52
Vermont Way L20: Boot . . . 2J 67
Verne Wlk. WN4: Ash M . . . 2H 63
Verney Cres. L19: Aller . . . 1A 130
Verney Cres. Sth. L19: Aller . . . 1A 130
Vernon Av. CH44: Wall . . . 5D 86
CH66: Hoot . . . 1C 160
Vernon Ct. PR8: South . . . 3K 11
Vernon Rd. PR9: South . . . 7C 8
Vernon St. L2: Liv . . . 5J 87 (4E 4)
WA1: Warr . . . 4B 118
WA9: St. H . . . 2E 74
Verona St. L5: Liv . . . 1B 88
Veronica M. WA8: Wid . . . 7K 113
Veronica Way CH66: Lit Sut . . . 4F 161
Verulam Cl. L8: Liv . . . 1C 108 (10N 5)
Verulam Rd. PR9: Chu . . . 4D 8
Verwood Cl. CH61: Irby . . . 2B 124
Verwood Dr. L12: Crox . . . 3E 70
Veryan Cl. L26: Halew . . . 7K 111
Vescock St. L5: Liv . . . 2K 87
Vesta Rd. L19: Gars . . . 5B 130
Vesuvian Dr. L19: Gars . . . 5B 130
Vesuvius Pl. L5: Kirk . . . 1K 87
Vesuvius St. L5: Kirk . . . 1K 87
Vetch Cl. WA3: G'brk . . . 2K 101
Viaduct St. WA8: Wid . . . 5C 134
WA12: New W . . . 3E 76
Viallage Way WN8: Skel . . . 3D 36
Vicarage Cl. CH42: Tran . . . 7B 106
L18: Moss H . . . 6K 109
L24: Hale . . . 1E 150
L37: Form . . . 6H 19
L40: Westh . . . 7F 25
Vicarage Dr. WA11: Hay . . . 6J 61
Vicarage Gdns. *WN5: Orr* . . . *7F 39*
(off Sandy La.)
Vicarage Gro. CH44: Wall . . . 2C 86
Vicarage Hill WA6: Hel . . . 7J 165
Vicarage La. L40: Westh . . . 7F 25
PR9: Banks . . . 1H 9
WA6: Frod . . . 4E 166
WA6: Hel . . . 7J 165
Vicarage Lawn L25: Gate . . . 3G 111
Vicarage Pl. L34: Prsct . . . 1C 92
Vicarage Rd. L37: Form . . . 6H 19
WA8: Wid . . . 2C 134
WA11: Hay . . . 6J 61
WN4: Ash M . . . 3F 63
WN5: Orr . . . 7F 39
Vicarage Subway WA2: P'gate . . . 6G 99
Vicarage Wlk. L39: Orm . . . 5C 24
WA4: S Hth . . . 1C 138
Vicar Rd. L6: Liv . . . 7E 68
Viceroy Ct. PR8: South . . . 2G 11
Viceroy St. L5: Liv . . . 1B 88
Vickers Dr. WN8: Skel . . . 3A 38
Vickers Rd. WA8: Wid . . . 4A 134
Vicoria Leisure & Fitness . . . 7H 7
Victoria Av. CH60: Hes . . . 4E 142
L14: B Grn . . . 5B 90
L15: W'tree . . . 7H 89
L23: Blun . . . 1C 52
WA4: Grap . . . 6G 119
WA5: Gt San . . . 2B 116
WA8: Wid . . . 5C 114
WA11: St. H . . . 5C 60
Victoria Bri. Rd. PR8: South . . . 2J 11
Victoria Bldgs. L37: Form . . . 5J 19
Victoria Cl. L17: Aig . . . 5G 109
Victoria Ct. L15: W'tree . . . 7H 89
L17: Aig . . . 4D 108
PR8: B'dale . . . 4F 11
(not continuous)
WN8: Skel . . . 2C 36
Victoria Dr. CH42: R Ferr . . . 7G 107
CH48: W Kir . . . 6C 102
L9: Walt . . . 7B 54
Victoria Falls Rd. L27: N'ley . . . 4K 111
Victoria Flds. CH42: Tran . . . 4C 106
Victoria Gdns. CH43: O'ton . . . 4B 106
Victoria Gro. WA8: Wid . . . 5C 114
Victoria Hall L2: Liv . . . 4E 4
Victoria Ho. L34: Prsct . . . 1D 92
WA11: R'ford . . . 5F 47
Victoria La. CH43: O'ton . . . 4B 106
Victoria Leisure & Fitness . . . 7K 19
Victoria M. CH65: Ell P . . . 6K 161
Victoria Mt. CH43: O'ton . . . 4B 106
Victoria Pde. CH45: New B . . . 5C 66
VICTORIA PARK
Bootle . . . 6A 54
Liverpool . . . 7H 89
Victoria Pk.
Birchfield Rd. . . . 6C 114
City Rd. . . . 7B 60
Knutsford Rd. . . . 4D 118
Victoria Pk. WN8: Skel . . . 2C 36
Victoria Pk. Arena . . . 4D 118
Victoria Pk. Glasshouses . . . 7C 114
Victoria Pk. Rd. CH42: Tran . . . 6D 106
Victoria Pl. CH44: Wall . . . 5E 86
L35: R'hill . . . 4J 93
WA4: S Hth . . . 7C 118
Victoria Prom. WA8: Wid . . . 5C 134
Victoria Rd. CH42: Tran . . . 4C 106
CH45: New B . . . 6A 66
CH48: W Kir . . . 7D 102
CH63: High B . . . 3D 126
CH64: Lit N . . . 5K 157
CH65: Ell P . . . 6K 161
L13: Liv . . . 1G 89
L17: Aig . . . 5G 109
L22: Water . . . 5E 52
L23: C'by . . . 1D 52
L36: Huy . . . 5K 91
L37: Form . . . 5F 19
L38: Ince B . . . 1E 40
L39: Augh . . . 7A 24
WA4: Grap . . . 6F 119
WA4: S Hth . . . 7D 118
WA5: Gt San . . . 4F 117
WA5: Penk . . . 4B 116
WA7: Run . . . 7C 134
(not continuous)
WA8: Wid . . . 2C 134
WA12: New W . . . 2G 77
WN2: Platt B . . . 3K 51
WN4: Gars . . . 2B 62
Victoria Rd. W. L23: Blun . . . 1C 52
Victoria Sq. WA4: S Hth . . . 7C 118
WA8: Wid . . . 2C 134
WA10: St. H . . . 2C 74
Victoria St. CH62: Port S . . . 4H 127
L1: Liv . . . 5J 87 (6E 4)
L2: Liv . . . 6J 87 (6E 4)
L35: R'hill . . . 4J 93
PR9: South . . . 7H 7
WA1: Warr . . . 3C 118
WA8: Wid . . . 2D 134
WA10: St. H . . . 1C 74
WA11: R'ford . . . 5F 47
Victoria Ter. *L15: W'tree* . . . *2J 109*
(off Pearson Ct., not continuous)
L35: R'hill . . . 4J 93
Victoria Trad Est. L35: R'hill . . . 4J 93
Victoria Trad. Est. WA8: Wid . . . 3C 134
Victoria Vs. L35: R'hill . . . 4J 93
Victoria Way L37: Form . . . 5H 19
PR8: South . . . 1F 11
Victor St. L15: W'tree . . . 7F 89
Victory Av. PR9: South . . . 1C 12
Victory Cl. L30: Boot . . . 5A 54
Vienna St. L5: Liv . . . 1B 88
Viennese Rd. L25: Gate . . . 2F 111
Viewpark Cl. L16: Child . . . 1D 110
View Rd. L35: R'hill . . . 5J 93
Viking Cl. L21: Lith . . . 6G 53
PR8: B'dale . . . 4G 11
Villagate La. WA4: App T . . . 5K 139
Village, The CH63: Beb . . . 3G 127
WA3: Ris . . . 2B 100
Village Cl. CH45: Wall . . . 1J 85
WA4: Thel . . . 4A 120
WA7: Cas . . . 2J 153
WN8: Skel . . . 3D 36
Village Ct. CH61: Irby . . . 3B 124
L17: Aig . . . 6E 108
Village Courts L30: N'ton . . . 7B 42
Village Grn. Ct. CH43: Bid . . . 7G 85
Village M. CH45: Wall . . . 1J 85
Village Nook L10: Ain . . . 3G 55
Village Rd. CH43: O'ton . . . 4A 106
CH48: W Kir . . . 6E 102
CH60: Hes . . . 3D 142
CH63: High B . . . 3D 126
WA6: Dun H . . . 7E 172
Village Sq. CH64: Will . . . 3F 159
Village St. L6: Liv . . . 3B 88 (1K 5)
WA7: Nort . . . 7B 136
Village Vw. WN5: Bil . . . 7G 49
Village Way CH45: Wall . . . 1J 85
L38: High . . . 5F 29
Villa Gloria Cl. L19: Aig . . . 1J 129
Villars St. WA1: Warr . . . 3C 118
Villas Rd. L31: Mag . . . 3K 43
Villiers Ct. L34: Know . . . 1F 71
Villiers Cres. WA10: Eccl . . . 1F 73
Villiers Rd. L34: Know . . . 7F 57
Vincent Cl. WA5: Old H . . . 7G 97
Vincent Ct. L1: Liv . . . 7K 87 (9G 4)
Vincent Naughton Ct. CH41: Birk . . . 3E 106
Vincent Rd. L21: Lith . . . 4J 53
L35: R'hill . . . 3H 93
Vincent St. CH41: Birk . . . 2D 106
L13: Liv . . . 6H 89
WA10: St. H . . . 2C 74
Vine Cres. WA5: Gt San . . . 2D 116
Vineries, The L25: Wltn . . . 5C 110
Vine Rd. CH66: Gt Sut . . . 3H 169
Vineside Rd. L12: W Der . . . 2B 90
Vine St. CH41: Birk . . . 1C 106
L7: Liv . . . 7B 88 (9M 5)
WA7: Run . . . 7C 134
WA8: Wid . . . 2C 134
Vine Ter. WA8: Wid . . . 6G 113
Vineyard St. L19: Gars . . . 4C 130
Vining Rd. L35: Prsct . . . 1F 93
Vining St. L8: Liv . . . 2B 108
Viola Cl. L33: K'by . . . 7B 44
Viola St. L20: Boot . . . 5J 67
Violet Cl. WA3: Bchwd . . . 3J 99
(not continuous)
Violet Rd. CH41: Birk . . . 1K 105
L21: Lith . . . 7H 53
Violet St. WA8: Wid . . . 2C 134
WN4: Ash M . . . 3J 63
Virgil St. L5: Liv . . . 3K 87 (1G 4)
WA10: St. H . . . 2A 74
Virginia Av. L31: Lyd . . . 1E 42
Virginia Gdns. WA5: Gt San . . . 7F 97
Virginia Gro. L31: Lyd . . . 1E 42
Virginia Rd. CH45: New B . . . 5B 66
Virginia St. L3: Liv . . . 5H 87 (4C 4)
PR8: South . . . 2J 11
Virginia Ter. CH66: Chil T . . . 3D 160
Virgin's La. L23: Thorn . . . 5F 41
Viscount Cen. L24: Speke . . . 4H 131
Viscount Dr. L24: Hale . . . 7J 131
Viscount Rd. WA2: P'gate . . . 5E 98
Vista Av. WA12: New W . . . 2E 76
Vista Rd. WA7: Run . . . 2C 152
WA11: Hay . . . 6E 62
WA12: New W . . . 2E 76
Vista Way WA12: New W . . . 2E 76
Vitesse Rd. L24: Speke . . . 3D 130
Vittoria Cl. CH41: Birk . . . 1D 106
Vittoria Ct. CH41: Birk . . . 1D 106
Vittoria St. CH41: Birk . . . 1C 106
Vivian Av. CH44: Wall . . . 5E 86
Vivian Dr. PR8: B'dale . . . 6G 11
Vixen Gro. WA8: Wid . . . 4B 114
Voce's La. L39: Bic . . . 1F 45
Voelas St. L8: Liv . . . 2C 108
Vogan Av. L23: C'by . . . 2G 53
Volunteer St. WA6: Frod . . . 2F 167
WA10: St. H . . . 2B 74
Vose Cl. WA5: Gt San . . . 2H 117
Vronhill Cl. L8: Liv . . . 2C 108
Vue Cinema
Birkenhead . . . 2D 106
Cheshire Oaks . . . 2B 170
Marine Dr. . . . 7G 7
Vulcan Cl. CH41: Birk . . . 7K 85
WA2: P'gate . . . 5F 99
WA12: New W . . . 5G 77
Vulcan Ct. PR9: South . . . 1J 11
Vulcan Gym & Fitness . . . 4G 77
Vulcan Ind. Est. WA12: New W . . . 5H 77
Vulcan St. CH41: Birk . . . 7K 85
L3: Liv . . . 3H 87 (1B 4)
L19: Gars . . . 5A 130
L20: Boot . . . 2G 67
PR9: South . . . 1J 11
Vyner Cl. CH43: Noct . . . 2J 105
Vyner Ct. CH43: Noct . . . 2J 105
Vyner Rd. CH45: Wall . . . 2K 85
Vyner Rd. Nth.
CH43: Bid . . . 1H 105
L25: Gate . . . 3E 110
Vyner Rd. Sth.
CH43: Bid . . . 2H 105
L25: Gate . . . 3E 110
Vyrnwy St. L5: Liv . . . 7B 68

W

WADDICAR . . . 1K 55
Waddicar La. L31: Mell . . . 2J 55
Waddington Cl. WA2: P'gate . . . 6F 99
Wadebridge Rd. L10: Faz . . . 7J 55
Wadeson Rd. L4: Walt . . . 4F 69
Wadeson Way WA3: Croft . . . 7H 79
Wadham Pk. L20: Boot . . . 4J 67
Wadham Rd. L20: Boot . . . 5J 67
Wagon La. WA11: Hay . . . 2J 75
Waine Gro. L35: Whis . . . 2G 93
Waine St. WA9: St. H . . . 2F 75
WA11: Hay . . . 7H 61
Wainfleet Cl. WN3: Wins . . . 1C 50
Wainwright Cl. L7: Liv . . . 7D 88
Wainwright Gro. L19: Gars . . . 3K 129
Wakefield Dr. CH46: Leas . . . 3D 84
Wakefield Rd. CH66: Gt Sut . . . 3G 169
L30: N'ton . . . 3C 54
Wakefield St. L3: Liv . . . 4A 88 (3H 5)
WA3: Golb . . . 6K 63
Walby Cl. CH49: W'chu . . . 6G 105
Walcot Pl. WN3: Wigan . . . 2D 50
Walden Cl. WA4: Thel . . . 5K 119
Walden Dr. CH1: W'bnk . . . 4A 168
Walden Rd. L14: K Ash . . . 4A 90
Waldgrave Pl. L15: W'tree . . . 6K 89
Waldgrave Rd. L15: W'tree . . . 6J 89
Waldorf Cl. WN3: Wins . . . 2B 50
Waldron WN8: Skel . . . 3D 36
Waldron Cl. L3: Liv . . . 4J 87 (3E 4)
Walford Cl. CH63: Spit . . . 7F 127
Walford Rd. WN4: Ash M . . . 2G 63
Walk, The L24: Speke . . . 7D 130
L28: Stock V . . . 7G 71
PR8: B'dale . . . 4G 11
Walkden Ho. WN4: Ash M . . . 7D 50
Walker Av. WA9: Sut M . . . 4D 94
Walker Cl. L37: Form . . . 1K 29
Walker Dr. L20: Boot . . . 6J 53
Walker Gallery, The . . . 5K 87 (4G 4)
Walker M. CH42: Tran . . . 5D 106
Walker Pl. CH42: Tran . . . 5D 106
Walker Rd. L21: Lith . . . 6G 53
Walker's Cft. CH45: Wall . . . 2K 85
Walkers La. CH66: Lit Sut . . . 5E 160
WA5: Penk . . . 5C 116
WA9: Sut M . . . 4C 94
Walker St. CH42: Tran . . . 5D 106
CH47: Hoy . . . 1D 102
CH62: Port S . . . 3H 127
L6: Liv . . . 4C 88 (3M 5)
WA2: Warr . . . 2A 118

234 A-Z Merseyside

Walker Way—Weller St.

Walker Way L9: Walt 7B **54**
Wallace Av. L36: Huy 3A **92**
Wallace Dr. L36: Huy 3K **91**
Wallace St. L9: Ain 7C **54**
WA8: Wid 1C **134**
Wallacre Rd. CH44: Wall 3J **85**
WALLASEY 2J **85**
Wallasey Bri. Rd. CH41: Birk 6K **85**
Wallasey Grove Road (Rail) 1J **85**
Wallasey Rd. CH44: Wall 3K **85**
CH45: Wall 3K **85**
Wallasey Village CH44: Wall 2J **85**
CH45: Wall 1J **85**
Wallasey Village Station (Rail) 2J **85**
Wallbrook Av. WN5: Bil 3F **49**
Wallcroft CH64: Will 4G **159**
Wallcroft St. WN8: Skel 3E **36**
Waller Cl. L4: Kirk 7A **68**
Waller St. L20: Boot 7G **53**
Wallgarth Cl. WN3: Wins 2C **50**
Wallgate Rd. L25: Gate 1D **110**
Wallgate Way L25: Gate 2D **110**
Wallingford Rd. CH49: Upton 4D **104**
Wallis St. WA4: Warr 5B **118**
Wallrake CH60: Hes 3D **142**
Wallsend Ct. WA8: Wid 5B **114**
Walmer Ct. PR8: B'dale 4F **11**
Walmer Rd. L22: Water 5E **52**
PR8: B'dale 5G **11**
Walmersley Dr. WA11: R'ford 7G **47**
Walmesley Rd. WA10: Eccl 1G **73**
Walmsley St. CH44: Wall 2C **86**
WA8: Wid 1E **134**
WA12: New W 2H **77**
Walney Rd. L12: W Der 6J **69**
WN3: Wins 2B **50**
Walney Ter. L12: W Der 6J **69**
Walnut Av. L9: Walt 3E **68**
Walnut Cl. WA1: W'ston 1A **120**
Walnut Gro. CH66: Whit 3H **169**
L31: Mell 2J **55**
WA9: St. H 6D **74**
Walnut St. L7: Liv 6B **88** (7L **5**)
PR8: South 4J **11**
Walnut Tree La. WA4: App 5F **139**
Walpole Av. L35: Whis 4F **93**
WN3: Wigan 1D **50**
Walpole Gro. WA2: Warr 5C **98**
Walpole Rd. WA7: Run 3D **152**
Walro M. PR9: Chu 4C **8**
Walsham Gdns. WA9: St. H 1A **94**
Walsh Cl. L5: Liv 3J **87** (1E **4**)
WA12: New W 1G **77**
Walsh Rd. L14: B Grn 5A **90**
(not continuous)
Walsingham Ct. *CH44: Wall 4D 86*
(off Liscard Rd.)
Walsingham Dr. WA7: Nort 7B **136**
Walsingham Rd. CH44: Wall 4D **86**
L16: Child 6C **90**
WA5: Penk 3D **116**
Walter Beilin Ct. L17: Aig 3G **109**
Walter Gro. WA9: St. H 7H **75**
Walters Grn. Cres.
WA3: Golb 3K **63**
Walter St. L5: Liv 2H **87**
WA1: Warr 1E **118**
WA8: Wid 7F **115**
WN4: Ash M 7H **51**
Waltham Ct. WA7: Nort 5C **136**
Waltham Rd. L6: Liv 1E **88**
WALTHEW GREEN 1E **38**
Walthew Ho. La. WN5: Wigan 2K **39**
(not continuous)
Walthew La. WN2: Platt B 1K **51**
(not continuous)
Waltho Av. L31: Mag 3G **43**
WALTON
Liverpool 4C **68**
Warrington 1A **138**
Walton Av. WA5: Penk 3C **116**
Walton Breck Rd. L4: Walt 7B **68**
Walton Hall Av. L4: Walt 4C **68**
L11: N Grn. 3F **69**
Walton Hall Gardens & Childreb's Zoo
. . . . . 2A **138**
Walton Heath Rd. WA4: Walt 7B **118**
Walton La. L4: Walt 7B **68**
WA3: Ris 2A **100**
Walton Lea Crematorium
WA4: H Walt 2A **138**
Walton Lea Rd. WA4: H Walt 2K **137**
(not continuous)
Walton Lodge Rd. L9: Walt 2B **68**
Walton Pk. L9: Walt 2C **68**
Walton Pk. Gdns. L4: Walt 4C **68**
Walton Rd. L4: Walt 7A **68**
WA3: Cul 3B **80**
WA4: Walt 1B **138**
WA10: St. H 7K **59**
Walton Sports Cen. 4D **68**
Walton Station (Rail) 2B **68**
Walton St. CH41: Birk 2E **106**
PR9: South 7J **7**
WA7: Run 7C **134**
Walton Va. L9: Walt, Ain 7C **54**
Walton Village L4: Walt 4B **68**
(not continuous)
Wambo La. L25: Gate 3G **111**
Wandsworth Rd. L11: N Grn. 5H **69**
Wandsworth Way WA8: Wid 3B **134**
Wango La. L10: Ain 4G **55**
Wanishar La. L39: Has 5C **22**
Wansfell Pl. WA2: Warr 4A **98**
Wantage Vw. L36: Roby 6G **91**
Wapping L1: Liv 7J **87** (8E **4**)
Wapping Quay L3: Liv 1J **107** (10E **4**)
Wapshare Rd. L11: N Grn. 5G **69**
Warbler Cl. L26: Halew 6H **111**
Warbreck Av. L9: Walt, Ain 6C **54**
Warbreck Moor L9: Ain 6D **54**
WARBRECK PARK 6D **54**
Warbreck Rd. L9: Walt 7C **54**
WARBURTON 7K **101**
Warburton Bri. Rd. WA3: Rix 6J **101**
Warburton Bri Rd. WA13: Warb 6J **101**
Warburton Cl. WA13: Lymm 4J **121**
Warburton Hey L35: R'hill 3H **93**
Warburton St. WA4: S Hth 7D **118**
Warburton Vw. WA3: Rix 5J **101**
Ward Av. L37: Form 1H **29**
Ward Cl. WA5: W'brk 6F **97**
Warden St. L4: Kirk 6A **68**
Wardgate Av. L12: Crox 3C **70**
Ward Gro. CH42: R Ferr 1F **127**
Wardley Rd. WA4: Walt 7B **118**
Wardley St. WN5: Wigan 6K **39**
Wardlow Av. WN5: Orr 2J **39**
Wardour St. WA5: Warr 2J **117**
Ward Rake L30: N'ton 1K **53**
Ward Rd. L23: Blun 7A **40**
Ward St. L3: Liv 5A **88** (5H **5**)
L34: Prsct 7D **72**
WA10: St. H 2C **74**
Ware Cl. WN4: Ash M 1H **63**
Wareham Cl. WA1: W'ston 7J **99**
WA11: Hay 7A **62**
Wareing Rd. L9: Ain 7E **54**
Waresley Cres. L9: Faz 2G **69**
WARGRAVE 3G **77**
Wargrave M. WA12: New W 5G **77**
Wargrave Rd. WA12: New W 3F **77**
Warham Rd. L4: Walt 7E **68**
Waring Av. CH42: Tran 6D **106**
WA4: Westy 3F **119**
WA9: St. H 4K **75**
Warkworth Cl. L36: Huy 7B **92**
WA8: Wid 5J **113**
Warkworth Ct. CH65: Ell P 1C **170**
Warmington Rd. L14: K Ash 4A **90**
Warminster Gro. WN3: Wins 2B **50**
Warner Dr. L4: Walt 6E **68**
Warnerville Rd. L13: Liv 6K **89**
Warnley Cl. WA8: Wid 5K **113**
Warren, The CH49: Upton 3F **105**
WA12: New W 3E **76**
Warren Ct. CH66: Gt Sut 1F **169**
PR8: B'dale 3E **10**
WA6: Frod 5F **167**
Warren Cft. WA7: Nort 3A **154**
Warrender Dr. CH43: Bid 7K **85**
Warren Dr. CH43: Bid 2G **105**
CH45: Wall, New B 6K **65**
CH66: Ell P 4G **161**
WA4: App 1C **138**
WA12: New W 2K **77**
Warren Grn. L37: Form 6H **19**
Warren Hey CH63: Spit 7G **127**
Warrenhouse Rd. L22: Water 3B **52**
L33: K'by 1E **56**
Warren Hurst CH45: New B 6A **66**
Warren La. WA1: W'ston 7K **99**
Warren Pk. CH45: Wall 7K **65**
Warren Rd. CH47: Hoy 1C **102**
L23: Blun 7A **40**
PR9: South 7C **8**
WA2: Warr 6D **98**
WA4: App 2C **138**
Warren St. L3: Liv 6A **88** (6J **5**)
Warren Way CH60: Hes 1B **142**
Warrington Av. CH65: Whit 2K **169**
Warrington Bank Quay Station (Rail)
. . . . . 4K **117**
Warrington Bus. Pk. WA2: Warr 6C **98**
Warrington Central Station (Rail)
. . . . . 2B **118**
Warrington Central Trad. Est.
WA2: Warr 2A **118**
Warrington Corporate Bus. Cen.
WA1: Warr 3B 118
(off Westminster Pl.)
Warrington New Rd. WA9: St. H 3D **74**
Warrington Old Rd. WA9: St. H 4D **74**
Warrington RLFC 2A **118**
Warrington Rd. L34: Prsct 1D **92**
L35: Prsct, Whis 1D **92**
L35: R'hill 3H **93**
WA3: Bchwd 4J **99**
WA3: Cul, Ris, G'bury 1E **80**
(not continuous)
WA4: Hatt, H Walt 4J **137**
WA5: Penk 4B **116**
WA7: Cas 7G **135**
WA7: Mnr P 5J **135**
(not continuous)
WA8: Bold H 7B **94**
WA8: Wid 1E **134**
WA12: New W 1A **78**
WA13: Lymm 5C **120**
WN3: Wigan 1D **50**
WN4: Ash M 3F **63**
Warrington Sports Club 2A **138**
Warrington St. CH41: Tran 4E **106**
Warton Cl. L25: Wltn 6G **111**
WA5: Penk 5E **116**
Warton St. L20: Boot 7G **53**
Warton Ter. L20: Boot 7H **53**
Warwick Av. L23: C'by 2D **52**
WA5: Gt San 1B **116**
WA5: Warr 1K **117**
WA12: New W 4H **77**
WN4: Ash M 3H **63**
Warwick Cl. CH43: O'ton 3C **106**
CH64: Nest 6J **157**
L36: Huy 4A **92**
PR8: South 4H **11**
Warwick Ct. CH65: Ell P 2C **170**
L8: Liv 2C **108**
Warwick Dr. CH45: Wall 1C **86**
CH48: W Kir 1E **122**
Warwick Gro. WA7: Cas 1H **153**
Warwick Rd. CH49: Upton 3C **104**
L20: Boot 2K **67**
L36: Huy 4A **92**
Warwick St. L8: Liv 2K **107**
PR8: South 4H **11**
WA10: St. H 3K **73**
Wasdale Av. L31: Mag 2G **43**
WA11: St. H 5D **60**
Wasdale Rd. L9: Walt 1C **68**
WN4: Ash M 4E **50**
Washbrook Av. CH43: Bid 6G **85**
Washbrook Cl. WA10: Eccl 2H **73**
Washbrook Way L39: Orm 6C **24**
Washington Cl. WA8: Wid 5B **114**
Washington Dr. L33: K'by 6B **44**
WA5: Gt San 1G **117**
Washington Pde. L20: Boot 2J **67**
Washington Rd. L27: N'ley 4K **111**
Wash La. WA4: Latch 5E **118**
Washway La. WA10: St. H 6B **60**
WA11: St. H 6C **60**
Wasley Cl. WA2: Fearn 4F **99**
Wastdale Ct. CH46: More 6A **84**
Wastdale Dr. CH46: More 6A **84**
Wastdale M. CH46: More 6A **84**
Wastle Bri. Rd. L36: Huy 2J **91**
Watchyard La. L37: Form 7A **20**
Waterbridge Ct. WA4: App 1D **138**
WA13: Lymm 5E **120**
Waterdale Cres. WA9: St. H 7F **75**
Waterdale Pl. WA9: St. H 7F **75**
Waterfall Dr. L4: Walt 3C **68**
L9: Walt 3C **68**
Waterfield Cl. CH63: High B 4D **126**
Waterfield Way L21: Lith 4G **53**
Waterfoot Av. PR8: Ains 6B **14**
Waterford Cl. WN2: Platt B 1K **51**
Waterford Dr. CH64: Lit N 4A **158**
Waterford Rd. CH43: O'ton 3K **105**
L27: N'ley 2G **111**
Waterford Way WA7: Murd 4A **154**
(not continuous)
Waterfront WA4: Pres H 4D **154**
Waterfront Bus. Area Parliament St. Nth.
L1: Liv 10G **4**
L1: Liv 1K 107
(off Bird St.)
Waterfront Bus. Area Parliament St. Sth.
L8: Liv 1K **107**
Watergate La. L25: Wltn 6F **111**
Watergate Way L25: Wltn 6F **111**
Waterhouse Cl. L6: Liv 1D **88**
Waterhouse St. L5: Liv 2B **88**
Waterland La. WA9: St. H 4H **75**
Water La. L35: Tar G 4C **112**
PR9: Cros 2F **9**
WA8: Cron 4C **112**
WATERLOO 4E **52**
Waterloo Cen. WA8: Wid 3C **134**
Waterloo Cl. CH65: Ell P 6A **162**
L22: Water 5D **52**
Waterloo Ct. CH63: Beb 3G **127**
Waterloo Docks L3: Liv 4H **87** (2B **4**)
WATERLOO PARK 4F **53**
Waterloo Pl. CH41: Birk 3E **106**
Waterloo Quay L3: Liv 4G **87** (2B **4**)
Waterloo Rd. CH45: New B 5B **66**
L3: Liv 3H **87** (1B **4**)
L21: Sea 6F **53**
L22: Water 5E **52**
PR8: B'dale 6E **10**
WA7: Run 7B **134**
(not continuous)
WA8: Wid 4C **134**
Waterloo Station (Rail) 4E **52**
Waterloo St. L15: W'tree 1J **109**
WA10: St. H 3B **74**
Watermead Dr. WA7: Pres B 5D **154**
Watermede WN5: Bil 1G **49**
Waterpark Cl. CH43: Pren 7K **105**
Waterpark Dr. L28: Stock V 6D **70**
Waterpark Ho. CH42: Tran 6B **106**
Waterpark Rd. CH42: Tran 6A **106**
CH43: Pren 7K **105**
Watersedge WA6: Frod 1F **167**
Watersedge Apartments
CH45: New B 5C **66**
Waterside L30: N'ton 7A **42**
WA4: App 1D **138**
WA9: St. H 2D **74**
Waterside Ct. WA7: Run 6A **134**
WA9: St. H 2D **74**
Waterside Dr. WA6: Frod 1E **166**
Waterside La. WA8: Hale B 4J **133**
Waterside Pk. L36: Roby 5H **91**
Waterstone Cl. L11: N Grn. 3K **69**
Water St. CH41: Birk 2F **107**
CH44: Wall 3D **86**
CH62: Port S 4J **127**
L2: Liv 6H **87** (6C **4**)
L3: Liv 6H **87** (6C **4**)
L22: Water 5D **52**
L23: Thorn 6H **41**
WA7: Run 6C **134**
WA8: Wid 3C **134**
WA10: St. H 3B **74**
WA12: New W 2G **77**
Water Tower Rd. CH64: Nest 2J **157**
Waterway Av. L30: N'ton 2D **54**
Waterways WA5: Gt San 2H **117**
Waterworks Dr. WA12: New W 2K **77**
Waterworks La. CH66: Hoot 2A **160**
WA2: Win 1B **98**
Waterworks Rd. L39: Orm 4E **24**
Waterworks St. L20: Boot 2K **67**
Watery La. WA2: Win 1J **97**
WA6: Frod 5G **167**
WA9: St. H 6G **75**
WA10: Windle 7H **59**
WA11: Windle 6F **59**
Watford Rd. L4: Walt 7C **68**
Watkin Cl. L30: N'ton 4D **54**
Watkins Av. WA12: New W 3D **76**
Watkinson St. L1: Liv 1K **107** (10F **4**)
Watkinson Way WA8: Wid 7B **94**
Watkin St. WA2: Warr 1B **118**
Watling Av. L21: Lith 4G **53**
Watling Way L35: Whis 1G **93**
Watmough St. L5: Liv 3A **88** (1J **5**)
Watson Av. WA3: Golb 4K **63**
WN4: Ash M 2G **63**
Watson St. CH41: Birk 1D **106**
Watton Beck Cl. L31: Mag 2H **43**
Watton Cl. L12: Crox 4E **70**
WA4: Thel 5J **119**
Watts Clift Way WA9: St. H 3D **74**
Watts Cl. L33: K'by 1E **56**
Watts La. L20: Boot 7A **54**
Wauchope St. L15: W'tree 7G **89**
Wavell Av. PR9: South 1D **12**
WA8: Wid 1J **133**
Wavell Cl. PR9: South 1D **12**
Wavell Rd. L36: Huy 3J **91**
Waverley WN8: Skel 2D **36**
Waverley Av. WA4: App 1D **138**
Waverley Ct. WN3: Wins 1B **50**
Waverley Dr. L34: Prsct 2K **91**
Waverley Gro. CH42: Tran 6C **106**
Waverley Ho. L19: Aig 2H **129**
Waverley Rd. CH47: Hoy 1E **102**
L17: Aig 4E **108**
L23: Blun 1C **52**
Waverley St. L20: Boot 3H **67**
PR8: South 1G **11**
Waverton Av. CH43: O'ton 6J **105**
Waverton Rd. CH66: Gt Sut 6G **161**
WAVERTREE 1G **109**
Wavertree Athletics Cen. 1H **109**
Waver Tree Av. WA8: Wid 1B **134**
Wavertree Av. L13: W'tree 6G **89**
Wavertree Blvd. L7: Liv 6F **89**
Wavertree Blvd. Sth. L7: Liv 6G **89**
Wavertree Bus. Pk. L15: W'tree 7H **89**
Wavertree Ct. CH66: Ell P 4H **161**
Wavertree Gdns. L15: W'tree 1H **109**
WAVERTREE GREEN 2J **109**
Wavertree Grn. L15: W'tree 1J **109**
Wavertree Ho. *L13: Liv 6J 89*
(off Binns Rd.)
Wavertree Nook Rd. L15: W'tree 6K **89**
(not continuous)
Wavertree Retail Pk. L7: Liv 6E **88**
Wavertree Rd. L7: Liv 6D **88** (6P **5**)
Wavertree Technology Pk.
L7: Liv 5G **89**
L13: W'tree 6G **89**
Wavertree Technology Park Station (Rail)
. . . . . 6H **89**
Wavertree Trad. Est.
L15: W'tree 1G **109**
Wavertree Va. L15: W'tree 7F **89**
Wayfarers Arc. PR8: South 1H **11**
Wayfarers Dr. WA12: New W 4J **77**
Wayford Cl. WA6: Frod 2D **166**
Waylands Dr. L25: Hunts X 2F **131**
Wayside Cl. WA13: Lymm 6F **121**
Wayville Cl. L18: Moss H 6J **109**
Waywell Cl. WA2: Fearn 4F **99**
Weald Dr. CH66: Lit Sut 5C **160**
Weardale Rd. L15: W'tree 2G **109**
Wearhead Cl. WA3: Golb 6K **63**
Weasdale Cl. WA9: St. H 7F **75**
Weaste La. WA4: Thel 7K **119**
Weates Cl. WA8: Wid 5G **115**
Weatherby CH49: W'chu 4F **105**
Weaver Av. L33: K'by 6D **44**
L35: R'hill 4H **93**
Weaver Ct. L25: Gate 5G **111**
Weaver Cres. WA6: Frod 2F **167**
Weaver Gro. WA9: St. H 3J **75**
Weaver Ho. *L25: Gate 5G 111*
(off Woodsome Pk.)
Weaver Ind. Est. L19: Gars 5A **130**
Weaver La. WA6: Frod 1D **166**
Weaver Pk. Ind. Est. WA6: Frod 1F **167**
Weaver Rd. CH65: Ell P 1A **170**
WA3: Cul 4C **80**
WA6: Frod 2F **167**
WA7: West 4C **152**
Weavers Fold WA1: Warr 2C **118**
Weaverside Av. WA7: Sut W 6H **153**
Weavers La. L31: Mag 6H **43**
Weaver St. L9: Walt 3B **68**
Weaver Vw. WA7: West 4B **152**
Webb Cl. L7: Liv 6E **88**
Webb Dr. WA5: B'wood 1D **96**
Webber Rd. L33: Know I 4F **57**
Webb St. L7: Liv 1E **108**
WA9: St. H 5F **75**
Web Complex L33: Know I 5G **57**
Webster Av. CH44: Wall 2D **86**
L20: Boot 2A **68**
Webster Dr. L32: K'by 3C **56**
Webster Rd. L7: Liv 1E **108**
Websters Holt CH49: Upton 2D **104**
Websters La. CH66: Gt Sut 2H **169**
Webster St. L3: Liv 5K **87** (4F **4**)
L21: Lith 6H **53**
WN2: Platt B 1K **51**
Weddell Cl. WA5: Old H 1H **117**
Wedge Av. WA11: Hay 1J **75**
Wedgewood Gdns. WA9: St. H 1H **93**
Wedgewood St. L7: Liv 5D **88**
Wedgwood Dr. WA8: Wid 3D **114**
Wednesbury Dr. WA5: Gt San 2D **116**
Weedon Av. WA12: New W 1F **77**
Weightman Gro. L9: Ain 7C **54**
Weint, The WA3: Rix 4K **101**
Weir La. WA1: W'ston 2A **120**
WA4: Warr 4D **118**
Weirside WA9: St. H 1F **95**
Weir St. WA4: Warr 7A **118**
Welbeck Av. L18: Moss H 3H **109**
WA12: New W 4H **77**
Welbeck Ct. *L22: Water 4D 52*
(off Mt. Pleasant)
Welbeck Rd. PR8: B'dale 4F **11**
WN3: Wigan 1C **50**
WN4: Ash M 7G **51**
Welbeck Ter. PR8: B'dale 4G **11**
Welbourne WN8: Skel 3D **36**
Welbourne Rd. L16: Child 6A **90**
Welburn Cl. WN5: Orr 6G **39**
Weldale Ho. *PR8: B'dale 4F 11*
(off Chase Cl.)
Weld Blundell Av.
L31: Lyd 6D **32**
Weld Dr. L37: Form 6H **19**
Weldon Dr. L39: Orm 6D **24**
Weldon St. L4: Walt 4B **68**
Weld Pde. PR8: B'dale 4F **11**
Weld Rd. L23: Blun 2C **52**
PR8: B'dale 3E **10**
Welfield Pl. L8: Liv 4C **108**
Welford Av. CH43: Pren 6K **105**
Welham Rd. WN3: Wigan 1F **51**
Welland Cl. L26: Halew 3J **131**
Welland Rd. CH63: High B 4D **126**
WN4: Ash M 7J **51**
Wellbank Dr. L26: Halew 7A **112**
Wellbrae Cl. CH49: Upton 3B **104**
Wellbrook Cl. L24: Speke 5H **131**
WA7: Brook 5A **154**
Wellbrook Grn. L24: Speke 6H **131**
Wellbrow Rd. L4: Walt 4C **68**
Well Cl. CH64: Ness 7A **158**
Wellcroft Rd. L36: Huy 3J **91**
Wellcross Rd. WN8: Uph 5D **38**
Weller St. L8: Liv 3B **108**

Wingfield Cl.—Wrenbury Cl.

Wingfield Cl. L29: Seft . . . 4K 41
Wingrave Way L11: N Grn. . . . 5K 69
Winhill L25: Wltn . . . 4E 110
Winifred La. L39: Augh . . . 2J 33
Winifred Rd. L10: Faz . . . 6K 55
Winifred St. L7: Liv . . . 6D 88 (6P 5)
WA2: Warr . . . 1C 118
Winkle St. L8: Liv . . . 3B 108
Winmarleigh St. WA1: Warr . . . 3A 118
Winmoss Dr. L33: K'by . . . 7D 44
Winnington Rd. CH47: Hoy . . . 3C 102
Winnipeg Dr. L27: N'ley . . . 3J 111
Winnows, The WA7: Run . . . 1F 153
Winser St. CH62: Port S . . . 3H 127
Winsford Cl. WA11: Hay . . . 6D 62
Winsford Dr. WA5: B'wood . . . 7C 76
Winsford Gro. CH66: Gt Sut . . . 1E 168
Winsford Rd. L13: Liv . . . 1G 89
Winsham Cl. L32: K'by . . . 5C 56
Winsham Rd. L32: K'by . . . 5C 56
Winskill Rd. L11: N Grn. . . . 5J 69
Winslade Ct. L4: Walt . . . 4D 68
Winslade Rd. L4: Walt . . . 5D 68
Winslow Cl. WA7: Nort . . . 2B 154
Winslow St. L4: Walt . . . 5B 68
WINSTANLEY . . . 2B 50
Winstanley College Sports Cen. . . . 1G 4
Winstanley Cl. WA5: Gt San . . . 3G 117
Winstanley Ho. *CH62: New F* . . . *2H 127*
(off Winstanley Rd.)
Winstanley Ind. Est. WA2: Warr . . . 6B 98
Winstanley Rd. CH62: New F . . . 2H 127
CH64: Lit N . . . 6J 157
L22: Water . . . 3E 52
WN2: Bam . . . 4K 51
WN5: Ash M, Bil . . . 7G 39
(not continuous)
Winstanley Shop. Cen. WN3: Wins . . . 2B 50
Winster Dr. L27: N'ley . . . 4A 112
WN2: Platt B . . . 2K 51
Winster Ho. WN5: Wigan . . . 4K 39
Winsters, The WN8: Skel . . . 2F 37
Winston Av. WA9: St. H . . . 4K 75
WA12: New W . . . 3G 77
Winstonb Cres. PR8: South . . . 6A 12
Winston Cres. PR8: South . . . 6A 12
Winston Dr. CH43: Noct . . . 3G 105
Winstone Rd. L14: K Ash . . . 3E 90
Winston Gro. CH46: More . . . 7C 84
Winterburn Cres. L12: W Der . . . 7A 70
Winterburn Hgts. *L12: W Der* . . . *7B 70*
(off Winterburn Cres.)
Winter Gdns., The *CH45: New B* . . . *6A 66*
(off Atherton St.)
Winter Gro. WA9: St. H . . . 3K 75
Winterhey Av. CH44: Wall . . . 4B 86
Winterley Dr. L26: Halew . . . 3A 132
Winter St. L6: Liv . . . 4C 88 (3M 5)
Winthrop Pk. CH43: O'ton . . . 3J 105
Winton Cl. CH45: New B . . . 6K 65
Winton Gro. WA7: Wind H . . . 1B 154
Winton Rd. WA3: Low . . . 1E 78
WINWICK . . . 1B 98
WINWICK GREEN . . . 7A 78
Winwick La. WA3: Croft . . . 5D 78
WA3: Low . . . 1E 78
Winwick Link Rd. WA2: Win . . . 1B 98
Winwick Parish Leisure Cen. . . . 1B 98
Winwick Pk. Av. WA2: Win . . . 2A 98
WINWICK QUAY . . . 4A 98
Winwick Rd. WA2: Warr . . . 3A 98
WA12: New W . . . 4J 77
Winwick St. WA2: Warr . . . 2B 118
Winwick Vw. WA5: C Grn . . . 5B 76
Winwood Hall L25: Wltn . . . 7E 110
Wirral Bus. Cen. CH41: Birk . . . 6C 86
Wirral Bus. Pk., The
CH49: Upton . . . 5D 104
Wirral Cl. CH63: Beb . . . 6F 127
WA3: Cul . . . 2A 80
Wirral Country Pk. . . . 6J 123
Wirral Country Pk. Vis. Cen. . . . 6H 123
Wirral Cres. CH64: Lit N . . . 6K 157
Wirral Dr. WN3: Wins . . . 2A 50
Wirral Gdns. CH63: Beb . . . 6F 127
Wirral Intl. Bus. Pk.
CH62: Brom . . . 1B 146
Wirral Leisure Pk. CH62: Brom . . . 6A 128
Wirral Little Theatre . . . 3C 106
Wirral Mt. CH45: Wall . . . 2K 85
CH48: W Kir . . . 6F 103
Wirral Mus. . . . 2F 107
Wirral Sailing Cen. . . . 6B 102
Wirral Tennis & Sports Cen. . . . 5H 85
Wirral Transport Mus. . . . 1E 106
Wirral Vw. L19: Gras . . . 3H 129
Wirral Vs. CH45: Wall . . . 1J 85
Wirral Way CH43: Noct . . . 3G 105
Wisenholme Cl. WA7: Beech . . . 6G 153
Wisteria Way WA9: Bold . . . 7J 75
Witham Cl. L30: N'ton . . . 1C 54
Witham Rd. WN8: Skel . . . 2C 36
Withburn Cl. CH49: Upton . . . 3C 104
Withens, The L28: Stock V . . . 7F 71
Withensfield CH45: Wall . . . 1B 86
Withens La. CH45: Wall . . . 1B 86
Withens Rd. L31: Lyd . . . 1F 43
Withers Av. WA2: Warr . . . 7D 98
Wither's La. WA16: H Legh . . . 3D 140
(not continuous)
Withert Av. CH63: High B . . . 1D 126
Witherwin Av. WA4: App, Grap . . . 2E 138
Withington Av. WA3: Cul . . . 2C 80
Withington Rd. CH44: Wall . . . 4C 86
L24: Speke . . . 6K 131
Withins Fld. L38: High . . . 6F 29
Withins La. L38: Gt Alt . . . 4F 31
Withins Rd. WA3: Cul . . . 3B 80
WA11: Hay . . . 5C 62
Within Way L24: Hale . . . 1E 150
Withnell Cl. L13: Liv . . . 5K 89
Withnell Rd. L13: Liv . . . 5K 89
Withy Cl. WA6: Frod . . . 3E 166
Withycombe Rd. WA5: Penk . . . 4C 116
Witley Av. CH46: More . . . 6C 84
Witley Cl. CH46: More . . . 6C 84
Witney Cl. CH49: Grea . . . 5A 104
Witney Gdns. WA4: App . . . 3E 138
Wittenham Cl. CH49: Upton . . . 4D 104
Wittering La. CH60: Hes . . . 2B 142
Witterings, The CH64: Nest . . . 2J 157
Witton Rd. L13: Liv . . . 1F 89
Witton Way WA11: R'ford . . . 5F 47
Witt Rd. WA8: Wid . . . 2C 134
Wivern Pl. WA7: Run . . . 6D 134
Woburn Av. WA12: New W . . . 4H 77
Woburn Cl. L13: Liv . . . 2H 89
WA11: Hay . . . 6D 62
Woburn Dr. WA8: Cron . . . 2K 113
Woburn Grn. L13: Liv . . . 3H 89
Woburn Hill L13: Liv . . . 3H 89
Woburn Pl. CH42: R Ferr . . . 6F 107
Woburn Rd. CH45: Wall . . . 1B 86
WA2: Win . . . 3A 98
Wokefield Way WA10: St. H . . . 2J 73
Wokingham Gro. L36: Huy . . . 7J 91
Wolfe Cl. WA4: Grap . . . 1G 139
Wolfenden Av. L20: Boot . . . 1A 68
Wolfe Rd. WA9: St. H . . . 4G 75
Wolferton Cl. CH49: Upton . . . 1F 105
Wolfe St. L8: Liv . . . 3A 108
Wolfrick Dr. CH63: Spit . . . 1H 145
Wolfson Sq. WN4: Ash M . . . 1D 62
Wollaton Dr. PR8: South . . . 5B 12
Wolmer St. WN4: Ash M . . . 1E 62
Wolseley Rd. WA10: St. H . . . 1B 74
Wolsey Cl. WN4: Ash M . . . 7E 50
Wolsey St. L20: Kirk . . . 5J 67
Wolstenholme Sq. L1: Liv . . . 7K 87 (8G 4)
WOLVERHAM . . . 7B 162
Wolverham Rd. CH65: Ell P . . . 1A 170
Wolverton WN8: Skel . . . 3F 37
Wolverton Dr. WA7: Wind H . . . 1B 154
Wolverton St. L6: Liv . . . 1D 88
Womack Gdns. WA9: St. H . . . 1A 94
Woodacre Gro. CH66: Ell P . . . 3H 161
Woodacre Rd. CH66: Ell P . . . 3G 161
Woodale Cl. WA5: Gt San . . . 1C 116
Woodall Dr. WA7: Run . . . 1D 152
Wood Av. L20: Boot . . . 1A 68
WOODBANK . . . 6A 168
Woodbank Cl. L16: Child . . . 7D 90
Woodbank La. CH1: W'bnk . . . 7A 168
Woodbank Pk. CH43: O'ton . . . 4K 105
Woodbank Rd. CH65: Whit . . . 2K 169
WA5: Penk . . . 4E 116
Woodberry Cl. CH43: Noct . . . 4H 105
L33: K'by . . . 6D 44
Woodbine Rd. WA13: Lymm . . . 4K 121
Woodbine St. L5: Kirk . . . 7K 67
Woodbourne Rd. L14: K Ash . . . 3B 90
Woodbridge Av. L26: Halew . . . 6H 111
Woodbridge Cl. WA4: App . . . 5E 138
Woodbrook Av. L9: Walt . . . 6B 54
Woodbrook Dr. WN3: Wigan . . . 1B 50
Woodburn Blvd. CH63: High B . . . 1E 126
Woodburn Dr. CH60: Hes . . . 4D 142
WOODCHURCH . . . 6F 105
Woodchurch Ct. CH42: Tran . . . 5C 106
Woodchurch La. CH42: Tran . . . 6B 106
CH49: W'chu . . . 1G 125
CH66: Ell P . . . 5G 161
Woodchurch Leisure Cen. . . . 5G 105
Woodchurch Rd. CH41: Birk . . . 5C 106
CH42: Tran . . . 5C 106
CH43: Pren . . . 7F 105
CH49: W'chu . . . 7F 105
L13: Liv . . . 3J 89
Woodchurch Sports Barn . . . 4G 105
Wood Cl. CH41: Birk . . . 1D 106
CH66: Hoot . . . 2C 160
L32: K'by . . . 3B 56
Woodcote Av. CH65: Whit . . . 2K 169
Woodcote Bank CH42: R Ferr . . . 2F 127
Woodcote Cl. L33: K'by . . . 1E 56
WA2: Warr . . . 6D 98
Woodcotes, The CH62: Brom . . . 4K 145
Woodcot La. CH60: Hes . . . 1D 142
Woodcroft WN8: Skel . . . 3F 37
Woodcroft Dr. CH61: Hes . . . 7D 124
Woodcroft La. CH63: High B . . . 1E 126
Woodcroft Rd. L15: W'tree . . . 1F 109
Woodcroft Way WA9: Clock F . . . 3E 94
Woodedge WN4: Ash M . . . 2D 62
WOODEND . . . 3D 134
Woodend CH61: Pens . . . 4D 124
L35: Whis . . . 7E 92
WA7: Murd . . . 3C 154
Woodend Av. L23: C'by . . . 6E 40
L24: Speke . . . 3G 131
L25: Hunts X . . . 3G 131
L31: Mag . . . 5E 42
Woodend Ct. WA8: Wid . . . 6F 115
Woodend Ind. Est. L24: Speke . . . 4H 131
Wood End La. CH64: Burt . . . 7E 158
Woodend La. L24: Speke . . . 5G 131
WA3: Rix . . . 5E 100
WOOD END PARK . . . 2H 129
Woodend Rd. CH65: Ell P . . . 5H 161
Woodene Cl. L32: K'by . . . 6E 56
Woodfall Cl. CH64: Lit N . . . 5A 158
Woodfall Gro. CH64: Lit N . . . 5A 158
Woodfall La. CH64: Lit N . . . 5K 157
Woodfarm Hey L28: Stock V . . . 6E 70
Woodfield Av. CH63: High B . . . 1E 126
Woodfield Cres. WN4: Ash M . . . 3E 62
Woodfield Rd. CH61: Pens . . . 5C 124
CH63: Beb . . . 6G 127
CH65: Ell P . . . 6A 162
L9: Walt . . . 1B 68
L36: Huy . . . 5G 91
L39: Orm . . . 7B 24
Woodfield Rd. Nth. CH65: Ell P . . . 6A 162
Woodford Cl. WA4: Thel . . . 5J 119
WA6: Hel . . . 2H 173
WA7: Run . . . 4D 152
Woodford Rd. CH62: New F . . . 1H 127
L14: K Ash . . . 3C 90
WA10: Windle . . . 7J 59
Woodford St. WN5: Wigan . . . 5K 39
Woodgate L27: N'ley . . . 2G 111
Woodger St. L19: Gars . . . 4A 130
Wood Grn. CH43: Bid . . . 7G 85
L34: Prsct . . . 1C 92
Woodgreen Rd. L13: Liv . . . 3J 89
Wood Gro. L13: Liv . . . 5H 89
Woodhall Av. CH44: Wall . . . 3D 86
Woodhall Cl. WA5: Gt San . . . 7E 96
Woodhall Rd. L13: Liv . . . 4J 89
Woodham Gro. CH64: Lit N . . . 6K 157
Woodhatch Rd. WA7: Brook . . . 5J 153
Woodhead Gro. WN3: Wigan . . . 2F 51
Woodhead Rd. CH62: Port S . . . 3J 127
Woodhead St. CH62: New F . . . 2H 127
Wood Heath Way CH62: East . . . 3C 146
WOODHEY . . . 2E 126
Woodhey Ct. CH63: High B . . . 1F 127
Woodhey Gro. CH63: High B . . . 2F 127
Woodhey Rd. CH63: High B . . . 2F 127
L19: Gras . . . 1J 129
Woodholme Ct. L25: Gate . . . 4F 111
Woodhouse Cl. L4: Walt . . . 7A 68
WA3: Bchwd . . . 4A 100
WOODHOUSES . . . 6B 166
Woodhouses L38: High . . . 6F 29
Woodhouses La. WA6: Frod . . . 6B 166
Woodhouses Pk. WA6: Frod . . . 6B 166
Woodhurst Cl. L36: Huy . . . 1G 91
Woodhurst Cres. L14: K Ash . . . 3E 90
Woodin Rd. CH42: R Ferr . . . 1G 127
Woodkind Hey CH63: Spit . . . 7G 127
Woodland Av. CH47: Meols . . . 6F 83
L40: Scar . . . 2H 17
WA8: Wid . . . 7B 114
WA12: New W . . . 3K 77
WA13: Lymm . . . 6J 121
Woodland Dr. CH45: New B . . . 7C 66
CH49: W'chu . . . 5E 104
WA13: Lymm . . . 6H 121
WN4: Ash M . . . 7F 51
Woodland Gro. CH42: R Ferr . . . 1F 127
Woodland Path L37: Ains, Form . . . 1K 19
Woodland Rd. CH42: R Ferr . . . 1F 127
CH48: W Kir . . . 6G 103
CH49: W'chu . . . 5E 104
CH65: Whit . . . 2J 169
L4: Walt . . . 6E 68
L21: Sea . . . 6F 53
L26: Halew . . . 2J 131
L31: Mell . . . 1J 55
Woodlands, The CH41: Birk . . . 3D 106
CH49: Upton . . . 3D 104
L34: Ecc P . . . 7F 73
PR8: Ains . . . 4C 14
Woodlands Cl. CH64: Park . . . 3H 157
L37: Form . . . 7H 19
L39: Orm . . . 6E 24
PR9: South . . . 7K 7
Woodlands Cres.
WA16: H Legh . . . 5K 141
Woodlands Dr. CH61: Barn . . . 5G 125
WA4: Thel . . . 5K 119
Woodlands La. CH48: W Kir . . . 7F 103
Woodlands Pk. L12: W Der . . . 2J 89
WA12: New W . . . 7G 63
Woodlands Rd. CH61: Irby . . . 4B 124
CH64: Park . . . 3H 157
L9: Ain . . . 6F 55
L17: Aig . . . 6G 109
L36: Huy . . . 5F 91
L37: Form . . . 1H 29
WA11: St. H . . . 7D 60
Woodlands Sq. *L27: N'ley* . . . *4A 112*
(off Winster Dr.)
Woodland Vw. CH66: Chil T . . . 3D 160
L23: Thorn . . . 5G 41
Woodland Wlk. CH62: Brom . . . 1J 145
WA7: Cas . . . 1J 153
Wood La. CH45: Wall . . . 1J 85
CH49: Grea . . . 3B 104
CH64: Park . . . 7G 143
CH64: Will . . . 2G 159
L27: N'ley . . . 3K 111
L34: Prsct . . . 2B 92
L36: Huy . . . 5B 92
L37: Gt Alt . . . 2J 31
L39: Down . . . *2J 31*
WA4: App . . . 1E 138
WA7: Murd . . . 4A 154
WA7: Sut W . . . 6H 153
WN8: Parb . . . 1K 27
Wood Lea L12: Crox . . . 3C 70
Woodlea Cl. CH62: Brom . . . 5K 145
PR9: Cros . . . 2F 9
Woodlee Rd. L25: Gate . . . 4G 111
Woodleigh Cl. L31: Lyd . . . 6D 32
Woodley Fold WA5: Penk . . . 4D 116
Woodley Pk. Rd. WN8: Skel . . . 6H 27
Woodley Rd. L31: Mag . . . 6E 42
Wood Moss La. L40: Scar . . . 5F 13
Woodpecker Cl. CH49: Upton . . . 3B 104
L12: W Der . . . 5D 70
WA3: Bchwd . . . 3B 100
Woodpecker Dr. L26: Halew . . . 6J 111
Woodridge WA7: Wind H . . . 1A 154
Wood Rd. L26: Halew . . . 2J 131
Woodrock Rd. L25: Wltn . . . 6F 111
Woodrow WN8: Skel . . . 3E 36
Woodrow Dr. WN8: Newb . . . 1F 27
Woodruff St. L8: Liv . . . 4B 108
Woods Cl. L39: Has . . . 6C 22
Woodside CH65: Whit . . . 2A 170
Woodside Av. CH46: More . . . 1C 104
PR8: Ains . . . 6B 14
WA6: Frod . . . 4F 167
WA11: St. H . . . 5B 60
WN4: Ash M . . . 4E 50
Woodside Bus. Pk. CH41: Birk . . . 1F 107
Woodside Cl. L12: W Der . . . 6K 69
WN8: Uph . . . 3E 38
Woodside Ferry App.
CH41: Birk . . . 1F 107
Woodside La. WA13: Lymm . . . 7K 121
Woodside Rd. CH61: Irby . . . 3C 124
WA5: Gt San . . . 2D 116
WA11: Hay . . . 6C 62
Woodside St. L7: Liv . . . 6D 88 (7P 5)
Woodside Way L33: K'by . . . 7D 44
Woods La. WN4: Ash M . . . 1H 63
Woodsome Cl. CH65: Whit . . . 3K 169
Woodsome Dr. CH65: Whit . . . 3K 169
Woodsome Pk. L25: Gate . . . 5G 111
Woodsorrel Rd. CH41: Birk . . . 1K 105
L15: W'tree . . . 1K 109
Woodstack St. WA9: St. H . . . 7G 75
Woodstock Av. WA12: New W . . . 4H 77
Woodstock Dr. PR8: B'dale . . . 1F 15
Woodstock Gdns. WA4: App . . . 3F 139
Woodstock Gro. WA8: Wid . . . 6K 113
Woodstock Rd. CH44: Wall . . . 4A 86
Woodstock St. L5: Liv . . . 2K 87
Wood St. CH41: Birk . . . 1D 106
CH47: Hoy . . . 1D 102
CH62: Port S . . . 4H 127
L1: Liv . . . 6K 87 (7G 4)
L19: Gars . . . 3A 130
L21: Lith . . . 6H 53
L34: Prsct . . . 1D 92
WA1: Warr . . . 2D 118
WA8: Wid . . . 7E 114
WA9: St. H . . . 2E 74
Woodthorn Cl. WA4: Dares . . . 5D 136
WOODVALE . . . 6C 14
Wood Va. WA9: St. H . . . 1A 94
Woodvale Cl. CH43: Bid . . . 7G 85
WA2: P'gate . . . 6E 98
Woodvale Ct. CH49: W'chu . . . 7E 104
PR9: Banks . . . 2J 9
Woodvale Rd. CH66: Lit Sut . . . 5F 161
L12: Crox . . . 3D 70
L25: Wltn . . . 6F 111
PR8: Ains . . . 7C 14
Woodvale Sidings PR8: South . . . 1D 20
Woodview L34: Know . . . 3J 71
Woodview Av. CH44: Wall . . . 5D 86
Woodview Cres. WA8: Wid . . . 1G 133
Woodview Rd. L25: Wltn . . . 4D 110
WA8: Wid . . . 1G 133
Woodville Av. L23: C'by . . . 2D 52
Woodville Pl. WA8: Wid . . . 7K 113
Woodville Rd. CH42: Tran . . . 4C 106
WN3: Ince M . . . 1K 51
Woodville St. WA10: St. H . . . 2D 74
(not continuous)
Woodville Ter. L6: Liv . . . 2D 88
Woodward Rd. CH42: R Ferr . . . 1G 127
L33: Know I . . . 1G 57
Woodway CH49: Grea . . . 4C 104
Woodyear Rd. CH62: Brom . . . 3A 146
Woolacombe Av. WA9: Sut L . . . 2E 94
Woolacombe Cl. WA4: Latch . . . 6D 118
Woolacombe Rd. L16: Child . . . 2B 110
Woolden Rd. M44: Cad . . . 6K 81
Wooler Cl. CH46: More . . . 7A 84
Woolfall Cl. L36: Huy . . . 3F 91
Woolfall Cres. L36: Huy . . . 3F 91
WOOLFALL HEATH . . . 2G 91
Woolfall Heath Av. L36: Huy . . . 2G 91
Woolfall Hgts. L36: Huy . . . 2G 91
Woolfall Ter. L21: Sea . . . 7G 53
Woolhope Rd. L4: Walt . . . 4D 68
Woollam Dr. CH66: Lit Sut . . . 4F 161
Woolley Cl. WA6: Frod . . . 1F 167
Woolmer Cl. WA3: Bchwd . . . 1D 100
Woolmoore Rd. L24: Speke . . . 3G 131
WOOLSTON . . . 1J 119
Woolston Grange Av. WA1: W'ston . . . 6K 99
WA2: P'gate . . . 5J 99
Woolston Rd. WA11: Hay . . . 6B 62
WOOLTON . . . 6E 110
Woolton Cinema, The . . . 6E 110
Woolton Cl. WN4: Ash M . . . 7D 50
Woolton Ct. CH66: Ell P . . . 3H 161
WOOLTON HILL . . . 5C 110
Woolton Hill Rd. L25: Wltn . . . 4C 110
Woolton M. L25: Wltn . . . 6D 110
Woolton Mt. L25: Wltn . . . 5E 110
WOOLTON PARK . . . 4E 110
Woolton Pk. L25: Wltn . . . 4E 110
Woolton Pk. Cl. L25: Wltn . . . 5E 110
Woolton Rd. L15: W'tree . . . 1J 109
L16: Child . . . 1J 109
L19: Aller, Gars . . . 3A 130
L25: Aller . . . 1C 130
Woolton St. L25: Wltn . . . 6E 110
(not continuous)
Woolton Swimming Pool . . . 6E 110
Woolton Views L25: Hunts X . . . 1H 131
Worcester Av. L13: Liv . . . 7F 69
L22: Water . . . 3C 52
Worcester Cl. WA5: Gt San . . . 3G 117
WA10: St. H . . . 4B 74
Worcester Ct. L20: Boot . . . 3K 67
Worcester Dr. L13: Liv . . . 7F 69
Worcester Dr. Nth. L13: Liv . . . 7F 69
Worcester Rd. CH43: Bid . . . 7H 85
L20: Boot . . . 2K 67
Worcester St. CH65: Ell P . . . 5A 162
Worcester Wlk. CH65: Ell P . . . 5A 162
Wordsworth Av. CH42: R Ferr . . . 7F 107
WA4: Warr . . . 5B 118
WA8: Wid . . . 1B 134
WA9: Sut M . . . 4C 94
WN5: Bil . . . 3F 49
WN5: Orr . . . 5H 39
Wordsworth Cl. L39: Orm . . . 4B 24
Wordsworth St. L8: Liv . . . 1D 108
L20: Boot . . . 1G 67
Wordsworth Wlk. CH48: W Kir . . . 1D 122
Wordsworth Way CH66: Gt Sut . . . 3G 169
L36: Huy . . . 6K 91
Wordworth Ct. L32: K'by . . . 5A 56
World of Glass, The . . . 3C 74
Worrow Cl. L11: N Grn. . . . 3K 69
Worrow Rd. L11: N Grn. . . . 3K 69
Worsborough Av. WA5: Gt San . . . 3F 117
Worsley Av. WA4: Westy . . . 4F 119
WORSLEY BROW . . . 5G 75
Worsley Brow WA9: St. H . . . 6G 75
Worsley Cl. WN5: Wigan . . . 6K 39
Worsley Grn. WN5: Wigan . . . 6K 39
Worsley Rd. WA4: Walt . . . 7B 118
Worsley St. WA5: Warr . . . 1K 117
WA11: Hay . . . 7H 61
WN5: Wigan . . . 6K 39
Worthing Cl. PR8: B'dale . . . 5F 11
Worthing St. L22: Water . . . 3C 52
Worthington Cl. WA7: Pal F . . . 3J 153
Worthington St. L8: Liv . . . 2K 107
Worthington Way WN3: Wigan . . . 2C 50
Wortley Rd. L10: Faz . . . 6G 55
Wotton Dr. WN4: Ash M . . . 2H 63
Wray Av. WA9: Clock F . . . 3F 95
Wrayburn Cl. L7: Liv . . . 7E 88
Wray Ct. WA9: Clock F . . . 3F 95
Wrekin Cl. L25: Wltn . . . 7F 111
Wrekin Dr. L10: Ain . . . 3G 55
Wrenbury Cl. CH43: O'ton . . . 6K 105
WA7: Sut W . . . 6H 153
WN5: Wigan . . . 5K 39

HOSPITALS and HOSPICES
covered by this atlas

N.B. Where Hospitals and Hospices are not named on the map, the reference given is for the road in which they are situated.

ALDER HEY CHILDREN'S HOSPITAL 3A **90**
Eaton Road
West Derby
LIVERPOOL
L12 2AP
Tel: 0151 2284811

ARROWE PARK HOSPITAL 7E **104**
Arrowe Park Rd.
WIRRAL
CH49 5PE
Tel: 0151 6785111

ASHTON HOUSE HOSPITAL 4B **106**
26 Village Road
Oxton
PRENTON
CH43 5SR
Tel: 0151 653 9660

ASHWORTH HOSPITAL 1K **43**
Parkbourn
LIVERPOOL
L31 1HW
Tel: 0151 4730303

BROADGREEN HOSPITAL 5A **90**
Thomas Drive
LIVERPOOL
L14 3LB
Tel: 0151 7062000

CARDIOTHORACIC CENTRE
(BROADGREEN HOSPITAL), THE
.................................5A **90**
Thomas Drive
LIVERPOOL
L14 3PE
Tel: 0151 2281616

CLAIRE HOUSE CHILDREN'S HOSPICE
.................................1D **144**
Clatterbridge Rd.
WIRRAL
CH63 4JD
Tel: 0151 3344626

CLATTERBRIDGE HOSPITAL 1E **144**
Clatterbridge Rd.
WIRRAL
CH63 4JY
Tel: 0151 3344000

ELLESMERE PORT HOSPITAL 2J **169**
114 Chester Road
Whitby
ELLESMERE PORT
CH65 6SG
Tel: 01244 365000

FAIRFIELD HOSPITAL 3A **60**
Crank Road
Crank
ST HELENS
WA11 7RS
Tel: 01744 739311

HALTON GENERAL HOSPITAL 4H **153**
Hospital Way
RUNCORN
WA7 2DA
Tel: 01928 714567

HALTON HAVEN 5A **154**
Barnfield Av.
Murdishaw
RUNCORN
WA7 6EP
Tel: 01928 719454

HESKETH CENTRE, THE 6J **7**
51-55 Albert Road
SOUTHPORT
PR9 0LT
Tel: 01704 383600

HOLLINS PARK HOSPITAL 1K **97**
Hollins Lane
WARRINGTON
WA2 8WA
Tel: 01925 664000

HOSPICE OF THE GOOD SHEPHERD ...7K **169**
Gordon La.
Backford
CHESTER
CH2 4DG
Tel: 01244 851091

LIVERPOOL WOMEN'S HOSPITAL
.................................7C **88** (9N **5**)
Crown Street
LIVERPOOL
L8 7SS
Tel: 0151 7089988

LOURDES HOSPITAL 3H **109**
57 Greenbank Road
LIVERPOOL
L18 1HQ
Tel: 0151 7337123

MARIE CURIE CENTRE, LIVERPOOL ...6F **111**
Speke Road
Woolton
LIVERPOOL
L25 8QA
Tel: 0151 801 1400

MOSSLEY HILL HOSPITAL 4G **109**
Park Avenue
Mossley Hill
LIVERPOOL
L18 8BU
Tel: 0151 2503000

MURRAYFIELD BUPA HOSPITAL 4H **125**
Holmwood Drive
Heswall
WIRRAL
CH61 1AU
Tel: 0151 6487000

NEWTON COMMUNITY HOSPITAL 4F **77**
Bradlegh Road
NEWTON-LE-WILLOWS
WA12 8RB
Tel: 01925 222731

NORTH CHESHIRE BUPA HOSPITAL ...7J **139**
Fir Tree Close
WARRINGTON
WA4 4LU
Tel: 01925 265000

ORMSKIRK AND DISTRICT
GENERAL HOSPITAL 6E **24**
Wigan Road
ORMSKIRK
L39 2AZ
Tel: 01695 577111

PARK LODGE HOSPITAL 2F **89**
Orphan Drive
LIVERPOOL
L6 7UN
Tel: 0151 3308934

QUEENSCOURT HOSPICE 4B **12**
Town Lane
SOUTHPORT
PR8 6RE
Tel: 01704 544645

RATHBONE HOSPITAL 5J **89**
Mill Lane
Old Swan
LIVERPOOL
L13 4AW
Tel: 0151 2503000

RENACRES HALL HOSPITAL 4D **16**
Renacres Lane
Halsall
ORMSKIRK
L39 8SE
Tel: 01704 841133

ROYAL LIVERPOOL DENTAL HOSPITAL
.........................5B **88** (5L **5**)
Pembroke Place
LIVERPOOL
L3 5PS
Tel: 0151 7062000

ROYAL LIVERPOOL UNIVERSITY HOSPITAL
.........................5B **88** (4L **5**)
Prescot Street
LIVERPOOL
L7 8XP
Tel: 0151 7062000

ST BARTHOLOMEW'S DAY HOSPITAL ...5G **91**
Station Rd., Huyton
LIVERPOOL
L36 4HU
Tel: 0151 4896241

ST CATHERINE'S HOSPITAL (BIRKENHEAD)
.................................4D **106**
Church Rd.
BIRKENHEAD
CH42 0LQ
Tel: 0151 6787272

ST HELENS HOSPITAL (MERSEYSIDE)
.................................5E **74**
Marshalls Cross Road
ST HELENS
WA9 3DA
Tel: 0151 4261600

ST JOHN'S HOSPICE IN WIRRAL 1E **144**
Mount Road, Higher Bebington
WIRRAL
CH63 6JE
Tel: 0151 3342778

ST JOSEPH'S HOSPICE 4F **41**
Ince Road
LIVERPOOL
L23 4UE
Tel: 0151 9243812

ST JOSEPHS HOSPICE (HETTINGA HOUSE)
.................................4F **25**
Dark Lane, Lathom
ORMSKIRK
L40 5TR
Tel: 01695 578713

ST ROCCO'S HOSPICE 1J **117**
Lockton Lane
WARRINGTON
WA5 0BW
Tel: 01925 575780

SCOTT CLINIC 2J **93**
Rainhill Road
ST HELENS
WA9 5BD
Tel: 0151 4306300

SIR ALFRED JONES MEMORIAL HOSPITAL
.................................3A **130**
Church Road, Garston
LIVERPOOL
L19 2LP
Tel: 0151 2503000

SMITHDOWN HEALTH PARK 2F **109**
Smithdown Road
LIVERPOOL
L15 2HE
Tel: 0151 33080/54/74/10

SOUTHPORT AND FORMBY
DISTRICT GENERAL HOSPITAL
.................................4A **12**
Town La.
SOUTHPORT
PR8 6PN
Tel: 01704 547471

SOUTHPORT GENERAL INFIRMARY
.................................3K **11**
Scarisbrick New Rd.
SOUTHPORT
PR8 6PH
Tel: 01704 547471

UNIVERSITY HOSPITAL AINTREE 6G **55**
Longmoor La.
LIVERPOOL
L9 7AL
Tel: 0151 525 5980

VICTORIA CENTRAL HOSPITAL 3B **86**
Mill La.
WALLASEY
CH44 5UF
Tel: 0151 6785111

WALTON HOSPITAL 3B **68**
Rice Lane
LIVERPOOL
L9 1AE
Tel: 0151 525 3611

WARRINGTON HOSPITAL............2K **117**
Lovely Lane
WARRINGTON
WA5 1QG
Tel: 01925 635911

WATERLOO DAY HOSPITAL 4E **52**
Park Rd.
Waterloo
LIVERPOOL
L22 3XR
Tel: 0151 9287243

WHISTON HOSPITAL 3F **93**
Warrington Rd.
PRESCOT
L35 5DR
Tel: 0151 4261600

WILLOW HOUSE RESOURCE CENTRE
.................................4E **92**
168 Dragon La.
PRESCOT
L35 3QY
Tel: 0151 4306048

WILLOWBROOK HOSPICE 7G **73**
Portico Lane
PRESCOT
L34 2QT
Tel: 0151 4308736

WOODLANDS HOSPICE 7F **55**
Longmoor La.
LIVERPOOL
L9 7LA
Tel: 0151 5292299

ZOE'S PLACE - BABY HOSPICE 2C **90**
Yew Tree La.
LIVERPOOL
L12 9HH
Tel: 0151 2280353